Walford's Concise Guide
to Reference Material

WALFORD'S CONCISE GUIDE TO REFERENCE MATERIAL

SECOND EDITION

EDITED BY

Anthony Chalcraft BA, MA, ALA
Alan Day MA, MPhil, PhD, DipLib, FRGS, FLA
Joan M. Harvey MA, FLA
Marilyn Mullay MA
Ray Prytherch MA, MPhil, ALA
Priscilla Schlicke BA, ALA
Stephen Willis BA, DipLib, ALA

THE LIBRARY ASSOCIATION
LONDON

© The Library Association 1992

Published by
Library Association Publishing Ltd
7 Ridgmount Street
London WC1E 7AE

First published 1981
This second revised edition 1992

British Library Cataloguing in Publication Data

Walford, A. J.
  Walford's Concise Guide to Reference Material.
  — 2Rev.ed
  I. Title   II. Chalcraft, Anthony
  011.02

  ISBN 1-85604-042-9

Computer production software by LIBPAC (Computer Services)
Ltd, Whittle le Woods, Lancs.
Typeset in 7/8pt Times by Spottiswoode Ballantyne Printers Ltd,
Colchester.
Printed and made in Great Britain by Butler & Tanner Ltd,
Frome, Somerset.

Contents

		Page
	Introduction	ix
	The editors	xi
	Abbreviations	xiii
0	GENERALITIES	1
001	Knowledge	1
01	Bibliography & Bibliographies	5
015	National Bibliographies	6
02	Librarianship & Information Studies	17
026/027	Libraries	21
028	Reading	23
03	Reference Books	25
030	Encyclopaedias	27
04	Essays, Reprints, Theses, Reviews	31
05	Periodicals	35
06	Organizations & Associations	41
07	Journalism & Newspapers	45
08	Polygraphies	48
087.7	Government Publications	50
09	Rare Books & Manuscripts	53
1	PHILOSOPHY & PSYCHOLOGY	55
101	Philosophy	55
159.9	Psychology	58
164	Logic	59
17	Ethics	59
2	RELIGION	60
22	Bible	61
23/28	Christianity	63
29	Non-Christian Religions	69
3	SOCIAL SCIENCES	73
301	Sociology	74
31	Statistics	77

32	Politics	80
33	Economics	85
331	Labour & Employment	87
332	Land & Property	88
334	Business Relationships & Organization	88
336	Finance & Banking	89
338	Economic Surveys, etc.	91
339	Trade & Commerce	93
65	Business & Management	95
34	Law	99
35	Public Administration	106
36	Social Services & Welfare	111
37	Education	115
39	Customs & Traditions	119
5/6	SCIENCE & TECHNOLOGY	125
51	Mathematics	133
52/529	Astronomy & Surveying	135
53	Physics	141
54	Chemistry	144
55	Earth Sciences	148
56	Palaeontology	157
572	Anthropology	159
573	Biology	162
58/59	Natural History	166
58	Botany	168
59	Zoology	173
6	TECHNOLOGY	179
608	Patents & Inventions	180
61	Medicine	182
62	Engineering	192
629	Transport Vehicles	210
63	Agriculture & Livestock	213
64	Household Management	220
654/656	Communication	224
66	Chemical Industry	231
67/68	Manufactures	238
68	Industries, Trades & Crafts	241
69	Building Industry	246
7	THE ARTS	248
7.011	Design	252
7.074.0	Antiques	253
71	Town & Country Planning. Landscapes	254

72	Architecture	256
73	Sculpture, Plastic & Metal Arts	259
737	Coins – Numismatics	259
738	Ceramics & Pottery	259
74	Decorative Arts & Drawing	262
749.1	Furniture	263
75	Painting	264
76/77	Graphics & Photography	266
76	Graphic Arts	266
77	Photography	267
78	Music	268
789.90	Sound Recordings (Discography)	274
79	Entertainment & Leisure	276
791.4	Films & Videos	277
792	Theatre	280
794/799	Games & Sport	284
8	LANGUAGE & LITERATURE	286
8.0	Languages & Linguistics	286
800	Languages	286
801	Linguistics	288
801.31	Proper Names	288
802.0	English Language	291
803	Germanic Languages	299
804/806	Romance Languages	301
804.0	French Language	301
805.0	Italian Language	302
806.0	Spanish Language	302
807/808	Classical & Slavonic Languages	304
807	Classical Languages	304
808	Slavonic & Baltic Languages	305
808.2	Russian Language	305
809	Oriental, African, etc. Languages	308
82/89	Literature	313
82-1/82-9	Literary Genres	318
820	English Literature	323
820.7/820.9	American & Australasian Literature	331
83	Germanic Literatures	335
84	Romance Literatures	338
840	French Literature	338
850	Italian Literature	339
860	Spanish Literature	340
87	Classical Literature	343

88	Slavonic Literatures	344
882	Russian Literature	344
89	Oriental, African, etc. Literature	346
9	GEOGRAPHY, BIOGRAPHY, HISTORY	351
90	Archaeology	351
908	Area Studies	356
91	Geography, Exploration, Travel	367
912	Maps & Atlases	370
914/919	Gazetteers & Guide Books	375
92	Biography	378
929.5/.9	Genealogy & Heraldry	387
93/99	History	392
931	Ancient History & Ancient Peoples	394
94	Mediaeval & Modern History	396
940	History − Europe	397
95	History − Asia	413
96	History − Africa	416
97/980	History − America	417
99	History − Australasia, Polar Regions	426
	Author−Title Index	423
	Subject Index	475

Introduction

This is a shortened version of the three-volume *Walford's guide to reference material*, 5th edition: Volume 1, *Science and technology* (1989), Volume 2, *Social and historical sciences, philosophy and religion* (1990), and Volume 3, *Generalia, language and literature, the arts* (1991). There are more than 3,000 entries, forming an updated compilation of what are considered to be the basic items in the main volumes, plus some more recent material up to April 1992.

From its first edition the purpose of *Walford* has been to identify and evaluate the widest possible range of reference materials. In addition to the expected bibliographies, indexes, dictionaries, encyclopaedias and directories a number of important textbooks and manuals of general practice are included. Although the majority of items are reference 'books', *Walford* is a guide to reference 'material'. Thus periodical articles, microforms, online and CD-ROM sources are all represented. Foreign-language works have been included where there is no satisfactory English alternative.

Targeted users of the parent three-volume edition 'include librarians developing and revising reference collections, staff on enquiry desks needing advice on further sources when local stock has been checked, research workers in the preliminary stages of projects, and students of library and information studies'. The main aim of the *Concise* is to include the *key* works in each subject area.

Entries in the *Concise* follow a subject arrangement based on the Universal Decimal Classification International Medium Edition of 1985 (BS1000M). Subject access for users unfamiliar with UDC can be gained either by checking the contents page to find the relevant section and then browsing through the entries, which are subdivided by form, place etc., or by using the subject index. Terms in this index are generated by the classification numbers given to the entries. Each entry is allocated a running serial number in the text to provide easy access from both the subject and author/title indexes. Full details on the structure and use of the indexes can be found in their introductions.

Individual entries are nearly always based on examination of the actual item and include full bibliographical detail. Annotations are provided, giving, in most cases, summary publishing history, outline of contents, comparison with other works, especially notable features and a brief general assessment of overall value, often illustrated by quotations from or references to reviews.

The example below shows the general layout of entries.

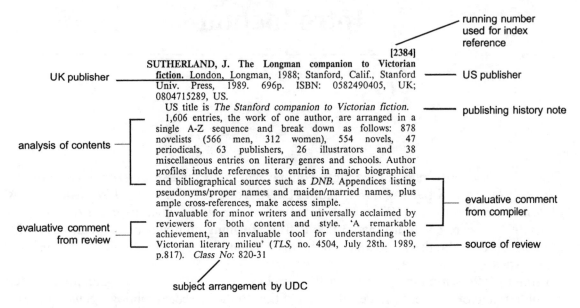

This volume is the work of seven compilers, whose responsibilities for the various classes were as follows:

Anthony Chalcraft
  0   Generalities

Joan Harvey
  1   Philosophy and Psychology
  2   Religion
  3   Social Sciences
  65 Business and Management

Marilyn Mullay and Priscilla Schlicke
  5   Science
  6   Technology

Ray Prytherch
  7   The Arts

Stephen Willis
  8   Language and Literature

Alan Day
  9   Geography, Biography and History

The project was overseen by Barbara Jover of Library Association Publishing. Joan Bibby constructed a thesaurus based on the UDC classification scheme. Martin Harrison of LIBPAC Computer Services automated the data capture and indexing. The compilers are indebted to John Walford for his continuing interest in this work and his contributions in the form of notes on new material.

August 1992

Anthony Chalcraft
Alan Day
Joan Harvey
Marilyn Mullay
Ray Prytherch
Priscilla Schlicke
Stephen Willis

The Editors

Anthony Chalcraft is Information and Systems Librarian at the University of Ripon and York St John. He contributes reviews to the journal *Reference reviews*.

Alan Day was Head of the Department of Library and Information Studies, Manchester Polytechnic, 1979−90. He has published reference handbooks on *History* (1976), *Archaeology* (1977), and *Discovery and exploration* (1980); *J. B. Priestley: an annotated bibliography* (1986); and *The British Library: a guide to its structure, publications, collections, and services* (1988); and was joint editor of *Printed reference material* (3rd edition, 1990). He is a regular contributor to *Reference reviews*. In 1989 he was President of the North Western Branch of The Library Association.

Joan M. Harvey lectured in librarianship at both Loughborough Technical College and Loughborough University until retirement, latterly specializing in business information. She has published textbooks on special librarianship and contributed to several reference works in the field. Currently, she is engaged on a sixth edition of *Statistics Europe: sources for social, economic and market research*.

Marilyn Mullay is Assistant Librarian at the Scottish Agricultural College in Edinburgh. Author of several publications on agricultural literature and online services, she also edits and contributes material to the database, Agdex Information Services.

Ray Prytherch is an information consultant specializing in information management, bibliography and training. His recent publications include the *Handbook of library cooperation* (1991) and the *Children's fiction sourcebook* (1992). He is co-editor of *Library and information work worldwide: an annual survey* (1991−), and editor of the monthly newsletter *Information management report*. He has also held appointments as Music and Sound Recordings Librarian at Leeds City Libraries, and as Senior Lecturer at the Leeds School of Library and Information Studies.

Priscilla Schlicke is Senior Lecturer in the School of Librarianship and Information Studies at Robert Gordon's University, Aberdeen, and Course Leader of the BA/BA(Hons) degree course in Publishing Studies. She is the author (with Paul Schlicke) of *The Old Curiosity Shop: an annotated bibliography* and writes regularly on new developments in CD-ROM for *Information management report*. Her current research interests include the acquisition of materials from Scottish publishers by libraries in Scotland and the problem of wasteful publication in scholarly journals.

Stephen Willis has worked for Manchester City Council's Libraries and Theatres Department since 1975 and is currently Group Manager: Humanities at the Central Library. His previous posts have included Language and Literature Librarian and Social Sciences Librarian.

Abbreviations

Listed below are the chief bibliographical abbreviations used in the *Guide*. Generally accepted abbreviations such as Co., Corpn, *e.g.*, *i.e.*, Inc., Ltd, and *q.v.* are not included.

AG [German] − Aktiengesellschaft: Co.
ALA − American Library Association
Abt. [German] − Abteilung: part
ampl. [Italian] − ampliata: enlarged
    [Spanish] − ampliado: enlarged
Aufl. [German] − Auflage: edition
augm. [French] − augmenté: enlarged
aum. [Portuguese] − aumentada: enlarged
    [Spanish] − aumentado: enlarged
Ausg. [German] − Ausgabe: printing, edition

BS − British Standard
Bd [German] − Band: volume
BFr − Belgian francs
bearb. [German] − bearbeitet: compiled, edited
Belg. − Belgian

c − copyright date
C. Cd. Cmd. Cmnd. − Command papers
ch. − chapter(s)
chron. − chronology
col. − colour, coloured
cols. − columns
comp. − compiler
corr. − corrected
    [French] − corrigé: corrected
    [Spanish] − corregido: corrected
    [Portuguese] − corrigida: corrected

DFl − Dutch florins
Dan. − Danish
diagrs. − diagrams
distr. − distributed
DM [German] − Deutsche Mark
druk [Dutch] − edition

ea. − each

ed. − edition, editor(s)
    [Italian] − edizione
    [Spanish] − edición
    [French] − édition
    [Portuguese] − edicao: edition
enl. − enlarged
erw., erweit. [German] − erweiterte: enlarged
exp. − expanded

FID − Fédération Internationale de Documentation
facsim(s). − facsimile(s)
fasc(s). − fascicule(s)
fig. − figures
fldg − folding
FFr − French francs
front. − frontispiece

ganz. [German] − gänzlich: complete
glav.red. [Russian] glavnyi redaktor: editor-in-chief
Gld. [Dutch] − guilders
GmbH [German] − Gesellschaft mit beschränkter Haftung: Ltd
Gosud. [Russian] − Gosudarstvo: State

HMSO − Her [His] Majesty's Stationery Office
Hft [German] − Heft: part number
hrsg. [German] − herausgegeben: edited, published

illus. − illustrations, illustrated
imp. [French] − imprimé, imprimerie: printed, printing firm
izd. [Russian] − izdanie: edition
    [Serbo-Croat] − izdanje: edition
Izdat. [Russian] − Izdatel': publisher

Jahrg. [German] — Jahrgang: annual publication

kiad. [Hungarian] — kiadás: edition
Kr [Danish, Norwegian, Swedish] — kroner

L [Italian] — lire
l. — leaves
Lfg. [German] — Lieferung: number, part

m.fl. [Danish] — med flere: and others

n.d. — no date
neubearb. [German] — neubearbeitet: revised
no. — number
Nor. — Norwegian
nouv. [French] — nouvelle: new (edition)
n.p. — no place of publication
Nr [Danish, German] — Nummer: number

n.s. — new series
NV [Dutch] — naamloze vennootschap: limited
    company

o.p. — out of print
omarb. [Swedish] — omarbetad: revised
opl. [Danish] — oplag: edition

p. — page(s)
pl. — plate(s)
port. — portrait(s)
pt(s) — part(s)
pub. — publisher
pubn. — publication

réd. [French] — rédigé: edited, compiled
repr. — reprinted
rev. — revised, revision
        [French] — révisé: revised
        [Portuguese] — revistada: revised

riv. [Italian] — riveduto: revised
R [South African] — rands
Rs — rupees

Sch — Schillings
ser. — series
sér. [French] — série: series
SFr — Swiss francs
supp. — supplementary, supplement(s)
Sw. — Swiss
Swed. — Swedish

t. [French] — tome(s): volume(s)
T. [German] — Teil(e): part(s)

u. [German] — und: and
UDC — Universal Decimal Classification
udg. [Danish] — udgave: edition
uit. [Dutch] — uitgaaf: publication
uitg. [Dutch] — uitgegeven: published
umgearb. [German] — umbearbeitete: revised
Univ. — University
unveränd. [German] — unverändert: unaltered
uppl. [Swedish] — upplaga: edition
utg. [Norwegian] — utgave: edition

v. — volume(s)
v. p. — various pagings
VEB [German] — Volkseigener Betrieb:
    People's Concern
verand. [German] — verandert: revised
verb. [German] — verbesserte: improved
verm. [German] — vermehrte: enlarged
vyd. [Czech] — vydání: edition
        [Slovak] — vydanie: edition

wyd. [Polish] — wydanie: edition

0 GENERALITIES
001 Knowledge

Intellectual Work

Research Methods

[1]
BERRY, R. **How to write a research paper.** 2nd ed. Oxford, Pergamon Press, 1986. v,116p. ISBN: 0080326811.
First published 1966.
A well-written, concise guide 'designed to be relevant to students at all levels of higher education' (Introduction p.1). Contents: 1. The choice of subject: using the library - 2. Preparing a bibliography - 3. Taking notes - 4. Composing the paper - 5. The final version - 6. Specimen paper - 7. Some errors to avoid - 8. Publication in a learned journal. Appendix: American Psychological Association guidelines for non-sexist language. Specimen paper (p.65-98), well-annotated. Written from the British perspective, a good alternative to the many US guides. *Class No:* 001.891

[2]
MANN, T. **A Guide to library research methods.** New York and Oxford, Oxford Univ. Press, 1987. xiv,199p. illus. ISBN: 0195049438.
Contents: Initial overview - Encyclopedias - Subject headings and the card catalog - Systematic browsing and the use of the classification scheme - Subject headings and indexes to journals - Keyword searches - Citation searches - Higher level overviews: review articles - Published bibliographies - Computer searches - Locating material in other libraries - Talking to people - Hidden treasures: reference sources. A readable guide, of value as an introduction to research methods at all levels. The author is a librarian in the Main Reading Room of the Library of Congress. *Class No:* 001.891

Information Technology

[3]
Information sources in information technology. Haynes, D., ed.
London, Bowker-Saur, 1990. xiv,350p. (*Guides to information sources.*) ISBN: 0408032855.
Discursive treatment in 2 pts. I. 'Information sources by subject' has 8 chapters dealing with the topics considered to make up information technology (*e.g.* Input technologies; Software, computer languages and operating systems; Transmission of information). II. 'Sources of information' comprises 11 chapters on forms of information (*e.g.* Machine-readable sources; Trade statistics and market information; Periodicals and conferences). Index p.335-50. Rather chaotically organized. Part II contains much discussion of general sources with little apparent direct relevance to information technology. Does not form the incisive account the field requires. *Class No:* 002:60

[4]
LONGLEY, D. *and* SHAIN, M. **Macmillan dictionary of information technology.** 3rd ed. London, Macmillan, 1989. viii,566p. illus. ISBN: 0333449711.
1st ed. 1982; 2nd ed. 1985.
Adds 1,800 entries to the 2nd ed., bringing the total to 7,800. Coverage: data processing; communications; office systems; information systems; microelectronics; graphics; printing; consumer electronics. Entries generally short (*e.g.* 'compact disc', *c.*90 words; 'digital switching' *c.*30 words), but some extended definitions for major topics (*e.g.* 'local area networks', *c.*450 words with 2 diagrams). Carefully cross-referenced. Becoming established as a standard source of reference in the field. *Class No:* 002:60

Online Information Systems

[5]
COX, J. **Keyguide to information sources in online and CD-ROM database searching.** London, Mansell, 1991. xxiv,247p. ISBN: 0720120934.
Guide to the literature, reference aids and organizational sources of information about online and CD-ROM searching. In 3 main sections. I, 'Survey of information sources ...', contains 5 chapters identifying and evaluating the literature. Confined to general material, items such as host manuals and guides to individual databases excluded. II, 'Bibliography' (p.112-221), has 450 briefly annotated entries in 14 sections including Directories of online databases, End users, Microcomputer hardware and software, Search techniques and Telecommunications. III, 'Directory of organizations', lists 158 online hosts, CD-ROM publishers, advisory and membership organizations, etc. Index (p.235-47); glossary. The first such guide in the field, well-organized and presented. *Class No:* 002.0

[6]
Directory of online databases. Detroit, Cuadra/Gale, 1979-. Semi-annual. ISSN: 01936840.
Annual subscription previously comprised two directory issues and two interim supplements limited to new and revised information. From 1991 published by Gale, apparently on a semi-annual basis, each issue containing full information.
V.12(3 & 4), July 1991 (xi,910p.) has 4,498 entries describing 5,026 publicly available databases and distinctly named files available from 731 hosts worldwide. Information for each database includes type (*e.g.* numeric), subject, producer, online service, conditions, content, language, coverage, time span and updating frequency. Indexes: subject; vendor geographic (list of vendors by country); producer; online service/gateway; telecommunications; master (databases, producers, online services, gateways). Accessible online through Data-Star, ORBIT and Questel. The detailed database descriptions and international coverage make this the best directory of online databases available. *Class No:* 002.0

[7]
Information industry directory. Detroit, Gale, 1971-. Annual. ISSN: 10516239.

Subtitled *A Comprehensive international descriptive guide to more than 4,500 organizations, systems and services involved in the production and distribution of information in electronic form.*

Present title from 11th ed. 1991, formerly *Encyclopedia of information systems and services*. Published annually since 1987. Until 10th ed. issued in separate US and international volumes. Also available on diskette and magnetic tape.

Coverage includes databases and their producers, CD-ROM products and services, vendors, gateways and networks, library networks and management systems, information retrieval firms, associations, research organizations, publishers and consultants. 4,558 actual entries of variable length in v.1 of 1991 ed., (*e.g.* 'C.A.B. International', *c.*900 words, main headings: staff, related organizations, description, scope, input, holdings, publications, computer based products and services, contacts; 'R.H. Blackwell', *c.*250 words). V.2 comprises 8 main indexes: Master; Databases; Publications/microforms; Software; Function/service (23 sub sections: Abstracting and indexing ... Database producers and publishers ... Library and information networks ... Optical publishing applications); Personal name; Geographic; Subject. US based entries predominate, but geographic coverage extends to 70 countries, UK well represented. The most comprehensive source in the field, enhanced by the thorough indexing. *Class No:* 002.0

[8]
Manual of online search strategies. Armstrong, C.J. *and* Large, J.A., *eds.* Aldershot, Gower, 1988. xv,831p. tables, diagrs. ISBN: 0566050587.

Aimed at the reasonably experienced database searcher seeking information on databases in unfamiliar subject areas. 19 chapters, 16 subject based (*e.g.* 5. Biological sciences; 9. Engineering; 12. Law-British and European legal systems). Initial chapter on general aspects of search strategy, chapters 16-19 on databases for home use, quick reference and electronic journals. Frequent use of examples, drawn from a wide range of databases. Appendices: 1. Databases and their hosts; 2. A selective list of directories, bibliographies and reference works. Indexed. A 'vade mecum for anyone interested in information sources and resources' (*Program*, v.23(1), January 1989, p.108). *Class No:* 002.0

[9]
UNITED KINGDOM ONLINE USER GROUP. UKOLUG quick guide to online commands. Webber, S. *and* Baile, C., *comps.* 3rd ed. London, UKOLUG, 1991. ix,82p. ISBN: 1870254058.

1st ed. 1987; 2nd ed. 1989.

Covers 33 commands from the following hosts: BLAISE-Line, BLAISE-Link/MEDLARS, BRS, Data-Star, Dialog, DIMIDI, ECHO, ESA-IRS, FIZ Technik, FT PROFILE, Kompass Online, NEXIS, ORBIT, PFDS (Pergamon Financial Data Services), Questel, STN International, TEXTLINE, TOXNET, Wilsonline. Not intended to replace host documentation but nonetheless "invaluable for regular searchers" (*Current awareness bulletin* (Aslib), v.8(7), September, 1991, p.365). *Class No:* 002.0

CD-Rom Information Systems

[10]
CD-ROM: a practical guide for information professionals. Gunn, A. *and* Moore, C., *eds.* London, Library Information Technology Centre and UK Online User Group, 1991. 50p. ISBN: 0951241230.

Basic 9 chapter guide aimed at librarians and others with no experience of CD-ROM. Concentrates on the practical aspects of setting up and operating CD-ROM technology; does not evaluate individual products or list suppliers, hardware, etc. Brief bibliography p.45-46. Index. 'For an information professional needing to 'gen up' quickly this is both an excellent starting point and a useful signpost to further publications" (*Aslib information*, v.19(4), April 1991, p.145). *Class No:* 002.00

[11]
The CD-ROM directory. 1986/87-. London, Task Force Pro Libra Publishing, 1986-. Annual.

1st ed. as *The International directory of information products on CD-ROM.*

The main section of the 5th ed. for 1991 (1990. 606p.) lists 1,532 CD-ROM products by title. Standard information, *e.g.* publisher, information provider, subject, description, hardware requirements, updates, price. Includes information on products in preparation. Further section, Company information, providing brief details of 1,840 businesses involved in the CD-ROM industry. Other sections: CD-ROM drives; Conferences and exhibitions; Books; Journals. Various indexes including subject, software and geographic. Also available as a CD-ROM disc. Wider in scope than the other CD-ROM directories and especially valuable in the UK. *Class No:* 002.00

[12]
CD-ROMs in print: an international guide. Westport, Conn., Meckler, 1987-. Annual. ISSN: 08918198.

The 1991 ed. (Desmarais, N. comp. xxiv,450p.) has over 1,400 entries for commercially available CD-ROMs A-Z by title. Information given includes provider/publisher/distributor, hardware/software, update frequency, time span, subject scope, printed equivalent and brief general description. Comprehensively indexed by data provider, publisher, distributor (US and non-US), software provider and subject. Good international coverage and reasonably priced. Probably the best all round source for those requiring basic information on the availability of CD-ROMs. *Class No:* 002.00

[13]
Directory of portable databases. New York, Cuadra/Gale, 1990-. Semi-annual. ISSN: 10458352.

Companion publication to *Directory of online databases* (*q.v.*).

Portable databases defined as those available on CD-ROM, diskette or magnetic tape. Separate sequences for each media, 958, 541 and 417 entries respectively in v.3(1), April 1991, (xiv,788p.). Each issue contains completely revised information including vendor, format, system requirements, software, price, description of contents, language, coverage, time span and updating frequency. Indexes: subject; database provider; vendor; online equivalent; printed or other equivalent; master. *Class No:* 002.00

[14]
ENSOR, P. CD-ROM research collections: an evaluative guide to bibliographic and full-text CD-ROM databases. Westport, Conn., Meckler, 1991. ix,302p. (*Supplements to computers in libraries.*) ISBN: 0887367798.

Covers 114 periodically updated CD-ROM databases. Numeric and directory CD-ROMs excluded. Entries, A-Z,

....(contd.)

average 2½p. with the heading scope and content often accounting for half the length. Further information includes publisher, equipment and software requirements, price, arrangement and control, search software and capabilities and print/online/other media counterparts. Many entries cite and draw on published reviews. Broad term subject and publisher/producer indexes; list of publishers with addresses. A valuable source, covering most of the major CD-ROM databases found in general libraries in greater depth than in directory publications such as the same publisher's *CD-ROMs in print* (*q.v.*). Further editions are planned. *Class No:* 002.00

Scripts, Symbols, etc.

Transliteration

[15]
BRITISH STANDARDS INSTITUTION. Transliteration of Cyrillic and Greek characters. London, B.S.I., 1958. 24p. (*BS:2979.*)

Section 1: British traditional-type system, Table A Cyrillic-to-English transliteration, Table B English-to-Cyrillic; Section 2: International system for modern Cyrillic, Table C Cyrillic-to-Latin, Tables D and E for Church Slavonic and Rumanian Cyrillic, Table F back-transliteration (Latin-to-Cyrillic, for tables C, D and E); Section 3: rule-of-thumb system for Greek, without regard to phonetic peculiarities of Ancient or Modern Greek, in line with international practice.

Other British Standards concerning transliteration are: *Transliteration of Arabic characters* (BS 4280:1968); *Specifications for the romanization of Japanese* (BS 4812:1972); *Guide to the romanization of Chinese* (BS 7014:1989), giving description and comparison of existing systems especialy Wades-Giles and Pinyin; *Guide to the romanization of Korean* (PD 6505:1982). *Class No:* 003.034

Abbreviations

[16]
Acronyms, initialisms & abbreviations dictionary. Detroit, Gale, 1960-. Annual. ISSN: 02704404.

First published 1960 as *Acronyms dictionary*, then issued on an irregular basis. Now published annually in 3v., each available for separate purchase.

Covers 'aerospace, associations, banking, biochemistry, business, data processing, domestic and international affairs, economics, education, electronics, genetics, government, information technology, investments, labor, law, medicine, military affairs, periodicals, pharmacy, physiology, politics, religion, science, societies, sports, technical drawings and specifications, telecommunications, trade, transportation and other fields' (subtitle, 15th ed. 1991). Main section (v.1, issued in 3 pts.), has definitions for over 500,000 acronyms, etc. (increase of 25,000 over the 14th ed) While the emphasis is on terms associated with the US, numerous terms of foreign origin likely to be encountered by Americans are also included. The remaining components of the 3v. set are *Reverse acronyms, initialisms and abbreviations* (publ. as v.3, also in 3 pts.), presenting the same terms as in v.1, but arranged alphabetically by complete word or phrase with the acronym as the definition, and *New acronyms, initialisms and abbreviations* (v.2), an inter-edition supplement usually containing c.12-15,000 new entries. *Class No:* 003.083

[17]
BUTTRESS, F.A. World guide to abbreviations of organizations. Heaney, H.J., *ed.* 9th ed. Glasgow, Blackie, 1991. 875p. ISBN: 0216930472.

....(contd.)

1st ed. 1954; 8th ed. 1988.

Well over 50,000 entries, 20% revised since the previous ed. Scope extends across the whole range of human activity, including commerce, industry, administration, education, journalism, politics, technology, medicine and recreation. Especially strong on the EEC and member states; improved coverage for Eastern Europe. Features include cross-referencing between acronyms of identical organizations in different languages (*e.g.* NATO=OTAN), bracketed addition of acronyms of parent bodies to entries for subsidiary organizations and, new to this ed., cross-referencing between defunct organizations and their successors. A major abbreviations dictionary, regularly updated. *Class No:* 003.083

[18]
DE SOLA, R. Abbreviations dictionary. 7th augm. international ed. New York, Elsevier, 1986. xviii,1240p. ISBN: 0444008071.

1st ed. 1958; 6th ed. 1981.

Over 23,000 new and augmented entries in this ed., bringing the total to over 250,000. Main body of the dictionary (p.1-1029) includes abbreviations, acronyms, appellations, computer technology, contractions, eponyms, government agencies, initialisms, nicknames, signs and symbols and slang. Some entries add brief definitions (e.g. Defense et Sécurité du Territoire (French equivalent of FBI)). A further 48 supplementary sections (p.1030-240) group abbreviations by subject (*e.g.* airlines, British counties, international vehicle licence letters, zodiacal signs). The only source to approach the Gale dictionaries and Wennrich (below) in breadth of coverage, and the better buy if cost rather than currency is the major consideration. *Class No:* 003.083

[19]
International encyclopedia of abbreviations and acronyms of organizations. [Internationale Enzyklopädie der Abkürzungen und Akronyme von Organisationen.] Wennrich, P. *and* Spiller, P., *eds.* 3rd rev. & enl. ed. München, Saur, 1990-. (*Handbook of technical documentation and bibliography,* v.9.) ISBN: 3598221606.

First published 1968 as *Internationales Verzeichnis von Abkürzungen von Verbänden Behörden und Organisationen.* 2nd ed. in 3v. 1970-72 as *Internationales Wörterbuch der Abkürzungen von Organisationen.* This ed. to be completed in 6v.

When complete will contain 'nearly half a million abbreviations of names, organizations, confederations, clubs, government offices, universities, and other teaching and research establishments as well as diverse other types of institutions. Where it was deemed appropriate, technical abbreviations which do not necessarily refer to an organization or an institution have also been included' (Preface p.vii, v.1). Limited to languages using the Roman alphabet. Includes common vernacular abbreviations in general use and historical abbreviations. Entries in one A-Z sequence give expansion with code indicating the area or sphere (*e.g.* country, language, etc.) in which the abbreviation is used. The only source to seriously rival the Gale dictionaries in terms of size. *Class No:* 003.083

[20]
PAXTON, J. The Penguin dictionary of abbreviations. Harmondsworth, Penguin, 1989. 385p. ISBN: 0140512292.

First published as *Everyman's dictionary of abbreviations* by Dent 1974. Rev. eds. 1981, 1983, 1986.

About 27,000 entries with over 37,000 definitions. Abbreviation followed by definition and English translation if foreign. Occasional entries supplemented by a phrase or sentence of explanation or subject reference (*e.g.* chem

....*(contd.)*
(chemistry)). Cross-references to related entries. British and Commonwealth slant. Some unique entries. *Class No:* 003.083

Standards

[21]
BRITISH STANDARDS INSTITUTION. BSI standards catalogue. Milton Keynes, British Standards Institution, 1984-. Annual. ISSN: 09530339.

Continues *British Standards yearbook*, 1937-83 (ISSN 00682578).

The 1990 ed. (xvi,610p.) lists BSI publications current at 31 December 1989 and gives a brief description of each. Arranged in numerical order within series: General series (prefix BS, p.1-361) ... Automobile series - Marine series - Aerospace series ... Drafts for development, etc. Detailed analytical index (p.454-610) of *c.*7,000 headwords. 'Sets of British Standards in the United Kingdom' (p.xi-xvi); 'Corresponding International/British Standards' (p.437-53). Also available online as *BSI standardline* through Pergamon Financial Data Services.

The monthly *BSI news* records new British standards as well as revisions and amendments. *Class No:* 006

The Humanities

[22]
Arts and humanities citation index. 1976-. Philadelphia, Institute for Scientific Information, 1978-. Semi-annual. ISSN: 01628445.

Companion publication to *Science citation index* and *Social sciences citation index.* Now published semi-annually in 3v.: v.1 Citation index. Guide to lists of source publications; v.2 Source index. Corporate index; v.3 Permuterm subject index.

Covers archaeology, architecture, art, Asian studies, classics, dance, film, TV and radio, folklore, history, language and linguistics, literature, music, philosophy, theatre, theology and religious studies. 6,100 journals indexed, approx. 1,000 fully, 5,100 selectively. The source index comprises an author index giving full reference, author's address (where available), language, selected key terms (where not obvious from the title) and brief bibliographical descriptions of all works cited in footnotes or bibliographies. The citation index is an alphabetical list by author of the cited items; the permuterm subject index covers every significant English word in the title of source items; the corporate index has geographic and organization sections. Wide coverage, but small type, difficult for the uninitiated to use and expensive. Also available online through Dialog (File 439) and BRS, updated every two weeks. *Class No:* 009

[23]
BLAZEK, R. *and* **AVERSA, E.S. The Humanities: a selective guide to information sources.** 3rd ed. Englewood, Colo., Libraries Unlimited, 1988. xvii,382p. (*Library science text series.*) ISBN: 087287558x.

First published 1974; 2nd ed., by A.R. Rogers, 1979.

Covers philosophy, religion, mythology and folklore, visual arts, performing arts and language and literature. Comparative and evaluative notes on 973 sources in even numbered chapters. Briefer odd numbered chapters 'relate to accessing information' in each discipline (*e.g.* computer sources, major organizations etc.). Some areas (*e.g.* Italian literature with only one entry) given cursory treatment. Author/title index to the source chapters; Subject index. Overall 'upholds the fine traditions and standards of its predecessors' (*RQ,* v.28(2), Winter 1986, p.275). A useful introduction to research in the humanities, but with a US slant. *Class No:* 009

[24]
Current research in Britain. The humanities. 4th ed. Boston Spa, British Library Document Supply Centre, 1991. xvi,447p. ISBN: 0712320865.

Published biennially, 1st ed. 1985. Companion volumes *Biological sciences, Physical sciences* and *Social sciences* published annually. *Current research in Britain* replaces *Research in British universities, polytechnics and colleges (RBUPC).*

Contains submissions from 621 academic departments and other bodies in sections for universities, polytechnics, colleges and museums and other institutions. For each research project gives name(s) of researcher(s), description of topic, start and estimated conclusion dates, sponsoring bodies (if any) and proposed form of publication. Compiled from information collected in late 1990. Indexed by researcher's name, study area and keyword. Also available online as part of the *Current research in Britain* database through Pergamon Financial Data Services. *Class No:* 009

01 Bibliography & Bibliographies

Bibliography

[25]

ESDAILE, A. Esdaile's manual of bibliography. Stokes, R., *rev. & ed.* 5th rev. ed. Metuchen, N.J., Scarecrow, 1981. x,397p. illus., plates. ISBN: 0810814625.

First published 1931; 4th ed. 1967.

Sets out to teach the first elements of bibliography. 10 chapters: 1. The nature of bibliography - 2. The parts of a book -3. Landmarks in the development of the book - 4. Papyrus, parchment, vellum, paper - 5. Typography - 6. Composition and press work -7. Illustration - 8. Binding - 9. The collation of books - 10. The description of books. References at chapter ends. Glossary p.382-90. Index. An established and authoritative text. *Class No:* 01.0

[26]

STOKES, R. A Bibliographical companion. Metuchen, N.J. and London, Scarecrow Press, 1989. x,298p. ISBN: 0810821753.

A glossary of bibliographical terms intended for the student rather than the experienced bibliographer. Fills the gap between Carter's *ABC for book collectors*, with its emphasis on book collecting, and Glaister's *Glossary of the book,* with its concentration on book production. Around 600 well-written entries averaging 300 words in length. Omits entries for prominent bibliographies. Exhaustively cross-referenced. *Class No:* 01.0

Bibliographies

Bibliographies of Bibliographies

[27]

BESTERMAN, T. A World bibliography of bibliographies and of bibliographical catalogues, calendars, abstracts, digests, indexes and the like. 4th ed., rev. and greatly enl. throughout. Lausanne, Societas Bibliographica, 1965-66. 4v. and index.

First published 1939-40 (2v.); 3rd ed. 1955-56 (4v.).

Records over 117,000 separately collated volumes of bibliographies in more than 40 languages, published up to 1963 or 1964. Arranged by subjects A-Z under more than 16,000 headings. Excludes general library catalogues, but admits patent abridgements and lists of manuscripts. Cited material not described, but the estimated number of items listed in each volume is normally stated as an 'alternative to critical annotation'. Occasional bibliographical notes (*e.g.* number of copies printed). The entries under 'Education' (v.2, cols. 1825-1914) have 32 sub-headings; one of these 'Teaching of specific subjects' deals with 45 subjects A-Z. Author, editor, etc. and anonymous title index. A monumental compilation by a single bibliographer, which is unlikely to be surpassed. Note must, however, be made of the objectionable style of entry of authors' names, with forenames preceding surnames (all in capitals), a feature

....(contd.)

which does not make for rapid location. Further points are the absence of publishers from entries and the lack of full coverage for Oriental and Slavic items. *Class No:* 011/015(009)

[28]

—A World bibliography of bibliographies 1964-1974: a list of works represented by Library of Congress printed catalog cards: a decennial supplement to Theodore Besterman, *A World bibliography of bibliographies.* Toomey, A.F., *comp.* Totowa, N.J., Rowmann & Littlefield, 1977. 2v. ISBN: 0874719992.

18,000 titles under 6,000 headings based on Library of Congress subject headings (8th ed.). Includes reprints of pre-1964 titles and continuation volumes. All are separately published titles, apart from some offprints. Excludes lists of sound recordings (except for the blind), lists of works of art, stamp collections, film catalogues and periodical indexes. Additional information to that given on the cards for many entries (*e.g.* references to earlier eds. or related publications). 1,400 references; author/title index. *Class No:* 011/015(009)

[29]

Bibliographic index: a cumulative bibliography of bibliographies. 1937-. New York, Wilson, 1938-. 3pa., final issue bound cumulation. ISSN: 00061255.

Annual cumulations since 1969: earlier cumulations 1937/42, 1943/46, 1947/50, 1951/55, 1956/59, 1960/62, 1963/65 and 1966/68.

Subject list of bibliographies published separately or appearing as part of books, pamphlets and periodicals. To be included bibliographies must contain 50 or more citations. Concentrates on English language material, although Germanic and Romance languages are also represented. Particularly strong on bibliographies appearing in periodicals, 2,800 titles examined on a regular basis. No author index. Of 'recognized excellence and depth that fills a bibliographic need not covered by other publications' (*American reference books annual,* v.19, 1988, p.36). Also available online through Wilsonline for records 1984 to date. *Class No:* 011/015(009)

Translations

[30]

Index translationum: répertoire international des traductions. Paris, Unesco, 1932-. Annual. ISSN: 00736704.

English subtitle *International bibliography of translations.* 1932-40 issued quarterly, numbered as a separate series. New series covers from 1948 (1949-).

Entries arranged under country in which the translation was published (A-Z by French form of country name), then by the 10 major UDC classes. Gives author, title of translation, name of translator, imprint and collation,

....(contd.)

language in which originally written and original title (italics). Author index; statistical summary by countries and UDC classes. V.37 for 1984 (1989. xii,1099p.) catalogues 52,405 translations published in 53 countries. The standard source for general translations. *Class No:* 013

[31]
Journals in translation. 5th ed. Boston Spa, British Library Document Supply Centre; Delft, International Translations Centre, 1991. viii,286p. ISBN: 0712320733.

1st ed. 1976. 4th ed. 1988.

List of journals A-Z (p.1-146, 1,352 titles) giving translated title, original title, date translation began, frequency, additional details, publisher of translation and whether held by BLDSC or SRIS. Indexed by title keyword and original title. Key to publishes/distributors with addresses. Includes both cover-to-cover translations and journals carrying translations of selected articles. Omits journals published simultaneously in two or more languages. Nearly all translations are into English. *Class No:* 013

Anonyma & Pseudonyma

[32]
HALKETT, S. *and* **LAING, J. Dictionary of anonymous and pseudonymous English literature.** Kennedy, J., *and others.* New ed. Edinburgh, Oliver and Boyd, 1926-62. 9v.

First published 1882-88 in 4v. V.1-7 reprinted New York, Haskell, 1971. ISBN 0838312454. $490.

The main work (v.1-7, published 1926-34) is arranged A-Z by title. Entries (*c.*70,000) indicate size, pagination, place, date, and authors' names, and sometimes give authorities for its attributions, although usually in such general terms as 'B.M. Catalogue'. V.6 includes the first supplement; v.7 has indexes of pseudonyms and real names, plus a short second suppt.

V.8-9 (17,000 entries) list new material, 1900-50, plus corrigenda, and cover a rather wider field than English literature. Arranged as in the main work; index of authors and index of initials, pseudonyma, etc., in both volumes.

V.1 of a 3rd ed. was published 1980 (*A Dictionary of anonymous and pseudonymous publications in the English language,* Horden, J. ed., Longman, ISBN 0582555213) covering 1475-1640. No further volumes are now planned. *Class No:* 014.1

[33]
Handbook of pseudonyms and personal nicknames. Sharp, H.S., *comp.* Metuchen, N.J., Scarecrow Press, 1972-82. 2v. plus 2 supplements in 3v.

Original work published 1972 in 2v. (1104p. 0810804603). First supplement, 1975, 2v. (1395p. 0810808072). Second supplement, 1982, (289p. 0810815397).

The original volumes list *c.*15,000 real names and *c.*25,000 nicknames and/or pseudonyms with birth and death dates and brief descriptions. Mostly for the western world, living persons included. 'More comprehensive than other similar guides' (*Wilson library bulletin,* v.47(8), April 1973, p.703).

The First supplement adds a further *c.*18,000 real names and *c.*30,000 nicknames and/or pseudonyms. The much smaller Second supplement adds another *c.*7000 and *c.*10,000 entries respectively. 'No one is likely to supersede this tremendously useful compilation' (*American notes and queries,* v.14(5), January 1979, p.80). *Class No:* 014.1

[34]
Pseudonyms and nicknames dictionary: a guide to 80,000 aliases, assumed names, code names, cognomens, cover names, epithets, initialisms, nicknames, noms de guerre, noms de plume, pen names, pseudonyms, sobriquets and

....(contd.)

stage names of 55,000 contemporary and historical persons, including the subjects' real names, basic biographical information and citations from which the entries were compiled. Mossman, J., *ed.* 3rd ed. Detroit, Gale, 1987. 2v. ISBN: 0810305410.

1st ed. 1980. 2nd ed. 1982.

Predominant categories are authors and entertainers. Others include athletes, criminals, journalists, military leaders, and politicians. One A-Z sequence with main entries giving real names, dates, identification codes (8 maximum), nationality, occupation and assumed name(s) and assumed name entries referring to main entries. List of *c.*275 bibliographical sources including who's whos and subject encyclopedias, but not the British Library or Library of Congress catalogues. Coverage increased by 32% in this edition making this one of the largest works of its kind. Only derivatives of given names, initials that replace names and middle names used as pseudonyms are excluded. Many entries are for very obscure and difficult to trace people.

Supplement *New pseudonyms and nicknames* (1988. 306p. ISBN 0810305485), provides coverage of 9,000 additional pseudonyms and nicknames. *Class No:* 014.1

[35]
ROOM, A. A Dictionary of pseudonyms and their origins, with stories of name changes. Chicago and London, St. James Press, 1989. viii,342p. ISBN: 1558620532.

Originally published in the US by MacFarland, ISBN 0899504507. 2nd ed. of the same author's *Naming names: stories of pseudonyms and name changes...* (London, Routledge and Kegan Paul, 1981).

Main section (p.68-323) comprises A-Z list of about 4,000 pseudonyms giving real name, dates, country of origin, profession and 10-100 word notes. 7 introductory chapters; 3 appendices, including a list of 250 real names commonly considered to be assumed names. *Class No:* 014.1

National Bibliographies

Bibliographies

[36]
BELL, B.L. An Annotated guide to current national bibliographies. Alexandria Va., Chadwyck-Healey, 1986. xxvi, 407p. (*Government documents bibliographies.*) ISBN: 0859641236.

Earlier ed. as *Annotated guide to national bibliographies* ed. R.I. Korman, New York, Meckler, 1982.

Lists national bibliographies by country A-Z. Annotated entries giving information under heads; title, compiler, scope and coverage, contents, cataloguing rules and classifiction scheme, entry information, arrangement, indexes, notes and comments, promptness received/currency, availability from, footnotes and selected articles. Also lists regional bibliographies in separate section. Extensive bibliography on national bibliography p.358-401. A comprehensive and detailed guide, although some inconsistencies of treatment detected by *Journal of documentation* v.44(1) 1988 p.71-73. *Class No:* 015(01)

[37]
Inventaire général des bibliographies nationales rétrospectives. [Retrospective national bibliographies an international directory.] Beaudiquez, M., *ed.* München, Saur, 1986. 189p. (*IFLA publications, 35.*) ISBN: 3598203993.

Arrangement A-Z by country. For each provides brief introduction describing publishing and bibliographic situation followed by chronological listing of bibliographies. Entries give type of bibliography, full bibliographic citation and annotations indicating sources, scope, compilation

....(contd.)

mode and types of documents listed. Author and anonymous title index. Most entries in English, a few in French and German. Does not cover Soviet Bloc countries. "Fills a basic gap in the ability to gain access to retrospective bibliographic material" (*American reference books annual* 1987 p.5). *Class No:* 015(01)

Worldwide

English

[38]
Books in English. London, British Library Bibliographic Services, 1971-. 6pa. ISSN: 00452572.

Microfiche service produced every two months, each issue cumulative, with a final annual cumulation. Further cumulations available for 1971-80 (578 fiche) and 1981-85 (289 fiche).

Computer produced from records for English language titles created by the British Library and Library of Congress. All entries catalogued according to AACR2 with Dewey class nos. and Library of Congress subject data. 1971-80 cumulation contains more than 1,100,000 records, 1981-85 over 500,000 records. Useful for bibliographical checking and as a cataloguing aid. *Class No:* 015(100)=20

[39]
International books in print: English-language titles published in Africa, Asia, Australia, Canada, Continental Europe, Latin America, New Zealand, Oceania and Republic of Ireland. München, Saur, 1979-. Annual (initially irregular). ISSN: 01709348.

10th ed. (1991) published in 2 parts in 4 volumes: Pt.1 *Author title list*; Pt.2 *Subject guide* (first published 1983).

Covers currently available English language titles published outside the US and UK. The 10th ed. lists c.210,000 items available from 6,157 publishers. Includes works of fiction, microforms and some other non-book materials. Most publications under 32p., periodicals, school textbooks, musical scores and maps excluded. Author/title section contains a list of publishers/distributors. Subject section, arranged by broad Dewey class numbers, includes a 'Country index' and 'Index of persons as subjects'. Also available as a CD-ROM database updated annually. A useful one-stop source, but far from comprehensive. Other sources (e.g. *Canadian books in print, Indian books in print* (*qq.v.*)) give fuller coverage for individual countries. *Class No:* 015(100)=20

Great Britain

16th & 17th Centuries

[40]
POLLARD, A.W. *and* **REDGRAVE, G.R.** A Short-title catalogue of books printed in England, Scotland and Ireland: and of English books printed abroad 1475-1640. Pantzer, K.F., *and others comps.* 2nd ed. London, Bibliographical Society, 1976-1991. 3v. ISBN: 0197217907.

Begun by W.A. Jackson and F.S. Ferguson, completed by K.F. Pantzer. V.1 A-H (1986. iii,620p.); v.2 I-Z (1976. xi,494p.); v.3 *A printers and publishers index, other indexes and appendices, cumulative addenda and corrigenda, with a chronological index.* (1991. xix,405p.). First published 1926 in 1v., reprinted 1950.

An author list of c.37,000 items (1st ed. 26,500) including books in other British languages and books in which English is on a par with other languauges. Excludes works by English authors printed outside England which are not in English. Entries follow the format of the 1st ed., but with more expansive transcriptions of titles and fuller notes and cross-references. 'S.T.C.' numbering system retained

....(contd.)

unchanged, many interpolations for new and moved items. Nearly 500 library locations (1st ed. 148); 'up to five on each side [of the Atlantic] have been listed with a view to geographical distribution' (Locations). V.1 contains a detailed introduction (p.xix-xliii). V.3 provides comprehensive indexing, etc. Contents: Index 1. Printers and publishers, A-Z (p.1-193), with supplementary lists (*e.g.* Patrons/publishers; Patentees) and 6 appendices; Index 2. Places other than London (subdivided British Isles and Colonies; The Continent; Fictitious places); Index 3. Selected London indexes; Index 4. Anomalous imprints; Cumulative addenda and corrigenda (p.261-318); Concordances: Bosanquet, Duff, Gregg; Chronological index (p.325-405). The primary source for bibliographical information on early English books and a model catalogue of its kind. *Class No:* 015(410)"15/16"

17th Century

[41]
Short-title catalogue of books printed in England, Scotland, Ireland, Wales and British America and of English books printed in other countries 1641-1700. Wing, D.G., *comp.* 2nd rev. & enl. ed. New York, Index Committee of the Modern Language Association of America, 1972-88. 3v.

V.1: A1-E2926 (1972. xx,622p. ISBN 0873520440); v.2: E2927-01000 (1982. xvii,690p. ISBN 0873520459); v.3: P1-Z28 (1988. xxvii,766p. ISBN 0873520467).

First published in 3v. 1945-51. Various independent supplements were published to the 1st ed. These included Morrison, P.G. *Index of printers, publishers, and booksellers in Donald Wing's 'Short-title catalogue'* ... (Charlottesville, Bibliographical Society of the Univ. of Virginia, 1955. 217p); Hiscock, W.G. *The Christ Church holdings in Wing's 'Short-title catalogue, 1641-1700'* ... ([Oxford], Christ Church, 1965); Wolf, E. *A Checklist of books in the Library Company of Philadelphia in and supplementary to Wing's 'Short-title catalogue, 1641-1700'* (Philadelphia, 1959. viii,106p.).

Continues Pollard and Redgrave's *Short title catalogue ... 1475-1600* (above). About 120,000 entries (up from 50,000 in 1st ed.) structured on the basis of author, short title, edition statement, imprint, date, format and occasionally pagination. Excludes works by English authors printed in other languages and serially published items (now covered by *British newspapers and periodicals 1641-1700*). Up to 5 UK and 5 North American locations given for each item; overall number of library locations drastically increased in this ed. to well over 500. V.1 differs from v.2-3 in that 7-8% of the numbers from the 1st ed. ('Wing nos.') were reassigned. This practice, which shattered an established bibliographical reference system, was widely criticised and not continued. V.2 contains 'A list of changes in entry numbering from the first to the second edition of volume 1 of the Wing short-title catalogue' as an appendix (p.669-90). Overall, this ed. is a great improvement over the 1st which contained many omissions and errors. Even so 'Wing is in its present form a bibliographical patchwork ... trapped in an obsolete technology. It still hovers uneasily between STC ... and ESTC' (*Times literary supplement*, no.4159, 17th December, 1982, p.1403). V.1 of this ed. continues to contain a number of errors and a revised version is anticipated. *Class No:* 015(410)"16"

18th Century

[42]
Eighteenth century short title catalogue. London, British Library. Computer database.

Available online via BLAISE-Line, file updated monthly, and on CD-ROM. Known as 'ESTC'

An ongoing project to produce records for all letterpress printed material published 1701-1800 in the British Isles and British colonies, plus that published elsewhere in English or in a British language (*e.g.* Welsh, Irish, etc.). Wide range of publications covered, including handbills and circulars, songs and ballads, sale catalogues, etc., but with newspaper and periodical parts and certain other materials excluded. Records derived from 500 participating organizations worldwide, compilation from editorial offices at the British Library and the University of Louisiana, Baton Rouge. Entries, based on AACR, include library locations. Searchable by author, title, imprint, locations, etc., but not subject (data not collected). 318,494 records September 1991. Information on progress and development provided by *Factotum: newsletter of the eighteenth century STC* (ISSN 01413635). *Class No:* 015(410)"17"

[43]
—The Eighteenth century short title catalogue 1990: microfiche edition. London, British Library, 1990. Microfiche.

Comprises 219 fiche (author/title catalogue, 182 fiche, date of publication index 18 fiche, place of publication index 12 fiche, supplementary indexes etc. remaining fiche). Accompanied by a 30p. pamphlet. Earlier ed. in 113 fiche, 1983.

Based on entries input to *ESTC*. About 284,000 records (150,000 1983), with over 1,000,000 locations in 1,000 libraries worldwide. A further microfiche ed. is scheduled for 1995. *Class No:* 015(410)"17"

19th Century

[44]
Nineteenth century short title catalogue: extracted from the catalogues of the Bodleian Library, the British Library, Harvard University Library, the Library of Congress, the Library of Trinity College Dublin, the National Library of Scotland and the university libraries of Cambridge and Newcastle. Newcastle-upon-Tyne, Avero, 1984-. ISBN: 0907977103, Phase 1. 0907977329, Phase 2.

To be published in 3 series: Series I. Phase I. 1801-1815 (1984-85. 5v. (v.1-4 A-Z; v.5. *England, Ireland, Scotland, London, directories, ephemerides & periodical publications. Title index, First supplement cumulative imprint and subject indexes to volumes 1-4*)); Series II. Phase I. 1816-1870. (1986-, projected for 50v., publication reached v.24 *Lecon-Lorc* in 1991); Series III to cover 1871-1918.

An immense project which 'aims to provide an increasingly complete listing of books printed between 1801 and 1918 in order of authors, subjects, places of imprint, titles and date of publication. British books are taken to include all books published in Britain, its colonies and the United States of America; all books in English wherever published and all translations from English' (Introduction, Series II). Based on library catalogues, Series I excludes the Library of Congress and Harvard University Library. Entries are in form and order of the British Museum (Library) catalogue (GK3), with alternative headings in parentheses and cross-references as necessary. Author statements include epithet and lifespan. Subject indexing based on Dewey, each entry including up to 3 class nos. In Series I imprint and subject indexes are provided in every volume; in Series II this practice is discontinued, with indexes included in every fifth volume. An admirable project, but some items are entered twice and use of the

....(contd.)
classification scheme is inconsistent. Thoroughly reviewed in the *Times literary supplement* (no.4227, 6 April 1984, p.381-82 and no.4388, 8 May 1987, p.497). *Class No:* 015(410)"18"

Contemporary

[45]
British national bibliography. Boston Spa, The British Library National Bibliographic Service, 1950-. Weekly, etc. ISSN: 00071544.

Known as 'BNB'. Cumulated indexes 1950/54, 1955/59, 1960/64, 1965/67, 1968/70, 1971/73; cumulated subject catalogues 1951/54, 1955/59, 1960/64, 1965/67, 1968/70.

Based on items received by the Legal Deposit Office of the British Library. Excludes periodicals (other than first issues or the first issue of a changed title), music (covered by *British catalogue of music* (*q.v.*)), maps and most government publications, especially those of a routine or specialized nature. Main listing in the form of a 'Classified subject catalogue', cataloguing by AACR2, arrangement by 20th Dewey. Bibliographical description cutback in recent years, modern English fiction, children's books, material with 32p. or less and works of religion, science and technology reduced to AACR2 level 1 standard. Cataloguing-in-publication introduced in 1977 and now used extensively. From 1991 the weekly issues include a separate CIP based 'Forthcoming titles' section, preceeding the main 'Titles currently received on legal deposit'. Author/title index, including series and names as subjects, in every issue, cumulated with a subject index, in the final issue for each month. Interim cumulations issued for January-April and May-August, with a final 2v. annual cumulation (also available in microfiche) as 'Subject catalogue' and 'Indexes'. Two microfiche cumulations are available: 1981-85 full cumulation containing 190,000 records; 1950-84 author/title cumulation containing 2,500,000 records, designed to support retrospective conversion and bibliographic checking. *BNB* is available online through BLAISE-Line as *BNBMARC*. A CD-ROM version was launched in 1988 in 3 discs: backfile 1950-85 (two discs 1950-76 and 1977-85); current file 1986-, updated quarterly. Since its inception in 1950 *BNB* has been the primary source for bibliographical information on British published books. Coverage is fuller than *Whitaker's book list*, especially in respect of non-trade items. *Class No:* 015(410)"312"

[46]
Whitaker's book list. London, Whitaker, 1924-. Annual. ISSN: 0953041X.

Current title from 1987, previously *Whitaker's cumulative book list* (ISSN 04104229). Frequency varies; cumulations published 1939/43, 1944/47, 1948/52, 1953/57, 1958/62, 1963/67, 1968/72 and 1973/75.

Aims to provide a full annual record of books published in the UK available for sale. Books published overseas also included if they have an English language text and are readily obtainable through the trade. Represents the final cumulation of the 'Publications of the week' section of *The Bookseller* (below). Entries, similar to *Whitaker's books in print*, in one A-Z sequence of authors, titles and subjects (where this forms part of the title). The 1990v. (xxxv,1430p.) lists 71,331 items. The 1980 v. in comparison listed 48,158 titles.

The 'Publications of the week' section in *The Bookseller* (London, Whitaker, 1858-. Weekly ISSN 00067539) is arranged according to 138 subject sections Agriculture ... Zoology from 1989, rather than in dictionary format as previously. Until December 1969 listings cumulated monthly; from January 1970 this function was assumed by *Whitaker's books of the month ...* (below). *Class No:* 015(410)"312"

[47]

—Whitaker's books of the month and books to come: books published this month and forthcoming books. London, Whitaker, 1970-. Monthly. ISSN: 00681350.

Based on the 'Publications of the week' section of *The Bookseller*, but also including details of books omitted from this listing, plus a large number of entries for books announced to appear during the following months. Same format as *Whitaker's book list*. Entries for forthcoming books preceded by a star symbol. A weekly microfiche version is also published as *Whitaker's weekly list*. *Class No: 015(410)"312"*

[48]

Whitaker's books in print: the reference catalogue of current literature. London, Whitaker, 1874-. Annual. ISSN: 09530398.

Title varies: *The Reference catalogue of current literature*, 1874-1961; *British books in print* 1965-87. From 1874-1932 issued at irregular intervals comprising publishers' catalogues bound together (A-Z by publisher), plus an index by author and title. Irregular publication continued 1936-61, but in the form of consolidated author and title lists. Annual publication under the title *British books in print* from 1967. Issued as a 4v. set from 1984.

Aims to record all books in print in the UK. From 1971 in one A-Z sequence of authors and titles, the former distinguished by bold type, with the addition of keyword subject entries where the subject forms part of the title or subtitle. Entries include detail such as names of editors/ revisors/translators, edition statement, number of pages, illustrations, size, binding and series. Coverage extends to children's books (also listed in the separately published *Children's books in print* (q.v.)), coded for reading ability, content and age range. List of publishers and their addresses and ISBN prefixes in v.1. The 1991 ed. contains details of 514,013 titles from 17,894 publishers.

Whitaker's books in print is also issued as a monthly microfiche service and is searchable online through BLAISE-Line and Dialog (File 430). A CD-ROM version, *Bookbank* was launched in 1988. A further CD-ROM product *Bookbank OP*, lists over 640,000 titles in the Whitaker database published 1970 or later but now out of print. An annually updated microfiche listing of out of print titles (covering from 1975) is also available. *Class No: 015(410)"312"*

Ireland

[49]

Irish publishing record. Dublin, National Library of Ireland, 1967-. Annual. ISSN: 05794056.

Before 1989 published by University College, Dublin.

The Irish national bibliography, covering material published in the Republic and Northern Ireland. Lists books, pamphlets, new serials, yearbooks, maps and musical scores, and reprints of titles first published before 1967. Arranged by Dewey broad classes with separate lists for serials, juvenile literature and school textbooks. The 1989 issue (1990, 203p.) has 1,114 entries including 103 serials, 29 juvenile books and 42 school textbooks. *Class No: 015(415)*

Germany

[50]

Deutsche Nationalbibliographie: und Bibliographie der im Ausland erschienenen deutschsprachigen Veröffentlichungen. Frankfurt am Main, Buchhandler-Vereinigung, 1991-. Weekly, etc.

Combines the pre-unification national bibliographies of the Federal Republic, *Deutsche Bibliographie*, and the Democratic Republic, *Deutsche Nationalbibliographie*.

....(contd.)

Deutsche Bibliographie, first published 1947 as *Bibliographie der deutschen Bibliothek*, main title from 1952, was issued in two main series on a weekly basis with monthly indexes and semi-annual and quinquennial cumulations. *Deutsche Nationalbibliographie*, also issued weekly, had quarterly and, from 1984, annual indexes and quinquennial cumulations (*Deutsches Bücherverzeichnis*). First published 1931 (preceded by *Wöchentliches Verzeichnis* 1842-1930), *Deutsche Nationalbibliographie* covered the whole of Germany until 1945 and continued to include publications from the Federal Republic, Austria and Switzerland in the post-war period, but not on a comprehensive basis. Although the new national bibliography has the title *Deutsche Nationalbibliographie*, in structure and scope it closely resembles *Deutsche Bibliographie* and is probably best regarded as its continuation.

The new *Deutsche Nationalbibliographie* is published in 3 main series: Reihe A *Monographien und Periodika des Verlagsbuchhandels - Wöchentliches Verzeichnis*. (Weekly. ISSN 09390421); Reihe B *Monographien und Periodika ausserhalb des Verlagsbuchhandels - Wöchentliches Verzeichnis*. (Weekly. ISSN 0939043x); Reihe C *Karten*. (Quarterly. ISSN 09390553).

Reihe A covers books, pamphlets (over 6p.), periodicals (new and ceased), government publications, audio-visual materials, etc., available through the book trade. Reihe B covers similar non-book trade materials. Reihe C is confined to maps. Both A and B are main entry listings in 65 main class groups. Combined indexes to A and B, giving access by author, title, subject, keyword, ISBN and publisher, issued weekly and monthly. Further component parts of the German national bibliography are Reihe H *Hochschulschriften* (Monthly), covering dissertations, Reihe M *Musikalien und Musikschriften* (Monthly) and Reihe N *Vorankündigungen Monographien und Periodika (CIP)* (Weekly), a CIP listing. *Deutsche Nationalbibliographie* is also available online, incorporating records from *Deutsche Bibliographie* back to 1966, as part of Biblio-data through STN International. A CD-ROM version, containing records from Reihe A,B,C,H and N and giving coverage from 1986, is issued quarterly. *Class No: 015(430)*

[51]

—Deutsche Nationalbibliographie: und Bibliographie der im Ausland erschienenen deutschsprachigen Veröffentlichungen. Reihe D. Monographien und Periodika - Halbjahrverzeichnis. Frankfurt am Main, Buchhandler-Vereiningung, 1991-. Semi-annual.

Effectively continues *Deutsche Bibliographie Halbjahres-Verzeichnis*, 1951-90.

A further series of the new *Deutsche Nationalbibliographie* mainly serving as a semi-annual cumulation of the entries in Reihe A and B. Publication is in 2 pts. *Alphabetisches Titelverzeichnis*, containing full bibliographic citation, and *Schlagwort- und Stichwortregister mit Systematishcer Übersicht der Schlagwörter*, providing subject and keyword indexing.

The final cumulation of *Deutsche Bibliographie*, which will presumably also be continued under the title *Deutsche Nationalbibliographie*, was *Deutsche Bibliographie. Fünfjahres-Verzeichnis*. First published for 1945/50 in 1953, the last cumulation for 1981/85 was published in 35v. 1987-89, the final 17v. comprising indexes. *Class No: 015(430)*

[52]

Verzeichnis lieferbarer Bücher. Bücherverzeichnis im Autorenalphabet kumuliert mit Titel- und Stichwortregister mit Verweisung auf den Autor. [German books in print.] Frankfurt am Main, Buchhändler-Vereiningung, 1971-. Annual. ISSN: 00678899.

....(contd.)

The 21st ed. (1991/92. 6v.) has 548,918 entries representing the output of 9,616 publishers in Germany, Austria, Switzerland and in the German language elsewhere. Arranged in a single alphabetical sequence of authors and anonymous titles, with title and keyword entries in italics. Publisher and ISBN prefix listings in the final volume. Updating half yearly supplement published between editions. A separate *Verzeichnis lieferbarer Bücher. ISBN-Register* is also available. *Class No:* 015(430)

[53]

—Verzeichnis lieferbarer Bücher. Schlagwort-Verzeichnis. [Subject guide to German books in print.] Frankfurt am Main, Buchhändler-Vereinigung, 1979-. Annual.

The companion subject set. Entries under very specific headings. A CD-ROM version of *Verzeichnis lieferbarer Bücher* is also available. *Class No:* 015(430)

France

[54]

Bibliographie nationale française: notices établies par la Bibliothèque Nationale à partir des documents déposés auprès du Service du dépôt légal. Paris, Bibliothèque Nationale, Office Général du Livre, 1976-. Semi-monthly, etc.

Title and publisher varies: until 1989 as *Bibliographie de la France* issued by Éditions du Cercle de la Librairie.

Continues the earlier series *Bibliographie de la France - Biblio* (1972-79), a product of the combination of *Bibliographie de la France: journal générale de l'imprimerie et de la librairie* (1811-1971) and *Biblio: catalogue des ouvrages parus en langue française dans le monde entier* (1933-71).

Published in 5 series. The main series *Livres* is now issued every 15 days (weekly until 1989), with 3 cumulative indexes on microfiche and an annual printed index. Supplementary series: I. *Publications en série* (*q.v.*) (monthly); II. *Publications officielles* (bimonthly); III. *Musique* (3pa.); IV. *Atlas, cartes et plans* (annual). Based on legal deposit. 34,400 numbered entries in the *Livres* issues for 1990. Full cataloguing for each item with ISBN and price. Arrangement by simplified UDC classification; author, title and specific heading subject indexes in each issue, cumulated as outlined above. 1975 to date available on CD-ROM from Chadwyck-Healey. 380,000 records June 1989, updated quarterly. *Class No:* 015(44)

[55]

Les Livres disponibles: la liste exhaustive des ouvrages disponibles publiés en langue française dans le monde. Paris, Éditions du Cercle de la Librairie, 1977-. Annual.

English title *French books in print*. Continues *Le Catalogue de l'édition française,* published in 5 editions 1971-76.

Published as 3v. in 6 pts.: Author; Title; Subject.

The 1991 ed. lists 328,942 French language titles published anywhere in the world, including 31,000 published July 1989-June 1990. Full entry data in all 3 sequences: title, subtitle, statement of responsibility, edition, publisher, year, pagination, collection, notes, ISBN and price. Subject sequence arranged by UDC classification with 14,000 term keyword index. List of publishers/distributors and list of series and their publishers in each sequence. Also available in microfiche, updated quarterly and as a CD-ROM database. *Class No:* 015(44)

Italy

[56]

Catalogo dei libri in commercio. Milano, Editrice Bibliografia, 1970-. Annual.

As *Catalogo dei libri italiani in commercio* 1970-74.

A catalogue of Italian books in print, issued by the Associazione Italiana Editori. Published in 3v.: Autori, Titoli, Soggetti. 244,055 titles, available from 2,344 publishers, listed in the 1991 volume. Also available online as *ALICE* through CILEA, including recently out of print items, and as a CD-ROM database updated quarterly. *Class No:* 015(450)

Spain

[57]

Libros españoles en venta. Madrid, Agencia Española ISBN, Ministerio de Cultura Centro del Libro y de la Lectura, 1973-. Annual. ISSN: 02146304.

Title varies slightly. Frequency also varies; initially irregular, then biennial. Now issued on an annual basis in 3v.; *Autores; Títulos; Materias.*

A record of in print Spanish books. The 1990 ed. lists 337,711 titles available from 2,843 publishers. Includes 29,975 titles in Catalan, 4,807 in Basque and 3,378 in Galacian. Gives only very limited coverage of Spanish language Latin American books (for these titles see *Libros en venta: en Hispanoamérica y España*). Full citation in each volume, but tiny print in condensed 5 col. format. Subject volume arranged in 23 main classes. Updated by a monthly supplement. Also available as an online database. *Class No:* 015(460)

USSR

[58]

Knizhnaia letopis. Moskva, 'Kniga', 1907-. Weekly. ISSN: 01302310.

'Book record'. The basic component of the complex series of bibliographies that make up Soviet national bibliography. Based on legal deposit, encompassing books, pamphlets and government publications in all the languages of the USSR. Entries in Russian according to the 50 class BBK scheme (Dewey until 1940). Quarterly name, place and subject index, *Vspomogatel'nye ukazateli* (ISSN 0201629x) and annual publishers' series index *Ukazatel' seriinykh izdanni* (ISSN 02016133). The weekly issues for 1990 carry a total of 47,832 entries. *Class No:* 015(47)

Netherlands

[59]

Brinkman's cumulative catalogus van boeken. Nederlandse bibliografie bevattende de in Nederland en Vlaanderen uitgegeven of herdrukte boeken, die werden ontvangen door het Depot van Nederlandse Publikaties van de Koninklijke Bibliotheek te 'sGravenhage. Houten, Bohn Stafleu Van Loghum, 1846-. Monthly, with interim and annual cumulations.

Title and format varies: as *Brinkman's Alphabetische lijst* until 1930.

An author and title list. Includes Flemish titles published in Belgium and new periodicals. Contains 'Instanties en Verenigingen' (corporate body) and 'Onderwerpenregister' (subject) indexes. *Nederlandse bibliografie B lijst* (1984-) is a supplementary listing of non-trade publications (*e.g.* government documents, scientific papers, privately published dissertations etc.). *Class No:* 015(492)

Belgium

[60]

Bibliographie de Belgique. [Belgische bibliografie.] Bruxelles, Bibliothèque Royale Albert I, 1875-. Monthly, with annual cumulation. ISSN: 00061336.

The official national bibliography based on legal deposit. Also includes books by Belgian authors published abroad and books relating to Belgium obtained by the Bibliothèque Royale, categories covered 1959-1974 by the separately published *Bibliographie de Belgique. Fascicule spécial.* V.115 for 1989 carries 6,951 entries arranged by 32 broad subject groups with author, title and subject indexes. Separate supplements cover serials, maps and atlases and music. *Class No:* 015(493)

India

[61]

Indian books in print: a bibliography of Indian books published in English language. Singh, S., *comp.* Delhi, Indian Bibliographic Bureau, 1967-. Annual (previously irregular, then biennial).

V.1 Authors; v.2 Titles; v.3 Subject guide. 1st ed. covered 1955/67. Assumed current 3v. format from 1972/73.

The 1991 issue (12th ed. ISBN 818500434x), lists 100,000 titles from 2,500 publishers. Confined to monographs; prices given where available. Subject volume, arranged by Dewey classification, includes a directory of publishers. *Class No:* 015(540)

Canada

[62]

Canadian books in print. Toronto, Toronto Univ. Press, 1973-. ISSN: 00688398, Author & title; 03151999, Subject.

Published in 2v.: Author and title index; Subject index, the latter published from 1975. Updating microfice editions of author/title index issued April, July and October.

Supersedes *Canadian books in print/Catalogue des livres canadiens en librairie* (1967-72), which included French language titles.

Aims to list all English language books bearing the imprint of a Canadian publisher, or originated by Canadian subsidiaries of international publishing firms. Also covers French language titles published by predominantly English language publishers, or published outside Quebec. The 1991 ed. contains 31,040 titles. Subject index arranged by Library of Congress subject headings. Also available online through Info Globe, updated quarterly. *Class No:* 015(71)

[63]

Canadiana: Canada's national bibliography. Ottawa, National Library of Canada, 1950-. Monthly (11 issues pa.), with annual cumulation. ISSN: 00085391.

French subtitle *La bibliographie nationale du Canada.*

Succeeds *The Canadian catalogue of books published in Canada, about Canada, as well as those written by Canadians* ... (Toronto, Public Library, 1923-50. Annual).

Covers books, pamphlets, first issues of periodicals and newspapers, theses, atlases, microforms, sheet music and sound recordings. Film and filmstrips excluded, listed in the separate *Film Canadiana.* Arrangement has varied considerably over the years. From 1981 published in two sequences: Canadian imprints; Foreign imprints (of Canadian association). Both sequences in Dewey classified order; indexed by author/title/series, English and French subject headings and ISBN/ISSN. Also available in microfiche since 1978, issued as a register with 6 indexes, including Dewey classified. Microfiche cumulations are available for 1973-80, and 1981-85. *Class No:* 015(71)

Latin America

[64]

Libros en venta: en Hispanoamérica y España. 5.ed. San Juan, Puerto Rico, Melcher, 1990. 3v. ISBN: 0923737049.

V.1 *Autores con guía de editores;* v.2 *Títulos;* v.3 *Materias con guía de editores.*

First published 1964, 4th ed. 1988.

Lists *c.*165,000 titles available from 6,500 publishers. Main coverage for Spanish-speaking Latin America, but includes Spain and Spanish works published in the United States. Subject volume classified by Dewey. Entries do not give ISBNs, and often lack other basic bibliographical detail such as edition statement or publication date. Publisher listings in v.1 and v.3. More comprehensive coverage for works published in Spain provided by *Libros españoles en venta (q.v.). Class No:* 015(729.99)

USA

[65]

American bibliography: a preliminary checklist ... 1801-1819. Shaw, R.R. *and* Shoemaker, R.H., *comps.* New York, Scarecrow Press, 1958-83. 23v.

19 annual volumes for 1801-19; *Addenda. List of sources. Library symbols* (1965); *Title index* (1965); *Corrections. Author Index* (1966); *Printers, publishers and booksellers index. Geographical index* (1983. ISBN 0810816075).

Continues Evans (*q.v.*). Compiled from secondary sources, 50,192 entries 1801-19, plus 1,768 in the addenda. *Class No:* 015(73)

[66]

—A Checklist of American imprints ... 1820-. Metuchen, N.J., Scarecrow Press, 1964-.

Compiler varies; initially R.H. Shoemaker, now C. Rinderknecht. Volumes individually priced.

Issued in annual volumes as with the preceding series *American bibliography* (above), but with fuller detail. To continue through to 1875, thereby replacing Roorbach's *Bibliotheca Americana* covering 1820-60 and Kelly's *The American catalogue of books* covering 1861-65. Items numbered sequentially on a decennial basis. 41,633 entries 1820-29 (1964-71), with a *Title index* (1972) and an *Author index* (1973). 59,415 entries 1830-39 (1972-88), with a *Title index* (1989. 2v.) and an *Author index* (1990). 1840 and 1841 published 1990, but with numbering now on an annual basis, 1841 having 5,692 items. From the 1838 v. has ceased to include United States documents. *Class No:* 015(73)

[67]

American book publishing record cumulative 1876-1949: an American national bibliography. New York, Bowker, 1980. 15v. ISBN: 0835212459.

V.1-10 Classified sequence; v.11 Fiction. Juvenile fiction; v.12 Non-Dewey Decimal classified titles; v.13 Author index; v.14 Title index; v.15 Subject index.

625,000 entries arranged by Dewey classification. Compiled from *A Catalog of books represented by Library of Congress printed cards* 1898-1942 plus supplement 1942-47 and *The Library of Congress author catalog, 1948-1952.* Excludes federal and other government documents etc., as with the current *American book publishing record. Class No:* 015(73)

[68]

American book publishing record cumulative 1950-1977: an American national bibliography. New York, Bowker, 1978. 15v. ISBN: 0835210944.

V.1-10 Classified sequence; v.11 Fiction. Juvenile fiction; v.12 Non-Dewey Decimal classified titles; v.13 Author index; v.14 Title index; v.15 Subject index.

....(contd.)

900,000 entries. Includes records from Library of Congress MARC tapes 1968-77 for titles that did not appear in the previous cumulations of *American book publishing record*. V.12 includes records appearing in the *National union catalog* not assigned a Dewey class no. Some omissions from earlier cumulations and some duplication of entries resulting from the merging of computer tapes. Abbreviation of Dewey class nos. give rise to Dewey sequences of great length (*e.g.* '192', *c.*40 cols.; '973', *c.*110 cols.). Nonetheless, this and the 1876-1949 cumulation represent a major bibliographical resource; a convenient alternative to the *National union catalog* for US imprints.

American book publishing record index 1876-1981: author/title/subject index on microfiche (New York, Bowker, 1982. 650 fiche. ISBN 0835214354) indexes both the retrospective cumulations in one sequence. 1,700,000 entries. *Class No:* 015(73)

[69]
EVANS, C. American bibliography: a chronological dictionary of all books, pamphlets and periodical publications printed in the United States of America, from the genesis of printing in 1639 down to and including the year 1820, with bibliographical and biographical notes. Chicago, the Author, 1903-34. 12v.

Reprinted Magnolia, Ma., Peter Smith. ISBN 0844611735, v.1.

Originally intended to extend to 1820, and later limited to 1800. Evans himself completed up to 1799 (letter M) when he died in 1935.

35,854 items arranged under year of publication; frequently notes locations of copies (for key to locations, see *New York Public Library bulletin,* v.40(8), August 1936, p.665-68). Each v. has author, classified subject, and printer and publisher indexes. The basic bibliography of early US books. Rounded off to 1800 by:-

V.13: *1799-1800* by C.K. Shipton (Worcester, Mass., American Antiquarian Society, 1955. xiii,349p. Reprinted Peter Smith. ISBN 08444611743). Items 35855-39162. Titles not always recorded in full as in the previous 12v. Author and subject indexes.

V.14: *Index* by R.P. Bristol (Worcester, Mass., American Antiquarian Society, 1959. vii,450p. Reprinted Peter Smith. ISBN 0844611751). Cumulated author-title index, also including entries for names of people, ships, Indian tribes etc.

R.P. Bristol has also prepared an *Index of printers, publishers and booksellers indicated by Charles Evans ...* (Charlottesville, Va., Bibliographical Society of the Univ. of Virginia, 1961. iv,172p.). *Class No:* 015(73)

[70]
—BRISTOL, R.P. Supplement to Charles Evans' American bibliography. Charlottesville, Va., Univ. Press of Virginia for The Bibliographical Society of America and The Bibliographical Society of the University of Virginia, 1970. xix,636p. ISBN: 0813902878.

Adds 11,262 items in chronological arrangement. An author/title and printer/publisher/bookseller index, also by Bristol, published as *Index to Supplement to Charles Evans American bibliography* (Charlottesville, Va., Univ. Press of Virginia, etc., 1971. v,191p. ISBN 813903378). *Class No:* 015(73)

Contemporary

[71]
American book publishing record. New York, Bowker, 1960-. Monthly, with annual cumulation. ISSN: 00027707.

Annual cumulations from 1966. Quinquennial cumulations 1960/64, 1965/69, 1970/74, 1975/79, 1980/84; 1960/64-1970/74 superseded by *American book publishing record cumulative 1950-1977* (*q.v.*).

A record of books published in the US, based mainly on Library of Congress cataloguing, cumulating the listings in *Weekly record* (below). Excludes federal and other government documents, subscription books, new printings, pamphlets under 49 pages, specialized publications of a transitory nature, and most elementary and high school textbooks. Full cataloguing records, including imprint detail, series, notes, LC class and cat nos., subject tracings, ISBN and price. Arranged by Dewey classification with separate sections for adult and juvenile fiction. Author and title indexes; subject index to the classification. The 1989 annual (1990. vii,1438p.) has entries for 38,000 titles. The nearest equivalent to an official US national bibliography. *Class No:* 015(73)"312"

[72]
—Weekly record. New York, Bowker, 1974-. Weekly (51 issues pa). ISSN: 0094257x.

Prior to 1974 published as a section of *Publishers' weekly* (New York, Bowker, 1872-. ISSN 00000019).

Main entry listing of newly published titles. Around 800 entries in each issue. Includes annuals, reprints etc., not catalogued by the Library of Congress. *Class No:* 015(73)"312"

[73]
Books in print. New York, Bowker, 1948-. Annual. ISSN: 00680124.

Initially subtitled *An Author-title-series index to the Publishers' trade list annual.* 1990-91 issued in 8 volumes: v.1-3 Authors; v.4-6 Titles; v.7 Out of print. Out of stock indefinitely; v.8 Publishers. Also available in microfiche (1982-, updated quarterly).

The 1990-91 volumes list 854,771 titles available from 33,000 US publishers and distributors. Includes reprints, children's fiction and school textbooks. Main exclusions are pamphlets and booklets, calendar and appointment books, books only available to member organizations, books sold only to schools and sheet music, song books etc. Foreign books listed only where bibliographic information submitted by a US publisher. Brief entries include, as available, author/editor etc., title, no. of vols., edition, LC card no., series, no. of pages, grade range, date of publication, price and ISBN. V.8 includes separate listings of new and inactive/out of business publishers. The major source for US published books, 'no publication compares in magnitude or accessibility to the *Books in print* series' (*American reference books annual,* 1988, p.10). *Class No:* 015(73)"312"

[74]
—Subject guide to books in print. New York, Bowker, 1957-. Annual. ISSN: 00000159.

1990-91 issued in 5 volumes: v.1-4 Subjects A-Z; v.5 Subject thesaurus. Also available on microfiche (updated quarterly).

Lists all non-fiction works in the author/title volumes under Library of Congress based subject headings. 66,000 headings 1990-91, with 55,000 cross-references. Includes a limited number of briefly annotated entries using either reviews or promotional summaries supplied by publishers. *Class No:* 015(73)"312"

[75]

Books in print plus. New York, Bowker, 1987-. CD-ROM database, updated bimonthly.

Offers up to 18 search paths. A further CD-ROM version *Books in print with book reviews plus* offers unabridged reviews from sources such as *Library journal, Booklist, Choice* and *School library journal.*

Books in print is also available online through Dialog (File 470) and BRS, including out of print titles back to 1979. *Class No:* 015(73)"312"

[76]

The Cumulative book index: a world list of books in the English language. New York, Wilson, 1898-. Monthly. ISSN: 0011300x.

Frequency has varied. Now monthly (except August) with paperbound cumulations within the year and, since 1969, a bound annual cumulation. Biennial cumulations 1957/58-1967/68; earlier cumulations for 1928/32, 1933/37, 1938/42, 1943/48. 1949/52 and 1953/56. No cumulations prior to 1928, published as a supplement to *United States catalog: books in print ...* (4 eds. 1899, 1902, 1912 and 1928).

Author, title and subjects in one A-Z sequence, arranged by Library of Congress filing rules. Since 1928 has attempted to list all books published in the English language worldwide. Excludes government documents, most pamphlets, inexpensive paperbacks, maps, music scores, editions limited to 500 or fewer copies, privately printed genealogies, local directories and material of a local or ephemeral nature. About ½ the entries are compiled from examination of the actual books, the remainder from US and UK MARC or other secondary sources. Directory of publishers in each issue. Records 1982 to date searchable online through Wilsonline, database updated twice weekly. A CD-ROM version is also available.

Cumulative book index is best regarded as a checking tool for English language publications of the US and to a lesser extent Canada and the UK. Very selective for other countries. Accurate and fairly prompt, but cataloguing is less full than *American book publishing record.* In the US an 'important part of the national bibliographic apparatus... CBI is an old friend - steady, reliable, changing very gradually as needed' (*American reference books annual,* 1989, p.8). *Class No:* 015(73)"312"

New Zealand

[77]

New Zealand books in print: includes books published in the Pacific Islands. Melbourne, D.W. Thorpe, 1957-. Irregular, now annual. ISSN: 01577662.

Author, title and subject keyword list of in print books published in New Zealand, about New Zealand or by New Zealand authors published overseas, plus books published in the Pacific Islands. The 18th ed. (1990. xxx,280p.) also contains useful information on the New Zealand publishing and book world including listings of publishers, overseas publishers with New Zealand agents, New Zealand book award winners 1976-1989 and New Zealand public libraries. *Class No:* 015(931)

Australia

[78]

Australian books in print. Port Melbourne, D.W. Thorpe, 1956-. Annual (initially irregular). ISSN: 0067172x.

Author/title list of books published in Australia, by Australians published overseas, or about Australia. Additional information includes lists of book trade and literary associations, series (Australian and foreign), overseas publishers with Australian agents and Australian publishers. A separate *Subject guide to Australian books in print* is also published. Updating provided by the 'New Australian

....(contd.)

titles' section of the monthly *Australian bookseller and publisher.* Available as an online database through AUSINET and as a microfiche service, updated monthly. *Class No:* 015(94)

[79]

Australian national bibliography. Canberra, National Library of Australia, 1961-. Monthly, with annual cumulation. ISSN: 00049816.

Cumulations also available in microfiche for January-April, January-August, January-December.

Supersedes *Books published in Australia,* cumulated in the *Annual catalogue of Australian publications.*

Frequency varies: monthly 1961-66; 4 issues per month with fourth issue cumulating into a monthly issue 1967-80; 2 issues per month with second issue cumulating into a monthly issue 1981-85.

Lists books and pamphlets published in Australia, as well as books with a substantial Australian subject content, or written by Australians published overseas. Apart from books, also covers new serials and government publications, with the exception of Acts, bills and ordinances. Entries are in classified Dewey order with author/title/series and subject indexes, the latter under Library of Congress headings (previously PRECIS). Records 1972 to date also available online through OZLINE, updated monthly. 1961-71 cumulation also available on microfiche. *Class No:* 015(94)

Library Catalogues

[80]

BRITISH LIBRARY. The British Library general catalogue of printed books to 1975. London, Saur (initially Bingley), 1981-87. 360v. ISBN: 085157520x.

Preceded by several earlier catalogues. The first (GK1) was published as *Catalogue of printed books* (1881-1900) in 95v. with a *Supplement* (1900-5) of 13v. (both photographically reprinted Ann Arbor, Edwards, 1946-50, 58v. and 10v.). A new attempt at a catalogue *General catalogue of printed books* (GK2) began publication in 1931, but was abandoned in 1954 having covered A-Dez in 51v. The next catalogue, the monumental *General catalogue of printed books. Photolithographic edition to 1955* (GK3) (1960-66) 263v., contained 4 million entries in 133,000 pages, recording all printed books, periodicals and newspapers, in languages other than Oriental, catalogued by the British Museum up to the end of 1955. GK3 was supplemented by a *Ten year supplement 1956-1965* (1968) 50v., a *Five year supplement 1966-1970* (1971-72) 26v. and a further *Five year supplement 1971-1975* (1978-79) 13v. GK3 is still commonly encountered, as many libraries, largely for financial reasons, have chosen not to purchase the catalogue to 1975.

Incorporates in a single alphabetical sequence the Photolithographed ed. and its three supplements. Subsequent revisions, corrections, amendments and additions made by British Library staff are also included. Basically an author, or rather 'name' catalogue, it maintains the practices of GK3. Entries under authors list not only their works, but also (in the form of cross-references) biographical and critical works about them. Very long author sequences (*e.g.* Dickens, v.82, p.349-447) include brief indexes. Most corporate bodies are entered under the town or country in which they are located with a reference from the body name. Within many corporate headings, especially states, entries are subdivided according to type of publication (*e.g.* laws, treaties). The heading 'England' (v.96-100) is accompanied by separate title and subheading index volumes. Generic headings are widely used (*e.g.* catalogues, collections, dictionaries, encyclopaedias). Note especially the heading 'Periodical publications' (v.252-54), subdivided by place. Invaluable for British publications up to the

....(contd.)

appearance of *British national bibliography* (*q.v.*) and for its selection of major foreign publications, particularly from the nineteenth and early twentieth centuries. A 6v. *Supplement* (1987-88. ISBN 086291275x) contains 85,000 additions and amendments. Conversion of the entire catalogue to machine readable format is now nearly complete. Online access is offered via BLAISE-Line, the file containing 3,865,646 records as at September 1991. A CD-ROM version, marketed by Chadwyck-Healey, is also available. *Class No:* 017/019

[81]
—BRITISH LIBRARY. The British Library general catalogue of printed books. 1976-. London, Saur, 1983-.

Three separate sets issued to date: 1976-1982 (1983. 50v. ISBN 086291485x); 1982-1985 (1986. 26v. ISBN 0862915406); 1986-1987 (1988. 22v. ISBN 0862917301). Also available in microfiche: 1976-1985 (473 fiche) and 1986-1987 (86 fiche). Further microfiche coverage for 1988-1989, issued 1990, (121 fiche).

The current catalogue, recording books and periodicals catalogued since 1975. Science and technology publications, cartography and music materials not covered comprehensively, the former restricted to items listed in *British national bibliography* (*q.v.*). Continues to omit works in Oriental languages. Newspapers held at Colindale and items added to the collections of the British Library Information Sciences Service, National Sound Archive and Document Supply Centre also excluded. Cataloguing and headings now according to AACR2, entry arrangement by BLAISE filing rules. Access points include authors, editors, and responsible corporate bodies, persons, corporate bodies and publications as subjects, (denoted by an asterisk) and most importantly in contrast to the catalogue to 1975, all distinctive titles. Collectively the three sets 1976-88 record *c.*1,000,000 publications. Also available online through BLAISE as *British Library catalogue: humanities and social sciences*, containing 1,238,093 records September 1991, file updated weekly. *Class No:* 017/019

[82]
BRITISH MUSEUM. Department of Printed Books. **Subject index of the modern works added to the library.** 1881-1960. London, Trustees of the British Museum, 1902-74.

Title varies slightly. Initial set for 1881-1900 published 1902-3 in 3v. (replacing 3 previous 5 year indexes covering 1880-95). Further volumes issued on a quinquennial basis: 1901-1905 (1906); 1906-1910 (1911); 1911-1915 (1918. 2v.); 1916-1920 (1922. 2v., 2nd v. covering books relating to the First World War); 1921-1925 (1927); 1926-1930 (1933. 2v.); 1931-1935 (1937. 2v.); 1936-1940 (1944. 2v.); 1941-1945 (1953); 1946-1950 (1961. 4v.); 1951-1955 (1974. 6v. ISBN 07141034554); 1956-1960 (1965. 6v.).

A comprehensive alphabetical subject catalogue, *c.*1,260,000 entries 1881-1960. Excludes 'pure' literature and personal name headings (to be found in the *General catalogue*); biographies usually under the relevant subject. Gives author, short-title, date, place, pagination (occasionally), publishers (since 1906, if in English). Up to 1945 searching handicapped by frequent alphabetico-classed headings. More specific subject headings adopted from 1951-55 to break up long sequences. *Class No:* 017/019

[83]
—BRITISH LIBRARY. The British Library general subject catalogue 1975 to 1985. London, Saur, 1986. 75v. ISBN: 086291650x.

A major compilation on a much larger scale than the previous volumes. Modernises practice using PRECIS subject headings; extensively cross-referenced. Entries, well laid-out in 3 column format, include bibliographical detail, ISBN and BL shelf-mark. Lacks introductory notes.

....(contd.)

Also available in microfiche as *Subject catalogue of printed books 1975-1985* from the British Library comprising 437 fiche. In 1991 the British Library issued a further 261 microfiche set *Subject catalogue of printed books 1985-1990*. *Class No:* 017/019

[84]
—BRITISH LIBRARY. Subject index of modern books acquired. 1961-1975. London, British Library, 1982-86.

Published in two sets: 1961-1970 (1982. 12v. ISBN 0904654559); 1971-1975 (1986. 14v. plus supplement. ISBN 0712300902).

The last volumes compiled according to the traditional system begun with the 1881-1900 set. About 400,000 entries 1961-70, 470,000 1971-75. Continued by the *General subject catalogue* (above). *Class No:* 017/019

[85]
LIBRARY OF CONGRESS. A Catalog of books represented by Library of Congress printed cards issued to July 31, 1942. Ann Arbor, Edwards, 1942-46. 167v.

Reprinted, New York, Rowman and Littlefield. ISBN 0874717248.

Reproduces photographically cards printed by the Library of Congress as part of the programme initiated at the turn of the century to maintain 'depository sets' recording its own holdings and those of a number of major research libraries. A main entry catalogue with cross-references, cards give author's full names and dates, full title, place, publisher, date, collation, edition, series, subject and added entry tracings, LC and often Dewey classification numbers, LC card number and a contents note. Pagination of 'hidden' bibliographies is also stated.

A *Supplement: cards issued August 1, 1942-December 31, 1947* (Ann Arbor, Mich., Edwards, 1948. 42v. (also reprinted Rowman & Littlefield)) provides continuing coverage. The dates (1942 and 1947) are of cards rather than books, the supplement including cards for books printed before 1 August 1942 and revised entries. Also contains 26,000 title entries for anonymous and pseudonymous works, most of which have a main entry in the 167v. set.

Continued by *Library of Congress author catalog: a cumulative list represented by Library of Congress printed cards, 1948-1952* (Ann Arbor, Edwards, 1953. 24v.) and thereafter in the *National union catalog* (below). The 1948-52 set includes added entries for the first time and groups films and filmstrips in the final volume.

The *Catalog of books ... to July 31, 1942* the Supplement and the 1948-52 volumes are all now superseded by the *National union catalog, pre-1956 imprints* (below), but can still be found in those libraries which have not acquired this cumulation. *Class No:* 017/019

[86]
—LIBRARY OF CONGRESS. National union catalog: a cumulative author list representing Library of Congress printed cards and titles reported by other libraries. Washington, D.C., Library of Congress, Card Division, 1956-82. Monthly, with quarterly and annual cumulations. ISSN: 00280348.

Continues the *Library of Congress catalog. Books: authors.* Cumulative retrospective coverage back to 1952 provided by *National union catalog: 1952-1955 imprints: an author list representing Library of Congress printed cards and titles reported by other American libraries* (Edwards, 1961. 30v.).

Five commercially published quinquennial cumulations produced as follows: 1953-1957 (Edwards, 1958. 28v.); 1958-1962 (Rowman & Littlefield, 1963. 54v.); 1963-1967 (Edwards, 1969. 72v.); 1968-1972 (Edwards, 1973. 119v.); 1973-1977 (Rowman & Littlefield, 1978. 150v.). All

BIBLIOGRAPHY & BIBLIOGRAPHIES

....(contd.)
cumulations include separate volumes *Music and phonorecords* and *Motion pictures and filmstrips.* No further quinquennial sets after 1977, coverage 1978-82 provided by five annual cumulations comprising 16,16,18,15 and 21 volumes respectively.

Ceased publication in paper 1982. Continuing coverage provided by the microfiche *National union catalog. Books.* (below).

From 1956 reported the holdings of 500 North American libraries (a figure gradually increased), in addition to the Library of Congress. Material in all languages of the Roman, Cyrillic, Greek and Hebrew alphabets included from the outset, items in Arabic and Indic alphabets and Chinese, Japanese and Korean characters included from the 1958-62 cumulation. Overall, foreign language titles probably represent nearly 50% of the total recorded. The very comprehensive acquisitions policy of the Library of Congress and the other reporting libraries, makes the *National union catalog* and its microfiche continuation (below) the most extensive catalogue of modern works in existence. Valuable as a source of bibliographical verification and for author bibliography, the *National union catalog* is an essential tool in any research library. *Class No:* 017/019

[87]
—LIBRARY OF CONGRESS. National union catalog. Books. Washington, D.C., Library of Congress, 1983-. Monthly. (Microfiche).

Main records appear in 'Register' format in the order in which they were processed, each identified by an alpha-numeric code. Name (main and added entry), title, series and subject heading indexes, each giving brief bibliographial detail, act as a key. Indexes cumulative, with a final annual cumulation, plus a five year cumulation 1983-87.

Continues to be based on records prepared by the Library of Congress and reporting North American libraries (now *c.*1,100 in number). Full Library of Congress records provided as in the paper *National union catalog.* The introduction of series and especially title indexes, greatly increases the efficacy of the catalogue as a bibliographical tool. Complementary series include *National union catalog. Audiovisual materials.*

The *National union catalog* is available as an online database through BLAISE-line, Dialog and Wilsonline. The current database *LC MARC* covers English language records from 1968, French language from 1975, German, Portuguese and Spanish from 1976 and other languages from 1977. The retrospective database *REMARC* has *c.*5,500,000 entries. *Class No:* 017/019

[88]
—National union catalog, pre-1956 imprints: a cumulative author list representing Library of Congress printed cards and titles reported by other American libraries. London, Mansell; Chicago, American Library Association, 1968-81. 754v. ISBN: 0720100038.

Compiled and edited with the co-operation of the Library of Congress and National Union Catalog Subcommittee of the Resources and Technical Services Division, American Library Association. Main sequence v.1-685; supplement v.686-754.

Replaces *A Catalog of books ... to July 31, 1942,* the *Supplement ... August 1, 1942-December 31, 1947, Library of Congress author catalog ... 1948-1952* and *National union catalog ... 1953-1957.* The latter set entirely replaced for printed material as works with an imprint date 1956 and 1957 were included in the 1958-62 volumes in anticipation of this cumulation. As records for films etc. are excluded, v.24 of the 1948-52 and v.27-28 of the 1953-57 sets, which include these types of material, are not replaced.

....(contd.)
Entries for *c.*11,000,000 works, cumulating the earlier catalogues as outlined above, plus titles reported by more than 700 contributing libraries in the US and Canada. Includes books, pamphlets, maps, atlases, microforms and music. Serials also covered, but not as comprehensively as in *Union list of serials* and *New serial titles (q.v.).* Generally confined to works in the Latin alphabet, items in other scripts recorded only if represented by a Library of Congress printed card giving uniform transliteration (coverage of Cyrillic script works provided by *The Slavic Cyrillic union catalog of pre-1956 imprints*). The 69 supplementary volumes list further material accumulated since the editorial work began in 1967 and, in separate sequences, locations for titles in the main set that are sparsely located in the main set.

A further cumulation, effectively continuing the *National union catalog: pre-1956 imprints,* is *National union catalog, 1956 through 1967: a cumulative author list representing Library of Congress printed cards and titles reported by other American libraries* (Totowa, N.J., Rowman & Littlefield, 1970-72. 125v.). This set represents a combination of the 1958-62 (includes 1956 and 1957 imprints) and 1963-67 quinquennial cumulations of the *National union catalog. Class No:* 017/019

[89]
LIBRARY OF CONGRESS. The Library of Congress catalog. Books: subjects. Washington, D.C., Library of Congress, 1950-84. Quarterly, with annual and quinquennial cumulations.

Quinquennial cumulations: 1950-1954 (Edwards, 1955. 20v.); 1955-1959 (Pageant Books, 1960. 22v.); 1960-1964 (Edwards, 1965. 25v.); 1965-1969 (Edwards, 1970. 42v.); 1970-1974 (Rowman & Littlefield, 1976. 100v.).

Change of title from 1975, continuing as *Library of Congress. Subject catalog.* No further quinquennial cumulations. Ceased publication with the annual for 1982. Coverage now provided by the subject index to the microfiche *National union catalog. Books (q.v.).*

A subject index to works represented by Library of Congress printed cards. Cumulations include publications from 1945. Entries omit the notes and tracings given in the author catalogues. *Class No:* 017/019

Bibliographies

[90]
NELSON, B.R. A Guide to published library catalogs. Metuchen, N.J., Scarecrow Press, 1982. xvi,342p. ISBN: 0810814773.

Includes only modern catalogues of major collections (mostly multi-volume of the last 20 years). Author acknowledges Collinson's *Published library catalogues* and Thompson's *Checklist and union catalog of holdings of major published library catalogs in METRO libraries* (New York Metropolitan Reference and Research Library Agency, 1980). Lists in 33 subject categories, 429 catalogues mostly examined by the author. Lengthy descriptions. Indexes of subjects and libraries. *Class No:* 017/019(01)

Book-auction & Book Sales Catalogues

[91]
American book prices current. 1894/95-. New York, Bancroft-Parkman, 1895-. Annual. ISSN: 00919357.
Publisher varies.

Generally regarded as the most reliable of the Anglo-American series of book-auction records. Since 1958 has included records for a limited number of auctions held outside the US. V.96 September 1989-August 1990 (1990. xxii,1031p.) covers *c.*210 sales, including a number in the UK, plus a few in Australia, Germany, Italy and the

15

....(contd.)

Netherlands. Currently arranged in 2 main pts: I. Autographs and manuscripts; II. Books (atlases, books, broadsides, maps and charts). List of auction houses, consignors and season's sales precedes. Entries arranged alphabetically by author, detail verified rather than merely transcribed. Minimum sale price now $50. No indexes to individual volumes, but separate quinquennial indexes from 1941. Earlier indexes cover 1914-22, 1923-32 and 1933-40. Recent indexes issued on a quadrennial basis, (1983-87. 1988. 2v. 0914022210). Online coverage also available as *Bookline Utopia* from Infronics Inc. *Class No:* 018.3

[92]

Book-auction records: a priced and annotated annual record of international book auctions. 1902/12-. Folkestone, Dawson, 1924-. Annual. ISSN: 00680095.

Title varies slightly. Publisher has also varied, originally Karslake, then Stevens & Stiles. Published quarterly until 1940.

Now in 2 pts: I. Printed books and atlases; II. Printed maps, charts and plans. Records for books in alphabetical order of author, except for certain large categories *e.g.*, Atlases, Bibles, Hymnals. Fairly full bibliographical detail for each entry, with notes on binding, imperfections etc., plus sale information, including name of auction house, date of sale, lot no., buyer's name and price achieved. V.87 *August 1989-July 1990* (1990. xvi,658p.) has records for *c.*250 sales mainly in Great Britain, but also in North America, Europe, Australia and South Africa. Includes only lots which realised £70 or over, (£150 or over if sold with faults).

V.1-24 (1902-26/27) has articles on bibliographical subjects (indexed in *Subject index to periodicals*) and until 1939 there was a list of 'points' distinguishing editions.

A *General index* has been published covering 1902-72 in 9v. (1902-12, 1912-23, 1924-33, 1934-43, 1944-48, 1948-58, 1958-63, 1963-68 and 1968-72). A further *General index to Book auction records for the years 1979-1984 (volumes 77-81)* published Dawson, 1985 (vi,1008p. 0712910352). *Class No:* 018.3

02 Librarianship & Information Studies

Librarianship & Information Studies

Abbreviations & Symbols

[93]
Acronyms and abbreviations in library and information work: a reference handbook of British usage. Montgomery, A.C., *comp. and ed.* London, Library Association, 1990. 250p. ISBN: 0853659893.

1st ed. 1975; 3rd ed. 1986. Prelim. ed. in *Library and information bulletin*, no.22, (1973), p.1-35.

Expands over 7,000 acronyms and abbreviations used in the English language literature of librarianship and information work. Selective coverage of related areas such as archives and museums, book trade, education and computer and micrographic technology. Entries include country of origin if not clear from the expansion. Adequately cross-referenced between name changes etc. The established source for British librarians and information workers. *Class No: 02.0(003)*

Bibliographies

[94]
Library and information science abstracts. London, Bowker Saur, 1969-. Monthly. ISSN: 00242719.

Previously published by Library Association Publishing. Issued bimonthly 1969-82. Widely referred to as *LISA*.

Provides signed, indicative and informative *c.*100-125 word abstracts on new developments in thought and practice in all fields of librarianship and information science. About 350 periodicals currently scanned systematically, articles forming up to 80% of the abstracted items, research reports and conference proceedings, accounting for the remainder. Geographic coverage truly international, *c.*50% of the abstracted material being of Western European origin, 25% North American, 10% Soviet and Eastern European and 10% Asian, mainly Japanese. Abstracts in classified arrangement according to the unpublished draft of the Classification Research Group's *A Classification of library and information science* (core subjects, A-Z; fringe subjects, 1/9). Outline of the classification, name, subject and journal indexes in each issue. Separate annual index with further cumulations *e.g.* 1976-1980. The primary bibliographic source in the field, 8,141 items abstracted in the issues for 1990. Available online from Dialog, BRS and ORBIT for records 1969 to date. *LISA* was also one of the earliest databases to be made available in CD-ROM format. For a full review of the CD-ROM version, see *Program*, v.22(1), January 1988, p.72-76. *Class No: 02.0(01)*

[95]
Library literature. 1921/32-. New York, Wilson, 1934-. Bimonthly, with annual cumulation. ISSN: 00242373.

Published quarterly until 1968. Cumulations triennial

....(contd.)
1933/35-1967/69, then biennial 1970/71-1976/77.

Primarily an index to periodical literature, but also covers books, pamphlets, films, filmstrips, microfilms and library science dissertations. Author and subject entries in one A-Z sequence as with other Wilson indexes. Separate list of book reviews and a 'Checklist of monographs cited'. International, but with an American bias, *c.*130 of the *c.*200 periodicals currently indexed published in the US. More confined to traditional librarianship than *Library and information science abstracts* (above). Also available online through Wilsonline December 1984 to date and in CD-ROM format. *Class No: 02.0(01)*

[96]
PRYTHERCH, R.J. Sources of information in librarianship and information science. 2nd ed. Aldershot, Gower, 1987. x,153p. ISBN: 0566055090.

1st ed. 1983.

Intended as a practical brief introduction to the literature. Narrative format in 10 chapters of which ch.6 on abstracting and indexing services is by far the longest. Other chapters include theses, dissertations and reports, encyclopedic sources and keeping up to date. Basic details on approximately 250 information sources in all, with reproduced sample pages for the more important titles. References and bibliography, p.143-147. Index. *Class No: 02.0(01)*

[97]
PURCELL, G.R. and SCHLACHTER, G.A. Reference sources in library and information services: a guide to the literature. Santa Barbara, ABC-Clio, 1984. xxvi,359p. ISBN: 0874363551.

1,193 entries in 7 chapters: Bibliography - Terminology - Encyclopedias, yearbooks, handbooks and manuals - Biographical and membership directories - Directories of libraries and archives - Sources of library statistics - Special services and operations (about 40% of total entries subdivided into 103 subject categories Academic libraries ... Women in librarianship). Entries fully annotated. International in scope, including a good range of non-US material. Author/title and geographic indexes, but the contents list provides the only subject access. By far the most comprehensive source available. *Class No: 02.0(01)*

Encyclopaedias & Dictionaries

[98]
Elsevier's dictionary of library science, information and documentation: in six languages English/American, French, Spanish, Italian, Dutch and German. Clason, W.E., *comp.* 2nd ed. Amsterdam, Elsevier, 1976. [10],708p. ISBN: 0444414754.

1st ed. 1973.

5,439 numbered English terms A-Z with brief definitions,

....(contd.)
followed by equivalents in the other 5 languages. French, Spanish, Italian, Dutch and German indexes refering to the numbered English language sequence. The 2nd ed., otherwise unchanged from the 1st, includes an Arabic supplement by S. Salem (p.607-708). A valuable work, but lacks a clear statement of selection criteria and includes a number of definitions best described as unusual. *Class No:* 02.0(03)

[99]
Encyclopedia of library and information science. Kent, A., *and others eds.* New York, Dekker, 1968-. Illus., tables, diagrs.
V.1-33: A-Z; v.34-35: Indexes; v.36-45: Supplements; v.46-47: Indexes (Supplements, plus v.1-35); v.48-: Supplements.

An encyclopedia of substantial, signed articles, generally well-documented. In addition to treatment of a wide range of library and information science topics, there is coverage for individual libraries, prominent librarians, bibliographers, etc. and libraries/librarianship in individual countries and cities. As the only English language multi-volume encyclopedia in the field, this is a valuable tool much enhanced by the recent *c.*90,000 entry author and subject indexes in v.46-47. Coverage is, however, very uneven and unsystematic. Thus while Cambridge University Library is afforded *c.*20p. the Bodleian receives only 6p. Similarly *British technology index* is given 13p., but *British National Bibliography* only 2½p. Another major drawback is the appearance of many important articles in the individually alphabetized supplementary volumes. These articles are included on an apparently random basis, with no particular emphasis given to new or emerging topics. The most recent supplement (v.48) has 26 articles ranging from 'CD-ROM encyclopedias', 18p. to 'Library absenteeism'. 2½p. *Class No:* 02.0(03)

[100]
HARROD, L.M. Harrod's librarians' glossary: of terms used in librarianship, documentation and the book crafts, and reference book. Prytherch, R.J., *comp.* 7th ed. Aldershot, Gower, 1990. xi,673p. ISBN: 0566036207.
1st ed. 1938; 6th ed. 1987.

'The purpose of the Glossary is to explain and define terms and concepts, identify techniques and organizations, provide up-to-date summaries of the activities of associations, major libraries, Government and international' (Preface p.vii). Subject coverage extends to publishing, archive work, printing, binding, conservation and the book trade. About 9,000 entries, (800 completely new, 2,000 updated or revised). Includes some lengthy encyclopedia type entries (*e.g.* 'British Library' 1½p., 'Typefaces' 5p., 33 examples). International in scope, but with a British emphasis. Entries for new technology, databases, etc. tend to be brief. Unsurpassed, an essential reference work for any librarian. *Class No:* 02.0(03)

Yearbooks & Directories

[101]
The Bowker annual: library and book trade almanac. New York, Bowker, 1956-. Annual. ISSN: 00680540.
Title varies; first published 1950 as *American library annual.* The complete text of the almanac is also available as part of the CD-ROM database *Library reference PLUS.*

The 1990 ed. (S. Filomena *comp.* xii,795p.) has 6 main sections: 1. Reports from the field (reports from various organizations *e.g.* Federal Library and Information Center Committee) - 2. Legislation, funding, grants - 3. Library/information science education, placement, salaries (includes statistical data on placement of graduates and salaries for qualified staff) - 4. Research and statistics (includes prices of books, statistics of book output) - 5. Reference information (includes bibliographies of recent library science

....(contd.)
books) - 6. Directory of organizations. Indexed p.775-95. The pre-eminent handbook for US librarians, containing a wide range of information not found in any other single source. *Class No:* 02.0(058)

[102]
CONFEDERATION OF INFORMATION COMMUNICATION INDUSTRIES. CICI directory of information products and services. 2nd ed. Harlow, Longman, 1990. viii,273p. ISBN: 0582061326.
1st ed. 1988.

Covers 1,884 organizations providing products and services in the information sector, ranging from abstracting services to telecommunications agencies. Entries by title A-Z include address, year of foundation, no. of employees, brief details of activity and summary data for products and services. Index of products and services (p.3-42) under such headings as Abstracting, Gerontology, Reprographics. Also contains brief lists of relevant periodicals and directories, guides and yearbooks. A geographic index would be a helpful addition. Overall 'far superior to TPFL's *Inside information* as its coverage is more in-depth and its organization layout ... far better' (*Current awareness bulletin,* v.7(4), April 1990, p.18). *Class No:* 02.0(058)

Histories

[103]
British library history: a bibliography. 1962/68-. Keeling, D.F., *ed.* Winchester, St. Paul's Bibliographies (formerly Library Association, Library History Group), 1972-.
6v. published to date: 1962/68 (1972. x,164p. ISBN 0853653454); 1969/72 (1975. v,150p. ISBN 0853654174); 1973/76 (1979. 200p. ISBN 0853657815); 1977/80 (1983. ix,242p. ISBN 0853658056); 1981/84 (1987. x,190p. ISBN 0853658374); 1985/88 (1991. x,181p. ISBN 0906795958). 1962/68-1981/84 published by the Library Association, Library History Group.

Covers the history of libraries, librarianship and book collecting in the British Isles. In 5 sections: Librarians; Librarianship; Libraries (vast majority of entries); Reading; Study of library history. Author and subject indexes in each v. Items continuously numbered reaching 4,620 with the 1985/88v. Strong on the coverage of scattered references outside the literature of librarianship. Includes theses and obituaries. Many entries briefly annotated. *Class No:* 02.0(091)

[104]
DAVIS, D.G. and TUCKER, J.M. American library history: a comprehensive guide to the literature. 2nd ed. Santa Barbara, ABC-Clio, 1990. xxii,471p. ISBN: 0874361427.
1st ed. 1978 by Harris, M.H. and Davis, D.G. as *American library history: a bibliography.*

Unannotated listing of more than 7,150 entries (doubling the number in the 1st ed.) giving full coverage until the end of 1986. Includes journal articles, chapters in books, unpublished research etc. Sections: 1. Historiography and sources - 2. General studies - 3. Private libraries and reading tastes - 4. Predecessors of the public library - 5. Public libraries - 6. Academic libraries -7. School libraries - 8. State libraries - 9. Special libraries - 10. Archival enterprise - 11. Education for librarianship - 12. Library associations - 13. Special aspects of librarianship -14. Women in librarianship - 15. Bibliographies of individual librarians and library benefactors. Each section begins with an introductory essay highlighting the major sources. Author and institution index; index to the introductory essays. The journal *Libraries and culture* contains biennial bibliographies intended to act as updating supplements. *Class No:* 02.0(091)

Biographies

Information Management

Cataloguing

[105]
Who's who in the UK information world 1992. Finlay, M., *comp. & ed.* 3rd ed. London, TFPL, 1991. 459p. ISBN: 187088924x.

1st ed. 1988/89.

Questionnaire based directory of over 3,700 entries. Wide ranging, including company and government librarians, information specialists, library school staff, personnel in information related organizations and some senior public and academic librarians. Detail given includes qualifications, present post, relevant memberships and training, no. of years experience, previous positions and brief description of current responsibilities and interests. Indexed by employing organization, employing organization activity and library and information science training institution attended. Entries provide uneven detail; many well-known individuals omitted. *Class No:* 02.0(092)

Institutions & Associations

[106]
FANG, J.R. *and* SONGE, A.H. World guide to library, archive and information science associations. [3rd ed.]. München, Saur, 1990. xxvii,517p. (*IFLA publications 52/53.*) ISBN: 3598108141.

First preliminary ed. as *Handbook of national and international library associations* (Chicago, American Library Association, 1973). 1st standard ed. Bowker 1976; 2nd ed. 1980.

In 2 pts.: International associations, 76 entries; National associations, 511 entries arranged by country. Full data includes address, officers, staff, establishment date, activities, fields of interest, structure, sources of support, publications, activities and bibliography for 1981-90. Indexes: Official journals of associations; Official names of associations; Chief officers; Subject; Countries with international associations; Countries with national associations. List of acronyms p.xiii-xxvii. Fairly comprehensive and well produced. Some specialist associations are included (*e.g.* UK entries for Agricultural Libraries in Colleges and Universities and Society of County Librarians as well as Aslib, Library Association etc.). The earlier eds. retain some minor reference value for the bibliographies *e.g.* 1975-80 in the 2nd ed. *Class No:* 02.0:061:061.2

[107]
LIBRARY ASSOCIATION. Library Association yearbook. London, Library Association, 1891-. Annual. ISSN: 00759066.

Title and frequency varies; annual publication since 1964.

The 1991 ed. (416p.) is in 3 sections. The first includes details of officers, headquarters departments and staff, past presidents, branches, special interest groups and committees, and medals, grants and awards. The second section reproduces the Royal Charter and gives bye-laws, election regulations, code of professional conduct, etc. The third and longest section comprises a list of members as of March 1991, giving date of joining and associateship, current post and employing organization. Separate lists of overseas and institutional (UK and overseas) members. Contents have varied over the years (*e.g.* 1968-73 carried a register of research in progress, the forerunner of *Current research in library and information science. Class No:* 02.0:061:061.2

[108]
Anglo-American cataloguing rules. Gorman, M. *and* Winkler, P., *eds.* 2nd ed. 1988 revision. London, Library Association, 1988. xxv,677p. ISBN: 085365509x.

Prepared under the direction of the Joint Steering Committee for the Revision of AACR, a committee of the American Library Association, the Australian Committee on Cataloguing, the British Library, the Canadian Committee on Cataloguing, the Library Association and the Library of Congress. Published jointly by the Library Association, American Library Association and Canadian Library Association.

Originally published 1967 in separate British and North American texts. 2nd ed. 1978 in one text. This revision updates the 2nd ed., incorporating the amendments of 1981-85, and the revision of Chap. 9, Computer files, 1987.

Designed for use in general libraries of all sizes, the rules cover the description and provision of access points for any library materials commonly collected. Organized in 2 main sections. I. 'Description', contains 13 chaps., the first setting out rules of general applicability, 2-10 giving rules for specific types of material (*e.g.* 5. Music; 7. Motion pictures and videorecordings) and 11-13 covering rules of partial generality. II. 'Headings, uniform titles and references' has 6 chaps.: Choice of access points; Headings for persons; Geographic names; Headings for corporate bodies; Uniform titles; References. 4 appendices: Capitalization; Abbreviations; Numerals; Glossary. Exceptionally thorough index comp. by K.G.B. Bakewell p.625-77. Majority of the revisions in this ed. of a minor nature. Now by far the most commonly used cataloguing code in English speaking countries. Also translated into 15 other languages including French, Italian, Japanese and Spanish. *Class No:* 025.40

[109]
—GORMAN, M. The Concise AACR2. 1988 revision. London, Library Association, 1989. xi,161p. ISBN: 0853657998.

First published 1981.

Intended 'to convey the essence and basic principles of the second edition of the *Anglo-American cataloguing rules, 1988 revision* ... without many of that comprehensive work's rules for out-of-the-way and complex materials' (General introduction p.1). Rules retained rewritten, simplified and supplied with examples. Widely used in smaller libraries instead of the full version. *Class No:* 025.40

Indexing

[110]
LIBRARY OF CONGRESS. Office of Subject Cataloging Policy. Library of Congress subject headings. Washington, D.C., Library of Congress, 1908-. Annual. ISSN: 10489711.

First published in parts between 1908 and 1914. Present title from 8th ed. (1975). Now published annually in 3v.

Updated by weekly lists, distributed on a monthly basis. Also available in microfiche, (new cumulations quarterly) and on CD-ROM, as *CDMARC subjects,* updated quarterly. The 13th ed. (1990) contains headings established through December 1989. Approx 181,000 headings in dictionary format displayed in 3 columns. Relationships indicated in thesaurus style from the 11th ed. (UF, BT, NT, etc.). About 40% of headings followed by LC class nos. representing most common aspect of subject. Much fuller than its nearest rival *Sears' list of subject heading* and more suitable for academic libraries. *Class No:* 025.42

Classification Systems

[111]
DEWEY, M. Dewey Decimal Classification and relative index. Comaroni, J., *and others eds.* 20th ed. Albany, N.Y., Forest Press, 1989. 4v. ISBN: 0910608377.

V.1 Introduction. Tables; v.2-3 Schedules; v.4 Relative index. Manual. 1st ed. 1876; 19th ed. 1979.

Regularly revised by the Decimal Classification Policy Committee, which includes representatives from the LA and ALA, as well as drawing on the expertise of outside groups. Used in most countries, and in most libraries in the UK, especially public and smaller academic libraries. The 20th ed. includes a completely revised schedule for class 780 Music, and incorporates the amendments issued to the 19th ed. for 001-006 Computer science and 301-307 Sociology. The index is also revised and reduced in size by the removal of unlikely references, while v.4 includes a manual, previously published separately in 1982. Revisions between editions are notified in *Dewey Decimal Classification: additions, notes and decisions.*
Class No: 025.44

[112]
LIBRARY OF CONGRESS. Subject Cataloging Division. Processing Department. **Library of Congress Classification.** Washington, D.C., Library of Congress, 1917-.

Published in classes and subclasses in various edition states. Recent revisions include Class B, Subclass BX. Religion: Christian denominations (1985); Class KDZ-KG-KH. Law of the Americas, Latin America and West Indies (1984); Class L. Education (1984); Class R. Medicine (1986); Class Z. Bibliography and library science (1980).

Originated simply for the arrangement of the Library of Congress collection before it reached its present size, the classification has grown to be one of the most widely used in the US, and is commonly used in university libraries in the UK. Its structure is suited to the scholarly library where the catalogue is not called on to provide an index closely modelled on the classification schedules.

Kept up-to-date by *L.C. classification. Additions and changes* (Washington, D.C., Library of Congress, Office for Subject Cataloging Policy. Quarterly. ISSN 00417912).
Class No: 025.44

026/027 Libraries

Libraries

Great Britain

[113]

World guide to libraries. Lengenfelder, H., *ed.* München, Saur, 1966-. Biennial. (*Handbook of international documentation and information, vol. 8.*) ISSN: 00000221.

Frequency varies: recent editions issued biennially.

The 10th ed. (1991. xxviii,1039p.) contains 42,122 entries for libraries in 166 countries. Largely questionnaire based. Aims to cover all general libraries with holdings of more than 30,000 volumes and special libraries with more than 5,000 volumes. Arranged by country A-Z (under English form of name), then according to type of library: National libraries; General research libraries; University libraries; School libraries; Government libraries; Ecclesiastical libraries; Corporate, business libraries; Special libraries maintained by other institutions; Public libraries. Includes separate entries for departmental libraries of universities, etc. Complete entry gives name, address, year founded, name of director or head, important holdings and special collections, main departments, statistics by type of material, name of accessible databanks or hosts, inter-library participation and membership of associations. Indexed by library name. The fullest source available, but the data given for each library is limited, and in many cases incomplete, while there are many anomalies in the subject classifications within country headings. Additional indexes, *e.g.* subject, special collections, would also be a valuable enhancement. Best regarded as a worldwide checklist and source of addresses. For North America and much of Europe, national and regional directories usually give fuller detail. *Class No: 026/027*

Europe

[114]

Guide to libraries in Western Europe: national, international and government libraries. Dale, P., *ed.* London, British Library Science Reference and Information Service, 1991. 122p. ISBN: 0712307850.

Published as a companion to *Guide to libraries and information units in government departments and other organizations* (*q.v.*).

Covers 532 "libraries and information services in government departments and other 'official' organizations who perform a national role" (*Introduction* p.1). Main section, Libraries by country (sub-arranged by English library name), gives brief details including address, librarian, stock and coverage, hours, services and publications. Further sections: National libraries - National library associations - British Council libraries. Indexed by library name, organization and subject. *Class No: 026/027(4)*

[115]

The Aslib directory of information sources in the United Kingdom. Codlin, E.M., *ed.* 6th ed. London, Aslib, 1990. 2v. ISBN: 0851422225.

Pt. 1 *Main directory* (967p.); pt. 2 *Subject and abbreviations index* (266p.). First published 1928; 5th ed., also in 2v. 1982-84, but with v.1 covering science and technology and v.2 social sciences, medicine and the humanities.

5,780 entries for information disseminators of all types, ranging from major academic and public libraries (*e.g.* John Rylands University Library of Manchester; Westminster Public Libraries), to specialized commercial, government, research, professional and other organizations (*e.g.* Circus Friends' Association of Great Britain; Jute Importers' Association). Entries, arranged A-Z by name, give address, type of organization, and person to whom to address enquiries, with summary data on subject coverage (terms selected by organization), special information services, special collections and publications. Lacks other basic data (*e.g.* opening hours, stock totals). Subject index includes some very general headings (*e.g.* management *c.*130 entries). Abbreviations index (p.211-66 of v.2), but no other indexes. Revised format of this ed. avoids previous duplication of entries between volumes. The only comprehensive source of its kind for the UK and an essential resource in all medium to large general libraries. For smaller libraries the *Shorter Aslib directory* (1986. ISBN 0851421997), based on the 5th ed., with *c.*2,000 entries, is a cheaper but less up-to-date alternative. *Class No: 026/027(410)*

[116]

Guide to libraries and information units: in government departments and other organizations. Dale, P., *ed.* 29th ed. London, British Library, 1990. [3],99p. ISBN: 0712307729. ISSN: 90525416.

First published 1948; now published approximately biennially, 28th ed. 1988. Previous eds. under the title *Guide to government department and other libraries.*

485 entries (100 new to this ed.) in 40 subject sections. Remains largely confined to government libraries, academic and public libraries omitted. Includes national libraries and libraries of overseas government agencies and official bodies located in the UK. Data given: address; librarian; hours; stock and coverage (often lengthy descriptions); availability (admission); services; publications. Good layout. Organization and subject indexes. *Class No: 026/027(410)*

[117]

Libraries directory. 1985/87-. Cambridge, James Clark, 1989-. Biennial. ISSN: 09614575.

Present title from 1988/90, previous issue as *The Libraries year book.* Continues the *Libraries, museums and art galleries yearbook,* first published 1897, last issued for

....*(contd.)*
1978/79 in 1981.

No longer covers museums and art galleries. The 1988/ 90v. (viii,172p.) in sections: The British Library - Public libraries (by authority A-Z) - Special libraries (by town, 1,108 entries, including many academic libraries) - Republic of Ireland. The best source for information on public libraries detail including population served, chief librarian, divisional/branch library addresses, loan periods, hours, stock, issues, special collections, equipment and facilities, staff (by category) and expenditure. Less extensive data for special libraries. Indexed by subjects, special collections and library and institution names. *Class No:* 026/027(410)

[118]
Libraries in the United Kingdom and Republic of Ireland.
Harrold, A., *ed.* London, Library Association, 1960-.
Annual (Irregular).

18th ed. (1992. iv,186p. ISBN 0853658595) in 6 main sections: Public libraries in the United Kingdom, the Channel Islands and the Isle of Man (arranged by library authority) - Public libraries in the Republic of Ireland - Libraries in universities and institutes of technology in the United Kingdom - Libraries in institutes of higher education - Selected government, national and special libraries in the United Kingdom - Selected academic, national and special libraries in the Republic of Ireland. Entries for each library/library authority gives basic data of address, chief librarian, other senior personnel and major branch libraries only. Lacks any information on subject strengths, hours, etc. Perversely the section Libraries in institutes of higher education mainly covers polytechnic libraries, colleges of higher education being largely excluded.
Class No: 026/027(410)

USA

[119]
American library directory. New York, Bowker, 1923-. Annual.
ISSN: 0065910x.

Frequency varies: annual since 1978.

Lists libraries of all types in the US, Puerto Rico, other regions administered by the US, and Canada. Almost 35,000 entries in the 1990/91 ed., arranged by state then city. Information given varies, but includes address, names of key personnel and subject holdings and, for many entries, income, expenditure, subject interests, special collections and publications. 9 codes indicate library type (*e.g.* C=College, L=Law). Statistical data on public libraries precedes each state listing. Supplementary information includes networks, consortia and other cooperative library organizations, library school and training courses, library systems, state and provincial library agencies and United States Information Agency Centers. Indexed by library name in v.2. Also available online (Dialog File 460) and in CD-ROM format as a component of the *Library Reference PLUS* database including additional information on booksellers, publishers, etc. *Class No:* 026/027(73)

[120]
Directory of special libraries and information centers. Detroit, Gale, 1963-. Annual. ISSN: 0731663x.

First published 1963; 2nd ed. 1968. Recent eds. issued on an annual basis.

Present subtitle *A Guide to more than 19,800 special libraries, information centers, archives and data centers maintained by government agencies, business, industry, newspapers, educational institutions, nonprofit organizations and societies in the fields of science, engineering, medicine, law, art, religion the social sciences and humanities.*

The 14th ed. (DeMaggio, J.A. ed. 1991. 2v. in 3) has 19,843 entries, including 1,000 for significant information centres outside the US and Canada. Information given

....*(contd.)*
includes parent body, subject keywords, head librarian, founding date, no. of staff, subjects, special collections, holdings (quantitative data), services, automated systems, publications, former names and principal staff. V.1 pt.2 contains 6 appendices (Networks and consortia; Libraries for the blind; Patent depository libraries; Regional depository libraries; United Nations depository libraries; World Bank depository libraries) and a 4,000 term subject index. The separately available v.2 provides geographic (US; Canada; International) and personal name indexes. A supplement, *New special libraries* (ISSN 01934287), is issued between eds. *Class No:* 026/027(73)

028 Reading

Reading

[121]

An English library. Farrow, N., *and others eds.* 6th ed. Aldershot, Gower in association with the Book Trust, 1990. ix,385p. ISBN: 0566058189.

1st ed. 1943; 5th ed. 1963.

Compiled 'with one objective: to identify the books from the classical and modern heritage that will extend our enjoyment of reading' (Introduction p.vi). Over 2,500 titles, selected by 20 contributors. Briefly annotated entries in 15 categories (*e.g.* World literature in English, Children's literature, Drama, Biography, Travel, History, The Bible, Fine arts, Reference), each with an introductory section discussing the selection. Author and title index. Many entries omit publisher's name; prices not given. *Refer* (v.6(3), Autumn 1990, p.21-22) notes outdated editions in the reference books section. *Class No: 028*

[122]

The Reader's adviser: a layman's guide to the literature. Chernow, B.A. *and* Vallasi, G.A., *eds.* 13th ed. New York, Bowker, 1986-88. 6v. ISBN: 0835224287, set.

V.1 *The best in American and British fiction, poetry, essays, literary biography, bibliography and reference* (783p. ISBN 0835221458); v.2 *The best in American and British drama and world literature in English translation* (898p. ISBN 0835221466); v.3 *The best in general reference literature, the social sciences, history and the arts* (780p. ISBN 0835221474); v.4 *The best in literature of philosophy and world religion* (801p. ISBN 0835221482); v.5 *The best in the literature of science, technology and medicine* (725p. ISBN 0835221490); v.6 *Indexes* (594p. ISBN 0835223159).

First published 1921. Early eds. with title *Bookman's manual.* 12th ed. published in 3v. 1974-77.

Volumes divided into chapters contributed by academics, librarians, etc. Each has a brief introduction followed by listings, beginning with general and reference works, then more specific titles. Many entries give brief annotations in addition to bibliographic citation and price. Some out of print titles included. V.3-5 of this ed. represent a major expansion of v.3 of the 12th ed., doubling the number of works listed. Coverage of science in particular, is greatly increased. Each volume individually indexed by subject, author and title in addition to the collective indexes in v.6. Imprints are American, but the work, for long a standard and now greatly expanded, is valuable as a selection tool and reference aid in general libraries of all types which serve an adult population. *Class No: 028*

Children's Reading - Study & Criticism

[123]

CARPENTER, H. *and* **PRICHARD, M.** **The Oxford companion to children's literature.** Oxford, Oxford University Press, 1984. x,587p., illus. ISBN: 0192115820.

More than 900 biographical entries for authors, illustrators, printers, publishers and educationalists. A further *c.*2,000 entries for major works of fiction, characters from books, genres, organizations, children's literature of specific countries and children's play and learning. Equal attention given to British, American and Commonwealth works. Well-written entries; comprehensively cross-referenced. Short on bibliographical guidance for further reading. A major contribution containing an enormous amount of information not readily obtainable from any other source. *Class No: 028:087.5*

[124]

CHESTER, T.R. Children's books research: a practical guide to techniques and sources. Stroud, Thimble Press in association with Westminster College, Oxford, 1989. 76p. ISBN: 0903355329.

Emphasis is on research methods, sections including 'Choosing your project', 'Writing the research proposal' and 'Using the library'. Brief discussion of the more important sources in the text. Books mentioned (p.57-60); Current periodicals (p.61-63); Booklist (p.67-74), drawing on Salway's *Reading about children's books* and *The Signal review.* A compact, well-written guide for those embarking on children's literature research. Complemented by:- *Class No: 028:087.5*

[125]

—**Sources of information about children's books.** Chester, T.R., *comp.* Stroud, Thimble Press in association with Westminster College, Oxford, 1989. 78p. ISBN: 0903355337.

Intended as a supplement to *Children's books research.* Main section comprises a list of 157 British collections specializing in children's literature and related materials (p.2-35). Entries include succinct descriptions; indexed. Further sections on 'Organizations and societies' and 'Printed sources' (p.53-78), a classified, annotated listing of mainly British publications. *Class No: 028:087.5*

[126]

Children's literature: a guide to reference sources. Haviland, V., *comp.* Washington D.C., Library of Congress, 1966. x,341p., illus. ISBN: 0686979362.

First supplement. 1972. (vii, 316p. ISBN 08444022x); Second supplement. 1977. (x,413p. ISBN 084440215x).

The main v. has 809 entries under broad topics such as Authorship, Illustration, Bibliography, plus 183 entries on International studies and National studies. Includes periodical articles, unpublished theses, records and tapes, as

....(contd.)
well as books and pamphlets. Index of authors, titles and
subjects. The two supplements chiefly cover new material
1966-74, the latter having 929 entries in the same basic
format as the parent volume. *Class No:* 028:087.5

[127]
Children's literature abstracts. Llanbrynmair, Children's
Libraries Section of the International Federation of Library
Associations, 1973-. Quarterly. ISSN: 03062015.
About 200 indicative, signed abstracts per issue, drawing
on *c.*50 English language journals. Arranged in sections (*e.g.*
Audio-visual materials; History of children's books;
Adolescent fiction; Psychological, educational and social
criteria; Illustrators). Author and subject index issued
annually. A separate *Books and pamphlets* supplement is
also produced on an approximately annual basis. *Class
No:* 028:087.5

[128]
International directory of children's literature.
Dunhouse, M.B., *comp.* New York, Oxford, Facts on File,
1986. 129p. ISBN: 0816014116.
Data from 84 countries. Chapters: 1) Children's literature
publishers (over 50% of book) - 2) Children's magazines -
3) Children's literature magazines - 4) Children's literature
organizations - 5) Children's literature fairs, seminars,
conferences - 6) Children's literature prizes - 7) Major
children's libraries and special collections - 8) Statistics on
children's books. Information presented by country within
each chapter. "Useful and unique" (*Reference books
bulletin* 1986-1987, p.43), although some information is
incomplete or available elsewhere. *Class No:* 028:087.5

[129]
Twentieth-century children's writers. Chevalier, T., *ed. and*
Kirkpatrick, D.L., *consulting ed.* 3rd ed. Chicago and
London, St. James Press, 1989. xxi,1288p. ISBN:
0912289953.
1st ed. 1978; 2nd ed. 1984. Preface by N. Lewis p.vii-xi.
Covers "English language authors of fiction, poetry and
drama" (p.xvii). This ed. adds more than 120 authors,
bringing the total to nearly 800. Entries, arranged A-Z,
consist of biography, a complete list of all separately
published books by category, including works for adults,
critical assessments by contributors and, in the case of
some living entrants, comments by the authors themselves.
Appendix (p.1085-1118) covers some important
representative writers of the 19th century. 'Foreign language
writers' with selected books in English translation (p.1122-
25). Title index. A "remarkably comprehensive" work
(*Refer*, 6(l), Spring 1990, p.20). "(M)eets the requirements
of high scholarship" (while being) "a user-friendly book
which can also provide hours of pleasure for the interested
browser" (*Children's literature abstracts. Books and
pamphlets*, June 1990, p.7). *Class No:* 028:087.5

Children's Reading - Books

[130]
Best books for children: preschool through grade 6.
Gillespie, J.T. *and* Naden, C.J., *eds.* 4th ed. New York,
Bowker, 1990. 1002p. ISBN: 0835226689.
First published 1959. 1st ed. in revised format 1978; 3rd
ed. 1985.
A substantial and valuable classified listing of 11,299
titles, plus a further 1,083 citations in notes. Excludes out-
of-print titles. Annotated entries note grade levels and
price. Indexed by author, illustrator, title, subject and grade
level. *Class No:* 028-053

[131]
Children's books in print: a reference catalogue. London,
Whitaker, 1972-. Annual. ISSN: 0577781x.
Frequency varies: annual from 1984.
Derived from *Whitaker's books in print* (*q.v.*). Lists
about 30,000 (1990) currently available titles. Includes a
classified sequence using 98 subject categories and a
directory of over 1,000 publishers and distributors. *Class
No:* 028-053

[132]
Children's books of the year. 1970-. London, Andersen Press
in association with Book Trust, 1971-. Annual.
Supersedes *The best books of ...*
The 1990 ed. (comp. J. Eccleshare, 113p. illus. ISBN
0862643007) has 14 sections (*e.g.* Picture books; Fiction for
older readers; People and places). 300 books selected, each
descriptively annotated. Index of authors, and illustrators;
index of titles. *Class No:* 028-053

[133]
The Junior bookshelf: a review of children's books.
Huddersfield, 1936-. 6pa. ISSN: 00226505.
Almost exclusively devoted to reviews of new children's
books. About 250 titles included in each issue in sections:
For librarians; Picture books; For children under ten; For
children ten to fourteen; For the intermediate library.
Entries also give price and ISBN. *Class No:* 028-053

[134]
The Signal selection of children's books. 1982-. Stroud,
Thimble Press, 1983-. Annual. ISSN: 02642212.
Initially published as *The Signal review of children's
books.*
The 1989 ed. (1990. 98p. ed. N. Chambers) has 237
brief, critically annotated entries for more than 350 titles.
Main sections: Picture books - Fiction - Traditional tales -
Information books - Books about children's books. Indexed.
Class No: 028-053

03 Reference Books

Reference Books

Bibliographies

[135]
BRITISH COUNCIL. Libraries Books and Information Division. Bibliographical Section. **Reference works (including CD-ROM).** London, The British Council, 1990. 84p. (*Core lists of library material.*) ISBN: 0863551068.

Lists 505 basic reference items, nearly all published in the UK, by Dewey classification giving bibliographic detail, ISBN, price, very brief annotation and grading (essential, recommended, useful, extra). Title index. "(B)iased towards British Council target users and therefore all subject areas are not covered to the same depth" (p.3). Nonetheless, a useful and up-to-date guide and a partial replacement for *Basic stock for the reference library* (1981). *Class No:* 03(01)

[136]
Guide to reference books. Sheehy, E.P., *ed.* 10th ed. Chicago, American Library Association, 1986. xiv,1560p. ISBN: 0838903908.

Originated in A.C. Kroeger's *Guide to the study and use of reference books* (1902). 3rd-6th eds., (1917-36) by I.G. Mudge; 7th-8th eds. by C.M. Winchell (1951-67); 9th ed. by E.P. Sheehy (1976).

A further thorough revision of the standard US guide to reference books. *c.*16,000 main entries (33% increase on 9th ed.) amended up to 1984, with some publications from 1985. 5 main sections (A. General reference works (including language dictionaries, biography, genealogy) - B. The humanities - C. Social and behavioral sciences - D. History and area studies - E. Science, technology and medicine), with 48 subsidiary subject divisions. Well set-out in 2 col. format with clear type; most subject divisions include introductory notes. Index (p.1299-1560) of *c.*28,000 entries for authors, editors, compilers, sponsoring bodies, titles and subjects.

While the work has an understandable US slant, scope is international, with a fair proportion of foreign language works. Strong coverage of the humanities, but science, technology and medicine (p.1132-1298) comparatively neglected. Entries lack full pagination, price and ISBN/ISSN. Databases are also inadequately treated, publications available online being indicated by symbol only, with no detail of vendor, time-span etc. Despite these limitations 'no other guide combines such breadth, inclusiveness, currentness and usefulness' (*Wilson library bulletin,* v.61(7), March 1987, p.64-65). '(C)omprehensive, conservative and scholarly', long review in *Choice,* (v.24(9), May 1987, p.1361-64).

Previous eds. were updated by supplements (*e.g.* 9th ed. supplements 1980 and 1982). A supplement to this ed., to contain about 4,500 entries, is scheduled for publication in 1992. The next full edition, to be produced from the

....(*contd.*)
Choice (*q.v.*) editorial office, is projected for 1995. Updating articles are also published in *College and research libraries.* The article *Selected reference books of 1989-90,* (v.52(2), March 1991, p.177-93) has *c.*25 new entries with 3p. of notes on new editions and supplements. *Class No:* 03(01)

[137]
MALCLÈS, L-N. Manuel de bibliographie. Lhéritier, A., *ed.* 4. éd. Paris, Presses Universitaires de France, 1985. vi,448p. ISBN: 2130389848.

First published 1954 as *Cours de bibliographie.* 3rd ed. 1975.

Around 4,000 entries, those for basic works being asterisked and briefly annotated. 32 chapters: 1-2, Bibliographie; 3-10, Bibliographies générales (including chapter 10 Encyclopédies et dictionnaires biographiques); 11-31 Bibliographies specialisées (12-21: Sciences humaines; 22-31: Sciences fundamentales); 32, Bibliographies de bibliographie, bibliologie. Index of authors and anonyma; index of subjects. Chapter introductions; also introductions to some sections. Helps to update Malclès's classic *Les Sources du travail bibliographique* (1950-58. 3v. in 4), but geographic coverage is limited to Western Europe and North America, with an emphasis on French sources. *Class No:* 03(01)

[138]
Printed reference materials: and related sources of information. Lea, P.W. *and* Day, A., *eds.* 3rd ed. London, Library Association, 1990. xxv,589p. ISBN: 1856040186.

First published 1980; 2nd ed., Higgens, G. ed., 1984. Full title of both eds. *Printed reference material.*

19 contributors, 20 sections: 1. Introduction - 2. Dictionaries - 3. General encyclopaedias - 4. Subject encyclopaedias - 5. Biographical reference works - 6. Business and company information - 7. News and current events - 8. Periodicals - 9. Reports and theses, conferences and symposia, standards and patents - 10. Maps, atlases and gazetteers - 11. Local history - 12. Current and retrospective bibliographies - 13. Subject bibliographies - 14. Community information - 15. Audiovisual materials - 16. Electronic publishing - 17. Indexes - 18. Government publications - 19. Statistical sources - 20. Official publications of international organizations. Each section comprises a short general/historical introduction followed by brief descriptive and comparative annotations of individual items. References and citations, and usually further reading, at section ends. The index p.527-89 provides access by author, organizations, subjects, countries and titles. Effectively updates A.D. Robert's classic *Introduction to reference books* (3rd ed. 1956). Despite some unevenness and a reduction in size of this ed., provides an excellent survey and remains the standard one volume British guide to reference material. *Class No:* 03(01)

[139]
TOTOK, W. *and* WEITZEL, R. Handbuch der bibliographischen Nachschlagewerke. Kernchen, H-J. *and* Kernchen, D., *hrsg.* 6., völlig neu bearb. Aufl. Frankfurt am Main, Klostermann, 1984-85. 2v. ISBN: 3465015924, v.1; 3465015940.

V.1 *Allgemeinbibliographien und allgemeine Nachschlagewerke* (xvi,472p.); v.2 *Fachbibliographien und fachbezogene Nachschlagewerke* (xviii,684p.). First published 1954; 5th ed. 1977.

About 6,000 entries, including subsumed references, mostly briefly annotated. V.1, in 17 main sections, covers general sources such as bibliographies of bibliographies, library catalogues, national bibliographies, theses, official publications, incunabula, encyclopedias, and biographical dictionaries. V.2 has 22 main subject sections each further subdivided. Includes major treatises and some leading periodicals. Author, title and subject index in each volume. Emphasises bibliographical sources including some 'hidden' and serial bibliographies. Primary German-language material, but English and other European languages are also fairly well represented. Strong on the general works covered in v.1, especially for European sources, but weaker in some subject areas, notably science and technology, where the sub-section for chemistry has only 34 entries. Nonetheless, a major tool for librarians and students of librarianship. *Class No:* 03(01)

Reviews & Abstracts

[140]
American reference books annual. Englewood, Colo., Libraries Unlimited, 1970-. Annual. ISSN: 00659959.

Aims to 'provide reviews of the complete spectrum of English language reference books published in the United States and Canada'. New monograph reference works covered comprehensively, indexing and abstracting services and other serials reviewed at 4-5 yearly intervals. Recent annuals have also included increasing numbers of British, Australian and Indian English language publications. Selective treatment of government publications and reports; works of less than 48 pages and highly specialized material excluded. The 1991 ed. (v.22. xxvi,825p.) has 1,833 signed, critical reviews in 37 main subject sections, with references to previous reviews and reviews in other periodicals. Indexed by author, title, subject and review contributor; quinquennial cumulated indexes 1970/74-1985/89. Widest coverage of the US reference reviewing sources and a valuable selection tool for English-language materials, especially specialized titles. *Class No:* 03(048)

[141]
Reference books bulletin: a compilation of evaluations appearing in Reference books bulletin. Chicago, American Library Association, 1970-. Annual. ISSN: 87550962.

Issued under the auspices of the Reference Books Bulletin Board of the ALA.

Present title from 1983/84; previously *Reference and subscription book reviews.* Continues *Subscription books bulletin reviews,* published in 5v. for 1956/60-1966/68, (1961-68).

Extracted from the *Reference books bulletin* section of the bimonthly *Booklist* (*q.v.*). The 21st ed. for 1988/89 (ix,210p.) contains 436 reviews of 250-500 words, occasionally longer, and 6 review articles p.1-28 (*e.g.* Medical reference tools for the layperson; 1988 encyclopedia round up (a regular feature from 1984/85); Sports reference books). Arrangement is by 17 Dewey based subject groups; subject, type of material and title indexes. Not as comprehensive as *American reference books annual* (above), but the reviews are generally longer, better written and more considered. *Class No:* 03(048)

[142]
Reference reviews: reviews of new reference materials prepared by librarians for librarians. Bradford, MCB University Press, 1987-. Quarterly. ISSN: 09504125.

Publisher varies.

Contains signed reviews of *c.*400-500 words in broad subject sections (*e.g.* General works, Business, Science, Literature, Children's books), with author and title indexes in each issue. The only British journal devoted to reviewing reference material. Unfortunately, the number of titles reviewed is limited (404 in 1991), many important items escaping attention. *Class No:* 03(048)

030 Encyclopaedias

Encyclopaedias

Multi-Volume Works

[143]
The Buyer's guide to encyclopedias. Tucker, N. *and* Timms, H., *comps*. Rev. ed. Cheltenham, Simply Creative, 1989. 38p. tables. ISBN: 1871327008.
First published 1988.
Reviews and compares most of the multi-volume encyclopedias that are 'widely purchased in Britain'. 7 titles treated in depth: *Children's Britannica, New Encyclopaedia Britannica, Encyclopedia Americana, Grolier academic encyclopedia/Macmillan family encyclopedia, New book of knowledge, Oxford illustrated encyclopedia* and *The World book encyclopedia*. Tables (p.30-35), contain comparative statistical data on price, pages articles, words, illus., maps, index entries, etc.; includes details for a number of sets not reviewed (*e.g. Colliers encyclopedia*). A handy, concise guide, effectively replacing J.M. Walsh's *Encyclopedia ratings*, last published 1982, which evaluated 20 British and US sets. *Class No: 030*

[144]
KISTER, K.F. Best encyclopedias: a guide to general and specialized encyclopedias. Phoenix, Oryx, 1986. xii,356p. tables. ISBN: 0897741714.
Replaces Kister's *Encyclopedia buying guide: a consumer guide to general encyclopedias in print*, 3rd ed. (Bowker, 1981. First published 1976). This title succeeded *General encyclopedias in print* by S.P. Walsh, 9th ed. (Bowker, 1973. First published 1963).
In depth reviews of 52 general English language encyclopedias. Each review divided into two sections: Facts (publishing history, description, price) and Evaluation (critical and comparative analysis, review citations, purchasing information). 5 appendices: A: General encyclopedia comparison chart - B: Specialized encyclopedias (annotated list of 450 subject encyclopedias under 32 subject headings) - C: Foreign language encyclopedias (annotated list of major Dutch, French, German, Italian, Japanese, Russian and Spanish general encyclopedias) - D: Encyclopedia bibliography (40 items) - E: Encyclopedia publishers and distributors (North American data only). Title/subject index. 'Excellent assessments of all available English language sets' (*Refer* v.4(3), Spring 1987, p.16), but sketchy on subject encyclopedias and not fully up to date on foreign language titles. *Class No: 030*

[145]
Collier's encyclopedia: with bibliography and index. New York, Macmillan Educational Co.; London, Collier-Macmillan. Annual revision. 24v. illus., maps, tables.
First published 1949-51 (20v.).
For both adults and advanced students, the editors having 'included the essential content of the curriculum of colleges and secondary schools as well as the upper grades' (Preface v.1). About 25,000 articles, nearly all signed, the work of *c*.5000 editors, advisors and contributors. Includes many lengthy articles (*e.g.* 'Libraries', v.14 p.559-99, *c*.40 illus., 1 chart). Biographical and geographical articles tend to be especially thorough and well-shaped (*e.g.* 'Leningrad', $3\frac{1}{2}$p., 2 illus., 1 map). The *c*.17,000 illus. are a less satisfactory feature for an encyclopedia at this level, Despite 3,000 new illus. in the 1991 revision, the majority remain in black and white. The 1,450 Rand McNally maps, while plentiful, some with gazetteer entries on the verso, are also of a variable standard. Limited use of references, the set depending on the index in v.24. At 400,000 clearly displayed entries, including illustrations and bibliography items, this is one of the most extensive of any English language encyclopedia. The other feature of *Collier's* which sets it apart from its rivals, is the 12,000 item bibliography, also in v.24 (p.1-201). Extensively revised in recent years, entries are in classified arrangement, some with one sentence annotations. While the whole set has an appreciable US slant, this is a valuable second-string encyclopedia. An alternative to the *Britannica* and *Americana* for smaller public libraries and home use.
Collier's international yearbook is primarily concerned with the events of the previous year. The 1990 yearbook (620p. illus.) is in basic A-Z arrangement with articles for countries, US states, major subjects and topical concerns. Includes 'Obituaries' p.463-505 and 'World facts and statistics' p.580-96. A number of feature articles, *e.g.* 'The greenhouse effect', 'Hispanic Americans', are also provided (p.1-96). One of the best encyclopedia yearbooks. *Class No: 030=20(003.8)*

[146]
The Encyclopedia Americana. International ed. Danbury, Conn., Grolier. Annual revision. 30v. illus., ports., tables, maps.
First published 1829-33. The earliest US encyclopedia and largely based on *Brockhaus Konversations - Lexikon* (7th ed. 1827-29).
Over 6,000 contributors, *c*.52,000 articles (40% biographies) *c*.900p. per volume. Articles are signed and briefly state qualifications of contributor. Stronger emphasis on North America than in comparable multi-volume sets, especially history, place-names and people (*e.g.*

....(contd.)

'Massachusetts': v.18 p.448-73; 7 sections, plus boxed information, illus. of state seal, 15 illus., double spread map backed by a gazetteer, 14 references). Also strong on science and technology (e.g. 'Aluminium': v.1 p.641-46; 8 illus., 2 diagrs., 6 references). Nearly 23,000 illus., judiciously placed, but with sparing use of colour. The index (v.30) is comprehensive with 350,000 entries, compensating for a lack of cross-references in the text. Remains one of the most authoritative and scholarly general encyclopedias, but revision is not as far-reaching as it might be and the physical appearance is unattractive. Overall 'today's set looks very old fashioned ... compressed columns, dated bibliographies and somewhat flimsy paper all work against a coverage that is in fact extremely thorough and comprehensive' (*The buyer's guide to encyclopedias* 1989 ed. p.22).

The Americana annual (1923-) is divided into 4 major sections: Year in review; Feature articles; Alphabetical section; Statistical and tabular data. *Class No:* 030=20(003.8)

[147]
The Macmillan family encyclopedia. London, Macmillan. Annual revision. 21v. illus., ports., diagrs., tables, maps. ISBN: 0333420519.

First published 1980. Published by Grolier in the US as *Academic American encyclopedia.*

The most recently established of the English language multi-volume general encyclopedias. '(C)reated for students in junior high school, high school or college and the inquisitive adult' (Preface). About 2,350 contributors, 29,000 articles, 17,000 illus. (predominantly col. and of a high standard) and 1,100 maps. Articles are brief to medium in length, often signed, over ½ with short appended bibliographies. Cross-references widely used in the text; v.21 *Index* has 200,000 entries, one of the fullest of its kind. A particular feature worthy of note is an attention to objectivity in dealing with controversial topics and a relative freedom from US bias. Currency is also good, the 1991 revision having 2,750 amended, plus 100 new articles. Negative features are closely spaced text and some lack of depth in the treatment of more complex subjects, especially those of a technical nature. The encyclopedia was one of the first to experiment with online availability. A CD-ROM version including 1,300 selected illus. has also been released. A full review appears in *Reference books bulletin* (in *Booklist*, v.87(8), 15 December 1990, p.575-76). *Class No:* 030=20(003.8)

[148]
The New Encyclopaedia Britannica. 15th ed. Chicago and London, Encyclopaedia Britannica. Annual revision. 32v. illus., ports., tables, maps.

From the 1985 printing comprises: Micropaedia (v.1-12); Macropaedia (v.13-29); Propaedia (1v.); Index (2v.).

The *Encyclopaedia Britannica* was first published in Edinburgh 1768-81. Further editions were produced throughout the nineteenth and early twentieth centuries, the most notable being the 24v. 9th ed. (1875-79) and the 26v. 11th ed. (1910-11). From the 24v. 14th ed. (1929) features of the modern Britannica such as continuous revision and the *Britannica book of the year* were gradually established.

The 15th ed. of the *Britannica* was first published in 1974 in 30v. comprising Micropaedia (10v.), Macropaedia (19v.) and Propaedia (1v.). The Micropaedia containing 100,000 brief entries, none longer than 750 words, was intended for ready reference, the bulk of the set being formed by the 4,200 lengthy articles of the Macropaedia. As then constituted the *Britannica* had no index, this function being performed by the Micropaedia. With the 1985 printing the *Britannica* was restructured, the main changes being a drastic reduction in the number of

....(contd.)

Macropaedia articles, the addition of two further Micropaedia volumes and most importantly, the provision of an index.

The 17v. Macropaedia 'Knowledge in depth' has 671 lengthy, scholarly articles covering 30p., with some much longer (e.g. Literature, the art of', 140p.). Generally confined to broad subjects (e.g. 'Chritianity'; 'Reproduction and reproductive systems'), the Macropaedia also has articles for countries and regions (e.g. 'Norway', 15p. (subdivided) full page col. map, 2 illus., 1 further map, 1¼ columns of bibliography) and c.100 biographies (e.g. Darwin, Freud, Johnson, Lincoln, Rembrandt). Many of the articles, especially those on technical or complex subjects, are written at a level which put them beyond the understanding of the layperson. Lengthy bibliographies are appended (e.g. the 68p. article 'Food processing' has 3¾p. of references).

The Micropaedia has c.65,000 entries averaging 275-300 words in length. Many biographical articles are included, the more substantial of which have bibliographies (e.g. 'Nkrumah, Kwame', 1p., 8 references; 'Stresemann, Gustav', 1½p., 1 port., 9 references). Subjects treated in the Macropaedia also have entries, a policy which allows the Micropaedia to stand alone, but results in much unnecessary duplication. The final part of the *Britannica*, the 2v. index, has c.500,000 references and cross-references. This recently introduced feature is a vital component of the whole enabling the set to function much more effectively as a reference tool and should be the user's first port of call.

Revised on an annual basis, the 1991 printing having 8 rewritten and 65 revised Macropaedia articles and 385 new and 1,475 revised Micropaedia entries, the *Britannica* is kept impressively up-to-date. Illustrations may be sparse, paper quality relatively poor and the price well in excess of rivals, but when it comes to major considerations such as comprehensiveness and authority the *Britannica* is unbeatable. *Class No:* 030=20(003.8)

[149]
—Britannica book of the year. Chicago and London, Encyclopaedia Britannica, 1938-. Annual. Illus., ports., tables., maps. ISSN: 00681156.

Spine title *Britannica world data.*

The 1991v. (910p.) is in 5 sections. The first contains a feature article 'Global environment - a planet in stress', the second is a chronology of 1990 (p.16-36) and the third 'Britannica update' (p.37-63), reproduces selected Macropaedia articles or parts of articles which have been revised or re-written. The main section, 'The year in review' (p.64-528) is divided topically (e.g. Agriculture and food supplies; Disasters; Fashion and dress; Literature; Sports and games), with biographies and obituaries following. The final section, 'World data' (p.529-880, grey edged paper), provides demographic, economic, transport, education, military, etc., statistics by country (p.538-739) and comparative national statistics (p.740-877). Indexed. One of the best encyclopedia yearbooks, and an important reference source in its own right, especially for the statistical information collected under 'World data'. *Class No:* 030=20(003.8)

Single-Volume works

[150]
The Cambridge encyclopedia. Crystal, D., ed. Cambridge, Cambridge Univ. Press, 1990. ix,1334[128]p., 16p. of plates, diagrs., tables, maps. ISBN: 0521395283.

Reprinted with updates and corrections 1991.

Slightly more entries (30,000 claimed) than the other British published one volume encyclopedias, achieved at the expense of text illustrations (only 750 diagrams and maps). Concise, well-written articles (e.g. 'Jupiter', c.400 words;

....(contd.)

'Venezuela', c.250 words, 1 map; 'Royal Opera House', 35 words), including 5,500 biographies and 4,000 geographical entries. Aims to give special emphasis to technology, computer science, the environment, medicine and leisure interests. A unique and valuable feature is the 128p. 'Ready reference' section containing largely tabulated data in 11 groupings. Individual tables include 'Largest deserts', 'UK road distances', 'Counties of England' (area, population, administrative centre), 'Political leaders, 1900-1990' (by country), 'Religious symbols', 'Sports and games' (winners by sport) and 'Common abbreviations'. 16p. of grouped col. plates, but no other col. illus. and no separate atlas section. Extensive use of cross-references (c.75,000) including references to 'Ready reference' data. In many ways similar to *The Longman encyclopedia* (q.v.), but overall, especially when the 'Ready reference' section is taken into account, the superior product. *Class No:* 030=20(003.9)

[151]

The Guinness book of records. Enfield, Guinness Publishing, 1955-. Annual.

Records included are those 'which improve upon previous records or which are newly significant in having become the subject of widespread and preferably international interest. ...(U)nique occurences, interesting peculiarities or 'firsts' are not necessarily records. Records in our sense are both measurable and comparable' (Introduction). 11 sections: The human being (e.g. longevity) - The living world - The natural world and space (e.g. weather, stars) - Science and technology - Buildings and structures - Transport - The business world (e.g. coins, postal services) - The arts and entertainment (e.g. best selling books) - Human achievements (e.g. longest walks, deepest dives) - The human world (e.g. politics, awards, religion) - Sports and games. Separate stop press section by chapter. Analytical index. The standard guide and one of the most familiar general reference tools, translated into 35 languages. A CD-ROM version, including sound and visual effects, is also available from Pergamon Compact Solution. *Class No:* 030=20(003.9)

[152]

The Hutchinson encyclopedia. 9th ed. London, Hutchinson, 1990. 1241p. illus., maps, ports, tables. ISBN: 0091745527.

First published 1948. Title varies, as *The Hutchinson 20th century encyclopedia* until 1981. 8th ed. 1988.

The longest established British one volume encyclopedia. Contains more than 25,000 short entries (e.g. 'Caxton, William', c.150 words; 'Italy', 3 cols., basic statistical tables and chronology; 'Reagan, Ronald' c.400 words), with 2,500 supporting illustrations, mainly in colour. Pronunciation and stress shown for entry words as necessary. Lacks a separate index but extensively cross-referenced. Good currency e.g. 'Acid house', 'Satellite TV'. 3 column format and smaller print size than most other one volume encyclopedias giving the text and somewhat cluttered appearance. Despite the recent publication of rival works remains one of the better buys. *Class No:* 030=20(003.9)

[153]

The Longman encyclopedia. Briggs, A., ed. Harlow, Longman, 1989. x,1178p. illus.,diagrs.,tables, maps. ISBN: 0582916208.

Based on the *Concise Columbia encyclopedia* with extensive revisions to give a greater British orientation. c.17,000 undocumented entries from 120 contributors, all approved by a distinguished editorial board including Sir Herman Bondi, Stuart Hall and Mary Warnock. Average article length only 86 words, but countries and major topics given extended treatment (e.g. 'New Zealand' c.500 words, 1 map, list of post-war prime ministers; 'Magnetism', c.550 words). Closely spaced text in two column format

....(contd.)

supported by 500 illus., 250 diagrs., 36 tables and 150 text maps, all black and white. Separate 16p. col. atlas section. Suitable for GCSE, A level and beyond, and as a quick reference tool. Fewer entries than some of the other one volume encyclopedias and visually not one of the most appealing, the *Longman's* main strength lies in the eminence and authority of the editors. *Class No:* 030=20(003.9)

Children

[154]

Children's Britannica. Sutton, M., ed.   4th ed. London, Encyclopaedia Britannica, 1988. 20v. illus., diagrs., maps. ISBN: 085229218X.

First published 1960; 3rd ed. 1973. Extensively revised and reset for this ed. Minor updating and revision on an annual basis.

About 3 million words in 4,230 articles. Generously, but not particularly attractively, illustrated with c.5,000 photographs (less than $\frac{1}{2}$ in colour) and c.1,500 diagrams. Articles are lengthy where necessary (e.g. 'Aircraft', 8p., 2p. of diagrs., 6 illus.), but typically less than 1p. V.19 contains a 40 map atlas section with a gazetteer. V.20 (633p.) comprises a *Reference index* of 30,000 dictionary entries, both for topics treated in the text (e.g. 'Matterhorn' c.25 words with 2 references) and those not covered (e.g. 'Homs' (Syria) c.30 words). Intended for a slightly younger age group than most of the other major children's encyclopedias and not a junior/adult set in the manner of *World book*. One of the most widely sold multi-volume encyclopedias for home use, also found in school and children's libraries. A particular advantage for British users is the relative freedom of US bias, the set being edited from London with many UK contributors. *Class No:* 030=20-0053

[155]

Compton's encyclopedia and fact-index. Chicago, Encyclopaedia Britannica. Annual revision. 26v. illus., (incl. col.), diagrs., charts, maps.

First published 1922.

Intended for US junior and senior high school and middle elementary school students. Articles are generally curriculum orientated, and although often lengthy, written in a controlled vocabulary appropriate to the audience level. The 1989 revision contains 5,200 text articles, supported by 20,000 illus. (a large number black and white) and 2,000 maps. Major articles are documented. A feature of *Compton's* is the 'Fact index' placed at the end of each volume. This functions as an index, as a means of refering to related articles in other volumes, and through dictionary type entries, as a source of information on topics considered too minor to warrant a full article. The final volume contains a cumulation of all 63,000 fact index entries. *Compton's* began an extensive updating programme from 1983, now completed. Currency and coverage is thereby further improved, confirming its position as second only to *World book encyclopedia* (q.v.) as a leading set for the 9-18 age group and beyond.

Compton's has been one of the first encyclopedias to exploit the potential of CD-ROM. *Compton's multi-media encyclopedia*, launched in 1989, contains not only the 8,000,000 words of text of the printed version, but 15,000 illus., 45 animated sequences and 60 minutes of sound. The entire *Merriam-Webster intermediate dictionary* is also incorporated. Various search paths are available, through the use of mouse-driven commands. As with the printed set, of most value to school and college libraries. *Class No:* 030=20-0053

[156]
Oxford children's encyclopaedia. Worrall, M., ed. Oxford, Oxford Univ. Press, 1991. 7v. Illus., diagrs., maps. ISBN: 0199101396.

An encyclopedia for younger children ages 7-13. Vols. 1-5 contain c.2,250 heavily illustrated articles, e.g. 'American Indians', 2p., 4 illus; 'Cassette players', c.150 words, 1 illus. 2 col. format with wide margins imaginatively used for additional information, references and captions to the illustrations. V.6 is a separate biography v. with c.600 entries. V.7 *Index* has c.15,000 entries, plus 'Lists of biographies by category' and a few tables e.g. 'Prime ministers of Great Britain and the United Kingdom'. Not a substitute for the much larger *Children's Britannica* (q.v.), but attractively produced and especially appealing to the younger child. *Class No:* 030=20-0053

[157]
World book encyclopedia. Chicago & London, World Book Inc. Annual revision. 24v. illus., diagrs., tables, maps.
First published 1917.
V.1-21 A-Z; v.22 *Research guide and index*; v.23-24 *Britain and Ireland.*

17,500 articles; 3,000 contributors and consultants; 29,000 illus. (24,000 in col.); 2,300 maps. Mostly short, signed aritcles written at the most appropriate vocabulary level for the anticipated readership. Thus 'Mouse' is written with the younger reader in mind, while 'Cell' is aimed at the older reader. Longer articles are carefully structured, with topical outlines, study questions, cross-references and lists of further reading. V.21 has a detailed analytical index with over 150,000 entries, 200 boxed reading and study guides on major topics in situ and 'A student's guide to better writing, speaking and research skills'. V.23-24, marketed specifically in the British Isles (v.23-24 marketed as *Australasia* in Australia and New Zealand), is not self-contained, but deals with Britain and Ireland in much greater detail than in the main volumes (e.g. 'Doncaster' 100 words; 'Hampshire' 4p., 2 illus., 1 map; 'Hardie, Keir' c.90 words). Extensively updated annually, the 1991 revision including 111 new, 416 re-written and 2,900 amended articles, *World book* is indisputably the leading all-purpose junior encyclopedia for those aged 10 and upwards.

The *World book year book* (first published 1922) is primarily an account of the events of the past year under the heading 'The world on file'. Also contains 'World book supplement', reprinting revised articles from the latest ed.

World Book Inc. have also released *Information finder* which contains the text and tables of the printed version on CD-ROM disc. Searching is by topic using the *World book* index or keywords. *Class No:* 030=20-0053

German

[158]
Brockhaus Enzyklopädie in vierundzwanzig Bänden. 19., völlig neubearb. Aufl. Mannheim, Brockhaus, 1986-. Illus., tables, diagrs., maps. ISBN: 3765311006.

To be completed in 24v. First published 1796-1808, as *Brockhaus' Konversations-Lexikon*. First post-war ed. (16th) as *Der Grosse Brockhaus*, 1952-63. 18th ed. issued in 15v. 1977-82, being a condensed version of the 25v. 17th ed. published 1966-81.

Continues the *Brockhaus* tradition of many short articles and small but plentiful illustrations. When complete this ed. is to contain 260,000 entries and have 33,000 illus., maps and tables. Longer articles for countries and major topics (e.g. 'Ägypten' (Egypt), 17 cols., 2 maps, 3 illus., 3 tables, c.25 item bibliography). Especially well documented (e.g. short article 'Knossos' (2 cols.) has 5 references), all bibliographies revised. Kept fully up-to-date by supplementary entries in every sixth volume. Publication reached NOS-PER in 1991. *Class No:* 030=30

French

[159]
Grand dictionnaire encyclopédique Larousse. Paris, Larousse, 1982-85. 10v. illus., facsims., diagrs., maps. ISBN: 2031023004.

A dictionary encyclopedia in the Larousse tradition. Encyclopedia entries are largely based on those in *La Grande encyclopedie* (1971-78. 21v.) but updated and condensed. c.190,000 mainly short articles in a 3 column format (e.g. 'Orwell, George', c.240 words; 'Maroc', 5 pages). Liberally illustrated, with c.12,000 photographs and 11,000 diagrams. Heavy and effective use of c.1,300 maps to present economic, demographic and historical data. Bibliographies provided for major articles, but filed at the end of each letter.

The earlier *Grand Larousse encyclopédique en dix volumes* (Paris, Larousse, 1960-64. 10v. Supplements 1968 and 1975), is on much the same plan. The progenitor *Grand dictionnaire universel du XIXe siècle* (Larousse, 1865-85. 17v.) is an outstanding example of the encyclopedia dictionary, still having some value as a source of biographical and historical data. *Class No:* 030=40

Italian

[160]
Grande dizionario enciclopedico UTET. Fondato da P. Fedele. 4 ed. Torino, Unione Tipografico-Editrice, 1984-91. 21v. Illus., plates, diagrs., maps. ISBN: 8802039216, v.1.
First published 1933-40. 3rd ed. 1966-75 in 20v.

Bears some resemblance to the 36v. *Enciclopedia italiana di scienze, lettre ed arti* (1929-39) in format and of similar standing as one of the major established and authoritative Italian encyclopedias. Contains mainly short articles, but with some longer for major subjects or countries (e.g. 'Nuova Zelanda' (New Zealand) 5½p., boxed statistical data, 5 refs). Longer articles are signed and have appended bibliographies. Impressive international coverage (e.g. 'Hamilton, Lady Emma' c.220 words, 4 refs.; Amundsen, Roald Engelbert' c.400 words, 3 refs., port). Well cross-referenced between articles. Illustrations are mostly black and white and of somewhat disappointing quality. V.21, *Grande atlante geografico e storico* contains 357p. of general and 173p. of historical maps. *Class No:* 030=50

04 Essays, Reprints, Theses, Reviews

Essays & Festschriften

[161]
Essay and general literature index. 1900/1933-. New York, Wilson, 1934-. Semi-annual, with cumulations. ISSN: 0014083x.

Continues *A.L.A. index to general literature*, (2nd ed. 1901-14), covering (with a supplement) up to 1910.

Basic publication on a semi-annual basis with a paper issue in June, followed by a bound annual cumulation. Permanent cumulation published every 5 years, first issued 1955/59. Earlier 7 year cumulations, 1934/40, 1941/47 and 1948/54.

Author and subject index in one sequence to essays published in collections, with particular emphasis on the humanities and, since 1970, the social sciences. Each issue currently indexes about 2,000 essays in around 175 collections. With the publication of the 1985/89 cumulation (J. Greenfieldt *ed.* 1990. 2031p.), indexing 19,579 essays in 1,593 collections, the total number of essays indexed since 1934 is approaching 275,000. Also available online through Wilsonline, December 1985-, updated every two weeks. *Class No:* 04.0

[162]
—**Essay and general literature index: works indexed 1900-1969.** New York, Wilson, 1972. 437p. ISBN: 0824205030.

Lists, under authors, the 9,917 collections indexed. Cross-references from titles, pseudonyms, translators, joint authors and editors. *Class No:* 04.0

[163]
LEISTNER, O. Internationale Bibliographie der Festschriften von der Anfängen bis 1979 mit Sachregister. [International bibliography of Festschriften from the beginnings until 1979 with subject index.] 2nd ed. Osnabrück, Biblio Verlag, 1984-89. 3v. ISBN: 3764812753.

1st ed. 1976 (1v.) gave coverage to 1974.

Considerably expands the coverage given by the 1st ed., listing over 30,000 Festschriften. The main body of the work comprises entries under persons honoured, giving basic bibliographical detail and birth and death dates, but with no attempt to list contents or contributors. Includes Festschriften dedicated to corporate bodies or published as issues of periodicals. V.3 includes a subject index, German language headings only, and supplementary entries to v.1-v.2. *Class No:* 04.0

[164]
—**Internationale Jahresbibliographie der Festschriften.** 1980-. [International annual bibliography of Festschriften. 1980-.] Osnabrück, Biblio Verlag, 1982-. Annual. ISSN: 07242298.

Continues Leistner's 2nd ed. (above), but provides more detail and greater depth of indexing. Now arranged in 5 sections published in 3 volumes: A. Festschriften in the alphabet of the honoured (including full list of contents

....(contd.)
with name of contributor) - B. Festschriften by fields of knowledge (classified) - C. Contributions by keywords (in German with English and French references) - D. Keyword index of contributions (refering to C) - E. Author index of contributors. Over 500 Festschriften indexed annually. *Class No:* 04.0

Reprints

[165]
Guide to reprints: an international bibliography of scholarly reprints. Kent Ct., Guide to Reprints Inc., 1967-. Annual. ISSN: 00728667.

A cumulating bibliography of currently available photo-offset reprints from around 450 publishing firms worldwide. To be included reprints must be full or not less than 75% of original size and published in an edition of 200 or more copies. Journals, government publications and collections covered as well as monographs. Information, as supplied by publisher, includes author, title, no. of vols., original publication date, ISBN, publisher and price. Date of reprint not given. *Class No:* 04.04

Theses & Dissertations

[166]
Comprehensive dissertation index, 1861-1972. Ann Arbor, Xerox University Microfilms, 1973. 37v. ISBN: 0835700801.

Contents: v.1-4: Chemistry; v.5: Mathematics and statistics; v.6: Astronomy and physics; v.7: Physics; v.8-10: Engineering; v.11-13: Biological sciences; v.14: Health and environmental sciences; v.15: Agriculture; v.16: Geography and geology; v.17: Social sciences; v.18-19: Psychology; v.20-24: Education; v.25-26: Business and economics; v.27: Law and political science; v.28: History; v.29-30: Language and literature; v.31: Communication and the arts; v.32: Philosophy and religion; v.33-37: Author index.

Entries for more than 417,000 dissertations. Based on *Dissertations abstracts, Doctoral dissertations accepted by American universities, List of American doctoral dissertations* and various lists, often unpublished, of individual universities. Aims at full coverage for the US, with some Canadian and foreign dissertations included. Within each subject volume the listing is A-Z by keyword, entries giving citation to *Dissertation abstracts* and other sources.

Continued by *Comprehensive dissertation index: supplement* (1973-. Annual). Cumulations provided as *Comprehensive dissertation index: ten year cumulation, 1973-1982* (1984. 38v., superseding earlier cumulation 1973-1977) and *Comprehensive dissertation index: five year cumulation, 1983-1987* (1989. 22v.). Both arranged by subject in similar sequence to the 1861-1972 cumulation, with author indexes. *Class No:* 043

[167]
Dissertation abstracts international. Ann Arbor, University Microfilms International, 1938-. Monthly.

Title varies: *Microfilm abstracts*, 1938-51; *Dissertation abstracts*, 1952-1969.

Published in 3 sections: A: *The humanities and social sciences* (Monthly. ISSN 04194209); B: *The sciences and engineering* (Monthly. ISSN 04194217); C: *Worldwide* (Quarterly. ISSN 10427279, until 1989 as *European abstracts* ISSN 03076075). A and B as separate sections from 1966; C published from 1977. All dissertations included in *Dissertation abstracts international* are microfilmed and available for purchase from University Microfilms International.

Sections A and B cover *c.*35,000 dissertations annually from *c.*550 institutions. Abstracts, average length 350 words, in classified arrangement with author's name, year, awarding institution and identification number. British doctoral dissertations from nearly 50 participating institutions now included, but the vast majority of dissertations remain of North American origin. Title keyword and author indexes in each monthly issue cumulated annually. Section C covers dissertations in all subject areas. Coverage extended 1989, although the total number of participating institutions remains small in comparison with A and B and is still predominantly European.

Dissertation abstracts is available online through BRS and Dialog, records extending back to 1861 (based on *Comprehensive dissertation index*). Abstracts available for dissertations from 1980, citations only prior to this date. Also available in CD-ROM format as *Dissertation abstracts on disc*, issued as 3 discs, 1861-June 1984, July 1984-1987 and 1988-, the latter updated every six months.

Retrospective index [to] *v.1-29*, (1970. 9v. in 11), is arranged by subject areas with author index. Now effectively replaced by *Comprehensive dissertation index* (above). *Class No: 043*

[168]
A Guide to theses and dissertations: an international bibliography of bibliographies. Reynolds, M.M., *ed.* 2nd ed. Phoenix, Oryx, 1985. vii,263p. ISBN: 0897741498.

1st ed., Detroit, Gale, 1975.

Identifies and annotates nearly 3,000 bibliographies (some hidden in journals) of US and foreign theses and dissertations. Arranged in 17 subject groups with subdivisions. Universal and national lists precede (p.1-19), of 34 and 165 entries respectively. Indexes of institutions, names and journal titles and subjects. Excludes general bibliographies of a single university, although institution specific subject bibliographies are covered. *Class No: 043*

Great Britain

[169]
Index to theses: with abstracts accepted for higher degrees by the universities of Great Britain and Ireland and the Council for National Academic Awards. 1950/51-. London, Aslib, 1953-. Quarterly. ISSN: 00736066.

Frequency varies: annual to 1975, then semi-annual; quarterly publication from 1986.

From v.35 (1986) includes 200-500 word abstracts and a greatly enhanced subject index. Previous volumes gave bibliographical citation only, with *Abstracts to theses* available as a separate microfiche service from v.26. About 9,000 theses abstracted annually. Excludes degrees awarded soley for published work and those dissertations submitted in partial fulfilment of a higher degree in conjunction with another examination. Classified arrangement in 11 major classes Arts and humanities ... Civil and chemical engineering. Author index and subject index, including references to terms in the abstracts. First edition of a CD-

....(contd.)
ROM version issued 1991 providing coverage of 163,000 theses 1970-1990. Two further CD-ROM versions scheduled for release, the first covering 1950-1991, to be followed by 1756-1992 (incorporating records from *Retrospective index to theses* (below)). *Class No: 043(410)*

[170]
Retrospective index to theses of Great Britain and Ireland, 1716-1950. Bilboul, R.R. *and* Kent, F.L., *eds.* Santa Barbara, Ca. and Oxford, ABC-Clio , 1975-77. 5v. & addendum. ISBN: 090345002x.

V.1 *Social sciences and humanities* (1975. (7),x,393p.); v.2 *Applied sciences and technology* (1976. (7),xii,159p.); v.3 *Life sciences* (1977. (7),xii,327p.); v.4 *Physical sciences* (1976. (7),xii,99p.); v.5 *Chemical sciences* (1976. (7),xii,251p.); *Addendum* (1977. 26p.).

Designed to precede *Index to Theses* (above). Includes *c.*50,000 theses in all; *c.*13,000 in v.1. Each v. has subject and author indexes. *Class No: 043(410)*

Reports

[171]
AUGER, C.P. Information sources in grey literature. 2nd ed. London, Bowker-Saur, 1989. ix,175p.illus. (*Guides to information sources.*) ISBN: 0862918715.

1st ed. 1975 as *Uses of reports literature.*

Grey literature not precisely defined, but considered to include material such as technical reports, trade literature and official publications. 12 chapters: 6 general (1. The nature and development of grey literature ... 3. Bibliographical control, cataloguing and indexing ... 5. Theses, translations and meeting papers); 6 specialised (aerospace, life sciences, business and economics, education, energy, science and technology). 3 appendices: A. Keys to report series codes; B. Trade literature; C. Addresses of organizations mentioned in the text. Index. A wide-ranging, well-executed survey of a complex field. *Class No: 047*

[172]
British reports, translations and theses. Boston Spa, British Library Document Supply Centre, 1981-. Monthly. ISSN: 09594922.

Supersedes *BLLD announcement bulletin.*

Lists British report literature and translations produced by British government organizations, local government, universities and learned institutions and most doctoral theses accepted by British universities and polytechnics. Also covers reports and unpublished translations from the Republic of Ireland and selected British official publications of a report nature that are not published by HMSO. All the material listed appears in the SIGLE (System for information on grey literature in Europe) database available through BLAISE and STN. Entries in broad classified arrangement; microfiche author, report number and key term indexes issued quarterly, cumulating annually. Inconsistencies in computer-generated key term indexing can hamper subject retrieval. The major source for British 'grey literature', all items included are available from the Document Supply Centre. *Class No: 047*

Abstracts

[173]
The Index and abstract directory: an international guide to services and serials coverage. Birmingham, Ala., EBSCO, 1989-. Annual. ISSN: 10411321.

Based on EBSCO's serials database, also used to compile the companion publication *The Serials directory (q.v.).*

2nd ed. (1990. xlviii,2784p.) in two sections. The first 'Serials listing' arranges 35,000 serials under subject headings (Aeronautics ... Zoology). Similar entry detail to

....(contd.)
The Serials directory, with coded data indicating coverage by indexing and abstracting services. The second section 'Index and abstract services listing' has information for 700 services. Entries, by title A-Z, indicate serials covered including dates, plus further detail such as online and CD-ROM availability. Includes some obscure and ceased indexes and abstracts; ISSN index. The second section is valuable as the most up-to-date general guide to the coverage of abstracting and indexing services; 'another weapon in the war to contain serials' (*Choice*, v.27(4), December 1989, p.612). *Class No:* 048.3

[174]
STEPHENS, J. **Inventory of abstracting and indexing services produced in the UK.** 3rd ed. London, British Library, 1986. viii,238p. (*British Library information guide, 2.*) ISBN: 0712330801.
1st ed. 1978 by G. Burgess and others (BL Research and development report, no.5420); 2nd ed. 1983 by G. Stephens (BL Library and information research report, no.21).
Lists 430 services A-Z. Includes all types of secondary services from card files to machine readable databases. Entries give producer, contact, subject scope, subject classification, sources (type of material covered), languages, geographic area, cost, start date, frequency/size of updates, online access, availability and additional notes. Broad and specific subject heading indexes. Further indexes of responsible authorities and database hosts. *Class No:* 048.3

Book Reviews

[175]
Booklist. Chicago, American Library Association, 1905-. Semimonthly, (monthly July and August). ISSN: 00067385.
Incorporates *Subscription books bulletin* from September 1956 and issued under the title *The Booklist and subscription books bulletin* until 1969.
'The purpose of *Booklist* is to provide a guide to current print and non-print materials worthy of consideration for purchase by small and medium-sized public libraries and school library media centers. A review in *Booklist* constitutes a recommendation for purchase'. Signed, measured reviews in sections for fiction and non-fiction. Extensive coverage of children's books (Adult books for young adults; Books for older readers; Books for middle readers; Books for the young; Series roundup). Reviews of audio-visual material included since 1969. Index in each issue cumulated semi-annually.
Each issue also contains *Reference books bulletin*, providing longer in depth reviews of new reference material, overseen by the ALA's Reference Books Bulletin Editorial Board. Cumulations of this section, which continues *Subscription books bulletin*, are published annually, also under the title *Reference books bulletin* (*q.v.*). *Class No:* 048.83

[176]
British book news: the British Council's monthly survey for book buyers throughout the world. London, British Council, 1940-. Monthly. ISSN: 00070343.
Published as *Selection of books* 1940. Subtitle varies. The monthly parts cumulated annually until 1950.
As from April 1987 practice of providing signed critical reviews discontinued. Instead an expanded 'Forthcoming books' section lists new titles (*c.*700 per issue) in 10 subject sections. Entries give basic bibliographical detail, Dewey class no., indication of readership level and a brief descriptive annotation only. Includes sections 'General reference and information science' and 'Secondary school textbooks'. Other children's material no longer covered, (included in separate *British book news children's book review*, 1983-88, now incorporated in *Books for keeps*

....(contd.)
(*q.v.*)). Continues to carry specialist book surveys and regular features *e.g.* 'Company profile' and 'Periodicals and journals' (reviews of new titles). Of diminished value since the dropping of critical reviews, but still useful as a basic selection tool. *Class No:* 048.83

[177]
Choice: current reviews for college libraries. Middletown, Conn., Association of College and Research Libraries, 1964-. Monthly, (except July/August). $135pa. ISSN: 00094978.
Each issue covers *c.*500 books with carefully, concisely written 250 word critical and comparative reviews, signed since 1984. Subject arrangement in main sections: General; Humanities; Science and technology; Social and behavioral sciences; Non print. Author and title indexes, cumulated annually. Issues also normally contain a feature article and a bibliographic essay (*e.g.* 'Career literature' and 'Child sexual abuse' October 1990). A major selection tool for US publications. *Class No:* 048.83

[178]
TLS. The Times literary supplement. London, Times Supplements, 1902-. Weekly. ISSN: 0307661x.
About 2,500 reviews pa., often a model of their kind, 'detached, measured and intelligent'. Emphasis on the humanities; subjects normally covered: art, bibliography, biography and memoirs, education, fiction, history, literature, natural history, poetry, politics, religion and travel. Reviews (now signed) do not invariably appear promptly and two or three books on the same subject may well and effectively be dealt with together. In addition to reviews each issue also contains a 'Listings', section giving bibliographical detail of *c.*50-100 new works, and an author index of books reviewed. Since 1973 the *TLS* has been indexed in *The Times index* (*q.v.*). Cumulated indexes have also been published as *The Times literary supplement index: 1940-1980* and *The Times literary supplement index: 1902-1939.* *Class No:* 048.83

Indexes

[179]
Book review digest. New York, Wilson, 1905-. Monthly (except February and July), annual cumulation. ISSN: 00067326.
A digest and index of book reviews in *c.*90 US and British periodicals (including *English historical review, New statesman and society, Times literary supplement*). To be eligible for inclusion a work must be distributed in the US and Canada and have been reviewed by at least two of the periodicals indexed if a non-fiction title, or three if a work of fiction. Includes reviews of children's books; government publications, textbooks and technical works in science and law excluded. Reviews arranged by author A-Z; subject and title indexes in each issue. About 6,000 books covered annually. Also available online through Wilsonline and on CD-ROM for records 1983 to date. Mainly useful for the digests, as the range of periodicals indexed is restricted compared with other sources such as *Book review index.* *Class No:* 048.83:014.3

[180]
—Book review digest: author/title index, 1905-1974. Dunmore-Leiber, L., *ed.* New York, Wilson, 1976. 4v. ISBN: 0824205898.
Author/title index in one sequence with cross-references from joint authors, pseudonyms etc. About 300,000 books covered.
A further cumulation *Book review digest: author/title index 1975-1984* (R.E. Klaum ed. 1986. 1488p. $65. 0824207297), covers 60,000 books. *Class No:* 048.83:014.3

[181]
Book review index. Detroit, Gale, 1965-. Bimonthly. ISSN: 05240581.

Frequency varies. Monthly, with quarterly and annual cumulations 1965-69, then suspended. Resumed with 6 issues pa. 1972 (issues 2,4 and 6 cumulating the preceding issue) and an annual cumulation. 1970-71 cumulations published retrospectively.

Indexes reviews of books and periodicals in more than 470 publications ranging from scholarly journals to general interest magazines such as *Newsweek.* Includes a number of titles published in the UK *e.g., Critical quarterly, Times literary supplement.* Reviews broadly defined to encompass all critical statements, even if in the form of brief annotations or listings. Entries, by author A-Z, omit reviewer's name. Reviews of children's literature extracted for inclusion in two companion series *Children's book review index* and *Young adult book review index.* Also available online through Dialog (File 137) for citations 1969 to date. *Class No:* 048.83:014.3

[182]
—Book review index: a master cumulation 1965-1984: a cumulated index to more than 1,605,000 reviews of approximately 740,500 titles. Tarbert, G.C. *and* Beach, B., *ed.* Detroit, Gale, 1985. 10v. ISBN: 0810305771.

Supersedes *Book review index: a master cumulation 1969-1979* (1980. 7v.).

Cumulative indexes for periodicals and reference books also published as *Book review index: periodical reviews 1976-1984* and *Book review index: reference books 1965-1984. Class No:* 048.83:014.3

[183]
Internationale Bibliographie der Rezensionen Wissenschaftlicher Literatur. [International bibliography of book reviews of scholarly literature.] Zeller, O., *hrsg.* Osnabrück, Dietrich, 1971-. Semi-annual. ISSN: 0020918x.

Each semi-annual issue in 3v. A companion publication to *Internationale Bibliographie der Zeitschriftenliteratur* (*q.v.*). Revives *Bibliographie der Rezensionen und Referate* (below).

Revised format from v.13(2) 1983. Remains in 5 pts., but pt.A is now a subject index listing reviewed works under German keywords, (English and French references) with bibliographical detail and review citation (title coded). Other parts comprise keyword index (keywords divided into 16 fields of knowledge), index of reviewed works by author, reviewer index (a useful feature not found in most other book review indexes) and list of periodicals in which the reviews cited can be located. Comprehensive international coverage, especially valuable for tracing reviews of scholarly works and non-English language titles. *Class No:* 048.83:014.3

05 Periodicals

Periodicals

[184]

British union-catalogue of periodicals: a record of periodicals of the world, from the seventeenth century to the present day, in British libraries. Stewart, J.D., *and others eds.* London, Butterworths, 1955-58. 4v .

Edited for the Council of the British Union-Catalogue of Periodicals. Supersedes *Union catalogue of the periodical publications in the university libraries of the British Isles ...* (London, Joint Standing Committee on Library Co-operation, 1937. xii,712p.), which locates 23,115 titles in 113 university libraries.

Lists more than 140,000 titles permanently filed in 441 libraries in the UK. Includes annuals, but excludes newspapers after 1799, directories and time-tables, and some ephemera. Includes complete holdings of many general libraries, with specialized material from special libraries and selected items from a great many other sources (this policy of partial coverage causes much unevenness in reports of holdings). Arrangement is by earliest title (or by earliest form of society), with liberal references. Gives changes of title, volume numbering and dates, and notes existence (but not locations) of cumulated indexes. V.4 includes a separate list of numerical titles (*e.g.* 24th Battalion).

A *Supplement to 1960*, Stewart, J.D. ed. (1962. 991p.), includes new periodicals, amended entries and titles not reported in the earlier volumes. Continued by:- *Class No:* 050

[185]

—British union-catalogue of periodicals, incorporating 'World list of scientific periodicals'. New periodical titles. 1960/68-80. London, Butterworths, 1964-81. Quarterly, with annual cumulations.

A cumulative issue for 1960-68 was published 1970. ISBN 0408700300. Ceased publication 1980; continued in part by *Serials in the British Library (q.v.).*

The incorporated *World list of scientific periodicals* was published by Butterworths in 4 eds. 1925/27-1963/65. *Class No:* 050

[186]

KATZ, B. *and* KATZ, L. **Magazines for libraries.** 6th ed. New York, Bowker, 1989. xxi,1159p. ISBN: 0835226328.

1st ed. 1969; 5th ed. 1986.

Annotates and evaluates periodicals that 'represent what the editors and consultants believe to be the best and most useful for the average elementary, secondary school, public, academic or special library' (Preface p.ix). 6,521 numbered entries, 30% new to this ed., 95% revised. Arranged in 139 subject sections (Abstracts and indexes - Women) on a similar basis to the same publisher's *Ulrich's international periodical directory (q.v.)*. In addition to standard bibliographic detail, entries include data on price, audience

....(contd.)
level, where indexed and online availability. Annotations sometimes rather sketchy, occasionally inaccurate (*e.g. British book news* fails to mention recent changes in format). Nonetheless, an established reference tool in the US which, despite some North American bias in title selection, 'increasingly deserves attention outside the country of origin' (*Reference reviews,* v.3(4), December 1989, p.154). A 7th ed. is to be published during 1992 (ISBN 0835231666). *Class No:* 050

[187]

Keyword index to serial titles. Boston Spa, British Library Document Supply Centre, 1980-. Microfiche. Quarterly. ISSN: 01439553.

Keyword-out-of-context listing, based on the Document Supply Centre's (DSC) master file of serials, non-current records included unlike in *Current serials received.* Also covers titles held by the British Library Science Reference and Information Service, Science Museum Library, British Library Humanities and Social Sciences and Cambridge University Library. 410,000 records, including cross-references, at the end of 1990. Holdings statements for DSC stock only; many records provide notes on changed titles, cessation of publication etc. Useful both as a unified key to the vast serial holdings of the British Library and as a source of basic bibliographical data. *Class No:* 050

[188]

—Boston Spa serials. Boston Spa, British Library Document Supply Centre, 1989-. CD-ROM database. Updated discs issued semi-annually.

Based on the DSC serials holdings file, including, as with *Keyword index to serial titles,* records for the Science Reference and Information Service, Science Museum, Humanities and Social Sciences (BL) and Cambridge University. Features Boolean searching, browse options, novice and expert search levels and save and print options, employing the same search software as *BNB on CD-ROM. Class No:* 050

[189]

—Current serials received. Boston Spa, British Library Document Supply Centre, 1965-. Annual. ISSN: 03090655.

First published as *Current serials received by the N.L.L.* Issued annually from 1978.

The 1991 ed. (654p.) lists 72,000 titles in all subject areas currently received by the Document Supply Centre and Science Reference and Information Service (SRIS). In 3 pts.: Current serial titles except for Cyrillic - Cyrillic titles (transliterated) - Cover to cover translations of Cyrillic titles. Entry consists simply of title and DSC shelf-mark. Titles held at SRIS indicated by codes. Primarily for inter-library loan use, but also functions as a handy checklist. *Class No:* 050

[190]
New serial titles: a union list of serials held by libraries in the United States and Canada. Washington, D.C., Library of Congress, Cataloguing Distribution Service, 1953-. Monthly. ISSN: 00286680.

Current subscription includes 8 monthly and 3 quarterly issues with an annual cumulation. Prepared by the Serial Record Division of the Library of Congress, based on the CONSER cooperative project since 1981.

Lists periodicals received by the Library of Congress and 600 other libraries. Titles covered are those which meet the AACR2 definition of a serial. Each issue arranged A-Z by title, with entries in the form of catalogue records, including ISSN and subject tracings. Until 1981 covered only records for periodicals that began publication after 1950, but now includes all serials regardless of date of initial issue. A major tool for the bibliographic control of serials.

Quinquennial cumulations are available for 1971/75 (2v.), 1975/80 (2v.) and 1981/85 (6v.) Further cumulation 1986/89 (6v.). Earlier cumulation provided by the set below:- *Class No:* 050

[191]
—New serial titles: a union list of serials commencing publication after December 31, 1949; 1950-1970 cumulative. Washington, D.C., Library of Congress, New York, Bowker, 1973. 4v. ISBN: 0835205568.

More than 250,000 entries with an average of 6 locations for each title. Incorporates 13,000 revisions and numerous new locations, plus ISSN's and country codes. V. 4 concludes with a 'Changes in serials' section. *Class No:* 050

[192]
The Serials directory: an international reference book. Birmingham, Ala., Ebsco Publishing, 1986-. Annual. ISSN: 08664179.

Issued in 3 volumes: v.1-2 Serials listing A-Z (subjects); v.3 Alphabetical title index; Ceased title index; ISSN index.

A new serials directory based on EBSCO's (subscription agents) internal database, the Library of Congress CONSER file and questionnaire returns. 130,000 entries in the 5th ed. (1991), under 147 major and 137 subsidiary headings. Standard data, including date first published, publisher, ISSN, frequency, language, price, editors, where indexed/abstracted, Library of Congress, Dewey, UDC and NLM class nos., CODEN, index availability, advertising acceptance, whether peer reviewed, circulation and availability in other forms. Two updating supplements issued between eds. Also available as a CD-ROM database, updated quarterly, with full CONSER MARC records for each citation. The inevitable comparison is with *Ulrich's international periodicals directory* (q.v.). The *Serials directory* includes more titles (130,000 as against 116,000) and has slightly fuller information for most entries. On the negative side it is less well laid out and is not as fully indexed. Overall *Ulrich's* probably remains the better source and certainly continues to be preferred by most UK libraries. *Class No:* 050

[193]
Serials in the British Library. London, British Library, 1981-. Quarterly, 4th issue annual cumulation. ISSN: 02600005.

Continues in part *British union-catalogue of periodicals: incorporating 'World list of scientific periodicals'. New periodical titles* (q.v.). Until the end of 1986 annual cumulation issued separately on microfiche.

Revised coverage from the first issue for 1987. Now consists of records for all new serial acquisitions of the British Library's London based reference collections, including titles received on legal deposit. About 4,000 titles catalogued annually, records derived from the *British*

....(contd.)
national bibliography and the current catalogues of the Humanities and Social Sciences and the Science Reference and Information Service. Definition of serial based on ISO:3297. Entries arranged alphabetically by cataloguing headings according to BLAISE filing rules. Computer-produced keyword index in each issue, includes many insignificant access points.

A microfiche cumulation, *Serials in the British Library 1976-1986* (57 microfiche.), lists 57,000 titles. *Class No:* 050

[194]
Ulrich's international periodicals directory: now including Irregular serials and annuals. New York, Bowker, 1932-. Annual. ISSN: 00000175.

Title varies: *Periodicals directory*, 1932-38; *Ulrich's periodicals directory*, 1943-63. Frequency also varies; irregular until 1969, then biennial. From the 27th ed. 1988/89 merged with *Irregular serials and annuals* (first published 1967) and issued annually as a 3v. set.

The most widely used directory of current serials based on Bowker's international serials database. Includes 'all publications that meet the definition of serial except general daily newspapers, newspapers of local scope or local interest, administrative publications of major government below state level that can easily be found elsewhere, membership directories, comic books and puzzle and game books' (Preface p.vii, 1990/91 ed.). Includes annuals and other less frequently published titles since the incorporation of *Irregular serials and annuals*. V. 1-2 comprise a 'classified list' (A-Z by title under subject headings), entries including Dewey class no., LC card no., ISSN, CODEN, frequency, date first published, publisher, price, editor, where indexed, online availability and vendor, title changes, whether refereed and, for an increasing number of titles, 10-40 word descriptive annotations. V.3 has sections: Refereed serials (A-Z list); Serials available on CD-ROM; Serials available online, with separate vendor listings; Cessations (A-Z title list of serials reported ceased in the last 3 years); Index to publications of international organizations; ISSN index; Title index. Cross-index and preliminaries in v.1. 29th ed. 1990/91 lists more than 116,000 current titles under 668 subject headings (62,000 entries updated from the previous ed.), plus 6,191 cessations. Kept up to date with the quarterly *Ulrich's update*, issued from the 17th ed. Available online through BRS, Dialog (File 480) and ESA-IRS (File 103), updated monthly. Also available on microfiche (quarterly cumulative issues) and as a CD-ROM database *Ulrich's plus*. (For a comparative review of the CD-ROM version see *RSR*, v. 18(2), 1990, p.81-86.) Well-organized, generally accurate and with wide international coverage, *Ulrich's* remains the pre-eminent serials directory, despite the recent launch of competitors. *Class No:* 050

[195]
Willings press guide: a guide to the press of the United Kingdom and to the principal publications of Europe, the Americas, Australasia, the Far East, Africa and the Middle East. East Grinstead, Reed Information Services, 1874-. Annual. ISSN: 00000213.

Publisher varies.

Covers newspapers, periodicals, magazines and some annuals. The 117th ed. (1991) is in 2v., *United Kingdom* (1556p.) and *Overseas* (649p.). The UK v. has c.13,000 entries A-Z by title, information given including foundation date, frequency, former title, circulation, publisher and editor. Separate lists of new, forthcoming and recently ceased titles. Classified index to titles (p.3-43), newspaper index (p.45-66) under headings National dailies, Regional dailies (by county), National Sundays, Regional Sundays and Weekly local newspapers (by county) and publisher

....(contd.)

index. The *Overseas* v. is arranged by country in regional sections *e.g.* Europe, The Americas, with a classified index of *c.*250 headings. Invaluable for library and desk use. Especially strong on British local newspapers (2,157 entries 1991) and general interest magazines. *Class No: 050*

Great Britain

[196]

Current British journals: a bibliographical guide. Woodworth, D.P. *and* Goodair, C.M., *eds.* 5th ed. Boston Spa, British Library Document Supply Centre, 1989. vii,740p. ISBN: 0712320539.

Sponsored by the UK Serials Group. 1st ed. 1970; 4th ed. 1986.

Extensively revised since the previous ed. including 1,700 new titles bringing the total to 8,160. Entries, in abridged UDC classified order, give title, year of first issue, frequency, price, indication of subject content (*c.*20-50 words), no. of pages per issue, policy on advertising, whether book reviews included, circulation, availability of indexes, ISSN, publisher name and address, previous title(s), other formats (*e.g.* microform), and indexing/abstracting services in which covered. Title and subject indexes. Excludes newspapers. A standard tool with full information for each title, but other sources *e.g. Willing's press guide* or *Benn's media directory* (*qq.v.*) are equally comprehensive, more frequent in publication and include newspapers. *Class No: 050(410)*

[197]

The Waterloo directory of Victorian periodicals 1824-1900. Phase I. Wolff, M., *and others eds.* Waterloo, Ont., Wilfrid Laurier Univ. Press for the Univ. of Waterloo, 1976. xxvii,1187p. ISBN: 0889200262.

Sponsored by the Research Society for Victorian Periodicals and Waterloo Computing in the Humanities.

Checklist of 28,995 entries, including about 4,000 cross-references. 'The conditions for inclusion are only that a periodical be published in Great Britain ... or be related to one that was. The definition of a periodical ... is a publication intended to be produced at regular intervals, for an indefinite period of time. So newspapers, magazines, reports of societies, monthly bulletins, annuals and almanaks are included' (p.xvi). Entries arranged by title A-Z: variable descriptive data from subtitle, numbering, dates, editor(s), place of publication, publisher, printer, price, size, frequency, illustrations, circulation, issuing body, indexing, notes, mergers and subsidiary and alternate titles. The most comprehensive source, more than doubling the *c.*11,000 entries for Victorian periodicals in the *Tercentenary handlist of English and Welsh magazines and newspapers (1920).* Forms the basis for the more extensive Phase II, two volumes of which, *The Waterloo directory of Irish newspapers and periodicals* (1987) and *The Waterloo directory of Scottish newspapers and periodicals* (1989), have so far been published. *Class No: 050(410)*

Germany

[198]

Deutschsprachige Zeitschriften: Deutschland - Österreich - Schweiz. Internationale Fachzeitschriften mit deutschen Beiträgen - Fremdsprachige Zeitschriften aus dem deutschen Sprachraum. Köln, Verlag der Schillerbuchhandlung, 1956-. Annual. ISSN: 04190054.

Until 1967 published as *Anschriften deutschsprachigen Zeitschriften.* Subtitle also varies.

Jahr. 35 (1991. 602p.) lists 10,000 periodicals published in Germany, Austria and Switzerland. Information for each entry includes publisher, frequency, foundation date, price and ISSN. Plentiful cross-references from alternate and

....(contd.)

abbreviated titles. Separate section (p.497-564) lists periodicals by subject groups. ISSN index. *Class No: 050(430)*

France

[199]

Bibliographie nationale française. Supplément I. Publications en série. Paris, Bibliothèque Nationale, 1977-. Monthly, with annual index. ISSN: 11423269.

Title and publisher varies. As *Bibliographie de la France. Supplément I. Publications en série* (01501399), until 1989.

UDC classified list of new serial titles, entries giving full bibliographical citation including frequency statement, ISSN and Bibliothèque Nationale call numbers. Title, collective author and subject indexes in each issue: annual cumulated index. *Class No: 050(44)*

Spain

[200]

Periodicos y revistas españolas e hispanoamericanos. Barcelona, Centro de Investigaciones Literarias Españolas e Hispanoamericanos, 1989. 2v. ISBN: 8487411010.

Intended for biennial publication.

V.1 comprises an A-Z list of Spanish language serials, regardless of place of publication. Entry detail includes frequency, start date, price, contents, publisher/distributor, subjects and editorial personnel. V.2 provides a subject index, additional sections on Catalan, Basque and Galician titles and a listing of reference serials, directories etc. *Class No: 050(460)*

USA

[201]

The Standard periodical directory. New York, Oxbridge Communications, 1964-. Annual. ISSN: 00856630.

Published annually from 1987, previously irregular.

The 14th ed. 1991 has entries for more than 75,000 periodicals published in the US and Canada. Periodical defined as any publication having a frequency of issue at least once every two years. Includes consumer magazines, trade journals, newsletters, government publications, house organs, directories, yearbooks, etc. Data for each title includes publisher, editor and other senior personnel, where indexed/abstracted, subscription rates, circulation, physical characteristics, availability in other media and ISSN. Entries in 230 subject sections Accounting-Zoology. Title index and cross-index to subjects. Geared to the general public, but gives wider coverage of North American titles than either *Ulrich's international periodicals directory* or *The serials directory* (*qq.v.*). *Class No: 050(73)*

Australia

[202]

Australian periodicals in print. Melbourne, D.W. Thorpe, 1981-. Annual (initially irregular). ISSN: 10302474.

First published under title *Australian serials in print.* Replaced National Library's *Current Australian serials* 1963-75, which in turn succeeded the selected list of Australian periodicals, annuals and serials in *Annual catalogue of Australian publications.*

Provides comprehensive coverage of Australian periodical publications, including magazines, newspapers, directories, yearbooks and trade publications. The 7th ed. (1989. 624p.) has one A-Z sequence with entries under title, subject keyword and publisher. Data includes subtitle, editor, description, year first published, microform availability, price, frequency, circulation, advertising acceptance, ISSN and distributor. *Class No: 050(94)*

Indexes

[203]
Humanities index. New York, Wilson, 1974-. Quarterly, with annual cumulation. ISSN: 00955981.

Continues in part *Social sciences and humanities index* (below).

Cover to cover indexing of 345 English language periodicals in the fields of archaeology and classical studies, area studies, folklore, history, language and literature, performing arts, philosophy, religion and theology. Includes numerous British titles *e.g. Contemporary review, Mind, Past and present.* Arranged in standard Wilson format, subject and author entries in one A-Z sequence. Separate list of book reviews. Records 1984 to date searchable online through Wilsonline. Also available on CD-ROM. *Class No: 050:014.3*

[204]
—Social sciences and humanities index: formerly *International index.* 1907/15-64. New York, Wilson, 1916-74. Quarterly, with cumulations.

As *Readers' guide to periodical literature supplement,* (covering 1907-19), 1916-20; as *International index to periodicals* 1916-65.

Up to 1928 *International index* covered education periodicals, now indexed in *Education index* (1929-), and up to 1945 also covered a number of foreign-language periodicals. As *Social sciences and humanities index* covered about 200 titles of which around 30 were British. From 1974 divides into *Humanities index* (above) and *Social sciences index.* (q.v.). *Class No: 050:014.3*

[205]
Internationale Bibliographie der Zeitschriftenliteratur aus allen Gebieten des Wissens. 1963/64-. [International bibliography of periodical literature covering all fields of knowledge. 1963/64-.] Osnabrück, Dietrich, 1965-. Semi-annual. ISSN: 00209201.

Also known as 'IBZ'. Three sister publications, *Internationale Bibliographie der Rezensionen, Internationale Jahresbibliographie der Festschriften* and *Internationale Jahresbibliographie der Kongressberichte,* cover book reviews, Festschriften and conference proceedings respectively.

Continues *Bibliographie der fremdsprachigen Zeitschriftenliteratur* (1911-64) and *Bibliographie der deutschen Zeitschriftenliteratur* (1896-1964).

Indexes *c.*200-300,000 articles in about 7,000 periodicals. Revised format from v.19(2) 1983. Each semi-annual issue in 6v.: v.1-4 Index rerum; v.5 Index systematicus. Autores; v.6 Periodica. Index rerum (subject index) comprises German language keyword index (English and French keywords refer to German entries), giving coded references to periodical titles and article citations. The Index systematicus organizes the keywords used into 16 fields of knowledge, the Autores section provides an author index, while the Periodica volume lists periodicals indexed by the code number quoted in the Index rerum entries. The only general periodical index providing international coverage on such a scale. Remains of some value in larger academic libraries, especially for German language material, but for most uses increasingly eclipsed by the growth of indexing and abstracting services devoted to specific subject fields. *Class No: 050:014.3*

[206]
Poole's index to periodical literature. 1802-1906. Boston, Mass., Osgood; London, Turner, 1882-1908. 6v.

V.1 1802-81; 1st Suppl. 1882-86; 2nd Suppl. 1887-92; 3rd Suppl. 1892-96; 4th Suppl. 1897-1901; 5th Suppl. 1902-6.

Original v. and suppls. available as reprints (Magnolia, Mass., Peter Smith ISBN 084465695x).

....(contd.)
The only general periodical index covering so long a period. Confined to American and English titles. Indexes nearly 600,000 articles in 479 periodicals. Invaluable within its limits as a key to 19th century magazine literature. A subject index only with title entries for works of fiction etc. No author entries, except for biographical or critical works, although the author's name does appear in parentheses in each subject entry. Entries do not give full pagination or date of articles. This deficiency is met by *Poole's index: date and volume key.* M.V. Bell and J.C. Bacon (Chicago, Association of College and Research Libraries, 1957. 61p. (ACRL monograph, 19)). *Class No: 050:014.3*

Great Britain

[207]
British humanities index. 1962-. London, Bowker-Saur, 1963-. Quarterly, with separate annual cumulation. ISSN: 00070815.

Published by Library Association Publishing until January/March 1990. Issued in 3 quarters with an annual cumulation until 1968. Continues in part *Subject index to periodicals* (below).

Indexes *c.*325 British journals and newspapers under specific subject headings A-Z, with a separate author index in each annual cumulation. Short explanatory notes attached to entries where the subject content is not clear from the title. Humanities interpreted broadly to include the arts, economics, history, philosophy, politics and society. Also indexes selected non-specialist articles of popular interest in science and technology. Newspaper coverage restricted to comment and features on current affairs and political and social criticism in the *Times, Guardian, Observer* etc. Particularly valuable for indexing local history and related titles *e.g. Derbyshire archaeological journal, North Staffordshire journal of field studies, Northamptonshire past and present.* A very valuable source for a wide range of British periodical literature, exhibiting a consistently high standard of indexing and production. To be available on CD-ROM from early 1992, with quarterly updating, as *BHI PLUS. Class No: 050:014.3(410)*

[208]
—Subject index to periodicals. 1915-61. London, Library Association, 1919-62. Annual, (quarterly issues 1954-61).

As the *Athenaeum subject index to periodicals* 1915-16. Frequency varies: annual 1915-22, 1926-53; quarterly with annual cumulations, 1954-61. 1923-25 partly compiled, but never published.

Issued as class lists with author indexes 1915-22, those for 1915-16 cumulated and published in 1v. 1919. Published as a subject index from 1926. From 1947 confined almost entirely to British periodicals (foreign titles dropped during World War II, except for some US titles discontinued 1947). During the 1950's indexed about 325 periodicals annually. With cessation of publication in 1961 continued by *British humanities index* (above) and *British technology index,* later *Current technology index.* (q.v.). *Class No: 050:014.3(410)*

[209]
Wellesley index to Victorian periodicals, 1824-1900: tables of contents and identification of contributors with bibliographies of their articles and stories and an index of initials and pseudonyms. Houghton, W.E., *ed.* Toronto, Univ. of Toronto Press; London, Routledge & Kegan Paul, 1966-89. 5v. ISBN: 0802027199, set.

Identifies nearly 12,000 authors as the anonymous or pseudonymous contributors to 43 major British monthlies and quarterlies. Titles indexed include: *The contemporary review, The Edinburgh review* (from 1802), *The quarterly review* (v.I); *The fortnightly review, The London review*

....(contd.)
(v.II); *Westminster review* (v.III); *British quarterly review, London quarterly review* (v.IV). V.I-v.IV each in 3 pts: A. 'Table of contents and identification of contributors (introductory essay for each title followed by table of contents for every issue, including the authorial signature, the *Index* attribution and evidence for that attribution); B. Bibliography of contributors (bibliographies of the identified contributors, together with biographical data and source of that data); C. Index of pseudonyms and initials (alphabetical table of identified and unidentified pseudonyms and initials). V.V *Epitome and index* consolidates the entries from part B of v.I-v.IV in one A-Z sequence. Also includes appendices: I. Items in part A of volumes I-IV altered in their appendices; II. Corrections and additions to volumes I-IV. *Class No:* 050:014.3(410)

Canada

[210]
Canadian periodical index. [Index périodiques canadiens.] Toronto, Info Globe, 1949-. Monthly, with annual cumulation. ISSN: 00084719.
Published by the Canadian Library Association until 1986. As *Canadian index to periodicals and documentary films* 1949-63. Cumulation 1948-59 (1962. 1180p.).
Coverage much expanded since the take over by Info Globe. Now indexes *c.*370 Canadian and 17 major US titles. Author, corporate name and subject entries in a single alphabetical sequence. Book and other reviews listed under form heading by title. The 1990 cumulation (v.43 1991. xiv,1614p.) has over 52,000 citations. Also available online through Info Globe 1977 to date. *Class No:* 050:014.3(71)

USA

[211]
Magazine index. Foster City, Ca., Information Access Corp., 1977-. Monthly.
Microfiche. Monthly fiches cumulate for 5 years.
Indexes 435 popular magazines published in the US and Canada, including sports and children's titles. Complete indexing of the titles covered *e.g.* reviews, editorials, product evaluations. Includes all the titles indexed in Wilson's *Readers' guide to periodical literature* (below).
Magazine index is also searchable as an online database through Dialog (File 47) and BRS. Contains over 2.5 million records, greatly extending the coverage of the microfiche service. Database updated monthly, records added daily to the *Newsearch* file. Two CD-ROM versions are also available *Magazine index plus*, corresponding to the microfiche service, and *Magazine index select*, covering a subset of 200 periodicals. *Class No:* 050:014.3(73)

[212]
Readers' guide to periodical literature (Unabridged): an author subject index to selected general interest periodicals of reference value in libraries. 1900-. New York, Wilson, 1905-. Monthly (except March, April, September, October, December semi-monthly), with quarterly and annual cumulations. ISSN: 00340464.
Annual cumulations began 1965, earlier cumulations cover longer periods; v.1 covers 1901-04.
Indexes *c.*200 titles nearly all published in the US. In one A-Z sequence of authors and subjects, except for book review citations indexed in a separate section. Valuable for its coverage of popular periodicals (selection of titles accomplished by vote), sound indexing and frequency. Records 1983 to date also available online through Wilsonline and on CD-ROM, abstracts included as in *Readers' guide abstracts* (below). *Class No:* 050:014.3(73)

[213]
—Abridged readers' guide to periodical literature: author and subject index to a selected list of periodicals. New York, Wilson, 1936-. Monthly (except June to August), with annual cumulation. ISSN: 0001334x.
Indexes *c.*60 of the titles covered in the main *Readers' guide.* Intended for school and smaller public libraries. *Class No:* 050:014.3(73)

[214]
—Readers' guide abstracts to periodical literature. New York, Wilson, 1984-. Microfiche and printed formats. ISSN: 08860092.
Orignally launched as a microfiche service. Printed ed. from 1988. According to publisher's literature from 1992 printed version to be published under title *Readers' guide abstracts school and public library edition* containing a subset of *c.*25,000 abstracts of the *c.*60,000 provided annually.
Abstracts are short, averaging *c.*125 words. *Class No:* 050:014.3(73)

Directories

[215]
Current British directories: a guide to directories published in the British Isles. Henderson, C.A.P., *ed.* 11th ed. Beckenham, CBD Research, 1988. xviii,355p. ISBN: 0900246502.
First published 1953; 10th ed. 1985.
Directories defined as 'any works which enable a searcher to locate, identify or obtain further information about a person, organization or other unit, or which provide the searcher with a list of persons, organizations or other units in a particular industry, trade or group, or in a specific area' (p.vii). Excludes works produced in other countries issued in Britain with a British imprint. In 2 main pts: 1. Local directories, listing general directories of specific areas or places, arranged by town; 2. Specialized directories, listing directories of specific industries, trades professions etc., arranged by title. About 3,500 titles listed, 600 new to this ed. Data includes publisher, date of first ed., frequency, price, no. of pages, ISSN, description of contents and former title(s). Publisher index; subject index p.283-354. The standard British guide to directories. *Class No:* 058

[216]
Directories in print. Detroit, Gale, 1980-. Annual. ISSN: 0899353x.
Published as *Directory of directories* until 1987. 8th ed. 1991 2v. has subtitle: *An annotated guide to over 14,000 directories published worldwide, including business and industrial directories, professional and scientific rosters, entertainment, recreation and cultural directories, directory databases and other non-print products and other lists and guides of all kinds.*
13,990 actual entries the majority for titles published in the US. Arranged under 26 subject groupings General business ... Retail, wholesale and service industries ... Publishing and broadcasting media ... Science and technology ... Education ... Hobbies and leisure activities. Up to 26 data elements for each entry including title, publisher, coverage, language, description, arrangement, indexes, former title, price, and online availability. V.2 contains a subject index (*c.*3,700 terms) and a title and keyword index (includes entries for titles in the same publisher's *City and state directories in print*). Unrivalled coverage, the essential key to directories and a useful pointer to sources for many reference enquiries. *Class No:* 058

[217]

The Top 3,000 directories and annuals. Reading, Dawson, 1980-. Irregular. ISSN: 02689928.

9th ed. (1991. [8],374p.). Eds. 1-8 (1980-87) published by Alan Armstrong; initial issues as *The Top 1,000 directories and annuals.*

9th ed. has exactly 3,000 entries by title A-Z (p.3-234). Gives title, publisher, distributor, date (current and next eds.), price, ISBN and a brief description rarely exceeding 50 words. Includes 'a selection of reference titles and guides which while not strictly directories or annuals, nonetheless remain invaluable to research and information specialists' (Introduction). Useful supplementary lists: titles available on alternative media (microfiche, online, CD-ROM); titles by month or year of issue; titles by publisher. Subject index (p.295-348) under detailed headings. List of publishers and their addresses. Not as comprehensive for British published directories as *Current British directories* (*q.v.*). *Class No:* 058

06 Organizations & Associations

Organizations & Associations

[218]

Yearbook of international organizations. Union of International Associations, *ed.* München, Saur, 1948-. Annual. ISSN: 00843814.

Published annually since 1983 (previously approximately biennial) in 3 volumes: 1. *Organizations descriptions and index*; 2. *Geographic volume. International organization participation; country directory of secretariats and membership*; 3. *Subject volume. Global action networks: classified directory by subject and region.*

The 27th ed. for 1990/91 has information for 26,656 international organizations. Main descriptive listing in v.1 arranged in 7 groups: Federations of international organizations; Universal membership organizations; Intercontinental membership organizations; Regionally defined membership organizations; Organizations emanating from places, persons, other bodies; Organizations having a special form, including foundations and funds; Religious orders, fraternities and secular institutions. Entries, based largely on information supplied by organizations, vary in length from 3 to 500 lines. Over 10,000 organizations have detailed entries providing descriptions of activities, aims, history, structure, membership and publications. Other information normally available includes address, name of executive officer, foundation date and former titles. Index in v.1 contains over 110,000 entries including organization names (all working languages of the organization), former names and abbreviations and initialisms. V.2 in 2 main sections, 'International organizations by country of membership' (M), with addresses and reference to entry no. in v.1 'and Secretariat countries' (S). Subject index in v.3 also in 2 main sections: Title and keyword index; Subject category index. The major source for international organizations, more comprehensive and detailed than Gale's *International organizations*. A CD-ROM version is to be made available during 1992. *Class No:* 061

Europe

[219]

Pan-European associations: a directory of multi-national organisations in Europe. Henderson, C.A.P., *ed.* 2nd ed. Beckenham, CBD Research, 1991. x,207p. ISBN: 0900246545.

1st ed. 1983.

Covers European voluntary organizations which represent membership, either throughout Europe, or in a significant number of countries. Also includes international voluntary organizations whose membership is almost exclusively European. About 1,600 entries (p.1-161) Action Committee for Europe ... Youth Forum of the European Communities, with 3,300 cross-references mainly to names in other languages. Excludes organizations concerned with specific geographic areas (*e.g.* Benelux, Scandinavia). Data includes

....(contd.)
activities, membership, affiliations, languages, publications and former names. Separate list of 'Unverified and lost associations' (p.163-68). Abbreviations index (p.171-79); subject index (p.181-201). Incudes some bodies not in the *Yearbook of international organizations* (above). *Class No:* 061(4)

Great Britain

[220]

Councils, committees & boards: a handbook of advisory, consultative, executive and similar bodies in British public life. Sellar, L., *ed.* 7th ed. Beckenham, CBD Research, 1989. xiv,403p. ISBN: 0900246529.

First published 1970; 6th ed. 1985. Eds. 1-5 ed. by J.G. Anderson. A companion volume to *Directory of British associations*.

Arranged A-Z by names of bodies. Wide ranging coverage, c.1,500 entries including Central Council for Education and Training in Social Work, National Health Service, Sports Council, Transport User Consultative Committees. Excludes local government councils and other purely local bodies, sub-committees responsible to a superior committee and organizations which include the words 'council', 'committee' or 'board', but which are associations having a voluntary membership. Data for each body includes address, establishment and membership, terms of reference, objects and duties, activities and publications. Cross references to entries in *Directory of British associations*. Abbreviation, chairmen and subject indexes. *Class No:* 061(410)

[221]

Directory of British associations: and associations in Ireland. Henderson, G.P. *and* Henderson, S.P.A., *eds.* 10th ed. Beckenham, CBD Research, 1990. xvi,547p. ISBN: 0900246537.

First published 1965; 9th ed. 1988.

The major British directory of associations covering 'national associations, societies, institutions and similar organizations which have voluntary membership in all fields of activity. Regional and local organizations concerned with important industries and trade ... are included as are local chambers of commerce and trade and county agricultural, archaeological, historical, natural history and similar organizations' (Introduction p.vii). Questionnaire based, about 8,000 organizations included. Entries, A-Z by name, give address, etc., name of secretary or chief executive, branches, organization type (coded, with brief explanation where necessary), activities, affiliations, publications, membership and former names. Separate list of 'Unverified and lost associations' (blue pages). Abbreviation index. Subject index under detailed headings; ample cross-references. *Class No:* 061(410)

USA

[222]
Encyclopedia of associations. Detroit, Gale, 1956-. Annual.
Title varies: early editions as *Encyclopedia of American associations*. Now published in 3 volumes: v.1 *National organisations of the US*; v.2 *Geographic and executive indexes*; v.3 *New associations and projects*.
Subtitle of 1990/91 ed. *A guide to over 30,000 national and international organizations, including: trade, business and commercial; agricultural and commodity; legal, governmental, public administration and military; scientific, engineering and technical; educational; cultural; social welfare; health and medical; public affairs; fraternal, foreign interest, nationality and ethnic; religious, veterans, hereditary and patriotic; hobby and vocational; athletic and sports; labor unions, associations and federations; chambers of commerce and trade and tourism; Greek letter and related organizations, and fan clubs.*
V.1 *National organizations of the US* in 3 pts. Pts.1-2 contain entries for 23,000 non-profit American membership organizations of national scope. Arranged according to 18 subject groups, up to 28 categories of information given for each entry, including address, chief official and title, number of members, staff, budget, regional state and local groups, description, computerized services, committees, sections and divisions, affiliated organizations, name changes, publications and conventions/meetings. Pt.3 of v.1 comprises an *Alphabetical index to organization names and keywords*. V.2 of the set offers further indexing by city and state and by executive name. The *New associations and projects* volume provides information on newly formed organizations not included in v.1, while a two issue inter-edition *Updating service* lists revised data.
The entire set, together with Gale's associated publications *International organizations* and *Regional, state and local organizations*, is searchable online through Dialog (File 114). Also available in CD-ROM format as *Gale global access associations*, offering menu based searching on up to 15 data fields. Replacement discs issued every 6 months. *Class No:* 061(73)

Non-Government Organizations

Learned Societies

[223]
Directory of European professional and learned societies. Adams, R.W., *ed.* 4th ed. Beckenham, CBD Research, 1989. xlix,380p. ISBN: 0900246510.
Distributed in the US by Gale. Title, introductory matter and subject indexes also in French and German. Replaces *Directory of European associations. Part 2. National learned, scientific and technical societies*, 1st ed. 1975, 3rd ed. 1984.
Excludes British, pan-European or international associations. About 3,000 entries arranged under more than 500 subject headings Academies of arts and letters ... Zoology. A full entry provides name, acronym, foundation date, address, objectives and fields of interest, membership, activities, membership of international organizations and publications. Indexed by subject, organization name and abbreviation. *Class No:* 061.22

[224]
The 1990 British club year book and directory. 7th ed. London, Eagle Commercial Publications, 1990. vii,612p. ISBN: 0951558307.
First published 1961, 6th ed. 1982.
Coverage includes sports clubs (*e.g.* bowls, golf, rugby) leisure interest clubs (*e.g.* antiques, camera, horticulture), social clubs, political clubs and various other general clubs and similar organizations. Brief entries, arranged in 120 categories Alcuin ... YWCA, giving address, tel. no. and contact (secretary etc.) only. Includes full listings of branches of nationally organized clubs (*e.g.* English Golf Union). Listing of working men's clubs p.128-73. A useful source, worthy of more regular updating. *Class No:* 061.237

Conferences

[225]
International congress calendar. Union of International Associations, *ed.* Brussels, Union of International Associations, 1961-. Quarterly. ISSN: 05386349.
Issued in 4 editions annually, each of which supersedes the last.
Covers conferences of international organizations and important national bodies. In geographical and chronological sections each giving date and place of conference, address of organizing body, estimated number of participants, number of countries represented, concurrent exhibitions and references to organization entries in the *Yearbook of international organizations* (*q.v.*). Subject/organization index based on significant keywords in the organization name or name of principal conference theme. *Class No:* 061.3

Conference Proceedings

[226]
Index of conference proceedings. Boston Spa, British Library Document Supply Centre, 1964-. Monthly, with annual cumulation. ISSN: 09594906.
Title varies slightly: as *Index of conference proceedings received* until the end of 1987.
Based on the comprehensive conference proceedings acquisition programme of the Document Supply Centre. Covers proceedings in all subject areas, languages and formats except audiovisual, including those published as books or as parts of normal serials. Indexing by subject key term derived from conference title and organizing/sponsoring body. Entry detail includes date and name of conference, title, meeting and document description, sponsoring/organizing body and DSC stock no. About 18,000 proceedings indexed annually. Also available in microfiche, online through BLAISE and on CD-ROM as *Boston Spa conferences*. *Class No:* 061.30

[227]
—Index of conference proceedings received, 1964-1988. London, Saur, 1989. 26v. ISBN: 0862918987.
Also available in microfiche from the Document Supply Centre.
Indexes more than 270,000 proceedings under 750,000 subject key terms. 'Although now the largest bibliography in its field, this remains essentially a finding list to such material held by the Document Supply Centre, and must be accepted as such' (*Reference reviews* v.3(4), December 1989, p.153). Major limitations include identification of books and serials containing proceedings by DSC stock no., rather than title, and key terms based strictly on title and organizing/sponsoring body. *Class No:* 061.30

[228]
Index to social sciences and humanities proceedings.
Philadelphia, Institute for Scientific Information, 1979-.
Quarterly, final issue annual cumulation. ISSN: 01910574.

Indexes published proceedings of conferences, seminars, symposia, colloquia, conventions, etc. International in scope, including some non-English language material. Excludes proceedings in which the majority of the material is not printed for the first time, or is in the form of abstracts. Main listing gives conference, location and date, bibliographical detail of proceedings and titles and authors of papers. 6 indexes: category (69 broad categories); permuterm subject; sponsor; author/editor; meeting location; corporate (geographic and organization sections). 22,609 proceedings indexed to the end of 1990. *Class No: 061.30*

[229]
Proceedings in print. Halifax, Mass., Proceedings in Print, 1964-. Bimonthly. ISSN: 00329568.

Initially confined to science and technology proceedings, but since 1967 has covered all subject areas and all languages. Now indexes about 3,500 proceedings annually. Conference proceedings defined to include symposia, lecture series, hearings, seminars, courses, colloquia and meetings. Entries, under conference title, give place, date and sponsoring agency, details of proceedings, where published, order information and price. Index of corporate authors, sponsoring agencies, editors and subject headings, cumulated annually. *Class No: 061.30*

Research Establishments

[230]
Centres and bureaux: a directory of concentrations of effort, information and expertise. Sellar, L., *ed.* Beckenham, CBD Research, 1987. xi,214p. ISBN: 0900246472.

Distributed in US by Gale.

Questionnaire based directory, predominantly of research organizations, but also including information and advice agencies and training institutions. With a few exceptions all organizations included have 'centre' or 'bureau' as part of their title (*e.g.* Cognac Information Centre; National Children's Bureau; Victorian Studies Centre). Includes some organizations previously listed in *Directory of British associations* (*q.v.*). Approximately 600 entries arranged alphabetically by title giving address, key personnel and total staffing, date of establishment, financial data, objectives, activities and publications. Indexed by abbreviation, sponsor and participating organization and subject. Lacks an index by geographic location. A useful addition to the CBD family of directories, including organizations not readily found elsewhere. *Class No: 061.62*

[231]
International research centers directory. Detroit, Gale, 1982-. Biennial. ISSN: 02782731.

5th ed. 1990-1991 (1990. Smith, D.L., ed. v.1327p.) has subtitle: *A World guide to government, university, independent non-profit and commercial research and development centers, institutes, laboratories, bureaus, test facilities, experiment stations, research parks and data collection and analysis centers, as well as foundations, councils and other organizations which support research.*

6,600 entries for research centres in 145 countries (332 for UK). Excludes US and Canada, covered in *Research centers directory* (below). Entries include name (English and indigenous), acronym, address, organization head, staff, description of activities, special facilities, publications and services, library and affiliates/subsidiaries. Multi-national section precedes country listings. Name and keyword, country and subject indexes. *Class No: 061.62*

[232]
Research centers directory. Detroit, Gale, 1960-. Annual (formerly irregular). ISSN: 00801518.

1st ed. 1960 as *Directory of university research bureaux and institutes.* Now published annually. 16th ed. (1992. 2v. Hill, K., ed.) has subtitle *A Guide to over 12,000 university-related and other non-profit research organizations established on a permanent basis and carrying on continuing research programs in agriculture, astronomy and space sciences, behavioral and social sciences, biological sciences and ecology, business and economics, computers and mathematics, education, engineering and technology, government and public affairs, humanities and religion, labor and industrial relations, law, medical sciences, physical and earth sciences and regional and area studies.*

US companion v. to *International research centers directory.* Coverage includes Canada. Entries in 17 subject sections: 5,000 heading subject index; geographic index, master index. *Class No: 061.62*

Museums

[233]
HUDSON, K. *and* **NICHOLLS, A. The Directory of museums and living displays.** 3rd ed. Macmillan, Basingstoke; Stockton Press, New York, 1985. xvii,1047p. ISBN: 0333362659, UK; 0943818176, US.

1st ed. 1975 and 2nd ed. 1981 as *The Directory of world museums.*

Claims to list 35,000 museums, with 'living displays', defined as 'zoos, aquaria, botanical gardens and living history farms', included for the first time in this edition. Listing by country in three-column A4 format. General note on each country, museums listed under town, then A-Z. Entries give only address and brief uncritical note on museum holdings. No subject index. Unfavourably compared with other museum directories by *Choice* (V24(1), September 1986, p.86), but still considered a 'valuable reference source'. *Class No: 069*

[234]
WOODHEAD, P. *and* **STANSFIELD, G. Keyguide to information sources in museum studies.** London, Mansell, 1989. xiv,194p. ISBN: 072012025x.

Provides 'an integrated guide to the documentation, reference aids and key organizational sources of information about museums and museum studies worldwide' (Introduction p.xi). In 3 pts: I. Overview of museum studies and its literature (8 discursive chapters, each with references) - II. Bibliographical listing of sources of information (329 annotated entries, a high proportion for works discussed in pt.I) - III. Listing of selected organizations (93 entries, also annotated). Pt.II, subdivided by form of material, includes entries for 54 museum directories. Entries in III list publications. Index p.165-94. A valuable new resource in museum studies, well-researched and presented. *Class No: 069*

Europe

[235]
HUDSON, K. *and* **NICHOLLS, A. The Cambridge guide to the museums of Europe.** Cambridge, Cambridge Univ. Press, 1991. xxvi,509p. illus., maps. ISBN: 0521371759.

Contains *c.*2,000 entries. Intended primarily for "more active and independent tourists" (p.vii), aiming to cover all the major national and regional museums with a selection of special interest collections. Most local museums of a general nature excluded. Confined to Western Europe; 380 UK museums included. Arranged by country then town, entries give address, hours, admission details, facilities etc., and a descriptive note of 50-300 words. 500 illus.; 12 locational maps. Indexes of subjects, museum names and

....(contd.)

museums associated with individuals. The first guide to European museums and "outstanding for its range, balance and quality of entries" (*Reference reviews*, v.5(3), 1991, p.8). *Class No:* 069(4)

Great Britain

[236]

HUDSON, K. *and* **NICHOLLS, A. The Cambridge guide to the museums of Britain and Ireland.** Rev. paperback ed. Cambridge, Cambridge Univ. Press, 1989. x,[16],452p. illus., maps. ISBN: 0521322723.

Hardback ed. 1987 (0521322723).

Aimed at 'absolute completeness' of coverage (Introduction p.ix). Entries for over 2,000 museums, art galleries and historic houses arranged under towns A-Z. Gives address, opening hours, name of curator, symbols to indicate visitor facilities and brief description of museum contents. Over 400 illustrations, some in colour; 16p. map section locates towns with museums. Indexes of museum names, subjects and museums associated with individuals. *Class No:* 069(410)

[237]

Museums yearbook: including a directory of museums and galleries of the British Isles. London, Museums Association, 1955-. Annual. ISSN: 03077675.

Title varies, previously *Museum calendar*.

The main body of each yearbook comprises the directory of museums (p.38-243 1990/91 ed.), listing museums by town A-Z. Information given includes governing body, admission charges, facilities, reports, catalogues, opening hours and a full list of senior staff with post held and qualifications. Name index of museums. No detail on collections. Other sections of the yearbook include: Useful addresses and related organizations; Area Museum Councils; Regional federations of British museums; Other museum associations (overseas); List of Museum Association institutional and personal members. Further information on the Museums Association in the introductory chapters, including policy statements and code of practice. *Class No:* 069(410)

USA

[238]

The Official museum directory. Wilmette, Ill., American Association of Museums and National Register Publishing, 1961-. Annual. ISSN: 00906700.

As *Museum directory of the United States and Canada* 1961-65. Annual since 1980.

The 1992 ed. (1991. [69],1474p.) has entries for more than 7,000 US museums (coverage of Canadian museums discontinued from 1984 ed.). Fairly brief information on personnel, governing authority, type of museum, collections, research fields, facilities, activities, publications, hours and admission prices. Lacks detailed descriptions of museum contents. Arranged by state, then city, with museum name, personnel and subject category indexes. Introductory information on the American Association of Museums, overseas museums associations, etc. A separate *Products and services directory* (1992 ed. [12],209p.) is also available. *Class No:* 069(73)

07 Journalism & Newspapers

Journalism & Newspapers

Mass Media

[239]
Benn's media directory. Tonbridge, Benn Business Information Services, 1846-. Annual. ISSN: 02698366.

Title varies: as *Newspaper press directory* until 1977, then *Benn's press directory* until 1985. Publisher also varies: Mitchell 1846-1948. Not published 1941-44.

Issued in 2 volumes: *United Kingdom edition* and *International edition.*

Still primarily a directory of periodicals and newspapers, despite recent title change. The UK v. (138th ed. 1990. 904p.) has sections for publishing houses, newspapers (national, then local A-Z by town), periodicals (A-Z by title preceded by a classified index) and directories and other reference sources. Also covers broadcasting and other communications agencies and media organizations. Overall includes 135 daily newspapers, 836 weekly newspapers, 1,167 free and local papers, 8,037 periodicals, 530 free magazines and 2,221 directories. The International v. of the same ed. (676p.) is arranged in area sections, then by country. Includes detail of 9,056 newspapers, 23,303 periodicals and 2,013 radio and television stations. Entries include coded references to UK advertising representatives. Fuller information than *Willing's press guide,* (*q.v.*), but somewhat cumbersome to use. *Class No:* 070.0

[240]
BLUM, E. *and* **WILHOIT, F.G. Mass media bibliography:** an annotated guide to books and journals for research and reference. 3rd ed. Urbana, Univ. of Illinois Press, 1990. viii,344p. ISBN: 0252017064.

1st ed. 1972 (itself a reworking of Blum's *Reference books in the mass media,* 1962) and 2nd ed. 1980 as *Basic books in the mass media.*

'All titles give information about some aspect of mass communication - theory, structure, economics, function, research, content, effects. Many are reference works. ... All entries have one common factor: they treat the subject in broad general terms' (Preface p.vii). Expanded from 1,179 to 1,947 entries in this ed. 9 main sections: General communications - Broadcasting media - Print media - Film - Advertising and public relations - Bibliographies - Directories and handbooks - Journals - Indexes to the mass communication literature. Well-written *c.*150 word evaluative annotations. Author, title and subject indexes. US bias and confined to English language material, but an excellent, established source. *Class No:* 070.0

[241]
BRAD/British rate and data: media facts at your fingertips. London, MacLean Hunter, 1954-. Monthly. ISSN: 02633515.

Sections (December 1991, v.38(12), xxiv,612p.):

....(contd.)
Newspapers (p.1-152), including national, regional, local paid and local free; Consumer and special interest publications (p.153-282), in sections Antiques...Woodworking; Business and professional publications (p.283-580) in sections Accountancy...Wine and spirit trade; Broadcast and electronic media (p.581-604); Outdoor and poster media (p.605-9); Advertising trade associations, societies and clubs (p.610-12); alphabetical title index (p.ix-xxiv). Primarily for advertisers, but also useful for basic current information on British newspapers and periodicals. The longest established and still most widely known British media guide. *Class No:* 070.0

[242]
Gale directory of publications and broadcasting media: an annual guide to publications and broadcasting stations, including newspapers, magazines, journals, radio stations, television stations and cable systems. Detroit, Gale, 1987-. Annual. ISSN: 10487972.

Issued in 3v. Continues the long established *Ayer directory of publications,* first published 1880 (as *IMS/Ayer directory of publications,* 1983-86).

Coverage extended to radio and television stations and cable systems from the 122nd ed. 1990. Excludes house organs and newsletters. Geographic coverage confined to the US, Canada and Puerto Rico. 36,000 entries in v.1-2 of the 124th ed. 1992, arranged geographically by state and town, print and broadcasting media listed in separate sequences. Print entries include publisher, address, description, establishment date, frequency, personnel, ISSN, subscription rates and advertising data. To be included publications must be issued four or more times annually. V.3 contains maps, statistical tables, classified lists and a master name and keyword index. An inter-edition supplement *Gale directory of publications update* reports changes and adds new entries. *Class No:* 070.0

The Press

[243]
The Newspaper press in Britain: an annotated bibliography. Linton, D. *and* Boston, R., *eds.* London, Mansell, 1987. xvii,361p. ISBN: 0720117925.

The first significant bibliography of the British newspaper press. 2,909 critically annotated entries for books, articles and theses on 'printed news journalism' from the earliest times to the present. Coverage includes photojournalism, cartoon illustration and news agencies. Arranged A-Z by author with an index of subjects, newspaper titles and persons. Appendices on the chronology of British newspaper history 1476-1986 and archival sources for *c.*155 individual newspapers and authors. A 'useful and comprehensively analytical work' (*Refer,* v.4(4), Autumn 1987, p.18). *Class No:* 070.1

[244]
SCHWARZLOSE, R.A. **Newspapers: a reference guide.** New York and London, Greenwood, 1987. xxxvii,417p. (*American popular culture.*) ISBN: 0313236135.

Selective guide to the literature on US newspapers from the beginning to the mid 1980s. Presentation as narrative essays, each with attached bibliography: 'Providing newspapers' - 'Newspapers and society' - 'Newspapers and the law' etc. Approximately half the coverage is for newspaper history. Includes appendix on major research collections. Well indexed p.337-417. Warmly received, 'no comparable book about the press' (*Choice*, v.25(10), June 1988, p.1546). *Class No: 070.1*

[245]
World press encyclopedia. Kurian, G.T., *ed.* London, Mansell, 1982. 2v. (xix,1202p.). ISBN: 0720116465.
Published in the US by Facts on File (0871966212).
Intended as a 'definitive survey of the press in 180 countries' (Preface v.1 p.xiii). 4 main sections. The first, 'The international press', comprises 6 essays including, 'Comparative press laws' and 'Press councils of the world'. The second and main section, 'The world's developed press', covers 83 countries Albania-Zimbabwe. Each country dealt with under headings: Basic data; Economic framework; Press laws; Censorship; State-press relations; Attitude towards foreign media; News agencies; Electronic news media; Education and training; Summary; Chronology; Bibliography. The remaining sections, 'Smaller and developing press systems' (33 countries) and 'Minimal and underdeveloped press systems' (65 countries) give similar, but much briefer, information. 4 appendices including 'News agencies of the world', a 4p. A-Z list by country. Detailed index (p.1171-202). No other source provides such a wealth of comparative information on the press in so many countries. *Class No: 070.1*

Newspapers

[246]
Bibliography of British newspapers. Toase, C.A., *gen. ed.* London, British Library, 1975-.
V.1 *Wiltshire* Bluhm, R.K. ed. (1975. 28p. 0853650381); v.2 *Kent* Bergess, W.F. and others eds. (1982. xviii,139p. 0712300014); v.3 *Durham and Northumberland* Manders, F.W.D. ed. (1982. xvi,65p. 0712301240); v.4 *Derbyshire* Mellors, A. & Radford, J. eds. (1987. xv,74p. 0712301240); v.5 *Nottinghamshire* Brook, M. ed. (1987. xvii,62p. 0712300619); v.6 *Cornwall: Devon* Rowles, J. & Maxted, I. eds. (1991. xiv,123p. 0712302239). V.1 published as a pamphlet by the Library Association Reference, Special and Information Section.
Eventual objective is to cover the entire British Isles based on pre-1974 county boundaries. Confined to newspapers providing general news. Format of volumes varies. Latest has main section listing newspapers A-Z by title. Separate section by town A-Z locates files in libraries, publisher's offices, record offices and other collections. Further 'Chronologies' section listing newspapers by town and date. Historical accounts and indexes also noted. *Class No: 070.2*

[247]
BRITISH LIBRARY. Newspaper Library. **Catalogue of the Newspaper Library, Colindale.** London, British Museum Publications for the British Library, 1975. 8v. ISBN: 0714103527.
V.1: London. (654p.); v.2: England and Wales, Scotland, Ireland. (672p.); v.3: Aden-New Guinea. (416p.); v.4: New Zealand-Zanzibar. (320p.); v.5: Titles, A-E. (600p.); v.6: Titles, F-L. (604p.); v.7: Titles, M-R. (604p.); v.8: Titles, S-Z. (604p.). Supersedes *Catalogue of printed books.* *Supplement: Newspapers published in Great Britain and*

....(contd.)
Ireland, 1800-1901. (London, British Museum, 1908. 532 cols.).
Compiled from the working catalogue of the Colindale collection. UK titles and amendments included up to the end of 1970, overseas titles and amendments up to the end of 1971. Covers 'London newspapers and journals from 1801 onward, English provincial, Scottish and Irish newspapers from about 1700 onward and large collections of Commonwealth and foreign newspapers' (Introduction). Excludes London newspapers published before 1801 (in separate BL Burney Collection) and newspapers in oriental languages. V.1 includes national newspapers published in London. Entries give title, dates, notes on changed titles etc. and extent of the Library's holdings. *Class No: 070.2*

Indexes

Great Britain

[248]
BNI: British newspaper index. Reading, Research Publications, 1991-. CD-ROM database. Quarterly updating.
Covers *The Times, Sunday times, Times educational supplement, Times higher education supplement, Times literary supplement* and *Financial times* 1990 onwards and *The Independent* and *Independent on Sunday* 1991 onwards. Features browsable 17,000 term index plus searching by a variety of variables including newspaper name, publication date, headline and journalist. Lacks coverage of *The Guardian* and expensive in comparison with basic paper alternatives such as *Clover newspaper index* (below). *Class No: 070.2:014.3(410)*

[249]
Clover newspaper index. Biggleswade, Clover Publications, 1986-. Weekly, (46 issues pa.), with half-yearly cumulated indexes.
Covers the *Daily telegraph, Financial times, Guardian, Independent, Observer, Times* and *Sunday times.* Includes magazines, but not supplements *e.g., Times educational supplement.* Index entries under detailed subject headings, reference to article title, newspaper, date, page and column. Reviews entered under headings Book reviews, Film reviews etc. Very promptly produced, normally available within two weeks of the issue indexed. *Class No: 070.2:014.3(410)*

[250]
The Times index. Reading, Research Publications (formerly Newspaper Archive Developments), 1973-. Monthly, with annual cumulation. ISSN: 02600668.
Quarterly 1973-76; annual cumulation from 1977.
Compiled from the final edition of each day. Also covers *The Sunday Times, The Times literary supplement, The Times educational supplement, The Times Scottish educational supplement* and *The Times higher educational supplement.* Entries under *c.*350 main subject headings, subdivided as necessary. Some group headings (*e.g.,* Books (titles and reviews), Theatrical productions). References to date, page and column. Several months time lag in appearance. During the suspension of publication of Times newspapers from 1st December 1978-12th November 1979 indexing was for the *Daily telegraph* and *Sunday telegraph.* Preceded by:- *Class No: 070.2:014.3(410)*

[251]
—THE TIMES. **Index to The Times.** London, The Times, 1906-72. Frequency varies.
Title varies: *The Annual index to The Times*, 1906-13; *The Official index to The Times*, 1914-January/February 1957. Frequency: monthly, with annual cumulations 1906-13: quarterly July 1914-56; bi-monthly, 1957-.

....(contd.)

Much the same format as the current index. Covered *The Times literary supplement*, 1906-21. *Class No:* 070.2:014.3(410)

USA

[252]

National newspaper index. Foster City, Ca., Information Access Corporation, 1979-. Microfilm service, updated monthly.

Indexes the *Christian Science monitor, New York times* (including *New York times book review* and *New York times magazine*), *Wall Street journal* and from 1982 the *Los Angeles times* and *Washington post.* Each monthly issue cumulative. Full indexing for each title, only weather charts, horoscopes, editorial cartoons etc. excluded. Also available online through BRS and Dialog (File 111), updated monthly. Daily updates available through the *Newsearch* database (Dialog File 211). A CD-ROM version gives coverage back to 1986, updated replacement discs provided monthly. *Class No:* 070.2:014.3(73)

Journalism

[253]

CATES, J.A. Journalism: a guide to the reference literature. Englewood, Colo., Libraries Unlimited, 1990. xvii,214p. (*Reference sources in the humanities.*) ISBN: 0872877167.

Selective guide to the English language reference literature on print and broadcast journalism. Includes bibliographies, dictionaries, encyclopedias, indexes and abstracts, biographical sources, directories, handbooks and manuals, style books, etc. 503 numbered entries with well-written evaluative annotations; a further 200 entries for core periodicals, societies and institutions, and research centers, archives and media institutes. Appendix: Database service suppliers and vendors. Author/title and subject indexes. Much more detailed and up-to-date than *The Journalist's bookshelf,* (8th ed. 1986) but 'would have been enhanced by a more detailed subject index' (*Choice,* v.28(3), November 1990, p.451-2). *Class No:* 070.4

News Digests

[254]

Facts on file: world news digest with cumulative index. New York, Facts on File, 1940-. Weekly. ISSN: 00146641.

Weekly looseleaf issues for insertion in binder. Twice monthly cumulating indexes (yellow pages), consolidated quarterly. Full colour Rand McNally quick reference atlas issued annually. Bound annual volumes available for separate purchase. Five yearly indexes published from 1946/50 onwards.

Based on the contents of more than 50 US and foreign newspapers and magazines including *The Times, Guardian* and *Economist.* Wide-ranging coverage, extending to economics and business, science and technology and social developments, as well as general news stories. Less detailed treatment of diplomatic topics and more popular in style than *Keesings.* Also available online through Dialog (file 264) and in CD-ROM format for 1980-88. *Class No:* 070.40

[255]

Keesing's record of world events. Cambridge, Longman, 1931-. Monthly. ISSN: 09506128.

Looseleaf with annual binder. Frequency weekly 1931-72. Published as *Keesing's contemporary archives* 1931-86.

Records national and international affairs, 'based on constant monitoring of the world's press and information services by experienced research editors'. Revised format from 1989. Each issue now begins with full coverage of

....(contd.)

major world news stories of the previous month. This is followed by a news digest section containing up to 100 concise, factual articles. Complemented by a reference section which includes cross-indexed and up-to-date background briefing documents. In the course of a year this section aims to cover every country and principal organization of the international political system. November 1990 issue (72p.) has full coverage of the CSCE Paris Summit, replacement of Thatcher by Major and the Polish presidential elections. 35p. of news digest items arranged Africa, America, Asia-Pacific, Europe, Middle East and International, and a reference section covering Pacific-Australasia and international bodies. Periodic subject and name indexes cumulated annually (subject yellow pages; name pink pages). Stronger on international affairs than its main rival *Facts on file* (above), but economics and business are comparatively neglected. Also available in microfiche and online through Profile Information, 1983 to date. *Class No:* 070.40

[256]

Keesing's UK record. Cambridge, Longman, 1988-. Bimonthly. ISSN: 0952195x.

Gives more extensive coverage of the UK than the main *Keesing's.* Nov/Dec 1990 issue in sections: Events of the month (calendar of principal occurrences); Government and politics; External affairs; Local government and regional affairs; Economic affairs; Social affairs; Obituaries; Legislative summary; Economic survey. Cumulated subject/name index published six monthly and annually. *Class No:* 070.40

08 Polygraphies

Publishers' Series

[257]

Books in series: original, reprinted, in-print, and out-of-print books, published or distributed in the US in popular, scholarly and professional series. 4th ed. New York, Bowker, 1985. 6v. ISBN: 0835219380.

Contents: v.1 *Series heading index. Subject index to series. Series index AAAS-Introductory handbook to art & design;* v.2 *Introductory mathematics for scientists and engineers - Zurich. Jung Institut Studies;* v.3 *Authors index. AB to Konig, H.W.;* v.4 *Authors index. Koo, Robert to Zzizinga, A.;* v.5 *Titles index. A.A. Milne-Mechanics of materials;* v.6 *Titles index. Mechanics of particular materials to ZZ.* Directory of publishers and distributors in v.4. First published 1976; 3rd ed. 1980.

286,754 titles in 26,642 series. Definition of series based on the Anglo-American cataloguing rules, entries mainly derived from Bowker's *American book publishing record* and *Books in print* databases. Includes discontinued/closed series. Excludes series for children, school textbooks in series, US government documents in series and series included in *Books in series 1876-1949* (1982. 3v.).

Continued by *Books in series, 1985-1988* (New York, Bowker, 1989. 2v. ISBN 0835226794, v.1). *Class No: 082.1*

Audio-Visual Materials

[258]

AVMARC. London, British Library, 1981-. Computer database.

Online equivalent of the *British catalogue of audiovisual materials* (below). The database was expanded in 1989 by the addition of some 16,000 records taken from the ILEA's LOCAS file, bringing the total number to 25,000 (*BLAISE newsletter,* no. 96, January/February 1989, p.5). *Class No: 084/086*

[259]

British catalogue of audio-visual materials: a subject catalogue of audio-visual materials processed by the British Library/Inner London Education Authority Learning Materials Recording Study. London, British Library, Bibliographic Services Division, 1979. 487p. ISBN: 0900220775.

Designated '1st experimental ed.'. Supplements 1980 (220p. ISBN 0900220856) and 1983 (147p. ISBN 0712310096).

Reflects the collection of the ILEA's Central Library Resources Service Reference Library. Includes slides, filmstrips, spoken word sound recordings, tape slides, overhead projections and educational kits, as well as some print materials such as wall charts. Major exclusions are 16mm films (apart from those provided by the British Universities Film Council), videorecordings and musical sound recordings. About 5,300 entries in Dewey classified

....(contd.)

arrangement; author/title/series and subject (PRECIS) indexes.

The two supplements, similarly arranged, add 2,300 and 1,200 items respectively. Records are largely derived direct from publishers, rather than from the ILEA as previously. *Class No: 084/086*

[260]

CORNISH, G.P. Archival collections of non-book materials: a listing and brief description of major national collections. Boston Spa, British Library, 1986. vii,41p. (*British Library information guide, 3.*) ISBN: 071233081x.

Updates J. Line's *Archival collections of non-book materials: a preliminary list indicating policies for preservation and access* (1977. BL R & D Report 5330).

Briefly describes 22 major national archives of non-book materials including sound recordings, visual recordings (film, video, photographs and slides) mixed media and graphics. Excludes collections which are specialized both by subject or format. *Class No: 084/086*

Illustrations

[261]

MCKEOWN, R. National directory of slide collections. London, British Library, 1990. viii,310p. (*British Library information guide, 12.*) ISBN: 0712332081.

Compiled from data collected for the *National survey of slide collections* (1989. British Library research paper, 67).

A first attempt at establishing a complete listing of UK slide collections. Coverage mainly of non-commercial collections in academic and public libraries, museums and galleries, research units, professional associations, teaching hospitals etc. About 950 entries in A-Z order of holding institution, giving data on collection size, subject coverage, opening hours, access conditions and contact person. Subject and geographical indexes. *Class No: 084*

[262]

Picture researcher's handbook: an international guide to picture sources - and how to use them. Evans, H. *and* Evans, M., *comps.* 4th ed. Wokingham, Van Nostrand Reinhold, 1989. 498p. ISBN: 0747600384.

1st ed. 1975. 3rd ed. 1986.

Sources include picture libraries, general libraries, museums, commercial picture and press agencies, art galleries, archives and historical societies. In 4 sections: General 285 entries; Regional (material covering several countries) 89 entries; National (material relating to a particular country) 266 entries; Specialist 466 entries (subdivided in 11 subject categories). Entries give address, description of material held, stock size, research facilities, hours, loan procedures/fees etc. Subject and sources indexes. More comprehensive coverage of British sources available

....*(contd.)*
in *Picture sources UK* (below), but valuable for better currency and good coverage of other countries. *Class No:* 084

[263]
Picture sources UK. Eakins, R., *ed.* London, Macdonald, 1985. 474p. ISBN: 0356100782.
Replaces Nunn, G.W.A. ed. *British sources of photographs and pictures,* 1952.
Information on 1,141 collections of photographs, prints and other visual material presented in 14 subject chapters. For each collection gives address, approximate no. of items held, dates of subject matter, detailed listing of subjects covered and access conditions. Collection and subject indexes. Worthy of regular updating. *Class No:* 084

Microfilms

[264]
Guide to microforms in print: incorporating International microforms in print. Author/title. Westport, Conn., Meckler, 1961-. Annual. ISSN: 01640747.
Title varies slightly; as *International microforms in print* 1974/75.
Covers microfilmed books, journals, newspapers, government publications, archival material, collections etc. Excludes theses and dissertations. Entries give basic bibliographical detail, type of microform and price only. Directory of publishers. Introductory matter also in French, German and Spanish. *Class No:* 084.0

[265]
—Guide to microforms in print: incorporating International microforms in print. Subject. Westport, Conn., Meckler, 1962-. Annual. ISSN: 01638386.
Companion volume to the above, arranged under *c.*140 broad subject headings derived from the Library of Congress classification.
Guide to microforms in print. Supplement (1979-) appears approximately 6 months after the annual volumes, listing newly available microforms in author/title and subject sequences. *Class No:* 084.0

Sound Recordings

[266]
British words on tape 1991: a directory of spoken word cassettes available in the UK. Voeglin-Carleton, A., *ed. and* Dixson, D., *comp.* London, Meckler, 1990. x,161p. ISBN: 0887366198.
From the same publisher as *Words on tape: an international guide to the audio cassette market,* issued annually from 1984 (ISSN 87553579).
Lists 6,700 cassettes available from 125 publishers. Covers "works both popular and esoteric orignally published in book form, lectures and seminars, dramatic performances and works newly created for the audio cassette medium. Subject areas represented include classical works, novels, children's fiction, Shakespearian plays, short stories, self help and inspirational works, business-related coursework, poetry readings, history, biography and language courses" (p.vii). Main entry by title gives author and reader, plus further information on contents, playing time, price etc., as available. Cross-references from individual titles in collections; author and subject indexes. *Class No:* 086.7

[267]
Directory of recorded sound resources in the United Kingdom. Weerasinghe, L., *comp. and* Silver, J., *researcher.* London, British Library, 1989. xxii,173p. ISBN: 0712305025.
Based on the *National register for collections of recorded sound* database maintained by the British Library. Covers

....*(contd.)*
489 collections of music, spoken literature and history, speeches, dialects, recordings for the blind, and transport, machinery and wildlife noises. Standard information for each collection including details of available written transcripts, finding aids, publications and complimentary non-sound resources. Repository organizations include libraries, museums, archives, learned societies and radio stations. Indexed (p.143-73) by topics, genres, events, geographic regions and corporate and individual names. A valuable and much-needed tool, although far from comprehensive in coverage. *Class No:* 086.7

087.7 Government Publications

Government Publications

Great Britain

[268]

AMERICAN LIBRARY ASSOCIATION. Government Documents Round Table. **Guide to official publications of foreign countries.** Bethesda, Congressional Information Service, 1990. xxi,359p. ISBN: 0886922038.

Contains annotated entries for the major official publications of 157 states, with the emphasis on current materials, serials strongly represented. Up to 17 categories of publication for each country including general guides, bibliographies and catalogues, government directories and organization manuals, statistical yearbooks, legislative proceedings, census reports and publications on economic affairs, health, labour, etc. About 3,250 entries overall giving title with English translation, publication date(s), place of publication, name of responsible agency, frequency of issue, availability and brief annotation. No indexes, but "superbly executed ... fills a major gap in the reference literature and will be an invaluable resource wherever the publications of foreign governments are utilized for research" (*Choice*, v.28(10), June 1991, p.1616). *Class No:* 087.7

Europe—Western

[269]

Official publications of Western Europe. Johansson, E., *ed.* London, Mansell, 1984-88. 2v. ISBN: 0720116236, v.1; 0720116627, v.2.

V.1 *Denmark, Finland, France, Ireland, Italy, Luxembourg, Netherlands, Spain and Turkey.* (xvi,313p.).
V.2 *Austria, Belgium, Federal Republic of Germany, Greece, Norway, Portugal, Sweden, Switzerland and United Kingdom.* (x,278p.).

Intended 'to present a state-of-the-art record of government publishing in the late twentieth century and to provide a practical reference work of lasting value' (Preface v.2 p.x). Separate chapters for each country, contributed by specialists, in standard format with slight variations: 1. Introduction - 2. Principal government publications (central government) - 3. Manner of publication - 4. Bibliographic control - 5. Local government publications - 6. Library collections and availability - 7. Bibliography. V.1 includes chapter 'The art and acquisition of foreign official publications'. Both volumes indexed by organization/title and subject. A 'must for most reference shelves as a starting point for tracing the source of any official publication' (*Library review*, v.37 (4), 1988, p.60); shows 'little overlap with other works in English' (*Choice*, v.26(4), December 1988, p.631). *Class No:* 087.7(400)

[270]

British government publications: an index to chairmen and authors. Richard, S., *comp.* London, Library Association, 1974-84. 4v.

V.I 1800-1899 (1982. ix,196p. ISBN 0853657432); v.II. 1900-1940 (1974, reissued 1982. iii,174p. ISBN 0853654271); v.III 1941-1978 (1982. vii,152p. ISBN 085365753x); v.IV 1979-1982 (1984. vii,95p. ISBN 0853657564).

Compiled for the Reference, Special and Information Section of the Library Association. V.I has variant subtitle *An Index to chairmen of committees and commissions of inquiry.* V.III cumulates earlier indexes for 1941-66 (2nd ed. 1973) and 1967-71 (1976) compiled by A.M. Morgan and L.R. Stephen.

Identifies government reports which are often known only by chairman's or author's name. Excludes annual and other periodic reports, accident inquiry reports and reports prepared by government officials in the course of their duties. Coverage in v.4 extended to non-HMSO publications. Arrangement is A-Z by latest form of chairman's name with chronological suborder. Cross-references from earlier forms of name. Entries give report title, date, responsible department and, if a Parliamentary paper, the Parliamentary reference, including volume number in the official bound set. No subject or other indexes. *Class No:* 087.7(410)

[271]

BRITISH LIBRARY. **Checklist of British official serial publications** 1987. Finnie, H., *comp.* 12th ed. London, British Library, 1987. viii,74p. ISBN: 0712300171.

1st ed. 1967, then approx. annual to 11th ed. 1980.

Lists A-Z by title 'serials issued by the United Kingdom central government departments and other agencies, and by bodies established, controlled or financed by the UK government' (Introduction). Exclusions: Parliamentary papers; publications of nationalised industries, public corporations, bodies with regional responsibilities only, tourist boards and museums and galleries; local interest publications; offprints, forms and examination questions. Brief entries giving issuing body, frequency and availability data only. Index of issuing bodies (new to this ed.). *Class No:* 087.7(410)

[272]

BUTCHER, D. **Official publications in Britain.** 2nd ed. London, Library Association, 1991. xiii,192p. ISBN: 085157422x.

1st ed. 1982.

"(E)xamines the nature and organization of official publishing in Britian at national, regional and local levels, the extent and adequacy of bibliographical control and the ways in which these publications may be selected and

....(contd.)

acquired" (*Preface* p.ix). 7 documented chapters: 1. The scope and structure of official publishing in Britain - 2. Parliamentary publications - 3. Government department publishing - 4. National and regional public bodies - 5. Bibliographic control and selection sources (p.125-49) - 6. The availability of official publications - 7. Local government publishing. Index p.185-92. Includes coverage of online and CD-ROM sources. Concise and up-to-date, providing a useful overview for the student and non-specialist librarian. *Class No:* 087.7(410)

[273]
Catalogue of British official publications not published by HMSO. Cambridge, Chadwyck-Healey, 1980-. Bimonthly, with annual cumulation. ISSN: 02605619.

Covers publications of organizations financed or controlled completely or partially by government, which are not published by HMSO. 'These organizations divide broadly into government departments, nationalized industries, research institutes, quangos ... and other non-official bodies' (1989 cumulation, p.7). Material covered includes periodicals, newspapers, single sheet updates and appendices, posters and audio-visual aids. Ephemeral material, circulars, internal memoranda and reports and material well catalogued elsewhere (*e.g.* Ordnance Survey maps, patents) excluded. Arranged A-Z by publishing body, entries give full bibliographical information, purchase detail and price. Indexed by personal name, corporate author and subjects in one sequence. Further microfiche identification number and source of publication indexes. Number of publications catalogued has gradually increased, the 1989 cumulation (1990. 527p.) containing 12,190 entries from 500 publishing organizations. Also available in CD-ROM format. Many of the documents listed are available in microfiche from Chadwyck-Healey, either on demand or on a subscription basis (subject based subscriptions available). *Class No:* 087.7(410)

[274]
—Keyword index to British official publications not published by HMSO. Cambridge, Chadwyck-Healey, 1983-. Bimonthly.

Bimonthly cumulating issues with final annual cumulations.

Indexes significant words from the titles of publications in the main *Catalogue* (above). *Class No:* 087.7(410)

[275]
The Catalogue of United Kingdom official publications. Cambridge, Chadwyck-Healey; London, HMSO, 1989-. CD-ROM database (quarterly replacement disks).

Amalgamates HMSO's catalogues with Chadwyck-Healey's *Catalogue of British official publications not published by HMSO*. Includes publications of international organizations as in *HMSO agency catalogue*. At set up contained around 160,000 records. Searchable fields include corporate author, personal author, title, series title, subject and keyword, chairman, date and price. Searches can be limited (*e.g.* in-print or out-of-print; HMSO publications or non-HMSO publications). Some indexing inadequacies noted by *Refer* (v.6(1), Spring, 1990 p.30), but 'will prove of immense value'. *Class No:* 087.7(410)

[276]
Directory of British official publications: a guide to sources. Richard, S., *comp.* 2nd ed. London, Mansell, 1984. xxxvi,431p. ISBN: 0720117062.

1st ed. 1981.

A directory of 1,283 official publishing bodies. Wide ranging coverage including organizations as diverse as the Arts Council, Commonwealth Secretariat, National Gas Consumers' Council and the Weed Research Organization. 15 sections: I/VI UK, Great Britain, England and Wales

....(contd.)

(central government; libraries, museums and galleries; research councils; nationalised industries; executive bodies and tribunals; advisory bodies) - VI/IX Northern Ireland - X/XIII Scotland - XIV Wales - XV Isle of Man and Channel Islands. Entries for each body provide a general overview of publishing activity, with the emphasis on publication lists and serial titles, and note whether publications indexed in *Catalogue of official publications not published by HMSO* (*q.v.*). Organization and subject indexes. An 'essential guide' (*Refer*, v.3(3), Spring 1985, p.18). *Class No:* 087.7(410)

[277]
GREAT BRITAIN. Her Majesty's Stationery Office. **HMSO annual catalogue.** 1922-. London, HMSO, 1923-. Annual. ISSN: 09518584.

Cumulates *HMSO daily list* and *HMSO monthly catalogue* (below). Published as *Government publications* 1972-84. Earlier titles: *Consolidated list of government publications* (1922-53); *Government publications catalogue* (1954-55); *Catalogue of government publications* (1956-71). Preceded by a *Quarterly list*, 1897-1921.

Lists all of the 8-9,000 items published by HMSO annually, except statutory instruments and statutory rules of Northern Ireland (separately covered, see below). In 3 main sections: Parliamentary publications, listed numerically by type of publication (House of Lords;. House of Commons; Command Papers; Public General Acts; Local Acts); Classified section, including all non-Parliamentary publications and Parliamentary publications (excluding bills, acts, debates and measures), listed under the responsible department or body; Northern Ireland HMSO publications. Index of subjects and names of authors, chairmen and editors; ISBN index. Supplementary sections on 'Periodicals and subscription rates' and 'Holdings of HMSO publications', listing UK libraries receiving the full HMSO subscription service. Also available online for records 1976 to date through BLAISE and Dialog (File 227), updated monthly.

HMSO monthly catalogue (ISSN 02637197) is in much the same format as the annual. *HMSO daily list* (ISSN 9051843x) usually has c.4p. with sections: Parliamentary publications; Non-Parliamentary publications; Northern Ireland publications; Agency publications; Statutory rules of Northern Ireland; Statutory instruments. Statutory instruments included in the daily list are cumulated in *List of statutory instruments together with the list of statutory rules of Northern Ireland for the month of ...* (ISSN 02672979), with annual cumulation.

Other supporting publications include *HMSO in print on microfiche* (Quarterly. ISSN 02671727) and *HMSO agency catalogue* (Annual, formerly *International organizations catalogue*,) listing publications of Europe and international organizations for which HMSO is the UK agent. *Class No:* 087.7(410)

[278]
RODGERS, F. A Guide to British government publications. New York, H.W. Wilson; London, Mansell, 1980. xviii,750p. ISBN: 0824206177.

3 parts (29 chapters): I. General (*e.g.* The evolution of official printing and publishing; General catalogues and indexes) - II. Parliamentary (*e.g.* Reports of debates; Parliament and its committees; Statutes and Statutory Instruments) - III. Executive agencies (*e.g.* Central control (including the Cabinet Office, Civil Service Department); Financial control; Industrial resources (including British Aerospace, Post Office); Education and libraries; Scotland; Wales and Northern Ireland; Miscellaneous agencies (*e.g.* HMSO). Glossary p.687-90. Detailed analytical index p.691-750. Brief historical notes precede discussion of the most important publications of each department/agency. Selected

....(contd.)
references at chapter ends. Remains one of the best and most extensive surveys of British official publishing available. *Class No:* 087.7(410)

USA

[279]
Index to US government periodicals. 1972-. Chicago, Infordata International, 1974-. Quarterly, 4th issue annual cumulation. ISSN: 00984604.

Annual volumes for 1972-73 published retrospectively.

Aims 'to provide access to every one of the US government periodicals which offer substantive articles of lasting research or reference value' (Notes to users). Now indexes 170 titles, author and subject entries in one A-Z sequence. Also available in microfiche and online through BRS and Wilsonline 1980-, updated monthly. *Class No:* 087.7(73)

[280]
Monthly catalog of United States government publications. Washington D.C., Government Printing Office, 1895-. Monthly. ISSN: 03626830.

Title varies: originally *Catalogue of United States public documents*, then *Monthly catalog; United States public documents* and *United States government publications: monthly catalog;* current title since 1950.

Since 1976 arranged by Superintendent of Documents classification (previously department or bureau), with full Anglo-American cataloguing for each entry. Comprehensively indexed by author, title, subject (Library of Congress headings), series/report no., contract no., stock no. and title keyword. Indexes cumulated annually.

Records 1976 to date available online through BRS, Dialog (File 166) and Wilsonline. A number of CD-ROM products covering the same time span are also available (*e.g.*, *GPO* (Silver Platter); *Le Pac: Government documents option* (Brodart); *US government Printing Office Monthly catalog* (Wilson)).

A separate *Periodicals supplement* (previously *Serials supplement*) is also issued. The *GPO sales publications reference file* is a catalogue of all publications and subscription services currently available: issued monthly on microfiche; also available on magnetic tape or online (*e.g.*, Dialog File 166).

Since 1975 the Superintendent of Documents has issued *Subject bibliographies* (previously *Price lists*), listing publications on a single subject or field of interest. *Class No:* 087.7(73)

[281]
WILLIAMS, W.J. Subject guide to major United States government publications. 2nd ed. Chicago, American Library Association, 1987. xi,257p. ISBN: 0838904750.

1st ed. by E. Jackson, 1968. Earlier work with same title by Melinat & Hirsberg, 1947.

Covers from the inception of federal government to 1986. 60% new material in this ed., titles selected 'with an eye to their enduring significance' (p.ix). Briefly annotated entries, many for serial publications, arranged by modified Library of Congress subject headings. 2 valuable appendices: I. Guides, catalogs and indexes and directories; II. Subject bibliographies (lists over 250 bibliographies published by the Superintendent of Documents). Title index. Well received, 'selection of titles is excellent' (*American reference books annual,* 1988, p.32), 'a tremendous improvement over its predecessors' (*Government publications review,* v.15(5), Sept/Oct. 1988, p.493). *Class No:* 087.7(73)

09 Rare Books & Manuscripts

Manuscripts

[282]
BRITISH MUSEUM. Catalogue of additions to the manuscripts in the British Museum. London, British Museum, 1843-.

Preceded by Ayscough, S. *A catalogue of the manuscripts preserved in the British Museum hitherto undescribed ...* (London, 1782. 2v.) and *Index to the additional manuscripts with those of the Egerton Collection preserved in the British Museum and acquired in the years 1783-1835* (London, 1849). A new catalogue of the manuscripts described in Ayscough has been published as *Catalogue of additions to the manuscripts 1756-1782* (London, British Library, 1977. 0714104906).

Catalogue of additions series published as follows: 1836-40 (1843); 1841-45 (1850); 1846-47 (1864); 1848-53 (1866); 1854-75 (1877-80); 1876-81 (1882); 1882-87 (1889); 1888-93 (1894); 1894-99 (1903); 1900-5 (1907); then on a quinquennial basis with the exception of 1935-45 (1970). Reprints available from the British Library.

The 'Additional' series is by far the largest collection of manuscripts and comprises all acquisitions since 1756 with the exception of those which form closed collections. Numbers begin at 4101, following the Sloane MSS 1-4100. *Catalogue of the additions to the manuscripts 1951-1955* (1982. 2v. (Pt.1 Descriptions. Pt.2 Index) 0904654699) brings the number of manuscripts to 48988. For more recent acquisitions see the List and Index Society's *Rough register of acquisitions of the Department of Manuscripts.*

Catalogues of special collections of manuscripts include *Index to the Sloane manuscripts in the British Museum* (1904), *Catalogue of the Stowe manuscripts in the British Museum* (2v. 1895-96) and *Catalogue of the Western manuscripts in the Old Royal and King's collections* (4v. 1921). The most recent 'additions' catalogue published is *Catalogue of additions to the manuscripts: the Blenheim Papers* (London, British Library, 1985. 3v. 0712300198).
Class No: 091

[283]
—BRITISH LIBRARY. Department of Manuscripts. **Index of manuscripts in the British Library.** Cambridge, Chadwyck-Healey, 1984-86. 10v. ISBN: 0859641406.

The product of over twenty years' editorial work consolidating the indexes to over 30, mostly published, catalogues including the 'Additional' series to 1950, *Index to charters and rolls in the Department of Manuscripts ...* (1912), *Catalogue of manuscripts in the Cotton Library ...* (1812), *Catalogue of the Stowe manuscripts* (1895) and *Index to the Sloane manuscripts ...* (1904). Personal and place-name index only, all subject entries removed unless they could be relocated under the name of a place. Form of entry for personal names based on the *Dictionary of national biography*. Entries give name of manuscript, name of collection in abbreviated form, number within collection

....(contd.)
and folio number. 4 column format, index slips photographically reproduced. Well over 1,000,000 entries. A 'marvellous key with which to unlock the British Library's great manuscript collections ... it will be used by some as a substitute for, rather than a key to, the catalogues' (*Times literary supplement*, no.4269, January 25th 1985, p.103).
Class No: 091

[284]
LIBRARY OF CONGRESS. SPECIAL MATERIALS CATALOGING DIVISION. MANUSCRIPTS SECTION. National union catalog of manuscript collections. 1959/61-. Washington D.C., Library of Congress, 1962-. Frequency varies, mostly annual. ISSN: 00900044.

Based on holdings reported to the Library of Congress by repositories throughout the United States. Manuscripts reported are largely personal papers, manuscripts or typescripts, originals or copies, of letters, memoranda, diaries, log books, drafts and the like. From 1970 also includes oral history transcripts and collections containing sound recordings. The initial 1959/60 volume catalogued 12,324 collections in *c.*400 co-operating libraries. Separate name, repository and subject index. The 1988/89 issue (1991. lxx,286p.), the 25th in series, reports 2,038 collections held by 45 repositories, 15 reporting for the first time. This brings the total to 60,565 collections located in 1,350 different repositories. Quinquennial cumulated subject, personal, family and corporate name and place indexes for 1975-79 and 1980-84, with separate paperbound index 1985 and further cumulation 1986-89 (1991. vii,410p.). Earlier indexes for 1963-66, 1967-69 and 1970-74 in volumes for 1966, 1969 and 1974 respectively. *Class No: 091*

[285]
—LIBRARY OF CONGRESS. **Index to personal names in the National union catalog of manuscript collections 1959-1984.** Alexandria, Va. and Cambridge, Chadwyck Healey, 1988. 2v. ISBN: 0898870372.

'(B)rings together for the first time in one alphabetical sequence all the personal and family names appearing in the descriptions of manuscript collections catalogued from 1959 to 1984' (Introduction p.vii). Around 200,000 entries; includes many corrections and revisions. *Class No: 091*

Incunabula

[286]
BRITISH MUSEUM. Department of Printed Books. **Catalogue of books printed in the XVth century** now in the British Museum. London, 1908-.

Pt.1. *Xylographica and books printed with types at Mainz, Strassburg, Bamberg and Cologne.* (1908. xxviii,312p.); pt.2. *Germany: Eltvil-Trier.* (1912. xvii,313-620p.); pt.3. *Germany: Leipzig-Pforzheim; German-speaking*

....(contd.)
Switzerland and Austria-Hungary. (1913. xl,621-864p.); pt.4.
Italy: Subiaco and Rome. (1916. xvi,145p.); pt.5. *Venice*
(1924. [lv],147-598p.); pt.6. *Italy: Foligno, Ferrara, Florence,
Milan, Bologna, Naples, Perugia and Treviso.* (1930. 1,599-
899p.); pt.7. *Italy: Genoa-Unassigned Addenda.* (1935.
lxxxviii,901-1213p.); pt.8. *France: French-speaking
Switzerland.* (1949. lxxxvii,441,21p.); pt.9. *Holland and
Belgium.* (1962. lxi,222p.); pt.10. *Spain, Portugal.* (1971.
lxxv,92[2]p.); pt.12. *Italy (Supplement)* (1985. x,93p.).
A photolithographic reprint of pts.I-VIII, (London, British
Museum, 1963) reproduces the Museum's working copy
which contains numerous manuscript additions and
corrections. Pt.9 separately reprinted 1967.
Gives full bibliographical descriptions, each volume
including excellently reproduced facsimiles of a sampling of
the characteristic types in use. Arranged by 'Proctor order'
i.e. by countries, towns and presses chronologically. Pt.3
has an introduction to the whole of the German section
with a typographical map and indexes to Hain's and
Proctor's numbers. Pt.7 has an introduction to the whole of
the Italian section with similar indexes. The 1985
supplement to the Italian section corrects some entries and
adds 216 editions acquired 1935-84. *Class No:* 093

[287]
Gesamtkatalog der Wiegendrucke. Kommission für der
Gesamtkatalog der Wiegendrucke, *hrsg.* Leipzig, then
Stuttgart, Hiersemann, 1925-.
7 complete volumes and Bd.8 Lfg.1 covering A-Federicis
issued to 1940. Publication then interrupted by World War
II. A new ed., compiled at the Deutschen Staatsbibliothek,
Berlin, and published from Stuttgart by Hiersemann,
commenced 1972 with a revised Bd.8 Lfg.1. Bd.8
completed 1978. Bd.9, also initially issued in parts,
completed 1991 covering Fogeda-Grassus. Bd.1-7 reprinted
without revisions, Kraus 1968-81.
Intended to be an author union catalogue of all known
incunabula estimated at some 40,000. When complete will
effectively replace Hain's *Repertorium bibliographicum* and
its supplements. Entries slightly fuller than in the British
Museum *Catalogue of books printed in the XVth century*
(above). References given to Hain, Copinger, Reichling,
Proctor, British Museum catalogue and national catalogues
of incunabula. From Bd.8 attempts to locate all recorded
copies, locations previously being selective for items
available in multiple copies. The completion of Bd.9 brings
the total number of entries to 11,338. *Class No:* 093

[288]
GOFF, F.R. Incunabula in American libraries: a third census
of fifteenth century books recorded in North American
collections. New York, Bibliographical Society of America,
1964. xviii,798p.
Supersedes the *First census* of 1919 and M.B. Stillwell's
Second census, 1940.
An author list, recording 47,188 copies of 12,599 titles,
held by 464 institutions and 296 private collections.
Abbreviated entries give short title, place, printer, date,
physical description, references to printed catalogues and
locations. Register of owners (p.xxiii-li); list of sources
(p.liii-lxiii). Appended: tables of variant author forms and
entries; index of printers and publishers; concordances to
the *Gesamtkatalog,* Hain, Proctor and Stillwell's *Second
census*; list of deletions from the *Second Census*; addenda.
A Supplement, (New York, Bibliographical Society of
America, 1972. xii, 104p. 0914930028), adds 324 titles in
3,560 copies.
A reprint of the 1964 ed., (Millwood, N.Y., Kraus
Reprint, 1973. 0527342009), is reproduced from a copy
annotated by Goff, and includes handwritten corrections
and notes on dealers' and auction house prices. *Class No:*
093

[289]
Incunabula short title catalogue. London, British Library,
1984-. Computer database.
Online access via BLAISE-LINE. File updated monthly.
An ongoing project to record in short-title form all books
and other material printed with movable type before 1501.
Based on two major national union catalogues of
incunabula, Goff's *Third census* and the *Indice generale
degli incunaboli delle biblioteche d'Italia.* These sources
supplemented by records for incunabula held by the British
Library and a number of other libraries including the
Bodleian, John Rylands University Library (Manchester),
the National Library of Scotland and the national libraries
of Holland and Belgium. By the end of 1991 the file
contained over 24,500 records. *Class No:* 093

Private & Small Presses

[290]
Private press books 1959-. Pinner, Private Libraries
Association, 1960-. Annual (Irregular).
Publication on a regular basis now resumed. Earlier
issues seriously delayed, (*e.g.,* 1978 published 1982, 1980
not appearing until 1986), reducing the work's value as a
selection tool. Delay overcome by the issue of combined
volumes covering 1981-84 (1987) and 1985-86 (1988).
Checklist of books issued by private presses during the
year. International in scope, but usually confined to English
language texts. Arranged by press, entries give full
bibliographical detail, physical description and price.
Author/title index. The 1989 annual (1991. 72p.
0900002956) carries 185 entries. Each issue also contains a
very useful feature, 'The literature of private printing',
listing books and journal articles relating to private presses
published during the year (49 entries 1989). Reviews of
individual titles excluded. *Class No:* 094.1

[291]
Small press record of books in print. Fulton, L., *ed.* Paradise
Ca., Dustbooks, 1966-. Annual.
1st issue 1966-68, 2nd issue 1969-72; then annual. The
same publisher also issues *International directory of little
magazines and small presses.*
The 20th ed. (1991-92. 1073p.) lists 33,000 books,
pamphlets, broadsides, posters and poem cards available
from 3,000 small publishers worldwide. Main sequence of
entries A-Z by author, some briefly annotated. Title,
publisher and subject indexes, the latter under broad
headings (*e.g.* 'Feminism'). *Class No:* 094.1

Illustrated Books

[292]
HODNETT, E. Five centuries of English book illustration.
Aldershot, Scolar Press, 1988. 364p. illus., plates. ISBN:
0859676978.
Aims to 'present the first one-volume, selective,
comprehensive and critical record of literary illustration in
England' (Introduction). In 2 parts: Pt.1 a critical account
in 11 chronological sections; Pt.2 a selective catalogue of
250 illustrators and 2,700 books. Limited to artists resident
in England or books printed in England. Children's books
excluded. Index of illustrators. 'Large impressive and
expensive' with 'highly subjective judgements on the merits
of individual authors' (*Library Association Record,* v.90(10),
October 1988, p.598); 'rich but fragmented treatment of
periods' (*Times Literary Supplement,* no.4467, 11-17
November 1988, p.1261). *Class No:* 096

1 PHILOSOPHY & PSYCHOLOGY

Philosophy

[293]

BYNAGLE, H.E. Philosophy, a guide to the reference literature. Littleton, Col., Libraries Unlimited, 1986. x, 170p. ISBN: 0872874648.

An annotated listing of general and specialized, mainly English-language, reference works in philosophy and related areas. Arranged in 14 numbered sections by type of reference work (indexing, abstracting and reviewing publications; directories and biographical sources; concordances: indexes; works of individual philosophers; computer databases), with general sources preceding specialized works. Author/title and subject indexes. '... detailed and judicious guide ...' (*Bulletin of the ABTPL*, no. 40, November 1987, p.2). DeGeorge's '*The philosophers' guide*' Lawrence, Kans, Regents Press of Kansas, 1980, is more comprehensive but less up-to-date. *Class No: 101*

[294]

PARKINSON, G.H.R., *and others, eds.* **The Handbook of Western philosophy.** New York, Macmillan, 1988. 935p. ISBN: 0029495938.

Aims to give an account of the present state of philosophical thinking, mainly in British philosophy, European philosophy being treated only as necessary. 37 scholarly articles are grouped in 6 sections (Meaning and truth - Theory of knowledge - Metaphysics - Philosophy of mind - Moral philosophy - Society, art and religion). Each section has an introduction; each article has endnotes and an annotated bibliography. Several appendices, including a glossary of philosophical terms and a chronological chart. Subject and name indexes. 'The handbook will become a standard source of reference ... complementing the bibliographic essays in Tice and Slaven's *Research guide to philosophy* (1984)' (*Choice*, v.26(5), January 1989, p.782). *Class No: 101*

[295]

The Philosopher's index: an international index to philosophical periodicals. Bowling Green, Ohio, Bowling Green University, 1967-.v.1,no.1-, Quarterly. ISSN: 00317993.

*c.*2000 indicative and informative abstracts each year of articles in *c.*300 major journals in English, French, German, Spanish and Italian. Subject index. Arrangement is under authors. Includes books and dissertations as well as journal articles. *The philosopher's index: a retrospective index to US publications from 1940* (1978. 3v.) includes entries for *c.*15,000 articles and *c.*6000 books, 1940-76. 'Philosopher's index' database covers international philosophical periodicals 1967-, and US philosophical periodicals, 1940-. Also available online (DIALOG). *Class No: 101*

[296]

SPARKES, A.W. Talking philosophy: a wordbook. London, Routledge, 1991. [v],307p. ISBN: 0415042224.

Attempts to give an account of the more important components of the vocabulary of philosophy in 10 chapters: 1. Saying things - 2. Meaning - 3. Nonsense, necessity, and possibility - 4. Inferring, implying, arguing, and 'if' - 5. Investigating - 6. Symbols: basic propositional forms; basic argumental forms - 7. of isms, ists, and ologies - 8. Arguing and investigating again - 9. Doing - 10. Relations. Notes (p.262-3). Bibliography (p.264-291). Index (p.292-307). 'A wonderful book to read' (*Choice*, v.28(10), June 1991, p.1624). *Class No: 101*

[297]

World philosophy: essay reviews of 225 major works. Magill, F.N. *and* McGreal, I.P., *eds.* Englewood Cliffs, N.J., Salem Press, 1982. 5v.

An expansion of *Master pieces of world philosophy in summary form* (1961. 2v.).

A chronological series of essay-digests of major philosophical treatises, explaining basic themes. Each essay carries further readings (briefly annotated). Western philosophical works preponderate. *Class No: 101*

Encyclopaedias

[298]

BULLOCK, A., *and others.* **The Fontana dictionary of modern thought.** 2nd ed. completely rev., expanded & updated. London, Fontana Press, 1988. xxvi,917p. ISBN: 0006861296.

First published 1977, ed. by A. Bullock & O. Stallybrass. Published in New York, by Harper & Row as *The Harper dictionary of modern thought.*

About 230 contributors. A dictionary-encyclopedia, it assembles some 5000 key terms from across the whole range of modern thought, sets them within their context, and offers short explanatory accounts (anything from ten to a thousand words), written by experts, but in language as simple as can be used without over-simplification or distortion (according to the preface to the 1st ed.). Cross-references. Companion volume to *The Fontana biographical companion to modern thought. Class No: 101(031)*

[299]

The Encyclopedia of philosophy. Edwards, P., *ed.* New York, Collier-Macmillan, 1973. 4v. (2400p.). ISBN: 0028949501.

First published in 1967 in 8v.

1450 comprehensive signed articles (over 900 on individual thinkers). 500 contributors from 24 countries; international editorial board of 153. Some Western slant. Systematic bibliographical coverage is a feature. Copious cross-references. Detailed subject index with 38,000 entries. Articles are scholarly but readable. 'A valuable, definitive encyclopedia' (*ARBA*, 1975, item 1287). *Class No: 101(031)*

[300]
PARKINSON, G.H.R., *ed.* **An Encyclopaedia of philosophy.**
London, Routledge, 1988. xi, 935p. ISBN: 0709940246.

Designed to provide a survey of current philosophical
thought which will not merely provide information but will
also help the reader to understand the nature of the subject
(*Preface*). 37 self-contained articles are grouped in 6
sections (A: Meaning and truth - B: Theory of knowledge -
C: Metaphysics - D: Philosophy of mind - E: Moral
philosophy - F. Society, art and religion). Each section
includes notes and a bibliography for further reading. The
work is prefaced by a survey of various views of the nature
of philosophy, and completed by a glossary of philosophical
terms (p.885-908); a chronological survey, 1600-1960; an
index of names (p.921-925); and an analytical subject index
(p.926-935). *Class No:* 101(031)

Histories

[301]
Dictionary of the history of ideas: studies of selected pivotal
ideas. P.P. Weiner, editor-in-chief. New York, Scribner's,
1968-73. 4v. & index. ISBN: 0684164183.

V.1. Abstraction in the form of concepts - Design
argument; 2. Despotism - Law, Common; 3. Law, Concept
of - Protest movements; 4. Psychological ideas - Zeitgeist;
5. Index. About 250 contributors. Preface outlines 'domains
and disciplines' involved in the history of ideas: the
external order of nature, anthropology, psychology, religion
and philosophy; literature and the arts; historical criticism;
economics, law and politics; mathematics, logic, linguistics.
Articles A-Z on 311 selected 'pivotal ideas' (*e.g.,* 'Baroque
in literature', 'Buddhism', 'Cosmology from antiquity to
1850', 'Faith, hope and charity', 'Welfare state', 'Relativity',
'Game theory'). Index ([lx], 479p.) is fully analytical (*e.g.,*
'Evil'; over 5 columns). *Class No:* 101(091)

[302]
GUTHRIE, W. K. C. **A History of Greek philosophy.**
Cambridge, Cambridge University Press, 1962-81. 6v. ISBN:
0521051592 V.1; 0521051606 V.2; 0521075661 V.3;
0521200024 V.4; 0521200032 V.5; 0521235731 V.6.

V.1: *The earlier Presocratics and the Pythagoreans*(1962);
V.2: *The Presocratic tradition, from Parmenides to
Democritus*(1965); V.3: *The fifth-century
enlightenment*(1969); 4: *Plato. The man and his Dialogues:
earlier period* (1975); 5: *The later Plato and the
Academy*(1978); 6: *Aristotle: an encounter*(1981). The
study of Anaxagoras in v.2.(p.266-344) provides a detailed
analysis of his writings, with citations and footnote
references. Each volume has an index of passages quoted or
referred to, and a general, analytical index, plus a
bibliography (unhelpfully arranged A-Z by authors: only
v.5,p.493-514). The section on Plato's *Apology* (v.5. p.70-
93) gives date, historicity, summary and comment, with 30
footnotes. V.3. deals fully with the Sophists, their
contemporaries, and Socrates. One reviewer (*Philosophy*
v.39.no.148, April 1964, p.184-5) notes the paucity of
Greek quotations, confined to footnotes and appendices. A
scholarly survey, by the Professor of Ancient Philosophy in
Cambridge University. 'Indispensable' (*British book news,*
December 1976, p.892). *Class No:* 101(091)

[303]
A History of Western philosophy. Oxford, Oxford University
Press, 1985-.

A comprehensive and up-to-date survey of philosophical
ideas from earliest times to the present day, for students of
philosophy and the general reader. 8 volumes are planned:
No.1. Classical thought, by T. Irwin (1989 ISBN
0192191969). No.2. Medieval philosophy, by D. Luscombe.
No.3. Renaissance philosophy, by C. Schmitt. (1988. ISBN
0521251044). No.4. The Rationalists, by J. Coningham

....(contd.)
(1988. ISBN 0192192094). No.5. The Empiricists, by R.S.
Woolhouse (1988. ISBN 0192192075). No.6. English-
language philosophy, 1750 - 1945, by J. Skorwski. No.7.
Continental philosophy since 1750, by R. Solomon (1985.
ISBN 0192192167) No.8. English-language philosophy since
1945, by D. Stroud. *Class No:* 101(091)

Biographies

[304]
BULLOCK, A. *and* WOODINGS, R.B., *eds.* **The Fontana
biographical companion to modern thought.** London, Collins,
1983. xxv,867p. ISBN: 0002163292.

Cover title: *The Fontana dictionary of modern thinkers.*
Over 1500 entries, each by an authority on the subject,
giving biographical details and an assessment of career and
work. A list of contributors precedes the biography
(AALTO ... ZWICKY); entries include subject, details of
birth and death, subject's category, publications,
bibliography (restricted to critical studies relating to
subject's life and work and limited to 2 titles. Details of
the subject's own publications are included in the entry
itself. Entries average about a column in length. Cross-
references. *Class No:* 101(092)

Asia

[305]
FAKHRY, M. **A History of Islamic philosophy.** 2nd ed. New
York, Columbia University Press; Harlow, Essex, Longman
Group, 1983. xxx,394p. (*Columbia studies in oriental
culture.*) ISBN: 0231055323, US; 0582783240, UK.

First published 1970.
A detailed survey, in chronological order, from the 7th
century to the present. 'Fakhry's book should now be
considered the best comprehensive book ever written on the
history of Arabic philosophy' (*Journal of the history of
philosophy,* v.10(2), April 1972, p.223, of the first edition).
Class No: 101(5)

[306]
FU, C.W. *and* CHANG, W. **Guide to Chinese philosophy.**
London, C. Prior; Boston, Mass., G.K. Hall, 1978.
xxxi,362p. (*The Asian philosophies and religious resources
guides.*)

About 1500 entries, with evaluative annotations. 16
closely divided chapters (*e.g.* 1. Confucius and Lao-Tza; 14.
Companion with Western philosophy; 16. Authoritative
texts and their philosophical significance). English
translations of original Chinese classics, plus secondary
books and articles about Chinese philosophy, with some
important French and German items. Numerous cross-
references. 'An indispensible guide' (*RQ,* v.18(3), Spring
1979, p.306). *Class No:* 101(5)

[307]
GRIMES, J. **A Concise dictionary of Indian philosophy:**
Sanscrit terms defined in English. New York, State
University of New York, 1989. 440p. ISBN: 0791401006.

'It is basic in that (i) it includes virtually all the words
basic to the various Indian philosophical systems, and (ii)
it defines those terms, in their dictionary or common and
literal meanings. The book is comprehensive in that it
defines many of its terms with the specific meaning that a
word has for a specific school' (*Preface*). Sanscrit terms are
given in Devanagari script and transliterated. '... a kind of
"ready reference" which will be found useful both by
scholars and generalists' (*Choice,* v.27(5), January 1990,
p.768). *Class No:* 101(5)

[308]
NAUMANN, St. E., *jr.* **Dictionary of Asian philosophies.**
London, Routledge & Kegan Paul, 1979. xxi,372p. tables.
ISBN: 0415039711.

Abhidharma ... Zoroastrianism. Entries for terms (giving
pronunciation), philosophies and thinkers. Sufism: p.316-21;
Mao Tse-tung: p.248-59; Indian philosophy (p.171-93: 7
sections). Text interspersed with quotations. Cross-
references. Preliminaries include 'Chronology of Asian
philosophers', p.xiii-xvii. 'No doubt it could be better, but
in any case, it is the best there is' (*American reference
books annual*, v.10, 1979, item 1082). 'The best source [for
Eastern philosophers] is still the *Encyclopedia of
philosophy*, edited by Paul Edwards' (*Choice*, v.16, no.1,
March 1979, p.57). *Class No:* 101(5)

Occultism & Parapsychology

[309]
GETTINGS, F. **Dictionary of occult, hermetic and alchemical
sigils.** London, Routledge & Kegan Paul, 1981. 410p. ISBN:
0710000952.

Designed as a reference, guide and sourcebook for those
involved in general occult studies. 1500 headings. Meanings
of over 9000 sigils (line patterns with magical significance)
which appear in European alchemical, astrological, geomatic
and related hermetic sources, plus a unique graphic index
of sigils by number of strokes, p.323-410. Bibliography,
p.293-312. Dating of sigils, p.239-291. 7 appendices (7,
'standard' sigils in modern astrology from Deutsche [*Die
Deutsche Ephemeride*, 1980). *Class No:* 133

[310]
SHEPARD, L.A., *ed.* **Encyclopedia of occultism and
parapsychology.** 3rd ed. Detroit, Mich., Gale Research Co.,
1991. 2v. (2008p.). ISBN: 0810349078.

First published in 1978, 2nd ed. 1984-85. Adapted from
L. Spence's *Encyclopaedia of the occult* (1920) and N.
Fodor's *Encyclopaedia of psychic science* (1934).

Over 5000 entries, varying from 1 sentence to many
pages in length in one A-Z sequence. Scope includes the
occult, magic, miracles and witchcraft, as well as numerous
paranormal events previously regarded as supernatural.
Prominent individuals in the field are covered. Many
entries include a wide range of bibliographical references.
Comprehensive general index and 9 topical indexes. 'Can
be faulted in many cases by its ignoring of evidence and
conclusions ... Would be a valuable resource if
supplemented by the use of critical studies' (*Choice*,
v.28(10), June 1991, p.1615). *Class No:* 133

Occultism

[311]
WOLMAN, B.B., *ed.* **Handbook of parapsychology.** New York,
Van Nostrand, Reinhold, 1977 (reprinted by McFarland &
Co., 1986). xxiv, 1007p. illus. ISBN: 0899501869.

31 contributors. 11 parts: 1. History of parapsychology -
2. Research methods - 3. Perception, communication, and
parapsychology - 4. Parapsychology and physical systems -
5. Parapsychology and altered states of consciousness - 6.
Parapsychology and healing - 7. Survival of bodily death -
8. Parapsychology and other fields (*e.g.*, anthropology) - 9.
Parapsychologic models and theories - 10. Social research
in parapsychology - 11. Suggested readings (annotated
bibliography, p.907-20). Glossary, p.921-36. Parts 1-10 each
have appended bibliogaphies. Name and subject indexes.
Class No: 133.2

Witchcraft & Magic

[312]
GUILEY, R.E. **The Encyclopedia of witches and witchcraft.**
New York, Facts on File, 1989. 421p. illus. ISBN:
081601793x.

Arranged A-Z by subjects and covering the history of
witchhunts, beliefs of witches, their organizations, folk
magic, pagan deities, sorcery, occultism, shamanism, etc.
Includes biographies. The length of citations varies from a
paragraph to several pages. 100 black-and-white illus.
Bibliography of 355 items, and also a list of works
mentioned in the text. Cross-references. '... comprehensive
coverage of terminology, biography and history make this
work an important addition to the reference works
available on the topic' (*Reference books bulletin*, November
1989, p.604). '... fills a unique niche. While covering the
history of witchcraft in a serviceable and accurate way, it
also includes a large amount of material, mostly
biographical, on modern witches' (*Choice*, v.27(5), January
1990, p.768). *Class No:* 133.4

Alchemy

[313]
HAEFFNER, M. **The Dictionary of alchemy:** from Maria
Prophetinsa to Isaac Newton. London, Aquarium Press,
1991. 272p. illus. ISBN: 1855380854.

A glossary of alchemical terms, concepts and symbols,
and main practitioners. Includes Western, Indo-Tibetan and
Chinese Taoist traditions. *Class No:* 133.5

Astrology

[314]
SAKOIAN, F. and ACKER, L.S. **Astrologer's handbook.** New
ed. Harmondsworth, Herts., Penguin Books Ltd., 1981.
xiv,461p. ISBN: 0140053360.

Originally published by Harper & Row, 1973.

16 chapters in two parts: I. Basic astrology; II.
Interpreting the aspects. '... designed to provide the layman,
the astrological student, and the practitioner of astrology
with the information necessary for interpreting horoscopes'.
(Section on 'How to read this book'). Glossary, p.441-442.
General index, p.443-449. Cross index of aspects, p.450-
461. Paperback issued by Mandarin, 1991. *Class No:*
133.52

Philosophical Systems

Socialist Systems

[315]
WALICKI, A. **A History of Russian thought:** from the
enlightenment to Marxism. Oxford, Clarendon Press, 1980
(reprinted as a paperback, 1988). xvii,456p. ISBN:
0198277040.

First published in Polish in 1973 as *Rosyjska filozofia i
myśl społeczna od oświecenia do marksizmu*. First
published in English, translated by H. Andrews-Rusiecka, by
Oxford University Press in 1980.

18 chapters (1. Trends in enlightenment thought ... 6.
The Slavophiles - 7. The Russian Hegelians ... 10. The
origins of Russian socialism ... 12. Populist ideologies - 13.
Anarchism ... 18. From populism to Marxism). Footnotes.
Index of names, p.449-456. '... excellent and brilliant work'
(*Political studies*, September 1989, p.476-7). *Class No:*
141.8

Communism. Marxism. Leninism

[316]
A Dictionary of Marxist thought. Bottomore, T., *ed.* Oxford, Basil Blackwell Publishers Ltd., 1983; Cambridge, Mass., Harvard University Press, 1984. xii, 587p. ISBN: 0631128522, UK.

Provides clear accounts of concepts, schools of thought and individual Thinkers by *c.*80 eminent scholars of Marxism, taking account of different interpretations and criticisms. Each entry is a short essay, followed by a short bibliography or guide to further reading. Includes an editorial article on critics of Marxism. Also includes a list of contributors, with affiliations; a consolidated bibliography, A-Z by author (p.533-66); a chronological list of writings by Marx and Engels; and a subject index (p.567-87). '... an excellent guide'. (*College and research libraries,* v.45(4), July 1984, p.293). 'Definitely supersedes Russell's *Marx-Engel's dictionary'* (1981) (*Library journal,* 15 October 1983, p.1955). *Class No:* 141.82

[317]
GORMAN, R.A., *ed.* **Biographical dictionary of Marxism.** London, Mansell Publishing; Westport, CT., Greenwood Press, 1986. x, 389p. ISBN: 0720118190, UK; 0313248516, US.

Focuses on materialist or orthodox Marxism. Selective biographies of over 210 major twentieth-century philosophers throughout the world. Each entry, ranging from ½-page to 3 pages in length, has biographical data on the individual, a summary of his/her significant contributions to Marxist theory and practice, and a bibliography of primary and secondary sources for research. Appendix: Entrants by nationality contribution. Index (p.371-388, double-column).' ... eminently readable ...' (*Library journal,* 1 February 1986, p.73). '... clearly written and concise entries ...' (*Choice,* July/August 1986, p.1651). *Class No:* 141.82

[318]
GORMAN, R.A., *ed.* **Biographical dictionary of Neo-Marxism.** London, Mansell Publishing Ltd.; Westport, CT., Greenwood Press, 1986. x, 464p. ISBN: 0720118204, UK; 0313235139, US.

Companion volume to the author's *'Biographical dictionary of Marxism'* (qv).

A useful introduction, outlining the origins and several key components of Neo-Marxist thought and action, precedes more than 205 biographical entries and 10 entries describing important groups, movements and journals. Cross-references. Selective bibliography of primary and secondary sources. Two appendices: Entrants by nationality; List of contributors. Good subject index (p.447-463 double-column). '... a valuable reference for the study of Neo-Marxism'. (*Choice,* v.23(9), May 1986, p.1368). *Class No:* 141.82

Psychology

[319]
Bibliographic guide to psychology. The Research Libraries of the New York Public Library and the Library of Congress. Boston, Mass., G.K. Hall, 1974-. Annual. ISSN: 0360277x.

Formerly *Psychology book guide.*

Each annual volume lists all materials catalogued during the previous year by the N.Y.P.L. Research Libraries, with additions from Library of Congress MARC tapes. Covers all aspects of psychology, as well as parapsychology and the occult sciences. *Class No:* 159.9

[320]
BORCHARDT, D.H. *and* **FRANCIS, R.D. How to find out in psychology:** a guide to the literature and methods of research. Oxford, Pergamon Press, 1984. xi,189p. 17 illus. ISBN: 0080312802.

First published in 1968 as *How to find out in philosophy and psychology,* by D.H. Borchardt.

'... eleven chapters. The first two deal with what psychology is about and its major theories, and chapters III-VI deal with the bibliographic aids used by psychologists ... How one gathers and presents such material is the subject of chapters VIII-X ... Chapter XI is concerned with professional matters and includes information on psychological organizations ...' (*Preface*). 5 appendices A. A guide to library searches ... E. Psychological societies). Bibliography, p.175-186. A-Z by author; journals A-Z by title. Subject index, p.187-189. *Class No:* 159.9

[321]
Handbook of developmental psychology. Wolman, J.B., *ed.* Englewood Cliffs, NJ., Prentice Hall, 1987. xv,953p. ISBN: 0133725995.

In 6 parts, each subdivided: 1. Research methods and theories - 2. Infancy - 3. Childhood - 4. Adolescence - 5. Adulthood - 6. Aging. *c.*75 contributors. Deals with fundamental concepts and research findings. Author index, p.937-953 (*c.*7000 entries). *Class No:* 159.9

[322]
PsycBooks: books and chapters in psychology, 1987-. Arlington, VA., American Psychological Association, 1989-. Annual. 5v. each year. ISSN: 10441514.

Psychological abstracts ceased to include books in 1980. In 1984 an effort was made to rectify this deficiency, resulting in this title.

Gives access to the latest books and chapters in psychology. V.I. Experimental psychology: basic and applied - II. Developmental, personality, social psychology - III. Professional psychology, disorders and treatment - IV. Educational psychology and health psychology - V. Author and subject indexes. *Class No:* 159.9

[323]
Psychological abstracts: non-evaluative summaries of the serial literature in psychology and related disciplines. Arlington, VA., The American Psychological Association Inc., 1927-. Monthly. ISSN: 00332887.

Over 3000 entries in each issue, from over 1400 journals, arranged in a classified order: General psychology - Psychometrics - Human experimental psychology - Animal experimental and comparative psychology - Psychological psychology - Psychological intervention - Communication systems - Developmental psychology - Social processes and social issues - Social psychology - Personality - Physical and psychological disorders - Treatment and prevention - Professional personnel and professional issues - Educational psychology - Applied psychology - Sport psychology and leisure. Brief subject index; author index. Available online. Vendors: BRS, DIMDI, Data-Star (PSYC), DIALOG, Orbit Information Technologies. Also on CD-ROM (American Psychological Association, Silver Platter (PsyclLIT). *Class No:* 159.9

Encyclopaedias

[324]
CORSINI, R.J., *ed.* **Encyclopedia of psychology.** New York, John Wiley & Sons, 1984. 4v. (1988p.). tables, charts. ISBN: 047186594x.

V.1. A - Eysenck, Hans; v.2. Fabre, Jean Maris - Perception; v.3. Perceptual - Zubin, Joseph; v.4. Bibliography. Name index. Subject index (analytical). Includes 1500 signed topical articles and 650 biographical

....(contd.)
articles, with references at the end of some entries. Cross-references. Length of entries varies (*e.g.,* 'Chomsky': 28 lines; 'Chromosome disorders': 2½ cols.; 'Comparative psychology': 6½ cols., in sections including 2 references and 9 cross-references to other subject entries). *RQ* (v.24(3), Spring 1985, p.356-7) complains that bibliographical references give inadequate detail and that biographical entries are sparse. A skillful abridgement, cutting out many of the biographical entries is *Concise encyclopedica of psychology* (Wiley, 1987. xxi,1242p. ISBN 0471010685).
Class No: 159.9(031)

Dictionaries

[325]
ENGLISH, H.B. *and* **ENGLISH, A.C. A Comprehensive dictionary of psychological and psychoanalytical terms: a guide to usage.** New York, Longmans Green, 1958 (reprinted by Mackay). xiv. 594p. diagrs. ISBN: 0679300333.
More than 13,000 terms and abbreviations are explained. The aim (*Preface*) is to include all terms frequently used in a special or technical sense by psychologists, with one set of definitions for the comparative layman and another set for the person working in the field of psychology. Pronunciation is given for unusual or difficult words. The inclusion of compound-word terms is a feature (*e.g.* 'Reinforcement' and its compounds occupy 5 pages). Extensive cross-references. *Class No:* 159.9(038)

[326]
Psychoanalytic terms and concepts. Moore, B.E. *and* Fine, B.D., *eds.* 3rd ed. New Haven, Co., American Psychoanalytic Association/Yale University Press, 1990. xxv,210p. ISBN: 0300045778.
First published 1967; revised ed. 1968 as *A glossary of psychological terms and concepts.*
Nearly 300 concepts defined, the long definitions containing both historical and current aspects of many of the terms. Includes references to cited works. 'See' references. *c.*200 experts contributed. 'This is a fine reference tool' (*Choice,* v.27(11/12), July/August 1990, p.1810). *Class No:* 159.9(038)

[327]
SUTHERLAND, S. Macmillan dictionary of psychology. London, Macmillan Press, 1989. [7],491p. diagrs. ISBN: 0333388291.
Published in the US by Crossroad/Continuum in 1989 with the title *The International dictionary of psychology* (ISBN 0826404405).
Intended as a dictionary for psychologists, including terms from neurology, linguistics, artificial intelligence, sociology, anthropology, statistics and philosophy. Includes *c.*10,000 terms, A-Z, with entries varying in length from *c.*5-120 words (averaging 20-50 words). Liberal cross-references. Examples are given in many cases. The 5 appendices are maps of the brain. Author is Professor of Experimental Psychology at the University of Sussex. '... for the most part, definitions succeed in fulfilling the book's purpose' (*Reference books bulletin,* v.81(21), July 1989, p.1884). *Class No:* 159.9(038)

[328]
WOLMAN, B.B., *comp. and ed.* **Dictionary of behavioral science.** 2nd ed. London, Academic Press; New York, Van Nostrand Reinhold, 1989. 370p. ISBN: 0127624554.
First ed. published 1973.
*c.*10,000 terms in all areas of theoretical, experimental and applied psychology and psychiatry. Includes biographical notes. *Class No:* 159.9(038)

Psychoanalysis

[329]
LAPLANCHE, J. *and* **PONTALIS, J.-B. The Language of psychoanalysis.** Translated by Donald Nicholas-Smith. London, Hogarth Press and the Institute of Psychoanalysis, 1973. xv, 510p. ISBN: 0701203439.
Originally as *Vocabulaire de la psychoanalyse* (Paris, Presses Universitaires de France, 1967; 5 éd. 1976). Paperback published in 1988 (London, Karnac House. 510p. ISBN 0946439494).
Entries (Abreaction ... Working-through) give German, Spanish, French, Italian and Portuguese equivalents of terms, plus definitions, discussion and references. 'Unconscious': 3p.: 3 main definitions, plus sub-entries: 4 references: 4 cross-references. Bibliography, p.491-7 (works by Freud cited: other authors: journals). Indexes of German and English terms. Intended for readers of Freud's writings.
Class No: 159.964.2

Logic

[330]
GREENSTEIN, C.H., *ed.* **Dictionary of logical terms and symbols.** Rev. ed. New York, Van Nostrand Reinhold, 1982. 188p. ISBN: 0442228341.
First published 1978.
Aims 'to present compactly, concisely and side by side a variety of alternative notational systems currently used by logicians, computer scientists, and engineers' (*Preface*). Glossary of logical terms, p.111-177. Bibliography, p.179-188. *Class No:* 164

Ethics

[331]
A Companion to ethics. Singer, P., *ed.* Oxford, Blackwell, 1991. xxii,565p. (*Blackwell companion to philosophy.*) ISBN: 0631162119.
47 original essays, arranged in 7 parts, dealing 'with the origins of ethics, with the great ethical traditions, with theories about how we ought to live, with arguments about specific ethical issues, and with the nature of ethics itself' (*Intro.*). Detailed analytical index, p.547-565. *Class No:* 17

Business Ethics

[332]
MCHUGH, F.P. Keyguide to information sources in business ethics. London, Mansell Publishing Ltd.; New York, Nichols Publishing, 1988. viii,173p. ISBN: 0720118492, UK; 0893973270, US.
An overview and survey in 3 parts: 1. Review of business ethics and its literature - 2. Bibliographical listing of sources - 3. Directory of selected organizations. Part 1 is a narrative account of the historical development of the subject in 5 chapters. Part 2 has 685 items, unannotated, of books and journal articles in a classified arrangement, and with an emphasis on contemporary literature. Part 3 (items 686-922) lists academic centres, business organizations, centres and organizations for professional ethics, and libraries, all subdivided by country, A-Z. Index, p.151-173. *Class No:* 174.4

2 RELIGION

Religion

[333]
ADAMS, C.J., *ed.* **A Reader's guide to the great religions.**
2nd ed. New York, Collier Macmillan, 1977. xvii, 521p.
ISBN: 0029002400.

First published 1965.

14 contributors (13 of them North American). 13
chapters: 1. Primitive religion - 2. The ancient world - 3.
The religions of Mexico and of Central and South America
- 4. The religions of China - 5. Hinduism - 6. Buddhism -
7. The Sikhs - 8. The Jainas - 9. The religions of Japan -
10. Early and Classical Judaism - 11. Medieval and modern
Judaism - 12. Christianity (p.345-406) - 13. Islam.
Appendix: 'The history of religions'. Running commentary.
Chapter 9 (p.247-82) has appended lists: 1. Reference books
relevant to religions of Japan - 2. Published bibliographies
(5 sections) - 3. Periodicals relevant to religions of Japan.
Author index; analytical subject index (p.494-521). 'It is
hard to fault such an excellent work' (*American reference
books annual.* 1978, v.9, entry no.969). *Class No:* 20

[334]
ELIADE, M. **A History of religious ideas.** Translated from
the French. Chicago, Ill., 1979-83. 3v. (*c*.1500p.). ISBN:
0226204006, v.1; 0226204022, v.2; 0226204049, v.3.

Translated from *Histoire des croyances et des idéas
religieuses* (Paris, Payot).

V.1. *From the Stone Age to the Eleusinian mysteries*
(1979) 15 footnoted chapters on Sumerian, ancient
Egyptian, Hittite and Canaanite, Vedic and Indian religions
before Buddha, with several chapters on Greek religion. 125
sections, each with bibliography. V.2. *From Gautama
Buddha to the triumph of Christianity* (1985) progresses
through the history of religious ideas, covering the religions
of ancient China, Brahminism and Hinduism, Buddha and
his contemporaries, Roman religion, Celtic and German
religion, Judaism, the Hellenistic period, the Iranian
syntheses, and the birth of Christianity. V.3 *From
Muhammed to the age of reforms* (1986) examines the
movement of Jewish thought out of ancient Eurasia, the
Christian transformation to the Mediterranean area and
Europe, and the rise and diffusion of Islam from
approximately the sixth century through the 17th century.
Each volume has a bibliography and index. *Class No:* 20

[335]
Religion index one: periodicals: a subject index to periodical
literature, including an author/editor index and Scripture
index. Evanston, Ill., American Theological Library
Association, v.13(1977-78)-. Irregular. ISSN: 01498428.

Previously as *Index to religious periodical literature*, v.1-
12, 1949-76. V.22 (1990) has a list of periodicals indexed;
a subject index of 407 double-column pages; an author and
editor index; and a Scripture index. ATLA religion database

....(contd.)
includes this title, and is available through BRS
Information Technologies; DIALOG; and WILSONLINE;
also a CD-ROM through H.W. Wilson Co. *Class No:* 20

[336]
—**Religion index two: multi-author works, 1976-.** Evanston,
Ill., American Theological Library Association, 1978-.
Annual. ISSN: 01498436.

The 1987 v. indexes 412 books and the 6113 articles/
parts they contained. In addition 32 festschriften and
collections of conference proceedings are indexed at book
level. Contents: List of titles indexed; Subject index;
Author/editor index; Scripture index.

Both series are online in the ATLA Religion database:
RIO v.1-4 (1949-1959) & v.2 (1975)-; RIT from 1960.
Class No: 20

[337]
Religious books in print: a reference catalogue, 1991. London,
J. Whitaker, 1991. 700p. ISBN: 0850212162. ISSN:
0305960x.

First published 1974. Annual.

Lists over 22,000 in-print titles plus a directory of their
1400 publishers and distributors. Author, title and keyword
index. Classified index of 18 principal subjects and 127
subsidiaries. *Class No:* 20

Encyclopaedias

[338]
MELTON, J.G. **Encyclopedia of American religions.** Revised
2nd ed. Detroit, Mich., Gale Research Co., 1988. 1102p.
ISBN: 0810328410.

First published 1980; first 2nd ed. with supplement,
1986/87.

Detailed information on 1588 individual churches,
religious bodies and spiritual groups, ranging from
Adventists to Zen Buddhism, organized into 22 religious
families of churches related to one another through
similarities of creed. In two sections: Part 1 is a series of
essays on the historical development of the American
religions; part 2 has entries on each religious group,
including information on beliefs and practices of the
religion, publications produced, headquarters or contact
address, number of congregations and membership, and list
of sources for further information. There are six separate
indexes: Religious organizations and institutions -
Educational institutions - Personal name - Publications -
Geographic - Subject. 'Authoritative and readable. Especially
valuable for its exhaustive coverage of religious bodies
outside the main stream' (*Reference books bulletin*, 1986/
87, p.53-4). Complemented by the author's *Encyclopedia of
American religions: religious creeds.* (*q.v.*). *Class No:*
20(031)

[339]

MELTON, J.G. Encyclopedia of American religions: religious creeds. Detroit, Mich., Gale Research Co., 1988. 838p. ISBN: 0810321327.

A collection of over 450 creeds, confessions, and statements of belief of America's religious groups (not only Christian, but also Jewish, Islamic, Scientology, Wiccan (witches), etc., and even 'Flying saucer' groups), arranged in 23 chapters, representing religious families, each sub-divided by names of religious groups. Information for each group includes historical notes and comments as well as the texts of the creeds, etc. Detailed table of contents, name and keyword index. Complements the author's *Encyclopedia of American religions* (*q.v.*). *Class No:* 20(031)

Dictionaries

[340]

Abingdon dictionary of living religions. Crim, K., *ed.* Nashville, Tenn., Abingdon Press, 1981. 864p. illus. ISBN: 0687004098.

1600 keywords and phrases. Concentrates on religions currently practiced in the world today. Over 150 American scholars contributed, providing comprehensive articles on the historical development and current status of the religions, describing the doctrines, sects, movements, significant personalities, sacred writings, religious practices, and holy sites and objects. Pronunciations given where not in general English usage. Complements Brandon's *Dictionary of comparative religion* (1970), which has fewer non-Christian religion entries. 'A good buy' (*RQ*, v.21(3), Spring 1982, p.296). *Class No:* 20(038)

[341]

BRANDON, S.G.F., *ed.* **A Dictionary of comparative religion.** London, Weidenfeld & Nicolson; New York, Scribner, 1970. viii, 704p. ISBN: 0684155613.

4 section editors; 28 contributors. About 4000 concise signed articles (*e.g.,* 'Scandinavian religion': p.159-64; 25 lines of bibliography. 'Buddhism. General survey', p.157-60). Adequate cross-references. General index, p.680-704. List of main sources, p.9-15. A standard dictionary to update Hastings' *Encyclopaedia of religion and ethics* (Edinburgh, T.& T. Clark Ltd; New York, Scribner, 1908-26) in this field. *Class No:* 20(038)

[342]

HINNELLS, J.R., *ed.* **The Penguin dictionary of religions.** London, Allan Lane/Penguin Books; New York, Facts on File, 1984. 550p. illus., diagrs., maps. ISBN: 0713915145, UK; 0871968622, US.

Mainly concerned with 'living' religions, including new religious movements, astrology, magic, the occult, as well as secular alternatives to religion, such as Marxism and humanism. A-Z arrangement and ample cross-references. The 29 international contributors have written entries ranging from *c.*40 to *c.*1500 words in length. Valuable scholarly bibliography is arranged under 30 broad subject headings and keyed to the dictionary entries (p.382-446). Also includes maps (p.366-381); a general index (p.465-550); and a synoptic index (p.447-464). Flowing, readable text, and the work's strength is in its coverage of Eastern religions and concepts. *Class No:* 20(038)

[343]

PYE, M. Macmillan dictionary of religion. London, Macmillan, 1991. 500p. ISBN: 033345409x.

Based on 'concepts drawn partly from the various religious traditions and partly from the historical and reflective study of religion as a modern academic discipline'. Gives concise explanations of nearly 6000 terms covering all aspects of the subject, and distinguishing between religious and theological terminology. Subject

....(contd.)

arrangement (Extinct and ancient religions - Israelite religion and Judaism - Islam - Christianity - Indian religions ... Sociology of religion - Psychology of religion ... Religions in various cultural disciplines). *Class No:* 20(038)

Quotations

[344]

PARRINDER, E.G., *comp.* **A Dictionary of religious and spiritual quotations.** London, Routledge; New York, Simon & Schuster, 1990. xi,218p. ISBN: 0132101211, US; 0415041287, UK.

Over 3000 quotations, arranged under 18 broad headings, with 177 subdivisions. Author and title index. Subject index. Eastern religions are well represented. Wider in scope than Pepper. *Class No:* 20(082.2)

[345]

PEPPER, M., *comp.* **Dictionary of religious quotations.** London, André Deutsch, 1989. 496p. ISBN: 0233983732.

Paperback ed. as *The Pan dictionary of religious quotations* (London, Pan Books, 1991. ISBN 0330315005). American ed. as *The Harper religious and inspirational quotation companion* (Harper, 1989. ISBN 0060161795).

Over 4000 quotations under topics, A-Z, with two or more quotations for each subject, spanning the world's major religions from classical times to the present. Includes unusual and entertaining quotations. Subject index, p.461-468. Index of authors and major works, p.469-496. *Class No:* 20(082.2)

Rationalism

[346]

STEIN, G., *ed.* **The Encyclopedia of unbelief.** Buffalo, NY, Prometheus Books, 1986. 2v. (819p.). ISBN: 0879753072.

Over 100 articles, including short bibliographies, covering philosophy, history and biography of the various branches of unbelief from scepticism to atheism. Cross-references. 5 appendices include 'Periodicals of unbelief' with nearly 500 periodical and newspaper titles. 'There is no comparable work' (*Library journal,* 1 November 1985, p.87). *Class No:* 211.5

Bible

[347]

The Zondervan pictorial encyclopedia of the Bible. Tenney, M. and Barabas, S., *eds.* New York, Zondervan Press, 1977. 5v. illus (some col.). ISBN: 0310331889.

7500 signed articles, contributed by 238 scholars - an international team. 32p. of full-colour maps (with index in v.5); 48p. of colour plates, unfortunately unnumbered and lacking text cross-references. Truly pictorial. Conservative standpoint. Compared with *The interpreter's dictionary of the Bible* (*qv*) in *American reference books annual 1976* (entry 1104) and considered 'particularly valuable for its supplementary information and alternative viewpoints.' *Class No:* 22

Dictionaries

[348]

The Eerdmans Bible dictionary. Myers, Allen C., *and others, eds.* Grand Rapids, Missouri, W. Eerdmans, 1987. 1094p. maps. ISBN: 0802824021.

Based on the highly respected Dutch *Bijbelse encyclopedie* (rev. ed. 1975).

About 5,000 entries and many cross-references. Uses the Revised Standard Version of the Bible as authority for quoted passages and forms of names. This American edition adds about 300 new articles and revises many

....*(contd.)*
others, but retains the Protestant evangelical flavour of the
earlier work. Includes basic information concerning people,
places and things of the Bible; surveys all the books of the
Bible; includes articles on the animals, jewels, birds, etc.,
mentioned; and investigates the chief themes and ideas.
Bibliographies are somewhat sketchy. 'Entries reflect
modern biblical scholarship and archaeological research. An
excellent and inexpensive study aid ...' (*Library journal*,
August 1987, p.115). *Class No:* 22(038)

Commentaries

[349]
Harper's Bible commentary. Mays, J.L., *ed.*   New York,
Harper & Row, 1988. xviii,1328p. illus. (mostly coloured).
ISBN: 0060655410.
   Introductory matter (p.1-84) is followed by the Books of
the Bible, Genesis ... Revelations, including the Apocrypha,
each with an introduction, commentary and bibliography.
4p. index precedes an appendix of coloured maps (16p.)
*c.*70 contributors. *Class No:* 22.07

[350]
The Interpreter's Bible: the Holy Scriptures in the King James
and Revised Standard Versions, with general articles and
introduction, exegesis, exposition for each book of the
Bible. Harmon, N.B., *ed.*   New York, Abingdon-Cokesbury
Press, 1952-57. (Reprinted by Abingdon Press, 1984).
Originally in 12 vols. Reprint in 8 vols. ISBN: 0687192315,
set.
   V.1. The Pentateuch ... - 2. Old Testament history ... - 3.
Wisdom, literature and poetry - 4. The major prophets - 5.
The minor prophets and the Apocrypha ... 6. The Gospels -
7. Acts and Paul's letters ... - 8. Revelation and the general
Epistles. Contributors (including eminent British theologians
and Biblical scholars) represent almost every branch of the
Christian Church: consulting editors, from larger Protestant
groups. Each page has text of A.V. and R.S.V. in parallel
columns, with exegesis and exposition below. Aimed at the
general reader, teacher and preacher of the Bible.
Indispensible, although some volumes are now dated. *Class
No:* 22.07

23/28 Christianity

Christianity

[351]

BARRETT, D.B., *ed.* **World Christian encyclopedia:** a comparative survey of churches and religions in the modern world, AD 1900-2000. Nairobi, Oxford University Press, 1982. [12], 1010p. illus., maps., tables. ISBN: 0195724356.

Covers 20800 denominations. 14 parts (1. Status - 2. Chronology - 3. Methodology - 4. Culture - 5. Evangelization - 6. Codebook - 7. Survey (a survey of Christianity and religions in 223 countries, A-Z by country, p.131-771) - 8. Statistics - 9. Dictionary - 10. Bibliography (selective listing, p.839-861) - 11. Atlas - 12. Who's who - 13. Directory - 14. Indexes (polyglot glossary of religious terminology; names of countries in 6 languages; names of God in 900 languages; index of people and languages; Christian abbreviations, acronyms and initials; photographic index; standard and definitive locations index). *Class No:* 230

[352]

HASTINGS, A. **A History of English Christianity, 1920-1985.** London, Collins, 1986. 720p. ISBN: 0002152118.

42 chapters in 7 parts: I. 1920 and before - II. The 1920s - III. The 1930s - IV. 1939-1945 - V. 1945-1960 - VI. The 1960s - VII. 1970-1985. Includes many portraits of personalities. Notes (p.673-703) are mainly references and arranged in chapter order. Index (p.704-720) includes 'see' references. '... this finely printed, vigorously written, industrially researched, sensibly opinionated yet cosmically fair survey of a very complex and hard-to-judge phenomenon... ' (*Church times,* 3 October 1986, p.6). *Class No:* 230

[353]

LATOURETTE, K.S. **Christianity in a revolutionary age:** a history of Christianity in the nineteenth and twentieth centuries. London, Eyre & Spottiswood, 1959-63. (Reprinted Greenwood Press, 1973). 5v. ISBN: 0837157005.

1: *The nineteenth century in Europe: background and the Roman Catholic phase* (xiv, 498p.); 2. *The nineteenth century in Europe: the Protestant and Eastern churches* ([1], [1], 532p.); 3: *The nineteenth century outside Europe: the Americas, the Pacific, Asia and Africa* (viii, [1], 527p.); 4: *The twentieth century in Europe: the Roman Catholic, Protestant and Eastern churches* (viii, 568p.); 5: *The twentieth century outside Europe: the Americas, the Pacific, Asia and Africa; the emerging world Christian community* (viii, 568p.).

Discusses all aspects of Christianity throughout the world since 1815 - theology, organization, devotional life and influence on the social, political and education scene. Well documented (*e.g.,* the chapter on Latin America in v.3 has 187 footnotes); each volume carries an annotated bibliography of *c.*17 pages of works cited more than once. Analytical index. *Class No:* 230

Theology

[354]

FORD, D.F., *ed.* **The Modern theologians:** an introduction to Christian theology in the twentieth century. Oxford, Basil Blackwell Ltd., 1989. 2v. (xvi,342; xii,330p.). ISBN: 0631153713, v.1; 0631168079, v.2.

'Aims to introduce the thought of most leading 20th-century Christian theologians and movements in theology' (*Preface*). Each volume has 14 chapters in 5 parts. V.1. Part 1. Corresponding to Revelation - 2. Existentialism and correlation - 3. Transcendential theology - 4. Tradition and beauty - 5. History and eschatology. V.2. Part 1. British theologies - 2. Theology in the United States - 3. Evangelical and orthodox theology - 4. New challengers in theology - 5. Theology and religious diversity. Each volume has a list of dates, a glossary, and an analytical index. *Class No:* 230.1

[355]

RAHNER, K. and VORGRIMLER, H., *eds.* **Concise theological dictionary.** 2nd ed. Tunbridge Wells, Kent, Burns & Oates, 1983. [8], 541p. ISBN: 0860121097.

First English edition 1965. Translated from *Kleines Theologisches Wörterbuch* (10th ed. Verlag Herder, Freiburg, 1976).

A revised and amplified edition, containing brief explanations (6 or 7 lines to 2p.) of the most important concepts of modern Catholic dogmatic theology. Entries arranged A-Z (Absolute ... Yahweh), with 'see' references. *Class No:* 230.1

[356]

Theological book review. October 1988-. Guildford, Surrey, Feed the Mind, 1988-. 3pa. ISSN: 09542191.

Claims to cover about 250 books from the UK, US and Third World in each issue. Subject arrangement. Author index and list of publishers in each issue. Michael Walsh found the entries in v.1(1) 'rather too uniformly fulsome' (*Bulletin of the ABTPL,* v.2(5), June 1989, p.35). *Class No:* 230.1

Saints

[357]

METFORD, J.C.J. **The Christian year.** London, Thames & Hudson, 1991. 144p. ISBN: 0500110212.

A companion to the holy days, festivals and seasons of the ecclesiastical year. Select bibliography, with some comment, p.129-30. Glossary, p.131-40. Detailed index. Scholarly discussion of origins, reasons and theological background. A calendar of saints' days would have been a helpful addition! *Class No:* 235.3

[358]

The Oxford dictionary of saints. Farmer, D.H. 2nd ed. Oxford, Oxford University Press, 1987. xxviii, 478p. ISBN: 0198691491.

First published 1978; reprinted with corrections 1979, 1980.

Concise accounts of the lives, cults, and artistic associations of *c*.1100 saints who lived or died or have been venerated in Great Britain and Ireland. Increased coverage of Greek and Russian saints in the 2nd ed. Arranged A-Z ('Joan of Arc': 3 columns; 10 references). 3 appendices (I. Some unsuccessful English candidates for canonization; II. Principal patronages; III. Principal iconographical problems). Index of places in Great Britain and Ireland associated with particular saints. Calendar of feasts. Valuable introduction refers to the 1969 reform of the Roman Calendar. 'Excellent value and as a single volume work based on critical principles is unlikely to be rivalled' (*Heythrop journal*, v.20, 1979, p.466, on the first edition). *Class No*: 235.3

[359]

WALSH, M., *ed.* Butler's lives of the saints: concise edition. London, Burns & Oates, 1985. 484p. ISBN: 0860121402.

One-volume abridgement of the original 12v. work. For each day of the year one saint is given, suitable for devotional reading as well as for historical background to Church history. Also reproduces full index from complete edition, with saints included in this volume highlighted in bold type. Contains the most recent canonizations as well as revised dating. *Class No*: 235.3

Creeds

[360]

CURTIS, W.A. A History of creeds and confessions of faith in Christendom and beyond. Edinburgh, Clark, 1911. xx, 502p.

An admirable survey of religious creeds throughout the ages, with extensive and representative quotations from the authoritative documents, bibliographies, and appendices of historical tables. Index.

The 3rd ed. of J.N.D. Kelly's *Early Christian creeds* was issued in a new edition in 1982 (Longman, 460p. 058249219x). *Class No*: 238

Ethics

[361]

MACQUARRIE, J. *and* CHILDERS, J.F., *eds.* A New dictionary of Christian ethics. London, S.C.N. Press; Philadelphia, Pa., Westminster Press, 1986. xvii, 678p. ISBN: 0334022053, UK; 0664209408, US.

First published 1967 as *A dictionary of Christian ethics* in the UK and as *Westminster dictionary of Christian ethics* in US.

167 contributors, representing Protestant, Anglican, Roman Catholic, Orthodox and Jewish faiths. Signed articles and brief follow-up bibliographies for longer items (*e.g.*, 'Jesus, Ethical teachings of': $7\frac{1}{2}$ cols; 4 references). Wide range of subjects (*e.g.*, Pride; Prison reform; Hippocratic oath; Industrial relations; Neoplatonism), including entries under moralists (*e.g.*, Schleiermacher). Many additional entries in the new edition; articles updated; bibliographies revised; more cross-references. '... major contribution that reflects contemporary ideas on Christian ethics and moral theology ... distinguished reference work'. (*Reference books bulletin*, 1986/87, p.52-53). 'Major omission is biographical entries, though movements associated with individuals remain' (*Library journal*, 15 March 1986, p.62). *Class No*: 241

Spirituality

[362]

WAKEFIELD,, G.S., *ed.* A Dictionary of Christian spirituality. New ed. London, SCM Press, 1983 (reprinted in paperback, 1988). xvi.400p. ISBN: 0334019672.

First published 1971. Published by Westminster Press in the US as *Westminster dictionary of Christian spirituality*.

The standard reference work on the subject. Includes 358 articles, written by a team of 153. Entries are signed, include bibliographical references, and are often lengthy (*e.g.* 'Asceticism': 6 cols., 5 references; 'Penitence': 2 cols., 6 references; 'Ecstasy': $1\frac{1}{4}$ cols., 4 references). Includes biographies. Cross-references. Clearly and concisely written, defining spiritual concepts, practices, schools and important persons. 'A fascinating exposition ... ' (Theology, v.87(717), May 1984. p.207-9). *Class No*: 248

Christian Church

[363]

CROSS, F.L. *and* LIVINGSTONE, E.A. The Oxford dictionary of the Christian Church. 2nd ed. London, Oxford University Press, 1974. xxxi, 1518p. ISBN: 0192115456.

First published 1957.

About 6000 entries particularly strong on biographies (*e.g.*, Zwingli: 2 cols., including $\frac{1}{2}$ col. of bibliography). Appended 'Chronological list of popes and antipopes'. Some 250 contributors. A corrective to the High Anglican stance, 'establishmentarianism and antiquarian attachment to the ways of the Western Church; (*T.L.S.*, 20 April 1973, p.448) of the 1st ed. Thus, the 2nd ed., while allotting 'Church of England' 6 cols. (including nearly 1 col. of bibliography), more justice is done to, for example, the Eastern Orthodox Church (3 cols. including $\frac{2}{3}$ of bibliography). The 2nd ed. was designed to take full account of recent years (*e.g.*, Pope Paul VI: $1\frac{3}{4}$ cols.; Vatican Council, The Second: '$1\frac{1}{2}$ cols. (14 lines of bibliography); World Council of Churches: $1\frac{1}{4}$ cols.; 10 lines of bibliography). Addressed 'to the educated public as a whole' (*Preface* to the 1st ed). 'The most useful quick-reference tool for the teachers of theology, and their hard-pressed students' (*Heythrop journal*, v.15, 1974, p.362).

The Concise Oxford dictionary of the Christian Church, edited by E.A. Livingstone (O.U.P., 1977. vi, 570p. ISBN 0192830147), based on the above, has over 5000 brief entries, shortened and modified to suit the lay reader. *Class No*: 26/28

Liturgy & Worship

[364]

A Bibliography of Christian worship. Thompson, B., *ed.* Metuchen, N.J. and London, American Theological Association and Scarecrow Press, 1989. xiii,786p. (*ATLA bibliography series, 25*.) ISBN: 0810821540.

51 sections arranged in 6 parts: 1. Reference works and general works - 2. Worship and the liturgy in the Christian tradition (covering more than half the book) - 3. Word and sacraments: theology, liturgy and spirituality - 4. The daily office and the church year - 5. Worship and the arts - 6. Church music and hymnology. Includes periodical articles as well as books. Author/editor, p.741-782. Church bodies/conference/organizations index, p.783-786. 'International in scope, its comprehensiveness and depth make this a truly outstanding work' (*Choice*, v.27(10), January 1990, p.1645). *Class No*: 264

[365]

DAVIES, J.G. A New dictionary of liturgy and worship. Rev. & expanded ed. London, S.C.M. Press; Philadelphia, Pa., Westminster Press, 1986. xv, [1], 544p. ISBN: 033402207x, UK; 0664212700, US.

First published 1972. Title in US is *The new*

....*(contd.)*

Westminster dictionary of liturgy and worship.

Over 100 contributors, Emphasis is on Christian worship (baptism, eucharist, etc.), with brief treatment of other religions. 'The separate articles are not confined to simple definitions but give the historical background to the subject treated and seek to relate this to the contemporary scene' (*Preface* to 1st ed.). Signed articles; references in text and/ or appended. It strikes a more ecumenical note than the *Oxford dictionary of the Christian church.* 'Students will come to find it extremely useful (especially in revision), both for its factual material and for the stimulation of faith' (*Heythrop journal*, v.15, 1976, p.240). '... will prove invaluable ...' (*British book news,* April 1986, p.211). *Class No:* 264

Hymns

[366]

JULIAN, J. **A Dictionary of hymnology**, setting forth the origin and history of Christian hymns of all ages and nations ... Rev. 2nd ed., with new supplement. London, Murray, 1907 (Reprinted, 1958, 2v.; Gordon Press, 4v. 1977). ISBN: 884901719x.

First published 1892.

Includes biographical and critical notices of authors and translators, historical articles on national and denominational hymnody, breviaries, etc., the English language being the keynote. Lists of contributors, MSS., abbreviations; indexes of first lines and names. Still the standard work. *Class No:* 264-068

Missionary Work (Christian Church)

[367]

LATOURETTE, K.J. **A History of the expansion of Christianity.** London, Eyre & Spottiswoode, 1938-47. 7v.maps.

1. *The first five centuries, to 500 A.D.* 2. *Thousand years of uncertainty, 500-1500 A.D.* 3. *Three centuries of advance, 1500-1800 A.D.* 4. *The Great Century: Europe and the U.S.* 5. *The Americas, Australasia and Africa.* 6. *North Africa and Asia.* 7. *Advance through storm, 1914 and after.*

A work of encyclopaedic range, by a well-known authority on Christian missions, likely to remain the standard history for many years to come, on the missionary enterprise of Christianity from its earliest times up to the present day. Each volume has its own index, full bibliography, and maps. 'Latourette handles temperately, charitably and with immense erudition every part of Christian expansion - Roman Catholic, Protestant, and Orthodox' (Neill, S. *A History of Christian missions* (1965), p.579). *Class No:* 266

Religious Associations & Societies

[368]

NATIONAL CENTRE FOR CHRISTIAN COMMUNITIES AND NETWORKS. **Directory of Christian groups, communities and networks.** 2nd ed. London, the Centre, 1984. vi, 94p.

First published in 1980, as *A directory of Christian communities and groups.*

A selective list of 384 groups, arranged A-Z by name in two sections - More recently established groups - Religious orders and congregations. Information includes name and address, telephone number, ecumenical date, numbers of staff and residents, brief description of denominational allegiance, aims, etc. Geographical index (by country, A-Z). Subject index (p.38-94). *Class No:* 267

Salvation Army

[369]

The Salvation Army year book, 1992. London, International Headquarters of the Salvation Army, 1992. [4], 270p. illus. Annual. ISBN: 0854125914. ISSN: 0080567x.

First published 1906.

Part 1 has 4 articles of special interest; pt.2. Facts and figures; pt.3 Reports, staff lists and addresses; 4. Rolls of Honour; Who's who in The Salvation Army. Index. *Class No:* 267.12

Church History

[370]

Encyclopedia of early Christianity. Ferguson, E., *and others,* eds. New York, Garland, 1990. 983p. illus. (*Garland reference library of the humanities, 846.*) ISBN: 0824057457.

997 entries by 135 scholars, covering persons, places, doctrines, practices, art, liturgy, heresies, and scisms of the first 600 years of Christianity. Entries vary in length from a few lines to *c.*4000 words. Cross-references. Bibliographies appended to most entries. *Class No:* 27

[371]

Oxford history of the Christian Church. Chadwick, H. *and* Chadwick, O., eds. Oxford, Clarendon Press, 1976-.

To be in some 20 volumes, published over several years. 'It will certainly be one of the largest and most comprehensive church histories of our time' (*The Church times,* 20 March 1981, p.6).

Intended to provide a full survey of the Christian Churches and their part in the religious heritage of humanity, particular attention being paid to the place of the churches in surrounding society, the institutions of church life and the manifestations of popular religion, the link with forms of national culture, and the intellectual tradition within and beyond Europe. So far published are: *A history of the churches in the United States and Canada,* by R. Handy (1976. 486p. maps. ISBN 0198269102); *The Frankish church,* by J.M. Wallace-Hadrill (1983. 472p. map. ISBN 0108269064); *Religion in England, 1688-1791,* by Gordon Rupp (1986. 596p. ISBN 0198269188); *The Orthodox Church in the Byzantine Empire,* by I.M. Hussey (1986. 428p. ISBN 0198269013); *The Popes and European revolution,* by Owen Chadwick (1981. 656p. ISBN 0198269196); and *The Papal monarchy: the Western Church from 1050 to 1250,* by Colin Morris (1989. 688p. ISBN 0198269072). *Class No:* 27

[372]

The Oxford illustrated history of Christianity. McManners, J., *ed.* Oxford, Oxford University Press, 1990. xi,726p. illus., maps. ISBN: 0198229283.

19 chapters arranged in 3 parts: From the origins to 1800; Christianity since 1800; Christianity today and tomorrow. Contributions, by a team of 18 leading scholars, based on latest research. Further readings, p.667-685 (by chapter). Chronology, p.680-705. 150 illustrations, 32 colour plates, and 12 maps. Sources are given. Detailed analytical index, p.707-724. Editor is Regius Professor of Ecclesiastical History, Oxford University. *Class No:* 27

[373]

Religion and society in North America: an annotated bibliography. Brunkow, R. de V., *ed.* Santa Barbara, CA., ABC-Clio Press, 1983. xi,515p. (*Clio bibliographical series, no.12.*) ISBN: 0874360420.

4304 annotated entries selected from v.11-18 of *America: history and life,* arranged in 21 sections: 1. United States and Canada - 2. Americanizations of institutions - 3. Business (including Protestant ethic) - 4. Communal

....(contd.)
movements and utopian thought - 5. Ecumenism and intergroup relations - 6. Education - 7. Family - 8. Government and politics - 9. Health - 10. Labour - 11. Missionary impulse ... 21. Religious groups (37 + anti-religious movements). Annotations between 50 to 100 words in length. Subject index, p.323-501; author index, p.502-510; list of periodicals, p.511-513. *Class No: 27*

Religious Orders & Communities

[374]
CONSTABLE, G. **Medieval monasticism:** a select bibliography. Toronto, University of Toronto Press, 1976. [xxi], 171p. (*Toronto medieval bibliographies, 6.*)
1036 references. Parts: 1. Reference - 2. Monastic history - 3. Monastic life and institutions. Closely subdivided. Includes a section on women in religious life. 'A standard reference tool for the study of many aspects of medieval culture' (*Library journal*, v.101(12), 15 June, p.1406). *Class No: 271*

[375]
KNOWLES, D. **The Religious orders in England.** Cambridge, Cambridge University Press, 1948-59. 3v.
1. The old orders, 1216-1314. 2. The end of the Middle Ages. 3. The Tudor age. Includes the history of the Friars of England. V.3 has a bibliography and detailed index, plus valuable appendices (*e.g.*, 2. Religious houses suppressed by Wolsey; 10. Regulars as bishops (a list). *Bare ruined choirs: the dissolution of the English monasteries*, by D. Knowles (C.U.P. 1976. illus. ISBN 0521707126) is an abridged and illustrated edition of v.3.
The standard work, making use of many published records of episcopal visitations. *Class No: 271*

Patrology (Church Fathers)

[376]
ALTANER, B. **Patrology.** Freiberg, Herder; Edinburgh & London, Nelson, 1960. xxiv,660p.
A translation by Hilda C. Graef, based on the 5th German edition of *Patrologie* (1958), revised and augumented.
Not a 'mere bibliography of patrology', but rather a literary history, with brief biographies and extensive bibliographical references. The section of St. Jerome, for example, covers p.462-77. Index. 'This indispensable manual for patristic studies is notable for the completeness of coverage and for its separate bibliographies for individual writers and subjects' (*Heythrop journal*, v.1(3), October 1960, p.359). *Class No: 276*

Christian Churches

[377]
BURGESS, S.M., *and others, eds.* **Dictionary of Pentecostal and charismatic movements.** Grand Rapids, MI., Zondervan, 1989. 914p. illus. ISBN: 0310441005.
Some 800 entries by 66 contributors focusing on movements in North America and, to some extent, in Europe. Includes biographies of people and descriptions of specific denominations with over 2000 members. Lengthy articles are prefaced by outlines of the text. All entries have bibliographies. Cross-references, but no index. *c.*200 black-and-white photographs, mainly portraits. '... successful both as a reference source ... and as a broadly based introduction to a religous movement ...' (*Reference books bulletin*, September 1989, v.86(1), p.102-3). *Class No: 28*

[378]
The Good church guide, 1989. London, Marshall Pickering, 1988. x,527p. ISBN: 0551017694.
Brings together details of more than 2000 churches throughout the United Kingdon, collected by questionnaire. Arrangement is geographical: England (subdivided by county, A-Z; London; Northern Ireland; Scotland; Wales; Isle of Man; Channel Islands; English-speaking churches abroad (by country, A-Z). Information given includes church name, denomination, address, historical interest, membership, worship, and symbols showing services conducted. *Class No: 28*

[379]
LIPPY, C.H. *and* WILLIAMS, P.W., *eds.* **Encyclopedia of the American religious experience:** studies of traditions and movements. New York, Macmillan/Charles Scribner's Sons, 1988. 3v. (xvli, 1872p.). ISBN: 0684180626.
105 commissioned essays on topics dealing with all aspects of the religious experience in the US (and to a limited extent in Canada), both historical and current, and including all denominations, faiths and sects. Arranged in 9 sections organized by broad topic and theme. Essays are lengthy, averaging 12-pages long and include excellent bibliographies. Good cross-references. Exhaustive index. '... valuable as a reference source for information about religious leaders, churches and sects.' (*Reference books bulletin*, 15 May 1988, p.1579-80). 'An outstanding achievement ... will become the standard reference tool in American religion'. (*Choice*, v.25(9), May 1988, p.1380). *Class No: 28*

[380]
UK Christian handbook, 1989/90. Bromley, Kent, MARC Europe, 1989. 807p. tables, maps. ISSN: 09476971.
First published 1964. Annual.
Sections on: Accommodation - Bookshops - Churches - Education - Leadership - Media - Overseas - Services - other useful addresses. Personnel index (p.643-695). Location index (p.697-736). Organization index (p.737-807). *Class No: 28*

Eastern Churches

[381]
ELLIS, J. **The Russian Orthodox Church:** a contemporary history. London, Croom Helm, 1986. [4],531p. (*Keston book, 22.*) ISBN: 0709915675.
13 chapters in 2 parts: part 1 (1. Churches and dioceses - 2. Parish life - 3. The clergy - 4. Theological education - 5. Monasticism - 6. Publications - 7. The laity - 8. The episcopate - 9. Church and state relations). Part 2 (Prologue - 10. The rise of orthodox dissent: up to 1974 - 11. The growth of orthodox dissent, 1974-6 - 12. The flowering of orthodox dissent, 1976-9 - 13. The repression of orthodox dissent, 1976-80. Concluding summary: up to 1985). Notes, p.455-507, by chapter. Bibliography, p.508-539, of books, periodicals, samizdat (selected), legislation, and archives. Analytical index, p.520-531. A new ed. was published by Routledge in 1990. (544p. ISBN 0415034671). *Class No: 281*

Roman Catholic

[382]
Catholic almanac, 1971-. Huntington, Indiana, Our Sunday Visitor, 1969-. Annual. (1992 ed. published 1991). 600p. ISBN: 0879732679.
Previously as *National Catholic almanac* (1904-1970).
Although primarily for the US, it covers the Catholic church worldwide. Includes a chronology and glossary, list of periodicals and encyclicals, statistics, and patron saints, popes, etc. Extensive index precedes. *Class No: 282*

[383]

HARDON, J.A., *S.J.* **Modern Catholic dictionary.** London, Robert Hale, 1981. xiii, 619p. ISBN: 0709193815.

An abbreviated ed., *Pocket Catholic dictionary* was issued in 1985 by Doubleday Image. (ISBN 038523281).

In two parts; part 1 is a dictionary of 5000 terms, directly or indirectly dealing with Catholic faith, worship, morals, history, canon law, and spirituality. The terms, even those from psychology and the social sciences, are described from the Roman Catholic point of view. Includes biographies, some 50 organizations and societies. Cross-references. Entries vary in length from 2-3 lines to a column or more. Part 2 is an appendix, containing the Credo of the People of God; a listing of popes from Peter to John Paul II; updated ecclesiastical calendars of both the Roman and Byzantine rites with saints for each day of the year; and a listing of religious communities and secular institutes in the United States and Canada. *Class No: 282*

[384]

MCCABE, J.P. **Critical guide to Catholic reference books.** 3rd ed. Englewood, Co., Libraries Unlimited, 1989. xiv,323p. (*Research studies in library science, no.20.*) ISBN: 0872876217.

First published 1971; 2nd ed. 1980.

Over 1500 main entries for publications on the teaching, history and mission of the Roman Catholic Church. 5 chapters, each closely subdivided: General; Theology; Humanities; Social science; History. Most entries are annotated, all are in European languages and available in North America. '...continues to be a mainstay for libraries supporting scholarly research on Catholicism' (*Reference books bulletin*, 1989-1990, p.37). *Class No: 282*

[385]

New Catholic encyclopedia: an international work of reference on the teachings, history, organization and activities of the Catholic Church, and on all institutions, religions, philosophies, and scientific and cultural developments affecting the Catholic Church from its beginning to the present. Catholic University of America, editorial staff. New York, McGraw-Hill, 1967; supplements, 1974-79 (Reprinted Palatine, Ill., Publishers Guild, 1981). 15v. (15,350p.), illus., maps. Plus 3 supplementary vols. ISBN: 007010235x.

About 17,000 articles by *c.*4,800 contributors; 7,400 illus. (32 col.pl.) and 300 maps. V.15 is an index of 300,000 entries (including entries for maps and illus.). All articles carry select bibliographies, some briefly annotated. 'St. Anselm of Canterbury': 5½ cols,; 2 illus.; 15 lines of bibliography. Wide coverage (*e.g.,* 'Psychiatry': 13 cols.; 'Zionism': 3 cols.; 'Hungarian art': 6p.; 20 lines of bibliography). Some unusual articles (*e.g.,* 'Translation literature, Greek and Arabic'). No biographies of living persons. Especially valuable on scholastic philosophy and theological writers. Excellently produced and illustrated. V.16-18 update and supplement. *Class No: 282*

[386]

Sacramentum mundi: an encyclopaedia of theology. Rahner, K., *ed. and others.* New York, Herder & Herder; London, Burns & Oates, 1968-70. 6v.

About 1000 signed articles, A-Z, on the central themes of modern religious thought, by over 600 specialists. Bibliographies are appended (*e.g.,* 'Zionism': v.6, p.393-6; ½ col. of bibliography; 'Islam;: v.3, p.165-70, 5 sections; ½ col. of bibliography). Short general index in v.6. An international theological dictionary, published in English, Dutch, French, German, Italian and Spanish. A significant contribution to the field of Roman Catholic lexicography. *Class No: 282*

The Popes

[387]

KELLY, J.N.D. **The Oxford dictionary of Popes.** Oxford, Oxford University Press, 1986. xiii,347p. ISBN: 0192139649.

'A Papal who's who' (*Preface*) precedes short biographies of 266 officially recognised Popes and 39 antipopes, arranged in chronological order (St. Peter ... John Paul II). Entries include birth and death dates, details of family background, pre-Papal career and activities in office, plus bibliographical sources. There is an appendix on Pope Joan. Extensive index, p.331-347, has cross-references. 'The entries themselves are little gems of concise and pungent scholarship' (*British book news*, May 1986, p.283-4). *Class No: 282POP*

Protestant

[388]

The Church of England year book, 1992. The official year book of the General Synod of the Church of England. 108th ed. London, Central Board of finance of the Church of England, 1992. Annual. xxxvii, 448p. ISBN: 0715180797. ISSN: 00693987.

2 main parts. 1. The Church of England (The General Synod - Parochial fees - The Central Board of Finance - Advisory committees and permanent commissions - Other boards, councils, commissions, etc. - The Convocations - The Ecclesiastical Courts - Provinces of Canterbury and York: diocesan lists ... The religious communities. - 2. The Anglican Communion (including Churches, provinces and dioceses overseas ... The ecumenical movement ... List of organizations (p.279-329) - Who's who (p.330-401) - General index. Index to advertisements. A *Statistical supplement,* showing latest trends in ordination, confirmation and baptism, is issued separately every two years. *Class No: 283/289*

Anglican

[389]

Crockford's clerical directory, 1991/92: a directory of the clergy of the Church of England, the Church of Wales, the Scottish Episcopal Church, the Church of Ireland. 92nd issue. London, Church House Publishing, 1991 (previous editions published by Oxford University Press), for the Church Commissioners for England and the Central Board of Finance of the Church of England. 68p. (adverts.), 1088p, maps. ISBN: 0715180762.

First published 1858. Preceded by *Clerical guide,* 1817-36, and *Clergy list* (1840?-).

Biographical notes under clergy (*c.*22,000), A-Z, p.1-815. Index of English benefices and churches; Index of Welsh benefices; of Scottish incumbencies; Irish benefices. Index of cathedrals and collegiate churches. Service, prison and hospital chaplains. Bishops of Anglican dioceses overseas. Addresses of provincial offices, Episcopal succession lists. An essential source on all matters relating to Anglican clergy; primarily concerned with those ordained in the British Isles. *Class No: 283*

[390]

STEPHENS, W.R.W. and HUNT, W., *eds.* **A History of the English Church.** London, Macmillan Press, 1899-1910 (and reprints). 8v. in 9. maps.

The standard history, based on a careful study of original authorities, and the best ancient and modern writers, in moderate-sized volumes. Goes beyond purely ecclesiastical history (*e.g.,* v.2, chapter 16: 'Popular religion, learning and art'). Each volume is by a specialist in the period covered, with its own analytical index, chronological tables and maps. A list of sources is appended to each chapter. *Class No: 283*

Lutheran

[391]
BODENSIECK, J.H., *ed.* **The Encyclopedia of the Lutheran Church.** Minneapolis, MN., Augsburg Publishing House, 1965. 3v.

Published under the auspices of the Lutheran World Federation.

*c.*3000 entries (A-E,F-M,N-Z), contributed by 723 Lutheran scholars and specialists from 34 countries. Includes 1000 biographical sketches and articles on places, etc., pertinent to Lutherism. Bibliographies. *Class No:* 284.1

Non-Conformist

[392]
BROWN, K.D. A Social history of the Nonconformist Ministry in England and Wales, 1800-1930. Oxford, Clarendon Press, 1988. xi, 244p. tables. ISBN: 0198227639.

An investigation into the private and professional lives of protestant nonconformist ministers, based on the statistical analysis of a sample of several thousand ministers of 5 denominations (Baptist, Congregational, Wesleyan, Primitive and United Methodist). 7 chapters: 1. Origins - 2. Training, 1800-*c.*1860 - 3. Training, *c.*1860-1914 - 4. An unsettled ministry? - 5. Private lives - 6. Public lives - 7. Postscript. Footnotes throughout. Select bibliography, p.235-241, by chapter. Index, p.241-244. '...an important contribution to British social and religous history ... most fascinating and scholarly study of a group of individuals who at one time wielded immense influence in society' (*Economic history review,* v.42(3), August 1989, p.411-2). *Class No:* 285/288

[393]
The Church of Scotland year-book, 1990. Edinburgh, Saint Andrew Press for the Church of Scotland, 1990. Annual. 390p. illus. ISBN: 0861531167.

First published 1884.

Directory information on synods, presbyteries and parishes; alphabetical list of ministers, probationers and lay missionaries. Index of personnel; index of places; index of subjects.

The United Free Church of Scotland issues *The handbook* biennially (Glasgow, United Free Church of Scotland, 1930-. *Class No:* 285/288

[394]
DEXTER, H.M. The Congregationalism of the last 300 years, as seen in its literature. New York, Harper, 1880. (2-vol. reprint, B. Franklin, 1970). 2v. (xl, 716, 326p.). ISBN: 0833708511.

Consists of 12 lectures, with a bibliographical appendix (326p.): 'Collections toward a bibliography of Congregationalism'. *Class No:* 285/288

United Reformed Church

[395]
The United Reformed Church year book, 1991/92. London, United Reformed Church in the United Kingdom, 1991. Annual. 216p. map. ISBN: 0853461198. ISSN: 00698849.

First published 1973.

Includes sections: Assembly officers, committees and departments - Provincial moderators, past moderators, recognised colleges and affiliations - List of churches in provinces and districts (p.16-129) - Summary of statistics - Roll of Ministers - Deaconesses - U.R.C. personnel serving overseas - Deceased Ministers and obituaries - Index of churches. *Class No:* 285.42

Methodist

[396]
DAVIES, R. *and* **RUPP, G.,** *eds.* **A History of the Methodist Church in Great Britain.** London, Epworth Press, 1965-1988. 4v. (c.2000p.). ISBN: 0716203960, v.1; 0716209014, v.2; 0716203871, v.3; 0716204444, v.4.

V.1 has 10 contributors and covers the 18th century in 9 chapters; bibliography of primary and secondary sources, p.317-9. Indexes of subjects, names and places. V.2 has 7 contributors and covers the first half of the 19th century; ample footnote references, but no bibliography. Analytical index. V.3 covers in depth the years from the middle of the 19th century to 1932 and the coming into operation of the Methodist Church Act in 1976. V.4 assembles primary documents of Methodist history from its beginnings, sections arranged chronologically; and includes a bibliography (p.650-800) arranged in 7 subject sections, all subdivided. Two appendices: 1. Chapter conversion table; 2. Index of authors and editors (p.803-830). Index of documents and source material (p.831-838). *Class No:* 287

Other Churches & Sects

Quakers (Society of Friends)

[397]
RELIGIOUS SOCIETY OF FRIENDS. Handbook of the Religious Society of Friends, 1982. 8th ed. London, Friends World Committee for Consultation, 1982. 128p. ISBN: 0901856061.

First published 1955. Issued 5-yearly since 1962.

Subtitled 'Finding friends around the world'. Lists Societies of Friends around the world, arranged geographically. Data on meetings, lists of Quaker schools, study centres, publications, libraries. *Class No:* 289.6

29 Non-Christian Religions

Non-Christian Religions

[398]
MELTON, J.G. Encyclopedic handbook of cults in America. New York, Garland Publishing Inc., 1986. x,272p. (*Garland reference library of social science, 213.*) ISBN: 0824090365.

Aims to be a concise summary of the most accurate information available on the more important of the alternative or non-conventional religious movements. 6 sections, each having an appended short bibliography (1. What is a cult? [surveys the broad range of issues surrounding the topic] - 2. The established cults - 3. The new age movement - 4. The newer cults - 5. Counter-cult groups - 6. Violence and the cults) Index, p.265-272. *Class No:* 29.0

[399]
PARRINDER, G. Dictionary of non-Christian religions. 2nd ed. Amersham, Bucks, Hulton Educational Publications Ltd., 1981. 320p. illus. ISBN: 0717509729.

First published 1971.

'This dictionary covers the whole field of the religions of the world, with the exception of Christianity and the Bible' (*Introduction*). About 3000 brief entries, including biographies. Special attention is paid to Hinduism, Buddhism and Islam, and other Far Eastern religions; also Near Eastern, Celtic, Teutonic and Scandinavian religions, the beliefs and customs of ancient American culture, Mayas, Aztecs and Incas, plus those of Australasia and Africa. Judaism is referred to in detail in the post-Biblical period. Ample cross-references. Over 300 drawings and photographs. No references to authorities consulted. Further reading list, p.318-9. Well produced. For undergraduates and the general reader. *Class No:* 29.0

[400]
PARRINDER, G., ed. An Illustrated history of the world's religions. London, Newnes, 1983. 528p. illus. ISBN: 0600337982.

21 chapters (1. Prehistoric religions ... 21. Islam. Conclusion). 20 specialist contributors. Bibliography, by chapters, p.516-9. Marginal text references to illustrations. Index (tiny print). Comparative religion for the new comer as well as the scholar. *Class No:* 29.0

Mythology

[401]
GRAY, I.H., ed. Mythology of all races. Boston, Mass., Archaeological Institute of America, Marshall Jones Co., 1916-32. (Reprinted New York, Cooper Square Publishers, 1964. 13v. illus.

Contents: V.1: *Greek and Roman,* by W.S. Fox (1916); 2: *Eddic,* by J.A. McCulloch (1930); 3: *Celtic,* by J.A. McCulloch; *Slavic,* by J. Machal (1918); 4: *Finno-Ugric, Siberian,* by U. Holmberg (1927); 5: *Semitic,* by S.H.

....*(contd.)*
Langdon (1931); 6: *Indian,* by A.B. Keith; *Iranian,* by A.J. Carnoy (1917); 7: *Armenian,* by M.H. Ananikian; *African,* by A. Werner (1925); 8: *Chinese,* by J.C. Ferguson; *Japanese,* by M. Anesaki (1928); 9: *Oceanic,* by R.B. Dixon (1916); 10: *North American,* by H.B. Alexander (1916); 11: *Latin American,* by H.B. Alexander (1920). 12. *Egyptian,* by W.M. Müller; *Indo-Chinese,* by J.G. Scott (1918). 13. Complete index to v.1-12 (1932). Each volume carries some 20-50 plates, in addition to figures in the text; also some 20 pages of bibliography. The detailed index runs to 477 pages,. Valuable for its truly extensive geographical coverage, backed by a full index. *Class No:* 292/293

[402]
HART, G. Dictionary of Egyptian gods and goddesses. London, Routledge & Kegan Paul, 1986. A paperback ed. was issued in 1990. ISBN 0415059097. 229p. illus. ISBN: 0710209657.

An outline time-chart and 2 maps precede the dictionary, arranged by name A-Z (Aken ... Yamm). The author has 'tried to include all the important deities that figure in magical medicine and daily life' (*Preface*). Entries are detailed and clearly written; some lengthy. (e.g., 'Aten': 10 pages; 'Osiris': 15 pages) but others only 2 or 3 lines. Short 'Select further reading' (p.227) and 'Alternative renderings of divine names' (p.229) complete the book. *Class No:* 292/293

[403]
Indian mythology: an encyclopedia of myths and legends. Knappert, J. London, Aquarium Press, 1991. 287p. illus. (*World mythology.*) ISBN: 1855380404.

Draws on a 5,000 year history of Indian culture, looking at mythology in both the Hindu and Buddhist traditions. Includes the deities, epic heroes, prophets and saints; the creation of the world; and religious concepts of the afterlife. The encyclopedia, arranged A-Z, is preceded by 7 introductory sections (p.9-27): The myths - The language - Prehistory - The peoples - Literature - The sources - History - Further reading - A guide to pronunciation. *Class No:* 292/293

[404]
Larousse world mythology. Grimal, P., ed. Rev. ed. London, Hamlyn, 1982. 569p. illus., (incl.col.pl.).

Translated from the French by G.P. Beardmore. Originally published as *Mythologies* (Paris, Larousse, 1963).

23 specialist contributions (Prehistory - Egypt - Sumer - Babylon - The Hittites - Greece - Rome - Persia - India - The Celts - Germans - Slavs - Ugric Finns - China - Japan - North America - Siberia). Profusely illustrated with 40p. of colour plates and 600 black-and-white illus. Bibliography of selected readings, p.546-7. Index. Lacks maps. *Class No:* 292/293

[405]
SOUTH, M., *ed.* **Mythical and fabulous creatures:** a source book and research guide. New York, Greenwood Press, 1987. xxxv, 393p. illus. ISBN: 0313243387.

The editor's introduction, which includes a bibliographic essay, is followed by 20 chapters on individual creatures arranged in 4 sections: Birds and beasts - Human-animal composites - Creatures of the night - Giants and fairies. The chapters are written as bibliographic essays. The second part of the book includes 'A Miscellany' and 'A Taxonomy' which have information on another 43 creatures. Glossary. General bibliography. Index with 'see' references. '... a breadth of coverage that is both impressive and delightful' (*Choice*, v.24(11/12), July/August 1987, p.1678). *Class No: 292/293*

Dictionaries

[406]
CRAIG, R.D. **Dictionary of Polynesian mythology.** New York, Greenwood Press, 1989. 456p. map. ISBN: 0313258902.

Covers an area from Hawaii in the north to New Zealand in the south and Easter Island in the east. A nearly comprehensive listing of the goddesses, gods and ancient heroes chronicled in the legends of the Polynesians. Bibliography of almost 300 sources. Highly recommended as a 'significant new work ... for Pacific studies and comparative mythology collections' (*RQ*, v.30(1), Fall 1990, p.112. from which this entry is taken). *Class No: 292/293(038)*

[407]
LURKER, M. **Dictionary of gods and goddesses, devils and demons.** New York, Routledge & Kegan Paul, 1987. 451p. ISBN: 0710208774.

First published in Stuttgart in 1984 as *Lexikon der Götter und Däomen: Namen, Funktionen, Symbole/ Attribute.*

c.1800 articles, their length proportionate to their importance, on the gods, and other supernatural persons from all the world's religions. Followed by indexes of varient names, secondary names, and by-names; of functions, aspects and areas of influence; and of symbols, attributes and motives; and a select bibliography. *Class No: 292/293(038)*

Ireland

[408]
ELLIS, P. B. **A Dictionary of Irish mythology.** Santa Barbara, CA., ABC Clio, Oxford, University Press, 1989. 240p. ISBN: 0874365538, US; 0192828711, UK.

Aimed at the enthusiast and the lay reader, but academics could find it useful. A lengthy introductory essay on the history of the Celts, the sources of their sagas and romances, precedes the dictionary, which covers gods, human heroes, titles, sites, objects, etc. A select bibliography is appended. *Choice* (v.27(2), October 1989, p.285) suggests an indication of pronunciations should be considered for a later edition. *Class No: 292/293(415)*

Classical Mythology

[409]
MORFORD, M.P.O. *and* LENARDON, R.J. **Classical mythology.** 3rd ed. New York, Longman Group Ltd., 1985. xvi, 576p. illus. ISBN: 0582285410.

First published 1971.

3 parts (26 chapters): 1. The myths of creation; The Gods - 2. The Greek sagas; Greek local legends - 3. The survival of classical mythology (*e.g.*, 26. Classical mythology in music and film). Select bibliography, p.541-544; also bibliographies at the end of the introduction (p.23-25) and

....(contd.)
appended to chapters. Indexes: A. Mythological and historical persons, subjects and placenames; B. Authors, artists, composers, subjects and titles. A 4th ed. was published in 1991 (703p. ISBN 0801304652). *Class No: 292*

[410]
TRIPP, E. **Dictionary of classical mythology.** Rev. ed. London, Collins, Publishers, 1988. [14], 631p. maps & geneological charts. ISBN: 0004343808.

First published 1970.

Over 2000 entries, A-Z, varying in length from 2 or 3 lines to 5 pages. Includes names of people and places as well as terms. Includes stories telling of the myths of Greece and Rome in readable and convenient form (*e.g.*, 'Oedipus': $2\frac{1}{2}$p.; 'Pan': $1\frac{1}{4}$p.; 'Media': $4\frac{1}{4}$p.; 'Zeus': 5p.). 'See' references. Pronouncing index. 5 maps of the classical world. 5 genealogical charts of great royal lines. *Class No: 292*

Eastern Religions

[411]
The Rider encyclopedia of Eastern philosophy and religion: Buddhism, Hinduism, Taoism, Zen. Schumacher, S. *and* Woerner, G., eds. London, Rider Books, 1989. xv,[i],468p. illus., tables. ISBN: 0712611924.

Originally published in German by Otto-Wilhelm-Barth Verlag in 1986.

The A-Z encyclopedia (p.1-444) has over 4000 entries and over 100 illustrations (*e.g.* 'Nirvana': $3\frac{1}{4}$ columns. illus.). Appendix: Ch'an/Zen lineage chart; bibliography, p.457-468 (grouped: Buddhism-Zen; subdivided into primary and secondary sources). 4 contributors: I. Fischer-Schreiber (Buddhism & Taoism); F.K. Ehrhard (Tibetan Buddhism); K. Friedrichs (Hinduism); M.S. Diener (Zen). A scholarly survey of the teachers, traditions and literature of Asian writers. *Class No: 294/299*

[412]
WINTERNITZ, M., *comp.* A Concise dictionary of Eastern religion: being the index volume to The sacred books of the East. Oxford, Clarendon Press, 1910, (reprinted 1925). xvi, 683p.

Forms V.50 of *The Sacred books of the East*. A remarkably detailed analytical index (*e.g.* 'Prayers': 15 columns, set solid). Many cross-references. Designed on the basis of a 'scientific classification of religious phenomena'. *Class No: 294/299*

Hinduism

[413]
STUTLEY, M. *and* STUTLEY, J. **A Dictionary of Hinduism:** its mythology, folklore and development, 1500 B.C. - A.D. 1500. London, Routledge & Kegan Paul, 1977 (Paperback ed. published 1985). xvii,372p. map. ISBN: 0710205872.

Published by Harper & Row in the US as *Harper's dictionary of Hinduism.*

c.2500 subject entries ('Jaina': 2 cols., 10 references). Bibliography, p.353-68. Diacriticals are shown. 'This outstanding work will be a standard reference tool in libraries for many years to come' (*American reference books annual*, 1978, entry no. 983). *Class No: 294*

Buddhism

[414]
HUMPHREYS, C.A. **A Popular dictionary of Buddhism.** Rev. ed. London, Curzon Press, 1976. (Reprint 1984). 224p. ISBN: 0700701842.

First published 1962.

Gives definitions and brief explanations of *c.*1000 terms (*e.g.,* 'Four Paths': ½p.). Includes brief biographies; references to the literature. Modified diacriticals. Author is Founder-President of the Buddhist Society. *Class No:* 294.3

[415]
International Buddhist directory. London, Wisdom Publications, 1985. 120p. (*A Wisdom reference book.*) ISBN: 0861710258.

In 2 parts: part 1: Confirmed addresses; pt.2: Unconfirmed addresses. Lists some 1800 Buddhist centres in 63 countries. 500 confirmed addresses include name and address, telephone number, which tradition of Buddhism, the spiritual director, whether centre is in city or country, or has resident teacher, accommodation, regular teachings, meditation and retreat facilities, library, bookshop, newsletter. Unconfirmed list includes some 1300 names and addresses. Arranged A-Z in both sections; tabular data in section 1. *Class No:* 294.3

Sikhism

[416]
COLE, W.O. *and* SAMBHI, P.S. **The Sikhs: their religious beliefs and practices.** London, etc., Routledge & Kegan Paul, 1978. xxvii, 210p. illus., maps. ISBN: 0710088434.

9 chapters (*e.g.,* 2. The place of the Ten Gurus in the Sikh religion; 6. Daily life, ceremonies and festivals: 8. The attitude ot Sikhism towards other religions. 'Primary sources for the study of Sikhism, p.xv-xvii. Glossary. Secondary sources (running commentary) and additional bibliography, p.196-204. Detailed non-analytical index. A new ed. was published in 1991 (ISBN 0415040280). *Class No:* 294.51

Yoga

[417]
ELIADE, M. **Yoga:** immortality and freedom. Trask, W.R., *translator.* 2nd ed. Princeton, N.J., Princeton University Press, 1970 (Reprinted 1991); London, Arkana (Penguin Group), 1989. xxii,536p. (*Bollinger series, v.56.*) ISBN: 0691017646, (US); 0140191585, (UK).

First published in US in 1958; 2nd ed. in 1969.

'A scholarly treatment of yoga philosophy, which gives an exhaustive survey of the history and main schools of thought' (Thompson, I. *Alternative medicine* (1981)). List of works cited, p.433-480. Index p.481-536. *Class No:* 294.527

[418]
FEUERSTEIN, G. **Encyclopedic dictionary of Yoga.** New York, Paragon House, 1990. 430p. illus. (90 black & white photographs). (*Living traditions series.*) ISBN: 155778244x.

Defines more than 2000 words, expressions and concepts found in the study of Yoga, arranged in English A-Z order. Entries range in length from a few lines to several pages. English keywords refer to Sanscrit equivalents. Includes brief biographies. Bibliography (p.427-430) is in two parts: 1. Reference; 2. Recommended reading. *Class No:* 294.527

Zoroastrianism

[419]
BOYCE, M. **Zoroastrians:** their religious beliefs and practices. London, Routledge & Kegan Paul, 1979. 252p. (*Library of religious beliefs and practices.*) ISBN: 0710001215.

14 chapters (2. Zoroaster and his teaching - 3. The establishment of Mazda worship ... 5. Under the Achaemenians - 6. Under the Seleucids and Sassanids ... 10. Under the Caliphs ... 13. Under the Qajars and British - 14. In the twentieth century. Chapter bibliographies, p.229-36 (with some notes). Glossary, p.xv-xvii. *Class No:* 295

Jewish Religion (Judaism)

[420]
COHN-SHERBOK, D. **A Dictionary of Judaism and Christianity.** London, SPCK, 1991. [v],180p. ISBN: 0281045380.

Aims to provide vital information about Judaism and Christianity in direct and simple language, making important connections between the two faiths. Entries vary in length from a few lines to 3 columns or more. Cross-references. For the general reader. 'The first dictionary to explain and compare key concepts, beliefs and practices of both Judaism and Christianity' (*British book news,* September 1991, p.607). *Class No:* 296

[421]
WIGODER, G., *ed.* **Everyman's Judaica:** an encyclopedic dictionary. London, W.H. Allen, 1975. xi,673p. illus. (incl. col. pl.). facsims, ports, tables, maps.

15,000 short entries. 'A guide to the Bible, to Israel old and new, to Jewish communities throughout the world, to famous Jews, to Jewish concepts and customs, to Jewish history and literature' (*Introduction*). 65 lists and tables (*e.g.,* List of Kibbutz, p.339-40; Common Jewish abbreviations, p.3-5; Blessings and benedictions, p.73). Appendices include 'Hebrew-English basic vocabulary'; 'Daily calendar'. Many brief biographies. 200 illus. (many in colour). Planned as complimentary to the 16v. *Encyclopedia Judaica* and its *Yearbooks.* *Class No:* 296

Islam

[422]
MIR, M. **Dictionary of Qur'ānic terms and concepts.** New York, Garland, 1987. 244p. (*Garland reference library of the humanities, 693.*) ISBN: 0824085469.

Lists over 500 terms found in the Qur'ān. English translations of the terms are arranged A-Z with cross-references from the transliterated Arabic. Definitions vary in length from several lines to 2 or more pages. Entries refer to specific passages in the Qur'ān where the term is used and explain its significance. A 20-page list of terms included follows the text. *Class No:* 297

[423]
The Shorter encyclopedia of Islam. Gibb, H.A.R. *and* Kramer, J.H., *eds.* Leyden, Brill, 1953 (Reprinted 1974). vii,671p. 7 pl., 2 plans. ISBN: 9004006818.

Comprises all the articles in the 1st ed., and supplement of the *Encyclopaedia of Islam* (1913-33) relating particularly to the religion and law of Islam. Most of these articles have been reproduced without material alteration; some have been shortened or revised; a few new entries have been added. Bibliographies have been brought up-to-date. Included is a 'Register of subjects', which gives the English translation of Arabic words used as headings. A-Z index of articles, stating authors. Invaluable. *Class No:* 297

Celtic Cults

[424]
GREEN, M. **The Gods of the Celts.** Totowa, N.J., Barnes & Noble Books; Gloucester, A. Sutton Publishers, 1986. [8], 257p. 103 illus. ISBN: 0389206725, US; 0862992923, UK.

A guide to Celtic beliefs in Britain and Europe 'drawing on the latest research and covering all aspects of the gods' ritual customs, cult objects, and sacred places. 7 chapters: The Celts and religion - Cults of sun and sky - Fertility and the Mother-Goddesses - War, death and the underworld - Water-gods and healers - Animals and animism - Symbolism and imagery in Celtic cult expression. Notes/references (p.226-235), bibliography (p.236-249), Index (p.250-257). *Class No:* 299.16

Chinese Religions

[425]
YU, D.C. *and* THOMPSON, L.G. **Guide to Chinese religion.** Boston, Mass., G.K. Hall, 1985. 200p. (*Asia philosophies and religious resource guide.*) ISBN: 0816179026.

Deals with religions that originated on Chinese soil, and includes material from 1500B.C. to 1977. *c.*3000 short annotated entries, covering all aspects and periods of religion from folk beliefs to rituals to Maoism and to conflicts between religious institutions. Index. *Class No:* 299.5

Japanese Religions

[426]
JAPAN. AGENCY OF CULTURAL AFFAIRS. **Japanese religion:** a survey. Tokyo & Palo Alto, Kodansha International Ltd., 1972 (reprinted 1981). 276p. illus. ISBN: 0870111833.

9 contributors (all Japanese). Part 1: Description and interpretation (2. Shinto; 3. Buddhism; 4. Christianity; 5. New religious movements; 6. Confucianism; 7. Folk religion...) - Part 2: Specific religious organizations - Part 3: Statistical tables. Index, p.265-72, includes Japanese characters. A survey of major religious organizations, with particular reference to their present circumstances. *Class No:* 299.52

[427]
READER, I. **Religion in contemporary Japan.** London, Macmillan, 1991. xv,277p. ISBN: 0333523210.

Aims to give the reader an overview of the contemporary nature of religion in Japan, in particular looking at religious behaviour and the ways in which religious themes are found in the lives of Japanese people. Notes (p.244-259); references cited (p.260-267); index (p.268-277). *Class No:* 299.52

African Religions

[428]
PARRINDER, G. **Africa's three religions.** 2nd ed. London, Sheldon Press, 1976. 256p. map. ISBN: 0859690962.

First published 1969 as *Religion in Africa.*

4 parts (20 chapters): 1. Traditional religions - 2. Christianity - 3. Islam - 4. Conclusion (18. Other religions; 19. Relationship of Africa religions; 20. Characteristics of religion in Africa). Bibliography, p.239-42 (3 sections). Non-analytical index. *Class No:* 299.6

Oceanic Religions

[429]
POIGNANT, R. **Oceanic mythology:** the myths of Polynesia, Micronesia, Melanesia, Australia. 2nd rev. ed. London, Newnes, 1985. 144p. illus. (incl.col.pl.). ISBN: 0600342832.

4 regional sections, as in title, with subdivisions. Many sub-sections. 148 illustrations, 48 in colour. 'Further reading list'. Index. *Class No:* 299.9

3 SOCIAL SCIENCES

Social Sciences

[430]
International current awareness services/ICAS. British Library of Political and Economic Science, at the London School of Economics, *comp.* London, Routledge, November 1991-. 4 series, each monthly. ISSN: 09601511, Anthropology; 0960152x, Economics; 09601538, Political science; 09601546, Sociology.

Aims to provide rapid international coverage of the world's most significant social science literature. Entries are drawn from a total of 13000 current serials, plus an extensive monograph collection. Coverage is worldwide, in 30 languages from over 60 countries. *Class No: 30*

[431]
PAIS bulletin: a selective subject list of the latest books, pamphlets, government publications, reports of public and private agencies, and periodical articles, relating to business, economic and social conditions, public administration and international relations, published in English throughout the world. New York, Public Affairs Information Service, 1915-. v.1, no.1-. Monthly, with 3 quarterly and annual cumulations. ISSN: 08982201.

Previously titled *Public affairs information service bulletin.*

Indexes more than 1000 English-language periodicals. The annual volume carries an author index. The annual entry 'Directories' provides a handy check-list directory of publishers and organizations in cumulations. Because of its frequent cumulation and wide coverage of English-language material, it is the major indexing service in the social sciences. Complemented by *PAIS foreign language index* (1972-. Quarterly, with annual cumulations), which covers publications and periodicals in 5 European languages, and *PAIS international in print* (1991-. Monthly), a current awareness journal of selected items. *PAIS international* is the PAIS online database, covering *PAIS bulletin* from 1976 and *PAIS foreign language index* from 1972; PAIS on CD-ROM is available from 1972. *Class No: 30*

[432]
Social sciences index. New York, H.W. Wilson, 1974-. v.1-. Quarterly, with bound cumulation. ISSN: 00944920.

One of two indexes superseding *Social sciences & humanities index* (1916-1974).

Author and subject entries to English-language periodicals in anthropology; area studies; community health and medical care; geography; gerontology; law & criminology; minority studies; planning and public administration; police science and corrections; policy sciences; psychiatry; psychology; social work and public welfare; sociology; urban studies, and related subjects. Author listing of citations to book reviews. 342 key periodicals currently indexed. Clear typography: good paper. *Class No: 30*

[433]
WEBB, W., *and associates.* **Sources of information in the social sciences:** a guide to the literature. 3rd ed. Chicago, Ill., American Library Association, 1986. x, 777p. ISBN: 083890405x.

Supersedes C.M. White's *Sources of information in the social sciences* (Chicago, A.L.A., Preliminary ed. 1959; 1st ed. 1964; 2nd ed. 1973. xviii, 702p.).

A thorough updating of White's standard sources, describing the literature; some sections reworked, others merely updated. 8110 numbered entries (2nd ed. 4527), mostly annotated, in 9 main classes: 1. Social science literature - 2. History - 3. Geography - 4. Economics and business administration - 5. Sociology - 6. Anthropology - 7. Psychology - 8. Education - 9. Political science. 20 contributors. Each chapter commences with a survey of the field, followed by a survey of the reference works, subject grouped. Cross-references. Extensive index (p.585-776) has subject, author-title and title entries. 'Focuses on form rather than function' (*Choice*, v.24(5), January 1987, p.749). *Class No: 30*

Dictionaries

[434]
GOULD, J. and **KOLB, W.K.,** *eds.* **A Dictionary of the social sciences.** London, Tavistock Publications, 1964. xvi, 761p.

Compiled under Unesco auspices.

About 270 British and US social scientists treat 1022 terms and concepts, especially in political science and sociology. Aims at extended discussion of each concept, its role in the social sciences and its historical development. Signed articles, sectionalized for different meanings; literature references in text; cross-references (*e.g.*, 'Gold standard': nearly 4 columns; sections A-D; 3 references in text; cross-references). Well produced. 'Undoubtedly the best one-volume dictionary of the language of the social scientist available today' (*Library journal*, v.90(2), 15 January 1965, p.231). *Class No: 30(038)*

[435]
KOSCHNICK, W.J. Standard dictionary of the social sciences. München, K.G. Saur, 1984-88. 2v. (x,664p.; x,680p.). ISBN: 3598105266, v.1; 3598105274, v.2.

V.1: English-German; v.2: German-English *c.*20,000 terms from all areas of the social sciences, particularly sociology, psychology, statistics, communications research, psychiatry. anthropology, political science and research methodology. Definitions range in length from a few words to a paragraph or more. Identifies authors who originated or were closely associated with particular terms. Cross-references. '... likely to be the standard English-German social science dictionary for some time' (*Choice*, v.23(5), January 1986, p.728). *Class No: 30(038)*

Yearbooks & Directories

[436]
Directory of alternative communities in the British Isles; compiled by Michèle and Kevin of The Teachers, Bangor, North Wales. 4th ed. Bangor, North Wales, Teacher Printing and Publishing, 1983. 199p.

First published 1977.

A list of over 100 communities operating in the British Isles, arranged A-Z by name of community (Ampleforth Abbey - Whitbourne Hall Community). Contains both a discussion of community life and details of size, social and economic organization, as well as a general description of aims and activities of each community. *Class No:* 30(058)

[437]
WHITAKER, J. An Almanack for the year of Our Lord ... 1868- (Annual). 124th., 1991. London, Whitaker, 1991. 1247p. illus., maps. ISBN: 0850212200.

Sub-title: 'containing an account of the astronomical and other phenomena and a vast amount of information respecting the government, finances, population, commerce, and general statistics of the various nations of the world, with an index containing nearly 10,000 references'. Includes British government and public offices (ministers and senior civil servants, with their salaries), lists of peers, baronets, knights, M.P.'s, judges, sheriffs (county and borough), holders of the V.C. and George Cross, societies. Data on churches, armed forces, education (public schools, universities, professional education), insurance companies and their rates, postal regulations, tide tables, income tax, national insurance, legal notes, conservation and heritage, etc. Index using computer technology, at end of volume (p.1193-1247). Still no cross-references. Invaluable in any library or home; particularly useful for the variety of miscellaneous information available through the detailed index. *Class No:* 30(058)

[438]
The World almanac & book of facts, 1991. New York, World Almanac, 1991. 960p. illus., maps. Annual. ISBN: 0886875803. ISSN: 00841382.

First published 1868.

Similar content to *Whitaker's almanak* and equally dependent on a detailed index (p.3-31). Includes a full annual chronology, memorable dates, US associations and institutions, US population statistics for places of 2500 or more, and has sections on noted personalities (not all US), foreign countries, A-Z, and sporting events. Quotes sources of statistics. 16p. of coloured flags and maps. The nearest approach to a general US yearbook. *Class No:* 30(058)

Institutions & Associations

[439]
World directory of social science institutions, 1990: research, advanced training, documentation, professional bodies. 5th ed. Paris, Unesco, 1990. xv,1211p. (*World social science information directories:* 2.) ISBN: 9230025526.

First consolidated ed., 1977, from basic loose-leaf index of 1970, plus updatings in the quarterly *International social science journal*. 4th ed. produced from Unesco's DARE BANK.

In 4 parts: - Section I is an alphabetical index of official names and acronyms of institutions, with the relevant entry number; Section II has full details of each institution, listed A-Z, preceded by international and regional organizations, with address, date of establishment, name of head, senior researchers, staff, subject coverage, type of organization, activities, finance, research facilities, method of data processing, and publications; Section III is an index, A-Z by name of head of institution; Section IV is an index by subject and geographic coverage, with indication of the host country of the institution. *Class No:* 30:061:061.2

Research Projects

[440]
BRITISH LIBRARY. Current research in Britain: social sciences. 6th ed. Boston Spa, West Yorks., British Library, 1991. xxi,714p. ISBN: 0712320857. ISSN: 02671964.

Supersedes *Research in British universities, polytechnics and colleges, government departments and other institutions,* v.3: *Social sciences,* which superseded the British Library's (and earlier the Department of Education and Science's) *Scientific research in British universities and colleges.* V.3 *Social sciences,* which in turn superseded in part Warren Spring Laboratory's *Register of research in the human sciences,* first published in 1967.

A register of current research in every university and polytechnic, many colleges and other institutions. An introduction is followed by a Department index and a List of universities, polytechnics, colleges and other institutions. The main sequence, Research in progress, is arranged in subject groups, and is followed by name, study area, and keyword indexes. *Class No:* 30:061:061.62.005

Sociology

[441]
ABY, S.H., *comp.* **Sociology: a guide to reference and information sources.** Littleton, Col., Libraries Unlimited, 1987. xv, 231p., (Reference sources in the social sciences series). ISBN: 0872874982.

659 entries in 3 parts - General social science reference sources (71 entries for guides, bibliographies, indexes and abstracts, handbooks and yearbooks, dictionaries and encyclopedias, statistics, directories, biographies); social science disciplines (69 entries in the fields of education, economics, psychology, social work, anthropology and history; and sociology (519 general reference sources and sources in sociological fields, *e.g.,* clinical sociology, population and demography, race and ethnic relations, women's studies). Entries are annotated. Up-dates Charles Mark's *Sociology of America* (Gale, 1976). Author/title index, p.203-16; subject index, p.217-31. '... an excellent up-to-date guide to the major reference sources of sociology ...' (*Choice,* v.24(11/12), July/August, 1987. p.1671). *Class No:* 301

[442]
Collins dictionary of sociology. Jary, D. *and* Jary, J. London, Harper Collins Publishers, 1991. 768p. illus. ISBN: 0004343735.

Includes terms most likely to be met from associated disciplines (*e.g.* psychology, economics, anthropology and political science), and methodological terms and research techniques. Also biographical entries. Cross-references. *Class No:* 301

[443]
Handbook of sociology. Smelser, N. J., *ed.* Newbury Park, CA., Sage Publications Ltd., 1988. 824p. ISBN: 0803926650.

Aims to supersede *Handbook of modern sociology* by R. E. L. Faris (1964).

22 Chapters arranged in 4 parts: 1. Theoretical and methodological issues - 2. Bases of inequality in society - 3. Major institutional and organizational settings - 4. Social process and change. Each chapter contains a lengthy, up-to-date bibliography. Subject index, p.775-791. Name index, p.792-824. US view of sociology. ' ... an excellent collection ... no better handbook of contemporary sociology' (*Choice* V.26 (7) March 1989, p.1122). ' ... uniformly high quality of contributions ... exceptionally rich in its coverage of fields of sociological specialisation, data sources, bibliographical material and theoretical expositions' (*The Sociological review,* v.37 (3), August 1989, p.551-3). *Class No:* 301

[444]

International bibliography of sociology ... British Library of Political and Economic Science, *comp.* London and New York, Routledge, 1952-. v.1-. Annual. ISSN: 00852066.

References to books, periodical articles, and documents, arranged in 11 sections, each subdivided: A. Social sciences. Research. Documentation - B. Methodology. Theory - C. Individuals, groups, organizations - D. Culture. Socialization. Social life - E. Social structure - F. Population. Family. Ethnic group - G. Environment. Community: Rural, Urban - H. Economic life - I. Labour - J. Politics. State. International relations - K. Social problems. Social service. Social work. Author and subject indexes. V.37: 1987 published in 1991 (lxxviii, 335p. ISBN 0415038804). Supported by *Thematic list of descriptors: sociology, 1989* (Routledge, 1989. xix,475p. ISBN 0415017793) and updated by *International current awareness service: sociology and related disciplines* (November 1990-. monthly). *Class No:* 301

[445]

Macmillan student encyclopedia of sociology; ed. by Michael Mann. London, Macmillan Press, 1983 (Reprinted 1987). xii, 434p. (Macmillan dictionary series). ISBN: 0333281934.

Aimed at all students of social science, with over 2000 entries, A-Z, of all important sociological terms, theories, concepts, and proper names. Entries vary from 100 to 300 or more words. Cross-references. '...wide-ranging... in fact, encyclopedic'. (*The Times educational supplement*, 18 March, 1984, p.36). *Class No:* 301

[446]

Sociological abstracts. Brooklyn, N.Y., subsequently San Diego, CA., Sociological Abstracts, Inc., 1952-. v.1, no.1-. 5 issues pa. ISSN: 00380202.

Sponsored by the International Sociological Association. About 4000 indicative and informative abstracts pa. Main sections: 0100. Methodology and research technology - 0200. Sociology: history and theory - 0300. Social psychiatry ... 0800. Mass phenomena ... 1000. Social differentiation ... 1900. The family and socialization ... 2100. Social problems and social welfare ... 2400. Policy, planning, forecasting ... 2900. Feminist/gender studies - 3000. Marxist sociology - 9000. Papers presented at sociology meetings. Supplement section (International review of publications in sociology) contains book abstracts and a listing of book reviews that appear in the serials abstracted in the issue). Subject, author and periodical indexes. Also online from 1961, updated quarterly. (BRS(SOCA), DIMDI, DIALOG and CD-ROM). *Class No:* 301

Great Britain

[447]

ABERCROMBIE, N., *and others.* **Contemporary British society:** a new introduction to sociology. Cambridge, Polity Press, 1988. 538p. illus., diagrs., graphs, tables, maps. ISBN: 074560220x.

12 chapters: 1. Introduction - 2. Work - 3. Class - 4. Gender - 5. Ethnicity and racism - 6. Families and households - 7. Towns, cities and the countryside - 8. Education - 9. Health - 10. Culture and media - 11. Deviance, crime and control - 12. Politics. Bibliography, p.520-531. Detailed order. Boxed information and summaries are a feature of this textbook. *Class No:* 301(410)

Public Opinion

[448]

Pros and cons: a debater's handbook. Jacobson,, M.D., *ed.* 17th ed. London, Routledge & Kegan Paul, 1987. x, 278p. ISBN: 0710210442.

First published 1896.

Objective is to give debaters a useful guide to for-and-against arguments on a wide range of controversial issues. Topics A-Z ('Advertising, public control and taxation' ... 'Written constitution'). Pro and con points on each topic in adjacent columns per page. The index groups topics under 21 heads (Agriculture ... Women). *Class No:* 301.153

Adolescents

[449]

Encyclopedia of adolescence. Lerner, R.M., *and others*, eds. New York, Garland, 1991. 2v. (c.1223p.). ISBN: 0824043782.

Over 200 articles (2 to 10 pages each) surveying the emotional upheaval and transformations that mark the passage from childhood to young adulthood. Bibliographies included at end of each article. Cross-references. Subject index. 'Highly recommended' (*Library Journal*,, 15 May 1991. p.77). *Class No:* 301.18-053.7

Aged People

[450]

Directory of services for elderly people in the UK. Lodge, K., *ed.* Harlow, Essex, Longman and Public Service Management in collaboration with the Centre for Policy on Aging, 1990. xxxvi,236p. (*Community information guides.*) ISBN: 0582055121.

Aims to bring together information on organizations which provide care, support and facilities for the elderly. Arranged in 7 sections, with full contact details. Index. *Class No:* 301.18-053.9

[451]

MADDOX, G.L., *and others.* **The Encyclopedia of aging.** New York, Springer Publishing Co., 1987. 890p. illus., tables. ISBN: 0826148409.

Concise, descriptive articles on *c.*500 subjects in the field, including biological, psychological and sociological aging, life experience of the elderly. Written for the non-specialist, it lists references to classical and recent works. Over 200 contributors from academic, medicine and health-related agencies. Entries, arranged A-Z, vary in length from 1-7 pages. Cross-references. Bibliography of over 2000 references to sources cited in the text. Comprehensive index. '... an authoritative reference source ...' (*Library journal*, 15 April 1987, p.75). *Class No:* 301.18-053.9

[452]

New literature on old age: a guide to new publications, courses and conferences on aging, 1977- no. 1-. London, Centre for Policy on Aging. 6pa. ISSN: 01402447.

About 100 entries (often briefly annotated) per issue. Covers new books and periodical articles, central and local government reports and circulars, statistical reports, semi-published research documents, and informal publications issued by voluntary groups, Mainly British literature. Cross-references. Headings: General - Attitudes to aging - Women - Health - Physical disability - Falls - Nutrition - Psychology - Mental illness and services to the mentally ill - Alcohol and aging - Social characteristics - Retirement - Education in later life - Leisure - Services - Social work - Income maintenance - Housing - Residential care - Health services - Primary health care - Medications - Community care - Family care - Ethnic minorities - Crime/security/abuse - Reference works - Annual reports. *Class No:* 301.18-053.9

Race Relations

[453]
AMIN, K., *and others*. **Racism and discrimination in Britain:** a select bibliography, 1984-1987. London, Runnymede Trust, 1988. [3], 98p. ISBN: 0902397753.

Lists books, pamphlets, offical reports and journal articles in 12 subject sections, each subdivided and subdivided again by form. Contents: 1. Racism and discrimination - 2. Politics and race - 3. Immigration and nationality - 4. Women, race and racism - 5. Employment and unemployment - 6. Education - 7. Housing and inner city - 8. The Health Service - 9. Social and welfare services - 10. Policing, racial violence and urban disorder - 11. Criminal justice and the legal system - 12. The media. Appendix lists addresses of publishing organizations. Supplements *Racism and discrimination in Britain: a select bibliography,* by P. Gordon and F. Klug, which covered 1970-83. No annotations and no index. *Class No:* 301.18-054

[454]
KALLEY, J.A. **South Africa under Apartheid:** a selected and annotated bibliography. Westport, CT., Meckler, 1989. 544p. ISBN: 088736506x.

1123 references to books and articles produced over the last 30 years, with emphasis on the last decade. Good author index and useful subject index arranged in broad categories. Fuller than S.E. Pyatt's *Apartheid: a selective annotated bibliography, 1979-1987* (Garland, 1990. 160p.), although the latter has an appendix on major South African laws and regulations. *Class No:* 301.18-054

[455]
KLEIN, B.T. **Reference encyclopedia of the American Indian.** 4th ed. New York, Todd Publications, 1986. 2v. ISBN: 0915344068, v.1; 0915344076, v.2.

First published 1967.

V.1 has a series of directories relating to native Americans (government agencies; reservations; museums, monuments & parks; Indian health services, etc.) with minimal information, and also a bibliography of *c.*4000 important books. V.2 is a biographical guide to contemporary American Indians and to non-Indians active in work related to the Indians. *Class No:* 301.18-054

[456]
The **Negro almanac:** a reference work on the Afro-American. Ploski, H.A., *and others, eds.* 5th ed. Boston, Mass., Gale Research, 1989. 1622p. illus., tables, graphs. ISBN: 0810377063.

First published 1967. First 4 eds. published by Wiley Interscience.

A massive compilation of information on all aspects of black life in America and around the world. Treats nearly 500 years of history with an emphasis on the current situation of blacks in American society in 33 chapters. Includes a 100-page chronology of black history to 1989. *Class No:* 301.18-054

[457]
Sage race relations abstracts. London, Sage Publications, on behalf of the Institute of Race Relations, 1975-. v.1-,no.1-. Quarterly. ISSN: 03079201.

Formerly *Race relations abstracts* (1968-74).

Over 1,000 indicative and informative abstracts pa, drawing on books and *c.*200 journals. 33 sections (Bibliographies - Adjustment and integration - Area studies ... Culture and identity ... Education (general, pre-school; further; higher; policy and planning; syllabuses) - Employment ... Housing ... Race relations (general; law and legislation; history and ideologies) ... Young people ... Ephemera. List of journals abstracted. Author and subject indexes. *Class No:* 301.18-054

Hunger

[458]
BALL, N., *ed.* **World hunger:** a guide to the economic and political dimensions. Oxford, Clio Press; Santa Barbara, CA., ABC-Clio, 1981. xxii,386p. 6 charts. (*War/peace bibliography series, no. 15.*) ISBN: 087436308x.

Explains and chronicles the literature of food production and distribution from economic and political perspectives. Items mostly in English. Introductions to the chapters on the major elements of the topic, highlighting particular problems, 'Highly recommended...' (*RQ*, v.21(2), Winter 1981. p.207). *Class No:* 304.9

Social Climate

Developing Countries

[459]
Third world resource directory. Fenton, T.P. *and* Heffron, M.J., *eds.* Maryknoll, N.Y., Orbis Books, 1984. 283p. illus. ISBN: 0883445093.

A guide to organizations and publications. In 3 parts: pt.1. Areas (ch.1. Third world - 2. Africa - 3. Asia and the Pacific - 4. Latin America and Caribbean - 5. Middle East); pt.2. Issues (*e.g.,* 6. Food, hunger, agribusiness - 7. Human rights - 8. Militarism, peace, disarmament - 9. Transnational corporations - 10. Women); pt.3. Indexes (Organizations - Books - Periodicals, pamphlets and articles - Audiovisuals - Audiovisual bibliographies, catalogues and guides - Bibliographies, directories and curriculum resources - Simulated games). 'The book is a guide to resources about the Third World and the United States involvement in the affairs of the Third World nations and peoples' (*Preface*). *Class No:* 308(4/9-77)

Great Britain

[460]
Atlas of British social and economic history since c.1700. Pope, R., *ed.* London, Routledge, 1990. xiii,250p. diagrs., maps. ISBN: 0415056330.

Maps and text illustrating historical development. 12 sections: 1. Agriculture - 2. The textile and chemical industries - 3. Metal, vehicle and engineering industries - 4. Coal, gas and electricity - 5. Transport and trade - 6. Demographic changes, 1901-1981-7. Employment and unemployment - 8. Urbanization and living conditions - 9. Labour movements - 10. Education - 11. Religion - 12. Leisure. Further reading, p.236-45 (by chapter). Detailed, analytical index ('Education': 1 column), p.246-50. 255 diagrs. and maps. A neat production. *Class No:* 308(410)

[461]
The **Cambridge social history of Britain, 1750-1950.** Thompson, F.M.L., *and others, eds.* Cambridge, Cambridge University Press, 1991. 3v. ISBN: 0521257883, v.1; 0521257891, v.2; 0521257905, v.3.

V.1 Regions and communities - v.2. People and their environment - v.3. Social agencies and institutions. Each volume has 6-8 contributions. V.3 includes chapters on education, health and medicine; crime, authority and the policeman's work; religion; philanthropy; clubs, societies and associations. Each volume has bibliographies and an index. *Choice* (v.28(6), February 1991, p.982) considers it serves best as a reference work to be dipped into selectively. A comprehensive index to all three volumes is called for. *Class No:* 308(410)

31 Statistics

Statistics

[462]
'The Economist' book of vital world statistics: a portrait of everything significant in the world today. Smith-Morris, M., *ed.* London, Hutchinson Business Books Ltd., 1990. 256p. tables, map. ISBN: 0091746523.

A view of how countries of the world compare on everything. Sections: Demography - Economic strength - Agriculture and food - Energy - Commodities - Transport and communications - Government finance - Inflation and finance - Trade and balance of payments - Debt and aid - Employment - Education - Health - Family life - Environment. Glossary, p.255. Sources, p.256. *Class No:* 310

[463]
UNITED NATIONS. DEPARTMENT OF INTERNATIONAL ECONOMIC AND SOCIAL AFFAIRS. Statistical Office. **Statistical yearbook/Annuaire statistique, 1987.** 36th ed. New York, UN., 1990. xxii,799p. ISBN: 9210611314.

First published 1949. Continues *Statistical year-book of the League of Nations,* 1926-42/44 (Geneva, 1927-45).

Covers over 200 countries and areas. 139 tables; time series: 1975, 1980-1987 usually. Sections: World summary - 2. General socio-economic statistics (population and manpower; national accounts; wages, prices and consumption; balance of payments; finance; health; education; culture; science and technology; development assistance; industrial property - 3. Statistics of basic economic activity (agriculture, forestry, fishing, industry, mining and quarrying, manufacturing, energy, external trade, transport, communications, international tourism). Sources, notes appended to tables. Annex 1: Country nomenclature; 2. Conversion coefficients and factors. In English and French. Supplemented by *Monthly bulletin of statistics* (1947-). Each issue has *c.*250p. of tables. Special tables feature regularly. A *Supplement* of definitions and notes is issued every few years. *Class No:* 310

[464]
UNITED NATIONS EDUCATIONAL, SCIENTIFIC AND CULTURAL ORGANIZATION. **Unesco statistical yearbook, 1990.** Paris, Unesco, 1990. [*c.*700p.], chiefly tables. ISBN: 9230027081.

First published, 1964. Annual. Continues the biennial *Basic facts and figures* (Unesco, 1952-62).

The 1990 edition covers *c.*200 countries; computer-produced tables. Sections: Reference tables - Education - Educational expenditure - Science and technology - Culture and communications - Libraries - Book production - Newspapers and other periodicals - Cultural paper (*e.g.* newsprint) - Archives - Museums and related institutions - Film and cinema - Broadcasting - International trade in printed matter. *Class No:* 310

[465]
—Unesco statistical digest: a statistical summary of data on education, science and technology, culture and communication, by country, 1988. Paris, Unesco, 1988. xxiv,335p. tables. ISBN: 9230025623.

First published 1982. Annual.

Basic statistics on a country-by-country basis. *Class No:* 310(100)(058)

[466]
World tables, 1991. World Bank. 6th updated ed. Baltimore, MD., Johns Hopkins University Press, for the World Bank, 1991. xvi,655p. ISBN: 0801842520. ISSN: 10435573.

First published 1971.

Collections of economic and social time series data for most countries of the world. Topical pages have 20 tables by subject, subdivided by country with data for 1970-1989 or 1990. Country pages include data on national accounts, foreign trade, balance of payments, external debt, manufacturing, money and fiscal, social indicators. *Class No:* 310

Europe

[467]
HARVEY, J.M. **Statistics Europe:** sources for social, economic and market research. 5th ed. Beckenham, Kent, CBD Research Ltd., 1987. xii, 320p. ISBN: 0900246480.

First published 1969.

2427 entries for Europe as a whole and for individual countries of Europe, both East and West, (*e.g.,* Sweden: p.261-268: Central Statistical Office; Libraries; Libraries and information services abroad; Bibliographies; Statistical publications (nos. 2159-2218). UK: nos. 1167-1553). Data include bibliographical information; time factor; price; pagination. Arranged in 9 subject groups for each country (general, production, external trade, internal distribution and service trades, population, social and political, finance, transport and communications, environment) many subdivided. Indexes of organizations, titles, and subjects. New ed. in progress. *Class No:* 310(4)

Great Britain

[468]
Annual abstract of statistics, 1991. Central Statistical Office. No.127. London, HMSO, 1991. Annual. x,349p. tables. ISBN: 011620446x.

First published 1946. Continues *Statistical abstract,* 1st, 1840/53- 83rd, 1924/38, compiled by the Board of Trade.

The 1991 ed. gives annual figures, so far as available, for 1978-89. 18 chapters: 1. Area and climate - 2. Population and vital statistics - 3. Social conditions - 4. Law enforcement - 5. Education - 6. Employment - 7. Defence - 8. Production - 9. Agriculture, fisheries and food - 10. Transport and communications - 11. Distributive trades.

....(contd.)

Research and development - 12. External trade - 13. Balance of payments - 14. National income and expenditure - 15. Personal income, expenditure and wealth - 16. Home finance - 17. Banking, insurance, etc. - 18. Prices. Sources appended to tables. Index of sources (by chapters), p.334-340. Index. Indispensable for British libraries. *Class No:* 310(410)

[469]
GREAT BRITAIN. CENTRAL STATISTICAL OFFICE. **Guide to official statistics.** 5th ed. London, HMSO, 1986. (Revised in 1990). v,191p. ISBN: 0116203943.

First published 1976.

Meant to cover all official and significant non-official sources published in the last 5 years. Annotated entries; also running commentary. 16 sections: 1. General - 2. Area, climate, environment - 3. Population, vital statistics - 4. Social statistics - 5. Labour - 6. Agriculture - 7. Production industries - 8. Transport - 9. Distribution and other services - 10. Public services - 11. Prices - 12. The economy - 13. General and public finance - 14. Business and financial institutions - 15. Overseas transactions - 16. Isle of Man & Channel Islands. Bibliography (titles, A-Z), p.143-156. Government department contact points (name & address; telephone no.). Alphabetical keyword index (analytical; 'Agriculture': nearly 1 column). *Class No:* 310(410)

[470]
MITCHELL, B.R. British historical statistics. Cambridge, Cambridge University Press, 1988. 886p. 322 tables. ISBN: 0521330084.

Supplants the author's two previous volumes, *Abstract of British historical statistics* and *Second abstract of British historical statistics.*

Contains the major economic and social statistical series for the British Isles from the earliest available, in the 12th century to 1980/81. Tables are grouped under 16 subject headings: Population and vital statistics - Labour force (including wages) - Agriculture - Industry (5 sections) - External trade - Transport and communications - Public finance - Financial institutions - Consumption - Prices - Miscellaneous (inc. crime and education) - National accounts. Subject index. A standard reference work. *Class No:* 310(410)

[471]
MORT, D. Sources of unofficial UK statistics. University of Warwick Business Information Service, *ed.* 2nd ed. Aldershot, Hants., Gower Publishing Co. Ltd., 1990. xi, 413p. ISBN: 056602795x.

First published 1986, compiled by D. Mort and L. Siddell.

A detailed guide to the main unofficial statistical sources in the UK of interest to business and industry. Part 1: The Statistics (Abacus Data Services ... Zinc Development Association). Data on 1077 sources/services (organization; title; coverage; availability; cost; comments; address; telephone number). Part 2: Title index. Part 3: Subject index. Patchy on issues, but excellent annotations, according to a review in *Library Association record,* (v.92(8), August 1991). *Class No:* 310(410)

[472]
Social trends, [no] 22, 1992. Central Statistical Office. London, HMSO., 1992. 255p. diagrs., graphs, tables, maps. ISBN: 0116205016. ISSN: 03067744.

First published 1970. Annual.

Sections: Population - Households and families - Education - Employment - Income and wealth - Expenditure and resources - Health and personal social

....(contd.)

services - Housing - Environment - Leisure - Participation - Law enforcement - Transport. Appendix: definitions and terms. Subject index, p.247-255. *Class No:* 310(410)

[473]
—Key date. Great Britain. Central Statistical Office. 1991/92 ed. London, HMSO, 1991. 110p. illus., charts, tables, maps. ISBN: 0116204508.

Published annually as a student version of *Social trends.* Cover title adds 'UK business and social statistics ...'.

Over 130 tables, maps and coloured charts, accompanied by reference sources. Data is for several years to 1990. Index. Also includes *Government statistics: a brief guide to sources,* p.89-110. *Class No:* 310(410)

USA

[474]
UNITED STATES. BUREAU OF THE CENSUS. Statistical abstract of the United States, 1991. 111th ed. Washington, US Government Printing Office, 1991. xxiv,986p.

First published for 1878. Annual.

*c.*1500 tables and charts arranged in 31 sections: 1. Population ... 3. Health and nutrition ... 9. State and local government finances and employment ... 16. Banking, finance and insurance ... 19. Energy ... 25. Mining and mineral products ... 27. Manufactures - 28. Domestic trade and services ... 29. Foreign commerce and aid ... 30. Outlying areas - 31. Comparative international statistics. 6 appendices: (1. Guide to sources of statistics ... 3. Statistical methodology and reliability). Detailed index, p.936-986. A basic statistical tool. *Class No:* 310(73)

Population

[475]
BOGUE, D.J. The Population of the United States: historical trends and future projections. New York, Free Press, 1985. 728p. tables. ISBN: 0029047005.

An eminently readable portrait of the people of the United States from 1790 to 1980 in 20 chapters. Includes detailed bibliographies, clear definitions of terms, and a guide to obtaining further information. Hundreds of charts, graphs, pie charts, etc. are included. 'An excellent accompaniment to the *Statistical abstract* and *Historical statistics of the United States (Library journal,* 15 April 1986, p.36). *Class No:* 312

[476]
Population index. Princeton, N.J., Office of Population Research (previously School of Public Affairs), for Population Association of America, 1935-. v.1-. Quarterly. charts, tables. ISSN: 00324701.

Fall 1991 issue has 842 indicative, analytical abstracts. Contents include 'Current items' (documented), 'Bibliography': A. General population studies and theories - B. Regional population studies - C. Spatial distribution - D. Trends in population growth and size - E. Mortality - F. Fertility - G. Nuptiality and the family - H. Migration - I. Historical demography and demographic history - J. Characteristics - K. Demographic and economic interrelations and natural resources - L. Demographic and non-economic interrelations - M. Policies - N. Methods of research and analysis including models - O. The production of population statistics - P. Professional meetings and conferences - Q. Bibliographies, directories, and other information services - R. New periodicals - S. Official statistical publications - T. Machine-readable data files. Geographical and author indexes (cumulated annually). A first-class example of an annotated bibliography in a special field, covering periodical articles, monographs, statistical yearbooks and new journals. *Class No:* 312

[477]

UNITED NATIONS. STATISTICAL OFFICE. Demographic yearbook, 1989. 41st ed. New York, United Nations, 1990. x,926p. ISBN: 9210510747.

First published for 1949. Annual.

Returns from over 220 countries or areas. Group 1: Tables published annually (tables 1-25); World summary - Population - Natality ... Infant and maternal mortality ... Divorce. Group 2: Special topic table (tables 26-35) on international migration. Technical notes on the statistical tables. Subject matter index, p.874-926. *Demographic yearbook: historical tables* was published in 1981 (1178p.). *Class No:* 312

Births & Deaths

[478]

ALDERSON, M. International mortality statistics. London, Macmillan; New York Facts on File, 1981. 524p. (380p. of tables). £45. $55. ISBN: 0871965143.

Comparative international data on causes of death during the 20th-century for 33 countries (US, Canada, Australia, New Zealand, Japan, Chile, Turkey, Europe, except Germany) and 178 causes of death. Mainly computer-produced serial mortality tables containing data in the form of age-standardized indexes. Each table devoted to a single cause of death for one sex. Preceded by explanatory material and state-of-the-art reviews on trends in mortality statistics, and on validity of data. Extensive bibliographical citations. *Class No:* 312.1/.2

32 Politics

Politics

[479]
ENGLEFIELD, D. *and* DREWRY, G., *eds.* **Information sources in politics and political science: worldwide.** London, Butterworths, 1984. xviii, 509p. (*Butterworths guides to information sources.*) ISBN: 0408114703.

Aims to be a critical assessment of a large English library on both the study and the practice of the subject (*Preface*). In 4 parts: 1. Resources - 2. Approaches to the study of politics and government - 3. Politics and government: United Kingdom - 4. Politics and government: overseas. The 24 contributors are academics and librarians, and the chapters are essays covering the various aspects of political studies (*e.g.*, political behaviour, political thought, comparative politics), of government, and of politics in the UK and the rest of the world by regions. Subject index, p.503-509. *Class No: 320*

[480]
EVANS, G. *and* NEWNHAM, J. **The dictionary of world politics:** a reference guide to concepts, ideas and institutions. Hemel Hempstead, Herts., Harvester Wheatsheaf; New York, Simon & Schuster, 1991. xiv,449p. ISBN: 0745002749, UK; 0132105276, US.

Over 600 entries, ranging from a few lines to 2 pages, providing information on concepts and institutions essential to an understanding of contemporary politics, including important terms likely to be found only in specialized texts or journals. Cross references. Omits South Africa, Iran and Cambodia. Well-designed and up-to-date. Usable in conjunction with Munro and Day's *A world record of major conflict areas* (*q.v.*). 'An essential purchase for most libraries' (*Library journal*, December 1990, p.116). *Class No: 320*

[481]
HOLLER, F.L. **Information sources of political science.** 4th ed. Santa Barbara, CA., ABC-Clio, 1986. xvii, 417p. ISBN: 0874363756.

First published 1971; 3rd rev. ed. 1981.

2423 annotated citations of printed and computerized reference works in political science and related social sciences and humanities. In 3 parts: Pt. 1 is an extended discussion of the author's political reference theory. Pt. 2 is the main body of the work, with citations covering general references; the social sciences; American government, politics and public law; international relations and organizations; comparative government and area studies; political theory; and public administration. Citations are numbered and listed A-Z within the sections, containing bibliographical information and descriptive annotations of 1-2 paragraphs. Pt.3 has author, title, subject and typology indexes, the latter identifying reference sources by their genre (*e.g.*, abstracts, bibliographies, directories, etc.). 'Every possible type of reference source is included, fully

....(contd.)
annotated, and easily located ... All in all, an indispensible volume for anyone doing political research'. (*College & research libraries*, v.48(1), January 1987, p.69). *Class No: 320*

[482]
International bibliography of political science. British Library of Political and Economic Science, *comp.* London and New York, Routledge 1954-. v.1-. Annual. ISSN: 00852058.

References to books, periodical articles, and documents, arranged in 6 subject sections, each subdivided: A. Political science. General studies and methods - B. Political thought - C. Political systems - D. Political life - E. Government policy - F. International life. Author and subject indexes. V.37: 1987 was published in 1991 (xxvi,316p. ISBN 0415064732). Supported by *Thematic list of descriptors: political science, 1989* (Routledge 1989. 480p. ISBN 0415017785) and updated in *International current awareness service ...* (*q.v.*). *Class No: 320*

[483]
People in power. Harlow, Essex, Longman Group, 1987. 1v. loose-leaf. ISBN: 0582017831.

A directory of the current political leadership in the sovereign countries of the world. Arranged by country, A-Z, outlines the current political system, including details of the head of state, full composition of the cabinet or council of ministers, and, where relevant, the leadership of the ruling party, ruling council, or military junta. Name and address of each country's ambassador or high commission in the UK also included. *Class No: 320*

[484]
Political handbook of the world, 1990. Annual. Banks, A.S., *ed.* 62nd ed. Binghamton, N.Y., C.S.A. Publications, for Center for Education and Social Research, State University of New York, 1990. 956p. ISBN: 0933199066. ISSN: 0193175x.

First published in 1927 as *Political handbook of Europe.* Title varies. Until recently, sponsored by the Council on Foreign Relations.

Covers government and intergovernmental organizations as of March 1988 (with major political developments noted to 1 Jan 1990). Reports for each country include general data, the constitution, foreign relations, current issues, political parties, the legislature, the cabinet, news media, and inter-governmental representation of each country. A second part deals with intergovernmental organizations, including their history, structure, activities, official and/or working languages. Appendices: A chronology of major events, 1945-1989. Chart showing membership of the United Nations and agencies. A convenient source for quick reference. *Class No: 320*

[485]
YORK, H.E. **Political science:** a guide to reference and information sources. Englewood Cliffs, Co, Libraries Unlimited Inc., 1990. 249p. (*Reference services in the social sciences, 4.*) ISBN: 0872877949.

650 evaluative as well as descriptive entries, 80-200 words each, arranged in 6 chapters. Sources include databases, periodicals and organizations. Author, title and subject indexes. 'This is an easily accessible, well-developed tool' (*Choice*, v.28(9), May 1991, p.1471) '... first choice guide for introducing students to political science reference literature and for evaluating political science reference collections' (*Wilson library bulletin*, v.65(8), April 1991, p.121). *Class No:* 320

Quotations

[486]
BAKER, D.B., *ed.* **Political quotations.** Detroit, Mich., Gale Research International Ltd, 1990. 508p. ISBN: 0810349205.

More than 5000 notable quotations on politics, from antiquity to the present, with emphasis on the 20th century. Author and keyword indexes. '... indisputably useful in its field ...' (*Wilson library bulletin*, v.65(4), December 1990. p.155). *Class No:* 320(082.2)

Europe

[487]
COOK, C. *and* PUGH, G. **Sources in European political history.** London, Macmillan Press, 1987-90. 3v. (749p.). ISBN: 0333239962 v.1; 0333277759 v.2; 0333423690 v.3.

V.1. *The European left;* v.2. *Diplomacy and international affairs;* v.3. *War and resistance* V.1. is a wide-ranging guide to the surviving personal papers of over 1000 individuals active on the European Left during the last century, including anarchists, syndicalists, pacifists, trade unionists, socialists and communists. Arrangement is A-Z (Abate ... Zyromsky), with brief information on the person and notes on the papers. V.2. provides a wide-ranging guide to the surviving private papers of over 1000 statesmen, politicians and diplomats who played a part in the shaping of modern Europe. Each volume includes a select bibliography. *Class No:* 320(4)

Great Britain

[488]
BUTLER, D. *and* BUTLER, G. **British political facts, 1900-85.** 6th ed. London, Macmillan Press Ltd., 1986. xix, 536p. tables. (*Macmillan historical and political facts.*) ISBN: 033339948x.

First published 1963.

23 sections: Ministers - Parties - Parliament - Elections - Political allusions - Civil Service - Royal Commissions, Committees of inquiry and tribunals - Administration of justice - Social conditions - Employment and trade unions - The economy - Nationalisation - Royalty - British Isles - Local government - The Commonwealth - International relations - Britain and Europe - Armed forces - The press - Broadcasting authorities - Religion - Bibliographical note (sources, p.519-522). Analytical index (p.523-536). A valuable compendium of data. 'Itself a national institution' (*TLS*, no.4021, 18 April, p.1148, on 5th ed.). *Class No:* 320(410)

[489]
COOK, C. **Sources of British political history, 1900-1951.** London, Macmillan Press, 1976-85. 6v. ISBN: 0333387899, set; 0333150368, v.1; 0333150376, v.2; 0333150384, v.3; 0333191609, v.4; 0333221249, v.5; 0333265688, v.6.

V.1. *A guide to the archives of selected organizations and societies;* v.2. *A guide to the papers of selected public*

....(*contd.*)
servants; v.3. *A guide to the private papers of Members of Parliament, A-K;* v.4. *...L-Z;* v.5. *A guide to the private papers of selected writers, intellectuals, and publicists;* v.6. *First consolidated supplement.* *Class No:* 320(410)

Asia—Middle & Near East

[490]
SHIMONI, Y., *ed.* **A Political dictionary of the Arab world.** Rev. ed. New York, Macmillan, 1988. 520p. illus., tables, charts, maps. ISBN: 0029164222.

Revised and updated version of *Political dictionary of the Middle East in the 20th century* (1972 & 1974).

600 entries prepared by a team of specialists from Tel Aviv University Centre for Middle Eastern and African Studies. Covers 21 Arab countries. Entries are arranged A-Z on a wide range of subjects from biographies to national political histories, movements and conflicts. 'Generally well researched and documented, the book is a useful tool for a wide ranging audience...' (*Library journal*, 15 February 1988p. p.161). *Class No:* 320(53+56)

Africa

[491]
PHILLIPS, C.S. **The African political dictionary.** Santa Barbara, CA., ABC-Clio, 1984. xxvii,245p. (*Clio dictionaries in political science, 6.*) ISBN: 0874360366.

Over 225 terms grouped in chapters by subject, subdivided A-Z. Each term has a 'definition' and a 'significance' paragraph, highlighting the historical, geographical, economic, sociological, philosophical and religious characteristics. Cross-references. Index. *Class No:* 320(6)

Institutions & Associations

[492]
BOGDANOR, V., *ed.* **The Blackwell encyclopedia of political institutions.** Oxford, Basil Blackwell Ltd., 1987. xvi, 667p. ISBN: 0631338412.

Contains 247 contributions from 13 Western industrialized countries. As well as political institutions, includes entries on many concepts and on deceased key political thinkers. Entries range from short paragraphs to 4-page articles (e.g., 'Civil rights': 3 cols.; 'European Community': 3 cols.; 'Monnet, Jean': 2 cols). Cross-references. Bibliographical references follow most entries. Contributors focus on their own world plus USSR and Eastern Europe. Index, p.647-667. '... the work is valuable because its main stream approach is more extensive and comprehensive than the various political science dictionaries available.' (*Choice*, v.26(1), September 1988, p.74). *Class No:* 320:061:061.2

Political Theory

[493]
The Blackwell encyclopaedia of political thought. Miller, D., *ed.* Oxford, Blackwell, 1987. xiii,570p. ISBN: 0631140115.

350 entries, both substantial articles and brief definitions, analysing concepts in political thought that influence the contemporary world, and outlining the thought of leading political theorists, past and present. Mainly Western traditions. Cross-references. 134 contributors. '... a solid reference work' (*Reference books bulletin*, 1987/88, p.591). *Class No:* 320.001

[494]
SABINE, G.H. **A History of political theory.** 4th ed., rev. Hinsdale, Ill., Dryden Press, 1973. [xvii], 871p. ISBN: 0030803055.

First published 1937.

3 parts: 1. The theory of the city state - 2. The theory of the universal community - 3. The theory of the national state (p.311-849). 36 chapters (35. Communism; 36. Fascism and National Socialism). Each chapter has footnotes and 'Selected bibliography'. Analytical index. Standard text-book, giving acceptable short analyses of major works concerned. *Class No:* 320.001

Internal Relations

Minorities

[495]
World directory of minorities. Minorities Rights Group, *ed.* Harlow, Essex, Longman; Chicago, Ill., St. James Press, 1990. xvi,427p. 29 maps. (*Longman international reference.*) ISBN: 1558620168, US; 0582036194, UK.

Updates the MRG's *World minorities* (Quartermaine House Ltd., Minorities Rights Group, 1977-80. 3v.) and their 80 plus MRG reports.

11 regional groupings, each region introduced by Patrick Thornberry. Within the groups, more than 150 ethnic or radical minorities are listed, A-Z, with a few salient facts (alternative names - location - population - percentage of population - religion - language) in 200-5000 words. Appendices are abstracts from original documents. Index, p.419-427. Essential for locating individual minority groups. *Class No:* 323.1

Resistance & Revolution

[496]
MUNRO, D. *and* DAY, A.J. **A World record of major conflict areas.** London, Edward Arnold Publishers Ltd.,; Chicago, Ill., St. James Press, 1990. [vi],374p. maps. ISBN: 0340522976.

'The purpose is to describe and elucidate, in an easy reference format, some 28 current conflicts in different parts of the world' (*Preface*). Arranged in 5 regions (1. Africa - 2. Middle East - 3. Asia/Far East - 4. Americas - 5. Europe), each subdivided by country. Chapters on specific conflicts follow a standard structure, beginning with a map and profile of the relevant country or territory, historical background, current status of conflict with chronology of events, followed by directory sections. General bibliography. p.374. *Class No:* 323.2

Terrorism & Persecution

[497]
THACKRAH, J.R. **Encyclopedia of terrorism and political violence.** London, Routledge & Kegan Paul, 1987. xi, 308p. ISBN: 0710206593.

Designed to provide information about theories and terms used in the rapidly growing academic study of terrorism and political violence. 200 entries of which about half focus on specific events, individuals, groups and nations. Virtually all entries relate to the post-World War II era, and vary in length from about 500 to 1000 words. Arranged A-Z (Abu Nidal ... Zimbabwe African People's Union (ZAPU). References and select bibliography of books and articles from the 1970s to 1986, with 'see also' references also after entries. Index, p.295-308. '... will be of use to researchers studying terrorism and to anyone trying to make some sense of terrorist activities reported in the daily press'. (*Reference books bulletin,* 1 March 1988, p.1119). *Class No:* 323.28

Elections

[498]
MACKIE, T.T. *and* ROSE, R. **The International almanac of electoral history.** 3rd complete rev. ed. London, Macmillan, 1990. [9], 448p, tables. ISBN: 0333452798.

First published 1974.

Sections on 24 countries (1. Australia since 1901 ... 23. United Kingdom since 1828; 24. United States of America since 1828). 19 of the countries are in Western and Northern Europe; the others are Australia, Canada, Israel, Japan, New Zealand and US. The section on Italy (p.216-227) contains a brief history, political parties in Italy, 1895-1979, data on elections, 1895-1979, statistics of total votes, party votes, number and percentage of seats won; 9 tables in all. Sources are cited at the end of each section. *Class No:* 324

Colonial Administration

[499]
Colonialism in Africa, 1870-1960. Stanford, CA., Hoover Institution on War, Revolution and Peace, 1969-75. 5v. tables, maps. ISBN: 0521073731, v.1; 052107732x, v.2; 052107844x, v.3; 0521086418, v.4; 0521078598, v.5.

1: *The history and politics of colonialism. 1870-1914;* edited by L.H. Gann and P. Duignan. 1969. 532p. 2: *The history and politics of colonialism, 1914-1960;* edited by L.H. Gann and P. Duignan. 1970. 563p. 3: *Profiles of change: African society and colonial rule;* edited by V. Turner, 1971. 455p. 4: *The economics of colonialism;* edited by P. Duignan and L.H. Gann. 1975. 719p. 5: *A bibliographic guide to colonialism in sub-Saharan Africa,* by P. Duignan and L.H. Gann. 1973. 552p. V.5 (2,516 entries) ranges over anthropology, law, literature, medicine, natural science, politics and religion, as well as including *c.2,000* items, arranged by colonial power, region and colony. General introductory section (*c.*300 entries) on general reference material, bibliographies, etc. Index of authors, titles, organisations, agencies, colonies and main geographical areas. Includes an amount of non-English language material. 'In all this is a scholarly work which will be invaluable to anyone studying Africa over the last hundred years' (*International affairs,* v.50, no.3, July 1974, p.517). *Class No:* 325.3

Slavery

[500]
MILLER, J.C. **Slavery:** a worldwide bibliography, 1900-1982. White Plains, NY, Kraus International Publications, 1985. xxvii, [1], 451p. ISBN: 0527636592.

5177 consecutively numbered entries grouped in 11 sections (General and comparative; North America; Spanish mainland; Brazil; Caribbean; Africa; Muslim; Ancient; Medieval and early modern Europe; other areas; the slave trade). Includes books, chapters in books, journal articles, and doctoral dissertations, mainly in Western European languages. No annotations. Author index, p.391-423. Subject/keyword index, p.425-451. Annual supplements planned for publication in the journal *Slavery and abolition.* *Class No:* 326

[501]
SMITH, J.D., *comp.* **Black slavery in the Americas:** an interdisciplinary bibliography, 1865-1980. Westport, CT., Greenwood Press, 1982. 2v. (1847p.). ISBN: 0313231184.

15667 unannotated citations arranged in 25 chapters (*e.g.,* African background, slave trade, geography, economics, Indian slave owners, conditions of slave life, family, religion, culture, resistance). Author and subject indexes (subject index weak: needs sub-divisions). 4394 cross-references. A massive bibliography, but computer-printout is

....(contd.)

difficult to read, however '... will surely be the most comprehensive compilation on slavery for a long time to come'. (*Choice*, v.20(10), June 1983, p.1438). *Class No:* 326

Foreign Relations

[502]

International affairs. Guildford, Surrey, Butterworths (previously Oxford University Press), for the Royal Institute of International Affairs, 1922-. v.1, no.1-. Quarterly. ISSN: 00205850.

About a quarter in each issue comprises review articles, book reviews, 'Other books received' and an author index of books reviewed. V.67(4), October 1991 has 6 main articles, plus 126 signed book reviews (p.769-845) in sections: International relations and organizations - Defense and disarmament - Politics, social issues and law - Economics - Energy and environment - History - Western Europe ... Latin America and the Caribbean - Bibliography and reference. 'Other books received'.

Cumulative index, 1922-76 to *International affairs*, edited by L. Adolphus and F.L. Kent (Abingdon, Oxford, Learned Information (Europe), 1978. 78p. ISBN 0904933121) is noted. *Class No:* 327

[503]

PLANO, J.C. *and* **OLTON, R. The International relations dictionary.** 4th ed. Santa Barbara, CA., ABC-Clio, 1988. xxiii,446p. ISBN: 0874364779, US; 058203096x, UK.

First published 1969 by Holt, Rinehart & Winston Inc., New York.

A 'Guide to major concepts' (p.xiii-xxiii) precedes the 12 subject chapters of the dictionary: 1. Nature and role of foreign policy - 2. Nationalism, imperialism and colonization - 3. Ideology and communication - 4. Geography and population - 5. International economics - 6. War and military policy - 7. Arms control and disarmament - 8. Diplomacy - 9. International law - 10. International organizations - 11. American foreign policy - 12. Patterns of political organization. For each there is a paragraph of definitions and one headed 'significance'. 570 entries in all, ranging in length from a half page to a page. No bibliographies. Index, p.423-446. *Class No:* 327

Great Britain

[504]

ASTER, S., *comp.* **British foreign policy, 1918-1945: a guide to research and research materials.** Wilmington, DE., Scholarly Resources, 1984. 324p. ISBN: 0842021760.

5 main chapters: I. Introduction (provides the historical background, including lists of Secretaries of State and Ambassadors to selected countries) - II. The Foreign Office and foreign policy - III. Research libraries and archives (A. Information and publications; B. General guides, directories, and union lists; C. Manuscript research) - IV. Bibliography of over 1600 selected references (A. General; B. Parliamentary and government; C. Memoirs, biographies; D. Secondary literature; E. Peacemaking and detente, 1918-1933; F. Diplomacy in crisis; G. The approach of war, 1937-1939; H. The Second World War, 1939-1945) - V. Index of authors, editors and compilers, p.301-324. Many entries are annotated. Mainly British publications, but some German and French. 'An important handbook ...' (*Choice*, v.22(5) January 1985, p.657). A revised ed. was published in 1991 (382p. ISBN 0842023100). *Class No:* 327(410)

[505]

The Cambridge history of British foreign policy, 1783-1919. Ward A.W., Sir *and* Gooch, G.P., *eds.* Cambridge, Cambridge University Press, 1922-23. 3v.

....(contd.)

Modelled on the *Cambridge modern history.* A connected narrative based on official documents which gives the history of British foreign policy from the national point of view. Each volume has appendices of supporting documents and chapter bibliographies, and an index. Chapter 8 of v.3 deals with the history of the Foreign Office during the whole period. *Class No:* 327(410)

USA

[506]

FINDLING, J.E. Dictionary of American diplomatic history. 2nd rev. & expanded ed. Westport, CT., Greenwood Press, 1989. xviii,622p. ISBN: 0313260249.

First published 1980.

Attempts to provide 'basic factual information on over 500 persons associated with US foreign policy from the Revolution through 1978, and descriptions or definitions of more than 500 non-biographical items connected with American diplomacy, ranging from crises to catchwords' (*Preface*). Entries average $\frac{1}{2}$p. in length. 5 appendices (A. Chronology of American diplomatic history - B. Key diplomatic personnel listed by presidential administration - C. Initiation, suspension, and termination of diplomatic relations - D. Place of birth - E. Locations of manuscript collections and oral histories). Index, p.591-622. *Class No:* 327(73)

Espionage

[507]

BURANELLI, V. *and* **BURANELLI, N. Spy/counterspy:** an encyclopedia of espionage. New York, McGraw-Hill Book Company, 1982. 361p. ISBN: 0070089159.

Profiles of the major figures and organizations of international intelligence from the Renaissance to the present. Over 400 articles on espionage and related information, arranged A-Z, including biographical sketches of spymasters and spies, descriptions of intelligence organizations, indentification of networks and secret societies, explanations of historical events, clandestine techniques, and vocabulary. Information is authoritative, accurate, complete with dates. Many articles cite suggestions for further reading. Extensive index. *Class No:* 327.84

[508]

O'TOOLE, G.I.A. The Encyclopedia of American intelligence and espionage: from the Revolutionary War to the present. New York, Facts on File, 1988. 539p. ISBN: 0816010110.

Nearly 700 articles arranged A-Z and cross-referenced. Some 70% of entries are biographical and include biographee's full name, birth and death dates, education, and intelligence and non-intelligence careers. Biographical and other sources appended. Remaining entries are on intelligence organizations, major events, techniques and devices, and the role of strategic/tactical intelligence and espionage in both peace and war. Longest article is an 18-page one on the CIA. Extensive subject index. 400-item unannotated bibliography of English-language books, articles and government documents. *Class No:* 327.84

[509]

ROCCA, R.G. *and* **DZIAK, J.J.,** *and others.* **Bibliography on Soviet intelligence and security services.** Boulder, Col., and London, Westview Press, 1985. xi, 203p. (*Westview special studies.*) ISBN: 0813370485.

A guide to Russian activities in intelligence, espionage, propaganda and psychological warfare. Includes 518 English-language sources, some translated Russian-language works, published since the Russian revolution. Sources grouped under 5 main headings (Selective bibliographies and other works; Russian/Soviet accounts; Defector/First-hand

....(contd.)

accounts; Secondary accounts; Congressional and other government documents). Each entry is numbered for reference from the indexes. Detailed annotations. Appendices: Glossary of abbreviations and terms; KGB and GRU leadership; and a chart depicting the growth of Soviet intelligence and security services. Author/source index, p.174-186. Title index, p.187-203. 'Strength lies not in its comprehensiveness ... but in extremely informative analysis provided in the extremely detailed annotations'. (*Choice*, v.23(2) October 1985, p.276). *Class No: 327.84*

Parties & Movements

[510]
BALL, A.R. **British political parties:** the emergence of a modern party system. 2nd ed. London, Macmillan, 1987. xviii, 268p. ISBN: 0333445015.
First published 1981.
A historical account of the development of the modern British party system from its origins to the late nineteenth century, written for students and others with little prior knowledge. 12 chapters in 4 parts: Part 1: The making of the British party system, 1867-1922 - pt.2: The inter-war party system, 1922-40 - pt.3: The party system and consensus politics, 1940-64 - pt.4: The challenge of the two-party system after 1964. Appendices list important dates since 1867, and leaders of British political parties. Select bibliography (subject grouped), p.251-261. Index, p.262-268. *Class No: 329*

[511]
The **Blackwell biographical dictionary of British political life in the twentieth century.** Robbins, K., *ed.* Oxford, Blackwell Reference, 1990. 449p. illus. ISBN: 0631157689.
Main focus is on politicians, but also includes information on the careers of church leaders, writers, the Royal Family, scientists, soldiers and businessmen, including some pre-1900 and Irish figures. Gives guidance on further reading. Has fewer facts than in *Dod's Parliamentary companion* or the *Civil Service yearbook,* but has much more qualitative comment. Full index. *Class No: 329*

[512]
DAY, A.J., *and others.* **Political parties of the world.** 3rd ed. rev. & updated. Harlow, Essex, Longman Group; New York, St. Martin's Press, 1988. x, 776p. (*A Keesing's reference publication.*) ISBN: 0582026261, UK; 0912289945, US.
First published 1980.
A guide to over 2000 political parties (Bangladesh has 127) worldwide, arranged A-Z (Afghanistan ... Zimbabwe), with brief introduction on each country. Little data given for some parties but the aim is to give information on historical development; structure; leadership; membership; policy; publications; international affiliations when available. Appendices on international party organizations. Index of people, organizations & countries, p.649-776. *Class No: 329*

[513]
REES, P. **Biographical dictionary of the extreme right since 1890:** an international biographical dictionary. Hemel Hempstead, Herts, Harvester Wheatsheaf, 1990. xx,418p. ISBN: 0710810199.
Profiles of 500 major figures on the radical right, extreme right and revolutionary right from 1890 to the present, arranged A-Z by surname. Entries include short bibliographies. *Class No: 329*

Socialism

[514]
NICHOLLS, D. *and* MARSH, P., *eds.* **Biographical dictionary of modern European radicals and socialists:** Vol.1: 1780-1815. New York, St. Martin's Press, 1988. 291p. ISBN: 0312019688.
To be in 7 vols.
187 biographies of political radicals who helped to transform Europe's social and political order. 48 contributors. Each biography commences by giving the subject's nationality, occupation, and membership or role in radical groups, then summarizes the subject's life and radical activities, and analyses his/her political philosophy and its relationship to others' ideas, concluding with suggestions of books by or about the person. The biographies are arranged A-Z by name of biographer. '... a high standard ...' (*Wilson library bulletin*, October 1988, p.106). *Class No: 329SOC*

33 Economics

Economics

[515]

Economic titles/abstracts: semi-monthly review (with annual index) providing concise information of interest to business, trade, industry, economic libraries and research institutes. Dordrecht, Netherlands, Martinus Nijhoff, for the Netherlands Foreign Trade Agency EVD of the Ministry of Economic Affairs, 1974-. ISSN: 01665057.

First published 1971 as *The use of economics literature.*

A continuation of *Economic abstracts* 1953-1973) and *Economic titles* (1973).

Compiled by the staff of the Library of the Economic Information Service, the Netherlands Ministry of Economic Affairs. About 500 abstracts per issue, arranged by UDC, of items in more than 1800 of the world's leading economic journals, trade journals, bank letters, and professional journals of all sectors and branches of industry, as well as books, special studies, and reports in the same fields. Bibliographical data for entries is 1-4 keywords in English and an abstract in the original language of the publication. Analytical subject index in each issue and cumulative annual subject index. The printed version of the online Foreign Trade & Economic Abstracts database, *Economic abstracts international.* Vendors: Belindis, Data-Star, DIALOG. *Class No:* 330

[516]

FLETCHER, J., *ed.* **Information sources in economics.** 2nd ed. London, Butterworth, 1984. xii, 339p. (Butterworths guides to information sources). ISBN: 0408114711.

First published 1971 as *The use of economics literature.*

24 chapters (2. Libraries and making a literature search - 3. Using the economics library - 4. Reference and bibliographic tools - 5. Periodicals - 6. Unpublished material ... 13. History of economic thought - 14. Economic history - 15. Economic theory ... 19. Labour economics ... 23. International economics - 24. Social economics. Index, p.333-39. British slant. *Class No:* 330

[517]

International bibliography of economics. British Library of Political and Economic Science, *comp.* London and New York, Routledge, 1955-. v.1-. Annual. ISSN: 0085204x.

References to books, periodical articles, and documents, arranged in 15 sections, each subdivided: A. Preliminaries - B. Methods - C. General and basic works - D. History of economic thought - E. Economic history - F. Economic activity - G. Organization of production - H. Production (goods and services) - I. Prices and markets - J. Money and finance - K. Income and income distribution - L. Demand (use of income) - M. Social economics and policy - N. Public economy - O. International economics. Author and subject indexes. V.36: 1987 was published in 1991 (xxxii,450p. ISBN 0415052416). Supported by *Thematic list of descriptors: economics, 1989* (Routledge, 1989. 494p. ISBN 0415017777) and updated by *International current*

....(contd.)
awareness service: economics and related disciplines (November 1990-. Monthly. ISSN 0960152x). *Class No:* 330

[518]

PALGRAVE, R.H.I. **The New Palgrave: a dictionary of economics.** Eatwell, J., *and others, eds.* London, Macmillan Press; New York, Stockton Press, 1988. 4v. (3500p.). ISBN: 0333372352, UK; 0935859101, US.

First published 1894-96 as the *Dictionary of political economy,* reprinted 1984, 1896 & 1899; new ed. published 1923-26 as *Palgrave's Dictionary of political economy.*

The new edition 'like its predecessor, attempts to define the state of the discipline by presenting a comprehensive and critical account of economic thought' (Publisher's note, v.1, p.vii). About 900 scholars participated. *c.*2000 signed entries in the 4 volumes (1300 subject entries and 900 biographical entries). Length of articles varies (*e.g.,* 'Econometrics', 11p.; 'Mathematical economics', 4p.) as do the bibliographies at the end of each article (less than 10 to over 200 items). The biographies, of economists born before 1st January 1916, list both selected works of the biographee and works about him/her. Extensive cross-references. Detailed analytical index, and appendix classifying entries by major subject area. '... succeeeds in its attempt to be a modern treatise on economics. It will undoubtedly become the classic for this century that its predecessor was for the preceding one. However, its scholarly and mathematical approach to the material means its usefulness is limited to serious researchers in economics and related social sciences'. (*Reference books bulletin,* 1st April 1988, p.1320). *Class No:* 330

Dictionaries

[519]

BANNOCK, G., *and others.* **Dictionary of economics.** 4th ed. London, Hutchinson, in association with Economist Books, 1989. 428p. ISBN: 0091743451.

First published 1972.

Comprehensively revised, extended and reset (*Foreword*) Over 1600 entries (definitions and short articles, *e.g.,* 'International liquidity': $1\frac{3}{4}$p.; 'Inflation accounting': 1p.). Biographies included (*e.g.,* 'Keynes': 2p.). Aimed at both the general reader and at students up to the second year of a university course in the subject. Extensive cross-references. *Class No:* 330(038)

[520]

EICHBORN, R., *von.* **Cambridge-Eichborn German dictionary:** economics, law, administration, business, general. Cambridge, Cambridge University Press, 1983. 2v. (xii,1163p.viii,1399p.). ISBN: 0521258456, v.1; 0521258464, v.2.

First published as *Wirtschaftswörterbuch* 1947; later

....(contd.)

editions titled *Der Grosse Eichborn* (Düsseldorf, Econ-Verlag GmbH.).

V.1: English-German; v.2: German-English. About 50,000 main entry words in each volume, the most comprehensive English-German/German-English dictionary of legal, economic, business and administrative terms and phrases available to date. A particular strength lies in the distinctions given between the British and American equivalents of German words and their different usages. Also includes a large number of common or specialized phrases and colloquialisms. *Class No:* 330(038)

[521]
KOHLS, S., *ed.* **Dictionary of international economics:** German, Russian, English, French, Spanish. Leiden, Netherlands, Sijthoff & Noordhoff International Publishers, 1976. 620p. ISBN: 9028605053.

Main part has 6500 German entries, A-Z, with equivalents in the other languages (9700 in Russian, 9300 in English, 9500 in French, & 9400 in Spanish). Indexes in the other languages refer to the German entries. *Class No:* 330(038)

[522]
The Macmillan dictionary of modern economics. Pearce, D.W., *ed.* 3rd ed. London, Macmillan Press, 1986. 472p. (*Macmillan dictionary series.*) ISBN: 033341747x, UK.

First published 1981. *Published in USA by MIT as The MIT dictionary of modern economics.* (3rd ed. ISBN 0262161044 (USA).

Designed for the needs of students of economics, and useful to students of business and the social sciences. Over 2,500 entries and 14 contributors. Entries (A-Z) include biographies (*e.g.,* 'J.M. Galbraith': over $1\frac{1}{2}$ col., including brief summaries of major works. 'International Monetary Fund': $3\frac{1}{2}$ cols.). No bibliographies. Review of the American edition states 'For currency and readability, this work supersedes Douglas Greenwald's 'McGraw-Hill dictionary of modern economics' (3rd ed., 1983) and Douglas A.L. Auld's 'American dictionary of economics' (1983) (*Choice,* v.24 (11/12), July/August 1987, p.1678). *Class No:* 330(038)

[523]
Oriental economist's new Japanese-English dictionary of economic terms. Tokyo, Oriental Economist, 1977. 561,79p.

Earlier eds. published 1970 and 1974.

Both Roman and Japanese characters, with English translations of the terms. Reported to be of high quality. *Class No:* 330(038)

[524]
The World Bank glossary... 3rd rev. ed. Washington, D.C., The World Bank, 1986. 2v. (429 + 360p.). ISBN: 082130819x, v.1; 0821308203, v.2.

Intended to assist the Bank's translators and interpreters, and other Bank staff. Includes terms used in economics and finance plus terminology common in such sections of Bank work as agriculture, education, energy, urban development, public health, transport, etc. Also lists acronyms frequently found in Bank texts and has a list of international, regional and national organizations. *Class No:* 330(038)

Developing Countries

[525]
Dictionary of development: Third World economy, environment, society. Welsh, B.W.W. *and* Butorin, P., *eds.* New York, Garland, 1990. 2v. (lxv,1194p.). ISBN: 0824014472.

V.1: A-I; v.2: I-Index. Introduction and 'Developing countries indicators' (by countries, A-Z, providing economic and statistical data concerning Third World societies and economies) precede the dictionary, which contains short definitions of terms, with origins, plus articles. Profuse cross-references. List of periodicals devoted to development topics, with publishers' addresses, completes the volume. *Class No:* 330(4/9-77)

[526]
Third world economic handbook. Sinclair, S. 2nd ed. London, Euromonitor Publications, 1989. 250p. tables. ISBN: 0863381634.

First published 1986.

Covers major economic developments and opportunities in third world countries and highlights short and long term economic opportunities. Regional analysis over 4 groups (Latin America, West Asia, South Asia, East Asia) is followed by detailed overviews for each country. Includes *c.*150 statistical tables. *Class No:* 330(4/9-77)

Great Britain

[527]
Bank of England quarterly bulletin. London, Economics Department of the Bank, 1960-. ISSN: 00055166.

First published 1960.

Invaluable on the British economy. Includes articles and an annex of statistics, some of which are not available elsewhere. *Class No:* 330(410)

[528]
Who's who in British economics: a directory of economists in higher education, business and government. Sturges, P. *and* Sturges, C., *eds.* Aldershot, Hants, Edward Elgar Publishing Ltd., 1990. ix,627p. ISBN: 185278105x.

For each name included gives address, post, qualifications, offices, expertise, publications, the information provided by the people themselves. Nearly 1700 entries. Subject index, p.563-627. *Class No:* 330(410)

Poverty

[529]
Human resources abstracts. Newbury Park, CA., Sage Publications Inc., 1975-. Quarterly. ISSN: 00992453.

Continues *Poverty and human resources abstracts.* v.1-9, 1966-74. Published with the co-operation of the Institute of Labor and Industrial Relations, University of Michigan and Wayne State University.

About 200 journals, mainly US, are scanned and each issue contains *c.*250 abstracts of journal articles, books and reports on employment and related topics such as economic structure and planning, labour markets and participation, labour and industrial relations, earnings and benefits, human resources and society, immigration and migration. Broadly classified arrangement in *c.*15 categories. Author and subject indexes in each issue and cumulated annually. 'A reference tool of high quality' (*Reference services review,* v.7(4), 1979, p.70). *Class No:* 330.16

Labour & Employment

[530]

Employment gazette. Department of Employment. London, HMSO., 1971-. tables. Monthly. ISSN: 03095045.

Succeeds *Ministry of Labour gazette* (1893-1968), thereafter as *Employment and productivity gazette* (1968-1970) and *Department of Employment gazette* (1971-1979).

V.100(1), January 1992, includes News brief; Special features (2 items); Questions in Parliament; Labour market data (on centre pages on tinted paper) with information on employment, unemployment, vacancies, industrial disputes, earnings, retail prices, tourism, other facts and figures. Index. *Class No: 331*

[531]

INTERNATIONAL LABOUR OFFICE. Yearbook of labour statistics, 1991. 50th issue. Geneva, ILO., 1991. xvii,1131p. ISBN: 9220073390. ISSN: 00843857.

First published 1936 (for 1935/36).

30 tables, with explanatory notes, in 9 chapters (1. Total and economically active population - 2. Employment - 3. Unemployment - 4. Hours of work - 5. Wages - 6. Labour cost - 7. Consumer prices - 8. Occupational injuries - 9. Strikes and lockouts). Statistics (1970-100) cover 1981-1990. Covers c.180 countries. Appendix includes International standard industrial classification of all economic activities (ISIC) and International classification of occupations (ISCO). References and sources, p.1093-1120. Index of countries, territories and areas.

Complemented by data presented each quarter in the *Bulletin of labour statistics.* (ISSN 00074950). *Class No: 331*

[532]

WALTON, F., comp. & ed. The Encyclopedia of employment law and practice. 2nd ed. London, Professional Publishing, 1985. loose-leaf. ISBN: 094655921x.

A guide to aspects of employment legislation in the UK, kept up-to-date by a quarterly amendment service. Main index (31p.) and table of cases (21p.) are followed by the encyclopedia, A-Z (Advisory, Conciliation and Arbitration Service (ACAS) ... Youth training scheme). As an example, the entry for 'Lock-out' is in 6 sections: 1. Definition - 2. Lock-outs as breaches of contracts of employment - 3. Dismissal of lock-out employees - 4. Meaning of 'directly interested' in a dispute - 5. Status of the contract of employment during lock-outs - 6. Action by an employer contemplating a lock-out. *Class No: 331*

Industrial Relations

[533]

GREAT BRITAIN. DEPARTMENT OF EMPLOYMENT. Directory of employers; associations, trade unions, joint organisations, etc. London, HMSO. Semi-annual. ISBN: 0113613210, April 1991 issue.

'Provides comprehensive lists of United Kingdom organizations whose objects include the negotiation of, or making of recommendations on wages and working conditions, or which provide representatives of organizations which are so concerned (*Introduction*). Organizations are grouped according to industries in which they function (SIC 1980 revision). Main sections: Employers' Associations - Trade union federations, trade union and other employees associations - Joint organizations, wages, councils, and arbitration boards, etc. Index. *Class No: 331.1*

[534]

International handbook of industrial relations: contemporary developments and research. Blum, A.A., *ed.* Westport, CT., Greenwood Press; London, Aldwych Press, 1981. xiv, 690p.

....(contd.)
illus., tables. ISBN: 0313213038, US; 0861720105, UK.

27 essays, arranged A-Z by country, attempt 'to describe how workers and managers around the world deal with their problems at the workplace' (*Preface*). Includes both Western European countries and developing countries. 29 contributors. Select bibliography on comparative industrial relations. Index, p.679-696. *Class No: 331.1*

Salaries & Wages

[535]

New earnings survey. Department of Employment. London, HMSO, 1968-. Annual. 6 parts each year. ISSN: 02620553.

Contents: A: Streamlined and summary analyses. Description of the survey; B: Analysis of agreement; C: Analysis of industry; D: Analysis by occupation; E: Analysis by region. Analysis by age group; F: Distribution of hours. Joint distributions of earnings and hours. Analysis of earnings and hours for part-time women employees. *Class No: 331.2*

Occupations & Careers

[536]

Careers encyclopedia. Segal, A., *ed.* 13th ed. London, Cassell, 1991. xxiv, 1280p. ISBN: 030431675x.

First published 1952.

Designed to be read to provide a broad general survey of the state of careers and employment, and the related areas of education and training. 11 sections (each subdivided, with appended 'Further reading',and 'Further information'): Academic and vocational qualifications - Academic and vocational studies and where they can lead - The world of work. The information society - Commerce, administration and finance - Creative, cultural and entertainment work - Land- and environment-related work - Central and local government and the armed forces - Manufacturing and production - Professional, scientific and social services - The service industries - Working overseas. 2 appendices: I: Organizations providing further information; II: Higher and further education institutions. Index to advertisers. Index, p.1231-1244. *Class No: 331.5*

[537]

The Directory of jobs and careers abroad. Lipinski,, A., *ed.* 7th ed. London, Vacation work, 1989. x,342 p. ISBN: 1854580132. ISSN: 01433482.

First published 1971.

In 3 parts: The general approach (Discovering your employment potential - Getting the job - Rules and regulations - Learning the language - Preparation and follow-up - Home letting) - Specific careers (17 sections, all subdivided) - Worldwide employment (by regions, subdivided by country; contacts; etc.). 5 appendices, including a Bibliography (p.327-328); Application procedure; Worldwide taxation; Worldwide living standards; Key to company classifications. Index to organizations, p.336-341. *Class No: 331.5*

[538]

Occupations, 92. Davies, K. Sheffield, Careers and Occupational Information Centre (COIC), 1990. 634p. ISBN: 0861106059.

Entries for c.600 jobs and careers, with information on the work involved, the work environment, pay and conditions, vacancies, prospects for promotion, entry requirements, training courses, and address for further information. Subject index. *Class No: 331.5*

Trade Unions

[539]
PELLING, H. **A History of British trade unionism.** 4th ed. London, Macmillan Press Ltd., 1987. xiii, 344p. 8 illus., 1 table. ISBN: 0333442857.

First published 1963.

A standard work, revised and updated to take account of recent research and to explain the course of events up to the 1980's. In 3 main parts: 1. The emergence of trade unions; 2. The consolidation of labour; 3. Problems of national integration. A statistical table covering the years 1893-1985 has numbers of trade unions, members, affiliations to the TUC, stoppages, and working days lost. Further reading (p.322-333) is in 3 sections: 1. General; 2. Histories of individual unions; 3. Additional sources for particular topics (by chapters). There is a detailed index (p.335-344). *Class No:* 331.881

[540]
Trade unions of the world, 1992-93. Upham, M., *ed.* 3rd ed., rev. & updated. Harlow, Essex, Longman Group, 1991; (distributed by Gale Research Co., in US and Canada). viii, 579p. (*Longman current affairs.*) ISBN: 0582081947, UK.

First published 1987.

An international guide to trade unions and their activities. Arrangement is by country and territory, and for each there is background information, a discussion of trade unionism there, and full details of the central trade unions and other unions active there. For each trade union the information given includes the original and English translation of title; address; leadership; telephone, fax., telex, cable numbers; history and character; structure; publications; and international affiliations. A separate section gives information on international organizations. There is also a select index of acronyms, and an index of trade union organizations. 'A handy compendium of basic information on the worldwide status of the labor movement' (*Choice*, v.25(7), March 1988, p.1072, review of the first edition). *Class No:* 331.881

Land & Property

[541]
Webster's new world illustrated encyclopedic dictionary of real estate. Gross, J.S., *ed.* 3rd ed. Englewood Cliffs, N.J., Prentice-Hall, 1987. 418p. illus. ISBN: 0139473181.

Previous ed. was *Illustrated encyclopedic dictionary of real estate.*

Includes a 251-page dictionary and 165-page portfolio of real estate forms. Entries in the dictionary are for real estate jargon, construction terms, and legal terminology for the layman; they vary in length from a sentence to a third of a page, and many have simple line-drawings for illustration. US-slanted. *Class No:* 332

Property Market

[542]
Property information source book, 1989. Moody, M., *comp.* London, Estates Gazette Ltd., 1988. 128p. ISBN: 0728201275.

'... identifies and describes reports, surveys and services which contribute to our knowledge about the way the communal property market works, and how it performs'. (p.5). 14 sections: Office markets; Detail markets; Industrial markets; Leisure; Agriculture; Topical issues; Property finance and investment; Independent research companies; Online databases and information services; Marketing services and the players in the market; Property law; Auctions; Property press surveys; the Development Corporations. No index. *Class No:* 332.72

Business Relationships & Organization

[543]
BALL, S. **The Directory of international sources of business information.** London, Pitman/Longman Group, 1989. vi,698p. ISBN: 0273030477.

Arranged in 3 main sections: country data sources; industry data sources; online data bases; preceded by an introduction and a section on European business information brokers and Euro-Info centres. The section on country data sources covers 29 countries, mostly European, arranged A-Z, with each entry including stock exchange members, chambers of commerce, embassies, major government offices devoted to commerce, and sources of statistics. The industry data sources section is arranged in 11 broad industrial groups, listing major international associations dealing with each group, directories, market research services, and journals. 4 appendices (1. Publishers of market research reports - 2. Data base hosts and producers - 3. Data base country coverage - 4. International telephone codes, etc.). 'The descriptions are well-written and provide sufficient information for users to make basic evaluative decisions' (*Choice*, v.27(2), October 1989, p.278). *Class No:* 334.7

[544]
Kelly's business directory, 1992. 105th ed., redesigned and updated. East Grinstead, W. Sussex, Reed Information Services Ltd, 1991. xlv,2251p. ISBN: 0610006304. ISSN: 02699265.

Over 84000 industrial, commercial and professional organizations in the UK are listed. Arranged in 4 sections: Reader reply section (reply paid cards for product literature); Classified section (with details of manufacturers, merchants, wholesalers and firms offering an industrial service, arranged under classified trade and professional headings); Oil and gas industry section (arranged similarly); Company information section (companies listed A-Z, with trade description, address and telecommunications details). *Class No:* 334.7

[545]
Kompass United Kingdom: register of British industry and commerce, 1991/92. East Grinstead, Reed Information Services, in association with the Confederation of British Industry (CBI), 1991. 4v. ISBN: 0862682134.

First published 1962. Annual.

Lists manufacturers, suppliers, distributors, products and services. V.I has *c.*41,000 different products and services offered by British industrial companies; v.II. Corporate information on 42,000 leading companies in British industry; v.III. Financial information, taken from last 3 years filed accounts on *c.*30,000 companies; v.IV. Details of 100,000 parents and their subsidiaries, showing their corporate structure. Also available on CD-ROM. *Class No:* 334.7

[546]
TUDOR, J. **Macmillan directory of business information sources.** 2nd ed. London, Macmillan Publishers, 1989. xi,464p. ISBN: 0333489829.

First published 1987.

A compendium of sources and resources: How to use this book; Finding business information; Directory of business information sources and centres; Foreign trade organizations of the UK (A-Z); British trade publications and their editorial offices (subject arrangement); Alphabetical indexes to Standard Industrial Classification (SIC codes) and organization sources (both of these serve as indexes); and main directory, arranged by subject (SIC), subdivided by UK and European sources and information centres, with names, addresses, telephone numbers, contacts, and brief indication of activities in some entries. *Class No:* 334.7

Dictionaries

[547]

Harrap's dictionary of business and finance. London, Harrap Ltd., 1988. [5],369p. ISBN: 0245545719, HB; 024554⌣60x, pbk.

'... concentrates on words and phrases in everyday business usage, and endeavours to make clear not only their meaning, but also, where appropriate, the way in which they are used'. (*Preface*). *Class No:* 334.7(038)

[548]

Harrap's five-language business dictionary. Angerer, M., *and others.* London, Harrap, 1991. 448p. ISBN: 0245603476.

Arranged in one A-Z sequence, the dictionary has 20,000 key business words from English, French, German, Italian and Spanish. *Class No:* 334.7(038)

[549]

Law and commercial dictionary in five languages: definitions of the legal and commercial terms and phrases of American, English and civil law jurisdictions. English, German, Spanish, French & Italian. Epstein, R., *ed.* St. Paul, MN, West Publishing Company, München, Beck, 1985. 2v. (xvi,885p.; xvi,899p.).

One volume has a pronunciation guide followed by the dictionary, A-J; the other continues the dictionary, K-Z and includes a list of legal abbreviations. Entries are for the English terms and phrases, with definitions, with the German, Spanish, French and Italian equivalents listed below. Includes terms related to systems in the other four countries. '... most unusual, but most practical ...' (*International journal of legal information,* v.15(5 & 6), p.77). *Class No:* 334.7(038)

Quotations

[550]

A Dictionary of business quotations. James, S. *and* Parker, R., *comps.* London, Routledge; New York, Simon & Schuster, 1990. vii,172p. ISBN: 0415020301, UK; 0132101548, US.

Over 2500 quotations from across the globe, for browsing and reference. Arranged by 215 topics, A-Z (Accounts ... Workers). Includes 'see-also' references under topic headings. Very wide coverage. Index of authors and sources. Index of keywords. *Class No:* 334.7(082.2)

Private Firms

[551]

Macmillan's unquoted companies, 1992. ICC Business Publications Ltd., *comp.* London, Macmillan Press, 1992. 2v. (xxiii,826;x,823p.). ISBN: 0333564014, set. ISSN: 02674378.

V.1: A-I; v.2: M-Z. Alphabetical listing of the top 20,000 companies. Include only companies with individual turnovers in excess of £3m. pa., and data reflects a 3-year trading period with individual sector performance tables to enable comparisons between companies. Geographical and SIC index. *Class No:* 334.722

Multinationals

[552]

Macmillan directory of multinationals. Stafford,, D. *and* Purkis, R., *eds.* New ed. London, Macmillan, 1989. 2.v. (1500p.). ISBN: 0333483863.

Information on 450 industrial companies with global turnover in excess of £1 billion. Company profiles include name, address, directors, structure, products and services, background and current situation, 5-year financial summary, major shareholders, principal subsidiaries and affiliates. *Class No:* 334.726

Small Businesses

[553]

The London Business School small business bibliography. Edwards, H. *and* Hughes, D., *eds.* 1989 ed. London, London Business School Library, 1990. xii,153p. ISBN: 0902583204.

First published 1980.

A listing of *c*.1500 items, adding to the 12,000 collected in the five previous volumes. Arranged in 3 main parts: Part 1. Literature review on employment and unemployment relations in the small enterprise. Part 2. Subject bibliography in 15 sections, mostly subdivided (1. Entrepreneurship - 2. Starting new businesses - 3. Managing the on-going small business - 4. Business policy and organizational development - 5. Education, training, information, advice and consultancy. 6. Financing the small business ... 11. Particular types of small business - 12. Employment and small business ... 14. The small firm and its environment in the UK - 15. The small firm and its environment in other countries). Part 3. Author bibliography. Appendices: List of journals from which articles have been included; List of institutions. *Class No:* 334.746.4

[554]

MORGANO, M. How to start and run your own business. 7th ed. London, Graham & Trotman, 1989. vii,158p. (*Better business series.*) ISBN: 1853332887.

A practical handbook of essential advice and information. 11 chapters: 1. Making a start - 2. Investigating the market - 3. Finding start-up money and using it effectively - 4. Getting the business going - 5. Taking professional advice - 6. Sales and marketing - 7. Exporting - 8. Planning and financial control - 9. Obtaining further finance - 10. The importance of people - 11. Growing larger. Useful addresses. Appendix: Budget update. Index, p.155-158. *Class No:* 334.746.4

Finance

[555]

CROPLEY, J. Directory of financial information sources. London, Woodhead-Faulkner, 1991. xii,308p. ISBN: 0859415643.

Each entry provides data on institutions, databases and publications. Arrangement is in 10 sections, mostly subdivided: 1. The financial scene - 2. Markets - 3. Financial institutions and credit operations - 4. Corporate institutions and operations - 5. Investment media - 6. Trade - 7. Law and regulations - 8. Economics - 9. People, systems and services - 10. Addresses. Author and title index, p.264-302. Subject index, p.303-308. *Class No:* 336

[556]

Financial statistics. Central Statistical Office. London, HMSO, 1962- no.1-. tables. Monthly. ISSN: 0015203x.

Prepared in collaboration with the Statistics Divisions of government departments and the Bank of England.

Brings together key financial and monetary statistics of the United Kingdom. 14 sections: 1. Financial accounts ... 3. Central government ... 6. Banks and building societies - 7. Other financial institutions - 8. Companies - 9. Personal sector - 10. Overseas sector ... 13. Exchange rates, interest rates and security prices - 14. Sectoral balance sheet. Supplementary tables. data and information (for figures in CSO databank). Index. *Financial statistics: explanatory handbook* is published annually. *Class No:* 336

[557]

GARNER, P., *and others, eds.* **Financial management handbook.** 3rd ed. Brentford, Middx., Kluwer Publishing Ltd., 1988. Loose-leaf, with updates. ISBN: 0903393336.

....(contd.)

First published in 1977, edited by G.M. Dickinson and J.E. Lewis.

Part 1: Corporate strategy and financial planning - 2: Evaluation of capital outlays - 3: Financing and dividend policy - 4: Sources of external funds - 5: The management of working capital - 6: Financial control systems and the measurement of performance - 7: Mergers and takeovers - 8: International financial management - 9: Financial management and its economic environment - 10: Using business computers. Each part contains several signed contributions, many by well-known contributors, which include bibliographies. The loose-leaf format is for regular updating. 30-page index. *Class No: 336*

[558]
MUNN, G. G. Encyclopedia of banking and finance. Woefel, C.J., *ed.* 9th ed. New York & London, McGraw-Hill Book Company 1991. xxvi,1097p. tables, charts. ISBN: 0077073940.

First published 1924; 8th ed. 1983.

c. 4200 lengthy entries, in addition to thousands of basic banking, business and financial terms. 'The in-depth entries provide a wealth of valuable information, such as historical background, analysis of recent trends, illustrative examples, statistical data, and citations to applicable laws and regulations (*Publisher's foreword*). Cross-references, but no index to this edition. *Class No: 336*

[559]
ROWLEY, E.E. The Financial system today: understanding financial information. Manchester, Manchester University Press, 1987. ix,228p. tables. ISBN: 0719014875.

A practical guide in 9 sections: 1. British government securities - 2. Measuring share price changes - 3. The retail price index - 4. The European currency unit - 5. Evaluation of a company - 6. London traded share options market - 7. Investment trusts and unit trusts - 8. The markets for foreign currencies - 9. The Eurocurrencies market. Index, p.223-228. Notes follow each chapter and include references. *Class No: 336*

Dictionaries

[560]
AVEYNON, E.A., *ed.* **Dictionary of finance.** New York, Collier-Macmillan, 1988. 486p. illus., tables, charts. ISBN: 0029164206.

Definitions for over 6000 terms in the area of finance and topics relating to finance (*e.g.,* banking, law, marketing, economics). Entries include multiple meanings for many terms. Cross-references. *Class No: 336(038)*

[561]
BANNOCK, G. *and* **MANSER, W. International dictionary of finance.** London, Hutchinson, in association with Economist Books, 1989. 220p. ISBN: 0091743443.

Concerned not only with international finance but with domestic financial matters in major countries, particularly UK and US. Main subjects covered are money markets, commodity markets, securities markets, banking and insurance, and terms and phrases are limited to the specialized terminology of finance. Entries vary in length from 2 lines to ½-page. Cross-references. List of abbreviations precedes the dictionary. 'Comprehensive and concise reference guide for those wanting to be well-informed about the international world of finance' (*British book news,* January 1990, p.38). *Class No: 336(038)*

[562]
DE MUNTER, M. *and* **BAUDUIN, C. Elsevier's fiscal and customs dictionary in five languages:** English/American, French, Dutch, and German. Amsterdam, Elsevier Science

....(contd.)

Publishers, 1988. xxxii,718p. ISBN: 0444428917.

Aimed at theoreticians and practitioners of fiscal law (including customs law), officials of tax administration, etc. 4845 numbered terms (words and phrases) in the English language, followed by French, Dutch and German equivalents. A bibliography (p.xv-xxxi) precedes, with dictionary item numbers in brackets for connection with legal, etc., documents. Includes certain legal and economic as well as purely fiscal terms. Indexes in all 4 languages. *Class No: 336(038)*

[563]
GUNSTON, C.A. *and* **CORNER, C.M. German-English glossary of financial and economic terms.** 8th ed. Frankfurt am Main, Knapp, 1983. xviii,918p.

First published 1953.

About 20,000 main entries, including abbreviations and names of German associations and organizations. Swiss, US, etc. terminology is differentiated. Some explanation of scope of terms. Well spoken of by translators. *Class No: 336(038)*

Public Finance

Accounts

[564]
UNITED NATIONS. DEPARTMENT OF INTERNATIONAL ECONOMIC AND SOCIAL AFFAIRS. Statistical Office. **Yearbook of national accounts statistics, 1988:** main aggregates and detailed tables. New York, United Nations, 1990. 2v. ISBN: 9211613256.

First published 1957. Annual.

International coverage of statistical data on national accounts estimates for 170 countries and areas, giving specific data on gross domestic product, national income and capital transactions, government and consumer expenditures, social security and household funds. One volume devoted to main aggregates; the other to detailed tables. Issued separately is *National accounts statistics: analysis of main aggregates,* presenting in the form of statistical tables, a summary of main national aggregates. *Class No: 336.126*

Taxation

[565]
HART, G. Dictionary of taxation. London, Butterworth, 1981. v, 236p. (*Butterworth's professional dictionaries series.*) ISBN: 040652159x.

Defines about 900 words and phrases, including definitions from the Finance Act, 1981. Entries vary from 2 lines to 2 pages in length, and sources (*e.g.,* Acts, etc.) are given. Cross-referenced. *Class No: 336.2*

Commercial Finance

[566]
GEISST, C.R. A Guide to financial institutions. London, Macmillan, 1987. 144p. tables. ISBN: 033338623x.

Provides a description of the major types of financial institution in both the United States and the United Kingdom, showing the inter-relationship between the major types of institution beginning with international financial institutions, and continuing with commercial banking, investment banking, building associations, life insurance companies and pension funds, and American federal agencies. There is also an 11-page index. *Class No: 336.6*

Capital & Investment

[567]
ROSENBERG, J.M. **The Investor's dictionary.** New York & Chichester, Sussex, John Wiley & Sons, 1986. xii,513p. ISBN: 0471836788.

*c.*8000 terms used by the securities exchange system, the commodity and futures exchange system, and the more recent development in US financial markets, are defined. Also includes commonly-used symbols, acronyms and abbreviations. Cross-references. Many words given multiple definitions based on their utilization in various fields of activity. Short definitions (*c.*2 to *c.*15 lines). '... both current and comprehensive'. (*RQ,* v.26(4), p.517). *Class No:* 336.60

Banking

[568]
PERRY, F.E. **Dictionary of banking.** 3rd ed. revised by G. Klein. London, Pitman Publishing, in association with The Chartered Institute of Bankers, 1988. [4], 356p. ISBN: 0712107657.

First published 1977, by Macdonald & Evans.

A comprehensive dictionary of *c.*7000 words and expressions, including jargon, a wide selection of French and German terms, and many cross-references. Fully updated, and directed towards bankers in any position, with particular emphasis on British bankers serving abroad in one or other countries of the European Community. *Class No:* 336.71

Building Societies

[569]
NORKETT, P. **The Building societies facts file.** Harlow, Essex, Longman Group Ltd., in conjunction with Tekron Publications Ltd., 1987. [4], 232p. ISBN: 0582022363.

Designed to give a complete overview of the financial performance of all building societies in the United Kingdom. Arranged in three categories: large (total assets over £250m), medium (£25m-£250m), and small (under £25m). The societies are ranked according to total assets, and there is a financial data sheet for each, giving annual results for 5 years to 1986 in a standard format for easy comparison, and percentage analyses of income, expenditure and balance sheet items. An appendix lists all societies, A-Z. *Class No:* 336.732

Stock Markets & Exchanges

[570]
The International Stock Exchange official yearbook, 1934-. 1990-1991 ed. London, Macmillan, 1991. vi, 1139. ISBN: 0333517245, UK; 1561590045, US. ISSN: 09536329.

Published by Skinner, 1934-1980; Macmillan 1981. Annual. Title was *The Stock Exchange official yearbook* until 1987.

Contains details of all officially listed securities, fully indexed. Main sections are: The securities market in the UK; Trading, settlement and transfer; Taxation; Trustees; British, Commonwealth, provincial and foreign government securities; Companies and public corporations in alphabetical order; Register of defunct and other companies; List of registrars; Supplement (of late material). Index (p.1125-1139). *Class No:* 336.76

Economic Surveys

[571]
Chisholm's handbook of commercial geography. Entirely rewritten by Sir Dudley Stamp. Blake, G.N. *and* Clark, A.N., *eds.* 20th ed. London & New York, 1980. xxxii,984p. tables, maps.

First published 1889.

4 main sections: 1. General factors affecting the production and distribution of commodities - 2. Circumstances connected with the exchange of commodities (transport, etc.) - 3. Commodities - 4. Regional geography (Europe ... Australia, New Zealand and the Pacific Islands, p.319-905). 6 appendices (1. Distribution maps (13); 3. International trade (statistics); 6. Conversion tables. Analytical index, p.933-84. 106 tables in main text. Standard text-book. *Class No:* 338

[572]
ECONOMIST INTELLIGENCE UNIT. **Country reports.** London, the Unit, 1952-. diagrs., charts, tables.

Early title was *Quarterly economic review series.*

There are reviews for 165 countries, each containing an executive summary; an outlook section on political and economic prospects for the next 12-18 months; a 10-20p. review section analysing political developments, government policies, trends in production and demand, monetary and fiscal conditions, etc.; statistical appendices. Valuable, if expensive, economic digests. *Class No:* 338

[573]
ORGANISATION FOR ECONOMIC CO-OPERATION AND DEVELOPMENT. **OECD economic surveys.** Paris, OECD, 1953-. illus., tables. Annual. ISSN: 03766438.

Previously as *Economic conditions in member and associated countries* and originally part of the O.E.C.D. annual report, 1949-52.

Country surveys, mostly north and western European, but including Japan, US, Canada, Yugoslavia, Turkey, Australia and New Zealand in a full year, although some countries are surveyed every other year (*e.g.,* 17 countries were surveyed in 1989/90). Such published reports are agreed documents, and analyse recent developments and immediate prospects (demand; output; wages and prices; money and capital markets; balance of payments; government policies and the problems facing them. *Class No:* 338

[574]
UNITED NATIONS. DEPARTMENT OF INTERNATIONAL ECONOMIC AND SOCIAL AFFAIRS. **World economic survey, 1991.** New York, United Nations, 1991. xi,239p. ISBN: 9211091209.

First published 1949-. Annual. Initially *World economic report,* a continuation of the League of Nations *World economic survey* (1927-44. 11v.).

9 chapters: 1. The state of the world economy - 2. Trends in global output and policies - 3. International trade - 4. International finance and net resource transfers - 5. Energy - 6. Implications of the transformation in Eastern Europe and the Soviet Union for economic relations among east, west and south - 7. International policy for reducing developing country debt, 1990-1991 - 8. Some economic aspects of military expenditure in the light of the end of the Cold War - 9. Special issues (A. Poverty and the socio-economic attainment of women - B. Environmental accounting and the system of national accounts - C. Selected demographic indicators). Annex: 39 tables. Explanatory notes precede, and sources are given in footnotes. *Class No:* 338

Maps & Atlases

Great Britain

[575]
Oxford economic atlas of the world. Jones, D.B., *ed.* 4th ed. London, Oxford University Press, 1972. viii, 239p. tables, maps. ISBN: 0198941064.

Prepared by the Cartographic Department of the Clarendon Press, and first published 1954.

91p. of maps in colour. 13 sections: Environment - Crops - Livestock - Forestry and fishing - Fibres and textiles - Energy - Minerals and metals - Transport industries - Manufacturing industries - Demography - Disease - Society and politics - Surface and air communications. Index-gazetteer of *c.*4000 names of places and specific sites (*e.g.*, mines, dams). Statistical supplement, p.117-239): countries, A-Z; statistics largely for 1963-65, with 1953-9 comparisons. Page size, 37.5 x 28.5 cm. Oxford regional economic atlases: *Western Europe* (1971. 162p.);*U.S.S.R. and Eastern Europe* (New ed., 1971. 140p.); *India and Ceylon* (1953. 141p.); *Pakistan* (1955. 142p.); *Middle East and North Africa* (1960. 143p.); *Africa* (1971. 230p.); *United States and Canada* (2nd ed. 1975. 176p. *Class No:* 338(084.3)

Histories

[576]
The Cambridge economic history of Europe. Cambridge, Cambridge University Press, 1941-89. 8v. in 9v. illus., tables, maps. ISBN: 0521045053, v.1; 0521087090, v.2; 0521045061, v.3; 052104507x, v.4; 0521087104, v.5; 0521045088, v.6; 0521215900 & 0521215919, v.7-2 vols; 0521225043, v.8.

1: The agrarian life of the Middle Ages (2nd ed. 1966) 2: Trade and industry in the Middle Ages (2nd ed. 1987) 3: Economic organization and policies in the Middle Ages 1963) 4: The economy of expanding Europe in the sixteenth and seventeenth centuries (1967) 5: The economic organization of early modern Europe (1977) 6: The industrial revolutions and after: incomes, population and technical change (1965) 7: The industrial economies: capital, labour and enterprise. 1. Britain, France, Germany and Scandinavia (1978) 2. The United States, Japan, and Russia (1978) 8: The industrial economies: the development of economic and social policies (1989). Originally planned by Sir John Clapham and Eileen Power, aiming to provide an authoritative survey of an aspect omitted from the Cambridge medieval and modern histories. Terminal date is mid-20th century. *Class No:* 338(091)

Europe

[577]
UNITED NATIONS. ECONOMIC COMMISSION FOR EUROPE. Economic survey of Europe, 1990-1991. New York, United Nations, 1991. ix,255p. tables, map. ISBN: 9211165083. ISSN: 00708712.

First published for 1946/47. Annual.

5 chapters: 1. The transition economies in 1990-1991: an overview - 2. Macro-economic developments and outlook - 3. International economic relations - 4. The hard road to market economy: problems and policies - 5. Explaining unemployment in the market economies: theories and evidence. 6. Statistical appendices (A. Western Europe and North America; B. Eastern Europe with the Soviet Union; C. International trade and payments). Tables and charts throughout. Data for 1990. Kept up-to-date by the *Economic Bulletin for Europe* (1948-. Quarterly). *Class No:* 338(4)

[578]
FLOUD, R. *and* **MCGLOSKEY, D.,** *eds.* **The Economic history of Britain since 1700.** Cambridge, Cambridge University Press, 1981. 2v. (xvii,485p.;xv,323p.). tables. ISBN: 0521298423, v.1; 0521298431, v.2.

V.1. 1700-1860; v.,2 1860 to the 1970s. V.1 has 13 chapters in 5 overlapping chronological divisions corresponding to the periods 1700-1800, 1780-1860, 1860-1914, 1900-1945, 1945 to present day. Each division, except the last, begins with a general survey followed by a number of chapters which consider the main problems which have arisen in the historical interpretation of that period. Each division, except first and last, conclude with chapters dealing with the social history of the period in relation to economic change. V.2 has 16 chapters for the earlier years, following the same pattern. Both volumes have bibliographies, indexes and glossaries. *Class No:* 338(410)

[579]
MORT, D., *comp.* **The Counties and regions of the United Kingdom:** a statistical and economic review. Warwick Statistics Service. Rev. ed. Aldershot, Hants., Gower Publishing Company Ltd., 1988. 224p. ISBN: 0566027550.

First published 1983.

A study of the main demographic, economic and employment trends in the 54 countries of England and Wales, the 12 regional and island areas of Scotland and Northern Ireland and its districts. Provides key statistics on population trends and characteristics, district sizes, unemployment, earnings, housing, industrial structure, and local authority expenditure. Bibliography. List of selected libraries/information services. *Class No:* 338(410)

USA

[580]
PORTER, G., *ed.* **Encyclopedia of American economic history.** New York, Scribner's, 1980. 3v. (xii,1286p.). ISBN: 0684162717.

In 5 sections: 1. The historiography of American economic history - 2. The chronology of American economic history - 3. The framework of American economic growth - 4. The institutional framework - 5. The social framework. Includes 72 interpretative and signed articles (e.g., on slavery, prices and wages, the automobile, immigration, women). Glossary. Comprehensive index. 'A superb addition to the reference literature on American economic history' (*RQ,* v.20(1), Fall 1980, p.93). *Class No:* 338(73)

[581]
Survey of current business. US Department of Commerce. Bureau of Economic Analysis. Washington, DC., the Department, 1921-. Monthly. ISSN: 00396222.

Consists of a general survey and articles, with invaluable centre pages on blue-tinted paper - 'Current business statistics'. Each issue carries a detailed subject index to sections and individual series of statistics. *Class No:* 338(73)

Economic Policies & Controls

Economic Development

[582]
Development index. East Kilbride, Glasgow (previously London), Overseas Development Administration, Library Services. 1967-. Monthly.
A list of periodical articles indexed by the Library of the Overseas Development Administration for current awareness. About 150 briefly annotated entries per issue, arranged under topics (*e.g.* Agricultural credit ... Women workers), on Third World countries. The country index is no longer provided. *Class No:* 338.1

[583]
Industrial development abstracts. United Nations Industrial Development Organization (UNIDO), Vienna. New York, United Nations, 1971-. 2-4pa. (*UNIDO industrial information system INDIS.*) ISSN: 03782654.
About 200 indicative abstracts per issue of 'printed publications, such as major studies and reports, publications in series, and selected articles; from the reports and proceedings of expert working groups, workshops and seminars; internal studies; public information series; and reports related to technical assistance'. (*Introduction*). Arranged by computer access number. Subject and personal author indexes precede. *Class No:* 338.1

[584]
International development abstracts. Norwich, Geo Abstracts, 1982-. 6pa. ISSN: 02620855.
Compiled by members of the staff at the Centre for Development Studies, University College of Swansea.
Arranged in 22 subject sections, including urbanization, regional and spacial planning; education and training; international relations, conflict, cooperation and aid; and trade. Worldwide coverage. The annual *International development index* has author, subject and regional indexes. *Class No:* 338.1

Production

[585]
UNITED NATIONS. DEPARTMENT OF INTERNATIONAL ECONOMIC AND SOCIAL AFFAIRS. Industrial statistics yearbook, 1988. 22nd ed. New York, United Nations, 1990. 2v. ISBN: 9211613205 v.1; 9210611373 v.2; 9211613213 set.
First published for 1938/62. Early title was *Growth of world industry* then *Yearbook of industrial statistics.*
V.1. *General industrial statistics*; v.2. *Commodity production statistics, 1979-1988.* V.1. contains general industrial statistics providing the basic country data as well as a selection of indicators showing global and regional trends in industrial activity. V.2. deals specifically with annual statistics of production of individual commodities. *Class No:* 338.3/.4

Tourism

[586]
Travel trade directory. 33rd ed. London, Business Information Services/Morgan-Grampion plc., 1991. viii,824p. ISBN: 0862131197. ISSN: 02681207.
Sections, each starting with A-Z index: Travel agents - Car travel - Coach travel - Sea travel - Media - Air travel - Travel trade information (National tourist and information offices; visa and passport offices; U.K. resort and regional information offices; associations, organizations and societies; national travel association) - Travel trade services - Tour operators - Hotels. *Class No:* 338.48

Trade & Commerce

[587]
MILLARD, P., *ed.* **Trade associations and professional bodies** of the United Kingdom. 10th ed. London, Gale Research International, 1991. ix,420p. ISBN: 0810383853.
First published 1962. First 9 editions by Pergamon Press.
Arranged in 3 parts: 1. Alphabetical list of trade associations and professional bodies 2. (A) Chambers of commerce, trade, industry and shipping; (B) United Kingdom offices of overseas chambers of commerce. Indexes: Subject (p.323-386); Geographic index by town (p.387-420). The Part 1 listing is arranged by name, with address and telephone/telex/fax numbers. A few entries include brief indications of what the organization is or does. *Class No:* 339

[588]
Multilingual dictionary of commercial international trade and shipping terms: English-French-Spanish-German. Branch, A.E., *and others.* London, Witherby, 1990. 255p. ISBN: 0948691905.
Lists some 2200 English terms used in the daily conduct of international trade and commerce with, under each term, the French, Spanish and German equivalents. *Class No:* 339

Businesses

[589]
DERDAK, T., *ed.* **International directory of company histories.** Chicago, Ill., St. James Press, 1987-. To be in 5v. ISBN: 0912289104, v.1; 1558620125, v.2; 1558620591, v.3; 0810398787, v.4; 1558620346, set.
Compiled with the assistance of the Faculty of History, University of Chicago.
Basic information and short company histories for *c.*1250 leading companies in the United States, Canada, Great Britain, Europe and Japan, arranged A-Z by business category (Advertising ... Utilities). Each entry is about 1500-3000 words in length and includes basic information (Headquarters, capitalization, subsidiaries, etc.) and a company history written by a trained historian. *Class No:* 339.1

[590]
The Directory of directors ... a list of the directors of the principal public and private companies in the United Kingdom, with the names of the concerns with which they are associated, 1992. 113th ed. East Grinstead, West Sussex,Reed Information Services Ltd., 1992. 2v. ISBN: 0611007908.
First published 1880.
V.1 lists *c.*59,000 directors, A-Z, the name being followed by companies of which the person is a director. V.2 lists *c.*16,000 companies and *c.*85,000 board members. Company information includes name, subject, address, telephone number, telex number, parent company, directors, date of accounts, financial data showing up to 3 years of accounts. *Class No:* 339.1

[591]
Major companies of Europe, 1991/92. 11th ed. London, Graham & Trotman, 1991. 3v. (1030; 360; 380p.). (*Major companies of the world series.*) ISBN: 1853335975, set; 1853335983, v.1; 1853335959, v.2; 1853335967, v.3. ISSN: 0266934x, v.1; 02684667, v.2; 02684675, v.3.
First published 1980.
A directory of 8000 of Europe's largest companies. V.1: Major companies of the Continental European Community; v.2: Major companies of the United Kingdom; v.3: Major companies of Western Europe outside the European Community. Data includes addresses; telephone/cable/telex/

....*(contd.)*

fax numbers; board of directors; senior executives; principal activities; trade names; subsidiary companies; principal bankers; financial information; and number of employees. *Class No:* 339.1

[592]

The Times 1000 ... 1991-1992. London, Times Books, 1991. Annual. 105p. ISBN: 0723004129. ISSN: 00824429.

First published for 1979-1980.

Listings of 1. Top 1000 European companies - 2. 500 leading British companies - 3. 50 most profitable UK companies - 4. Top 100 American companies - 5-11. (other countries) - 12. Top rest of the world - 13. British banks - 14. European banks - 15. Largest unit trusts - 16. Life insurance companies - 17. Non-life insurance companies - 18. Property companies - 19. Building societies - 20. Investment trusts. Data includes ranking, company name, main activity, chairman and managing director, turnover, capital employed, net profit, etc. Index, p.92-104. *Class No:* 339.1

[593]

Who owns whom, 1991: United Kingdom and Republic of Ireland. High Wycombe, Bucks, Dun & Bradstreet International, 1991. 2v. (xxiii,960p.;v,1371p.). ISBN: 0900625988. ISSN: 01404040.

First published 1958. Annual, with quarterly supplements.

Designed to help anyone needing to know about company connections. V.1 lists parent companies in A-Z order by company name with H.O. address and a guide to main business activities of the group, together with complete breakdown and 'family tree' of the subsidiary and associate companies. Also a separate listing of consortia. V.2 is an A-Z index of subsidiary and associated companies, showing their parents. Parent companies are also listed and marked 'Parent entry'. Who owns whom online is also available via the publisher.

Similar volumes are published for Continental Europe, North America, and Australia and the Far East. *Class No:* 339.1

Foreign Trade

[594]

BROOKE, M.Z. *and* **BUCKLEY, P.J.,** *eds.* **Handbook of international trade.** London, Macmillan Press, 1988. xiv,460p. ISBN: 0333453336. ISSN: 09536248.

First published 1982.

A survey of sources of information arranged in 9 sections: 1. Strategic issues - 2. Export and import - 3. Licensing, franchising, and other contractual arrangements - 4. Foreign investment - 5. Key markets - 6. Special industrial sectors - 7. Influence of treaty organizations - 8. Sources of information - 9. Indexes (subjects; abbreviations; countries and regions; treaties; companies and other relevant organizations; publications). *Class No:* 339.5

[595]

UNITED NATIONS. STATISTICAL OFFICE. International trade statistics yearbook, 1989. New York, United Nations, 1991. 2v. ISBN: 9210611403.

First published for 1950. Annual.

V.1, Trade by country; v.2. Trade by commodity matrix tables. International coverage of foreign trade statistics through summary tables showing overall trade by regions and countries; world exports by origin and area of destination as well as by product. *Class No:* 339.5

Exports

[596]

British exports, 92. 24th ed. East Grinstead, West Sussex, Kompass-Reed Information Services, 1991. 2v. ISBN: 0862682118, v.1; 0862682126, v.2; 086268210x, set. ISSN: 02683105.

Prior to this edition, title was *Kelly's United Kingdom exports.*

Lists more than 10,000 major UK exporters under 16,500 product and service classifications. V.1. Products and services (Indices to products. Product and service section). V.2. Company information (Product information pages. Trade names section. Company information section, with their overseas agents, branches and subsidiaries). *Class No:* 339.564

65 Business & Management

Business Methods & Organization

[597]
Business acronyms. Towell, J.E., *ed.*   Detroit, Mich., Gale, 1988. xxiv, 414p. ISBN: 0810325497.

25,000 acronyms and abbreviations, drawn from the 450,000-entry *Acronyms, initialisms and abbreviations dictionary*, plus additions. Two sequences, one arranged by acronyms, the other by definitions. *Class No: 650.011*

[598]
Business periodicals index. New York, H.W. Wilson, 1958-. 11pa.; cumulated 4pa. and annually. ISSN: 00076961.

Its parent is *Industrial arts index*, 1913-57, from which both *Business periodicals index* and *Applied science and technology index* have stemmed.

Subject index to articles in over 250 English-language periodicals of which *c.*12 are British. Full cross-references. Appended 'Book reviews'. Available online through WILSONLINE and also available on CD-ROM. *Class No: 650.011*

[599]
DANIELLS, L.M. **Business information sources.** 2nd rev. ed. Berkeley, Calif., Univ. of California Press, 1985. xv, 673p. ISBN: 0520053354.

First published 1976.

21 chapters (1. Methods of locating facts ... 3. US business and economic trends ... 5. Foreign statistics and economic trends ... 10. Management ... 16. International management ... 20. Production and operations management - 21. A basic bookshelf, p.549-54 (briefly annotated)). Detailed analytical index. Confined to English-language sources. A standard work, US-slanted. *Class No: 650.011*

[600]
Encyclopedia of business information sources: a bibliographic guide to approximately 22,000 citations covering more than 1,100 primary subjects of interest to business personnel. Woy, J., *ed.*   7th ed. Detroit, Mich., Gale, 1988. 1000p. ISBN: 0810327643.

Arranged under topics, Abbreviations ... Zinc industry. Sources in each case include 'Abstract services and indexes', 'Online data bases', 'Research centers and institutes', 'Statistics sources', 'Trade associations and professional societies'. Numerous cross-references. Index of headings precedes, p.11-37. *Class No: 650.011*

[601]
Information sources in management and business. Vernon, K.D.C., *ed.*   2nd ed. London, etc., Butterworths, 1984. xviii, 346p. tables. (*Butterworths Guides to information sources.*) ISBN: 0408013451.

First published as *The use of management and business literature* (1975).

14 contributors. 3 parts (19 chapters, mostly with

....(contd.)
appended references): 1. The literature, the library and bibliographical tools for finding information - 2. Business information in various forms (company information; statistical publications, online services; market research reports; research in progress) - 3. Subject surveys of the literature (accounting and finance; organization studies; market; strategic management and planning; operations management; quantitative business analysis; business law). A basic guide on the subject. *Class No: 650.011*

[602]
The International directory of business information sources and services. London, Europa Pubns., Ltd., 1986. ix, 578p. ISBN: 0946653186.

A directory of business organizations in 23 countries (Australia - USA), plus international organizations. Subdivisions: Chambers of commerce; International trade; Government organizations; Independent organizations; Research organizations; Sources of statistical information; Business libraries. Data on each organization include date of founding; chief staff; activities, statistics; publications. Detailed index, p.353-78. *Class No: 650.011*

Dictionaries

[603]
ADAM, J.H. **Longman dictionary of business English.** 2nd rev. ed. Harlow, Essex, Longman, 1989. xvi, 564p. ISBN: 0582050294.

Defines *c.*2,000 words and phrases used in current business and commerce. Includes abbreviations, organizations and brief biographical notices. Full cross-references. Appended 'Useful information' (15 tables of measures, weights, etc.). Clear and simple definitions, showing terms in context. Specially suitable for students of English. *Class No: 650.011(038)*

Biographies

[604]
Dictionary of business biography: a biographical dictionary of business leaders active in Britain in the period 1860-1980. Jeremy, D.J., *ed.*   London, Butterworth, 1984-86. 5v. & Supplement. facsims, ports. ISBN: 0406273413, v.1; 0406273421, v.2; 040627343x, v.3; 0406273448, v.4; 0406273456, v.5; 0406273405, 5v, with supplement.

.   5v.: A-C, D-G, H-L, Mc-R, S-Z. Supplement: Indexes, contributors, errata. About 1,000 signed biographies in all, with emphasis on business careers. V.1, p.547-54 is devoted to George Cadbury, with appendix on writings and sources (unpublished and published). Living businessmen are included only if they have now retired from full-time office. Serves to supplement entries in *The Times* obituary columns and the *Dictionary of national biography*, which

....(contd.)
tend to pass over businessmen. The editor: Research Fellow, Business History Unit, London School of Economics and Political Science. *Class No: 650.011(092)*

[605]
Dictionary of Scottish business biography, 1860-1960.
Slaven, A *and* Checkland, S., *eds.* Aberdeen, Aberdeen University Press, 1986 - 1989. 2v. illus. ISBN: 0080303986 v.1; 0080303994 v.2.
V.1.:*The staple industries* is arranged in 9 sections, by industry (Extractive industries - Metals ... Shipbuilding ... Clothing ... Leather and footwear), each section having an essay, followed by a bibliography, A-Z by biographee. Personal name and subject indexes. V.2. *Processing, distributing, services* is arranged in 10 chapters (Food, drink and tobacco ... Construction ... Distributive trades - Banking, insurance and finance). *Class No: 650.011(092)*

Office Practice

[606]
BATE, J. St. J. Management guide to office automation. London, Collins, 1987. 228p. diagrs., tables. ISBN: 0003833534.
16 chapters: 2. Management's role in office management projects; 8. Technologies in the office; 14. Office automation as a support function: 16. Office automation - a threat or an opportunity? Glossary, p.218-26. Brief index. Aimed at senior and middle management in commercial, administrative and financial organizations. *Class No: 651*

[607]
GARTSIDE, L. Modern business correspondence: a comprehensive business guide to business writing and related office services. 4th ed. London, Pitman, 1986. x, 529p. illus. ISBN: 0273025759.
3rd ed., 1976.
2 parts (23 chapters): 1. The English background (principles of good business writing: style; presentation; spelling) - 2. Business correspondence (including filing and indexing systems; office machine systems; typing; letter styles). 4 appendices (C. Glossary of business terms, p.429-97; D. Abbreviations used in business). Detailed, analytical index. 48 illus. *Class No: 651*

[608]
HUTCHINSON, L. Standard handbook for secretaries. 8th ed. New York, etc., McGraw-Hill, 1969. x, 638p.
A mine of information on a variety of topics: letter and letter writing; dictation; typewritten work; copy for the press; filing; legal papers; patents and trademarks; copyright; government information; business and banking papers; securities; foreign exchange; financial statements; petty cash; insurance. Abbreviations; various tables; reference books. Detailed, analytical index. A basic title on the more conventional aspects of secretarial work. *Class No: 651*

Correspondence

[609]
The Multilingual business handbook: a guide to international correspondence. Ferney, D., *and others.* 2nd rev. ed. London, Macmillan, 1990. 352p. illus. ISBN: 0333512480, HB; 0333512499, pbk.
First published in 1983 by Pan Books, edited by P. Hartley and others.
A glossary of commercial expressions used in business correspondence in English, French, German, Spanish and Italian. Covers sales and distribution, agencies, customers, property, sales, rentals, hotel and travel reservations, and vocabulary relating to banking, post office, telephone, etc. *Class No: 651.7*

Accountancy

[610]
FRENCH, D. Dictionary of accounting terms. London, Financial Training Publications, 1985. xii, 300p. ISBN: 0906322677.
Defines more than 3,400 words and expressions used with a special meaning in accountancy. Includes abbreviations, synonyms. 'Profit and loss account': nearly ½p.; 'Holding company': ⅔p. *Class No: 652.7*

Book-keeping

[611]
Spicer and Pegler's book-keeping and accounts. Spicer, E.E. *and* Pegler, E.C. 20th ed., by P. Gee. London, Butterworth, 1988. xiv, 566p. ISBN: 040667812x.
26 chapters (1. Incomplete records ... 26. Special reports including Stock Exchange situations). Detailed contents. Detailed, analytical index, p.557-66. 'Prepared with the examination needs of the student primarily in mind' (*Preface*). *Class No: 652.71*

Management

[612]
ARMSTRONG, M. A Handbook of management techniques. London, Kogan Page, 1986. 578p. diagrs., graphs, tables. ISBN: 1850910774.
10 parts (124 sections): 1. Introduction - 2. Corporate management - 3. Marketing management - 4. Operations management - 5. Financial management - 6. Personal management - 7. New technology (section 103: The electronic office) - 8. Management science - 9. Planning and resource application - 10. Efficiency and effectiveness. Each section starts with a definition of the technique and continues with application, appraisal, and - at times - further reading (*e.g.* 101. Systems analysis: p.440-50; 4 diagrs.). Detailed, analytical index, p.561-74. Highly organized study of management skills, procedures and activities. *Class No: 652.8*

[613]
The Encyclopedia of management. Heyel, C., *ed.* 3rd ed. New York, Van Nostrand Reinhold, 1982. xxx, [1], 1371p. diagrs., graphs, tables, maps. ISBN: 0442251653.
Over 200 contributors. More than 350 documented articles, A-Z, ranging in length from half a page to 30p. 'Quality control and quality assurance': p.998-1009, carrying 7 exhibits, 35 references and 5 cross-references. 3 appendices: A. Universities and colleges (all US); B. Sources of information (organizations, A-Z); C. Sources of information (journals cited). Detailed analytical index, p.1361-71. 'A much-needed compendium of management information' (*Reference books bulletin*, 1983-1984, p.84). *Class No: 652.8*

[614]
FRENCH, D. and SAWARD, H. Dictionary of management. 2nd ed. London, Pan Books, 1984. x, 470p. ISBN: 0330285122.
First published 1975.
Defines *c.*4,000 terms 'that are likely to be encountered or read about, or discussing, management topics'. Reference in text to 70 sources. Entries include abbreviations and organizations. *Class No: 652.8*

[615]
Information sources in management and business. Vernon, K.D.C., *ed.* 2nd ed. London, etc., Butterworths, 1984. xviii, 346p. tables. (*Butterworths Guides to information sources.*) ISBN: 0408013451.
First published as *The use of management and business*

....(contd.)
literature (1975).

14 contributors. 3 parts (19 chapters, mostly with appended references): 1. The literature, the library and bibliographical tools for finding information - 2. Business information in various forms (company information; statistical publications, online services; market research reports; research in progress) - 3. Subject surveys of the literature (accounting and finance; organization studies; marketing; strategic management and planning; operations management; quantitative business analysis; business law). A basic guide on the subject. *Class No: 652.8*

Reviews & Abstracts

[616]
The ANBAR management bibliography: a guide to recent management books. Wembley, Middx., ANBAR Management Publications, 1987-. Quarterly. ISSN: 09535713.

Continues *Anbar management publications.*

October 1988 issue (61p.) has *c.*500 annotated entries, evaluative and sometimes recommending for purchase. About 30 sections, classified, covering both books and audiovisual material. Highlights 'top twenty' items and mentions well-known authors featuring in the issue. Includes quotations from reviews. Prices are usually given. *Class No: 652.8(048)*

[617]
SCIMP [Selective cooperative index of management periodicals]: European index of management periodicals. European Business School Librarians Group. Helsinki, Helsinki School of Economics Library, previously Manchester, Manchester Business School Library, 1978-. 10pa. ISSN: 07822979.

Over 5,000 references pa.; *c.*150 journals scanned. Subject classes (100 General management; 200 Finance and economics; 300 Industry and marketing; 400 Associated subjects (*e.g.*, Psychology; Communications). Author, company, and permitted subject indexes per issue, cumulated 3 times a year. A truly international effort: indexing is shared amongst 7 different countries; the database functions at Helsinki, editing at Delft, printing at Manchester, and the *SCIMP/SCAMP thesaurus* at the London Business School Library. *Class No: 652.8(048)*

Personnel Management

[618]
ARMSTRONG, M. A Handbook of personnel management. 3rd ed. London, Kogan Page, 1988. xix, 712p. tables. ISBN: 1850913366.

7 sections: 1. Personnel management - an overview - 2. Organizational behaviour - 3. Organizational planning and development - 4. Employee resourcing - 5. Employment and personnel administration - 6. Reward management - 7. Employee relations. Appendices A-L (A. Personnel policies ... H. Disciplinary procedure ... L. Assessment centres). Bibliographies throughout. *Class No: 652.83*

Production Management

Quality Control

[619]
EUROPEAN ORGANISATION FOR QUALITY CONTROL. Glossary Committee. **Glossary of terms used in quality control,** with their equivalents in Arabic, Czech, Danish, Dutch, Finnish, French, German, Italian, Norwegian, Polish, Russian, Serbo-Croatian, Spanish, Swedish. 4th ed., edited by C.E. Pollington. Rotterdam, the Organisation, 1976. xii, 670p.

....(contd.)
First published in 1965.

457 English-based terms, with definitions (p.9-82), and equivalents and indexes in the other 13 languages. *Class No: 652.856*

[620]
LOCK, D., *ed.* **Gower handbook of quality management.** Aldershot, Hants, Gower, 1990. xxi,649p. ISBN: 0366027704.

Contributions by professionals on a broad range of issues. 'It provides a full and instructive discussion of quality programmes and their implementation. Comprehensive'. (*British book news,* September 1990, p.575). *Class No: 652.856*

Marketing & Sales

[621]
Compendium of marketing information sources. London, Euromonitor Publications, 1989. xi,258p. ISBN: 0863382495. ISSN: 09572376.

'... a comprehensive one-stop guide to assessing the UK marketplace with classified entries identifying primary sources of market information available from official and unofficial sources on UK markets' (*Foreword.* In 7 sections, all subdivided and with brief annotations or descriptions: 1. Libraries and information services - 2. Abstracts and indexes - 3. Online databases and databanks - 4. Official sources - 5. Non official sources - 6. Market research agencies - 7. Company information. Products and services index; General index. *Class No: 652.88*

[622]
European marketing data and statistics, 1991. 26th ed. London, Euromonitor Publications, Ltd., 1991. Annual. [xii],463p. tables, maps. ISBN: 0863383955. ISSN: 00712930.

First published 1964.

Covers the 33 countries of Eastern and Western Europe. Profiles of the countries are followed by some 24 subject areas containing statistics on marketing geography, demographic trends and forecasts, economic indicators, finance and banking, external trade, labour force indicators, industrial resources and output, energy resources and output, defence, environmental data, consumer expenditure patterns, retailing, advertising, consumer markets, housing, health, education, agriculture, telecommunications, transport, tourism and culture. *Class No: 652.88*

[623]
HART, N.A. and **STAPLETON, J. Glossary of marketing terms.** 3rd ed. London, Heinemann, on behalf of the Institute of Marketing and the CAM Foundation 1987. 226p. ISBN: 0434918598.

First published 1977.

Contains *c.*2,500 terms on research, management, export, packaging, advertising, raw materials, selling, public relations, law, etc. Aimed at students taking diploma and degree examinations in the marketing field. *Class No: 652.88*

[624]
Macmillan dictionary of marketing and advertising. Baker, M.J., *ed.* 2nd ed. London, Macmillan Press, 1990. [vi],271p. ISBN: 0333516044.

First published in 1984.

About 2000 initialled entries, by 26 contributors, of terms commonly used in marketing and advertising, including thumb-nail sketches of key concepts and ideas. Fully cross-referenced. Intended readership: practitioners, managers, students and lay persons. *Class No: 652.88*

Market Research

[625]
BRITISH LIBRARY. Science Reference and Information Service. **Market research: a guide to British Library holdings.** Leydon, M., *ed.* 7th ed. London, SRIS, 1991. ix, 194p. (*Key to British Library holdings series.*) ISBN: 0712307745.

Sub-title varies.

Lists over 2000 current reports, arranged by subject. Subject index precedes (p.v-ix) the list of research reports, industry surveys and country profiles (p.1-168). Publishers' directory, p.169-194. British Library reference and loan copies (from the British Library Documents Supply Centre) are indicated. *Class No: 652.880*

Retail Selling

[626]
Markets yearbook. 31st ed. Oldham, The 'World's Fair' Ltd., 1991. 224p.

A list of markets in England, Wales and Scotland, with market days, owners and superintendents, etc. Directory (one alphabetical sequence), Aberdare ... Ystradgyrlais, p.20-133. Wholesalers directory, p.135-202. List of market venues, p.203-216. Index to advertisers. *Class No: 652.887*

[627]
Retail directory 1992. 46th ed. London, Newman Books, Ltd., 1991. 1325p. maps. ISBN: 0707969565. ISSN: 03054012.

Earlier title: *Stores, shops, supermarkets: retail directory.*

2 major parts: *Company details*, by type of retail operation: stores, shops and hypermarkets. High Street and out of town. Specialized outlets and groups - *Shopping street areas*, in over 500 towns: England (9 areas), Wales, Scotland, Northern Ireland, Republic of Ireland. Index to advertisers. Outline maps and town plans. *Class No: 652.887*

Publicity

Advertising

[628]
Advertiser's annual, 1990-91. 65th ed. East Grinstead, Reed Information Services Ltd. 1990. 3v. (2473p.). ISBN: 0611007533. ISSN: 00653578.

First published 1915. (Business Pubns., Ltd.).

Data on over 2,500 advertising agencies, sales promotion consultants, sponsorship consultants, recruitment advertising agents, and public relations companies. V.1: Advertising planner - v.2: Media (newspapers and periodicals; TV and radio; outdoor advertising) - Overseas media - v.3: Overseas media planner. Index to classified headings. Services and supplies. *Class No: 652.91*

[629]
BRAD/British rate and data: media facts at your fingertips. London, Maclean Hunter, for British Rate and Data, 1954-. Monthly. ISSN: 02633515.

The November 1991 issue has 4 main sections: Newspapers - Consumer and special interest publications - Business and professional publications, subjects, A-Z) - Other media (*e.g.*, cinema advertising; radio stations; television data; video tape publications). Data include advertising rates per page, part of page, etc. Primarily for advertising, but also valuable for near-current facts on several thousand British newspapers and periodicals. Standard Rate and Data Service (Skorkie, Ill.) provides a more extensive US rate-and-advertising data, now in 13 sections, varying in frequency. The original *Standard rate and data service* ran between 1919 and 1950. *Class No: 652.91*

[630]
GRAHAM, I. **Encyclopedia of advertising:** an encyclopedia containing more than 1,100 entries relating to advertising, marketing, publishing, law, research, public relations, publicity and the graphic arts ... for everyday use by advertisers, agencies, advertising practitioners, businessmen and students. New York, Fairchild, 1969. xiii, 494p. illus. ISBN: 0317581651.

First published 1952.

3 sections: 1. Advertising terminology, A-Z - 2. Terms grouped according to subject matter - 3. Directory of associations. No index. 'A useful source of information about graphic arts, commercial TV, copywriting and other aspects of advertising' (*Library journal*, 1 March 1970, p.864). *Class No: 652.91*

Public Relations

[631]
Hollis press & public relations annual, 1991-92. 23rd ed. Sunbury-on-Thames, Mddx., Hollis Directories Ltd., 1991. lxxxvii,1011p. ISBN: 0900967765. ISSN: 00733059.

First published 1967 as 'Contact'.

Arranged in 6 sections, each on a different tinted paper: 1. New contacts - commercial, industrial, consumer, professional, financial - 2. Official, public and corporate information sources - 3. Public relations consultancies (UK, Ireland, Overseas) and PR regional guide - 4. Reference and research addresses for communications - 5. Services and supplies - 6. Hollis sponsorship. Subject index (classification guide). Master index (p.897-1011). *Class No: 652.94*

34 Law

Law

[632]
Index to legal periodicals, 1908-. New York, H.W. Wilson Company, in co-operation with the American Association of Law Libraries, 1909-. Monthly (except September), cumulating quarterly, annually and 3-yearly. ISSN: 00194077.
  Subject and author index to more than 400 legal periodicals from common-law countries (US and Commonwealth). Separate indexing of legal cases commented on (under plaintiff's name A-Z) and of book reviews. Pronounced US slant. Also available online, WESTLAW, Wilsonline and CD-ROM. *Class No:* 340

[633]
WALKER, D.M. The Oxford companion to law. Oxford, Clarendon Press, 1980. ix,[1],1366p. ISBN: 019866110x.
  Concise information 'about some of the principal legal institutions, courts, judges and jurists, systems of law, branches of law, legal ideas and concepts, important doctrines and principles of law, and other legal matters ...' (*Preface*). Coverage extends to English-speaking and Western European countries. 'South African law' (sectionalised): p.1159-62; 9 references. Brief biographies (*e.g.,* Montesquieu: ½ column; 1 reference). Appendix 1: 'List of the holders of various offices since 1660' (UK, p.1316-62); 2: 'Bibliographical notes' (p.1363-66: 1. Bibliographies - 2. Indexes to periodical literature - 3. Legal biography and profession - 4. Legal history - 5. Jurisprudence - 6. Comparative legal studies - 7. International law and institutions - 8. European Communities law - 9. Commonwealth law - 10. Particular countries (Australia ... USA). Not a concise legal encyclopaedia of the law of any country; 'still less ... a layman's Home Lawyer' (*Preface*). Note occasional double entries, *e.g.,* both 'Tender, legal' and 'Legal tender' - by different contributors. *Class No:* 340

Databases

[634]
RAPER, D., *ed.* **Law databases, 1988.** London, Aslib, 1988. [3],70p. (*An Aslib online guide.*) ISBN: 0851422284.
  First published 1983.
  Details of 35 databases 'from the material supplied, in the main, by database producers' (*Introduction*). Information includes name, content, period of coverage, updating, producer, host, cost. There is a list of countries covered by the databases, and a list of host/producer addresses. A bibliography of 23 items completes the book. *Class No:* 340(003.4)

Dictionaries

[635]
EUROPEAN PARLIAMENT. Legal terminology of the European Communities. Luxembourg, Office for Official Publications of the European Community, 1976. 2v. (873 p.).
  Terms in French-Italian-English-German-Dutch-Danish, arranged under 632 classified French keywords, followed by equivalents in the other languages. V.2. is the index. *Class No:* 340(038)

[636]
LE DOCTE, E. Dictionnaire de termes juridiques en quatre langues ... Legal dictionary in four languages. 4th ed. Antwerp, Maklu; London, Sweet & Maxwell Ltd., 1987. [16], 822p. ISBN: 0421378204, UK; 9062151639, Belgium.
  First published 1978.
  *c.*12,000 words & phrases: French-base, with Spanish, English and German equivalents across a double-page. Very brief definitions, but includes alternative terms. Indexes in Spanish, English and German refer to page numbers. A section on judicial systems of Spain, Belgium, Luxembourg, Netherlands, Germany, Austria, England, Ireland, US and Canada, p.731-749. *Class No:* 340(038)

[637]
SAUNDERS, J.B., *ed.* **Words and phrases legally defined.** 3rd ed. Butterworth and Co., (Publishers) Ltd., 1988-89. 4v. ISBN: 0406080402, Set; 0406080410, v.1; 0406080429, v.2; 0406080437, v.3; 0406080445, v.4.
  First published about 1950.
  An A-Z listing over the four volumes (e.g., v.1: A-C) aiming at accurate definitions of legal terms. Scope of the 3rd ed. broadened by the addition of selections of statutory definitions and extracts from textbooks (*e.g., Halsbury's laws of England*). Cross-references. Indications given when a term relates to a particular country such as Canada or Australia. A useful companion to *Halsbury's laws ....* *Class No:* 340(038)

[638]
—**Mozley & Whiteley's law dictionary.** Ivamy, E.R.H., *ed.* 10th ed. London, Butterworth & Co., (Publishers) Ltd., 1988. vii,511p. ISBN: 0406625263.
  First published 1876.
  A concise legal dictionary with over 3000 entries and cross-references. Its purpose is to give an exposition of legal terms and phrases of past and present use. 10th ed. adds definitions of terms used in the commercial and business world. *Class No:* 340(038)

[639]
STROUD, F. Stroud's judicial dictionary of words and phrases. James, J.S., *ed.* 5th ed. London, Sweet & Maxwell, 1986. 6v. ISBN: 0421366303; 0421389109, supplement.

LAW

....(contd.)

First published 1890; 4th ed. 1971-75, with supplements.

A dictionary of words and phrases that have been interpreted by the judges, giving their interpretations. Statutory definitions not judicially interpreted are referred to. Cross-references. V.1: A-C; v.2: D-H; v.3: I-O; v.4: P-R; v.5: S-Z; v.6: Tables of cases and statutes. The first supplement includes developments from July 1985 to July 1987 and it is intended to issue a cumulative supplement annually (1991 supplement. 175p. ISBN 0421429909). Rearrangement of the articles has improved access to the contents. 'This dictionary enjoys a well-merited reputation and the frequently heard question 'have you checked Stroud?' is a tiny indication of this. It has the authority of reliability and comprehensiveness achieved over nearly one hundred years and through five editions ...' (*Law librarian*, v.18(2), August 1987, p.68-69). *Class No: 340(038)*

Great Britain

[640]
All England law reports. London, Butterworths, 1936-. Weekly.

A series of reports of decisions of all the courts; in suitable cases editorial notes are given, explaining the legal significance. Cases are speedily reported. Annual cumulative index and 'noter-up'. This also contains a table of cases, a table of statutes judicially considered, and a table of cases judicially noticed in later editions.

All England law reports reprint, 1558-1935 (London, Butterworths, 1966-68. 36v. and index. ISBN 040600000x) is a selection in the same styles as the *All England law reports*.

LEXIS, a computer-based legal research service, launched by Butterworths in 1980, contains the full text of all English cases reported in the main series of law reports since 1945. *Class No: 340(410)*

[641]
Every man's own lawyer, by 'A barrister'. 71st ed. London, Macmillan Press, 1981. vp. ISBN: 0333318358.

First published 1863.

A short elucidation of those parts of English law that are of most interest to the private citizen and written for the non-specialist. In general, 'the law ... in force during the first half of the year 1979' (*Preface*). 25 chapters (*e.g.*, 2. Personal rights and remedies; 7. The law of property; 10. Criminal law; 15. Wills and trusts; 25. A short dictionary of legal terms). Table of cases; table of Statutes. Analytical index. Well-sectionalised and footnoted. *Class No: 340(410)*

[642]
GREAT BRITAIN. Statutory Instruments. 1890-. London, HMSO, 1890-.

Initially (and until 1947) as *Statutory Rules and Orders* ('S.R. & O.'). Cumulation, to December 31, 1948 (HMSO, 1949-52. 25v.), as *S.R. & O. and S.I. revised*.

Statutory Instruments ('S.I.'),. each issued separately and cumulated annually (less local S.I.s and revocations), consist of subordinate legislation, - Orders in Council and Orders, rules, regulations, etc. made by Ministers and others. A biennial subject index is provided in *Index to Governmental Orders in force* ... The annual *Table of Government Orders* is in numerical order. *Class No: 340(410)*

[643]
GREAT BRITAIN. STATUTORY PUBLICATIONS OFFICE. The Public General Acts and General Synod Measures. London, HMSO, [1831]-. Annual (formerly sessional).

Early title was *The Public General Acts and Church Assembly Measures*. *Class No: 340(410)*

[644]
GREAT BRITAIN. STATUTORY PUBLICATIONS OFFICE. Statutes in force. London, HMSO, 1972-. Loose-leaf, with 64 binders.

Replaces *The Statutes revised*.

A series of booklets, in subject groups, A-Z. *Class No: 340(410)*

[645]
Halsbury's Statutes of England and Wales. 4th ed. London, Butterworths, 1985-. To be in 50v. (v.40 postponed). ISBN: 0406214093.

First published 1930. Companion to *Halsbury's Laws of England*.

Aim is to provide the user with an up-to-date version of the amended text of every Public General Act or Ecclesiastical Measure in force in England and Wales, with detailed annotations to each section and schedule. Arrangement is A-Z by subject and there is an index to each volume. V.50 includes Treaties of the European Communities. *Cumulative supplement, 1989* (1989. ISBN 0406043442). *Tables of Statutes and general index, 1989-90* (1989. ISBN 0406214727) refers to v.1-39 & 41.50. 'Particularly useful for tracing Acts on a particular subject' (Dane, J., and Thomas, P.A. *How to use a law library* (1979),p.51) of the 3rd ed. *Class No: 340(410)*

Scotland

[646]
WALKER, D.M. The Scottish legal system: an introduction to the study of Scots law. 5th ed. rev. Edinburgh, W. Green, 1981. xliii,526p. 8 illus. ISBN: 0414006836.

First published 1959.

Written primarily as a textbook for the introductory course in the legal curriculum of Glasgow University. 15 chapters, each with 'further readings' (3. The branches of legal science - 4. The development of Scots law ... 7. The modern judicial system ... 10. The sources of Scots law - 11. The repositories of Scots law ... 14. The administration of criminal justice - 15. The making of new law). Many footnotes referring to books, articles, case law, and Statutes. *Class No: 340(411)*

Libraries

[647]
MISKIN, C., *ed.* **Directory of law libraries in the British Isles.** 3rd ed. Hebden Bridge, West Yorks, Legal Information Resources Ltd., 1988, for the British and Irish Association of Law Libraries. ix,120p. ISBN: 1870369025.

First published 1976 by the Association and edited by B. Mangles.

Entries for 317 libraries, based on replies to a postal questionnaire, with supplementary information. Arranged by place (England; Ireland; Scotland; Wales; Channel Islands and other islands). Data: name and address; telephone-telex-fax numbers; opening hours; terms of admission; loans; facilities and services; stock; subject coverage; affiliation, etc. 4 indexes - by name of organization, type of organization, contact name, special collection name. 'Presentation and layout is excellent; (*The Law librarian*, v.20(2), May 1989, p.71). *Class No: 340:061:026/027*

Legal Aid

[648]
Legal aid handbook. Legal Aid Board. 1991 ed. London, Sweet & Maxwell, 1991. vii,402p. ISBN: 0421450002.
First published 1950 by HMSO. From 1990 ed. by Sweet & Maxwell.
Sets out the 1988 Legal Aid Act and the references, together with eligibility tables, list of legal aid forms, and an updated version of the Law Society's *Notes for guidance*. Index. *Class No: 340.028*

Comparative Law

[649]
DAVID, R. and BRIERLEY, J.E.C. Major legal systems of the world today: an introduction to the comparative study of law. 3rd ed. London, Stevens & Sons, 1985. xvi,624p. ISBN: 0420473408.
First published 1978. Translation of *Les Grands systèmes de droit contemporains*.
4 parts: 1. The Romano-Germanic family - 2. Socialist laws - 3. The common law (English law; law of the US) - 4. Other conceptions of law and the social order (Muslim law; Law of India; Laws of the Far East; Laws of Africa and Malagasy). Appendix 1: 'Bibliographical information' (brief notes; 9 sections: Bibliographical tools ... Unification and harmonisation of law), p.577-609. Appendix 2: 'Useful information and references' (Centres of comparative law; Comparative law studies; Comparative law libraries). Bibliography, p.577-613. Index, p.615-624. *Class No: 340.5*

International Law

[650]
BLEDSOE, R. and BOCZEK, B.A. The International law dictionary. Santa Barbara, CA., ABC-Clio, 1987. 422p. (*Clio dictionaries in political science series, no.11.*) ISBN: 087436406x.
368 key terms in international law, including concepts, major treaties, international conventions, and theories. Organized thematically in 12 chapters. The 2-part entries first define the term and then explain its significance and implications through historical and current examples. Most entries are brief essays. 'See also' references. Good index. 'A must for law collections ...' (*Wilson library bulletin*, November 1987, p.94). *Class No: 341*

[651]
Encyclopedia of public international law. Bernhardt, R. Amsterdam, North-Holland Publishing Company, 1981-. To be in 12 instalments, and ultimately in 4v.
Published under the auspices of the Max-Planck-Institute for Comparative Public Law and International Law.
First issued in subject instalments: 1. Settlement of disputes - 2. Decisions of international courts ... - 3. & 4. Use of force ... - 5. International organizations in general ... - 6. Regional co-operation ... - 7. History of international law ... - 8. Human rights and the individual in international law. International economic relations - 9. International relations ... - 10. States. Responsibility of States ... - 11. Law of the sea - 12. Geographical issues. Instalment 8 (1985. xv,551p.) has 129 entries by 87 authors. 'Lists of articles' in each instalment is a subject list relating to the complete work. Articles are signed and include bibliographies. Cross-references. *Class No: 341*

Law of International Organizations

League of Nations

[652]
WALTERS, F.P. A History of the League of Nations. London, Oxford University Press, under the auspices of the Royal Institute of International Affairs, 1952 (Reprinted in one vol. in 1986 by Greenwood Press). xvi,833p. ISBN: 0313250561.
First published 1952 in 2v.
The standard work on the League of Nations. An objective account by a member of the Secretariat, 1919-40. 67 chapters, taking the narrative up to 1946. No bibliography, but a rather general appendix note on sources. Supported by a very good analytical index. *Class No: 341.121*

United Nations

[653]
The Encyclopaedia of the United Nations and international agreements. Osmánczyk, E.J. 3rd ed. London & Philadelphia, Taylor & Francis, 1985. xv, 1059p. ISBN: 0850663121.
First published 1974 in Polish (Warsaw); 2nd ed. in Spanish, 1976.
A compendium of political, economic and social information, including data on the structure of the United Nations; its specialised agencies, and the many intergovernmental and non-governmental organizations that co-operate with the UN. Over 7000 entries, more than half of them having short explanations of words or names; other entries comprise descriptions of all the States in the world, and vary in length from a third to a full page. Sources are given for most entries. Also includes 'World population statistics, 1985-2025'; a list of acronyms and abbreviations; a selective index (p.975-1046); and an index to agreements, conventions and treaties (p.1047-1059). *Class No: 341.123*

[654]
UNDOC: current index. United Nations documents index. New York, and Geneva, United Nations Publications, 1979-. v.1, no.1/2-. 10pa. ISSN: 02505584.
Comprehensive coverage of UN documentation, including full bibliographical descriptions. Subject, author and title indexes. Also a check-list of new UN documents received at headquarters. *Class No: 341.123*

European Community

[655]
Encyclopedia of European Community law. Simmonds, K.R., *ed.* London, Sweet & Maxwell, 1973-. 3v.(loose-leaf). ISBN: 0421193506, v.A; 0421193603, v.B; 0421207604, v.C.
Vol. A: United Kingdom sources (2 loose-leaf binders); v.B: European Community treaties (3 loose-leaf binders); v.C: Community Secondary legislation (7 loose-leaf binders). Text, with commentary in smaller type; definitions. Brief bibliographies. Kept up-to-date with amendments.
Secondary legislation (regulations, directories, decisions, recommendations and opinions made by the Council of the European Communities) is published in *Official journal of the European Communities*). *Class No: 341.174*

[656]
The European Communities encyclopedia and directory, 1992. London, Europa, 1991. (distributed in US and Canada by Gale Research Ltd.). xix,390p. tables. ISBN: 0946653658.
In 4 parts: 1 has information on the European Communities, arranged A-Z, covering personalities, politics, programmes, reports and committees, acronyms, catch terms

....(contd.)

and phrases, etc. Pt.2 is a collection of essays by British academics on the political, legal, and social activities of the EC. Pt.3 is a detailed statistical survey. Pt.4 is a directory of EC institutions, including MEPs. Appendices summarize 3 original treaties, list measures involved in the implementation of the internal market, and give information on EC databases. *Class No:* 341.174

[657]

The European Community 1991/92: the professional reference book for business, media and government. Morris, B., *ed.* 3rd ed. London, Macmillan, 1991. 500p. tables. ISBN: 0333398386.

First published 1981.

The essential guide to what's what and who's who in the E.C. The introduction is followed by sections on: Europe 1990 - Member States of the European Community - The European Community framework - A-Z of European Community issues - European directory. Index. The first ed. was named best new business reference book of the year by Aslib. *Class No:* 341.174

[658]

LEONARD, D. Pocket guide to the European Community. Oxford, Basil Blackwell Ltd; London, Economist Publications, 1988. xiii,210p. tables, graphs. ISBN: 0631162844.

An introduction to the history, institutions and functions of the European Community. 4 sections: The background - The institutions - The competances - Special problems. Cross-references. 8 appendices (1. Basic statistics of member states; 2. Presidents of the High Authority and the Community; 5. Elections to the European Parliament; 7. The single European Act; 9. Eurojargon). Suggestions for further reading, p.201-202. Index, p.203-210. *Class No:* 341.174

[659]

PAXTON, J., *ed.* **A Dictionary of the European Communities.** 2nd ed. London, Macmillan Press, 1982. 240p. ISBN: 0333334388.

First published in 1977 as *A dictionary of the European Economic Community.*

Entries A.A.S.M. ... Zollverein. Lengthier articles (*e.g.,* 'Rome, Treaty of' p.219-221) are sectionalised. That on 'Referendum, United Kingdom, p.222-226, has detailed breakdown by counties of voting. Includes brief biographies, and abbreviations. Cross-references, *e.g.,* from French terms to English. Select bibliography (grouped), p.279-282. A handy quick-reference tool. *Class No:* 341.174

Alliances & Treaties

[660]

GRENVILLE, J.A.S. The Major international treaties, 1914-1945 a history and guide with texts. London, Methuen, 1987. xviii,268p. 4 maps. ISBN: 0416080928.

Supersedes, in part, Grenville's *The major international treaties, 1914-1973 ...* (1974).

An introduction is followed by 10 chapters: 1. Secret agreements and treaties of the first world war - 2. The peace settlements and the League of Nations - 3. France, Britain, Italy and Germany, 1921-33 - 4. France and the eastern allies, 1921-39 - 5. The Soviet Union and her neighbours, 1919-37 - 6. The collapse of the territorial settlements of Versailles, 1931-8 - 7. From peace to world war in Europe and Asia, 1937-41 - 8. The Grand Alliance: Britain and the United States and the Soviet Union, 1941-45 - 9. The Allied conferences and the political settlement of Europe, 1943-5 - 10. The alliance and alignments of the United States from the League of Nations to the United Nations. Source references for the principal treaties, p.256-261. Analytical index, p.263-268. *Class No:* 341.232/.24

[661]

—GRENVILLE, J.A.S. *and* WASSERSTEIN, B. The Major international treaties since 1945: a history and guide with texts. London, Methuen, 1987. xiv,528p. ISBN: 0416380808.

Supersedes, in part, J.A.S. Grenville's *The major international treaties, 1914-1973 ...* (1974).

An introduction on international treaties is followed by 10 chapters: 1. The foundations of post-war diplomacy - 2. The United States treaty system - 3. The Soviet treaty system - 4. The German question - 5. West European integration - 6. South and East Asia and the Pacific - 7. Africa - 8. The Middle East and East Mediterranean - 9. Latin America and the South Atlantic - 10. Détente and arms control. Appendix: Multilateral treaties on human rights and the environment. Sources for treaty texts, p.500-506. Analytical index, p.507-528. *Class No:* 341.232/.24

[662]

Treaties and alliances of the world. Rengger, N., *ed.* 5th ed. Harlow, Essex, Longman Current Affairs, 1990. x,579p. diagrs., tables, maps. ISBN: 0582057337.

First published 1968. H.W. Degenhardt edited the first four eds.

Compiled with the cooperation of the editorial team of Longman and *Keesing's Contemporary archives* (now *Keesing's Record of world events*). 5 parts: 1. The analysis of treaties and alliances in world politics - 2. International organizations - 3. Treaties and alliances of the Cold War - 4. Regional agreements - 5. Trans-regional and informal groupings. 13 maps. Grouped bibliography, p.567-70. Index. *Class No:* 341.232/.24

Disarmament

[663]

ELLIOT, J.M. *and* **ELLIOT, R.R. The Arms control, disarmament and military security dictionary.** Santa Barbara, CA, ABC-Clio, 1989. 349p. ISBN: 0874364302.

268 numbered entries, designed to complement by definition and organization those terms noted in standard texts on the topics. Arrangement is A-Z within subject-matter chapters. Extensive cross-references. US slant. Includes 24p. of notes. *Class No:* 341.67

[664]

SIPRI: yearbook: world armaments and disarmament, 1991. Stockholm International Peace Research Institute. 22nd ed. Oxford, Oxford University Press, for SIPRI, 1991. xxxviii,741p. tables. ISBN: 0198291450. ISSN: 09530282.

1st issue (1970) covered 1968/69.

20 chapters in 4 parts: 1. Weapons and technology - 2. Military expenditure, the arms trade and armed conflicts - 3. Developments in arms control - 4. Special features. Annexes: A. Major multilateral arms control agreements; B. Chronology, 1990. Abstracts, p.723-727. Index, p.729-741. *Class No:* 341.67

[665]

World encyclopedia of peace. Laszlo, E. *and* Yoo, J.Y., *eds.* Oxford, Pergamon Press, 1986. 4v. (1930p.). illus. ISBN: 0080326854.

Over 3000 literary references by over 200 experts from more than 30 countries, predominantly Western European and American. V.1-2 has a 36p. essay of introduction and history of peace encyclopedias, followed by a series of *c.*500 articles arranged A-Z by subject. V.3 has reprints of texts of peace treaties and conventions since 1919, a chronology of the peace movement, and Nobel Peace Prize laureates. V.4 lists peace organizations and institutions, A-Z by country; a bibliography arranged thematically (p.69-135); a list of journals arranged thematically (p.136-155) and devoted to peace research, peace activism, and international

....(contd.)
relations; and a list of contributors. Also a name index (p.173-230) and an analytical subject index (p.231-294) to the whole work. 'As the introductory essay ... suggests, this is a unique endeavor in many ways: it is also a fair achievement and deserves a place in all but the smallest reference collections' (*College & research libraries,* v.48(4), July 1987, p.358). '... includes some noteworthy flaws' (*Choice,* October 1987, p.292). *Class No:* 341.67

Constitutional Law

[666]
BLAUSTEIN, A.P. *and* **FLANZ, G.H. Constitutions of the countries of the world.** Dobbs Ferry, N.Y., Oceana, 1971-77. 17 binders. Loose-leaf. ISBN: 0379004674.
Each binder has full text (translated, as necessary) of *c.*10 constitutions. Each text is accompanied by a concise chronology of events leading up to its adoption and a brief annotated bibliography for further reference. *Historic constitutions* (1971-79. 10v.) is arranged under countries, A-Z. *Class No:* 342

[667]
DERBYSHIRE, J.D. *and* **DERBYSHIRE, I. Political systems of the world.** London, Chambers, 1989. xii,932p. tables, maps. ISBN: 0550210083.
A guide to the political philosophies, systems and structures of every country of the world. In 3 parts: 1. The comparative approach; 2. Political systems of the world's nation-states (p.136-762); 3. Towards one world. Appended: Data sources. Detailed analytical index (p.895-904). 165 notes on geographical regions plus 55 semi-sovereign states, colonies and dependencies. A 'political system' implies operation of a statistical office, a legislative body, and a national bank. *Class No:* 342

Parliaments

[668]
Parliaments of the world: a comparative reference compendium, prepared by the Inter-Parliamentary Union. 2nd ed. Aldershot, Hants, Gower Publishing Company Ltd; New York, Facts on File, 1986. 2v. (1440p). tables. ISBN: 0566053810, (UK); 0810611869, (US).
First published in 1976 by Macmillan Press.
A comparative study of the structure and operation of parliaments throughout the world. An introduction is followed by chapters on The parliaments of the world - Parliament and its membership - Parliamentary procedure - Proceedings and debates - Parliamentary groupings - Parliamentary committees - Parliament and its means of information - Parliament and the media - Legislation - The budget - Parliament and the Government - Parliament and emergency - Constitutionality of laws - Dissolution of Parliament - Judicial and other functions of Parliament. Index. ' ... a potpourri of useful and otherwise difficult-to-locate information about this branch of government in 83 countries ...' (*Reference books bulletin,* 1986/7, p.68). *Class No:* 342.53

[669]
WILDING, N. *and* **LAUNDY, P. An Encyclopaedia of Parliament.** Completely rev. 4th ed. London, Cassell, 1971. ix,931p.
First published 1958.
'Abjuration Act' ... 'Zinoviev letter'. Covers British and Commonwealth Parliaments, giving definitions of terms (*e.g.,* 'Closure'), background history (*e.g.,* 'Elizabeth I (1533-1603) and Parliament'), and notes on procedure, privileges and customs of Parliament. Lengthier articles have brief bibliographies, for further reading. 34 appendices (2. Salaries of Ministers, Speakers and Members ... 34.

....(contd.)
Bibliography, p.892-931 with subdivisions). Well produced. Both authors were members of the Federal and Southern Rhodesian Parliaments. The standard work. *Class No:* 342.53

Great Britain

[670]
Dod's parliamentary companion, 1991. 159th year; 172nd issue. Hurst Green, Sussex, Dod's Parliamentary Companion Ltd., 1991. xi,1000p. ports. ISBN: 0905702174. ISSN: 00707007.
Established 1832.
Sections: The Royal Family - Biographies of Peers (A-Z, p.1-330) - Composition of the House of Lords - Biographies of Peers of Ireland who are not Peers of Parliament - Precedence - Addressing letters - Biographies of Members of the House of Commons (A-Z, p.391-607) - Constituencies and polling, etc. - The Ministerial responsibilities - Government and public offices. Index. *Class No:* 342.53(410)

[671]
Erskine May's Treatise on the law, privileges, proceedings and usage of Parliament. Boulton, C., *ed.* 21st ed. London, Butterworths, 1989. xliv,1079p. ISBN: 0406114714.
First published 1844; 18th ed. 1971.
Parts: 1. Constitution, powers and privileges of Parliament (chapters 1-11) - 2. Proceedings in Parliament: public business (12-34) - 3. Proceedings in Parliament: private business. Table of abbreviations (references to sources), p.xxxix-xliv. Detailed table of contents. Appendix: House of Commons Standing Orders relative to public business. Detailed, analytical, index, p.1025-1079. 'Erskine May' is not official; next to the *Journals* of both Houses, it is accepted as the great secondary authority. For the parliamentary and constitutional specialist; whereas *Abraham and Hawtrey's Parliamentary dictionary* (3rd ed., by S.C. Hawtry and H.M. Barclay. London, Butterworth, 1970. viii,248p.) is for the general political audience (*T.L.S.* no.3625, 20 August 1971, p.985).
For the historical development of parliamentary procedure: Campion, G.F.M., 1st baron Campion. *An introduction to the procedure of the House of Commons* (2nd ed. London, Macmillan, 1950. 348p.); and, complementary, from the historical viewpoint, to Erskine May, - Redlich, J. *The procedure of the House of Commons: a study of its history and present form* (London, Constable, 1908. 3v.). *Class No:* 342.53(410)

[672]
FORD, P. *and* **FORD, G. A Guide to Parliamentary Papers;** What they are, how to find them, how to use them. 3rd ed. Shannon, Irish University Press, 1972. 87p. (*Southampton University Studies in Parliamentary Papers.*) ISBN: 0716514184.
First published 1955.
'Our main aim is to familiarise the researcher with the different kinds of papers, to explain the apparatus for finding them and to indicate the most profitable way of extracting information from them' (*Preface to the third edition*). Bibliographical aids, p.71-80; index, p.81-85. A valuable introduction to a complex subject. *Class No:* 342.53(410)

[673]
Manual of procedure in the public business: laid on the table by Mr. Speaker for the use of Members. House of Commons. 13th ed. London, HMSO, 1984. xix, 287 p. ISBN: 0108360156.
Contents of chapters: 1. Meetings of Parliament - 2. Election and admission of Members - 3. The Speaker and Chairmen of Committees - 4. Officers and Departments of

....(contd.)

the House - 5. Sittings of the House and arrangement of business - 6. Matters taken ... - 7. General rules of procedure - 8. Public bills - 9. Committees - 10. Financial business - 11. Relations between the two Houses - 12. Communications between the Crown and the House - 13. Witnesses ... - 14. Accounts and papers - 15. Records of the House - 16. Miscellaneous - 17. Private bills - 18. Special procedure orders - 19. Procedure under the Parliament Acts of 1911 and 1949 - 20. European legislation and international assemblies. *Class No:* 342.53(410)

USA

[674]
Congressional quarterly's guide to the Congress of the United States. 3rd ed. Washington, Congressional Quarterly Inc., 1982,. xx, [1],1185p. illus. ISBN: 0871872390.

First published 1971.

Carefully defines and explains, with full footnotes, the complex procedures and issues of the US House of Representatives and Senate. 7 chapters: 1. The origins and development of Congress - 2. Powers of Congress - 3. Congressional procedures - 4. Housing and support of Congress - 5. Congress and the electorate - 6. Pressures on Congress - 7. Qualifications and conduct. Several appendices (Biographical index of members, 1789-1982; Constitution; Documents of the pre-Constitutional period; Congressional statistics; Congressional rules; Glossary of Congressional terms; Lobbying; etc.). Detailed index. 'An essential reference work' (*Choice,* May 1977, p.344, of the 2nd ed.). *Class No:* 342.53(73)

Human Rights

[675]
ANDREWS, J.A. and HINES, W.D. Keyguide to information sources on the international protection of human rights. London, Mansell; New York, Facts on File, 1987. 169p. ISBN: 0720118735, UK; 0816018227, US.

An introduction to the international and regional protection of human rights, and to its literature. Part 1. General background, has overviews of the history of human rights, international treaties and conventions, and individual rights; pt.2 is an annotated bibliography arranged by general topics (*e.g.,* treaties, constitutional protection) and by format (*e.g.,* by law reports, bibliographies); and pt.3 has brief descriptions of a wide range of organizations. Index to authors, titles, subjects and organizations. 'An essential and timely research tool' (*International affairs,* v.63(4), Autumn 1987, p.725). 'Highly recommended' (*Choice,* v.25(6), February 1988, p.881). *Class No:* 342.7

[676]
World human rights guide. Humana, C., *comp.* 2nd ed. New York, Facts on File; London, Hodder & Stoughton, 1986. xviii,344p. tables, charts, maps. ISBN: 0816014043, US; 0850580757, UK.

First published 1983.

Assesses information about human rights in 120 major countries, from data compiled from a 40-item questionnaire based on 3 UN documents (Universal Declaration of Human Rights. International Covenant on Economic, Social and Cultural Rights. International Convenant on Civil and Political Rights). Arranged A-Z by country and including human rights rating; life expectancy; infant mortality; form of government; UN covenants ratified; income per head; percentage of gross national product on military; state of health; education; factors affecting human rights; summary. The amount of information depending on what could be collected by questionnaire and extensive literature search. *Class No:* 342.7

Citizens Rights

[677]
Reader's Digest you and your rights: an A to Z guide to the law. Williams, D.W., *ed.* 9th ed. London, Reader's Digest Association Ltd., 1986. 752p. illus.

A to Z entries (Abandoned vehicle ... Zebra crossing). Written in simple language and well sectionalised, it makes good use of two-colour illustrations, facsimiles, and cross-references. Quotes cases and decisions. 'How to make a complaint', p.736-752. Index. A 10th ed. was published in 1991 (ISBN 0276420055). *Class No:* 342.71

Criminal Justice

[678]
Criminology and penology: an international abstracting service covering the etiology of crime and juvenile delinquency, the control and treatment of offenders, criminal procedure and the administration of justice. Criminologica Foundation, the University of Leiden, and Joint Bureaus for Dutch Child Welfare (WIJN), Utrecht., *eds.* Amstelveen, Netherlands, Kugler Publications b.v., for the Criminologica Foundation, London, 1961-. v.1-. 6pa. ISSN: 01666231.

Formerly *Excerpta criminologica* (v.1-8. 1961-68) and *Abstracts on criminology and penology...* (v.9-19. 1969-79).

*c.*500 indicative and informative abstracts in each issue, arranged in 13 sections, further subdivided. Each issue has author and subject indexes, the last issue each year having annual cumulated indexes. *Class No:* 343.1

[679]
Encyclopaedia of world crime. Nash, J. R. Wilmette, Il., Crime Books Inc. (distributed by Marshall Cavendish), 1990. 6v. illus. ISBN: 0923582002.

V.1-4 have over 50000 articles, with 4000 illustrations, including stories of criminals, prosecutors, executioners, legal theorists, assassination victims, notorious prisons, organized crime syndicates, crime fighters, and fictional works based on real crime. Length of articles varies from a few sentences to several pages. V.5 is a dictionary of 20000 terms from law enforcement, the underworld, current slang, etc., and also includes summaries of court decisions and legislation. V.6 has an index of proper names; a subject index, and a bibliography of over 25000 books. 'An important work ...' (*RQ* v.30(3), Spring 1991, p.416). *Class No:* 343.1

[680]
KADISH, S.H., *ed.* **Encyclopedia of crime and justice.** New York, Collier Macmillan, 1983. 4v.(1790p.). ISBN: 0029181100.

286 articles organized topically, which present all sides of the cogent arguments. Reading lists are given after each article. Several multi-articles on the biggest problem areas (*e.g.,* sentencing (10 articles); police (9 articles); prisons (6 articles)) All are well-written. Cross references. Glossary of terms, and excellent index. 'An invaluable interdisciplinary study of the field of criminal justice.' (*Library journal,* v.109(1) January 1984, p.74). *Class No:* 343.1

Commercial Law

[681]
IVAMY, E.R.H. Dictionary of company law. 2nd ed. London, Butterworth, 1985. 264p. (*Butterworths professional dictionary series.*) ISBN: 0406681635.

First published 1983.

Words and phrases used in company law, each entry containing a concise statement of the relevant provisions of the Companies Acts and of significant case law. Entries vary in length (*e.g.,* Debenture, $6\frac{1}{2}$ pages; Deed of settlement, $3\frac{1}{2}$ lines; Fraudulent trading, *c.* 600 words).

....(contd.)
Cross-references. This second edition brings the dictionary up-to-date with the Companies Act, 1985, Companies Securities (Insider Dealing) Act, 1985, and the Business Names Act, 1985. *Class No:* 347.7

Copyright

[682]
Copyright laws and treaties of the world. Unesco *and* World Intellectual Property Organization (WIPO), *and others.*
Paris, Unesco; Washington, Bureau of National Affairs Inc., 1956-. Annual Supplements. 3v. (loose-leaf).
'A compilation of the laws, orders, rules, regulations, conventions and treaties which establish, in and between the different countries of the world, the legal provisions for the protection of copyright' (*Explanatory notes*). Arranged by countries. A-Z. *Class No:* 347.78

Legal Procedures & Personnel

[683]
Stone's justice's manual, 1991. Richman, J. *and* Draycott, A.T., *eds.* 123rd ed. London, Butterworth & Co (Publishers) Ltd.; Shaw & Sons Ltd., 1991. 3v. ISBN: 0406386927.
First published 1842.
Detailed authoritative information. 10 parts in 3v. V.1. Part 1. Magistrate's Courts, procedure - II. Evidence - III. Sentencing - IV. Family law - V. Juvenile Courts - VI. Licensing. V.2. Part VII. Offences, matters of complaint, etc. V.3. Part VIII. Transport - IX. Precedents and forms - X. Miscellaneous legislation. Table of Statutes. A-Z table of Statutory Instruments. Chronological list of S.I.'s. Table of cases. Index, p.401-715. *Class No:* 347.9

Courts

[684]
The County court practice, 1991. Thompson, P.K.J., *ed.*
London, Butterworth, 1991. Annual. clxxxv,2023,57p. ISBN: 0406163278.
Part 1: General jurisdiction (relevant Acts; County court rules, 1981; County court forms; costs and fees; Procedural tables) - 2. Special jurisdiction (Admiralty ... Consumer credit ... Water). Appendix (County court directory; Scales of costs). Analytical, index, 57p. The Law is generally stated as at 1 January 1991. *Class No:* 347.97/.99

[685]
A Reference guide to the United States Supreme Court.
Elliott, S.P., *ed.* New York, Facts on File, 1986. 476p. illus. ISBN: 0816010188.
6 major sections: The role of the Supreme Court - The constitutional powers of the branches of federal government - Division of power - Individual rights - Landmark cases - Biographies of the Justices (a concise biography, A-Z, of every Justice who has served on the Supreme Court). Several appendices of chronological listings. The bibliography includes books on the Court itself as well as on individual Justices. Index to cases, individuals and subjects. Supplements Congressional Quarterly's *Guide to the United States Supreme Court*(1979). *Class No:* 347.97/.99

35 Public Administration

[686]
COLLIN, P.H. **Dictionary of government and politics.** Teddington, Mddx., Peter Collin Publishing, 1988. [3],225,[23]p. ISBN: 094854905x.

c.5000 main words and phrases covering national legislatives, elections, local government, parliamentary and council procedure, international affairs and political parties and theories. Aims to cover both British and American terminology. A supplement gives information about the political and legislative systems in both Britain and the United States, together with the reproduction of relevant documents. Examples given. *Class No:* 350

[687]
The Scottish government yearbook, 1992. Paterson, L. *and* McCrone, D., *eds.* Edinburgh, University of Edinburgh, Unit for the Study of Government in Scotland, 1992. 282p. ISBN: 0951805304.

First published 1979.

20 sections. The editors' introduction is followed by '2. The political year in Westminster, 3-8 are articles on constitutional issues, 9-11 on education, 12-15 on general matters, 16-19 on reference (opinion polls, Scottish legislation, structure of the Scottish Office, Parliamentary by-elections. 20 is on recent publications (452 items on Scottish government and politics). *Class No:* 350

Government Bodies

[688]
Councils, committees & boards: a handbook of advisory, consultative, executive & similar bodies in British public life. Sellar, L., *ed.* 7th ed. Beckenham, Kent, CBD Research Ltd., 1989. xiv,403p. ISBN: 0900246529.

First published 1970.

About 1270 entries (Aberdeen and District Milk Marketing Board ... Youth Committee for Northern Ireland). Includes Crown Agents, BBC and National Health Service (p.210-218). Data on each body: name; abbreviation; validity indication; address; telephone & telex number; establishment and membership; terms of reference, objects or duties; activities and supplementary information; publications; notes re imminent or proposed changes which will affect status/functions. Cross-references. Abbreviations index; index of chairmen, presidents and chief executives; subject index. 'An essential reference tool' (*Trade and industry*, 25 November 1977, p.386, on the 3rd ed.). *Class No:* 350.07

[689]
The Civil Service year book, 1991. Cabinet Office. London, HMSO., 1991. xi,1018,xiii-xlxp. ISBN: 011430047x.

Issued annually.

6 chapters: 1. The Royal Household - 2. Parliamentary Offices - 3. Ministers, Departments and Executive Agencies - 4. Libraries, museums and galleries. Research councils. Other organizations - 5. Departments and other organizations (Northern Ireland; Scotland; Wales) - 6. Salary tables. Entries briefly state scope of office and give telephone numbers for contacting. Index to individual officers. Index to departments and sub-departments precedes. Essential to any reference library. *Class No:* 350.08

[690]
DREWRY, G. *and* BUTCHER, T. **The Civil Service today.** Oxford, Basil Blackwell, 1988. x,259p. tables. ISBN: 0631154280.

A prologue: some crises of the 1980s, precedes 11 chapters (1. Charting the territory - 2. How things came to be - 3. Some facts and figures - 4. The universal department - 5. Recruitment and training - 6. Conditions of service - 7. The working context - 8. Ministers and civil servants - 9. The public face of private government - 10. Slimmer and fitter: the quest for efficiency and effectiveness - 11. Conclusion: the Civil Service at the crossroads?. 422 notes, by chapter headings, p.222-244. Select bibliography, by subject sections with no annotations, p.245-252. Index, p.253-259. *Class No:* 350.08

Housing

[691]
Housing year book, 1992. 9th ed. Harlow, Essex, Longman Group (UK) Ltd., 1991. xv,467p. ISBN: 0582086779. ISSN: 02645181.

First published 1983.

A guide to local and central government departments, institutions, and people concerned with housing issues and problems in the UK. Preliminaries, including a gazetteer, are followed by 22 sections relating to local authorities, housing, rent and rates, etc., and including 20: Sources of information; and 21: Guide to government legislation and reports. Index, p.452-467; Advertisers' index. *Class No:* 351.778.5

Local Government

[692]
HARRISON, T. **Access to information in local government.**
London, Sweet & Maxwell, 1988. xv,107p. ISBN:
0421384107.
'Designed as a concise and practical guide to the law
governing access to information held by local authorities
and access to meetings generally'. Contents: 1. Access by
the public (I. The Local Government (Access to
Information) Act, 1985; II. Access to outside the 1985 Act)
- 2. Access by local authority members - 3. Personal
information - access and confidentiality - 4. The Data
Protection Act, 1984 - 5. The Access to Personal Files Act,
1987. App.1: Text of the 1985 Act; App.2: List of
enactments conferring rights to attend meetings or inspect
documents. *Class No:* 352

[693]
The **Municipal year book and public service directory.** 1991
ed. London, Municipal Journal Ltd., 1991. 2v. maps.
Annual. ISBN: 090055262x. ISSN: 03055906.
First published 1898.
46 sections of general information on public services.
V.1. Functions and officers (35 sections: 1. Administrative
and legal services ... 31. Water - 32. National associations
of local authorities - 33. Organizations - 34. Maps - 35.
Late information). V.2 Authorities and members (sections
36 to 46: 36. County councils of England ... 46. Central
government of England).General index; index to local
authorities; index to advertisers. *Class No:* 352

[694]
YOUNGS, F.A. **Guide to the local administrative units of
England.** London, Royal Historical Society, 1980-1991. 2v.
(xx,830p.;xx,919p.). ISBN: 0901050679, v.1; 0861932781,
v.2.
Vol I. Southern England; vol II. Northern England. Each
volume in 4 parts: 1. The parishes of England (V.I p.1-554;
v.II. p.1-635) - 2. Local government units - 3.
Parliamentary constituencies - 4. The dioceses of England.
Parts 2-4 summarise the information in pts. 1 of each
volume. Dividing line between volumes is roughly from the
Severn to the Wash. Detailed lists of sources. *Class No:*
352

Urban Areas (Towns & Cities)

[695]
GROSS, C. **A Bibliography of British municipal history.** 2nd
ed. Leicester, Leicester University Press, 1966 (Reprinted
New York, B. Franklin). vi,xvi,vii,xxxiv,461p. ISBN:
8833714651.
First published 1897 by Harvard University Press.
3092 numbered items (with interpolations) - books,
pamphlets, articles - on the constitutional history of British
boroughs. Introductory 'Survey of principal public and local
records for municipal history and town chronicles'. Part 1:
General works (including bibliographies, sources, secondary
works) on municipal history (including countries), arranged
by period and by subject. Part 2: Works on individual
towns, A-Z (p.150-430). Particularly important items (*e.g.*,
Anderson) are asterisked. Index, p.433-461. A basic critical
bibliography. The 2nd ed. is a reprint, with an essay on
Gross and his contributions to urban studies, by G.H.
Martin. *Class No:* 352.075.1

[696]
GUTKIND, E.A., *and others.* **International history of city
development.** London, Collier-Macmillan, 1964-72. 8v. illus.,
facsims., plans, maps. ISBN: 0029132509, v.1; 0029132606,
v.2; 0029132703, v.3; 0029132800, v.4; 0029133009, v.5;
0029133106, v.6; (no information on v.7); 0029133300, v.8.

....*(contd.)*
Contents: v.1. Urban development in Central Europe
(1964); v.2 Urban development in the Alpine and
Scandinavian countries (1965); v.3. Urban development in
Southern Europe: Spain and Portugal (1967); v.4. Urban
development in Southern Europe: Italy and Greece (1969);
v.5. Urban development in Western Europe: France and
Belgium (1970); v.6. Urban development in Western
Europe: the Netherlands and Great Britain (1971); v.7
Urban development in East-Central Europe: Poland,
Czechoslovakia and Hungary (1972); v.8 Urban
development in East Europe: Bulgaria, Romania and the
U.S.S.R. (1972). V.6 (xv,512p.) devotes p.127-473 to Great
Britain (chapters: 5. Origin and spread of settlement; 6.
The Roman interlude; 7. Invasion and settlements; 8. The
Middle Ages; 9 Utopia. Reality. Subtopia; 10. City survey
(24 cities); bibliography, p.492-504). V.6 has 294 captioned
illus. in all. *Class No:* 352.075.1

Central Government

[697]
Countries of the world and their leaders, 1991. Detroit, Mich.,
Gale Research Company, 1991. Annual. 2v.(1858p.). illus.,
70 maps and other illus. ISBN: 0810348411. ISSN:
01962809.
Basic social, political and economic data for 170
countries of the world, provided by the US State
Department and other government sources. Also other
information of use to American businessmen and other
travellers, including the CIA's list of 'Chiefs of State and
Cabinet members of foreign governments' and reports on
OAU, NATO, OECD, UN, ASEAN and the EC.
Supplement published 1991 updates. *Class No:* 354

[698]
'The Economist' dictionary of political biography. London,
Economist Books Ltd., 1990. 335p. ISBN: 009174847x.
Over 2000 entries, including brief biographies (*e.g.*
'Mitterand': 1¾ columns. A glossary and list of
abbreviations follow. The index arranges entries under
countries, Afghanistan ... Zimbabwe. Very readable text.
Class No: 354

[699]
**Political leaders of the contemporary Middle East and North
Africa:** a biographical dictionary. Reich, B., *ed.* Westport,
CT., Greenwood Press, 1990. 557p. ISBN: 0313262136.
Profiles 70 men and women who have had a significant
impact on the political development of the Arabic-speaking
countries of the area since World War II. Each entry (7-
10p.) is signed and concludes with a list of additional
sources as well as noting the political leader's own writings.
A chronology of the region, up to 1989, precedes a
bibliography of general sources and a detailed index.
'Strongly recommended'. (*Choice*, v.27(11/12), July-August
1990, p.1810). *Class No:* 354

[700]
Who's **who in European politics.** New York and Borough
Green, Kent, Bowker-Saur, 1990. xxi,760p. ISBN:
0862919118.
Section 1 has over 6000 short biographies of active
politicians (heads of state; members of government, national
legislatures, political parties, trade unions, and prominent
regional leaders) arranged A-Z in one sequence. Section 2 is
a political directory by countries. Geographically limited to
the two dozen member nations of the Council of Europe
(*i.e.* Western Europe). *Class No:* 354

Diplomatic Service

[701]
The Diplomatic Service list, 1991. Foreign and Commonwealth Office. 26th ed. London, HMSO., 1991. vi,344p. ISBN: 011591708x.
Succeeds *The Foreign Office list* (1806-1965). Issued twice a year.
In 4 parts: 1. Home departments - 2. British representatives overseas - 3. Chronological lists, from 1971, of Secretaries of State, Ministers of State, Permanent Under-Secretaries, Ambassadors, High Commissioners and permanent representatives to international organizations - 4. Biographical notes, and lists of staff (of Senior Grade to Grade 10 of the Diplomatic Service, officers of Grades S1-S3 of the Secretarial Branch and officers of the Security Officer Branch). *Class No:* 354DIP

[702]
FELTHAM, R.G. Diplomatic handbook. 5th ed. London, Longman Group (UK) Ltd., 1988. ix,180p. ISBN: 0582494613.
First published 1970.
10 sections: 1. Diplomatic relations (*e.g.,* the establishment of diplomatic missions and of permanent diplomatic missions) - 2. The Ministry of Foreign Affairs - 3. The diplomatic mission - 4. Protocol and procedure - 5. Diplomatic privileges and immunities - 6. Consular offices and consular posts - 7. The United Nations - 8. International organizations and agreements outside the UN - 9. International law and practice - 10. Conferences. Appendices A-E (E: Glossary of diplomatic, consular, legal and economic terms). Analytical index. Author is former Director of the Foreign Service Programme at the University of Oxford. 'An exceptionally handy little book' (*International affairs,* v.56(4), Autumn 1980, p.682) of the 3rd ed. *Class No:* 354DIP

Armed Forces

[703]
Brassey's multilingual military dictionary. Oxford, Pergamon & Brassey's Defence Publications, 1987. xvii,815p. ISBN: 0080270328.
c.7000 key military words and phrases in the English language, with definitions in English, numbered, and followed by equivalents in French, Spanish, German, Russian and Arabic. 6 indexes, one in each of the languages, including English, refer to the numbered items. Index of definitions and equivalents in British English and US usage, p.447-457. Appendices (*e.g.,* A. Ranks; B. Units/formations). *Class No:* 355

[704]
The Military balance, 1991-92. Oxford, Brassey's for the International Institute for Strategic Studies, 1991. Annual. 252p. illus., tables. ISBN: 0080413242. ISSN: 04597222.
First published 1959 as *The Soviet Union and the NATO powers: the military balance.*
In 2 parts: 1. Countries and principal facts - 2. Tables and analysis. Provides an authoritative assessment of the military strength and defence spending of every country possessing armed forces. Country entries detail military organization and list equipment holdings, manpower and relevant economic data. *Class No:* 355

[705]
WISE, T. A Guide to military museums. 5th rev. ed. Doncaster, S. Yorks., Athena Books, 1988. [80]p.
First published 1969.
211 main entries, arranged under regiments (descriptive notes; hours, curator, approaches; marginal badges of

....(contd.)
regiments). Index of special museums (*e.g.* German occupation: Channel Islands). 72 entries on 'other places of interest'. *Class No:* 355

Quotations

[706]
A Dictionary of military quotations. Royle, T., *comp.* London, Routledge; New York, Simon and Schuster, 1990. [xii],210p. ISBN: 0415041384, UK; 0132101130, US.
Nearly 3500 quotations arranged in 5 major categories: 1. Captains and kings - 2. Battles and wars - 3. Armies and soldiers - 4. War and peace - 5. Last post. Author index, p.191-198. Subject index, p.199-210. *Class No:* 355(082.2)

Great Britain

[707]
GORDON, L.L. British battles and medals: a description of every campaign medal and bar awarded since the Armada, with the historical reasons for their awards, and the names of all the ships, regiments and squadrons of the Royal Air Force whose personnel are entitled to them. Joslin, E.C., *ed.* 6th ed. London, Spink & Son, 1988. viii,299p. illus. (some col.). ISBN: 0907605257.
First published 1947.
10 sections: Campaign medals from 1588 to 1982 listed in chronological order - Polar medals - United Nations medals - Indian Army ranks and British equivalents - List of regiments and corps as at 1987 - Precedence of corps and infantry regiments - Cavalry and infantry regiments - Bibliography - Index of medals - Index of bars. Profusely illustrated in black-and-white, and 4 pages of bars in colour. A standard reference work for medal collectors. *Class No:* 355(410)

[708]
HIGHAM, R., ed. A Guide to the sources of British military history. London, Routledge; Berkeley, CA., University of California Press, 1971. xxi,630p. (*Conference in British studies, no.1.*) ISBN: 0710072511, UK; 0520016742, US.
25 chapters, by various hands (1. Introduction - 2. Military developments from prehistoric times to 1485 - 3. Military developments of the Renaissance - 4. The Navy, to 1714... 11. Colonial warfare, 1815-1970... 16. The development of the Royal Air Force, 1909-1945... 24. The evolution of naval medicine - 25. The history of military and martial law. Includes information on access to special collections and private archives. Appended bibliography of 362 items. No index. 'Nearly all 25 chapters are very good and some are outstanding' (*Journal of modern history,* v.45(1), March 1973, p.92-93. *British military history: a supplement to Robin Higham's guide...* (New York, Garland, xii,586. ISBN 0824084500) was published in 1988. *Class No:* 355(410)

Uniforms & Insignia

[709]
KNÖTEL, R. Uniforms of the world: a compendium of army, navy and air force uniforms, 1700-1937. Knötel, H. *and* Sieg, H., *eds.* Rev. & enl. ed. New York, Scribner; London, Arms and Armour Press, 1980 (reissued by Arms and Armour Press in 1988). 483p. illus. ISBN: 0684103047, US; 1850791090, UK.
Originally published 1896. Translated from the 1956 ed. by R.G. Bell.
Broad chronological and geographical coverage. 1600 illus. 'Leans rather heavily on the uniforms of the preunified states of Germany ... Recommended for all libraries' (*Choice,* v.18(4), December 1980, p.507-8). *Class No:* 355.14

Battles & Battlefields

[710]
LAFFIN, J. **Brassey's battles:** 3,500 years of conflict, campaigns and wars from A to Z. London, Oxford, Brassey's Defence Publications: Pergamon Press, 1986. 500p. 80 illus., maps. ISBN: 0080311857.

A dictionary of over 7000 entries for battles, campaigns and wars. Contents: Chronicle from Greek-Persian wars to W.W.II (p.1-21); Major wars and 'incidents' since 1945 (p.24). List of battles, campaigns and wars (p.27-482) A-Z by name of battle. 'Textual entries are clear, concise and informative and quality of design and production is first class' (*British book news*, May 1986, p.293). *Class No:* 355.422

[711]
SMURTHWAITE, D., *ed.* **Ordnance Survey complete guide to the battlefields of Britain.** Exeter, Devon, Webb & Bower, 1984. 224p. 140 illus. (50 col.), 133 maps (col.). ISBN: 0863501575.

Chronological arrangement (The Romans in Britain, 55 BC-AD 409 - Early England, 410-1060 - The Middle Ages, 1066-1450 - The age of the Wars of the Roses, 1450-1550 - The English Civil War, 1642-51 - Warfare in the age of reason, 1660-1746 - The Battle of Britain: the Royal Air Force, 1918-40). Tables of regiments. Gazetteer. Glossary. Further reading (p.221). Analytical index, p.222-224. *Class No:* 355.422

Strategy

[712]
ROBERTSON, D. **A Dictionary of modern defense and strategy.** London, Europa Publications, 1987. xii,324p. ISBN: 0946653712, UK; 0810350432, US.

Distributed in US & Canada by Gale Research Co., under the title *Guide to modern defense and strategy.*

Over 400 entries describing the terms, tactics, organizations, and accords governing today's defence. Entries arranged A-Z and each defined by an essay of *c*.350 words. Extensive cross-references. Uses non-technical language. British bias. A new ed. was published in 1990 (ISBN 0946653674). *Class No:* 355.43

Army

[713]
The Army list. 1814-. London, HMSO, 1814-. Frequency varies. 2v. (xiv,579p.;774p.). ISBN: 0117727067, Part 1 (1991 ed.); 0117726710, Part 2 (1990 ed.).

Part 1 is in 4 sections: 1. Queen and Royal Family; 2. Defence councils, Army commands, Establishments; 3. Regular Army; 4. Territorial Army. Index of names (p.445-577). Subject index (p.578-9). Part 2 lists officers in receipt of retired pay. *Class No:* 356

Histories

[714]
BARTHORP, M. **The Armies of Britain, 1485-1980.** London, National Army Museum; Guernsey, Seagull S.A., [1981]. 296p. illus., maps.

A popular account in 22 chapters. Appendices: 1. Regiments and corps of the British army in 1979 and their chief forbears; 2. Command of the army, 1485-1980. Chapter references, p.290-8. Index to text and illus.

For detailed period histories of army organization and administration, best sources are: Cruickshank, C.G. *Elizabeth's army* (1946); Fifth, Sir C.H. *Cromwell's army* (3rd ed., 1932); Walton, C. *History of the British standing army, 1660-1700* (1894); Curtis, E.E. *The organization of the British army in the American revolution* (1926); Oman,

....(contd.)
Sir C. *Wellington's army* (1912); and Dunlop, J.K. *The development of the British army, 1899-1914* (1938). *Class No:* 356(091)

Great Britain

[715]
GRIFFIN, D. **Encyclopaedia of modern British army regiments.** Wellingborough, Northants. P. Stephens, 1985. 236p. illus. ISBN: 0850597080.

Deals, in order of seniority, with each of the regiments left in the modern army. Includes information on insignia, honours, anniversaries, customs, mascots, dress distinctions, marches, etc., plus a 'family tree' for each regiment showing its lineage. Many photographs and other illustrations. *Class No:* 356(410)

USA

[716]
HIGHAM, R., *ed.* **A Guide to sources of US military history.** Hamden, CT., Archon: Shoestring Press, 1981. xiii,559p. ISBN: 0208014993.

19 chapters - bibliographical essays on major sources by specialists: 1. Introduction - 2. European background of American military affairs - 3. Colonial forces, 1607-1776 - 4. The American revolution ... 6. The Navy in the nineteenth century, 1789-1889 ... 10. Science and technology in the twentieth century ... 12. Military and naval medicine ... 17. The Army, 1945-1973 - 18. The Navy, 1941-1973 - 19. Museums as historical resources. Lengthy bibliographies after each essay (*e.g.*, 17. The Army: 390 references, A-Z). Introductory essay ends with suggestions for further research, then a bibliography. 6431 bibliographical references in all.

2 supplements have been published - 1. by Shoestring Press (1981. xiv,332p. ISBN 020801750x); 2. by Archon Books (1986. xiii,352p. ISBN 0208020721). *Class No:* 356(73)

Air Force

[717]
The Air Force List, 1991. London, HMSO, 1991. viii,519p. ISBN: 011772646x. ISSN: 02668610.

First published 1949. Annual. Previously *The Monthly Air Force list* February, 1919-1939.

Arranged by Commands/Branches, etc.; R.A.F. Voluntary Reserve. Index of names. Also 'The Royal Air Force retired list' (1990. [4],392p. ISBN 0117726168). *Class No:* 358.4

[718]
TAYLOR, M.J.H. **Encyclopedia of the world's air forces.** New York. Facts on file; Wellingborough, Northants. Patrick Stephens Ltd., 1988. 216p. ISBN: 0816020043 US; 1852601353 UK.

Largely updates M. Hewish's *Air forces of the world* (1979).

'Details of the world's aircraft from single aircraft operated by the Comores Air Force to the many thousands operated by the super powers' (*Stephen's catalogue*). Arranged A-Z by country, each country entry includes a map showing geographical location and a brief history of its air force, followed by information on current strength, air bases, commitments, budgets, and air policies, etc., Comparative specifications for aircraft types are in data tables at the end of the book. The author is a noted British aviation authority. *Class No:* 358.4

Navy

Histories

[719]
BEAVER, P., *ed.* **Encyclopaedia of the modern Royal Navy:** including the Fleet Air Arm and Royal Marines. 3rd ed. Wellingborough, Northants, Patrick Stephens, 1987. 329p. illus., maps, tables. ISBN: 0850598605.

First published 1982.

'Aims to illustrate the many facets of the modern Royal Navy ... remains the only comprehensive guide to all these elements' (*Introduction*). The introduction is followed by essays on the Royal Navy since 1945, organization and role, Royal Navy warships, the Fleet Air Arm, the Royal Marines, auxiliary services, other services, naval equipment weapons and services, uniforms and insignia. Also a glossary and an index. *Class No:* 359

[720]
GREAT BRITAIN. MINISTRY OF DEFENCE. Navy Department. **The Navy list:** containing lists of ships, establishments and officers of the Fleet, 1991. London, HMSO, 1991. vi,362p. ISBN: 0117726818. ISSN: 01416081.

First published April 1814. Annual. Not published for sale between September 1939 and May 1949. July and January supplements cover selective promotions, Queen's Birthday and New Year honours, and changes.

Contents include: 2. Alphabetical list of officers - 3. Seniority lists of officers on active list - 4. Key Royal Navy personnel - 5. Ships and units of the fleet and establishments - 6. Key addresses - 7. Reserves - 8. Obituary ... Also *The Navy list of retired officers* ... (1989. xii,215p., ISBN 0117726141). *Class No:* 359

[721]
OBIN, A. **Bibliography of nautical books, 1991.** 6th ed. Warsash, Southampton, Warsash Nautical Bookshop, 1991. 478p. ISBN: 0948646063.

First ed. published 1985. Computer printout, one line per title. 2 supplements issued for this edition.

11 sections: 1. Books, main listing by title (p.9-120) - 2. Books, main listing by author - 3. Books, main listing by subject - 4. Hydrographic Department (Admiralty) - 5. International Maritime Organization - 6. Statutory instruments - 7. M notices (Department of Transport) - 8. British standards - 9. Journals and periodicals - 10. Video cassettes - 11. Publishers and suppliers (addresses and telephone numbers). Coverage of shipping, naval, maritime, yachting, and marine engineering items in print, forthcoming, and out of print. *Class No:* 359

[722]
PALMER, J., *comp.* **Jane's dictionary of naval terms.** London, Macdonald & Jane's. 1975. [iv],342p. ISBN: 035608258x.

Over 6000 entries for maritime military terms, terms of general seamanship and some purely mercantile terms ('Davit': ¾col.; 'Shackle': 1 column). Different meanings are numbered. Many cross-references. Sources (p.2) include Royal Navy, US Navy and NATO manuals. *Class No:* 359

[723]
PEMSEL, H. **Atlas of naval warfare:** an atlas and chronology of conflict at sea, from the earliest times to the present day. London, Arms and Armour Press, 1977. 176p. illus., tables, maps.

First German ed. 1975.

4 sections: The age of galleys - The age of sail - The iron and steel - The nuclear age. Traces events up to 1973 (the Arab-Israeli 'Yom Kippur' war). 'The war in the Pacific', 1941-42: p.125-8; 8 maps; 8 illus. of ships. 9 appendices (*e.g.,* 'The world's naval powers', by number of ships, 1859-1977). Select bibliography, p.165-6. Index. 'An excellent work, well researched and attractively put together' (*American reference books annual*, 1979, v.10, item 1604). *Class No:* 359

[724]
ALBION, R.G. **Naval and maritime history:** an annotated bibliography. 4th ed. rev. & expanded. Mystic, CT., Munson Institute of American Maritime History, the Marine Historical Association, Inc., 1972. ix,370p. ISBN: 0913372056.

First published 1951.

Lists *c.*5000 books in English, plus PhD. theses. In 7 main sections: 1. Reference works (A-G, including F: Lists of ships; G: Lists of men) - 2. Merchantmen and warships - 3. Captains and crews - 4. Maritime science, exploration and expansion - 5. Commerce and shipping - 6. Navies (naval history, by periods, p.229-302) - 7. Special topics (*e.g.,* Auxiliary services; Main American maritime museums). Books asterisked represent 'the select minority of the more substantial and useful'. Author and subject indexes. 'An indispensable companion to any writer on maritime subjects' (E.G.R. Taylor, on the 3rd ed., in *Journal of the Institute of Navigation*, v.17(2), April 1964, p.211). US-slanted. *Class No:* 359(091)

[725]
MARCUS, G.J. **A Naval history of England.** London, Allen & Unwin, 1961-71. 2v. (xii,494p.; 523p.). maps.

V.1: *The formative years [to 1973]*; v.2: *The age of Nelson.* V.2. is well formulated and has chapter bibliographies. p.505-20. Non-analytical index, but ships are listed in detail. Very readable narrative. Aims to be a compromise between the short and the full-scale history. '... a must for all secondary schools and libraries' (*British book news*, June 1971, p. 498). *Class No:* 359(091)

[726]
SWEETMAN, J., *ed.* **American naval history:** an illustrated chronology of the U.S. Navy and Marine Corps, 1775 - present. Annapolis, Md., Naval Institute Press, 1984. 330p. illus., maps. ISBN: 0870212907.

Year-by-year summary of major events in the history of the US Navy and Marine Corps from the American Revolution through 1984. Covers battles, warships, personnel, exploration, etc. *c.*200 illustrations and several specially drawn maps. Bibliography. Calendar, vessel and general indexes. A 2nd ed. was published in 1991 (384p. ISBN 1557507856). *Class No:* 359(091)

36 Social Services & Welfare

Charities & Foundations

[727]
Charities digest: an alphabetical digest of charities, 1991. 97th ed. London, Family Welfare Association, 1991. Annual. 354p. ISBN: 0900954442.
First published 1882 as *The annual charities register and digest*. Title varies.
A detailed directory of *c.*2000 charitable trusts and associations for special and general classes. Sections: Charities in the UK - Registry of Friendly Societies - Giving to charity - Alphabetical list of charities registered under the Act - Some organizations not registered - Adoption societies - Almshouses - C.A.B. - Councils for voluntary service - Legal advice centres - Local associations for the deaf - Local associations for disabled people - Local associations for the blind - Subject index - Advertisers' index. *Class No:* 36.075

[728]
Directory of grant-making trusts, 1991. 12th ed. Tonbridge, Kent, Charities Aid Foundation, 1991. xxvi, 1038p. ISBN: 0904757528.
First published 1968 by National Council of Social Service, Charities Aid Fund.
4 parts: 1. Classification of charitable purposes - 2. Trusts listed under classifications (p.7-19). Alphabetical list of trusts empowered to give to general charitable trusts - 3. Register of grant-making charitable trusts (p.351-983). Trusts deleted from Part III - 4. Geographical index of trusts (p.986-1024). Alphabetical index of subjects (p.1025-1038). Some entries include titles of publications (*e.g.,* Oxfam, p.776). *Class No:* 36.075

[729]
The International foundation directory. Hodson, H.V., *ed.* 5th ed. London, Europa Publications Ltd.; Detroit, Mich., Gale Research Co., 1991. xxvii,526p. ISBN: 0946653666, UK.
First published 1974.
A directory of about 900 institutions in 50 countries, A-Z, covering foundations, trusts and similar non-profit institutions in many fields. Data on each: name and address; founding data; brief history; activities; finance; names of officers; publications (if any). Bibliography: index. Coverage is wide-ranging, including science, medicine, education, social welfare, the arts and humanities, aid to less-developed countries, and international relations. *Class No:* 36.075

Social Services

[730]
BUNCH, A. **Community information.** In *Printed reference material* (3rd ed., 1990, edited by P.W. Lea and A. Day), p.324-359.
General sources - Government publications - Subject areas (careers ... women). 6 references. An important and timely contribution. *Class No:* 362

[731]
CANS (Citizens Advice Notes): a service of information ... compiled from authoritative sources. Cumulative ed. to 1991. London, NCVO (National Council for Voluntary Organisations), CANS Department, 1991. 2v. plus supplements.
First published as *Notes on new emergency regulations, 1939.*
Continuously updated digest of social legislation. 16 sections: 1. Administration of justice ... 3. British nationality and migration - 4. Business and industry - 5. Consumer protection ... 7. Education - 8. Employment ... 11. Housing, general - 12. Housing: Rent Acts - 13. Local government and public health - 14. Married persons and children ... 17. Personal health and welfare services ... 21. Town and country planning - 22. Transport (Roads). Index precedes, p.1-101. *Class No:* 362

[732]
Social service abstracts: monthly summaries of selected documents. Department of Health and Social Security Library Services. London, HMSO (previously the Library), 1972-. Monthly. ISSN: 03094693.
Includes over 2000 abstracts a year. Sections: Social policy - Social services - Social work - Services for the elderly and the handicapped - Services for children and young people - Services for other special needs - DHSS circulars - Bibliographies. Author and analytical subject index per issue; cumulated annually. Covers the whole range of the personal social services, with particular emphasis on literature originating in Britain. *Class No:* 362

[733]
Social services year book, 1991/92. London, Longman Group (UK) Ltd., 1991. Annual. lii,802p. ISBN: 0582078695. ISSN: 0307093x.
First published 1972 (for 1972/73).
31 sections (*e.g.,* 7. County Council social services and allied departments ... 9. London - 10. Scotland - 11. Northern Ireland ... 16. Health authorities ... 19. Advice and counselling - 20. Voluntary service - 21. Elderly people's welfare organizations ... 30. Social services and allied organizations - 31. Buyer's guide. Index, p.778-800. Bibliography precedes, p.xlii-xlvii, arranged by subjects. A mine of information. *Class No:* 362

[734]
Voluntary agencies directory, 1991. 12th rev. ed. London,
Bedford Square Press, 1991. xi,238p. ISBN: 0719912865.

Previously as *Voluntary social services: a directory of
national organisations* (first published 1928) and *Voluntary
organizations: an NCVO directory.*

A directory of over 2000 organizations, including
voluntary organizations, charity and pressure groups,
arranged A-Z. Data: address; chairman's name; contact
name; date of foundation; objectives; activities; publications;
etc. Useful addresses, p.167-170; abbreviations and
acronyms, p.171-177; classified index, p.179-224. *Class No:*
362

Health & Welfare

[735]
ELLING, R.H., *ed.* **Cross-national study of health systems -
countries, world regions, and special problems:** a guide to
information sources. Detroit, Mich., Gale Research Co.,
1980. xviii,687p. (*Health affairs information guide series,
v.3.*) ISBN: 0810314533.

Complementary to *Cross-national study of health systems
- concepts, methods and data sources.* (Transaction Books,
1980).

Identifies 17 types of special problems in health systems.
Specific countries (including Canada, Cuba, People's
Republic of China, Sweden, UK and USSR - but not USA,
dealt with elsewhere in the Health affairs series), and other
world regions are then covered. The annotated bibliography
records research monographs, periodical articles, official
reports and unpublished dissertations. *Class No:* 362.1

[736]
Health service abstracts. London, Department of Health and
Social Security Library, 1974-. no.1-. Monthly. ISSN:
02680459.

Succeeds *Current literature on personal social services*
and, later, *Current literature on health services.* As from
May 1985 incorporates *Hospital abstracts* and *Current
literature on general medical practice* also.

About 150 brief summaries of journal articles, reports,
books, and references per issue. Headings: Services for
special groups (Maternity - Children - Elderly - Terminally
ill - Physically handicapped - Psychiatric services - Mentally
handicapped - Ethnic minorities - Prison medical services);
Services for special diseases; NHS reports; DHSS
publications; Circulars and other guidance material. Cross-
references. Author and subject indexes. Database is
DATASTAR. *Class No:* 362.1

[737]
HOGARTH, J. **Glossary of health care terminology.**
Copenhagen, World Health Organization, Regional Office
for Europe, 1975. 476p.

About 350 main entries with references to many other
terms; designed to promote the standardization of public
health terminology. Coverage: health services; resources;
finance; manpower; buildings; drugs; management; planning;
statistics. Detailed index. *Class No:* 362.1

Great Britain

[738]
Croner's care homes guide. New Maldon, Croner Publications,
1987. 2v. ISBN: 0900319518, South; 0900319526, North &
Midlands. ISSN: 09525157.

One volume covers the South of England, the other the
North and Midlands. Each volume is arranged by counties
and then alphabetically by town in postal address. Together
they list over 10,000 homes. Each entry includes full name
of home, date established, full postal address, telephone
number, name of proprietor, ownership status, special

....*(contd.)*
services offered, visiting arrangements, fees, number of
residents, conditions of acceptance, licensing authority,
details of accommodation available, arrangements for meals,
lifts, TV, telephone, heating, etc. A-Z index by names of
homes. *Class No:* 362.1(410)

[739]
**The Hospitals and health services yearbook ... and directory of
hospital suppliers;** an annual record of the hospitals and
health services of Great Britain and Northern Ireland,
incorporating *Burdett's Hospitals and charities,* founded
1889. 1991 ed. London. Institute of Health Services
Management, 1991. xxvii,[5026]p. ISBN: 0901003727.

21 sections, including directories of health authorities in
England, in Wales and in Scotland; Statutory instruments
and circulars; Summaries of reports; Health Service
literature; a short bibliography; and Directory of hospital
suppliers. Indexes (on green paper); Health authorities,
hospitals; general index; advertisers. *Class No:* 362.1(410)

[740]
LAING, W. **Laing's review of private health care ... and
directory of independent hospitals,** residential and nursing
homes and related services 1990/91. 3rd ed. London, Laing
& Buisson Publications, 1990. 1220p., tables, map. ISBN:
1854400193. ISSN: 09539050.

Lists *c*12,000+ private and voluntary homes for the
elderly, plus independent hospitals, screening clinics, and
homes and hospitals for the mentally ill. *Class No:*
362.1(410)

[741]
The NHS handbook. National Association of Health
Authorities and Trusts. 7th ed. London, Macmillan Press,
1991. xxiii,267p. ISBN: 033353736x.

First ed. published 1980.

Aims 'to make N.H.S. easily understood by those without
prior knowledge of its structure and to provide an up-to-
date reference document for those already working in the
N.H.S. and related fields ...' (*Publisher's catalogue*).
Sections: The N.H.S. today - Management - Funding -
Trends in health care - Health care provision - Support
services - Personnel - Care in the community - Partnerships
with the N.H.S. Also a quick reference section and an
index. *Class No:* 362.1(410)

[742]
Registered Nursing Home Association: reference book, 1990/91:
registered nursing homes, clinics and hospitals in the UK.
15th ed. Birmingham, the Association, 1990. 210p. maps.

Contents: Summary of National Health Service beds -
List of N.H.S. in region/district order - Regional health
authorities/boards - Alphabetical list of members of the
R.N.H. Association - Town/district locations of members of
the R.N.H. Association. *Class No:* 362.1(410)

Libraries

[743]
**Directory of medical and health care libraries in the United
Kingdom and Republic of Ireland, 1990.** Wright, D.J., *for
the Medical, Health and Welfare Libraries Group of the
Library Association.* 7th ed. London, Library Association
Publishing Ltd., 1990. xiv,295p. ISBN: 0853657793.

First published 1957, the 1st-4th editions being titled
Directory of medical libraries in the British Isles.

Lists over 600 specialist libraries, with details of address,
telephone and fax numbers, electronic mailing addresses,
librarian, readers, stock policy, opening hours, publications,
branches, holdings, etc. 2 appendices, including 1. List of
members of NHS Regional Libraries Group. List of
libraries arranged A-Z by town. Indexes of personal names,

....(contd.)
establishments, counties, and named collections. Subject index to special collections. Selected subject index to libraries. *Class No:* 362.1:061:026/027

Hospitals

[744]
Hospital literature index. Chicago, Ill., American Hospital Association, 1945-. Quarterly (from 1945 to 1961, 2pa.) 4th quarter is annual hard-bound issue. 5-year cumulations. ISSN: 00185736.
From 1978 compiled with the co-operation of the National Library of Medicine.
About 10,000 references pa from *c.*500 English-language journals. An A-Z author-subject index of literature about hospital administration, planning and financing, and administrative aspects of medical, paramedical, etc., fields. Includes references to significant books as well as periodical articles. Also available online; Vendors: DIMDI; National Library of Medicine. *Class No:* 362.11

Family Planning

[745]
LOUDON, N. *and* **NEWTON, J.,** *eds.* **Handbook of family planning.** Edinburgh, Churchill Livingstone, 1985. xiv,334p. illus. ISBN: 0443024804.
17 chapters: 1. Family planning - The United Kingdom: services and training - 2. Choice of method ... 4. Combined oral contraceptive pills ... 7. Intrauterine contraceptive devices ... 10. Sterilization ... 14. Medicolegal aspects of family planning ... 17. Family planning in general practice. Addresses. Analytical index, p.327-334. A 2nd rev. ed. was published in 1991 (484p. illus. ISBN 044303964x). *Class No:* 362.178

Disabled & Handicapped

[746]
Directory for the disabled: a handbook of information and opportunities for disabled and handicapped people. Darnborough, A. *and* Kinrade, D., *comps.* 4th ed. Cambridge, Woodhead-Faulkner, in association with the Royal Association for Disability and Rehabilitation, 1985. x, 358p. ISBN: 0839412555.
First published 1977.
16 sections ... 2. Financial benefits and allowances - 3. Aids: their provision and availability ... 7. Employment - 8. Mobility and motoring ... 11. Sport and leisure ... 16. Helpful organizations. 2 appendices: A. Selected further information, including bibliographies; B. Addresses of publishers and stockists mentioned. Index, p.349-53). *Class No:* 362.4

Child Welfare

[747]
UNICEF. State of the world's children, 1992. Adamson, P. *and* Adamson, L. Oxford, Oxford University Press for UNICEF, 1992. [xi], 96p. tables, charts. ISBN: 0192622285. ISSN: 0265718x.
Annual, first published 1980.
In 2 parts: A report submitting 10 specific propositions for ending the poverty of one quarter of mankind, and a section of statistical tables (p.69-89); footnotes to tables (p.90-96). *Class No:* 362.7

Youth Welfare

[748]
Directory of youth services and child care in the UK. 2nd ed. Harlow, Essex, Longman, 1992. xvii,346p. (*Longman community information guide.*) ISBN: 0582087864.
First published 1990.
A comprehensive, detailed listing of local authority, independent and voluntary organizations. In 2 parts: 1. Public and statutory services, central and local government, England, Wales, Scotland and Northern Ireland - 2. Voluntary, private and non-statutory services. Index, p.340-345. *Class No:* 362.8

[749]
Youth movements of the world. Angel, W.D. Harlow, Essex, Longman, 1991. 700p. illus. (*Longman current affairs.*) ISBN: 0582062713.
Lists over 1000 youth organizations and government and non-government agencies under countries A-Z. Introduction on each country gives statistics (demography, education, employment and health) and information on government youth ministries and youth policies. On each organization: contact; office holders; membership; history; aims; activities; affiliations. *Class No:* 362.8

Insurance

[750]
COCKERELL, H. Dictionary of insurance. 2nd ed. London, Witherby & Co. Ltd., 1987. viii,235p. ISBN: 0900886501.
First published 1980 as *Witherby's dictionary of insurance.*
About 2000 terms, with brief (*c.*20-word) definitions. List of abbreviations precedes. Appendix. 'Institutions of insurance', p.207-35. 'Intended to help people who practice insurance or who need to read about it, to understand the terms and abbreviations they may encounter. It is not encyclopedic' (*Preface*). *Class No:* 368

[751]
Financial times world insurance year book, 1991. Harlow, Essex, Longman Group (UK) Ltd.; Chicago, Ill., St. James Press, 1991. xxi,594p. ISBN: 0582067154, UK; 1558621091, US.
Entries for 1170 companies in 82 countries, arranged geographically (Argentina ... Zimbabwe). Each country section is prefaced by selected statistics and details of leading national insurance associations and institutes. Information for each insurance firm is foundation, head office, directors, management, classes written, activities, capital, ownership, financial results (data for the last three years available). Preliminary sections are: Currency: conversion rates and abbreviations - Company designations - Financial terms defined - Lloyds of London. Indexes of classes written (p.493-522), companies (p.523-589), international professional services (p.590-594), and advertisers (p.594). *Class No:* 368

Social Security

[752]
Social security statistics, 1991. Department of Social Security. London, HMSO, 1992. 379p. tables, map. ISBN: 0117619272.
First published for 1972. Annual. Replaces tables previously included in the annual report of what was then the Department of Health and Social Security.
In 8 sections: A. Income related benefits - B. Elderly - C. Unemployment - D. Incapable of work because of sickness - E. Disabled and carers - F. War pensions and industrial injuries - G. Mothers, widows and families - H. Other statistics. Data is for several years to 1990. 6 appendices

....(contd.)

(*e.g.,* 2. Sources of statistics - 3. Useful publications - 4. Description of social security regions - 5. Description of standard regions). *Class No:* 368.4

37 Education

Education

[753]

British education index. 1954-.v.1-. Leeds, University of Leeds (previously London, Library Association, then British Library Bibliographic Division), 1954-58; 1968-. 3 quarterly issues and annual cumulation. ISSN: 00070637.

An index of articles of permanent educational interest, published in a wide range of English-language periodicals. Arranged by author, with full bibliographical citations, then by subject. List of indexed journals. Also available online. Vendors: DIALOG. *Class No:* 370

[754]

CLARKE, P.B. Finding out in education: a guide to sources of information. Harlow, Essex, Longman, 1990. ix,217p. ISBN: 0582067545.

Annotated entries, arranged in form rather than subject sections. 29 sections in all: 1. Introduction ... 3. Guides to libraries ... 7-17 General reference sources - 18-20. Bibliographies - 21-24. Periodicals - 25-26. Educational research - 27. Conclusion - 28. Title index (p.194-211) - 29. Subject index (p.212-217). No author index. Author was formerly librarian at Jordanhill College of Education, Glasgow. *Class No:* 370

[755]

Core list of books & journals in education. O'Brien, P. *and* Fabiano, E., *eds.* Phoenix, Ariz., Oryx, 1990. 125p. ISBN: 0597745590.

Mainly limited to English-language imprint material. Entries have detailed annotations. 3 indexes: author/title; title; subject. *Class No:* 370

[756]

Education index. New York, H.W. Wilson, 1932-. v.1-. Monthly (except July and August), cumulates quarterly and annually (July-June). ISSN: 00131385.

An index to *c.*350 selected educational journals, proceedings and yearbooks. A-Z order of subjects and authors, list of book reviews appended. Journals covered are predominantly US. Also available online. (Vendors: Wilsonline (EDI)) and on CD-ROM. *Class No:* 370

[757]

The International encyclopedia of education: research and studies. Huson, T. *and* Postlethwaite, T.N., *eds.* London, Pergamon Press, 1985. 10v. (6068p.). 500 illus. ISBN: 0080281192.

15,000 entries cover 17 major areas of education (adult education, counselling, curriculum, economics, administration, policy, educational technology, evaluation, higher education, national systems, pre-school education, education research, special education, teaching, vocational education, and industrial education). Strong US emphasis. Lengthy entries (*e.g.*, 'Adolescence': $10\frac{1}{4}$ cols., 8 sections, 8

....(contd.)
references; 'Audiovisual equipment': over 8 cols., 7 sections, 3 references). Vol. 10 contains a classified list of entries, a list of contributors, author and subject indexes, and a list of major educational journals. *Supplementary volume 1* (1989. xxvi,864p. ISBN 0080349749) is the first of a series intended to extend and update the work. *Class No:* 370

[758]

PAGE, G.T. *and* **THOMAS, J.B. International dictionary of education.** London, Kogan Page, 1977. 381p. diagrs. ISBN: 0850383013.

Over 10,000 entries, ranging from the fine points of curriculum development and educational research to the colloquialisms of the classroom and lecture theatre (*Introduction*). Brief definitions (maximum: *c.*150 words); numbered meanings. Very concise bibliographies; entries for international organizations and major national institutions and associations. Appendix of abbreviations, and of American honor societies, professional fraternities and sororities. British and US emphasis. *Class No:* 370

Yearbooks & Directories

[759]

The Education authorities directory and annual, 1991. 88th year of publication. Merstham, Redhill, School Government Publishing Ltd., 1991. lxxx,1280p. ISBN: 0900640243. ISSN: 00709131.

First published 1909.

Various sections: Government departments, public offices, examination organizations - Local education authorities - Secondary and middle schools (p.156-559) - Teachers' centres - Further education - Polytechnics and Scottish central institutions - Institutes/colleges of higher education (teacher training) - Universities - Special schools and homes for the handicapped - Special community homes - Directors of social services - Educational psychological service - Careers centres - Public library authorities - Organizations concerned with education (p.1198-1249) - Education publishers and equipment suppliers - Commonwealth education departments and universities (p.1264-1280). Preliminary pages include: Index to local education authorities and secondary schools; General index (p.xi-xxvi); Index to place names; Index to advertisers; Buyer's guide; 'Coming events in education, 1991'. *Class No:* 370(058)

Histories

[760]
ARMYTAGE, W.H.G. Four hundred years of English education. Cambridge, Cambridge University Press,1964. viii,353p.
Covers the period 1563-1963 in 12 chapters. Chapter notes, p.270-324; references to general sources used, p.vii-viii. Analytical index. Author was Professor of Education, University of Sheffield. *Class No:* 370(091)

Research Projects

[761]
MITZEL, H.E., *and others, eds.* **Encyclopedia of educational research.** 5th ed. London, Collier Macmillan; New York, Free Press, 1982. 4 v. (2126 p.) illus. ISBN: 0029004500.
First published in 1941. Sponsored by the American Educational Research Association.
Presents a critical synthesis and interpretation of reported research in the field. 256 lengthy articles by 300 specialists, with extensive bibliographies (*e.g.,* 'Bilingual education': 18 cols., with 'see also' references and 39 bibliographical references; 'Computer-based education': 29 cols. in 15 sections, with 'see also' references and including $7\frac{1}{2}$ columns of bibliographical references. Cross references. ' ... an essential purchase for libraries serving students and professionals in education' (*Library journal*, 1 January, 1983, p.42). *Class No:* 370:061:061.62.005

Teaching Materials

Education Technology

[762]
International yearbook of educational and training technology, 1991. Osbourne, C., *ed.* 9th ed. London, Kogan Page, in association with the Association for Educational and Training Technology, 1991. Annual. 508p. ISBN: 0749403780. ISSN: 03709732.
First published in 1976. Previously as *APLET yearbook of educational and instructional technology, 1972/73* (1972).
Arranged in 4 parts: 1. International and regional centres of activity - 2. Centres of activity in the United Kingdom - 3. Centres of activity in the United States (by State, A-Z) - 4. Centres of activity worldwide (by country, A-Z). Each section lists organizations actively involved in the development of educational and training technology and includes addresses, telephone and telex numbers, contact names, area of interest, details of current and future research and development projects, main services offered, keywords summarizing the organization's activities, and recent publications by staff or personnel. Index of institutions. *Class No:* 371.68/69

Schools

Yearbooks & Directories

[763]
Independent schools yearbook, 1991: girl's schools: the official book of reference of the Girls' Schools Association and the Independent Schools Association Inc. 85th year. London, A. & C. Black, 1991. Annual. xl,615p. ISBN: 0713634168.
Previously titled *The Girl's school yearbook.*
Contents: 1, Schools belonging to The Girl's Schools Association - 2. Other senior schools - 3. Preparatory school entries - 4. The Independent Schools Association Inc. - 5. Tutors, tutorial colleges and other independent institutions - 6. Universities and colleges - 7. Careers. *Class No:* 373(058)

[764]
—**Independent schools yearbook, 1991:** boy's schools, co-educational schools and preparatory schools: the official book of reference of The Headmasters' Conference ... 101st year. London, A. & C. Black, 1991. Annual. xliv,965p. ISBN: 0713634154.
Formerly *The Public preparatory schools yearbook.*
Similar information to the above. *Class No:* 373(058)

Primary Schools

[765]
The Routledge compendium of primary education. Campbell, R.J., *ed.* London, Routledge & Kegan Paul, 1988. x,250p. ISBN: 0415002206.
Designed as a guide and reference source to the theory, practice and policy in primary education. Part 1 consists of 14 extended analyses and discussions of the main ideas in the field, such as classroom processes, home-school relationships, and children's development and learning. Part 2 is a glossary, including definitions of complex or controversial ideas; a list of 'Further reading', and outlines of important reports, surveys, Education Acts, and leading figures in primary education. *Class No:* 373.3

Adult Education

[766]
DRODGE, S. Adult education. Newcastle-under-Lyme, AAL Publishing, 1988. [2],53p. ISBN: 0900092696.
Sections: Information about adult classes - Providing resources for adult classes - Adult basic education - Provision for independent learners - Supporting open learning packages - Education guidance services - Twenty-five practical ways to work with adult learners - References and further reading (p.52-3). *Class No:* 374.7

Open Learning

Yearbooks & Directories

[767]
Open learning directory, 1989. Brooke Association (Manchester) Ltd. Bradford, Training Agency, 1989. xvi,484,[7]. ISBN: 0863922910.
Designed for use by employers, training advisers, etc. Details of over 1500 open learning training courses, arranged in 4 sections: 1. Open learning delivery centres and consultancy services - 2. Open learning support services - 3. Other institutions - 4. Open learning packages (arranged A-Z by subject, Agriculture ... Transport, and subdivided again). Bibliography, p.457. Indexes (p.462-484) by subject (principal topics), by names (organizations), by courses (A-Z), by qualifications, and advertisers. *Class No:* 374.7OPE(058)

Special Education

[768]
Exceptional child education resources. Reston, VA., Council for Exceptional Children, 1968-. Quarterly. ISSN: 01604309.
As *Exceptional child education abstracts* until May 1977.
Abstracts periodical articles from over 250 journals, as well as books, reports, surveys, doctoral dissertations, and nonprint professional media. Covers education of both handicapped and gifted children. Numerical order, with author, subject and title index, per issue and annually. The Council acts as a clearinghouse for ERIC programmes in this field. On-line database available, 1966- (updated quarterly). *Class No:* 377

[769]

Handbook of special education: research and practice. Wang, M.C., *and others, eds.* Oxford, Pergamon Press, 1987. 3v. (xi,387p.;xi,392 p.;ix,376 p.). ISBN: 0080333834 Vol.1; 0080333842 Vol.2; 0080333850 Vol.3.

V.1. Learner characteristics and adaptive education; v.2. Mildly handicapped conditions; v.3. Low incidence conditions. The 3 vols. contain 45 chapters in 9 sections, each summarizing the well-confirmed knowledge in a particular area, giving attention to the research literature, tested experience and practice of leading professionals. Each vol. has a bibliography, author and subject index. Synthesis of findings published 1990 (236p. ISBN 0080402380; 0080402372). *Class No:* 377

Further & Higher Education

[770]

The International encyclopedia of higher education. Knowles, A.S., *ed.* Washington, Jossey-Bass Publishers, 1977. 10v. (5208p.). ISBN: 0875893236.

V.1. *Contents. Contributors, Acronyms. Glossary.* v.2-9. A-Z entries. v.10. *Index.* About 500 named contributors. Appended to each substantial article are lists of (a) major international and national organizations; (b) principal information sources. 'Adult education': v.2. p.120-73: 7 sections, plus two appendices (p.168-73). Country entries are a feature. V.9 concludes with 'International directory' (p.4477-4588). V.10: *Index* comprises a name index and a subject index (p.4633-5208). Somewhat elaborate layout. For the very large reference library. 'A unique source for state-of-the-art surveys, and particularly for comparative studies ... (*Library journal*, 15th April 1979, p.886). *Class No:* 378

[771]

MOHR, B., *ed.* **Higher education in the European Community:** student handbook. 6th ed. Luxembourg, Office for Official Publications of the European Communities; London, Kogan Page, 1990. 516p. ISBN: 9282607399, EC; 0749401281, UK.

First published 1977.

A directory of courses and institutions in the 12 countries. Arranged by country, information for each is organizations of higher education (type, student statistics, organization and validity of courses); admission and registration; knowledge of the language of instruction, language courses, and other courses; financial assistance and scholarships; entry and residence regulations; social aspects (social security and health insurance, advisory services, student employment, cost of living, accommodation, etc.). Appendix to each entry lists organizations and institutions from which further information and application forms may be obtained, a bibliography of national information material and, in most cases, a table of subjects taught at each institution. Also includes information on the European University Institute, Florence; College of Europe; Bruges; and information on the Erasmus programme, ECTS, Comett, Lingua and Naric. Note: the manuscript was completed in May 1989. *Class No:* 378

[772]

Research into higher education abstracts. Abingdon, Oxon, Carfax Publishing Co., for the Society for Research into Higher Education, 1967-. v.1,no.1-. 3pa (previously quarterly). ISSN: 00345426.

About 200 abstracts per issue. Sections: A. General - B. Systems and institutions - C. Teaching and learning - D. Students - E. Staff - F. Student assessment and course evaluation - G. Continuing education - H. Information technology and networks. Over 500 journals scanned. Author and subject indexes each issue, cumulating in the 3rd issue each year. *Class No:* 378

Academic Dress

[773]

HAYCRAFT, F.W., *comp.* **Degrees and hoods of the world's universities and colleges.** 5th ed., rev. and enl. by F.R.S.Rogers and others. Hassocks, Sussex, C.A.H.Franklyn, 1972. xvii,162p.illus.

First published 1923.

Short historical introduction. Main section gives, under each country, its universities and under each university its degrees and details of the shape and colours of its degree hoods. Separate sections for theological colleges and learned societies. Illus. include hoods in full colour and a section showing hood shapes. A comprehensive index is provided. *Class No:* 378:391

Degrees & Qualifications

[774]

British qualifications. 21st ed. London, Kogan Page, 1990. Annual. lvii,740p. ISBN: 0749402814.

First published 1966.

A comprehensive guide to educational, technical, professional and academic qualifications in Britain. 7 parts: 1. Teaching establishments - 2. Secondary school examinations - 3. Further education examinations - 4. Awards made by universities and polytechnics - 5. Qualifications, listed by trade & professions (c.200 career fields and professions (Accountancy ... Youth and community service) - 6. Accrediting bodies - 7. Membership of professional associations. Detailed index, p.711-740, preceded by index of advertisers. *Class No:* 378.2

[775]

Which degree? a comprehensive guide to all full-time and sandwich degree courses offered in the UK, 1992. 23rd ed. London, The Newpoint Publishing Company Ltd., 1991. Annual. 5v. ISBN: 0862633397, full set; 086263332x, v.1; 0862633338, v.2; 0862633346, v.3; 0862633354, v.4; 0862633362, v.5.

Successor to *Which university?*.

A subject listing of over 12,000 degree courses in the UK, stating content and entrance requirements followed by sections on universities, polytechnics and colleges, stating amenities, etc. Volumes are arranged by subject: 1: Arts, humanities, languages - 2. Engineering, technology, the environment - 3. Mathematics, medicine, sciences - 4. Business, education, social sciences - 5. Universities, polytechnics, colleges: a guide to institutions. Essential reading. Indexes to all 5 vols. *Class No:* 378.2

Scholarships & Postgraduate Awards

[776]

Study abroad: international scholarships and courses. 27th ed. Paris, Unesco, 1991. xvii,1276 p. ISBN: 9230027154.

First published 1948.

A directory of more than 3000 opportunities for further study and training in all academic and professional fields, offered by international organizations, governments, private and public foundations, universities and other institutions in more than 124 countries. *Class No:* 378.3

Universities, Polytechnics & Colleges

[777]

Commonwealth universities yearbook, 1991: a directory to the universities of the Commonwealth and the handbook of the Association. 67th ed. London, Association of Commonwealth Universities, 1991. 4v. ISBN: 0851431313. ISSN: 00697745.

First published 1914.

V.1: Australia ... Britain ... Brunei & Darussalam. V.2:

....(contd.)
Canada ... Hong Kong. v.3: India ... Nigeria. v.4: Pakistan
... Zimbabwe. 6 appendices, including university admissions
requirements and a select bibliography (p.2792-2818). Index
of institutions and topics and name index. *Class No:*
378.4/.6

[778]
International handbook of universities. International
Association of Universities. 12th ed. London, Macmillan
Press, for the Association, 1990. 1302p. ISBN: 0333436431.
First published 1959.
Includes over 6500 universities in 115 countries, arranged
A-Z by country, with brief descriptions of faculties and
departments, names of deans and principals, admission
requirements, degrees and diplomas awarded, publications,
number of academic staff, student enrollment, library (stock
and publications). Index. *Class No:* 378.4/.6

[779]
The World of learning, 1991. 41st ed. London, Europa
Publications, 1990. Annual. xv,1987p. ISBN: 0946653623.
ISSN: 00842117.
A directory of universities, colleges, libraries, learned
societies, museums, art galleries and research institutes in
more than 150 countries, arranged A-Z (International -
Afghanistan ... Zimbabwe). Includes over 26,000
institutional names, addresses, etc., and lists more than
150,000 individuals. The international section has details of
more than 400 international educational, scientific and
cultural organizations. Includes 'open' and 'free' universities.
Index of institutions, p.1885-1987. *Class No:* 378.4/.6

Great Britain

[780]
British universities guide to graduate study, 1991-92. 7th ed.
London, Association of Commonwealth Universities, 1991.
358p. ISBN: 0851431291.
First published 1973. Formerly *Postgraduate courses in
United Kingdom universities* and *Schedule of post graduate
courses in the United Kingdom.*
A directory of c.3,000 graduate courses lasting at least six
months, arranged in 54 subject groups. Short descriptions
of course content, method of assessment, length, fees, grants
and awards. *Class No:* 378.4/.6(410)

[781]
Polytechnic courses handbook, 1992 entry: higher education:
full-time and sandwich courses in England, Wales and
central institutions in Scotland. 21st ed. London, The
Committee of Directors of Polytechnics, 1991. xvii,728p.
ISBN: 1872007031.
Sections: 1. Polytechnics (A-Z, places, p.1-71) - 2. First
degree courses (Multidisciplinary studies - p.74-523) - 3.
Higher national diploma courses - 4. Advanced non-degree
courses - 5. Second-stage advanced courses. Appendix A:
Taught higher degrees and CNAA diplomas; B. Other
postgraduate courses. Course index (to all main subjects
available in the courses). *Class No:* 378.4/.6(410)

[782]
University entrance, 1992: the official guide. 5th ed. London,
Association of Commonwealth Universities, for the
Committee of Vice-Chancellors and Principals of the
Universities of the United Kingdom, 1991. 472p. illus.,
tables. ISBN: 0851431305.
First published in 1987. Successor to *Compendium of
university entrance requirements.*
Lists over 11000 courses and their entrance requirements.
Also profiles and pictures of 80 admitting universities and
university colleges in the UK. Subject index. *Class No:*
378.4/.6(410)

USA

[783]
American universities and colleges. 13th ed. New York,
deGruyter, 1987. 2024p. ISBN: 089925179x. ISSN:
00660922.
First published 1928.
Describes over 1900 institutions in detail. Profiles are
arranged by state and include information on history,
admission requirements, programmes offered, degrees
conferred, enrollment, fees and financial aid, faculty size,
administration, buildings and grounds, etc. Institution and
general indexes. *Class No:* 378.4/.6(73)

39 Customs & Traditions

Costume

[784]
ANTHONY, P. *and* **ARNOLD, J. Costume: a general bibliography.** London, Costume Society, c/o Department of Textiles, 1974. vi,42p. ISBN: 090340706x.
First published 1966.
A selection of *c*.500 periodical articles, books and journals, mainly published after 1900, dealing primarily with the history of Western European costume. (*Introduction*). 35 sections of briefly annotated entries (sections by form and by subject). No index. *Class No:* 391

[785]
ARNOLD, J. A Handbook of costume. London, Macmillan Press, 1973 (Reprinted 1978). 336p. illus., facsims., ports. ISBN: 0333244893.
1. Primary sources (1. Paintings - 2. Sculpture... 6. Monumental brasses... 9. Dolls - 10. Tapestries, embroidery, printed and woven textiles - 11. Archival material, literary sources, periodicals and newspapers) - 2. Dating costumes from construction techniques - 3. Costume conservation, storage and display - 4. Costume for children and students (use of library and museums; collection of reproductions showing primary source material) - 5. Costume for the stage - 6. Costume bibliography (p.217-32; 18 sections; *c*.500 items) - 7. Collections of costume and costume accessories in England, Scotland and Wales (over 80 collections under places, A-Z, p.233-336). Each part of section 1 has list and notes of books with 'useful' illustrations or a list of primary source books. Over 240 illus. (photography; line drawings) in all. No index. A valuable guide to sources. *Class No:* 391

[786]
Fairchild's dictionary of fashion. Calasibetta, C.M. 2nd ed. New York, Fairchild, 1988. 749p. illus. ISBN: 0870056352.
First published 1976.
A significantly revised and updated edition of 10,000 entries, A-Z, for organizations, persons, slang terms, trademarks, clothing, hair styles, jewelry and fabrics. Numerous cross-references. Black-and-white drawings illustrate the terms, and there are 16 full-colour pages with 50 illustrations of costume from Ancient Egypt to 1988 America. An appendix of 171 brief biographical entries for fashion designers is followed by black-and-white portraits of some 64 of them. 'Authoritative, well-designed ...' (*Reference books bulletin*, 15 December 1988, p.690). *Class No:* 391

[787]
IRELAND, P.J. Encyclopedia of fashion details. London, Batsford, 1987. 264p. 314 illus. ISBN: 0713448040.
Fashion details (*e.g.*, pleats, tucks, piping, pockets,

....(contd.)
collars). Arrangement is A-Z and illustrates some of the ways in which style and decorative effects may feature in the design of a garment. *Class No:* 391

[788]
PICKEN, M.B. The Fashion dictionary: fabric, sewing and apparel in the language of fashion. Rev. & enl. ed. New York, Funk & Wagnall, 1973. xii,[1],434p. illus.
First published 1939 as *The Language of fashion*. Rev. ed. 1957.
More than 10,000 words briefly defined, with pronunciation. 109 group terms (*e.g.*, Linens, Heels). Includes obsolete terms. 'Sleeves': $5\frac{1}{2}$ columns in the 1959 ed., describing *c*.50 types of sleeve, with 11 small line-drawings. 202 half-tones, plus *c*.2 line-drawings per page. Analytical index of illustrations. Adequate cross-references. A standard work in its field. *Class No:* 391

[789]
YARWOOD, D. The Encyclopedia of world costume. London, Batsford, 1978. (Reprinted 1986). 472p. illus. ISBN: 0713413409.
This work, in A-Z order, has 2164 careful line-drawings and 8p. of coloured illustrations. 'Sleeves' (p.377-84): 39 illus.; 'Lace' (p.264-72) includes specific laces and lace terms. Bibliography (grouped), p.454-9. Detailed index. 'This book should be in every school and public library' (*New history*, no.11., 1979, p.8). *Class No:* 391

Histories

[790]
GORSLINE, D. A History of fashion. London, Fitzhouse Books (an imprint of B.T. Batsford), 1991. xiii,266p. illus. ISBN: 0713465921.
First published in 1953; first published in Great Britian by Batsford in 1955.
A historical and visual study of dress from the ancient world to the middle of the 20th century. In 3 parts, all subdivided: I. Costume of the ancient world; II. European costume; III. American costume. Detailed contents list precedes. *c*.1800 ilustrations. Bibliography, p.249-256. Sources, p.257-266. Essentially pictorial with a minimum amount of explanatory material. 'A reference for professionals and students alike' (*British book news,* January 1991, p.64). *Class No:* 391(091)

[791]
A Visual history of costume. London, Batsford, 1984-86. 6v. illus. ISBN: 0713440937; 0713440953; 0713448571; 0713448598; 0713440996; 0713440910.
Devised for those who need reliable, easy-to-use reference material on the history of dress. The central part of each volume is a series of illustrations taken from the time of the dress itself. Clothes described and significance

....*(contd.)*
explained. Arranged chronologically. Glossaries designed to
also act as indexes. Volume titles: *14th & 15th centuries*,
M. Scott. (1986. 152p. 150 illus); *16th century*, by J.
Ashelford. (1983. 144p. 156 illus (8 col.)); *17th century*
(1983. 144p. 158 illus (8 col.)); *18th century*,by A. Ribeiro
(1983. 144p. 156 illus (8 col.)); *19th century* (1984. 144p.
158 illus (8 col.)); *20th century*, by P. Byrde (1986. 152p.
162 illus.). *Class No:* 391(091)

20th Century

[792]
The Guinness guide to 20th-century fashion. Bond, D. 2nd
ed. Enfield, Middx., Guinness Publishing Ltd., 1985
(Reprinted 1988). 240p. illus (some col.). ISBN:
0851123562.
First published 1981.
Chapters for each of the decades from the 1900s to the
1980s, the text describing the decade and fashions,
supported by the many illustrations. Index, p.237-240.
Class No: 391"19"

Children's Fashions

[793]
CUNNINGTON, P. and BUCK, A. **Children's costume in
England, 1300-1900.** London, Black, 1965. 236p. 15 illus.
ISBN: 0713603712.
One chapter per century; many contemporary quotations.
Deals with children from infancy to the age of *c.16*.
Particularly rich in illus. Bibliography, p.226-9 (manuscript
sources; printed manuscripts and books; dress and domestic
economy; journals; secondary sources). Non-analytical index.
Class No: 391.31

Customs

[794]
KIGHTLY, C. **The Customs and ceremonies of Britain:** an
encyclopaedia of living traditions. London, Thames &
Hudson, 1986. 248p. illus., map. ISBN: 0500250960.
Over 200 entries describing English, Scottish and Welsh
customs and ceremonies (*e.g.*, 'Pig-face Sunday', 'Cheese
rolling', 'Whuppity Stourie') arranged A-Z by name of
custom or ceremony (or under a group title whenever a
custom does not warrant a separate entry). Entries include
dates, times and locations of the ceremonies when
appropriate. Over 200 illus. (12 in col.). Cross-references.
Includes a calendar of customs; a select (brief) bibliography
(1p.); a regional map; and a regional gazeteer (England
divided into 12 regions; Scotland and Wales separate)
listing customs and places where they occur. '... fascinating
...' (*Choice*, v.24(2), October 1986, p.280). *Class No:* 392

Festivals

[795]
MCNEILL, F.M. **The Silver bough:** a four-volume study of
the national and local festivals of Scotland. Glasgow.
Maclellen, 1957-90. 4v. ISBN: 0853351619, v.1;
0948474041, v.3; 0853350027, v.4.
V.1: *Scottish folk-lore and folk-belief* (1957); 2: *A
calendar of Scottish national festivals, Candlemas to
Harvest Home* (1959); 3: *A calendar of Scottish national
festivals, Halloe'en to Yule* (1990); 4. *The local festivals of
Scotland* (1970). V.2-4 deal with festivals in calendar order.
V.1 carries a brief bibliography; that in v.2 is a little fuller
(but authors and titles only). V.2 is well illustrated and
carries many quotations. 'A valuable compendium of
information' (*Scottish studies*, v.4, 1960, p.219-22). *Class
No:* 394.2

[796]
SPICER, D.G. **The Book of festivals.** Detroit, Mich., Gale
Research Co., 1969 (Reprinted by Omnigraphics Inc.,
1990). xiv,429p. ISBN: 1558888411.
Part 1: The festivals of different peoples (p.3-347; A-Z;
'Festivals of Albania' ... 'Festivals of Yugoslavia'). Pt.2: The
story of the calendars (Armenian, Chinese, Gregorian,
Hindu, Jewish, Julian, Mohammedan). Appendix: 'Glossary
of familiar religious and festival terms'. Selected
bibliography on festivals, p.389-420 (by countries). Index of
festivals. *Class No:* 394.2

[797]
SPICER, D.G. **Yearbook of English festivals.** New York,
Wilson, 1954 (Reprinted Westport, CT. Greenwood Press,
1973). xxv,298p. map. ISBN: 0837161320.
Part 1: Chronological survey; part 2: The Easter cycle. In
calendar order; gives very readable, rather popularised
accounts of current festivals, thus supplementing Chambers;
Book of days. Glossary; bibliography; indexes of customs,
counties and regions. *Class No:* 394.2

[798]
WHISTLER, L. **The English festivals.** London, Heinemann,
1947. 241p. illus.
The calendar festivals described in some detail, with
helpful bibliographical footnotes. An appendix indexes
carols in several collected volumes. *Class No:* 394.2

Special Days

[799]
Holidays and anniversaries of the world. Mossman, J., *ed.*
2nd ed. Detroit, Mich., Gale Research Co., 1990. 1080p.
ISBN: 0810348705.
First published 1985.
Lists 23000 regional, national and international holidays
and anniversaries for each of the 366 days of the
Gregorian year. Includes birthdates of famous people of all
ages; days of the Saints, Holy Days and other days of
religious significance; historical events; etc. Glossary of time
words. Index. *Class No:* 394.268

Official Ceremonies

[800]
MILTON, R. **The English ceremonial book:** a history of
robes, insignia and ceremonies still in use in England.
Newton Abbot, Devon, David & Charles, 1972. 216p. illus.
6 chapters: The heralds and the college of Arms - 2. The
coronation: the royal robes and regalia - 3. Robes and
coronets of the peers - 4. Robes of judges, serjeants and
barristers - 5. Knighthood: insignia and robes of orders of
chivalry - 6. Civic robes and insignia. Chapter notes and
short bibliography, p.208. Authorities personally consulted,
p.209. Detailed index. 61 illustrations (8 in colour). *Class
No:* 394.4

Chivalry

[801]
BROUGHTON, B.B., *comp.* **Dictionary of medieval
knighthood and chivalry:** concepts and terms. New York,
Greenwood Press, 1986. 614p. illus. ISBN: 0313245525.
Intended as a resource for medievalists at all levels and
areas of interest. Topical arrangement of entries, which
have quick definitions and in-depth discussions of chivalry
and knighthood as practiced in England and France.
Extensive cross-referencing. Most entries include one or
more bibliographical references and there is also a lengthy
bibliography. Calendar of feast days and saint's days. Index.
Class No: 394.7

[802]

BROUGHTON, B.B., *comp.* **Dictionary of medieval knighthood and chivalry:** people, places and events. New York, Greenwood Press, 1988. 774p. charts. ISBN: 0313253471.

Companion volume to *Dictionary of medieval knighthood and chivalry: concepts and terms* (1986) above.

Over 700 entries with wide coverage of Britain and France. Extensive cross-reference to items in both this and the previous volume. Entries are fairly short and include bibliographical references. Separate bibliography of 249 items of mainly secondary sources. Appendices include genealogical charts of reigning families. 70-page double-column index. *Class No: 394.7*

Etiquette

[803]

Debrett's etiquette and modern manners: current behaviour for every sphere of social and business life. Donald, E.B., *ed.* Exeter, Webb & Bower, in association with Debrett's Peerage Ltd., 1990. 400p. illus. ISBN: 0863503667.

First published 1981.

16 sections, giving precise guidance: 1. Births and the ceremonies of childhood ... 3. Weddings ... 6. Table manners - 7. Parties - 8. Invitations, letters and talk - 9. Visitors and houseguests ... 11. Public occasions and events ... 13. Courtship - 14. Household staff - 15. Sports and games - 16. Dress. Appendix: Initials and abbreviations of rank, honours and degrees: Precedence in England and Wales; Scotland. Analytical index (p.391-399). 'The first comprehensive book of etiquette to be issued since the social revolution of the sixties' (*The Times,* 25 June 1981, p.1). *Class No: 395*

[804]

POST, E.P. **Emily Post's etiquette.** 14th ed. New York, Harper, 1984. 1018p. ISBN: 0061816833.

First published 1922.

The standard US handbook, legislating for every conceivable social occasion. This edition updates the 1975 ed. (published by Funk & Wagnell), paying more attention to behaving on the job and to business situations than earlier editions, and less attention to dress. Includes a new section on unmarried couples living together and expands the section on divorce. *Class No: 395*

Forms of Address

[805]

Debrett's correct form: Standard modes of address for everyone from peers to presidents. Montague-Smith, P., *comp. & ed.* New rev. ed. Exeter, Webb and Bower, 1990. (Distributed by Penguin Books Ltd.). [viii],423p. ISBN: 0863503659.

First published 1970.

7 parts: 1. The Royal Family - 2. The Peerage - 3. Other titles and styles - 4. Styles by office (*e.g.,* Legal) - 5. Official and social occasions - 6. American usage - 7. Usages in other foreign countries. Appendices: Rules for hoisting flags ... Pronunciation of titles and surnames. Detailed, analytical index, p.413-423. *Class No: 395.6*

[806]

Titles and forms of address: a guide to their correct use. 19th rev. ed. London, A & C Black, 1990. xxxviii,185p. ISBN: 0713631325.

First published 1918.

Sections: Royalty - The peerage - Dukes and duchesses - Marquesses and marchionesses - Earls and countesses - Viscounts and viscountesses ... Chiefs of Scottish clans ... Ecclesiastical - The Royal Navy - The Army - The Royal Air Force ... Law, diplomatic and government - Honours,

....(contd.)

qualifications and appointments - The universities. Some pronunciations of proper names. Analytical index, p.179-185. Confined to English titles, including those of the church and civic dignitaries. *Class No: 395.6*

Women & Society

[807]

CARTER, S. *and* RITCHIE, M. **Women's studies:** a guide to information sources. London, Mansell; Jefferson, NC., McFarland, 1990. 278p. ISBN: 0720120586, UK; 0899505341, US.

Over 1000 English-language works published mainly between 1978 and 1988. Arranged in 3 main sections: General material (*e.g.* reference sources, biographies, women's studies) - Women in the world (subdivided geographically) - Special subjects (13 topics). Annotations vary in length from two lines to two paragraphs. Indexed by author, title and subject. Updates S.E. Searing's *Introduction to library research in women's studies* (1985) and K. Loeb's *Women's studies: a recommended core bibliography* (1987). *Class No: 396*

[808]

CHARLES, N. *and* JAMES, J. **The Rights of women:** the essential question and answer guide to women's legal problems. London, Arrow Books, 1990. 224p. ISBN: 0099662302.

Gives answers to queries about women's legal problems, from sexual harassment at work to compensation claims. *Class No: 396*

[809]

HUMM, M. **The Dictionary of feminist theory.** Hemel Hempstead, Herts., Harvester Wheatsheaf Publications; Columbus, Ohio, Ohio State University Press, 1989. xvi,278p. ISBN: 0710811489 UK; 0814205062, US.

'A broad, cross-cultural and international account of contemporary feminist thought' (*Preface*). Claims to be the first fully cross-referenced guide to bring together, clarify and explain the concepts and ideas about women and their views of the world. Bibliography, p.251-278. *Class No: 396*

[810]

TUTTLE, L., *ed.* **Encyclopedia of feminism.** Harlow, Essex, Longman Group UK Ltd.; New York, Facts on File, 1986. 399p. ISBN: 0582893461, UK; 0816014248, US.

Aims to provide, in one volume, ready access to major events, people, ideas, organizations and publications in the contemporary and past women's movements. Emphasis on America and Western Europe. Arrangement is A-Z, length of entries varying from *c.*30 words to $2\frac{1}{4}$ columns (*e.g.,* 'Holloway brooch':1 col; 'Housework': $2\frac{1}{2}$ cols.' 'Liberal feminism': $2\frac{1}{2}$ cols.). Many entries are about people. Good cross-reference structure. Extensive bibliography, p.375-399, by authors, A-Z. 'An excellent reference guide to a vast body of information;' (*Choice,* v.24(8), April 1987, p.1204). *Class No: 396*

[811]

Women's studies encyclopedia. Tierney, H., *ed.* Westport, CT., Greenwood Press, 1989-. v.1. 433p. v.2. 384p. ISBN: 0313267251, v.1; 031327357x, v.2.

To be in 3v.

V.1 Views from the sciences; v.2. Literature, art and learning. Focuses on recent feminist research in the natural, behavioural and social sciences, health and medicine, economics, linguistics, political sciences, and the law. Articles provide a definitive historical overview and current research findings. Most articles include selected references. *Class No: 396*

Reviews & Abstracts

[812]

Studies on women abstracts. Abingdon, Oxon, Carfax Publishing Co., 1983-. v.1, no.1-. 6pa. ISSN: 02625644.

*c.*800 indicative and informative abstracts pa. Covers books and journal articles in all main areas of women's studies (education, employment, women in the family and community, medicine and health, female sex and gender role socialization, social policy, social psychology of women, female culture, media treatment of women, biography, literary criticism, and historical studies. List of books received for inclusion. List of journals covered (396). Author and subject indexes, cumulated annually. *Class No:* 396(048)

[813]

Women studies abstracts. Rush, N.Y., Rush Publishing Co., 1972-.no.1-. Quarterly. ISSN: 00497835.

About 200 indicative and informative abstracts per issue, arranged in 22 subject sections: Education, localization - Sex roles, characteristics, differences and similarities - Employment - Sexuality - Family ... History - Literature and art ... Women's Liberation Movement. Appended is an extensive listing of book reviews. Author and subject indexes, cumulating in the 4th issue each year. 'Recommended for the basic women's studies collection in college libraries (*Choice*, v.12(12), February 1976, p.1544). *Class No:* 396(048)

[814]

—**Women's studies index.** 1989-. Boston, Mass., G.K. Hall, 1991-. Annual.

Covers over 100 journal titles, ranging from popular to scholarly. Whereas *Women's studies abstracts* offers depth, this index offers breadth. Author and subject access. *Class No:* 396(048)

Quotations

[815]

PARTNOW, E. **The Quotable woman ... 1800-1981.** New York, Facts on File, 1983. 608p. ISBN: 0871965801.

Organized chronologically by birthdates, subdivided by speakers. Headers for each section list only names and dates. The biographical indexes to each volume provide alphabetical access and identify each of the women's nationality, occupation, and family ties to other women in the books. 6000 quotations. *Class No:* 396(082.2)

Histories

[816]

FREY, L., *and others, comps.* **Women in Western European history:** a select chronological, geographical and topical bibliography from antiquity to the French Revolution. Westport, CT., Greenwood Press, 1982. lv,760p.

A historical outline and topical guide to citations, p.xv-l, (serves as a detailed contents list) is followed by a Guide to quotations (names A-Z & pages on which quoted). The bibliography is arranged in 6 sections: 1. Historical surveys - 2. Antiquity - 3. Middle Ages - 4. Renaissance/ Reformation - 5. Seventeenth century - 6. Eighteenth century. Entries are numbered and arranged by subject in each section, subdivided by authors, A-Z. No annotations. Subject index, p.633-639; name index, p.641-660; author index, p.661-760. *Class No:* 396(091)

[817]

—FREY, L., *and others, eds. & comps.* Women in Western European history: a select chronological, geographical and topical bibliography, the nineteenth and twentieth centuries. Westport, CT., Greenwood Press, 1984. liv,1025p. ISBN:

....(contd.)

0313228590.

Similar arrangement to the above, with 4 sections: 1. Nineteenth and twentieth centuries - 2. Nineteenth century (*c.*1789-1914) - 3. Early twentieth century, 1914-1945 - 4. Twentieth century since 1945. A first supplement (1986. 699p. 0313251098) supplements the two earlier volumes, with more recently discovered or published material. *Class No:* 396(091)

[818]

KANNER, B., *ed.* **The Women of England,** from Anglo-Saxon times to the present: interpretative bibliographical essays. Hamden, CT., Archon; Shoestring, 1979; London, Mansell, 1980. 429p. ISBN: 0208016392, US; 0720115647, UK.

13 contributors. 12 bibliographical essays (*e.g.,* 'Women in Norman and Plantagenet times', p.83-123; 55 notes; bibliography, p.113-23. 'A survey of primary sources and archives for the history of early twentieth-century English women', p.388-409; 21 notes; bibliography (*i.e.,* library and society sources), p.410-8). Index. 'This belongs in any library used by students of literature, history, or the social sciences. (*Library journal,* v.104(14), August 1979, p.1552). *Class No:* 396(091)

Gypsies

[819]

BINNS, D. **A Gypsy bibliography:** a bibliography of recent books, pamphlets, articles, broadsheets, theses and dissertations pertaining to gypsies and other travellers that the author is aware of at the time of printing. Manchester, Dennis Binns Publications, 1982. [108]p. ISBN: 0950829005.

1306 items (1289 arranged A-Z by author; the rest are of records currently available). Includes materials from 1500 to the present day, but pre-1914 titles are omitted if unattainable or obscure or in a foreign language. *Class No:* 397

Folklore & Folktales

[820]

Internationale volkskundliche Bibliographie/International folklore and folklife bibliography/... 1939/41-. Bonn, (previously Basle), Rudolf Habelt Verlag GmbH, for Société Internationale d'Ethnologie et de Folklore, 1949-.Biennial. ISSN: 00749737.

Under the auspices of the Conseil International de la Philosophie et des Sciences Humaines, with Unesco support. Continues *Volkskundliche Bibliographie* (Berlin, de Gruyter, for Verband Deutsche Vereine für Volkskunde, 1919-41. v.1-13: 1917-36, which itself continues *Catalogus van Volklorein de Koninklijke Bibliotheek* (The Hague, Drukkerij 'Humanitas', 1919-22. 3v. in 2).

The 1985-1986 volume, published 1991, has *c.*11,600 items in 21 classes (1. Folklore and folklife in general - 2. Settlement - 3. Buildings - 4. Objects - 5. Signs - 6. Technology, arts and crafts, industries - 7. Characteristics and types of people - 8. Costume, - 9. Food - 10. Manners and customs, festivals, pastimes - 11. Social groups, common law - 12. Popular beliefs - 13. Folk medicine - 14. Popular science - 15. Folk literature - 16. Popular poetry - 17. Music and dance - 18. Folk-tales, myths, legends ... 21. Popular speech. List of periodicals precedes. Author and subject indexes. *Class No:* 398

[821]

THOMPSON, S., *ed.* **Motif-index of folk-literature:** a classification of narrative elements in folk tales, ballads, myths, fables, medieval romances, exempla, fabliaux, jest books, and local legends. Rev. ed. Copenhagen, Rosenkilde & Bagger; Bloomington, Indiana State University Press,

....*(contd.)*
1955-58. 6v. ISBN: 0253338875.
First published Bloomington, 1932-36. 6v.
A systematic thematic index, covering a vast collection of
folk-literature; references and some source material are
cited. A-Z index and list of sources. The scope of the
revised ed. is extended to include Icelandic sagas, early
Irish literature, and oral tales of India. V.6, as before,
provides a detailed A-Z index of motifs. An indispensable
study of the subject. *Class No:* 398

Great Britain

[822]
ALEXANDER, M. British folklore, myths and legends.
London, Weidenfeld & Nicolson, 1982. 224p. 90 illus. (24
in colour). ISBN: 0297781510.
Examines the survival of different legends and customs
and charts the evolution of folk belief. 9 sections: The
magical island - Stones, graves and chalk images - 'There
were giants in the earth' - The fabulous bestiary - The
secret commonwealth - The Devil's congregation - The
ghostlore of Britain - Rebels and champions - The Pagan
inheritance. Picture sources. Index. *Class No:* 398(410)

[823]
**BRIGGS, K.M. A Dictionary of British folk-tales in the
English language,** incorporating the F.J. Norton Collection.
London, Routledge & Kegan Paul, 1970-71. 4v. ISBN:
0710002076.
A: Folklore narratives (2v. v,580p.; v.580p.). B: Folk
legends (2v. lxvi,623p.; v,774p.). Pt.A, v.1: Fables and
exempla, includes a list of books, cited and consulted, tale-
type index and index-to-story titles. Pt.A, v.2: *Jocular tales.
Novelle. Nursery tales.* Pt.B, v.1 includes list and index, as
in pt.A, v.1. Folk legends are subdivided alphabetically by
types (*e.g.,* Black dogs; Bogies; Devils; Dragons ... Witches;
Miscellaneous legends). Folk-tales are narrated in full and
embrace verse tales (*e.g.,* Child's *English and Scottish
ballads*), giving source, type and motifs and comment, if
considered necessary. 'Recommended for public and
academic libraries' (*Library journal,* 1 December 1976,
p.2470). *Class No:* 398(410)

[824]
Folklore, myths and legends of Britain. 2nd ed. London,
Reader's Digest Association, 1977. 552p. illus. (some in
colour). ISBN: 0340163979.
First published 1973.
In 3 parts: 1. Lore of Britain - 2. Romance of Britain -
3. People of myth. 28 contributors. Detailed index, p.542-
550. Lavishly illustrated. *Class No:* 398(410)

Ireland

[825]
O SÚILLEABHÁIN, S. A Handbook of Irish folklore.
Dublin, Educational Co. of Ireland, Ltd., for the Folklore
of Ireland Society, 1942 (Reprinted Detroit, Mich., Singing
Tree: Gale Research Co., 1971). xxxi,699p. ISBN:
6810335611.
14 chapters (1. Settlement and dwelling ... 13. Popular
oral literature - 14. Sports and pastimes). No index, but a
detailed contents list (p.xix-xxxi); no sources. 'The main
purpose ... is to serve as a guidance for collectors of Irish
oral tradition' (*Introduction to collectors*). A mine of
information and also, because of the many questions listed,
a guide for further research. *Class No:* 398(415)

Wales

[826]
OWEN, T.M. Welsh folk customs. 4th ed. Llandysul, Dyfed,
Gomer Press, 1987. 197p. 16p. of plates (black & white).
ISBN: 0863833470.
First published 1959, 1st to 3rd eds. published by the
National Museum of Wales, Cardiff.
Chapters: 1. The Christmas season - 2. Candlemas and
the movable festivals - 3. May and midsummer - 4.
Harvest and winter's eve - 5. Birth, marriage and death.
Select bibliography (p.187-189) A-Z by author. Index
(p.190-197). 'The text provides an integrated study of the
subject based on the literature, on replies to questionnaires
and on information collected in the field' (*Foreword* to an
earlier edition). Well documented. *Class No:* 398(429)

America

[827]
FLANAGAN, C.C. and **FLANAGAN, J.T. American folklore:**
a bibliography, 1950-1974. Metuchen, N.J., Scarecrow Press,
1977. vi,406p. ISBN: 0810810735.
3639 numbered entries, with very brief annotations for
some 16 sections: 1. List of magazines and abbreviations -
2. Festschriften, symposia, collections - 3. Bibliography,
dictionaries, archives - 4. Folklore: study and teaching - 5.
General folklore - 6. Ballads and songs - 7. Tales and
narrative material - 8. Legends (theory; history; collections)
- 9. Myth and mythology - 10. Beliefs, customs,
superstitions, cures - 11. Folk heroes - 12. Folklore in
literature - 13. Proverbs, riddles, Wellerisms, limericks - 14.
Speech, names, cries, etc. - 15. Minor genres (*e.g.,* rhymes;
graffiti) - 16. Obituaries (of prominent folklorists). Includes
some Canadian, Mexican and Caribbean material. *Class
No:* 398(7)

Metrical Romances

[828]
LACY, N.C., and others, eds. **The New Arthurian
encyclopedia.** 2nd ed., completely rev. and expanded. New
York, Garland, 1991. xxxviii,577p.100 black & white illus.
(*Garland reference library of the humanities, v.585.*) ISBN:
0824043774.
First ed. published in 1986.
Over 1200 essay entries and a large number of brief and
informative entries, by 130 contributing scholars. Treats
major authors and texts as well as broad subjects, covering
the Arthur legend from the earliest tales to the present day
in literature, history, art, music, films, etc. Each essay has
a short bibliography of 1-4 items appended. Cross-
references. Subject list of entries by category, p.xiii-xxv.
Index, including all authors, artists, and important themes
and motifs, p.535-577. Recommended as 'an important
beginning in Arthurian studies' (*Library journal,* 1 Sept.,
1991, p.182). *Class No:* 398.22

Superstitions

[829]
OPIE, I. and **TATEM, M.,** eds. **A Dictionary of superstitions.**
Oxford, Oxford University Press, 1989. xiii,[1],494p. ISBN:
0192115979.
1600 entries, arranged A-Z by subject, that treat
superstitions of the British Isles that have survived to the
nineteenth and twentieth centuries. Each superstition is
illustrated by one or more quotations in chronological order
to show the history and development of the superstition,
the quotations being from a wide range of published and
unpublished sources. Geographical locations and other
clarifying information is given in brackets. Extensive cross-
references. Entries vary in length from 2 or 3 lines to over

....(contd.)

a column. Select bibliography of 16th to 20th-century books and periodicals, p.455-462. Analytical index, p.463-494. *Class No:* 398.3

Fairies & Goblins

[830]
BARBER, R. *and* **RICHES, A. A Dictionary of fabulous beasts.** New ed. Ipswich, Boydell Press, 1975. 168p.

First published 1971 by Macmillan Press.

Fabulous beasts, A-Z, from the Asbaia to the Zû. Bibliography of over 200 items, with references from the text, is arranged chronologically. The black-and-white illus. are few and far between, and *RQ* (v.12(1), Fall, 1972, p.86) recommends, for illus., *A fantastic bestiary.* by Ernest Lehner, with over 300 illus. *Class No:* 398.43

[831]
EASTMAN, M.H. Index to fairy tales, myths and legends. 2nd ed. Boston, Faxon, 1926. Supplement, 1937; 2nd supplement, 1952. ix,610p. (1st supplement, ix,566p.; 2nd supplement, 370p.). ISBN: 0873050282.

About 30,000 references in an alphabetical analytical index, with list of books analysed; geographical list; bibliography of books on the art of story telling. Includes some modern stories. Continued by: *Class No:* 398.43

[832]
—IRELAND, N.O. Index to fairy tales, 1949-1972 including folklore, legends and myths in collections. Westwood, Mass., Faxon, 1973. (Available Metuchen, N.J. Scarecrow). 741p. Supplements, 1973-77 (1979. 259p.) and 1978-1986 (1989, 575p.), both published by Scarecrow. ISBN: 0810820110; 0810818558; 081082194x.

Main work indexes 406 books. Innovations are the comprehensive subject index of stories and the single A-Z sequence. *Class No:* 398.43

Proverbs

[833]
WHITING, B.J. *and* **WHITING, H.W. Proverbs, sentences and proverbial phrases, from English writings mainly before 1500.** Cambridge, Mass., Belknap Press of Harvard University Press; London, Oxford University Press, 1968. li,733p. ISBN: 0674719506.

About 10,000 entries, A-Z by keyword, and then chronologically, with exact citation to source. Where appropriate, references to other standard collections are cited. Indexes: important words; proper nouns. 'It will not be superseded' (*Library journal,* v.93(21), 1 December 1968, p.4543). *Class No:* 398.9

[834]
—WHITING, B.J. Modern proverbs and proverbial sayings. Cambridge, Mass., Harvard University Press, 1989. 709p. ISBN: 0674580532.

5567 entries of material published between *c.*1930 to the early 1980s, arranged by keyword, with bibliographical sources indicated. A very wide variety of sources were scanned throughout the years for this compilation. Unfortunately, only one keyword, usually the first noun, is used for each proverb; no definitions are given, even for abstract or metaphorical proverbs; and no oral proverbs are included. However, 'No other compilation of proverbs covers the twentieth century with such comprehensiveness ... Whiting's crowning work will become a standard reference source for proverbs and should delight both the scholar and the casual browser' (*Reference books bulletin,* November 15, 1989, p.696). *Class No:* 398.9

5/6 SCIENCE & TECHNOLOGY

Government Policies

Worldwide

[835]
Longman Guide to world science and technology. Harlow, Essex, Longman Group, 1982-.
Science and technology in the United Kingdom, by R. Nicholson. 1991. xv,312p. ISBN 0582900514.
Science and technology in Eastern Europe, edited by G. Darvas. 1988. *c.* 350p. ISBN 0582900549.
Science and technology in France and Belgium, by E.W. Kellerman. 1983. 140p. ISBN 058290084X.
Science and technology in the USSR, edited by M.J. Berry. 1986. 424p. ISBN 0582900530.
Science and technology in Scandinavia, by G. Férne. 1988. ISBN 0582018927.
Science and technology in China, by T.B. Tang. 1984. 278p. ISBN 0582900565.
Science and Technology in Japan, by A.M. Anderson. 1984. 421p. ISBN 0582900158.
Science and technology in the Middle East, by Z. Sardar. 1982. 335p. ISBN 0582900522.
Science and technology in Africa, by J.W. Forje. 1987. ISBN 0582000866.
Science and technology in the USA, by A.H. Teich and J.H. Pace. 1986. 427p. ISBN 0582900611.
Science and technology in Latin America, by Latin American Newsletters, Ltd. 1983. 373p. ISBN 0582900573.
Science and technology in Australasia, Antarctica and the Pacific Islands. (Forthcoming).
Science and technology in the Federal Republic of Germany, by F. Krahmer. 1990. ISBN 0582054397.
Chapters in each volume concern the organizational sectors, followed by specific areas (*e.g.*, agriculture). Appended directory of sources. Establishments and subject index. *Class No:* 5/6.0(100)

Science

Abbreviations & Symbols

[836]
BRITISH STANDARDS INSTITUTION. Specification for quantities, units and symbols. London, BSI, 1979-82. 14 pts. (*BS 5775.*)
Replaces BS 1991: *Letter symbols, signs and abbreviations* (1961-).
0 *General principles.* 1982. 16p. £25.60 1. *Space and time.* 1979. 20p. £25.60. 2. *Periodic and related phenomena.* 1979. 12p. £16.20. 3. *Machines.* 1979. 24p. £25.60. 4. *Heat.* 1979. 20p. £25.60. 5. *Electricity and magnetism.* 1980. 28p. £25.60. 6. *Light and related electromagnetic radiations.* 1982. 16p. £25.60. 7. *Acoustics.* 1979. 20p. £25.60. 8. *Physical chemistry and molecular physics.* 1982. 20p. £25.60. 9. *Atomic and nuclear physics.*

....(contd.)
1982. 20p. £25.60. 10. *Nuclear reactions and ionizing radiations.* 1982. 24p. £25.60. 11. *Mathematical signs and symbols for use in the physical sciences and technology.* 1979. 36p. £25.60. 12. *Dimensionless parameters.* 1982. 12p. £19.10. 13. *Solid state physics.* 1982. 24p. £25.60. *Class No:* 5(003)

[837]
OCRAN, E.B. Ocran's acronyms: a dictionary of abbreviations and acronyms used in scientific and technical writing. London, Routledge & Kegan Paul, 1978. xiv, 262p. (reprinted with corrections, 1980).
About 7,000 entries in the main A-Z sequence, p.1-184, followed by 47 subject sections (Aeronautics... Transportation). Excludes most associations and government bodies. Aeronautics and computer services figure prominently. 'Compiled to fulfil a subject approach' (*Introduction*). 'Reference librarians will find this volume very useful' (*Choice*, v.16(1), March 1979, p.58). *Class No:* 5(003)

Databases

[838]
Brit-line: directory of British databases. V.4, no.1. London, McGraw-Hill Book Company, 1989. xiii,408p. ISBN: 0077071689.
First published 1986.
4 sections: 1. Databasics - 2. Database directory - 3. Indexes - 4. Prepaid reply card. The database directory contains details (producer, subject, type, database content, host, file details, restrictions, printed version, sample record) of 375 databases. Subjects covered include agriculture, aviation, chemistry, earth sciences, energy, engineering, food science and technology, general science and technology, health and safety, medical science, patents, shipping and veterinary medicine. There are five indexes: producer; host; cross; entry; address - the last two being the most reliable. *Class No:* 5(003.4)

[839]
HALL, J.L. Online bibliographic databases. 4th ed. London, Aslib, 1986. ISBN: 0851422020.
First published 1979.
A 63-page commentary precedes the directory of 250 bibliographic databases that are readily available and mostly in English. Data on each include subject index, printed and online versions, online file details, online service suppliers, indicative access charges, references. Appended bibliography of 1,011 references. Appendices: Data producers; Online service suppliers; Most important word(s) in bibliography; Broad subject headings. Author index; detailed, analytical general index, p.469-508. Prelims. feature sample search templates for 9 leading systems, *eg*, BLAISE, DIALOG, BRS, INFOLINE. A well organised and documented guide.
5th ed. due to be published in 1992. *Class No:* 5(003.4)

Bibliographies

[840]
GROGAN, D. **Science and technology: an introduction to the literature.** 4th ed. London, Bingley, 1982. 400p. ISBN: 0851573150.

First published 1970.

Concerns the kinds of sources. 22 chapters (usually with 'Further reading'): 1. The literature - 2. Guides to the literature - 3. Encyclopedias - 4. Dictionaries - 5. Handbooks - 6. Directories and yearbooks - 7. Books 'in the field' - 8. Bibliographies - 9. Periodicals - 10. Indexing and abstracting services - 11. Computerized databases - 12. Reviews of progress - 13. Conference proceedings - 14. Research reports - 15. Patents and trademarks - 16. Standards - 17. Translations - 18. Trade literature - 19. Theses and research in progress - 20. Non-print media - 21. Microforms - 22. Biographical sources. Analytical index of subjects and forms; titles mentioned in text - merely examples of their kind - are not included. An impressive survey, 'written primarily for students, not practitioners' (*Introduction*). *Class No:* 5(01)

[841]
PARKER, C.C. *and* TURLEY, R.V. **Information sources in science and technology:** a practical guide to traditional and online use. 2nd ed. London, etc., Butterworths, 1986. [viii], 328p. diagrs., tables, charts. ISBN: 0408014679.

First published 1975.

Main sections: Choosing sources of information and their guides - People - Organizations - The literature (p.37-138) - Information services (p.139-210) - Searching: the literature and computer databases - Obtaining literature in a usable form - Organizing and presenting information - Current awareness. Appendix: Helping the library user. Detailed, analytical index. A feature is the graphic use of charts for comparison and rating purposes (*e.g.,* chart 1, Information sources and guides versus coverage). The index (p.302-28) includes authors and titles. Good use of bold type. Admirably meets the authors' objective: 'to produce a text which is suitable for beginners, but which will also serve as a handy reference work for the more experienced' (*Preface*). *Class No:* 5(01)

[842]
SCICAT: Science Reference and Information Service Catalogue. London, British Library, Science Reference and Information Service, 1990. 4 issues pa. Negative microfiche.

Author/title catalogue. Classified catalogue.

Contains additions to SRIS stock from 1974 plus many items published earlier, including all serials held by SRIS. The *Classified catalogue* is arranged according to the SRIS classification scheme and has an index. *Class No:* 5(01)

[843]
Scientific and technical books and serials in print. New York, Bowker, 1972-. Annual. 3v.

1. *Books: Subject index.* 2. *Books: Author index.* 3. *Books: Title index. Serials: Subject index. Serials: Title index.*

The 1991 volumes (4850p.) provide bibliographical and ordering information for over 130,000 books and 18,000 periodicals. More than 11,000 new entries. Directory of over 4,000 publishers and distributors. V.1 employs over 13,000 subject categories. Includes serials translated from Russian. *Class No:* 5(01)

Encyclopaedias

[844]
Encyclopedia of physical sciences and technology. Meyers, R.A.M., *ed.* San Diego, Academic Press, 1987-88. 15v. 11000p.

Coverage includes chemistry, physics, geology, astronomy, computer science, meteorology and mineralogy. 4,200 glossaries accompany the articles. Includes 6,000 figures and 2,000 tables. Bibliographies consist of 4,000 titles. V.15. *Subject index* contains 45,000 entries. A scholarly encyclopaedia, recommended for academic, rather than school, libraries. *Class No:* 5(031)

[845]
McGraw-Hill encyclopedia of science and technology. 6th ed. New York, etc., McGraw-Hill, 1987. 19v. & index. illus., diagrs., tables, maps. ISBN: 0070792925.

First published 1960.

About 4,000 contributors; *c.*8,000 articles, A-Z, on all branches of pure and applied science. Signed contributions, averaging *c.*5 references, plus cross-references (*e.g.,* 'Geomagnetism': v.8, p.38-45; 6 references to books and articles; 5 maps; 3 diagrams; 1 table, 1 cross-reference). V.20 (624p.) lists contributors and provides both topical and analytical (p.121-624) indexes. A major US encyclopedia, although bibliographies need to be more current.

Annual updates, between editions: *McGraw-Hill Yearbook of science and technology.* The *Encyclopedia* (6th ed., 1987) has provided several encyclopedia spin-offs, on astronomy, physics, chemistry, electronics, engineering.

7th ed., due to be published 1992, is to contain 7,500 articles, 13,000 illus. and an analytical index with 160,000 entries. *Class No:* 5(031)

[846]
Van Nostrand's scientific encyclopedia. Considine, D.M., *ed.* 7th ed. New York, Van Nostrand Reinhold, 1988. 2v. xvi,1628+1629-3180p. illus., diagrs., graphs, tables, maps. ISBN: 0442217501, set; 0442318146, v.1; 0442318162, v.2.

First published 1968.

The 6,773 alphabetically arranged entries include 800 which are new or revised. Subject coverage includes chemistry, biosciences, plant sciences, physics, mathematics and medicine. Over 3,000 black-and-white illustrations and 500 tables. New to this edition is a 109-page, 45,000-entries index. Brief bibliographies. *Class No:* 5(031)

Dictionaries

[847]
McGraw-Hill dictionary of scientific and technical terms. Parker, S.P., *ed.* 4th ed. New York, McGraw-Hill, 1989. xvii,2088, 49p. illus., figs., diagrs. ISBN: 0070452709.

First published 1974.

Contains *c.*100,000 terms (7,600 new to this edition). Pronunciation given for all terms for the first time. Entries include synonyms, abbreviations and acronyms. Brief definitions. *c.*3,000 illustrations in the margins. Appendices include SI conversion tables, the Greek alphabet, the periodic table of the elements, schematic electronic symbols and the classification of living organisms. The last apendix is a biographical dictionary of over 1,200 eminent historical and contemporary scientists. Thumb-indexed. *Class No:* 5(038)

Polyglot

[848]

FEUTRY, M. Technological dictionary/ Dictionnaire technologique/Technologisches Wörterbuch. Paris, La Maison du Dictionnaire, 1976-78. 3v.

1. *Mechanics, metallurgy, hydraulics and related industries.* 1976. *Supplemento español.* 1976. 2. *Les ressorts.* 1978. 3. *Aeronautique.* 1978.

V.1 has 14,051 numbered entries, English-French-German, in 3 columns, with French and German indexes. Well spoken of. *Class No:* 5(038)=00

English

[849]

BALLENTYNE, D.W.G. *and* **LOVETT, D.R. A Dictionary of named effects and laws in chemistry, physics and mathematics.** 4th ed. London, Chapman & Hall, 1980. 346p. ISBN: 0412223902.

First published 1958.

About 14,000 entries, A-Z, for effects and laws best known by the name of the person(s) who discovered or propounded them (*e.g.,* Guy Lussac's law, - under 'G'). Formulas and chemical structures; cross-references. Definitions are clearly stated, but omit biographical data and bibliographies.

Ruffner, J.A. *Eponyms dictionary index* (Detroit, Mich., Gale, 1977. xxxi, [1], 734p. Supplement no.1, 1985. 248p.) covers a much wider field. *Class No:* 5(038)=20

[850]

Chambers science and technology dictionary. Cambridge, Chambers, 1988. xvi,1008p. figs., tables. ISBN: 1852961503.

First published as *Chamber's technical dictionary* in 1940.

About 45,000 entries, arranged A-Z, followed by 10 appendices, (Paper tables ... Animal kingdom ... Physical constants, standard values and equivalents). Alternative forms, terms derived from the headword and variables in mathematical formulae are in italics while bold type is used for cross-references and vector notation. Trade names are also indicated in the text. General, not intended to replace specialist dictionaries.

A Spanish ed. appeared in 1979. *Class No:* 5(038)=20

[851]

UVAROV, E.B. *and* **ISAACS, A. The Penguin dictionary of science.** 6th ed. Harmondsworth, Middx., Penguin Books, 1986. [v], 466p. diagrs., tables, chemical structures. ISBN: 0670807168.

5th ed., 1979.

About 5,000 terms are defined, with numerous cross-references. Entries average *c.*50 words in length. 11 appended tables (*e.g.,* 6-figure conversion factors). 'In this edition, as in previous editions, the general principle of selecting predominantly scientific terms, as opposed to technical words, has been maintained' (*Foreword to the 1986 edition*). A long-established 'standard work of reference' (*The History of science,* v.24(4), December 1986, p.442). *Class No:* 5(038)=20

German

[852]

DE VRIES, L. German-English science dictionary, updated and expanded by L. Jacolev and P.L. Bolton. 4th ed. New York, London, etc., McGraw-Hill, 1978. xxxviii, 628p. ISBN: 0070166021.

First published 1939.

About 65,000 entries; Addendum, p.559-628: *c.*7,000 entries. Coverage: mathematics, physics, chemistry, biology, botany, zoology, anatomy, agronomy, horticulture. Sub-

....(contd.)
entries in bold type. 'Keim' (germ) and compounds: $1\frac{1}{2}$ columns. Preliminary essay: 'Suggestions for translators'. Appended lists of geographical names, abbreviations, chemical elements, weights and measures, etc. *Class No:* 5(038)=30

[853]

DORIAN, A.F. Dictionary of science and technology, German-English. 2nd rev. ed. Amsterdam, etc., Elsevier, 1981. x, 1119p. ISBN: 0444419977.

First published 1970.

About 100,000 entries. Terms in the 1st ed. 'regarded as ballast' have been dropped and 20,000 new headwords added. *Class No:* 5(038)=30

[854]

—DORIAN, A.F. Dictionary of science and technology, English-German. 2nd rev. ed. Amsterdam, etc., Elsevier, 1978. xii, 1402p. ISBN: 0444416498.

First published 1967.

Has *c.*100,000 entries, with definitions and explanations of many of the English terms. Well thought of by translators, although the tendency to enter under the qualifying adjective and not the noun qualified should be noted. *Class No:* 5(038)=30

[855]

ERNST, R. Wörterbuch der industriellen Teknik. [Dictionary of engineering and technology.] 4. Aufl. Wiesbaden, Brandstetter, 1975-80. 2v.

First published 1948.

1. *Deutsch-Englisch.* 4. Aufl. 1980. 1092p. 2. *Englisch-Deutsch.* 4. Aufl. 1975. 1146p.

V.1 has 149,400 entries, bringing it into line with the latest French-German volume in the series. 'A revised edition of this well-tried and proven work'. (*The Incorporated Linguist,* v.20(1), Winter 1981, p.28). V.2 has an introduction on 'The nature of technical English'. Regarded (Picken, C. *'The translator's handbook,* p.209) as the standard work in the field. *Class No:* 5(038)=30

[856]

KUČERA, A. The Compact dictionary of exact science and technology. Wiesbaden, Brandstetter, 1982-89. 2v.

1. *English-German.* 2nd ed. 1989. 2. *German-English.* 1982.

V.1 offers *c.*50,000 headword entries; v.2, over 67,000. Gives not merely equivalents but also frequently refers to *Chambers Dictionary of science and technology* (for fuller definitions) and to the German DIN standards. Appendices on German, British and US standards, etc. 'Few dictionaries succeed in putting so much solid, reliable information in so little space. Invaluable not only for anyone working in the field, but also can serve as a model for other bilingual terminological dictionaries' (*ARBA,* 1984, entry 1232). *Class No:* 5(038)=30

Norwegian

[857]

ANSTEINSSON, J. English-Norwegian technical dictionary. [Engelsk-norsk teknisk ordbok.] 3rd rev. ed. Trondheim, Brun; Vero Beach, Fla, Vanous, 1984. 541p.

First published 1948; 2nd ed. 1950.

At head of title-page: 'Norwegian Council for Technical Terminology'.

About 20,000 entries. Clear layout; compounds are picked out in bold type. *Class No:* 5(038)=396

[858]
ANSTEINSSON, J. Norsk-engelsk teknisk ordbok. Ny utg. av O. Peiersen. Trondheim, Brun; Vero Beach, Fla, Vanous, 1985. 223p. ISBN: 8270284742.
About 20,000 entries for Norwegian terms, with English equivalents.
The two dictionaries are intended for Norwegian technical colleges and do not cater for the foreigner's lack of knowledge of stress, pronunciation of syllabification of Norwegian words. The specialized vocabularies are, however, recommended by translators. *Class No:* 5(038)=396

Swedish

[859]
ENGSTRÖM, E. Engelsk-svensk teknisk ordbok. 13. uppl. Stockholm, Travaru-Tidning Förlaget; New York, French and European, 1978. 1026, [2]p. ISBN: 0828806756, US ed.
Over 100,000 entries (including subentries). 'Safety': nearly 2 columns. Includes abbreviations. About 200 categories, etc. are applied to terms. American technical terms receive special attention. *Class No:* 5(038)=397

[860]
ENGSTRÖM, E. Svensk-engelsk teknisk ordbok. [Swedish-English technical dictionary.] 10. uppl. Stockholm, Svensk Trävarutidning Förlaget; New York, French and European, 1977 (1984 printing). 973, [1]p. ISBN: 0828806764, US ed.
About 100,000 entries and subentries. 'Kraft' (power): 3 columns. Appended list of sources. *Class No:* 5(038)=397

[861]
GULLBERG, I.F. Svensk-engelsk fackordbok för näringsliv, fövaltning, undevisning och forskning. [A Swedish-English dictionary of technical terms used in business, industry, administration, education and research.] 2. revid. uppl., med suppl. Stockholm, Norstedt, 1977. xix, [1], 1722p.
First published 1964 (xvi, 1246p.).
The 2nd ed. has an extensive supplement of *c.*40,000 new terms, giving a total of *c.*175,000 categorized terms, A/Z. Rich in idioms. Includes many proper names ('Internationella...': nearly 36 columns). British and US usages not differentiated. Includes abbreviations. List of important dictionaries in 50 languages. Well-produced and a fine example of its kind. *Class No:* 5(038)=397

Danish

[862]
WARRERN, A. Dansk-Engelsk teknisk ordbog. 6. udg. Copenhagen, Clausen Bøger, 1981. 393p. ISBN: 8711040270.
First published 1949; 5th ed., 1976 (385p.).
About 15,000 word-for-word entries. Many compounds. British and US usage differentiated; terms categorized. Entry under qualifying adjective. Abbreviations not included. *Class No:* 5(038)=398

[863]
WARRERN, A. Engelsk-dansk teknisk ordbog. 6. udg. Copenhagen, Clausen Bøger, 1974. 383p.
15,000 word-for-word entries, compounds being given separate entries. *Class No:* 5(038)=398

French

[864]
DE VRIES, L. French-English science and technology dictionary. 4th ed., rev. and enl. by S. Hochman. New York, etc. McGraw-Hill, 1976. xiii, 683p. ISBN: 0070166293.
First published 1940; 3rd ed; 1962.
About 52,500 entries, including a supplement of *c.*4,500 new terms added to 3rd ed. Emphasises new developments (*e.g.*, in automotive technology, astronautics, electronics, electronic data processing). 'All the terms published by the French Ministry of National Education, in January 1973 have been included' (*Library journal*, v.101(13), July 1976, p.1516). *Class No:* 5(038)=40

[865]
ERNST, R. Comprehensive dictionary of engineering and technology, with extensive treatment of the modern techniques and processes. Cambridge, University Press; New York, French and European, 1982-1984. 2v. ISBN: 052130377x; 0521303788; 082880611x, v.1, US ed; 0828806101, v.2, US ed.
1. *Français-Anglais*, viii, 1085p. 2. *English-French*. xxiii, 1399p.
V.1 has 159,142 entries; v.2 195,546 entries. Each term is categorized. 'Deals with all branches of modern industry involving chemistry, electrical engineering, electronics, commerce, space travel, telecommunications, data processing, & microprocessors. Though expensive, the set belongs in all comprehensive science and technology collections and in the hands of serious translators' (*New technical books*, v.70(8), October 1985, item 1056). *Class No:* 5(038)=40

Italian

[866]
DENTI, R. Dizionario tecnico, italiano-inglese, inglese-italiano. 11. ed. riv., ampliata ed aggiornata. Milan, S.F. Vanni, 1985. [xvi], 2023p. ISBN: 882031052x.
First published 1946.
About 105,500 entries. Italian-English, p.1-835; English-Italian, p.837-1916. Many sub-entries are given separate entries. 'Leva' (lever), over 1½ columns. Appendices include technical abbreviations in common use, conversion factors, mathematical symbols, British and American measures and metric equivalents. *Class No:* 5(038)=50

Spanish

[867]
Diccionario de términos científicos y técnicos. Lapedes, D.N., *redactor jefe*. Barcelona, Marcombo; New York, French and European, 1981. 5v. illus. ISBN: 0070791724; 0828806683, US ed.
Spanish translation of *McGraw-Hill Dictionary of scientific and technical terms* (2nd ed., 1978), with its categorized 108,000 entries. V.1-4 provide the translation, adding English term. V.5 provides the English original, with Spanish equivalent. *Class No:* 5(038)=60

Portuguese

[868]
DE PINA ARAÚJO, A. De Pina's technical dictionary / Dicionário técnico. São Paulo, McGraw-Hill do Brasil, 1978. 2v. (616p. + 495p.).
1. *English-Portuguese*. 616p. 2. *Portuguese-English*. 493p. Reprint of the 1964 ed.
About 75,000 translated terms in all, mostly equivalents. American English used (*e.g.*, 'aluminium'). Tendency to

....(contd.)
enter under qualifying word instead of noun (*e.g.,* 'high tide' - under 'high' and not 'tide'). No less than *c.*500 categories applied to terms. *Class No:* 5(038)=690

Russian

[869]
CALLAHAM, L.I. Russian-English chemical and polytechnical dictionary. 3rd ed. New York, London, etc., Wiley, 1975. xxvii, 852p. ISBN: 0471129984.
First published 1947; 2nd ed., 1962.
'A technical as well as a chemical dictionary...' (*Preface,* 1st ed.). About 100,000 Russian entries and sub-entries. Terms are categorized, genders given; abbreviations, prefixes and common Russian word-endings included. Good typography for cyrillic characters. Particularly helpful on pure and applied chemistry. *Class No:* 5(038)=82

[870]
CHERNUKHIN, A.E., *ed.* Anglo-russkiĭ politekhnicheskiĭ slovar': 80,000 terminov. Izd. 3. Moscow, Ruskiĭ Iazyk, 1976. 647p. ISBN: 0080219365.
2nd ed. 1971 (671p.).
'English-Russian polytechnical dictionary' has entries for *c.*80,000 terms. Coverage excludes medicine, mathematics, pure and natural sciences. Appendices: abbreviations; conversion tables. While recommending it, *Choice* (v.15(3), May 1978, p.371), complains of the crowded 3-column page, poor typography and inferior paper, - a sharp contrast to Callaham. *Class No:* 5(038)=82

Arabic

[871]
AL-KHATIB, A.Sh., *comp. and ed.* A New dictionary of scientific and technical terms, English-Arabic, with illustrations. 6th ed. Beirut, Librairie du Liban, 1985. xv, 751p. illus., tables.
First published 1971 (xv, 751p).
About 50,000 entries; 3 columns, with about one illus. per column. 17 appendices (conversion tables, etc.). Bibliography, p.750. A reprint of the 1971 edition in quarto format. *Class No:* 5(038)=927

Chinese

[872]
Han ying kung cheng chi shu tzu hui. [Chinese-English dictionary of engineering technology.] Pei-ching, Hai yang chu pan she, 1986. 892p.
Includes *c.*107,000 terms on technological subjects, including astronautics and telecommunications. Radical index, p.7-13 and index of syllables of Hanyupinyin, p.14-21. *Class No:* 5(038)=951

[873]
Modern Chinese-English technical and general dictionary. New York, etc., McGraw-Hill, 1963. 3v.
1. *Tables* (Wade-Giles - Pinyin conversion table, etc.). Radical stroke index, in alphabetical sequence, - the real key to the dictionary. 2. *Standard telegraphic code, in numerical sequence.* 1900p. 3. *Pinyin romanization in alphabetical sequence* (permuted index). 188p.
About 212,000 entries, over 80% of them common scientific and technical terms. 'The main emphasis is on information not readily available in existing dictionaries' (*Introduction*). Proper names and vocabulary of Chinese Communism are included. Each Chinese character is represented by a 4-digit code (0001-), adapted from the Standard Telegraphic Code. V.2-3 both give English equivalents. Recent linguistic reforms are included. *Class No:* 5(038)=951

Reports Literature

[874]
Government reports announcements & index. Springfield, Va., National Technical Information Service (NTIS), 1975-. Semi-monthly.
Succeeds *Government research announcements* (1971-75). Orignally as *Bibliography of scientific and industrial reports* (1946-49), then as *Bibliography of technical reports* (1949-54), then as *US government research reports* (1954-64) and then as *US government research and development reports* (1965-71). Title and frequency vary.
About 2,500 abstracts per issue, including patents. 22 subject fields, further divided. Indexes: subject, personal author, corporate author, contract number, accession/report number. Covers government sponsored R & D reports, government analyses, etc. NTIS database is available online and CD-ROM. *Class No:* 5(047)

Reviews & Abstracts

[875]
Aslib book list: a monthly list of recommended scientific and technical books, with annotations. London, Aslib, 1935-. v.1(1)-. Monthly.
Quarterly until March 1948.
About 500 entries pa., with 50-60 word evaluative annotations in UDC order. Books are graded: 'A', elementary level; general readership; 'B', intermediate level; university textbook; 'C', advanced level; specific readership; 'D', reference books. Broad subject index and author or title index per issue and cumulated annually. A reliable current book-selection tool, normally restricted to books in English. *Class No:* 5(048)

[876]
New technical books: a selective list with descriptive annotations. New York Public Library, Science & Technology Research Center, 1915-. 10pa.
1985: 1,500 annotated entries for noteworthy books, mostly in English. Entries, in broad Dewey Decimal Classes feature two paragraphs: 'Content' and 'Note', the latter indicating readership, level and standing. Parts of continuing multi-volume works (*e.g.,* Kirk-Othmer) and annual review series (*e.g., Advances in ...*) receive attention. The annual author and catchword indexes occupy middle pages of the December issue each year. Larger format and 6 pa. as from 1988. A valuable selection tool, although somewhat late in appearance. *Class No:* 5(048)

[877]
Pascal [formerly Bulletin signalétique]. Paris, Centre National de la Recherche Scientifique, 1984-.
65 sections, replacing the 49 of the *Bulletin signalétique,* with its monitoring of over 5,000 periodicals worldwide. The PASCAL series has been on line since 1973 (accessible on ESA-IRS, TÉLÉSYSTÈMES-QUESTEL, DIALOG), a bilingual database having 'more than five million entries with an annual update of over half a million' (Anthony, L.J. *Information sources in engineering.* 2nd ed., 1985, p.148).
PASCAL has three main groups: 'Explore', 'Folio', 'Théma', with sections as follows:
PASCAL Explore, pt. 11. *Physique atomique et moléculaire, Plasmas.* 12. *État condensé.* 13. *Structure des liquides et des solides, cristallographie.* 20. *Électronique et télécommunications.* 27. *Méthodes de formation et traitement des images.* 30. *Microscopie électronique et diffraction électronique.* 32. *Metrologie et appareillage en physique et physiochimie.* 33. *Informatique.* 34. *Robotique, automatique automatisation des processes industriels.* 36. *Pollution de l'eau, de l'air et du sol.* 48. *Environment cosmique terrestra, astronomie et géologie extraterrestre.* 49.

....(contd.)
Météorologie. 60. *Génétique.* 61. *Microbiologie.* 62.
Immunologie. 63. *Toxicologie.* 64. *Endocrinologie humaine.*
65. *Psychologie, psychopathologie, psychiatrie.* 71.
Ophtamologie. 72. *Otorhinolaryngologie, stomatologie,
pathologie cerviofaciale.* 73. *Dermatologie, maladies
sexuellement transmissibles.* 74. *Pneumologie.* 75.
Cardiologie et appareil circulatoire. 76. *Gastroentérologie,
foie, pancreas, abdomen.* 77. *Néphrologie, voies urinaires.*
78. *Neurologie.* 79. *Pathologie et physiologie
ostéoarticulaires.* 80. *Hématologie.* 81. *Maladie
métabolique.* 82. *Gynécologie, obstetique, andrologie.* 83.
Anesthétic et réanimation. 84. *Genie biomédical,
informatique biomédicale.* 99. *Congrès. Rapports. Thèses.*
   Folio, pt. 10. *Mécanique et acoustique.* 16. *Chimie
analytique, minérale et organique.* 17. *Chimie générale,
minérale et organique.* 21. *Electrotechnique.* 23. *Génie
chimique, industries chimique et paractionique* 24.
Polymères, peintures, bois 25. *Transports terrestres et
maritimes.* 40. *Mineralogie.* 41. *Gisements métalliques et
non-métalliques, économie miniere.* 42. *Roches cristallines.*
43. *Roches sedimentaires, geologie marine.* 44. *Stratigraphie,
géologie régionale, géologie générale.* 45. *Tectonique,
geophysique interre.* 46. *Hydrologie, géologie de l'ingénieur,
formations superficialles.* 47. *Paléontologie.* 52. *Biochimie.*
54. *Reproduction des vertébrés, embryologie.* 55. *Biologie
végétale.* 56. *Écologie animale et végétale.* 64, *Anatomie et
physiologie des vertébrés.* 70. *Pharmacologie, traitements,
médicamenteux.*
   Théma, pt. 195. *Bâtiment, travaux publics.* 205. *Sciences
d'information, documentation.* 210 *Industries agrimentaires.*
215. *Biotechnologie.* (French ed.). 216. *Biotechnology.*
(English ed.). 230. *Énergie.* 235. *Médicine tropicale.* 240.
Métaux, métallurgie. 245. *Soudage, brasage et techniques
connexe.* 251. *Cancérologie.* 260. *Zoologie fondamentale et
appliqué des invertébrés. Class No:* 5(048)

[878]
Science citation index. Philadephia, Pa., Institute for Scientific
Information, 1961-. 6pa., with annual and 5-yearly
cumulations for the period 1969-79.
   Citation index. Source index. Permuterm subject index.
   The *Citation index* records, A-Z, authors of papers,
monographs, etc., followed by a list of later writers who
have cited/quoted those originals. The *Source index* has
entries for those citing/quoting writers, while the
Permuterm subject index based on relevant words in titles
of papers etc., provides the subject approach. *SCI* covers
c.3,800 journals, monographs etc. SCISEARCH database.
   Available online via DIALOG, Data-Star; CD-ROM
(Institute for Scientific Information). *Class No:* 5(048)

Periodicals

[879]
Science & technology libraries. New York, Haworth Press,
1980-. Quarterly. ISSN: 0194262x.
   Each issue has contributions on a particular theme (*e.g.,*
'Role of computers in sci-tech libraries', v.6(4); 'Role of
translations in sci-tech libraries', v.3(2)). Also featured are
special papers, *e.g.,* 'Information sources in laser science
and technology'. A regular section: 'New reference works in
science and technology' (*e.g.,* v.7(1), Fall 1986, devotes 40p.
to c.80 initialled reviews in 5 subject groups). Reviews are
descriptive but do indicate readership. *Class No:* 5(051)

Yearbooks & Directories

[880]
Directory of scientific directories: a world bibliographic guide
to medical, agricultural, industrial and natural science
directories. 4th ed. Harlow, Essex, Longman, 1986. [vii],
232p. ISBN: 0582901510.
   First published 1969 (Hodgson).
   International guide to c.1,250 published and forthcoming
directories of organizations and individuals involved in
research and education in science and technology. 7
geographical sections, each with 10 subject subsections.
Indexes of publishers, directory titles, and editors/compilers.
   Class No: 5(058)

[881]
McGraw-Hill yearbook of science and technology:
Comprehensive coverage of the important events of the
year, as compiled by the staff of the McGraw-Hill
Encyclopedia of Science and Technology. New York, etc.,
McGraw-Hill, 1961-. Annual. illus., diagrs., graphs, tables,
maps.
   The 1992 annual (1991. [xii],523p. ISSN 00762016) has
c.250 contributors. Entries, A-Z (Acid rain ... Zooplankton).
'Queuing theory' (p.377-83) has 15 references. Detailed,
analytical index. *Class No:* 5(058)

Teaching Materials

[882]
The New illustrated science and invention encyclopedia. Rev.
ed. London, Marshall Cavendish, 1988. 27v. illus. (incl.
col.).
   Based on *How it works: the illustrated encyclopedia of
science and technology* (1978), but simplified and
Americanised for children.
   Concerns the 'hows', 'whats' and 'whys' of the scientific
world. V.1-23 consist of an A-Z sequence of c.40 topics.
V.24 contains brief biographical sketches of c.100 scientists;
v.25 looks at inventors and inventions; v.26 contains a
glossary and index to the set; v.27, careers in science. Of
the previous ed., 'An up-to-date inviting set of scientific
and technical information for elementary and junior high
school children, with a good emphasis on graphics'
(*Reference books bulletin,* 1984/1985, p.66). *Class No:*
5(072)

Tables & Data Books

[883]
KAYE, G.W.C. *and* **LABY, T.H.,** *comps.* **Tables of physical
and chemical constants,** and some mathematical functions.
15th ed. London & New York, Longman, 1986. [viii],
477p. graphs, tables. ISBN: 0582463548.
   59 contributors. 4 main sections: 1. General physics - 2.
Chemistry - 3. Atomic and nuclear physics - 4.
Mathematical functions. Analytical index. Subsection
references. All tabulated values appear in SI units. Essential
for any reference library. *Class No:* 5(083)

Histories

[884]
BYNUM, W.F., *ed.* **Dictionary of the history of science.**
Princeton, N.J., Princeton Univ. Press; London, Macmillan,
1981. xxxi, 494p.
   700 articles by 95 scholars, plus 10 subject editors,
mostly British. Coverage: pure science, human science and
medicine. Basically a dictionary of the leading ideas and
concepts of Western science developed over the last five
centuries. Entries usually carry brief references. Appended
list of 800 scientists, cross-referenced to entries.

....*(contd.)*
Bibliography of 130 reference works and monographs. 'This scholarly, high quality dictionary' (*Wilson Library bulletin*, March 1982, p.542). *Class No:* 5(091)

[885]
CORSI, P. and WENDLING, P. **Information sources on the history of science and medicine.** London, Butterworth Scientific, 1983. xvi, 531p. facsims., diagrs. (*Butterworths Guides to information sources.*)
21 contributors; 24 documented chapters, in 4 parts. Part 1 consists of general chapters on the history of science and relations with associated areas (*e.g.,* anthropology, religion). Part 2, on major institutions and research methods. Part 3 (chapters 11-19), historical range of modern sciences and developments. Part 4 reviews status of non-European developments -US, Indian, Islamic and Chinese, African. Chapter 8: 'Guide to bibliographical sources', p.137-56; Chapter 19: Medicine since 1500, p.378-407, has bibliography, p.393-407. List of journals, p.501-8. Analytical subject index, including names of authors and institutions, p.509-31. 'Highly recommended' (*Choice,* v. 21 (1), September 1983, p.64). *Class No:* 5(091)

[886]
ISIS **cumulative bibliography:** a bibliography of the history of science, formed from *ISIS* critical bibliographies 1-90, 1913-65. Whitrow, M., *ed.* London, Mansell, in conjunction with the History of Science Society, 1971-84. 6v.
1. *Personalities, A-J.* 1971.
2. *Personalities, K-Z, and institutions, A-Z.* 1971.
3. *Subjects.* 1976. 772p. £50.
4. *Civilizations and periods, Prehistory to Middle Ages.* 1982.
5. *Civilizations and periods, 18th to 19th centuries.* Addenda to v.1-3, 1982.
6. *Author index.* 1984. 350p. £40.
'The result of weeding, tidying and sorting the *ISIS* Critical Bibliographies 1-90' (Jayawardene,S.A. *Reference books for the historian of science*). The *Personalities* section has nearly 40,000 entries for 10,000 individuals. 'Aristotle': *c.*450 entries; 'Royal Society': 123 entries. 'The whole series will be an essential purchase for any library catering for the needs of historians of events' (*British Book News,* August 1977, p.598).
Supplementary vols. covering the periods 1966-75 and 1976-85 have been published. *Class No:* 5(091)

[887]
RONAN, C.A. **The Cambridge illustrated history of the world's science.** Cambridge Univ. Press; London, Newnes, 1983. 543p. illus., facsims, maps. ISBN: 0521258448.
10 chapters: 1. The origins of science - 2. Greek science - 3. Chinese science - 4. Hindu and Indian science - 5. Arabian science - 6. Roman and medieval science 7. From Renaissance to scientific revolution ... 10. Twentieth-century science. Bibliography (by chapters), p.528-9. Index, p.532-43, includes references to the illus. *Class No:* 5(091)

Biographies

[888]
ABBOTT, D., *ed.* **The Biographical dictionary of scientists.** London, Blond Education, 1984-5. 6v. diagrs.
Mathematicians. 1984. [vii], 175p. *Astronomers.* 1984. 204p. *Physicists.* 1984. 212p. *Chemists.* 1984. 203p. *Biologists.* 1984. 194p. *Engineers and inventors.* (Mullen) 1985. 188p.
Each volume provides *c.*200 biographical sketches of scientists, past and present. No recommended further reading, but major primary works are cited. Glossary and index for each volume. No criteria for inclusion are stated.

....*(contd.)*
Very readable, like Asimov's *Biographical encyclopedia of science and technology.* Mainly for school use. *Class No:* 5(092)

[889]
American men and women of science, 1989-90: a biographical directory of today's leaders in physical, biological and related sciences. Daley, B., *ed.* 17th ed. New York, Bowker, 1989. 8v. (7,775p.). ISBN: 0835225682.
First published 1906, as *American Men of science.*
Biographical sketches on over 125,000 active US and Canadian scientists working in over 164 sub-specialities. Almost 4,000 new entries. Separate discipline index (A-Z by specialty). 'A truly indispensable directory for reference collections of all levels' (*Science and technology libraries,* v.10(4) Summer 1990, p.123). Available online via DIALOG. *Class No:* 5(092)

[890]
Dictionary of scientific biography. Gillespie, C.C., *ed.* New York, Scribner's, 1970-80. 16v. (8v. reprint, 1981).
Edited under the auspices of the American Council of Learned Societies.
1-14. A-Z. 1970-76.
15. *Supplement 1. Biographies and topical essays.* 1978. xi, [1], 518p.
16. *Index.* 1980. 510p.
Bibliographical entries for *c.*5,000 deceased scientists, from Thales to Bernal. A panel of 39 consultants for the main volumes; several hundred contributors per volume. Contributions focus on the biographee's place in the history of science rather than on his or her life story. All entries are signed and fully documented. 'Bacon, Francis': v.1, p.372-85, with 51 references (bibliography of 2½ columns: 1. Original works; 2. Secondary): 'Wallace, Alfred Russell': v.14. p.133-40; 1½ columns bibliography). V.15 includes 6 topical essays on Indian, Babylonian, Assyrian, Egyptian, early Japanese and Mayan science. V.16, name and subject index, includes persons not the subject of biographical articles, mustering 45,000 names in all. Separate lists of contributors and biographies, societies, periodicals, scientists (by field). At least comparable, for the historiographer of science, to the *Dictionary of American biography* and *Dictionary of national biography.* The 'single most valuable reference work in the history of science' (Jayawardene, S.A. *Reference books for the historian of science* (1982), p.19).
The *Concise dictionary of scientific biography* (1981) retains entries for the 5,000 scientists, but with a text reduced to about 10% of the original. 'Highly recommended' (*Choice,* January 1982, p.603). *Class No:* 5(092)

[891]
OGILVIE, M.B. **Women in science:** antiquity through the nineteenth century; a biographical dictionary, with annotated bibliography. Cambridge, Mass., & London, MIT Press, 1986. xi, [1], 254p.
Biographical accounts of more than 150 women scientists, p.22-187. The annotated bibliography has sections A-G (A. Bibliographies and reference works; abstracts, bibliographies, catalogues, guides and biographical dictionaries and encyclopedias, p.189-96 ... G. Nineteenth and early twentieth centuries, p.225-9). List of subjects of biographical accounts, p.240-5. Detailed index, p.246-54. Supplements the major multi-volume biographical dictionaries. *Class No:* 5(092)

Europe

[892]
Who's who in science in Europe: a biographical guide in science, technology, agriculture and medicine. 5th ed. Harlow, Essex, Longman Group. 1987. 3v. (2880p). ISBN: 0582901146.

First published 1967; 3rd ed. (Hodgson), 1978; 4th ed., 1984.

About 21,000 biographical entries for scientists from 30 countries (USSR: only 2 names). Data include titles of major publications and research interests. The main sequence, A-G, H-P, Q-Z is supported by a country and subject index, in which the scientists feature under the country in which they work subdivided into 8 subject specializations. *Class No:* 5(092)(4)

USA

[893]
ROTHENBERG, M. The History of science and technology in the United States: a critical and selective bibliography. New York, Garland, 1982. (*Bibliography of the history of science and technology, 2. Garland reference library of the humanities, 308.*) ISBN: 0824092783.

832 annotated entries in 6 sections, on bibliographies and general studies; the physical sciences; the biological sciences; the social sciences; technology and agriculture. Most of the references concern items published 1940-80. Author and subject indexes. 'An excellent overview of the role science and technology have played in American history' (*Choice*, v.20(8), April 1983, p.114). *Class No:* 5(73)

Translations

[894]
PICKEN, C., *ed.* **The Translator's handbook.** London, Aslib, 1983. vii, 270p. illus., facsims., tables. ISBN: 0851421733.

Rev. and enl. ed. of *Technical translation mannual,* edited by J.B. Sykes (Aslib, 1971. xvii, 173p.).

24 contributors (biographical notes on p.247-52). 8 parts (17 sections): 1. Introductory survey - 2. People who do the job - 3. How is the job done? (chapter 5: The practical tools employed, p.47-79, with bibliography; 5ii: Machine translation) - 4. Kinds, types and categories of translation - 5. The world view (*e.g.,* Relations between languages) - 6. International and national professional organizations - 7. Bibliography of technical translation and sources of information (bibliographies, dictionaries, glossaries, p.201-13) - 8. Glossary, p.217-38. Appendices: A. Cover-to-cover translation; B. Transliteration of Russian; C. Proof correction marks, British and US. Detailed, analytical index. Authoritative; good value. *Class No:* 5=03

Writing & Lecturing

[895]
AUSTIN, M., *ed.* **The ISTC handbook of technical writing and publication techniques:** a practical guide for managers, engineers, scientists and technical publishers. London, Heinemann, 1985. 213p.

8 contributors. Chapter 1: 'Choosing language for effective technical writing'. Other chapters on preparation for writing, editing , illustration, translations and printing. British Standard requirements are considered. Index. 'A work which should be available in all scientific and professional libraries' (*Library review*, v.35(2), Summer 1986. p.149-50). *Class No:* 5:001.81

Information Services

[896]
European sources of scientific and technical information. Harvey, A.P., *ed.* 9th ed. Harlow, Essex, Longman Group, 1991. viii, 402p. ISBN: 058207150x.

First published 1957.

A guide to more than 1,300 organizations, including patent and standard offices, national and special bodies and their library facilities (including access to online and CD-ROM databases). 25 subject sections, subdivided under countries. Subject index; organization and keyword index. Includes Eastern Europe, but not the former USSR. *Class No:* 5:061:025.5

Conferences

[897]
Forthcoming international scientific and technical conferences. London, Aslib, 1924-. 4pa. (Main list is in February, updated by supplement in May and cumulative supplements in August and November). ISSN: 00464686.

Records more than 1,000 conferences pa., arranged in chronological order. Data on each: date; title of conference; location; address for enquiries. Subject, location and organization indexes. *Class No:* 5:061:061.3

Research Establishments

[898]
European research centres: a directory of organizations in science, technology, agriculture and medicine. 8th ed. Harlow, Essex, Longman Group, 1990. 2v. (2453p.).

6th ed., 1985. Combines what were previously *European research index* (4th ed. Hodgson, 1977) and *East European research index* (4th ed. Hodgson, 1977).

Directory of *c.*20,000 research laboratories in science, technology, agriculture and medicine. Covers both Western and Eastern countries, but not the former USSR. Data note size of establishment, key personnel, research activities, interests and major projects. Title and subject indexes. *Class No:* 5:061:061.62

[899]
Industrial research in the United Kingdom: a guide to organizations and programmes. 14th ed. Harlow, Essex, Longman, 1991. 592p.

First published 1946 as *Industrial research in Britain* (Guernsey, Hodgson). 13th ed., 1989.

Details of *c.*3,000 laboratories active in agricultural and environmental sciences, chemical and materials sciences, earth and astronomical sciences, electronics and computer sciences, pharmaceutical, biomedical and biological sciences, and engineering and transportation. 6 sections: 1. Industrial firms - 2. Research associations and consultancies - 3. Government departments and their laboratories - 4. Universities and polytechnics - 5. Trade and development associations - 6. Personal name index. Title of establishment index. Detailed, non-analytical index. *Class No:* 5:061:061.62

51 Mathematics

Mathematics

Databases

[900]

Mathfile. Providence, R.I., American Mathematical Society, 1973-.

MATHFILE is a database equivalent of *Mathematical reviews*, with records from 1973 onwards and available on DIALOG and BRS hosts. A rival is MATHEMATICS ABSTRACTS database, corresponding to *Zentralblatt für Mathematik;* available on INKA. Because of the strong connection between mathematics and physics, INSPEC is 'probably the best source before MATHFILE was available' (Hawkins, E.T., in *Database*, v.8(1), February 1985, p.16). Available on CD-ROM (Silver Platter) as *MathSci Disc*, 1982-. *Class No:* 510(003.4)

Encyclopaedias

[901]

Encyclopaedia of mathematics. Hazewinkel, M., *ed.* Dordrecht, Netherlands, Reidel, 1988-. v.1-. Formulas; equations. ISBN: 0155608010, set.

To be completed in 10v. (*e.g.* v.7. Orb-Ray ... v.10. Index).

A translation, with updates and editorial comments, of The Soviet *Mathematical encyclopaedia* ('Soviet Encyclopaedia Publishing House', 1977-85. 5v.).

Three kinds of articles: 1. Surveys of main directions in mathematics - 2. Detailed discussion of concrete problems, results and techniques - 3. Short (reference) definitions. Many include annotations or editorial comment and references (to both Soviet and Western literature). Entries classified by AMS numbers from the 1980 scheme. *Class No:* 510(031)

[902]

Encyclopedic dictionary of mathematics. Mathematical Society of Japan. 2nd ed., edited by K. Itó. Cambridge, Mass., & London, MIT Press, 1987. 4v. (2,120p.). diagrs, graphs, tables formulas. ISBN: 0262090260.

First published 1934. 2nd ed. is English translation of the 3rd Japanese ed. (1985), with references to English-language textbooks in place of the original Japanese textbooks.

V.1-3 (A-E, F-N, O-Z) comprise 450 articles (Abel ... Zeta functions). V.4 includes 23 appendices (1. Algebraic functions ... 23. Statistical estimation and statistical hypothesis testing), as well as numerical and statistical tables, a list of journals, systematic and A-Z lists of the articles. Name index; detailed, analytical subject index (p.1917-2148). 'An essential buy for every library and for many private bookdealers' (*Nature*, v.330, 26 November 1987. p.322). *Class No:* 510(031)

Handbooks & Manuals

[903]

TUMA, J.J. Engineering mathematics handbook. 3rd ed. New York, Chichester, etc., McGraw-Hill, 1987. 512p. tables. ISBN: 0070650433.

First published 1970.

A compendium, in logical sequence of sections, from algebra, geometry and trigonometry to Laplace transforms and tables of definite integrals. 3rd ed. adds 2 chapters, on plane curves and areas, space curves and surfaces. Bibliography; index. For engineers, architects, teachers and students. *Class No:* 510(035)

Dictionaries

[904]

Webster's new world dictionary of mathematics. Karush, W., *ed.* New York, Prentice-Hall, 1989. 317p. illus., diagrs., graphs, tables. ISBN: 0131926675.

Defines over 1400 mathematical terms. Includes arithmetic, algebra, geometry, trigonometry and analytical geometry. Appended: Brief biographies of famous mathematicians, a chart of mathematical symbols and tables of powers, roots, logarithms and trigonometric functions. Much overlap with *Facts on file dictionary of mathematics* (2nd ed., 1988). 'For high school and college students' ('Reference books bulletin', *Book list,* December 15, 1989, p.860). *Class No:* 510(038)

Reviews & Abstracts

[905]

Current contents: CompuMath. Philadelphia, Pa., Institute for Scientific Information. 1981-. Monthly. ISSN: 0276220x.

Contents-list of *c.*250 issues of journals per issue (*c.*120p.). Subjects: science & technology; mathematics; operations; research & management science; statistics & probability. Available online via DIALOG, file 151/ CompuMath. *Class No:* 510(048)

[906]

Mathematical reviews. Providence, R.I., American Mathematical Society, 1940-. v.1-. Monthly.

About 45,000 abstracts pa. 94 sections (as in *Zentralblatt für Mathematik,*): 00. General ... 01. History and biography ... 03. Mathematical logic and foundations ... 11. Number theory ... 20. Group theory and generalizations ... 26. Real functions ... 40. Sequences, series ... 51. Geometry ... 60. Probability theory and stochastic processes ... 70. Mechanics of particles and systems ... 80. Chemical thermodynamics, heat transfer ... 90. Economics, operational research, programming games ... 94. Information and communication circuits. Author index; key index; serial additions and changes. Annual index: *Index of mathematical papers* (1973-). *Mathematical reviews cumulative index, 1973-1979*

....(contd.)
covers v.45-58 in 12v., with *c*.300,000 entries. The basic
reviewing service in mathematics. Database: MATHFILE;
CD-ROM: *MathSci Disc. Class No:* 510(048)

Histories

[907]
**DAUBEN, J.W. The History of mathematics, from antiquity to
the present:** a selective bibliography. New York & London,
Garland, 1985. xxxv, 467p. ISBN: 0824092848.

2,400 entries, mostly annotated, with numerous cross-
references. 6 sections: 1. General reference works - 2.
Source materials - 3. General histories of mathematics - 4.
The history of mathematics: Chronological periods (p.29-
215) - 5. The history of mathematics: sub-disciplines
(algebra ... topology) - 6. The history of mathematics:
selected topics (*e.g.,* Mathematics education; Regional
studies; Women in mathematics). Author and subject (non-
analytical) indexes. 'An excellent addition to existing
bibliographical sources in the history of mathematics' (*ISIS,*
v.76, December 1985, p.595). The author is editor of
Historia mathematica. Class No: 510(091)

Recreational Mathematics

[908]
**EISS, H.E. Dictionary of mathematical games, puzzles and
amusements.** New York, Greenwood Press, 1988. xiv,278p.
illus. ISBN: 0313247145.

A-Z sequence of mathematical games, both classical and
modern, with detailed explanations, line drawings and
cross-references. Mathematic theories, underlying the games,
feature throughout; chapters include brief bibliographies.
Criticized in *Choice* (July/August, 1988, p.1273) for
omission of 'significant terms' and poor illustrations. *Class
No:* 510-8

Analysis

Functions

[909]
CRC handbook of mathematical sciences. Beyer, W.H., *ed.*
6th ed. Boca Raton, Florida, CRC Press, 1987. 860p.
diagrs., graphs, tables, formulas.

5th ed. 1978, and formerly as *CRC Handbook of tables
for mathematics.*

Compendium on mathematical and statistical functions,
logically arranged in 13 sections. 1. Constants and
conversion factors - 2. Algebra - 3. Combinatorial analysis -
4. Geometry - 5. Trigonometry - 6. Logarithmic exponential
and hyperbolic functions - 7. Analytical geometry - 8.
Calculus - 9. Differential equations - 10. Special functions -
11. Numerical methods 12. - Probability and statistics - 13.
Aerodynamics. Appendix: Mathematic symbols and
abbreviations. Detailed index, p.249-60. *Class No:* 517.5

Statistics

[910]
TIETJEN, G.L. A Topical dictionary of statistics. London,
Chapman & Hall, 1986. ix, [i] 171p. ISBN: 0412012014.

15 topical chapters, each with short annotated
bibliography: Summarizing data - Random variables and
probability distribution - Some useful distributions -
Estimation and some hypothesis testing - Regression - The
design of experiments and the analysis of variants -
Reliability and survival analysis - Order statistics -
Stochastic processes - Time series - Categorical data -
Epidemiology - Quality control and acceptance sampling -
Multivariate analysis - Survey sampling. Index of specific
terms. Detailed, analytical index. *Class No:* 519.22

52/529 Astronomy & Surveying

Astronomy

Bibliographies

[911]
KEMP, D.A. **Astronomy and astrophysics: a bibliographical guide.** London, Macdonald, 1970. xxiii, 584p. (*Macdonald bibliographical guides.*) ISBN: 0356030113.

Annotated entries for 3,642 numbered items (with interpolations). 75 sections, systematically arranged (1. Reference media - 2. Star catalogues, ephemerides, etc.... 25. Origin of the solar system... 49. Stellar evolution... 73. Cosmology - 74. Abundance and origin of the elements. - 75. Cosmic rays and gamma - and X-ray astronomy). Periodical articles are included. Entries (in column form): running number, title, author, etc; number of items and years covered; annotations (sometimes evaluative). Entries go up to 1969. Author and subject indexes, p.533-84. The author was at one time librarian of the Royal Observatory, Edinburgh. 'An invaluable reference source for astronomers, other scientists working in the fringe areas of astronomy, and librarians' (*The Recorder*, no.271, 15 February 1971, p.2). *Class No:* 520(01)

[912]
SEAL, R.A. **A Guide to the literature of astronomy.** Littleton, Colo., Libraries Unlimited, 1977. 306p.

578 numbered entries, with evaluative comments of a high standard. 4 sections: 1. Reference material in astronomy - 2. General materials (*e.g.,* history; textbooks) - 3. Descriptive astronomy - 4. Special topics (*e.g.,* space science and aerodynamics). Appended 'Bibliography of basic reference material in astronomy' (p.238-9) - 80 items, including 31 atlases and star catalogues. Items are coded as recommended for A. Astronomy libraries; B. Public libraries; C. College/university libraries. Author-title and subject indexes. Excludes astronautics. For the non-specialist. *Class No:* 520(01)

[913]
—LUSIS, A. **Astronomy and aeronautics: an enthusiast's guide to books and periodicals.** London, Mansell, 1986. xx, 292p. ISBN: 072011795x.

968 annotated and numbered entries. 7 sections: 1. General astronomy - 2. Practical astronomy - 3. History of astronomy - 4. Astronomy plus ... (multi-and interdisciplinary works) - 5. Astrophysics - 6. The solar system - 7. Astronautics (p.198-255). Items asterisked were not available for inspection. Author index; Title index: books; Title index: periodicals; Subject index (analytical). Annotations are often evaluative and may cite reviews in *Sky and telescope*, etc. Attempts to provide a comprehensive annotated list in English 'for anyone ... below professional or undergraduate level' (*Introduction*). Claims to be in some ways a successor to Seal's *Guide* (*qv*). *Class No:* 520(01)

Encyclopaedias

[914]
Encyclopedia of astronomy and astrophysics. Meyers, R.A., *ed.* San Diego, Academic Press, 1988. xiv,807p. illus., diagrs., tables. ISBN: 0122266900.

41 articles, arranged A-Z (Astronomy, Infrared ... X-ray Astronomy), averaging 20 pages in length. Each article has a glossary and bibliography appended. *c.*300 photographs and illustrations. Cross-references and analytical index. *Class No:* 520(031)

[915]
MOORE, P., *ed.,*. **The Astronomy encyclopaedia.** London, Mitchell Beazley, 1987. 464p. illus. (incl. col.), ports., diagrs., tables. ISBN: 0855336048.

About 100 contributors. A-Z sequence of 2,500 entries (50-3,000 words in length), including 7 essays on major topics (*e.g.,* 'The big bang'; 'Exploring space'; 'Interstellar matter'; 'Pulsars'). 570 illus. (170 in colour), well captioned. Cross-references. Low priced. No bibliographies. 'A volume that will remain a popular reference source for many years to come' (*New scientist*, no.1589, 3 December 1987, p.67). *Class No:* 520(031)

Handbooks & Manuals

[916]
RONAN, C., *ed.* **Encyclopedia of astronomy:** a comprehensive survey of our solar system, galaxy and beyond. London, New York, etc., Hamlyn, 1979. 240p. illus. (incl. coloured), star charts, diagrs., graphs.

6 contributors. Chapters : Introduction - The stars - The solar system - Extragalactic astronomy - Theories of the universe - Observing the universe - The amateur observer - Star charts. 13 appendices (6. Star catalogues; 10. Comparative data on the planets; 12. Names of stars). Appended glossary, short bibliography and index (in tiny print). Like the *Cambridge Encyclopedia of astronomy*, fully illustrated, making good use of a large format. Praised in *New scientist* (29 November 1979, p.710) for its in-depth treatment of galaxies. 'The pictures and diagrams are as good as the text'. *Class No:* 520(035)

[917]
SIDGWICK, J.B. **Amateur astronomer's handbook.** 4th ed., prepared by J. Muirden. London, Pelham Books, 1979. xxix, 508p. diagrs., tables. ISBN: 0720711649.

1st ed., 1955.

41 sections on the instrumental and theoretical background of practical astronomy (40. Manufacturers and suppliers; 41. Bibliography, p.521-52, under 29 heads). Index, partly analytical, p.555-68. A classic in its field. Although the 4th ed. shows extensive revision, the text retains its original flavour. *Class No:* 520(035)

[918]
—SIDGWICK, J.B. Observational astronomy for amateurs. 4th ed., prepared by J. Muirden. London, Pelham Books, 1982. xix, 348p. ISBN: 0720713781.

Intended as a sequel to Sidgwick's *Amateur astronomer's handbook,* and first published in 1957. The 19 sections (1. Solar observation... 19. Nebulae and clusters) are followed by a lengthy bibliography (p.299-337) under 27 heads, and an analytical index. 'It is a sound reference for established and would-be practising astronomers, even if they have an earlier edition, and also for all amateurs interested in the real basics of solar system astronomy' (*Sky and telescope,* v.65, January 1983, p.40). *Class No: 520(035)*

Dictionaries

[919]
ILLINGWORTH, V., *ed.* The Macmillan dictionary of astronomy. 2nd ed., (1st ed., 1979, has U.S. title *The Facts on File dictionary of astronomy*). London, Macmillan, 1985. [v], 437p. diagrs., tables. (*Macmillan reference books.*) ISBN: 0333390628.

1st ed., 1979.

19 contributors. Over 2,300 entries, generous in length (*e.g.,*'Saturn' : 2 columns; 'Black hole' : 2½ columns). Ample cross-references. 12 appended tables (*e.g.,* 'Planetary satellites; 12. Recent successful planetary probes). 'The book walks the fine line between dictionary and encyclopaedia, but it does it very well' (*New scientist,* 5 September 1985, p.57). *Class No: 520(038)*

Reviews & Abstracts

[920]
Astronomy and astrophysics abstracts. Berlin, Springer-Verlag for Astronomisches Rechen-Institut, Heidelberg, 1969-. v.1(1)-. 2pa.

Prepared under the auspices of the International Astronomical Union. Continues *Astronomisches Jahresbericht* (v.1-68, 1900-68).

V.51B: Literature, 1990, pt.1 has 566p. of entries. Parts A and B of v.51 comprise together 11,423 brief abstracts and references. The 13 main classes (001-015) comprise: 001-015: Periodicals, proceedings, books, activities - 021-022: Applied mathematics, physics - 031-036: Astronomical instruments and techniques - 041-046: Positional astronomy, celestial mechanics - 051-053: Space research - 061-067: Theoretical astrophysics - 071-080: Sun - 081-085: Earth - 091-107: Planetary system - 111-126: Stars - 131-134: Interstellar matter, nebulae - 041-144: Radio sources, X-ray sources, cosmic rays - 151-161: Stellar systems, galaxy, extragalactic objects, cosmology. Author, subject and object indexes. A major abstracting and indexing service. *Class No: 520(048)*

Histories

[921]
GINGERICH, O., *ed.* Astrophysics and twentieth-century astronomy to 1950. Cambridge Univ. Press, 1984. 198, lvip. illus., ports., facsims, graphs, tables. (*The General history of astronomy, v.4A.*) ISBN: 0521242568.

Two parts (11 sections, each with further reading): 1. The birth of astrophysics and other late nineteenth century trends (*c*.1850-*c*.1950) - 2. Observatories and instrumentation. Appendix: The world's largest telescopes, 1850-1950. Index, p.li-lvi. Well illustrated, and intended for a wide audience.

V.4B is to cover: 3. Modern astrophysics - 4. The structure of the universe (1900-1950) - 5. The sociology of astronomy. 'These are going to be books that every astronomer and many non-astronomers will wish to possess for themselves'. (*History of science,* v.23(1), no. 59, March 1985, p.122). *Class No: 520(091)*

Institutions & Associations

[922]
Earth and astronomical sciences research centres: a world directory of organizations and programmes. 2nd ed. Harlow, Essex, Longman, 1991. v [vi],623p. (*Reference on research.*) ISBN: 0582082749.

First published 1984.

Guide to over 3,000 technology and research laboratories in more than 100 countries, arranged A-Z (Algeria ... Zimbabwe). Subject coverage includes geochemistry; petrology; mineralogy; planetary and galactic observations; meteorology. Data include title of establishment in original language, acronym and English translation; senior staff; research expenditure; publications; research activities; affiliation. New to this edition is a list of the main national and international trade associations and societies. (466 entries). Titles of establishments index; subject index. *Class No: 520:061:061.2*

[923]
Handbook for astronomical societies. Jones, B., *ed.* Plymouth, Federation for Astronomical Societies, 1977-. Annual. diagrs. tables.

Contents of the 12th ed., 1989: 4 articles - FAS list of officers - The Federation of Astronomical Societies - FAS slide list - Other astronomical organizations - List of local astronomical societies - Regional groups - Periodicals (26) - Equipment suppliers - Places to visit - Speakers - Information sources - Visual aid sources - Sources of astronomical software - Additions and amendments - Index to articles in previous handbooks. A very useful quick-reference tool. *Class No: 520:061:061.2*

Astrophysics

Tables & Data Books

[924]
ALLEN, C.W. Astrophysical quantities. 3rd ed. London, Univ. of London, 1973. 310p. tables. ISBN: 000485111500.

First published 1955.

15 sections, data being largely numerical and tabular: 2. General constants and units - 3. Atoms - 4. Spectra - 5. Radiation - 6. Earth - 7. Planets and satellites - 8. Interplanetary matter - 9. Sun - 10. Normal stars - 11. Stars with special characteristics - 12. Star population and the solar neighbourhood - 13. Nebulae, sources and interstellar space - 14. Clusters and galaxies - 15. Incidental tables (*e.g.,* annual variations). Analytical index, p.303-30. 'The most widely used source of astrophysical data' (Coblans, H., *ed. Use of physics literature* (1975), p.124). Allen : Emeritus Professor of Astronomy, Univ. of London. *Class No: 520-1(083)*

Astronomical Instruments

Observatories

[925]
Directory of European observatories 1988. Vercoutter, P.A.J., *comp.* 3rd ed. Ieper, Astronomical Contact Group, 1988. 432p. tables. (*Philippe's astronomical series, v.3.*) ISBN: 907247001x. ISSN: 07757085.

729 entries for observatories and institutions (1. Austria ... 27. Yugoslavia). 'Great Britain', 42 entries; 'France', 57 entries. Omits CIS. 6 types of observatory are differentiated. Data on each observatory appear under 19 heads (*e.g.* library; regular publications; observatory information; instruments). *Class No: 520.1*

Solar System

[926]
BEATTY, J.K. *and* **CHAIKIN, A.,** *eds.* **The New solar system.** 3rd ed. Cambridge, University Press; Cambridge, Mass., Sky Publishing Corporation, 1990. viii,326p. illus. (incl. col.), maps (incl. col.). ISBN: 0521361621.

First published 1982.

Major revision of the previous edition, published in 1982, and incorporating new information collated from *Voyager* and the 1985/86 Halley's Comet visit, among other things. 23 chapters: 1. The golden age of solar-system exploration ... 7. Surfaces of the terrestrial planets ... 12. Planetary rings ... 17. Comets ... 20. Small bodies and their origins ... 23. Putting it all together. Also includes planet, satellite and small-body characteristics, glossary, author biographies and suggested further reading, planetary maps and index. Excellent illustrations. Recommended for public and academic libraries. *Class No:* 523

[927]
KUIPER, G.P. *and* **MIDDLEHURST, B.M.,** *eds.* **The Solar system.** Chicago, Ill. (and later, London), Univ. of Chicago Press, 1953-63. 4v. illus., diagrs., maps, charts, tables.

V.1: *The sun.* 1953. xx, 746p. v.2: *The earth as a planet.* 1955. xviii, 752p. v.3: *Planets and satellites.* 1961. xx, 601p. v.4: *The moon, meteorites and comets.* 1963. xxii, 820p.

V.4 has 22 chapters, each with its own contributors; references appended. Thus, chapter 1: 'The lunar surface: introduction (p.1-56) has references (p.47-50) up to 1962. The analytical 'index of subjects and definitions' (p.799-810) has 76 sub-entries under 'Lunar craters'. A standard work of reference, now somewhat dated. *Class No:* 523

Stars & Galaxies

Handbooks & Manuals

[928]
KUIPER, G.P. *and* **MIDDLEHURST, B.M.,** *eds.* **Stars and stellar systems:** compendium of astronomy and astrophysics. Chicago, Ill., & London, Univ. of Chicago Press, 1961-75. 9v. illus., tables, maps.

V.1: *Telescopes.* 1961. v.2: *Astronomical techniques.* 1962. v.3: *Basic astronomical data.* 1963. v.4: *Clusters and binaries.* (Cancelled). v.5: *Galactic structures.* 1965. v.6: *Stellar atmospheres.* 1960. v.7: *Nebulae and interstellar matters.* 1968. v.8: *Stellar structure.* 1965. v.9: *Galaxies and the universe.* 1975.

Intended as an extension to the 4-v. *Solar system* series (*qv*), to cover astrophysics and stellar astronomy. Separate editors are appointed for each volume. V.2 has 24 main chapters, each by an expert, with extensive references (chapter 17, 'Photographic photometry', has 111 references). Subject index. 'The aim of the series is to present stellar astronomy and astrophysics as basically empirical sciences, co-ordinated and illustrated by the application of theory' (*Preface to the Series*). 'A landmark series' (*New technical books*, July 1978, entry 777). Supported in part by the National Science Foundation. *Class No:* 524(035)

[929]
RIDPATH, I. Collins' guide to stars and planets. London, Collins, 1984. 384p. illus., (incl. colour), star charts. ISBN: 0002190710.

88 star charts by W. Tirion, depicting the constellations A-Z, form the core of this pocket-sized volume, with descriptive text facing. A further section provides over 35 coloured plates. Analytical index. 'Warmly recommended (in a fairly crowded field) to any would-be astronomer' (*British book news*, April 1985, p.226).

....(contd.)
The night sky, by I. Ridpath and W. Tirion (London, Collins, 1985. 240p.) also makes good use of the 88 constellation charts. *Class No:* 524(035)

[930]
The Webb Society deep sky observer's handbook. Hillside, N.J., Enslow, 1980-90. 8v. ISBN: 0718824334, v.1; 0718824342, v.2; 0718824687, v.3; 0718825276, v.4; 0718825527, v.5; 0894901338, v.6; 0894901346, v.7; 0894902083, v.8.

1. *Double stars.* 1986. £14.95. 2. *Planetary and gaseous nebulae.* 1980. £13.95. 3. *Open and globular clusters,* 1980. £15.95. 4. *Galaxies.* 1982. £16.95. 5. *Clusters of galaxies.* 1982. £16.95. 6. *Anonymous galaxies.* 1987. £13.95. 7. *The southern sky.* 1987. £15.97. 8. *Variable stars.* 1990. £15.95.

The *Handbook's* aim is 'to provide a series of observer's manuals that do justice to the equipment that is available today and to cover fields that have not been adequately covered by other organizations of amateurs. The manuals are designed primarily for the more experienced amateur' (*General preface*). Intended to replace Revd. T.W. Webb's classic *Celestial objects for common telescopes* (first published 1839, reaching 6 editions by 1917, and still in print). The new *Handbook,* with its appendices and bibliographies, 'will justly have a special place in any amateur's bookshelf as the most comprehensive guide' (*British book news,* August 1982, p.466). *Class No:* 524(035)

Tables & Data Books

[931]
HIRSHFELD, A. *and* **SINNOTT, R.,** *eds.* **Sky catalogue 2000.0:** stars to visual magnitude 2000.0. Cambridge Univ. Press, 1982-5. 2v. (604 + 444p.). tables. ISBN: 0521247101.

1: *Stars to magnitude 8.0.* 1982. 2: *Double stars, variable stars and nonstellar objects.* 1985.

Companion volumes to Tirion's *Sky atlas 2000.0.* V.1 tabulates 45,269 stars, listed in order of increasing sight ascension. 91% of the stars in the catalogue have their distances given, apart from other data. Both the *Sky atlas* and the *Catalogue* (v.1) are considered 'essential acquisitions for all active astronomical observers' (*Nature,* v.298, 5 August 1982, p.588). V.2 (15 main data sections) covers more than 28,000 celestial objects not in v.1. A 2nd ed. of v.1 is to be published in 1992. *Class No:* 524(083)

Illustrations

[932]
The Cambridge atlas of astronomy. Audouze, J. *and* Israël, G., *eds.* 2nd ed. Cambridge, University Press, 1988. 432p. illus., charts, tables. ISBN: 0521363608.

Translation of *Le grand atlas de l'astronomie* (Encyclopaedia Universalis, 1986).

26 contributors, plus 3 consultant editors. Main sections: Sun (28p.); The solar system (180p.); Stars and the Galaxy (82p.); The extragalactic domain (64p.). 770 photographs (350 in colour) and 350 colour diagrams. There are no great changes from the previous edition, although the introduction is new and there are results of recent space missions, *e.g. Voyager 2* and the *Giotto* mission to Halley's comet. There are only 2p. of maps covering the entire sky, treatment being in the form of 2, 4 or 6-page topics. Of the earlier edition, 'It is an unexcelled reference for the astronomy enthusiast' (*British book news,* September 1985, p.541). Page size: 36.8 x 26.8cm. *Class No:* 524(084.1)

[933]
HENBEST, N. *and* **MARTEN, M. The New astronomy.** Cambridge Univ. Press, 1983. 240p.

Has 267 full-colour illus., ranking it 'among the most

....(contd.)

comprehensive of modern astronomical picture albums. Topics and text develop around roughly three-dozen celestial objects' (*Sky and telescope,* v.65, October 1982, p.323). 'Images of astronomical objects taken over the whole band starting with gamma-rays, X-rays and ultraviolet radiation and finishing with the infrared, millimetre waves and radio...' (*New scientist,* 12 January 1984, p.43). *Class No:* 524(084.1)

Maps & Atlases

[934]

NORTON, A.P. **Norton's 2000.0:** star atlas and reference handbook (epoch 2000.0). Ridpath, I., *ed.* 18th ed. Harlow, Essex, Longman Scientific & Technical; New York, John Wiley, 1989. xii,179p. maps, diagrs., tables. ISBN: 058203163x.

First published 1910. 17th ed. entitled *Norton's star atlas and reference handbook.*

18 maps, plus Northern and Southern hemisphere index map, together indicate the position of *c.*8,700 stars and 600 nebulae. 5 sections: 1. Star charts - 2. Position and time - 3. Practical astronomy - 4. The solar system - 5. Stars, nebulae and galaxies. Appendix includes units and notation, astronomical constants, symbols and abbreviations and useful addresses. Text has been almost entirely rewritten for this edition. The best atlas for amateurs. *Class No:* 524(084.3)

Navigation

[935]

The **Astronomical almanac** for the year 1992: data for astronomy, space sciences, geodesy, surveying, navigation and other applications. Washington, U.S. Government Printing Office; London, H.M. Stationery Office, 1991. Tables. Annual. ix,546p. tables. ISBN: 0118869426.

'Beginning with the edition for 1981, the title *The Astronomical Almanac* replaced both the title *The American Ephemeris and Nautical Almanac* and the title *The Astronomical Ephemeris,* unifying the two series' (*Preface, 1992*).

'The principal ephemerides in this Almanac have been computed from fundamental ephemerides of the planets and the moon prepared at the Jet Propulsion Laboratory, California, in cooperation with the U.S. Naval Observatory' (*Preface 1992*). Sections A-N. (D. Moon, 1992 ... E. Saturn, 1992 ... J. Observatories, 1992 ... N. Index). *Class No:* 527

[936]

GREAT BRITAIN. MINISTRY OF DEFENCE. Navy. **Admiralty manual of navigation.** Rev. ed. London, H.M. Stationery Office, 1954-73. 5v. illus., diagrs., tables, maps. (*B.R.45.*) ISBN: 0117707686; 0117714674.

First published 1914.

V.1 (rev. consolidated ed., incorporating changes 1-4. 1971) is a practical guide for executive officers; v.2 (rev. ed. 1973) provides a textbook of nautical astronomy and off-shore navigation; v.3 (1954) is based on the navigation syllabus for officers qualifying in navigation and direction, and deals with advanced subjects and mathematical proofs not included in v.1-2. Admiralty charts and publications are covered in v.1, chapter 2. V.4 (1962), on certain navigational equipment and techniques used by H.M. ships, is not available to the public. V.5 (6 bound parts) provides exercises on the use of tables (*e.g.* astronomical, Great Circle, tidal and tidal streams, time and chronometer, relative velocity questions).

The 1987 revised ed. of v.1 (xviii, 697p.) is entitled *General navigation, coastal navigation and pilotage,* with 19 chapters, a bibliography (p.675-7) and index (p.677-97).

....(contd.)

The Admiralty issues updates and amendments for mariners in its weekly publication, *Admiralty notice to mariners. Class No:* 527

Air & Nautical Almanacs

[937]

The **Air almanac.** London, H.M. Stationery Office, 1933-. Now annual. (*A.P. 1602.*) ISBN: 011772517x.

Produced jointly by H.M. Nautical Almanac Office, Royal Greenwich Observatory, and Nautical Almanac Office, U.S. Naval Observatory.

'The object of the *Air Almanac* is to provide in a convenient form the astronomical data for air navigation' (*Explanation*). Tables show daily position of the sun, Aries, planets and moon. A folding navigational star chart is appended. Aimed to meet the general requirement of the military forces in the UK, US, Australia, Canada and New Zealand. *Air almanac 1992* (1991. 168p. £39). *Class No:* 527.05

[938]

The **Nautical almanac** for the year 1992. London, H.M. Nautical Almanac Office; Washington, Nautical Almanac Office, U.S. Naval Observatory, 1991. 318p. ISBN: 0117725935.

The detailed calendar of tables for the sun, moon, planets and stars for the year is followed by 'Explanation', standard times, star charts, etc. 'This Almanac, with minor modifications and changes of language, has been adopted for the Brazilian, Danish, Greek, Indian, Indonesian, Italian, Korean, Mexican and Norwegian almanacs' (*Preface*). *Class No:* 527.05

Tide Tables

[939]

GREAT BRITAIN. HYDROGRAPHIC DEPARTMENT. **Tide tables** for the year ... London, Hydrographic Department, 1977-83. 3v. illus., forms, tables, maps. (*NP 201-203.*)

First published 1833.

V.1: *European waters, including Mediterranean Sea.* 1983. l, 434p. £7.50. v.2: *Atlantic and Indian Oceans, including tidal stream tables.* 1980. xlviiip. £5.75. v.3: *Pacific Ocean and adjacent seas, including tidal stream tables.* 1981. [469]p. £6.50.

V.1 has 3 parts: 1. Prediction of high and low water for standard ports; 2. Non-harmonic data; 3. Harmonic constants. Geographical index, p.415-20. List of tidal publications. *Class No:* 527.08

Surveying. Geodesy

[940]

BANNISTER, A. *and* RAYMOND, S. **Surveying.** 5th ed. London, Pitman, 1984. x, 510p. illus., diagrs., tables. ISBN: 0273020064.

13 chapters: 1. Introductory - 2. Chain surveying - 3. Levelling - 4. The theodolite and its use - 5. Optical distance measurement - 6. Electronic and electro-optical distance measurement - 7. Survey methods - 8. Areas and volumes - 9. Curve surveying - 10. Analysis and adjustments of measurements - 11. Orientation and postition - 12. Hydrographic surveying - 13. Photogrammetry. Chapter exercises. Marginal headings. Partly analytical index. Emphasis is on modern equipment and techniques. The two authors, formerly readers in civil engineering, Univ. of Salford, are now directors, Georesearch, Ltd., Stockport. *Class No:* 528

[941]
BOMFORD, G. **Geodesy.** 4th ed. Oxford, Clarendon Press, 1980. vii, 855p. diagrs., tables. ISBN: 019851946x.
First published 1952.
7 Chapters: 1. Triangulation, traverse and trilateration (field work) - 2. Computation of triangulation, traverse and trilateration - 3. Heights above sea-level - 4. Geodetic astronomy - 5. Gravity observations - 6. Physical geodesy - 7. Artificial satellites. 10 appendices. Bibliography (620 items), p.800-28. Analytical index. Chapter 7, on Satellite geodesy, because of the great advances during the last ten years, has been much expanded. A standard text. *Class No:* 528

Photogrammetry

[942]
SLAMA, C.C., *ed.* **Manual of photogrammetry.** 4th ed. Falls Church, Va., American Society for Photogrammetry and Remote Sensing, 1980. 1056p. ISBN: 0937294012.
'The definitive work on the use of photogrammetric techniques to extract quantitative information from vertical and oblique aerial photography' (Harris, C.D. *ed. Geographical bibliography for American libraries* (1985), entry 375). *Class No:* 528.7

Remote Sensing

[943]
HYATT, E. **Keyguide to information sources in remote sensing.** London, Mansell, 1988. xiv, 274p. ISBN: 0720118549.
The largest and most up-to-date English-language guide to its subject. 3 parts: 1. Survey of remote sensing and its literature. 2 chapters outline the development of remote sensing, the technology, the systems and the satellites, in general and regionally by continent. 2 further chapters provide an in-depth analysis of the literature of the subject, covering the conventional categories (books, reports, trade literature, etc.) and the secondary sources (bibliographies, abstracts, reviews, databases). Chapter 5 covers language factors and dictionaries; chapter 6 details sources of remotely sensed imagery; chapter 7, 'Audio-visual material', includes slides, videocassettes, maps and atlases). Part 2 (p.127-249) is an annotated bibliography of 819 items. Of the 493 published information sources, over 100 journals and 100 books are listed, and more than 20 entries each for literature guides, abstracts and indexes and databases. Finally, 326 organizations, grouped under 81 countries, with addresses, are listed. This is an immensely impressive guide, well written, clearly set out - the work of an information specialist in a remote sensing research unit. *Class No:* 528.71

Cartography

Bibliographies

[944]
Bibliographia cartographica ... Hrsg. von der Staatsbibliothek Preussischer Kulturbesitz in Verbindung mit der Deutschen Gesellschaft für Kartographie. [International documentation of cartographical literature.] Munich, etc., K.G. Saur, 1974-. v.1-. Annual. v.15. 1989). ISSN: 03400409.
Supersedes *Bibliotheca cartographica* (v.1-29/30. 1946/47). Contains *c.*2,500 numbered items. 12 sections: 1. Bibliographies. Map collection. Documentation - 2. General publications - 3. History of cartography - 4. Institutions and organizations of cartography - 5. Theoretical cartography - 6. Cartographic technology - 7. Topographic and landscape cartography - 8. Thematic maps and cartograms - 9. Atlas cartography - 10. Use and application of maps. General purpose maps - 11. Reliefs and other forms of cartographic representation - 12. Globes. List of

....(contd.)
periodicals (*c.*300); List of abbreviations; Concordance of the UDC and of the chapter headings of the *Bibliotheca cartographica*, Index of authors. *Class No:* 528.9(01)

[945]
PARRY, R.M. *and* PERKINS, C.R. **World mapping today.** London, Butterworths, 1987. [x], 583p. diagrs., maps. ISBN: 0408028505.
7 General chapters (*e.g.,* 2. The state of world mapping - 3. Map acquisition - 4. Map evaluation - 5, Maps and remote sensing - 6. Digital mapping - 7. Future trends in digital mapping). World mapping, p.61-568: The world; Africa; The Americas; Australia; Europe; The oceans. ('Philippines', p.340-2: Mapping - Further information - Addresses; Catalogue; Atlases and gazetteers; General. 2 map keys, 1:50,000.). 'List of geographic indexes' [*i.e.,* of 200 map keys] precedes text. Glossary, p.569-72. Geographical index. Publishers index. Well organised and well produced. For all map libraries as well as for most non-specialist libraries. *Class No:* 528.9(01)

Handbooks & Manuals

[946]
GREAT BRITAIN. MINISTRY OF DEFENCE. **Manual of map reading and land navigation.** 2nd ed. London, H.M. Stationery Office, 1989. various pagings, 5 folding maps. (*Army code 70947.*) ISBN: 0117726117.
1st ed. published as *Manuel of map reading,* 1973.
13 chapters: 1. Introduction - 2. Scale - 3. Marginal information - 4. Representation of detail - 5. Representation of relief - 6. Referencing systems - 7. Direction - 8. Compasses and their use - 9. Land navigation - 10. Tactical information printing systems - 11. Map substitutes - 12. Special maps - 13. Map supply. 'Produced primarily to provide instructors in the Armed Services with a comprehensive source of reference on which to base training' (*Publisher's description*). *Class No:* 528.9(035)

[947]
LOCK, C.B.M. **Modern maps and atlases:** an outline guide to twentieth century production. London, Bingley, 1969. 619p. ISBN: 0851570720.
A manual in five sections: 1. The techniques of modern cartography - 2. International maps and atlases - 3. National and regional maps and atlases (p.109-403) - 4. Thematic maps and atlases - 5. Map librarianship. The detailed analytical index has *c.*6,000 main entries. A solid contribution on 20th-century mapping (despite absence of map specimens) and an essential reference.
Modern maps and atlases is not fully incorporated into Dr. Lock's later *Geography and cartography* (Bingley, 1976); 'only a few entries (*i.e.,* map librarianship) have been included' (*RQ,* v.16(3), Spring 1977, p.259). *Class No:* 528.9(035)

Yearbooks & Directories

[948]
MAIZLISH, A. *and* HUNT, W.S. **The World map directory, 1989.** Santa Barbara, Map Link, 1988. 278p. maps. ISBN: 0929591003.
A catalogue of maps available from the publisher. Lists 46,000 titles, including thematic and topographic maps. International in scope though not all-inclusive - coverage of Eastern Europe, the CIS and developing countries is limited. Each entry includes sheet name, Map Link code, price, scale, date and an estimation of the quality of the map. Annotations of variable length are provided for most maps. Contains a list of publisher abbreviations (no addresses) and a geographic index. '*The World Map*

....(contd.)

Directory is a must for all map collections and map libraries' (*Reference books bulletin,* 1 May 1989, p.1531). *Class No:* 528.9(058)

Maps & Atlases

[949]

World directory of map collections. Compiled by the [IFLA] Section of Geography and Map Libraries. 2nd ed.; edition, J.A. Wolter and others. Munich & London, K.G. Saur, 1986. xliii, 405p. (*IFLA publication, v.31.*) ISBN: 3598203748.

Lists 670 collections, in 65 countries. Arrangement is by countries. Data on each collection include size and nature, the type and availability of catalogues. Name index of institutions and person in charge. *Class No:* 528.9(084.3)

Histories

[950]

The History of cartography. Chicago, Ill., Univ. of Chicago Press, 1987-. v.1-. illus., maps. ISBN: 0226316333.

1. *Cartography in prehistoric, ancient and medieval Europe, and the Mediterranean.* 1987. 599p. £78.95.

To be in 6v. V.1 carries the narrative up to *c.*1470. V.2-6 are to extend coverage both chronologically and geographically. 'No large library can afford to be without this' (*Library journal,* 15 September 1987, p.79). *Class No:* 528.9(091)

[951]

TOOLEY, R.V. Maps and map-makers. 6th ed. London, Batsford, 1978. xii, 140p. illus., facsims. ISBN: 0713413956.

First published 1949.

Treatment is by schools of geography. Chapters: Pre-Christian geography - The Arabs and medieval Europe - Italy - Germany - Holland and Belgium - French cartography - English map-makers. English maritime atlases - The country maps of England and Wales - Scotland and Ireland - Africa - Asia - America - Australia - Scandinavia. Extensive chapter bibliographies; many reproductions of maps. 140 illus. Detailed index. A popular work on the history of cartography. *Class No:* 528.9(091)

Biographies

[952]

TOOLEY, R.V. Tooley's dictionary of mapmakers. Tring, Herts., Map Collector Publications, 1979. xii, 684p. Supplement, 1985. ISBN: 0845117012; 0845117033, suppl..

Brief biographical data on over 20,000 mapmakers, from earliest times to 1900: name; date of birth and death (when known), titles of honour (if any), working address and changes of address (which often enables the user to establish the approximate date of publication of a map), main output of maps or atlases, with dates and editions whenever known. Includes a list of 'Works consulted', revealing surprising omissions. The *Supplement* adds *c.*4,000 names to the dictionary. Nevertheless, a standard work and attractively produced. *Class No:* 528.9(092)

Time

[953]

PARISE, F., *ed.* **The Book of calendars.** New York, Facts on File, 1982. [vii], 387p. tables. ISBN: 0871964678.

Main sections: Ancient calendars (p.1-122) - Africa - Modern Near East - India - Southeast Asia - Far East - Central America - Western calendars (p.291-379, including Calendar of saints; French Revolutionary calendar; Soviet calendar [discontinued in 1940]). Non-analytical index. A handbook that offers basic information on the structure of

....(contd.)

the calendar and extensive tables for quick conversions. More than 40 ancient peoples' calendars; over 60 calendars 'enabling the reader to translate one calendar date to its appropriate Julian or Gregorian date' (*Introduction*). *Class No:* 529

53 Physics

Abbreviations & Symbols

[954]
INTERNATIONAL UNION OF PURE AND APPLIED PHYSICS. Commission for Symbols, Units and Nomenclature. **Symbols, units, nomenclature and fundamental constants in physics.** London, The Union, through the Royal Society of London, 1987. 67p. tables. (*Document IUPAP 25*.)
First published 1978 as *Symbols, units and nomenclature in physics.*
As well as thoroughly covering physics, lists embrace mathematical terminology and symbols. 'Strongly recommended for libraries serving physical sciences' (*Science and technology libraries,* V.11(1), Fall 1990, p.740).
Class No: 530(003)

Databases

[955]
INSPEC. Hitchin, Herts., Institution of Electrical Engineers, 1969-. Updated biweekly.
INSPEC database provides online access to *Physics abstracts, Electrical and electronic abstracts,* and *Computer and control abstracts,* through DIALOG from 1969, and through BRS since 1970. Available on CD-ROM. D.T. Hawkins notes both bibliographic (INSPEC, PHYS, SPIN, Atomicindex and Nuclear science) and numeric (Superindex, PHYSCOMP, OECD Nuclear Energy Agency database, and GAPHYOR) databases covering physics (*Database,* v.8(1), February 1985, p.15-16, with a comparison table and references, p.17-18). *Class No: 530(003.4)*

Bibliographies

[956]
SHAW, D.F., *ed.* **Information sources in physics.** London, Butterworth, 1985. xii, 456p. graphics, tables. (*Butterworths guides to information sources.*) ISBN: 0408014741.
Supersedes *Use of physics literature,* edited by H. Coblans (Butterworth, 1975. xii, 290p.). 21 contributors, 20 documented chapters. 1. Introduction - 2. The scope and control of physics and its literature - 3. Science libraries, reference material and general treatises - 4. Abstracting, indexing and on-line services - 5. Atomic and molecular physics ... 8. Crystallography ... 10. Electronics and computer hardware ... 12. Geophysics, astrophysics and meteorological physics ... 15. Nuclear and particle physics ... 19. Grey literature (*e.g.,* reports) - 20. Patent literature. 3 appendices (A: the most important physics journals according to INSPEC; C: Publishers; abbreviations and addresses). Name index; subject and title index. Editor is Keeper of Scientific Books, Radcliffe Science Library, Oxford University. 'The standard work on the literature of

....(contd.)
physics for both the librarian and the physicist for some considerable time to come' (*Library review,* v.35(2), Summer 1986, p.137). *Class No: 530(01)*

Encyclopaedias

[957]
BESANÇON, R.M., *ed.* **The Encyclopedia of physics.** 3rd ed. New York, Van Nostrand Reinhold, 1985. [xix], 1378p. diagrs., graphs, formulas. ISBN: 0442257783.
First published 1966; 2nd ed., 1974 (xv, 1067p.).
More than 300 A-Z entries, by *c.*250 contributors. 'Quantum theory': p.985-1000, with 21 references, 7 cross-references. Detailed index, p.1347-78. A substantial revision, aimed at a wide public: physicists, teachers and librarians, students, engineers and scientists. Handy for basic, up-to-date information. *Class No: 530(031)*

[958]
KNIGHT, D. **A Companion to the phyiscal sciences.** London, Routledge, 1989. 177p. ISBN: 0415009014.
An encyclopedic dictionary (terms, concepts, theories and individuals). Includes some citations to additional in-depth readings. *Class No: 530(031)*

[959]
MEYERS, R., *ed.* **Encyclopedia of modern physics.** San Diego, Ca., Academic Press, 1990. 773p. ISBN: 0122266927.
34 entries, A-Z, surveying the state-of-the-art, traditional and applied physics (*e.g.* holography, quasi-crystals and superconductivity). Each entry has cross-references; brief glossary; index. 'Suitable for advanced undergraduate and graduate students as well as professional scientists and engineers' (*New technical books,* Jan/Feb, 1991, p.1045). *Class No: 530(031)*

Handbooks & Manuals

[960]
A **Physicist's desk reference.** Anderson, H.L., *ed.* New York, American Institute of Physics, 1989. 356p. ISBN: 0883186202.
Updated edition of *Physics vade mecum.* (1981).
22 fields of physics (*e.g.* acoustics, cryogenics, crystallography, elementary particles, fluid dynamics, spectroscopy and structure, nuclear physics, optics, plasma physics, surface physics). Chapters on fundamental constants, conversion factors, basic mathematical and physics formulas. Each chapter by an expert. 'An indispensable handbook for all libraries serving readers who need physics information' (*Science and technology libraries,* v.11(1), Fall 1990, p.139). *Class No: 530(035)*

Dictionaries

[961]
DAINTITH, J. **The Pan dictionary of physics.** London, Pan, 1990. 240p. illus. ISBN: 0330314521.
Defines 3000 commonly used physics terms. *Class No:* 530(038)

[962]
LORD, M.P. **Macmillan dictionary of physics.** London, Macmillan, 1986. xx, 330,[1]p. diagrs., tables. ISBN: 0333390660, HB; 0333423771, PB.
Enlarged and updated version of the physics content of *Dictionary of physical science*, edited by J. Daintish (Pan Books, 1978).
Over 4,000 entries, averaging *c.*50 words but occasionally of column length (*e.g.,* 'Laser'). 7 tables precede (*e.g.* 'Symbols and SI units for some physical quantities'). 'Further reading suggestions' (undergraduate level: 2 items; pre-postgraduate level: 2). Adequate cross-references; *c.*200 small diagrams. 'Will be of use to Physics students at first year undergraduate and lower levels, and also to amateur enthusiasts and lay persons' (*Preface*). *Class No:* 530(038)

Reviews & Abstracts

[963]
Physics abstracts. Science abstracts. Section A. London, INSPEC (The Institution of Electrical Engineers), 1898-. Bimonthly. ISSN: 00368091.
1991: 151,994 abstracts and references. Main sections (Closely subdivided): 00.00 General - 10.00 The physics of elementary particles and fields - 20.00 Nuclear physics - 30.00 Atomic and molecular physics - 40.00 Classical areas of phenomenology (*e.g.,* electricity and magnetism) - 50.00 Fluids, plasmas and electric discharge - 60.00 Condensed matter: structure, thermal and mechanical properties - 70.00 Condensed matter: electronic structure, electrical, magnetic, and optical properties - 80.00 Cross-disciplinary physics and related areas of science and technology - 90.00 Geophysics, astronomy and astrophysics. Author index: subsidiary indexes: bibliography; book; conference; corporate author. Subject indexes, 2pa. List of journals scanned in half-yearly author index. Four or five-yearly cumulative indexes. The major English-language physics abstracting service. Available online via DIALOG, BRS and Data-Star; CD-ROM. *Class No:* 530(048)

Tables & Data Books

[964]
JERRARD, H.G. *and* MCNEILL, D.B. **A Dictionary of scientific units,** including dimensionless numbers and scales. 5th ed. London & New York, Chapman & Hall, 1986. 222p. ISBN: 0412280906.
First published 1963.
The dictionary (*c.*400 entries, Abampere ... Zhukov scale), p.9-165. 5 appendices (2. Standardization commmittees and conferences; 4. Conversion tables). References, p.194-212. Analytical index, p.213-222. Compared with the 1963 ed., 'incorporates more precise values of the fundamental physical constants, as well as more exact definitions of other words' (*Journal of chemical education*, v.64, July 1987, p.A174). *Class No:* 530(083)

Thesauri

[965]
INSPEC thesaurus, 1991. 9th ed. London, Institution of Electrical Engineers, 1991. v, 547,61p. ISBN: 0852964897.
First published 1973.
The 9th edition contains *c.*13,000 terms (6,000 'preferred terms' and 7,000 cross-references). Terms range over fields of physics, electronics, communications, electrical engineering, information technology, computing and control systems. Alphabetical display of terms (547p.) is followed by a hierarchical display of used terms. *Class No:* 530:025.43

Physical Measurement

[966]
SYDENHAM, P.H., *and others.* **Handbook of measurement science.** New York, Wiley, 1982-83. 2v. (1413p.).
1. *Theoretical fundamentals.* 1982. xxiv, 654p.
2. *Practical fundamentals.* 1983. xxii, p.655-1413.
V.1 has 18 contributors; v.2, 17. 32 documented chapters, in all (*e.g.,* 7. Pattern recognition (6 contributors), v.1, p.277-330, including 5p. of references; 32. Sources of information measurement, v.2, p.1363-89, with 7 references). Index. 'No measurement or control enquirer should be without it' (*Measurement and control,* v.16, February 1983, p.47-48).
A new ed. appeared in 1992. *Class No:* 530.08

Mechanics

Aerodynamics

[967]
GUNSTON, B. **The Guinness book of speed.** Enfield, Middx., Guinness, 1984. 192p. illus. ISBN: 0851122671.
Pt.1: The living world. Pt.2: The technical world. Index to text and illus., p.189-92. *Class No:* 533.6

Sound. Vibrations

[968]
Acoustics abstracts. Brentwood, Essex, Multi-Science Publishing Co., Ltd., 1967-. pts. A,B. ea. 6pa. ISSN: 00014974.
About 3,000 abstracts pa. Sections: Fundamental acoustics - Solid state acoustics - Liquid state acoustics - Gaseous state acoustics ... Ultrasonic applications - Audio frequencies - Noise - Architectural acoustics - Vibration and shock - Review and miscellaneous. Annual indexes. *Class No:* 534

[969]
HARRIS, C.M., *ed.* **Shock and vibration handbook.** 3rd ed. New York, etc., McGraw-Hill, 1987. v.p. diagrs.
First published 1961.
44 sections, each with references. Section 44: Effects of shock and vibration on man (55p.; 111 references, plus 2p. of additional references). 29p. index. Particularly intended to be used as a working reference by engineers and scientists in the mechanical, civil, acoustical, aeronautical, electricity, air-conditioning, transportation and chemical fields' (*Preface*). *Class No:* 534

Optics

Microscopy

[970]
Dictionary of light microscopy. Bradbury, S., *and others,* comps. Oxford Univ. Press; Royal Microscopical Society, 1989. x,139p. diagrs., tables. (*Microscopy handbooks 15.*) ISBN: 0198564139, pbk.

Covers *c*.1250 terms: A (symbol for absorbance, etc.) ... Zoom. Entries range from 2 to *c*.15 lines. Non-preferred terms are indicated as such. Numerous cross-references. Appendices give equivalent terms in English, French and German. Compiled by the Nomenclature Committee of the Royal Microscopical Society. Well-produced. *Class No:* 535.083.98

Reflection. Emission.

Lasers

Spectral Data

[971]
CRC atlas of spectral data and physical constants for organic compounds. Grasselli, J.G. *and* Ritchey, W.M. 2nd ed. Cleveland, Ohio, CRC Press, 1975. 6v. (4688p.). tables, formulas. ISBN: 0878193170.

First published 1973.

1. *Name. Synonym directory. Structures. Spectroscopic aids. Special cross-correlation tables.* 2/4. *Data tables: Compounds , A-B, C-D, P-Z.* 5. *Indexes* for molecular formulas, molecular weights, physical constants, WLN [Wiswesser Line Notation], Mass spectra 6. *Special data indexes.*

Spectral data and physical constraints for *c*.21,000 organic compounds. Bibliographic references, for further reading. *Class No:* 535.330

Colours

[972]
Colour index. 3rd ed. (2nd revision). Bradford, Society of Dyers and Colourists, 1971-82. Additions and amendments, 4pa. 7v. (7304p). tables.

First published 1924-28.

V.1-5 (1971 ed.) record 7,898 generic names of individual dyes and pigments. V.1-3: Colorants classified according to their usage; v.4: Colorants classified according to their chemical constitution; index of intermediate compounds; index of formulae. V.5: Code letters for colorant manufacturers; index of *Colour index* generic names, with colorants listed under each; index of commercial names of colorants. V.6-7 are supplements to V.1-4, 6. Supplement 1988: Pigments and solvent dyes. *Class No:* 535.6

[973]
HOPE, A. *and* **WALCH, M. The Color compendium.** New York, etc., Van Nostrand Reinhold, 1990. 360p. illus.

An encyclopedia of topics on colour, ranging from art and history to the social sciences and technology. Each entry is cross-referenced. Includes bibliographies. Colour illus. and photographs throughout. Wide appeal. *Class No:* 535.6

Heat

Heat Transfer

[974]
ROHSENOW, W.M. *and* **HARTNETT, J.P.,** *eds.* **Handbook of heat transfer applications.** 2nd ed. New York, etc., McGraw-Hill, 1985. 1440p. illus. ISBN: 0070535531.

First published 1975.

Sections : Basic concepts of heat transfer - Mathematical methods - Thermophysical properties - Conduction - Numerical methods in heat transfer - Natural convection - Forced convection - Internal flow in ducts ... Rarsfield gases - Electric and magnetic fields - Condensation - Boiling - Two-phase flow - Radiation. 691 illus. Numerous references. *Class No:* 536.2

Heat Effects on Bodies

[975]
CHANEY, J.F., *and others, eds.* **Thermophysical properties research literature retrieval guide, 1900-1980.** New York, Plenum Press, 1982. 7v. tables. (*First published 1964-70. 2v.*)

1. *Elements.* 2. *Inorganic compounds.* 3. *Organic compounds and polymeric materials.* 4. *Alloys, intermetallic compounds and cermets.* 5. *Oxide mixtures and minerals.* 6. *Mixtures and solutions.* 7. *Coatings, systems, composites, foods, animal & vegetable products.*

Covers world literature on 14 thermodynamic and physical properties of 44,300 substances. Over 75,000 references. Each volume has a materials directory (A-Z), search parameters (substances, numerically), a bibliography and author index. An important research tool for the physical chemist. *Class No:* 536.4

Electricity

Measurements

[976]
Key abstracts: Electrical measurements and instrumentation. London, INSPEC; New York, Institute of Electrical and Electronic Engineers, 1976-. Monthly. (*Key abstracts.*) ISSN: 03077977.

About 150 abstracts per issue. 7 main sections: 1. Measurement science - 2. Measurement equipment and instrumentation systems - 3. Measurement of specific electric and magnetic variables - 4. Measurement of specific nonelectric variables - 5. Biomedical instrumentation and measurement - 6. Aerospace instrumentation - 7. Geophysics instrumentation and measurement. No indexes. A current awareness service. *Class No:* 537.083

54 Chemistry

Chemistry

Databases

[977]
CA SEARCH. Columbus, Ohio, American Chemical Society, Chemical Abstracts Service; 1967-.

CA SEARCH is a major database, derived from the weekly *Chemical abstracts*. It now carries *c.*6 million citations, giving CA Registry Numbers, but omitting the abstracts (except on DIALOG). The latter are covered by CAS ONLINE.

Hawkins, D.T. 'A review of online physical sciences and mathematics databases. Part 2: Chemistry' (*Database,* v.8(2), June 1985, p.31-41) consists of 1. Introduction; 2. Bibliographic databases (2.1 Chemical abstracts; 2.2 Other bibliographic databases); 3. Name directories and substructure searching systems. 4. Numeric databases; 5. Full text databases. Appended chart of relevant databases, with headings: Chemical databases; Major subject(s), Producer, Starting date. 41 references. *Class No:* 540(003.4)

Bibliographies

[978]
MAIZELL, R.E. How to find chemical information: a guide for practicing chemists, educators and students. 2nd ed. New York, Chichester, etc., Wiley, 1987. xvii,402p.

First published 1979.

19 chapters: 1. Basic concepts - 2. Information flow and communication patterns in chemistry - 3. Search strategy - 4. Keeping up to date - current awareness programs - 5. How to get access to articles, patents, translations, specifications, and other documents quickly and efficiently - 6. 'Chemical abstracts' service - history and development - 7. Essentials of 'Chemical abstracts' use - 8. Other abstracting and indexing services of interest to chemists - 9. Some US government technical information centers and sources - 10. Online databases, chemical structure searching, and related topics - 11. Reviews - 12. Encyclopedias and other major reference books - 13. Patents - 14. Safety and related topics - 15. Location and using physical property and related data - 16. Chemical marketing and business information sources - 17. Process information - 18. Analytical chemistry - a brief review of some of the literature sources - 19. Summary of representative major trends and development in chemical information. Indexes (name; subject), p.377-402. A practical approach, with 'pros and cons' for many sources described. *Class No:* 540(01)

[979]
WIGGINS, G. Chemical information sources. New York, McGraw-Hill, 1991. 352p. 2 disks (IBM-PC). ISBN: 0079099394.

Covers databases including citation, subject and patent

....(contd.)
searching, with emphasis on online sources. Includes more traditional printed ones (dictionaries, handbooks, etc.) as well. An innovation in this type of work is the floppy disks (3.5 inch) containing over 2100 records with citations for, among other things, the complete reference collection of the Indiana University Chemical Library. 'Recommended very highly' (*Choice,* February 1992, p.920). *Class No:* 540(01)

Encyclopaedias

[980]
CONSIDINE, D.M. *and* **CONSIDINE, G.D.,** *eds.* **Van Nostrand encyclopedia of chemistry.** 4th ed. Princeton, N.J., Van Nostrand Reinhold, 1984. [viii], 1082p. diagrs., tables. ISBN: 0442225725.

About 1,300 entries, 'Absolute zero' ... 'Zymolytic reaction'. 112 contributors, although entries are not usually signed. Longer articles are documented (*e.g.,* 'Phosphorous': $9\frac{1}{2}$ columns, with 7 references). Analytical index, p.1039-82. Nearly 80% of the text is completely new. 'Designed for ready comprehension by anyone with a general background in chemistry' (*Journal of chemical education,* December 1984). *Class No:* 540(031)

Dictionaries

[981]
BENNETT, H., *ed.* **Concise chemical and technical dictionary.** 4th ed. London, E. Arnold, 1986. xxxviii, 1271p. ISBN: 0713135840.

First published 1974.

Some 85,000 brief definitions, with many cross-references. Includes abbreviations and chemical structures. Prelims. on nomenclature, pronunciation, names and formulas of radicals occurring in organic compounds. The 4th ed. is enlarged with definitions of new trademark products, chemicals, drugs and terms coined to cover the latest technical developments. Prelims. have a section, 'The pronunciation of chemical words'. Intended for use by both professionals and laymen. *Class No:* 540(038)

[982]
Grant and Hackh's chemical dictionary. Grant, R.L. *and* Grant, A.C., *eds.* 5th ed. New York, etc., McGraw-Hill, 1987. xii, 641p. diagrs., charts, tables.

First published 1929; 4th ed. 1969.

More than 55,000 entries, including terms in such related fields as physics, medicine, biology, agriculture, pharmacy and mineralogy. Emphasis on chemical nomenclature. A standard chemical dictionary. *Class No:* 540(038)

Reviews & Abstracts

[983]

Chemical abstracts. Columbus, Ohio, American Chemical Society, 1907-. v.1 Weekly. $8,500pa. ISSN: 00092258.

Chemical abstracts provides over 500,000 abstracts pa., taken from over 14,000 journals worldwide, plus patents, conference proceedings, government research reports, books and dissertations. Coverage in 80 sections. Odd-numbered weekly issues feature organic and biochemical sections; even-numbered issues cover applied chemistry, chemical engineering. Weekly keyword, patent and author indexes; half-yearly author, general subject, chemical substance, formula and patent indexes. The earlier 10-yearly cumulative indexes (1907-56) became 5-yearly 1957-. (The 7th Collective index, for 1962-66, occupied 24v., with extremely detailed indexing, - c.650 entry-words per 1,000 words in the abstracts).

Chemical abstracts is also available in 5 fortnightly index groupings (1963-): *Applied chemistry and chemical engineering* sections (CAAS), *Biochemical sections* (CABS), *Macramolecular sections* (CAMS), *Organic chemistry* sections (CAOS), and *Physical and analytical chemistry* sections (CAPS). (No volume indexes are included in section subscriptions). Other features available: *Index guide; Ring index handbook;* and a chemical-compound *Registry* (1974), assigning CAS Registry Numbers to unique compounds. *Using chemical abstracts* comprises a cassette and workbook.

CA selects offers a current-awareness service, reproducing 100-200 CA abstracts per bi-weekly issue in 36 areas (*e.g., Chemical hazards, Forensic chemistry, Liquid crystals,* and *New books in chemistry*). *Chemical Abstracts Service source index* (CASSI) lists periodicals abstracted. Other titles include *Chemical titles.*

Chemical abstracts is the most widely used abstracting service in English that covers the whole field of chemistry, pure and applied, and including biochemistry. All science libraries should provide at least some parts of the Chemical Abstracts Service.

CA SEARCH corresponds as a database to *Chemical abstracts. Class No: 540(048)*

Progress Reports

[984]

ROYAL SOCIETY OF CHEMISTRY. Specialist periodical reports: reviews of the chemical literature. London, the Society [formerly Chemical Society], 1967-. 45 series, usually annual.

Alicyclic chemistry.
Aliphatic, alicyclic and saturated heterocyclic chemistry.
Aliphatic and related natural product chemistry.
Aliphatic chemistry.
The alkaloids.
Amino-acids, peptides and proteins.
Aromatic and heteroaromatic chemistry.
Biosynthesis.
Carbohydrate chemistry. 2 pts.
Catalysis.
Chemical physics of solids and their surfaces.
Chemical thermodynamics.
Colloid science.
Dielectric and related molecular processes.
Electrochemistry.
Electron spin resonance.
Electronic structure and magnetism of inorganic compounds.
Environmental chemistry.
Fluorocarbon and related chemistry.
Foreign compound metabolism in mammals.
Gas Kinetics and energy transfer.
General and synthetic methods.

....(contd.)
Heterocyclic chemistry.
Inorganic biochemistry.
Inorganic chemistry of the main group elements.
Inorganic chemistry of the transition elements.
Inorganic reaction mechanisms.
Macromolecular chemistry.
Mass spectroscopy.
Molecular spectroscopy.
Molecular structure by diffraction methods.
Nuclear magnetic resonance.
Organic compounds of sulphur, selenium and tellurium.
Organometallic chemistry.
Organophosphorous chemistry.
Photochemistry.
Radiochemistry.
Reaction kinetics.
Saturated hetrocyclic chemistry.
Spectroscopic properties of inorganic and organometallic compounds.
Statistical mechanics.
Surface and defect properties of solids.
Terpenoids and steroids.
Theoretical chemistry.

The reports are critical in-depth accounts of the progress in specific areas by acknowledged authorities, normally appearing within 12 months after the period of literature coverage. *Class No: 540(055)*

Tables & Data Books

[985]

CRC handbook of chemistry and physics. Lide, D.R., ed. 71st ed. Boca Raton, Florida, CRC Press, 1990. v.p. diagrs., charts, tables, chemical structures. ISBN: 0849304711.

First published 1914.

This new edition of a classic reference source (the 'Rubber Bible') has been substantially reorganized by a new editor into an arrangement which facilitates browsing. About 20% of the tables are completely new/updated. Includes more tables on health and the environment than earlier versions. An invaluabe mine of information which 'remains the essential reference tool for physical data, required in virtually all libraries' (*Choice*, September 1991, p.56). *Class No: 540(083)*

[986]

LANGE, N.A., ed. Lange's handbook of chemistry. 13th ed., by J.A. Dean. New York, etc., McGraw-Hill, 1985. v.p. tables, chemical structure. ISBN: 0070161925.

First published 1934.

11 sections, mainly tables: 1. Mathematics - 2. General information and conversion tables - 3. Atomic and nuclear structure - 4. Inorganic chemistry - 5. Analytical chemistry - 6. Electrochemistry - 7. Organic chemistry - 8. Spectroscopy - 9. Thermodynamic properties - 10. Physical properties - 11. Miscellaneous (*e.g.,* Glossary). 38p. detailed analytical index, including formulas. Section 7 (153p.) includes description of 7,000 organic compounds. A classic tool for chemists. The 14th ed. was due in August 1992. *Class No: 540(083)*

Patents

[987]

GRUBB, P.W. Patents in chemistry and biotechnolgy. 2nd ed. Oxford, Clarendon Press, 1986. xii, 335p. ISBN: 019855222x, HB; 0198552211, PB.

First published 1982 as *Patents for chemists.*

A guide to the lay reader of the patent systems of the UK, US and Europe. Contains sections on general principles of patenting, inventions in chemistry,

....(contd.)
pharmaceuticals and biotechnology, patenting for the
chemical inventor and the politics of patents. Also has a
glossary of terms and list of cases. *Class No:* 540(088.8)

Writing & Lecturing

[988]
DODD, J.S., *ed.* The ACS style guide: a manual for authors
and editors. Washington, American Chemical Society, 1986.
264p. diagrs., tables. ISBN: 0841209170.
Contents: The scientific paper - Grammar, style and
usage - Illustrations and tables - Copyright and permissions
- Manuscripts submissions in machine-readable form - The
literal literature: becoming part of it and using it - Making
effective oral presentations. 'This is a true *vade mecum,* in
the best sense of the word' (*New technical books,* January
1986, entry 831).
The ACS also publishes *Handbook for authors of papers
in American Chemical Society publications* (Washington,
1978, vi, 122p). *Class No:* 540:001.81

Theoretical Chemistry

Physical Chemistry

Electrochemistry

[989]
HIBBERT, D.B. *and* JAMES, A.M. Dictionary of
electrochemistry. 2nd ed. London, Macmillan, 1984. ix,
308p. diagrs., graphs, tables, chemical structures. ISBN:
0333349830.
First published 1976.
Several hundred electrochemical terms and concepts. 'pH':
$3\frac{1}{2}$p. Numerous cross-references. 'References and methods',
p.298-9; 'Electrochemical journals', p.300; 'Tables of useful
data', p.301-8. Further reading, on occasion. Eponyms. 130
diagrams. *Class No:* 541.13

Radiation Chemistry

[990]
CRC handbook of radiation chemistry. Tabata, V., *and others.*
Boca Raton, Fl., CRC Press, 1990. 936p. graphs, tables.
ISBN: 0849429957.
18 chapters, some with references. Much tabular data.
Index, p.921-36. *Class No:* 541.15

Laboratory Tools & Techniques

Work with Liquids

[991]
VISWANATH, D.S. *and* NATARAJAN, G. Data book on the
viscosity of fluids. New York, Hemisphere, 1989. 990p.
ISBN: 0891167781.
Includes organic compounds, inorganic liquids, liquid
metals, plasticizers and foods like soybean oil. For each
compound one primary journal reference and *Chemical
abstracts* CAS Registry number. Common name index. 'A
major source for viscosity data' (*Science and technology
libraries,* v.10(2), Winter 1989, p.138). *Class No:* 542.6

Analytical Chemistry

[992]
Analytical abstracts. London, Royal Society of Chemistry,
1954-. 12pa. ISSN: 00032689.
About 12,000 abstracts pa. Classes A-J: A. General
analytical chemistry - B. Inorganic chemistry - C. Organic
chemistry - D. Biochemistry - E. Pharmaceutical chemistry
- F. Food - G. Agriculture - H. Environmental chemistry -
J. Apparatus and technique. Cross-references. Subject index.
Annual subject and author indexes. *Analytical abstracts* is
online, January 1982-. *Class No:* 543

[993]
CRC handbook of basic tables for chemical analysis.
Bruno, T.J. *and* Svornos, P.D.N. Boca Raton, Fl., 1989.
[viii],517p. tables, chemical structures, graphs. ISBN:
0849339359.
11 chapters, closely sub-divided (*e.g.* 'Thin layer
chromatography' (p.129-59): 5 sections; 243 references).
Index, 28p. *Class No:* 543

Organic Chemistry

[994]
Dictionary of organic compounds: the constitution of physical,
chemical, and other properties of the principal carbon
compounds and their derivatives, together with the relative
literature. Buckingham, J., *ed.* 5th ed. London, Chapman
& Hall, 1982. 7v. (7848p.). Annual supplements, 1983-.
£1,175. ISBN: 0412170000.
First published 1934-37; 3rd ed., edited by Sir I.
Heilbron and H.M. Bunbury (1953. 4v.).
The main work has data on 150,000 of the most
common and important organic compounds for chemists,
biochemists, pharmacologists and biologists. Documented.
Five indexes: Name index; Molecular formula index;
Heteroatom index; Chemical Service Registry number;
Cumulative structure. Known as 'DOC 5'. 'An essential
adjunct wherever organic compounds are used' (*Nature,*
v.300, 25 November 1982, p.336). Supplements have
cumulative indexes.
Heilbron database (online via DIALOG) is the source
from which the Chapman & Hall chemical dictionaries are
compiled. *Class No:* 547

Compounds

[995]
BARTON, Sir D. *and* OLLIS, W.D. Comprehensive organic
chemistry; the synthesis and reactions of organic
compounds. Oxford, etc., Pergamon Press, 1979. 6v.
(*c.*8,000p).
1. Stereochemistry, hydrocarbons, halo compounds,
oxygen compounds. 2. Nitrogen compounds, carboxylic
acids, phosphorous compounds. 3. Sulphur, silenium,
silicon, boron, organometallic compounds. 4. Heterocyclic
compounds. 5. Biological compounds. 6. Author, formula,
subject, reagent, reaction indexes.
Emphasises throughout the properties and reactions of all
the important classes of organic compounds, including those
compounds prepared by synthesis as well as natural
products created by biosynthesis. Over 100 contributors;
over 20,000 literature references. Actual coverage of v.6
(xii, 1,628 p.): formula, subject, author, reaction and
reagent. 'A must for all chemistry collections of importance'
(*New technical books,* v.64(10), December 1979, entry
1493). *Class No:* 547.2

Crystallography

[996]
International tables for crystallography. 2nd rev. ed. Dordrecht, Reidel, for the International Union of Crystallography, 1987-. (*3rd series of International tables*; 1st series, 1935.) ISBN: 9027722809.

A. *Space group symmetry.* 1987. xvi, 878p. Brief teaching edition (120p.) was published in 1988.

Volume A (pt.1: Tables for plane groups and space groups has 15 documented sections, plus subsections) treats the symmetries of one-, two- and three-dimensional space groups and point groups in direct space. Detailed features of each space group appear under 13 heads.

Volumes B (*Reciprocal space*) and C (*Physical and chemical information data of interest to crystallographers*) are in preparation. *Class No:* 548

Mineralogy

Encyclopaedias

[997]
The Encyclopedia of gemstones and minerals. Holden, U. *and* Mathez, E.A., *eds.* New York, Facts on File, 1992. 320p. illus. ISBN: 0876021775.

Properties/values of over 200 rocks, stones, jewels and other mineral substances. 400 illus. Data on characteristic form, specific gravity, symmetry, system, refraction, location, use and commercial value. 'Highly recommended for all types of libraries' (*Library Journal*, 15 February 1992, p.160). *Class No:* 549(031)

[998]
ROBERTS, W.L., *and others.* **Encyclopedia of minerals.** New York, Van Nostrand Reinhold, 1990. xxiii,979p. illus. (some col. pl.). ISBN: 0442276818.

First published 1974.

Item-by-item description of more than 2,500 minerals, Abelsonite ... Zykaite. Data include crystal system, space group, lattice constants, hardness, desnity, cleavage, habit, colour-lustre, mode of occurrence, strongest diffraction lines and selected references. Glossary, p.xix-xxiii. 237 colour photos. *Class No:* 549(031)

Handbooks & Manuals

[999]
PELLANT, C. Rocks, minerals and fossils of the world. Boston, Mass., Little, Brown, 1990. 175p. illus. ISBN: 0316697966.

Contents: Glossary - Geological time scale - Igneous rocks - Metamorphic rocks - Sedimentary rocks - Fossils. Further reading. Index. Over 300 colour illus. 'A basic reference work for college and research libraries' (*New Technical Books*, Nov./Dec. 1990, 1734). *Class No:* 549(035)

Reviews & Abstracts

[1000]
Mineralogical abstracts. London, Mineralogical Society of Great Britain, and Mineralogical Society of America, 1920-. Quarterly. £95.

Earlier (1920-58) published in *The mineralogical magazine.*

About 5,500 abstracts and references pa. 18 sections, A-V: Age determination - Apparatus and techniques - Book notices ... Economic minerals and mineral deposits ... Experimental mineralogy ... Geochemistry ... Meteorites and tektites ... Mineral data ... Petrology ... Various topics. Index of authors per issue; annual author and subject indexes. *Class No:* 549(048)

Gemmology

[1001]
SMITH, G.F.H. Gemstones. Revised by F.C. Phillips. 14th ed. London, Chapman & Hall, 1972. xii, 580p. illus. (incl. col.), diagrs., tables. ISBN: 0412108909.

First published 1912.

Four parts (41 footnoted chapters): 1. Physical character - 2. Technology and history - 3. Description (A. Principle stones; B. Other gem materials; C. Ornamental stones; D. Organic products, *e.g.,* pearl, ivory, resin) - 4. Classification tables. Appendices include bibliography (12 groups), p.544-56. Index, p.559-80. Still the most complete scholarly work in English. *Class No:* 549.091

55 Earth Sciences

Earth Sciences

Databases

[1002]
GEOBASE. Norwich, Geo Abstracts Ltd., 1980-.
Over 380,000 references on geography, geology, ecology and related disciplines, with 40,000 additonal records each year. Includes abstracts as well as bibliographic citations. Covers over 2,000 science and technology journals and books; reports; monographs; theses. Includes *International development abstracts; Geographical abstracts; Mineralogical abstracts; Ecological abstracts*. Available via DIALOG and ORBIT, and on CD-ROM. *Class No: 550(003.4)*

Bibliographies

[1003]
Bibliography and index of geology. Alexandria, Va., American Geological Institute, 1969-. 12pa. ISSN: 00982784.
Succeeds *Bibliography of North American geology* (U.S. Geological Survey, 1931-72, which included literature 1785-1970), and *Bibliography and index of geology exclusive of North America* (Geological Society of America), 1933-68. 32v.
References photocomposed from citations in GeoRef, the AGI database. 29 fields of interest (01 Mineralogy and crystallography - 02. Geochemistry - 03. Geochronology - 04. Extraterrestrial geology - 05/06. Petrology - 07. Marine geology and oceanography - 08/11. Paleontology - 12. Stratigraphy, historical geology and paleoecology... 16. Structural geology - 17/20. Geophysics - 21. Hydrogeology and hydrology - 22. Engineering and environmental geology - 23/25. Surficial geology - 26/29. Economic geology). Profuse cross-references. Omits geography and meteorology, both well covered elsewhere. List of serials precedes. Analytical subject and author indexes; annual cumulative index in 4 pts. Available on microfiche, online and CD-ROM. The major indexing service for geology. *Class No: 550(01)*

[1004]
Information sources in the earth sciences. Wood, D.N., *and others, eds.* 2nd ed. London, Bowker Saur, 1989. 518p. (*Guides to information sources.*)
First published as *Use of earth sciences literature* (Butterworth, 1973).
20 chapters: 1. Introduction - 2. Earth science libraries and their use ... 6. Computerized information services and geological databases/databanks ... 9. Palaeontology ... 12. Petrology ... 16. Engineering and environment geology ... 18. Meteorology and climatology ... 20. History of geology. The chapter on computerized bibliographic and data retrieval is new to this edition. Aimed at students and practising geologists. *Class No: 550(01)*

Encyclopaedias

[1005]
FAIRBRIDGE, R.W., *ed.* **Encyclopedia of earth sciences.** New York, Van Nostrand Reinhold.
1. *The encyclopedia of oceanography.* 1966. 2. *The encyclopedia of atmospheric sciences and astrogeology.* 1967. 3. *The encyclopedia of geomorphology.* 1968. 4A. *The encyclopedia of geochemistry and environmental sciences.* 1972. 4B. *The encyclopedia of mineralogy,* edited by K. Frye. 1981. 6. *The encyclopedia of sedimentology,* edited by R.W. Fairbridge and J. Bourgeois. 1978. 7. *The encyclopedia of paleontology,* edited by R.W. Fairbridge and D. Jablanski. 1979. 8(1). *The encyclopedia of world regional geology: Western hemisphere.* 1975. 11. *The encyclopedia of climatology,* edited by R.W. Fairbridge and J.E. Oliver. 1986. 12(1). *The encyclopedia of soil science: Physics, chemistry, biology, fertility and technology,* edited by R.W. Fairbridge and C.W. Finkl, Jr. 1979. 15. *The encyclopedia of of beaches and coastal environments,* edited by M.L. Schwartz. 1982. 16. *The encyclopedia of solid earth geophysics,* edited by D.E. James. 1989. *The encyclopedia of igneous and metamorphic petrology,* edited by D.R. Bowes. 1989. (Unnumbered volume).
Planned in 24v. An ambitious, comprehensive series of encyclopaedias, alphabetically-arranged. Lengthy, documented articles preponderate, each beginning with a simple explanation, expanding into detailed treatment. Inter-volume cross-references. Detailed indexes. *Class No: 550(031)*

Dictionaries

English

[1006]
The Concise Oxford dictionary of earth sciences. Allaby, A. and Allaby, M., *eds.* Oxford, University Press, 1990. xxi,410p. ISBN: 0198661460.
One-third of the *c.*8,000 entries are taken from *The Oxford dictionary of natural history,* (1985). Entries, AA ... Zosterophyllophytina, include abbreviations, *e.g.* FFT, and short biographies, *e.g.* Holmes, Buffon, Thomson. Many cross-references. 11-page bibliography. 'A mine of information' (*Nature,* v.344, 29 March 1990, p.391). *Class No: 550(038)=20*

Reviews & Abstracts

[1007]
Current contents: Physical, chemical and earth sciences. Philadelphia, Pa., Institute for Scientific Information, 1961-. v.1(1)-. Weekly. ISSN: 01632574.

Each issue contains the title pages of *c.*150 journals. Also has current book contents; title word index; author index and address directory; publishers address directory. Online, CURRENT CONTENTS SEARCH and available on diskette. *Class No:* 550(048)

Tables & Data Books

[1008]
CLARK, S.P., *Jr. ed.* **Handbook of physical constants.** Rev. ed. New York, Geological Society of America, 1966. 587p. tables. (*Geological Society of America. Memoir 97.*) ISBN: 0813710979.

First published 1942.

Data, in 27 sections, on the physical constants of all subjects and substances relating to earth sciences. 30 contributors; over 200 tables. 'A "must" for all geological and chemical libraries and reference shelves' (*Economic geology,* v.61(6), September/October, 1966, p.1164). *Class No:* 550(083)

Histories

[1009]
PORTER, R. The Earth sciences: an annotated bibliography. New York & London, Garland, 1983. xxxiv, 192p. illus. (*Bibliography of the history of science and technology, v.3.*) ISBN: 0824092678.

808 briefly annotated entries in 10 sections: 1. Bibliography and reference works - 2. General histories - 3. Specialist histories (C. Geomorphology; D. Palaeontology; I. Mineralogy) - 4. Cognate sciences (*e.g.,* Natural history) - 5. Studies by area - 6. Biographical studies - 7. Institutional histories - 8. The social dimension - 9. Geology, culture and the arts. Entries average *c.*50 words. Author and subject index. 'A valuable bibliographical source book... About ⅓ of titles are in a major Western language other than English' (*Natural history book reviews,* v.7(3), 1984, p.171). *Class No:* 550(091)

Institutions & Associations

[1010]
Earth and astronomical sciences research centres: a world directory of organizations and programmes. 2nd ed. Harlow, Essex, Longman, 1991. v [vi],623p. (*Reference on research.*) ISBN: 0582082749.

First published 1984.

Guide to over 3,000 technology and research laboratories in more than 100 countries, arranged A-Z (Algeria ... Zimbabwe). Subject coverage includes geochemistry; petrology; mineralogy; planetary and galactic observations; meteorology. Data include title of establishment in original language, acronym and English translation; senior staff; research expenditure; publications; research activities; affiliation. New to this edition is a list of the main national and international trade associations and societies. (466 entries). Titles of establishments index; subject index. *Class No:* 550:061:061.2

Geophysics

Encyclopaedias

[1011]
The Encyclopedia of solid earth geophysics. James, D.E., *ed.* New York, Van Nostrand Reinhold, 1989. xvi,1328p. figs. (*Encyclopedia of earth sciences, 16.*) ISBN: 0442243669.

160 articles, arranged A-Z (Absolute age determination: radiometric ... Viscous remanent magnetization (VRM) and viscous remagnetization) covering seismology, gravity, geodesy tectonophysics, geomagnetism and related subjects. Short bibliographies and cross-referenced list of related entries. Subject and author citation indexes. Aimed at both the academic and layperson. *Class No:* 550.3(031)

Geochemistry

[1012]
FAIRBRIDGE, R.W., *ed.* **The Encyclopedia of geochemistry and environmental sciences.** New York, etc., Van Nostrand Reinhold, 1972. xxi, 1321p. diagrs., graphs, tables, maps. (*Encyclopedia of earth sciences, v.4A.*)

378 articles, A-Z, by 237 specialists. Broad scope, embracing all elements in nature, all the more important cycles and processes, mineral groups, and all economic ore deposits. Each contribution has references and cross-references (*e.g.,* 'Groundwater motion in draining basins', p.478-87, has 3 columns of references, plus cross-references to other volumes in the series. 'Hydrocarbons', p.495-503; 2p. of references). A major reference source. *Class No:* 550.4

[1013]
WEDEPOHL, K.M., *ed.* **Handbook of geochemistry.** Berlin, New York, Springer-Verlag, 1969-74. 2v. in 6. diagrs., graphs, tables, Loose-leaf.

About 70 contributors. V.1 'contains fundamental facts of geochemistry, geophysics and cosmochemistry, together with definitions, dimensions, methods of evaluation, etc.' (*Preface*). V.2 (5v., *c.*3300p.) has data on 'each element, with the exception of the noble gases, the lanthanides and the platinum elements'. *Class No:* 550.4

Prospecting & Exploration

Remote Sensing

[1014]
COLWELL, R.N., *ed.* **Manual of remote sensing.** Falls Church, Va., American Society of Photogrammetry, 1983. 2v. (xvii, xvii, 2440p.). illus. (incl. col.). ISBN: 0937294527.

First published 1975.

V.1: Theory, instruments and techniques; v.2: Interpretation and applications. 36 documented chapters; 279 col. plates. 'The most comprehensive work on remote sensing to date' (Harris, C.D. *Geographical bibliography for American libraries* (1985, item 356)). *Class No:* 550.81

Geothermal Exploration

[1015]
ARMSTEAD, H.C. Geothermal energy: its past, present and future contributions to the energy needs of man. 2nd ed. London & New York, Spon, 1983. xxxviii, 404p. illus., diagrs., tables. ISBN: 0419122206.

First published 1978.

19 chapters (1. Historical note... 4. The heat energy of the earth - 5. The nature and occurrence of geothermal fields - 6. Exploration - 7. Drilling - 8. Bore characteristics and their measurement - 9. Fluid collection and transmission - 10. Electric power generation from geothermal energy - 11. Direct applications of earth heat...

....(contd.)
14. Some economic considerations... 18. The future - 19. Epilogue: the frame of the geothermal picture). 257 references, p.377-88. Detailed, partly analytical index, p.389-404. A comprehensive treatment; the standard textbook. *Class No:* 550.836

[1016]
EDWARDS, L.M., *and others, eds.* **Handbook of geothermal energy.** Houston, Texas, Gulf Publishing Co., 1982. ix, 613p. illus., diagrs., graphs, tables. ISBN: 0872013227.
15 contributors. 10 chapters: 1. Introduction - 2. Worldwide geothermal resources - 3. Geology of geothermal systems - 4. Exploration for geothermal energy - 5. Geothermal well drilling and completion - 6. Casing and tubular design concepts - 7. Geothermal cementing - 8. Formation evaluation - 9. Reservoir engineering concepts - 10. Energy conversion and economic issues for geothermal energy. Statistics, to 1982. Detailed, analytical index, p.599-610. Aims at 'a comprehensive review of significant developments in the location and production of geothermal energy' (*Foreword*). Complementary to Armstead in stressing practical aspects. *Class No:* 550.836

Geology

Encyclopaedias

[1017]
FINKL, C.W., *ed.* **The Encyclopedia of applied geology.** Princeton, N.J., Van Nostrand Reinhold, 1984. xxviii, 832p. illus., diagrs., graphs, tables, maps. (*Encyclopedia of earth sciences, v.13.*) ISBN: 0442225377.
82 contributors. 87 main entries, well subheaded and documented (*e.g.*, 'Geochronology': 8p.; subsections, 3 tables, 3 graphs; 55 references. 'Geomorphology, applied': p.243-70; nearly 5p. of references). Valuable preface, with sections on abstracting and indexing services, computerised databanks,. periodicals, texts and reference works. Adequate cross-references. Samples a wide range of interrelated topics in geology in the service of man. *Class No:* 551(031)

Handbooks & Manuals

[1018]
PUTNAM, W.C. **Putnam's geology.** Birkeland, P.W. *and* Larson, E.E. 5th ed. New York, Oxford University Press, 1989. 646p. illus. (incl. col.), diagrs., maps. ISBN: 0195056302.
First published 1964.
19 chapters: 1. The planetary system ... 8. Volcanism ... 11. Mass movements and related geological hazards ... 15. Shore processes and landforms ... 19. Resources and energy. References appended to each chapter. Conversion table and glossary. Analytical index, p.635-46. A detailed textbook, with numerous black-and-white illustrations. *Class No:* 551(035)

Dictionaries

Polyglot

[1019]
ZYLKA, R. **Geological dictionary:** English, Polish, Russian, French, German. Warsaw, Wydawnictwa Geologiczne, 1970. 1439p.
About 25,000 numbered English-base entries, with Polish, Russian, French and German equivalents (and synonyms) and indexes. 'One of those rare multilingual dictionaries of technical terms that will please a geologist, a translator, and a graduate student faced with any important piece of geological literature from Europe' (*Choice,* v.9, November 1972, p.1116). *Class No:* 551(038)=00

English

[1020]
BATES, R.L. *and* JACKSON, J.A. **Glossary of geology.** 3rd ed. Amsterdam, Elsevier, 1987. 754p. ISBN: 0913312894.
First published 1957. Published in the US and Canada by the American Geological Institute.
Contains *c.*37,000 terms, covering subject areas which include geology; geophysics, sedimentology; hydrogeology; mineralogy; plate tectonics. For the first time, pronunciation is given. Includes abbreviations and dates when terms were first used. There are *c.*2,000 bibliographic references. The definitive geology glossary. *Class No:* 551(038)=20

Reviews & Abstracts

[1021]
Geological abstracts. Norwich, Elsevier, Geo Abstracts, 1989-. 12pa. ISSN: 09540512.
Previously *Geophysics and tectonic abstracts* (1982-85), originally *Geophysical abstracts* (1977-81).
1986-1988, split into 4 series: *Economic geology (qv)*; *Sedimentary geology (qv)*; *Palaeontology & stratigraphy*; *Geophysics & tectonics.*
Divided into 16 subject areas: Mineralogy - Geochemistry - Geochronology - Igneous and metamorphic geology - Sedimentary geology - Stratigraphy - Quarternary geology - Palaeontology - Regional geology - Geophysics - Structural geology and tectonics - Seismology - Engineering and environmental geology - Economic geology - Extra-terrestrial geology - General texts. Monthly, annual and regional indexes. Available online on the GEOBASE database. *Class No:* 551(048)

Yearbooks & Directories

[1022]
The Geologist's directory: a guide to geological services, equipment and sources of geological information. McInairnie, E., *ed.* 4th ed. London, Institution of Geologists, 1988. ix,219p. ISBN: 0950690651.
3rd ed., 1985.
9 sections: 1. The Institution of Geologists - 2. Geology in government (*e.g.* 'Local government in England', 'County Councils in Ireland') - 3. Geology in education - 4. Geology in industry - 5. Consultants (*e.g.* 'Consulting geochemists', 'Consulting mining engineers') - 6. Specialist services - 7. Buyers guide - 8. Geological information sources - 9. Companies working overseas. *Class No:* 551(058)

Biographies

[1023]
SARJEANT, W.A.S. **Geologists and the history of geology:** an international bibliography from the origins to 1978. London, Macmillan, 1980. 7v. in 6 (4526p.) + Supplement, 1979-84. 2v. (1691p.). ISBN: 0333293638, set.
V.1 (5 sections) provides an introduction and records histories of geology and related sciences; v.2-3 (sections 6-7): The individual geologists, A-Z; v.4 (sections 8-9): Index of geologists by nationality and country; index of geologists by speciality; v.5 (section 10): Index of authors, editors and translators, p.3535-4515. 'This bibliography attempts to bring together details of all those works in languages using the Latin alphabet which deal with the history of geology' (section 1, *General introduction*). Bibliographies of about 10,000 geologists, - a mammoth undertaking. 'It merits unqualified recommendation to those libraries serving users interested in the history of science' (*Choice,* v.18(4), December 1980, p.510). New supplements are planned at 5-yearly intervals. *Class No:* 551(092)

Worldwide

[1024]
Beiträge zur regionalen Geologie der Erde. Berlin & Stuttgart, Borntraeger, 1961-. illus., maps.
1. *Die Geologie Mittelamerikas.* R. Weyl. 1961. xvi, 226p.
2. *Die Geologie von Paraguay.* H. Poutzer. 1962, xii, 184p.
3. *Geologie von Chile.* W. Zeil. 1964. xi. 233p.
4. *Geologie der Antillen.* R. Weyl. 1966. viii, 410p.
5. *Rocky Mountains.* D.H. Roeder. 1966. xiv, 316p.
6. *Geologie von Syrien und dem Libanon.* R. Wohlfart. 1967. xii, 326p.
7. *Geologie von Jordanien.* F. Bender, 1968. xi, 230p. Supplementary ed. in English, with revisions. 1974, xi, 196p.
8. *Geologie von Ungarn.* L. Trunko. 1969. x, 258p.
9. *Geologie von Brasilien.* K. Beurlen. 1970. viii, 444p.
10. *Geology of the South Atlantic Islands,* R.C. Mitchell-Thomé. 1970. x, 368p.
11. *Geologie von Ecuador.* W. Sauer. 1971. ix, 316p.
12. *Geology of the Middle Atlantic Islands.* R.C. Mitchell-Thomé, 1976. ix, 382p.
Volumes 13-17 deal with the Andes (1979), Afghanistan (1980) Central America (2nd ed. 1980), Burma (1983), the USSR (1985), N.W. Germany (1986) and Greece (1986), respectively. An excellent series of regional geologies. *Class No:* 551(100)

[1025]
FAIRBRIDGE, R.W., *ed.* **The Encyclopedia of world regional geology.** Part 1: Western Hemisphere (including Antarctica and Australia). Stroudsburg, Pa., Dowden, Hutchinson & Ross, 1975. xv, 704p. illus., tables, maps. (*Encyclopedia of earth sciences, v.8.*)
88 contributors; *c.*150 signed entries, with references and cross-references. Entries are under countries A-Z. 'United States of America', p.502-641 ('Alaska', p.513-22: climatology and biogeography; physiography and geomorphology; tectonic framework; stratigraphy; geological history; mineral resources. 52 references, 2 illus., 2 maps). 'West Indies', p. 658-66; 20 cross-references. Author and subject indexes. Well illustrated. A major work of reference of considerable value to all levels of enquirer. *Class No:* 551(100)

Great Britain

[1026]
BRITISH GEOLOGICAL SURVEY. British regional geology. 2nd-4th ed. London, H.M. Stationery Office, 1935-.
Scotland:
Orkney and Shetland, by W. Mykura. 1976. £2.25.
The Northern Highlands, by G.S. Johnstone and W. Mykura. 4th ed. 1990. £6.
Grampian Highlands. 3rd ed., by G.S. Johnstone, 1966. £1.75.
The Tertiary volcanic districts. 3rd ed., by J.E. Richey. 1961. £1.
The Midland Valley of Scotland. 3rd ed., by I.B. Cameron and D. Stephenson. 1985-. £5.
The South of Scotland. 3rd ed., by D.C. Greig and others. 1971. £0.50.
England:
Northern England. 4th ed., rev. by B.J. Taylor, and others. 1971. £2.50.
The Pennines and adjacent areas. 3rd ed. by W. Edwards and F.M. Trotter. 1954. £2.50.
Eastern England from the Tees to the Wash., 2nd ed., by P. Kent, 1980. £4.50.
Central England. 3rd ed., by B. Hains and A. Horton. 1969. £2.50.

....(contd.)
East Anglia and adjoining areas. 4th ed., by C.P. Chatwin, 1961. £2.50.
Bristol and Gloucester district. 2nd ed., by G.A. Kellaway and F.B.A. Welsh. 1948. £3.25.
London and Thames valley. 3rd ed., by R.L. Sherlock, 1930. £0.80.
The Wealden district. 4th ed., by R.W. Gallois. 1965. £2.50.
The Hampshire basin and adjoining areas, by R.V. Melville and E.C. Freshney. 1982. £4.50.
South-west England. 4th ed., by E.A. Edmonds and others. 1975. £5.
Wales:
North Wales. 3rd ed., by T.N. George. 1961. £1.75.
South Wales. 3rd ed., by T.N. George. 1970. £2.50.
The Welsh Borderland. 3rd ed., by J.B. Earp and B.A. Hains. 1971. £3.50.
A series of pamphlets handbooks that include maps based on the 1:250,000 scale maps of the Geological Survey. *Class No:* 551(410)

Earth Structure

[1027]
HOLMES, A. Holmes' principles of physical geology. 3rd ed., revised by D.L. Holmes. London, Nelson, 1978. [xv], 730p. illus., diagrs., maps. ISBN: 0177612983.
First published 1944.
31 sections, each with selected references (*e.g.,* 5. Igneous rocks: volcanic and plutonic ... 12. Volcanoes and their products (p.188-229). 47 illus. and diagrs.; 15 references ... 21. Ice Ages and their problems ... 27. Magnetism, palaeomagnetism and drifting continents ...). Analytical index. Very well illustrated. Excellent value; standard text. *Class No:* 551.1

Geodynamics

Volcanoes

[1028]
SIMKIN, T., *and others.* **Volcanoes of the world:** a regional directory gazetteer and chronology of volcanism during the last 10,000 years. Stroudsburg, Pa., Hutchinson Ross, and the Smithsonian Institution, 1981. vii, 233p. ISBN: 0879334088.
3 parts: a directory of volcanoes (1,343 active; 5,564 dead); chronology of eruptions; gazetteer. Based on the computerized database at the Smithsonian Institution. The 30p. introduction outlines the catalogues' background, sources and significance of the various categories of information utilised. 709 references. 'This is a truly monumental work which, it is hoped, will be updated from time to time' (*Natural history book reviews,* v.7(4), 1985, p.258). *Class No:* 551.21

Tectonics

[1029]
SEYFERT, C.K., *ed.* **The Encyclopedia of structural geology and plate tectonics.** New York, Van Nostrand Reinhold, 1987. 576p. illus., diagrs., graphs, maps. (*Encyclopedia of earth sciences, v.10.*) ISBN: 0442281250.
About 90 contributors. 119 main entries, A-Z, Many cross-references 'Gondwanaland', p.309-14; 6 references. 'Rift valleys', p.671-88; 3 columns of references. Author citation index. Detailed, non-analytical subject index. A well-organized treatment, typical of this continuing series. 'Highly recommended' (*Choice* v.23(7), March 1988, p.1062). *Class No:* 551.24

Sedimentation

[1030]
FAIRBRIDGE, R.W. *and* BOURGEOIS, J., *eds.* The Encyclopedia of sedimentology. Stroudsburg, Pa., Dowden, Hutchinson & Ross, Inc., 1978. xvi, [1], 901p. illus., graphs, tables, maps. (*Encyclopedia of earth sciences, v.6.*)
193 contributors from 23 countries. Entries. 'Abrasion pH' ... 'Zebra dolomite' - each signed, with references and cross-references. 'Estuarine sedimentation': p.288-93, with 1½ cols. of bibliography and 6 drawings. Analytical index, p.875-90. 'An essental reference book for geologists, oceanographers, and scientists, hydrologists and others in related fields' (*Choice*, v.16(2), April 1979, p.202). *Class No:* 551.3

Glaciology

[1031]
Advances in periglacial geomorphology. Edited by M.J. Clark, for the International Geophysical Union Commission on the Significance of Periglacial Phenomena. Chichester, Wiley, 1987. xxiv, 481p. illus., diagrs., graphs, maps. ISBN: 0471909815.
18 contributors. 4 parts (17 documented chapters): 1. Weathering, erosion and related sedimentary features - 2. Frozen ground and active layer processes - 3. Process and form: the example of frost mounds - 4. Perspectives on the periglacial system. Chapter 6.: Ground ice and permafrost; p.113-49, has 6½p. of references. Abstracts in English, French and German precede each chapter text. Detailed, analytical index, p.475-81. Well organized; authoritative. *Class No:* 551.32

[1032]
Antarctic bibliography. Prepared by the Library of Congress. Washington, Library of Congress, 1965-. v.1-. Annual (irregular). ISSN: 00664626.
Each issue contains *c.*2,000 abstracts. 13 subject areas: A. General - B. Biological sciences - C. Cartography - D. Expeditions - E. Geological sciences - F. Ice and snow - G. Logistics, equipment and supplies - H. Medical scientists - I. Meteorology - J. Oceanography - K. Atmospheric physics - L. Terrestrial physics - M. Political geography. Author-title, analytical subject, geographic and grantee indexes.
The *Antarctic bibliography, 1951-1961 (1970)* extends cover retrospectively.
Antarctic bibliography (1962-) is the printed version of COLD database (Cold Regions Research and Engineering Laboratory). *Class No:* 551.32

Geomorphology (Earth's physical forms)

Bibliographies

[1033]
HARRIS, C.D., *and others, eds.* A Geographical bibliography for American libraries. Washington, Association of American Geographers, 1985. xxiii, 437p. ISBN: 089291193x.
A joint project of the Association of American Geographers and the National Geographic Society.
71 contributors. 7 parts: 1. General aids and sources - 2. History, philosophy and methodology, - 3. Systematic fields of physical geography - 4. Systematic fields of human geography - 5. Applied geography (*e.g.*, Planning; Military geography) - 6. Regional geography (worldwide) - 7. Publications suitable for school libraries. 2,903 concise, well-annotated entries. Analytical index, p.384-437. An important aid, 'to assist libraries in the United States, Canada, and other countries to identify, select and secure publications of value in geography that are appropriate to the purposes and resources of each collection' (*Introduction*). *Class No:* 551.4(01)

Dictionaries

Polyglot

[1034]
MEYNEN, E., *ed.* International geographical glossary. [Internationale geographische terminologie.] International Geographical Union *and* Commission on International Geographical Terminology. Deutsche Ausgabe. Wiesbaden, F. Steiner, 1985. 1479p. DM288.
About 2,400 German-base geographical terms, with equivalents in English, French, Italian, Spanish, Russian and Japanese. Terms are also grouped by categories for English, German and French. 'The product of international collaboration' (*A geographical bibliography for American libraries;* edited by C.D. Harris, 1985, entry 102). *Class No:* 551.4(038)=00

English

[1035]
CLARK, A.N. Longman dictionary of geography, human and physical. Harlow, Essex, Longman, 1985. ix, 724p.
About 8,000 shortish entries for terms 'commonly used in geographical writing over the past 100 years' (*Preface*), with claims to be the first dictionary to deal with the major aspects of geography in one volume. Entries for terms covered by Stamp and Clark are cited as 'G' and those in Chisholm's *Handbook of commercial geography* (20th ed. Longman, 1980) as 'C'. Includes terms for commodities; also, brief biographies. 'The book is a valuable addition to geographical literature and will be an asset to many people, by no means only geographers' (*Geographical journal*, v.152(2), July 1986, p.257). *Class No:* 551.4(038)=20

[1036]
STAMP, Sir D. *and* CLARK, A.N., *eds.* A Glossary of geographical terms, based on a list prepared by a Committee of the British Association for the Advancement of Science. 3rd ed. London, Longman, 1979. xxix, [1], 571p.
First published 1961.
57 correspondents and collaborators. Coverage: physical, human, economic and political geography. Terms are given various definitions, drawn freely from leading works, with acknowledgements, and 'Comment' added, as necessary. Thus the entry 'Savannah, Savanna, Savana' cites 6 sources plus comments on derivation, spelling, meaning etc. Appendix 2 lists words in foreign languages that have been absorbed into English literature; Appendix 3: 'Some stratigraphical terms'. 'List of standard works', p.xvii-xxv. 'A valuable work of reference, with its most useful features preserved' (*Geographical magazine*, January 1980, p.316). *Class No:* 551.4(038)=20

Reviews & Abstracts

[1037]
Geographical abstracts. Physical geography. Norwich, Elsevier; Geo Abstracts. v.1-. 1989-. 12pa. ISSN: 09540504.
Contains *Geographical abstracts*, series A. *Landforms and the Quaternary; Climatology and hydrology; E. Sedimentology; G. Remote sensing, photogrammetry and cartography*, 1986-88.
Covers over 1,000 geographical journals, books, conference proceedings, reports and theses. Subject coverage includes sedimentology; tectonics; landforms and the Quaternary; hydrology; remote sensing, photogrammetry and cartography; meteorology and climatology. Each issue contains a regional index. Separately published index issue arranged by subject, authors, and geographical areas. Online GEOBASE (*q.v.*). *Class No:* 551.4(048)

Periodicals & Progress Reports

[1038]
HARRIS, C.D. and FELLMANN, J.D., comps. **International list of geographical serials.** 3rd ed. Chicago, Ill., University of Chicago, Dept. of Geography, 1980. [iv], 457p. (*Research paper no.193.*) ISBN: 0890651000.
First published 1960.
'A comprehensive retrospective inventory of 3,445 geographical serials from 107 countries [International. Afghanistan ... Zimbabwe] in 55 languages with locations in union lists' (sub-title). A list of principal sources precedes and 'Lists of titles in non-Roman scripts' follows the definitive inventory. Index and cross-reference, p.399-457. *Class No:* 551.4(05)

Europe

[1039]
EMBLETON, C., ed. **Geomorphology of Europe.** New York, Wiley, 1984. [x], 465p. illus., maps. ISBN: 0471800708.
20 chapters by members of the Commission on Geomorphological Survey and Mapping of the International Geographical Union. 1. Structural and tectonic framework of the continent of Europe - 2. Principal structural and tectonic features of ocean floors around Europe - 3. Exogenic landforms of Europe - 4. Iceland ... 16. Balkan Peninsula ... 19. Ural mountains - 20. Submarine morphology around Europe (8 maps; 1 cross-section). References (A-Z authors), p.431-47. Detailed, analytical index, p.449-65. 'The first comprehensive survey of the geomorphology of Europe'. (*New technical books*, February 1986, item 285). *Class No:* 551.4(4)

Islands

[1040]
HUXLEY, A., ed. **Standard encyclopedia of the world's oceans and islands.** London, Weidenfeld & Nicolson, 1962. 383p. illus. (incl. col.), maps.
A-Z sequence of more than 350 articles (Aden ... Zuyder Zee), with geographical and background data on the world's oceans, channels, straits, gulfs, currents, islands, capes, etc. (Greenland is ranked as an island, but Australia not). 'Galapagos Islands': location, area, map reference, plus $1\frac{1}{2}$ columns of description. Gazetteer of *c.*2,000 entries, p.325-64. 10 location maps; 16 col. plates. No bibliographies. Evidently for popular consumption. *Class No:* 551.42

Coastlines

[1041]
SCHWARTZ, H.L. **The Encyclopedia of beaches and coastal environments.** Stroudsburg, Pa., Hutchinson Ross, 1982. 940p. illus., maps. (*Encyclopedia of earth sciences, v.15.*) ISBN: 0879332131.
184 contributors. Articles A-Z, usually documented. Cross-references. Coverage: geomorphology; ecology; coastal engineering; continental, regional and specific types of coast. Well illustrated. 'The most thorough glossary of its kind' (*A geographical bibliography for American libraries*, edited by C.D. Harris (1985), p.96). *Class No:* 551.435.36

[1042]
STEERS, J.A. **The Coastline of England and Wales.** 2nd ed. Cambridge, University Press, 1964. xxviii, 762p. diagrs., tables, maps.
First published 1946.
8 of the initial 19 chapters give detailed geomorphological data on the coast, working anticlockwise from 'The Solway to the Dee', and ending with 'The North-East Coast'. Chapters 20-27 add data on the same regional pattern, noting the great damage done to the east

....(contd.)
coast on 31 January and 1 February 1933. 163 diagrs., tables and maps. Numerous footnotes, including references to the plates in Steers' *The coast of England and Wales in pictures* (2nd ed., 1960). Index, p.721-50. 'He has given us what is, perhaps, the most important physiographic monograph since geography attained full status in the British universities' (*Geographical journal*, v.109(1/3), July 1947, p.109, on the 1946 ed.).
The coastline of Scotland, by J.A. Steers (C.U.P., 1973. xvi, 325p. illus., maps) is the companion volume. *Class No:* 551.435.36

Caves

[1043]
Current titles in speleology: bibliographical details of papers published throughout the world on caving topics. London, British Cave Research Association, 1972-. Annual.
Continues *Speleological abstracts* (1964-70).
No. 23: The literature of 1990 (1991. [x],112p.) has *c.*3,000 entries in 6 main sections: Generalia - Africa (Algeria ... Zaire) - America (Anguilla ... Venezuela) - Asia (Burma ... Vietnam) - Australasia and Pacifica (Australia ... Pitcairn Island) - Europe (Austria ... Yugoslavia). A list of periodicals consulted and addresses precedes the sections. '1990 sees the smallest number of titles in *CTS* since 1982' (*Editorial*). *Class No:* 551.44

Oceanography

Encyclopaedias

[1044]
FAIRBRIDGE, R.W., ed. **The Encyclopedia of oceanography.** New York, Van Nostrand Reinhold, 1966. 1056p. illus. (incl.pl.), diagrs., tables, maps. (*Encyclopedia of earth sciences, v.1.*)
245 signed articles, A-Z, by 135 specialists, on all aspects of oceanography and submarine geology. 'Atlantic Ocean': 30p.; 'Sea ice': 5p.; 'Mineral potential of the oceans': 8p.; 'Gulf Stream': 5p.). Short selected bibliograhies follow most articles; well illustrated. The first of a series, each volume being automatic but cross-indexed. The general editor is Professor of Geology, Columbia Univ. Aimed at high-school students, teachers and specialists. *Class No:* 551.46(031)

Handbooks & Manuals

[1045]
HILL, M.N., ed. **The Sea:** ideas and observations in progress in the study of the sea. New York, Interscience: Wiley, 1962-83. 6v. in 10. illus., diagrs., tables, maps.
1. *Physical oceanography.* 1962. xv, 564p.
2. *The composition of sea water. Comparative and descriptive oceanography.* 1963. xv, 554p.
3. *The earth beneath the sea.* History, 1963. xvi, 963p.
4.(2pts.) *New concepts of sea floor evolution;* edited by A.E. Maxwell. 1971.
5. *Marine chemistry,* edited by E.D. Goldberg. 1974. xiv, 895p.
6. *Marine modeling;* edited by E.D. Goldberg. 1977. xxv, 1045p.
7.(2pts.) *The oceanic lithosphere,* edited by C. Emiliane. xii, [i], 1728p.
8. *Deep-sea biology;* edited by G.T. Rowe. 1983. ix[i], 560p. (*qv*).
V.1 has 33 contributors; v.2:29. V.3 (39 contributors) is the first comprhensive work of its kind. 3 sections: 1. Geophysical exploration - 2. Topography and structure - 3. Sedimentation. Chapter 34, 'The Pleistocene period' has $6\frac{1}{2}$p. of references. Well illustrated throughout. Each volume has author and subject indexes. An authoritative, critical

....(contd.)
and detailed survey that attempts to be 'a balanced account of how oceanography and the thoughts of oceanographers were moving' (*Preface*). *Class No:* 551.46(035)

Reviews & Abstracts

[1046]
Aquatic sciences and fisheries abstracts. Bethesda, Md., Cambridge Scientific Abstracts, 1978-. Monthly 2pts. (*Formerly part of Aquatic sciences and fisheries abstracts, 1971-77.*)
Pt.1: *Biological sciences and living resources.*
Pt.2: *Ocean technology, policy and non-living resources.*
Pt.2 carries *c.*10,000 abstracts pa. Coverage: oceanography, limnology, geochemistry, underwater optics and acoustics, geology and geophysics, marine technology and engineering resources (including oil, minerals, desalination and energy, pollution policy and sea law, documentation). Monthly and annual subject and author indexes. Microfiche and magnetic tapes available. ASFA database available on CD-ROM. Available online via BRS(CSAL), CISTI, DIMDI, DIALOG and ESA. *Class No:* 551.46(048)

Maps & Atlases

[1047]
The Times atlas and encyclopaedia of the sea. Couper, A.D. 2nd ed. London, Times Books, 1989. 272p. illus. (col.), diagrs., tables, maps. ISBN: 0723003181.
First published as *The Times atlas of the oceans* (Times Books, 1983).
Comprehensive but unconventional (neither a detailed atlas nor an alphabetically-arranged encyclopaedia) treatment of the world's oceans, written and cartographed by 28 contributors. 5 sections: The ocean environment (incl. the ocean basins, p.26-43) - Resources of the ocean (incl. fisheries, p.90-101) - Ocean trade (incl. shipping routes, p.146-59) -, The world ocean (incl. strategic use of the oceans, p.178-91). 11 appendices, glossary, index, p.258-72. With *c.*400 illustrations and maps, all in colour, it should serve a wide readership. *Class No:* 551.46(084.3)

Meteorology

Encyclopaedias

[1048]
FAIRBRIDGE, R.W., *ed.* **The Encyclopedia of atmospheric sciences and astrogeology.** New York, London etc., Reinhold, 1976. xv, 1200p. illus., diagrs., tables, maps. (*Encyclopedia of earth sciences, v.2.*)
About 150 contributors. Signed articles, A-Z, with references appended. Lengthier articles preponderate, beginning with a simple explanation and proceeding to detailed technical data (*e.g.,* 'Radar astronomy', p.786-91; 3 figures, 1 table, ½ col. of references, 25 cross-references). Well illustrated. Intended for all scientists, for those still in high school to the emeritus professor (*Preface*). A comprehensive reference work on astronomy, climatology, meteorological and related sciences. *Class No:* 551.5(031)

Handbooks & Manuals

[1049]
HOUGHTON, D.D., *ed.* **Handbook of applied meteorology.** New York, etc., Wiley, 1985. xv, 1461p. illus., diagrs., graphs, charts, tables, maps. ISBN: 0471084042.
54 contributors. 5 parts: 1. Fundamentals - 2. Measurements - 3. Applications - 4. Societal impacts - 5. Resources (data; books and journals; education; research centers and libraries; directory sources). 46 documented

....(contd.)
chapters in all (*e.g.,* ch. 4: 'Weather forecasting', p.205-79, including 4p. of references and bibliography). Appendices: A. Glossary and units; B. Climatic data (monthly; 147 locations, worldwide), p.1369-1431. A massive compendium; North American slant. 'Designed for professionals and technicians outside the meteorological profession.' (*New technical books,* January 1986, p.101). *Class No:* 551.5(035)

Dictionaries

[1050]
GREAT BRITAIN. METEOROLOGICAL OFFICE. Meteorological glossary. Lewis, R.P.W., *comp.* 6th ed. London, H.M. Stationery Office, 1991. 335p. illus. (incl. col. pl.). ISBN: 0114003637.
About 2,300 technical terms used in meteorology are concisely defined and discussed, with profuse cross-references. The publisher claims that 'many new terms and definitions have been introduced as a result of research and developments in meteorology, climatology, hydrology and from increasing research into the greenhouse effect (given 110 words) and global warming', (although there is no entry for latter term). Attractively produced, although the use of lower case typeface slightly irritates. *Class No:* 551.5(038)

Reviews & Abstracts

[1051]
Meteorological and geoastrophysical abstracts. Boston, Mass., American Meteorological Society, 1950-. v.1(1)-. Monthly. ISSN: 00241130.
Formerly *Meteorological abstracts and bibliography,* 1950-59.
Each issue contains *c.*600 abstracts and references. 6 sections: A. Environmental sciences - B. Meteorology - C. Astrophysics - D. Hydrosphere. Hydrology - E. Glaciology - F. Physical oceanography. Author subject and geographic indexes, cumulated annually and at longer intervals, *e.g.,* for v.21-26. Online on DIALOG.
Cumulated bibliography and index to 'Meteorological and geoastrophysical abstracts', 1950-1969: classified subject and author arrangements (Boston, Mass., G.K. Hall, 1972. 8v.) is made up of a 4-v. subject sequence of 138,000 entries, classified by UDC and a corresponding 4-v. author sequence. *Class No:* 551.5(048)

Vapours

Clouds

[1052]
SCORER, R. Clouds of the world: a complete colour encyclopedia. Melbourne, Victoria, Lothian Publishing Co. (Pty.), Ltd.; Newton Abbot, Devon, David & Charles, 1972. 176p. illus. (incl. col. pl.).
14 sections (1. Cumulus ... 4. Cirrus ... 7. Altocirrus (p.100-5; 4 black-and-white illus.; 14 col. illus.) ... 8. Warm sector cloud ... 11. Condensation trails ... 13. Optical phenomena - 14. Rotation. Appendix: Photogrammetry and stereoscopic photography. Bibliography, p.172. Detailed, non-analytical index. 14 col. plates, each with 5-8 photos., lengthy descriptive captions facing. 'The text is admirably clear ... The book can be heartily recommended to all those whose business involves clouds, particularly meteorologists and aviators' (*British book news,* January 1973, p.35). *Class No:* 551.576

Climate

[1053]
GREAT BRITAIN. METEOROLOGICAL OFFICE. Tables of temperature, relative humidity, precipitation and sunshine for the world. London, HM Stationery Office, 1958-.
1. *North America and Greenland*, (including Hawaii and Bermuda). 1981. (Met. O. 856a). £21.
3. *Europe and the Azores*. (Met.O. 856c). £15.
4. *Africa; the Atlantic Ocean south of 35 degrees north and the Indian Ocean*. 1983. (Met. O. 856d). £23.
V.2, 5 & 6 bear the older series title, - *Tables of temperature, relative humidity and precipitation of the world*.
2. *Central and South America, the West Indies and Bermuda*. 1959. (Met. O. 617b). £1.50.
5. *Asia*. 2nd ed. 1966. (Met. O. 617c). £3.75.
6. *Australasia and the south Pacific Ocean, the corresponding sectors of Antarctica*. 1958.
Monthly data (average and extremes for about 1,000 carefully selected and well distributed stations throughout the world). *Class No: 551.58*

[1054]
PEARCE, E.A. and SMITH, C.G. The World weather guide. 2nd ed. London, Hutchinson, 1990. 480p. graphs, tables, maps. ISBN: 0091745357.
First published 1990.
Continent and country data schedules: Africa - North America - Central and South America - Asia - Australia - Caribbean islands - Europe - Oceanic islands. (Australia, p.298-308, is divided into 4 climatic regions, with 19 weather stations listed. Data: temperature (highest recorded; average daily; lowest recorded); relative humidity; precipitation. Analytical index, p.473-80). Impressive, useful for both the actual and armchair traveller. *Class No: 551.58*

Stratigraphy (Historical Geology)

[1055]
Geologic time scale 1989. Harland, W.B., *and others*. Cambridge, Cambridge University Press, 1990. xvi,263p. figs., tables. ISBN: 0521383617.
Revised edition of *A geologic time scale 1982*.
7 sections: 1. Introduction - 2. The chronometric (numerical) scale - 3. The chronostratic scale - 4. Isotopic methods, dates, precision and database - 5. Chronometric calibration of stage boundaries - 6. The magnetostratigraphic time scale - 7. Geologic events and the time scale. 6 appendices, *e.g.* 2. Recommended three-character abbreviations for chronostratic names with alternative symbols. References and selected bibliography, p.223-46. General index, p.243-48. Stratigraphic index, p.249-63. *Class No: 551.7*

Petrology

[1056]
CRC handbook of physical properties of rocks. Carmichael, R.S., *ed.* Boca Raton, Florida, CRC Press, 1982-84. 3v. (1089p.). tables, graphs. ISBN: 0849302269, v.1; 0849302277, v.2; 0849302285, v.3.
16 contributors. V.1: Mineral composition of rocks. Electrical and spectroscopic properties of rocks and minerals - V.2: Seismic velocities. Magnetic and engineering properties of rocks and minerals - V.3 Density of rocks and minerals. Elastic constants of minerals. Inelastic properties of rocks and minerals: strength and sheology. Radioactivity properties of minerals and rocks. Seismic attenuation. All chapters have appended bibliography. Each volume carries an index. 'The intent is to bridge the gap between individual reports with only specific limited data, and

....(contd.)
massive assemblies of data which are uncritically presented' (*Preface*).
An updated and abridged edition of this work appeared in 1989, *CRC practical handbook of physical properties of rocks and minerals* (741p. CRC Press). *Class No: 552*

Rocks

[1057]
SUTHERLAND, D.S., *ed.* Igneous rocks of the British Isles. New York, etc., Wiley, 1982. 645p. ISBN: 0471278106.
37 contributors. 7 sections, reviewing the major occurrences of igneous rocks in Great Britain and Ireland. 'An obligatory purchase for any geological institution library, and will find itself constantly thumbed through by students, teachers and research workers' (*Geological magazine*, v.120, July 1983, p.407). *Class No: 552.1/.4*

Meteorites

[1058]
BRITISH MUSEUM (NATURAL HISTORY). The Catalogue of meteorites, with special reference to those represented in the collection of the British Museum (Natural History). 4th ed., edited by A.L. Graham, and others. London, British Museum (Natural History), with the Univ. of Arizona Press, Tucson, 1985. 464p. ISBN: 0565009419.
3rd ed., 1966; Appendix, 1977. M.H. Hey was the compiler of the 3rd ed.
Data on each meteorite name; place where found (or place of impact), plus co-ordinates; chemical content (with citations to the original literature); weight; present owner; specimen number (if appropriate). The British Museum (Natural History)'s collection runs to *c*.2,784 meteorites (*Astronomy*, v.14 , March 1986, p.72). A standard work of reference, the definitive list of all well-documented meteorites known worldwide.
Next edition of the *Catalogue* is not until 1992. Meanwhile an updating set of floppy discs is available. *Class No: 552.6*

Economic Geology

[1059]
Bibliography of economic geology. Didcot, Systems Publications, 1982-. 6pa. ISSN: 00167053.
Formerly *Geocom bulletin*, 1968-81.
Over 5,000 references pa. Classes 100000-900000, 'arranged by subject according to the economic geology subset of *Geosaurus: Geosystems thesaurus of geoscience*,' in 32 sections (General publications ... Geoscience information). Each issue has subject, locational, stratigraphical, geographical and author indexes. *Class No: 553*

Minerals & Ores

[1060]
RENSBURG, W.C.J., van. Strategic minerals. Englewood Cliffs, N.J., Prentice-Hall, 1986. 2v. (xvi, [1], 552p. + xiii, 362p.). diagrs., graphs, tables. ISBN: 0138513872, v.1; 0138514119, v.2.
V.1: *Major mineral exporting regions of the world: issues and strategies* has 6 parts: Canada; Southern Africa; Australia; Latin America; China; The oil-crop economies. Bibliography (6 parts), p.527-42. Detailed index. V.2: *Major mineral consuming regions of the world* covers 4 parts: United States; Japan; Western Europe; USSR. Bibliography (4 parts), p.331-47. Detailed index. p.349-62. A major aim was to analyze 'the effects of government policies, laws and regulations on the availability, reliability, and cost of producing minerals' (*Preface*). *Class No: 553.2/.4*

[1061]

RIDGE, J.D. Annotated bibliographies of mineral deposits in Europe. Oxford, etc., Pergamon Press, 1984-1989. ISBN: 0080302424, v.1; 0080302432, v.2; 0080240224, set.

Pt.1. *Northern Europe including examples from the USSR in both Europe and Asia.* 1984. viii,778p. Pt.2. *Western and south central Europe.* 1989. viii,473p.

Pt.1 covers Ireland; Great Britain; Norway; Sweden; Finland; Poland; USSR. Pt.2 covers Portugal; Spain; France; Belgium-Germany-Netherlands; Switzerland; Italy; Iran. References in Pt.1 are mostly in English, while Pt.2 references are made up of the major European languages. Pt.2 has only an author index, thus greatly reducing its usefulness, while Pt.1 has an index to authors; A/Z index of deposits; index of deposits (according to metals and minerals produced; according to age of mineralization; according to the modified Lindgren classification).

The 5v. *Mineral deposits of Europe* (Institution of Mining and Metallurgy; the Mineralogical Society, 1978-89) is arranged by country, with bibliographies appended to each chapter. Name and subject indexes. 'Some national chapters are landmarks, being the first comprehensive descriptions in English (or any other language) of their ore deposits' (*Foreword*). *Class No:* 553.2/.4

[1062]

RIDGE, J.D. Annotated bibliographies of mineral deposits in the Western Hemisphere. Boulder, Colo., Geological Society of America, 1972. xiv, 681p. maps. Supplement, 1974. 8p. (*Geological Society of America. Memoir* no.131, - revision and expansion of *Memoir* no.75, 1958.) ISSN: 00107053.

Covers North and South America; arrangement, under country/US state/Canadian province, is by deposit. For each deposit: minerals mined; age and position in the Lindgren classification, plus bibliography and notes. Indexes of authors and deposits (A-Z, by age, by metals and minerals produced, by Lindgren classification). Appendices provide a classification of ore deposits, and topics for consideration. Aimed, like the other two volumes, at the economic geologist in his study of specific deposits. *Class No:* 553.2/.4

Hydrology

[1063]

Selected water resources abstracts (SWRA). Reston, Va., Water Resources Scientific Information Center, U.S. Geological Survey., 1968-. Monthly. ISSN: 0037136x.

About 2,000 abstracts per issue. Subject fields and groups: 01. Nature of water. 02. Water cycle; 03. Water supply augmentation and conservation; 04. Water quantity management and control; 06. Water resources planning; 07. Resources data; 08. Engineering works; 09. Manpower, grants and facilities; 10. Scientific and technical information. Subject and author indexes; organizational index; accession number index. Available on CD-ROM. *Class No:* 556

Rivers & Lakes

[1064]

CZAYA, E. Rivers of the world. Translated from the German by S. Furness. Cambridge, University Press, 1983. 248p. illus. (incl. col.), diagrs., tables, maps. ISBN: 0521258359.

8 chapters: 1. Arteries of the continents - 2. Rivers shape their valley - 3. Cataclysmic events in river history - 4. Waterfalls and rapids - 5. Pluvial lakes - 6. Inland drainage - 7. Lowland rivers and river mouths - 8. Rivers in harness. Bibliography, p.233-5 (authors, A-Z). Detailed, non-analytical index, p.236-48. 192 illus. A mass of factual information, clearly presented. *Class No:* 556.5

56 Palaeontology

Palaeontology

Bibliographies

[1065]
LUM, A. 'Palaeontology'. in *Information sources in the earth sciences*, edited by D.N. Wood *and others*. 2nd ed. London, Bowker-Saur, 1989. p.236-273.

Readable and authoritative review of major works in the subject. Headings, after general historical survey, are: Taxonomy - Palaeontological texts (including techniques, and popular to advanced textbooks) - Palaeoecology & palaeoclimatology - Evolution & the fossil record - Micropalaeontology - Palynology - Palaeobotany - Invertebrate palaeontology - Vertebrate palaeontology (including brief review of popular books on dinosaurs) - Abstracting & indexing services. Appendix lists 132 currently published palaeontological periodicals. The author is on the staff of the Palaeontology library at the British Museum (Natural History). *Class No:* 560(01)

Encyclopaedias

[1066]
The Macdonald encyclopedia of fossils. Arduini, P. *and* Teruzzi, G. London, Macdonald, 1986. 317, [3]p. col. illus., diagrs. ISBN: 035612367x.

Has text and illus. on 260 fossils; Plants, entries 1-16; invertebrate fossils, 17-186; vertebrate fossils, 187-260. Text, including symbols for geological eras and habitats, faces text. Glossary, p.307-17. Index. A neat, small-format guide. *Class No:* 560(031)

Handbooks & Manuals

[1067]
FORTEY, R. Fossils: the key to the past. 2nd ed. London, British Museum (Natural History), 1991. 187p. illus. (incl. col.). ISBN: 0565011073.

First published 1982.

Provides a lively yet authoritative, fully-illustrated survey for the amateur palaeontologist. The 10 chapters include 'How to recognise fossils', 'Making a collection' (with notes on collecting, preserving and identifying), and a new chapter recounting the identification of a new dinosaur from recently-discovered fossil remains. 'In this book I have tried to show how fossils, far from being mere dry bones, can be used to reconstruct the history of the Earth' (*Preface*). *Class No:* 560(035)

Reviews & Abstracts

[1068]
Geographical abstracts. Physical geography. Norwich, Elsevier; Geo Abstracts, 1989-. ISSN: 09540504.

Succeeds *Geological abstracts*: palaeontology & stratigraphy.

This journal, which abstracts 'over 1,000 leading geographical journals, plus books, conference proceedings, reports and theses' (*Editorial introduction*) includes in its subject coverage such relevant headings as Palaeogeography; Sedimentation and tectonics; Systematic palaeoecology; Quarternary. Mainly author abstracts listed, up to 300 words each. 12 issues pa., each with regional index, plus separately published index issue arranged by subject, authors, and geographical areas. Online GEOBASE, availabe on DIALOG. *Class No:* 560(048)

Maps & Atlases

[1069]
HALLAM, A., *ed.* Atlas of palaeobiogeography. Amsterdam, Elsevier, 1973. xii, 531p. illus., maps. ISBN: 0444409750.

47 contributions, by specialists, on distribution of a wide variety of fossil groups during the last 600 million years (*e.g.,* Ondovician trilobites; articulate brachiopods; graptolites; corals; conodonts, p.13-58. Jurassic plants, p.329-38; Jurassic and cretaceous dinosaurs, p.339-52). Chapter bibliographies. Index of genera and references. Authoritative; assumes some geological and palaeontological knowledge. *Class No:* 560(084.3)

Great Britain

[1070]
BRITISH MUSEUM (NATURAL HISTORY). British Caenozoic fossils (Tertiary and Quaternary). 5th ed. London, British Museum (Natural History), 1975. vi, 132p. illus. (pl.), map. ISBN: 0565055402. *Class No:* 560(410)

[1071]
—BRITISH MUSEUM (NATURAL HISTORY). British Mesozoic fossils. 6th ed. London, British Museum (Natural History), 1983. xi, 207p. illus. (pl.), map. ISBN: 0565008722. *Class No:* 560(410)

[1072]
—BRITISH MUSEUM (NATURAL HISTORY). British Palaeozoic fossils. 4th ed. London, British Museum (Natural History), 1975. vi, 203p. illus. (pl.), map. ISBN: 0565056247.

Each volume includes explanatory notes on the plates, a coloured distribution-map, bibliography and index. Simply written, attractively produced and inexpensive booklets, 'to enable the young, or those without experience, to know

....(contd.)

about fossils they may expect to find and to identify for themselves those they have collected' (Preface to *British Mesozoic fossils*). *Class No:* 560(410)

Fossil Invertebrates

[1073]

MOORE, R.C., *ed.* **Treatise on invertebrate paleontology.** Prepared under the guidance of the Joint Committee on Invertebrate Paleontology. New York, Geological Society of America; Laurence, Kansas, Univ. of Kansas Press, 1953-.

Sponsored by the Geological Society of America, the Paleontographical Society, the Paleontological Society and the Society of Economic Paleontologists and Mineralogists.

1. A. *Introduction.* B-D *Protista* (C. pt.2, 1964; D. pt.3, 1954). E. *Archaeocyatha, porifera.* 1955. Rev. ed. 1972. F. *Coelenterata.* 1956. G. *Bryozoa.* 1953. H. *Brachiopoda.* 1965. 2v. I-N. *Mollusca* (I. 1960; K. 1964; L. 1957; N. 1969-71. 3v.). O-R. *Arthropoda.* 1955-69. 5v. S-U. *Echinodermata* (S. 1967. 2v; U. 1966. 2v.). V. *Graptolithina.* 1955. 2nd ed. 1970. W. *Miscellanea.* 1962. Suppt. 1: *Trace fossils and problematica.* 2nd ed., 1975. Suppt. 2. 1981. X. *Addenda. Index.*

Aims 'to present the most comprehensive statement of knowledge concerning invertebrate fossil groups' up to 1950 (*Editorial preface*). Each volume contains detailed descriptions; section references; detailed index. A feature is the wealth of line-drawings and diagrams. Part F. *Coelenterata* (1956. xx, 498p.) has 358 diagrs. According to P.-M. Guelpa (Malclès, L.-M. *Les sources du travail bibliographique,* v.3, p.250), Moore is stronger on systematics than is Piveteau (*Traité de paléontologie).* The standard work on invertebrate palaeontology, written by the world's leading authorities (about 150 contributors).

The revised and enlarged editions of certain of the volumes (Boulder, Colo., Geological Society of America) began in 1970. *Class No:* 562

Fossil Vertebrates

[1074]

CAMP, C.L., *and others.* **Bibliography of fossil vertebrates, 1928/1933-.** New York, Geological Society of America, 1940-73. 9v. 5 yearly.

Preceded by O.P. Hay's *Bibliography and catalogue of the fossil vertebrates of North America* (Washington, Geological Survey, 1902. *Bulletin* no.179) and his *Second bibliography* (Washington, Carnegie Institution, 1929-30. Publication no.390).

Camp's *Bibliography of fossil vertebrates, 1969-72* (1973, xlvi, [i], 733p. Geological Society of America. *Memoirs*) is an author catalogue subarranged chronologically, with *c.*7,500 entries. Subject index (p.388-575) has detailed subdivision under countries and includes obituaries. Systematic index, p.577-733. Supplementary list of serials, p.xi-xxxix.

Continued in *Bibliography of fossil vertebrates, 1973-1977,* by M. Green and others (South Dakota School of Mines and Technology, 1979), and now annually by *Bibliography of fossil vertebrates,* 1978-, by J.T. Gregory (Falls Church, Va., American Geological Institute, 1981-). *Class No:* 566

Dinosaurs

[1075]

LAMBERT, D. *and* **THE DIAGRAM GROUP. Dinosaur data book:** the definitive, fully illustrated encyclopedia of dinosaurs and other prehistoric reptiles. New York, Facts on File with the British Museum (Natural History), 1990. 320p. figs., maps. ISBN: 0816024316.

7 chapters: 1. The age of dinosaurs - 2. The A to Z of dinosaurs - 3. Dinosaurs classified - 4. Dinosaur life - 5. Dinosaurs worldwide - 6. Dinosaurologists - 7. Dinosaurs revived. Bibliography, p.306-10. Authoritative and lively text, with illustrations and maps on virtually every page. *Class No:* 568.19

Mammals

[1076]

SAVAGE, D.E. *and* **RUSSELL, D.E. Mammalian paleofaunas of the world.** Reading, Mass., & London, Addison-Wesley, 1983. 432p. ISBN: 0201064944.

Lists more than 3,000 genera and at least twice that number of species over a 200-million year time-span. 'A highly reliable work, an indispensible reference source and a monumental data base from which to test our theories, be they evolutionary, faunal or geographical' (*Nature,* v.304, 4 August 1983, p.471). *Class No:* 569

Man

[1077]

DAY, M.H. Guide to fossil man. 4th ed. London, Cassell; Chicago, University Press, 1986. xv, [i], 432p. illus., diagrs., tables, maps. ISBN: 0304312886; 0226138895, US ed..

First published 1965.

Three parts. 1: The anatomy of fossil man - 2. The fossil hominids (Europe, plus country division; Near East; Northwest Africa; East Africa; Southern Africa; The Far East; Oceania), p.16-401 - 3. Essays on fossil man (with references). Records new evidence from 34 sites featured in previous editions, plus details of 15 new sites. Appended 'Geologic and palaeomagnetic time scales'; Glossary. Partly analytical index. Author is Professor of Anatomy, United Medical and Dental Schools of Guy's and St. Thomas's Hospital, Univ. of London. *Class No:* 569.9

572 Anthropology

Anthropology

Bibliographies

[1078]
International bibliography of social and cultural anthropology.
[Bibliographie internationale d'anthropologie sociale et culturelle.] London, Tavistock Publications, 1955-. v.1-.
Annual. (*International bibliography of the social sciences.*)
Prepared by the International Committee for Social Science Information and Documentation.
Each issue contains *c.*1,700 entries. 10 sections: A. Anthropology: general studies; B. Materials and methods of anthropology; C. Morphological foundations; D. Ethnographic studies of people and communities; E. Social organisation and relationships; F. Religion, magic, witchcraft; G. Problems of knowledge, arts and science, folk traditions; H. Studies of culture and personality. 'National character'; I. Problems of acculturation and social change; contact situations; J. Applied anthropology. Author and analytical subject indexes. *Class No:* 572.0(01)

[1079]
SPENCER, F., *comp.* **Ecce homo: an annotated bibliographic history of physical anthropology.** New York & London, Greenwood Press, 1986. xiii, [1], 459p. illus., facsims. (*Bibliographies and indexes in anthropology, no.2.*) ISBN: 0313240566.
2,340 annotated entries. 4 parts: 1. Ancient, medieval, Renaissance and early modern literature - 2. Eighteenth century - 3. Nineteenth century (945 entries) - 4. Twentieth century (1,168 entries: Human population biology; Primatology; Paleoprimatology; Paleo-anthropology - Old World; New World). Name and subject indexes. *Class No:* 572.0(01)

Encyclopaedias & Dictionaries

[1080]
HUNTER, D.E. *and* **WHITTEN, P.,** *eds.* **Encyclopedia of anthropology.** New York, Harper & Row, 1976. xi, 411p. illus., tables, maps. ISBN: 0060470941.
About 1,400 entries, by 87 contributors. 'Monotheistic religions': 2 columns; 4 references. Includes brief biographies (*e.g.,* Levi-Strauss: nearly 1 column). Well illustrated, with *c.*200 photographs and line drawings. Cross-references, and subject index, less adequate. Some US slant. Aims to be a 'compact, comprehensive, accessible reference source' (*Preface*) and largely succeeds. Reasonably priced.
Fuller in coverage and more comprehensive than *Dictionary of anthropology,* edited by C. Winwick (New York, Philosophical Library, 1956. vii, 579p). *Class No:* 572.0(03)

Reviews & Abstracts

[1081]
Anthropological index to current periodicals in the Museum of Mankind Library (incorporating the former Royal Anthropological Institute Library). London, the Museum, 1963-. 4pa. ISSN: 00035467.
As *Index to current periodicals received in the Library of the Royal Anthropological Society,* 1963-67.
About 10,000 numbered references pa. Sections: 1. General - 2. Africa - 3. Americas - 4. Asia - 5. Australasia. Pacific - 6. Europe. Subdivisions (where appropriate): General; Physical anthropology; Archaeology; Cultural anthropology; Ethnography; Linguistics. The first issue of each volume lists additions and amendments to current periodicals, while a revised list of current periodicals, with abbreviations, is published separately. Annual author index, but no subject index. Excellent for current awareness. *Class No:* 572.0(048)

Somatology (Anatomy of Man)

[1082]
BROTHWELL, D.R. Digging up bones: the excavation, treatment and study of human skeletal remains. 3rd ed. London, British Museum (Natural History); Oxford University Press, 1981. 208p. illus. ISBN: 0198585047.
1. Notes for guidance in excavating and reporting on human remains - 2. Description and study of human bone - 3. Demographic aspects of selected biology - 4. Measurement and morphological analysis of human bones - 5. Injuries and marks on bone - 6. Ancient disease - 7. Concluding remarks. For the layperson as well as the specialist. Bibliography, p.179-99. Index, p.201-8. 17 plates. *Class No:* 572.5

Ethnology (Races)

Encyclopaedias

[1083]
Encyclopedia of world cultures. V.1: North America. O'Leary, T.J. *and* Levinson, D., *eds.* Riverside, N.J., G.K. Hall, 1991. 424p. maps. ISBN: 0816118086.
V.1. *North America.* 424p. maps.
First volume of a projected 10-volume set due to be completed in 1993. 223 articles arranged alphabetically on cultures in the US, Canada and Greenland, varying in length from a few lines, *e.g.* 'Koyukon', to six pages, *e.g.* 'Apache'. Data in each entry include ethnonyms, history and cultural relations, linguistic and geographic orientation, economy, kinship, marriage and family, and religion. Short bibliographies of six or seven items are appended to each entry. Appendix lists extinct native American tribes. Glossary and ethnonym index. Filmography lists *c.*300 films and videos. No illustrations. 'When complete, the

....(contd.)

Encyclopedia of world cultures will be unique in its provision of concise summaries for almost all cultural groups' (Booklist, v.87(21), July 1991 p.2062). Class No: 572.9(031)

[1084]

The Illustrated encyclopedia of mankind. Carlisle, R., *and others, eds.* London, Marshall Cavendish, 1990. 22v. illus., maps. ISBN: 1854350323.

First published 1978, 2nd ed. 1984.

V.1, 2-15 contain A-Z treatment of racial, ethnic and cultural groups and nationalities. V.16-20 cover general themes (unchanged from the 1984 ed.), *e.g.* 'Costume'; 'Social organization'; 'Beliefs of the world'. There is a new *Origins of mankind* volume with its own index. V.22 contains general, thematic and geographic indexes; population charts; bibliography; glossary. Over 3,000 colour photographs. Recommended for public and school libraries which do not already possess the 1984 ed. Otherwise the 1984 ed. would suffice. *Class No: 572.9(031)*

Tables & Data Books

[1085]

MURDOCK, G.P. Atlas of world cultures. Pittsburgh, Univ. of Pittsburgh Press, 1981. 151p. ISBN: 0822934329.

Revision of his *Ethnographic atlas* (1967).

Not an atlas but coded data on 563 cultures 'most fully described in the ethnographic literature', applying 76 factors. (The 1967 *Atlas* coded 862 cultures). 'Although the coded format requires skill to utilize, the mass of information presented makes the effort worthwhile' (*Library journal,* 1 June 1981, p.1210). *Class No: 572.9(083)*

[1086]

—MURDOCK, G.P., *and others.* Outline of cultural materials. 4th ed. New Haven, Conn., Human Relations Area Files Press, 1982. 247p.

Delineates the basic HRAF classification scheme placing data into 79 major and 619 major subject divisions, plus cross-references. *Class No: 572.9(083)*

[1087]

—MURDOCK, G.P., *and others.* Outline of world cultures. 6th ed. New Haven, Conn., Human Relations Area Files Press, 1983. xii, 359p. ISBN: 0875366643.

The companion volume, takes a geographical/historical stance. 8 main regions: World; Asia; Europe; Africa; Middle East; North America; Oceania. Detailed index, p.195-259. Aims to provide 'an outline organization and classification of the known cultures of the world'. *Class No: 572.9(083)*

USA

Black Races

[1088]

DAVIS, N., *ed.* Afro-American experience. Westport, Conn., Greenwood Press, 1985. 288p. (*Bibliographies and indexes in Afro-American studies, no.9.*) ISBN: 031324930x.

An annotated guide to 105 general reference works on black studies, plus topical chapters on 537 books covering slavery, sociology, family, etc. 'A boon to public and academic libraries' (*Wilson library bulletin,* April 1986, p.62). *Class No: 572.9(73)(=96)*

Amerindians, North

[1089]

STURTEVANT, W.C., *ed.* Handbook of North American Indians. Washington, Smithsonian Institution, 1978-. illus., maps.

1. *Introduction.* 2. *Indians and Eskimos in contemporary society.* 3. *Environment, origin and population.* 4. *History of Indian-white relations.* 1991. 5. *Arctic;* edited by D. Damas, 1984. 6. *Subarctic;* edited by J. Helm. 1981. 7. *The Northwest Coast;* edited by W.C. Sturtevant and W. Suttles. 1990. 8. *California;* edited by R.F. Heizer. 1978. 9/10. *Southwest;* edited by A. Ortiz, 1979-83. 11. *The Great Basin;* edited by W.L. D'Azevedo. 1989. 12. *The Plateau.* 13. *The Plains.* 14. *The Southeast.* 15. *Northeast;* edited by B.G. Tripper. 1978. 16. *Technology and the visual arts.* 17. *Native languages.* 18/19, *Biographical dictionary.* 20. *Consolidated index.*

Planned in 20v. V.15, *Northeast,* (1978. 924p.), comprises 54 contributors by specialists on 75 Indian tribles who lived (and may still live) in south-east Canada and north-east USA. Profusely illustrated; well documented and indexed. Authoritative. 'The unrelenting excellence of these volumes marks on editorial achievement of the first rank' (Webb, W.H., and associates. *Sources of information in the social sciences* (3rd ed., 1986. item F989)). *Class No: 572.9(=97)*

[1090]

WAUCHOPE, R., *ed.* Handbook of Middle American Indians. Austin, Univ. of Texas Press, 1964-76. 16v. Supplements, 1981-.

1. *Natural environment and early cultures.* 1964. 2-3. *Archaeology of Southern Mesoamerica.* 1965. 3. *Archaeological frontiers and external connections.* 1966. 5. *Linguistics.* 1967. 6. *Social anthropology.* 1967. 7-8. *Ethnology.* 1969. 9. *Physical anthropology.* 1970. 10-11. *Archaeology of Northern Mesoamerica.* 1971. 12-15. *Guide to ethnohistorical science.* 1973-75. 16. *Sources cited and artifacts illustrated.* 1976. Supplement.

Each volume consists of specialist contributions on the life, customs, culture, milieu, etc., plus an extensive bibliography and detailed index. Lacks any preface or formal introduction to the work as a whole. Covers the area South of F.W. Hodge's *Handbook of American Indians (qv),* and updates J.H. Steward's *Handbook of South American Indians.* 'It would be hard to exaggerate the importance of this series' (*American anthropologist,* v.67, 1965, p.1333).

Supplements are promised. *Class No: 572.9(=97)*

Amerindians, South

[1091]

STEWARD, J.H., *ed.* Handbook of South American Indians. Washington, Smithsonian Institution, 1946-59. 7v. illus., maps.

1. *The marginal tribes.* 1946. 2. *The Andean civilizations.* 1946. 3. *The tropical forest tribes.* 1948. 4. *The circum-Caribbean tribes.* 1948. 5. *The comparative ethnology of South American Indians.* 1949. 6. *Physical anthropology, linguistics and cultural geography of South American Indians.* 1950. 7. *Index.* 1959.

A truly comprehensive study, with extensive chapter bibliographies. V.7, the general index, has *c.*20,000 entries. Some of the volumes have glossaries. *Class No: 572.9(=98)*

Aborigines

[1092]

TINDALE, N.B. Aboriginal tribes of Australia: their terrain, environmental controls, distribution, limits and proper names. Berkeley, Calif., University of California Press, 1974. 2v. (Text; Maps). ISBN: 0520020057.

10,283 numbered entries. Text (xii, 404p) has 4 parts: 1. The people and the land - 2. Catalogue of Australian aboriginal tribes (by states, then by tribes, A-Z, with references, p.161-262) - 3. Alternatives, variant spellings and invalid terms. Appendix: 'Tasmanian tribes'. Bibliography, p.389-401. Non-analytical index, p.389-401. Non-analytical index, p.389-401; Tasmanian tribe index, p.402-4. V.2 consists of 4 folding location maps. *Class No:* 572.9(=995)

573 Biology

Biology

Abbreviations & Symbols

[1093]
DUPAYRAT, J. **Dictionary of biomedical acronyms and abbreviations.** 2nd ed. Chichester, John Wiley & Sons, 1990. 162p. ISBN: 0471926493.
First published 1984.
About 7,000 definitions for the 4,000 most common biomedical acronyms. Increase in the number of basic acronyms is 30% up on the previous edition. Intended primarily for researchers, physicians and translators. *Class No:* 573.0(003)

Bibliographies

[1094]
WYATT, H.V., *ed.* **Information sources in the life sciences.** 3rd ed. London, etc., Butterworths, 1987. xiv, 191p. tables. (*Butterworths Guides to information sources.*) ISBN: 040811472x.
First published 1966, as *Use of biological literature;* edited by R.T. Bottle and H.V. Wyatt; 2nd ed. 1971 (392p.).
9 contributors. Introduction; 13 chapters (6 by H.V. Wyatt): 1. Reading for profit: current awareness - 2. Literature searching by computer - 3. Secondary sources: abstracts, indexes and bibliographies - 4. Databanks; collections [of specimens] - 5. Guides to the literature - 6. Biochemical sciences - 7. Microbiology - 8. Biotechnology - 9. Genetics - 10. Zoology - 11. Ecology - 12. Botany - 13. History of biology. Index, p.187-91.
This 3rd ed. is only half the size of the 2nd, and users are referred to the 2nd ed. on foreign serials, patents, botanical taxonomy, history and biography of biology. Aimed at working scientists and information specialists; 'a guide rather than a compendium'. Good on databanks. Up-to-date, but marred by an inadequate index, and exorbitantly priced. 4th ed. due to be published in 1992. *Class No:* 573.0(01)

Handbooks & Manuals

[1095]
The Cambridge encyclopedia of life sciences. Friday, A. *and* Ingram, D.S., *general eds.* Cambridge Univ. Press, 1985. 432p. illus. (incl. col.), diagrs., tables, maps. ISBN: 0521256968.
Three major parts (15 chapters), each with further reading. 1. Processes and organization (1. The cell ... 5. The geology) - 2. Environments (6. Marine environments ... 10. Living organisms and environments) - 3. Evolution and the fossil record (11. The evolutionary process ... 15. Recent history of the fauna and flora). 31 contributors. Species index; subject index (in tiny print). The book's

....(contd.)
central theme is 'the adaptations of plants and animals to their environments and their relations with other organisms within those environments' (*Foreword*). Well integrated and well illustrated. *Choice,* (v.23(5), January 1986, p.724) finds coverage uneven, although the book - as much a textbook as an encyclopaedia - is 'highly recommended for undergraduate and public libraries'. *Class No:* 573.0(035)

Dictionaries

English

[1096]
Chambers biology dictionary. Walker, P.M.B., *ed.* Cambridge, W.R. Chambers; University Press, 1989. xii,324p. diagrs. ISBN: 185296152x.
Derived from *Chambers science and technology dictionary* (*q.v.*). Contains *c.*10,000 definitions, including *c.*3,000 in zoology, *c.*2,500 in botany, and *c.*1,200 in biochemistry, molecular biology and genetics. Definitions are concise, with some terms given fuller treatment in a series of over 100 special articles, *e.g.* genetic manipulation, poison. Synonyms and cross-references are indicated in italic and bold type. Largely a duplication of the same subject areas in the parent dictionary but has a good, clear layout and would be useful for the more specialized life sciences library. *Class No:* 573.0(038)=20

[1097]
HENDERSON, I.F. *and* HENDERSON, W.D. **Henderson's dictionary of biological terms.** 10th ed., by E. Lawrence. Harlow, Longman Scientific and Technical, 1989. xi, 636p. ISBN: 0582463629.
First published 1920; as *A directory of scientific terms.* (1st-8th eds.).
Over 18,000 headwords. Updates existing definitions and incorporates many new terms *e.g.,* AIDS, gene therapy, biotechnology, ribozyme. Revised and simplified outline classification of the Plant and Animal Kingdoms, the Fungi and Monera (prokaryotes). New appendix of *c.*60 structural formulae of important biotechnical compounds. *Class No:* 573.0(038)=20

[1098]
International dictionary of medicine and biology. Landau, S.I., *ed.-in-chief.* New York, Wiley, 1986. 3v. (li, 3200p.). ISBN: 047101849x.
Over 100 contributors; more than 150,000 entries, thanks to the inclusion of biology. Among the subjects most extensively covered are ecology, environmental health, infectious diseases, occupational medicine, toxicology. A concise guide to usage precedes. Highly recommended as 'indispensable for medical and science libraries' (*Library journal,* 15 June 1986, p.61). *Class No:* 573.0(038)=20

Reviews & Abstracts

[1099]
Biological abstracts. Philadelphia, Pa., BioScience Information Service (BIOSIS), 1926-. Semi-monthly. ISSN: 00063169.

The world's leading abstracting service in biology and biomedicine. Over 235,000 abstracts pa. from *c*.9,500 journals. Arranged in 84 sections, A-Z, including Aerospace and underwater biological effects; Cardiovascular system; Ecology (Environmental biology); Genetics and Cytogenetics; Immunology; Neoplasms and neoplastic agents; Nervous system; Pharmacology; Public health; Toxicology; Virology. Author index; Biosystematics index; Generic index; Subject index - per issue. Cumulative indexes, 2pa., and 5-yearly (on microfiche, *e.g.*, 1975-79).

Reprints from *Biological abstracts* include *Abstracts of mycology* and *Abstracts of entomology*.

Biological abstracts/RRM (*qv*) is complementary to *Biological abstracts* in its coverage. Both services feed into *BIOSIS PREVIEWS* database (1969-). *Class No:* 573.0(048)

[1100]
Biological abstracts/RRM: reports, reviews, meetings. Philadelphia, Pa., BioScience Information Services (BIOSIS), 1980-. Fortnightly. ISSN: 01926985.

As *Bioresearch index,* v.1-17 (1965-79).

About 235,000 references pa. (No abstracts, despite the title, but keywords are appended to entries). Coverage: symposia, meetings, reviews, monographs, book chapters, etc., - thus complementary to the coverage of *Biological abstracts.* Author, biosystematic, generic and subject indexes. *BIOSIS PREVIEWS* database (1969-). *Class No:* 573.0(048)

[1101]
Current contents: Life sciences. Philadelphia, Pa., Institute of Scientific Information, 1958-. Weekly. ISSN: 00113409.

Provides contents lists of *c*.250 journal issues. (multidisciplinary; chemistry ... neurosciences & behavior; animal & plant science). Author, title and address directory; Publishers address directory. Request-a-print service available. Available online and on diskette. *Class No:* 573.0(048)

Tables & Data Books

[1102]
FISHER, Sir R.A. *and* **YATES, F. Statistical tables for biological, agricultural and medical research.** 6th ed. Edinburgh & London, Oliver & Boyd, 1963. x, 146p. tables.

First published 1948; 5th ed. 1956.

50 tables (numbered 1-34, with interpolations). Main additions to the 6th ed. are: v, 'Fiducial limits for a variance component', and xvii, 'Balanced incomplete blocks-combinatorial solutions'. The valuable introduction give examples of the ways in which the tables can be used and includes 82 references to books, monographs and papers on statistic methods up to 1963. No index. A standard source. *Class No:* 573.0(083)

Institutions & Associations

[1103]
DARNAY, B.T. *and* **YOUNG, M.L.,** *eds.* **Life sciences organizations and agencies directory:** a guide to approximately 8,000 organizations and agencies providing information in the agricultural and biological sciences. Detroit, Mich., Gale. 1988. xxi, 864p. ISBN: 0810318261.

7,662 numbered entries. 18 chapters (*e.g.,* 5. Computer information services: international; 6. Consulting firms; 10. Research centers: international; 16. US federal government research centers). Basic data on each organization include

....(contd.)
date of foundation and name of contact, research activities and fields. Master name and keyword index. US emphasis. *Class No:* 573.0:061:061.2

Research Projects

[1104]
Current research in Britain. Biological sciences. Boston Spa, British Library. Annual. ISBN: 0712320873, 1991 ed. ISSN: 02671956.

Replaces *Research in British universities, polytechnics and colleges* (RBUPC). First published 1985.

One of a set covering 4 subject areas, registering research in every British university and polytechnic, many colleges and other institutions, with details of *c*.60,000 projects in all. *Biological sciences* lists *c*.20,000 projects. 'Research in progress' (p.1-500) lists universities, polytechnics, colleges (other than univ. colleges), and other institutions (including government depts.) numerically. Data number, name, and dept., address, head of dept., researches and title of project, dates, bequests, etc. Name, study area and keyword indexes. The standard British research tool in biological sciences. *Class No:* 573.0:061:061.62.005

Ecology

Bibliographies

[1105]
Environmental periodicals bibliography. Baltimore, Md., National Information Services Corporation, 1990.

Compiled by the Environmetal Studies Institute of the International Academy of Santa Barbara. International in scope, covering scientific, technical and popular journals. Contains over 400,000 citations collected since 1972. Subject areas include human ecology, water and land resources, nutrition, air and energy. Available on CD-ROM. *Class No:* 574(01)

Encyclopaedias & Dictionaries

[1106]
ALLABY, M. Macmillan dictionary of the environment. 3rd ed. London, Macmillan, 1988. [v], 423p. ISBN: 0333455614.

First published 1977 ([v], 532p.).

About 5,000 interdisciplinary terms, straying into many fields, - botany, zoology, chemistry, physics, mathematics, economics (*e.g.*, ½p. each on Ice Age, nuclear reactor, mangrove). Includes a few biographical entries, for Darwin, Malthus, Lamarck, etc. 'Soil classification': 1p. Profuse cross-references. *Class No:* 574(03)

[1107]
McGraw-Hill encyclopedia of environmental science. Parker, S.P., *editor-in-chief.* 2nd ed. New York, etc., McGraw-Hill, 1980. x, 858p. illus., diagrs., graphs, tables, maps. ISBN: 0070452644.

First published 1974.

Over 250 contributors. 'Surveying the environment' (5 essays) precede the A/Z sequence of signed articles on environmental science and engineering. 'Sea water': p.634-57 (with 15 figures, 7 references); 'Radiation biochemistry': p.588-92; 6 references). Many of the articles were written specially for this volume; some were taken from the *McGraw-Hill Encyclopedia of science and technology* (4th ed. 1977). Analytical index, p.839-58. 650 illus. in all. 'A very valuable basic reference for libraries without the multi-volume encyclopedia' (*Library journal,* 1 April 1975, p.653, on the 1974 ed.). *Class No:* 574(03)

Handbooks & Manuals

[1108]
GRZIMEK, B., *and others, eds.* **Grzimek's encyclopedia of ecology.** English ed. New York, London, etc., Van Nostrand Reinhold, 1976. 705p. illus. ISBN: 0442229488.
Originally published Zurich, Kindler Verlag AG, 1971. A supplement to *Grzimek's Animal life encyclopedia (qv).*
42 contributors. Part 1: The environment of animals (1. Adaptations to the abiotic environment; 3. Habitats and their fauna; 4. Man as a factor in the environment of animals) - Part 2. The environment of man. Many coloured plates; excellent coloured maps. 'A worthy purchase' (*New technical books,* November 1977, entry 1564). *Class No: 574(035)*

Yearbooks & Directories

[1109]
Directory for the environment: organisations, campaigns and initiatives in the British Isles. Frisch, M., *ed.* 3rd ed. London, Green Print, 1990. 320p. ISBN: 1854250361.
Previously published as *Directory for the environment,* 2nd ed. 1986.
Lists local and national organizations, campaigns and government bodies concerned with the human and natural environment. Coverage includes consultancies, charities, research institutes, campaigning groups, learned societies, and commercial enterprises throughout Britain and Ireland. *Class No: 574(058)*

[1110]
FITCH, J.M., *ed.* **Environmental and international sciences research centres:** a world directory of organizations and programs. Harlow, Essex, Longman, 1984. 742p.
Data on *c.*3,500 industrial, governmental and academic organizations, plus libraries and observations in *c.*130 countries. Index of establishments and an extensive subject index. *Class No: 574(058)*

Worldwide

[1111]
Ecosystems of the world. Goodall, D.W., *ed.* Amsterdam, etc., Elsevier, 1977-. illus., diagrs., tables, maps.
1. *Wet coastal ecosystems;* edited by V.J. Chapman, 1977. 4. *Mires: swamp, bog, fen and moor;* edited by A.J.P. Gore. 4A. *General studies,* 1983. 4B. *Regional studies,* 1983. 5. *Temperate deserts and semi-deserts;* edited by N.E. West. 1983. 9. *Heathlands and related shrublands;* edited by R.L. Specht. 2v. 1979-81. 10. *Temperate broad-leaved evergreen forests;* edited by J.D. Ovington. 1983. 11. *Mediterranean-type shrublands;* edited by F. Di Castri, etc. 1981. 12. *Hot deserts and arid shrublands;* edited by M. Evenari. 1985-6. 2v. 13. *Tropical savannas;* edited by F. Bourlière. 1983. 14A. *Tropical rain forest ecosystems;* edited by F.B. Golley. 1983. 14B. *Tropical rain forest ecosystems;* edited by H. Lieth and M.J.A. Werger. 1989. 15. *Forested wetlands;* edited by A. Lugo. 1989. 17A. *Managed grasslands: regional studies;* edited by A. Breymeyer. 1989. 17B. *Managed grasslands;* edited by R.W. Snaydon. 1987. 18. *Field-crop ecosystems;* edited by C.J. Pearson. 1991. 21. *Bioindustrial ecosystems;* edited by D.J.A. Cole and G.C. Brander. 1986. 23. *Lakes and reservoirs;* edited by F.B. Taub. 1984. 26. *Estuaries and enclosed seas;* edited by B.H. Ketchum. 1983. 27. *Continental shelves;* edited by H. Postma and J.J. Zijlstra. 1987. 29. *Managed aquatic ecosystems;* edited by R.G. Michael. 1987.
Each volume is the work of a team of specialists. Extensive bibliographies.
Monumental compendium of information about processes and characteristics of ... ecosystems of the world ... 'The

....(contd.)
most thorough treatment of its kind to date' (*Geographical bibliography for American libraries;* edited by C.D. Harris (1985), p.76-77). *Class No: 574(100)*

Hydrobiology (Marine Biology)

[1112]
Aquatic sciences and fisheries abstracts. Bethesda, Md., Cambridge Scientific Abstracts, 1978-. Monthly. 2pts. ISSN: 01405373.
Replaces *Aquatic sciences and fisheries abstracts,* 1971-77 (an amalgamation of *Aquatic biology abstracts* and *Current bibliography for aquatic sciences and fisheries*).
Pt.1. *Biological sciences and living resources.* Pt.2. *Ocean technology, policy and non-living resources, (qv).* Pt.1, 1985: 24,100 abstracts. Main parts: 1. General aspects; 6-7. Biology; 74-194. Ecology, ecosystems and pollution; 195-245. Fisheries. Author and subject indexes per issue and annually. CD-ROM and online BRS(CSAL), CISTI, DIMDI, DIALOG, ESA. *Class No: 574.5*

Genetics

[1113]
KING, R.C. *and* STANSFIELD, W.D. **A Dictionary of genetics.** 4th ed. New York, Oxford University Press, 1990. 406p. illus., diagrs., chemical structures. ISBN: 0195063708.
First published 1968.
7,100 concise definitions, 20 per cent of which are new or updated. 250 illustrations. 4 appendices: A. Classification - B. Domesticated species - C. Chronology; Index of scientists (1,010 entries); Bibliography - D. Periodical list; Multijournal publishers; Foreign words in scientific titles. A German edition (Verlagsgesellschaft, 1990) contains a German/English index. *Class No: 575*

[1114]
RIEGER, R.O., *and others.* **Glossary of genetics and cytogenetics, classical and molecular.** 4th rev. ed. Berlin, etc., Springer Verlag, 1976. 647p. diagrs., tables.
First published 1954 as *Genetisches und cytogenetisches Wörterbuch.*
About 4,000 entries, stating first use of term (author; date). 'Inheritance': 2p. Addenda, p.638-47. Bibliography. p.573-637. 100 diagrams, etc. 'Remains the outstanding reference glossary of genetics' (*Heredity,* v.41(1), 1978, p.115-6). The *Glossary* has also been translated into Russian and Polish.
A 5th ed., *Glossary of genetics: classical and molecular,* was published in 1991. *Class No: 575*

Evolution

[1115]
Encyclopedia of human evolution and prehistory. Tattersall, I., *and others, eds.* Chicago and London, St. James Press, 1988. xxxv,603p. illus., diagrs., tables. ISBN: 1558621172.
*c.*2,000 entries, arranged A-Z. Extensive coverage of all aspects of evolutionary theory, primatology, evolutionary and prehistoric hominid research, genetics, primate palaeontology and palaeontology. Many cross-references and references for further reading. Numerous clear illustrations. Useful for lay persons or undergraduates. 'An excellent reference tool, and the only one of its type' (*Science and technology libraries,* v.10(1), 1989, p.125). *Class No: 575.8*

[1116]
SMITH, F.H. *and* SPENCER, F. **The Origins of modern humans:** a world survey of the fossil evidence. New York, Wiley, 1985. $76. ISBN: 047183419x.
11 contributors, of which 9 concern skeletal remains

....(contd.)
found in Europe, Western Asia, East Asia and Australasia, China, and the Americas. While conceding that the text is refreshingly free from the Eurocentric bias, the review in *Nature* (v.314, 18 April 1985, p.649) quarrels with the maps and quality of photographs and drawings. Nevertheless, 'An invaluable source of reference for those already familiar with the fossil record, anatomy and population genetics'. *Class No: 575.8*

Biochemistry

[1117]
SCOTT, T. *and* EAGLESON, M. **Concise encyclopedia of biochemistry.** 2nd ed. Berlin, Walter de Gruyter, 1988. 649p. diagrs., tables, charts, formulas. ISBN: 0899254578.

First ed. (1983) based on 2nd ed. of *Brockhaus ABC Biochimie* (1981).

Extensive revision brings in new material covering enzymology, molecular biology, metabolism, metabolic regulation and natural products. Entries, A-Z, vary in length from one paragraph to several pages ('Evolution': 4 columns, 2 charts, 1 table; 'Recombinant DNA technology': 8p., 12 diagrs.). Each enzyme is given its Enzyme Commission number. Adequate cross-references. An excellent aide-mémoire. *Class No: 577.1*

Vitamins

[1118]
MACHLIN, L.J., *ed.* **Handbook of vitamins:** nutritional, biochemical and clinical aspects. New York, Dekker, 1984. 614p. (*Food science and technology, v.13.*) ISBN: 082477091x.

Detailed data on all known vitamins, including chemistry, food content, metabolism, functions and deficiency symptoms. A final chapter considers substances lacking vitamin status. Appendix: 'Recommended daily allowances for vitamins (revised 1983)'. An authoritative and comprehensive source of information. 'For nutritionists, biochemists and even the interested lay person' (*Science & technology libraries,* v.5(4), Summer 1985, p.98).

A 2nd ed. was published in 1990. *Class No: 577.16*

Viruses (Virology)

[1119]
NICHOLAS, R. *and* NICHOLAS, D. **Virology: an information profile.** London, Mansell, 1983. viii, 236p. ISBN: 0720116732.

3 parts. 1. Overview of virology and its literature (history and scope; organizations; conferences; the literature; searching the literature), p.1-168 - 2. Bibliography (392 unannotated entries), p.169-95 - 3. Directory of organizations, culture collections and libraries, p.197-223. Analytical index, p.227-36. Excludes biochemistry and genetics. Despite some omissions (*e.g.,* Science Reference Library), it is a 'very good analytical critical work that fills a gap in the literature available' (*British book news,* March 1984, p.162). *Class No: 578*

Microbiology

[1120]
Annual review of microbiology. Palo Alto, Calif., Annual Reviews, Inc., 1947-. Annual. illus., diagrs., tables. ISSN: 00664227.

V.45, 1991 (x,657p.) has 23 articles which include 'Techniques for selection of industrially important microorganisms' (with 3p. of refs.) and 'Plant genetic control of nodulation' (with 13p. of refs.). Analytical subject index, p.637-48. Cumulative indexes to contributing authors, v.41-45, chapter titles, v.41-45. *Class No: 579*

[1121]
SINGLETON, P. *and* SAINSBURY, D. **Dictionary of microbiology and molecular biology.** 2nd ed. Chichester, New York, Wiley, 1987. xii, 1019p. illus., diagrs., charts, tables, chemical structures. ISBN: 0471911143.

First published 1978 as *Dictionary of microbiology* (viii, 481p.).

About 10,000 terms; many cross-references. 'AIDS': 3 columns; 'Salmonella': over 2 columns; 'Electron microscope': over 4p. plus keyed diagrams. 5 appendices (*e.g.,* Biosynthesis). Key to journal-title abbreviations. Key to book references (202 in all), p.1011-19. For undergraduates and postgraduates in this field, primarily. *Class No: 579*

Bacteria

[1122]
Bergey's manual of systematic bacteriology. 2nd ed. Baltimore, Md., Williams & Wilkins 1984-89. 4v. illus., tables. ISBN: 0683041088, v.1; 0683078933, v.2; 0683079085, v.3; 0683090615, v.4.

Replaces *Bergey's Manual of determinative bacteriology* (8th ed. 1974).

V.1 by N.R. King. 1984, xxvii, 964p. V.2 by H.A. Sneath, 1984. xviii, 634p. V.3 by J.T. Staley, 1989. xxviii, 714p. V.4 by S.T. Williams, 1989. xxii,420p.

Projected in 4 volumes, with 205 contributors and 17 main sections in all. Each volume contains an extensive bibliography (*e.g.,* v.1: p.837-942) and an index of scientific names of bacteria. V.1 covers the Gram-negative bacteria; v.2, the Gram-positive bacteria; v.3, the archaebacteria, cyanobacteria and remaining Gram-negatives; v.4, the actinomycetes. *Class No: 579.8*

58/59 Natural History

Nature Study

Bibliographies

[1123]
FREEMAN, R.B. British natural history books, 1495-1900: a
handlist. Folkestone, Kent, Dawson, 1980. 437p. ISBN:
0712909710.
Two parts: 1. Alphabetical list (4,206 numbered entries);
2. List of titles in date order from 1495-1800. Subject
index, partly analytical, p.403-37. Numbers in italics
indicate 'those works which, in the opinion of the author,
are the most important contributions to the subject of the
entry'. 'Something more than a short title list and
something more than a bibliography' (*Introduction*). It
reveals 'an unassailable completeness, scrupulous care over
minor details, and a seemingly total freedom from printers'
slips' (*British journal for the history of science,*) v.14(2),
no.46, March 1981, p.86-87). *Class No: 58/59:502(01)*

Encyclopaedias & Dictionaries

[1124]
ALLABY, M., ed. The Oxford dictionary of natural history.
Oxford University Press, 1985. xiv, 688p. ISBN:
0192177206.
56 countributors and consultants. More than 12,000
entries, A-Z, listing taxa of animals and plants down to
family level, including 'any lower taxa of particular interest'
(*Preface*). Numerous cross-references, especially from
common to scientific name. 'Felidae (cats)': $\frac{2}{3}$ column;
'Dance language': $\frac{3}{4}$ column. A few brief biographies (*e.g.*,
Darwin: $\frac{1}{2}$ column). Failure to give priority to common-
name entry is criticized in *New scientist* (10 April, 1986,
p.68). However, 'It's an essential book to have about the
classroom, laboratory, library or study' (*British book news,*
March 1986, p.165). *Class No: 58/59:502(03)*

Reviews & Abstracts

[1125]
Natural history book reviews: an international bibliography.
Berkhamstead, Herts., AB Academic Press, 1976-. v.1, no.1-
. Quarterly, (originally 3pa). illus., facsims. ISSN: 1308180x.
V.10(1), 1990 contains a bibliographic essay. 'First
readings in charology', p.1-4. Reviews arranged in 14
categories: General (10 items) ... Ecology (3) ... Mammals
(5) ... The Young Naturalist (1). Full bibliographical details
precede each review. Apparent lack of index for recent
volumes reduces the value of this work which is an
important current source in its field. *Class No: 58/59:502(048)*

Yearbooks & Directories

[1126]
MEENAN, A., comp. and ed. Directory of natural history and
related societies in Britain and Ireland. London, British
Museum (Natural History), 1983. vii, 407p. ISBN:
0565008595.
Nearly 1,000 entries, Aslib Biological and Agricultural
Sciences Group ... Zoological Society of Northern Ireland.
Data on each society include aims, membership, meetings,
publications, additional information (*e.g.,* library). Arranged
under English and Welsh counties, Scotland, Ulster, and
Eire. Appended geographical and subject indexes. A much-
needed comprehensive and up-to-date directory, superseding
A. Lysaght's *Directory of natural history and other field
study societies in Great Britain* (1959). *Class No: 58/59:502(058)*

Europe

[1127]
The Natural history of Britain and Northern Europe. London,
Hodder and Stoughton; 1978-9. 5v., ea.224p. illus, (mostly
col.), maps. ISBN: 0340226145; 0340231548; 0340226153;
0340231556; 034023153x.
1. *Mountains and moorlands,* by A. Darlington. 1978. 2.
Towns and gardens, by D. Owen, 1978. 3. *Fields and
lowlands,* by D. Boatman. 1979. 4. *Coasts and estuaries,* by
R. Barnes. 1979. 5. *Rivers, lakes and marshes,* by B.
Whitton. 1979.
The 5 volumes cover the whole of the northern half of
Europe west of Russia and the Baltic states, and include
Iceland. V.3 has 2 parts: 1. Ecological survey, with map of
lowland vegetation of Northern Europe; 2. A field guide to
a representative selection of plants and animals. Plates
(p.74-213) of plants, invertebrates, amphibians, reptiles,
birds, mammals. Detailed index. Entry is under the
vernacular names of plants and animals. Aimed at the
traveller-naturalist. *Class No: 58/59:502(4)*

America—North & Central

[1128]
COLLINS, H.H. Harper & Row's complete field guide to
North American wildlife. Eastern edition. New York, Harper
& Row, 1981. 714p. illus. (incl. col.). ISBN: 0690019696.
Earlier ed. as *Complete field guide to American wildlife,
central and north* (1959).
'Covering 1500 species of birds, mammals, reptiles,
amphibians, food and game birds of both fresh and salt
waters, mollusks, and the principal marine invertebrates
occurring in North American east of the 100th meridian
from the 55th parallel to Florida north of the Keys'
(*Subtitle*). Data include appearance, behaviour, habitat.
Index. *Class No: 58/59:502(71/73)*

[1129]

RANSOM, J.E. **Harper & Row's complete field guide to North American wildlife. Western edition.** New York, Harper & Row, 1981. 809p. illus. (incl. col.). ISBN: 0690019696.

'Covering 1800 species of birds, mammals, reptiles, amphibians, food and game fishes of both salt and fresh waters, mollusks, and the principal marine invertebrates occurring in North America west of the 100th meridian from the 55th parallel to the border of Mexico' (*Subtitle*). Data include appearance, behaviour, habitat. Index. *Class No:* 58/59:502(71/73)

Nature Reserves

[1130]

International handbook of national parks and nature reserves. Allin, C.W., *ed.* Westport, Conn., Greenwood Press, 1990. 560p. tables, maps. ISBN: 0313249024.

Describes and evaluates national parks and nature reserves in 25 nations and one regional cluster. Data include history of park preservation and administrative structures concerned with park protection. Bibliography appended to each chapter. Suitable for academic libraries. *Class No:* 58/59:502.4

[1131]

The Macmillan guide to British nature reserves. Hywell-Davies, J., *and others.* 2nd ed. London, Macmillan, 1989. xii,654p. col. illus., maps. ISBN: 0333467906.

First published 1984.

Arranged under English and Welsh counties, and Scottish regions. About 3,000 entries (some regrettably brief) for nature reserves and wildlife sites throughout the British Isles (excluding Eire). Data on each: location, type of reserve; features; visiting seasons; description. List of contributors. No bibliography. Well illustrated in colour. The most comprehensive of British nature reserve gazetteers, although bulky as a guide. *Class No:* 58/59:502.4

Nature Conservation

[1132]

Directory for the environment: organisations, campaigns and initiatives in the British Isles. Frisch, M., *ed.* 3rd ed. London, Green Print, 1990. 320p. ISBN: 1854250361.

Previously published as *Directory for the environment,* 2nd ed. 1986.

Lists local and national organizations, campaigns and government bodies concerned with the human and natural environment. Coverage includes consultancies, charities, research institutes, campaigning groups, learned societies, and commercial enterprises throughout Britain and Ireland. *Class No:* 58/59:502.6

[1133]

World plant conservation bibliography. [London], Royal Botanic Gardens, Kew; World Conservation Monitoring Centre, 1990. xv,645p. ISBN: 0947643249.

Designed to complement *Plants in danger; what do we know?* (World Conservation Monitoring Centre, 1986). Contains over 10,000 citations to published literature, ranging from specific to general, local to international. Includes data from the late 1970s onwards. Includes references on conservation of rare and threatened plants; erosion and conservation of plant genetic resources; extent and loss of habitats and vegetation; a selection of forestry papers; role and work of botanical institutions in plant conservation; conservation thinking and policy; protected areas. 3 indexes: 1. Plant names - 2. Plant families - 3. Geographical. Supplements and revisions are planned. *Class No:* 58/59:502.6

Wildlife Conservation

[1134]

BAKER, S. **Endangered vertebrates:** selected, annotated bibliography, 1981-1988. New York, Garland, 1990. xv,197p. (*Garland reference library of social science, no.480.*) ISBN: 0824047966.

International in scope and includes a wider range of publications than *Official World Wildlife Fund guide to endangered species of North America.* Coverage includes books, symposia, journal articles, and dissertations. Appendix gives names and serial publications of appropriate organizations. Indexes allow access by common name, scientific name, author or geographic area. Has both academic and general appeal. *Class No:* 58/59:502.7

[1135]

GRIMMETT, R.F.A. *and* JONES, T.A., *comps.* **Important bird areas in Europe.** Cambridge, International Council for Bird Preservation, 1989. x,888p. tables, maps. (*ICBP technical publication no.9.*) ISBN: 0946888175.

Inventories arranged A-Z by country, Albania ... Yugoslavia. Describes 2,444 sites and provides an indication of the extent to which they are unprotected or threatened. The chapter on each country is subdivided into sections on general information, ornithological importance, conservation infrastructure and protected-areas system, international resources relevant to the conservation of sites, overview of the inventory, glossary, inventory and main references. Maps showing the sites are also included. 6 appendices: 1. Numerical criteria used to select sites for migratory species ... English names of species mentioned in the text. 'It is intended for international agencies, governmental and non-governmental nature conservationists, land-use planners and professional and amateur ornithologists' (*Introduction*). *Class No:* 58/59:502.7

58 Botany

Botany

Bibliographies

[1136]
STAFLEU, F.A. *and* COWAN, R.S. **Taxonomic literature:** a selective guide to botanical publications and collections, with data, commentaries and types. 2nd ed. Utrecht, Bohn, Scheltema and Holkema, 1976-88. 7v. 6250p. (*Regnum vegetabile, 94, 98, 105, 110, 112, 115, 116.*)

Arranged under authors, A-Z, with brief biographical notes. 16,614 items from 6,186 authors are contained in v.1-6. Also, information on composite works, herbaria with collections, sources of bibliographical and biographical notes, annotated list of authors, most important works, etc. Name and title indexes per volume. *Class No:* 580(01)

[1137]
SWIFT, L.H. **Botanical bibliographies:** a guide to bibliographic materials applicable to botany. Minneapolis, Minn., Burgess, 1970. xxxix, 804p.

5 main sections: general bibliography; background literature (*e.g.,* biological), botanical literature (general and reference works; taxonomic, ecological and physiological botanical works); literature of applied botany (plant cultivation, etc.); literature of auxiliary studies (style manuals; botanical illustration, etc.). 'Highly recommended for all reference libraries' (*Library journal,* v.96(11), 1 June 1971, p.1963-4). *Class No:* 580(01)

Encyclopaedias & Dictionaries

[1138]
JACKSON, B.D. **A Glossary of botanic terms,** with their derivation and accent. 4th ed., rev. and enl. London, Duckworth, 1928. x, [ii], 481p.

First published 1900.

Latin equivalents accompany most of the 10,000 terms defined. Sub-entries are grouped under the generic term (*e.g.,* the entry for 'Cryptanthous' occupies one column and has 23 sub-entries). Appendix D: Bibliography of botanical dictionaries (40 annotated items), p.478-81. The standard English-language botanical glossary. *Class No:* 580(03)

Handbooks & Manuals

[1139]
STRASSBURGER, E. **Strassburger's textbook of botany.** Denffer, D. von, *and others.* New English ed., translated from the 10th German ed., by P. Bell and D. Coombe. London, Longman, 1976. xvi, 877p. illus., diagrs., tables, maps.

First published 1894.

4 parts: 1. Morphology - 2. Physiology - 3. Systematics and evolution - 4. Plant geography. Chronology, p.xv-xvi. References (by parts and sections), p.798-816. Excellent

....(contd.)
analytical index, p.817-77. Claimed to be the most comprehensive and up-to-date textbook of plant science in a single volume. *Class No:* 580(035)

Dictionaries

[1140]
STEARN, W.T. **Botanical Latin:** history, grammar, syntax, terminology and vocabulary. 3rd ed., rev. Newton Abbot, Devon, David & Charles, 1983. xiv, 566p. illus. ISBN: 0715385488.

First published 1966 (London, Nelson, xiv, 566p.).

About 80p. of concise grammar, extensive vocabulary of *c.*6,000 terms and a general bibliography and list of references. Intended primarily to help botanists to read the extensive literature of their subject, and to describe new species in language that is correct, lucid and unambiguous. *Class No:* 580(038)

Nomenclatures

[1141]
International Code of Botanical Nomenclature, adopted by the 14th Botanical Congress, Berlin, July-August 1987. Greuter, W., *and others, eds.* Königstein, Koeltz, 1988. xiv,328p. (*Regnum vegetabile, v.118.*) ISBN: 3874292789.

Consists of authoritative rules for the codifying of plants, the main part of the volume, p.80-289, delineating plant families in detail. English language only. The quarterly *Taxon* reports changes in the *Code.* *Class No:* 580(083.72)

Biographies

[1142]
DESMOND, R. **Dictionary of British and Irish botanists and horticulturists,** including plant collectors and botanical artists. 3rd ed. London, Taylor & Francis, 1977. xxvi, 747p. ISBN: 0850660890.

The *Dictionary* is the latest revision of *A biographical index of British and Irish botanists,* by J. Britten and G.E.S. Boulger (1893), revised by A.B. Rundle (1931).

About 10,000 entries, A-Z, for deceased people, mainly those born in the British Isles. Data: name, date and place of birth and death; education; qualifications; honours officeship in relevant societies; brief details of career; serial publications; editorship of periodical(s); biographical references in books and periodicals; location of plant collections, herbaria, manuscripts, drawings, portraits, state of collections, any plant commemorating the individual, and that person's name. Subject index classifies many of the entries under profession, plants on the country where the flora were collected and studied. 'This new Dictionary is by any standards a remarkable piece of work, reflecting an immense labour on its compiler's part, and shedding light into many very obscure corners' (*American scientist,* v.35(1) 1978, p.84). *Class No:* 580(092)

Botanical Gardens

[1143]
International directory of botanical gardens V. Heywood, C.A., *and others.* 5th ed. Königstein, Koeltz, 1990. 1019p. ISBN: 387429319x.

First published 1963.

1,400 entries, under countries A-Z. Data: status (*e.g.,* governmental); date of foundation; co-ordinates; rainfall; taxa (number of species and varieties grown); herbarium; publications; greenhouses; hours open to the public; name of director and staff). 'USSR': p.849-938. The new computerized format makes the book needlessly bulky and there are no page headings for guidance. *Class No:* 580:061:061.6

Practical Work

Collections

[1144]
Index herbariorum: a guide to the location and contents of the world's public herbaria. 8th ed. New York, New York Botanical Gardens for the International Association for Plant Taxonomy, 1990. 693p. (*Regnum vegetabile, v.120.*) ISBN: 0893273589. ISSN: 00800694.

First published 1952.

Pt.1: *The herbaria of the world.* 8th ed., by P.K. Holmgren and others. 1990.

Covers *c.*1,800 herbaria worldwide. Arranged A-Z by country (10 appearing for the first time), with sites arranged alphabetically within each country. Data: addresses, important collections, sponsoring organizations, geographical arrangement, herbarium abbreviations, name of director and staff. Indexes include important collections; staff; cities, p.615-93. Indispensable and well-organized. *Class No:* 580.082

[1145]
KENT, D.H. *and* ALLEN, D.E., *comps.* British and Irish herbaria: an index to the location of herbaria of British and Irish vascular plants. 2nd ed. London, Botanical Society of the British Isles, 1984. *c.*350p. ISBN: 0901158089.

First published 1958.

8 sections, especially 2: 'Universities, museums and other institutions possessing herbaria': principal collections and contributions (over 630 institutions, under locations, A-Z). Section 3: Collectors. Privately owned herbaria are listed in a further section. Extensive bibliography, p.317-31. Classified index to locations of collections. *Class No:* 580.082

Plants (Flora)

Worldwide

[1146]
FRODIN, D.G. Guide to standard floras of the world: an annotated, geographically arranged systematic bibliography of the principal floras, enumerations, checklists and chronological atlases of different areas. Cambridge Univ. Press, 1984. xx, 619p. ISBN: 0521236886.

Combined a thorough analysis of floras and floristics with a geographically arranged guide to the most useful floras and checklists of vascular plants of the world (*Nature,* v.315, 2 May 1985, p.2). Systematic bibliography (999 entries) has 10 divisions (0. World floras; 1. North America; 6. Europe; 9. Melanesia and Oceania). Appendix A: Major general bibliographies; B. Abbreviations of serials cited. Geographical and author index. Expensive. *Class No:* 581.1(100)

Europe

[1147]
BLAMEY, M. *and* GREY-WILSON, C. The Illustrated flora of Britain and Northern Europe. London, Hodder & Stoughton, 1989. 544p. illus. (incl. 446 col. pls.). ISBN: 0340401702.

A copiously illustrated handbook of *c.*2,500 flowering wild plants from Britain and Northern Europe, comprising specially-commissioned colour paintings to aid identification. (With up to 10 species shown per page, a larger page-size might have been advisable, as the book is already too bulky as a field guide). Detailed family descriptions, preceded by helpful introduction (p.9-30)and glossary (p.31-38). Some tree families included (p.41-59). Key to plant families (p.489-518) and English and Latin indexes. An attractive flora aimed at the serious amateur botanist. *Class No:* 581.1(4)

[1148]
TUTIN, T., *and others.* Flora europaea. Cambridge Univ. Press, 1964. 6v. illus., maps.

1. *Lycopodiaceae to Platanacea.* 1964. xxxii, [1], 464p. £70. 2. *Rosaceae to Umbelliferae.* 1968. xxvii, 454p. £70. 3. *Dispensiceae to Myoporaceae.* 1972. xxix, 370p. 4. *Plantaginaceae to Compositae (and Rubiacead).* 1976. xxix, 505p. £70. 5. *Alismataceae to Orchidaceae.* 1980, xxxviii, 452p., £70. *Checklist and chromosome index.* 1982. 440p £39.50. *Consolidated index.* 1982. 212p. £50.

The first complete flora of Europe. The project is sponsored by the Linnean Society of London and is based on studies in herbaria and in the field. Systematic descriptions of all flowering plants and ferns in Europe and intended primarily for professional botanists. Handsomely produced. *Class No:* 581.1(4)

Great Britain

[1149]
British plant communities. Rodwell, J.S., *and others, eds.* Cambridge, University Press, 1991-. ISBN: 0521235588, v.1.
V.1. *Woodlands and scrub.* 1991. x,395p. V.2. *Mires and heaths.* V.3. *Grasslands and montane vegetation.* V.4. *Aquatic communities, swamps and tall-herb fens.* V.5. *Maritime and weed communities.*

A projected set of 5 volumes, which aims to describe over 250 plant communities in Great Britain (excluding Northern Ireland). V.1 contains an introduction, a key, and 25 community descriptions. Each community description contains data on synonymy, constant species, physiognomy, sub-communities, habitat, zonation and succession, distribution, affinities, floristic tables, and distribution maps. Index of synonyms to woodlands and scrubs, p.369-76. Index of species in woodlands and scrub, p.377-84. Bibliography, p.385-95. Culmination of 15 years' detailed survey and analysis of British vegetation by those involved in the National Vegetation Classification. *Class No:* 581.1(410)

[1150]
CLAPHAM, A.R., *and others.* Flora of the British Isles. 3rd ed. Cambridge Univ. Press, 1987. ISBN: 0521309859.

First published 1952; 2nd ed., 1962.

Main sections: Pteridophyta - Gymnospermae - Angiospermae (Dicotyledons. Monocotyledons). Data on habit; whether native/introduced; ecology; geographical distribution; evolutionary history; agricultural significance, etc. Bibliography, p.633. Notes on families and life forms. 'Likely to be the standard British flora well into the next century' (*Nature,* v.328, 27 August, p.772). *Class No:* 581.1(410)

[1151]

—CLAPHAM, A.R., *and others.* Flora of the British Isles: illustrations. Drawings by S.I. Roles. Cambridge Univ. Press, 1957-65. 4v. illus.

Follows the sequence and nomenclature of the parent work. 1,910 black-and-white drawings. *Class No:* 581.1(410)

[1152]

MCCLINTOCK, D. and FITTER, R.S.R. **The pocket guide to wild flowers.** London, Collins, 1956. xii, 340p. illus.

Main purpose is to enable anyone to name any wild flower, grass, sedge, tree or shrub that he or she is likely to see in the British Isles. 112 plates (64 in colour and arranged in colour sequence, blue ... yellow). Glossary. Indexes to English and Latin names 'One of the most successful attempts made in recent years to put down our Flora inside a single manageable volume'. (*Journal of the Royal Horticultural Society*, v.85(8), August 1960, p.375). *Class No:* 581.1(410)

[1153]

—MCCLINTOCK, D. Supplement to 'The pocket guide to wild flowers'. Platt, Kent, D. McClintock, [1959]. ix, 89p.

Describes 450 further species. The *Supplement* also adds a long list of hybrids not recorded in the parent work; a valuable list of albinos, a bibliography and a list of county floras and checklists. *Class No:* 581.1(410)

[1154]

ROSS-CRAIG, S. **Drawings of British plants;** being illustrations of species of flowering plants growing naturally in the British Isles. London, Bell, 1964-74. 31pts. and index (pts.1-9 in 3v.; pts.10-23.

Systematic arrangement (*e.g.,* pts.8-9: Rosaceae; 15-18: Compositae), giving brief description of the plant and its common name. Partly replaces Fitch and Smith's *Illustrations of the British flora* and R.W. Butcher's *Further illustrations of British plants* (1930). The drawings (*c.*30 plates per part) of inflorescence, the plant's constituent parts and its general habit are of a high standard, and the reproductions are uniformly excellent. *Class No:* 581.1(410)

USA

[1155]

RICKETT, H.W. **Wild flowers of the United States.** New York, McGraw-Hill, 1966-75. 6v. and index. illus. (pl.), maps.

Publication of the New York Botanical Garden.

1. *The Northern states.* 1966. 2pts. 2. *The Southeastern states.* 1967. 2pts. 3. *Texas.* 1969. 2pts. 4. *The Southwestern states.* 1970. 2pts. 5. *The Northwestern states.* 1972. 6. *The Central mountains and plains.* 1973. 3pts. *Complete index.* 1975.

V.1 (2pts. 559p.) has 180 plates, with concise systematic description, plus distribution, facing. End-paper maps. Each volume carries an index. *Class No:* 581.1(73)

Australasia & Oceania

[1156]

HARRIS, T.Y. **Wild flowers of Australia.** 8th ed. London, Sydney, etc., Angus & Robertson, 1979. xiii, 207p. illus. (*Australian natural science library.*) ISBN: 0207136440.

First published 1938.

Part 1: Popular descriptions, with plates. Part 2: Key to the families of plants. Technical descriptions of plants, p.76-184. Glossary of botanical terms, p.185-94. Books of reference (24 titles). Names of authors and abbreviations. Analytical index, p.198-207. Descriptions face illus. A standard guide. *Class No:* 581.1(9)

Diseases

[1157]

BUCZACKI, S.T. and HARRIS, K.M. **Collins' guide to the pests, diseases and disorders of garden plants.** London, Collins, 1981. 512p. illus., (incl. col.). ISBN: 0002191032.

General introduction - A/Z key to symptoms - 24 col. plates (captions facing) - Pests (eelworms ... mammals), p.132-264 - Diseases (rusts ... viruses), p.267-471. - Disorders (mineral nutrient; non-nutritional disorders (*e.g.,* drought; pollution)). Data: symptoms; biology; treatment. Grouped bibliography, p.493-5. Glossary. Index, p.500-12. 'Highly practical, authoritative and free from waffle' (*Natural history book reviews*, v.6 (1/2), 1982, p.78).

Shorter guide to pests, diseases and disorders of garden plants (Collins, 1983. 320p. illus (incl. col.)) is by K.M. Harris, and others. *Class No:* 581.2

Economic Aspects

[1158]

UPHOF, J.C.T. **The Dictionary of economic plants.** 2nd ed. Lehre, Cramer, and New York, Stechert-Hafner, 1968. [viii], 591p.

First published 1959.

The 2nd. ed. adds over 3,000 species, bringing total different species of economic plants briefly described to 9,500. Entry is under Latin name, with reference from common name. Data on geographical distribution, products and principal uses. Bibliography, systematically arranged, p.453-91. Helpful group references (*e.g.,* from 'Confectionery, Plants used in'). A valued reference tool. *Class No:* 581.6

[1159]

—USHER, G. A Dictionary of plants used by man. London, Constable, 1974. 619p. ISBN: 0094579202.

Comparable in scope to Uphof. Main entries are under genera. While Usher is fuller than Uphof in providing cross-references from common names, Uphof is richer in local names and plants and their uses (*e.g.,* by North American Indians). *Class No:* 581.6

Systematic Botany (Categories of Plants)

Flowerless Plants (Cryptogams)

Algae, Seaweeds, etc.

[1160]

BRITISH MUSEUM (NATURAL HISTORY). Seaweeds of the British Isles. London, British Museum (Natural History), 1977-. diagrs., tables.

1. *Rhotophyta.* 1977-. (pt.1 1977. £13.75; pt.2A. 1983. £13). 2. *Chlorophyta.* (1991-. £27). 3. *Fucophyceae* (Phaeophyceae) (pt.1. 1987. £30). 4. *Tribophyceae* (Xanthophyceae) (1987. £7.50).

The result of many years' research carried out by the British Museum (Natural History) and the British Phycological Society. Bibliographical references. The series is to cover all the British and the majority of northern Atlantic seaweeds. Description of each species incorporates notes on ecology and distribution, plus 1 or more illus. *Class No:* 582.26

Fungi, Moulds

[1161]
AINSWORTH, G.C. **Ainsworth & Bisby's dictionary of the fungi.** 7th ed., by D.L. Hawksworth. Farnham Royal, Commonwealth Agricultural Bureaux, 1983. 412p. illus., diagrs., tables. ISBN: 0851985157.

First published 1943; 6th ed., 1971.

c.16,500 entries. Covers more than the taxonomy of the fungi; morphology, structure, spore types and various aspects of physiology, metabolism and ecology are also treated. 'The *Dictionary* is the place to begin any enquiry concerning the fungi,' (*Natural history book reviews,* v.7(3), 1984, p.169). *Class No: 582.28*

[1162]
AINSWORTH, G.C. *and* SUSSMAN, A.S., *eds.* **The Fungi: an advanced treatise.** New York & London, Academic Press, 1965-73. 4v. in 5.

1. *The fungal cell.* 1965. 748p. 2. *The fungal organism.* 1966. 805p. 3. *The fungal population. Ecology.* 1966. 738p. 4A. *A taxonomic review, with keys. Ascomycetes and fungi imperfecti.* 1973. 621p. 4B. *A taxonomic review with keys. Lower fungi and busiodimycetes.* 1973. 536p.

A well-documented treatise, the work of numerous specialist contributors. V.1, chapter 12. 'Carbohydrate metabolism' (p.302-47) has references, p.338-47. V.1 has author and subject indexes, index to fungi and actinomycetes. *Class No: 582.28*

Yeasts

[1163]
ROSE, A.H. *and* HARRISON, J.S., *eds.* **The Yeasts.** 2nd ed. London & New York, Acaedemic Press, 1987-91. 4v. ISBN: 0125964110, v.1; 0125964129, v.2; 0125964137, v.3; 0125964145, v.4.

Previously published in 3v., 1969-71.

1. *Biology of yeasts.* 1987. xii,423p. 2. *Yeasts and the environment.* 1987. xvi,309p. 3. *Metabolism and physiology of yeasts.* 1989. xxiv,635p. 4. *Yeast organelles.* 1991. xxx,765p.

17 contributors in v.4. Chapter 5: 'Cell walls', p.199-277 includes references (264-277). Author and analytical subject indexes. A detailed, authoritative, treatise. *Class No: 582.282*

Mushrooms & Toadstools

[1164]
LANGE, M. *and* MORA, F.B. **Collins' guide to mushrooms and toadstools;** with 96 colour plates from *Flora agaricina danica,* by J.E. Lange. London, Collins, 1963. 257p. illus. (col.).

A reliable handbook for rigid identification, thanks to ingenious keys and splendid illus. Bibliography, p.234-5. Index entries include descriptive notes. Some omitted species are noted in *Nature,* v.200, 10 November 1963, p.823. *Class No: 582.287*

[1165]
PHILLIPS, R. **Mushrooms and other fungi of Great Britain and Europe.** London, Ward Lock & Pan Books, 1981. 288p. illus. (col.). ISBN: 0330264419.

Contents: Introduction; Visual index; Glossary. Agarics - Gomphediaceae - Chanterelles - Bolates - Polypores - Ascomycetes. Bibliography, p.282. Full colour illus., with descriptive captions, identifying over 900 specimens, showing the various stages of growth. A handsome quarto that deserves a place in every public library at least. *Class No: 582.287*

Mosses

[1166]
WATSON, E.V. **British mosses and liverworts:** an introductory work, with full descriptions and figures of over 200 species and keys for the identification of all except the very rare species. 3rd ed. Cambridge Univ. Press, 1981. xviii, 519p. illus. (incl. pl.). ISBN: 0521285364.

First published 1955.

Main sequence: Musci (p.124-401); Hepaticae (p.401-498). Introduction includes notes on works of reference. Appended habit lists, p.1-24. Detailed index, p.511-9. Well illustrated, with descriptive captions. A standard work. *Class No: 582.34*

Vascular Plants

Ferns

[1167]
JONES, D.L. **Encyclopaedia of ferns:** an index to ferns, their structure, biology, economic importance, cultivation and propagation. London, British Museum (Natural History), 1987. xvii, 433p. illus. (incl. col.), diagrs. ISBN: 0565010190.

7 parts (1. Introduction; structure and botany of ferns - 2. The cultural requirements of ferns - 3. Pests, diseases and other ailments of ferns - 4. Propagation and hybridisation of ferns ... 6. Ferns to grow (p.202-385) - 7. Appendices (*e.g.,* Ferns for wet soils)). Glossary. Bibliography, p.417-20. Fern societies and study groups. Detailed index, p.422-33. 400 illus. (250 in colour). Well produced; by a professional Australian horticulturalist. *Class No: 582.350*

Flowering Plants (Seed Plants & Phanerogams)

Dictionaries

[1168]
WILLIS, J.C. **A Dictionary of flowering plants and ferns.** 8th ed., student ed., rev. by H.K.A. Shaw. Cambridge Univ. Press, 1985. xxii, 1245, lxvip. ISBN: 0321313953.

First published 1897.

Over 50,000 entries, giving for every genus an outline of its distribution, family and often some additional facts. 'It is good value and all serious students of botany should have a copy' (*Natural history book reviews,* v.8(2), 1986, p.115-6). *Class No: 582.4(038)*

Nomenclatures

[1169]
HUTCHINSON, J. **The Families of flowering plants,** arranged according to a new system based on their phylogeny. 3rd ed. Oxford, Clarendon Press, 1973. xviii, [1], 908p. illus., diagrs., tables, maps.

First published 1926.

Part 1: Dicotyledones (descriptions of orders and families of dicotyledones, with keys to genera of smaller families), p.153-634 - Part 2: Monocotyledones. Glossaries, p.126-8, p.906-7. 430 figures. Hutchinson (who died in 1972) rearranged the families of plants - under dicotyledones and monocotyledones - in ascending order. *Class No: 582.4(083.72)*

Grasses

[1170]

HUBBARD, C.E. Grasses: a guide to their structure, identification, uses and distribution in the British Isles. 3rd ed., revised by J.C.E. Hubbard. Harmondsworth, Penguin Books, 1984. 476p. illus. ISBN: 0140222790.

2nd ed. 1968 (462p.).

Description and illus. of individual grass, p.59-372, with text facing illus. page. Introduction includes 'Key for naming wild and agricultural grasses'. Appendices include 'The uses of grass' and a classification. Bibliography, p.47-52. Indexes to common and botanical names. A standard work.

International in scope is *Genera graminum: grasses of the world,* by W.D. Clayton and S.A. Renvoize (HM Stationery Office, 1986. 389p.). Containing 651 entries, data for each entry include bibliographic references; description; anatomy; habitat; geographical distribution. *Class No:* 582.542

59 Zoology

Zoology

Bibliographies

[1171]
BRITISH MUSEUM (NATURAL HISTORY). Animal identification: a reference guide. London, British Museum (Natural History); Chichester, Wiley, 1980. 3v. ISBN: 0471277657; 0471277665; 0471277673.

1. *Marine and brackish water animals;* edited by R.W. Sims, 1980. vi, 111p. £14.55. 2. *Terrestrial and freshwater animals,* (not insects); edited by R.W. Sims. 1980, x, 120p. £14.55 3. *Insects;* edited by D. Hollis. 1980. viii, 160p. £20.95.

Systematically arranged. V.3 (Insects, general) (Thysanura ... Hymenoptera), with regional grouping as necessary; *c.*4,500 references. 'This work should be of immense value to applied biologists, biologists working a poorly worked region of the world, expedition zoologists or amateur naturalist collecting on an overseas holiday' (*Natural history book reviews,* v.5(3/4), 1982, p.128-9). *Class No:* 590(01)

Dictionaries

[1172]
ALLABY, M., *ed.* **A Dictionary of zoology.** Oxford, University Press, 1991. viii,508p. ISBN: 0198661622.

Intended for the zoologist or zoology student, this reference work consists of *c.*8,000 entries, including cross-references. Definitions vary from 10-400 words, covering taxa (down to familial level for vertebrates, but with less complete coverage of other phyla); earth history; ecology; evolutionary concepts; genetics; physiology; taxonomic principles; zoogeography; as well as some biographical material on individuals distinguished in the science. Taxonomic names are given in Latin with common names cross-referenced. Comprehensive and workmanlike subject dictionary. *Class No:* 590(038)

Reviews & Abstracts

[1173]
The Zoological record, being the record of zoological literature relating to the year... York, BIOSIS, UK, and London, Zoological Society, 1865 (covering 1864)-. v.1-. Annual parts. ISSN: 01443607.

V.1-6 as *Record of zoological literature;* v.43-52 (1906-15) formed Section N of the *International catalogue of scientific literature.* Since v.115 (covering 1978) published jointly by BIOSIS UK and the Society.

1. *Comprehensive zoology.* 2. *Protozoa* (1. Recent; 2. Fossil). 3. *Porifera.* 4. *Coelenterata.* 5. *Echinodermata.* 6. *Platyhelminthes, annelida, conodonta* (A,B,C). 7. *Brachiopoda.* 8. *Bryozoa* (Polyzoa). 9. *Mollusca.* 10. *Crustacea* (1. Recent; 2. Fossil). 11. *Trilobita.* 12. *Arachnida.* 13. *Insecta* (A,B,C,D,E,F). 14. *Protochordata.* 15.

....(contd.)
Pisces (1. Recent; 2. Fossil). 16. *Amphibia.* 17. *Reptilia.* 18. *Aves.* 19. *Mammalia.* 20. *List of new genera and subgenera.*

About 80,000 references pa. (27 parts). Each part consists of author list of papers and books, with subject, geographic, palaeontological and systeamtic indexes. The most important record for retrospective searching in systematic zoology (including palaeontology). Online database, 1978-, via DIALOG, BRS. *Class No:* 590(048)

Nomenclatures

[1174]
International code of zoological nomenclature. 3rd ed. London, International Trust for Zoological Nomenclature, in association with British Museum (Natural History), etc., 1985. xx, 338p. ISBN: 085301003x.

Adopted by the 20th General Assembly of the International Union of Biological Sciences. Previous ed., 1964.

The Code (in French and English facing) occupies 18 sections, p.3-179. Appendices A-F include A. Code of ethics; D. Recommendations on the formation of names. Glossary, p.251-97. Index of scientific names; English index. The new Code came into force on 1 January 1983. An important key. *Class No:* 590(083.72)

Zoos

[1175]
International zoo yearbook. London, Zoological Society of London, 1961-. Annual. ISSN: 00749664.

V.29, 1990 (vii,412p.) has 3 sections by various hands: 1. Horticulture in zoos (p.1-52) - 2. New developments in the zoo world (p.53-243: nutrition; exhibits; breeding and reproduction; housing; animal welfare) - 3. Reference section (*e.g.* Species of fishes bred in captivity during 1987 and multiple generation births; Census of rare animals in captivity 1988). Appendix 1: Taxonomic authorities consulted in the *Yearbook.* Author index, v.27-29; Subject index, v.27-29. Articles are documented. *Class No:* 590:061.3

Animals (Fauna)

Handbooks & Manuals

[1176]
GRZIMEK, B., *ed.* **Grzimek's animal life encyclopedia.** New York, London, etc., Van Nostrand Reinhold, 1972-74. 13v. illus., maps.

Originally Kindler Verlag AG, Zurich, 1966-70.

About 150 contributors, mostly German. Coverage: v.1. Lower animals - v.2. Insects - 3. Mollusks - 4/5. Fishes. Amphibians - 6. Reptiles - 7/9. Birds - 10/13. Mammals. Each volume has an index and appendices (including a

....(contd.)
four-language dictionary in English, German, French and Russian; conversion tables; supplementary readings). Well illustrated. 'Emphasis is on what animals do, their habitats, behaviour, feeding and breeding biology ... Anatomy, physiology and ethnology take second place' (*TLS*, no.3669, 23 June 1972, p.729). 'The single most complete source on the animal kingdom' (*RQ*, v.25 (1), Fall 1985, p.146). *Class No:* 591.1(035)

[1177]
Remarkable animals: a unique encyclopaedia of wildlife wonders. Sundén, U., *ed.* Enfield, Middx., Guinness Superlatives Ltd., 1987. 239p. illus. (col.). ISBN: 085112867x.
Contents: Mammals (p.7-81) - Birds (p.82-129) - Fishes (p.130-65) - Amphibians and reptiles (p.166-205) - Insects and arachnids (p.206-35). Popular, almost sensationalistic, treatment of zoology, but well-produced and highly readable. *Class No:* 591.1(035)

Behaviour

[1178]
The Audubon Society encyclopedia of animal life. Buettmer, G., *ed.* New York, Clarkson Potter (distributed by Crown), 1982. 606p. illus. (incl. col.).
6 major sections (Animals; Birds; Reptiles; Amphibians; Fishes; Invertebrates), subdivided mostly by families. Data on physical characteristics, social habits, range, habitat and reproductive behaviour. Over 1,000 illus., well captioned and cross-referenced from text. 'Even libraries that own the 13v. Grzimek (1972) will want this harmony of words and pictures' (*Wilson library bulletin*, January 1983, p.428). *Class No:* 591.5

Geographic Distribution of Animals

[1179]
KERRICH, G.J, *and others, eds.* **Keyworks to the fauna and flora of the British Isles and Northwestern Europe.** London, Systematics Association, 1978. xii, 179p.
First published 1942.
About 2,500 entries, with occasional annotations, covering books and periodical articles. Systematic arrangement. Supersedes the Systematics Association's *Bibliography of key works for the identification of the British fauna and flora*, by J. Smart and G. Taylor (1953). No index. For more specialized scientific libraries. 'Graduate and professional levels' (*Choice*, v.16(1), March 1979, p.54,56). *Class No:* 591.9

[1180]
LEVER, C. **The Naturalized animals of the British Isles.** London, Hutchinson, 1977. 600p. illus., tables, maps. ISBN: 0091277906.
4 parts (59 sections): 1. Mammals - 2. Birds - 3. Amphibians and reptiles - 4. Fish. Section 29: 'Mandarin ducks', p.282-98 (with 2 illus., 1 location map). Chronological table of introduction of animals. Chapter bibliography, p.521-56; general bibliography, p.557-8. Indexes of people, species and places. End-paper maps. 'The first comprehensive account of the exotic vertebrates of the British Isles' (*Foreword*). 'A work of formidable scholarship' (*British book news*, January 1986, p.37). *Class No:* 591.9

Systematic Zoology (Categories of Animals)

Invertebrates

[1181]
BARNES, R.D. **Invertebrate zoology.** 5th ed. Philadelphia, Pa., W.B. Saunders, 1987. ix, 893p. illus., diagrs. ISBN: 003008914x.
First published 1963.
A textbook on major, minor and even some fossil invertebrate phyla. Reduction of c.170p. on the 4th ed., although new material is incorporated, plus an expanded glossary, index and 'boxed essays' on topics. Each of the 20 chapters has an appended bibliography, sometimes briefly annotated. Authoritative, readable and finely illustrated by photographs and drawings. 'So Barnes is better than ever, though it's still the case that only 3 per cent of the space is given to the insect' (*Nature*, v.332, 10 March 1988, p.184). *Class No:* 592.0

Molluscs. Shellfish & Shells

[1182]
The Macdonald encyclopedia of shells. London, Macdonald, 1982. 512p. col. illus., tables, maps. ISBN: 0356085759.
5 chapters: Soft surface mollusks (entries 1-133) - Firm surface mollusks (134-221) - Coral dwellers (222-302) - Other marine mollusks (303-35) - Land and fresh water mollusks (336-57). Classified table of the species mentioned in text. Glossary. Detailed index of entries, p.503-12. Data on appearance, size, geographical occurrence and ecological environment; symbols roughly indicate dimensions. Small format. 1,230 col. illus.; distribution maps. *Class No:* 594

Spiders

[1183]
ROBERTS, M.J. **The Spiders of Great Britain and Ireland.** Colchester, Essex, Harley Books, 1985. 3v. (2v. of text; v.3: Colour plates). ISBN: 0946589054, v.1; 0946589062, v.2; 0946589070, v.3.
1. *Atypidae - Therdiosomatidae.* 1985. 250p. 2. *Linyphiidae.* 3. *Colour plates.* 1985. 250p.
V.1 includes a general introduction to arachnology, including morphology and behaviour, classification and nomenclature. V.3 has 237 colour plates illustrating 307 species (in some cases, both sexes). An authoritative textbook for identification, supplementing both J. Blackwall's pioneer work, *A history of the spiders of Great Britain and Ireland* (1861-64). and *British spiders*, by G.H. Locket and A.F. Millidge. *Class No:* 595.4

Insects

Bibliographies

[1184]
GILBERT, P. *and* HAMILTON, C.J. **Entomology: a guide to information sources.** 2nd ed. London, Mansell, 1990. [viii],259p. ISBN: 0720120527.
First published 1983.
8 chapters: 1. Introduction - 2. Naming and identification of insects - 3. Specimens and collections - 4. The literature of entomology (p.72-147: primary journals; review journals; monograph series) - 5. Searching and locating the literature - 6. Keeping up with current events (newsletters, c.80 entries) - 7. Entomologists and their organizations - 8. Miscellaneous services (translation services and guides; apicultural information). 1,822 entries for books, periodical articles, journals and organizations. Detailed analytical index, p.243-59. Of the 1st ed., 'A most useful reference work, well ordered, judiciously annotated ...' (*Natural history book reviews*, v.7(3), 1984, p.156). *Class No:* 595.7(01)

Handbooks & Manuals

[1185]
IMMS, A.D. Imms' general textbook of entomology. 10th ed,
by O.W. Richards, and R.G. Davies. London, Chapman &
Hall, 1977. 2v. (1354p.).
9th ed. 1964 (London, Methuen).
1. *Anatomy and physiology. Development and
metamorphosis.* 2. *The orders [1-29] of insects.*
A comprehensive treatise, well documented (*e.g.*, v.2.
Order 26; Diptera, p.951-1071, has bibliography, p.1046-71).
Detailed index to v.2 (p.1281-1304), including authors of
articles. 'A workmanlike updating by two of the most
experienced general entomologists of the day' (*Journal of
natural history*, v.12(2), March/April 1978, p.233). *Class
No:* 595.7(035)

[1186]
ROYAL ENTOMOLOGICAL SOCIETY OF LONDON.
Handbooks for the identification of British insects. London,
the Society, 1949-. 11v. illus.
1. 16pts. (General introduction. Thysanura ...
Siphonaptera). 1949-57. 2. *Hemiptera.* 8pts. 1965-84. 3.
Lepidoptera. 4/5. *Coleoptera.* 15pts. 1952-77. 6/8.
Hymenoptera. 5pts. 1951-78 9/10. *Diptera.* 10pts. 1949-88.
11. *Check list of British insects.* 2nd ed. 5pts. 1964-78.
A detailed, invaluable series, with clear illus., systematic
descriptions, and bibliographies. Indispensable for
entomologists. *Class No:* 595.7(035)

Reviews & Abstracts

[1187]
Entomology abstracts. Bethesda, Md., Cambridge Scientific
Abstracts, 1969-. Monthly. $465pa. ISSN: 00138924.
About 950 abstracts per issue. Sections: General.
Bibliography - Systematics - Techniques - Morphology -
Physiology, anatomy, histology & biochemistry -
Reproduction & development - Behaviour, biology &
ecology - Genetics - Evolution - Geography & present-day
faunas - Fossil forms & faunas. Notification of proceedings.
Book notices. Detailed author and subject indexes per issue.
Reprinted from *Biological abstracts,* with its BIOSIS
PREVIEWS database. Available on CD-ROM. *Class No:*
595.7(048)

Europe

[1188]
CHINERY, M. A Field guide to the insects of Britain and
Northern Europe. 2nd ed. London, Collins, 1976. 352p.
illus. (mostly col.). ISBN: 0002192160.
First published 1962.
Preliminary text concerns the biology of insects, collecting
and preserving, classification, and a key to the orders of
European insects. Two main orders - Apterygote and
Pterygote - are then considered in detail. Glossary, p.323-
36; bibliography (grouped, p.337-41). Entomological
suppliers. Detailed index (in tiny print). Over 1,000 illus.
(788 in colour). Small format. *Class No:* 595.7(4)

Butterflies & Moths

[1189]
D'ABRERA, B. Butterflies of the world. Faringdon, Oxon., &
Melbourne, Lansdowne Editions, 1977-. 5v. illus., maps.
1. *Butterflies of the Australian region.* 1971. 2nd ed.
1977-. 415p. 2. *Butterflies of the Afro-tropical region.* 1980.
593p. 3. *Butterflies of the Neo-tropical region.* 1981. 4pts.
4. *Butterflies of the Oriental region.* 5. *Butterflies of the
Holarctic region.*
V.1 includes New Zealand, Papua, New Guinea, Timor,
Solomon Islands, and surrounding areas. Arranged in

....(contd.)
taxonomic sequence. Lavishly illustrated. Bibliography,
p.397-4001. Index, p.403-15. No geographical index. Only 3
maps. Large format. An identification guide, produced
without access to collections held by the Commonwealth
Scientific and Industrial Research Organisation, Canberra.
Class No: 595.78

[1190]
HEATH, J. and others. The Moths and butterflies of Great
Britain and Ireland. Colchester, Essex, Harley Books, 1976-.
illus. (incl. col.), maps.
V.1. *Micropterigidae to heliozelidae.* 1976. 343p. V.2.
Cossidae to heliodinidae. 1985. 460p. V.7. Pt.1 *Hesperiidae
to nymphalidae.* 1987. 370p. V.7. Pt.2. *Lasiocampidae to
thyatiridae.* 1991. 400p. V.9. *Sphingidae to noctuidae.* 1983.
288p. V.10. *Noctuidae (Cuculliinae to hypeninae) and
agaristidae.* 1983. 459p.
Projected in 11v. V.10: *Noctuidae (part 2) and
Agaristidae* (1983) features 225 distribution maps (although
lacking a situation map covering the whole area) and 13
superb colour plates, with 23 text figures. A check list of
species is not included. 'Despite these criticisms, this
volume *is* a definitive work and is far superior to anything
currently available on the group, although the price may be
prohibitive' (*Natural history book reviews*, v.7(3), 1984,
p.157-9). V.1,2,7,9 and 10 have so far appeared. Aims 'to
provide a complete, fully illustrated, and up-to-date work of
identification' (*Introduction*). A standard work. *Class No:*
595.78

Vertebrates

[1191]
YOUNG, J.Z. The Life of vertebrates. 3rd ed. Oxford,
Clarendon Press, 1981. xx, 645p. illus., diagrs., graphs.
ISBN: 0198571720.
First published 1950.
33 chapters. Includes the embryology, anatomy,
physiology, biochemistry, palaeontology and ecology of all
vertebrates. 'The whole book is organized around the theme
that mechanisms of homeostasis have become increasingly
more complex during vertebrate evolution, allowing life to
continue under conditions not possible before' (*Preface to
the third edition*). Chapter references, p.586-608. Author
index; analytical subject index (p.613-43). *Class No:* 596

Fishes

[1192]
NELSON, J. Fishes of the world. 2nd ed. New York, Wiley,
1984. 523p. illus., maps. ISBN: 0471864757.
First published 1976.
Systematic treatment of fishes, - orders, sub-orders and
families, and listing genera. Anatomical data; ecological
status, 45 distribution maps of classes/families worldwide.
The clear drawings are well linked to the text. Readership:
museum systematists (for the classification) and 'fishery
biologists whose trade is population dynamics' (*Nature*,
v.312, 13 December 1984, p.679). *Class No:* 597

[1193]
WHEELER, A. The World encyclopedia of fishes. London,
Macdonald, 1985. xiv, 368p. illus. (incl. col.). ISBN:
0356107159.
Describes nearly 1,500 species individually (A-Z), with
entry under scientific names. Data include size, distribution
and colour. Glossary and plates (96p.) precede. These
colour plates - 50 in all - are arranged in systematic order
of families. Some 700 fine line-drawings in text. The
author, Principal Scientific Officer at the British Museum
(Natural History). *Class No:* 597

ZOOLOGY

Reptiles & Amphibians

[1194]
ARNOLD, E.N. *and* BURTON, J.A. **A Field guide to the reptiles and amphibians of Britain and Europe.** London, Collins, 1978. 272p. illus. (incl. col. pl.). ISBN: 0002193183.

Coverage is Europe west of Moscow. 5 sections: Salamanders and newts; Frogs and toads; Tortoises, terrapins and sea turtles; Lizards and amphisbaenians (7 areas); Snakes. Glossary, p.243-7; Bibliography (grouped), p.248-52. 126 small distribution maps. 35 illus. (257 in colour). Concise, synoptic text, but remarkably readable. 'This book is a very real contribution to herpetology and will be of great value not only to the travelling naturalist but to all students of the subject' (*Journal of natural history*, v.19(1), January/February 1979, p.126). *Class No:* 598.1

[1195]
FROST, D.R., *ed.* **Amphibian species of the world:** a taxonomic and geographical reference. Lawrence, Kansas, Allen Press, and the Association of Systematics Collections, 1985. 732p. ISBN: 0942924118.

Data on 4,014 named species, with taxonomic index. 'Compiled for the Parties to the Convention on International Trade in Endangered Species of Wild Fauna and Flora to serve as a standard reference to amphibian nomenclature ...' *Class No:* 598.1

Snakes

[1196]
MATTISON, C. **Snakes of the world.** Poole, Dorset, Blandford Press, 1986. 190p. illus. (mostly col.), chart, maps. £10.95. ISBN: 0713714638.

9 chapters (2. Size, shape and function - 3. Colour and markings - 4. Reproduction - 5. Food and feeding ... 7. Ecology and behaviour ... 9. Snake families (p.124-79)). Bibliography, p.180-3 (5 sections, each with short introduction). Detailed analytical index to text and illus. Well balanced, with good quality illustrations. *Class No:* 598.12

[1197]
PARKER, H.W. **Snakes - a natural history.** 2nd ed., rev. and enlarged, by A.G.C. Grandison. London, British Museum (Natural History), with Ithaca, N.Y., Cornell Univ. Press, 1977. iv, 108p. illus. (incl. col. pl.). ISBN: 0565056387.

Replaces his *Natural history of snakes* (1965). Includes glossary and bibliography. 16p. of colour plates; 29 figures. 'The illustrations are quite outstanding' (*Journal of natural history*, v.11(8), November/December 1977, p.719). *Class No:* 598.12

Birds

Encyclopaedias & Dictionaries

[1198]
CAMPBELL, B. *and* LACK, E., *eds.* **A Dictionary of birds.** Calton, England, T. & A.D. Poyser, for the British Ornithologists' Union, 1985. 670p. illus. ISBN: 0856610399.

Contributed by *c.*280 specialists. Entries, A-Z, are under English names of birds chosen. Data: definition; general characteristics; mode of life, distribution; familial taxonomy, 'Cuckoo': p.123-6, with 6 references; 'Poetry, Birds in': p.475-8, with 15 references. Many cross-references. Over 500 photographs, drawings, etc. (*Nature*, v.317, 3 October 1985, p.392, finds the drawings disappointing, failing to complement the text.) The *Dictionary* is in line of succession from A. Newton and H. Gadow's *Dictionary of birds*. Intended as a greatly expanded updating of H.F.

....(contd.)
Witherby's *Handbook of British birds* (London, Witherby, 1938-41. 5v. illus., maps). The illus. are a definite improvement on Witherby's tiny quarter-page illus. 'Highly recommended for college, university and public libraries' (*Choice*, v.23(5), January 1986, p.724-5). *Class No:* 598.2(03)

Tables & Data Books

[1199]
HOWARD, R. *and* MOORE, A. **A Complete checklist of the birds of the world.** 2nd ed. London, Academic Press, 1991. xxxiv,622p. ISBN: 0123569109.

Arranged by orders and families, Struthioniformes ... Passeriformes, p.1-542. References, by families, p.8-47. Indexes of Latin and English names, p.543-622. As a checklist, goes down to subspecies. Preceded by J.L. Peters' *Checklist of birds of the world* (1931-87. 16v.) which it, in part, updates, but lacks Peters' taxonomic notes, references and distribution notes. *Class No:* 598.2(083)

Worldwide

[1200]
CRAMP, S. *and* SIMMONS, K.E.L., *and others, eds.* **Handbook of the birds of Europe, the Middle East and North Africa:** the birds of the Western Palearctic. Oxford Univ. Press, 1977-. col. illus., diagrs., tables, maps.

1. *Ostrich to Ducks.* [ix], 722p. 1977. £70. 2. *Hawks to Bustards.* 696p. 1980. £70. 3. *Waders to Gulls.* 1000p. 1983. £70. 4. *Terns to Woodpeckers.* 970p. 1985. £70. 5. *Tyrant flycatchers to Thrushes.* 800p. 1987. £75.

The Western Palearctic includes all Europe, plus the Middle East to Turkey, Iraq and Jordan, and North Africa down to 19°N. The 7v. will describe all 795 species of birds, of which *c.*600 are breeding species. V.1 has 56 colour plates and 350 text figures. The text consists mainly of accounts of species, under orders. 'Mute swan' (*cygnus olor*) occupies, p.372-9, with 1 col. pl., 8 other illus., 2 distribution maps. Field characteristics: Habitat, distribution, population, movement, social pattern and behaviour, voice, breeding, plumages, etc. Plates include illus. of eggs and nest down. References, p.701-14; glossary; index. *Class No:* 598.2(100)

[1201]
SIBLEY, C.G. *and* MONROE, B.L., *Jr.* **Distribution and taxonomy of birds of the world.** New Haven; London, Yale University Press, 1990. xxiv,1111p. maps. ISBN: 0300049692.

Taxonomic listing covering 9,672 living species of birds. Data in each species entry include scientific name; author of the name and year of description; standardized English name; coded world number; a brief description of preferred habitats; detailed description of species distribution; alternative common names. Also contains a world numbers cross-listing, 24 maps, gazetteer, p.875-906, bibliography, p.907-39 and an index which includes common and scientific names. Authoritative. *Class No:* 598.2(100)

Europe

[1202]
PETERSON, R., *and others.* **A Field guide to the birds of Britain and Europe.** London, Collins, 1983. 239p.

First published 1954.
77 colour plates, with brief data facing, depict more than 1100 birds of 505 species. Main sequence: Divers ... Buntings. p.36-210. Prelims. 'How to identify books', 'European check-list', 'The ornithological societies'. 362 small distribution maps. Index, p.227-39. Small format.

176

SECOND EDITION

....*(contd.)*
Excludes CIS. 'Basic stock item for all libraries and schools' (*Library world*, March 1966, p.279, on the 1965 ed.). *Class No:* 598.2(4)

Great Britain

[1203]
BANNERMAN, D.A. The Birds of the British Isles. Edinburgh & London, Oliver & Boyd, 1952-63. 12v. illus. (pl.), maps.

Systematically arranged. Entry for each bird species includes notes on identification, occurrence in Britain, distribution, habits and migration, breeding and nesting habits. The accurately coloured plates are a feature, each volume containing about 30 such plates. Footnote references. V.12 includes a short comparative list of Celtic bird-names of the British Isles (p.405-23), and an index of scientific names in the 12v. A classic work. *Class No:* 598.2(410)

[1204]
—**WITHERBY, H.F.,** *ed.* **The Handbook of British birds.** London, Witherby, 1938-41. 5v. illus., maps.

Arranged by families. For each species details concern habitat, characteristics, distribution (in Britain and abroad), and descriptions, plus a col. illus. 520 numbered entries. V.5 includes general indexes of English and scientific names in the 5v., and each volume has an index of English names and a glossary of terms. 'A standard work of reference for British and, indeed, European ornithologists' (*Nature*, v.196, 17 November 1962, p.610). *Class No:* 598.2(410)

America—North & Central

[1205]
The Audubon Society encyclopedia of North American birds. Terres, J.K. New York, Knopf, 1980. 1109p. illus. (incl. col.). ISBN: 0394466519.

A compendium on the 847 species of birds recorded in the USA and Canada. About 6,000 entries, A-Z, on the life histories of the bird species, biographical notes on American ornithologists, articles on avian biology (*e.g.*, courtship, migration, song), definitions of terms, organizations. Full cross-references. Bibliography. 'By far the most ambitious and extensive book of its kind' (*Reference books for small and medium-sized libraries* 4th ed. ALA, 1984, item 1064). *Class No:* 598.2(71/73)

Mammals

Encyclopaedias

[1206]
Grzimek's encyclopedia of mammals. Grzimek, B., *ed.* New York, McGraw-Hill Publishing Company, 1990. 5v. illus. maps. ISBN: 0079095089, set.

Based on *Grzimek's animal life encyclopedia (q.v.)*.
More than 200 contributors. Entries in each volume are arranged by order and suborder. Each entry has an introductory section, with a map showing geographical distribution, followed by chapters discussing specific families or species. Standardized summary charts include data on scientific name; number of species and sub-species; size; life span; food; habitat; enemies. Outstanding feature is the 3,500 colour photographs which have been laser-scanned. Bibliography and index at the end of each volume, although there is no index for the complete set. Recommended for school, public and academic libraries. *Class No:* 599(031)

Handbooks & Manuals

[1207]
MACDONALD, D., *ed.* **The Encyclopedia of mammals.** London, Allen & Unwin; New York, Facts on File, 1984. 2v. (895, xxxi, xxxiip.). col. illus.; col. diagrs. ISBN: 004500028x.

About 200 contributors in all. 1: The carnivores (7 families: the cat family ... the hyena family), sea mammals, primates, etc. V.2 covers herbivores, insectivores, bats and marsupials. Each quarto volume carries a grouped bibliography, glossary and analytical index. The entry 'Squirrel': p.612-27; 25 col. illus; 2 col. diagrs. 1,200 col.illus., superbly presented. 'Its main market is likely to be naturalists, yet the technical detail should appeal to students and biologists' (*British book news*, February 1985, p.100, on v.2). *Class No:* 599(035)

Tables & Data Books

[1208]
HONACKI, J.H., *and others, comps. & eds.* **Mammal species of the world:** a taxonomic and geographic reference. With the assistance and cooperation of the American Society of Mammalogists. Lawrence, Kansas, Association of Systematics Collections, in conjunction with Allen Press, 1981. 694p.

Compiled for the Parties to the Convention on International Trade in Endangered Species of Wild Fauna and Flora.

Lists *c.*4,170 specis, in taxonomic order. Data: scientific name and authority; type locality; geographical distribution; legal status of endangered species and controlled species. Bibliography of cited sources. Taxonomic index. Aims to provide a standard reference to mammalian nomenclature. *Class No:* 599(083)

Worldwide

[1209]
CORBET, G.B. *and* **HILL, J.E. A World list of mammalian species.** 3rd ed. Oxford, University Press; Natural History Museum Publications, 1991. viii,243p. figs. ISBN: 0198540175.

First published 1980.
Systematic list of 4,327 species. Data: Latin name; common name; distribution. Bibliography (general works; geographical sources; taxonomic sources), p.213-31. Detailed index, p.232-43. *Class No:* 599(100)

[1210]
NOWAK, R.M. *and* **PARADISO, J.L. Walker's mammals of the world.** 4th ed. Baltimore, Md., Johns Hopkins Press, 1983. 2v. (1362, xlvi, viiip.) illus., charts, tables.

First published 1964.
V.1: Monotremata ... Rodentia; v.2: Rodentia ... Artiodactyla. V.2 includes a bibliography of literature cited, p.1307-62 (A-Z authors), - a major contribution. V.1 has an analytical index of orders, families and genera, with bold type for scientific names. Numerous black-and-white illus. (*c.*1 per page), substantial revision of a classic. 'This monumental work is indispensable' (*Library journal*, 15 April 1984, p.784). A 5th ed. was published in 1991. *Class No:* 599(100)

Europe

[1211]
CORBET, G. *and* OVENDEN, D. The Mammals of Britain and Europe. London, Collins, 1980. 253p. illus. ISBN: 000219774x.

'Includes all species of mammals that occur in a wild state in Europe West of the USSR, including Spitzbergen and Iceland, and in the northeastern Atlantic north of 35 degrees north' (*Preface*). Excludes extinct species of the region. Colour plates and drawings of 190 species are followed by 15 sections: 1. Tracks and signs - 2. Skulls and teeth - 3. Antlers and horns - 4. Marsupials - 5. Insectivores - 6. Lagomorpha - 7. Rodents - 8. Primates - 9. Carnivores - 10. Pinnipedes - 11. Odd-toed ungulates - 12. Even-toed ungulates - 13. Cetaceans - 14. Checklist of European mammals - 15. Mammals in Britain and Ireland (plus distribution maps of British and Irish species). *Class No:* 599(4)

Great Britain

[1212]
CORBET, G.B. *and* HARRIS, S. The Handbook of British mammals. 3rd ed. Oxford, Blackwell Scientific Publications for the Mammal Society, 1991. xiv,588p. illus., maps. ISBN: 0632016914.

First published 1964 (edited by H.N. Southern).

An extensive revision of the previous edition. A systematic account of the 98 species known to be feral in the British Isles and surrounding seas. Data include: recognition; sign; description; relationships; measurements; variation; distribution; habitat; feeding; population. 3 appendices: 1. Extinct species - 2. Ephemeral introductions and escapes - 3. Sound recordings. Items in the bibliographies appended to each chapter total 3,186. Glossary, list of abbreviations and index. 'It will definitely be the standard work for the next two decades' (*Reference reviews*, v.5(2), 1991, p.24). *Class No:* 599(410)

Whales, etc.

[1213]
WATSON, L. Sea guide to whales of the world. London, etc., Hutchinson, 1981. 302p. illus. (col.), charts, maps. ISBN: 0091466008.

7 chapters: 1. Cetology and cetologists - 2. The origin and distribution of whales - 3. Description - 4. Standard cetaceans - 5. Natural history - 6. Status [population] - 7. Distribution. 3 appendices (3. Biography, p.285-6: 100 selected 2-4 line notes). Bibliography, 287-97 (A/Z; including many periodical articles). 76 species are listed, p.10-11; 96 species illus., 167 col. diagrs., 82 distribution maps (for dolphins and purpoises, as well as whales). Non-analytical index, p.298-302. 'An outstanding work' (*Library journal*, 1 February 1982, p.249). *Class No:* 599.5

Primates

[1214]
NAPIER, J.R. *and* NAPIER, P.H. A Handbook of the living primates. London & New York, Academic Press, 1967. xiv, 456p. illus. (pl.), tables.

Three parts: 1. Functional morphology of primates - 2. Profiles of primate genera - 3. Supplementary and comparative data (*e.g.*, taxonomy and nomenclature; habitats of primates; limbs and locomotion). References (A/Z authors; *c.*900 items), p.417-46. 113 plates. Index to illus. and plates, p.447-56. 'A work of great scholarship' (*Science journal*, v.4(3), March 1969, p.92). *Class No:* 599.8

Apes & Monkeys

[1215]
TUTTLE, R.H. Apes of the world: their social behavior, communication, mentality and ecology. Park Ridge, N.J., Noyes, 1987. 421p. illus, tables. ISBN: 0815511043.

Data provide readable, succinct accounts of the taxonomy, locomotion, feeding, nesting, tool use, cognition and communication, sociobiology. Extensive bibliography. 'Tuttle has written a scholarly work that could serve as a standard reference for many years'. (*Nature*, v.328, August 1987, p.678). *Class No:* 599.82

6 TECHNOLOGY

Biotechnology

[1216]
BAJAY, Y.P.S., *and others*. Biotechnology in agriculture and forestry. Berlin, etc., Springer Verlag, 1986-. illus., micrographs, tables. ISBN: 0387518096.

An important, comprehensive work. So far (1986-91) 16v. have appeared. Trees (1986-91. 3v.); Crops (1986-88. 2v.); Potato (1987); Medical and cosmetic plants (1988-91. 3v.); Plant, protophasts and genetic engineering (1989. 3v.); Legumes and oilseed crops (1990-); Somaclonal variation in crop improvement (1990-); Wheat (1990); Rice (1990). Full sub-section references. Each volume carries a subject index. *Class No:* 6:573

[1217]
COOMBS, J. The International biotechnology directory, 1991. Alston, Y.R. 7th ed. Basingstoke, Macmillan, 1990. xv,674p. ISBN: 0333538870.

Covers Western Europe, North America, Brazil, Australasia and Japan. 3 parts: International organizations and information services - Government organizations and societies - Companies and organization; products and areas of research (by country, A-Z). Indexes: Companies; buyers' guide; products. *Class No:* 6:573

[1218]
Current biotechnology abstracts. Nottingham, Royal Society of Chemistry, 1983-. Monthly. ISSN: 02643391.

About 5000 abstracts pa. 4 parts (15 sections): Technocommunications (*e.g.*, 2. Legal issues and safety) - Techniques (*e.g.*, Fermentation technology) - Industrial areas (8. Pharmaceutics; 9. Energy production; 10. Agriculture; 11. Chemical industry; 12. Food) - Information (14. Forthcoming events; 15. Books, reviews, etc.). Subject, substance, and company indexes per issue and annually. No author index. Online access: CURRENT BIOTECH, DATA-STAR. Worldwide coverage of relevant patents and journals. *Class No:* 6:573

[1219]
DOWNS, L.J. The Biotechnology marketing sourcebook. London, British Library, Science Reference and Information Service, Biotechnology Information Service, 1990. [iv],137p.

Introduction - Record structure - Alphabetical list of journals (p.1-120; 251 titles) - Publishers' addresses - Keyword index. The first of a new series. Worldwide listing of 251 English-language periodicals, newsletters and abstracts for workers in 'biotechnology, the life sciences, health care, biochemistry and related fields' (*Introduction*). Details include advertising contact/scope/readership. For marketing managers, science, technology and medical publishers, conference organizers and information officers. *Class No:* 6:573

[1220]
EUESDEN, M., *ed*. Introduction to biotechnology information. London, British Library, Science Reference and Information Service, 1991. 90p. ISBN: 0712307621.

5 sections: 1. Scientific information - 2. Biotechnology - patents - 3. Online databases - 4. British official publications - 5. Business information in biotechnology. 9 appendices, A-I (I: Further reading). Detailed, analytical index, p.83-88. *Class No:* 6:573

Technology

Abbreviations & Symbols

[1221]
PUGH, E., *comp*. Pugh's Dictionary of acronyms and abbreviations: abbreviations in management, technology and information science. 5th ed. London, Library Association Publishing, 1987. ISBN: 0853655375.

First published 1968.

More than 28,000 entries, stating country of origin or organization, as considered necessary. Unlike the wide-ranging *Acronyms, initialisms and abbreviations dictionary* with its 500,000 odd terms, plus *International acronyms, initialisms and abbreviations dictionary* (2nd ed. Gale, 1987), for terms of foreign origin, Pugh concentrates largely on management, technology and information science. *Class No:* 60(003)

Reviews & Abstracts

[1222]
Applied science and technology index. New York, H.W. Wilson, 1913-. 11pa.; quarterly, annual cumulations. ISSN: 00036986.

As *Industrial arts index*, 1913-57.

Subject index to *c*.350 English-language journals, mostly US. Closely subdivided (*e.g.*, 'Electronics industry' (December 1991: 15 subject and country subheadings, plus cross-references). Appended 'Book reviews'. Selection of periodicals for indexing ... is accomplished by subscriber vote. Time-lag about 4 months. Also available online in WILSONLINE, covering the H.W. Wilson index series and via BRS; CD-ROM. *Class No:* 60(048)

[1223]
Current contents: Engineering, technology & applied sciences. Philadelphia, Pa., Institute for Scientific Information, 1975-. Weekly. ISSN: 00957917.

Preceded by *Current contents: Engineering & technology*. (1970-74).

Reproduces contents pages of *c*.100 journal issues each week, covering some 700 journals during the year. 13 disciplines (*e.g.*, management, aerospace, chemistry, metallurgy, nuclear power, optics and acoustics). Prelim.

....(contd.)
pages note journal coverage changes, book announcements, etc. Title index; author index, plus address dictionary; publishers address directory. *Class No:* 60(048)

[1224]
Current technology index. London, Bowker-Saur, 1981-. 6pa., with annual cumulation. ISSN: 02606593.
Formerly *British technology index*, 1962-80. Published by the Library Association until 1990.
Indexes *c.*20,000 items pa. Arranged under subjects/topics A-Z. A feature is the use of chain subject headings (*e.g.,* 'Petroleum, Pipelines, Repair, Freezing, Carbon dioxide' - virtually a highly compressed descriptive annotation). Coverage: general technology, applied sciences, engineering, chemical technology, manufactures and technical services. 316 journals are currently scanned. Time lag: 5-7 weeks. *CTI* is available online through DIALOG and on CD-ROM. *Class No:* 60(048)

Histories

[1225]
HERRING, S.D. From the Titanic to the Challenger: an annotated bibliography on technological failures of the twentieth century. New York, Garland, 1989. 486p. ISBN: 0824030435.
Evaluative annotations; indicates inclusions of photographs/drawings. 'Has no comparable equivalent' (*RQ,* v.29(3), Spring 1990, p.440). *Class No:* 60(091)

[1226]
MCNEILL, I., *ed.* **An Encyclopedia of the history of technology.** London, Routlege, 1990. 1085p. illus., diagrs., charts. ISBN: 0415013062.
22 contributions, each with further reading, by an international team of specialists. Theme: important inventions and their development, from Stone Age to Space Age. Subject and name indexes. 150 black-and-white illus. Editor was formerly Executive Secretary of the Newcomen Society for the Study of the History of Science and Technology. Detailed index of topics and names. *Class No:* 60(091)

[1227]
SINGER, C., *and others, eds.* **A History of technology.** Oxford, Clarendon Press, 1954-84. 8v. illus. (incl. pl.), tables, maps. ISBN: 019858105x.
1. *From early times to the fall of the ancient empires.* 1954, iv, 627p.
2. *The Mediterranean civilizations and the Middle Ages, c.700 BC to c.1500.* 1956. ix, 802p.
3. *From the Renaissance to the Industrial Revolution, c.1600-c.1750.* 1957. 804p.
4. *The Industrial Revolution, c.1750-c.1850.* 1958. xxxiii, 728p.
5. *The late nineteenth century, c.1850-c.1900.* 1958. xxxviii, 888p.
6-7. *The twentieth century (c.1900-c.1950),* edited by T.I. Williams. 1978. 2v.
8. *Consolidated indexes.* 1984. 232p.
Intended as a comprehensive history of the 'methods and skills by which man has attained a gradual easing of his earthly lot through mastery of his natural environment' (*Preface*). Technology as an aspect of history, especially social history, and as an influence on the development of civilization. Each chapter is by a specialist, and each volume is well equipped with illus. (incl. plates), tables, maps and bibliographies. V.8 comprises 4 parts: 1. List of contents for v.1-7; 2. Index of names; 3. Index of place-names; 4. Index of subjects (p.127-232). 'An interesting authoritative account of inestimable value' (*Aslib book list,* May 1979, item 199). *Class No:* 60(091)

Developing Countries

[1228]
HEAWOOD, R. *and* **LARKE, C. The Directory of appropriate technology.** London, Routledge, 1989. xi,[i],317p. ISBN: 0415627016.
Originated in the Work of the Alternate Technology Information Group (1976-).
Sections include: General/multi-disciplinary organizations; Ecology/environment; Education. Appended lists cite reference material, serial publications, audiovisual aids, etc. Intended for people - young and old - who want to explore options. *Class No:* 60(4/9-77)

Patents & Inventions

Trade Names, Trade Marks, Brand Names

[1229]
A-Z of European brands. London, Euromonitor Pubs., 1991. 400p. ISBN: 0863384004.
Over 5000 brands, considered by country, product sector and owner. Leading brands sold in the European market, both US and European. *Class No:* 608(088.7)

[1230]
NEWTON, D.C. Trade names: an introductory guide and bibliography. London, British Library, 1991. [ii],202p. ISBN: 0712307532.
Part 1 (p.7-59): 8 chapters on legal aspects and international agreements; 6 appendices (6: Periodicals); Index. Part 2: Introduction; Directory of literature of trade marks; Index. Includes some guidance on databases. Sources are based on the Science Reference and Information Service (SRIS) collection of the British Library. *Class No:* 608(088.7)

[1231]
The Trade mark journal. London, Patent Office, 1976-. Weekly.
Contains official notices, applications for trade marks advertised before registration, marks registered, renewals and other proceedings. Trade mark applications are arranged in classified order. *Class No:* 608(088.7)

[1232]
WOOD, D., *ed.* **Trade names dictionary.** Detroit, Mich., Gale, 1974-. 2v. ISSN: 02728818.
7th ed. 1989. 1,952p. $320.
A-Z list of about 206,000 US consumer-oriented trade names, brand names, etc., with names and addresses of 44,000 manufacturers and suppliers. Companion vol. *Trade names dictionary: company index* (7th ed. 1989. $320). *New trade names* is a supplement to both. *Class No:* 608(088.7)

Inventions

[1233]
GISCARD D'ESTAING, V-A., *ed.* **The Book of inventions and discoveries.** London, Queen Anne Press, 1990. 291,[i]p. col. illus., facsims., tables. ISBN: 0356188353.
Based on *Le livre mondial des inventions.*
Transport - Warfare - Science - Space - Medicine - Information technology - Ecology and the environment - Power and industry - Everyday life - Games, toys, sport - The bizarre - Media and Communications - The arts. Index of inventors and of inventions. Dates are given throughout; boxed information. Excellent for quick reference, teenagers and browsers. *Class No:* 608.1

[1234]
WILLIAMS, T.I. **Science: invention and discovery in the twentieth century.** London, Harrap, 1990. 256p. illus. (mostly col.), facsims., ports., diagrs., graphs. ISBN: 0245600248.

4 consultant editors. 6 periods: 1900/1914 ... 1973/1989. Appended: Biographies, p.228-49 (c.200 major Scientists and technologists); Glossary; Further reading, p.250. Detailed, analytical index. Text includes 12 'special features' (e.g. 'The structure of the nucleus', p.120-37). Covers physical sciences, biological and medical sciences and technology. About 350 illus., many in colour. For the lay person. *Class No:* 608.1

Patents

Databases

[1235]
MARCHANT, P. **Online patents and trademarks databases:** 1989. 3rd ed. London, Aslib, 1988. [iv],52p. ISBN: 0851422489.

First published 1983 as *Patents databases.* 2nd ed. 1987. Describes 55 patents and trademark databases, including updating, producer, host, costs, conditions, search aids, language. Also 8 'planned' databases. Directory of hosts and producers. Useful but inevitably dated. *Class No:* 608.3(003.4)

Bibliographies

[1236]
BRITISH LIBRARY. Science Reference and Information Service. **International guide to official industrial property publications.** Rimmer, B. 2nd ed., revised and updated. London, British Library, SRIS, 1988, with 1990 updating supplement. loose-leaf. ISBN: 0712307540. ISSN: 03064301.

5 parts: British industrial property publications - European patent publications - International patent publications - Search services (secondary services; computer databases; *Patent information and documentation handbook.* A brief guide to Science Reference and Information Service holdings of official publications on patents, designs, trade marks and plant breeders rights for the UK, and the patent publications arising from the European Patent Convention and Patent Cooperation Treaty (both of which the UK has acceded to). Index. The 2nd ed., rev. by S. van Dulken, adds a Chapter on the People's Republic of China. *Class No:* 608.3(01)

Handbooks & Manuals

[1237]
LEVY, R.C. **Inventing and patenting sourcebook:** how to sell and protect your ideas. Huffman, R.J., *ed,*. New York, Gale, 1990. 922p. ISBN: 0810348713.

Supplies a wealth of directory-type information from a US angle. *Class No:* 608.3(035)

Periodicals

[1238]
Official gazette of the United States Patent and Trademark Office: Patents. Washington, US Patent and Trademark Office, 1872-. Weekly.

Includes offical notices, abstracts of reexamination, reissue, utility, plant and design patents; abstracts of statutory invention registrations.

Annual index published separately. Part I: cumulated lists of applicants for patents, reexaminations, etc. Part II: index to subjects of invention - separate classified listings of patents, design patents, etc., and summary of publication statistics. *Class No:* 608.3(051)

[1239]
Official journal (patents). London, Patent Office, 1854-. Weekly.

Contents: official notes; details of applications for patents; applications published; granted patents (including European patents designating the UK); details of designs registered and renewed; progress of patents and legal proceedings; receipts of foreign patents in the Science Reference and Information Service. Appended list of additions to the Science Reference Library (Holborn). Annual cumulated name index, annual cumulated subject-matter indexes in each volume of abstracts of patent applications. *Class No:* 608.3(051)

Information Services

[1240]
EISENSCHITZ, T.S. **Patents, trade marks and designs in information work.** London, Croom Helm, 1987. 236p. ISBN: 0709909586.

Introductory section on the concepts behind industrial property followed by sections on patents, industrial copyright and designs, trade marks and EEC competition law. The book is intended as a source book for information workers, with details of the documentation particularly of the UK and US. *Class No:* 608.3:061:025.5

Patent Law

[1241]
PATERSON, G. **The European patent system.** London, Sweet & Maxwell, 1992. 600p. ISBN: 0421430508.

Commentary on case law developed by the Board of Appeal following introduction of the European Patent Convention. *Class No:* 608.3:347.77

61 Medicine

Medicine

Abbreviations & Symbols

[1242]

LOGAN, C.M. *and* **RICE, M.K. Logan's medical and scientific abbreviations.** Philadelphia, Pa., J.B. Lippincott Co., 1987. xix, 673p. ISBN: 0397545894.

Compiled from over 60 sources. 6 sections: 1. Abbreviations - 2. Symbols - 3. Chemotherapy regimes - 4. Latin terms: charting and prescriptions - 5. Cancer staging abbreviations - 6. Elements. Extensive coverage, *e.g.,* the single letter A has 53 terms. Useful bibliography, p.671-3. *Class No:* 610(003)

[1243]

MASA: medical acronyms, symbols and abbreviations. Hamilton, B. *and* Guidos, B., *eds.* 2nd ed. New York, Neal-Schuman, 1988. 277p. ISBN: 1555700128.

First published 1984.

Over 32,000 entries, 12,000 added since the previous edition. Terms found in older literature and medical records are included in addition to current abbreviations. Numerous cross-references. *Class No:* 610(003)

Databases

[1244]

LYON, E. Online medical databases 1991. 5th ed. London, Aslib, 1991. 96p. (*Aslib online guide.*) ISBN: 0851422748.

First published 1983.

A list of 135 bibliography or full-text databases, all commercially available online. Data include content; producer; text; costs. The addresses of hosts, producers and suppliers are listed. Bibliography and index. *Class No:* 610(003.4)

[1245]

MEDLINE [Medical Analysis and Retrieval Service On-Line]. Washington, National Library of Medicine, 1971-.

Database, with full coverage of *Index medicus* by 1974, with monthly update of *c.*25,000 entries. Search aids: MESH [Medical Subject Headings], an annual thesaurus of headings used in *Index medicus,* and Permuted Mesh headings. The UK contribution to MEDLINE is provided by the British Library, Boston Spa. Available on CD-ROM. The corresponding database for *Excerpta medica* abstracts (*qv*) is EMBASE (1974-), which covers 4,000 biomedical journals and includes 100,000 records pa. which don't appear in the printed journals. *Class No:* 610(003.4)

[1246]

Online databases in the medical and life sciences. New York, Cuadra/Elsevier, 1987. xxi, 170p.

Descriptions of 795 online databases, p.1-128. Data on each: type; subject; producer; online service; content;

....(contd.)

language; coverage; countries; time span; updating. Addresses of online services and gateways, p.129-36. Subject index; online service/gateway index; master index. *Class No:* 610(003.4)

Bibliographies

[1247]

BLAKE, J.B. *and* **ROOS, C.,** *eds.* **Medical reference works, 1679-1966:** a selected bibliography. Chicago, Ill., Medical Library Association, 1967. viii, 343p. Supplements 1-3, 1970-75.

2,703 numbered entries, concisely annotated, in the main volume. Nos.1-413: Medicine, general (indexes and abstracts; reviews; bibliographies; translations; theses; congresses; dictionaries; periodicals; directories; encyclopedias. - Nos.414-832: History of medicine - Nos.833-2073: Special subjects, A-Z (Aerospace and submarine medicine ... Zoology)). Excludes bibliographies of individuals, etc. Basic reference works for the smaller medical library are asterisked. A primary selection tool in its day.

Supplements 1-3 carry 1,059 items. Further supplements are due from National Library of Medicine computer bases. *Class No:* 610(01)

[1248]

Current bibliographies in medicine. Washington, D.C., US Government Printing Office, 1991-.

Compiled by the National Library of Medicine. Each issue varies in length from 14 to 50 pages and contains lists of books, periodicals and audio-visual materials on topics of current popular interest. Recent titles include: 'Medical waste disposal'; 'Laboratory animal welfare'; 'Nutrition and AIDS'. *Class No:* 610(01)

[1249]

MORTON, L.T. *and* **WRIGHT, D.J. How to use a medical library.** 7th ed. London, Library Association Publishing, 1990. v,88p. ISBN: 0851574661.

First published 1934.

10 sections: 1. Introduction - 2. Finding your way around the library - 3. Periodicals - 4. Indexes and abstracts - 5. Searching the literature - 6. Basic reference works - 7. Aids for writers and speakers - 8. Historical and biographical sources - 9. Audio-visual aids - 10. Biomedical library facilities in Britain. References, p.78-82. Analytical index, p.83-88. Written as a guide for medical practitioners, research workers and those who are training for a career in medical librarianship. *Class No:* 610(01)

[1250]

MORTON, L.T. *and* **GODBOLT, S.,** *eds.* **Information sources in the medical sciences.** 3rd ed. London, Butterworths, 1984. xviii, 534p. (*Butterworths Guides to information*

....(contd.)
sources.) ISBN: 0408114738.
First published 1974, as *Use of medical literature*.
29 contributors. 24 chapters: 1. Libraries and their use - 2. Primary sources of information - 3. Indexes, abstracts, bibliographies and reviews - 4. Standard reference sources - 5. Mechanized sources of information retrieval - 6. Anatomy and physiology - 7. Biochemistry, biophysics and molecular biology - 8. Public health ... 22. Historical, biographical and bibliographical sources - 23. Audio-visual materials - 24. The organization of personal files. This authoritative, well-balanced guide, with its three additional chapters, lacks only one feature (in common with some other volumes in the series), - an author index. *Class No:* 610(01)

Encyclopaedias

[1251]
Butterworth's medical dictionary. 2nd ed. Editor-in-chief, M. Critchley. London, Butterworths, 1978. xxxii, 1942p.
First published as *The British medical dictionary*, edited by Sir A.S. McNally (1961; rev. ed., 1965).
About 58,000 entries, revised by a team of 50 consultants. 'Paralysis': $5\frac{1}{2}$ columns; 'Spasm': 2 columns. Very brief biographical data under eponyms. Pronunciation of entry-words; chemical structures. Appendix: 'Anatomical nomenclature', tabulated. Regarded as a landmark in British medical lexicography. '99.9% of the time this lexicon does exactly what one would expect of it' (*The Lancet*, no.8063, 11 March 1978, p.536). *Class No:* 610(031)

[1252]
Dorland's illustrated medical dictionary. 27th ed. Philadelphia, Pa., W.B. Saunders, 1988. xxxii, 1888p. illus., tables. ISBN: 0721631541.
1st-23rd eds. as *The American illustrated medical dictionary*.
17 consultants. Over 80,000 entries, including abbreviations. 'Cell' (with subentries for types of cell in bold): 15 columns. Claims to establish 'certain standards of etymological propriety' by including 'Fundamentals of medical etymology', p.xvii-xxxii. Occasional small line-drawings in addition to the more detailed 53 plates. Generally considered to be reliable. *Class No:* 610(031)

Dictionaries

Polyglot

[1253]
DORIAN, A.F., *ed.* **Elsevier's encyclopaedic dictionary of medicine.** Amsterdam, etc., Elsevier, 1987-. ISBN: 0444872930, Pt.C; 0444428267, Pt.D; 0444428232, Pt.A; 0444428240, Pt.B.
A. *General medicine.* 1987. ix, 1175p. B. *Anatomy.* 1987. ix, 601p. C. *Biology, genetics and biochemistry.* 1989. xii,708p. D. *Therapeutic substances.* 1990. x,492p.
Projected in 4v. In 5 languages: English, French, German, Italian and Spanish. About 17,000 terms in v.A-B. Concise English definitions, with equivalents in the other 4 languages. 'Based on the English equivalents of the Nomina Anatomica as set forth by the sixth International Congress of Anatomists in Paris in 1955' (*Preface*). *Class No:* 610(038)=00

English

[1254]
Concise medical dictionary. 3rd ed. Oxford, University Press, 1990. 759p. illus. ISBN: 0192619314.
First published 1980.
About 10,000 entries. 33 contributors and advisers. 'Each entry contains a basic definition, followed - where appropriate - by a more detailed explanation or description' (*Preface*). For this edition, many new terms relating to prenatal diagnosis, molecular genetics and infertility treatment have been included. Adequate cross-references. Entries range in length from a few words to $\frac{2}{3}$ column (*e.g.* 'Leprosy'; 'Sickness benefit'). Good value. *Class No:* 610(038)=20

[1255]
International dictionary of medicine and biology. Landau, S.I., *ed.-in-chief.* New York, Wiley, 1986. 3v. (li, 3200p.). ISBN: 047101849x.
Over 100 contributors; more than 150,000 entries, thanks to the inclusion of biology. Among the subjects most extensively covered are ecology, environmental health, infectious diseases, occupational medicine, toxicology. A concise guide to usage precedes. Highly recommended as 'indispensable for medical and science libraries' (*Library journal*, 15 June 1986, p.61). *Class No:* 610(038)=20

Reviews & Abstracts

[1256]
Excerpta medica. Amsterdam. Excerpta Medica-Embase Publishing, 1947-. 45 sections, 6-32pa. Dfl.196-1736.
The most comprehensive medical abstracting service. The 45 sections contain 250,000 abstracts pa. in English from *c.*3,500 medical journals. Monthly and annual author and subject indexes. Computerized indexing since 1969.
54. *AIDS.* 1989-. 1. *Anatomy, anthropology, embryology and histology.* 1947-. 24. *Anesthesiology.* 1966-. 31. *Arthritis and rheumatism.* 1965-. 27. *Biophysics, bio-engineering and medical instrumentation.* 1967-. 16. *Cancer.* 1953-. 18. *Cardiovascular disease and cardiovascular surgery.* 1957-. 15. *Chest diseases, thoracic surgery and tuberculosis.* 1948-. 29. *Clinical biochemistry.* 1948-. 13. *Dermatology and venereology.* 1947-. 21. *Developmental biology and teratology.* 1961-. 40. *Drug dependence, alcohol abuse, and alcoholism.* 1973-. 3. *Endocrinology.* 1947-. 46. *Environmental health and pollution control.* 1971-. 50. *Epilepsy abstracts.* 1971-. 49. *Forensic science abstracts.* 1975-. 48. *Gastroenterology.* 1971-. 5. *General pathology and pathological anatomy.* 1948-. 20. *Gerontology and geriatrics.* 1958-. 36. *Health policy, economics and management.* 1971-. 25. *Hematology.* 1967-. 22. *Human genetics.* 1963-. 26. *Immunology, serology and transplantation.* 1967-. 6. *Internal medicine.* 1947-. 4. *Microbiology, bacteriology, mycology and parasitology.* 1948-. 151. *Mycobacterial diseases, leprosy, tuberculosis and related subjects.* 1979-88. 8. *Neurology and neurosurgery.* 1948-. 23. *Nuclear medicine.* 1964-. 10. *Obstetrics and gynecology.* 1948-. 35. *Occupational health and industrial medicine.* 1971-. 12. *Ophthalmology.* 1947-. 33. *Orthopedic surgery.* 1956-. 11. *Otorhinolaryngology.* 1948-. 7. *Pediatrics and pediatric surgery.* 1947-. 30. *Pharmacology.* 1948-. 2. *Physiology.* 1948-. 34. *Plastic surgery.* 1970-. 32. *Psychiatry.* 1948-. 17. *Public health, social medicine and epidemiology.* 1955-. 14. *Radiology.* 1947-. 19. *Rehabilitation and physical medicine.* 1958-. 9. *Surgery.* 1947-. 52. *Toxicology.* 1983-. 28. *Urology and nephrology.* 1967-. 47. *Virology.* 1971-.
Excerpta Medica Foundation also issues monthly current bibliographies, and 2 indexing services: *Adverse reaction titles* and *Drug literature index.* Online, EMBASE. *Class No:* 610(048)

[1257]
Index medicus. Washington, National Library of Medicine, 1960-. 12pa. ISSN: 00193879.

Covers *c*.3,000 journals. Each issue has subject and author sections, plus - since 1967 - 'Bibliography of medical reviews' (articles are all well documented surveys of the recent biomedical literature'). A comprehensive index to the world's medical literature. Annual cumulation as *Cumulated index medicus*. The computerized information retrieval service, MEDLINE (*qv*), is associated with *Index medicus*. Indispensable in its field. *Class No:* 610(048)

Yearbooks & Directories

[1258]
The Medical directory, 1991. 147th ed. 2v. (xix,3966+287p.). ISBN: 058207665x.

First published 1845.

The main sequence (v.1: A-L, v.2: M-Z) covers medical practitioners registered to practise in the UK. Data include qualifications, appointments (past and present) and publications. V.2 has appended: local lists; hospitals; university and medical schools; Royal Colleges in England and Scotland; postgraduate institutions; postgraduate medical centres; research institutions; coroners (England & Wales); government departments and statutory bodies; royal appointments; medical MPs, and titled members of the profession. Index; index to advertisements. For most purposes the *Directory* is preferred to the *Medical register*, because of its additional listings. *Class No:* 610(058)

Quotations

[1259]
Medical quotes: a thematic dictionary. Daintith, J. *and* Isaacs, A., *eds.* Oxford, New York, Facts on File, 1989. 260p. ISBN: 0816020949.

Published in paperback as *Dictionary of medical quotations* (Collins. 1989).

About 1,600 quotations, arranged A-Z by theme (Abortion ... Youth), ranging from old favourites through to film, television and radio broadcasts. Cross-references given to related topics. 2 indexes keyword-key phrase and author. 'Every waiting room should have one' (*Library Association record,* January 1990, p.68). *Class No:* 610(082.2)

Tables & Data Books

[1260]
Geigy scientific tables. 8th rev. and enl. ed., edited by C, Lentner. West Caldwell, N.J., Ciba-Geigy Corpn., 1981-. ISBN: 0914168509, v.1; 0914168517, v.2; 0914168525, v.3; 0914168533, v.4; 0914168541, v.5.

7th ed., edited by K. Diem and C. Lentner.

1. *Units of measurement; body fluids; composition of the body; nutrition.* 1981. 295p. 2. *Introduction to statistics; statistical tables; mathematical formulae.* 1982 240p. 3. *Physical chemistry; composition of blood; hematology; somatometric data.* 1984. 359p. 4. *Biochemistry; metabolism of xenobiotics; inborn errors of metabolism; pharmacogenetics and ecogenetics.* 1986. 330p. 5. *Heart and circulation.* 1990. 280p.

Further volumes are in preparation. Ready reference souce of basic data in biomedicine. *Class No:* 610(083)

Histories

[1261]
MORTON, L.T. Morton's medical bibliography: an annotated checklist of texts illustrating the history of medicine (Garrison and Morton). 5th ed., by J.M. Norman. Aldershot, Scolar Press, 1991. 1267p. ISBN: 0859678970.

First published 1943.

8,927 main entries (1,051 of them new), arranged by subject, *e.g.,* biology, epidemiology, leprosy, obstetrics, then chronologically. Includes translations and reprints. Sections on medical biography, medical bibliography and medical lexicography. Indexes of personal names and subjects. Unrivalled. *Class No:* 610(091)

Biographies

[1262]
Dictionary of American medical biography. Kaufman, M., *and others.* Westport, Conn., Greenwood Press, 1984. 2v. (1027p.). ISBN: 031321378x.

Continues H.A. Kelly and W.L Bussage's *Dictionary of American medical biography* (1928).

Records more than 1,000 medical personalities of the 17th-20th centuries who died before 31 December 1976. Includes references to other sources (*e.g., Dictionary of American biography*). Nearly 100p of appendices, listing biographees by date and place of birth, by state where prominent, by speciality/occupation, by medical school attended. Extensive index. *Class No:* 610(092)

[1263]
Medical sciences international who's who. 4th ed. Harlow, Essex, Longman Group, 1990. vi,1341p. (*Reference on research.*) ISBN: 0582041937.

First published 1980. 2nd ed. as *International medical who's who*.

Biographical details of *c*.8,000 senior medical and biomedical scientists from over 90 countries. 2 parts: 1. Biographical profiles (A to Z, p.1-1306) - 2. Country and subject index. *Class No:* 610(092)

[1264]
MORTON, L.T. *and* **MOORE, R.J. A Bibliography of medical and biomedical biography.** Aldershot, Hants., Scolar Press, 1989. ix,208p. ISBN: 0859677974.

Originally intended as 3rd ed. of J.L. Thornton's *Select bibliography of medical biography;* (2nd ed. Library Association, 1970).

1,600 individuals listed (Abano ... Zuckerman). Biographies restricted to English language and translations. Locations of archival material are also listed. Collective biographies, p.173-77. Short list of books on the history of medicine and related subjects, p.178-88. Discipline index of biographees, p.189-208. *Class No:* 610(092)

Research Establishments

[1265]
Medical research centres: a world directory of organizations and programmes. 9th ed. Harlow, Essex, Longman, 1990. vi,877p. (*Reference on research.*) ISBN: 0582061237.

Succeeds *Medical research index* (5th ed. Hodgson, 1979); *Medical research centres* (8th ed. Longman, 1988).

Arranged A-Z by country, Angola ... Zimbabwe. A guide to *c*.6,000 organizations and laboratories which conduct or finance medical or biological research and development. Data: name and address; telephone, telex and fax numbers; names of key personnel; finance; activities; publications; clients. Indexes of establishments and subject. *Class No:* 610:061:061.62

Ethics

[1266]
DUNCAN, A.S., *and others,* eds. **Dictionary of medical ethics.** 2nd ed. London, Darton, Longman and Todd, 1981. xxxi, 459p. diagrs., tables. ISBN: 0232514925.

First published 1977.

About 150 contributors. All articles are signed, with references (*e.g.,* 'Mental illness, Certification of': $2\frac{1}{2}$ columns, 12 references; 'Psychiatry, Misuse of': 4p. 17 references). 'The work is of high standard and includes questions of social as well as purely medical importance ... Can be unreservedly recommended' (*British book news,* March 1978, p.196-7). 'This much needed and valuable book' (*British medical journal,* 5 November 1977, p.1218-9), on the 1st ed. *Class No:* 610.17

Anatomy

[1267]
Gray's anatomy. 36th ed., edited by P.L. Williams and R. Warwick. Edinburgh, Churchill Livingstone, 1989. xvi, 1578p. illus. (incl. col.), tables. ISBN: 0443025886.

First published 1858.

8 subject sections: Introduction - Cytology - Embryology - Osteology - Arthrology - Myology - Angiology - Neurology - Splanchnology. Bibliography (authors, A/Z), p.1477-1548. Analytical index, p.1549-98. Excellent keyed line-drawings, well captioned. The classic textbook on anatomy. The two editors are former professors of Anatomy, Guy's Hospital Medical School, Univ. of London. *Class No:* 611

Physiology

[1268]
AMERICAN PHYSIOLOGICAL SOCIETY. Handbook of physiology: a critical comprehensive presentation of physiological knowledge and concepts. Rev. ed. Baltimore, Md., Williams & Wilkins, for the Society, 1977-. illus.

First published 1959-83 (10 sections). Rev.

1. *The nervous system.* 5v. (8pts.). 1977-87. 2. *The cardiovascular system.* 4v. (6pts.). 1979-84. 3. *The respiratory system.* 4v. 1985-88. 4. *Adaptation to the environment.* 1964. 6. *The gastrointestinal system.* 4v. 1989-90. 7. *Endocrinology.* 7v. 1972-76. 8. *Renal physiology.* 2v. 1991. 9. *Reactions to environmental agents.* 1977. 10. *Skeletal muscle.* 1983.

The revised ed. was started in 1977 before completion of the earlier ed. The latter's intention was 'to cover the physiological sciences in their entirety and in about 10 years, and to repeat the process periodically thereafter' (*Foreword,* v.1, Section 1). Well documented multivolume treatise. *Class No:* 612

[1269]
EMSLIE-SMITH, D., *and others.* **Textbook of physiology** (BDS). 11th ed. Edinburgh, Churchill Livingstone, 1988. xii,548p. illus., diagrs., tables. ISBN: 0443034125.

First published 1950 as *Textbook of physiology and biochemistry.*

Has 21 contributors. 41 chapters (The blood ... Energy balance and exercise ... Thermoregulation). Numerous half-tones, line-drawings, and tables. Standard text, with many chapters completely rewritten, and with the medical student mainly in mind. Some references follow each chapter. Index p.535-548. 'BDS' is the book's 'affectionate nickname' (*Preface* to 11th ed.) and comprises the initials of the first editors' surnames. *Class No:* 612

Health & Hygiene

[1270]
SMITH, T. **The New Macmillan guide to family health.** 2nd ed. London, Macmillan, 1987, 848p. ilus. (incl. col.), charts, tables. ISBN: 0333455258.

29 contributors. 4 parts: 1. The healthy body - 2. Symptoms and self-diagnosis - 3. Diseases, disorders and other problems - 4. Caring for the sick. Boxed information, a feature. Appended: Helpful organizations, p.762-3; drug index, p.792-801. Glossary. 'Accidents and emergencies', p.815-32. Detailed, analytical index, p.833-46. Designed for use in both sickness and health. *Class No:* 613

Food

[1271]
BENDER, A.E. **Dictionary of nutrition and food technology.** 6th ed. London, Butterworths, 1990. [vi], 336p. tables. ISBN: 0408037539.

First published 1960.

About 4,000 entries and cross-references, p.1-309. Entries for abbreviations and trade names. Includes 300 new terms; 300 entries revised. Bibliography (now separated from entries), p.310-24 (Additives and ingredients ... Toxicology). Tables, p.327-36. Aims 'to assist the specialist from one field to understand the technical terms used by the variety of specialists in the food fields' (*Preface* to 5th ed.). Author was Professor of Nutrition, Queen Elizabeth College, Univ. of London. *Class No:* 613.2

[1272]
MCCANCE, R.A. and WIDDOWSON, E.M. **The Composition of foods.** 5th rev. and extended ed. London, Royal Society of Chemistry; Ministry of Agriculture, Fisheries and Food, 1991. xiii,462p. tables. ISBN: 0851863914.

3 sections: 1. Introduction - 2. Tables, p.21-388 (*e.g.,* Milk and milk products; Herbs and spices; Nuts; Beverages) - 3. Appendices (*e.g.* Organic aids; Recipes; References; Index). Supplements are to be published in 1992. The standard work. *Class No:* 613.2

[1273]
TVER, D.F. *and* RUSSELL, P. **Nutrition and health encyclopedia.** Princeton, N.J., Van Nostrand Reinhold, 1981. v. 569p. illus., diagrs., charts, tables. ISBN: 0442248598.

A-Z definitions and longer articles, the latter on carbohydrates, toxins, drugs, bodily functions, etc. Tabular data on food, caloric and vitamin values. 'Should become a standard ready-reference in this field' (*Choice,* v.19(3), November 1981, p.362). *Class No:* 613.2

Physical Welfare

Sports Medicine

[1274]
Encyclopaedia of sports medicine. Dirix, A., *and others,* eds. Oxford, Blackwell Scientific Publications, 1988-. ISBN: 0632019638, v.1.

V.1. *The Olympic book of sports medicine.* xii,692p.

Produced by the International Olympic Committee's Medical Commission and the International Federation of Sports Medicine. V.1 has over 50 contributing authors and 13 sections: 1. Introduction ... 3. Assessment of physical and functional capacity - 4. Environmental conditions ... 8. Female athletes - 9. Sport and physical activities in older people ... 13. Doping and doping control. A bibliography is appended to each chapter. Abundant figures and graphs, with easy to read text. *Class No:* 613.70

Physical Education

[1275]
Sports documentation monthly bulletin. Birmingham, Sports Documentation Centre, Univ. of Birmingham, 1971-. Monthly. ISSN: 01421794.

About 3,500 abstracts pa. Two main parts. *General* (25 headings: Administration... Women, including Physical education and Sports injuries). *Individual sports and activities* (8 grouped headings: Association football, Australian Rules football ... Triathlon, Volleyball, Weightlifting, Wrestling). Author and subject indexes per issue, cumulated annually. *Class No:* 613.72

Alcoholism

[1276]
O'BRIEN, R. *and* **CHAFETZ, M. The Encyclopedia of alcoholism.** 2nd ed. New York, Facts on File, 1991. 346p. tables. ISBN: 081601955x.

First published 1982.

Over 500 entries, A-Z, covering a wide variety of aspects of alcohol and alcoholism: production, consumption by ethnic groups, regulations and customs worldwide, medical aspects, psychological theories, treatment of alcoholism, organizations, and slang. Many statistical tables; 24p. of bibliographies. Subject index. Of the first ed., 'Clear, concise style; useful to both the layperson and the professional' (*Library journal,* 1 April 1983, p.733). US-slanted. *Class No:* 613.81

Drugs (Narcotics)

[1277]
The Encyclopedia of drug abuse. Evans, G., *and others.* 2nd ed. New York, Facts on File, 1991. 370p. tables. ISBN: 0816019568.

First published 1984.

Over 500 entries, ranging in length from several lines to several paragraphs. Covers political and legal aspects of drug abuse as well as medical and psychological issues. 4 appendices, including lists of drug slang, statistical tables, and a directory of relevant agencies. Extensive bibliography; index. Designed as a companion to *The encyclopedia of alcoholism,* by R. O'Brien and M. Chafetz (1991) (*qv*). Of the first ed., 'No library should be without this comprehensive and timely resource on drug abuse' (*Choice,* v.22(3), November 1984, p.405-6). *Class No:* 613.83

Smoking

[1278]
ROYAL COLLEGE OF PHYSICIANS OF LONDON. Smoking or health: the third report from the Royal College of Physicians of London. London, Pitman Medical, 1977. 128p. ISBN: 0272794126.

First published 1962.

10 sections: 1. Tobacco consumption, promotion and control in Britain ... 3. Pharmacology and toxicology ... 4. Smoking and cancer ... 6. Smoking, bronchitis and other conditions ... 9. The smoking habit - 10. Prevention of disesase due to smoking. Appended: 'Summary of recommendations for action'. 3p. of references, p.125-7. *Class No:* 613.84

Public Health

[1279]
Oxford textbook of public health. Holland, W.W., *and others,* eds. 2nd ed. Oxford, University Press, 1991. 3v. diagrs., graphs, tables. ISBN: 0192617060, v.1; 0192617079, v.2; 0192617087, v.3; 0192619268, set.

First published 1984-85 as a revision of W. Hobson's *The theory and practice of public health* (1961).

1. *Influences of public health.* xix,561p. 2. *Methods of public health.* xxii,563p. 3. *Applications in public health.* xix,657p.

Over 100 contributors. Extensive coverage, relating to developed countries, and including more examples from non-English speaking countries than in the previous edition. Includes sections on public health policies and strategies, provision of public health services, epidemiological approaches, health service planning and evaluation and needs of special client groups. Bibliographies are appended to each chapter and each volume has an index covering the set. *Class No:* 614

Public Safety

Industrial & Occupational Safety

[1280]
HSELINE. Sheffield, Health and Safety Executive, 1981-.

A database and major source of bibliographical references to published documents on health and safety at work. About 100,000 references by December 1988, adding *c.*1,000 entries monthly. Coverage emphasizes mining, nuclear technology, explosions, explosives, hazardous chemicals, occupational hygiene, industrial pollution, occupational safety and agricultural safety. Online access, ESA-IRS, Pergamon INFOLINE. Available on CD-ROM. *Class No:* 614.8-027

Encyclopaedias

[1281]
INTERNATIONAL LABOUR OFFICE. Encyclopaedia of occupational health and safety. Permeggiani, L., *technical ed.* 3rd (revised) ed. Geneva, ILO, 1983. 2v. (xxiv, xxiii, 2538p.). illus. (incl. col. pl.), diagrs., plans, tables. ISBN: 9221032892.

First published 1930.

V.1: A-K; v.2: L-Z. About 1,000 contributors, on a wide range of topics, from accident causation, ergonomics and occupational cancer to lighting, psychology, and statistics. 'Mines, ventilation of' occupies nearly 3p. in v.1, with 5 references, 5 figures. 'Shift work': $3\frac{1}{2}$p., 7 references. Appendices: Basic data; International documentation. Some operational guidelines. Analytical index, p.2447-2533. Despite uneven treatment of subjects and restricted documentation, a major contribution. 'A practical guide ... particularly [for] those in developing countries and those without access to adequate library facilities' (*Science & technology libraries,* v.5(2), Winter 1984, p.75). *Class No:* 614.8-027(031)

Fires & Fire Prevention

[1282]
GREAT BRITAIN. HOME OFFICE. Fire Department. **Manual of firemanship.** New series. London, HM Stationery Office, 1974-. Books 1-12, illus. (incl. pl.).

1. *Elements of combustion and extinction.* 1974. 128p. £4.95. 2. *Fire brigade equipment.* 1974. 224p. £5.95. 3. *Hand pumps, extinguishers and foam equipment.* 2nd ed. 1988. xiii,102p. £5.50. 4. *Incidents involving aircraft, shipping and railways.* 1985. xxvii, 266p. £7.50 5. *Ladders and appliances.* 1984. 204p. £6.50. 6. *Breathing apparatus*

....(contd.)

and resuscitation. 2nd ed. 1989. xiii,123p. £5.95. 7. *Hydraulics, pumps and pump operation.* 2nd ed. 1986. xvi,208p. £6.50. 8. *Building construction and structural fire protection.* 1976. 200p. £5.50. 9. *Fire protection of buildings.* 2nd ed. 1990. xii,208p. £5.50. 10. *Fire brigade communications and mobilizing.* 2nd ed. 1991. xvi,149p. £5.95. 11. *Practical firemanship. 1.* 1981. 192p. £5.50. 12. *Practical firemanship. 2.* 1983. 276p. £7.95.

Covers both theory and practice. Book 9 has 3 parts: Fire extinguishing systems; Fire alarm systems; Fire-venting systems. 21 chapters. Glossary and terminology. Further reading, p.181-3. 46 plates. Includes concise practical instructions. *Class No: 614.84*

Hazardous Chemicals

[1283]
SAX, I. *and* LEWIS, R.J. **Dangerous properties of industrial materials.** 7th ed. New York, Van Nostrand Reinhold, 1989. 3v. ISBN: 0442280203.

V.1 includes 3 articles on toxicology and carcinogenicity, and the indexes. *c.*3,500 new entries. The synonym index lists French, German, Italian, Dutch and Polish synonyms in addition to English. Also contains a CAS Registry No. index and a CODEN index. V.2 and v.3 contain chemical data and hazard potential for 20,000 substances. Some entries have structural drawings. Clinical data on animals and humans have been expanded and updated. *Class No: 614.878*

First Aid

[1284]
Baillière's handbook of first aid. 7th ed, revised by N.G. Kirby and S.J. Mather. London, Baillière Tindall, 1985. vii, 360p. illus. ISBN: 0702010979.

First published 1941.

3 parts (36 sections): 1. Assessment of the casualty and casualty report - 2. Structure and function - 3. Clinical practice (15. Asphyxia and respiratory disorders ... 36. Transport by stretcher (p.331-52. 27 line-drawings)). Detailed, analytical index, p.353-60. Improved line-drawings. 'This book is intended for instructors and for those who will practise advanced first aid' (*Preface*). *Class No: 614.88*

Pharmacology

[1285]
Information sources in pharmaceuticals. Pickering, W.R., *ed.* London, Bowker-Saur, 1990. xvii,566p. tables. ISBN: 0408025182.

International in scope. 28 contributors. 3 parts (20 documented chapters). General appendix to Part 3 contains sections on literature sources; online databases; centres of excellence; health statistics. Index, p.554-66. Editor is in charge of the Wellcome Foundation's central R & D information function. *Class No: 615*

Homeopathy

[1286]
SMITH, T. **An Encyclopaedia of homoeopathy:** a comprehensive reference book and survey of the subject from its beginnings to the present day. Worthing, Sussex, Insight Editions, 1983. [viii], 283p. ISBN: 0946670013.

About 1,000 entries, A-Z. Highlights history, philosophies, major personalities, remedies and illnesses. Cites major works by homeopathic practitioners. *Class No: 615.015.32*

Pharmacopoeias

Great Britain

[1287]
British pharmacopoeia, 1988. Published on the recommendation of the Medicines Commission pursuant to the Medicines Act, 1968. 2nd ed. London, HM Stationery Office, 1988. 2v. (740 + 400p.). graphs. ISBN: 0113208375, set.

Contains 2,100 monographs for items and substances used in medicine. V.1 features medicinal and auxiliary substances, plus infra-red spectra. V.2 contains the formulary, blood products, immunological products, radiopharmaceutical preparations, and surgical materials. Formulary extensively revised. 24 appendices, *e.g.,* 6. Qualitative sections and tests; 18. Methods of sterilisation. V.2 has index to both volumes. Updated by an annual addendum. *Class No: 615.11(410)*

[1288]
DPF/BNF: Dental practitioners' formulary together with British national formulary, for use in the National Health Service. London, British Medical Association & The Pharmaceutical Press. 1990. Irregular. ISBN: 0853692408, DPF; 0853692009, BNF. ISSN: 02636419, DPF; 0260535x, BNF.

Previously published separately up to 1990 as *British national formulary* and *Dental practitioners' formulary.*

No. 20, 1990-92 comprises two formularies in a single volume. DPF (x,36p.) is divided into 4 sections (guidance on prescribing); classified notes on drugs and preparations; appendices (5, interactions ... breast-feeding); and list of dental preparations. BNF (xiv,562p.) consists of 'Guidance on prescribing, emergency treatment of poisoning', then 15 sections of 'Classified notes on drugs and preparations' (12: ear, nose, and oropharynx, p.349-354). 8 appendices and index (p.523-562). Poor cover design over-emphasises dental content. *Class No: 615.11(410)*

USA

[1289]
Physicians' desk reference / PDR. Oradell, N.J., Medical Economics. Annual.

First published 1947.

The 1989 ed. (2418p. illus.) contains a 'Production information section' (*c.*1700p.). It concerns over 2,500 pharmaceuticals, A-Z. Data: indicates usage, dosage, description, clinical pharmacology, supply, warnings, contraindicators, adverse reactions, overdose and precautions. Appendices: Conversion tables ... Guide to management of drug overdose. Comprehensive. Prepared by drug manufacturers and their consultants. For the American practitioner. *Class No: 615.11(73)*

Medications & Drugs

[1290]
The British Medical Association guide to medicines and drugs. London, Dorling Kindersley, 1988. 432p. illus., diagrs. ISBN: 0863182984.

Structured information (general; quick reference; information for users; special precautions; possible adverse effects) on 213 of the most widely used drugs. 5 parts: 1. Understanding and using drugs - 2. Drug finder index - 3. Major drug groups - 4. A-Z of drugs - 5. Glossary and index. Appended drug poisoning emergency guide. *Class No: 615.2*

Origins of Medicines & Therapy

Plant Medicines

[1291]
CRC handbook of medicinal herbs. Duke, J.A. Boca Raton, Florida, CRC Press, 1985. [xi], 677p. illus, tables. ISBN: 0849336309.

Catalogue of herbs, p. 1-516, with details of 365 medicinal species (uses, folk medicinal applications, chemistry and toxicity). 5 tables, p.517-98 (*e.g.,* 1. Medicinal herbs, toxicity ranking and price list). References, p.585-594. *Class No:* 615.32

Therapeutic Treatments

[1292]
STANWAY, A. Alternative medicine: a guide to natural therapies. Rev. ed. Harmondsworth, Penguin Books, 1986. 319p. diagrs. ISBN: 0140085610.

Information on 32 therapies, arranged A-Z (*e.g.,* Acupuncture; Biofeedback; Naturopathy, Yoga). Each entry carries a definition, background, how it's done, how it works, why does it work, what's it used for, does it work etc. Useful bibliography, p.50-63. Index. *Class No:* 615.8

Psychotherapy

[1293]
WALROND-SKINNER, S. A Dictionary of psychotherapy. London, Routledge & Kegan Paul/Methuen, 1986. [xi], 379p. ISBN: 0710099789.

About 850 documented entries (*e.g.,* 'Cartesian': $1\frac{1}{2}$ columns; 6 references, 2 cross-references; 'Leadership': $1\frac{1}{2}$ columns, 6 references, 3 cross-references) Brief biographies (*e.g.,* Jung). Embraces classical concepts as well as new psychotherapies. The author is currently Associate Director of Ordinands and Tutor in Pastoral Studies for the Diocese of Bristol. 'This new dictionary definitely fills a gap in the field' (*Choice,* v.24(2), October 1986, p.288). *Class No:* 615.851

Toxicology (Poisons)

[1294]
SITTIG, M. Handbook of toxic and hazardous chemicals and carcinogens. 2nd ed. Park Ridge, N.J., Noyes Data, 1985. 950p. illus. ISBN: 0815510098.

Aims to 'present concise chemical and safety information on nearly 800 toxic and hazardous chemicals' (*Preface*). Each chemical is classified as a carcinogen, hazardous substance, hazardous potential and/or priority toxic pollutants. An excellent source of economic information. *Class No:* 615.9

[1295]
WEXLER, P. Information resources in toxicology. 2nd ed. New York, Elsevier, 1988. xxiv,510p. ISBN: 0444012141.

First published 1982.

2 sections: 1. United States resources (16 chapters, *e.g.* 'History'; 'Journals'; 'Audiovisuals'; 'Poison control centres') - 2. International organizations (20 chapters, *e.g.* 'International Union of Toxicology'; 'China'; 'Italy'; 'Sweden'). Entries on books, journals, etc. are annotated. Concentrates on health effects. Topics not stressed include management of hazardous wastes, aspects of pollution control, drug, alcohol and tobacco abuse. Heavy US slant. *Class No:* 615.9

Diseases (Pathology)

[1296]
ALTMAN, P.L. *and* **KATZ, D.D.,** *comps. and eds.* **Human health and disease.** Bethesda, Md., Federation of American Societies for Experimental Biology, 1977. xxi, [i], 435p. diagrs., graphs, tables. (*Biological handbooks, 2.*) ISBN: 0913822116.

More than 300 contributors. 7 parts (186 sections): 1. Infectious diseases - 2. Immunological factors - 3. Metabolic disorders - 4. Organ system diseases -5. Neurologic diseases - 6. Endocrinology and endocrinopathies - 7. Radiation. Numerous tables and references ('Adrenal hormones', p. 328-32; 40 references). Detailed, analytical index (p.375-435) includes entries for diagrams, footnote and headnote items). A mine of information; for specialists. *Class No:* 616.01

[1297]
International nomenclature of diseases. Geneva, Council for International Organizations of Medical Sciences; World Health Organization, 1979-. 4v.

V.2. *Infectious diseases.* 208p. 1987. V.3. *Diseases of the lower respiratory tract.* 1979. V.4. *Diseases of the digestive system.* 269p. 1991. V.5. *Cardiac and vascular diseases.* 113p. 1991.

'The principle objective of IND is to provide, for every morbid entity, a single recommended name' (*Introduction*). *Class No:* 616.01

Worldwide

[1298]
HOWE, G.M., *ed.* **A World geography of human diseases.** London, New York, etc., Academic Press, 1977. xxviii, [2], 621p., diagrs., tables, maps. ISBN: 0123571502.

22 contributors, nearly all British. States 'what is known about a selected range of important diseases in terms of pattern, distribution and trend' (*Foreword*). 20 sections (1. Schistosomiasis ... 20. Deficiency diseases), with appended references. Some of the maps are adapted from American Geographical Society's *Atlas of diseases*, 'It is a book which will become not only a standard work of reference, but also provoke debate on the major issues of world health and the provision of health services in the future' (*International affairs,* v.54(3), July 1978, p.475-6). 'Should be available to all students of medicine' (*British medical journal,* no.6114, 18 March 1978, p.708). *Class No:* 616.01(100)

Tropical Diseases

[1299]
Manson's tropical diseases. 19th ed., by P.E.C. Manson-Bahrs, D.R. Bell. London, Baillière Tindall, 1987. xxii, 1557p. illus., diagrs., tables, maps.

First published 1898. 18th ed. 1980 (xiv, 843p.).

17 sections, *e.g.,* 1. Diseases commonly presenting as fever; 2. Diseases commonly presenting as diarrhoea; 15. Clinical problems in the tropics; 16. Protecting the traveller; 17. Drugs. 4 appendices (3. Medical entomology, p.1381-1488, with 123 references). Detailed analytical index. A well-established classic. *Class No:* 616.01-036.21

Patient types

Geriatrics

[1300]
CRC handbook of physiology in aging. Masoro, E.J., *ed.*
Boca Raton, Florida, CRC, 1981. 502p. tables. ISBN:
0849331439.
A compendium of lists, tables, etc. summarizing data,
with full references. 'It deserves a place on the desks of all
those who practice geriatric medicine as well as those who
teach or study the physiologic processing of aging' (*Journal
of the American Geriatric Society,* v.30, March 1982,
p.225). *Class No: 616.01-053.9*

Syndromes

[1301]
Dictionary of medical syndromes. Magalini, S.I., *and others.*
Philadelphia, Pa., J.B. Lippincott, 1990. xiii,1042p. ISBN:
0397508824.
First published 1971.
Entries for *c.*3,000 syndromes. 'Riley-Day': synonyms;
symptoms; signs; etiology; pathology; diagnostic procedures;
therapy; prognosis; bibliography (3 references). Detailed
analytical index, p.957-1042. *Class No: 616.01-06*

Symptoms & Diagnosis

[1302]
French's index of differential diagnosis. 12th ed., edited by
F.D. Hart. Bristol, J. Wright, 1985. xii, 1032p. illus. (incl.
col.) tables. ISBN: 0723607850.
First published 1912.
18 contributors. A classic encyclopaedic dictionary of
diagnosis. 'Abdomen, rigidity on' ... 'Yawning'. The article
'Joint, infection of' has 14 sections, p.453-73, with 18 illus.
334 of the 739 illus. are in colour. The detailed, analytical
index, on blue-tinted paper, p.897-1032, is a quick-reference
bonus. *Class No: 616.01-07*

Treatment

Nursing

Encyclopaedias & Dictionaries

[1303]
Baillière's encyclopaedic dictionary of nursing and health care.
Weller, B.F., *ed.* London, Baillère Tindall, 1989.
xxvi,1042p. figs. ISBN: 0702011967.
Aimed at the UK-trained and practising nurse and
compiled by 45 specialists. Over 32,000 main and sub-
entries (A ... Zymosis). Definitions vary in length, *e.g.*
Balm, 1 line; Intracranial, 3 columns, and include
pronunciation. 3 appendices: 1. Degrees, organizations and
abbreviations - 2. Units of measurement and table of
chemical elements - 3. Useful addresses. *Class No: 616.01-
083(03)*

[1304]
Mosby's medical, nursing, and allied health dictionary. 3rd ed.
St. Louis, Mo., C.V. Mosby Company, 1990. xx,1608p.
illus. (incl. col.), diagrs., graphs, tables. ISBN: 0801632277.
First published 1983.
64 consulting contributors. About 26,000 entries, 3,000
new to this edition. Length of entries varies from a few
words to several columns, *e.g.* 'Burn therapy': method;
nursing orders; outcome criteria; 2 columns. 44-page colour
atlas of human anatomy. 21 appendices, p.1267-1608 (*e.g.*
Pharmacology; Directory of nursing organizations and
health care workers; Leading health problems and
communicable diseases). Pronunciation and stress of terms
is given. 10,000 cross-references. Well produced; careful
line-drawings; thumb ed. *Class No: 616.01-083(03)*

Reviews & Abstracts

[1305]
International nursing index. New York, American Journal of
Nursing Co., 1966-. 4pa.; annual cumulation. ISSN:
00208124.
Published in co-operation with National Library of
Medicine.
Indexes over 270 nursing journals published worldwide,
as well as nursing articles in the 2,600 biomedical titles
indexed in *Index medicus.* A list of current books
published by and for nurses is appended to each issue and
the cumulation. Online access is available through
MEDLINE. 'This is the master index to nursing literature'
(*Reference Service Review,* v.9(4), October/December 1981,
p.22). Available on CD-ROM. *Class No: 616.01-083(048)*

[1306]
Nursing bibliography: a monthly list of current publications
on nursing and allied subjects. London, Royal College of
Nursing, 1972-. Monthly. ISSN: 03009947.
8-9,000 references pa. under subjects, Abortion ...
Wounds. Selectively indexes more than 200 English-language
periodicals. Coverage: books, reports, articles, pamphlets
and theses. Each issue carries an author index. The
separate list of subject headings and of journals indexed is
revised annually. *Class No: 616.01-083(048)*

Education Courses

[1307]
**WELL, J. The Directory of continuing education for nurses,
midwives and health visitors.** London, Newpoint Publishing
Company, 1990. 239p. ISBN: 0862631297.
14 sections: 1. Introduction - 2. Statutory control of
nursing education ... 8. Courses for midwives ... 11. Higher
education courses - 12. Teacher preparation courses - 13.
Management courses - 14. Open and distance learning. 5
appendices (*e.g.* 'Alphabetical list of courses'; 'Useful
addresses'). *Class No: 616.01-083:377.3*

Immunology

[1308]
Excerpta medica. 26. Immunology, serology and transplantation.
Amsterdam, Excerpta Medica, 1967-. ISSN: 00144304.
About 9,000 abstracts pa. 15 sections: 1. General aspects
- 2. Laboratory methods and techniques - 3. Treatment ...
7. Antibodies - 8. Cell-mediated immune responses - 9.
Modulation of immune responses ... 15. Transplantation
immunology. Subject and author indexes per issue and
annually. Online, EMBASE. Available on CD-ROM. *Class
No: 616.01-097*

Special Pathology

Hearing (Otology)

[1309]
Gallaudet encyclopedia of deaf people and deafness. Van
Cleve, J.V. New York, etc., McGraw-Hill, 1987. 3v.
(1400p.). ISBN: 0070792291, set.
Sponsored by Gallaudet College, Washington, D.C.
271 articles, most of them documented, on sign language,
audiology, auditory disorders organizations, deaf community
publications, rehabilitation, demographics, biographies of
distinguished deaf individuals, educational programmes,
conditions and status of the deaf community in most major
countries, etc. 250 illus. 8,000-entry index. 'Likely to
become the standard work in its field' (*Choice,* v.24(8),
April 1987, p.1198). *Class No: 616.28*

Dentistry

[1310]
CLENNETT, M.A. **Keyguide to information sources in dentistry.** London, Mansell, 1985. 287p. facsim. (*Keyguide series.*) ISBN: 072011747x.

Part 1: Survey of dentistry and its libraries (8 sections, *e.g.*, 5. Finding out about the literature; 7. Sources of special information: patents, audiovisual material, etc., 8. Language problem) - Part 2: Bibliography (666 annotated entries, under subjects: anaesthesia ... radiography; miscellaneous subjects) - Part 3: Directory of organizations (selected list of dental libraries; national dental associations; dental associations and societies; schools and university depts.; publications). 1,445 numbered entries in all. Detailed and analytical index, p.273-87. Well researched. Intended for the information worker or non-dental researcher. *Class No:* 616.314

Reviews & Abstracts

[1311]
Index to dental literature, 1939-. Chicago, Ill., American Dental Association, 1943-. 4pa. ISSN: 00193992.

Initially (1939-61) as *Index to dental literature in the English language.*

About 10,000 references pa. Contents: Dental books published; Dissertations and theses; Serials indexed; Dental descriptors; Cross-references; Qualifiers; Bibliography of dental reviews (subject and name sections); Index to dental literature (subject and name sections). Annual cumulation. Available online on MEDLINE database and on CD-ROM. *Class No:* 616.314(048)

Psychiatry

[1312]
AMERICAN PSYCHIATRIC ASSOCIATION. Joint Commission on Public Affairs. **A Psychiatric glossary.** 6th ed. Washington, D.C., American Psychiatric Association, 1989. ix, 142p. tables. ISBN: 0880480270.

First published 1957.

Defines *c.*1,500 terms, plus brief notes on 'prominent names' and schools of psychiatry. Nearly all the terms derive from 'dynamic psychiatry'. 7 extensive tables on drugs, psychological tests, research terms, etc. Full cross-references. Aimed at personnel in the mental health field, whereas *Chambers' dictionary of psychiatry,* by J.A. Bressel and G. La Fond Cantzlaar (1967. xiv, 234p.), with *c.*2,000 terms, is intended primarily for the general public. *Class No:* 616.89

[1313]
CAMPBELL, R.J. **Psychiatric dictionary.** 6th ed. New York, Oxford University Press, 1989. 811p. ISBN: 0195052935.

First published 1940.

Encyclopaedic dictionary of *c.*10,000 terms and cross-references, covering relevant terms in both technical language (using DSM-III-R nomenclature - thus, 7p. on different types of 'schizophrenia') and popular usage ('gay', 'moron'). Very brief biographical entries. Preceded by 'Key to pronunciation', book references (1p.) and abbreviations (9p.). The standard dictionary in its field. *Class No:* 616.89

[1314]
SHEPHERD, M., *ed.* **Handbook of psychiatry.** Cambridge Univ. Press, 1982-85. 5v.

1. *General psychopathology.* 1983. xi, 307p. £37.50; £13.50. 2. *Mental disorders and somatic illness.* 1983. 337p. £17.50. 3. *Psychoses of uncertain etiology.* 1982. xiv, 313p. £40; £13.95. 4. *The neuroses and personality disorders.* 1983. xviii, 500p. £22.50. 5. *The scientific foundations of*

....(contd.)
psychiatry. 1985. xiv, 359p. £45; £20.

Each volume carries an extensive bibliography (*e.g.*, v.3, *c.*1,300 references). Chapters include such topics as 'The historical background'; 'Neurological disorders'; 'Affective psychoses'; 'Philosophy and psychiatry'. Cross-references between the volumes. Author and subject indexes. *Class No:* 616.89

Communicable Infections & Fevers

[1315]
MANDELL, G.L., *and others eds.* **Principles and practice of infectious diseases.** 3rd ed. New York, etc., Churchill Livingstone, 1990. 2340p. illus., diagrs., graphs, tables, chemical structures, maps. ISBN: 0443086869.

First published 1979.

Over 240 contributors. 4 parts (297 documented chapters): 1. Basic principles in the diagnosis and management of infectious diseases - 2. Major clinical syndromes - 3. Infectious diseases and their etiologic agents - 4. Special problems. Chapter 149: 'Poliovirus', p.1359-67, with 94 references. Detailed 106-page index. 'This expanded and extensively rewritten 3rd ed. ... all of the chapters have been revised, rewritten and updated' (*Preface*). *Class No:* 616.9

AIDS

[1316]
AIDS information sourcebook 1989-1990. Malinowsky, H.R. *and* Perry, G.J., *eds.* 2nd ed. London, Oryx Press, 1990. 224p. ISBN: 0897445442.

First published 1988.

600 new or updated lists of testing, treatment and counselling centres. Chronology of significant AIDS-related events. Annotated bibliography contains AIDS-related books, pamphlets, films, videotapes and online databases. *Class No:* 616.98

[1317]
Virology and AIDS abstracts. Cambridge, University Press, 1988-. 12pa. (*Cambridge scientific abstracts.*) ISSN: 08965910.

Originally as *Virology abstracts* (1967-87).

1991: *c.*8,800 abstracts drawn from *c.*5,000 primary sources. Author and subject indexes per issue and annually. Online: DIALOG, ORBIT, etc. *Class No:* 616.98

Surgery

[1318]
Recent advances in surgery. Edinburgh, etc., Churchill Livngstone, 1992. illus., diagrs., graphs, tables. ISBN: 0443045690. ISSN: 01438395.

First published 1965.

The 1992 volume (250p.) has 25 contributors. The 14 documented articles include: 'Surgical management of ulcerative colitis' (p.23-38); 'Blood transfusion: indications and hazards' (p.119-36); 'Fluid balance and electrolytic disturbance' (p.209-24). Analytical subject index. *Class No:* 617

Ophthalmology

[1319]
MILLODOT, M. **Dictionary of optometry.** 2nd ed. London, Butterworth, 1990. 221p. ISBN: 0407022112.

About *c.*3,000 terms used in optometric practice, with definitions, synonyms, abbreviations, examples, and cross-references. Intended for students and practitioners. *Class No:* 617.7

[1320]
Ophthalmic literature. Oxford, Butterworth-Heinemann, 1947-.
4pa. ISSN: 00303720.

More than 4,000 abstracts specially-commissioned pa.
V.44(5), 1991 contains c.500 abstracts, divided into 2
sections: 1. The eye (18 sections: 1. Lids ... 18. Ocular
motility) - 2. General sections (e.g. 3. Pathology; 10.
Veterinary ophthalmology). Author and subject indexes.
New format planned for 1992 onwards and a change of
title to New ophthalmic literature. Class No: 617.7

62 Engineering

Engineering

Abbreviations & Symbols

[1321]
Dictionary of engineering acronyms and abbreviations. Keller, H. *and* Erb, U. London, Adamintine, 1989. [v],312p. ISBN: 074490014x.
  About 30,000 entries. Aims to cover the major fields of engineering. Some North American bias (*e.g.* DTI is identifed as 'Department of Trade and Industry [US]', but not for the UK). Well-produced with bold type for entry terms. *Class No:* 620(003)

Databases

[1322]
Compendex. New York, Engineering Information Inc., 1970-.
  COMPENDEX is the machine-readable database for *Engineering index* (now *Engineering index monthly, qv*). Among its hosts are BRS and DIALOG. Connect charges are fairly high. V.N. Anderson's 'Searching the engineering databases' (*Database*, v. 10(2), April 1987) gives a brief comparative survey. CD-ROM (Dialog).
  SHE subject headings in engineering supplies the terms used in *Engineering index* and its associated COMPENDEX database. *Class No:* 620(003.4)

Bibliographies

[1323]
ANTHONY, L.J., *ed.* **Information sources in engineering.** 2nd ed. London, Butterworths, 1985. [x], 579p. (*Butterwoths Guide to information sources.*)
  First published as *The use of engineering literature*, K.W. Mildren (1976. [viii], 621p.).
  26 contributors; 28 chapters. 4 main sections: Introduction - Primary infomation sources (Reports ... Trade catalogues) - Secondary information sources (Abstracting and indexing services; bibliographies and reviews ... standard reference sources) - Specialized subject fields (chapters 11-28; 11. Stress analysis ... 28. Nuclear power engineering, with 5p. of references). 'Index to subjects, information services and organizations', detailed and analytical, p. 563-79. An outstanding contribution to the series.'No other source provides such comprenhensive coverage of the literature of engineering' (*Special libraries*, v. 78(2), Spring 1987, p.152. *Class No:* 620(01)

Handbooks & Manuals

[1324]
Eshbach's handbook of engineering fundamentals. Tapley, B.D., *ed.* 4th ed. New York, Wiley, 1990. [2368p.] diagrs., charts, tables. ISBN: 0471890847.
  3rd ed. 1975.
  Some 78 contributors. 16 documented sections (*e.g.* 12. Electronics: 174p. 50 references). Many formulas. Detailed, analytical index. Covers mechanical, electrical, chemical and civil engineering. Significantly revised, with an added chapter on computer science, and a much expanded chapter on automatic control. Equations, definitions and explanations are a feature. Bibliographies, although updated, rarely list post-1980 publications. *Class No:* 620(035)

Reviews & Abstracts

[1325]
The Engineering index monthly: the index to the world's engineering developments. New York, Engineering Index, Inc., (now Engineering Information), 1884-. 12 pa. with annual cumulation. ISSN: 01683036.
  Until September 1962 as *Engineering index.*
  Now produces *c.*22,000 abstracts pa. Coverage includes some conference proceedings. About 75% of articles are English-language material. Author and subject indexes per issue. *The Engineering index annual* (with 4-year cumulations) includes author, author affiliation and cumulative subject indexes, as well as the abstracts themselves. The *Index* is available online as COMPENDEX [COMPuterized ENgineering InDEX], 1970-. A major abstracting service. On CD-ROM (Dialog). *Class No:* 620(048)

Tables & Data Books

[1326]
Kempe's Engineer's year-book, 1991. Sharpe, C., *ed.* 96th ed. London, Morgan Grampian, [1991]. 2v. [xxii, 3500p.] illus., diagrs., graphs, tables.
  About 100 contributors. V.1 has 46 sections, A1-F5 (B6, 'Numerical engineering', has 36p. with ½p. of bibliography). V.2 has 45 sections, F6-L10 (H4, 'Line communication', has 27p. with a brief bibliography). This ed. includes new chapters on 'Brazing', 'Intellectual property law for the engineer' and 'Radio communication underground'. Chapters on 'Microprocessors', 'Radio Communication', 'Airports and air transport' have been dropped. 'Chapter guide to information on environmental issues', p.ix. A major engineering reference tool. *Class No:* 620(083)

[1327]
McGraw-Hill handbook of essential engineering information and data. New York, McGraw-Hill, 1991. 1072p. illus. ISBN: 0070227640.

....(contd.)

A collection of basic engineering information, data and principles for day-to-day problem solving. Drawn from various McGraw-Hill engineering handbooks, supplemented by explanatory comments. About 50 sections. 760 illus. 'Highly recommended' (*Choice*, March 1991, p.1102). *Class No:* 620(083)

Standards

[1328]
KVERNELAND, K.O. World metric standards for engineering. New York, Industrial Press, 1978. xi, [735p.] diagrs., tables. ISBN: 0831111135.

Aimed to assist engineers, manufacturers, designers, and draughtsmen in North American and other countries where transition to the metric system is taking place; this work provides comparisons of the standards in 8 of the largest industrial countries of the world and is thus of value even in areas where SI units are already in use. 16 of its 20 sections cover components, systems, materials and practices of general engineering interest, but 6 in particular concern mechanical engineering: 8. Seven threads - 9. Fasteners ... 12. Bearings - 13. Mechanical power transmission systems - 14. Fluid power systems and components ... 17. Metal cutting tools. Text, tables and illustrations are adequate for their intended purpose and impressive in coverage. *Class No:* 620(083.74)

Research Establishments

[1329]
Engineering research centres: a world directory. Archbold, T., *and others eds.* 2nd ed. Harlow, Essex. Longman Group, 1988. viii,599p. ISBN: 0582017785.

Data on more than 3,500 official laboratories, industrial research centres, and educational establishments with research and development programmes. Subject areas extend to standards, metrology, computer theory and software, and transport engineering. Arranged by countries, then bodies A-Z. Data include names of senior staff, number of graduate research staff, annual expenditure, activities, publications, products. Index of establishments; subject index. *Class No:* 620:061:061.62

Engineering Design

[1330]
CULLUM, R.D. Handbook of engineering design. London, Butterworths, 1988. [vii], 303p. illus., diagrs. graphs. ISBN: 0408005580.

19 contributors. Part 1 (chapters 1-11, each with bibliography: 1. Stages in design; 2. Engineering materials; 3. Stress analysis; 4. Bearings; 5. Fastenings; 7. Design aspects of production processes) - Part 2 (chapters 12-16; *e.g.*, 13. Structure and organization in design offices). Directory; addresses. Detailed analytical index, p.301-3. Well illustrated. *Class No:* 620.001.6

Materials Science

Encyclopaedias

[1331]
BEYER, M.B., *ed.* Encyclopedia of materials science and engineering. Oxford, etc. Pergamon Press, 1986. 8v. (6105p.). illus., diagrs.

More than 1,400 contributors. 1,580 signed, documented articles on 45 broad subject areas (*e.g.*, metals, ceramics, polymers magnetic materials, welding). Some articles, designated 'An overview', introduce and survey a subject, furnish systematic and comprehensive bibliographic references to the entire subject, and are extensively cross-

....(contd.)

referenced (*e.g.*, 'Advanced ceramics: an overview', v.1, p.98-105: 4 sections, 3 diagrs., 9 illus., 16 references). V.8, *Index*, includes systematic outline of the *Encyclopedia*, list of contributors, citation index, subject index (*c.*50,000 entries), materials information sources (p.527-42, supplementing article references), and list of acronyms. Aims to produce a comprehensive work to 'serve the needs of education and industry' (*Introduction*). Supplementary v.2 (1990) carried 130 articles (*e.g.* 'Germanium', p.931-35, with a bibliography of 18 items). *Class No:* 620.02(031)

[1332]
International encyclopedia of composites. Lee, S.M., *ed.* New York, etc., VCH, 1990-. v.1-. ISBN: 0895732904, set.

1. *Acetal resins and composites to Cynate ester resins.* xvi,563p. ISBN: 0895737310.

2. *Damage control to Joining polymeric adhesives.* xii,524p. ISBN: 0895737329.

The completed work will include more than 300 contributors. Lengthy, documented articles ('Aramid fiber composites', p.37-56, 120 references), with cross-references. Each volume includes a list of 'main entries'. Topics covered fall into 4 groups: Special types, *e.g.* engineering materials; Behaviour under varying conditions; Those with special properties; Design aspects. Of value to practising scientists and engineers and advanced-level students. A major work. *Class No:* 620.02(031)

Handbooks & Manuals

[1333]
BOLTON, W. Newnes engineering materials pocket book. Oxford, Heinemann Newnes, 1989. diagrs., tables. xiii,194p. (*Pocket Book.*) ISBN: 043490113x.

Covers materials - ferrous; aluminium; copper; magnesium; nickel; titanium; polymeric; ceramic; composite - in separate chapters. Each includes discussion of material itself, details of coding systems and compositions, heat treatment information, properties, typical uses. Appendix: conversion tables. Index, 6p. Small format. Intended for students with project work and practising engineers. *Class No:* 620.02(035)

Tables & Data Books

[1334]
CRC handbook of materials science. Lynch, C.T., *ed.* Boca Raton, Florida, CRC Press, 1974-80. 4v. illus., tables.

1. *General properties.* 1974. 782p.

2. *Metals, composites, and refractory materials.* 1975 [vi], 440p.

3. *Nonmetallic materials and applications.* 1975. [xi], 642p.

4. *Wood.* 1980. [xi], 459p.

Mostly tabular data. Thus, v.4 has tables on p.72-402, standard definitions of wood terms, and forest product associations (USA). Each volume has an analytical index, with a general index and an index to specific names. *Class No:* 620.02(083)

[1335]
HOULDCROFT, P.T., *ed.* Materials data sources. Compiled for the Materials Group, the Institution of Mechanical Engineers, and sponsored by the Institute of Metals. London, Mechanical Engineering Pubns, for the Institution of Mechanical Engineers, 1987. vi, 111p. tables. ISBN: 085298636x.

6 sections: 1. Metals and alloys - 2. Refractories, ceramics, glasses and hardmetals - 3. Polymers and composites - 4 Timber - 5. Databases and materials selectors - 6. Educational establishments. Appendices: A.

....(contd.)

Addresses of standards organizations; B. Joining and adhesive bonding consumables. Small format. For quick-reference. *Class No:* 620.02(083)

Energy (Sources)

[1336]
ANTHONY, L.J., *ed.* **Information sources in energy technology.** London, etc., Butterworths, 1988. xii, 324p. (*Butterworths Guides to information sources.*) ISBN: 040803050x.

11 contributors. 3 parts (16 documented chapters): 1. Energy in general - 2. Fuel technology - 3. Specific energy sources (solid, liquid and gaseous fuels; nuclear energy; solar and geothermal energy; alternative energy sources). Detailed, analytical 'Index to subjects, information services and organizations'. Well up to the Butterworths' series standards. Some overlap with the companion *Information sources in engineering*. *Class No:* 620.9

[1337]
Energy and the environment in the 21st century. Tester, J.W., *and others.* Cambridge, Mass., MIT Press, 1991. xix,1006p. ISBN: 0262200783.

Proceedings of the conference held at the Massachusetts Institute of Technology. The 2 plenary sessions comprise sections A-F: A. Transport systems - B. Industrial processes - C. Building systems - D. Electric power for the developing countries - E. Economics and policy - F. Advanced energy supply technologies. Detailed, analytical index. *Class No:* 620.9

[1338]
World energy and nuclear directory. 8th ed. Harlow, Essex, Longman, 1990. 574p. ISBN: 0582079330.

Combines former *World energy directory* (2nd ed. 1985) and *World nuclear directory* (7th ed. 1985).

Records 1,500 research and technology laboratories in the nuclear sciences, plus 2,000 industrial, official, academic and independent organizations, laboratories and consultancies carrying out or promoting development work in non-atomic energy generation and distribution. Establishment and subject indexes. *Class No:* 620.9

Energy Conservation & Exploitation

Alternative Sources

[1339]
BRITISH LIBRARY. Science Reference and Information Service. **Sources of information on alternative energy technology held at the Science Reference and Information Service.** Dunning, P.H., *comp.* London, British Library, Science Reference and Information Service, 1986. 52p. ISBN: 071230732x.

A briefly annotated guide to the holdings of the Science Reference Library during the last ten years. Coverage: biomass energy, energy recycling, geothermal energy, solar energy, wave and wind energy. Arrangement is by form of material (*e.g.,* books, directories, business reports). Shelf-marks are given. Index to list of organizations with an interest in alternative energy technologies. 'A most useful guide in its field' (*Aslib information*, v.14(10), October 1986, p.235). *Class No:* 620.97

[1340]
GRAYSON, L., *ed.* **Recycling: energy from community waste:** a guide to sources. 2nd ed. London, British Library, Science Reference and Information Service, 1991. iv,143p. ISBN: 0712307618.

International survey in 4 sections: 1. Legislative background - 2. Energy recovery options - 3. Bio-conversion

....(contd.)

- 4. Thermo-chemical conversion (p.68-126). Indexes of personal authors, corporate bodies, subjects. 576 numbered references under sub-sections. *Class No:* 620.97

Mechanical Engineering

[1341]
CARVILL, J. **Mechanical engineer's data book.** Oxford, Butterworth-Heinemann, 1991. 352p., illus., tables. ISBN: 075061014x.

Extensive use of illus. and tables. Includes information on manufacturing processes. *Class No:* 621

[1342]
ISMEC: mechanical engineering abstracts. Bethesda, Md., Cambridge Scientific Abstracts, 1973-. v.1(1)-. Bi-monthly. ISSN: 03060039.

Originally published by the Institute of Mechanical Engineering as an index to current literature. Published monthly. 2 vols. per year before 1979. Subsequently published by Data Courier Inc., the present publishers took over in 1981 and, in 1982, v.15, began to publish abstracts. Groups contents into 9 sections, (*e.g.,* 1000. Management and production; 3000. Mechanics, materials and devices; 4000. Production processes, tools and equipment) with sub-sections (*e.g.,* 3600. Tribology) also sub-divided (*e.g.,* 3610. Bearings). Each issue (bi-monthly from 1987) has author and subject indexes. Cumulative annual indexes. Scope: 250 journals, theoretical and applied, plus many conferences and books. Each entry has unique identifier and full citation. Abstracts of variable quality and efficiency - often verbose. Annual content has been diminishing from 15,000 in 1982 to 9,600 in 1991. Also available as a computerized database, ISMEC online via established hosts *e.g.,* DIALOG, ESA-IRS, or through leased tapes. *Class No:* 621

[1343]
KUTZ, M., *ed.* **Mechanical engineer's handbook.** New York, etc., Wiley, 1986. xix, 2,316p. illus., diagrs., graphs, tables. ISBN: 047108817x.

Intended, as an independent work, to complement the last (12th) edition of Kent's *Mechanical engineers' handbook* (Wiley, 1950). 82 contributors. 78 chapters in 6 parts, with emphasis on Materials and mechanical design (630p.) and Energy and power (800p.). Other parts: Digital computers - Manufacturing engineeering - Systems, controls and instrumentation - Management and research. An extremely wide-ranging work, covering theory, practice, engineering, management in all their aspects, some inevitably thinly. Despite the Editor's rightful criticism of wholesale reproduction of tables of data ('Why destroy forests to make paper for printing tables ...?') the work contains many hundreds, of necessity, supported by numerous graphs. Chapter references and bibliographies and a 60-page index complement well-organized and pleasingly displayed text and data. *Class No:* 621

[1344]
Machinery's handbook: a reference book for the mechanical engineer, draftsman, toolmaker and machinist. Oberg, E., *and others, eds.* 23rd ed. New York, Industrial Press, 1988. 2500p. diagrs., graphs, tables. ISBN: 083111200x.

First published 1914. Previous edition 1984.

A comprehensive data book of 147 sections. Main sections: Mathematical tables; Tribology and bearings; Gearing; Machine elements; Machinery and forming; Iron and Steel; Alloys; Joining; Casting; Properties of materials. Covers American and British practice and standards. Analytical index. Separate, additional metric index, and Ready Reference Index of frequently used tables and

....*(contd.)*
formulas on endpapers. Companion vol.: *'Machinery's handbook' guide to the use of tables and formulas.* 1988. 230p. $12.95. ISBN 0851112018. The 24th ed. is due in 1992. *Class No: 621*

[1345]
NAYLER, G.H.F. Dictionary of mechanical engineering. 3rd ed. London, etc., Butterworths, 1985. 394p. diagrs. ISBN: 0408015055.
First published 1967. Previous ed. 1975.
'Previous editions have concentrated on terms relating to moving parts, machines, and the production of power and its adoption in transport and mechanisms. This edition has added terms relating to both mechanical engineering design and manufacture, typified by the field of robotics' (*Author's Preface*). *Class No: 621*

Maintenance Engineering

[1346]
Standard handbook of plant engineering. Rosaler, R.C. *and* Rice, J.O., *eds.* New York etc., McGraw-Hill, 1983. xv, [1,824]p. diagrs., graphs, tables. ISBN: 0070521603.
Supersedes *Facilities and plant engineering handbook* (1973), edited by B.T. Lewis and J.P. Marron.
678 contributors. 4 parts, 20 sections. A. The basic plant facility: construction, equipment and maintenance - B. Plant operation equipment: selection and maintenance - C. The maintenance function: basic equipment and supplies - D. Supplementary technical data. Appendices contain brief guide to mainly non-published US sources of information and metric conversion tables. Brief glossary and good, 43-page index. Almost 900 diagrs., graphs, tables, etc.
'Presents a wealth of information on planning, construction, operation and maintenance of manufacturing and service facilities' (*Welding design & fabrication*, v.57, Mar. 1984, p.232). (Another favourable review in *Civil engineering - ASCE*, v.52, Dec. 1982, p.22). *Class No: 621-7*

Protection of Machinery

Fluid Sealing

[1347]
Seals and sealing handbook. 2nd ed. Morden, Surrey, Trade and Technical Press, 1986. xviii, 535p. illus., diagrs., graphs, tables. ISBN: 0854611010.
First published 1981, 'Compiled by the editors of the Trade & Technical Press Ltd'.
Aims to provide comprehensive information (basics, principles, selection criteria, applications, data, suppliers). 11 sections (1. Fundamentals and principles - 2. Static seals - 3. Dynamic seals - 4. Oil seals ... 6. Special seal types ... 8. Seals for special applications - 9. Materials - 10. Data (and glossary) - 11. Buyer's guide and indexes of subjects and advertisers). *Class No: 621-762*

Nuclear & Atomic Engineering

Bibliographies

[1348]
CHESTER, K., *comp.* **Nuclear energy and the nuclear industry:** a guide to selected literature and sources of information. 2nd ed. London, Science Reference and Information Service, 1986. 44p. ISBN: 0712307427.
Previous ed. 1982.
A valuable guide, with annotations, to over 100 publications in the subject field: 30 abstracting/indexing services; almost 60 periodicals; 12 directories and yearbooks; 4 publications with data on nuclear reactors; 4

....*(contd.)*
bibliographies series. Also contains list of 35 organizations and 19 suppliers, companies and consultants, plus 12 publications giving market research and survey information. Notes about books, reports, conference and patents are included, but no entries. No index. *Class No: 621.039(01)*

[1349]
JEDRUCH, J. Nuclear engineering databases, standards and numerical analysis. New York, Van Nostrand Reinhold, 1985. xix, 295p. illus., diagrs., graphs, tables. ISBN: 0442245742.
A guide to sources of information, data projects and collections, computerized databases, regulations, standards, computer-aided design methods, property and performance data centres and bases, government bodies and engineering societies and their publications, concerned with nuclear reactor engineering. Heavily orientated to the US. Many useful lists and tabulations. Classified bibliography (p.267-81). Extensive references. 'Nuclear engineers, public utilities personnel and government regulatory officials will find this guide to the software of nuclear engineering an indispensable on-the-job tool' (*Mechanical engineering*, v.107, August 1985, p.72). *Class No: 621.039(01)*

Reviews & Abstracts

[1350]
INIS Atomindex. Vienna, International Nuclear Information System, International Atomic Energy Agency, 1920-. v.1(1)-. 24pa. ISSN: 00047139.
Successor to *Nuclear science abstracts* (ceased 30 June 1976). V.1-20 as *List of bibliographies on nuclear energy*.
About 90,000 indicative and informative abstracts pa. Classified order: A00. Physical sciences - B00. Chemistry, materials and earth sciences - C00. Life sciences - D00. Isotopes, isotope and radiation applications - E00. Engineering and technology - F00. Other aspects of nuclear energy. Each section subdivided in detail, *e.g.*, E10.00 Engineering - 16.00 Accelerators - E16.30. Components and auxiliaries - E16.31. Ion sources. Each abstract lists subject headings used in indexes. Each issue has personal author, corporate entry, subject, conference date, conference place and report, standard and patent number indexes. (*N.B.,* No index of conference *names.*) Semi-annual indexes cumulative annually. English abstracts and translations of foreign-language titles. Covers reports, conference papers, patents, journal articles and books (in that order for each section). Also available on magnetic tape (from which the printed version is prepared), and online via DIALOG, ESA-IRS, INKA, BELINDIS and STN, and on CD-ROM (BRS Europe). First issue in each volume (1st January) contains list of over 4,300 journals scanned regularly. *Class No: 621.039(048)*

Tables & Data Books

[1351]
Nuclear data sheets. Duluth, Minn., Academic Press, 1969-. Monthly. (3v. pa). tables.
Produced and edited by the National Nuclear Data Center for the International Network for Nuclear Structure Data Evaluation, assembled from ENSDF (Evaluated Nuclear Structure Data File), the computerised data bank, maintained by the Center, which is based at the Brookhaven National Laboratory, Upton, New York. Provides data on nuclear structure and radioactive decay for all known isotopes, critically evaluated by scientists supplying the data from 11 countries. There are indexes of references every four months - one for each vol. - with annual cumulations since 1978 and cumulations for 1969-74 and 1975-77. *Class No: 621.039(083)*

[1352]
INIS: Thesaurus. Vienna, International Atomic Energy Agency, 1987. (*INIS reference series.*) ISBN: 9201781873.

First published 1970 and based on the 1969 ed. of *EURATOM Thesaurus.*

Contains 17,243 accepted terms (descriptors) and 5,803 forbidden terms (non-descriptors) from the fields of nuclear physics and reactor technology and related topics. Identifies deleted and added terms (since previous ed.) in separate lists, and arrows in main alphabetical sequence also identify added terms. Scope notes for many terms. Appendix gives full listings of narrower terms in certain cases. *Class No:* 621.039:025.43

Reactors

[1353]
MARSHALL, W., *ed.* Nuclear power technology. Oxford, Clarendon Press, 1983. 3v. illus., diagrs. (*Oxford science publications.*)

1. *Reactor technology.* xv, 503p. £50. ISBN 0198519486.
2. *Fuel cycle.* xv, 456p. £50. ISBN 0198519583.
3. *Nuclear radiation.* xv, 363p. £50. ISBN 0198519591.

32 contributors in 24 chapters cover all aspects of nuclear power from 'How reactors work', through various types of fission reactor (with one chapter on fusion), fuel (design, reprocessing, etc.), waste, with a separate vol. on radiation, its risks and its applications in medicine and dating. Chapter references, suggestions for further reading and glossaries are valuable adjuncts. Separate volume indexes.

Various reviews from within the industry pay tribute to content, style, range, clarity, with isolated criticisms about the book's treatment of waste and costings, but an independent authority should be cited: 'A noble effort, which has produced a fine work of science' (*Nature*, v. 309, June 7, 1984, p. 565). *Class No:* 621.039.4

Electrical Engineering

Abbreviations & Symbols

[1354]
BRITISH STANDARDS INSTITUTION. Guide for graphical symbols for electrical power, telecommunications and electronics diagrams. London, BSI, 1985-86. 13 pts. (*BS 3939:1985-1986.*)

Supersedes BS108 and BS530.

Pt. 1: General information, general index. 1986. 35p.

Pt. 2: Symbol elements, qualifying symbols and other symbols having general applications. 1985.

Pt. 3: Conductors and connecting devices. 1985. 8p.

Pt. 4: Passive components. 1985. 8p.

Pt. 5: Semiconductors and electron tubes. 1985. 24p.

Pt. 6: Production and conversion of electrical energy. 1985. 16p.

Pt. 7: Switchgear, controlgear and protective devices. 1985. 28p.

Pt. 8: Measuring instruments, lamps and signalling devices. 1985. 12p.

Pt. 9: Telecommunications: switching and peripheral equipment. 1985. 16p.

Pt. 10: Telecommunications: transmission. 1985. 32p.

Pt. 11: Architectural and topographical installation plans and diagrams. 1985. 12p.

Pt. 12: Binary logic elements. 1985. 88p.

Pt. 13: Analogue elements. 1985. 12p.

Over 2,000 symbols for use in draughting throughout the field. *Class No:* 621.3(003)

[1355]
ARDIS, S.B. A Guide to the literature of electrical and electronics engineering. Poland, J.M., *ed.* Littleton, Colorado, Libraries Unlimited Inc., 1987. xx, 190p. (*Reference sources in science and technology series.*) ISBN: 0872874745.

The first English-language, wide-ranging and substantial guide to the field since Burkett and Plumb's *How to find out in electrical engineering* (1967), and therefore very welcome. Its subject range extends to communications and computing engineering and includes microwaves, radar, materials science and satellite technology. Excluded are robotics, electrical wiring and construction and applications of electronic devices in music, biomedicine and avionics. Coverage is restricted to English-language reference material published post-1978. Arrangement is by type of material (bibliographies, abstracts, data bases, patents, standards, etc.). 8 parts, 25 chapters, with annotated entries for almost 700 publications and information sources.

British users will note omission, over-brief treatments, mis-spelling of some British sources of information, and will be disadvantaged by the American publisher and price data given, but will still find this a valuable guide overall, especially its strong coverage of the many handbooks in this subject area. *Class No:* 621.3(01)

Dictionaries

[1356]
INSTITUTE OF ELECTRICAL AND ELECTRONICS ENGINEERS. IEEE Standard dictionary of electrical and electronic terms. Jay, F., *ed.* 4th ed. New York, IEEE/ Wiley, 1988. 1270p. illus.

First published 1972.

About 24,000 entries, including almost 9,000 new or revised terms, with separate list of *c.*15,000 acronyms, abbreviations, etc. All definitions are derived from IEEE or other standards (about 450 sources) and are thus authoritative. *Class No:* 621.3(038)

Reviews & Abstracts

[1357]
Electrical and electronics abstracts. Science abstracts. Section B. London, INSPEC/Institution of Electrical Engineers, in association with the Institute of Electrical and Electronics Engineers, Inc., New York, 1898-. v.1-. Monthly.

Currently more than 70,000 abstracts pa. and still growing! Classifed into 8 major categories (*e.g.,* 10.00: Circuit theory and circuits - 20.00: Components, electronic devices and materials; ... 80.00: Power systems and applications), subdivided (*e.g.,,* 12.00: Electronic circuits; 12.70: Filters; 12.70F: Digital filters). Each issue has 6 indexes (subjects, authors, bibliographies, books, conferences, corporate authors). Half-yearly indexes, plus cumulative 4-5 year indexes. The major abstacting service in its field. Available on-line as part of the INSPEC data base. Also INSPEC magnetic tapes are available twice monthly. CD-ROM. *Class No:* 621.3(048)

Yearbooks & Directories

[1358]
Electrical and electronics trades directory: 1991. 109th ed. Stevenage, Herts., Peregrinus, 1991. Annual. v.p. ISBN: 086341236x.

First published 1883.

The 'Blue Book' offers 'a comprenhsive guide to companies in the electrical and electronics industries, showing their main sources of manufacture and supply' [*Foreword*]. Lists *c.*4,000 organizations. Covers

....(contd.)

manufacturers, suppliers, servicing companies, representatives, wholesale distributors. A classified list of products and materials comprises half the content. Indexes of firms and persons and of trade names. Emphasis is British. *Class No:* 621.3(058)

Tables & Data Books

[1359]

FINK, D.G. and BEATY, H.W., *eds.* **Standard handbook for electrical engineers.** 12th ed. New York, etc., McGraw-Hill, 1987. xvi, [2210]p. illus., diagrs., graphs, circuits, tables. ISBN: 0070209758.

First published 1907; 11th ed., 1978.

A companion to Fink and Christiansen's *Electronic engineers' handbook.* 115 contributors. 28 sections. Scope: generation, transmission, distribution, control, conservation and application of electrical power with relevant supporting material. Major sections: 2. Electric and magnetic circuits - 3. Measurements and instruments - 4. Properties of materials - 5. Steam generation ... 10. Power system components - 11. Alternative power sources ... 14. Transmission systems ... 18. Power distribution ... 20. Motors ... 22. Electronics - 23. Electricity in transportation. Considerable revision and much new material. Complete chapter on standards, with full list of US standards in alphabetical subject order. Almost all sections have reference lists and bibliographies, but many citations are elderly or ancient (pre-World War II). The contents of each section are better displayed but identification of topics by paragraph number makes location more difficult. Worse: the index practice is inconsistent in referring - conventionally - to pages. *Class No:* 621.3(083)

[1360]

LAUGHTON, M.A. and SAY, M.G., *eds.* **Electrical engineer's reference book.** 14th ed. London, etc., Butterworths, 1985. [xii, 980]p. illus., diagrs., graphs, tables. ISBN: 0408004320.

First published 1945. M.G. Say's editorship has been continuous since then. Previous ed. 1973.

36 chapters by 72 specialist contributors grouped in: Fundamentals - Energy supply - Power plant - Application. Separate chapters on education and training and on standards. Many new chapters - *e.g.,* Control systems and analysis; Power electronics; HUDC - and expansion into self-contained chapters of some topics - *e.g.,* turbines; nuclear reactor plant; road, railway and marine transportation. Greater depth of coverage of most topics, with updated illustrative matter.

'Impressively produced in a clear, double column format, the book was a pleasure to handle ... close attention to indexing and contents listing ... prevent the reader becoming overwhelmed by the sheer scale. A minor criticism is the uneven distribution of suggested further reading ... This is a book for quick answers and also for more relaxed browsing. It is highly recommended' (*Electronics and power,* v.32(9), Sept. 1986, p.681). *Class No:* 621.3(083)

[1361]

SUMMERS, W.I., *ed.* **American electricians' handbook.** 11th ed. New York, etc., McGraw-Hill, 1987. [1664]p. illus., diagrs., tables. ISBN: 0070139326.

First published 1913. Previous ed. 1981.

Long-established compendium previously edited by T. Croft. Aims to give complete guidance on selection, installation, maintenance and operation of all types of electrical equipment and wiring. Extensively revised to incorporate developments in electronics and solid-state circuits and computing. 11 Divisions, *e.g.,* 1. Fundamentals ... 4. General electrical equipment and batteries ... 7. Generators and motors ... 9. Interior wiring (315p.). - 10.

....(contd.)

Electric lighting (205p.). In addition to the 100's of tables throughout the work, Division 11 collects 116 tables of general application. There are over 1,500 illus., clear and apposite. *Class No:* 621.3(083)

Power Supply

Hydroelectric Power

[1362]

GULLIVER, J.S. and ARNDT, R.E.A., *eds.* **Hydropower engineering handbook.** New York, McGraw-Hill, 1991. illus., diagrs., graphs, tables. v.p. ISBN: 0070251932.

Emphasises design aspects and cost estimates, with some attention to the environmental effects of hydropower plant. Case studies and examples feature. Chapters carry references. Index. *Class No:* 621.311.21

Transmission

Cables

[1363]

Electric cables handbook. Bungay, E.W.G. and McAllister, D., *eds.* 2nd ed. Oxford, BSP Professional Books, 1990. xiv,977p. illus., diagrs., graphs, tables. ISBN: 063202299x.

First published 1982.

28 contributors, almost all from BICC. 5 parts: 1. Theory, materials, design - 2. Wiring cables - 3. Supply distribution cables - 4. Transmission cables - 5. Submarine cables. Appendices (p. 707-941) contain tables of data on all commonly used cable types. Classified bibliography (25p.), index and chapter references.

'... gives a comprehensive and authoritative account of the state of the art ... [and] ... has the merit of presenting much good explanatory material rather than merely giving factual information...' (*Electrical review* of the first ed.). *Class No:* 621.315.2

Measurement

[1364]

NOLTINGK, D.E., and *others.* **Instrumentation reference book.** London, Butterworth, 1988. v.p. illus., diagrs. ISBN: 0408015624.

6 parts: 1. Mechanical measurement - 2. Measurement of temperature and chemical composition - 3. Electrical and radiation measurement - 4. Instrumentation systems - 5. Further scientific and technical information - 6. Directories and commercial information (1-10. 10: Master address list). Index. About 30 main contributors with chapters by various hands. 'Mainly applications oriented' (*Introd.*). Well produced. *Class No:* 621.317

Batteries

[1365]

CROMPTON, T.R. **Battery reference book.** London, etc., Butterworth, 1990. xii,v.p. illus., diagrs., graphs, tables. ISBN: 0408007907.

2 introductory chapters (technology; selection), then chapters 3-63 in 6 parts: 1. Characteristics - 2. Theory and design - 3. Performance evaluation - 4. Applications - 5. Charging - 6. Suppliers (types of batteries). Appendices: suppliers (manufactuers; international; A-Z by country); glossary (*c.*225 terms; 'Activated stand life' - 'yield'); Standards (British; IEC); bibliography (3p.). Detailed, analytical index. 'Of interest to battery manufacturers and users and the manufacturers of equipment using batteries' (*Preface*). *Class No:* 621.355

Waves & Oscillations

Microwaves

[1366]
Microwave handbook. Potters Bar, Radio Society of Great Britain, 1989-. V.1-. illus., diagrs., graphs, tables.
V.1. *Components and operating techniques.* M.W. Dixon, ed. 1989. v.p. (0990612886).
To be in 3v. V.1 has 5 contributors; 6 chapters. Apart from much referenced information, it is a timely collection of practical diagrams, hints and tips. 2-page index. *Class No:* 621.37.029

Pulses

Amplifiers

Lasers

[1367]
Laser handbook. Amsterdam, etc., North-Holland, 1972-90. 6v. diagrs., graphs, tables.
1-2., edited by F.T. Arecchi and E.O. Schulz-Dubois. 1972. xxvii, 1947p. £181.25. ISBN 0720402131.
3., edited by M.L. Stitch. 1979. v, 878p. £129.69. ISBN 0444852719.
4., edited by M. Bass and M.L. Stitch. 1985. x, 594p. £90.63. IBSN 0444869271.
5., edited by M. Bass and M.L. Stitch. 1985. ix, 692p. £102.13. ISBN 0444869344.
6., edited by W.B. Colson and C. Pellegrini. 580p. £107.90. ISBN 0444869530.
A series of 'expository monographs' (*Preface*) on laser technology and applications by specialists, no longer (since v.3) limited by length of article. V.3 has 11 articles; v.5 has 5. 'With the increasing use of lasers in such a wide variety of scientific applications, this book [v.3] will be a valuable reference for advanced students and practising scientists in physics, chemistry and engineering' (*Philosophical magazine,* part B, v.41(6), 1980, p.706). A review in *Physics today* (Dec. 1980, p.59-60) draws attention to inevitable omissions of recent information in v.3. but commends the series, and ends: 'Every research group in quantum mechanics should have access to this set of references'. *Class No:* 621.375.826

Electronics

Abbreviations & Symbols

[1368]
BROWN, P. Electronics and computer acronyms. 2nd ed. London, etc., Butterworths, 1988. [vii], 272p. diagrs. ISBN: 0408023988.
First published 1985 as *Dictionary of electrical electronics and computer abbreviations.*
Nearly 400 new entries, bringing the total to almost 2,500, shift the emphasis heavily to the title subjects, although telecommunications, microprocessors, lasers, fibre optics, radio, television, audio and general electrical engineering terms are also included. Definitions and explanations range from one line to fifteen, are often illustrated and are clear and concise. Unexpected entries include whole words, *e.g.,* jack, tweeter, X-ray, whilst the Appendix (p.270-2) oddly concentrates entirely on battery choice and use. *Class No:* 621.38(003)

Databases

[1369]
ELCOM. Bethesda, Md., Cambrige Scientific Abstracts.
Covers 1980 to date. A bibliographic database providing references, with abstracts, to world literature on electronics, computing and communications, including research, commercial and marketing information. Sources include journal articles, government reports, conference papers, theses, patents. File size: 100,000 citations. Updated bi-monthly; *c.*10,000 additions pa. Hosts: ESA-IRS; BRS. Printed versions: *Electronics and communications abstracts* and *Computer and informative systems abstracts journal.* 'ELCOM ... might be the best choice for the undergraduate student or computer hobbyist who is not interested in exotic foreign language materials ... Elcom covers newspapers and trade literature that may not be considered scholarly enough [for INSPEC and COMPENDEX]' (*Database,* v.4(2), June 1981, p.13-29). *Class No:* 621.38(003.4)

Encyclopaedias

[1370]
GIBILISCO, S. and SLATER, N., eds. Encyclopedia of electronics. 2nd ed. Blue Ridge Summit, Pa., TAB Books, 1990. 960p. illus., diagrs., graphs, circuits, tables. ISBN: 0830633898.
First published 1985.
A collection of over 3,000 short articles, A-Z, presenting clear definitions and explanations, with appropriate illustrations (nearly 2 per page), from the whole field of electronics and related subjects. The entries are also listed under 17 categories which alphabetically display the scope (Antennas and feed lines - Audio electronics - Broadcasting and communications ... Computers and digital electronics - Electricity and magnetism ... Switching and control ... Wiring and construction). A specific subject index of 5,500 entries facilitates reference to relevant articles for terms not found in the main encyclopaedia section. 'A good book for public, high school and college libraries' (*Choice,* v.28(6), December 1990. p.607). *Class No:* 621.38(031)

[1371]
McGraw-Hill encyclopedia of electronics and computers. Parker, S.P., ed. 2nd ed. New York, London, etc. McGraw-Hill, 1988. [x], 964p. illus., diagrs., graphs, tables. ISBN: 007045499x.
First published 1984.
'Much of the material ... has been published previously in the *McGraw-Hill Encyclopedia of science and technology,* 6th edition [1987]' (t.p. verso.). Contains 520 articles, 120 of them 'completely revised' (*Preface*), by 328 contributors, alphabetically arranged by topic. Conveniently collects articles from three main areas: principles of electronics; science and technology of electronic devices; applications of devices, with emphasis on computing. Extensive analytical index facilities retrieval. Useful article bibliographies. 1250 illus. *Class No:* 621.38(031)

Handbooks & Manuals

[1372]
COLLINS, T.H. Analog electronics handbook. New York, Prentice-Hall, 1989. xxiv,460p. diagrs., graphs, tables. ISBN: 0130331198.
28 chapters, each in numbered sections. Chapters 1-6 cover background theory and mathematics; 7-28 cover applications (*e.g.* 7. Passive components; 15. Active filters; 23. Modulation; 27. Microwaves and radar principles). Worked examples and over 500 diagrs., etc. Includes glossary of symbols (letter and graphic); Tables (*e.g.* Laplace

....*(contd.)*
transforms); analytical index. No bibliography or 'further reading'. 'A useful and well-written book' (*Choice,* May 1989, p.1548). *Class No: 621.38(035)*

[1373]
FINK, D.G. *and* CHRISTIANSEN, D., *eds.* **Electronic engineers' handbook.** 3rd ed. New York, etc., McGraw-Hill, 1989. xvi, [2528]p. illus., diagrs., graphs, circuits, tables. (*McGraw-Hill handbooks.*) ISBN: 0070209812.
First published 1975. 2nd ed. 1982.
'New edition now covers the entire range of electronics' (*Preface*). About 170 contributors; 29 sections (including revised, expanded or new sections on power electronics, pulsed circuits, CAD programs and languages, and standards). Detailed, analytical index, 81p. Contains over 2,000 illustrations and over 3,000 references. *Class No: 621.38(035)*

[1374]
MAZDA, F., *ed.* **Electronic engineer's reference book.** 6th ed. London, etc., Butterworth, 1989. v.p. illus., diagrs., graphs, circuits, tables. ISBN: 0408054301.
First published 1958 by Haywood Books. 5th ed. 1983.
85 contributors. Follows the five-part arrangement of the 5th ed.: 1. Mathematical and electrical techniques - 2. Physical phenomena - 3. Materials and components - 4. Electronic circuit design and instrumentation - 5. Applications (including communication satellites, networks, computers, videotape). 6 added chapters on newer topics, *e.g.* application specific integrated circuits, computer aided design techniques, digital system analysis, software engineering, local area networks, integrated services digital network (ISDN). Clear text; attractively laid out; simple diagrams; excellent analytical index; useful reference and 'further reading' lists. *Class No: 621.38(035)*

Dictionaries

[1375]
AMOS, S.W., *ed.* **Dictionary of electronics.** 2nd ed. London, etc., Butterworths, 1987. [vii], 324p. diagrs., graphs, circuits. ISBN: 0408027509.
First published 1981.
2nd ed. includes new definitions, and revisions or expansions of some others. Aims to keep abreast of developments in semiconductor devices, digital techniques, computers and microprocessors. Target users: non-experts and workers in other fields. Deliberate overlap of coverage with *Dictionary of audio, radio and video,* by R.S. Roberts and *Dictionary of telecommunications,* by S.J. Aries. Approximately 2,300 entries (including cross-references) with terms defined informatively, many with lengthy descriptions and illustrations. *Class No: 621.38(038)*

[1376]
TURNER, R.P. *and* GIBILISCO, S. **Illustrated dictionary of electronics.** 5th ed. Blue Ridge Summit, Pa., TAB Books, 1991. 720p. diagrs., tables. (*TAB Professional and reference book series.*) ISBN: 0830673458.
4th ed. 1988.
More than 22,000 terms and abbreviations defined, briefly (*c.*3 to 4 lines). Numerous cross references. Appendices: schematic symbols; tables of data (*e.g.* resistor color codes; mathematical functions; electronics abbreviations). *Class No: 621.38(038)*

Reviews & Abstracts

[1377]
Electronics and communications abstracts. London, Multiscience Publishing, 1961-. v.1(1)-. Monthly. ISSN: 00135119.
6,000-7,000 indicative abstracts. Covers periodical articles, conference proceedings, reports and books. 6 sections: Electromagnetic wave techniques - Materials, devices and phenomena - Circuits and networks - Communications - Control - Computers - Measuring, recording and miscellaneous applications. Twice-yearly subject index and annual author index. No other indexes. *Class No: 621.38(048)*

Tables & Data Books

[1378]
CLIFFORD, M. **Master handbook of electronic tables and formulas.** 4th ed. Blue Ridge Summit, Pa., TAB Books, 1984. x, 382p. diagrs., tables. ISBN: 0830606254; 083061625x, pbk.
Aims to provide solutions to problems in electronics and communications by copious provision of tables giving data for the many hundreds of relevant formulas, obviating the need for calculations. 25 chapters cover basic concepts (resistance, inductance, power, etc.), applications (recording, video, antennas, etc.), computers, constants, conversions numbers. One chapter lists all formulas and an effective index leads directly to information required. *Class No: 621.38(083)*

Circuits

[1379]
GRAF, R.F. **The Encyclopedia of electronic circuits.** Blue Ridge Summit, Pa., TAB Books, 1985-1991. 3v. circuits, tables.
V.1 (1985. 760p. ISBN: 0830609385) presents *c.*1,300 circuits in an A-Z sequence, with a subject index.
V.2 (1988. 838p. ISBN: 083063183) includes alarm and security circuits, smoke, moisture and metal detectors, computer, fibre optic and laser circuits, among much else.
V.3 (1991. 838p. ISBN: 083063348) organizes circuits into 108 categories.
Almost 1,300 circuits presented in 98 alphabetically arranged sections (Alarms ... Metal detectors ... Zero crossing detectors). Brief descriptive notes for most circuits and sources (books, periodicals, trade literature) given for each. Specific index leads directly to required circuits. All 3v. are fully illustrated. *Class No: 621.38.04*

[1380]
HOLLAND, R.C. **Illustrated dictionary of microelectronics and microcomputers.** Oxford, etc., Pergamon Press, 1985. v, 162p. diagrs., tables. ISBN: 0080316344, Hardback; 0080316352, Flexicover.
About 850 terms, including cross-references, with definitions and explanations ranging from a few words to several hundred, supported by diagrams. Clear and simple. Includes a number of manufacturing terms from the trade literature. 'For those bewildered by the new language of microelectronics it is a very useful dictionary [which explains] often-used words, phrases and abbreviations' (*Aslib book list,* v.50(9), Sept. 1985, item 441). *Class No: 621.38.04*

Printed Circuits

[1381]
COOMBS, C.F., *Jr., ed.* **Printed circuits handbook.** 3rd ed.
New York, etc., McGraw-Hill, 1988. xxxvi, [884]p. illus.,
diagrs., graphs, tables. ISBN: 0070126097.
First published 1967.
Previous ed. 1979. 27 contributors. Aims to provide in
one volume the information needed to design, manufacture,
test and repair printed wiring boards and assemblies
(*Preface*). 8 parts, 35 chapters (1. Introduction to printed
wiring - 2. Engineering - 3. Fabrication (the largest part - 8
chapters, 241p.) - 4. Assembly and test - 5. Soldering - 6.
Quality and reliability - 7 Multilayer circuits - 8 Flexible
circuits). The newest techniques - *e.g.*, surface mount
technology (SMT) - are generously covered. Numerous
tables, chapter references and a glossary are valuable
adjuncts to a clear, logically-presented, essentially practical
text. Good index. Emphasis is heavy on US sources. *Class
No:* 621.38.049.75

Telecommunications

[1382]
FREEMAN, R.L. **Reference manual for telecommunications
engineering.** New York, etc., Wiley 1985. xv, 1504p., illus.,
diagrs., graphs, charts, tables, nomograms. ISBN:
0471867535.
Aims 'to provide a central source of basic information'
for designers and users of all kinds of telecommunications
systems. Content is assembled in 26 subject areas (*e.g.*,
Signaling, Fiber optics transmission, Radio transmission,
Electromagnetic interference), each type with introductory
material, essential information, references and, often, a
bibliography. Most of the material is drawn from
authoritative sources, which are identified. Index of more
than 3,000 entries. *Class No:* 621.39

[1383]
GRAHAM, J. *and* LOWE, S. **The Facts on File dictionary of
telecommunications.** 2nd ed. New York, Facts on File, 1991.
240p. diagrs., tables. ISBN: 0816020299.
First published 1983.
Covers acronyms, abbreviations, computer-related terms
and a few commercial products. Major concepts have
extended definitions. 'Highly recommended for academic
and technical libraries' (*Library Journal*, 1 July 1991,
p.86,88). *Class No:* 621.39

[1384]
PETERSEN, D. **Audio, video and data telecommunications.**
New York, McGraw-Hill, 1992. 344p. illus. ISBN:
0077074270.
The basic theories of telecommunications, with modern
applications. Practical examples and case studies. *Class
No:* 621.39

Wave Signals

[1385]
WEIK, M.H. **Fiber optics standard dictionary.** 2nd ed. New
York, Van Nostrand Reinhold, 1989. 352p. ISBN:
0444223876.
Updates *Fiber optics and lightwave communications
standard dictionary.*
Several thousand terms are defined and explained, with
liberal use of examples, illus. and cross-references. 12 pages
of bibliography. An essential dictionary in its specific field.
Class No: 621.391.6

Radio & Television Apparatus

[1386]
World radio TV handbook. London, Billboard, Ltd./Pitman,
1946-, v.1-. Annual. 576p. illus., diagrs., tables, maps.
Vol. 42, 1988 (ISBN 0902285130). First published 1946
as *World radio handbook.*
A guide to radio and television broadcasting stations
throughout the world, with data on frequencies, radiated
power, exact location, operating hours, frequency schedules,
languages broadcast, news bulletins, etc. Separate sections
for radio and television, each arranged by continent and
then alphabetically by country. Separate list of long and
medium wave stations and short wave stations. Information
about international organizations. Miscellaneous data: world
time; solar activity; reception conditions; receivers owned in
each country; suitable megahertz bands, etc. User's guide in
4 languages. Equipment test reports. Advertisements. *Class
No:* 621.396/.397

Radio

VHF

[1387]
JESSOP, G.R., *ed.* **VHF/UHF manual.** 4th ed. London,
Radio Society of Great Britain, 1983. [viii], [528]p. illus.,
diagrs., graphs, circuits, tables. ISBN: 0900612630.
First published 1969. Previous ed. 1976.
Covers the spectrum above 30 MHz. 11 chapters, *e.g.*, 2.
Propagation ... 4. Receivers - 5. Transmitters ... 8.
Antennas - 9. Microwaves - 10. Space communications.
Extensively illustrated.
'Previous editions ... gained worldwide acceptance as the
standard handbook for amateur radio on v.h.f. and u.h.f.
and microwaves. This fully revised and greatly expanded
fourth edition provides a wealth of design and
constructional information for a wide variety of equipments
...' (*Radio and electronic engineer*, v.54(5), May 1984,
p.214). *Class No:* 621.396.029

Space Radiocommunication

Satellites

[1388]
MORGAN, W.L. *and* GORDON, G.D. **Communications
satellite handbook.** New York, Wiley, 1989. 900p. illus.
ISBN: 0471316032.
5 main parts covering: teletraffic; communications;
satellite systems; multiple access techniques; space craft
technology; satellite orbits. Extensive chapter references.
Lists of symbols, constants and acronyms. *Class No:*
621.396.94.04

[1389]
WILLIAMSON, M. **The Communications satellite.** New York,
A. Hilger, 1990. 420p. ISBN: 0852741928.
Includes a case study of direct broadcasting by satellite
(DBS). Excludes electronic control systems design and
transmission and coding methods. *Class No:* 621.396.94.04

Television

[1390]
JACKSON, K.G. *and* TOWNSEND, B. **Television and video
engineer's reference book.** London, Butterworth Heinemann,
1991. 772p. illus., diagrs. ISBN: 0750610212.
Comprehensive, including television transmitters,
transformers, sound editing, audio recording, mixers and
special effects, studio lighting, lighting control, receiving
antennae, semiconductors and microelectronics. *Class No:*
621.397

[1391]
TRUNDLE, E. **Television and video engineer's pocket book.** London, Heinemann, 1986. 323p. illus., diagrs., circuits, tables. ISBN: 0434901970.

Outlines concisely 'the systems, formats and technology of contemporary TV and video equipment' (*Preface*) for the benefit of practising service engineers, before relating this essential background information to fault identification and repair techniques and the use of a wide variety of test equipment. A final chapter of reference data collects basic information, but much other data is to be found with the subject to which it relates elsewhere in the book. This book cannot give the serviceman all he needs for his work but can be a useful foundation. *Class No: 621.397*

Heat Engineering

[1392]
ELLIOTT, T.C., *ed.* **Standard handbook of powerplant engineering.** New York, McGraw-Hill, 1989. xiv,v.p. illus., diagrs., graphs, tables. ISBN: 0070191069.

46 chapters in 6 sections: 1. Steam generation - 2. Turbines and diesels - 3. Fuels and fuel handling - 4. Pollution control - 5. Plant electric systems - 6. Instrumentation and control. Analytical subject index. 40 contributors, from industry. A practical approach. *Class No: 621.4*

[1393]
GUYER, E.C., *ed.* **Handbook of applied thermal design.** New York, etc., McGraw-Hill, 1989. xv, v.p. illus., diagrs., graphs, tables. ISBN: 0070253536.

67 contributors. Intended to provide 'a general perpsective' (*Preface*) on heat transfer analysis, materials performance, heating and cooling technology and instrumentation and controls. 13 parts, each with a number of chapters: 1. Fundamentals of thermal design and analysis ... 4. Structural materials in thermal design - 5. Heat transfer fluids ... 9. Refrigeration ... 12. Thermal sensors - 13. Automatic temperature controls. Appendix: 'Classified unit conversions'. Detailed subject index (12p.). 'Recommended for libraries serving a technical clientele' (*Choice*, Feb. 1989, p.968). *Class No: 621.4*

Internal Combustion Engines

Diesel Engines

[1394]
LILLY, L.C.R., *ed.* **Diesel engine reference book.** London, Butterworths, 1984. [707]p. illus., diagrs., graphs. ISBN: 0408004436.

Successor to *Diesel engine principles and practice*, by C.C. Pounder, first published 1955. Previous ed. (2nd) 1962.

32 contributors and chapters, grouped into: Theory; Engine design practice; Lubrication; Environmental pollution; Crankcase explosions; Engine types; Engine testing; Maintenance. Chapter references. Index (*c*.1,700 entries). Lists of engine types and manufacturers, institutions, and fuel injection equipment manufacturers.

'A comprehensive work on the design, operation and maintenance of all types of diesel engines ... Ranges through subjects which will be of long-term use to engine designers, installation engineers and ... enormous number of users ...' (*Automotive-engineering*, v.92, Dec. 1984, p.102). *Class No: 621.436.1*

Pneumatic Energy Machines

[1395]
BARBER, A. **Pneumatic handbook.** 7th ed. Morden, Surrey, Trade & Technical Pr., 1989. 640p., xv. illus., diagrs., tables. ISBN: 0854611374.

First published 1965. Previous ed. 1982.

Standard reference work for pneumatic and compressed air engineering. 12 sections cover principles, compressors, air lines, valves, actuators, circuits, tools, techniques, devices and machines, miscellaneous data, lists of standards and symbols and buyers' guide, glossary and index. Copious illustrations and many tables. Interspersed advertisements. *Class No: 621.5*

Refrigeration

Yearbooks & Directories

[1396]
The **Refrigeration and air conditioning year book.** Croydon, Maclaren, 1987. Annual. 366p. illus. ISSN: 02685361.

Published since 1975 as part of subscription to *Refrigeration and air conditioning and heat recovery*; also available separately. Previously as *Refrigeration and air conditioning year book*.

8 sections: 1. Company information - 2. Classified guide to manufacturers and suppliers - 3. Contractual and specialist services - 4. Geographical guide - 5. Trade names - 6. Foreign brand names and UK agencies - 7. UK agencies for foreign firms - 8. Profession and other organizations. Full-page advertisements by categories: (industrial, commercial refrigeration; air conditioning; instrumentation and control; insulation). *Class No: 621.56(058)*

Fluids Handling Engineering

[1397]
FLUIDEX. **BHRA Fluid engineering abstracts.** Cranfield, Beds., BHRA Fluid Engineering.

Covers 1973 onwards. References, with abstracts, to literature of fluids, including aerodynamics, fluid flow, fluid engineering, offshore technology and rheology. Updated monthly. 15,000 additions pa. Hosts: DIALOG and ESA-IRS. Cost per connect hour: $69 and £52.65. Available on magnetic tape. Publications: *BHRA Fluid Engineering thesaurus*; *Guide to the Fluidex database*, *Fluidex Notes*, *Fluidex Newsline*. Printed versions: several abstracts journals covering the various fields of interest, *e.g.*, *Tribos*, *Fluid-sealing abstracts*, *Pumps and other fluids machinery abstracts*, *Pipelines abstracts*. *Class No: 621.6*

Valves & Taps

[1398]
BARBER, M.J., *and others, eds.* **Handbook of power cylinders, valves and controls.** Morden, Surrey, Trade and Technical Press, 1986. ix, 364p. illus., diagrs., graphs, charts, tables. ISBN: 0854611002.

Aims to provide 'essential information on the principles and control of hydraulics and pneumatics, together with detailed coverage of all types of hydraulic and pneumatic cylinders, valves and their electronic controls'. 8 sections of text with information on theory, construction, operation, performance, selection, including relvant tables and graphs, followed by data section listing standards and symbols. Concise, but adequate index (8p.). *Class No: 621.646*

Pumps

[1399]

KARASSIK, I.J., *and others eds.* **Pump handbook.** 2nd ed. New York, etc., McGraw-Hill, 1986. xxii, [1351]p. illus., diagrs., graphs, tables. ISBN: 0070333025.

First published 1976.

72 contributors. Contents assembled in 13 sections. Major sections: 2. Centrifugal pumps (330p.) - 3. Displacement pumps - all types (127p.) - 6. Pump drivers (178p.) - 8. Pumping systems (118p.) - 9. Pump services, *i.e.,* applications and areas of use (317p). Other sections cover: materials; controls; intakes; selection and purchase; installation, operation and maintenance; testing. Extensive appendix of general technical data supplements hundreds of specialized tables in the text. Excellent index provides good access to well-organized and clearly presented contents. SI and US Customary units are used and bibliographial references are provided. 'Readers may be overwhelmed by the magnitude of the material. It is truly a matter of having access to more information on pumps than most people care to know or are able to absorb. But that is really the mark of a good reference text ... The editors have done an excellent job of providing an authoritative guide ...' (*Chemical engineering,* v.93, Nov. 10, 1986, p.140). *Class No:* 621.65

Production Engineering

Databases

[1400]

CAD/CAM online. New York, EIC/Intelligence Inc.

Covers 1983 to date. A bibliographic database providing references, with abstracts, to world literature on computer-integrated manufacturing, covering computer-aided design and and manufacture (CAD/CAM) and commercial and economic aspects. Sources include periodical articles, conference papers, research reports, government reports, patents and books. File size: more than 20,000 items. Updated monthly. 1,500 additions pa. Hosts: DIALOG; ESA-IRS. Printed version: *CAD/CAM abstracts. Class No:* 621.7/.9(003.4)

Bibliographies

[1401]

COX, J., *and others.* **Keyguide to information sources in CAD/CAM.** London, Mansell; Lawrence, KS, Ergosyst Associates, 1988. xxi,257p. ISBN: 072011974x, UK; 0916313158, US.

3 parts. I. Survey of CAD/CAM and its information sources (7 documented chapters, p.3-110). II. Bibliography (514 items). III. Directory of organizations (217 research centres, online hosts; international in scope). Detailed, analytical index, p.245-57. Glossary (AGV—Workstation), p.xv-xxi. An authoritative survey. *Class No:* 621.7/.9(01)

Laws

[1402]

DEVINE, J. and WATTS, A., *comps.* **Information pack on product liability.** London, Information and Library Service, Institution of Mechanical Engineers, 1987. vii,80p. (*Information pack, 6.*) ISBN: 0852986505.

3 parts: 1. Product liability information (abstracts and indexes - text books), p.1-41; 2. Recent liability coverage (26 items), p.42-48; Product liability references (122 items; aeronautical engineering - welding), p.49-73. Author and subject indexes. A useful series. *Class No:* 621.7/.9(01)(094.1)

[1403]

BENEDICT, G.F. **Nontraditional manufacturing processes.** New York, Dekker, 1987. xiii, 381p. illus., diagrs., graphs, tables. (*Manufacturing engineering and materials processing, no. 19.*) ISBN: 0824773527.

21 chapters cover the use of energy in new ways or the application of forms of energy preivously not used in manufacturing processes concerned with machining (removal processes), joining and forming. Each chapter deals with a different process in the same format: principles and equipment; capabilities and parameters; application; summary (succinct pros and cons); references. There are 8 chapters each for mechanical and thermal processes. 2 Appendices list US equipment manufacturers and acronyms. Each chapter has a list of references. Excellent illustrations. 'For those seeking a single volume of information, defining the principles and capabilities, together with advantages to be gained and pitfalls to be avoided, this book is to be recommended' (*Production engineer* v.66(7), July/August 1987, p.11). *Class No:* 621.7/.9(035)

[1404]

DROZDA, T.J., *ed.* **Tool and manufacturing engineers handbook.** 4th ed. Dearborn, Mich., Society of Manufacturing Engineers, 1983-86. 5v. illus., diagrs., graphs, tables.

First published as *Tool engineers handbook* in 1949. Previous ed. 1976.

1. *Machining.* 1983. [1484]p. ISBN 0872630854.

2. *Forming.* 1984. [900]p. ISBN 0872631354.

3. *Materials and finishing.* 1985. [864]p. ISBN 0872631761.

4. *Quality control and assembly.* 1986. [750]p. ISBN 087263177x.

5. *Manufacturing management.* 1988. [551]p. ISBN 0872633063. 6 sections, subdivided: 1. Operations and strategic planning - 2. Managerial leadership and its foundations - 3. Human resources - 4. Manufacturing/engineering interface - 5. Resource utilization - 6. Quality. Detailed, analytical index, 9p. *Class No:* 621.7/.9(035)

Dictionaries

[1405]

TVER, D.F. and BOLZ, R.W. **Encyclopedic dictionary of industrial technology:** materials, processes and equipment. New York, London, Chapman and Hall, 1984. [vi] 353p. diagrs., tables. ISBN: 0412005018.

Wide-ranging coverage of materials, machine tools, computers, robots, manufacturing processes and treatments, and equipment, handling, inspection and testing. Definition and description of *c.*1,800 terms vary from one line to fifty. Cross-references. Select bibliography p.349-53. *Class No:* 621.7/.9(038)

Workshop Practice

Powder Metallurgy

[1406]

FAYED, M.E. and OTTEN, L., *eds.* **Handbook of powder science and technology.** New York, etc., Van Nostrand Reinhold, 1984. xiv, 850p. illus., diagrs., graphs, tables. ISBN: 0442226107.

26 contributors from 7 countries. 19 chapters cover particle size analysis and measurement, fundamental properties of powders and their behaviour, size enlargement and reduction, mixing, storage, fluidization technology, pipeline transport, sedimentation, filtration, cyclones, wet scrubbers, etc. Chapter references.

'I definitely can recommend this handbook to all

....(contd.)

chemical engineers who are involved with the storage, handling and processing of particulate solids and powders' (*Chemical engineering*, v.92, Jan. 7, 1985, p.113). *Class No: 621.762*

[1407]
Powder metallurgy science and technology: abstracts of current journals, report and patent literature. Swarthmore, Pa., Peters Technology Transfer, 1968-. v. 1-. Monthly. ISSN: 00485020.

Coverage includes conference papers and book reviews. About 1,400 informative abstracts pa. Numbered consecutively from no.1, 1968. Classified arrangement: General information - Powder production - Powder properties - Compaction - Sintering - Forging, rolling and extrusion - Physical properties of sintered compacts - Ferrous metals and alloys - Non ferrous metals and alloys ... Fibre metallurgy - Refractories - Porous and friction materials -Nuclear applications ... Cermets and cemented carbides. *Class No: 621.762*

Boiler Making

[1408]
BEDNAR, H.H. Pressure vessel design handbook. 2nd ed. New York, Van Nostrand Reinhold, 1986. xi, 431p. diagrs., graphs, charts, tables. ISBN: 0442213859.

First published 1981.

Aimed as a practical aid to design in conformity with section 8 of the ASME Boiler and Pressure Vessel Code, there are chapters on loads and stresses; design for tall and short vertical vessels and supports for horizontal vessels; welds; materials; numerical methods for stress analysis. 10 Appendices include 172 bibliographical references, a list of relevant US standards and a glossary. Imperial units used.

'Should be a valuable resource not only to junior mechanical and vessel design engineers but also to practicing professionals who wish to expand their knowledge of the subject. Bednar has done a fine job in organizing and condensing much widely scattered information ...' (*Chemical engineering*, v.93, Oct. 13 1986, p.95). *Class No: 621.772*

Welding

[1409]
AMERICAN WELDING SOCIETY. Welding handbook. Kearns, W.H., ed. 7th ed. Miami, Florida, American Welding Society/London, Macmillan, 1975-85. 5v. illus., diagrs., graphs, tables.

1. *Fundamentals of welding*, ed. by C. Weisman. 1975. 373p. £34. ISBN 0333198743.

2. *Welding processes - arc and gas welding and cutting, brazing, and soldering.* 1978. 592p. £17.50. ISBN 0333256662.

3. *Resistance and solid-state welding and other joining processes.* 1980. 459p. £29. ISBN 0333273958.

4. *Metals and their weldability.* 1983. 582p. £39. ISBN 0333293428.

5. *Engineering, costs, quality and safety.* 1985. 456p. £68. ISBN 0333293436.

The major work of reference, with contributions by specialists from many countries. Revised volume by volume. Whole set currently in 7th ed. Extensively provided with bibliographical references. Generously illustrated. Separate indexes.

Publication of the 8th ed. began in 1987.

1. *Welding technology.* 1987. xiii,638p. £66. *Class No: 621.791*

[1410]
International standards index: welding and related processes. Abington, Woodhead, 1991. 646p. ISBN: 1855730219.

Loose-leaf. Bi-annual supplements planned.

Lists nearly 5000 standards on welding and allied techniques from 16 countries. Includes European and international standards. *Class No: 621.791*

[1411]
Welding abstracts. Oxford, Pergamon Press, for the Welding Institute, 1988-. Monthly. ISSN: 09520287.

About 500 abstracts per issue. Sections: Processes - Production - Equipment and materials - Properties and testing - Manufacturing and construction - General. Author and subject indexes per issue. Includes patents and standards. Online. *Class No: 621.791*

Packaging

[1412]
International packaging abstracts. Oxford, etc., Pergamon, 1981-. v.1-. Monthly. ISSN: 02607409.

Compiled by the Information Section of Pira (the Research Association for the Paper & Board, Printing & Packaging Industries). More than 4,000 informative abstracts pa., derived from over 250 periodicals, and from books, reports, standards, conference proceedings and newspapers. 8 sections (1. Packaging in general - 2. Materials - 3. Components - 4. Retail unit packages - 5. Transit packs - 6. Packaging for specific products - 7. Packaging operations and machinery - 8. Distribution), each subdivided (*e.g.*, 3.1 Labels; 6.13 Beverages). Author and subject indexes in each issue. Mean delay time for abstracts less than 3 months. Also available online through INFOLINE. *Class No: 621.798*

[1413]
PIRA Abstracts. Leatherhead, Surrey, PIRA, the Research Association for the Paper and Board, Printing and Packaging Industries.

Covers 1975 to date. A bibliographic database providing references, with abstracts, to the literature of paper and pulp manufacture, printing and packaging. Packaging materials, operations and equipment, products, markets and companies are covered. Sources: over 700 periodicals, books, reports, standards and conference papers. File size: 110,000 items (1986). Updated fortnightly. 10,000 additons pa. Available via INFOLINE. Cost per connect hour: $70. Printed version split between: *International packaging abstracts; Printing abstracts; Paper and board abstracts.* *Class No: 621.798*

Containerization

[1414]
Jane's Freight containers, 1987. 19th ed. London, Jane's Publishing Co., 1987. Annual. 712p. illus., diagrs., tables. ISBN: 0710608446.

16 sections grouped under 6 headings: Terminals (International ports, inland terminals and railway adminstrations) - Operators (Ship operators; Non-vessel operating carriers) - Air freight (Airports; International Air Transport Association; Major cargo-carrying airlines; Unit load devices manufacturers; Air cargo ground handling equipment manufacturers) - Manufacturers and services (Container leasing; Container manufacturers; Container handling; Container component manufacturers; Container filling and associated services; Container servicing) - International road and rail - International container standards. General index and ship index (over 2,000 entries). Standards section contains text of ISO 830, *Terminology relating to freight containers* (p.685-88). A

....(contd.)
combination of detailed illustrated descriptions of ports, airports, shipping fleets and a buyers' guide. Available online via DIALOG. *Class No:* 621.798.12

Machine Elements

[1415]
ROTHBART, H.A., *ed.* **Mechanical design and systems handbook.** 2nd ed. New York, etc., McGraw-Hill, 1985. xii, [1812]p. illus., diagrs., graphs, charts, tables. ISBN: 0070540209.
Previous ed. 1964.
52 contributors. This comprehensive handbook for machine design and dynamic analysis of mechanical systems groups its 43 sections into 5 main groups: Mechanical engineering fundamentals - Systems analysis and synthesis - Mechanical design fundamentals - Mechanical fastener components - Power-control components and subsystems. The influence of the computer is pervasive and has necessitated the re-writing of almost half the sections. Pertinent data for fabrication, function, stability, reliability, performance, machine life, are in profusion. Extensive reference lists. Detailed index (62p).
'Contains a wealth of information for mechanical, electrical, civil and chemical engineers ... An extensive and comprehensive reference for any engineering office' (*Public works*, v.117, August 1986, p.20). *Class No:* 621.8

Gears & Clutches

[1416]
DRAGO, R.J. **Fundamentals of gear design.** Boston, Mass., etc., Butterworth, 1988. xiii,560p. illus., diagrs., graphs, tables. ISBN: 040990127x.
Intended as a 'general design reference guide' for the 'beginning or occasional' gear designer (*Preface*, p.xi). 11 chapters (with references and sometimes bibliography) in 4 parts: I. Introduction (history; types of gears; theory) - II. Fabrication and inspection - III. Failure and load capacity evaluation - IV. Lubrication. 3 appendices (gear geometry; nomenclature; quality designations); index (15p.). Author is a practising and consulting engineer. Well-produced; extensively illustrated. 'An excellent general reference to the basics of gear design' (*Choice*, Feb. 1989, p.968). *Class No:* 621.833.3

Materials Handling

Fasteners

[1417]
Industrial fasteners handbook. 3rd ed. Morden, Surrey, Trade & Technical Press, 1985. vi, 650p. illus., diagrs., tables. ISBN: 0854610979.
Complete revision and updating of earlier editions to take account of new manufacturing techniques and new types of fasteners and materials. Attempts to provide detailed description and data for all known types, arranged logically in sections. 1. Review of mechanical fasteners (including design, performance, materials, manufacture) - 2. Bolts and machine screws - 3. Special duty fasteners (*e.g.*, vibration-resistant, fasteners for plastics, furniture, buildings) - 4. Special purpose fasteners (*e.g.*, rivets, plugs, pins, clips, staples) - 5. Tools used for fastening - 6. Data, standards, trade associations - 7. Buyers' guide (including trade names, classifed index, manufacturers' addresses). Well illustrated, copious data tabulations and effective index. Advertisements. *Class No:* 621.88

Lubrication

[1418]
CRC handbook of lubrication; (Theory and practice of tribology). Booser, E.R., *ed.* Boca Raton, Florida, CRC Press, 1984. 2v. illus., diagrs., graphs. ISBN: 0849339014 v.1; 0849339022 v.2.
1. *Application and maintenance.* [xiv], 600p. 2. *Theory and design.* [xiv], 689p.
Sponsored by the American Society of Lubrication Engineers as successor to McGraw-Hill *Standard handbook of lubrication engineering* (1968).
80 contributors. V.1. gives approximately equal treatment to: applications in automobiles, aircraft and machine tools; other industries; maintenance. V.2. is similarly divided between: friction, wear and lubrication theory; lubricants and their properties and uses; design principles. Chapter bibliographies. *Class No:* 621.89

[1419]
Tribos (Tribology abstracts). Cranfield, Beds., British Hydromechanics Research Association, 1968-. v.1-. ISSN: 00412694.
Continues *Tribology* (quarterly).
About 2,000 informative abstracts pa. of items drawn from over 1,000 journals, plus reports, standards and conference proceedings. Main sections: Testing and instrumentation - Materials - Friction - Wear - Lubrication - Lubricants - Machine components - Machinery and other applications.
Issue and cumulative annual indexes of personal and corporate authors and of subjects. Available online, as part of FLUIDEX database. *Class No:* 621.89

Mining

[1420]
IMM abstracts; a survey of world literature on economic geology, mining, mineral dressing, extraction metallurgy [and] allied subjects. London, Institution of Mining and Metallurgy, 1950-. 6pa. ISSN: 00190020.
About 3,000 abstracts per issue. 13 sections: Generalities - Mineral industry - Mathematical methods and computing - Physical and chemical studies - Analysis and instrumentation - Economic geology - Mining - Mineral processing - Metallurgy - Health and safety - Environment - General engineering - Civil engineering. No indexes. Microfiche and microfilm available. Online through IMM. *Class No:* 622

[1421]
The Mining directory, mines and mining equipment companies worldwide. 5th ed. London, Don Nelson Pubns., 1990. 722p. ISBN: 0946004021.
Main portion: A-Z listing of mines and mining equipment companies. Appended buyers' guide lists companies by subject. Geographical and company indexes. 5th ed. includes more companies and company specific data than did previous editions. *Class No:* 622

[1422]
STARK, M.M. **Mining and mineral industries:** an information sourcebook. Phoenix, Arizona, Oryx Press, 1988. [ix], 124p. (*Oryx sourcebook series in business and management.*) ISBN: 0097742958.
558 numbered entries, in 12 form sections: Core library collection (general; journals) - Dictionaries and encyclopedias - Handbooks and manuals- Directories - Bibliographies and literature reviews - Indexes and abstracts - Databases (items 221-68) - Industry surveys - Conferences and symposia - Texts and treatises - Journals - Maps and Atlases. 'Associations and research centers'. Sources. Section

....*(contd.)*

title and subject indexes. 'The literature selected varies from introductory to extremely technical and scholarly' *(Introduction).* *Class No: 622*

Methods

Oil extraction

[1423]
Petroleum engineering handbook. Bradley, H.B., *and others, eds.* Richardson, Tx., Society of Petroleum Engineers, 1987, second printing 1989. xxiv,v.p. illus., diagrs., graphs, tables. ISBN: 1555630103.

First published 1962 as *Petroleum production handbook.*

59 chapters, closely subdivided, in 3 sections: 1. Mathematics (basic tables; calculation procedures - 1 chapter) - 2. Production engineering (materials; methods; tools - 18 chapters) - 3. Reservoir engineering (properties; recovery data and methods; reserves; formation evaluation; etc. - 40 chapters). Author index (14p.); detailed, analytical index (59p.). Numerous tables and illustrative material; extensive chapter references. Comprehensive and invaluable. *Class No: 622.276*

Offshore

[1424]
Offshore engineering abstracts. Cranfield, Beds., BHRA, The Fluid Engineering Centre, 1986-. 6pa.

125 abstracts per issue. Coverage: design, construction, operation and maintenance of offshore structures and associated equipment. Sources: articles, monographs, reports, conference proceedings, patents. Author and subject indexes per issue and annually. FLUIDEX database, available on DIALOG and ESA-IRS. *Class No: 622.276.04*

Types of Mine

Oilfields

[1425]
TIRATSOO, E.N. Oilfields of the world. 3rd ed., rev. Beaconsfield, Berks., Scientific Press, 1986. xvi, [416]p. illus., maps, tables. ISBN: 090136018x.

First published 1973; 3rd ed., 1983 (xvi, 392p.).

Extensive data on the geology, history and economic geography of *c.*2,500 oilfields in some 90 countries. The 3rd ed., rev., includes a 24p. *Supplement* which incorporates new developments and updated statistical information. Appendices cover properties of crude oil and world oil reserves. Chapter references. 183 tables, 83 line-drawings, 4 plates and 8p. of maps. *Class No: 622.323*

Military & Naval Engineering

[1426]
PRETZ, B. Dictionary of military and technological abbreviations and acronyms. London, Routledge & Kegan Paul, 1983. [iv], 496p. ISBN: 0710092741.

Records *c.*50,000 acronyms and abbreviations used by the British, American, German and Soviet military. Bibliography, p.495-6. *Class No: 623*

Weapons & Arms

[1427]
Jane's Weapon systems, 1988-89. Blake, B. 19th ed. London, Jane's Publishing Co., 1988. Annual. [51], 1008p. illus., diagrms., tables. ISBN: 0710608551.

First published 1969.

3 main sections (p.34-904), subdivided by country: Strategic weapons and systems (land based) - Shipborne weapons and systems - Airborne weapons and systems. Glossary precedes. Analysis (tables, p.906-57): missiles; radar; sonar equipment; torpedoes; electronic warfare equipment; NATO designations of Soviet systems and equipment. Numerical list of entries. Index, p.995-1008. Online via DIALOG. *Class No: 623.4*

Small Arms

[1428]
EZELL, E.C. *and* **PEGG, T.M. Small arms of the world:** a basic manual of small arms. 12th ed. London, Arms and Armour Press, 1983. 894p. illus., diagrs, tables.

First published 1943 as *Basic manual of military small arms.* A completely new and revised version of the classic work by W.H.B. Smith.

Part 1. Small arms development since 1945 (Rifles and carbine development; Machine gun development; Submarine gun development; Handgun developments; Special purpose weapons development (*e.g.,* Grenade launches). Part 2: Description of small arms by nations (44) and a basic manual of recent weapons: Argentina ... Yugoslavia, p.194-843. Characteristic of each given. Appended: Small arms for outdoor sports. Small arms ammunition. Selected bibliography, p.883-5. Detailed, analytical index, p.889-94. 2,000 illus. *Class No: 623.44*

Field Engineering

Communications

[1429]
Jane's Military communications, 1991-92. Williamson, J., *ed.* 8th ed. London, Jane's Publishing Co., Ltd., 1991. [35], 894p. ISBN: 0710609582.

First published 1979 (for 1979/80).

Two main parts: Equipment (Radio communication ... Electronic warfare ... Laser and optical - Miscellaneous) - Systems. Addenda. Appendices (acronyms and code names; glossary; AN numbered communications equipment; director). Abundant technical data. Indexes: manufacturers; alphabetical. Online via DIALOG; CD-ROM. *Class No: 623.61*

Navies

[1430]
Conway's All the world's fighting ships. London, Conway Maritime Press, 1979-83. 4v. in 5. illus., diagrs. ISBN: 0870219235.

Conway's All the World's fighting ships, 1860-1905. 1979. [vii], 440p.

Conway's Fighting Ships, 1906-1921. 1983. [viii], 439p.

Conway's All the World's fighting ships, 1922-1946. 1980. [viii], 456p.

Conway's All the World's fighting ships, 1947-1982. pt.1: *The Western Powers;* pt.2: *The Warsaw Pact and non-aligned nations.* 1983. 2v.

The two 1947-1982 volumes aim to provide a coherent overview of the post-World War II naval revolution, using newly released information where possible (Foreword). Provides an historical survey (beginning with the introduction of ironclad ships), complementing *Jane's Fighting ships,* as well as correcting data in the latter's

....(contd.)

volumes. Each of the Conway volumes provides technical data on types of ships, photographs and line drawings, plus a detailed index. 'Conway's is an invaluable addition to naval reference collections of any size' (*Reference books bulletin, 1984-1985* (1986). p.42). *Class No: 623.8*

[1431]
FRIEDMAN, N. The Naval Institute guide to world naval weapons systems. Anapolis, MD, Naval Institute Press, 1989. 511p. photos, diagrs. ISBN: 0870212953.

Arranged by type of system. Sections: Surveillance and control - Strategic strike systems - Strikes - Surface warfare - Anti-aircraft warfare - Anti-submarine warfare - Mine warfare. Index. *Class No: 623.8*

Civil Engineering

Handbooks & Manuals

[1432]
BELL, F.G. Ground engineer's reference book. London, Butterworth, 1987. 1264p. illus., tables. ISBN: 0408011734.

About 70 contributors. 5 parts (59 chapters): 1. Properties and behaviour of the ground - 2. Investigation in ground engineering - 3. Treatment of the ground - 4. Construction in ground engineering - 5. Numerical methods and modelling in ground engineering. Chapter 11: 'Stability of soil slopes' (16p. 19 references; 2 items of further reading; 10 figures). 1,028 illus. in all. For practising civil engineers. *Class No: 624(035)*

[1433]
Structural engineering handbook. Gaylord, E.H., Jr. *and* Gaylord, C.N., *eds.* 2nd ed. New York, McGraw-Hill, 1990. v.p. diagrs., graphs, tables.

46 contributors. 30 sections. 763 illus. An authoritative reference work, for engineers, architects and students in these fields. Analytical index (over 2,000 entries). *Class No: 624(035)*

Dictionaries

[1434]
SCOTT, J.S. Dictionary of civil engineering. 4th ed. Harmondsworth, Penguin, 1991. 608p., illus. ISBN: 0140512462.

3rd ed. 1981.

About 5,000 terms are concisely defined. Includes a wide range of terms in soil mechanics, heavy construction and mining. 'Retaining wall': 1p. with illus. US usage is covered. For the layman and non-specialist engineer. *Class No: 624(038)*

Reviews & Abstracts

[1435]
International civil engineering abstracts. Dublin & London, CITIS, Ltd., 1982-. 10pa. ISSN: 03324085.

Formerly *ICE abstracts*, 1974-81.

About 3,000 abstracts pa. 10 sections: Structural engineering - Bridges - Buildings; materials; construction - Tunnels; underground structures; mechanics - Miscellaneous - Hydraulic power stations; dams - Coastal engineering; ports; waterways - Public health engineering; water supply; irrigation; hydrology - Highway and traffic engineering; transportation; airports. *Class No: 624(048)*

Yearbooks & Directories

[1436]
Ground engineering yearbook, 1991. Sanders, D.M. London, Thomas Telford, 1991. 712p. illus. ISBN: 0727716131.

Annual.

Usual directory type information on seven areas: 1. General information on ground engineering - 2. Standards and codes of practice - 3. Institutions and associations - 4. Materials and products - 5. Plant and equipment - 6. Contractors and specialist contracting services - 7. Consulting engineers. Indexes: Trade names; Company and personnel; Subject. *Class No: 624(058)*

Tables & Data Books

[1437]
HICKS, T.G. Civil engineering calculations reference guide. New York, etc., McGraw-Hill, 1987. xii, 291, [1]p. diagrs., graphs, tables. ISBN: 0070287988.

A condensation of Hick's *Standard handbook of engineering calculations* (2nd ed. 1985).

18 sections, closely subdivided (*e.g.*, Principles of statics; Geometric properties of areas; Analysis of stress and strain; Steel beams and girders; Timber engineering; Reinforced concrete, Prestressed concrete; Fluid mechanics; Soil mechanics). Coverage includes surveying and photogrammetry. References, p.286. Index, p.287-91. Calculations are in dual units. *Class No: 624(083)*

[1438]
Spon's Civil engineering and highway works price book, 1992. 6th ed. London, Spon, 1991. xxii,779p. ISBN: 0419173803. ISSN: 0957171x.

First published 1984.

13 parts: 1. General - 2. Preliminaries and general terms - 3. Resources - 4. Unit costs (civil engineering works) - 5. Unit costs (highway works) - 6. Oncosts and profits - 7. Costs and tender prices indices - 8. Daywork - 9. Professional fees - 10. Approximate estimates - 11. Outputs - 12. Tables and memoranda - 13. Updates. Detailed, analytical index, p.765-79. *Class No: 624(083)*

Structures

Concrete

[1439]
FINTEL, M.J., *ed.* Handbook of concrete engineering. 2nd ed. New York, Van Nostrand Reinhold, 1985. xiv [1], 892p. illus., diagrs., graphs, tables. ISBN: 0442226233.

First published 1974.

25 contributors. 27 mostly documented sections (6. Properties of materials for reinforced concrete; 8. Prestressed concrete (58 references); 11. Tabular structures for tall buildings; 16. Silos and bunkers (36 references); 19. Concrete pipes; 26. Computer applications; 27. Structural plain concrete). Detailed analytical index, p.575-92. *Class No: 624.012.3*

[1440]
REYNOLDS, C.E. *and* STEEDMAN, J.C. Reinforced concrete designer's handbook. 10th ed. London, Spon, 1988. xii,436p. diagrs., graphs, tables. ISBN: 0419145303, Hb; 0419145400, Pb.

First published 1932; 9th ed. 1981.

In 2 parts. Part I includes general and descriptive material (*e.g.* structural analysis; materials and stresses (p.36-48); electronic computational aids). Part II gives tables, data, worked examples for specific structures (*e.g.* continuous beams (p.150-72); columns (p.340-76)). 3 appendices: A. Mathematical formulae and data; B: Metric/

....(contd.)

imperial length conversions; C: Metric/imperial equivalents for common units. Analytical index, p.433-6. *Class No:* 624.012.3

Metal

[1441]
HAYWARD, A. and WEARE, F. **Steel detailers' manual.** Oxford, etc., BSP Professional Books, 1989. xii,203p. diagrs., illus., graphs, tables. ISBN: 0632018453.

6 sections (1. Use of structural steel - 2. Detailing practice - 3. Design guidance - 4. Detailing data - 5. Typical connection details - 6. Examples of structures). 'Further reading', 'Bibliography', Index. Frequent reference to British Standards and Codes of Practice. Of value to practising draughtsmen, engineers, students. Highly detailed. *Class No:* 624.014

Bridges

[1442]
WITTFOHT, H. **Building bridges:** history, technology, construction. Düsseldorf, Beton-Verlag 1984. 327p. illus. ISBN: 3764001703.

Translated and revised ed. of *Triumph der Spannweiter.*
Sections: Use of timber - Reinforced concrete - Launching the entire bridge - Prestressed concrete's limits - Lightweight concrete - Bridges of tomorrow. About 500 photographs. Portrays 'a level of professionalism and scholarship which makes it ideal not only for the most technical collections but also for a large readership who are non-specialists but just plain bridge lovers' (*New technical books,* v.71(3), March 1986, entry 464). *Class No:* 624.2

Railway Engineering

[1443]
Jane's World railways, 1991/92. Allen, G.F.   33rd ed. London, Jane's Publishing Co., 1991. [60], 964p. illus., diagrs., tables. ISBN: 0710608489.

Manufacturers (p.1-327) - Private freight car leasing companies - International rail services - International associations - Consultancy services - Railway systems - Rapid transit and underground railways. Detailed index, p.787-98. Online via DIALOG.

Incorporates *Jane's Urban transport systems* (3rd ed., 1984). *Class No:* 625.1

[1444]
UNION INTERNATIONALE DES CHEMINS DE FER. **Lexique général des termes ferroviaires.** 3. éd. Paris, The Union, 1975. 1602p.

First published 1957.

About 13,000 French-based railway terms, with German, English, Italian, Spanish and Dutch equivalents and indexes. The standard dictionary in its field. *Class No:* 625.1

[1445]
WESTWOOD, J.N. **The Railway data book.** Cambridge, P. Stephens, 1985. 224p. diagrs., tables, maps. ISBN: 0850596297.

23 chapters (2. Railway ownership and control; 4. Track and its terminology; 8. Signals; 11. Steam locomotive trends and trend-setters; 12. Electrification; 14. The diesel loco; 26. The passenger train; 23. A note on stations). 3 appendices (1. Preserved steam railways - 2. Major railway museums - 3. Railway enthusiast societies (British, French, German, US and Canadian)). Further reading (magazines, books, timetables). Non-analytical index. Concentrates on Western Europe (especially Britain) and North America. For the railway enthusiast. *Class No:* 625.1

Underground Railways

[1446]
CARRINGTON, B., *and others.* **Subways of the world.** In *Mass transit.* V.12(11), November 1985; v.12(12), December 1985. illus., diagrs.

Mass transit. v.12(11), November 1985, p.10-58, provides an A-Z guide to the world's operating metro systems. Details give population served, network length, system status, fare system, equipment used, etc. *Mass transit,* v.12(12), December 1985, p.44-54, lists A-Z world metro systems that are under construction and proposed systems. *Class No:* 625.42

Roads

[1447]
HRIS abstracts. Washington, Highway Research Information Service, National Research Council, 1968-. Quarterly. ISSN: 00176222.

About 1,800 abstracts per issue, covering research reports, technical papers in conference proceedings, and journal articles. Classified order (*e.g.*, 11. Administration; 17. Energy and environmental; 32. Cement and concrete; 51. Safety; 54. Operations of traffic control; 62. Foundations (soil); 90. Highway research, general). Source, author and retrieval term indexes.

TRIS (Transportation Research Information Service) is the online service, hosted by DIALOG, and available to US and Canadian users. *Class No:* 625.7

[1448]
OGLESBY, C.H. and HICKS, R.G. **Highway engineering.** 4th ed. New York, London, etc., Wiley, 1982. xiii, [1], 844p. illus., charts, tables. ISBN: 047102936x, HB; 0471871451, PB.

First published 1954; 3rd ed. 1975.

The new edition gives 'added attention' (*Preface,* p.vi) to rehabilitation and maintenance, efficient management, public transport, energy shortages and costs, safety, new materials and problems of developing nations. 21 chapters, each with problems: 3. Highway and urban transporation planning ... 8. Driver, vehicle, traffic and road characteristics - 9. Highway design ... 15. Constructing the road bed ... 19. Bituminous pavements ... 21. Highway maintenance and rehabilitation. Index, p.809-44. For practising engineers and administrators, for junior, senior and fifth-year college students, and as a starting point for advanced courses and individual study. A neat production. *Class No:* 625.7

Hydraulic Engineering

[1449]
MORGAN, N., *ed.* **Marine technology reference book.** Boston, Mass., Butterworth, 1990. v.p. tables. ISBN: 0408027143.

13 sections, with 'references and further reading': 1. Ocean environments - 2. Offshore structures ... 12. Electronic navigation and radar - 13. Maritime law. Well-produced. 17p. index. 109 photos; 750 line-drawings. 19 contributors. 'Designed to serve as a first point of reference' (*Preface*). *Class No:* 626

[1450]
TAYLOR, P.A. **Dictionary of marine technology.** Oxford, Butterworth, 1989. 244p.

Defines terms in marine and offshore engineering, naval architecture, shipbuilding, shipping and ship operations. Intended to displace the *Dictionary of marine engineering and nautical terms* (Newnes, 1965), emphasizing marine technology terms. 'See' references; some illus. *Class No:* 626

Underwater Work

[1451]
SOCIETY FOR UNDERWATER TECHNOLOGY. Advances in underwater technology, ocean science and offshore engineering. Dordrecht, etc., Kluwer, 1985-. illus., diagrs., tables.

25v. to date.

Volumes consider the entire field of offshore technology. V.25, *Safety in offshire drilling: the role of shallow gas surveys* (ed. D.A. Ardus and C.D. Green. 1990. viii,293p. £54.50. ISBN: 0792308991) has 13 chapters in 5 parts (Introduction - Acquisition - Processing, analysis and interpretation - Application of geophysical data - Procedures, regulations and guidelines). *Class No:* 626.02

Docks & Harbours

Cargo Handling

[1452]
INTERNATIONAL CARGO HANDLING COORDINATION ASSOCIATION. A Multilingual glossary of cargo handling terms. 3rd ed. London, the Association, 1987. 205p. illus. ISBN: 0906297974.

First published 1982; 2nd ed. 1984.

462 terms in 6 sections: 1. Transport vehicles - 2. Handling and securing equipment - 3. Goods and unit loads -4. Infrastructure and terminals - 5. Cargo Administration - 6. Abbreviations. English terms with Dutch, Finnish, French, German, Italian, Portuguese, Spanish and Swedish translations. Each entry has a brief definition in English. Language indexes. *Class No:* 627.35

Public Health Engineering

Databases

[1453]
ENVIROLINE. New York, Environment Information Center, 1971-.

ENVIROLINE is the database corresponding to *Environment abstracts.* Available through hosts DIALOG, ESA-IRS, ORBIT and SDC.

European Communities Commission's ENGUIDE (Munich, Franklin, 1980. EUR 6842) is a guide to bibliographical databases for users of environmental information. *Class No:* 628(003.4)

Encyclopaedias

[1454]
ASHWORTH, W. The Encyclopedia of environmental studies. New York, Facts on File, 1991. 424p. ISBN: 0816015317.

Describes related scientific terminology, regulatory agencies and environmental laws, individual environmentalists and events that have profoundly affected the environment. *Class No:* 628(031)

[1455]
Encyclopedia of environmental control technology. Cheremisinoff, P.N., *ed.* Houston, Texas, Gulf Publishing Co., 1989-. V.1-. diagrs., charts, tables.

V.1. *Thermal treatment of hazardous wastes.* 1989. 828p. $155.

V.2. *Air pollution control.* 1989. 1066p. $155.

V.3. *Wastewater treatment technology.* 1989. 684p. $155.

V.4. *Hazardous waste containment and treatment.* 1990. 776p. $155.

Each volume has chapter references and an index. V.1 covers current treatment methods in the field and projects future trends in research and technologies. Vols. 5-10 are forthcoming. *Class No:* 628(031)

Handbooks & Manuals

[1456]
CLAY, H.M. Clay's handbook of environmental health. 15th ed., edited by W.H. Basset and F.G. Davies. London, H.K. Lewis, 1981. viii, [2], 851p., illus., tables. ISBN: 0718604512.

First published 1933; 14th ed. 1977.

36 chapters in 6 parts: 1. Administration - 2. Construction technology - 3. Housing - 4. Health and safety - 5. Pollution control - 6. Food safety and hygiene. Most chapters have 'Further reading'. Changes in the 15th ed. include a new chapter on food hygiene and a rewritten chapter on occupational health and safety. Index, p. 821-51. Cites Acts in full. A basic handbook.

The 16th ed. was published in 1991. *Class No:* 628(035)

[1457]
JACKSON, M.H., *and others.* **Environmental health reference book.** London, Butterworths, 1988. c.600p. illus. ISBN: 0408026006.

15 sections: Introduction - Food poisoning and hygiene - Food control - Pathology of food animals - Housing administration - Building science and technology - Health and safety - Atmospheric pollution - Water quality and water supply - Sewerage and waste water disposal - Solid waste management - Noise control - Radiation - Pestology - Communicable diseases. Well illustrated. Emphasis is on the technical aspects rather than on legislation. *Class No:* 628(035)

[1458]
Standard handbook of environmental engineering. Corbitt, R.A., *ed.* New York, McGraw-Hill, 1990. v.p. illus., diagrs., graphs, tables. ISBN: 0070131589.

Comprehensive, covering technical aspects of air and water quality control standards and treatment, wastewater and solid waste disposal, and hazardous waste management. Separate legislation/regulations section. Over 900 tables, charts and diagrams. Extensive chapter references; lengthy subject index. US slanted. *Class No:* 628(035)

Reviews & Abstracts

[1459]
Environment abstracts. New York, Environment Information Center, 1971-. 10 pa. ISSN: 00933287.

About 5,000 abstracts pa. Sections (01. Air pollution ... 03. Energy ... 05. Environmental design & urban ecology... 09. Land use and misuse... 14. Radiological contamination ... 15/16. Renewal resources (terrestrial; water) ... 19. Water pollution ... 21. Wildlife. Conferences. Subject, industry and author indexes, cumulated in annual *Environment Index.* The leading abstracting service in the environment field. ENVIROLINE database. *Class No:* 628(048)

Maps & Atlases

[1460]
LEAN, G., *and others.* **Atlas of the environment.** London, Hutchinson, 1990. 192p. illus., tables, maps. ISBN: 0091747104.

Introduction and 42 articles (Major biomass - Climatic regions and land - Human numbers ... The Arctic-Antarctic). Compiled in collaboration with WWF/World Wide Fund for Nature. Only data from the 1980s and 1990 are included. Appended unit and conversion tables. Bibliography, p.187-92 (authors A-Z). Detailed contents but no index. Well illustrated in colour throughout. *Class No:* 628(084.3)

Water Supply

[1461]
Aqualine abstracts. Oxford, etc., Pergamon Press, on behalf of Water Research Centre, Medmenham, 1927-. Bi-weekly. ISSN: 02635534.
Formerly *WRC information* (1974-84), incorporating *Water pollution abstracts*, 1949-73.
1991: 4,815 abstracts. 8 sections: 1. Water resources and supplies - 2. Water quality - 3. Monitoring and analysis of water and wastes - 4. Water treatment - 5. Underground services and water use - 6. Sewage - 7. Industrial effluents - 8. Effect of pollution (sewage; heated discharges; metals; pesticides; fossil fuels; radio-activity). Annual author, subject and KWOC indexes.
AQUALINE database, available on Pergamon INFOLINE 1960-. 'The world's technical literature at your fingertips' by P. Russel and B. Wilkinson (*Water*, no. 37, March 1981, p. 26-28) discusses online information services on the water industry, particularly AQUALINE database. *Class No:* 628.1

Treatment

[1462]
LORCH, W., *ed.* Handbook of water purification. 2nd ed. Chichester, E. Horwood, 1987. 777p. illus., diagrs., tables. ISBN: 0853129916.
First published 1981.
19 editors and contributors. 3 parts (22 documented chapters): 1. Background to water purification - 2. Purification processes (membrane; distillation; disinfection) - 3. Purified water practice. Chapter 18: 'Sterile and apyrogenic water', p.640-92; 124 references. Detailed index, p.773-7. *Class No:* 628.16

Marine Pollution

[1463]
Wastes in the ocean. New York Wiley, 1983. 6v.
1. *Industrial and sewage wastes in the ocean;* edited by I.W. Duedall and others. 1983. xviii, 431p.
2. *Dredged material disposal in the ocean;* edited by K.P. Parr and others. 1983. xxii, 522p.
3. *Radioactive wastes in the ocean;* edited by K.P. Parr. 1983. xxii, 522p.
4. *Energy wastes in the ocean;* edited by I.W. Duedall. 1985. 818p.
5. *Deep-sea waste disposal,* edited by by D.H. Kester. 1985. 346p.
6. *Near-shore waste disposal,* edited by B.H. Ketchum and others. 1985. 534p. *Class No:* 628.394

Environmental Pollution Measures

[1464]
Acid rain abstracts annual. New York, Bowker A & I Publishing, 1989-.
1988,222p. (ISBN: 0835226409).
Bi-monthly issues. The 1988 annual reprints the 733 abstracts for the year. Focuses on the sources, causes and effects of acid deposition, and the economic, political, health and natural resource issues. Geographic index, geographic key term list and expanded subject keyterm list (plus author, subject and source indexes - as in the monthly issues). The annual appends a list of 'Conferences and events' and 2 articles. Available on CD-ROM. *Class No:* 628.5

[1465]
JOHNSON, C. Green dictionary. London, Optima, 1991. 320p. ISBN: 0356195688.
Simple explanations of over 400 terms, issues and ideas connected with the environmental debate. *Class No:* 628.5

[1466]
Pollution abstracts; with indexes. Bethesda, Md., Cambridge Scientific Abstracts, 1970-. 6 pa.
1,500 abstracts per issue. Sections: Air pollution - Marine pollution - Freshwater pollution - Sewage and wastewater treatment - Waste management - Lead pollution - Toxicology and health - Noise - Radiation - Environmental action. Analytical subject and author indexes per issue, cumulated annually. *Class No:* 628.5

Noise Abatement

[1467]
NELSON, P.M., *ed.* Transportation noise reference book. London, Butterworths, 1987. [492]p. illus., diagrs., graphs, tables. ISBN: 0408014466.
27 contributions. Main parts (24 documented sections): Introduction and physical assessment - The effects of transportation noise on man - Train noise - Aircraft noise - Decision making methods for transport noise control. 4 appendices (3. standards relating to traffic noise and its control; 4. list of addresses). Index. 405 illus., including 20 half-tones. 'Highly recommended' (*Choice*, March 1988, p.1126). *Class No:* 628.517

Industrial Effluents & Wastes

[1468]
ROBINSON, W.D., *ed.* The Solid waste handbook: a practical guide. New York, Chichester, etc., Wiley, 1986. xxvii, 811p., illus., diagrs., maps, tables. ISBN: 0471877115.
Concerned with solid waste management rather than engineering design. The emphasis is on public issues, legislation, regulation, finance, economics, waste recovery, and on the situation in the US. 21 chapters in 3 parts: 1. Public issues - 2. Implementation issues: systems, hardware, operations - 3. Hazardous solid wastes. 42 contributors. Index. Intended for use at all levels of government, national to local. *Class No:* 628.54

Lighting Engineering

[1469]
MURDOCH, J.B. Illumination engineering - from Edison's lamp to the laser. New York, Macmillan Publishing Co.; London, Collier Macmillan, 1985. xiv, [i], 541p. diagrs., graphs, tables. ISBN: 0029485800.
11 documented chapers, *e.g.*, 2. Lighting calculations and measurements; 5. Vision and color; 6. Lamps; 7. Interior lighting design: average illuminance; 9. Daylighting; 10. Optics and control of light; 11. Exterior lighting (11 references). Problems, p.491-526, with answers to selected problems, p.527-9. Detailed, analytical index, p.533-41. 'A scientific and technical treatment of lighting, rather than an architectural and design treatment' (*Preface*). *Class No:* 628.9

629 Transport Vehicles

Transport Vehicles

Motor Vehicle Engineering

[1470]
Automobile abstracts: a monthly survey of worldwide technical literature. Nuneaton, Warwickshire, Motor Industry Research Association, 1955-. Monthly. ISSN: 09090817.

Originally as *Monthly summary of automobile engineering literature*, 1955-67; as *MIRA abstracts* 1972-74.

About 2,700 abstracts pa., in 6 main sections: Vehicles (motor industry; operation; design; performance) - Components - Fluids - Materials (metals, plastics, glass, etc.) - Production - Research (R & D principles and organizations). Appended: Other SAE papers; Supplementary information; Forthcoming conferences, courses and motor shows. 'Periodicals held in MIRA Library' (*c.*350); occasional book reviews and surveys, and list of MIRA publications. *Class No:* 629.113

[1471]
BOSCH, R. Automotive handbook. 2nd ed. Düsseldorf, Robert Bosch, GmbH, 1986. 70p. diagrs., graphs, tables.

By a team of contributors. A compendium of technical data ('Internal combustion engine': p.282-337), from 'Bases and fundamentals' to 'Road traffic legislation'. Index of headings (*c.*2,000 entries), p.686-706. Cites DIN standards. *Class No:* 629.113

[1472]
SAE handbook. Warrendale, Pa., Society of Automotive Engineers, 1924-. Annual.

1. *Materials.* 2. *Parts & components.* 3. *Engines, fuels, lubricants, emissions, and noise.* 4. *On-highway vehicles & off-highway machinery. Index.*

Originally in 1v., now runs to 4v. Includes over 2,000 specifications and more than 1,000 standards, plus recommended practices and information reports on ferrous and nonferrous metals, nonmetallic metals, threads, etc. *Class No:* 629.113

Private Cars

[1473]
GEORGANO, N. The New encyclopedia of motorcars, 1885 to the present. New York, Dutton, 1983. 688p., illus.

First published 1968 as *The complete encyclopedia of motorcars 1885 to the present.* 2nd ed. 1973 (751p).

Includes profiles of about 4,300 cars built over the last century worldwide. One illustration per make, as far as possible. Data on each make: nationality; date(s); principal place of manufacture; history; technical information (selective). 'An excellent contribution to existing automotive historical materials' (*Antique Automobile* v.47, November/December 1982, p.17). *Class No:* 629.114.6

[1474]
Glossary of automotive terms. Warrendale, PA, Society of Automotive Engineers, 1988. [iv],609p. ISBN: 0898836778.

'A compendium of automotive engineering terms and related definitions which appear in SAE standards, Recommended practice and Information reports' (*Preface*). Numerous cross-references. *Class No:* 629.114.6

Sports Cars

[1475]
COTTON, M. Directory of world sportscars. Bourne End, Bucks., Aston Pubns., 1988. 216p. illus. ISBN: 094662738x.

Over 70 distinct car makes and models appearing since 1982 in world championships. 165 illus. *Class No:* 629.114.62

Motor Cycles

[1476]
CHRISTENSEN, R.D. Motorcycles in magazines, 1895-1983. Metuchen, N.J., Scarecrow Press, 1985. [viii], 342p. illus. ISBN: 081081756x.

2,503 numbered entries, usually with brief annotations. 3 parts: 1. General interest and popular technical magazines, 1895-1983 - 2. Automotive magazines, 1950-1983 - 3. *Cycle* magazines, 1978-83. Indexes: A. Motorcycle tests, impressions, descriptions and model announcements; B. Competition reports; C. General, p.333-42. *Class No:* 629.118

Shipbuilding

[1477]
BMT [British marine technology] abstracts. Wallsend, Tyne & Wear, BMT Ltd., Wallsend Research Station, 1946-. Monthly. ISSN: 02689650.

Previously as *Journal of abstracts of the British Ship Research Association* (1962-67), and originally as *Journal of the British Shipbuilding Research Association* (1946-62).

V.42(1), January 1987, carries 255 abstracts from current technical literature. Sections: Ship design - Ship construction - Ship machinery and systems - Ship operation - Fluid mechanics - Ocean engineering - Warships - Miscellaneous. Record of new or converted ships. Author and ship's name index. Online through BSRA database at Wallsend, which also covers the output of *Ship abstracts* (published by a consortium headed by the Norwegian Ship Research Institute). *Class No:* 629.12

[1478]
LAYTON, C.W.T. Dictionary of nautical words and terms. 3rd ed., revised by P. Clissold. Glasgow, Brown, Son, & Ferguson, 1987. [vi],397p. ISBN: 0851745369.

First published 1955.

8,000 definitions in navigation, seamanship, rigging,

....(contd.)
metrology, astronomy, naval architecture, ship economics, hydrography, cargo stowage, marine engineering, ice terminology, buoyage, yachting, etc. (*e.g.* 'Lloyd's Register of Shipping': 11 lines). Includes acronyms, organizations. Appended list of abbreviations. *Class No:* 629.12

[1479]
NOEL, J.V. The VNR dictionary of ships and the sea. New York, etc., Van Nostrand Reinhold, 1987. vi, 393p. illus. ISBN: 0442256310.
About 6,000 entries, including abbreviations and acronyms, briefly defined (*e.g.,* 'Gulf stream system': 9 lines; 'Beaufort scale': ½p). Cross-references. International code flags and pennants, on end papers. *Class No:* 629.12

Passenger Ships

[1480]
KLUDAS, A. Great passenger ships of the world. Cambridge, P. Stephens, 1975-77. 5v. illus.
First published as *Die grossen Passagierschiffe der Welt.* (Oldenbourg, 1972). V. 1: 1858-1912(1975); V. 2: 1913-1923(1976); V. 3: 1924-1935; V. 4: 1936-1950(1977); V. 5: 1951-1970(1977).
Deals with ships either in classes (*e.g.,* Elder Dempster liners) or individually (*e.g.,* 'Queen Elizabeth'). Covers passenger vessels of 10,000 gross tons or more. General data: chronology; yard number; launching and commissioning dates; handed over to ...; retired; rebuilt. Technical data: dimensions; propulsion; power; speed; passengers; crew. Historical data: owners; builders; completion; routes. V.5 (226p) carries a bibliography, p.212-3. Index of ships' names. Well illustrated, - about 1 per page. *Class No:* 629.123.3

Rail Vehicle Engineering

[1481]
HOLLINGSWORTH, B. An Illustrated guide to modern trains. London, Salamander, 1985. 235p. illus. (incl. col.). ISBN: 0861012208.
Concentrates on 80 powerful locomotives since 1945, tracing the cycle from steam to diesel, diesel electric and electric, then back to steam. Most of the illustrations are in colour. 'Very appropriate for public libraries and special collections on railroading' (*Science and technology libraries,* v.8(1), Fall 1987, p.172). *Class No:* 629.4

Aircraft Engineering

[1482]
GIBBS-SMITH, C.H. Aviation: an historical survey; from its origin to the end of World War II. 2nd ed. London, HM Stationery Office, 1985. xiv, 320p. illus., tables. ISBN: 0112904211.
First published 1970. At head of title: 'Science Museum'
18 chapters. 'Quotations on flying', p.221-229. Folding table on powered flight. 'A chronology of aviation from antiquity to 1945', p.239-52. Glossary. Bibliography, p.273-80. Conversion tables, etc. Addenda, p.289-92. Detailed, analytical index, p.293-320. Well illustrated (22 plates of small photographs; 128 line-drawings). A classic in the literature of aviation history. *Class No:* 629.7

[1483]
Jane's All the world's aircraft: 1991-92. Lambert, M., ed. 81st ed. London, Jane's Information Group, 1991. [40],807p. illus. ISBN: 0710609655.
Sections (mostly subdivided by countries, A-Z): Aircraft (Argentina ... Yugoslavia), p.1-531 - Sports aircraft - Microlights - Sailplanes - Hang gliders - Lighter than air:

....(contd.)
airships, balloons. Acronyms. Indexes to sections. Illus. (c.2 per page), diagrs., tables. Available online via DIALOG. *Class No:* 629.7

[1484]
Jane's Encyclopedia of aviation. London, Jane's Publishing Co. 5v. (1078p.). illus. (incl. col.), ports., diagrs. ISBN: 0710607105.
Aircraft, AAMSA ... Zlin, with data on about 5,000 different aeroplanes, including spacecraft and gliders. V.1 includes glossary, a world directory of airlines, world directory of air forces, aerospace world records, and the first part of the A-Z sequence of aircraft - AAMSA ... Antonov. Includes biographies. Index (tiny print) in v.5, p.1065-78. About 3,000 illus. in all. Online via DIALOG. *Class No:* 629.7

Astronautics (Space Craft)

[1485]
FURNISS, T. Space flight: the records. Enfield, Middx, Guiness Superlatives, 1985. 168p. illus., ports., tables. ISBN: 0851124518.
5 sections: 1. Manned space flight diary [12 April 1961 - 29 April 1985] - 2. Firsts in manned space flight - 3. Manned space machines - 4. An A to Z of space travellers (p.69-107) - 5. Manned space flight, tables (Manned space flight duration tables ... Space shuttle schedule). Postscript (latest flight 1985). Glossary. Detailed index, p.162-8. *Class No:* 629.78

[1486]
The Illustrated encyclopedia of space technology. Gatland, K.W., ed. 2nd ed. London, New York, Salamander Books, 1989. 306p. illus., diagrs., maps. ISBN: 0861014499.
First published 1981.
A popular history including weather patrols, manned flights, military systems, space cities, lunar and planetary probes. 'Space diary' (p.252-97) covers events from 360 BC to 1989. Glossary of terms; subject index. Lavishly illustrated, many in colour. *Class No:* 629.78

[1487]
International aerospace abstracts. New York, American Institute of Aeronautics and Astronautics Technical Information Service, for NASA, Scientific and Technical Information Branch, 1961-. 26p. (3 issues in January).
Replaces abstracts in *Aero/Space engineering* (formerly *Aeronautical engineering review*), 1942-60.
About 50,000 abstracts pa. Sections: Aeronautics - Astronautics - Chemistry and materials - Engineering - Geosciences - Life sciences - Mathematics and computer sciences - Physics - Social sciences - Space sciences - General. Coverage: periodicals (including government-sponsored), books, meetings, papers, conference proceedings, translations of journals, and journal articles. Indexes of subjects, personal authors, contract numbers, meetings papers and report numbers, accession number. A basic abstracting service. (Abstracts and indexes of report literature are the province of *Scientific and technical aerospace reports* (STAR)). *Class No:* 629.78

[1488]
Jane's Spaceflight directory, 1987. Turnill, R., ed. 3rd ed. London, Jane's Publishing Co., 1987. [32], 551p. illus., diagrs., tables. ISBN: 0710608381.
First published 1984. A complete revision of R. Turnill's *The Observer's spaceflight directory* (Warne, 1978, 384p.).
Main contents: National space programmes (p.1-282) - International space programmes - Military space - Launchers - The solar system - World space centres -

....(contd.)
Spacemen - Space industry. Notes, p.514-28. Addenda. Satellite launch tables. Detailed index, p.544-51. An up-to-date compendium. 'Should become the standard reference for aerospace information' (*Reference books bulletin 1984-1985*, p.76, on the 1984 ed). Online via DIALOG. *Class No:* 629.78

[1489]
WILLIAMSON, M. Dictionary of space technology. Bristol; New York, Adam Hilger, 1990. xi,401p. illus., diagrs. ISBN: 0852743394.
Over 1,600 entries ('Solar energy': $c.\frac{1}{2}$p.). Over 100 photos and diagrs. Final 3 sections: Physics and astronomy - Space Centres and organizations - Miscellaneous. Classified list of dictionary entries under 12 headings. Cross-references (plentiful). Good use of bold type and uncongested layout. *Class No:* 629.78

63 Agriculture & Livestock

Agriculture

Bibliographies

[1490]
LILLEY, G.P., *ed.* **Information sources in agriculture and food science.** London, etc., Butterworths, 1981. xiv, 603p. (*Guides to information sources.*) ISBN: 0408106123.

18 contributors. 2 parts: 1. General (chapters 1-7) - 2. Specialized areas (8. Soils and fertilizers; 9. Agricultural engineering; 10. Weed biology, weed control and herbicides; 12. Field crops and grasslands; 13. Temperate horticulture; 14. Tropical agriculture; 15. Animal production; 16. Veterinary science; 17. Forestry; 18. Food science; 19. Agricultural economics; 20. Agrarian and food history). Appendix: List of abbreviations used. Index (subjects, organizations, journal titles), p.591-603. Thin on coverage of fish and fisheries; omits beekeeping.

A new ed., *Information sources in agriculture and horticulture*, was due to be published by Bowker-Saur in 1991. *Class No: 63.0(01)*

Handbooks & Manuals

[1491]
FREAM, W. **Fream's principles of food and agriculture.** Spedding, C.R.W., *ed.* 17th ed. Oxford, Blackwell Scientific Publications, 1992. xxvii,308p. tables, graphs. ISBN: 0632029781.

First published 1892 as *Fream's elements of agriculture*, 16th ed. (1983), *Fream's agriculture*.

10 sections: 1. The food and agricultural industry - 2. Meeting human needs - 3. World agriculture ... 7. The inputs to agriculture - 8. The principles of processing of products ... 10. Feeding the world in the future. References, p.xi-xii. Glossary, p.xv-xxiv. Fewer than half the number of pages of the previous ed. and has only 10 contributors compared with 42. This edition 'builds on the principles of agriculture ... and relates these to a more international view of agriculture, and its past, present and future roles in society' (*Preface*). *Class No: 63.0(035)*

[1492]
MCCONNELL, P. **Primrose McConnell's 'The agricultural notebook'.** 18th ed., edited by R.J. Halley, R.J. Soffe. London, etc., Butterworths, 1988. xiv, 689p. illus., diagrs., tables. ISBN: 0408030607.

First published 1883.

29 contributors. 4 parts (29 documented chapters): 1. Crop production - 2. Animal production - 3. Farm equipment - 4. Farm management. Chapter 21: 'Farm machinery', p.503-536; 66 references. Glossary of units, p.668-70. Detailed, analytical index, p.671-89. Follows the completely new approach and format of the 17th ed. (1982). Facts and figures for farmers, students and all engaged or interested in farming. *Class No: 63.0(035)*

Dictionaries

Polyglot

[1493]
HAENSCH, G. *and* HABERKAMP DE ANTON, G. **Dictionary of agriculture in six languages:** German, English, French, Spanish, Italian, Russian. 5th completely rev. and enld. ed. Amsterdam, etc., Elsevier, 1986. xxix, 1264p. ISBN: 0444995129.

First published 1959; 4th ed., 1975 (xxiv, 1000p.).

11,163 numbered German-base entries, with equivalents in the other five languages. Subject sections A-Q (*e.g.,* A. Food and agriculture: general terms; D. Economics and sociology of agriculture; E. Processing of animal produce; J. Plant cultivation: special part; N-O. Animal breeding; P. Farm buildings; Q. Agricultural machinery). Genders given. German, English, French, Spanish, Italian, Russian and Latin indexes. *Class No: 63.0(038)=00*

English

[1494]
DALAL-CLAYTON, D.B. **Black's agricultural dictionary.** 2nd ed. London, A. & C. Black, 1985. xiii, 432p. illus., diagrs., tables. ISBN: 0713626798.

First published 1981.

About 4,000 entries (*e.g.,* 'Plough': nearly 1p., including keyed line-drawing; 'Chart of common sheep names', p.338). Ample cross-references. Appendix of abbreviations, acronyms and initials. Concerned essentially with agriculture in the UK. *Class No: 63.0(038)=20*

Reviews & Abstracts

[1495]
Bibliography of agriculture: data provided by National Agricultural Library, US Department of Agriculture. Phoenix, Arizona, Oryx Press, 1942-. 12pa. ISSN: 00061530.

Contains *c.*9,000 items per issue. Some 96 subject areas, further subdivided, record proceedings, annual and special reports, pamphlets and government publications, as well as periodical articles. Corporate author, personal author and analytical subject (based on title catchword) indexes per issue, cumulated annually (1985: 2v. - 4625p.). 'The most indispensable single source in the field' (*Library trends*, v.15(4), April 1967, p.882). Online database: AGRICOLA, and available on CD-ROM. *Class No: 63.0(048)*

[1496]
Current contents: Agriculture, biology & environmental sciences. Philadephia, Pa., Institute for Scientific Information, 1970-. Weekly.

Previously (1970-72) subtitled 'Agriculture, food and veterinary sciences'.

....(contd.)

Displays contents-pages of *c.*900 current issues of journals. (issue for 10 Feb 1992 contained contents pages from 114 journals). Sections: 'Features' (*e.g.,* Current book contents); 'Discipline guide', grouping contents-pages by areas of interest (*e.g.,* Multidisciplinary; Biology; ... Animal sciences; Veterinary medicine; Animal health). Weekly title word index. Author and address directory. Publishers' address directory. Available on diskette and online on the SCISEARCH database. *Class No:* 63.0(048)

Periodicals & Progress Reports

[1497]
BRITISH LIBRARY. Science Reference Library. **Index to periodicals on agriculture held by the Science Reference Library.** Jackson, G., *comp.* London, Science Reference Library, 1981-84. ISBN: 0902914650, set.
pt.1. *Agricultural research and industry.* 1981. [11], v, 143, [5]p. pt.2. *Agronomy and other aspects of plant science.* 1984. x, 206p.
Title entry. V.1 carries *c.*1,850 titles. V.2 *c.*2,500 titles. Annuals are included. Data: country, holding, class-mark. *Class No:* 63.0(05)

Yearbooks & Directories

[1498]
CAB INTERNATIONAL. Directory of research workers in agriculture and allied sciences. Vernon, R., *ed.* Wallingford, Oxon., CAB International, 1989. ix, 490p. ISBN: 0851986234.
Previous ed. 1982 as *List of research workers, 1981, in the agricultural sciences in the Commonwealth.*
4 sections: 1. Organisations and research workers, by country - 2. Subject index - 3. Index of persons - 4. Index of institutions. Data on approximately 29,000 research workers include name, educational qualifications, and studies. *Class No:* 63.0(058)

Tables & Data Books

[1499]
FOOD AND AGRICULTURE ORGANIZATION. FAO production yearbook. Rome, FAO, 1947-. Annual (v.44: 1990. 1991). tables.
Statistical data on all important aspects of food and agriculture, including land population, index numbers of agricultural production, food supplies, wages and freight rates. V.44 (xlix, 306p.) has 132 tables.
FAO quarterly bulletin of statistics (1988-) updates. *Class No:* 63.0(083)

Tropics

[1500]
Tropical agriculture series. Wrigley, G., *general ed.* London, etc., Longman Scientific & Technical, 1953-. Volumes in print:
Agriculture in the tropics, by C.C. Webster and P.N. Wilson. 2nd ed. 1980. *Bananas,* by N.W. Simmonds. 3rd ed., 1987. *The camel,* by R.T. Wilson. 1984. *Cattle production in the tropics.* v.1, by W.J.A. Payne. 1970. *Climate, water and agriculture in the tropics,* by I.J. Jackson, 2nd ed., 1989. *Cocoa,* by G.A.R. Wood and R.A. Lass. 4th ed., 1985. *Coffee,* by G. Wrigley. 1988. *Cotton,* by J.M. Munroe. 2nd ed., 1987. *An introduction to animal husbandry in the tropics,* by W.J.A. Payne. 4th ed. 1990. *East African crops,* by J.D. Acland. 1972. *Introduction to tropical agriculture,* by A. Youdeouwei, and others. 1986. *The oil palm,* by C.W.S. Hartley. 3rd ed. 1989. *Oilseed crops,* by E.A. Weiss. 1983. *Rice,* by D.H. Grist, 6th ed., 1986. *Rubber,* by C.C. Webster and W.J. Baulkwill. 1989.

....(contd.)

Sheep production in the tropics and sub-tropics, by R.M. Gatenby. 1986. *Sorghum,* by H. Doggett. 2nd ed. 1988. *Spices,* by J.W. Purseglove, and others. 1981. 2v. *Sugar cane,* by F. Blackburn. 1984. *Tobacco,* by B.C. Akehurst. 2nd ed. 1981. *Tropical crops* (v.1 *Monocotyledons;* v.2 *Dicotyledons*), by J.W. Purseglove. 1975. *Tropical fruits,* by J.A. Samson. 1986. *Tropical grassland husbandry,* by L.V. Crowder and H.R. Chheda. 1975. *Tropical oilseed crops,* by E.A. Weiss. 1983.
D.H. Grist's *Rice* (6th ed. 1986. xx, 599p. illus. (pl.) ISBN 058240402), was first published 1953. Its four parts (22 chapters) cover rice, the plant; genetics and breeding of rice; paddy and production; rice, the product. 4 appendices, including 1. 'Standardization of rice terminology; 4. Species of rice'. Bibliography, p.543-76. Detailed, analytical index. 49 plates. A definitive contribution. *Class No:* 63.0(213)

Great Britain

[1501]
GREAT BRITAIN. MINISTRY OF AGRICULTURE, FISHERIES AND FOOD. Agricultural statistics for the United Kingdom. London. HM Stationery Office. Annual. tables.
Agricultural section (Area of agriculture land ... Distribution of holdings by type of agricultural acitivity) - Horticultural series (*e.g.,* area of horticultural land; area of glasshouses) - English counties (county statistics) - Prices section (corn ... feedstuffs and fertilizers) - Prices indices. Five-year series of statistical data. *Class No:* 63.0(410)

Research Establishments

[1502]
Agricultural research centres: a world directory of organizations and programmes. 10th ed. Harlow, Essex, Longman Group, 1990. 987p. (*Reference on research.*) ISBN: 0582061229.
9th ed. 1988. Previously as *Agricultural research index* (F. Hodgson).
Arranged alphabetically by country, Albania ... Zimbabwe. Lists *c.*4,500 laboratories and departments that conduct or finance agricultural research. Covers *c.*140 countries, including those of the Third World. Food, environmental and biological sciences are included in the subject coverage. Data include affiliation, status, senior staff, annual expenditure and publications. Index of names of establishments. Non-analytical subject index. *Class No:* 63.0:061:061.62

Forestry

[1503]
FORD-ROBERTSON, F.C. and **WINTERS, R.K.,** *eds.* **Terminology of forest science, technology, practice and products:** English language version. Rev. ed. Washington, Society of American Foresters, 1983. xxi, 370p. illus. (*Multilingual forestry terminology series, no.1.*)
First of a series of multilingual forestry terminologies authorized by the joint FAO/IUFRO Committee on Forestry Bibliography and Terminology. This ed. is a reprinting of the 1971 ed. + an addendum.
*c.*7,000 entries, differentiating US usage. Includes abbreviations. Many cross-references. 6 appendices (*e.g.,* 1. Key to published sources drawn on; 4. Deprecated key and secondary terms with their preferred synonyms). *Class No:* 630

[1504]
Forestry abstracts. Prepared by the CAB International Forestry Bureau. Wallingford, Oxon., CAB International, 1939-. 12pa. ISSN: 00157538.

....(contd.)

About 10,000 abstracts pa. 16 sections: General publications and general techniques - General aspects of forestry - Silviculture - Forest mensuration and management - Physical environment - Fire - Plant biology - Mycology and pathology - Insects and other invertebrates ... Catchment management. Soil conservation - Other land use. Nature conservation - Arboriculture - Dendrochronology and dendroclimatology. Author and subject indexes per issue and annually. The major source.

Online through CAB ABSTRACTS database (covering the 19 major CAB abstract journals). Available on the CAB ABSTRACTS CD-ROM and TREECD. *Class No:* 630

[1505]
JAMES, N.D.G. **The Forester's companion.** 4th ed. Oxford, Basil Blackwell, 1989. xii, 310p. tables. ISBN: 0631167242.
First published 1955.
33 chapters (1. Forest trees grown in Britain ... 8. Forest management ... 12. Diseases and pests ... 16. Utilization ... 27. Societies, organizations, establishments, and trusts concerned with forestry work). 1. Appendix: Abbreviations. Index, p.302-10. Small format. *Class No:* 630

Trees (Silviculture)

Encyclopaedias

[1506]
BEAN, W.J. **Trees and shrubs hardy in the British Isles.** 8th ed. Chief editor, D.L. Clarke. London, Murray, 1970-80. 4v. illus. Supplement. 432p. 1988. ISBN: 0719524285; 0719517907, Supplement.
First published 1914-33.
Entries, A-C, D-M, N-Rh, Ri-Z, under Latin names. V.1 (Abelia-Cytisus. xx, 848p.) contains a glossary (p.112-20) and select bibliography, the descriptive list of genera and species (p.137-831), with 77 plates and 112 botanical drawings, and an index. Data: full description (corrected or updated) of species and varieties (but no keys to identification), common name, synonyms, distribution, date of introduction, features, merits and cultivation, plus 'references for illustrations'. V.4 (xv, 808p.) covers 115 genera, with 111 black-and-white photographs, and index, p.785-808. *Class No:* 630.2(031)

[1507]
The Oxford encyclopedia of trees of the world. Hora, B., *consultant ed.* Oxford Univ. Press, 1981. 288p. col. illus., tables. ISBN: 0192177125.
39 contributors. Devotes the main section to 149 wild and cultivated genera. Data: structure; distribution; history; ecology; cultivation; economic use. A further section concerns native trees of Asia, Africa and America. Appended keys to families, a general bibliography (p.277); glossary. Indexes to common and Latin names. 365 illus. well captioned. 'An excellent choice' (*RQ*, v.21(4), Summer 1982, p.420). *Class No:* 630.2(031)

Farms

Organic Farming

[1508]
LAMPKIN, N. **Organic farming.** Ipswich, Farming Press, 1990. xiii,701p. illus. (some col.), tables. ISBN: 0852361912.
15 chapters: 1. Organic farming-agriculture with a future - 2. The living soil ... 4. Management of manures, slurry and organic residues - 5. Rotation designs for organic systems ... 8. Livestock husbandry ... 12. Marketing and processing ... 14. Converting to organic farming - 15. The wider issues. 6 appendices (1. Standards for organic

....(contd.)

agriculture ... 4. Addresses ... 6. Some metric conversion factors). Sections on animal husbandry particularly useful. Bibliographies appended to each chapter. Author is lecturer in agricultural economics at the University College of Wales, Aberystwyth and Development Director of the Aberystwyth Centre for Organic Husbandry and Agroecology. Good value. *Class No:* 631.147

Management

[1509]
NIX, J. *and* HILL, P. **Farm management pocketbook.** 21st ed. Ashford, Kent, Department of Agricultural Economics, Wye College, 1990. vii, 216p. tables. ISBN: 0862660319.
First published 1966.
4 sections: 1. Gross margin data (1. General notes; 2. Cash crops; 3. Grazing livestock; 4. Pigs, poultry and fish) - 2. Labour - 3. Machinery; 4. Miscellaneous data (*e.g.*, 1. Fixed costs; 4. Buildings; 15. Farm records; 19. Useful addresses and telephone numbers). Index. Virtually annual update. J. Nix is National Westminster Bank Professor. *Class No:* 631.15

Agricultural Machinery

[1510]
CULPIN, C. **Farm machinery.** 11th ed. London, Collins, 1986. [x], 450p. illus. ISBN: 0003832228.
First published 1938.
24 documented chapters (2. Tractors: constructional features) ... 4. Ploughs: components and features ... 7. Equipment for sowing and planting ... 10. Pumps and irrigation machinery ... 15. Root-harvesting machinery - 16. Horticultural machinery ... 18. Equipment for livestock husbandry - 19. Equipment for milk production ... 22. Machinery for land drainage, reclamation and estate maintenance - 23. Environmental control in crop and stock building. 6 appendices (*e.g.*, 5. Electricity on the farm). Index. Well illustrated and captioned. A standard textbook, written for farmers and those who advise them. *Class No:* 631.3

[1511]
The Green book. Birmingham, Guardian Communications, 1951-. Annual. ISSN: 00173932.
First published 1951 as *British tractors and farm machinery: the Green book series.*
1991/92 edition has seven sections: 1990 review - Trade organizations, research and educational establishments - Alphabetical index to manufacturers and suppliers - Index to classifications - Classified section - Product analysis section, index to tables (Balers and bale handling equipment ... Cultivation equipment ... Grain and seed crop harvesting equipment ... Livestock husbandry equipment ... Power washers and steam cleaners ... Tractors, tracklaying) - Index to advertisers. At £75 for only 114p., this edition seems expensive. *Class No:* 631.3

Soil Science

[1512]
FAIRBRIDGE, R.W. *and* FINKL, C.W., Jr., *eds.* **The Encyclopedia of soil science.** Stroudsbourg, Pa., Dowden, Hutchinson & Ross, 1979. Part 1. xxi, 646p. illus., diagrs., graphs, tables, chemical structures. (*Encyclopedia of earth sciences, v.12.*) ISBN: 0897331763.
Part 1: *Physics, chemistry, biology, fertility and technology.* Entries: Acidity ... zero tillage. Documented articles (*e.g.*, 'Humus': $1\frac{1}{2}$ columns of references; 'Soil structure' ($5\frac{1}{2}$p.): 2 columns of references; 4 illus., 1 table). Cross-references to other volumes in the series. Subject

....(contd.)

(non-analytical) and author indexes.

Part 2, to cover soil morphology, genesis, classification and geography, is still in preparation. *Class No:* 631.4

Fertilizers

[1513]

Soils and fertilizers. Prepared by the CAB International Bureau of Soils. Wallingford, Oxon., CAB International, 1938-. 12pa. ISSN: 00380792.

About 17,000 abstracts pa. Classes: 0. Documentation - 1. Soil science - 2. Fertilizers. Soil management ... 6. Other agricultural topics ... 8. Botany. Ecology - 9. Other topics. Author and subject indexes per issue and annually. Online CAB ABSTRACTS database and CD-ROM. *Class No:* 631.8

Pests & Diseases

[1514]

SCOPES, N. Pest and disease control handbook. Stables, L., *ed.* 3rd ed. Thornton Heath, British Crop Protection Council, 1989. xiii, 732p. ISBN: 0948404280.

First published 1979.

16 chapters, by various hands. Chapters 5-15 concern pests and diseases of different types of crop plants (*e.g.,* chapter 10, - vegetables, p.261-321; 31 references). Chapter 16: 'Insect, mite and fungal pests of stored cereals and oilseed crops'. Detailed, analytical index. A mine of authoritative information. *Class No:* 632

Pesticides

[1515]

The Pesticide manual: a world compendium. Worthing, C.R., *ed.* 9th ed. Farnham, Surrey, British Crop Protection Council, 1991. xlvii,1141p. tables, chemical structures. ISBN: 0948404426.

First published 1968.

Details 670 chemical compounds or microbial agents used as active ingredients of pesticides. Part 1: Compounds in use: main entries (pesticides, A-Z; data: nomenclature; development; properties; formulations; uses; toxicology; analysis). Part 2: Superseded compounds (yellow pages). 4 appendices: Abbreviations; Bibliography; Names and addresses of firms mentioned in the text; Notes on common names, chemical nomenclature and structures. 4 indexes: *Chemical abstracts* Service Registry Numbers; Molecular formulae; Code numbers; Chemical, common and trivial names and trademarks. *Class No:* 632.95

Field Crops

[1516]

Field crop abstracts. Wallingford, Oxon., CAB International, 1948-. Monthly. ISSN: 0015069x.

About 10,000 abstracts pa. Sections: Cereals - Legumes - Root crops - Fibre plants - Oil plants - Miscellaneous crops - Green manures - Field crops, general - Crop botany - Weeds - Pests and diseases - Surveys and land use - Farming systems - Soil and water conservation - Agricultural meteorology - Miscellaneous. Appended: Reports. Conferences. Books. Author and subject indexes per issue and annually. Online CAB ABSTRACTS database and CD-ROM. *Class No:* 633

Horticulture

[1517]

Horticultural abstracts. Wallingford, Oxon., CAB International, 1931-. 12pa. ISSN: 00185280.

About 10,000 abstracts pa. 9 main sections: General aspects of research and its application - Temperate tree fruits and nuts - Small fruits - Viticulture - Vegetables, temperate, tropical and greenhouse - Ornamental plants - Minor temperate and tropical industrial crops - Subtropical fruit and plantation crops - Tropical fruit and plantation crops. Author and subject indexes per issue and annually. Online CAB ABSTRACTS database. *Class No:* 634

[1518]

SOULE, J. Glossary for horticultural crops. Sponsored by the American Society for Horticultural Science. New York, etc., Wiley, 1985. xxvi, [1], 898p. ISBN: 0471884995.

About 8,000 terms are defined. 6 broad categories (subdivided): 1. Horticultural crops - 2. Morphology and anatomy - 3. Horticultural taxonomy and plant breeding - 4. Horticultural physiology and crop ecology - 5. Propagation and nursery handling - 6. Post-harvest handling and marketing. Selected references, p.679-92 (authors, A-Z). Index of terms; index of crops. Over 300 line-drawings. Well constructed, but typography makes for reading difficulties. *Class No:* 634

Fruit & Vegetables

[1519]

Food from your garden: all you need to know to grow, cook and preserve your own fruit and vegetables. London, etc., Reader's Digest, 1977 (reprinted with amendment, 1987). [v], 380p. illus. ISBN: 0274001702.

20 contributors and advisers. Sections: A basic guide to the kitchen - Growing and cooking - Pests and diseases - Home preserving - Food from the countryside - Making your own wine - Keeping poultry and bees. Index, p.375-80. Oblong format. A well-illustrated step-by-step guide. *Class No:* 634.1/635.1

Gardening

Bibliographies

[1520]

ISAACSON, R.T. Gardening: a guide to the literature. New York, Garland Pubg. Co., 1985. xiii, 198p. ISBN: 0824090195.

784 annotated entries, in 7 sections (further subdivided): Reference - Landscape design - Ornamental garden plants - Methods of growing and using plants - Garden practices and plant problems - Miscellaneous gardening topics - Periodicals and catalogs ... List of libraries with extensive gardening collections. Name, title and subject indexes. 'Specially useful both to the serious gardener and to the librarian who wants to build a collection to support this subject' (*Reference books bulletin, 1985-86*, p.67). US-slanted. *Class No:* 635(01)

Encyclopaedias

[1521]

The Marshall Cavendish illustrated encyclopedia of gardening. Hunt, P., *ed.* New York, Marshall Cavendish Corporation, 1968-70. 20v. (iv, 2799p.). col. illus., diagrs., maps.

V.1-17: Aaron's beard ... Zygopetalum, including entries on gardening operations, pests and diseases, as well as featuring plants and flowers. V.17 has appended 'Great gardens of the world', p.2362-80. V.18-20: Garden calendar. Index (in v.20), p.2717-79. Numerous cross-references.

....(contd.)

Quality, number and generous size of coloured illus. are outstanding ('Dahlia', v.4, p.426-37, has 51 illus.). Quarto. *Class No: 635(031)*

[1522]
ROYAL HORTICULTURAL SOCIETY. Dictionary of gardening: a practical guide and scientific encyclopaedia of horticulture. Chittenden, F.J., *and others.* 2nd ed. prepared by P.M. Synge. Oxford, Clarendon Press, 1956. 4v. (2356p.). Supplement 2nd rev. ed. 1969. ISBN: 0198691068; 0198691165.

First published 1951.

Entry-words are given accentuation and etymology. Longer articles are signed. 'Scilla': 3p. (general description; hardy and greenhouse types; diseases; 64 species; brief botanical descriptions). 'Tomato': 3½p. (cultivation; diseases; pests). Illus. are line-drawings mostly made direct from living plants, with some adaptations from illus. to the *Botanical magazine.* Each volume lists *c.*120 works containing the illus. cited. A standard work for British gardeners.

The 1969 *Supplement* consists of pt.1, on flowers, fruit and vegetables, (A-Z in each case); pt.2, (p.153-354): additions and corrections to the main volumes.

Due in April 1992 is *The New Royal Horticultural Society dictionary of gardening* (4v. Macmillan Press), covering over 50,000 plants in cultivation throughout the world. *Class No: 635(031)*

[1523]
The Royal Horticultural Society gardeners' encyclopedia of plants and flowers. Brickell, C., *ed.* London, Dorling Kindersley, 1989. 608p. illus. (col.). ISBN: 0863183867.

Sections: How to use this book - Plant origins and names - Creating a garden - The planter's guide - The plant catalogue (p.38-400) - The plant dictionary (p.401-594, listing *c.*8,000 plants with their characteristics and cultivation). Glossary of terms. Index of common names. Lavishly illustrated, with *c.*4,000 colour photographs. *Class No: 635(031)*

Cacti

[1524]
LAMB, E. and LAMB, B. The Illustrated reference on cacti and other succulents. London, Blandford Press, 1955-78. 5v. illus.

Describes over 1,000 species (195 genera), with one page of brief descriptions per species. Note on culture could be fuller, especially on watering. The coloured plates provide excellent identification. V.4 has 280 illus. (94 in colour); v.5: 280 illus. (100 in colour).

Pocket encyclopaedia of cacti in colour (Rev. ed. London, Blandford Press, 1981, 28p. 326 col. illus.) was first published in 1970. *Class No: 635.92:582.85*

Veterinary Medicine

Encyclopaedias & Dictionaries

[1525]
BLOOD, D.C. and STUDDERT, V.P. Baillière's comprehensive veterinary dictionary. London, etc., Baillière Tindall, 1988. xii, 1124p. tables. ISBN: 0702011959.

8 consultants. The dictionary (p.1-997) has *c.*50,000 entries. 'Rabbit': 9 lines, *c.*20 cross-references to types, etc.; 'Manx': 17¼ lines. Basic scientific terms were drawn and adapted from Baillière's Dictionary database. Anatomical tables. Appendix comprises 18 tables (*e.g.,* laboratory services). 'Based on a survey of more than one hundred veterinary textbooks' (*Preface*). *Class No: 636.09(03)*

[1526]
BLOOD, D.C., *and others.* **Veterinary medicine:** a textbook of the diseases of cattle, sheep, pigs, goats and horses. 7th ed. London, etc., Baillière Tindall, 1989. xxiii, 1502p. illus. tables. ISBN: 0702012866.

First published 1960.

2 sections: 1. General medicine. 2. Special medicine. 35 chapters in all: 1. Clinical examination and making a diagnosis ... 7. Diseases of the liver and pancreas ... 10. Diseases of the respiratory system ... 15. Mastitis ... 25. Diseases caused by protozoa ... 28. Metabolic diseases ... 33. Diseases caused by allergy ... 35. Specific diseases of uncertain etiology. Conversion tables, p.1461-2. Normal laboratory values, p.1463-4. Index, p.1465-1502. 101 tables (1. Degrees of severity of dehydration and guidelines for assessment ... 78. Single and multiple host ticks). Numerous bibliographies throughout. Standard text. *Class No: 636.09(035)*

Reviews & Abstracts

[1527]
Index veterinarius. Wallingford, Oxon., CAB International, 1933-. Monthly. ISSN: 00194123.

Lists *c.*20,000 references pa., under subjects, A-Z. Supported by author index. 'Titles are selected from some 1,200 serial publications regularly scanned by the staff of the Bureau, and from books, annual reports, monographs, theses and other serial publications'. A list of the serials appears irregularly in the *Veterinary bulletin.* CAB ABSTRACTS database, and CD-ROM. *Class No: 636.09(048)*

Tables & Data Books

[1528]
British pharmacopoeia (veterinary), 1985. Published on the recommendation of the Medicines Commission pursuant to the Medicines Act 1968. Effective date, 1 September 1985. London, HM Stationery Office, 1985. xviii, 213 + 204p. plus Amendment inserts 1 & 2 (1985-86). ISBN: 0113208480.

The first part consists of monographs (*e.g.,* Immunological products). 25 appendices (*e.g.,* General reagents; Infra-red reference spectra). Detailed analytical index. Well produced. This pharmacopoeia provides standards for the quality of substances, preparations and immunological products used in veterinary medicine, plus information on action, use, dose, solubility, storage and labelling. *Class No: 636.09(083)*

[1529]
The Merck veterinary manual: a handbook of diagnosis, therapy, and disease prevention and control for the veterinarian. 6th ed. Rahway, N.J., Merck & Co., Inc., 1986. xxvii, 1677p. ISBN: 0911910530.

First published 1955; 5th ed. (xxxii, 1672p.), 1979.

About 350 contributors. 9 parts: 1. General (anatomy & physiology) - 2. Behaviour - 3. Clinical values and procedures - 4. Fur, laboratory and zoo animals - 5. Management, husbandry, and nutrition - 6. Poultry - 7. Toxicology - 8. Pharmacology - 9. Zoonoses. Detailed, analytical index, p.1611-77. *Class No: 636.09(083)*

Livestock

[1530]
BRIGGS, H.M. *and* **BRIGGS, D.M. Modern breeds of livestock.** 4th ed. New York, Macmillan; London, Collier-Macmillan, 1980. xiv, 802p. illus., charts, tables. ISBN: 002314730x.

58 chapters. 4 sections: 1. The breeds of cattle - 2. The breeds of swine - 3. The breeds of sheep and goats - 4. The breeds of horses. Introduced on individual classes and groups. Detailed index, p.777-802. US slanted. *Class No:* 636.1/.5

Horses & Ponies

[1531]
HOPE, C.E.G. *and* **JACKSON, G.N.,** *eds.* **The Encyclopedia of the horse.** London, Ebury Press/ Pelham Books, 1973. 336p. illus., maps.

121 contributors. Entries (signed), A-Z (broad headings), cover all aspects, including show jumping, associations, breeds, biographies, and the horse in prehistoric art. Occasional references appended to articles. Over 300 black-and-white illus. and 32 unusually fine colour plates; clear diagrams. A handsome quarto. 'An exceptionally good book', comments *British book news* (December 1973, p.817), while objecting to the double columns of small print. *Class No:* 636.1

Cattle

[1532]
PORTER, V. Cattle: a handbook to the breeds of the world. London, Christopher Helm, 1991. 400p. illus. (col. pl.), maps. ISBN: 0713680008.

7 sections: The cattle of Europe - Tropical cattle - The cattle of Africa - The cattle of Asia - The buffaloes - The cattle of America - The cattle of Australia and New Zealand. 6 appendices (1. Metrication table ... 3. Cattle breeds and their synonyms ... 6. Useful addresses). Bibliography. Index, p.392-400. Data for each breed include development, physical characteristics, historical and current role, special characteristics and, for the major breeds, a detailed history. Beautifully illustrated. Good value. *Class No:* 636.2

Sheep and Goats

[1533]
COOP, J.E., *ed.* **Sheep and goat production.** Amsterdam, etc., Elsevier, 1982. xiii, 492p. diagrs., tables. (*World animal series, C1.*) ISBN: 0444419896.

25 documented chapters (1. Ecology and distribution - 2. Breeding ... 7. Nutrition and diseases ... 12. Wool grading and marketing ... 15. Milk production in sheep and goats ... 16. Systems [of grazing] ... 25. Village and smallholding systems). 27 contributors; biographical notes, p.481-4. Subject index, p.485-92. Quarto. *Class No:* 636.3

Pets

[1534]
DIAGRAM GROUP. Pets: every owner's encyclopedia. London & New York, Paddington Press, 1978. 431p. illus.

7 sections: 1. Dogs; cats; mustelids (ferrets, skunks); rabbits; rodents; horses, ponies, donkeys; artiodactyls (goats, sheep, etc.) Wild mammals - 2. Fish (p.176-223) - 3. Invertebrates - 4. Amphibians (*e.g.,* frogs) - 5. Reptiles - 6. Birds - 7. Conservation. Reference (including classification). Further reading (p.422-3). Index, p.424-31. Comprehensive, covering selection, handling, care, food and feeding, housing and equipment, illness, breeding and showing. *Class No:* 636.596/.9

Cage & Aviary Birds

[1535]
RUTGERS, A. *and* **NORRIS, K.A.,** *eds.* **Encyclopedia of aviculture.** Translated from the Dutch. Poole, Dorset, Blandford Press, 1970-77. 3v.

V.1 deals mainly with aquatic species, birds of prey, pheasants, pigeons and doves. V.2, with parrots, budgerigars, cuckoos, nightjars, humming birds and owls. The *Passeriformes* order occupies most of v.3, with numerous varieties of canaries and finches. The *Encyclopedia* concludes with a bibliography of 160 items, and indexes of English and Latin names. It provides a wealth of information on captive birds, their adaptability and care of them. 44 col. illus. depict *c.*260 species (based on review in *Library review,* v.28, Spring 1979, p.53-54). *Class No:* 636.68

Dogs

[1536]
WILCOX, B. *and* **WALKOWICZ, C. Atlas of dog breeds of the world.** Neptune City, NJ, TFH Publications, 1989. 912p. illus. ISBN: 0866229302.

First section contains essays on different types of dogs, *e.g.* scenthounds, mastiffs, terriers, gun dogs. The second part consists of alphabetically arranged entries for 400 breeds of dogs worldwide. Affenpinscher ... Yugoslavian Hounds. Entries consist of country of origin, size, description of coat and colour, groups with which it can be registered, and the larger category to which it belongs. Glossary, extensive bibliography and index. More than 1,000 excellent photographs illustrating each breed. It is more comprehensive than *The Complete dog book* (Howell Book House, 1989). *Class No:* 636.7

Cats

[1537]
POND, G. *and* **RALEIGH, I.,** *eds.* **A Standard guide to cat breeds.** London, Macmillan, 1982. 318p. illus. (incl. col.). ISBN: 0333240420.

5 contributors. A general section concerns feline genetics, coat colours and patterns, eye colours. Glossary. Shorthair cats, p.38-177. Longhair cats, p.179-231. Appendices include such matters as show preparation, show rules, breeding, medicine and behaviour. Detailed, non-analytical index. Well illustrated. *Class No:* 636.8

Dairy Produce

[1538]
INTERNATIONAL DAIRY FEDERATION. Dictionary of dairy terminology, in English, French, German and Spanish. Amsterdam, etc., Elsevier, 1983. [xii], 323p. ISBN: 0444421017.

3,909 English-based terms (with explanations, as considered necessary), with equivalents and indexes in French, German and Spanish. Bibliography, p.[ix] - [x]. Includes pertinent vocabularies from chemistry, microbiology, engineering, physiology and agriculture. *Class No:* 637.1

Cheese

[1539]
ANDROUET, P. Guide to world cheeses. Githens, J., *tr.* English ed., revised. Henley-on-Thames, Oxon., Aidan Ellis, 1983. [v],561p. ISBN: 0856291794.

First published 1973. French title as *Guide du fromage.* 12 chapters (*e.g.,* 4. Selecting cheeses by flavour and season; 8. Dictionary of cheese, p.159-471; 9. Special cheeses and non-French cheeses; 12. Some cheeses to try

....*(contd.)*

outside France). 'New cheeses', p.549-61. Glossary, p.519-41. Descriptions of *c.*500 varieties, highlighting French cheeses.

Published as *Cheese guide* in 1988. 551p. *Class No:* 637.3

[1540]
FOX, P.F. **Cheese: chemistry, physics and microbiology.** London, Elsevier, 1987. 2v. ISBN: 1851660526, v.1; 1851660534, v.2; 1851660542, set.

V.1. *General aspects.* 400p. V.2. *Major cheese groups.* 393p.

V.1 has 14 contributors, 10 chapters, including 'The enzymatic coagulation of milk' and 'Nutritional aspects of cheese'. V.2 has 17 contributors, 11 chapters including 'Dutch-type varieties' and 'Processed cheese products'. An authoritative technical study, aimed at the cheese-manufacturer, or agricultural/nutritional student, rather than the gourmet. *Class No: 637.3*

Beekeeping

[1541]
CRANE, E. **Bees and beekeeping:** science, practice and world resources. Oxford, Heinemann Newnes, 1990. xii,614p. illus., figs., tables. ISBN: 0434902713.

6 sections: 1. The bees used in beekeeping, and background information - 2. Beekeeping with movable-frame hives - 3. Beekeeping with simpler and cheaper hives - 4. Maintaining honeybee health - 5. Honeybees' plant resources, and products from the hive - 6. Beekeepers. 2 appendices: 1. Important world honey sources and their geographical distribution - 2. Beekeeping gazetteer of individual countries. Bibliography, p.539-93. Plant, geographical name, and subject indexes. The author is a former Director of the International Bee Research Association and one of the foremost authorities on beekeeping and honey. With its readable text and clear illustrations, this book is essential for any library covering this area. *Class No: 638.1*

Fish & Fisheries

[1542]
CRC handbook of mariculture. McVey, J.P., *ed.* Boca Raton, Fla., CRC Press, 1983-. 2v. (*CRC series in marine science.*) ISBN: 084930220x, v.1; 0849302196, v.2.

V.1 *Crustacean aquaculture.* 1983. 442p. V.2. *Finfish aquaculture.* 1991. 256p.

V.1 has 4 sections: 1. Larval foods for crustaceans - 2. Maturation, spawning hatchery and grow-out techniques for crustaceans - 3. Pathology and disease treatments for crustaceans - 4. Crustacean nutrition. V.2 covers marine finfish culture in Europe, Japan, Taiwan and the US. Each chapter in the set has a bibliography appended. Because of the 8-year gap between the publication of v.1 and v.2, the former may have lost some of its value. *Class No: 639.2*

Fishing Gear

[1543]
BRANDT, A., von. **Fish catching methods of the world.** 3rd ed. Farnham, Surrey, Fishing News Books, Ltd., 1984. xiv, 418p. illus., diagrs. ISBN: 0852381255.

First published 1964.

31 detailed chapters (1. Introduction ... 31. Fishing systems and harvesting machines). Includes fishing gear and methods used by small-scale and subsistence-level fishermen. Appended: 'Classification of catching methods'. Bibliography of 690 entries, p.394-406 (A-Z, authors). Detailed, non-analytical subject index; Species and product index;

....*(contd.)*

Geographical index. The author was for many years head of Hamburg's Institute for Fishing Technology. *Class No:* 639.2.081

Deep-Sea Fishing

Maps & Atlases

[1544]
FOOD AND AGRICULTURE ORGANIZATION. Fisheries Department. **Atlas of the living resources of the seas.** 4th ed. Rome, FAO, 1981. 23p. + 60 col. maps (some folded). ISBN: 9250010001.

First published 1971. In English, French and Spanish editions.

Text: Introduction - Productivity of the seas - Exploitation and utilization of resources - Movements and migrations - Topography and nomenclature - Size and distribution of resources - Value of estimates. Alphabetical index of fish names (p.14-23). The maps illustrate geographical and vertical distribution, migration and existing state of exploitation. Oblong. 'A splendid example of the effectiveness of simplicity in compilation' (*Geographical journal*, v.140(1), February 1974, p.161, on 3rd ed., 1972). *Class No: 639.22(084.3)*

Aquaria

[1545]
MILLS, D. *and* VEVERS, G. **The Practical encyclopedia of freshwater tropical aquarium fishes.** 2nd ed. London, Salamander Books, 1989. 208p. illus. (col.). ISBN: 0861014901.

First published 1982.

2 sections: 1. Practical section (Selecting a tank ... Aquatic plants ... Basic fish anatomy ... Expanding the interest) - 2. Species guide (a survey of over 200 tropical freshwater fishes). Further reading; glossary; index. Many colour illustrations. Mills is a fishkeeping expert, while Vevers is a former Curator of the Aquarium at London Zoo. *Class No: 639.33/.34*

64 Household Management

Household Management

Catering Establishments

[1546]
CRACKNELL, H.L. *and* NOBIS, G. **The New catering repertoire.** London, Macmillan, 1989-90. 2v. illus., tables, maps. ISBN: 0333391659, v.1; 0333391667, v.2.
V.1. *Aide-mémoire du chef.* xiii,810p. 1989. V.2. *Aide-mémoire du restaurateur et sommelier.* xix,492p. 1990.
V.2 has 2 main sections: 1. The waiting staff handbook (1. Service procedures ... 4. Menus ... 9. Restaurant personnel ... 11. Eating habits of nations) - 2. The wine waiting and bar staff manual (12. Wine production and wine-making countries ... 15. Cocktails and mixed drinks ... 17. Cigars). 19 appendices (A. Glossary of restaurant terms for the service of wine ... E. Styles of folding table napkins ... I. The law and the restaurateur ... 5. Stills for making wines and spirits). Many black-and-white drawings. No index. *Class No:* 640.02

Hotels & Restaurants

Worldwide

[1547]
'Financial Times' world hotel directory, 1992: an essential aid for business travellers. Harlow, Essex, Longman Group, 1991. xlii, 646p. ISBN: 0582085063.
'Hotels and essential travel facts' (2,699 entries), p.1-620; with data on hotel reservation system; style (*e.g.*, traditional); location; manager; rooms and charges; services and facilities; conferences; period when hotel closed. Hotel groups and representatives. Incentive schemes for business travellers. 1-5 star gradings. Appended: City centre maps of key business districts. Geographical index. Executive selection. Advertisers' index. For the business executive. *Class No:* 640.024.1/.3(100)

Europe

[1548]
The Good hotel guide, 1992: Britain and Western Europe - also Morocco and Turkey. Rubenstein, H., *ed.* London, Papermac (Macmillan), 1991. 836p. maps. ISBN: 0333563387.
Recommends hotels chosen for excellence and value in all price brackets based on first-hand reports. Part 1: Great Britain and Ireland, p.3-314. Part 2: The continent: Austria ... Yugoslavia (18 countries), p.315-780. Alphabetical list of hotels, p.781-95. 19 location maps. Appended hotel report form. *Class No:* 640.024.1/.3(4)

[1549]
Les Guides rouges. Paris, Michelin. Annual. maps.
Benelux. Deutschland. España. Europe. France. Great Britain and Ireland. Italia. Portugal.
'Red guides', providing details of hotels, restaurants and garages in the countries concerned, under towns A-Z. About 70 symbols are applied; tariff ranges indicated. Keyed two-colour town plans are a feature. *France, 1992* (1991. 1300p.) includes 8p. of coloured maps and an index of localities listed by departments. *Class No:* 640.024.1/.3(4)

America—North & Central

[1550]
Hotel and motel red book. New York, American Hotel and Motel Association, 1886-. Annual. illus., maps. ISSN: 00733490.
Official directory of the Association's members, covering hotels, motels and resorts. Mainly for USA, Canada and Caribbean, with a brief international section. *Class No:* 640.024.1/.3(71/73)

Restaurants

[1551]
Egon Ronay's Cellnet guide, 1991. Hotels & restaurants in Great Britain and Ireland: 2,500 establishments. London, Egon Ronay's Guides, 1990. 796p. + 27p. of maps; town plans. ISBN: 1871784085.
1,492 hotels, 947 restaurants. 9 sections (London ... Republic of Ireland), p.160-681. Awards for excellence; restaurants, 1-3 stars. Prices: A-F categories for hotels. Quick reference lists. 27p. of maps. Concise, evaluative comments. *Class No:* 640.024.3

[1552]
The Good food guide 1991. Jaine, T., *ed.* London, Consumers' Association and Hodder and Stoughton, 1991. 769p. (*Which? book series.*) ISBN: 0340528168.
Covers 1,300 establishments, based on reports, by readers, of 10,000 meals. Arranged A-Z, by place. Maps. Aimed at the individual but would be a suitable addition to general library collections.
Complemented by *The Vegetarian good food guide* by the same publisher, which features nearly 900 cafés, pubs, hotels and restaurants in the UK. *Class No:* 640.024.3

Inns & Public Houses

[1553]
The Good beer guide, 1991. 18th ed. St. Albans, Campaign for Real Ale [CAMRA], 1990. 504p. maps. ISBN: 1852490039.

Has brief information (applying 15 symbols) on *c.*5,000 British pubs serving traditional 'real' ale and beer. Arranged under counties of England, Wales, Scotland, Isle of Man, Channel Islands, and Northern Ireland. A 'Breweries section', and a map section follow. Not to be confused with the fuller, more readable *Good pub guide* (*qv*). *Class No:* 640.024.4

[1554]
The Good pub guide 1992. Aird, A., *ed.* 10th ed. London, Ebury, 1992. 943p.+25p. maps. ISBN: 0712647279.

Independent evaluative guide to *c.*5,000 pubs in England (arranged by counties Berkshire-Yorkshire), Scotland, Wales, and Channel Islands, using reports from up to 8,000 contributors. Each geographical area opens with specifically recommended pubs, followed by a less-detailed 'lucky-dip' section for that area. Opening hours, food & drink specialists, entertainments, etc, are listed, with emphasis on value for money. Overseas 'lucky dip' appendix. *Class No:* 640.024.4

Clubs & Hostels

[1555]
YHA accommodation guide 1992 (England and Wales). St. Albans, Herts., Youth Hostels Association (England and Wales), 1991. Annual. 192p. town plans, maps.

Hostel entries in 28 areas (Northumberland and Roman Wall ... Northern Ireland), p.15-151. About 35 signs and symbols applied. Prelims. include notes on YHA activities, hostel information, membership, world travel, other services. Small town plans; map of England and Wales and Northern Ireland. Advertisers' index. General index. Hostel index.

Scotland (Stirling) and Eire (Dublin) each have a YHA, issuing an annual guide while the International Youth Hostel Association publishes a handbook covering Europe, Africa, Asia and Australasia. *Class No:* 640.024.6

Camps & Caravan Sites

[1556]
Europa camping + caravaning / Internationalen Führer/Guide international, 1991. 38. Ausg. Stuttgart, Drei Brunnen Verlag, GmbH, [1991]. 944p. illus. (mostly col.), maps. ISBN: 379560205x.

Guide to 5,500 camping sites, - Europe (30 countries, including CIS, Czechoslovakia, Hungary, Bulgaria, Rumania); Near East (4 countries); North Africa (5 countries). Heavy use of symbols to include information. Coloured maps, p.827-82. Many advertisements. *Class No:* 640.028

[1557]
ROYAL AUTOMOBILE CLUB. RAC camping and caravanning guide, 1991: Great Britain & Ireland. Croydon, RAC Publishing, 1990. 320p. tables, maps. ISBN: 0862110874.

Over 2,000 sites (England; Scotland; Scottish islands; Orkney and Shetland isles; Wales; Isle of Man; Channel Islands; Northern Ireland; Republic of Ireland), p.27-296. Preliminaries include hiring camp equipment, National Parks. Appended: Motorway service areas. Index of sites by county. 10p. of maps. *Class No:* 640.028

Consumers & Shopping

Bibliographies

[1558]
FOREMAN, S. Consumer monitor: an annotated bibliography of British government and other official publications relating to consumer issues. Aldershot, Hants., etc., Gower, 1987. vii, 450p. ISBN: 0566054019.

Compiled for the National Consumer Council.

About 2,500 annotated entries. 12 subject categories: 1. Housing - 2. The neighbourhood - 3. Transport - 4. Goods and services - 5. Fuel and water - 6. Personal finance and social security - 7. Health and safety - 8. Education - 9. Welfare - 10. Communications - 11. The legal system - 12. Leisure. References (some annotated). Author and detailed analytical subject indexes. *Class No:* 640.03(01)

Laws

[1559]
Encyclopedia of consumer law. Thomas, W.H., *general ed. and* Ervine, C., *Scottish ed.* London, Sweet & Maxwell/W. Green & Son, 1980-. Loose-leaf v. Updates issued twice-yearly.

5 parts: 1. Statutes (all relevant statutes, including Consumer Protection Act, 1987) - 2. Statutory instruments - 3. Cases (competition; contract; credit; criminal; sale of goods; Scottish; services) - 4. Circulars and notices - 5. European Economic Community material (Treaty of Rome, and relevant secondary legislation). Index. *Class No:* 640.03(094.1)

[1560]
NATIONAL FEDERATION OF CONSUMER GROUPS. A Handbook of consumer law. 3rd ed. London, Consumers' Association, and Hodder & Stoughton, 1989. 252p. tables. ISBN: 0340488778.

First published 1982.

15 chapters: 1. Consumer law - 2. Sensible buying and pursuing complaints - 3. Shops and shopping - 4. Prices - 5. Consumer safety - 6. Food - 7. Contracts, liabilities and exclusion clauses - 8. Misrepresentation - 9. Trade descriptions and labelling - 10. Defective goods - 11. Defective services - 12. Insurance - 13. Financial and professional services - 14. Consumer credit - 15. Fair trading. Appendices: 1. Useful addresses; 2. Suggestions for further reading, p.238 (5 evaluative annotated entries). Index, p.241-52. *Class No:* 640.03(094.1)

Great Britain

[1561]
Which? London, Consumers' Association, 1968-. 12pa.

Each issue contains advice for consumers and evaluative reports on products. Issue for December 1990 has 5 sections: 1. Regulars - 2. Home and leisure (Microwave ovens - Compact cameras ... Kettles) - 3. Your rights - 4. Money (Giving money to charity - Shares) - 5. Public interest (Pet shops - Drinking and driving). Companion publications include *Holiday Which?, Gardening from Which?, Which? wine monthly* and *Which? way to health. Class No:* 640.03(410)

Food & Drink

Cookery

Bibliographies

[1562]

BULSON, C. Current cookbooks. Middletown, Conn., Choice, 1990. ISBN: 091449208x.

Annotated list of 250 books, mostly published since 1970. Arranged alphabetically by cuisine, Armenian ... Vietnamese, cooking techniques, courses, foods and audience. *Class No:* 641.5(01)

Encyclopaedias & Dictionaries

[1563]

New Larousse gastronomique; the world's greatest cookery reference book. London, Hamlyn, 1977. [viii], 1064p. illus., maps.

Original French ed. 1938, as *Larousse gastronomique.* as *Nouveau Larousse gastronomique,* 1968.

Entries 'Abaisse' ... 'Zweiback'. ('Fritter', p.394-8, records nearly 100 recipes, with brief cooking instructions; 'Hors d'oeuvres', p.457-88). 'International cookery', p.501-12, is a very brief survey of national specialities. 'Many of the recipes in this encyclopedia cater for large numbers of people and it would be merely pedantic to try to standardise quantities' (*Introduction* to 1961 ed.). Small type and illus., some lush whole-page colour plates. Detailed analytical index, p.1008-64. For the skilled cook. *Class No:* 641.5(03)

[1564]

STOBART, T. The Cook's encyclopedia. Owen, M., *ed.* New York, Harper & Row, 1981. 547p. ISBN: 0060141271.

An A-Z encyclopaedia of ingredients and processes, with cross-references. Not another compilation of recipes. Simon, A.L., and Howe, R. *Dictionary of gastronomy* (McGraw-Hill, 1970. 400p.) describes more concoctions and ingredients; Stobart concentrates rather on explaining processes. Well organized. *Class No:* 641.5(03)

Handbooks & Manuals

[1565]

ESCOFFIER, A. The Complete guide to the art of modern cookery. Cracknell, H.L. *and* Kaufman, R.J., *tr.* London, Butterworth-Heinemann, 1991. ISBN: 0750602880.

Supersedes *A guide to modern cookery* (2nd ed. 1957). Originally as *Le guide culinaire* (1902).

5,011 recipes. 17 chapters (1. Sauces ... 3. Soups ... 6. Fish ... 12. Roasts ... 16. Sweets, puddings and desserts ... 17. Poached fruits (compotes), jams and drinks). Both imperial and metric measures given. Glossary, p.589-92. Specimen menus, p.593-609 (Christmas menu, 1906: 31 items). Detailed index. *Class No:* 641.5(035)

Condiments, Garnishes & Pickles

[1566]

The Complete book of herbs. Bremness, L., *ed.* London, Dorling Kindersley, 1988. 288p. illus. (col.). ISBN: 0863183131.

8 sections: Herbs in the garden - Herbal index - Using herbs (*e.g.* herbal decorations; herbs in the kitchen; herbs for the household) - Herbs for beauty - Essential oils - Herbs for health - Cultivating and harvesting herbs - A catalogue of herbs. Glossary. Useful addresses. Bibliography. Index. Many useful illustrations. *Class No:* 641.88

[1567]

NORMAN, J. The Complete book of spices. London, Dorling Kindersley, 1990. 160p. illus. (col.), maps. ISBN: 0863184871.

5 main sections: The spice trade past and present - Spice index (arranged by botanical name) - Spice mixtures (*e.g.* 'Sambal'; 'Berbere') - Cooking with spices, p.110-45 - Spices in the home. Index. Bibliography (85 items). Data for each spice include distribution; appearance and growth; aroma and taste; culinary, medicinal and cosmetic uses. Clearly and colourfully presented. *Class No:* 641.88

The Home

[1568]

BREMNER, M. Enquire within upon everything. 2nd ed. London, Century, 1990. viii,756p. figs. ISBN: 0091745535.

First published 1988.

16 sections: 1. Social behaviour - 2. Food ... 4. Domestic matters ... 9. Things mechanical - 10. Law - 11. Money - 12. In sickness ... 15. Organizations (Consumer bodies ... Medical - Police ... Travel and transport) - 16. Facts and figures. Bibliography. Index. 'It is a first source which will give the basics and provide pointers to where to find out anything else you want to know' (*Preface*). *Class No:* 643/645

Maintenance

[1569]

BRAGDON, A.D., *ed.* **The Homeowner's complete manual of repair & improvement.** New York, Arco, [c.1983]. 576p. illus. ISBN: 0668057378.

Originally as *Peterson's Home repair & maintenance guide.*

6 sections (subdivided into chapters): Interior repairs & decoration - Windows - Doors - Security & insulation - Furniture care & refinishing - Electrical fixtures, wiring and appliances - Plumbing and heating - Exterior maintenance & improvements. Excellent illus. and step-by-step instructions. Brief index. Given high marks for simplicity, completeness, accuracy and readability in *Reference books bulletin, 1983-1984,* p.102. *Class No:* 643.0045

[1570]

Reader's Digest new D-I-Y manual. London, Reader's Digest Association, 1987. 504p. illus. (col.), figs., diagrs. Loose-leaf.

2 sections: 1. Items for the home (*e.g.* Kitchens ... Bedrooms ... Outside the house) - 2. Techniques, tools and materials (*e.g.* Painting, wallpapering and tiling ... Home security ... Central heating ... DIY in the garden). Index, p.1-5. A step-by-step guide with numerous illustrations. A standard DIY title. *Class No:* 643.0045

Clothing

Sewing & Needlework

[1571]

CLABBURN, P. The Needleworker's dictionary. London, Macmillan, 1976. 296p. illus. (incl. col.), diagrs.

Nearly 2,000 entries, A-Z, including short biographies. Cross-references. Appended select list of museums and collections exhibiting textiles. Bibliography, p.288-92. 350 photographs, 300 line-drawings. 'Mainly for students of needlework, amateur and professional embroiderers, art and costume historians, and the fashion world... An invaluable work of reference' (*British book news,* April 1977, p.313). *Class No:* 646.2

[1572]

Reader's Digest complete guide to sewing. London, New York, etc., Reader's Digest Association, Ltd., 1978. 528p. illus., (incl. col.), diagrs.

Detailed, step-by-step approach. Sections: Sewing essentials - Patterns, fabrics and linings - Making clothes that fit - Designing your own patterns - Preparing to sew - Basic stitches - Seams - Darts and tucks - Pleats - Gathering, shirting, smocking and ruffles - Pockets - Hems and other edge finishes - Zip fasteners - Buttons and other fasteners - Tailoring - Sewing for the family - Sewing for the home (*e.g.,* bedspreads). Sewing projects (p.440-516; *e.g.,* dresses, dungarees). Over 2,000 two-colour illus. ('Collars', p.228-44; *c.*150 illus). Many patterns. Index, p.517-20. *Class No:* 646.2

Cleaning

[1573]

PHILLIPS, B. The Complete book of cleaning: how to clean everything - the right way, the lazy way, the green way. London, Piatkus, 1990. 154p. ISBN: 0749910178.

Concise update of the author's *Wonder worker's complete book of cleaning* (Sidgwick and Jackson, 1980).

15 chapters: 1. Laundering - 2. A-Z of fabrics and their care ... 6. Guidelines for housework ... 10. Cleaning windows and plate glass ... 15. A-Z of household products. Addresses, p.149-51. Detailed index, p.152-4. *Class No:* 648.5

654/656 Communication

Telecommunication Services

[1574]
WEIK, M.H. **Communications standard dictionary.** 2nd ed. New York, Van Nostrand Reinhold, 1989. 1219p. illus., diagrs., graphs. ISBN: 0442205562.

About 13,600 entries and cross-references concerning the science and technology of communications ('A-and-not-B gate' ... 'Zoom lens'). Claims to cover 64 fields. *Class No:* 654

The Book

[1575]
ABHB / Annual bibliography of the history of the printed book and libraries. The Hague, Nijhoff (now Dordrecht, Academic Publishers), 1973-. v.1-. Annual.

V.20 (1991, xi, 422p.) has 3,899 entries for items published in 1989 plus additions from the previous years. List of periodicals (*c.*2,000), p.1-41. Sections A-M (E. Book illustration; G. Book trade, publishing; J. Libraries; L. Newspapers, journalism). Indexes: Authors' names and anonyms; Geographical and personal names. 'A basic item for any bibliographical reference shelf' (*TLS*, no.3951, 15 December 1977, p.1484). *Class No:* 655.0

[1576]
GLAISTER, G.A. **Glaister's glossary of the book:** terms used in papermaking, printing, bookbinding and publishing, with notes on illuminated manuscripts and private presses. 2nd ed. London, Allen & Unwin, 1979. [xv], 551p. illus. (incl. col.), facsims. ISBN: 0040100065.

First published 1960.

3,932 entries, including biographies (*e.g.*, Gutenberg: nearly 2p.; 2 facsims.). Updated to include such entries as 'Computer assisted type-setting' ($1\frac{1}{2}$ columns; 7 cross-references). Covers all book-making processes, with a natural emphasis on the historical (*e.g.*, 'Islamic bookbinding: 2p.). Appendixes A-D (A. Some type specimens; D. A short reading list, p.547-51, grouped). 238 illus. 'Apart from specialist libraries, any general reference collection of any size must have a copy' (*Library Association record*, v.82(8), August 1980, p.370). *Class No:* 655.0

[1577]
JENNETT, S. **The Making of books.** 5th ed. London, Faber, 1973. 554p. illus. (incl. col.), facsims.

First published 1951.

2 parts (24 chapters): 1. Printing and binding (chapters 1-12) - 2. The design of books (13-24). This ed. includes new techniques and technologies. List of 'further reading and reference', p.517-23. 'A polyglot glossary of technical terms' (English, French, German, Italian), p.524-39. Detailed, non-analytical index. 200 illus. A standard work for students of bibliography, typography and printing. *Class No:* 655.0

Printing Industry

Dictionaries

[1578]
WIJNEKUS, F.J.M. *and* WIJNEKUS, E.F.P.H. **Elsevier's dictionary of the printing and allied industries,** in English, French, German, Dutch, Spanish and Italian. 2nd rev. ed. Amsterdam, etc., Elsevier, 1983. xxxvi, 1026p. ISBN: 0444422498.

First published 1967.

14,968 English-base terms, with equivalents and indexes in the other five languages. Spanish and Italian are added in this edition. *Class No:* 655.1(038)

Reviews & Abstracts

[1579]
Printing abstracts. Oxford, etc., Pergamon Press, 1945-. Monthly. ISSN: 0031019x.

Compiled by the Information Section of PIRA (Paper and Board, Printing and Packaging Industries Research Association).

January, 1992 issue contains 383 abstracts. 5 sections: 1. General - 2. Prepress and DTP(*e.g.*, photography) - 3. Printing processes - 4. Post press (*e.g.*, bookbinding) - 5. Products (*e.g.*, newspapers, books and periodicals; business forms and stationery). Author and subject indexes per issue only. Also online through Pergamon Orbit INFOLINE. *Class No:* 655.1(048)

Yearbooks & Directories

[1580]
Printers yearbook: BPIF guide to the printing industry. London, British Printing Industries Federation. Annual. illus., tables. ISSN: 02642387.

The 1991/92 yearbook (1991. 262p.) has 9 sections. 1. British Printing Industry Federation - 2. Printers' law - 3. Industrial relations (including national agreements)- 4. Education and training - 5. Technical information and buyers' guide - 6. Economics (*e.g.*, index of retail prices) - 7. International - 8. What's what/who's who (including associated organizations) - 9. Detailed, analytical index. *Class No:* 655.1(058)

Processes & Printing Surfaces

Copy Presentation

[1581]
BUTCHER, J. Copy-editing: the Cambridge handbook. 2nd ed. (desk ed.). Cambridge, Cambridge University Press, 1981. xii, 331p. illus., tables. ISBN: 0521238684.

15 chapters (3. Preparing the typescript for setting; 6. House style; 10. Bibliographical references; 13. Science and mathematics books; 15. Reprints and new editions). 8 appendices (7. French and German bibliographical terms and abbreviations). Glossary, p.294-311. Select bibliography. Detailed, analytical index, p.314-31.

A 3rd ed. is due to be published in 1992. *Class No:* 655.25

[1582]
HART, H. Hart's rules for compositors and readers at the University Press, Oxford. 39th rev. and updated ed. Oxford Univ. Press, 1983. 192p. ISBN: 019212983x.

First published 1893.

States Oxford University Press practice on spelling, pluralizing, syllabification, capitalizing, punctuation, abbreviation, etc. Includes a guide to the setting of Welsh, Dutch, Afrikaans, and a new section on Machine Reader Codes. All words are brought into line with the *Oxford dictionary for writers and editors* (1981). *Class No:* 655.25

Word Processing

[1583]
LANGMAN, L. An Illustrated dictionary of word processing. Phoenix, Arizona, Oryx, 1986. xiii, 289p. illus. ISBN: 0897742869.

Covers more than 500 word-processing terms and functions. Extensive cross-references. Appendices. 'Primarily of assistance to beginners' (*Choice*, v.24 (2), October 1986, p.282), as well as to the prospective purchasers of word-processing software. *Class No:* 655.254.4

Typography

[1584]
GARLAND, K. Graphics, design and printing terms: an international dictionary. 2nd ed. London, Lund Humphries, 1988. 264p. illus., facsims., diagrs. ISBN: 085331523x.

Defines *c*.2,000 terms, A-Z with many cross-references. Includes many computing terms, abbreviations and illustrations. A useful quick-reference tool. *Class No:* 655.26

[1585]
STEVENSON, G.A. Graphic arts encyclopedia. 2nd ed. New York, etc., McGraw-Hill, 1979. x, 483p. illus., diagrs., tables. ISBN: 0070612889.

First published 1968 (xiv, [1], 492p.).

3,000 terms, A-Z with many cross-references, p.1-420. 'Deals with (1) the products and tools with which the image is formed, (2) the kind of image, and (3) the surface or material upon which the image is produced' (*Preface*). Bibliography, p.421-2. Associations and societies (all in USA), p.423. Trade journals (US and British), p.426-8. Product, manufacturers; and general indexes. Clear, accurate and easy to use, with US slant.

A 3rd ed. is due to be published in 1992. *Class No:* 655.26

Techniques

[1586]
HUTCHINGS, E.A.D. A survey of printing processes. 2nd ed. London, Heinemann, 1978. x, 246p. illus., tables.

First published 1970.

14 chapters: 1. Type production - 2. Camera work and process engraving - 3. Letterpress relief plates - 4. Letterpress printing - 5. Offset lithographic plates - 6. Offset lithographic printing - 7. Reprography - 8. The photogravure process - 9. Screen process printing - 10. Flexographic printing - 11. Collotype printing - 12. Finishing processes, binding machines and methods of binding - 13. Comparison of printing processes - 14. Modern technical developments. V.13-14 are new. Glossary. Reading list, p.241. Index. Covers 'the technical subjects which form the syllabus for examinations in General Printing Knowledge' (*Preface*). *Class No:* 655.3

Book Trade

[1587]
American book trade directory. New York, Bowker, 1915-. Now biennial.

The 1989/90 directory (1989. 1805p.), lists 25,435 bookstores, jobbers, wholesalers and distributors in the US and Canada, noting subject specialities. Geographic and name indexes. (Firms are classified by category of books sold). *Class No:* 655.4

[1588]
International literary market place: the directory of the international book publishing industry, 1991. New York, Bowker, 1990. Biennial. 783p. ISBN: 0835221687. ISSN: 00746827.

First published 1965.

A directory of over 10,000 book publishers and book-trade organizations in more than 160 countries, other than the US and Canada. Arranged alphabetically by country, sections include publishers; book trade; libraries; literary associations. 90-page Yellow Pages acts as an index to the directory. Criticized in *Reference reviews*, v.5(3), 1991 for patchy coverage. Companion to *Literary market place* (q.v.). *Class No:* 655.4

[1589]
Literary market place: the directory of the American book publishing industry with industry Yellow Pages, 1991. New York, R.R. Bowker. Annual.

First published 1940.

The 1991 ed. (1657p. 1990.) contains a 330-page section on US and Canadian publishers which is followed by sections on editorial services and agents; advertising, marketing and publishing; book manufacturing; sales and distribution organizations; services and suppliers, associations, events, courses and awards; books and magazines for the trade. The index of *c*.500 pages includes a Yellow Pages section of all organizations and personnel with addresses and telephone numbers. Companion to *International literary market place* (q.v.). *Class No:* 655.4

Publishing

[1590]
5001 hard-to-find publishers and their addresses. 4th ed. London, Dawson, 1990. 147p. ISBN: 0946291217.

First published 1981.

Includes details of over 8,000 publishers. Concentrates on Western Europe, the Commonwealth and USA. Arranged A-Z by publisher. Designed to complement such directories as Bowker's *Literary market place* (qv). Considerably extended since the previous ed., its strength lies in listing specialized and small publishers. *Class No:* 655.41

[1591]
MÓRA, I., *comp.* **Publisher's practical dictionary in 20 languages.** 3rd rev. ed. Munich, K.G. Saur, 1983. ix, 418p. £38. ISBN: 3598104499.
First published 1974 (German-base terms).
About 1,000 English-base terms, with equivalents and indexes in other 19 languages, - German, French, Russian, Spanish, Bulgarian, Danish, Finnish, Dutch, Italian, Croat, Norwegian, Polish, Portuguese, Rumanian, Swedish, Serb, Slovak, Czech and Hungarian. 'Very easy to use' (*RQ*, v.10(1), Fall 1974, p.67-68). *Class No:* 655.41

[1592]
Publishers' international ISBN directory. Opitz, H. *and* Strasser, K.-H., *eds.* Munich, etc., K.G. Saur, 1991. Annual.
The 18th ed. (3v. 4624p. 1991) contains more than 220,000 entries from 200 countries, arranged under continents. Includes over 105,000 publishers with ISBN prefixes. Includes microfilm, video and computer software publishers, complete with ISBN. Supplements *British books in print*, etc. *Class No:* 655.41

Bookselling

Antiquarian & Second-hand Books

[1593]
Sheppard's book dealers in North America: a directory of antiquarian and secondhand book dealers in the USA and Canada. 11th ed. Old Woking, Surrey, Richard Joseph, 1990. 343p. ISBN: 1872699006. ISSN: 09500715.
First published 1954.
Sections (as in *Sheppard's Book dealers in the British Isles*): Miscellaneous information - Geographical directory of dealers - Alphabetical index - Speciality index - Index of advertisers. *Class No:* 655.425

[1594]
Sheppard's book dealers in the British Isles: a directory of antiquarian and secondhand book dealers in the United Kingdom, the Channel Islands, the Isle of Man and the Republic of Ireland, 1990-91. 15th ed. Farnham, Surrey, Richard Joseph, 1990. 576p. ISBN: 1872699014. ISSN: 09500715.
Contains over 2,300 entries. Geographical directory of book dealers, p.55-330 (English counties; Wales, Scotland; Isle of Man; Northern Ireland; Republic of Ireland; Channel Islands). 'Miscellaneous information' (*e.g.*, Book trade and literary periodicals; supplies and services) precedes. Alphabetical index (including dealer's addresses and 'phone numbers). Speciality index. List of dealers, grouped, Agriculture ... Topography and travel. Index of advertisers. *Class No:* 655.425

[1595]
Sheppard's European bookdealers 1989-90. 7th ed. London, Europa Publications, 1989. 300p. ISBN: 0946653402.
Bookdealers listed under 27 countries, Austria ... Yugoslavia. Periodicals, p.4-11; reference books, p.12-18 - Alphabetical index; speciality index; list of advertisers. *Class No:* 655.425

Transport Services

Encyclopaedias & Dictionaries

[1596]
Concise encyclopedia of traffic and transportation systems. Papageorgiou, M., *ed.* Oxford, Pergamon Press, 1991. xviii,658p. figs., illus. (*Advances in systems, control and information engineering.*) ISBN: 0080362036.
118 articles arranged A-Z (Air traffic control: an overview ... Visual and instrument flying rules), written by 135 contributors. Each article has a bibliography appended. Cross-references. Aimed at academics, managers, operators, managers, engineers and graduate students. Contains some updated and revised articles from *Systems and control encyclopedia*) (1987). *Class No:* 656(03)

Handbooks & Manuals

[1597]
HOMBURGER, W.S., *and others, eds.* **Transportation and traffic engineering handbook.** 2nd ed. Englewood Cliffs, N.J., Prentice Hall, Inc., 1982. 883p. illus., graphs, tables. ISBN: 0139330626.
First published 1976, edited by J.E. Baerwald.
28 well-documented sections, stressing traffic engineering rather than mass transportation. Geographical and detailed subject indexes. *Class No:* 656(035)

Great Britain

[1598]
GREAT BRITAIN. DEPARTMENT OF TRANSPORT. Transport statistics: Great Britain 1991. London, HM Stationery Office, 1991. xii, 302p. tables. ISBN: 0115510788.
Tables (each with commentary, notes and definitions, plus footnoted sources): 1. Transport: an overall view; 2. Road; 3. Rail; 4. Water transport; 5. Air transport; 6. International comparisons; 7. Selected historical series. 4 articles precede the tables (*e.g.*, A. Investment in transport ... D. Road accident fact sheets). Appendices. Detailed, analytical index. Data revised and updated quarterly in *Quarterly transport statistics. Class No:* 656(410)

[1599]
Reviews of United Kingdom statistical sources. Oxford, etc., Pergamon Press, for the Royal Statistical Society and the Social Science Research Council, 1978-.
V.7. Review 12: *Road passenger transport,* by D.L. Munby. 13: *Road goods transport,* by A.N. Watson. 1978. xii, 138p. 127p. v.10. Review 17: *Ports and inland waterways,* by R.E. Baxter. 18: *Civil aviation,* by C.M. Phillips. 1978. xii, 302p. v.14. Review 24: *Rail transport,* by D.H. Aldcroft. 1981. 280p. 25: *Sea transport,* by D. Mort. 1981. xii, 268p.
The aim of the series is 'to act as a work of reference to the sources of statistical material of all kinds, both official and unofficial' (*Introduction*, v.7). V.17, Review 18: *Civil aviation* (p.111-302) has 4 chapters, with appended quick-reference list; bibliography; coverage of publications; useful libraries and books; appendix of forms, and a subject index. Statistics are analysed in this *Review* up to September 1977. *Class No:* 656(410)

Routes & Services

Urban Transport

[1600]
INSTITUTION OF HIGHWAYS AND TRANSPORTATION
and **DEPARTMENT OF TRANSPORT. Roads and traffic
in urban areas.** London, HM Stationery Office, 1987. xxiv,
418p. illus. (incl. col.), diagrs., tables, maps. ISBN:
011550818x.
Replaces *Urban traffic engineering techniques* (1968) and
Roads in urban areas (1966).
Reflects the enormous changes in car ownership, lorry
weights, parking facilities, and many other recent trends.
'An important new standard reference work for traffic
engineers and road designers ...' (*British book news*, July
1988, p.577). *Class No: 656.022.9*

Road Transport

[1601]
**INTERNATIONAL ROAD UNION. Manuel du transport
routier international.** [Handbook of international road
transport.] 10th ed. Geneva, ITU, 1988. 494p. tables,
forms. Loose-leaf.
Countries, Austria ... Yugoslavia. Appendices: Customs
Convention, on the international transport of goods under
cover of TIR channels - Community transit systems - List
of the principal juridical texts on international road
transport - Table showing maximum size and weight
permissible for road vehicles in Europe. *Class No: 656.1*

[1602]
The Little red book 1991/92: road passenger transport
directory for the British Isles and Western Europe.
Booth, G., *ed.* London, Ian Allan, Ltd., 1991. 215p. ISBN:
0711019703.
5 sections: 1. Trade directory - 2. United Kingdom
operators, p.43-170 - 3. Tendering authorities, traffic
commissioners (Department of Transport) - 4. European
operators - 5. Index (British Isles operators). *Class No:
656.1*

Railway Transport

Worldwide

[1603]
Railway directory: a *Railway Gazette* yearbook. Sutton, Surrey,
Railway Gazette International. Annual.
First published 1894. Formerly *Railway directory & year
book.*
The 1992 ed. contains systems maps for all countries,
statistical data on every railway. Includes lists of 10,000
senior staff, data on 200 urban rail systems and lists of
1,200 manufacturers/suppliers. General, personnel,
manufacturers and advertisers index. Numerous maps.
Class No: 656.2(100)

Great Britain

[1604]
OTTLEY, G., *and others, comps.* **A Bibliography of British
railway history.** London, Allen & Unwin, 1965. 683p. +
Supplement (1988. 544p.).
1983 reprint (termed '2nd edition') by the Science
Museum (HMSO. £25. ISBN 0112903347).
7,950 entries, many annotated, with 1 location in 16
British libraries (particularly the British Museum) and
private collections. Excludes children's books (usually) and
highly technical specialized books, but includes spotters
books and others that contain useful railway history. Main
classes, A-T (B. Railway transport at particular periods - C.
Railway transport in particular areas ... T. General
directories, gazetteers, atlases, guide books, lists of stations,

....(contd.)
distance tables, time-tables). Entries state number of illus.
Appended lists and 'genealogies' of railway companies.
Extensive author-title and subject index, p.477-683.
Comprehensive, and a model of its kind. *Class No:
656.2(410)*

[1605]
THOMAS, D. St. J. *and* **PATMORE, J.A.,** *eds.* **A Regional
history of the railways of Great Britain.** Dawlish (later,
Newton Abbot), Devon, David & Charles, 1960-. 15v. illus.,
maps.
1. *The West country,* by D. St. J. Thomas. 6th rev. ed.
1988. 2. *Southern England,* by H.P. White. 1981 ed. 3.
Greater London. 3rd ed. by D. St. J. Thomas. 1989. 4.
North-east England, by K. Hoole. 3rd rev. ed. 1986. 5.
Eastern counties, by D.I. Gordon. 3rd ed. 1990. 6.
Scotland: the Lowlands and the Borders. 2nd ed., by J.
Thomas and A.J.S. Paterson. 1984. 7. *The West Midlands.*
2nd ed., by R. Christiansen. 1984. 8. *South and West
Yorkshire.* 2nd ed. by D.A.W. Joy. 1984. 9. *The East
Midlands,* New ed., by R. Leleux. 1984. 10. *The North-
west.* 2nd ed. by G.O. Holt. 1986. 11. *North and Mid
Wales,* by P.F. Baughan. 1980. 12. *South Wales,* by D.S.
Barrie. 1980. 13. *Thames and Severn,* by R. Christiansen.
1981. 14. *The Lake counties,* 2nd ed., by D. Joy. 1990. 15.
The North of Scotland, by J. Thomas and D. Turnock.
1989.
Each volume is self-contained and well-illustrated. V.4
has 44 good-quality half-tone plates, 9 text illus., 8 regional
maps, 1 folding map, plus a partly analytical index. *Class
No: 656.2(410)*

[1606]
**WIGNALL, C.J. Complete British railways maps and
gazetteers, 1825-1985.** Rev. ed. Oxford Publishing Co.,
1985. iv, 71, 79p. ISBN: 086093294x.
First published 1983.
Atlas of 2-colour maps (71p.) distinguishes between 6
types of railway, *e.g.,* Lines closed to passengers; Preserved
lines open to passengers; Lines underground at this point.
Gazetteer to maps (76p.) notes stations open or closed to
passengers and HQ of preserved railways, plus preservation
centres. Lists of mainland railway companies, p.77-79. A
well-produced quarto. *Class No: 656.2(410)*

Timetables

[1607]
ABC rail guide. Dunstable, Beds., ABC International Division,
Reed Travel Group. Monthly. tables, maps. ISSN:
00010472.
Contains an A-Z list of places in Great Britain served by
rail, with information on fares and train times to and from
London only, p.40-250; complete timetable for services in
London and SE England, p.251-600; provincial Intercity
section, p.601-750, arranged partly A-Z by 72 'important'
cities and towns, partly tabular; shipping and miscellaneous
tables, p.751-800; some European tables, p.801-16. Handy
guide but not comprehensive for stations outside Southern
England. *Class No: 656.222*

[1608]
British Rail passenger timetable. London, British Railways
Board. 2pa., plus supplements. tables, maps.
Established 1853.
The October 1991 - May 1992 issue 'contains all internal
rail services, coastal shipping information and connections
with Ireland, Isle of Man, the Isle of Wight, the Channel
Islands and certain continental services to France, Belgium,
etc'. Timetables, p.33-1570. Station index precedes. 'Other
useful information' (*e.g.,* InterCity sleepers; Private railway
systems). Local and suburban services are included. Unlike
ABC rail guide, includes connections. *Class No: 656.222*

[1609]
Thomas Cook European timetable: railway and shipping services throughout Europe. Peterborough, Thomas Cook. Monthly. tables, maps. ISSN: 0952620x.

September 1991 issue (544p. £6.50) contains a 32-page Winter Supplement. Information includes explanation of signs; city plans; car sleepers; airport links; holiday trains; public holidays; shipping services; books, guides and maps. The index now includes places which do not have a rail service. The section 'What's new this month' draws attention to any changes or alterations since publication of the previous issue.

Complemented by *Thomas Cook overseas timetable: railway, road and shipping services outside Europe. Class No: 656.222*

Marine Transport

Encyclopaedias

[1610]
The Oxford companion to ships and the sea. Kemp, P., *ed.* Oxford Univ. Press, 1976 (reissued 1988). ISBN: 0192820842.

3,700 articles on nautical terms, famous ships, seamen, navigators, ports, explorers, etc. 'Diving' (unassisted, assisted and free diving), p. 250-5; 5 illus., references to Bathyscaph, Bathysphere. Biographical sketches (*e.g.,* 'Tasman', 'Von Spee', 'Conrad'). Also, Maritime museums, naval instruments. Generally omits material on oceanography and small-boat pleasure sailing. 5 appendices (1. Equivalent ranks; 3. Rules of the road). 226 half-tones; 187 line-drawings. 'Highly recommended' (*Library journal,* 15 January 1977, p.188). *The Economist* (23 October 1976, p.142) finds that 'Modern technology has largely been sacrificed for the sake of history'. *Class No:* 656.6(031)

Dictionaries

English

[1611]
SULLIVAN, E. The Marine encyclopaedic dictionary. 2nd ed. London, Lloyd's of London Press, 1988. vii, 470p. ISBN: 1850441278.

About 15,000, entries, many for abbreviations. Some longer entries, *e.g.,* 'International shipping organizations': 5½ columns; 'Coastguard': 3 columns' 'SOLAS (Safety of life at sea)': 7p.; 'Lloyd's Register of shipping': 6 columns. Covers all the terminology in use in the marine transport and shipping industry. Well-produced. 3rd ed. to be published in 1992. *Class No:* 656.6(038)=20

Yearbooks & Directories

[1612]
Lloyd's nautical year book, 1979-. London, Lloyd's of London Press, 1979-. Annual. illus.

Originally as *Lloyd's Calendar,* established 1898.

A compendium that includes articles, a list of maritime organizations, data on safety at sea, shipping insurance and legal terms, calendar information, standard times, sea-distance tables, and much else. *Class No:* 656.6(058)

Ships' Flags

[1613]
WILSON, T. Flags at sea: a guide to the flags flown at sea by British and some foreign ships from the 16th century to the present day, illustrated from the collections of the National Maritime Museum. London, HM Stationery Office, 1986. 127p. illus. (incl. col.), charts. ISBN: 0112903894.

Concentrates on the sea flags of Britain, Spain, the Netherlands, France and the United States. Special chapters on flag signalling and the manufacturing of sea flags. *Class No:* 656.6:929.925

Maritime Navigation

Handbooks & Manuals

[1614]
GREAT BRITAIN. MINISTRY OF DEFENCE. Navy. **Admiralty manual of navigation.** London, HM Stationery Office. 5v. illus., diagrs., tables, maps. (*BR 45.*)

V.1 (Rev. ed. 1987. xviii, 697p.): *General navigation, coastal navigation and pilotage,* supersedes the edition of 1964. V.2 (1973, 348p.) is the text book of ocean navigation and nautical astronomy. V.3 includes chapters on radio aids, navigational instruments, logs and echo sounders, gyros and magnetic compasses, automated navigation and radar plotting systems. V.4 (classified) has data and information on navigation, fleetwork and shiphandling. V.5 (6 bound parts) provides exercises on the use of tables (*e.g.,* astronomical, Great Circle, tidal and tidal streams, time and chronometer, relative velocity questions).

V.1 has 19 chapters, with 7 appendices (*e.g.,* 4: Projections). Bibliography, p.675-7. Detailed, analytical index. Well produced. Written primarily for naval officers, but with a wider appeal.

The Admiralty issues updated information in its weekly publication, *Admiralty notice to mariners. Class No:* 656.61(035)

[1615]
GREAT BRITAIN. MINISTRY OF DEFENCE. Navy. **Admiralty manual of seamanship.** London, HM Stationery Office, 1951 (and reprints, incorporating amendments). v. illus., diagrs., graphs, tables, maps. ISBN: 0117722618, v.1; 0117722452, v.2; 0117722698, v.3.

1. *Basic seamanship.* 1979. xi, 509p. 2. *Intermediate level seamanship.* 1981. x, 435p. 3. *Shiphandling and navigational.* 1983.

V.1 has 4 parts (18 chapters); Ship knowledge and safety; Type of ship; Design and construction of warships; Ship handling, etc. - V. 2 concerns intermediate level seamanship - V.3 Advanced seamanship. *Class No:* 656.61(035)

[1616]
The Macmillan & Silk Cut nautical almanac. London, Macmillan Press, 1980-. Annual. illus., graphs, tables, maps.

1991 ed. (839p.) has 10 chapters: 2. General information - 3. Coastal navigation - 4. Radio navigational aids - 5. Astro-navigation - 6. Communications - 7. Weather - 8. Safety - 9. Tides - 10. Harbour, coastal and tidal information. 20 areas (SW England ... Federal Republic of Germany). Detailed index. Claims to be 'the first comprehensive almanac designed specifically in North-West Europe'. Attractively produced, with over 800 charts and diagrams. *Class No:* 656.61(035)

[1617]
TATE, W.H. A Mariner's guide to the rules of the road. 2nd ed. Annapolis, Md., Naval Institute Press, 1982. 169p. illus. ISBN: 0870213555.

First published 1974.

....(contd.)

Analyses and compares the 1972 International report for preventing collisions at sea, and the Inland Navigation Rules Act, which between them control the movement of vessels both on the high seas and on US inland waterways. 'Absolutely essential to professional mariners and serious marine hobbyists' (*Library journal,* 1 December 1982, p.2249). *Class No:* 656.61(035)

Signals

[1618]
GREAT BRITAIN. HYDROGRAPHIC DEPARTMENT. Admiralty list of radio signals. London, Hydrographic Office, 1985-86. 6v. *(NP 275(1)-(6).)*
1. *Coast radio stations.* 1986 ed. 2. *Radio navigational aids.* 1986 ed. 3. *Radio weather messages. Meteorological codes.* 1985 ed. Diagrams. 4. *Lists of meteorological observation stations.* 5. *Radio time signals. Radio navigation warnings and position fixing systems.* 1986 ed. Diagrams. 6. *Port operations. Pilot services and traffic surveillance.* 1985 ed.
Updated by corrections in section 6 of the weekly edition of Admiralty *Notices to mariners* until suspended. *Class No:* 656.61.054

Lights & Beacons

[1619]
GREAT BRITAIN. HYDROGRAPHIC DEPARTMENT. Admiralty list of lights and fog signals. Taunton, Hydrographer of the Navy. 1985-86 ed. 12v. tables, maps.
A. *British Isles and north coast of France.* 1986 ed. (NP 74). £8.50. 2. B. *Southern and eastern sides of the North Sea.* 1986 ed. (NP 75). £5. C. *Baltic Sea.* 1986 ed. (NP 76). £10. D. *Eastern side of Atlantic Ocean.* (NP 77). £4.50. E. *Mediterranean, Black Sea and Red Seas.* 1986 ed. (NP 78). £9.15. F. *Arabian Sea, Bay of Bengal and North Pacific Ocean.* 1986 ed. (NP 79). £10. G. *Western side of South Atlantic Ocean and East Pacific Ocean.* 1986 ed. (NP 80). £9.25. M. *Northern and eastern coasts of Canada.* 1985 ed. (NP 81). £4.75. J. *Western side of North Atlantic Ocean.* 1985 ed. (NP 82). £8.90. K. *Indian and Pacific Oceans, south of the Equator.* 1985 ed. (NP 83). £8.90. L. *Norwegian and Greenland Seas.* 1985 ed. (NP 84). £9.30. M. *Arctic Ocean.* 1985 ed. (NP 85). £8.90.
Mostly tables stating number, name and position, latitude and longitude, characteristics and intensity, elevation, range, structure, remarks. *Class No:* 656.61.057

Ports & Harbours

[1620]
Lloyd's maritime atlas of world ports and shipping places. New 16th ed. Editors, A.K.C. Beresford, and others. Colchester, Essex, Lloyd's of London Press, 1989. 145p. tables, col. maps. ISBN: 1850442266.
First published as *Lloyd's Maritime atlas,* 1951. Previously as *Lloyd's Book of ports and shipping places* (1937-).
Coloured maps, p.2-64; index to maps precedes. Appendix 1: Inland container depots; 2. Distance tables. Geographical index, p.68-117; alphabetical index, p.118-45. Includes *c.3,000* ports in index and/or maps. Designed for use with *Lloyd's ports of the world* (*q.v.*). *Class No:* 656.615

[1621]
Lloyd's ports of the world 1992. 10th ed. Colchester, Essex, Lloyd's of London Press, 1992. 863p. ISBN: 1850444382.
Directory of 2,800 ports worldwide, specifying anchorage and berthing details, possible hazardous approaches, loading facilities etc. Divided into Africa, North America, Central

....(contd.)

America & West Indies, South America, Asia, Australia and Pacific Islands, Europe, European Community (p.599-818), Internal Free Trades, with ports arranged A-Z. Indexes. *Class No:* 656.615

Canal & River Transport

[1622]
HADFIELD, C. The Canals of the British Isles. Newton Abbot, Devon, David & Charles, 1950-.
1. *British canals: an illustrated history* by C. Hadfield. 7th ed. 1984. 2. *The canals of south and south-east England.* 1969. 3. *The canals of south-west England.* 2nd ed. 1985. 206p. 4. *The canals of south Wales and the Border.* 2nd ed. 1967. 5. *The canals of the West Midlands.* 3rd ed. 1985. 352p. 6. *The canals of the East Midlands* (including part of London). 2nd ed. 1970. 7. *The canals of eastern England,* by J. Boyes and R. Russell. 1977. 8/9. *The canals of north-west England.* 1970. 2v. 10/11. *The canals of Yorkshire and north-east England.* 1970. 2v. 12. *The canals of Scotland,* by J. Lindsay. 1968. 13. *The canals of the north of Ireland,* by W.A. McCutcheon. 1965. 14. *The canals of the south of Ireland,* by T.H. and D.R. Delaney. 1973.
V.10/11, on Yorkshire canals, covers the periods, up to 1970, and 1970-72. V.11 (254p. has 16 plates, 22 text illus. and maps, plus combined analytical index). Appendices: 1. Summary of facts about the canals and navigation of the North-east. 2. Principal engineering works.
C. Hadfield, author of v.1-6, 8-11 in the series, provides a combined index to v.2-14. *Class No:* 656.62

[1623]
Inland waterways series. Huntingdon, Imray, Laurie, Norie & Wilson, 1950-. illus., maps, plans.
Inland waterways of Great Britain and Ireland; compiled by L.A. Edwards. 6th ed. 1985. *Inland waterways of France,* by D. Edwards-May. 5th ed. 1984. 292p. *Inland waterways of the Netherlands,* by E.E. Benest. 3v. 1966-72. *Inland waterways of Belgium,* by E.E. Benest. 1960.
The 5th ed. of *Inland Waterways of France* (1984. 289p.) features particulars of the waterways, with distance tables, p.27-270. Numerous plans; conversion tables; short glossary (French-English, English-French). Index, p.279-89. *Class No:* 656.62

Air Transport

Airports & Airfields

[1624]
Pooley's flight guide: United Kingdom and Ireland. Pooley, R. and Ryall,, W., *eds.* London, R. Pooley, Ltd., 1991. xvi,486p. tables, plans, maps. ISBN: 0902037234.
United Kingdom civil aerodromes, p.69-347. Preceded by sections on procedures, controlling authorities, navigational aids, and meteorological services, etc. Military and Ministry aerodromes. Private airfields. Helicopters. Aeronautical light beacons. Republic of Ireland, p.431-63. Appended conversion tables, etc. *Class No:* 656.71

Timetables

[1625]
ABC world airways guide. Dunstable, Beds., ABC International Division. Monthly. 2v. tables.
First published 1948.
V.1: Airlines of the world. International time calculator. Flight routings. Timetables, Aachen ... Mzuzu (Malawi). V.2: Timetables; Naberevnye Chelnye (CIS) ... Zurich. Includes fares section (p.1-286). *Class No:* 656.73.022

Postal Services

Postage Stamps

[1626]

Stanley Gibbons Great Britain specialised stamp catalogue.
London, Stanley Gibbons Publications, Ltd. 5v.

First published 1963.

1. *Queen Victoria.* 9th ed. 1989. 432p. 2. *King Edward VII to King George VI.* 8th ed. 1989. 448p. 3. *Queen Elizabeth II. Pre-decimal issues.* 8th ed. 1990. 456p. £12.95. 4. *Queen Elizabeth II. Decimal definitive issues.* 6th ed. 1991. 592p. £14.95. 5. *Decimal special issues.* 1991. 392p.

Each volume has introductory notes, appendices, and further reading. Thus, v.2 has sections M, N, P, Q for the four reigns, plus R: Postage due stamps; 6 appendices (E. Perforations) and 'Further reading' (Postal history ... Postmarks), p.400-3. *Class No:* 656.835

[1627]

Stanley Gibbons simplified catalogue. Stamps of the world.
1992 ed. London, Stanley Gibbons Publications, Ltd. 3v. illus.

1. *Countries, A-J.* 1064p. 2. *Countries, K-Z.* 1056p. 3. *Commonwealth countries.* 736p.

'An illustrated and priced three-volume reference to the postage stamps of the whole world, excluding changes of paper, perforation, shade and watermarks' (*subtitle*). Each volume has an index. *Class No:* 656.835

[1628]

Stanley Gibbons stamp catalogue. London, Stanley Gibbons.

1. *British Commonwealth.* 94th ed. 1992. 1304p. 2. *Austria & Hungary.* 4th ed. 1988. 233p. 3. *Balkans.* 3rd ed. 1987. x, 497p. 4. *Benelux.* 3rd ed. 1988. x, 261p. 5. *Czechoslovakia and Poland.* 4th ed. 1991. 240p. 6. *France.* 3rd ed. 1987. x, 336p. 7. *Germany.* 3rd ed. 1987. x, 288p. 8. *Italy & Switzerland.* 3rd ed. 1986. x, 292p. 9. *Portugal and Spain.* 3rd ed. 1991. 400p.

10. *Russia.* 4th ed. 1991. 400p. 11. *Scandinavia.* 3rd ed. 1988. 232p. 12/14. *Africa since independence.* 2nd ed. 1983. 3v. 15. *Central America.* 2nd ed. 1984. x, 526p. 16. *Central Asia.* 2nd ed. 1983. x, 212p. 17. *China.* 4th ed. 1986. 288p. 18. *Japan & Korea.* 2nd ed. 1984. x, 275p. 19. *Middle East.* 4th ed. 1990. 576p. 20. *South America.* 3rd ed. 1989. 736p. 21. *South-east Asia.* 2nd ed. 1985. x, 295p. 22. *U.S.A.* 3rd ed. 1990. x, 213p.

V.1 includes post-independence issues of Ireland, Pakistan and South Africa. Index precedes main sequence (Great Britain ... Zululand). Appended: Addenda and corrigenda; Stamps added; Catalogue numbers altered; General philatelic information. *Class No:* 656.835

66 Chemical Industry

Chemical Engineering

Encyclopaedias

[1629]
KIRK, R.E. *and* OTHMER, D.F., *eds.* **Encyclopedia of chemical technology.** 3rd ed. New York, Wiley, 1978-84. 26v. (24v. + supplement volume + general index).
First published 1947-60 (15v. & 2 suppts.); 2nd ed. 1963-71 (22v. & suppt.).
Over 1,300 contributors (an international team). About one half of the c.1,300 articles concern chemical substances. The article in the 2nd ed. on 'Literature on chemical technology' has been chopped in favour of 'Information retrieval' (with 34 references) and 'Patents literature' (v.16. p.889-945, with 80 references + 7 general references). Both SI and English units are used and Chemical Abstracts Service (CAS) Registry numbers cited to improve access to the literature. 'The ideal first source of reference for information on the properties, manufacture and use of any chemical; on industrial processes, on methods of analysis; and on scientific subjects allied to chemical technology' (*British chemical engineering*, v.10(1). January 1965, p.10, on the 2nd ed.).
Publication of the 4th ed. (27v.) began in September, 1991. Vols. are scheduled to appear every three months. *Class No:* 66.0(031)

[1630]
ULLMANN, F. **Ullmann's Encyclopedia of industrial chemistry.** 5th completely revised ed. Weinheim, VCH Verlagsgesellschaft, 1985-. (A19. 1991). illus., diagrs., graphs, tables. ISBN: 0895731576.
First published 1914; 4th ed. (1972-84. 24v.) as *Ullmanns Enzyklopädie der technischen Chemie.*
5th ed., the first in English, is planned in 2 series; A1-A28 (entries A-Z, *e.g.*, A1-A7: Abrasives ... Copper Compounds; Index to v.1-7. 1987. viii, 117p.); B1-B8 (basic topics, *e.g.*, B4: Materials science). Each volume in the A series has 20-30 articles. 'Copper compounds', in A7, has 9 sections, p.567-93, with 197 references. Comparable to Kirk & Othmer as a European counterpart. *Class No:* 66.0(031)

Handbooks & Manuals

[1631]
CHENIER, P.J. **Survey of industrial chemistry.** New York, etc, Wiley-Interscience, 1986. xiv, [1], 422p. ISBN: 0411010774.
27 chapters: 1. Introduction to the chemical industry: an overview ... 3. Leading chemicals and chemical companies ... 5. Industrial gas ... 11. Seven basic organic chemicals ... 16. Basic polymer chemistry - 17. Plastics ... 22. Pesticides ... 26. Surfactants, soaps and detergents - 27. The chemical industry and pollution. 'List of important references and their abbreviations' (p.xiii-xv). Appendix: 'Possible subjects for topics'. Index. *Class No:* 66.0(035)

[1632]
COULSON, J.M. *and* RICHARDSON, J.F. **Chemical engineering.** 4th ed. Oxford, Pergamon Press, 1990-. V.1-. illus., diagrs., graphs, tables.
First ed. (2v.) 1954-55.
V.1 (*Fluid flow, heat transfer and mass transfer.* xiii,708p. ISBN: 0080379508) has 13 sections. Detailed, analytical index, p.685-708. V.2-6 are to be: 2. Particle technology and separation processes - 3. Chemical and biochemical reaction engineering and control - 4/5. Solutions to the problems in volumes 1, 2 and 3 - 6. Chemical engineering design. *Class No:* 66.0(035)

[1633]
PERRY, R.H. *and* GREEN, D.W. **Perry's chemical engineers' handbook.** 6th ed. New York, etc., McGraw-Hill, 1984. [2336]p. illus., diagrs., graphs, tables. ISBN: 0070494797.
First published 1934; 5th ed., 1973.
About 130 contributors. 27 sections, each with contents page and references. Topics range from transport and storage of fluids and heat transfer equipment to process control and biochemical engineering. Section 19, 'Liquid-solid systems' (109p.) has 132 illus., diagrams and graphs, plus 18 tables. The 301p. on physical and chemical data include $4\frac{1}{2}$ columns of references. 1,848 illus., etc. in all. The 68p. of analytical index carry c.9,000 entries. This compendium is known as the chemical engineer's 'Bible'. Also in Spanish edition. *Class No:* 66.0(035)

Dictionaries

[1634]
GARDNER, W. **Gardner's Chemical synonyms and trade names.** Pearce, J., *ed.* 9th ed. Aldershot, Gower, 1987. [vi],1081p. Chemical formulas. ISBN: 0291397034.
First published 1924; 8th ed. 1978.
Some 12,000 new entries. In two parts: Trade names and synonyms (A-Z); Names and addresses of manufacturers (much expanded from earlier editions). Many cross-references. *Class No:* 66.0(038)

Reviews & Abstracts

[1635]
Chemical engineering abstracts. Nottingham, Royal Society of Chemistry, 1982-. Monthly.
1986: 4,516 abstracts. 22 sections (2. Process operation, loss prevention and optimization; 5. Heat transfer; 7/8 Diffusional operations; 12. Reactors, plant, equipment and techniques; 14. Computers and their applications; 21/22. Techno-commercial items (e.g., plant equipment)). Subject index per issue and annually. Available online as Chemical Engineering and biotechnology abstracts, via DIALOG. *Class No:* 66.0(048)

[1636]

Chemical industry notes. Columbus, Ohio, Chemical Abstracts Service, 1973-. Weekly. ISSN: 0045639x.

About 12,000 entries p.a. 8 sections: A. Production -B. Pricing - C. Sales - D. Facilities - E. Products and processes - F. Corporate activities - G. Government activities - H. People. Keyword and corporate named indexes per issue and annually. Carries 'business oriented articles of value to the chemical industry'. Online; host: DATASTAR, DIALOG. *Class No:* 66.0(048)

Yearbooks & Directories

[1637]

WHITESIDE, R. Major chemical and petrochemical companies of Europe, 1991-1992. 5th ed. London, Graham & Trotman, 1991. 272p. ISBN: 1859336203.

Nearly 1000 entries, with usual directory-type information. *Class No:* 66.0(058)

Tables & Data Books

[1638]

BENNETT, H., *ed.* **The Chemical formulary:** a selection of valuable, timely, practical, commercial formulae and recipes for making thousands of products in many fields of industry. New York, Chemical Publishing Co., Inc; London Chapman & Hall (now Godwin), 1933-. (v.28. 1989).

V.28 (1989. 438p. ISBN 0820603287) lists recipes for amateur or professional chemist. Appendix includes a list of trademark chemicals and their suppliers, information of federal food, drug and cosmetic laws, a list of incompatible chemicals and emergency first aid for chemical injuries. *Chemical formulary: cumulative index for volumes 1 through 25* (New York, Chemical Publishing Co., 1987. 474p. $75. ISBN 0820603193) provides many useful cross-references. *Class No:* 66.0(083)

[1639]

SHUGAR, G.J., *and others, eds.* **Chemical technicians' ready reference handbook.** 3rd ed. New York, etc., McGraw-Hill, 1990. 864p. illus., diagrs., tables. ISBN: 007037183x.

First published 1973; 2nd ed. 1981.

Emphasis on step-by-step procedures. In explaining frequently-used laboratory techniques, adds a new chapter on spectroscopy techniques (*e.g.* NMP, infrared). New sections stress laboratory safety. *Class No:* 66.0(083)

Processes

[1640]

MEYERS, R.A. Handbook of chemical production processes. New York, etc., McGraw-Hill, 1986. v.p. illus., diagrs., graphs, tables. ISBN: 0070417662.

Contributions from 19 firms located in the UK, the Federal Republic of Germany, Japan, Netherlands and the US. 3 parts (40 chapters): 1. Organic chemicals - 2. Polymers - 3. Inorganic chemicals. Abbreviations and acronyms. 10-p. index. Good layout. *Class No:* 66.02

Liquids

Solvents

[1641]

Industrial solvents handbook. Flick, E.W., *ed.* 3rd ed. Park Ridge, N.J. Noyes Data, 1985. 648p. diagrs., tables.

First two editions (1970, 1977) by I. Mellan.

About 1,000 tables of basic data (citing sources) of physical properties of most solvents and on solubilities of a variety of the materials in these solvents. Sections on halogenated hydrocarbons, polyhydric alcohols, ethers, acids, esters. *Class No:* 66.061

Chemical Products

[1642]

ASH, M. *and* **ASH, I.,** *comps.* **Concise encyclopaedia of industrial chemical additives.** London, E. Arnold, 1991. xi,859p. ISBN: 0304556226.

In four sections: Chemical trade names dictionary (p.1-611) - Chemical compound cross-references (p.612-709) - Functional classification of trade names - Chemical manufacturers directory (international). Over 18,000 entries for chemical trade name products currently used throughout the world. *Class No:* 661

[1643]

ASH, M. *and* **ASH, I.,** *eds.* **The Thesaurus of chemical products.** London, E. Arnold, 1986. 2v. ISBN: 0713136030; 0713136043.

1. *Generic-to-tradename.* 2. *Tradename-to-generic.*

Over 50,000 up-to-date national and international tradename entries. Each volume has appendix of chemical manufacturers (*c.*950) and of their addresses; also 'Books for consultation'. *Class No:* 661

[1644]

ASH, M. *and* **ASH, I. What every chemical technologist wants to know.** London, E. Arnold, 1988-90. 5v.

Emulsifier and welding agents. 1988 400p. £65.

Dispersants, solvents and solutions. 1988. 480p. £65.

Plasticizers, stabilizers and thickeners. 1989. 424p. £65.

Conditioners, emollients and lubricants. 1990. 412p. £65.

Resins. 1990. 400p. £65.

Each volume includes trade name products, generic chemical symbols and trade name product manufacturers. Indexes by trade names, formulas, synonyms, etc. *Class No:* 661

[1645]

The Merck index: an encyclopedia of chemicals, drugs and biologicals. 11th ed. Rathway, N.J., Merck & Co., 1989. *c.*2300p. tables.

First published 1889.

Monographs of *c.*10,000 chemicals, drugs and biologicals, with notes on preparation, boiling point, toxicity, uses, etc., plus chemical structure and references. Appended: organic name reactions; miscellaneous tables, Chemical Abstracts Service names and Registry names; Therapeutic category and biological activity index; Formula index; Cross-index of names (plus titles of deleted 9th and 10th ed. monographs), etc. Index of 315p. (*c.*70,000 entries). Online: CIS (Chemical Information Service). *Class No:* 661

Surface-active Agents

[1646]

World surface coating abstracts. Compiled by Paint Research Assoiciation, Teddington, Middx. Oxford, etc., Pergamon Press, 1928-. Monthly. ISSN: 75578409.

About 10,000 abstracts pa. 50 sections (01/02. Pigments, extenders, dyestuffs and phosphors; 23/24. Polymers containing silicon and other elements; 35/36. Water-borne paints and their components; 53/54. Weathering corrosion; 73/74. Industrial and other hazards; 87. Legislation and other official publications; 88. Standards and specifications. Books. Annual author and subject indexes. Online database. *Class No:* 661.185

Fuel Technology

[1647]
CLARK, G.H. Industrial and marine fuels reference book. London, etc., Butterworths, 1988. 528p. illus., diagrs. ISBN: 0408014881.

26 sections (The choice of fuels - The chemistry of petroleum - Crude oil refining - Laboratory tests on fuels - Natural gas and LPG ... General operating problems of large diesel engines - Deposit formation and corrosion in steam boilers - Chimney stack emissions). Appendix. 239 illus. For mechanical, marine and plant engineers, plus shipowners, engine-builders and designers. *Class No:* 662.6

[1648]
Fuel and energy abstracts: a bimonthly summary of world literature on all technical, scientific, commercial and environmental aspects of fuel and energy. Guildford, Butterworth Scientific, on behalf of the Institute of Energy, 1978-. 6pa. ISSN: 01406701.

Formerly *Fuel abstracts and current titles*/ FACTS (1960-), succeeding monthly *Fuel abstracts* (1945-58).

About 8,000 abstracts pa. Classified sections: 01. Solid fuels - 02. Liquid fuels - 03. Gaseous fuels ... 06. Electric power operation and utilization ... 15. Environment - 16. Fuel science and technology ... 18. Energy conversion and recycling. Subject and author indexes per issue and pa. Coverage: 'World literature on scientific, technical, commercial and environmental aspects of fuel and energy'. Highly regarded. *Class No:* 662.6

Coal

[1649]
Coal abstracts. London, IEA [International Energy Agency] / Coal Research. Technical Information Service, 1977-. Monthly. ISSN: 83094879.

1985: 10,853 abstracts. 12 sections: Coal industry - Reserves and exploration - Mining - Preparation - Transport and handling - Properties - Combustion - Waste management - Environmental aspects - Products - Health and safety. Author and cross-reference index. Annual author and subject indexes.

COAL DATABASE (IEA COAL), 1978-. *Class No:* 662.66

Beverages

Wines

[1650]
JOHNSON, H. Hugh Johnson's wine companion. 3rd ed. London, Mitchell Beazley, 1991. 526p. illus., tables, maps. ISBN: 085533892x.

First published 1971 as *The World atlas of wine.* 2nd ed. 1983.

Over 7,500 detailed profiles of chateaux, estates and negotiants, starting from France and Bulgaria to New Zealand and Chile. 'This is the definitive encyclopedia of the world's vinyards and winemakers' (*Good book guide,* V.A92, Annual selection, 1992). *Class No:* 663.2/.3

Food Industry

[1651]
CONSIDINE, D.M. and CONSIDINE, G.D., eds. **Food and food production encyclopedia.** Princeton, N.J., Van Nostrand Reinhold, 1982. xvi, 2305p. ISBN: 0442216122.

An impressive tome: *c.*1,200 articles, 1.9 million words, nearly 3,000 cross-references, 1,000 illus. 578 tables and a 6,200 entry-word index. Longer articles carry bibliographies. The editors identify three stages in food production: growth, nurture, processing. One of the appendices to the

....(contd.)
A-Z sequence tabulates data on additives (78p.). 'Because of its authority, currency and comprehensive scope, it promises to be of continuing value for some time to come' (*Reference books bulletin, 1983-1984.* p.92). *Class No:* 664

[1652]
Food science and technology abstracts. Wallingford, Oxon., CAB International: International Food Information Service (IFIS), 1969-. Monthly. ISSN: 00156574.

Over 2,000 abstracts per issue. Over 1,200 journals searched. Sections A-V (A. Basic food science ... V. Patents). Author and subject indexes per issue and annually. The main food science and technology abstracting service since 1969. Online access: DIALOG, ESA-IRS. CD-ROM (Silver Platter). *Class No:* 664

[1653]
GEAR, A. The New organic food guide; including a list of 600 outlets throughout Britain and Ireland. London, Dent, 1987. xvii, 232p. ISBN: 046002454x.

3 parts (10 chapters): 1. Modern farming: and indictment- 2. Organic farming: the biological alternative - 3. Where to buy organic food (p.59-197; chapters 8-10: 8. Organically grown foods to be found in the shops; 9. A guide to outlets (p.100-89: The South West ... The Channel Islands); 10. A guide to wholesalers). 4 appendices (2. Organizations; 4. References (64)). Detailed, analytical index, p.225-32. *Class No:* 664

Bibliographies

[1654]
GREEN, S. Keyguide to information sources in food science and technology. London, Mansell, 1985. viii, 231p. (*Keyguide to information sources.*) ISBN: 0720117488.

Part 1: Food science and technology and their literature, - a survey of the field in 7 narrative chapters, each with appended references. Chapter 5, 'The literature of food science and technology', p.71-95 discusses forms of material (*e.g.,* reports, dictionaries) - *Part 2:* Bibliography, consists of 715 briefly annotated entries (General aspects; Beverages ... Sugar sweetness, confectionary) - *Part 3:* Directory of selected organizations (by continent). Detailed index. Aimed at special librarians, lecturers and workers in the food industries, 'especially those involved in research and development' (*Preface*). *Class No:* 664(01)

Food Engineering

[1655]
HALL, C.W., and *others.* **Encyclopedia of food engineering.** 2nd ed. Westpoint, Conn., AVI Pubg. Co., 1986. x, [1], 882p. illus., diagrs., graphs, tables. ISBN: 0870551574.

First published 1971.

About 75 contributors. Entries (Absolute pressure controller ... Zinc) can be lengthy, *e.g.,* 'Energy conservation in food processing', p.293-320, with 29 references. This volume, first of a 3v. set, emphasizes equipment and facilities used in food handling and transportation. *Class No:* 664.0

[1656]
MCCANCE, R.A. and WIDDOWSON, E.M. The Composition of foods. 5th rev. and extended ed., by B. Holland and others. Cambridge, Royal Society of Chemistry, 1991. xiii,462p. tables. ISBN: 0851863914.

First published 1940; 4th ed. 1978.

Documented tables cover *c.*1,200 items, including such popular commodities as fish fingers, yogurt, oven chips and coca-cola. 21p. index. Supplements to this edition will cover fruit and nuts, vegetable dishes, fish and fish products and fatty acid composition of foods. A well-known compendium of data on food values. *Class No:* 664.0

Sugar Industry

[1657]
MARIE, S. *and* PIGGOTT, J.R., *eds.* **Handbook of sweeteners.** Glasgow and London, Blackie, 1991. xiv,302p. diagrs., graphs, tables. ISBN: 0216928362.
18 contributors. 11 well-documented chapters. Full contents list. Index, p.295-302. *Class No: 664.1*

Preservation & Treatments

Additives

[1658]
SMITH, J., *ed.* **Food additive user's handbook.** Glasgow and London, Blackie, 1991. 286p. tables. ISBN: 0216929113.
16 contributors. A concise handbook in 15 chapters, with 'Further reading' and, at times, references. Numerous tables. Analytical index, p.281-6. *Class No: 664.8.022*

Oils, Fats & Waxes

[1659]
HAMILTON, R.J. *and* BHATTI, A. **Recent advances in chemistry and technology of fats and oils.** London & New York, Elsevier, 1987. xii, 188p. illus., graphs, tables.
8 contributors; 8 contributions (*e.g.,* 'Physical properties of fats and oils' (15 references); 'The analysis of lipids with special reference to milk fat' (115 references)). Author and subject indexes. *Class No: 665*

Cosmetics & Perfumery

[1660]
MULLER, P.M. *and* LAMPARSKY, A., *eds.* **Perfumes: art, science and technology.** New York, etc., Elsevier, 1991. [viii],658p. illus., diagrs., tables, chemical structures. ISBN: 1851665730.
30 contributors. 7 parts (20 chapters plus 'Outlook'): 1. Perfumes as an art ... 4. Classification of odours ... 6. Production of perfume - 7. Topics in perfume research (Chapter 19 (94p.): 'Natural products'). Detailed, analytical index. 'A state-of-the-art compilation of the relevant know-how' (*Preface*). *Class No: 665.57/.58*

Petroleum Industry

Bibliographies

[1661]
PEARSON, B.C. *and* ELLWOOD, K.B. **Guide to the petroleum reference literature.** Littleton, Colo., Libraries Unlimited, 1987. xi, 193p. ISBN: 0872874737.
11 sections: 1. Guides to the literature and bibliographies - 2. Indexing and abstracting services - 3. Dictionaries - 4. Encyclopedias and yearbooks - 5. Handbooks, manuals and basic texts - 6. Directories - 7. Statistical sources - 8. Databases - 9. Periodicals - 10 Professional and trade associations - 11. Publishers. Sections 1-9 comprise 420 numbered entries. Author/title and subject index. 'For library school students new to the field' (*Marine and petroleum geology*, v.5(3), August 1988). *Class No: 665.6(01)*

Handbooks & Manuals

[1662]
JENKINS, G. **Oil economists' handbook.** 5th ed. London and New York, Elsevier, 1989. 2v. ISBN: 1851683452, set.
V.1. Statistics [to 1987]. xvi,467p. £110. 29 sections (1. Crude oil prices ... 29. Oil quality data and conversion factors).
V.2. vii,396p. £90. Dictionary: an encyclopedic glossary; Chronology of significant events (to January 1989); Directory of organizations, under countries. V.2 includes a bibliography, p.375-6. *Class No: 665.6(035)*

Dictionaries

[1663]
STEVENS, P., *ed.* **Oil and gas dictionary.** London, Macmillan, 1988. 270p. graphs, tables. ISBN: 033337844x.
About 2,000 entries, A-Z, some at length (*e.g.,* 'Crude oil prices', p.39-46). Includes financial, business and general economic terms. Cross-references; abbreviations. Chronology, 1859-1986, p.221-37. Appended 'Energy data conversion tables' (*e.g.,* 'Metric ton oil equivalents of gaseous fuels and electricity'). 'Highly recommended' (*Choice,* May 1989, p.1500). *Class No: 665.6(038)*

Reviews & Abstracts

[1664]
International petroleum abstracts. London, Wiley Heydon, Ltd, on behalf of the Institute of Petroleum, London, 1921-. Quarterly. ISSN: 03094944.
About 1,200 abstracts pa. Sections: Oilfield exploration and exploitation - Transport and storage - Refining and related processes - Products - Corrosion - Engines and automatic equipment - Safety and industrial hygiene - Economics and marketing - Politics and legislation - Pollution. Author index per issue; author and subject indexes annually. Online INFOLINE. *Class No: 665.6(048)*

[1665]
Petroleum abstracts. Tulsa, Oklahoma, University of Tulsa, 1961-. Weekly. ISSN: 00316423.
About 10,000 abstracts pa., on petroleum exploration and production of crude oil and gas. Includes patents. Online as 'Petroleum exploration and production', a restricted file on DIALOG. A leading current-awareness source of petroleum exploration and production. *Class No: 665.6(048)*

Yearbooks & Directories

[1666]
'Financial Times' Oil and gas international year book: 1991. 91st ed. Harlow, Essex, Longman Group, 1990. Annual. xxii,558p. tables. ISBN: 0582059607.
Companies : upstream (entries 1-443) - Companies: downstream (entries 444-702) - Brokers and traders (entries 703-786) - Associations (entries 787-861). Geographical and company indexes. Appended: 5 tables (*e.g.,* World oil consumption). International professional services. Suppliers directory and buyers' guide. Advertisers' index. *Class No: 665.6(058)*

Offshore Oil

[1667]
Offshore engineering abstracts. Cranfield, Beds., BSRA, The Fluid Engineering Centre, 1986-. 6pa.
125 abstracts per issue on offshore structures and equipment, their design, construction, operation and maintenance. Author and subject indexes per issue and annually. Online FLUIDEX, available via DIALOG, ESA-IRS. *Class No: 665.60*

Refining

[1668]
MEYERS, R.A. **Handbook of petroleum refining processes.**
New York, etc., McGraw Hill, 1986. [480]p. illus., diagrs.,
graphs, tables. ISBN: 0070417636.
22 contributors. 11 parts (some with brief bibliographies
appended): 1. Alkylation and polymerization - 2. Cracking
... 5. Isomerization ... 8. Separation processes ... 11.
Gasification. Glossary. Abbreviations and acronyms.
Detailed, analytical index (10p.). *Class No: 665.66*

Petrochemicals

[1669]
Worldwide petrochemical directory, 1992. 30th ed. Tulsa,
Oklahoma, Penn Well Publishing Co., 1962-. Annual. ISSN:
00842583.
Broad geographical regions: U.S.; Canada ; Latin
America; Europe; Africa; Middle East; Asia, Each company
entry includes list of key personnel, services, products.
Company and geographical indexes; advertisers' index.
Claims to identify all petrochemical projects under
construction worldwide. *Class No: 665.7*

Glues & Adhesives

[1670]
SKEIST, I., *ed.* **Handbook of adhesives.** 3rd ed. New York,
Van Nostrand Reinhold, 1990. ISBN: 0342280130.
47 chapters on the physics, chemistry and applications of
adhesives. Many diagrs., charts, tables. Chapter
bibliographies (some plus 'further readings'). Lists of
standards and commercial producers of materials. *Class
No: 665.93*

Glass Industry

[1671]
UHLMANN, D.R. and KREIDL, N.J., *eds.* **Glass science and
technology.** Orlando, Florida, Academic Press, 1980-. illus.,
tables. ISBN: 0127067051.
1. *Glass-forming systems.* 1983. 465p.
2. *Processing.* 1984. 360p. £73.50.
3. *Viscosity and relaxation.* 1986. 412p.
4A. *Structure, microstructure and properties.* 1990. 360p.
£88.50.
4B. *Advances in structural analysis.* 1990. 400p. £88.50.
5. *Elasticity and strength in glasses.* 1980. 282p. £47.50.
V.3 has 7 documented chapters (Viscoelasticity of glass -
Mechanical relaxation in inorganic glasses - Rheology and
relaxation in metal glasses - Technological aspects of
viscosity - Annealing of glass - Rheology of polymeric
fluids - Physical aging of polymer glasses). Index. 'For more
broad-based physical science collections in academe and
industry' (*Science & technical libraries,* v.8(2), Winter 1987/
88, p.138). *Class No: 666.1*

Ceramics

[1672]
Ceramic abstracts. American Ceramic Society, *comp.*
Colombus, Ohio, American Ceramic Society, 1918-. 6pa.
ISSN: 00959960.
Originally published in *Journal of the American Ceramic
Society.*
About 10,000 abstracts pa. 18 sections: 1. Abrasives ... 3.
Cements, limes and plasters ... 5. Glass ... 9. Electronics ...
15. Engineering materials - 16. Chemistry and physics - 17.
General - 18. Books. Keyword index per issue. Annual
author and subject indexes. *Class No: 666.3/.7*

[1673]
NEWMAN, A.C.D., *ed.* **The Chemistry of clays and clay
minerals.** London, Longman. 1987. 480p. (*Mineralogical
Society monograph, no. 6.*) ISBN: 0582301149.
Covers not only the chemical constitution of the silicate
clays, with associated iron, aluminium and manganese
oxides and hydroxides, but also the properties of those
materials most useful to man, - particularly industrially. 'A
major contribution to clay science' (*Nature,* v.328, 13
August 1987, p.588). *Class No: 666.3/.7*

[1674]
World ceramic abstracts. Oxford, Pergamon Press, 1989-.
Monthly. ISSN: 09578897.
Formerly *British ceramic abstracts* (1942-1988); originally
British Ceramic Society. *Abstracts* (1930-1941).
About 6,000 abstracts pa. 16 sections (*e.g.,* Intermediate
and semi-finished products; Processing and treatment
(including machines)). Subject index per issue and annually.
Online. *Class No: 666.3/.7*

Cement Industry

Concrete

[1675]
The Concrete year book, 1991. 67th ed. London, Palladian
Publications, Ltd., 1991. Annual. 560p. ISSN: 00698288.
General information on concrete and construction -
Institutions and associations - Consulting and structural
design - Site investigation - Contractors - Piling -
Tunnelling - Specialist services - Concrete repairs and
protection - Cement ... Products and equipment for
manufacturers - Reinforcement and prestressing ... Guide to
products in precast concrete - Trade names - Personnel in
the concrete industry. Indexes to advertisers. General index.
Class No: 666.97

[1676]
GAMBHIR, M.L. **Concrete technology.** New York, etc.,
McGraw-Hill, 1987. 304p. illus. £4.95. ISBN: 0074516442.
12 sections on manufacture and production of structural
concrete. Concrete-making materials (2 sections) - Properties
of fresh concrete - Properties of hardened concrete -
Statistical quality control of concrete - Proportioning of
concrete mixes - Production of concrete - Extreme weather
concreting - Special concrete and concreting techniques -
Form work - Inspection and testing - Repair technology for
concrete structures. 78 illus. *Class No: 666.97*

Colour

Dyes & Dyeing

[1677]
Sigma-Aldrich handbook of stains, dyes and indicators.
Green, F.J. Milwaukee, WI, Aldrich Chemical Co., 1990.
776p. ISBN: 0941633225.
Guide to 325 compounds used as stains, dyes and
indicators, A-Z by common name. Full data, plus reference
to other sources and spectra when easily available. *Class
No: 667.2*

Metallurgy

Databases

[1678]
METADEX database. Metals Park, Ohio, American Society for Metals; London, The Institute of Metals, 1966-.
METADEX is the major database for metals and metallurgy. The online version of *Metal abstracts*. Available from DIALOG, DATA-STAR, ESA and other hosts. *Class No:* 669(003.4)

Bibliographies

[1679]
PATTEN, M.N., *ed.* **Information sources in metallic materials.** London, etc., Butterworths, 1989. xvi,415p. tables. (*Guides to information sources.*) ISBN: 0408014911.
17 contributors; 18 chapters, sub-divided. 2 parts: I. Materials (1. General sources - 2. Extraction metallurgy - 3. Iron and steel ... 7. Lead ... 9. Zinc ...); II. Applications (11. Powder metallurgy ... 14. Design ... 18. Materials for the packaging industry). Appendices: abbreviations and addresses of organizations. Index, 8p. Forms of literature (*e.g.* reports, patents) are treated in their relation to a particular metal or application; *e.g.* chapter 13, 'Corrosion', p.253-63, covers learned societies, dictionaries, standards organizations, handbooks, data banks, marketing companies, trade associations, books, abstracts, journals, reviews. A valuable contribution to an important series, formerly *Butterworths guides to information sources. Class No:* 669(01)

Handbooks & Manuals

[1680]
Metals handbook. Prepared under the direction of the ASM International Handbook Committee. 10th ed. Metals Park, OH, American Society for Metals, 1990-. illus., diagrs., graphs, tables.
First published 1948; 9th ed. (17v.) 1978-1989.
1. *Properties and selection: irons, steels, and high-performance alloys.* 1990. 1063p.
2. *Properties and selection: nonferrous alloys and special purpose metals.* 1990. 1328p.
3. *Heat treating.* 1991. c.1200p.
4. *Friction, lubrication and wear technology.* 1991. c.1200p.
5. *Surface cleaning, finishing and coating.* Due 1992.
6. *Welding, brazing and soldering.* Due 1992.
7. *Microstructural analysis.* Due 1993.
V.2 is the work of over 400 authors, reviewers and contributors. 5 major sections (62 articles): 1. Specific metals and alloys - 2. Special-purpose materials - 3. Superconducting materials - 4. Pure metals - 5. Special engineering topics. Appended: Metric conversion guide; Abbreviations, symbols and trade names. Analytical index, p.1279-1328. Micrographs. Numerous tables. Written primarily for the industrial user of metals and alloys. *Class No:* 669(035)

[1681]
—Metals handbook. Boyer, H.E. *and* Gull, T.L., *ed.* Desk ed. Metals Park, Ohio, American Society for Metals, 1985. v.p.(c.1200p.). illus., diagrs., tables. ISBN: 087170188x.
4 parts (37 chapters): 1. General information (glossary; engineering tables, etc.) - 2. Properties and selection (chapters 4-20; *e.g.,* 4. Carbon and alloy steels; 20. Materials for special application) - 3. Processing - 4. Testing and inspection (*e.g.,* 37. Quality control). Some chapters have references appended. 61p. index. Aims 'to provide a single authoritative first-reference to all of metals technology' (*Preface*). *Class No:* 669(035)

Reviews & Abstracts

[1682]
Metals abstracts. London, Metals Information: Institute of Metals, and Metals Park, Ohio, ASM International, 12pa.
About 4,000 abstracts and references pa. 36 sections (*e.g.* 11. Construction - 12. Crystal properties ... 21. Metallography ... 31 Mechanical properties ... 41 Ores and raw materials ... 51. Foundry ... 61. Engineering components and structures ... 71 General and non-classified - 72. Special publications. Author index per issue. Online as METADEX.
Metals Information also publishes *Iron & steel industry profiles, Steel alert, Nonferrous alert,* and the annual *World calendar* (1976-). *Class No:* 669(048)

Yearbooks & Directories

[1683]
Industrial minerals directory: a world guide to producers of non-metallic, non-fossil minerals. 2nd ed. Worcester Park, Surrey, Metal Bulletin Books, Ltd., 1986. lvi, 642p. ISBN: 0900542993. ISSN: 01419263.
First published 1977.
A directory of producers, under countries Albania ... Zimbabwe. Buyers' guide, in a mineral-by-mineral guide to producers. Professional services directory. Index to advertisers. *Class No:* 669(058)

Tables & Data Books

[1684]
SMITHELLS, C.J. **Smithells' Metals reference book.** Brandes, E.A. *and* Brook, G., *eds.* 7th ed. London, etc., Butterworth Heinemann, 1992. xvi,[1664]p. illus., graphs, tables. ISBN: 0750610204.
First published 1949; 6th ed., 1983 (xiv,1600p.).
Includes data on isotopes, crystallography, gas-metal systems, electron emission, magnetic properties, heat treatment, corrosion control and superplasticity. A standard source of data on metals and alloys. *Class No:* 669(083)

Iron & Steel Industry

Steel

[1685]
Euro abstracts. Section 2: Coal and steel. Research programmes and agreements. Scientific and technical publications and patents in German, English and French. Luxembourg, Commission of the European Communities, 1975-. Monthly. ISSN: 03783472.
Formerly part of Euro abstracts: scientific and technical publications and patents, 1970-74.
Fairly lengthy abstracts covering research programmes, research agreements, scientific and technical publications, patents, training courses and seminars, forthcoming conferences and symposia. Annual index. *Class No:* 669.14

Non-Ferrous Metals

Aluminium

[1686]
HATCH, J.E., *ed.* **Aluminum: Properties and physical metallurgy.** Metals Park, Ohio, American Society for Metals, 1984. [ix], 424p. illus., diagrs., graphs, tables. ISBN: 0871701766.
Succeeds v.1 of the 3.v. series, *Aluminum* (1967).
53 contributors. 10 chapers: (1. Properties of pure aluminum & constitution of alloys ... 5. Metallurgy of heat treatment and general principles of precipitation hardening

....(contd.)
... 7. Corrosion behavior ... 10. Aluminum powder and powder metallurgy products (52 references)). Detailed, analytical index. Micrographs. *Class No:* 669.71

[1687]
World aluminum abstracts: a monthly review of the world's technical literature on aluminum. Sponsored jointly by the Aluminum Association (Washington), European Aluminium Association (Dusseldorf), Japan Light Metals Association (Tokyo). Metals Park, Ohio, American Society for Metals, 1970-. Monthly.
Previously as *Aluminum abstracts* (1963-69); originally as *Light metals bulletin* (1949-62).
About 600 abstracts per issue. 8 sections: 1. Aluminum industry - 2. Ores, alumina products extraction - 3. Melting, casting, foundry - 4. Metalworking, fabrication, fininishing - 5. Physical and mechanical metallurgy - 6. Engineering properties and tests - 7. Quality control and tests - 8. End uses. Subject, author and corporate author indexes per issue and annually. Online through DIALOG. *Class No:* 669.71

Rare Earth Metals

[1688]
GSCHNEIDNER, K.A., *Jr.* and EYRING, Le R., *eds.* **Handbook of the physics and chemistry of rare earths.** Amsterdam, etc., North-Holland Co., 1978-. graphs, tables.
1. *Metals.* 1978, xxv, 894p.
2. *Alloys and intermetallics.* 1979. xiii, 628p. £110.
3./4. *Non-metallic compounds.* 1979. xiii, 604p; xiii, 602p. £115; £105.
5. *Rare earth alloys and compounds.* 1982. x, 701p. £132.
10. *High energy spectroscopy.* 1987. 611p. £113.
11. *Two hundred year impact of rare earth on science.* 1988. xiv, 594p. £113.
Each volume carries documented chapters by specialists. V.5 is an expansion of K.A. Gschneidner's earlier *Rare earth alloys: a critical review of the alloy systems of the earth, scandium and yttrium metals* (1961). Chapter 71, in v.10: 'X-ray absorption and emission spectra,' p.453-549, has 6 pages of references. 'Indispensible for academic libraries and chemistry collections' (*New technical books,* June 1980, item 273). *Class No:* 669.85/.86

67/68 Manufactures

Jewellery

[1689]
BLAKEMORE, K. **The Retail jeweller's guide.** 5th ed. London, Butterworth, 1988. 432p. illus.

First published 1969,- designed to replace Selwyn, A. *The retail jeweller's handbook and merchandise manual for sales personnel* (7th ed. London, Heywood, 1962). 4th ed. 1983.

Sections: The metals - The gems - Antique silverwear - Boxes of the 18th and 19th centuries - How silverwares are made - Hallmarks on gold, silver and platinum - Jewellery of the past - The making of jewellery - The history of watches and clocks - Mechanical watches and clocks today - Electrical and electronic watches and clocks. Glossaries. Appendices. Both textbook and reference tool. *Class No:* 671.12

[1690]
UNTRACHT, O. **Jewellery: concepts and technology.** London, Hale, 1982. xxiv, 840p. illus. (incl. col.), diagrs., tables. ISBN: 0709196164.

19 sections (*e.g.*, 3. Metal, the jewel's raw material - 4. Basic techniques - 5. Sheet metal - 6. Wire - 7. Tubing - 8. Surface ornament, without heat - 9. Surface ornament, with heat - 10. Fabrication - 11. Casing - 12. Natural materials in jewellery - 13. Stones and their setting - 14. Metal finishing - 15. Metallic coating techniques - 16. Metallic build up - 17. Colouring - 18. Standard weights, measures and tables - 19. Glossaries (p.757-90)). Bibliography (grouped), p.791-8. Sources of tools, supplies and services (US, UK). Museums (p.vii). Analytical index (tiny print), p.808-40. Over 900 illus. in all, few in colour. A weighty, impressive volume, dealing with the work of 300 jewellers in 26 countries. *Class No:* 671.12

Iron & Steel Goods

Fasteners, Pins etc.

[1691]
PARMLEY, R.O., *ed.* **Standard handbook of fastening and joining.** 2nd ed. New York, etc., McGraw-Hill, 1989. [672]p. illus., tables. ISBN: 0070485224.

First published 1977.

15 sections: Threaded fasteners-description and standards - Standard pins ... Rope splicing and tying - Metrics and general data. Index. The 2nd ed. contains over 50% new or revised material. For engineers, machinists and technicians in all fields. 880 illus. *Class No:* 672.8

Timber

[1692]
Concise encyclopedia of wood and wood-based materials. Schniewind, A.P., *ed.* Oxford, Pergamon, 1989. 354p. illus., diagrs., tables. (*Advances in materials science and engineering.*) ISBN: 0080347266.

73 documented chapters (A-Z) by leading authorities in the field. Subject index. An updated supplement to *Encyclopedia of materials science and engineering,* edited by M.B. Beyer. *Class No:* 674

[1693]
CORKHILL, T., *comp.* **A Glossary of wood:** 10,000 terms relating to timber & its uses, explained and classified. London, Stobart, 1979. viii, 656p. illus. ISBN: 085442010x.

First published 1948 (London, Nema Press. viii. 656 p.).

Of the 10,000 terms mostly concisely defined, 1,000 are illustrated in clear line-drawings, some measured. Lengthier notes on major types of wood, *e.g.*, mahogany. 'Veneers': 1p., with 6 illus. All aspects of timber, from tree to finished product, especially the many uses and fabrication of wood. Abbreviations are included in the A-Z sequence. Keyed line-drawings (*e.g.*, roof trusses). A standard dictionary on wood. *Class No:* 674

[1694]
Forest products abstracts. Wallingford, Oxon., CAB International Forestry Bureau, 1978-. 6pa.

1991: 2,640 abstracts. 10 sections: General publications and general techniques. - General aspects of forest products and industry - Wood properties (including bark) - Timber extraction, conversion and measurement - Damage to timber and timber protection. Surface finishes - Utilization of wood as such - Veneers. Composite boards, laminated beams, panels, improved wood glues - Pulp industries and the chemical utilization of wood - Other uses of forest products - Competitive materials - Marketing and trade. Economics. Author and subject indexes. Occasional 'news items' precede abstracts.

Online through CAB ABSTRACTS database (covering the 19 major CAB abstract journals). Hosts include DIALOG, ESA-IRS. CD-ROM (Silver Platter). *Class No:* 674

[1695]
PATTERSON, D. **Commercial timbers of the world.** 5th ed. Aldershot, Gower Technical Press, 1988. x,339p. illus. ISBN: 0291397182.

First published 1948, by F.H. Titmuss.

An encyclopedia of over 350 species. 4 sections: 1. Structure and properties - 2. Wood: its preparation for use - 3. Hardwoods (Abura - Zebrawood) - 4. Softwoods (Alerce - Yew). Bibliography, p.322-25. Index of wood species. *Class No:* 674

Leather

[1696]
International leather guide: 1990. Tonbridge, Kent, Benn, 1990. x,500p. ISBN: 0863820832. ISSN: 09555080.

Sections: Tanners and merchants - Tanners and merchants buyers' guide - Hide and skin suppliers - Chemical suppliers - Chemical buyers' guide - Machinery manufacturers - Machinery buyers' guide - Consultants and technical assistance - Trade organizations - Five-language glossary of everyday leather terms (English; French; German; Spanish; Italian) - Index to advertisers. *Class No:* 675

Paper

[1697]
International pulp and paper information sources: an essential guide to the world of pulp and paper information. Farrell, S. Leatherhead, Surrey, Pira Information Services, 1988. [xii],379p. ISBN: 0902799185.

A range of information sources (*e.g.* published materials; organizations; markets; manufacturing standards and testing) on all aspects of paper, including raw materials and manufacturing equipment. 24 countries. Indexes: Country; Organizations; Publications; Subject. A wealth of information. *Class No:* 676

[1698]
Paper and board abstracts. Compiled by the Information Section of PIRA (Paper Industry Research Association). Oxford, etc., Pergamon Press., for the Paper and Board, Printing and Packaging Research Association, 1968-. Monthly. ISSN: 03070778.

About 4,000 abstracts pa. Some 20 sections (*e.g.*, Paper and board industry in general; company information; Nonfibrous raw material; Paper and board making; Machinery and equipment; Instrumentation and control; Properties and history of paper and board; Paper and board specialities; Synethetic paper and nonwovens. Book section). Available online. *Class No:* 676

[1699]
Thesaurus of pulp and paper terminology. 3rd ed. Atlanta, Ga., Institute of Paper Science and Technology, 1991. xvi,557p. ISBN: 0870100009.

First ed. 1965; 2nd ed. 1971.

Includes over 22,000 main entries (11,000 'key' terms and 11,000 cross-references). Terms include chemical, biological, industrial nomenclature. Alphabetical display of terms (540p.) is followed by a 'Microthesaurus' of well-known proper names (countries, professional societies, etc.). *Class No:* 676

Yearbooks & Directories

[1700]
Phillips International Paper directory, 1990. 87th ed. Tonbridge, Kent, Benn, 1990. xiv,594p. ISBN: 0863820417.

Contents: Mills of the world (countries, A-Z); Classified list of products - Merchants - Agents (paper; pulp) - Waste paper merchants and processors - Exporters and importers - Suppliers (machinery; equipment; materials) - Converters (packaging and other products) - Brand names and watermarks - Trade associations - Index to advertisers. *Class No:* 676(058)

Textiles

[1701]
ECONOMIST INTELLIGENCE UNIT. World textile trade and production trends. Anson, R. *and* Simpson, P. London, the Unit, June 1988. 343p. graphs, tables. (*Special report no. 1108.*) ISBN: 0850582075.

3 parts (16 chapters): 1. General trends in production - 2. International trade in textiles and clothing - 3. Textile prospects and clothing prospects, by country (p.161-342). Appendix: Exchange rates. Statistics usually for 1980, 1985/87. Numerous tables. *Class No:* 677

[1702]
WINGATE, I.B. Fairchild's dictionary of textiles. 6th ed. New York, Fairchild Pubrs., 1979. 691p. illus. ISBN: 0870051989.

First published 1915.

About 15,000 entries, including organizations. 7 sections: A. Textile fibers - B. Yarns - C. Fabric construction - D. Finishing - E. Finished products ready for sale - F. Inventors and development of textile technology - G. Trade and government standards and regulations. Includes brief biographies, trademarks. Cross-references. 'An indispensable source of reference to people in all branches of that industry and related ones ...' (*Choice*, v.16, July/August 1979, p.646). *Class No:* 677

[1703]
World textile abstracts. Manchester, Shirley Institute, 1969-. 24pa. £210pa. ISSN: 00439118.

About 400 abstracts per issue. 10 sections: 1/3. Fibres, yarns, fabrics: manufacture and properties - 4. Chemical and finishing processes - 5. Products: manufacture, properties, aftercare - 6. Plant services and environment - 7. Management - 8. Analysis, testing, quality control - 9. Polymer science - 10. Generalities. Author, patent and subject indexes per issue, cumulated annually.

World textile abstracts: register of keywords (Shirley Institute, 1983. 2v. 91p., 28p.) consists of *Keyword list* and *Auxiliary lists.*

Online access: DIALOG, INFOLINE. *Class No:* 677

Products

Carpets

[1704]
Carpet annual 1991. 55th ed. Tonbridge, Kent, Benn. xvi,396p. ISBN: 0863820891. ISSN: 00690767.

Manufacturers of carpets and rugs, smooth floor-coverings, underlays - Trade marks and specialist names - Manufacturers and suppliers of machinery, materials, accessories and services - Buyer's guide - Wholesalers, importers & agents - UK retailers - UK planners, fitters and contractors - Carpet trade organizations - Glossary of trade names (English, French, German) - Index to advertisers. *Class No:* 677.07.5

Textile Fibres

Man-made Fibres

[1705]
Moncrieff's Man-made fibres. McIntyre, J.E. 7th ed. Sevenoaks, Kent, Butterworth, 1988. 672p. ISBN: 0408005246.

6th ed. 1975 (1094p.).

Numerous sections, *e.g.*, Fundamental concepts and terminology ... The synthesis of fibre-forming polymers ... Viscose fibres ... Nylon ... Non-woven fabrics - Dyeing and finishing - Identification and estimation of man-made fibres - Economic and social aspects - List of man-made fibres.

....(contd.)
Index. A classic work of reference on the structure, manufacture, dyeing, finishing and processing of man-made fibres. *Class No:* 677.4

Plastics & Rubbers (Polymers)

[1706]
RAPRA abstracts: the abstracts journal designed for rubbers and plastics producers, processors and users. Shawbury, Shrewsbury, RAPRA Technology, Inc., 1968-. 12pa. ISSN: 00336750.

RAPRA: Rubber and Plastics Research Association of Great Britain. Originally RABRM (Research Association of British Rubber Manufacturers) *Summary of current literature* (1923-51. v.1-29), then *Rubber abstracts* (1952-65. v.30-42), which divided into *Plastics: RAPRA abstracts* (1965-67) and *Rubbers: RAPRA* (1965-67).

About 15,000 abstracts and references pa. Main sections: Generalia - Commercial and economic - Legislation - Industrial health and safety - Raw materials and monomers - Polymers and polymerization - Compounding ingredients - Intermediate and finished products - Relating to particular industries and fields of use - Applications - Processing and treatment - Properties and testing. Detailed, analytical subject index per issue; annual author and subject indexes. Online via ORBIT. *Class No:* 678

Rubber

[1707]
BLOW, C.M. *and* **HEPBURN, C. Rubber technology and manufacture.** London, Butterworth Scientific, for the Plastic and Rubber Institute, 1982. (Corrected reprint, 1985). 608p. illus., diagrs., graphs, tables. ISBN: 0408005874.

51 contributors. 12 documented chapters (1. History - 2. Outline of rubber technology ... 4. Raw polymeric materials ... 6. Materials for compounding and reinforcement ... 10. Manufacturing techniques - 11. Testing procedure; standards, specifications - 12. Organizations). Bibliography (general and by chapters), p.534-61. Literature and patent references. Index. *Class No:* 678.4

Plastics

[1708]
BROWN, R.P., *ed.* **Handbook of plastics test methods.** 3rd ed. Harlow, Essex, Longman; New York, Wiley, 1988. xiv,442p. illus., diagrs., graphs, tables. ISBN: 0582030153, UK; 0470211342, US.

First published 1971; 2nd ed. 1981.

21 documented chapters: 3. Preparation of test pieces ... 6. Polymer characterisation ... 10. Friction and wear - 11. Creep, relaxation and set - 12. Fatigue - 13. Electrical properties - 14. Optical properties - 15. Thermal properties ... 18. Fire testing of plastics ... 21. Testing products. Index, p.438-42. Emphasis is on testing of materials, not products. Tests related to 130 standards where possible. *Class No:* 678.5

[1709]
BRYDSON, J.A. Plastics materials. 5th ed. London, Butterworth Scientific, 1989. xix, 839p. ISBN: 0408007214.

First published 1966. 4th ed. 1982.

30 documented chapters, closely subdivided, on properties, processes and applications of plastics materials (e.g., 10. Polyethylene, p.196-234; 14 references, bibliography of 9 items). 'General properties of the nylons', p.460-65; 7 graphs, 5 tables. Includes recent production and consumption figures for the commercially important polymers. Detailed analytical index, p.823-39. Detailed contents list. *Class No:* 678.5

Synthetic Polymers & Rubbers

[1710]
ADKINS, R.T., *ed.* **Information sources in polymers and plastics.** London, etc., Bowker-Saur, 1989. xii,313p. Tables. (*Guides to Information Solurces.*) ISBN: 040802027x.

In 3 parts, each with several sections. Part I covers published formats (serials, books, patents, standards, grey literature, online databases); Part II, materials (polymer structures, properties, adhesives, fibres, rubber, etc.); Part III, geographical areas and translations. 18 contributors. Subject index, p.303-13. A comprehensive guide to the literature. *Class No:* 678.7

[1711]
BRANDRUP, J. *and* **IMMERGUT, E.H.,** *eds.* **Polymer handbook.** 3rd ed. New York, etc., Wiley, 1989. c.1870p. ISBN: 0471812447.

First published 1966. 2nd ed. 1975.

About 80 contributors. 8 sections: 1. Nomenclature rules. Units - 2. Polymerization and depolymerization - 3. Physical properties of monomers and solvents - 4. Physical data of oligomers - 5. Physical constants of some important polymers - 6. Solid state properties (6.1 'Crystallographic data for various polymers', 208p. 1,946 references) - 7. Solution properties - 8. Abbreviations of polymer names. About 30% more data than previous ed. Concentrates on synthetic polymers, poly (saccharides) and derivatives and oligomers. Index lists only physical constants of polymers. *Class No:* 678.7

[1712]
MARK, H.F., *and others, eds.* **Encyclopedia of polymer science and engineering.** 2nd ed. New York, etc., Wiley, 1985-90.

First published 1964-77 (16v. plus 2 suppt.) as *Encyclopedia of polymer science and technology.*

19v. (v.1-18: A-Z; v.19: Index), with c.600 contributors. Articles are lengthy, signed and documented. V.1: A to Amorphous (843p.) has 27 contributions. That on 'Amorphous polymers' occupies p.789-843, with 260 references. Cross-references. The standard work on polymers. Available online via DIALOG (File 322). *Class No:* 678.7

[1713]
—KROSCHWITZ, J.J. Concise encyclopedia of polymer science and engineering. New York, etc., Wiley-Interscience, 1990. 1341p. ISBN: 0491151253.

An abridgement of the 19v. *Encyclopedia* with many tabulated data and tables, but few illus. This work is much more thorough than M.S.U. Alger's comparable 1-v. *Polymer science dictionary* (1990), according to the reviewer in *Choice* (v.28(6), February 1991, p.910). *Class No:* 678.7

PVC

[1714]
NASS, L.I. *and* **HEIBERGER, C. Encyclopedia of PVC.** 2nd ed., revised and expanded. New York, Dekker, 1980-. illus. diagrs., graphs, tables. ISBN: 0824774272.

1. *Resin manufacture and properties.*

2. *Compound design and additives.*

3. *Compounding processes, product design, and specifications.*

4. *Conversion and fabrication processes.*

5. *Safety and environmental concerns.*

V.1 (1985. 702p.) has 15 contributors, 11 documented sections, with author and subject indexes. The bibliography in v.5 runs to 323 references, plus an appended glossary of acronyms. *Class No:* 678.743

68 Industries, Trades & Crafts

Industries, Trades & Crafts

[1715]
Directory of European industrial and trade associations.
Leigh, R., *ed.* 4th ed. Beckenham, Kent, CBD Research, 1986. lvi,405p. ISBN: 0900246464.

Editions 1-3 as part of *Directory of European associations* (1971, 1976, 1981), now split into the above and *Directory of European professional and learned societies.*
Over 5,000 titles of associations (Abattoirs ... Zip fasteners), with cross-references. Subject index precedes main text: English (orange-tinted pages); French (yellow); German (green). Much use of abbreviations and symbols. *Class No:* 680

Country Crafts

[1716]
HILL, J. The Complete practical book of country crafts.
Newton Abbot, Devon, David & Charles, 1979. 254p. illus., diagrs., tables. ISBN: 071537706x.

22 sections: Materials - Tools and devices - Hurdle making - Clog making - Wood carving - Chair making - Coopering ... Blacksmithing ... Basket making - Thatch and straw - Rope making - Bricks and pottery - Hedging and walling. 2 appendices: 1. Further information, displays, courses; 2. Addresses of suppliers. Bibliography (grouped), p.249-52. Index, p.253-4. *Class No:* 680.0

Clock & Watch Making

[1717]
BAILLIE, G.H. Clocks and watches: an historical bibliography. London, N.A.G. Press, 1951. (Reprinted London, Holland Press, 1978). xxv, 388p. illus.

The period covered is 1344 - 1799; the arrangement of entries, chronological. Major works are analysed in detail (*e.g.,* J.A. Lepaute's *Traité d'horlogerie* (1955) is alloted 2 pages, with 4 supporting diagrams). The bibliography 'is confined to mechanical timepieces and to everything connected with them' (*Foreword*). Name and subject indexes. The most important compendium of its kind. *Class No:* 681.11

[1718]
DE CARLE, D. Watch and clock encyclopedia. 3rd ed. Ipswich, Suffolk, N.A.G. Press, 1983. 326, [1]p. illus., diagrs., tables. ISBN: 0719801702.

First published 1950.
Definitions of c.3,000 antiquarian, technical and commercial terms. No less than 31 appendices follow, including 'Chimes' (with music examples), 'Clock hands', 'English period styles', 'French period styles', 'Horological dates', 'Watch part nomenclatures in 6 languages'. Bibliography of 19 items. 1,350 small line-drawings. A mine of specialized information. *Class No:* 681.11

Instrument Making

[1719]
EWING, G.W., ed. Analytical instrumentation handbook. New York, M. Dekker, 1990. 1088p. ISBN: 0824781848.

Detailed descriptions of the major techniques of spectrochemical, electrochemical and chromotographic analysis, and other technique (*e.g.* chapter of 73p. on nuclear magnetic resonance). This handbook can therefore 'serve as a one-volume resource in place of a number of monographs' (*Science and technology libraries,* v.11(1), Spring 1991, p.149). *Class No:* 681.2

[1720]
Jones' Instrument technology. Noltingk, B.E., *ed.* 4th ed. London, Butterworth, 1985-7. 5v. illus., diagrs., graphs, tables.

First published 1956.
1. *Mechanical measurements.* 1985. ix, 170p.
2. *Measurement of temperature and chemical composition.* 1985. [viii], 282p.
3. *Electrical and radiation measurement.* 1987. 220p.
4. *Instrumentation systems.* 1987. 168p.
5. *Automatic instruments and measuring systems.* 1986. 180p.
The 4th ed. reflects recent developments in electronics, gas analysis and other subjects. V.1 has 9 contributors, with 11 documented sections and a detailed subject index. *Class No:* 681.2

Computers

Abbreviations & Symbols

[1721]
TOWELL, J.E. and SHEPPARD, H.E., eds. Computer & telecommunications acronyms. Detroit, Mich., Gale, 1986. 391p. ISBN: 0810324911.

A dictionary of *c.*25,000 acronyms, terms, etc., in the computer and telecommunications fields. Entries are selected from *Acronyms, initialisms & abbreviations dictionary* (9th ed. Gale, 1984). Added to many definitions are subject categories, geographical locations and citation of sources. *Class No:* 681.3(003)

Bibliographies

[1722]
Computing information directory: a comprehensive guide to the computing literature. Hildebrandt, D.M., *ed.* 6th ed. Federal Way, Wash., Pedaro Inc., 1989. 410p.

First published 1981 as *Computer science resources.*
Revised annually. Master subject index, with subheadings, by type of literature, *e.g.* current books; computer-related journals; indexing and abstracting services; software resources; programming languages; etc. Well-produced and a valuable US-slanted source. *Class No:* 681.3(01)

Encyclopaedias

[1723]
RALSTON, A. *and* REILLY, E.D., *Jr., eds.* **Encyclopedia of computer science and engineering.** 2nd ed. New York, Van Nostrand Reinholt, 1983. xxix, 1664p. illus., diagrs., tables. ISBN: 0442244967.

First published 1976, as *Encyclopedia of computer science.*

301 contributors. 550 signed articles, - 90 of them new - arranged into 9 categories: 1. Hardware - 2. Computer systems - 3. Information and data - 4. Software - 5. Mathematics of computing - 6. Theory of computing - 7. Methodolgies - 8. Applications - 9. Computing milieux. 'Dataflow': 2½p., 5 references; 3 diagrs., 4 cross-references. 6 appendices (1. Abbreviations and acronyms, mathematical notation, units of measure; 2. Computer science and engineering research journals; 6. Glossary of major terms in five languages). Full index, p.1615-64. The standard one-volume reference work on computers. 'Clear, concise information for the non-specialist' (*American libraries,* v.15(5), May 1986, p.297). *Class No:* 681.3(031)

Handbooks & Manuals

[1724]
TOOLEY, M. **Newnes computer engineer's pocket book.** London, Heinemann, 1987. 203p. illus., diagrs., tables. ISBN: 0434919675.

Covers a range of topics (*e.g.* Basic logic gates, Boolean algebra, ASCII control characters), devoting 1-2 pages to each (although 74 series has nearly 20 pages). Extensively illustrated; list of abbreviations; index (5p.). Small format. 'Aims to provide ... everyday information' in an accessible format (*Preface*). *Class No:* 681.3(035)

Dictionaries

[1725]
ILLINGWORTH, V., *ed.* **Dictionary of computing.** 3rd ed. Oxford Univ. Press, 1990. [xi], 528p. illus., tables. ISBN: 0198538251.

First published 1983. 2nd ed. 1986.

Nearly 4,500 terms in computing. Includes technical terms in hardware and software, plus broader context of social and legal implications. 'Small flaws do not tarnish authoritative definitions, broad coverage and timeliness ... Highly recommended' (*Choice,* March 1991, p.1094). *Class No:* 681.3(038)

[1726]
LYNCH, D.B. **Concise dictionary of computing.** London, Chartwell-Bratt, 1991. 380p. ISBN: 0862382685.

Defines over 4,000 terms, A-Z. Comprehensive and non-technical reference source and guide for users of computers and IT in education and business. *Class No:* 681.3(038)

Reviews & Abstracts

[1727]
Computer and control abstracts. Science abstracts. Section C. London, INSPEC, 1969-. Monthly. ISSN: 00368113.

Formerly *Control abstracts,* 1966-68.

About 70,000 abstracts pa. Classes, closely subdivided: 00.00 General and management topics - 10.00 Systems and control theory - 30.00 Control technology - 40.00 Numerical analysis and theoretical, computer topics - 50.00 Computer hardware - 60.00 Computer software - 70.00 Computer applications. Author index per issue; Subject index, twice yearly; Subsidiary indexes, where appropriate; Bibliography index (for well-documented articles); Book index (for books received and abstracted); Corporate author

....(contd.)
index; Conference index. Indexes cumulated 2pa. and 4-yearly (*e.g.,* 1977-1980). INSPEC database. CD-ROM. *Class No:* 681.3(048)

Yearbooks & Directories

[1728]
Computers and computing information resources directory. Connors, M., *ed.* Detroit, Mich., Gale, 1987. x, 1271p. $160.

Directory of over 4,000 organizations (worldwide associations and user groups ... consultants and research centres). Also details of over 1,500 periodicals, directories, and abstracting/indexing services in the computer field. Master name and keyword index (28,000 entries); geographic index; personal name index. A comprehensive source book, particuarly for US users. *Class No:* 681.3(058)

Data Processing

Micros

Encyclopaedias

[1729]
Encyclopedia of microcomputers. Kent, A. *and* Williams, J.G., *eds.* New York, Dekker, 1981-. v.1-. illus., diagrs. ISBN: 0824727002.

1. 'Access methods' to 'Assembly language and assemblers'. 1988. 434p.

2. 'Authoritative systems for interactive video' to 'Computer design'. 1988. [vi], 452p.

To be completed in 10v., containing c.500 articles, and over 5000p. V.1 has 32 contributors, 26 articles. Well documented (*e.g.,* 'Artificial intelligence'; p.283-324, with 62 references plus 3p. bibliography. 'Aimed to the needs of microcomputer hardware specialists, programers, system analysts, engineers, operation recorders, and mathematicians' (*Preface,* v.1). *Class No:* 681.31-181.4(031)

Handbooks & Manuals

[1730]
BIRNES, W.J., *ed.* **Microcomputer applications handbook.** New York, etc., McGraw-Hill, 1989. x,645p. diagrs., tables. ISBN: 0070053979.

30 contributors. 6 chapters: 1. Hardware systems - 2. MOS memory - 3. Operating systems - 4. Networked systems - 5. Applications systems - 6. High-level programming languages. Glossary (abend-Z-net), p.475-634. Detailed, analytical index, p.635-45. A basic, comprehensive guide to PCs. *Class No:* 681.31-181.4(035)

[1731]
MONEY, S.A. **Newnes microprocessor pocket book.** Oxford, Heinemann Newnes, 1989. viii,252p. illus. (*Pocket Book.*) ISBN: 0434912905.

A basic survey in 15 chapters (*e.g.* 1. Integrated circuits ... 6. 16/32 bit processors ... 9. Parallel input and output ... 15. System development). Appendices: Abbreviations (5p.); Useful addresses (UK and US). Index (4p.). Concentrates on 'popular microprocessors in current use' (*Preface*). Small format. *Class No:* 681.31-181.4(035)

Dictionaries

[1732]
HORDESKI, M. **The Illustrated dictionary of microcomputers.** 3rd ed. Blue Ridge Summit, Pa., TAB Books, 1990. 445p. diagrs., flow charts. ISBN: 0830673687, HB; 0830633685, PB.

First published 1978. 2nd ed. 1986.

Several thousand entries, covering both hardware and software. Includes jargon. The publishers claim to have added nearly 4,000 entries. Some helpful diagrams and charts. *Class No:* 681.31-181.4(038)

Reviews & Abstracts

[1733]
Microcomputer index. Mountain View, Ca., Database Services, 1980-. 6pa.

Stable core of *c.*50 microcomputer journals on business, education and home computer uses. Subject indexing and abstracts. Coverage includes reviews of books, softare and hardware. Online via DIALOG. *Class No:* 681.31-181.4(048)

Tables & Data Books

[1734]
MONEY, S.A. **Microprocessor data book.** 2nd ed. Oxford, Blackwell Scientific, 1990. iv,316p. tables. ISBN: 0632020938.

Provides condensed data for most of the currently available microprocessor and microcomputer devices, with details of internal architecture, instruction set, electrical data and package details. 3 groups: 4-bit, 8-bit and 16-bit types. Also includes chapters covering input-output and other interfaces, peripheral control and support devices. Contains a directory of manufacturers (p.305-9) and glossary of terms. Useful as an aid to selecting appropriate device, to be followed up by consultation of manufacturers' data sheets and manuals. 'This is a useful volume for a wide range of practitioners' (*Electronics and Power,* v.29, Feb. 1983, p.181, of the first ed.). *Class No:* 681.31-181.4(083)

Computer Software

[1735]
The Software encyclopedia, 1990. New York, etc., Bowker, 1990. 2v. (2552p.). ISBN: 0835227626.

V.1: Title index; V.2: arrangement by system hardware (*e.g.* IBM, Unix). Within each system, software is arranged by subject and specific applications. Publisher index. Covers all subject areas, including engineering, science and medicine, but not software for schools (see Bowker's *Software for schools*).

The most up-to-date information appears in such online databases at the Microcomputer software guide (DIALOG file 278). *Class No:* 681.31.0

Security

[1736]
FLAHERTY, D.H., *ed.* **Privacy and data protection:** an international bibliography. London, Mansell, 1985. xxvi, 276p. ISBN: 0720117194.

1,862 references to works, published and unpublished, on the need to protect individuals from misuse of computer-stored data concerning those individuals. 6 sections (4. Legal aspects of privacy and data protection: Canada, Federal Republic of Germany, France, Sweden, UK, US, International ... 6. Selected bibliographic materials, p.241-7). Author index. A valuable research tool. *Class No:* 681.31.004.4

[1737]
JACKSON, K.M., *and others.* **Computer security reference book.** Oxford, Butterworth Heinemann, 1992. 800p. ISBN: 0750603577.

In-depth treatment of the entire field, including computer crime, data protection, EFTPOS schemes, evaluation of security products, hacking, public key cryptography, and other topical aspects. *Class No:* 681.31.004.4

Automation Technology

[1738]
CONSIDINE, D.M., *ed.* **Standard handbook of industrial automation.** London, etc., Chapman and Hall, 1987. xix, 460p. illus., diagrs., graphs, tables. (*Advanced industrial technology series.*) ISBN: 0412008319.

Over 70 contributors. A practical handbook concentrating on the implementation of automation: designing, specifying, using, evaluating equipment and systems. 5 sections: 1. Backdrop to automation systems (including annotated brief glossary) - 2. Sensors and measuring systems - 3. Control systems - 4. Actuators and materials (with much emphasis on robots) - 5. Interfaces and communications (including Local Area Networks and communication standards). Ample illustration (445 diagrams and half-tones) and 57 tables complement an excellent index as aids to use of a wide-ranging work.

'... the Handbook represents the best we have come to expect from the American technical publishing houses. The editors and their 73 contributors are to be congratulated on their endeavors' (*Production engineeers,* v.66(8), Sept. 1987, p.9). *Class No:* 681.5

[1739]
GRAHAM, G.A. **Encyclopedia of industrial automation.** Harlow, Longman and Society of Manufacturing Engineers, 1988. [xvi],597p. illus. ISBN: 058203566x.

US title: *Automation encyclopedia.*

About 700 entries, A-Z arrangement. Some definitions are very brief (*e.g.* 'comparator', 2 lines); others lengthy (*e.g.* 'numerical control', 31p.). Cross-references. Covers technologies, processes, techniques and applications. *Class No:* 681.5

[1740]
HAMILTON, L., *comp.* **Information pack including bibliography on advanced manufacturing technology.** London, Information and Library Service, Institution of Mechanical Engineers, 1986. vi,98p. (*Information pack, 1.*) ISBN: 0852986041.

2 parts: 1. AMT information (abbreviations; contacts; products; open learning; abstracts and indexes, etc.), p. 1-45; 2. References (236 items) with abstracts (key reports; general articles; applications of AMT), p.47-98. Most from the mid-1980s. Good value. *Class No:* 681.5

[1741]
HAMILTON, L. *and* HALLAM, L., *comps.* **Information pack on computer integrated manufacturing.** London, Information and Library Service, Institution of Mechanical Engineers, 1987. vi,89p. (*Information pack, 4.*) ISBN: 0852986459.

2 Parts: 1. CIM information (abbreviations - standards), p.1-60; 2. CIM references (108 items) with abstracts, p.61-81. Indexes: author, subject, company name. A useful series. *Class No:* 681.5

Cybernetic Technology

Artificial Intelligence. Expert Systems

[1742]
HANCOX, P.J., *and others*. **Keyguide to information sources in artificial intelligence/expert systems.** London, Mansell; Lawrence, KS, Ergosyst Associates, 1990. xii,300p. tables. ISBN: 0720120071, UK; 0916313182, US.
3 parts. I. Survey of artificial intelligence/expert systems and its literature (5 documented chapters, p.3-112). II. Bibliography (659 items): general sources, p.1133-55; component specialisms (automated theorem proving - robotics), p.155-84; applications (agriculture-space), p.184-212; directories and related sources, p.212-21. III. Organizations (includes research centres, online database hosts; international in scope), p.225-77. Detailed, analytical index, p.279-300. An authoritative survey. *Class No:* 681.51:007.510

[1743]
HUNT, V.D. **Artificial intelligence and expert systems sourcebook.** New York, London, Chapman & Hall, 1986. xi, 315p. diagrs., tables. (*Advanced industrial technology series.*) ISBN: 0412012111.
An illustrated dictionary of definitions (p.41-277), many of them extensive and including acronyms and system names. Preceding it: a review of developments in artificial intelligence and expert systems. Appended: a brief directory of organizations, manufacturers and consultants; a list of acronyms; a bibliography of *c.*250 references and a short trademarks list. No index. Has more to offer than does Rosenberg's *Directory of artificial intelligence. Class No:* 681.51:007.510

[1744]
RAGGETT, J. and BAINS, W. **Artificial intelligence from A to Z.** London, Chapman & Hall, 1992. x,246p. illus. ISBN: 0412379503, UK; 0442312008, US.
About 200 AI terms defined in non-technical language: Abduction - Zero Sum. Definitions range 6 lines to 2p. Simple diagrams serve to illustrate points; some cross-references. Appendices: 'Benchmark'; AI programs; Languages and environments. Index, 6p. For the layperson and likely to be warmly welcomed. *Class No:* 681.51:007.510

Robots

[1745]
Robot technology. London, Kogan Page, 1983-86. 8v. in 9.
1. *Modelling and control,* by P. Coiffet. 1983. ISBN: 0850385334. 156p. £25.
2. *Interaction with the environment,* by P. Coiffet. 1983. ISBN: 0850385342. 240p. £39.
3. *Teleoperation and robotics,* by J. Vertut and P. Coiffet. 1985. 2 parts. ISBNs: 0850385881; 0850389623. 332p; 256p. £65.
4. *Robot components and systems,* by F. Lhote and others. 1984. ISBN: 0850386497. 346p. £30.
5. *Logic and programming,* by M. Parent and C. Laurgeau. 1984. ISBN: 0850386500. 190p. £48.10.
6. *Decision and intelligence,* by J. Aleksander, H. Farrey and M. Ghallab. 1986. ISBN: 0850386519. 203p. £45.95.
7. *Performance and computer-aided design,* by A. Liegeois. 1985. ISBN: 0850386527. 268p. £44.90.
8. *Indexes and bibliography.* 1986. ISBN: 0850386977. 105p. £20.
'The series must constitute an essential element of any technical library worth its salt ... [and] ... will form an essential guide and reference source for all those in industry or research involved with robots and the related technology' (*Production engineer,* v.65(9) Oct. 1986, p.11). *Class No:* 681.51:007.52

[1746]
Robotics abstracts. New York, Bowker, 1983-. Monthly.
More than 1,600 abstracts pa., with world coverage of periodicals, reports, patents and conference papers. Available online via DIALOG (Supertech; File 238); CD-ROM. *Class No:* 681.51:007.52

[1747]
WALDMAN, H. **Dictionary of robotics.** New York, Macmillan; London, Collier-Macmillan, 1985. viii, [1], 303p. illus. ISBN: 0029485304.
Concise, readable definitions of over 2,000 terms in robot systems, actions and hardware. Sequence: AA series CNC robots ... Zoom. 'Spot welding': $\frac{1}{2}$p. Includes brief biographies. For students first exploring the subject, as well as for the researcher, the librarian and the business person. *Class No:* 681.51:007.52

Sound & Video Recordings

[1748]
BENSON, K.B., *ed.* **Audio engineering handbook.** New York, etc., McGraw-Hill, 1988. xxii,1040p. illus., diagrs., graphs, tables. ISBN: 0070047774.
33 contributors. 17 chapters, most with references, beginning with principles of sound and hearing (1); digital audio (4); amplification (6); sound reproduction systems and techniques (7-13); post-production and noise reduction systems (14-15); tests and standards (16-17). The chapter on standards concentrates on the US. 21p. index. Extensively illustrated. 'Both practical and theoretical ... a major work in its field' (*Choice,* April 1989, p.1360, which found this more comprehensive than G. Ballou's *Handbook for sound engineers: The new audio cyclopedia,* 1987). *Class No:* 681.8

Furniture

[1749]
Directory to the furnishing trade, 1990. Tonbridge, Kent, Benn, 1990. xiv,496p. ISBN: 0863820840. ISSN: 00706604.
Directory-type information for the UK and Eire. Sections: Manufacturers and wholesalers - Agents and distributors - Buyers' guide - Trademarks and brand names -Geographical guide - Business information - Index to advertisers. *Class No:* 684

Bookbinding

[1750]
ROBERTS, M.T. and ETHERINGTON, D. **Bookbinding and the conservation of books:** a dictionary of descriptive terminology. Washington, Library of Congress, 1982. 296p. illus. (incl. col. pl.). ISBN: 0313237182.
Defines *c.*3,000 terms and expressions, drawn from 373 listed sources. Coverage: bookbinding history, papermaking, some bibliographical terms and, particularly, the techniques, processes, equipment and materials of hand and machine binding, plus conservation. 'Provides an authoritative, comprehensive dictionary for bookbinders and conservators' (*Reference books bulletin, 1983-1984,* p.57). *Class No:* 686

Clothing

[1751]
The British clothing industry year book. 1990-91. Solihull, W. Midlands, Kemp Group (Printers & Publishers), Ltd., 1990. v.p. ISBN: 0862591678.
Sponsored by the British Knitting & Clothing Export Council (BKCEC).
15 sections: General information - Exhibitions - Index to classifications - Alphabetical section - Trade names - Menswear - Womenswear - Childrenswear - Fashion

....(contd.)

accessories - Fabrics and textiles - Trimmings - Machinery and ancillary equipment - Services - Buying offices, etc. Index to display advertisers. *Class No:* 687

[1752]
GIOELLO, D.A. *and* **BERKE, B. Fashion production terms.** New York, Fairchild Books and Visuals, 1979. 340p. illus. (*Language of fashion series.*) ISBN: 0870052004.

Grouped headings (*e.g.*, pattern layout; design control), covering both tools and techniques, and garment construction from design to completion. Each term is defined with photograph or line-drawing. Bibliography and index. 'An outstanding reference work for students or professionals in all facets of fashion' (*Choice*, v.16(7), September 1979, p.798). *Class No:* 687

69 Building Industry

Building

Encyclopaedias

[1753]

BROOKS, H. Encyclopedia of building and construction terms.
2nd ed. Englewood Cliffs., N.J., Prentice-Hall, 1983. [iv],
443p. illus., diagrs., charts. ISBN: 0132755114.
First published 1976.
Defines more than 2,800 terms, some at length (*e.g.,*
'Solar collectors': nearly 3p.). 'Index by function' (24
functions/subject areas) precedes, p.7-38: 178 illus. etc. Four
appendices: A. Construction centres (US); D. Conversion
factors. 'This is one of the best encyclopedias covering the
terminology associated with the building industry ...'
(*Reference books bulletin, 1984/1985* (1986), p.21). *Class
No:* 69.0(031)

Handbooks & Manuals

[1754]

CHANDLER, I. Building technology. London, Mitchell, for
Chartered Institute of Building. 3v. ISBN: 0713451785, v.1.
   1. *Site organization and method.* 1988.
   2. *Performance.* 1988.
   3. *Design, production and maintenance.* 1987.
   V.1 (176p.) has 5 parts, concentrating on production
services and systems installation, and the design/
construction interface. Part 5 deals with 3 case studies.
'References and further reading'. p.172-7. Index. *Class No:*
69.0(035)

Dictionaries

[1755]

BRETT, P. Building terminology: an illustrated reference guide
for practitioners and students. Oxford, etc., Heinemann
Newnes, 1989. [viii],339p. illus. ISBN: 0434901768.
   6 sections, each in alphabetical order: 1. Architectural
style - 2. Building construction - 3. Documentation,
administration and control - 4. General - 5. Materials and
scientific principles - 6. Services and finishes. Index, p.321-
39 (*c.*3,000 entries). Over 350 diagrams and photographs,
so much superior in this respect to the *Macmillan
dictionary of building* with its 12 appended pages of
diagrams. *Class No:* 69.0(038)

Reviews & Abstracts

[1756]

Current information in the construction industry (CICI).
Croydon, Surrey, Property Services Agency Library Service,
1946-. Fortnightly.
   Formerly *Library bulletin,* issued by Ministry of Public
Building and Works.
   Part 1 (yellow pages): 'Forthcoming meetings, conferences
and exhibitions'. Part 2 (white pages): 'New books,
pamphlets and periodical articles in the construction
industry' (*c.*100 brief annotated entries per issue, classified
by UDC). Prices of books and pamphlets are given.
Concentrates on the practical aspects of the industry. Half-
yearly cumulation as *Construction references.* Online
through INFOLINE, using PICA (construction and
architecture) database. *Class No:* 69.0(048)

Published Series

[1757]

Mitchell's Building series. London, Mitchell, 1979-88. 7v.
illus., diagrs., graphs, tables.
   Components. 1979. £9.95.
   Environment & services. 1988. £10.95.
   Finishes. 1979. £9.95.
   Materials, by A. Eycrett. 1986. £9.95.
   Structure & fabric. 1983. 2v., ea.£9.95.
   Water, sanitary and waste services for buildings, by A.
Wise. 1985. £12.95.
   The *Materials* volume (320p.), first published 1970, has
17 sections. 1. Properties generally - 2. Timber ... 4. Stones
... 6. Bricks and blocks ... 8. Concrete - 9. Metals ... 12.
Glass - 13. Plastics and rubbers - 14. Adhesives - 15.
Mortars for joining ... 17. Sealants. Detailed analytical
index. *Class No:* 69.0(082.1)

Standards

[1758]

SMITH, M., *ed.* **Manual of British Standards on building
construction and specification.** 2nd ed. London, BSI, in
association with Hutchinson, 1987. 334p. illus., tables.
ISBN: 0091707609.
   First published 1985.
   CI/Sf/B tables 0-4, further subdivided. 0. Physical
environment - 1. Building elements - 2. Contractors, firms -
3. Materials - 4. Activities, requirements. Analysis of
relevant standards, providing basic information. Index
precedes. 213 tables. *Class No:* 69.0(083.74)

Information Services

[1759]
CONSTRUCTION INDUSTRY RESEARCH AND INFORMATION ASSOCIATION. CIRIA guide to EC and international sources of construction information. Richardson, B.G., *comp.* London, CIRIA, 1989. 108p. (*CIRIA special publication 66.*)

Data on over 200 (non-UK) EC and other international organizations of interest to the UK construction industry. Gives original name, with English translation, if necessary. Subject index. There are also editions covering France, Germany and Spain. *Class No:* 69.0:061:025.5

Estimates

[1760]
Spon's Architects' and builders' price book, 1992. 117th ed. London, Spon, 1992. xxxix,1043p. tables. ISBN: 0419173609. ISSN: 03063046.

First published 1873.

5 parts: 1. Fees and daywork - 2. Rates of wages - 3. Prices for measured work - 4. Approximate estimating - 5. Tables and memoranda. Numerous tables. Detailed, analytical index (p.1023-43). *Class No:* 69.003.12

Building Materials

[1761]
TAYLOR, G.D. Construction materials. London, Longman, 1991. 544p. ISBN: 0582042992.

Covers properties of metals, concrete, ceramics, fibrous composites and siliceous materials. Includes standards. *Class No:* 691

Building Trades

Heating & Ventilation

[1762]
ASHRAE handbook. Atlanta, Georgia, American Society of Heating, Refrigerating and Air-Conditioning Engineers, 1982-85. 4v.

First published 1961. As *ASHRAE handbook and product directory,* 1974-77. 4v., now divided into *ASHRAE handbook* and annual *ASHRAE product information file. Fundamentals.* 1985. *Systems.* 1984. *Equipment.* 1983. *Applications.* 1982.

Fundamentals, by various contributors, concerns basic principles, general engineering data, load calculations, duct and pipe sizing. Indexes. A detailed survey of US practice. *Class No:* 697

Painting & Decorating

[1763]
GOODIER, J.H. Dictionary of painting and decorating, covering also allied industrial finishes. 3rd ed. London, C. Griffin, 1987. xi, 422p. ISBN: 0852642792.

First published 1961.

About 1,500 entries (*e.g.,* 'Metal spraying': 1p.; 'Lead paint - statutory regulations': 3p.). Conversion factors and tables precede. Cross-references. An encyclopaedic dictionary for craftsmen, students and teachers. *Class No:* 698.1

7 THE ARTS

Bibliographies

[1764]
ARNTZEN, E.M. *and* RAINWATER, R. **Guide to the literature of art history.** Chicago, American Library Association; London, Art Book Co., 1980. 616p. £50.00. ISBN: 0905309057.
A major guide, containing over 4,000 entries with descriptive critical annotations. Intended for scholarly researchers, but including all basic materials. Main subject areas: painting, sculpture, architecture, prints, drawings, photographs, decorative arts. Organized into four categories: general reference sources, general primary and secondary sources, the particular arts, and serials. Author/title index and detailed subject index. The cut-off date was 1977, but retrospective value is good. *Class No:* 7.0(01)

[1765]
Art index: an author and subject index to domestic and foreign art periodicals and museum bulletins covering archaeology, architecture, art history, arts and crafts, city planning, fine arts, graphic arts, industrial design etc. New York, H.W. Wilson, 1929-. ISSN: 00043222.
Now quarterly with annual cumulations; 3-year cumulations 1929-1953; 2-year cumulations 1953-1967, then annual. Available on WILSONLINE and CD-ROM from 1984.
Wide international coverage, and comprehensive in all aspects of visual arts. Covers 250 serials, bulletins, exhibitions. Subjects include archaeology, architecture, art history, film, industrial and interior design, landscape and town planning, photography, television etc. Single alphabetical sequence; separate index of book reviews. *Class No:* 7.0(01)

[1766]
Bibliography of the history of art. Bibliographie d'histoire de l'art. Vandoeuvre-les-Nancy, INIST Diffusion, 1990-.
Replaces *Répertoire d'art et d'archéolgie* and *Répertoire international de le litterature de l'art* (RILA). Issued quarterly, with annual cumulative index. Online access via DIALOG and QUESTEL.
24,000 citations per year expected; abstracts presented in French or English. Covers Western art from late antiquity to the present. Joint venture of INIST (CNRS Institut de l'Information Scientifique et Technique) and AHIP (The Getty Art History Program). *Class No:* 7.0(01)

Encyclopaedias & Dictionaries

[1767]
CHILVERS, I., *ed.* **The Concise Oxford dictionary of art and artists.** Oxford, OUP, 1990. 517p. ISBN: 0198661665.
An abridgement of the *Oxford Dictionary of Art,* revised and updated.
Alphabetical arrangement of names and terms; covers Western painting, sculpture, and graphic art. Artist biographies, groups, styles, movements, critics, patrons, dealers and collectors, museums and galleries; scope: fifth century to present. *Class No:* 7.0(03)

[1768]
CHILVERS, I. *and* OSBORNE, H. *and* FARR, D., *eds.* **The Oxford dictionary of art.** Oxford, OUP, 1988. 576p. ISBN: 0198661339.
Based on Oxford Companions to *Art, Twentieth-Century Art,* and *Decorative Arts.*
Entries cover major names in Western art including historians, artists, collectors, dealers, and terms, schools, techniques, styles and genres. Covers fifth century BC to present day. 3,000 entries in alphabetical arrangement include no artists born after 1945. "A second edition may modify the imbalances to attain an objectivity which should be the first aim". (*Apollo,* Sept. 1989. p.212). *Class No:* 7.0(03)

[1769]
MURRAY, P. *and* MURRAY, L. **The Penguin dictionary of art and artists.** 6th ed. Harmondsworth, Middx, Penguin, 1989. 464p. ISBN: 0140512101.
First published 1959.
Covers painting, sculpture and engraving in Western Europe and North America from c.1300 to the present. Alphabetical list of terms, processes, movements; biographical entries for 1200 artists with locations of works. Cross-references. *Class No:* 7.0(03)

[1770]
The Oxford illustrated encyclopaedia of the arts. Norwich, J.J., *ed.* Oxford, OUP, 1990. 512p. illus. ISBN: 0198691378.
Volume 5 of the *Oxford Illustrated Encyclopedia.*
Over 3000 A/Z entries on art, architecture, dance, sculpture, music, theatre, cinema, photography, literature and the decorative arts, from pre-history to the present. Entries vary in length from 50-1000 words; 350 illustrations, 175 in colour. 120 contributors. An excellently-produced and authoritative single-volume source. *Class No:* 7.0(03)

[1771]
STANGOS, N., *ed.* **Thames and Hudson dictionary of art and artists.** Rev. ed. London, Thames & Hudson, 1988. 208p. illus. ISBN: 0500234027.

....*(contd.)*

Covers individual artists, styles and movements, groups, critics, techniques and materials. Cross-references. 'An excellent, concise reference work' (*Choice* 22(11/12) July/ August 1985. p.1621). *Class No:* 7.0(03)

Handbooks & Manuals

[1772]
MAYER, R. **Artist's handbook of materials and techniques.** 5th ed. London, Faber, 1991. xv,761p. ISBN: 0571143318, pbk; 0571150675.

A thorough treatment; coverage includes pigments, oils, acrylics, tempera, grounds, watercolour, gouache, pastel, encaustic, mural, solvents and thinners, glues, wax, chemistry, conservation, inks, brushes etc. Numerous appendices and tables. Bibliography in category order (pp.675-711) and a good index (pp.713-761). *Class No:* 7.0(035)

Dictionaries

[1773]
LUCIE-SMITH, E., *ed.* **Dictionary of art terms.** London, Thames & Hudson, 1988. 208p. illus. ISBN: 0500233896.

Over 2,000 entries, including the vocabulary of the arts of India, China, Japan, Malaysia, Oceania, Africa, pre-Columbian America, as well as Western art. 'Almost everyone concerned with the history of art will find invaluable the clear, brief definitions' (*TLS* April 8, 1988,p.397). *Class No:* 7.0(038)

[1774]
WALKER, J.A. **Glossary of art, architecture and design since 1945;** terms describing movements, styles, groups and organizations derived from the vocabularies of artists, critics, and curators. 3rd ed. London, Library Association Publishing, 1992. 402p., illus. ISBN: 0851576398.

700 definitions of groups, styles etc. that have evolved since 1945; international in scope, and based on published literature. Concepts and theoretical ideas are a valuable feature; cross-references, indexes of artists, art groups, and art concepts. Bibliographies follow many entries. *Class No:* 7.0(038)

Periodicals

[1775]
Art documentation: the bulletin of the Art Libraries Society of North America. Tucson, Az, ARLIS/NA, 1982-. ISSN: 07307187.

Issued quarterly, formerly *ARLIS/NA Newsletter* (1972-81).

Excellent journal source for articles on art librarianship, slide and photography curatorship, art history, book publishing, art bibliography. Regular sections of book reviews and publications received. *Class No:* 7.0(051)

[1776]
Art libraries journal. London, ARLIS, 1976-. ISSN: 03074722.

Issued quarterly.

Good selection of articles on art librarianship, book reviews, bibliographies. 'Truly international rather than UK-oriented'. (*Art Documentation* 6,2. Spring 1987, p.42). *Class No:* 7.0(051)

Yearbooks & Directories

[1777]
Arts Review yearbook 1992. Hughes, G., *ed.* London, Arts Review (Starcity) Ltd., 1992. 168p.,illus. ISBN: 0904831167. ISSN: 03093611.

Directory of exhibitions held in the previous year and forthcoming; London & regional museums and galleries, societies and organizations. Lists fine art magazines, suppliers, print publishers, studios, auctioneers. Advertisers' index. *Class No:* 7.0(058)

[1778]
Writers' and artists' yearbook. 84th ed. London, A. & C. Black, 1991. 599p. ISBN: 0713632798.

Annual.

Part one (markets) includes sections relevant to performing arts and broadcasting (script markets for theatre, radio, television, and films; list of specialist agents). Sections on illustration & design, including art agents, & firms requiring drawings & designs; photography; picture research; music, including list of UK and US publishers. Part two of the yearbook gives general information on finance, law and regulations, publishing practice, preparation of materials. List of societies & prizes. *Class No:* 7.0(058)

Quotations

[1779]
CROFTON, I., *comp.* **A Dictionary of art quotations.** London, Routledge, 1988. 223p. ISBN: 0415003229.

Quotations from artists, and reactions to their work. Emphasis on Western fine arts, arranged in one alphabetical sequence of 371 topics. Minimal citation details; author and subject indexes. *Class No:* 7.0(082.2)

Histories

[1780]
HONOUR, H. *and* FLEMING, J. **A World history of art.** 3rd ed. London, Lawrence King, 1991. 766p. illus. ISBN: 1856690008; 1856690059, Pbk.

Published in the US by Prentice-Hall as *The visual arts: a history.*

Concise and well organized, and covering art of all countries and periods. An excellent single-volume source. *Class No:* 7.0(091)

[1781]
HOOKER, D., *ed.* **Art of the Western World.** London, Boxtree, 1991. 464p. illus. ISBN: 1852831626, pbk.

First published in hardback 1989.

Intended as a companion to the television series *Art of the Western World* produced by TVS for Channel 4 UK. 18 chronological chapters by well-known specialist contributors cover the major periods from Greek and Roman art to post-modernism. Excellent illustrations; each chapter also contains two double-page features examining in detail a crucial work of the period, in addition to its inclusion in the main text. Three 3-hour videotapes are available to accompany the book. *Class No:* 7.0(091)

[1782]
Pelican history of art. Harmondsworth, Penguin Books 1953-. To be completed in 50v.

30. *Prehistoric art in Europe,* by N.K. Sandars. 2nd ed. 1985. 0140561307.

41. *The arts in prehistoric Greece,* by S. Hood, 1978. 0140561420.

14. *The art and architecture of ancient Egypt,* by W. Stevenson-Smith. Rev.ed. 1981. 0140561145.

7. *The art and architecture of the ancient Orient,* by H.

....(contd.)

Frankfurt. 4th rev. ed. 1969.

11. *Greek architecture,* by A.W. Lawrence. 3rd ed. 1984. 0145061110.

42. *Etruscan art,* by A. Brendel. 1979. 014051439.

32. *Etruscan and early Roman architecture,* by A. Boëthius and J.B. Ward-Perkins 1970. 0140561447.

39. *Roman art,* by D.E. Strong. 1976. 2nd ed. 1980. 0140561390.

45. *Roman Imperial architecture,* by J.B. Ward-Perkins. 1980. 0240561455.

33. *Early Christian and Byzantine art,* by J. Beckwith. 2nd ed. 1980. 0140560335.

24. *Early Christian and Byzantine architecture,* by R. Krautheimer. 1965. 0140561684.

36. *Ars sacra, 800-1200,* by P. Lasko. 1972. 014056036x.

34. *Painting in Europe, 800 to 1200,* by C.R. Dodwell. 1971. 0140560343.

Pictorial arts of the West, 800 to 1200, by C.R. Dodwell. 1990. 0140560769.

13. *Carolingian and Romanesque architecture, 800-1200,* by K.J. Conant. 3rd ed. 1974. 0140560130.

19. *Gothic architecture,* by P. Frankl. 1962.

20. *Painting and sculpture in Europe, 1780 to 1880,* by F. Novotny. 2nd ed. 014056120x.

29. *Painting and sculpture in Europe, 1880 to 1940,* by G.H. Hamilton. Rev. ed. 1972. 0140561293.

15. *Architecture: nineteenth and twentieth centuries,* by H.R. Hitchcock. 4th ed. 1971. 0140561153.

12. *Architecture in Britain: the Middle Ages,* by G. Webb. 2nd ed. 1965.

9. *Sculpture in Britain: the Middle Ages,* by L. Stone. 2nd ed. 1972. 0140560092.

5. *Painting in Britain: the Middle Ages,* by M. Rickert. 3rd ed. 1969.

3. *Architecture in Britain: 1530 to 1830,* by I. Summerson. 5th ed. 1970. 014056103.

23. *Sculpture in Britain. 1530 to 1830,* by M.D. Whinney. New ed. rev. J. Physick. 1988. 0145060238.

1. *Painting in Britain 1530 to 1790,* by E. Waterhouse. New ed. 1978. 0140560017.

22. *Baroque art and architecture in Central Europe: Germany, Austria, Switzerland, Hungary, Czechoslovakia, Poland,* by E. Hempel. 1965.

31. *Painting and sculpture in Germany and the Netherlands, 1500-1600,* by G. Van der Osten and H. Vey. 1969. 0140560319.

4. *Art and architecture in France, 1500 to 1700,* by A. Blunt. 2nd ed. 1970. 0140560041.

37. *Art and architecture of the eighteenth century in France,* by M. Lewey and W. Kalnein. 1972.

28. *Art and architecture in Italy, 1250-1400* by J. White. Rev. ed. 1970. 0140561285.

38. *Architecture in Italy, 1400-1600,* by L.H. Heydenreich and W. Lutz. 1974.

16. *Art and Architecture in Italy, 1600 to 1750,* by R. Wittkower. 3rd ed. 1973. 0140561161.

26. *Sculpture in Italy, 1400 to 1500,* by C. Seymour, jr. 1966. 0140560262.

35. *Painting in Italy, 1500 to 1600,* by S.J. Freedberg. 1971. 0140561358.

17. *Art and architecture in Spain and Portugal, and their American dominions, 1500 to 1800,* by G. Kubler and M. Soria. 1959.

6. *The art and architecture of Russia,* by G.H. Hamilton. 2nd ed. 1976. 0140560068.

25. *Sculpture in the Netherlands, Germany, France and Spain, 1400 to 1500,* by T. Müller. 1966. 0140560254.

27. *Dutch art and architecture, 1600 to 1800,* by J. Rosenberg, and others. Rev. ed. 1972. 0140561277.

18. *Art and architecture in Belgium, 1600 to 1800,* by H. Gerson and E.H. ter Kuile. 1960.

10. *The art and architecture of China,* by L. Sickman and A. Soper. 3rd ed. 1968. 0140561102.

(contd.)

8. *The art and architecture of Japan,* by R.T. Paine and A. Soper. 2nd ed. 1974. 0140560084.

2. *The art and architecture of India: Buddhist, Hindu, Jain,* by B. Rowland. 3rd ed. 1971.

21. *The art and architecture of ancient America,* by G. Kubler. New ed. 1984. 0140560211.

40. *American art,* by J. Wilmerding. 1976.

An important, scholarly series. Each volume has excellent illustrations. Paperback versions of several of the more expensive volumes are also available. *Class No:* 7.0(091)

[1783]

World of art. London, Thames & Hudson. 126 vols.

Established as a major series of paperbacks - almost all at a bargain price - *World of art* combines specialist contributions in a compact format with very high quality illustrations. New titles are issued regularly and revisions of existing titles appear frequently. The titles are grouped into six categories: architecture and design, history of art, modern movements, painters and sculptors, special fields (for example posters, photomontage, furniture), and reference works. Wide coverage, reliable texts, and excellent value. *Class No:* 7.0(091)

Biographies

[1784]

CAPLAN, H.H. The Classified directory of artists' signatures, symbols and monograms. 2nd ed. London, Grahame, 1982. 873p. ISBN: 0860436586.

Several thousand artists are included; the first section presents signatures arranged alphabetically, the second monograms under first letter, the third illegible signatures under the first recognisable letter, and the fourth symbols arranged by general shape. *Class No:* 7.0(092)

[1785]

—CAPLAN, H.H. The Classified directory of artists' signatures, symbols and monograms: American artists with new UK additions. London, Grahame, 1987. 564p. ISBN: 0950889318.

Separate sections cover signatures, symbols, illegible and misleading signatures etc. Cross references, and formatted data pages. Includes 18th, 19th, and 20th century artists. *Class No:* 7.0(092)

[1786]

GOWING, L., *ed.* Biographical dictionary of artists. London, Macmillan, 1983. xvi,784p., illus.

90 contributors; 1,340 main entries for printers, sculptors, painters, architects worldwide. Chronology; glossary. Index includes 1,000 additional names with very brief details. 800 illustrations. *Class No:* 7.0(092)

[1787]

THIEME, U. and BECKER, F. Allgemeines Lexikon der bildenden Künstler von der Antike bis zur Gegenwart. Leipzig, Seemann, 1907-50. 37v.

Reprinted Seemann, 1965. Also Somerset House (Teaneck, NJ).

About 400 contributors; *c.*40-50,000 entries for painters and engravers, plus some architects and sculptors. V.37 covers anonymous artists and monogrammists. Longer articles are signed and well documented (*e.g.,* 'Sir Joshua Reynolds': 3 columns, - 1 col. of biographical data, listing and locating paintings; 2 cols. of bibliography: works by Reynolds, then material on him, - monographs, catalogues, periodical articles, etc.). That on Poussin, by Walter Friedlander, v.27, p.321-7, has sections on biography, artistic development, paintings (6½ cols.) and bibliography (1. col).

....(contd.)

The most extensive dictionary of its kind (each v. has *c.*600p., double column). Includes living artists, but in this respect is supplemented by: Vollmer, H. *Allgemeines Lexikon des bildenden Künstler des XX. Jahrhunderts.* Leipzig, Seemann, 1953-62. 6v. This is arranged on the same detailed pattern as Thieme and Becker. *Class No:* 7.0(092)

[1788]

Who's who in art: biographies of leading men and women in the world of art today - artists, designers, craftsmen, critics, writers, teachers, curators. 24th ed. London, Art Trade Ltd., 1990. xxiv, 566p. ISBN: 0900083131.

Covers some 3,000 names, mainly British but with a good international spread. Details of schools and academies; entries include awards, publications, agent addresses. Appendix of signatures and monograms. *Class No:* 7.0(092)

Great Britain

[1789]

BINDMAN, D., *ed.* **Thames and Hudson encyclopaedia of British art.** London, Thames & Hudson, 1985. 320p. illus. ISBN: 0500234205.

Paperback edition 1988 (050020229x).

Covers painting, sculpture, printmaking from Anglo-Saxon periods to the present day. Alphabetical arrangement for artists, styles, schools and groups, types of production, individual works and groups of works, techniques, galleries, societies, art schools, periodicals, patronage. Subject index; bibliography. World gazetteer of museums and galleries containing British art. 316 monochrome illustrations. *Class No:* 7.0(410)

[1790]

WADDELL, H. London art and artists guide. 5th ed. London, A & C. Black, 1989. ISBN: 0713630752.

Information on galleries and museums in London (over 600 entries), with further sections on art schools, studios, commerical galleries, art competitions. *Class No:* 7.0(410)

Yearbooks & Directories

[1791]

Arts festivals in Britain and Ireland 1989/90. Barbour, S., *ed.* London, Rhinegold Publishing, 1989. 240p.,illus. ISSN: 09511121.

Calendar of events, subject guide, and listing of festivals in England, Channel Isles, Isle of Man, Scotland, Wales, Northern Ireland, Republic of Ireland. Appendices give details of regional arts associations, committees etc. *Class No:* 7.0(410)(058)

[1792]

British art and antiques yearbook. London, Antique Collector Magazine, 1978-. ISSN: 01408763.

Directory and guide to over 5,000 antique and fine art dealers, auctioneers, and restorers. Indexes by place, speciality, business name. *Class No:* 7.0(410)(058)

[1793]

MARCAN, P., *comp.* **Arts address book:** a classified guide to national (UK and Ireland) and international organizations. 3rd ed. High Wycombe, Bucks, Peter Marcan Publications, 1989. 159p. ISBN: 1871811031.

Wide coverage of arts bodies, including drama, dance, cinema, music, literature, museums, cultural associations. Black and ethnic arts are represented, and new databases and archives. Professional, trade, research, educational and amateur bodies are given; 1443 entries. *Class No:* 7.0(410)(058)

Gazetteers

[1794]

JACOBS, M. *and* **WARNER, M. The Phaidon companion to art and artists in the British Isles.** London, Phaidon, 1980. 320p., illus.

'This is the first book about art written exclusively from the point of view of place' (*Preface*). Divides the British Isles into 9 regions, East Anglia; Ireland; London; The Midlands; The North; Scotland; The South-east; Wales; The West country and Channel Islands. Appendices: List of collections open to the public p.305-6; Bibliography, p.307-8 (regions; books/exhibition catalogues). Index of persons, works illustrated; places. 297 illus. 'The text associates localities with artists who have lived there at some time ..., as well as the patrons, who commissioned and bought their pictures ... A very attractively produced guide' (*British Book news*, April 1981, p.250). *Class No:* 7.0(410)(083.86)

Histories

[1795]

The Cambridge guide to the arts in Britain. Ford, B., *ed.* Cambridge, CUP, 1988-. 9v., illus.

Volume 1: Prehistoric, Roman & early Mediaeval (1988; 318p.; 0521309719) Volume 2: Middle Ages (1988; 312p.; 0521309751) Volume 3: Renaissance & Reformation (1989; 356p.; 052130976x) Volume 4: Seventeenth century (1990; 360p.; 0521309778) Volume 5: Augustan Age (1990) Volume 6: Romantics to early Victorians (1990; 352p.; 0521309794) Volume 7: Later Victorian age (1990; 363p.; 0521309808) Volume 8: Edwardian Age and the Inter-war years (1989; 367p.; 0521309816) Volume 9: Since the second world war (1988; 380p.; 0521327652). Chronological, cross-disciplinary account; separate chapters devoted to major branches of the arts: literature, music, drama, visual arts, crafts, architecture. Introductory chapter; detailed appendices with bibliographies, further reading, and brief biographies. *Times Literary Supplement* review (Feb.3 1989. p.116) calls it an 'ambitious venture', but comments on uneven treatment. *Class No:* 7.0(410)(091)

Ireland

[1796]

STRICKLAND, W.S. A Dictionary of Irish artists. Rev. ed. Dublin, Irish Univ. Press, 1969. 598,728p., (2v.). ISBN: 0716506025.

Originally published Dublin: Maunsel, 1913.

Includes 'not only every artist of any note who has worked in Ireland but those of Irish birth ... who have followed this profession in England and elsewhere' (*Preface*). Excludes architects. Entries carry detailed lists of works. V.2 has detailed index (p.665-728) of names and subjects of pictures, sculpture, etc. names of owners and places where pictures are; also an appendix; 'Art institutions in Ireland'. 150 portraits. *Class No:* 7.0(415)

USA

[1797]

KARPEL, B., *ed.* **Arts in America.** Washington, DC, Smithsonian Institution Press, 1979. 4v.

25,000 entries in 21 subject areas covering architecture, decorative arts, design, sculpture, painting, graphic arts, photographs, film, theatre, dance, music, art of Native Americans, art of the West, serials, periodicals, dissertations, theses, visual resources. Includes books, exhibition catalogues, bibliographies. Vol.4 contains indexes by authors, artists, subjects, selected titles. *Class No:* 7.0(73)

Yearbooks & Directories

[1798]

American art directory 1991-1992. Sevenoaks, Kent, Bowker-Saur, 1991. 780p. ISBN: 0835228967.

Lists over 7000 art institutions in the United States and Canada, including museums, art galleries, libraries, art schools, state art councils, and exhibition booking agencies. *Class No:* 7.0(73)(058)

Biographies

[1799]

FALK, P.H. Who was who in American art: compiled from the original 34 volumes of American Art Annual ... Madison, CT, Sound View Press, 1985. 707p. ISBN: 0932087000.

Alphabetical listing of artists, craftspeople, photographers, cartoonists, critics and historians taken from *AAA* 1898-1933 and *Who's Who in American Art* 1935-1947. 25,000 entries with wide range of data; 'an invaluable source' (*Choice* 23(6) Feb. 1986. p.855). *Class No:* 7.0(73)(092)

[1800]

Who's who in American art 1991-1992. Sevenoaks, Bowker, 1991. 1300p. ISBN: 0835228975.

Biennial.

Biographical details of over 11,000 artists, administrators, historians, educators, collectors, critics, curators, dealers in the US, Canada & Mexico. Geographic index; professional classification index. Obituaries section, cumulative from 1953. *Class No:* 7.0(73)(092)

Women

[1801]

CHIARMONTE, P. Women artists in the United States: a selective bibliography and resource guide on the fine and decorative arts, 1750-1986. Boston, G.K. Hall, 1990. 1024p. ISBN: 081618917x.

3,000 artists represented in entries covering almost 4,000 published items. Brief summaries of each publication. Part one - critics, organizations and resources, includes repositories and collections, biographical tools; part two examines the literature on women's art (painting, sculpture, photographs, performance, ceramics, crafts etc.) and lists documents on artists A/Z. Indexes by author/title, and artist name. *Class No:* 7.0(73)(092)-0055.2

Australia

[1802]

MCCULLOCH, A. Encyclopaedia of Australian art. 2nd ed. Hawthorn, Vic, Hutchinson, 1984. 668,560p. (2v.), illus. ISBN: 009148300x.

First published 1968; rev. ed. 1981.

Alphabetical listing of artists, galleries, museums, art centres, prizes, awards and exhibitions. Artist entries give brief biographical and professional data. 300 illustrations. *Class No:* 7.0(94)

20th Century

Biographies

[1803]

NAYLOR, C., *ed.* **Contemporary artists.** 3rd ed. London, St. James Press, 1989. 1,059p. ISBN: 0912289961.

850 entries, both established figures and newcomers who have attracted critical acclaim. No figure deceased prior to 1960 is included. Critical essay with personal data, and details of awards, exhibitions, etc. Retention of earlier editions recommended. *Class No:* 7.0"19"(092)

Libraries

[1804]

PACEY, P., *ed.* **Art library manual:** a guide to resources and practice. London, Bowker in association with ARLIS, 1977. xviii,423p.

21 contributors (20 of them British). 24 sections: 1. General art bibliographies - 2. Quick reference material - 3. The art book - 4. Museum and gallery publications - 5. Exhibition catalogues - 6. Sales catalogues and the art market - 7. Standards and patents - 8. Trade literature - 9. Periodicals and serials - 10. Abstracts and indexes - 11. Theses - 12. Primary sources - 13. Out of print materials - 14. Reprints - 15. Microforms - 16. - Sound recordings, video and films - 17. Slides and filmstrips - 18. Photographs and reproductions of works of art - 19. Photographs as works of art - 20. Printed ephemera - 21. Book design and illustration (p.337-54; 4p. of bibliography) - 22 Artists' books and book art - 23. Loan collections of original works of art - 24. Illustrations. Appendix 1: Other libraries and organizations as sources of information; 2. Conservation. Chapter references; appended bibliographies. Analytical index, p.404-23.

A most respected and valuable source; now in need of revision in many respects. *Class No:* 7.0:061:026/027

Yearbooks & Directories

[1805]

VIAUX, J., *comp.* **IFLA directory of art libraries.** New York, Garland, 1985. xxi, 480p. ISBN: 0824089138.

Lists libraries in over fifty countries, excluding US and Canada. Standardised data; subject index. Detailed review in *Art Libraries Journal* (v.11(1) 1986, p.36-38) commends the work but points out several faults and omissions. *Class No:* 7.0:061:026/027(058)

Design

Encyclopaedias & Dictionaries

[1806]

DALLEY, T., *ed.* **The Complete guide to illustration and design:** techniques and materials. New ed. Oxford, Phaidon, 1984. 224p.,illus.,tables. ISBN: 0714823473.

2 parts: Illustration (Introduction. 1. Pencils and other point media; 2. Pen and ink; 3. Oils and other paint media; 4. Printmaking; 5. Technical illustration) - Graphic design (Introduction. 6. Design equipment; 7. Copying and photoprinting; 8. Design and typography; 9. Design procedures; 10. Design and photography; 11. Reproduction and printing). Glossary, p.208-213. Paper and sizes. Manufacturers and suppliers. Index, p.218-24. Step-by-step instruction, profusely illustrated (550 illus., 250 in colour), with descriptive captions. *Class No:* 7.011(03)

[1807]

JERVIS, S., *ed.* **The Penguin dictionary of design and designers.** Harmondsworth, Penguin, 1984. 533p. ISBN: 0140510893.

Alphabetical arrangement, giving brief biographies and topical entries covering the applied arts 1450 to present. *Class No:* 7.011(03)

[1808]
The International design yearbook 1990/1991. Bellini, M.
London, Thames & Hudson, 1990. 239p. illus. ISBN:
0500236011. ISSN: 02692007.
Sixth volume of an annual series.
Illustrates the year's best work on furniture, lighting,
textiles, tableware, and industrial products. Biographical
index of designers represented, suppliers, list of museum
acquisitions. Bibliography of design publications. *Class No:*
7.011(058)

Biographies

[1809]
MORGAN, A.L. *and* **NAYLOR, C.,** *eds.* **Contemporary
designers.** 2nd ed. London, St. James Press, 1990. 1000p.,
illus. ISBN: 0912289694.
650 entries on graphic, industrial/product, fashion, textile,
interior, film, stage, set, and costume designers worldwide.
Alphabetically by name, with biographical details, statement
by contributor and designer, list of references. First edition
(1985) was well received (*Choice* 23(1) Sept., 1985, p.94).
Over 500 illustrations. *Class No:* 7.011(092)

Periods & Styles

Modern Art

Encyclopaedias & Dictionaries

[1810]
The Oxford companion to twentieth century art.
Osborne, H., *ed.* Oxford, OUP, 1981. 672p. illus. ISBN:
0192820761.
A/Z entries cover biographies, accounts of movements &
associations, elucidation of terms, historical perspectives.
300 reproductions in 8 plate sections (Expressionism;
Cubism; Surrealism; Constructivism; American art to 1960;
abstract art after 1960; Pop art; artists & countries outside
major movements). *Class No:* 7.036(03)

Ornamentation

Dictionaries

[1811]
LEWIS, P. *and* **DARLEY, G. Dictionary of ornament.**
London, Pantheon, 1986. 319p. ISBN: 0394509315.
European and North American material; covers styles,
patterns, motifs, techniques, and individuals. Over 1,000
entries, and valuable visual key. Photographic surveys of
significant motifs and techniques under such headings as
'animal forms', 'linear decoration'. Ranges from Renaissance
to present day with emphasis on use of treatises, pattern
and design books. *Class No:* 7.04(038)

Symbols & Allegories

[1812]
HALL, J., *ed.* **Dictionary of subjects and symbols in art.** 2nd
ed. London, Murray, 1979. 349p. illus. ISBN: 0719541476.
Paperback edition 1984 (0719541476).
Alphabetical sequence of entries with cross-references.
Small line drawings. Covers classical, Christian and
Renaissance symbols. *Class No:* 7.045

Collectors & Collecting

[1813]
Art sales index. Hislop, R., *ed.* Weybridge, Art Sales Index,
1968-. 2v. per annum. ISSN: 01430688.
Also available on microfiche (6pa.) and online as *Art
Quest,* continuously updated.
Printed volumes comprise:- vol.1, chronological list of
sales, index A-K by artist to oil paintings, watercolours and
drawings; vol.2, index L-Z, also index by author to
sculptures, bronzes and three-dimensional works. Entries
give full name, dates, nationality, prices in sterling and US
dollars, date and place of sale etc. Includes details of over
70,000 sale results from 1000 auctions. *Class No:* 7.074

Antiques

[1814]
MILLER, J. *and* **MILLER, M. Miller's antique price guide.**
13th ed. London, Hamlyn, 1992. 800p., chiefly illus. ISBN:
090587966x.
Illustrates & describes over 10,000 items grouped under
70 subject headings, with price guide. Directories of
auctioneers, specialists; index to advertisers. *Class No:*
7.074.0

Great Britain

[1815]
ADAMS, C., *comp.* **Guide to the antique shops of Britain -
1991.** 19th ed. Woodbridge, Antique Collectors Club, 1990.
1126p. illus., maps. ISBN: 1851491325.
First published 1972, issued annually.
7,000 dealers listed, with name, address, telephone
number, hours of opening, size of showroom. Type of
stock, price range, attendance at fairs etc. services offered.
Geographic arrangement. Index of packers, exporters,
auctioneers. List of fairs; index of names, subjects. Many
advertisements. *Class No:* 7.074.0(410)

71 Town & Country Planning. Landscapes

Town & Country Planning

Great Britain

[1816]
CULLINGWORTH, J.B. **Town and country planning in Britain.** 10th ed. London, Unwin Hyman, 1988. 460p. ISBN: 0044451180.

First published 1964.

Standard textbook on environmental planning, planning controls and legislation. References & further readings; index. *Class No:* 711(410)

[1817]
Directory of architecture and planning. Lodge, K., *ed.* Harlow, Longmans, 1990. 381p. ISBN: 0582067200.

Annual; first published 1956.

Details of local authorities in England, Wales, Scotland, Northern Ireland, Channel Islands, Isle of Man, Isles of Scilly. Development and planning bodies; public services; parks; tourist boards; universities, educational facilities; professional bodies. Sources of information p.350-5. Organizations listed p.356-71. Index. *Class No:* 711(410)

Town Planning

Histories

[1818]
GUTKIND, E.A., *and others.* **International history of city development.** London, Collier Macmillan. 1964-72. 8v. illus., maps.

1. *Urban development in Central Europe.* 1964. 2. *Urban development in the Alpine and Scandinavian countries.* 1965. 3/4. *Urban development in Southern Europe* [Spain and Portugal; Italy and Greece]. 1967-69. 5/6. *Urban development in Western Europe* (France and Belgium; Netherlands and Great Britain). 1970-71. 7. *Urban development in East-Central Europe: Poland, Czechoslovakia and Hungary.* 1972. 8. *Urban development in Eastern Europe: Bulgaria, Romania and USSR.* 1972. V.6 (xv, 512p.) devotes chapters 5-10 to Great Britain (5. Origin and spread of settlement - 6. The Roman interlude - 7. Invasion and settlement - 8. The Middle Ages - 9. Utopia. Reality. Subtopia - 10. City survey (24 cities).). 294 captioned illus. in all. Bibliography, p.487-504 (Great Britain: 492-504). Detailed index. *Class No:* 711.4(091)

Landscape Planning

[1819]
International yearbook of rural planning. Gilg, A.W., *ed.* London, Elsevier Applied Sciences, 1988. 386p., illus. ISBN: 1851663002.

Latest issue; intended to be annual.

Data on physical, social and economic planning of the countryside. 4 sections: Annual review, of current developments in UK, US and Europe; Legislative review (of new and proposed legislation); Literature review, of the year's publications; Substantive articles, providing a longer-term perspective on planning issues. *Class No:* 712.2

National Parks

Europe—Western

[1820]
DUFFEY, E. **National parks and reserves of Western Europe.** London, Macdonald, 1982. 228p., illus., maps.

Covers 19 countries. Norway and Iceland ... Yugoslavia, Greece. West Germany, p.76-99: 11 col. illus; 17 col. maps, mainly regional; marginal data on particular reserves, stating access, when open and facilities. UK and Eire: p.158-81. Appended glossary; map key; index to plants and animals; general index; addresses of conservation organizations; bibliography (p.287; general, and by countries). Particularly good colour illus.; 163 major maps. About 30 consultants. A guide to 344 of the most important sanctuaries. *Class No:* 712.23(400)

Gardens & Parks

[1821]
GOODE, P. *and* LANCASTER, M., *eds.* **The Oxford companion to gardens.** Oxford, OUP, 1986. 635p. illus. ISBN: 0198661231.

Alphabetical arrangement covering garden history, garden and landscape design and designers, concepts and technical terms. Over 1500 entries, more than 700 being for individual gardens. Entries for countries outline historical development. Cross-references; bibliography. 'The value of having access to information ... from all parts of the world capsulized in one volume cannot be overestimated' (*Art Libraries Journal* 12(3), 1987. p.50-52). *Class No:* 712.26

Great Britain

[1822]
HADFIELD, M. A History of British gardening. 3rd ed.
London, Murray, 1979. 509p. illus., plans. ISBN:
0719536448.
Paperback issue 1985. First published 1960 as *Gardening
in Britain.*
8 chapters: 1. From Eden to Utopia, to 1529 - 2. From
Utopia to Paradise, 1530/1629 - 3. From the knot to the
parterre, 1630/1659 - 4. France triumphant, 1660/1719 - 5.
The landskip, 1720/1780 - 6. From picturesque to
gardenesque, 1781/1840 - 7. The glorious Victorians, 1814/
1882 - 8. Nature returns as science advances, 1883-1939.
Footnotes. Appendix: 1939/1978 (p.431-54). Bibliographical
notes (by chapters), p.455-74. Detailed index (*c.*4,000
entries), p.475-507; index to Appendix, p.508-9. 'Will for
long be the standard work on gardening in England'
(*Journal of the Royal Horticultural Society,* on the 1st ed.).
Class No: 712.26(410)

[1823]
ROSE, G. *and* **KING, P.,** *eds.* **The Good gardens guide 1990.**
London, Barrie & Jenkins, 1990. 496p., maps. ISBN:
0712635068.
Details of over 1,000 gardens in the UK & Ireland, with
information on location, admission, facilities, description,
seasonal features, grading. Arranged by county. No name
index. *Class No:* 712.26(410)

Environmental Protection

Great Britain

Yearbooks & Directories

[1824]
Conservation sourcebook. New ed. London, HMSO for
Museums & Galleries Commission, 1991. 160p. ISBN:
0112904939.
Originally published by the Crafts Commission.
Details of UK national and regional organizations
involved in the conservation of buildings and objects,
including research bodies, societies, collectors' associations,
quangos. Data include name, address, aims, history,
publication, services, awards available. *Class No:*
719(410)(058)

[1825]
Who's who in the environment: England. Cowell, S., *ed.*
London, Environment Council, 1990. 337p. ISBN:
0903158353.
Similar publication for Scotland (1989; 2nd ed.). Wales
and Northern Ireland expected.
Lists organizations alphabetically (p.1-323) covering about
1,000 regional and national bodies. Contact name, address,
details of publications, membership total etc. *Class No:*
719(410)(058)

72 Architecture

Architecture

Bibliographies

[1826]
BRADFIELD, V.J., *ed.* **Information sources in architecture.** London, Butterworths, 1983. xvi,419p. ISBN: 0408107634.
12 contributors. 16 documented chapters: 1. Introduction: information for architects - 2. Libraries - 3. Information-retrieval techniques - 4. Computerized information retrieval - 5. Using and presenting information - 6. Sources and organization of information - 7. Periodicals - 8. Trade literature, technical information and standards - 9. Government publications, legislation and statistics - 10. Maps, drawings and slides - 11. Developing a design - 12. Executing a design - 13. Finishing a design - 14. Managing the design and the office - 15. Conservation - 16. Buildings, people, places: background information. Appendices: 1. Outline classification (Dewey, UDC L/Congress, CI/SfB); 2. Associations and abbreviations used. Analytical index, p.401-19. Covers information over the whole of the construction processes. Primarily for the architect and architecture student. *Class No:* 72.0(01)

Encyclopaedias

[1827]
Encyclopedia of architecture: design, engineering and construction. Wilkes, J.A., *ed.* New York, Wiley, 1988-1990. 4,000p. (5v). ISBN: 0471633518.
Sponsored by the American Institute of Architects, this set has become a standard source. Emphasizes processes and technology, but also covers history, aesthetics and biography. Specialist contributors, numerous bibliographies, illustrations and tables. Volume 5 (pp.442-659) contains an updating supplement and general index to the set. 'The range of subjects it attempts to cover is both disparate and questionable'. (*Architectural Review*, CLXXXIV, no.1102, Dec. 1988, p.10). *Class No:* 72.0(031)

[1828]
FLEMING, J., *ed.* **The Penguin dictionary of architecture.** 3rd ed. Harmondsworth, Middx, Penguin, 1980. 356p. illus., plans. ISBN: 0140510133.
First published 1966.
Over 2,000 entries for terms, countries, styles, movements, biographies, etc. and cross-references. 'Mansart, François': nearly 2 columns; 'Italian architecture': over 12 cols. 'Roof': 3½ cols., plus 'Roof elements': 4 keyed line-drawings; 88 small but clear line-drawings in all. No bibliographies. Additions to the 3rd ed. are particularly for English and American 19th- and 20th-century architects. A bargain. *Class No:* 72.0(031)

Dictionaries

[1829]
HARRIS, C.M., *ed.* **Dictionary of architecture and construction.** New York, McGraw-Hill, 1975. 553p., illus. ISBN: 0070268193.
The work of 52 expert contributors; 12,000 definitions illustrated by 1,700 line drawings. Covers design, appearance, installation, ceramic surfaces, landscape architecture, ancient and classical styles, mediaeval, renaissance, and modern periods. *Class No:* 72.0(038)

Histories

[1830]
FLETCHER, B. **A History of architecture.** Musgrave, J., *ed.* 19th ed. London, Butterworths, 1987. xxxi, 1621p., illus., maps, charts. ISBN: 040801587x.
First published 1896.
Sir Bannister Fletcher's work has been long regarded as the standard historical source; new edition is well illustrated and indexed. Seven sections cover Egypt and Near East, Europe to the Renaissance, Islam and early Russia, Pre-Colonial outside Europe, Renaissance Europe, Colonial outside Europe, and Twentieth Century. Glossary; bibliographies after each section. Detailed index p.1545-1621. 18 colour plates, and 850 pages of monochrome photographs and drawings; chronological tables. *Class No:* 72.0(091)

[1831]
PEVSNER, N. **An Outline of European architecture.** New ed. London, Penguin, 1990. 496p. illus. ISBN: 0140135243.
First published 1943. 7th ed. published 1963.
Chronological arrangement of chapters covering fourth century AD to the 1950s. A standard, authoritative work in a convenient, single-volume format. Excellent narrative text, but illustrations (monochrome) although adequate are poor by current standards. Glossary, with line drawings, p.473-5; bibliography p.457-470, arranged by period and country. *Class No:* 72.0(091)

[1832]
World atlas of architecture. London, Mitchell Beazley, 1984. 408p. illus., maps, charts, diagrams. ISBN: 0855335408.
First published 1981 as *Le Grand Atlas de l'Architecture Mondiale* (Paris) which was partly based on Mitchell Beazley's *Great Architecture of the world* (1975).
Six main sections: non-European civilizations, ancient world, late antiquity & early mediaeval, mediaeval, age of classicism, modern era. 725 photographs, 111 reproductions, 36 maps, 20 charts, 174 architectural plans. Glossary; index; chronological tables; subject index. *Class No:* 72.0(091)

Biographies

[1833]
PLACZEK, A.K., *ed.* **Encyclopedia of architects.** London,
Macmillan, 1982. 2,400p. (4v). ISBN: 0029250005.
A major source for all areas and periods; distinguished
panel of advisors. All aspects of work are covered,
including engineers, planners. Over 2,450 biographies;
signed entries by over 600 contributors, with list of main
works. Glossary: 1,000 illustrations; indexes contain over
20,000 entries. 'Will long stand as a basic reference work'.
(*Choice* 25(7) March 1988. p.1057). *Class No:* 72.0(092)

Great Britain

[1834]
LEVER, J. *and* **HARRIS, J. Illustrated dictionary of
architecture 800-1914.** London, Faber, 1991. 224p. illus.
ISBN: 0571137652; 0571137660, Pbk.
Alphabetically listed entries of UK buildings; excellent
photographs and drawings arranged chronologically by
building type or feature. *Class No:* 72.0(410)

Scotland

[1835]
PEVSNER, N., *ed.* **The Buildings of Scotland.**
Harmondsworth, Penguin, 1978.
Lothian, except Edinburgh, by Colin McWilliam. 1978.
523p.
The first volume of an 11 volume series. 6 general
chapters on types of building in the area are followed by a
descriptive gazetteer of buildings, towns and villages
(Abercorn ... Woodhouselee), *e.g.,* Haddington (p.230-45):
churches, public buildings, villas, farms. Glossary; index of
plates; index of artists; index of places. Pocket-sized. *Class
No:* 72.0(411)

Ireland

[1836]
PEVSNER, N., *ed.* **The Buildings of Ireland.** Harmondsworth,
Penguin. 1979-.
*North West Ulster: the counties of Londonderry,
Donegal, Fermanagh and Tyrone,* by Alistair Rowan. 1979.
First of a series of 9v. devoted to a comprehensive
survey of Ireland's buildings. Each of the country's 32
counties is dealt with, allowing 1v. to Dublin, city and
county, and 2v. each to Ulster, Munster, Leinster and
Connaught.
North-West Ulster is a detailed inventory, Aghadowey ...
White Island, with sub-entries for individual buildings.
Glossary, p.509-34; indexes of plates, artists, patrons and
clients, and places. *Class No:* 72.0(415)

England

[1837]
PEVSNER, N., *ed.* **Buildings of England series.**
Harmondsworth, Penguin, 1966-. 33v., illus.
Pocket-sized county series, each arranged A/Z by place
with descriptions of buildings. Glossary; indexes to plates,
persons, & places.
The standard series is gradually being revised and
republished in a larger format, with improvements to the
illustrations. *Class No:* 72.0(420)

Glossaries

[1838]
CURL, J.S. English architecture: an illustrated glossary. 2nd
ed. Newton Abbot, David & Charles, 1986. 192p. illus.,
plans. ISBN: 0715388878.
Concise alphabetical listing, illustrated with photographs,
drawings and diagrams. Includes many Scottish terms. Five-
column entry for *symbol* lists motifs, and their meaning or
referents. *Class No:* 72.0(420)(038.1)

Wales

[1839]
PEVSNER, N., *ed.* **The Buildings of Wales.** Harmondsworth,
Penguin, 1979-.
To be in 6v.
Powys (Montgomeryshire, Radnorshire, Breconshire), by
R. Haslam. 1979. 436p.
This first volume in the series has 3 main sections:
Prehistoric and Roman remains (p.19-26); Introduction,
p.27-68 (plus 'further reading' - running commentary, p.69-
71); Gazetteer of the three shires (features in caps.; Powys
Castle, p.188-96; 5 illus., 2 plans. Architectural glossary,
p.389-414, with diagrs.; Language glossary, p.415-20 (Welsh;
English). Indexes of plates; architects, etc.; plates (101).
Class No: 72.0(429)

USA

[1840]
HUNT, W.D. Encyclopedia of American architecture. New
York, McGraw Hill, 1980. 612p. ISBN: 0070312990.
A reliable, non-technical, general guide. About 200 briefly
documented articles (Airports ... Zoological gardens) on
every aspect of American architecture: history, building
types, materials, structures, architects, firms, systems,
trends. Fully illustrated. *Class No:* 72.0(73)

Periods & Styles

Classicism

[1841]
CHITHAM, R. The Classical orders of architecture. London,
Butterworth Architecture, 1985. 160p., illus. ISBN:
0851397794.
Covers elements, details, rules of composition, illustrated
by 50 line drawings. Introduction gives history, details of
the orders, use. Glossary p.145-59; brief bibliography p.160.
Class No: 72.035

Modern

[1842]
LAMPUGNANI, V.M., *ed.* **Thames and Hudson encyclopedia
of twentieth century architecture.** London, Thames &
Hudson, 1988. 384p., illus. ISBN: 0500202346.
Hardback edition 1986; German original (Stuttgart, 1983)
based on the *Encyclopedia of Modern Architecture*
(Munich, Zurich, 1963).
Distinguished contributors; includes biographies, surveys
of styles, movements etc. About 500 monochrome
illustrations. *Class No:* 72.038

ARCHITECTURE

Types of Buildings

Religious Architecture

Churches

England & Wales

[1843]
BETJEMAN, J., *ed.* **Collins guide to parish churches of England and Wales** including the Isle of Man. 4th ed. London, Collins, 1980. 528p. illus., maps. ISBN: 0002161664.

First published 1958; 2v. ed. (1968) as *Collins' Pocket guide to English parish churches. (The South.* 447p.; *The North.* 384p.).

A lengthy introduction (p.13-76) is followed by the guide proper, under 46 English counties (Avon ... West Yorkshire) and 6 Welsh counties, then under places A-Z. Glossary of architectural forms. Index of architects and artists, p.489-97; index of places, p.498-528 (including cross-references; *c.*4,000 entries, covering about 25% of the churches involved). 51 plates. *Class No:* 726.54(42)

Abbeys & Cathedrals

England & Wales

[1844]
NEW, A.S.B. **A Guide to the cathedrals of Britain.** London, Constable, 1980. 462p. illus., maps, plans.

A pocket guide to 106 cathedrals, - all the cathedrals of Britain, regardless of denomination, arranged under places, A-Z, p.16-444. Many small plans, indicating clerestory height, with a deeper shading for towers and domes. 'York Minster': p.433-41; 1 illus., 1 ground plan. Glossary, p.5-15. Appended lists: Some ex-cathedrals (27); Architects and designers; Embroiderers, tapestry-makers, illustrators; Furniture makers; Glass artists; Metalworkers; Mosaic and ceramic artists; Organ builders; Painters; Sculptors. Well-produced. *Class No:* 726.6/.7(42)

Domestic Architecture

Manor Houses & Stately Homes

Great Britain

[1845]
Historic houses, castles and gardens open to the public. Alcock, S., *ed.* East Grinstead, British Leisure Publications, 1992. 269p. illus. ISBN: 0948056193.

Published annually since 1954.

Useful introductory sections preface the main directory of over 1300 properties, and gardens, arranged in order of counties (England, Wales, Irish Republic, Northern Ireland) and by region (Scotland). Many entries feature colour photographs; standard data includes a brief description, access arrangements, charges, facilities, opening hours, telephone number. Supplementary sections cover Oxford and Cambridge universities, properties open by appointment only, specialist garden centres, index of properties, and maps. Numerous advertisements provide additional information. *Class No:* 728.8(410)

73 Sculpture, Plastic & Metal Arts

Sculpture

Histories

[1846]
POPE-HENNESSY, J., *ed*. **A History of Western sculpture.**
London, Michael Joseph, 1967-1969. 352, 368, 352, 352p.
(4v).
A monumental and excellent reference source: volume
one features classical sculpture (G.M.A. Hanfmann), two
mediaeval sculpture (R. Salvini), three renaissance to rococo
(H. Kentner), and four nineteenth and twentieth centuries
(F. Licht). Historical and social background explored;
excellent illustrations. *Class No:* 730(091)

Coins

[1847]
KRAUSE, C.L. *and* MISHLER, C. **Standard catalog of world
coins.** 16th ed. Iola, Wis, Krause Publications, 1989. 1856p.
illus., tables, maps. ISBN: 0873411234.
This edition revised by C.R. Bruce.
Alphabetically by country then chronologically by coin
denominations. Over 43,000 full size photographs. Full
details, current values, monogram chart, identification key.
Guide to Eastern mint names. *Class No:* 737

Encyclopaedias & Dictionaries

[1848]
JUNGE, E. **World coin encyclopedia.** London, Barrie &
Jenkins, 1984. 297p. illus. ISBN: 0091551404.
Over 1,500 entries and 450 illustrations covering names
of coins, terminology, persons and places, with emphasis on
classical and European coinage. Bibliography of 500 items.
'Scholarly reference source' (*Choice* 22(10) June 1985.
p.1474). *Class No:* 737(03)

Great Britain

[1849]
MITCHELL, B. *and* REEDS, B., *eds*. **Standard catalogue of
British coins:** coins of England and the United Kingdom,
1990. 25th ed. London, Seaby, 1989. xvi,352p. illus., maps,
chart. ISBN: 1852640413.
First published 1929. Original title *A Catalogue of coins
of Great Britain and Ireland.* A companion volume *Coins
of Scotland, Ireland and the Isles* was published in 1983.
(0900652640).
Chronological arrangement. Illustrates over 1500 coins
with revised market values. Bibliography; Latin legends;
mint marks. *Class No:* 737(410)

Medals

Yearbooks & Directories

[1850]
Medals year book 1989. Brant, J.G., *ed.*   London, BAC
Books, 1989. 240p.,illus. ISBN: 1870161076.
First published 1979.
Data, with reproductions, on 250 medals: background and
history; prices of issues. Dealer directory. Military book
stockists. Researchers. Auctioneers. Record offices.
Museums. Types of medals: Gallantry medals - Campaign
medals - Long-service medals - Coronation and Jubilee
medals - Naming on medals - Abbreviations of units found
on medals. Detailed index of medals precedes. *Class No:*
737.2(058)

Great Britain

[1851]
JOSLIN, E.C., *and others*. **British battles and medals.** 6th ed.
London, Spink, 1988. 299p. illus. ISBN: 0907605257.
This edition revised by L.L. Gordon.
Catalogue of every campaign medal and bar awarded
since the Armada. Details of military background. 'Drawing
extensively on existing reference sources, the information
has been updated and 'pruned'. and an extensive index
included to make the book as accessible as possible'
(*Antique Collector* November 1989, p.154). *Class No:*
737.2(410)

Ceramics & Pottery

Encyclopaedias & Dictionaries

[1852]
CAMERON, E. **Encyclopedia of pottery and porcelain:** the
19th and 20th centuries. London, Faber, 1986. 366p., illus.
ISBN: 0571113974.
Supplements Honey's *European ceramic art* (1949-52)
(*q.v.*).
Covers world ceramics 1800-1960; about 2500 cross-
referenced entries for factories, techniques, styles, designers,
potters and decorators. Selective bibliographies cover most
entries. Over 550 illustrations, and 155 potter's marks.
Class No: 738(03)

[1853]
HAMER, F. *and* HAMER, J. **The Potter's dictionary of
materials and techniques.** 3rd ed. London, A. & C. Black,
1991. 394p. illus. ISBN: 0713633379.
Standard reference book for craft potters; includes data
on behaviour of clays and glazes, sources and character of
materials, notes on historical development, and terminology.
Numerous excellent diagrams, drawings and photographs.
Bibliography; list of suppliers. *Class No:* 738(03)

[1854]

HONEY, W.B. **European ceramic art,** from the end of the Middle Ages to about 1815. London, Faber, 1949-52. 53,788p. (2v.).

Volume 1 is mainly plates (192, 24 colour) with introduction (Reissued in a second edition, 1963). Volume 2 contains alphabetical entries on factories, types of ware, artists, techniques, collectors. Bibliography p.17-27; index to marks p.683-788. Cameron continues where this work finishes. *Class No:* 738(03)

Great Britain

[1855]

GODDEN, G.A. **The Concise guide to British pottery and porcelain.** London, Barrie & Jenkins, 1990. 224p. illus. ISBN: 0712636005.

Revised edition of *The Observer's book of pottery and porcelain* by Mary & Geoffrey Payton (Warne, 1973).

Alphabetical arrangement of entries covering styles, potteries, types of ware. Bibliography p.206-213. 8 pages of plates; index. *Class No:* 738(410)

Ceramic Marks

[1856]

CHAFFERS, W. **Marks and monograms on European and Oriental pottery and porcelain.** 15th rev. ed. London, Reeves, 1965. 635,443p. (2v.) illus. ISBN: 0721100511.

First published 1863.

V.1: *Continental & Oriental pottery* - v.2: *British pottery.* (British pottery manufacturers in 1900, 1964, p.390-408. Selected bibliography (p.328-38) includes contents-listing of transactions. In the 15th ed. the accounts of Bow, Longton Hall and Lowestoft have been completely rewritten. The standard work on pottery marks. *Class No:* 738.0

Great Britain

[1857]

CUSHION, J.P. **Pocket book of British ceramic marks.** New ed. London, Faber, 1983. 439p.,illus. ISBN: 0571131085.

A very useful summary. 3,000 entries, with over 800 reproductions of marks under towns arranged alphabetically. Index of manufacturers, names, and initials. *Class No:* 738.0(410)

Porcelain

[1858]

HONEY, W.B. **Old English porcelain:** a handbook for collectors. Barrett, F.A., *ed.* 3rd ed. London, Faber, 1977. xxxiv,440p.,illus.

First published 1928.

17 sections: 1. Introduction - 2. Chelsea - 3. Bow - 4. Derby - 5. Longton Hall - 6. Lowestoft - 7. Lund's Bristol and early Worcester - 8. Worcester (p.229-85; 25 illus.) - 9. Caughley - 10. Liverpool - 11. Pinkton - 12. Nantgarw and Swansea - 13. Coalport - 14. Plymouth and Bristol - 15. Staffordshire - 16. Swinton (Rockingham) - 17. Miscellaneous factories... Appendix A: Marks; B. English porcelain bodies. Locations of collections referred to in the text. Bibliography (by sections). p.414-23. Many footnotes. 136 illus. Analytical index, p.425-50. The standard general guide to English porcelain, 1745-1850. *Class No:* 738.1

Metal Arts

Goldsmiths & Silversmiths

Encyclopaedias & Dictionaries

[1859]

NEWMAN, H. **An Illustrated dictionary of silverware.** London, Thames & Hudson, 1987. 367p. ISBN: 0500234566.

Covers UK and North America, and includes wares, techniques, designers, and makers, 1500 to the present. Well illustrated and with plentiful bibliographic notes. 'Excellent, much-needed work' (*Choice*, March 1988). *Class No:* 739.1(03)

Great Britain

[1860]

POOLE, T.R. **Identifying antique British silver.** London, Bloomsbury, 1988. 327p. illus., charts. ISBN: 0747500924.

Sections on hallmarks, punch shapes, date letters, styles, chronology. Alphabetical illustrated dictionary of artefacts (p.39-131), alphabetical and descriptive list of makers' marks (p.136-321). Bibliography; glossary. *Class No:* 739.1(410)

Hallmarks

[1861]

BRADBURY, F. **Book of hallmarks:** a guide to marks of origin on British and Irish silver, gold and platinum, and on foreign imported silver and gold plate 1544-1980. Old Sheffield plate-makers marks, 1743-1860. Rev. ed. Sheffield, J.W. Northend, 1989. 112p.,illus. ISBN: 0901100226.

Previous edition 1980.

Small format, comprehensive handbook. *Class No:* 739.10

Jewellery

[1862]

NEWMAN, H. **and** ROBERTSON, R. **An Illustrated history of jewellery.** Rev. ed. London, Thames & Hudson, 1987. 352p. illus. ISBN: 0500274525.

2500 entries include definitions of terms relating to materials, processes, and types, descriptions of named items, biographical entries for designers and makers, and topographical entries. 16 colour plates, and 632 monochrome illustrations. Line drawings. *Class No:* 739.2

Copper, Bronze etc.

Brass

[1863]

SCHIFFER, P. **and** SCHIFFER, N. **The Brass book:** American, English and European, fifteenth century through 1850. Exton, Penn, Schiffer, 1978. xii,447p.,illus. ISBN: 091683817x.

Re-issued 1987.

Historical introduction (p.15-32) followed by alphabetically arranged sections on brass objects (Andirons - warming pans). Large sections on andirons, candlesticks, fire-place accessories, kettles, tobacco boxes. Smaller sections include scientific instruments, lamps & lanterns, horse brasses, tableware etc. Dating charts; representative items described & illustrated. Catalogue of 18th century furniture brass reproduced p.413-43. Bibliography; index. *Class No:* 739.5BRA

Great Britain

[1864]
LESTRANGE, R. **British monumental brasses.** London,
Thames & Hudson, 1972. 150p., illus.
 A catalogue of over 9,000 brasses under countries,
counties and then churches, A-Z. Appendices on crosses,
chalice brasses, etc. 'General books of reference', p.149-50.
Class No: 739.5BRA(410)

Bronze

[1865]
MACKAY, J. **The Dictionary of Western sculptors in bronze.**
Woodbridge, Suffolk, Antique Collectors' Club, 1977. 414p.
ISBN: 0902028553.
 About 800 entries, A-Z, from the beginning of the 18th
century to about 1960, and covering 'Western Europe and
most westernised parts of the world, such as America and
Australia'. Oriental sculpture is included, if in the western
idiom. Lengthier entries have references (*e.g.,* John Gibson:
½ column, 2 references). Family trees, p.407-12. Select
bibliography (9 sections). p.413-4. 'The primary purpose ...
is to enable the collector, dealer and student to identify
bronzes that bear a signature' (*Author's preface*). No ports.
or illus. *Class No:* 739.5BRO

Pewter

[1866]
COTTERELL, H.H. **Old pewter:** its makers and marks in
England, Scotland and Ireland. London, Batsford, 1929.
xv,432p. plates, illus.
 Introduction on history, marks and collecting.
Alphabetical list of pewterers with illustration of their
marks where known. Alphabetical list of initialled marks,
obscure marks, devices, 'hall-marks'. Bibliography. 6 fold-
out plates of London and Edinburgh Touchplates. *Class
No:* 739.5PEW

Arms & Armour

Encyclopaedias & Dictionaries

[1867]
TARASSUK, L. *and* BLAIR, C., *ed.* **The Complete
encyclopaedia of arms and weapons.** London, Batsford, 1982.
544p. illus. ISBN: 0713415959.
 Alphabetical sequence covering weapons, styles of armour,
component parts; all periods and places. Nine named
contributors; numerous detailed & systematic illustrations
and diagrams. 90 colour plates. Good coverage of obscure
oriental & classical terms. Bibliography p.536-44. *Class
No:* 739.7(03)

Firearms & Pistols

[1868]
BLACKMORE, H.L. **A Dictionary of London gunmakers 1350-
1850.** London, Phaidon, 1986. 222p., illus. ISBN:
0714880213.
 Historical overview precedes the 170p. dictionary of
individual and company names. Each entry gives full name
and variants, trade, dates, address, and brief information
on significant designs, innovations, etc. 260 gunmakers'
marks illustrated; 9 brief appendices. 'Uniquely valuable
treasury' (*Antique Collector,* August 1986, p.63) 'of quite
outstanding importance' (*British Book News* October 1986,
p.596). *Class No:* 739.74

74 Decorative Arts & Drawing

Decorative Arts & Drawing

Encyclopaedias & Dictionaries

[1869]
FLEMING, J. and HONOUR, H. **The Penguin dictionary of decorative arts.** Rev. ed. London, Viking, 1989. 935p. illus. ISBN: 0670820474.

A concise guide to Western decorative arts from the Middle Ages to the present. Almost 5000 entries and over 1000 illustrations. Alphabetical arrangement of designers, craftsmen, movements, styles, techniques, materials, terms. Almost every entry has a bibliographic citation, and there are many cross-references. *Class No:* 740(03)

Drawing

[1870]
ASHWIN, C. **Encyclopedia of drawing:** materials, technique and style. London, Batsford, 1982. 264p., illus.

Entries: Abstraction ... Water colour. 'Caricature': p.42-47; 'Grip': p.110-3. Cross-references in bold. Index to artists, p.261-4. 258 illus. (incl. 19 in colour). The text is not confined to technical information in the narrow sense but approaches drawing also 'as a means of recording and communicating information, feelings and opinions' (*Preface*). *Class No:* 741

Technique

[1871]
HAYES, C., *ed.* **The Complete guide to painting and drawing techniques and materials.** New ed. Oxford, Phaidon, 1984. 224p.,illus. ISBN: 0714823481.

A step-by-step guide in 17 chapters, including: 3. Oils; 4. Acrylics; 5. Tempera; 6. Fresco; 7. Exterior painting; 8. Water colour; 9. Gouache; 10. Pastels; 11. Charcoal; 12, Pen and Ink; 13. Pencil; 14. Airbrushing; 15. Drawing aids; 16. Printmaking; 17. Presentation and storage. Glossary. Manufacturers and suppliers. Analytical index, p. 216-22. Attractively produced (817 illus., of which 341 are in colour). *Class No:* 741.02

Cartoons & Caricature

[1872]
GIFFORD, D. **Encyclopedia of comic characters.** Harlow, Longman, 1987. 256p. illus. ISBN: 0582892945.

Over 1200 entries covering 150 years of mainly British characters, but including well-known American and foreign names. Alphabetical arrangement, each entry with illustration. Details of illustrator, comic, dates, publisher etc. Index of comics and creators. *Class No:* 741.5

Textile Arts

Histories

[1873]
GEIGER, A. **A History of textile art.** London, Pasold Research Fund in association with Sotheby Parke Bernet, 1979. 317p., illus. ISBN: 0856670533.

Originally 1972 as *Ur Textilkonstens Historia.*

Discusses materials, implements, fabrics, development, Asia, Europe, Scandinavia, dyeing, printing, trade, conservation. Bibliography p.290-305. Line drawings in text, and 95 monochrome plates at end. *Class No:* 745.52(091)

Tapestries & Carpets

[1874]
BLACK, D., *ed.* **World rugs and carpets.** Feltham, Middx, Country Life Books, 1985. 256p., illus., maps. ISBN: 0600358968.

Published in the US as the *Macmillan Atlas of Rugs and Carpets.*

Chapters describe weaving methods, history, work of individual countries. Main function is a gazetteer arranged by geographical region. Excellent illustrations. *Class No:* 745.521

Needlework & Handicrafts

Encyclopaedias & Dictionaries

[1875]
DIAGRAM GROUP. **Handbook of arts and crafts:** the encyclopedia of the fine, decorative and applied arts. Lawther, G., *ed.* London, Harrap, 1981. 319p., illus.

'Examples from over 150 specialized fine and applied arts, involving the use of over 2000 tools. Each skill is illustrated by an example of the art form, or by a documentary illustration of the artists at work' (*Foreword*). Closely subdivided: Introduction - Writing on bone and stone ... Development of the pen ... Printing type ... Photography ... Oil painting ... Brass rubbing ... Pottery (p.86-109) ... Plaster ... Metal ... Wood sculpture ... Carving ... Glossary (p.180-201) ... Precious metals ... Beadmaking ... Weaving ... Crochet ... Millinery ... Leather decoration. Bibliography (general: 18 sections), p.310-1. Analytical index p.313-9. Over 4,000 illus., mainly two-colour. Well produced. *Class No:* 746(03)

[1876]
DILLMONT, T. **Encyclopaedia of needlework.** Rev. ed. London, Bracken Books, 1988. 830p. illus. ISBN: 1851700145.

Originally published 1886 and revised at intervals; available in several language versions.

....(contd.)

20 sections cover plain sewing, embroidery, tapestry, knitting, crocheting, openwork etc., with instructions or tracing. Abundant illustrations. *Class No:* 746(03)

Lacemaking

[1877]

EARNSHAW, P. Dictionary of lace. 2nd ed. Aylesbury, Bucks, Shire, 1984. 240p. illus. ISBN: 0852637004.

Alphabetical arrangement of terms covering materials, tools, techniques, proper names and broader areas such as design, dating, fashion. Cross references; bibliography. 48 pages of monochrome illustrations. *Class No:* 746.2

Embroidery

[1878]

SWIFT, G. Batsford encyclopedia of embroidery techniques. London, Batsford, 1984. 240p., illus. ISBN: 0713467819.

Covers styles, techniques, terms of hand and machine embroidery. 370 alphabetically arranged entries; 500 photographs and line-drawings. Good bibliography p.229-236; list of collections. *Class No:* 746.3

Crochet & Knitting

[1879]

COMPTON, R. The Illustrated dictionary of knitting. London, Batsford, 1988. 272p. diagrs., charts. ISBN: 0713448636.

Over 500 main entries arranged alphabetically; line illustrations and photographs. *Class No:* 746.4

Interior Decoration

[1880]

GORE, A. The History of English interiors. London, Phaidon, 1990. 192p. illus. ISBN: 0714826111.

Historical survey using newly commissioned photographs, and contemporary sources. Records all styles and periods from mediaeval times. *Class No:* 747

Glass & Crystal Ware

[1881]

NEWMAN, H. An Illustrated dictionary of glass. London, Thames & Hudson, 1987. 308p. illus. ISBN: 0500274517.

First published 1977.

Alphabetical entries for types, techniques, decorative styles, makers & manufacturers, including histories of major factories. Subtitle adds; 2442 entries, including definition of wares, materials, processes, forms and decorative styles ... from antiquity to the present. *Class No:* 748

Stained Glass

Great Britain

[1882]

COWEN, P. A Guide to stained glass in Britain. London, Michael Joseph, 1985. 280p., illus., charts, maps. ISBN: 0718125673.

First part contains an introduction on history and design (p.4-67); second part is county-by-county gazetteer. 600 main entries, & 1500 single-line entries. Glossary; thematic guide; bibliography; various indexes. 54 colour illustrations and numerous monochrome. *Class No:* 748.02(410)

Furniture

[1883]

ARONSON, J. The Encyclopedia of furniture. New ed. London, Batsford, 1989. 496p., illus. ISBN: 071345881x.

First published 1938. Re-issued as *The new encyclopedia of furniture* (New York, Crown, [1967]. ix,484p.).

Substantial articles, also c.2,500 separate descriptive definitions. 'A glossary of designers and craftsmen'. The examples are largely of US origin or in US museums. A popular standard work; 2000 illustrations. *Class No:* 749.1

[1884]

PAYNE, C., *ed.* **Sotheby's concise encyclopaedia of furniture.** London, Conran Octopus, 1989. 208p. illus. ISBN: 1850291977.

Covers earliest times to 1988; chronological arrangement of chapters, discussing styles, countries etc. Select bibliography, glossary, drawings and 300 colour photographs. *Class No:* 749.1

England

[1885]

EDWARDS, R. Shorter dictionary of English furniture. New ed. London, Hamlyn, 1987. 688p., illus. ISBN: 0600554015.

First published 1964.

Concentrates on domestic furniture. 'Standard reference work' (*Antique Collector* 1987, p.98). *Class No:* 749.1(420)

[1886]

MACQUOID, P. and EDWARDS, R. The Dictionary of English furniture, from the Middle Ages to the late Georgian period. 2nd ed. Woodbridge, Antique Collectors' Club, 1983-6. 3v., illus. ISBN: 185149037x.

First published 1924-7; this edition is a reprint of that published by Country Life Books, 1954.

Of particular value is the detailed attention paid, in text and illus., to different articles of furniture (*e.g.*, the articles on various types of table ('Tables, Artists and Reading' ... 'Tables, Work') occupy p.185-325, with 423 illus. Includes biographies; articles are signed; many cross-references; literature references in the text 43 col. plates. A most important work, textually and pictorially. *Class No:* 749.1(420)

Styles

USA

[1887]

BATES, E.B. and FAIRBANKS, J.L. American furniture, 1620 to the present. New York, Marek/Putnam, 1981. 561p.

Comprehensive coverage by period, with useful illustrations. Extensive social and historical commentary. Glossary of cabinet makers' terms, and bibliography. *Class No:* 749.1.03(73)

75 Painting

Painting

Yearbooks & Directories

[1888]
HISLOP, R., *ed.* **The Picture price guide 1990**: UK auction prices. 3rd ed. Weybridge, Art Sales Index, 1990. 450p. ISBN: 090387234x.
Gives details for each medium of number of works sold, total values, lowest, highest and medium prices. Includes 12,500 artists and sculptors of all periods and from all countries. *Class No:* 75.0(058)

[1889]
Lyle official arts review, 1991: the price guide to paintings. Curtis, T., *ed.* 17th ed. Galashiels, Lyle, 1990. 607p., illus. ISBN: 086248135x.
Arranged A/Z by artist, with over 2,000 illustrations. Individual paintings sold during the year are identified and the price paid indicated. Advice on styles and movements included in discussion of artists. *Class No:* 75.0(058)

Biographies

[1890]
COURTAULD INSTITUTE OF ART. London. **A Checklist of painters**. *c.*1200-1976. London, Mansell, 1978. xvi,337p.
'Today there are about 50,000 artists represented in the Witt Library and the number of reproductions is now in excess of 1,200,000' (*Foreword*). Data on each artist (A-Z): name; nationality; dates. 'It will be invaluable to students and to anyone in search of information about painters of fame or promise in reproductions of their works' (*British book news*, February 1979, p.165). *Class No:* 75.0(092)

Great Britain

[1891]
VINEY, N. *and* PIPER, D. **Shell guide to the great paintings of England**. London, Deutsch. 1989. ISBN: 0233984666.
Major collections examined in county-by-county arrangement; 300 entries, each giving principal attractions; location guide. *Class No:* 75.0(410)

Scotland

[1892]
HALSBY, J. *and* HARRIS, P. **Dictionary of Scottish painters**. 1600-1960. Edinburgh, Canongate, 1990. 304p.,illus. ISBN: 0862413281.
Over 2,000 entries with brief biographical details. 300 colour illustrations. *Class No:* 75.0(411)

Ireland

[1893]
CROOKSHANK, A. *and* FITZGERALD, D.J.V. **The Painters of Ireland**, *c.*1660-1920. London, Barrie & Jenkins. 1978. 303p., illus.
15 chapters: 1. The seventeenth century - 2. Portrait painters, 1700-1950 ... 4. The Dublin Society School and the Pastelists ... 8. Landscapes - 9. Foreigners in Ireland and decorative painters ... 14. The influence of Antwerp, Paris, Brittany and London - 15. Nineteenth-century subject pictures and portraits. Notes, p.287-91. Bibliography (books and pamphlets; catalogues). Appendix 1: The Dublin Society's Drawing Academy; 2. The Metropolitan School of Art, Dublin. Non-analytical index (p.299-303), but including names of paintings. *Class No:* 75.0(415)

Canada

[1894]
REID, D. **A Concise history of Canadian painting**. 2nd ed. Oxford, OUP, 1989. 432p. illus. ISBN: 0195406648.
First published 1973.
Covers early 17th century to 1980. Biographical data and critical appraisals. 200 illustrations, 37 colour. *Class No:* 75.0(71)

USA

[1895]
GERDTS, W.H., *ed.* **Art across America**: regional painting in America, 1710-1920. New York, Abbeville, 1990. 422,396, 396p. (3v.), illus. ISBN: 0558590331.
The work of many authoritative contributors. State-by-state overview, with annotations on individual artists; excludes New York City, Boston & Philadelphia. 800 artists are included; cross-references; bibliographies at the end of each volume. *Class No:* 75.0(73)

Materials & Paints

Water-colour Painting

Great Britain

[1896]
MALLALIEU, H.L. **Dictionary of British watercolour artists** up to 1920. 2nd ed. (vol.1). Woodbridge, Suffolk, Antique Collectors' Club, 1986, 1979, 1990. 298,557, 300p. (3v.), illus. ISBN: 1851490256, v.1; 0902028634, v.2; 1851491112, v.3.
Volume one lists over 6000 artists; bibliography; cross-references. Volume two gives 800 monochrome illustrations with dates, titles, sizes, commentary. Appendices include family trees. *Class No:* 75.023.2(410)

Periods & Styles

19th Century

[1897]
WOOD, C. **The Dictionary of Victorian painters.** 2nd ed. Woodbridge, Antique Collectors' Club, 1978. 764p. illus. ISBN: 0902028723.
First published 1971.
Covers 11000 artists working 1837-1901. Alphabetical arrangement with brief information, titles of exhibited works. Includes many minor or obscure figures. 540 illustrations giving title, date, size, and location. *Class No:* 75.035

20th Century

[1898]
Phaidon dictionary of twentieth-century art. 2nd ed. London, Phaidon, 1978. 420p.
First published 1973 as *Phaidon dictionary of modern art.*
40 contributors, covering painting, sculpture and architecture. Over 1,700 entries for 1,600 artists, Aaltonen ... Zwobada, plus over 140 groups of movements. Short bibliographies appended to many articles 'Picasso': $3\frac{1}{2}$ columns, 5 references; 'Pop art': $1\frac{1}{2}$ cols., 5 references; 'Expressionism': $1\frac{1}{2}$ cols., 5 references). 'Much of the material here presented was originally written in German (*Foreword*). Includes European, Australian, Japanese and Israeli artists, apart from British and American. *Class No:* 75.036

Painting Subjects

Portraits

Great Britain

[1899]
ORMOND, R. *and* ROGERS, M., *ed.* **Dictionary of British portraiture.** London, Batsford/National Portrait Gallery, 1979-81. 157,231,228,176p. (4v.). ISBN: 0713414685, v.1; 0713414707, v.2; 0713414723, v.3; 071341474x, v.4.
Vol.1 covers Middle Ages to the early Georgians; Vol.2 later Georgians and early Victorians; Vol.3 Victorians 1800-1860; vol.4 Twentieth century, born before 1900. The volumes list portraits in public galleries and institutions; arranged alphabetically by sitter with a list of known portraits in various media. Sitters name index in vol.4. 'Indispensible ... a very thorough guide' (*British Book News* Sept. 1982, p.563-4). *Class No:* 75.041(410)

Miniature Painting

[1900]
FOSKETT, D. **A Dictionary of British miniature painters.** London, Faber, 1972. 596,108p. (2v.), plates. ISBN: 0571082955, v.1; 0571097464, v.2.
Reprinted with the author's *Collecting miniatures* (1979) in one volume as *Miniatures: dictionary and guide* (Antique Collectors' Club, 1987).
Brief biographical details of 4,500 miniaturists 1520-1910. Entries give subjects, characteristics, signatures, important works. Bibliography p.592-6. Volume 2 contains the plates and index. 'Information is neither invariably complete nor accurate' (*Royal Society of Arts Journal* v.137, no.5391, Feb. 1989, p.181). *Class No:* 75.05

76/77 Graphics & Photography

Graphic Arts

Abbreviations & Symbols

[1901]
WALLIS, L.W. **Dictionary of graphic arts abbreviations.**
London, Lund Humphries, 1986. 139p. ISBN: 0853315000.
Over 5000 abbreviations and acronyms for organizations
& associations, equipment, processes & technical terms.
Class No: 76(003)

Encyclopaedias & Dictionaries

[1902]
DALLEY, T., *ed.* **The Complete guide to illustration and
design:** techniques and materials. New ed. Oxford, Phaidon,
1984. 224p.,illus.,tables. ISBN: 0714823473.
2 parts: Illustration (Introduction. 1. Pencils and other
point media; 2. Pen and ink; 3. Oils and other paint
media; 4. Printmaking; 5. Technical illustration) - Graphic
design (Introduction. 6. Design equipment; 7. Copying and
photoprinting; 8. Design and typography; 9. Design
procedures; 10. Design and photography; 11. Reproduction
and printing). Glossary, p.208-213. Paper and sizes.
Manufacturers and suppliers. Index, p.218-24. Step-by-step
instruction, profusely illustrated (550 illus., 250 in colour),
with descriptive captions. *Class No:* 76(03)

Handbooks & Manuals

[1903]
COTTON, B. **The New guide to graphic design.** London,
Phaidon, 1990. 192p. illus. ISBN: 0714826278.
Good overall guide to setting up in graphic design;
principles, client relationships, studio organization,
equipment, materials, case studies. Over 400 illustrations.
Class No: 76(035)

Dictionaries

[1904]
GARLAND, K. **Graphics, design and printing terms:** an
international dictionary. 2nd ed. London, Lund Humphries,
1988. 264p., illus. ISBN: 085331523x.
First edition (1980) as the *Illustrated Graphics Glossary.*
Defines over 2,000 terms, with ample cross-references.
US/UK usage discussed. Useful bibliography; over 300
illustrations. *Class No:* 76(038)

Histories

[1905]
MEGGS, P. **A History of graphic design.** New ed. London,
Viking, 1985. 511p.,illus. ISBN: 0670807214.
Five sections in part one cover the evolution of graphic
communications from ancient times to the invention of
movable typography. Part 2 (4 sections) examines early
typography in Europe, and design of the printed page. Part
3 (5 sections) discusses industrial revolution effects on
printing. Part 4 (10 sections) concentrates on 20th century
developments. Glossary p.492-496; bibliography p.492-502;
600 photographs & 400 line drawings. *Class No:* 76(091)

Great Britain

[1906]
MACKENZIE, I. **British prints:** dictionary and price guide.
Woodbridge, Suffolk, Antique Collectors' Club, 1987. 359p.
illus. ISBN: 0902028960.
Brief biographical data on over 2000 print-makers 1650-
1950, with description of characteristic work, guide to
market values. 706 illustrations. Bibliography. *Class No:*
76(410)

USA

[1907]
HORN, M., *ed.* **Contemporary graphic artists.** Detroit, Gale
Research, 1986-1988. 272, 288, 269p. (3v). ISSN:
08858462.
Particularly valuable for areas of work often omitted -
cartoonists, animators, comic strip artists, illustrators, poster
designers, computer graphic artists. Emphasis on modern
American names, but some historical and foreign figures.
'An indispensible reference source'. (*Art Documentation,*
5(3), Fall 1986, p.138). *Class No:* 76(73)

Commercial Graphics

[1908]
SIMPSON, I., *ed.* **The New guide to illustration.** London,
Phaidon, 1990. 192p. illus. ISBN: 0714826286.
Aimed at professional illustrators and showing working
practices and techniques. Includes computer-generated
images. Glossary of technical terms, addresses of
professional bodies, suppliers of materials. *Class No:* 766

Photography

[1909]
The Focal encyclopedia of photography. London, Focal Press, 1965. 1936p. (2v.), illus. ISBN: 0240506316.
First published 1956.
Scholarly & comprehensive guide mainly to the technical aspects of photography; A/Z of terms, processes, individual names. Obviously now dated, but retaining a value and status in the literature, and still in-print 1991. *Class No:* 77

[1910]
HEDGECOE, J. Complete guide to photography. London, Collins & Brown, 1990. 224p., illus. ISBN: 1855850001.
Techniques and elements explained for all types of work - people, places, natural world, action, still-life. 70 practical projects are described in detail. Glossary of terms. 500 illustrations (400 in colour). *Class No:* 77

Encyclopaedias & Dictionaries

[1911]
EDWARDS, M. Complete encyclopedia of photography. London, Multimedia Books, 1991. 191p. illus. ISBN: 1853750034.
Discusses equipment, films, cameras, lighting, darkroom practice, and photographic themes - portraits, still life, street life, sport etc. 250 good illustrations. *Class No:* 77(03)

Histories

[1912]
NEWHALL, B. History of photography, from 1839 to the present. Rev. 5th ed. London, Secker & Warburg, 1982. 319p., illus. ISBN: 0436305070.
First published 1937.
Considered one of the classic works in this field. Praised as a good, concise introduction, both 'readable' and 'engaging' (*Choice* February 1988). Illustrated with over 300 examples, newly selected for this edition. *Class No:* 77(091)

Biographies

[1913]
BROWNE, T. *and* **PARTNOW, E.,** *eds.* **Biographical encyclopedia of photographic artists and innovators.** London, Macmillan, 1983. 722p. ISBN: 0025175009.
Gives 2,000 names, living and dead, international coverage. Especially useful for the inclusion of less-well-known figures. Biographies p.3-684 with details of career, publications, locations, agents, etc. List of museums p.685-702, and photographic galleries p.703-721. 144 plates in centre section. *Class No:* 77(092)

Microphotography

Yearbooks & Directories

[1914]
Micrographics and optical recording buyer's guide. 9th ed. Bedford, Spectrum for G.G. Baker. 1990. 191p. ISBN: 0906635144. ISSN: 09513906.
Earlier editions as *Micrographics Yearbook* (1981-86).
Introductory sections cover document storage, videomicrographic systems, optical storage, software, costs, Associations and institutions listed (p.42-44), standards (p.45-49), publishers (p.50-53), equipment suppliers (p.58-89). Also materials suppliers, services, index to trade names, model names, agents. *Class No:* 778.14(058)

Film & Television Photography

Video

[1915]
HEDGECOE, J. Hedgecoe on video: a complete creative and technical guide to making videos. London, Pyramid, 1990. 254p., illus. ISBN: 1871307341.
Eight major projects examined, as a means of discussing equipment, accessories, techniques, editing, sound. *Class No:* 778.534

Photographic Collections

[1916]
HARRISON, H.P., *ed.* **Picture librarianship.** London, Library Association Publishing, 1981. 542p. ISBN: 0853659125.
Section 1: techniques and organizations (photographic sources p.35-54) selection, presentation & storage, arrangement & indexing, microforms, education & training. Section 2: case studies and surveys of picture libraries (national, government, special, institutional, educational, public, communcation industry). Bibliography p.495-517. Good index. *Class No:* 779

78 Music

Music

Abbreviations & Symbols

[1917]
THOMSETT, M.C. **Musical terms, symbols and theory:** an illustrated dictionary. London; St. James Press, 1990. 277p. illus. ISBN: 1558620540.

Comprises a glossary of terms; multi-language instrument guides; illustrated notation guide; scales, keys and chords. *Class No:* 780(003)

Bibliographies

[1918]
The British catalogue of music. London, British Library, 1957- . ISSN: 00681407.

Two interim issues and an annual cumulation each year; initially quarterly. Cumulation 1957-1985 published in 10 vols. (London, K.G. Saur, 1988). Available through BLAISE-LINE 1987-.

A record of new music published in the UK, foreign music available in the UK through a sole agent, music acquired from foreign publishers; based on receipts at the BL Copyright office. Classified section (now arranged by DDC 20; previously by a special BCM classification), title and composer index, subject index (arranged by musical forms). *Class No:* 780(01)

[1919]
DUCKLES, V.H. *and* KELLER, M.A. **Music reference and research materials.** 4th ed. New York, Schirmer, 1988. 714p. ISBN: 0028703901.

International coverage, including Asian sources; annotations mainly descriptive with some critical comment. Numbered entries arranged alphabetically within broad categories, in turn subdivided into narrower subject areas. Extensive, multi-access indexes. 'Best single guide to reference sources in the field of music' (*Reference Books Bulletin*, May 1, 1989). Heavily criticized for 'questionable bibliographic practices and poor proofreading' (*Choice*, June 1988, p.1658). *Class No:* 780(01)

[1920]
Music index: a subject-author guide to current music periodical literature. Warren, Michigan, Harmonie Park Press, 1949-. xxxvi,1156p. (latest cumulation). ISSN: 00274348.

Monthly, cumulating annually. Publishers' previous name *Information Coordinators* (Detroit). Available on CD-ROM from 1991; first disc covers 1981-88 and will be updated annually (UK agent: Cambridge, Chadwick Healey; annual subscription £690).

Alphabetical dictionary catalogue arrangement. Covers 350 periodicals, with an emphasis on US titles, and including

....(contd.)
several general publications. Also includes obituaries, review of books & performances. Cumulation 1983/4 (vols. 35 & 36) issued 1988. *Class No:* 780(01)

Encyclopaedias & Dictionaries

[1921]
BLOM, E. **The New Everyman dictionary of music.** Cummings, D., *comp.* 6th ed. London, Dent, 1988. 880p. ISBN: 046003037x.

This new revision retains the high standard of its predecessors; over 1,500 new entries compared with the previous edition. *Class No:* 780(03)

[1922]
KENNEDY, M. **The Oxford dictionary of music.** Oxford: OUP, 1985. xiv, 810p. ISBN: 0193113333.

Revised and enlarged edition of the *Concise Oxford Dictionary of Music* 3rd ed., 1980.

Thorough, low-priced and well produced, this revision contains 500 new entries, and amendments and corrections throughout, including worklists and dates of composition. Compact, two-column layout is easy to read, but information is brief and abbreviated. Good coverage of jazz, "light" music, as well as classical. Includes composers, conductors, performers, terms, named pieces; small number of musical examples, no illustrations. *Class No:* 780(03)

[1923]
New Grove dictionary of music and musicians. Sadie, S., *ed.* 6th ed. London, Macmillan, 1980. 20v.

First published 1871-1889; 5th ed. edited by E. Blom, 1954. Supplementary volume 1961.

6th ed. is virtually a new work; '97% of the material has not been derived from former editions' (*Acta musicologica*, v.54, 1982, p.4) of the 2,426 contributors, 34% are American, 20% British and 13% German. Its 22 million words compare strikingly with the 5th ed.'s 8 million. Of the 22,500 articles, 16,500 are biographical - chiefly on composers (*e.g.* 'Beethoven': 40p. of text; 24p. of lists of works and bibliography). 4,500 illus.; over 3,000 music examples; 9,000 cross-references (*e.g.* 'France', v.6, p.741-64: 28 cross-references), - compensating to some extent, for the lack of a general index.

Two leading features, then, of 'Grove 6': lengthy, signed and authoritative articles, prefaced by helpful outlines; and extensive work-lists and bibliographies (*e.g* J.S. Bach, v.1, p.785-840; works-list, p.818-36; bibliography, p.837-43. Dvorak, v.5, p.765-92; 14 sections; 8p. of works-list; 2½ columns of bibliography; 1 illus., 2 facsims., 3 ports., 8 musical examples).

For the librarian and musicologist/bibliographer: 'Bibliography of music', v.2, p.682-92; 'Periodicals', v.14, p.467-535 (*c.* 6,000 titles); 'Dictionaries and encyclopaedias', v.8, p.430-59; 'Libraries', v.10, p.719-821. *Class No:* 780(03)

[1924]

New Harvard dictionary of music. Randel, D.M., *comp.* Cambridge, Mass., & London: Belknap Press of Harvard University, 1986. xxi, 942p. ISBN: 0674615255.

Total revision of the 1969 edition by Apel.

Authoritative and respected, this edition is the work of nine advisers and seventy contributors. There are 6,000 entries, and musical examples, drawings and illustrations are featured. Coverage includes all countries and periods, from earliest times to jazz, rock etc., and styles, forms and instruments. There are no biographies. Major articles have brief bibliographies; bibliographical articles include *Dictionaries and Encyclopedias* pp226-230, and *Periodicals* pp625-628. *Class No:* 780(03)

[1925]

The New Oxford companion to music. Arnold, D., *ed.* Oxford, OUP, 1983. 2017p. (2v).

First published 1938; 10th ed. 1970 as *The Oxford companion to music*, by P.A. Scholes.

90 contributors; 6,000 entries (of which over 2,000 define musical terms), 'Brahms'; 2½p. incl. port., music example, 4 references); 'Jazz'; 5½p., incl. 5 illus.; 'Broadcasting of music': 8p. incl. 4 illus., facsim; 'Electronic music intruments'; 4p., 3 illus.; 'Copyright': 7p. Longer articles are sectionalised, with list of headings (*e.g.* 'Ballet and theatrical dance': 17p.; 11 illus., but no bibliography; 'Records and reproduction': 12p., 7 illus., 4 references; 'Japanese music': 17½p., 8 illus., 6 music examples). Some inconsistency in provision of plot-synopses for operas. Over 1,500 illus., and music examples in all.

'In no way a successor to that curious, infuriating, but lovable compilation, the original *Oxford companion to music.*' Rather, 'a thorough, impersonal, dispassionate and accurate dictionary ... The most readily available source of information (*Brio*, v.20, no.3, Autumn/Winter 1983, p.61). *Class No:* 780(03)

[1926]

SADIE, S. *and* **LATHAM, A.,** *eds.* **Grove concise encyclopaedia of music.** London, Macmillan, 1988. 850p. ISBN: 0333432363.

Based on the *New Grove Dictionary of music and musicians*, 1980.

High standards of production; mainly devoted to Western, classical music. Some 10,000 entries, but no bibliographic support, although work lists are included for major composers. *Class No:* 780(03)

[1927]

WESTRUP, J., *and others.* **Collins dictionary of music.** Rev. ed. London, Collins, 1988. 576p. ISBN: 0004343565.

A concise version of the *Collins Encyclopaedia of Music.* Good coverage of modern musical figures, and revisions of articles on composers, instruments, terms, performers, critics, orchestras, etc. *Class No:* 780(03)

Periodicals & Progress Reports

[1928]

Brio: journal of the United Kingdom Branch of the International Association of Music Libraries, Archives and Documentation Centres. Oxford, IAML (UK). ISSN: 00070173.

Issued twice per year.

Useful feature articles, listing of new publications received at the British Library Document Supply Centre (arranged in instrumental categories etc.), and a good selection of scholarly book reviews, supported by further short notices of new books. *Class No:* 780(05)

[1929]

Notes. Ochs, M., *ed.* Canton, MA, Music Library Association, 1942-. ISSN: 00274380.

Quarterly.

The Journal of the Music Library Association; excellent range and quality of book reviews in each issue, varying in length from 350-1,500 words. Vol. 47(3), March 1991, for example, contains 72 substantial book reviews, and 18 pages listing books received. Also reviews of new music, and an excellent index of CD and record reviews. *Class No:* 780(05)

Yearbooks & Directories

[1930]

Kemps international music and recording industry yearbook 1990. 22nd ed. London, Kemp Group, 1989. 533p. ISBN: 0862591619.

Directory of concert & tour managers, broadcast & video services, recording facilities, sound equipment, trade etc. Mainly UK, but international section p.389-533. *Class No:* 780(058)

Quotations

[1931]

WATSON, D., *ed.* **Chambers book of musical quotations.** London, Chambers, 1990. 256p. ISBN: 0550210121.

Ranges widely from jazz, pop and folk to opera and orchestral music. An extertaining collection. *Class No:* 780(082.2)

Histories

[1932]

ABRAHAM, G. The Concise Oxford history of music. London, Oxford University Press, 1979. 968p., illus. ISBN: 0193113198.

Unrelated to the *New Oxford History of Music.* Five main sections - rise of West Asian & East Mediterranean music, ascendancy of Western Europe, ascendancy of Italy, ascendancy of Germany, fragmentation of tradition. Subdivided into 41 chapters, the structure being clearly set out in the contents pages. Further reading & recommended editions, arranged by main sections, p.864-912. Thorough index. *Class No:* 780(091)

[1933]

GROUT, D. *and* **PALISCA, C. A History of Western music.** 4th ed. London, Dent, 1988. 928p. ISBN: 0460047701.

Substantially revised, and with a new format; analyses of style, commentaries on developments, and chronologies within chapters are key features. *Class No:* 780(091)

[1934]

The New Oxford history of music. London, OUP, 1954-. 10v. to date (*c.*950p. per vol.). ISBN: 0193163012, v.1; 0193163020, v.2; 0193163039, v.3; 0193163047, v.4; 0193163055, v.5; 0193163063, v.6; 0193163071, v.7; 019316308x, v.8; 0193163098, v.9.

Originally as the *Oxford History of Music* (1901-5; 6v.). To be completed in 11 vols. Vol.10 currently out-of-print.

1. *Ancient and Oriental music*; edited by E. Wellesz. 1957.

2. *Early medieval music, up to 1300*; edited by A. Hughes. 1954.

3. *Ars Nova and the Renaissance, 1300-1540*; edited by A. Hughes and G. Abraham. 1960.

4. *The age of humanism, 1540-1630*; edited by G. Abraham. 1967.

5. *Opera and church music, 1630-1750*; edited by A. Lewis and N. Fortune, 1975.

6. *The growth of instrumental music, 1630-1750.* 1986.

....(contd.)

7. *The age of enlightenment, 1745-1790*; edited by E. Wellesz and F.W. Steinfield. 1973.
8. *The age of Beethoven, 1790-1830*, by G. Abraham. 1982.
9. *Romanticism, 1830-1890*; edited by G. Abraham. 1990.
10. *The modern age, 1890-1960*; edited by M. Cooper. 1974.
11. *Chronological tables, bibliogaphies and index.*
The editor of each volume is assisted by specialists. V.2 has chapter bibliographies, footnotes, music examples and detailed indexes. While conceding that the then 4 new volumes stand favourably against all competition, *Library Journal* (v.93, no.8, 15 January 1968, p.1609-10) find that they are *isolated* music history and do not fulfil the stated objective - 'to present music ... as an art developing in constant association with every form of human culture and activity'. On v.10, *Music & letters* (v.56, no.2, April 1975, p.202) notes a 'prevailing tendency to survey rather than to excavate'. *Class No:* 780(091)

Biographies

[1935]
JACOBS, A. **The Penguin dictionary of musical performers:** a biographical guide to significant interpreters of classical music - singers, solo instrumentalists, conductors, orchestras and string quartets - ranging from the seventeenth century to the present day. London, Viking Penguin, 1990. 240p. ISBN: 0670807559.
Designed as a companion to Jacobs *New Penguin dictionary of music*, 1977.
25,000 entries, each giving name, dates, nationality, brief biography and major works premiered. Founding dates for orchestras & quartets, also personnel and history. Index of composers. Some inconsistencies have been noted (*Choice,* February 1991. p.916). *Class No:* 780(092)

[1936]
SLONIMSKY, N. **The Concise Baker's biographical dictionary of musicians.** London, Macmillan, 1988. 1407p. ISBN: 0028724119.
Based on *Baker's biographical dictionary of musicians,* 1984.
Half the size of the source volume, eliminating some less important categories of entry. Entries are short, but sound and well written. *Class No:* 780(092)

20th Century

[1937]
CUMMINGS, D. *and* MCINTIRE, D., *eds.* **International who's who in music and musician's directory 1990-91.** 12th ed. Ely, Cambs, Melrose Press, 1990. 1,300p. ISBN: 0948875208.
First published 1937.
Biographical information on 8,000 contemporary composers, arrangers, soloists, conductors, managers etc. in the classical and light classical fields. Appendices list societies, schools, awards, orchestras, opera companies. *Class No:* 780(092)"19"

Great Britain

Yearbooks & Directories

[1938]
British music yearbook 1991. Carter, A., *ed.* 17th ed. London, Rhinegold Publishing, 1990. 715p. ISBN: 0946890366. ISSN: 02662329.
Lists official organizations (p.7-38), artists & agents (39-238), also venues, promoters (clubs, festivals etc.). Covers classical music, folk, jazz, and light music. Sections on early music, recording & broadcasting, competitions & scholarships, education, libraries, museums, marketing, suppliers & services. Very brief subject index (p.309-12). *Class No:* 780(410)(058)

USA

Encyclopaedias & Dictionaries

[1939]
JABLONSKI, E. **Encyclopedia of American music.** New York: Doubleday, 1981. 629p. ISBN: 0385080883.
A chronological arrangement in seven major periods, from hymns of the Pilgrim Fathers to the present day; all types of music are included. Introductory sections are supported by some 1200 entries. Sometimes idiosyncratic, but an interesting approach. An appendix of recordings is provided on pp 579-592. *Class No:* 780(73)(03)

Biographies

[1940]
Who's who in American music: classical. Cattell, J., *ed.* New York: Bowker, 1983. xiii, 582p. ISBN: 0835217256.
Covers administrators, managers, composers, conductors, critics, directors, educators, instrumentalists, vocalists; 6,800 entries, included by invitation, not application. Indexes by geographical location and class of activity. Entries in alphabetical order, noting training, works, recordings, positions, teaching, awards. Bibliographies limited to three items; publications listed to a maximum of five. Agent's address given. *Class No:* 780(73)(092)

20th Century

Biographies

[1941]
LABLANC, M.L., *ed.* **Contemporary musicians:** profiles of the people in music. Detroit, Gale, 1989-. 253p. (vol.1). ISSN: 10442197.
Expected to appear twice each year.
Biographical and critical data on lyricists, performers, composers, in popular music, jazz, and contemporary classical. Each volume offers 80-100 names, with photographs, basic data, list of compositions, selected discography. Subject index, which will cumulate in future volumes. *Class No:* 780"19"(092)

Music Librarianship

[1942]
BRYANT, E.T. **Music librarianship:** a practical guide. 2nd ed. Metuchen NJ, London: Scarecrow Press, 1985. xiv, 449p. ISBN: 0810817853.
An authoritative and comprehensive guide, covering administration, reference books, periodicals, cataloguing, classification, sound recordings. Bibliography pp423-442. *Class No:* 780:02

Music Libraries

[1943]
Directory of music research libraries, including contributions to RISM. Benton, R., *ed.* Kassel, Bärenreiter, 1967-. 5v.

Published under the auspices of the International Association of Music Libraries, Archives and Documentation Centres: Commission of Research Libraries. Volume 1: (2nd ed. 1983) Canada & the US. (3761806841; 282p.). Volume 2: Thirteen European countries (1970) (Covers 784 libraries in Austria, Belgium, Denmark, Finland, E. & W. Germany, UK, Ireland, Luxembourg, Netherlands, Norway, Sweden, Switzerland). Volume 3: Spain, France, Italy, Portugal (1972; University of Iowa Press; republished by Bärenreiter, 1975). Volume 4: Australia, NZ, Japan, & Israel (1979). Volume 5: Czechoslovakia, Hungary, Poland, Yugoslavia (1985). Data: address; type and size of collection; lending library codes. Country index of libraries. Very favourably reviewed in *Brio*, Spring/Summer 1980, p.29. To be completed in 6v. *Class No: 780:061:026/027*

[1944]
PENNEY, B. Music in British libraries: a directory of resources. 4th ed. London, Library Association, 1992. 112p. ISBN: 0853657394.

Entries in alphabetical order of location giving details of collections of printed music and sound recordings in the UK. Coverage has been expanded from earlier editions to include university, polytechnic and college collections, music schools, cathedrals, private collections, in addition to public libraries. Standard range of data given. Indices by composer, collection names, etc. *Class No: 780:061:026/027*

Music Education

[1945]
British music education yearbook. 1990-91. Carter, A., *ed.* 3rd ed. London: Rhinegold Publishing, 1990. xi, 530p. ISBN: 094689034x.

Details of conservatories, universities, polytechnics, colleges, training facilities, local authority music centres, independent and special schools, scholarships, grants, examinations etc. Highlights new areas of interest, and new music resources - books and new music by category. *Class No: 780:37*

[1946]
USCHER, N. The Schirmer guide to schools of music and conservatories throughout the world. New York, Schirmer, 1988. 635p. ISBN: 0028730305.

Also published as *A Critical guide to music schools and conservatories throughout the world.*

Covers 750 institutions worldwide; gives academic information, entrance and degree requirements, specializations, fees. Arranged by country; indexes by name, areas of study, instruments taught. Excludes purely academic courses in US. *Class No: 780:37*

Music Theory

Thematic Catalogues

[1947]
BROOK, B.S. Thematic catalogues in music: an annotated bibliography, including printed, manuscript and in-preparation catalogues. Hillsdale, NY, Pendragon Press, 1972. xxxvi, 347p.

1,444 numbered, annotated entries, under composers A-Z. Symbols indicate 'in preparation', 'manuscript', 'literature'. Appendix A: Manuscript thematic catalogues before 1830 (p.xxi-xxv) - B. Printed thematic catalogues before 1830.

....*(contd.)*
p.xxvi-vii. The most comprehensive bibliography of thematic catalogues superseding the Music Library Association's *A check-list of thematic catalogues* (New York Public Library, 1954. 37p; 362 entries) and *Queen's College supplement* (1966). *Class No: 781.973*

Kinds of Music

Opera & Operettas

Encyclopaedias & Dictionaries

[1948]
ANDERSON, J. Bloomsbury dictionary of opera and operetta. London, Bloomsbury, 1989. 448p. ISBN: 0747504814.

US edition as the *Harper dictionary of opera & operetta.*

4,500 composers, singers, roles, arias, companies, terms, are included. Opera coverage is good; operetta - which does not include musical comedy - fills a gap in the literature. *Class No: 782(03)*

[1949]
GÄNZL, K. and LAMB, A. Gänzl's Book of the musical theatre. New York, Schirmer, 1989. 1353p. ISBN: 0028719417.

Includes 300 shows arranged by country; historical introduction to each section, then in chronological order of first performance. Basic production information, characters, and synopsis. Discography. *Class No: 782(03)*

[1950]
GREEN, S. Encyclopedia of the musical film. New ed. New York, OUP, 1988. 352p. ISBN: 0195054210.

Entries, A-Z, p.3-319. 'Wizard of Oz, The'; $2\frac{3}{4}$ columns (credits, cast, songs, history and synopsis, TV repeat, 2 references). 'Judy Garland': $1\frac{1}{2}$ columns, with over $\frac{1}{2}$p. list of parts played. 'Succinct information regarding the musical screen's most prominent individuals, productions, and songs. Though emphasis is on Hollywood output (including feature-length cartoons), British musical films and selected original television musicals are also covered' (*Preface*). *Class No: 782(03)*

[1951]
Kobbé's complete opera book. 10th ed. London, Bodley Head, 1987. xvii,1404p. illus. ISBN: 0370310179.

First published 1922. Edited & revised by the Earl of Harewood.

Wide coverage of works that remain in the repertory; three main sections cover opera before 1800 (120p.) the nineteenth century (670p.), and the twentieth century (550p.). Each section is subdivided either by national style (Italian opera, etc.) or by major figures (Wagner, Verdi). *Class No: 782(03)*

Dictionaries

[1952]
BARLOW, H. and MORGENSTERN, S. A Dictionary of opera and song themes: including cantatas, oratorios, lieder and art songs. Rev. ed. New York, Crown, 1976. $15.95. ISBN: 0517525038.

8,000 vocal themes arranged alphabetically by composer, title. Indexes by song title, first line, melody written in alphabetical notation. *Class No: 782(038)*

Histories

[1953]
GROUT, D.J. **A Short history of opera.** New York, Columbia University Press, 1988. xix,913p. ISBN: 0231061927.
First published 1947.
Six sections cover 16th, 17th, 18th, 19th centuries, Nationalism & opera, 20th century. Scholarly and authoritative; enormous bibliography p.731-825 arranged in chapter order. *Class No:* 782(091)

Great Britain

[1954]
GÄNZL, K. **The British musical theatre.** London: Macmillan, 1986. x, 1196, ix, 1258p. (2v). ISBN: 0333419545, set.
First colume covers 1865-1914 in a chronological arrangement; introduction to each year, then details of productions, first-performance cast lists. Appendices of published music and recordings. Index covers composers, authors, librettists, lyricists, producers, directors, and theatres. Second volume similar, covers 1915-1984. Winner of the McColvin Medal 1987. *Class No:* 782(410)

Sacred & Church Music

[1955]
DIEHL, K.S. **Hymns and tunes:** an index. Metuchen, NJ, Scarecrow, 1966.
Covers 78 Protestant hymnals with entries for 12,000 hymns by first line, author, composer, tune name, and opening notes. *Class No:* 783

[1956]
STUDWELL, W.E. **Christmas carols:** a reference guide. New York, Garland, 1984. 278p. ISBN: 0824088999.
Provides information and historical notes on over 700 carols. *Class No:* 783

England

[1957]
LONG, K. **The Music of the English church.** London, Hodder & Stoughton, 1991. 480p. ISBN: 0340149620.
Explores the growth and development of the art of liturgical music, the circumstances of its writing and performance, and its place in a wider European culture. *Class No:* 783(420)

Vocal Music

[1958]
LAX, R. *and* SMITH, F. **The Great song thesaurus.** 2nd ed. Oxford, OUP, 1988. 774p. ISBN: 0195054083.
Includes over 11,000 songs published up to 1986. Extensive system of cross references; indexes by key word, key line, lyricists, subject, and category. Inventory of significant songs 1558-1986. *Class No:* 784

USA

[1959]
EWEN, D. **American songwriters.** New York; H.W. Wilson, 1987. xi, 489p. ISBN: 0824207440.
Includes 146 biographies of composers and lyricists, covering 150 years. Ranges over folk music, country and western, rock, jazz, tin-pan alley, R & B, minstrelsy, shows, film music. Performance histories of over 5,000 songs. Brief bibliographies. *Class No:* 784(73)

Folk Songs

[1960]
The Oxford book of sea songs. Palmer, R., *ed.* Oxford, OUP, 1986. xxx,343p. illus. ISBN: 0192141597.
Useful introduction; 159 songs with sources noted. Bibliography; glossary of nautical terms; index of titles & first lines. *Class No:* 784.4

[1961]
POPSI: the popular song index. Boston Spa, British Library, 1990. 5 microfiche. ISSN: 09585702.
Intended to appear annually, cumulating; microfiche edition will continue, but from 1991 a microcomputer database is expected also.
Title index of songs in popular music anthologies held at BLDSC, 'from music hall to the current top ten'. Includes the contents of about 400 anthologies (BLDSC shelfmarks are given). Indexing on the database version should allow for searching by single words or parts of titles. *Class No:* 784.4

Encyclopaedias & Dictionaries

[1962]
GAMMOND, P. **The Oxford companion to popular music.** Oxford, University Press, 1991. 204p. ISBN: 0193113236.
Examines all aspects of Anglo-American popular music, from operetta to blues & folk. Includes historical material, performer and composer biographies, styles, instruments, songs, shows. *Class No:* 784.4(03)

[1963]
LOWE, L. **Directory of popular music 1900-1980.** 2nd ed. Droitwich, Worcs: Peterson Publishing Co, 1986. 1440p. ISBN: 0904702022.
Arranged in nine sections comprising a chronological list followed by stage shows, films, directory of publishers, award winners, song contest winners. Novello award nominations, theme & signature tunes, title index. *Class No:* 784.4(03)

USA

[1964]
SANJEK, R. **American popular music and its business:** the first four hundred years. Oxford, OUP, 1988. 469, 482, 734p. (3v). ISBN: 0195040287, v.1; 0195043103, v.2; 0195043111, v.3.
Concentrates on economic and business concerns, in classical and popular fields. Examines public concerts, religion, performing rights, recording industry, contracts, copyright, patronage, publishers etc. Excellent bibliographies. 'Unlikely to be superseded for many decades such is the range of scholarship and the depth and thoroughness of the examination.' (*Choice*, 1989, p.816). *Class No:* 784.4(73)

Children's Songs

[1965]
CUSHING, H.G., *comp.* **Children's song index:** an index to more than 22,000 songs in 189 collections. St. Clair Shores, MI, Scholarly Press; 1977. ISBN: 0403072107.
Reprint of 1936 edition.
Dictionary catalogue arrangement featuring titles, first lines, composers, lyricists, and subjects. *Index to children's songs* updates this volume. *Class No:* 784.67

[1966]
PETERSON, C.S. *and* FENTON, A.D., *comps.* **Index to children's songs: a title, first line, and subject index.** New York, Wilson, 1979. 318p. ISBN: 082420638x.
Continues Cushing's *Children's song index* and covers collections published 1909-1977. *Class No:* 784.67

National Anthems

[1967]
REED, W.L. *and* BRISTOW, M.J., *eds.* National anthems of the world. 7th ed. New York, Blandford Press, 1988. 513p. ISBN: 0713719621.

172 nations listed alphabetically; gives piano score, notes on composer, lyricist, transliterations, translations into English. *Class No: 784.71*

Instrumental Music

Brass Bands

[1968]
Directory of British brass bands: volume 6, 1990/91. Macclesfield, McMillan Martin for British Federation of Brass Bands, 1990. 108p.

Lists national organizations, associations, championships; contest calendar; area associations; directory of member bands. *Class No: 785.12*

[1969]
TAYLOR, A.R. Brass bands. London, Granada, 1979. x,356p. illus. ISBN: 0246110821.

3 parts: 1. History of the brass band movement (up to the 1970s) - 2. Events and occasions (festivals, contests and championships) - 3. Appendices; 1. Contest results; 2. A brass band contest calendar; 3. Discography; 4. B.B.C radio broadcasting. 5 Salvation Army. Detailed, partly analytical index. No bibliography. *Class No: 785.12*

Jazz & Blues Music

Encyclopaedias & Dictionaries

[1970]
CARR, I. *and* PRIESTLEY, B. *and* FAIRWEATHER, D. Jazz: the essential companion. London, Paladin, 1989. 562p. ISBN: 0135092744.

Published in US, by Prentice Hall, 1988.

1600 entries ranging over all types of jazz, from its origins to the present day; mainly biographical sketches with critical comments. Likely to become 'the standard one-volume reference source' (*Choice*, March 1989, p.1116). *Class No: 785.16(03)*

[1971]
CLARKE, D. The Penguin encyclopedia of popular music. Harmondsworth, Penguin, 1989. 1376p. ISBN: 0670803499.

Basic information on rock, country, jazz, gospel, heavy metal, reggae, rap, ragtime, new age, folk, zydeco, funk, punk and blues. 3,000 entries, cross references, and 90 page index. *Class No: 785.16(03)*

[1972]
HARDY, P. *and* LAING, D. Faber companion to twentieth century popular music. London, Faber, 1990. 875p.

Definition of popular music is difficult: seems to specialise in jazz and rock but with omissions. Readable and well-designed; no general index. The Penguin *Encyclopedia of Popular Music* has more entries, and perhaps more information but is poorly designed. *Class No: 785.16(03)*

[1973]
KERNFELD, B., *ed.* New Grove dictionary of jazz. London, Macmillan, 1988. 670, 690p. (2v). ISBN: 093585939x.

Although based on the 1980 edition of *Grove*, up to 90% of the material is new. 250 contributors; articles signed; bibliographies and discographies. 'Difficult to convey the scope and importance' (*Choice* April, 1989. p.1310). *Class No: 785.16(03)*

Pop Music

[1974]
GAMBACCINI, P. *and* RICE, J. The Guinness book of British hit albums. 4th ed. London, Guinness, 1990. 352p. illus. ISBN: 085112397x.

Reviews albums issued 1958-1989 with statistical data; alphabetical list of every soloist and group that has featured in the Top 100. *Class No: 785.19*

[1975]
GAMBACCINI, P. *and* RICE, J. *and* RICE, T. The Guinness book of British hit singles. 8th ed. London, Guinness, 1991. 406p. illus. ISBN: 0851129412.

Details of every hit single from 1952. Alphabetical index of names, title index. Miscellaneous information sections discuss specific trends and achievements. *Class No: 785.19*

[1976]
POPSI: the popular song index. Boston Spa, British Library, 1990. 5 microfiche. ISSN: 09585702.

Intended to appear annually, cumulating; microfiche edition will continue, but from 1991 a microcomputer database is expected also.

Title index of songs in popular music anthologies held at BLDSC, 'from music hall to the current top ten'. Includes the contents of about 400 anthologies (BLDSC shelfmarks are given). Indexing on the database version should allow for searching by single words or parts of titles. *Class No: 785.19*

Encyclopaedias & Dictionaries

[1977]
BARNARD, S. *and* HARDY, P. *and* LAING, D. Encyclopaedia of rock. London: MacDonald, 1987. 480p. ISBN: 0356142744.

Based on *Encyclopaedia of Rock* 3v. Panther Books, 1976.

Sound and up-to-date alphabetical summary of soloists, groups, technicians, producers, styles, record companies. 1,500 entries; well-produced. *Class No: 785.19(03)*

[1978]
GAMMOND, P. The Oxford companion to popular music. Oxford, University Press, 1991. 204p. ISBN: 0193113236.

Examines all aspects of Anglo-American popular music, from operetta to blues & folk. Includes historical material, performer and composer biographies, styles, instruments, songs, shows. *Class No: 785.19(03)*

[1979]
STAMBLER, I. Encyclopedia of pop, rock and soul. Rev. ed. New York, St. Martin's Press, 1989. 864p. ISBN: 0312025734.

About 500 entries on mainstream rock and pop, but with brief coverage of less well known areas. Lengthy entries give good background data, recording information, and critical comment. *Class No: 785.19(03)*

Chamber Music

[1980]
COBBETT, W.W., *ed.* Cyclopedic survey of chamber music. 2nd ed. London, OUP, 1963. 3v.

First published 1929-39 (2v.).

V.1-2 (A-H, I-Z) are a reprint of the original ed., with its signed analyses of all important works in the repertoire, plus numerous music examples and lists of works, with publishers. Biographical entries are fairly full (*e.g.* J.S. Bach: v.1, p.81-111; 48 music examples; list of chamber music works).

V.3 (ix, 211p.) consists of updating surveys: 'European

....(contd.)

chamber music since 1929' (p.1-81) - 'Chamber music in Britain since 1929' (p.82-111) - 'Russian chamber music (p.123-51) - 'Chamber music in America' (p.152-93). Bibliography, p.194-200. Additions and corrections to dates in v.1-2, compiled by N. Slonimsky, p.201-9.

The standard work, being the only comprehensive survey of its field. *Class No:* 785.7

Musical Instruments

[1981]
REMNANT, M. Musical instruments: an illustrated history from antiquity to the present. London, Batsford, 1990. 295p. illus. ISBN: 0713451696.

Ten chapters covering families of instruments, and a final chapter on orchestration. A useful survey with 240 photographs. *Class No:* 786/789

[1982]
SADIE, S., *ed.* **New Grove dictionary of musical instruments.** London, Macmillan, 1984. 3v., illus. ISBN: 0333378784.

Based on *New Grove* but with some significant revisions. Signed articles with bibliographies, illustrations and musical examples, cover Western instruments, makers, modern instruments, performing practice, and non-Western, and folk instruments. *Class No:* 786/789

Sound Recordings (Discography)

[1983]
CD guide. Peterborough NH, WGE Pub. Inc., 1989-.

Two issues pa. Various previous titles (*Green CD guide* etc.) and frequencies.

Some 26,000 titles per issue. Basic data given, and a valuable link to reviews of the recordings in this publication and other WGE publications. Performance & sound quality graded 1-10. *Class No:* 789.90

[1984]
—**CD guide optical edition.** Peterborough, NH, WGE Publishing, 1990-. 1CD.

Issued quarterly.

A CD-ROM version of a guide to all known music CDs worldwide. Contains information currently on over 40,000 titles; can be searched by title, composer, artist, record, label, CD number. Includes full-text reviews of over 4,000 items from standard sources, and 10,000 sound and performance ratings. *Class No:* 789.90

[1985]
The Classical catalogue: the most complete listing of currently available recordings on CD, LP, Cassette, VHS, Laserdisc, and DAT. Harrow, Middx., General Gramophone Publications. 711p. ISSN: 09615237.

Master Editions published in December and June; 10 monthly supplements are issued between these Editions.

Regarded as an outstanding and authoritative source. Subdivided into 6 indexes: composers, artist, opera, concert, video cassette & Laserdisc, Digital Audio Tape. The first section is further divided into orchestral, chamber, instrumental, vocal & choral, stage works. Full details are given in each entry, including record company, manufactuers' code etc., and date of review in the *Gramophone* magazine. Index of manufacturers' names, labels, distributors, classical nicknames, abbreviations. *Class No:* 789.90

[1986]
MUSIC MASTER. Master catalogue. Humphries, J., *ed.* London, Music Master/Harrap. 1856p.

First published 1974. Annual. Supplements issued monthly, & quarterly cumulations.

....(contd.)

Complete list of all singles, albums, cassettes, CDs and music videos available from British companies. A series of substantial paperback derivatives is also published, including-

Heavy metal catalogue.
Music on video.
Films & shows.
Singles catalogue.
Jazz catalogue.
Tracks catalogue.
CD catalogue.
Record catalogue.
British pop singles 1975-1984 (1985).
Country music catalogue.
Labels list. *Class No:* 789.90

[1987]
The Penguin guide to compact discs. Greenfield, E. *and* Layton, R. *and* March, I. London, Penguin Books, 1990. xix,1366p. ISBN: 0140468870.

Lists all recordings currently available with advice on interpretation, performance, recording quality, value for money. Composer arrangement with narrative discussion including the listings with manufacturers' catalogue numbers, star rating symbol. Sections also cover orchestral concerts, instrumental recitals, vocal & choral collections. *Class No:* 789.90

[1988]
—**The Penguin guide to compact discs and cassettes, Yearbook** 1991/92. Greenfield, E. *and* Layton, R. *and* March, I. London, Penguin Books, 1991. xvii,615p. ISBN: 0140153667.

Follows the pattern of the base volume above; comprehensive coverage of new releases, showing the enormous growth in CD production. From 1992/3 the yearbook will be issued in two volumes, of which one will concentrate on bargain price recordings. *Class No:* 789.90

[1989]
Schwann CD. Chatsworth CA, ABC Consumer Magazines Inc, 1985-.

Successor to the *Schwann Catalog* first issued in the early 1950s; from 1985-89 titled the *Schwann Compact Disc Catalog.* Issued monthly; a separately-published quarterly *Schwann Record & Tape Guide: Super Schwann* still appears for non-CD productions.

Currently lists some 20,000 items in each issue, divided by broad category (composers, pop/rock, jazz, musicals/movies/TV shows, etc.). Date of first listing given, and expanded entries for new releases. Covers CDs, 3-inch CDs, LPs, cassettes, videodiscs, and digital audio tapes (DAT). *Class No:* 789.90

Opera

[1990]
GÄNZL, K. The Blackwell guide to the musical theatre on record. Oxford, Blackwell, 1990. 556p. ISBN: 0631165177.

International coverage (British, US, French, Austrian, German recordings) and reliable in historical background. Written as a buyer's guide, comparing available recordings and suggesting a core collection. 'Highly recommended' (*Library Journal*, October 15, 1990, p.80). *Class No:* 789.90:782

Jazz

[1991]
KERNFELD, B., *ed.* **Blackwell guide to recorded jazz.** Oxford, Blackwell, 1991. 320p. ISBN: 0631171649.
Details of 150 outstanding performances/recordings of all styles, and periods, that would represent a basis for a comprehensive collection. Selection made by internationally renowned specialists. *Class No:* 789.90:785.16

[1992]
OLIVER, P., *ed.* **Blackwell guide to blues records.** Oxford, Blackwell, 1989. xiii,347p. ISBN: 0631165169.
Arranged in 12 chapters with an introduction to each, and discography giving details and annotation. Bibliography (p.321-3) and index. *Class No:* 789.90:785.16

Rock Music

[1993]
HOUNSOME, T. New rock records: a collectors' directory of rock albums and musicians. 3rd ed. Poole, Dorset, New York: Blandford Press, 1987. xii, 738p. ISBN: 0713719524.
First published as *Rockmaster* 1978, and as *Rockrecord* 1979.
Covers 45,000 albums, 7,500 bands, and indexes names of 80,000 musicians. Alphabetical arrangement by group name; includes only basic data, no commentary. *Class No:* 789.90:785.19

79 Entertainment & Leisure

Leisure

Dictionaries

[1994]
SMITH, S.L.J. **Dictionary of concepts in recreation and leisure studies.** Westport, CT, Greenwood Press, 1990. 372p. ISBN: 0313252629.

Definition of terms such as 'national park', 'environment', 'holiday', 'wilderness'; entries discuss historical development of the term, different current opinions, suggested standard definition, and a bibliography usually of 10-30 scholarly sources. Cross-references; index. *Class No:* 790(038)

Great Britain

[1995]
Leisure services yearbook. 1991/92. Brett, M., *ed.* Harlow, Longmans, 1991. 364p. ISBN: 0582071593.

Sections cover: Arts and entertainment - national & regional organizations; leisure provision, arts centres, music, drama, film/video. Sport - national & regional. Conservation & the Countryside. Tourism. Professional associations/institutes. Index. *Class No:* 790(410)

Performing Arts

Awards & Prizes

[1996]
KAPLAN, M., *ed.* **Variety presents:** the complete book of major US show business awards. New York, Garland, 1985. 564p., illus. ISBN: 0824089197.

Earlier version 1982.

Lists winners of all categories (over 4,000) of Oscars 1927-83, Emmys 1948-83, Tonys 1947-83, Grammys 1958-83, Pulitzer Prize Plays 1917-83. Index of winners and nominees, titles. *Class No:* 791/793(079.2)

Biographies

[1997]
Contemporary theatre, film and television. O'Donnell, M.M., *ed.* Detroit, Gale Research, 1983-. 522p.,illus.(vol.8). ISBN: 0810320711, vol.8. ISSN: 074906 4x.

Until 1981 titled *Who's who in the Theatre,* issued in 17 editions from 1912. *CTFT* volumes 1-7 remain in print.

Biographical and career information on currently popular figures, including performers, directors, writers, producers, designers, managers, choreographers, technicians, composers, dancers, critics. Each volume contains about 700 entries, about one third of which have a photograph. Heavy American emphasis.

Vol.6. contained a cumulative index for the series to that time and the seventeen editions of the previous title. *Class No:* 791/793(092)

[1998]
LA BEAU, T., *ed.* **Theatre, film and television biographies master index:** a consolidated guide to over 100,000 biographical sketches of persons living and dead, as they appear in over 40 of the principal biographical dictionaries devoted to the theatre, film and television. Detroit, Gale, 1979. xii,477p.

Entries, A.E. ... Stefan Zweig. Coverage: actors, actresses, directors, filmmakers, playwrights, lyricists, cinematographers, designers and others involved in these performing arts. Sources: over 40 biographical dictionaries and directories (largely US) devoted to the stage, screen, opera, popular music, radio and TV. *Class No:* 791/793(092)

Great Britain

[1999]
British performing arts yearbook, 1991. Barbour, S., *ed.* London, Rhinegold Publishing, 1990. 964p. ISBN: 0946890315. ISSN: 09515208.

Covers England, Scotland, Wales, Isle of Man, Channel Islands, Northern Ireland & Irish Republic. Details of venues (addresses etc., status, policy, administration, facilities, technical data, studios etc.) for London, and regionally (p.1-528) with indexes by town, type of venue, audience capacity. Directory of companies and individual performers, management, orchestras, arts festivals, arts councils, suppliers and services, agents. *Class No:* 791/793(410)

Broadcasting & Radio

[2000]
BARNOUW, E.A. **A History of broadcasting in the United States.** Oxford, OUP, 1966-85. 3v., illus. ISBN: 0195004744, v.1; 0195004752, v.2; 0195012593, v.3.

1. *A tower in Babel.* 1966. 344p.
2. *The golden web.* 1985. 398p.
3. *The image empire.* 1971. 402p.

Traces in v.1 the pre-1920 development of radio, its role in World War I and progress in the 1920s, up to the Depression of 1929. V.2 continues up to the 1950s, concentrating on the major broadcasting networks. V.3 covering 1953-69, concentrates 'on the emergence of television as a dominant force' (*RSR,*v.9, no.3,July/September 1981,p.37). Each volume has a bibliography and index. *Class No:* 791.096

[2001]
BRIGGS, A. **The History of broadcasting in the United Kingdom.** Oxford, OUP, 1961-79. 4v., illus.

1. *The birth of broadcasting.* 1961. xiii, 425p.
2. *The golden age of wireless.* 1965. xvi, 688p.
3. *The war of words.* 1970. xviii, [i], 766p.
4. *Sound and vision.* 1979. xiv, 1062p.

....(contd.)
'I have had the fullest access to all surviving archives' (*Preface*, v.1). V.1 covers the period up to 1926, when the BBC was formed; numerous footnote references; 50 illus., 'Bibliographical note', p.407-9. V.2: 1927-39; 54 illus.; 'Bibliographical note', p.660-3. V.3 is a detailed, critical and well-documented account; 24 plates; 'Bibliographical note', p.727-32. V.4 reaches the passing of the Independent Television Act, 1955; 7 sections: 1. News, views and perspectives - 2. Politics - 3. Drama, features and variety - 4. Sounds of music - 5. Religion - 6. Education - 7. Sport. Numerous footnote references; 'Bibliographical note', p.1025-31. Each volume has its own analytical index.

An authoritative account, relating the history of broadcasting to that of British society during the period. 'Historians working on the cultural and political life after the Second World War will find it [v.4] to be a marvellously well-ordered source of indispensable information' (*TLS*, no.4001, 23 November 1979, p.30). *Class No:* 791.096

[2002]
MACDONALD, B. **Broadcasting in the United Kingdom:** a guide to information sources. London, Mansell, 1988. 266p. ISBN: 0720119626.

Excellent, comprehensive survey; introductory history of broadcasting, then structure & organizations, including government bodies, councils, trade unions, professional associations, audience research groups, educational facilities, awards, festivals. Primary sources examined (p.128-154); printed & electronic sources (p.156-200) by category (dictionaries, periodicals, abstracts, online etc., etc.) each with annotations. Research sources; institutional sources (archives, libraries, museums). Further reading sections throughout; addresses quoted. Index. *Class No:* 791.096

Television

[2003]
HALLIWELL, L. **Halliwell's television companion.** 3rd ed. London, Grafton, 1986. 941p., illus. ISBN: 0246128380.

12,000 entries list A/Z actors, producers, writers, directors, technical terms, organizations, US series, miniseries, TV movies, and 'most British programmes worth remembering'. Entries for people are very brief; film & series entries give date, plot summary, cast, review quote. *Class No:* 791.097

Yearbooks & Directories

[2004]
BRITISH FILM INSTITUTE. **Film and television handbook, 1991.** London, BFI, 1990. 304p., illus. ISBN: 0851702775. Annual.

Reviews UK cinema 1989-90, examining production, distribution, exhibition, British films, TV programmes. Directory section p.68-304 is arranged by category and includes archives & libraries, awards, bookshops, cinemas, courses, festivals, laboratories, publications, studios, etc., etc. Excellent, comprehensive publication. *Class No:* 791.097(058)

[2005]
International television and video almanac 1990. Klain, J., *ed.* 35th ed. New York, Quigley Publishing 1990. 748p. ISBN: 0900610433. ISSN: 05390761. Annual.

Extensive subject list (p.6A-18A) leads to television year in review, statistics, awards, festivals, biographies (p.1-355) of film & TV personalities (*c*.5,000 entries) services; television is covered (p.388-618) through history, companies, programmes, stations, cable, advertising agencies, organizations, UK & Ireland industry, world

....(contd.)
market; home video (p.620-748) covers statistics, companies, retailers, consumer & trade publications, services, market & distributors. *Class No:* 791.097(058)

Biographies

[2006]
Who's who on television. 5th ed. London, Boxtree & ITV Publications, 1990. 224p., illus. ISBN: 1852831057.

Brief entries give credits and photograph for about 1,000 current names. 'Unforgetables' section lists great names no longer performing. Details of TV companies, agents, fan clubs. *Class No:* 791.097(092)

Great Britain

[2007]
SENDALL, B. *and* POTTER, J. **Independent television in Britain.** London, Macmillan, 1982-1990. 418,429,352,428p. (4v.). ISBN: 0333309413, v.1; 0333309421, v.2; 0333301956, v.3; 0333455436, v.4.

Volume 1 (Sendall): Origin & foundation, 1946-62.
Volume 2 (Sendall): Expansion & change, 1958-68.
Volume 3 (Potter): Politics & control, 1968-80.
Volume 4 (Potter): Companies and programmes, 1968-80.
The definitive history of independent TV; scholarly and comprehensive, with many references, and appendices giving the full texts of key documents etc. Fully indexed. Bibliography in vol. 4 (p.385-403) covers 1962-80. *Class No:* 791.097(410)

Films & Videos

[2008]
Bowker's Complete video directory 1990. Volume one: entertainment; volume two: education/special interest. New York, Bowker, 1990. 2,480p.(2v). ISBN: 0835228916.

Mid-year supplement issued. Annual publication of the main volumes is planned. Partially based on the earlier *Home Video Directory*.

41,000 titles listed in volume one; second volume covering educational and special-interest videos contains a further 20,000 items. Alphabetical arrangement with annotation, genre, date, awards, plot summary, running time, cast, director, price and availability etc. Several indexes, including cast names, director, genre, series, format. Addresses of manufacturers and distributors. *Class No:* 791.4

[2009]
ELLIOTT, J. **Elliott's Guide to films on video.** 2nd ed. London, Boxtree, 1991. ISBN: 1852831421.

Lists 10,000 feature films currently available on video; gives plot synopsis, cast list, production date, running time, star rating, format. *Class No:* 791.4

[2010]
MALTIN, L., *ed.* **TV movies and video guide, 1992.** New York, Signet/Penguin, 1991. xiii,1487p. ISBN: 0140158626. Annual.

18,500 brief entries by title, new and old, with details of director, cast, plot, date, running time, and 'capsule review'. Symbol indicates availability on videocassette; star-rating feature. Double column pages, small typeface. *Class No:* 791.4

Encyclopaedias & Dictionaries

[2011]
ALLAN, E., *ed.* **A Guide to world cinema:** covering 7,200 films of 1950-1984 including capsule reviews and stills from the programmes of the NFT, London. London, Whittet Books, 1985. vi, 682p. ISBN: 0905483332.
Major films of UK, US, major European countries, Japan, Australia, etc. All types of film are included with basic data and brief commentary. Title arrangement with director index. *Class No:* 791.4(03)

[2012]
HALLIWELL, L. Halliwell's film guide. Walker, J., *ed.* 8th ed. London, Harper Collins, 1991. xi,1234p. illus. ISBN: 0246137681.
First published 1977.
17,000 films are included (1,000 new to this edition) arranged A/Z by titles, giving country of origin, year of release, running time, b & w/colour, production credit, alternative titles, synopsis, assessment, credits for writer, director, photographer, music. Principal cast listed; brief review quote for many entries; note on awards nominations. Lists of alternative titles, translated titles. Illustrations are film stills, but few in number. *Class No:* 791.4(03)

[2013]
HALLIWELL, L. Halliwell's filmgoer's and video viewer's companion. 9th ed. London, Grafton, 1988. 800p. ISBN: 0246133228.
Incorporates *Movie Quiz* and *Book of Quotes.* Also paperback edition (Paladin, 1989; 0586088776).
General encyclopaedic guide to films; thorough, updated and extended. A/Z listing of actors, actresses, directors, scriptwriters, editors, cinematographers, studios, themes, key films, technical terms. Symbols in the text indicate complete filmographies, outstanding figures, quotations. *Class No:* 791.4(03)

[2014]
LYON, C. *and* **VINSON, J.,** *eds.* **International dictionary of films and filmmakers.** Chicago, St. James' Press, 1984-1988. 5vols. ISBN: 091228904x, v.1; 0912289058, v.2; 0912289082, v.3; 0912289090, v.4; 0912289864, v.5.
Also issued in the UK as the *Macmillan Dictionary of Films and Filmmakers.*
Scholarly team of advisers, consistent format; international but mainly western world. First volume examines 490 significant films, second directors and filmmakers, third actors and actresses, fourth writers and production arts; fifth volume is title index. 'Especially valuable for its bibliographic citations and its extensive filmographies' (*Reference Books Bulletin* August 1988).
2nd. ed. of vol.1, edited by N. Thomas (1990) examines 650 films. Improved format, especially in arrangement of bibliographies. Now provides cross-references to foreign titles. 'Major advance over the first edition, but it unaccountably omits the criteria for inclusion'. (*Library Journal* Sept 1. 1990. p.214). *Class No:* 791.4(03)

[2015]
NASH, J. *and* **ROSS, S.R.,** *eds.* **Motion picture guide.** Chicago, Cine Books, 1985-1987. 12 vols. ISBN: 0933997000.
Outstanding reference work on English language films, including details of duration, cast, synopsis, critical evaluation, and reviews. Several excellent indexes. Over 25,000 entries. Ten volumes of text, and two index volumes; continued by *Motion Picture Guide Annual.* *Class No:* 791.4(03)

[2016]
—NASH, J. *and* ROSS, S.R. Motion picture guide 1990 annual: (the films of 1989). Evanston, Ill., Cinebooks, 1990. 799p., illus. ISBN: 0933997175.
Update of the *Motion Picture Guide.* UK distributor Bowker-Saur.
1989 film reviews (p.1-340), people to watch, obituaries, awards, index of films by country, name index. Fifth in the annual series designed to continue the original work. *Class No:* 791.4(03)

Dictionaries

[2017]
KONIGSBERG, I. The Complete film dictionary. London, Bloomsbury, 1988. 432p. ISBN: 0747503028.
Comprehensive coverage of technical terms in filmmaking; genres, thematic topics, sources. *Class No:* 791.4(038)

Reviews & Abstracts

[2018]
MILNE, T., *ed.* **Time Out film guide.** 2nd ed. London, Penguin Books, 1991. 767p. ISBN: 0140145923.
Arranged A/Z by title giving brief details of director, cast, running time, video availability. Brief signed review. Appendices by genre (Action & adventure, children's, comedies, documentaries, epics, fantasy, film noir, gangster, historical & costume, horror, musicals, S.F. thrillers, war, westerns) list titles and function as a category index. Also appendices of key foreign films, index of directors, general subject index. *Class No:* 791.4(048)

Biographies

[2019]
Annual index to motion picture credits. Woodward, B., *ed.* Beverley Hills, Academy of Motion Picture Arts & Sciences, 1988. 374p. ISBN: 0942102088. ISSN: 01635123.
Issued annually, from mid-1930s; until 1978 titled *Screen Achievements Record Bulletin.*
1987 volume records 15,000 credits to 379 films open to entry for Academy Awards. 'Most reliable and complete source of information' (*Booklist,* Feb 1. 1989, p.922) especially for technical staff. Index to annual volumes 1976-87. *Class No:* 791.4(092)

[2020]
FILMER, A.J. *and* **GOLAY, A. Harrap's Book of film directors and their films.** London, Harrap, 1989. 491p. ISBN: 0245549420.
UK & US figures, also foreign names if they have made films in English. Lists names A/Z with simple list of film titles arranged by date. Indicates Oscar awards. Title index p.283-491. Contains about 3,300 names, and indexes 26,000 films. *Class No:* 791.4(092)

Great Britain

[2021]
British national film and video catalogue. London, British Film Institute, 1963-. £48pa.
Original title *British National film catalogue.* Issued quarterly with annual cumulations. 1963-1983 also available on microfilm.
Details of all films and videos made available for non-theatrical loan or, if British, loan or sale in the UK. Includes educational and training films, independent productions, documentaries, television programmes, & feature films. Arranged by subject using UDC, with A/Z index. Full details given including plot summary/contents note, intended audience. Annual volume also includes a

....(contd.)
production index (sponsors, directors, editors, production companies addresses).

Recent annual volumes contain *c*.3,500 items, of which 80% are video. Videodiscs now included also. *Class No:* 791.4(410)

Film Libraries

[2022]
THORPE, F., *ed.* **International directory of film and TV documentation centres.** 3rd ed. Chicago, St. James Press, 1988. ISBN: 0912289295.

Originally a publication of FIAF (International Federation of Film Archives).

Describes 104 sources worldwide with addresses, hours, access, size, facilities, holdings summary. Variable in data provided. *Class No:* 791.4:061:026/027

Film Festivals

[2023]
Directory of international film and video festivals 1991 and 1992. London, British Film Institute in association with the British Council, 1991. 160p. ISBN: 0851702864.

Published biennially.

Lists over 300 festivals, with details of participation. Arranged in country order, with indexes by category, and chronologically. *Class No:* 791.4:061.7

Genres of Films

Comedy films

[2024]
LANGMAN, L. **Encyclopedia of American film comedy.** New York, Garland, 1988. 639p. ISBN: 0824084969.

Wide coverage of history, personalities, and entries for 150 films 1912-1984 which exemplify American humour. Filmography after each entry. No full index. *Class No:* 791.43.0COM

Horror films

[2025]
HARDY, P., *ed.* **Encyclopedia of horror movies.** New York, Harper, 1986. xiii, 408p. ISBN: 0060550503.

Compiled with British Film Institute assistance; international coverage. Chronological arrangement with commentary. *Class No:* 791.43.0HOR

Musicals

[2026]
GREEN, S. **Encyclopedia of the musical film.** New ed. New York, OUP, 1988. 352p. ISBN: 0195054210.

Entries, A-Z, p.3-319. 'Wizard of Oz, The'; $2\frac{3}{4}$ columns (credits, cast, songs, history and synopsis, TV repeat, 2 references). 'Judy Garland': $1\frac{1}{2}$ columns, with over $\frac{1}{2}$p. list of parts played. 'Succinct information regarding the musical screen's most prominent individuals, productions, and songs. Though emphasis is on Hollywood output (including feature-length cartoons), British musical films and selected original television musicals are also covered' (*Preface*). *Class No:* 791.43.0MUS

Science fiction

[2027]
FULTON, R. **The Encyclopedia of TV science fiction.** London, ITV/Boxtree, 1990. 593p. ISBN: 1852832770.

250 entries A/Z cover series, individual plays, and cartoons. Details of cast, director, technical staff, plot, historical note. Covers UK & US work, and some other English-language material. Chronological table at end. *Class No:* 791.43.0SCI

Westerns

[2028]
BUSCOMBE, E., *ed.* **The BFI Companion to the Western.** New ed. London, Deutsch, 1990. 432p. ISBN: 0233983325.

In addition to lists of films, provides excellent biographical and thematic essays, filmographies for actors, directors, scriptwriters etc., and an extensive historical background. *Class No:* 791.43.0WES

Puppets

[2029]
CURRELL, D. **Complete book of puppet theatre.** London, Black, 1986. 352p.,illus. ISBN: 0713624299.

Revised and expanded edition of the *Complete Book of Puppetry.*

Excellent all-round introduction, illustrated with photographs, performance diagrams etc. Suitable for novices, teachers, and experienced practitioners. *Class No:* 791.5

Histories

[2030]
SPEAIGHT, G. **The History of the puppet theatre.** 2nd ed. London, Hale, 1990. 366p.

Ten chapters beginning with medieval mimes and tracing the history to the present day revival. Appendices list puppet shows in England, and plays performed by puppeteers in England. Extensive notes and references p.271-312. Index. *Class No:* 791.5(091)

Funfairs etc.

[2031]
Showman's directory 1990. 22nd ed. Godalming, Surrey, S. & J. Lance Publications, 1990. 423p. ISBN: 0946509255.

Directory of UK contractors and services, entertainment, etc. Covers all types of public events - concerts, fun fairs, car rallies, country shows. Alphabetical index and chronological list of 1990 shows, rallies, art shows, festivals, dog shows, Press, TV & radio contacts. Societies & organizations. *Class No:* 791.7

Circuses

[2032]
SPEAIGHT, G. **A History of the circus.** London, Tantivy Press, 1980. 216p., illus.

6 parts (37 chapters); 1. The origins of circus - 2. The early years - 3. The circus in Britain in the 19th century - 4. The circus in America - 5. The golden age of the circus in Europe - 6. The circus in the 20th century. Appendix: Circus buildings in London, New York and Paris. Chapter notes, p.199-210. Non-analytical index of performers and proprietors. Defines circus as 'that entertainment of human bodily skills and trained animals that is presented in a ring of approximately 13 metres in diameter, with an audience grouped all around it' (*Introduction*). Russian circus: only 1 column. *Class No:* 791.83

792 Theatre

Encyclopaedias & Dictionaries

[2033]
BANHAM, M., *ed.* **The Cambridge guide to world theatre.**
Cambridge, CUP, 1989. 1104p. ISBN: 0521265959.
Encyclopaedic and international with bibliographies for
major entries, and extensive cross referencing. Alphabetical
arrangement covering history, stage, television, actors,
directors etc. All entries signed. 'Enthusiastically
recommended' (*Choice*, June 1989). *Class No: 792.0(03)*

[2034]
The Oxford companion to the theatre. Hartnoll, P., *ed.* 4th
ed. Oxford, OUP, 1983. x,934p.,illus. ISBN: 0192115464.
First published 1951.
International in scope. 87 contributors. Entries, Abbey,
Henry Eugene ... Zweig. Stefan. 'Theatre buildings'; 6
columns; 'Italy'; 15 cols; 'Comédie Française': 1 col.;
'Society for Theatre Research': ½col.; 'Broadway Theatre,
New York': 1 col.; 'Theatre in the Round': 1 col.; 'Robson
Flora': nearly 1 col. No entry made under 'Periodicals', and
bibliographies are reserved for the appended, unannotated
'A guide to further reading', p.917-32 (reference works;
general histories; Great Britain; Ireland; Europe; US; Asia;
Dramatic forms; Technique of stagecraft; Acting; Theatre
criticism). 96 plates. 'Miss Hartnoll is to be congratulated
on the unabated excellence of the work she first launched
in 1951' (*British book news*, January 1984. p.44). *Class
No: 792.0(03)*

[2035]
THOMSON, P. and SALGADO, G. **Everyman companion to
the theatre.** London, Dent, 1985. 458p. ISBN: 0460044249.
Brief alphabetically-arranged entries, including playwrights,
actors, actresses, directors, buildings, companies, drama
genres and movements. Accurate, concise source. *Class No:
792.0(03)*

Handbooks & Manuals

[2036]
TURNER, B., *ed.* **The Actor's handbook, 1989.** London,
Bloomsbury, 1989. 400p. ISBN: 0747502498.
Lists drama schools, agents, theatres, critics, associations;
useful, reasonably priced compilation. *Class No: 792.0(035)*

Dictionaries

[2037]
HODGSON, T. **The Batsford dictionary of drama.** London,
Batsford; New York, New Amsterdam Books, 1988.
432p.,illus. ISBN: 0713446935.
US title is *The Drama dictionary.*
'The main intention ... is to provide useful working
definitions of terms used in the theatre and by theatre
critics. It does not aim to provide exhaustive information
about dramatists, plays, theatre companies and theatre
buildings' (*Preface*). The 1,300 entries, arranged A-Z, are
mainly brief (few run to a full page) and cover forms of
drama, kinds of stage, acting terms, dramatic movements
and styles, character types and dramatic structure. Entries
are fully cross-referenced and most include suggestions for
further reading, although there is no separate bibliography.
31 line drawings. *Class No: 792.0(038)*

[2038]
TRAPIDO, J., *and others.* **An International dictionary of
theatre language.** Westport, Conn., Greenwood Press, 1985.
xxxvi,1032p. ISBN: 0313229805.
Discusses 15,000 terms (English and foreign) from all
periods. Abundant cross-references, and a good
bibliography. *Class No: 792.0(038)*

Quotations

[2039]
SNELL, G. **The Book of theatre quotes:** notes, quotes and
anecdotes of the stage. London, Angus & Robertson, 1982.
ix,195p.,illus.
Entries under 88 headings. Abbey Theatre ... W.B. Yeats.
Each quotation (sometimes lengthy) has introductory
remarks in bold. Appended credits. Detailed non-analytical
index. Well illustrated. *Class No: 792.0(082.2)*

Great Britain

Yearbooks & Directories

[2040]
British alternative theatre directory, 1990/91.
McGillivray, D., *ed.* London, Conway McGillivray, 1990.
300p.,illus. ISBN: 0951228331. ISSN: 01425218.
First published 1979.
Contents: Alternative theatre companies - Young people's
theatre - Puppet companies (data on each include policy;
origins; subsidy; personnel; tours; audiences; equipment;
productions; other activities; contact) - Venues (London,
England, Scotland, Wales) - Arts Council and regional
associations - Theatre organizations - National centres of
the International Theatre Institute - Principal national
festivals. Index to advertisers and photographs; Index to
companies. Map and list of London fringe theatres.

....*(contd.)*

Very full and clear details are provided, and coverage now extends to cabaret venues, film & video facilities. *Class No:* 792.0(410)(058)

[2041]
British theatre directory 1990. Holland, A., *ed.* 18th ed. London, Richmond House, 1989. 547p. ISBN: 187032305x. ISSN: 03064107.

First published 1972.

Contents include details of theatres in London and provinces, concert venues, amateur theatres, arts centres (all with address, phone number, administration details, technical facilities), municipal arts and leisure departments, data on production companies, ballet & opera companies, orchestras, puppet theatres, circus etc.; lists of agents by speciality, directory of book and journal publishers, training & education facilities, advertisers' index. *Class No:* 792.0(410)(058)

[2042]
British theatre yearbook, 1990. Lemmon, D., *ed.* 2nd ed. London, Helm, 1990. 376p.,illus. ISBN: 0747020167.

Divided into 6 main sections: theatres in London, National Theatre, Royal Shakespeare Company, outer-London theatres, regional, touring companies. Details of productions given with cast lists, reviews. Index of plays. First edition criticised as 'patchy' (*Refer* 5(4) Autumn 1989). *Class No:* 792.0(410)(058)

Eire

[2043]
FITZ-SIMONS, C. The Irish theatre. London, Thames & Hudson, 1983. 202p.,illus. ISBN: 0500013004.

Unique picture of theatre history from the Middle Ages to the contemporary Dublin scene. *Class No:* 792.0(417)

Canada

[2044]
The Oxford companion to Canadian theatre. Benson, E. *and* Conolly, L.W., *eds.* Oxford, OUP, 1990. 662p.,illus. ISBN: 0195406729.

703 signed articles on genres, theatres, companies, biographies of dramatists, directors, designers and major plays. Lengthy section (25,000 words) devoted to history of drama in English & French speaking Canada. General index of names; cross-references; bibliographies follow many entries. *Class No:* 792.0(71)

USA

[2045]
BORDMAN, G. The Oxford companion to American theatre. Oxford, OUP, 1985. 734p. ISBN: 0195034430.

Biographies of authors, performers, composers, producers, directors etc., and forms of presentation. Good coverage of individual key works, and details of societies, organizations, journals etc. *Class No:* 792.0(73)

[2046]
—BORDMAN, G. The Concise Oxford companion to American theatre. Oxford, OUP, 1987. 448p. ISBN: 0195051211.

Based on the *Oxford Companion to American theatre* (1985). *Class No:* 792.0(73)

[2047]
BRONNER, E.J. The Encyclopedia of the American theatre, 1900-1975. London, Tantivy Press/New York, Barnes, 1980. 659p.,illus.

Data on over 2,000 plays produced on- and off-

....*(contd.)*

Broadway, 1900-75. The plays were written/adapted by American or Anglo-American authors. Titles A-Z, with appraisals. Excludes musicals. Appendices: 1. Theatre calendar (notable premières of the century: by months; by titles; leading perfomers); 2. Débuts: actors; 3. Débuts: playwrights; 4. The golden 100 ... 5. Statistical record (Broadway productions); 6. Awards (Pulitzer Prizes, etc.). Non-analytical index, p.587-659. *Class No:* 792.0(73)

Libraries

Great Britain

[2048]
HOWARD, D., *comp.* Directory of theatre resources: a guide to research collections and information services. 2nd ed. London, Library Association ISG and Society for Theatre Research, 1986. 144p. ISBN: 0946347085.

Three hundred entries cover UK libraries of all types, and societies and associations. Basic data and brief descriptions; excellent layout, and good indexes. *Class No:* 792.0:061:026/027(410)

America — North

[2049]
RACHOW, L.A., *ed.* Theatre and performing arts collections. New York, Haworth Press, 1981. 166p. ISBN: 091772447x.

Confined to North American collections, but covering holdings related to all countries. Includes substantial collections on British theatre. *Class No:* 792.0:061:026/027(71+73)

Amateur Theatre

[2050]
Amateur theatre yearbook 1989-90, incorporating community theatre and training. Vance, C., *ed. and* Hackworth-Young, J., *comp.* St. Albans, Herts., Platform Publications, 1989. ISBN: 0951499106.

First edition of a proposed regular series.

Geographical listing of UK amateur theatre, community theatre, and theatrical training facilities. Details of publishers & publications for the performing arts, specialist bookshops, theatrical suppliers, back-up services etc. *Class No:* 792.077

Musical Theatre

USA

[2051]
BLOOM, K. Broadway: an encyclopedic guide to the history, people and places of Times Square. Oxford, Facts on File, 1990. 432p., illus. ISBN: 0816012490.

Introductory history, then brief entries covering playwrights, composers, actors, producers, directors, restaurants, theatres (concise history of each one), jargon & slang, advertising etc. 'Essential for theatre collections' (*Library Journal*, November 1, 1990. p.80). *Class No:* 792.5(73)

[2052]
BORDMAN, G. American musical theatre: a chronicle. Oxford, Univ. Press, 1979. viii,749p. ISBN: 0195023560.

11 chapters. 1. Prologue: origins to 1866 ... 6. The birth of the modern musical, 1914-1921 ... 8. The golden age of the American musical, 1924-27 ... 10. The American musical as a conscious art form, 1942-1965 - 11. Epilogue: exhaustion and the search for new directions, 1965-1978. For each musical: plot synopses; physical production, and principal statistics; biographies of actors, songwriters,

....(contd.)
librettists and producers. Examples of lyrics and dialogue. Appendix, - adjunct to index of shows and sources. Non-analytical indexes of shows and sources, songs and people. *Class No:* 792.5(73)

Music Hall & Pantomime

Great Britain

[2053]
BUSBY, R. **British music hall:** an illustrated who's who from 1880 to the present day. London, Elek, 1976. 191p.,illus.
Who's who, A/Z, p.15-191. 'Marie Lloyd': 1¾p., 1 port.; 'Tony Hancock': 2 cols., 1 port. Includes entries for groups (*e.g.*, Morecambe and Wise) and families. Preceded by 'Introduction: From pleasure gardens to variety', and list of terms. Fully illustrated. *Class No:* 792.7(410)

Ballet

Encyclopaedias & Dictionaries

[2054]
BALANCHINE, G. *and* MASON, F. **Balanchine's festival of ballet.** London, W.H. Allen, 1978. xxv,838p.
First published 1954, as *Balanchine's Complete stories of the great ballets;* US revised edition under this title issued by Doubleday, 1977.
Part 1: 'Stories of the great ballets': scene-by-scene stories of 401 classic and contemporary ballets, A-Z by title. Parts 2-9: 2. How to enjoy a ballet - 3. A brief history of the ballet - 4. Chronology of significant events in the history of the ballet ... 6. Ballet for young children - 7. Careers in ballet - 8. Notes and comments on dancers, dancing and choreography - 9. Glossary (with line-drawings). Detailed, analytical index, p.689-805. 79 photographs. *Class No:* 792.8(03)

[2055]
KOEGLER, H. **The Concise Oxford dictionary of ballet.** 2nd ed. Oxford, OUP, 1982. 459p. ISBN: 0193113252.
Original German edition *Friedrichs Ballettlexikon* 1972.
5,000 entries covering all aspects of ballet over 400 years: dancers, choreographers, designers, ballets, theatres, schools, companies, and technical terms. Small print; heavily abbreviated. *Class No:* 792.8(03)

[2056]
ROBERTSON, A. *and* HUTERA, D. **Dance handbook.** Boston, G.K. Hall, 1990. 278p., illus. ISBN: 081619095x.
Confined to Western theatrical dance, the handbook contains entries for 200 major individuals, companies, choreographers, ballet and other dance works, arranged in chronological sections - romantic ballet, classical ballet, Ballets Russes, birth of modern dance, modern ballet, the dance explosion alternatives. Significance of items is explained, and links with related works. Sections contain glossaries, bibliographies, directories of journals, festivals etc. Indexes to persons, films, performances, terms. *Class No:* 792.8(03)

Dictionaries

[2057]
MARA, T. **Language of ballet:** a dictionary. Princeton, Princeton Book Co., 1987. vi, 120p. $18.95. ISBN: 0871271443.
Reprint of the 1966 edition.
Good definitions, particularly of technical terms, are a special feature of this concise, but authoritative volume on ballet terminology. *Class No:* 792.8(038)

Yearbooks & Directories

[2058]
PARRY, J., *ed.* **World ballet and dance 1990-91:** an international yearbook. New York, Dance Books, 1990. 302p. ISBN: 1852730277.
Second publication in the series; four parts comprise: feature articles, dance archives, review of dance around the world, data on dance companies including repertory, associated schools. Contributors are of high calibre. 'International review of dance activities in a single resource ... the editors are to be congratulated' (*Choice* September 1991, p.72). *Class No:* 792.8(058)

Histories

[2059]
BLAND, A. **The Royal Ballet:** the first fifty years. London, Threshold/Sotheby Parke Bernet, 1981. 320p.,illus. ISBN: 0901366110.
Covers both the Royal Opera House and Sadler's Wells Theatre. Contents include A-Z list of dancers (with dates of earliest traceable date of appearance) and choreographers who have worked with either company, plus a chronology of their ballets. Also, each company's repertory, A/Z (data on production, revival, revision and new dancers) and chronology of production, plus an itinerary, conjointly, - providing a virtually complete record of performances. An important source. *Class No:* 792.8(091)

[2060]
STEEN, J. **History of ballet and modern dance.** London, Hamlyn, 1982. 256p.,illus.
Arranged in four country groups: Italy, France, Russia (p.72-98), Great Britain (p.99-129), Australia and Canada - Denmark, Sweden, Finland, Norway - The Netherlands, Belgium - Austria, Germany, Czechoslovakia, Hungary, Poland, with biographical sketches of leading personalities, in each case. 'Modern dance', p.203-39. Chronology, 1480-1982. Non-analytical index. 70 illus., and ports. *Class No:* 792.8(091)

Biographies

[2061]
COHEN-STRATYNER, B.N. **Biographical dictionary of dance.** London, Macmillan/New York, Schirmer, 1982. 970p. ISBN: 0028702603.
Covers Europe and America from sixteenth century onwards; alphabetical listing of performers, choreographers, composers, designers, teachers, etc., giving standard data and career details and key roles. Includes all forms of dance from classical ballet, to variety shows. About 3,000 entries. *Class No:* 792.8(092)

Dancing

[2062]
MOORE, A. **Ballroom dancing.** 9th ed. London, A & C Black, 1986. 324p., illus. ISBN: 0713627948.
First published 1936.
The standard textbook on technique; charts illustrate patterns and foot positions. 'An indispensable work for all dancers and teachers' (*Guardian* obituary of the author, March 9. 1991). Sections cover Quickstep, Waltz, Foxtrot, Tango, competitions, popular dances, novelty dances & games. *Class No:* 793.3

Encyclopaedias & Dictionaries

[2063]
MCDONAGH, D. The Complete guide to modern dance. New York, Doubleday, 1976. xv,534p.,illus.

Sections: The forerunners (*e.g.*, Isadora Duncan) - The founders (*e.g.*, Martha Graham) - In and out of the steps of the founders (p.121-274) - Freedom and new formalism - Freedom and formalism (second generation; names, A-Z). Chronology of significant dates and events in modern dance development. 'Further reading' (p.509-13; briefly annotated; includes periodical articles). Detailed, non-analytical index. Excellent illus. 'This is the only existing book that gives the subject matter (or stories) for modern dance' [as opposed to ballet] (*Choice*, v.13, no.10, December 1976, p.1274). *Class No:* 793.3(03)

Yearbooks & Directories

[2064]
Dancing yearbook 1991. Dearling, J., *ed.* 34th. ed. Brighton, International Dance Teachers Association, 1989. 128p. ISBN: 0900326220. ISSN: 04046919.

Details of organizations, festivals, championships, teachers, rules, results. Bibliographies and journals listed p.9-10. *Class No:* 793.3(058)

Histories

[2065]
CLARKE, M. *and* **CRISP, C. The History of the dance.** London, Orbis Publishing, 1981. 256p.,illus.

10 chapters: 1. Primitive & ancient dance - 2. Religious dance - 3. European folk dance - 4. Eastern dance - 5. Social dance - 6. Ballet de cour - 7/8. History of dance - 9. Modern dance - 10. Stage & Screen. Appendix: Notation, Chapter notes, p.246-7. Bibliography, p.248-9 (authors, A/Z). Index (*c*.2,000 entries), p.230-6. Over 250 illus., well-captioned. 'An encylopaedic survey of the dance in virtually all its known forms ... 'Highly readable' (*British book news*, June 1981, p.367-8). *Class No:* 793.3(091)

Conjuring

[2066]
WATERS, T.A. Encyclopedia of magic and magicians. Oxford, Facts on File, 1988. 372p., illus. ISBN: 0816013497.

Also in paperback; (0816019819).

Alphabetical listing of technical terms (routines, effects) and 'performers and creators of magic past and present'. (Intro.). Cross-references; some entries have bibliographic notes. *Class No:* 793.8

794/799 Games & Sport

Games & Sport

Encyclopaedias & Dictionaries

[2067]
CUDDON, J.A. **The Macmillan dictionary of sports and games.** London, Macmillan, 1980. xxviii,870p. diagrs.

About 6,000 entries for sports (including many minor), events, awards and terms (*e.g.,* 'Bowling, tenpin': 10 columns, 1 diagr. with descriptive caption). Omits biographies and bibliographies. Numerous cross-references. 'Some major dates and events', p.xiv-xxviii (3200 B.C.-A.D. 1979). Typography does not make for easy reference, headwords being indistinct and text (in 3 columns) too solid. Diagrams and plans are only occasional. *Class No:* 794(03)

[2068]
The Oxford companion to sports and games. Arlott, J., *ed.* London, OUP, 1975. viii,1143p. illus.

Aims to 'help the reader understand a sport when he watches it for the first time'. Describes *c.*200 games, with historical notes. Entries cover biographies, techniques, equipment, outstanding performances, events, clubs, stadia. 100 contributors; but articles are not signed. Excludes board and table games, but includes table tennis. Karate and bullfighting are in, but not skiing, mountaineering and orienteering. Rules and records are not spelt out. British slant ('Cricket': p.183-214; 4 diagrams; 12 photographs; 11 lines of references). Cross-references. 200 clear diagrams; 400 good action half-tones. A compendium rather than a companion. 'The least satisfactory of Oxford's splendid *Companions*' (*The Times*, 21 November 1980, p.VI). *Class No:* 794(03)

Histories

[2069]
BOTERMANS, J., *and others.* **The World of games:** their origins and history. New York, Facts on File, 1989. 242p. ISBN: 0816021848.

Details of 150 board, dice, card, domino, and activity games are featured. Well illustrated. Playing rules are included. *Class No:* 794(091)

Indoor Games

[2070]
SCARNE, J. **Scarne's Encyclopedia of games.** London, Constable, 1973. xii,628p., illus. ISBN: 0094595208.

28 chapters on card games (1-22) and indoor games generally, *e.g.* 2.Draw poker ... 6. Canasta ... 11. Cribbage and how it is played ... 20. Miscellaneous card games .. 23. Tile games - 24. Dice and their many games - 25. Chess checkers and tecko - 26. Games requiring special equipment - 27. Lottery and guessing games - 28. Parlor games for all (*e.g.* charades). Glossary of game terms, p.589-608.

....(contd.)
analytical index. US slanted 'A very useful reference tool for all ages' (*Library journal*, v.99, 15 April 1974, p.1100). *Class No:* 794.0

Chess

[2071]
HOOPER, D. *and* WHYLD, K. **The Oxford companion to chess.** Oxford, OUP, 1987. 407p., illus. ISBN: 0192819860.

Includes terms, biographies of major players, openings, strategies, history etc. Detailed discussion of 200 games. Well indexed; multi-language glossary. *Class No:* 794.1

Card Games

[2072]
PARLETT, D. **The Oxford guide to card games:** a historical survey. Oxford, OUP, 1990. xii,361p., illus. ISBN: 0192141651.

A source of information on the history and evolution of card games; does not cover rules, strategies, tactics. International coverage of all types of games. Excellent illustrations; useful appendices; glossary; full bibliographical notes; indexes. 'Authoritative and erudite, yet attractively written and interesting' (*Reference Reviews* 4(4) 1990, p.29). *Class No:* 794.4

Laws

[2073]
GIBSON, W.B. **Hoyle's Modern encyclopedia of card games:** rules of all the basic games and popular variations. London, Hale, 1979. 398p. ISBN: 0709148410.

Definitive source for the rules of card games, including bridge, and other indoor games. Alphabetical arrangement with cross-references. Glossary-index. *Class No:* 794.4(094.1)

Word Games

[2074]
PARLETT, D. **The Penguin book of word games.** Harmondsworth, Middx., Penguin Books, 1982. 235p., illus.

Part 1: Spoken word games (*e.g.* Just a minute; Charades; Twenty questions) - Part 2: Written word games (*e.g.* Consequences; Scrabble; Anagrams). Data on each game: number of players; suitable age; whether serious or light-hearted. Postscripts. 'Acceptability of words games'; 'Some useful statistics for word-gamers' (*e.g.* letter-occurrence frequency), Solution to problems; Bibliography, p.230-1. Index, p.233-5. Over 100 games are described, with examples. *Class No:* 795

SECOND EDITION

Sport

Encyclopaedias & Dictionaries

[2075]
Encyclopedia of physical education, fitness, and sport. Cureton, T.K., *ed.* Washington, DC, American Alliance for Health, Physical Education, Recreation & Dance, 1977-85. 4v. ISBN: 0883142937.

Volume one covers philosophy, programmes and history; two training, environment, nutrition and fitness; three sports, dance and related activities; four human performance, efficiency, exercise & fitness. Scholarly, academic treatment by expert contributors. *Class No:* 796(03)

Dictionaries

[2076]
CONSIDINE, T. The Language of sport. Oxford, Facts on File, 1983. 355p. ISBN: 0871966530.

Definitions of over 5,000 terms, arranged alphabetically within groups by sport. Abundant cross-references, and a good index. *Class No:* 796(038)

Quotations

[2077]
JAMES, S., *comp.* **Chambers sporting quotations.** Edinburgh, Chambers, 1990. 250p. ISBN: 055020489x.

Some 1,500 quotations, arranged under 110 headings (names of sports). Cross references; dates are given for each item and a brief citation of where it can be found. *Class No:* 796(082.2)

Official Records

[2078]
MATTHEWS, P. *and* **MORRISON, I. The Guinness encyclopedia of international sports records and results.** 2nd ed. Enfield., Guinness Superlatives, 1990. 416p., illus. ISBN: 0851129102.

First edition 1987.

Introductory sections explain events; lists of winners, records, statistics. Covers national and world champions in over 100 sports. Well illustrated. *Class No:* 796(093.2)

Laws

[2079]
DIAGRAM GROUP. Rules of the game. Rev. ed. New York, St. Martins Press, 1990. 320p., illus. ISBN: 0312045743.

First edition 1974.

13 general categories of sport grouped (water, combat, etc.), with basic rules of 150 sports (13 new to this edition). Extensive use of drawings and diagrams; a useful source, but treatment is limited in scope and omits strategies, variations. *Class No:* 796(094.1)

Great Britain

[2080]
MASON, T., *ed.* **Sport in Britain:** a social history. London, CUP, 1989. 384p. illus. ISBN: 0521351197.

Nine experts examine major sports over the last 150 years, analysing origins, growth, organization, gambling, media coverage etc. Covers angling, athletics, boxing, cricket, football, golf, horse-racing, tennis, rowing, Rugby Union. Scholarly in intent, but interestingly written. *Class No:* 796(410)

Yearbooks & Directories

[2081]
Recreation management handbook. London, Spon, 1975-. ISSN: 0144624x.

Published biennially; previously *Recreation Management Yearbook.*

Compiled for the Institute of Leisure & Amenity Management (ILAM). Directory of sports associations (UK & international), recreation management, education & training, awards, law, equipment suppliers etc. *Class No:* 796(410)(058)

Olympic Games

[2082]
HUGMAN, B.J. *and* **ARNOLD, P. The Olympic Games:** complete track and field results 1896-1988. New York, Facts on File, 1989. 383p. ISBN: 0816021201.

Gives names of all participating athletes, details of country, event, time, distance, etc. Brief biographies of outstanding figures. *Class No:* 796.032

Outdoor Pursuits

Great Britain

[2083]
British outdoor amenities directory 1991/92. Sanders, H., *ed.* Over, Cambs, J.S. Turner, 1991. 624p. ISBN: 0951163884. ISSN: 09554025.

Lists local authority parks departments A/Z, open spaces, nurseries, golf courses, reserves. Glossary of terms; details of education and training courses available; buyers' guide. *Class No:* 796.5(410)

8 LANGUAGE & LITERATURE
8.0 Languages & Linguistics

[2084]
MODERN LANGUAGE ASSOCIATION OF AMERICA. **MLA international bibliography** of books and articles on the modern languages and literatures, 1921-. New York, MLA, 1922-. Annual.

The major English-language bibliography in its field. Known as *American bibliography* from 1921 to 1955, when it listed only writings by Americans on the literatures of various countries; then as *Annual bibliography,* 1956-62, with coverage extended to include foreign-language writers; present title since 1963.

In 5 parts since 1981: 1. *British Isles, British Commonwealth, English-Caribbean and American literatures* - 2. *European, Asian, African and Latin American literatures* - 3. *Linguistics* - 4. *General literature and related topics* - 5. *Folklore.* Since 1983 these have been published in 2 vols. with v.1 including the 5 parts and a document author index, and v.2 comprising a comprehensive subject index with many cross-references. Individual parts are available separately with their own author and subject indexes. The 1989 bibliography has nearly 47,000 entries and lists *c.*1,450 periodicals that have been analyzed.

Available online via DIALOG, with records back to 1963, and WILSONLINE back to 1981. Historical data is being added to the DIALOG database and eventually the whole file back to 1921 will be available online. Records from 1981 to the present are available on CD-ROM from H.W. Wilson, as part of their WILSONDISC programme. Over 375,000 citations currently accessible, updated quarterly. A detailed review of the CD-ROM version appears in *Choice,* v.26(1), Sept. 1988, p.94. *Class No:* 8.0

[2085]
The Year's work in modern language studies, 1929/30- . London, Oxford Univ. Press, 1931-40; Cambridge, Cambridge Univ. Press, 1951-63; London, Modern Humanities Research Association, 1964-. v.1-. Annual. ISSN: 00844152.

Annual bibliography, with running commentary, of studies in languages and literatures. V.51, *1989* (1990. x,1236p.) has sections for Latin, Romance, Celtic, Germanic, and Slavonic languages, with subdivisions by subject specialists on individual languages. Many thousands of studies cited. Indexes of names and subjects. *Class No:* 8.0

Language Teaching

[2086]
Language teaching: the international abstracting journal for language teachers and applied linguists. Cambridge, Cambridge Univ. Press, 1968-. v.1, no.1-. Quarterly. ISSN: 02614448.

Produced jointly by the Centre for Information on Language Teaching and Research (CILT) and the British Council, and formerly known as *Language Teaching Abstracts* and *Language Teaching and Linguistics: Abstracts.*

....(contd.)
Each issue carries over 130 abstracts, in English, in 4 main subject areas (1. Language learning and teaching: theory and practice - 2. Teaching particular languages - 3. Research in the supporting sciences - 4. Language description and use) plus ' a specially commissioned state-of-the-art survey article on an important aspect of language learning or teaching' (*e.g.* 'Reading in a foreign language' in the Oct. 1989 issue) with a full bibliography. Author and subject indexes in each issue. List of periodicals scanned in each January issue - over 350 in Jan. 1989. International coverage. *Class No:* 80:372.88

[2087]
The Working languages of the European Community: a guide to learning resources. Walford, A.J., *ed.* London, Library Assoc., 1991. vii,208p. ISBN: 0853658099.

Chapters by the editor and 5 contributors on French, Italian, Spanish, Portuguese, German, Dutch, Danish, Modern Greek, and English as a second language, in which language courses (including audio-visual materials), dictionaries (both general and specialized), grammars, and background materials are described and evaluated. Introductory chapter by the editor includes criteria for selecting dictionaries. Brief bibliography after each chapter. Appendix has lists of language bookshops and film and video sources in the UK. Index of titles and subjects.

Supersedes, as far as these languages are concerned, the 3rd ed. of *Guide to foreign-language courses and dictionaries,* edited by A.J. Walford and J.E.O. Screen (London, Library Assoc., 1977), which covered all the major European languages, plus Arabic, Japanese and Chinese, but is now out of print. *Class No:* 80:372.88

Languages

[2088]
CAMPBELL, G.L. **Compendium of the world's languages.** London, Routledge, 1991. 2v.(xxiv,1574p.). ISBN: 0415029376.

V.1 *Abaza to Lusatian.*
V.2 *Maasai to Zuni.*

Contains clearly presented accounts of over 300 individual languages — covering their history, writing system, sound system and grammatical system — plus 20 language-families. Most languages are illustrated by a translation of the first 8 verses of St. John's Gospel. Details of 38 scripts appended. Bibliography (14p.). List of languages and cross-references.

'Covers considerably more ground than Comrie, and differs from Ruhlen (*A Guide to the world's languages*) in providing much more data on individual languages, though it nowhere approaches Ruhlen's completeness. Of the three, Campbell has the most thorough discussion of the extinct languages (such as Sumerian, Urartian and Elamite), a field

....(contd.)
ignored almost entirely by Comrie and handled indifferently by Ruhlen' (*TLS* no. 4628, Dec. 13, 1991, p.24). *Class No: 800*

[2089]
CRYSTAL, D. The Cambridge encyclopedia of language. Cambridge, Cambridge Univ. Press, 1987. vii,472p. illus. ISBN: 0521264383.

The first attempt to cover the whole field of language in a single-volume encyclopedia is an unqualified success. A massive amount of information is organized in 11 chapters (called 'Parts'), which comprise 65 articles ('thematic sections') of between 2 and 20 pages, each of which is a self-contained presentation of a major theme in language study. The data is made accessible by means of a clearly presented table of contents, numerous cross-references and three indexes: languages, families, dialects and scripts; authors and personalities; topics. Attractively presented with many photographs, diagrams, maps and tables and intelligent use of a variety of typefaces.

Appendices include: glossary of over 1,000 terms; lists of special symbols and abbreviations; table of the world's languages, indicating family, where spoken and by how many, bibliography (8p.) with the emphasis on recent publications. Main text contains many statistical tables which will be invaluable in reference work, *e.g.* speakers of English throughout the world, mother tongues of US citizens, letter and word frequency, most popular names, etc.

Generously reviewed in *TLS* (no.4428, Feb.12, 1988, p.166) and *Language Monthly* (no.52, Jan. 1988, p.16-17) and rightly so, considering it is essentially the work of one author. *Class No: 800*

[2090]
GUNNEMARK, E. A Geolinguistic handbook. [2nd ed.]. Gothenburg, Gunnemark, 1985. 286p. maps. ISBN: 9178100917.

1st ed. 1983, as *What language do they speak? - a geolinguistic handbook.*

A very useful guide to the languages spoken in different countries. Main section arranged by country, with further sections on languages, scripts, classification, etc. Includes statistics of numbers of speakers. Bibliography (7p.). Indexes of terms and languages. *Class No: 800*

[2091]
The World's major languages. Comrie, B., *ed.* London, Croom Helm; New York, Oxford Univ. Press, 1987. xiii,1025p. illus. ISBN: 0415045169, UK; 0195205219, US.

50 essays (average 20p.) by 44 specialists on major languages and language groups, each one discussing the historical development of the language, its grammar, sound system and writing system, and sociological factors such as its use as a written or official language. Several maps and many tables. Selective bibliographies and lists of references follow each essay but these concentrate on grammars and histories and do not include dictionaries. Over half of the essays (26) are devoted to Indo-European languages.

A lengthy review in *The Linguist* (v.27(2), Spring 1988, p.90-91) suggests that while the work will be 'indispensable in libraries, as it brings together much knowledge not easily available elsewhere', it does not supersede Meillet and Cohen's *Les Langues du monde*, which covers practically all languages, nor does it replace the language articles in the *New Encyclopaedia Britannica*, which provide fuller comparative and historical information, but it complements both of them.

4 regional selections from the main work are available, all ed. by B. Comrie and published by Routledge:
The Major languages of East and South-East Asia. 240p. ISBN: 0415047390.

....(contd.)
The Major languages of Western Europe. 352p. ISBN: 0415047382.
The Major languages of Eastern Europe. 288p. ISBN: 041505771x.
The Major languages of South Asia, the Middle East and Africa. 336p. ISBN: 0415057728. *Class No: 800*

Translation & Translators

[2092]
Directory of translators and translating agencies in the United Kingdom. Morris, P. *and* Weston, G., *eds.* 2nd ed. London, Bowker-Saur, 1990. viii,299p. ISBN: 0862912776.

1st ed. Beverley, Merton Press, 1987, as *Register of translators and translating agencies in the United Kingdom.*

1. Individual translators, A-Z, has over 750 entries giving name, professional qualifications, address, telephone, fax and E-mail numbers, languages covered, subject specialisms, availability of interpreting services and any other relevant information provided by the translator - 2. Agencies, A-Z, gives similar information for *c*.150 agencies - 3. Index of subject specialisms (Abrasives to Zoology via Footwear and Real Estate) - 4. Index of 55 languages (Afrikaans to Welsh via Faroese and Putonghua), further divided by geographical area - 5. Agencies translating most languages. Entries based on returns from a questionnaire distributed May 1989, with all entries from 1st ed. updated. Essential for business information services, but will need to continue to be regularly updated. *Class No: 800:651.926*

Artificial Languages

Esperanto

[2093]
WELLS, J.C. Concise Esperanto and English dictionary: Esperanto-English/English-Esperanto. Reprint of 1969 ed. London, Hodder, 1981. ix,419p. (*Teach yourself books.*) ISBN: 0340275766.

Originally published London, English Univs. Press, 1969, as *The E.U.P. concise Esperanto and English dictionary.*

Has *c.*9000 entries in the first section and *c.*19,500 in the second. Based largely on the *Plena vortaro* (4th ed., with Supplement, 1954). Useful guide to pronunciation and summary of grammar (35p.). *Class No: 800.892*

Sign Language

[2094]
MILES, D. British sign language: a beginner's guide. London, B.B.C., 1988. 141p. illus. ISBN: 0563213957.

Fully illustrated introduction to British sign language (BSL). After a historical survey of the development of the deaf community, Chapter 3, 'How the language works' (p.46-106), gives a comprehensive survey of current practice with numerous illustrations and clear instructions. Glossary of terms, subject index and sign index. Designed to support the BBC TV series and video of the same name. *Class No: 800.95*

[2095]
WORLD FEDERATION OF THE DEAF. Gestuno: international sign language of the deaf. Carlisle, British Deaf Assoc., 1975. unpaged. illus. ISBN: 0950418706.

Illustrations of 1,470 sign-language gestures, arranged in subject categories with French and English parallel text and indexes in each language. *Class No: 800.95*

Linguistics

[2096]
CRYSTAL, D. A Dictionary of linguistics and phonetics. 3rd ed. Oxford, Blackwell, 1991. xiv,389p. ISBN: 0631178694.

1st ed. London, Deutsch, 1980, as *A First dictionary of linguistics and phonetics*; 2nd ed. Blackwell, 1985.

A well-established dictionary covering c.1,500 linguistic terms. Entries comprise definition, explanation, and examples, and all have references to one or more of the 40 standard textbooks listed in the select bibliography. Clearly laid out, with ample cross-references. Over 300 new terms listed in 3rd ed., and all old entries have been revised. *Class No:* 801

[2097]
International encyclopedia of linguistics. Bright, W., *ed.* New York, Oxford Univ. Press, 1991. 4v. illus. maps. ISBN: 0195051963.

A major new reference work compiled by over 400 contributors, under the direction of 25 topic editors, and covering all aspects of contemporary linguistics. Entries are arranged A-Z and fall into 3 categories: lengthy, signed essays (up to 5,000 words) on major topics (*e.g.* Phonetics); shorter essays (also signed) on more specific topics and on languages or language families; and shorter, unsigned articles on minor languages. Most entries have bibliographies and those on languages and language families are followed by very useful 'language lists' giving geographical, statistical and sociolinguistic information. Well illustrated with maps, tables, charts, etc. Glossary of linguistic terms (76p.). Extensive cross-references, synoptic table of contents and detailed index (104p.) provide full access. *Class No:* 801

[2098]
Linguistics and language behavior abstracts (LLBA). San Diego, Calif., Sociological Abstracts Inc., 1967-. v.1, no.1-. Quarterly. ISSN: 08888027.

Vols. 1-18 (1967-84) entitled *Language and language behaviour abstracts*.

A leading abstracting journal in the field, covering 1,800 international periodicals in a wide range of disciplines, including anthropology, education, medicine, psychology and philosophy, as well as those devoted solely to linguistics.

V.23(1), April 1989, has 2,002 abstracts under 30 broad subject headings with many subdivisions, followed by author index, source publication index and subject index, entries in the latter including brief abstracts of the abstracts.

Available online via DIALOG and BRS, the database currently containing c.110,000 records from 1973 onwards. Updated quarterly. *Class No:* 801

[2099]
The Linguistics encyclopedia. Malmkjaer, K., *ed.* London, Routledge, 1991. xx,575p. illus. ISBN: 0415029422.

Over 80 lengthy entries (average 6p.), by a team of 26 international specialists, on major and subsidiary areas of linguistic study, with applied linguistics (*e.g.* lexicography, speech therapy) particularly well covered. Entries are arranged A-Z, are extensively cross-referenced and followed by suggestions for further reading. Many are illustrated by diagrams and tables. Bibliography (39p.). Index. *Class No:* 801

Dictionaries

[2100]
GRANT & CUTLER LTD. Foreign language dictionaries: specialist and general, 1991-1992. London, Grant & Cutler, 1991. 107p.

A catalogue from the UK's largest foreign-language bookshop, listing c.1,000 specialist dictionaries between English and the main European languages under 50 subject headings. Also has sections on general dictionaries, business correspondence and translation. Some entries have brief annotations. Index of subjects and keywords. *Class No:* 801.3

Nicknames

[2101]
Names and nicknames of places and things. Urdang, L., *ed.* London, Grafton; Boston, Hall, 1987. 381p. ISBN: 0246132469, UK; 0816187800, US.

Defines and explains the connotations of the names given to c.1,500 real, legendary and fictional locales and landmarks. Includes buildings, businesses, and some objects as well as places. Very thorough index.

Reprinted in paperback, with revisions, by Oxford Univ. Press, 1991, under the title *A Dictionary of names and nicknames* (viii,326p. ISBN: 0192828576). *Class No:* 801.3:392.91

Proper Names

[2102]
PAYTON, G. The Penguin dictionary of proper names. Paxton, J., *ed.* Rev. ed. London, Viking, 1991. viii,563p. ISBN: 0670825735.

A long-awaited revision of *Payton's proper names* (London, Warne, 1969). An American version of the 1st ed. was published under the title *Webster's dictionary of proper names* (Springfield, Mass., Merriam, 1970), with many British-oriented entries dropped in favour of names more familiar to American users.

A dictionary of c.11,000 names which are regularly encountered in newspapers, literature, etc., including people and places (both real and fictional); titles of works of music, literature and art; historical events; ships, cars and planes; nicknames; political parties; religious groups; races and languages; sporting events; etc., etc. Entries contain brief explanatory notes and cross-references. 'A highly personal choice of names' (*Preface*) but nevertheless very useful. *Class No:* 801.31

[2103]
ROOM, A. Dictionary of translated names and titles. London, Routledge, 1986. xviii,460p. ISBN: 0710099533.

Lists over 4,000 well-known names and titles in English alphabetical order, followed by their equivalents in French, German, Italian, Spanish and Russian. This main sequence is numbered (1-4108) and followed by cross-indexes in the other 5 languages. Geographical names include countries, cities, seas, rivers, mountains and regions; personal names include historical personages, biblical, mythological and fictional characters, saints and popes. Titles cover works of art and literature, battles, treaties and international organizations. There is much additional information in the form of dates (for people, events and works) and locations (for geographical features). An appendix lists 75 common personal forenames and their equivalents. Invaluable. *Class No:* 801.31

Place Names

[2104]
EKWALL, E. The Concise Oxford dictionary of English place-names. 4th ed. Oxford, Oxford Univ. Press, 1960. li,546p. ISBN: 0198691033.
1st ed. 1936; 3rd ed. 1947.
Recognized as the standard work in the field and has entries for over 10,000 place-names, giving the following information: county, historical forms with dates, authorities, comments on etymological development and likely meanings. Includes a valuable introduction with list of works consulted (14p.). Incorporates many additions and corrections to 3rd ed.
Does not include many names originating after 1500, but these have been covered in recent works by A. Room.
Class No: 801.311

[2105]
Illustrated dictionary of place names: United States and Canada. Harder, K.B., *ed.* Reprint of 1976 ed. New York, Facts on File, 1986. 634p. illus. ISBN: 0816011435.
Originally published New York, Van Nostrand Reinhold, 1976.
Explains the names of *c.*15,000 places including cities, towns, provinces, states, counties, and natural features such as rivers, lakes and capes. Entries include variations of the name, and information about county and state capitals and emblems. All places whose name derives from the same source (*e.g.* the name of a president) are grouped within one entry. Bibliography (5p.). 200 illustrations. *Class No:* 801.311

[2106]
MILLS, A.D. A Dictionary of English place-names. Oxford, Oxford Univ. Press, 1991. xxxii,388p. maps. ISBN: 0198691564.
Over 12,000 concise entries, giving modern county; most likely meaning and derivation of the name; a typical earlier form with date; and the name's spelling in Domesday Book if it occurs there. Includes rivers and coastal features as well as towns, villages, counties and districts. Glossary of name elements (7p.). Bibliography (3p.). Introductory essay (20p.) describes the development, formation and significance of place-names. *Class No:* 801.311

[2107]
ROOM, A. Dictionary of place-names in the British Isles. London, Bloomsbury, 1988. xxvi,414p. ISBN: 074750170x.
Origins and history of over 4,000 familiar place-names. Introduction discusses role and lore of place-names, sources, naming patterns, river names, etc. List of place-name elements (6p.). Bibliographical essay (6p.). *Reference Reviews* (v.3(1), March 1989, p.41) prefers *Concise Oxford dictionary of place names* for its more comprehensive coverage of specific areas, but commends the 'clear, jargon-free style' of the very informative entries. *Class No:* 801.311

[2108]
ROOM, A. Place-names of the world: a dictionary of their origins and backgrounds. Rev. ed. North Ryde, New South Wales, and London, Angus & Robertson, 1987. 259p. ISBN: 0207155399.
1st ed. Newton Abbot, David & Charles, 1974.
More than 1,000 of the world's most familiar place-names explained with emphasis on foreign-language names (mostly entered under their English-language version). List of non-English name elements. Bibliography (4p.). Rev. ed. includes major place names created or adopted since 1974. *Class No:* 801.311

Personal Names

Forenames

[2109]
HANKS, P. *and* **HODGES, F. A Dictionary of first names.** Oxford, Oxford Univ. Press, 1990. xxxvi,443p. ISBN: 0192116517.
Main sequence covers names used in Britain, Europe and North America, tracing each name back to its linguistic root and listing pet and short forms, masculine and feminine forms, cognates, diminutives, and other variants. Highly readable entries include information about the fluctuations in popularity of individual names. Excellent introductory survey of naming practices in different countries, with bibliography. Supplementary sequences of names used in the Arab world (36p.) and the Indian subcontinent (57p.), each with introductory essay and bibliography. Covers *c.*7,000 names in all. *Class No:* 801.313.1

[2110]
STEWART, G.R. American given names: their origin and history in the context of the English language. New York, Oxford Univ. Press, 1979. viii,264p. ISBN: 0195024656.
A historical sketch of the use of given names in the US (40p.) precedes the main sequence of names (Aaron-Zureel), which provides the following information: male/female, language of origin, meaning, and notes on usage and popularity. Cross-references. *Class No:* 801.313.1

[2111]
WITHYCOMBE, E.G. The Oxford dictionary of English Christian names. 3rd ed. Oxford, Clarendon Press, 1977. xlvii,310p. ISBN: 0192812130.
1st ed. 1945.
Includes names found in England since the 14th century, giving etymology, meaning, and earliest usage. Appendix: 'Some common words derived from Christian names'. *Class No:* 801.313.1

Family Names

[2112]
HANKS, P. *and* **HODGES, F. A Dictionary of surnames.** Oxford, Oxford Univ. Press, 1988. liv,826p. ISBN: 0192115928.
Some 10,000 entries, dealing with *c.*70,000 common surnames of the English-speaking world and Europe, selected after an international scrutiny of telephone directories. 'Each entry explains the linguistic origins of each surname, together with peculiarities of its history, current distribution, and other relevant facts' (*Introduction*). Introduction includes a lengthy section on the typology of surnames and a 'Survey of national and cultural groups of surnames'. Bibliography (2p.). Index (over 200p.) lists all names included, whether as main entry, variant or cognate. 'Immediately becomes the standard reference source for the information it contains' (*Booklist*, v.85 (21), July 1989, p.1882). *Class No:* 801.313.2

[2113]
REANEY, P.H. A Dictionary of English surnames. 3rd ed., with corrections and additions by R.M. Wilson. London, Routledge, 1991. lxx,509p. ISBN: 041505737x.
1st ed. 1958; 2nd ed. 1976. Both by Reaney and entitled *A Dictionary of British surnames.*
The standard work in the field, giving the meanings of over 16,000 names (4,000 added for this ed.) and their variants, together with early forms, sources and origins, plus notes on etymology. Lengthy, scholarly introduction (60p.) includes bibliographic details of sources and other works consulted.

....(contd.)

'The change of title reflects a concentration on surnames of specifically English rather than Celtic origin which has become increasingly apparent in successive editions. As a rule, Scottish, Welsh and Irish names are only included when forms for them are found in English sources or when they coincide in form with specifically English surnames' (*Preface*). For full coverage of other British names, see:

The Surnames of Scotland, by G.F. Black (New York, N.Y. Public Library, 1946. lxii,838p. ISBN: 0871041723).

Welsh surnames, by T.J. and P. Morgan (Cardiff, Univ. of Wales Press, 1985. 211p. ISBN: 0708309364).

The Surnames of Ireland, by E. Maclysaght (7th ed. Dublin, Irish Academic Press, 1989. 320p. ISBN: 0716524414). *Class No:* 801.313.2

[2114]

SMITH, E.C. New dictionary of American family names. New York, Harper & Row, 1973. 570p.

A new ed. of *Dictionary of American family names* (1957).

Lists *c.*22,000 US surnames (a huge increase on earlier ed.) with brief notes on their origin and meaning but without detailed etymologies. *Class No:* 801.313.2

Eponyms

[2115]

MANSER, M.H. Dictionary of eponyms. London, Sphere, 1988. 307p. illus. ISBN: 0722163126.

Approx 1,000 eponyms are listed in a single A-Z sequence and explained in non-scholarly terms in this paperback. Concentrates on the more well-known eponyms in general use and includes brief biographical information. *Class No:* 801.313.9

Multilingual Dictionaries

[2116]

Harrap's CD-ROM multilingual dictionary database. London, Harrap, 1989. ISBN: 0245600256.

18 dictionaries on one CD-ROM, giving access to over 7 million words in 12 languages: English, French, German, Spanish, Italian, Dutch, Danish, Finnish, Norwegian, Swedish, Japanese, and Chinese. The dictionaries include both general works (*e.g. Il Nuovo Ragazzini*) and specialist lexicons (*e.g. Sansyusha's Dictionary of science and technology: English-German-Japanese*). 5 are Harrap publications. Updated according to dictionary revisions.

Searching can be confined to a single dictionary or several dictionaries can be searched at once. The price includes CD-ROM, search software on floppy disk, and user's manual. *Class No:* 801.323.9

Phonetics

[2117]

PULLUM, G.K. and LADUSAW, W.A. Phonetic symbol guide. Chicago, Univ. of Chicago Press, 1986. xxx,266p. ISBN: 0226685314.

Describes and explains the use of all phonetic symbols likely to be encountered in modern linguistic work, and also covers diacritical marks. Clearly presented entries include notes comparing usage under the European IPA tradition and the American tradition, the differences between these being explained in the introduction. Appendices include glossary of phonetic terminology, bibliography, and comparative charts of vowels and consonants. 'The book is unique. It is very competently done. The attention to detail is exemplary, as is the clarity of exposition' (*Journal of Linguistics,* v.24(2), Sept. 1988, p.570-71). *Class No:* 801.4

Semantics & Semiotics

[2118]

Encyclopedic dictionary of semiotics. Sebeok, T.A., *ed.* Berlin, de Gruyter, 1986. 3v. ISBN: 3110105594.

V.1, *A-M;* v.2, *N-Z;* v.3, *Bibliography.*

Vols. 1-2 have 426 lengthy, signed articles, by 236 contributors from many countries, giving 3 types of information: the historical background and present usage of semiotic terms; biographical information on and assessment of the work of leading figures in semiotic studies; and exposition of the impact of semiotics on various disciplines. V.3 lists *c.*5,500 works under authors, A-Z, which are cited in the dictionary. *Class No:* 801.54

802.0 English Language

Bibliographies

Anglo-Saxon

[2119]
Annual bibliography of English language and literature, 1920-. London, Modern Humanities Research Assoc., 1921-. v.1-. ISSN: 00663786.

Earlier published by Cambridge Univ. Press for M.H.R.A. V.61: *1986* (1990. xliv,915p.) has 14,892 entries for books, pamphlets and periodical articles (from *c.*1,400 journals), as well as unpublished British and Irish theses, covering the English language and English, American and Commonwealth literature. English language section (p.73-163) has 1,642 entries under 14 main headings and numerous subheadings. Cross-references. Index of authors and subjects. Index of scholars. More comprehensive than *The Year's work in English studies* (*q.v.*), but not annotated. *Class No:* 802.0(01)

[2120]
The Year's work in English studies, 1919-. Oxford, Blackwell; Atlantic Highlands, N.J., Humanities Press, for The English Association, 1921-. v.1-. Annual. ISSN: 00844144.

Earlier published by Oxford Univ. Press and J. Murray. V.68: *1987* (1990. lvii,933p.) has 19 chapters in which subject specialists survey the year's output of books and articles (from over 950 journals) on the English language and English, American and Commonwealth literature. Chapter 3, English language (p.59-120), has 9 sections, with references to periodical articles in the text and over 100 books listed at the end of the chapter. List of best books and articles. Index of critics. Index of authors and subjects. *Class No:* 802.0(01)

Histories

[2121]
BAUGH, A.C. *and* **CABLE, T. A History of the English language.** 3rd ed. Englewood Cliffs, N.J., Prentice Hall; London, Routledge, 1978. xvi,438p. ISBN: 0415050731, UK.

1st ed. 1951; 2nd ed. 1959.

Presents the historical development of English against the background of political, social and intellectual events. Includes a chapter on English in America. Extensive chapter bibliographies with evaluative commentary, plus footnote references. The 11 chapters have 256 numbered sections. Index. *Class No:* 802.0(091)

[2122]
BOSWORTH, J. Anglo-Saxon dictionary, based on the manuscript collections of the late Joseph Bosworth, ed. and enl. by T.N. Toller. Oxford, Clarendon Press, 1882-98 (repr. 1972). xii,1302p. ISBN: 0198631014.

— *Supplement,* by T.N. Toller. Oxford, Clarendon Press, 1908-21. 768p.

— *Enlarged addenda and corrigenda to the Supplement,* by A. Campbell. Oxford, Clarendon Press, 1972. viii,68p.

The *Supplement* and *Enlarged addenda* are now available in one vol. (ISBN: 019863112x).

The standard dictionary of Old English. About 60,000 entries in all, with many illustrative quotations, drawn from manuscripts and printed sources. In the main volume sources are listed on p.iii-xii. In the *Supplement*, letters A-G occupy over half the volume, representing the revision and enlargement which T.N. Toller was not able to make in the main work. *Class No:* 802.0-022

[2123]
HALL, J.R.C. A Concise Anglo-Saxon dictionary. 4th ed., with a supplement by H.D. Merritt. Cambridge, Cambridge Univ. Press, 1960. xv,432p.

1st ed. 1894; 3rd ed. 1931.

About 40,000 entries; aims to deal with all the words that occur in Anglo-Saxon poetry and prose. List of sources (7p.). It includes 12th-century words not in Bosworth and has references to Old English quotations in the *OED*. A standard dictionary for the non-specialist; the supplement covers 1,700 words. *Class No:* 802.0-022

Middle English Language

[2124]
STRATMANN, F.H. A Middle English dictionary, containing words used by writers from the twelfth to the fifteenth century. New ed., rearranged, rev. and enl. by H. Bradley. London, Oxford Univ. Press, 1891 (repr. 1963). xxiv,708p. ISBN: 0198631065.

Over 20,000 entry-words, with etymology, meanings and references to selected texts. List of sources (8p.). Remains the only comprehensive dictionary of Middle English in a completed form until Kurath's *Middle English dictionary* reaches an end.

For briefer coverage, see A.L. Mayhew and W.W. Skeat's *A Concise dictionary of Middle English, from AD1150 to 1580* (Oxford, Clarendon Press, 1888. xv,272p.). *Class No:* 802.0-023

Usage

[2125]
FOWLER, H.W. A Dictionary of modern English usage. 2nd ed., rev. by Sir. E. Gowers. Oxford, Clarendon Press, 1965 (repr. with corrections, 1983). xx,725p. ISBN: 0198691157.
1st ed. 1926.
Some 3,000 entries, A-Z, including c.400 extremely readable articles that embody Fowler's personal recommendations on usage in general and the use of common words. Many brief and more particularized entries on spelling, pronunciation, meaning or phraseology are interspersed. Adopts the Socratic method of teaching by wrong examples. Entry words are sometimes arbitrarily chosen although a classified guide, under four broad heads, precedes in the 2nd ed.
Still regarded as the classic guide, but essentially for British users despite some concessions to US practice in the 2nd ed. *Class No: 802.0-06*

[2126]
GREENBAUM, S. *and* WHITCUT, J. The Longman guide to English usage. Harlow, Longman, 1988. xiv,786p. ISBN: 0582556198.
An alphabetically-arranged guide with c.5,000 entries covering difficult words, grammatical problems, points of style, pronunciation, etc. Easy to use with clear page layout, full cross-references and a variety of typefaces. Addressed primarily to users of standard British English, but American usage is, nevertheless, well covered. *Class No: 802.0-06*

[2127]
MILLER, C. *and* SWIFT, K. The Handbook of non-sexist writing for writers, editors and speakers. 2nd ed. New York, Harper & Row, 1988; London, Women's Press, 1989. 178p. illus. ISBN: 0061816027, US; 0704338785, UK.
1st ed. 1980 (US) and 1981 (UK).
A well-established, concise manual which contains numerous examples of sexism in writing with suggestions for nonsexist alternatives. 2nd ed. has 46p. more than the first and includes a thesaurus of c.150 nonsexist terms, mainly occupational. Reference notes for each of the 6 chapters. Index. British edition has been suitably amended by The Women's Press. *Class No: 802.0-06*

[2128]
Webster's Dictionary of English usage. Springfield, Mass., Merriam-Webster, 1989. 978p. ISBN: 0877790329.
c.2,300 articles, A-Z, of varying length (up to a maximum of 4p.), which trace usage history and discuss contemporary usage. The entries include c.20,000 quotations (with details of author, source and date) from the vast Merriam-Webster files and also draw on the advice of some 275 other dictionaries and manuals. 'It is likely to become the first choice for most users due to its authority, recency, readability, summarization of other advice, and generous number of illustrative quotations' (*Booklist*, v.86(2), Sept. 15, 1989, p.210). *Class No: 802.0-06*

English Slang

[2129]
New dictionary of American slang. Chapman, R.L., *ed.* New York, Harper & Row, 1986; London, Macmillan, 1987. xxxvi,485p. ISBN: 0333441257, UK.
Based on Wentworth and Flexner's *Dictionary of American Slang* (New York, Crowell, 1960), which was enlarged and updated in 1967 and 1975.
An improvement on *DAS,* which is described by *English Today* (no.11, July 1987, p.41) as 'a lexicographical disaster', but not to be regarded as comparable to Partridge's monumental *Dictionary of slang and unconventional English* (*q.v.*), because it seldom gives even approximate dates for

....(contd.)
the appearance of particular terms, its illustrative quotations are undated, and it omits many etymologies that are by no means obvious. Over 17,000 entries (c.11,000 in *DAS*) with 'impact symbols' to denote vulgar and taboo terms. Fully cross-referenced. Drops *DAS*'s classified lists of slang terms. *Class No: 802.0-086*

[2130]
PARTRIDGE, E. A Dictionary of catch phrases: British and American, from the sixteenth century to the present. Beale, P., *ed.* 2nd ed. London, Routledge, 1985. xxv,384p. ISBN: 0710204957.
1st ed. 1977.
Over 5,500 entries, of which 2,500 remain intact from the 1st ed., the rest being amended or completely new. As well as the catch phrases of entertainers there are a wide range of popular sayings, greetings, toasts, clichés, proverbs, euphemisms, similes, etc., all explained in a mixture of anecdote and scholarship. Most sources quoted are 20th century. A fine reference book, but a name index would have made it even better. *Class No: 802.0-086*

[2131]
PARTRIDGE, E. A Dictionary of slang and unconventional English: colloquialisms and catch phrases, fossilised jokes and puns, general nicknames, vulgarisms and such Americanisms as have been naturalised. Beale, P., *ed.* 8th ed. London, Routledge, 1984. xxix,1400p. ISBN: 0415065682.
1st ed. 1937; 7th ed. 1970, in 2 vols.
Beale took over the editorship of this definitive work before Partridge's death in 1979 and has conflated the original text of the 1st ed. with all the subsequent addenda (which had appeared in a supplementary vol. in recent eds.), incorporated 5,000 new entries compiled by Partridge and over 1,000 of his own, and revised the whole. Some re-arrangement means that phrases are now entered under the term the user is most likely to turn to first. Entries comprise keyword, definition, register, dating, and sources, followed by editor's comments where appropriate. Approx. 55,000 entries in main sequence, plus Appendix of nearly 100 articles on particular topics, e.g. Nicknames, Back slang.
A Concise dictionary of slang and unconventional English, ed. by P. Beale (London, Routledge, 1989. xxvi,534p. ISBN: 0415028078) has c.15,000 entries, with coverage restricted to terms known to have arisen in the 20th century. *Class No: 802.0-086*

[2132]
THORNE, T. Bloomsbury dictionary of contemporary slang. London, Bloomsbury, 1990. vii,583p. ISBN: 0747501718.
'Aims to describe the core of English language slang in use between 1950 and 1990' (*Preface*) and has entries for over 5,000 words and phrases likely to be encountered in contemporary literature, popular music, the media and conversation. Compiled in the UK, but the US, Australia and the Caribbean are well represented. Entries comprise: headword, variants, part of speech, regional label, definition(s), explanation if required, and illustrative sentences, some invented and others from fully referenced sources. Clear layout, with good use of typefaces. *Class No: 802.0-086*

Dialects

[2133]
WRIGHT, J. The English dialect dictionary. London, Frowde, 1898-1905 (repr. Oxford, Oxford Univ. Press, 1981). 6v. ISBN: 019580497x.

Subtitle: 'Being the complete vocabulary of all dialect words still in use, or known to have been in use during the last two hundred years; founded on the Publications of the English Dialect Society and on a large amount of material never before printed'.

Covers over 100,000 words and phrases from England, Scotland, Wales and Ireland. Each entry gives regions in which found and variations, pronunciation, illustrative quotations and etymology. V.6 includes a supplement of 179p., a bibliography of works quoted classified by area and indexed, and 'The English dialect grammar'. *Class No:* 802.0-087

National Variants of English

Scotland

[2134]
The Concise Scots dictionary. Robinson, M., *ed.* Aberdeen, Aberdeen Univ. Press, 1985. xli,820p. ISBN: 0080284914.

An updated distillation of *The Scottish national dictionary* and *A Dictionary of the older Scottish tongue,* excluding illustrative quotations, rare items for which there is little evidence, obvious derivatives and Norse material from Shetland, Orkney and Caithness. A superbly laid-out introduction (33p.) gives a history of Scots, explains fully the relationship with the parent works and includes maps of dialect divisions and administrative regions. Approx. 25,000 entries, giving pronunciation, grammatical function, meaning, dating, geographical distribution and etymology.

Aberdeen Univ. Press have also published *The Scots thesaurus,* ed. by I. Macleod and others (1990. 536p. ISBN: 0080409261), which has a classified arrangement and a substantial English/Scots index. *Class No:* 802.0-087.41

South Africa

[2135]
BRANFORD, J. A Dictionary of South African English. 3rd ed., rev. and enl. Cape Town, Oxford Univ. Press, 1987. xxxi,444p. ISBN: 0195704274.

First published 1978; 2nd ed. 1980.

About 6,000 entries, including not only forms of English that are peculiarly South African, but also words absorbed from Afrikaans, native African languages and the local Malay, Indian and Jewish communities. Entries state pronunciation, part of speech, meaning(s) and etymology and are illustrated by often quite lengthy quotations from a wide variety of sources. The quotations make this scholarly reference work highly readable and many entries contain cross-references to quotations under other entries. Particularly long entries for 'boer', 'kaffir', 'kraal', 'veld' and their compounds. Clear introduction and pronunciation key; list of earliest recorded dates of selected items (2p.); list of word sources quoted, including individuals, newspapers and magazines (13p.). 3rd ed. contains many new entries from the vocabulary of civil disorder, 'chosen with sorrow and dismay' (*Preface*). 4th ed. due 1992 (ISBN: 0195705955).

Likely to remain the best guide to the subject until the longer *Dictionary of South African English on historical principles* appears in the 1990s. *Class No:* 802.0-087.468

Canada

[2136]
A Dictionary of Canadianisms on historical principles: produced by the Lexicographical Centre for Canadian English, University of Victoria, British Columbia. Avis, W.S., *ed.* Toronto, Gage, 1967. xxiii,927p. illus.

Over 10,000 entry-words, each being supported by dated evidence from printed sources, representing words originating in Canada, having a particular meaning there, or which are associated with an especially Canadian activity. Entries comprise headword, pronunciation (unusual words only), part of speech, etymology (if relevant), restrictive label (region, activity, etc.), definition, and quotations in chronological order. Many cross-references. Bibliography of sources and list of periodicals cited (47p.).

A Concise dictionary of Canadianisms, ed., by W.S. Avis and others, was published in 1973 (Toronto, Gage).

Avis has also edited (with others) the *Gage Canadian dictionary* (Toronto, Gage, 1983. 1313p. illus. ISBN: 077151980x), which claims to 'reflect the usage generally accepted by Canadians throughout the country' as regards spelling, pronunciation, vocabulary and style. *Class No:* 802.0-087.471

Caribbean

[2137]
CASSIDY, F.G. and LE PAGE, R.B. Dictionary of Jamaican English. 2nd ed. Cambridge, Cambridge Univ. Press, 1980. lxiv,509p. ISBN: 052122165x.

1st ed. 1967.

OED-style dictionary of words, meanings and pronunciations peculiar to Jamaica, originating there, or surviving there after being lost elsewhere. Entries give pronunciation, part of speech, etymology, definition and dated citations. Approx. 8,000 headwords. Bibliography of sources (12p.). Lengthy scholarly introduction.

2nd ed. adds information about usage elsewhere in the Caribbean to many entries and a Supplement with a further 380 entries. *Class No:* 802.0-087.472.9

USA

[2138]
MATHEWS, M.M. A Dictionary of Americanisms on historical principles. Chicago, Univ. of Chicago Press; London, Oxford Univ. Press, 1951. 1946p.

Only words or expressions originating in the United States being entered, this work is of narrower scope than Craigie and Hulbert's *Dictionary of American English,* (London, Oxford Univ. Press, 1936-44. 4v.) though it does not have the latter's chronological limitations. Brief etymology, pronunciation in a modified IPA notation and illustrative quotations are given. Carefully chosen line-block illustrations in the text. Bibliography of works cited, p.1913-46.

An abridged version, entitled *Americanisms,* was published by Chicago Univ. Press in 1966 (304p.). *Class No:* 802.0-087.473

[2139]
Webster's new world dictionary of American English. Neufeldt, V. *and* Guralnik, D.B., *eds.* 3rd college ed. New York, Simon & Schuster, 1988. 1600p. ISBN: 0139492801.

1st ed. 1953.

Claims 170,000 entries, of which 20,000 are new to this ed. As the title suggests, strong attention is paid to words and meanings of American origin, including colloquial and slang terms, and some 11,000 Americanisms are marked by an asterisk. Entries give syllabification of headwords and guidance on end-of-line word division, and American pronunciation is indicated using the publisher's own system.

....(contd.)

Senses are arranged historically (earliest first) and coverage of etymology is particularly good, extending even to place names. Some entries have usage notes and synonym lists and there are over 650 line drawings. Abbreviations, foreign terms, and proper names are treated in the main sequence. The list of colleges has been dropped, but the appended source documentation section has been expanded. Reviewers have welcomed the improved readability brought about by a change of typeface in this ed. *Class No:* 802.0-087.473

Australia

[2140]

The Australian national dictionary: a dictionary of Australianisms on historical principles. Ramson, W.S., *ed.* Melbourne, Oxford Univ. Press, 1988. xv,814p. ISBN: 0195547365.

OED-style dictionary of 10,000 Australianisms, which are defined as 'those words and meanings which have originated in Australia, which have a greater currency here than elsewhere, or which have a special significance in Australia because of their connection with an aspect of the history of the country' (*Introduction*). Approx. 6,000 main entries, comprising headword, pronunciation (International Phonetic Alphabet), part of speech, subject or restrictive label, variant spellings, etymology, definition, cross-references, variant forms and citations in chronological order. Combinations of which the headword is the main element are normally listed in a sub-section of the main entry. Over 60,000 dated and referenced quotations from 9,500 sources, the most frequently quoted being listed in the select bibliography (48p.). Map of 58 Aboriginal languages. 'Makes obsolete all earlier dictionaries of Australian English' (*Choice*, v.26(11/12), July/Aug. 1989, p.1806). *Class No:* 802.0-087.494

English as a Second Language

[2141]

HORNBY, A.S. The Oxford advanced learner's dictionary of current English. 4th ed. Oxford, Oxford Univ. Press, 1989. xix,1579p. ISBN: 0194311104.

1st ed. 1948 as *The Advanced learner's dictionary.*

The standard dictionary for students of English as a foreign language, with *c.*50,000 headwords and derivatives, 11,000 idiomatic expressions, 90,000 illustrative phrases and 1,000 line drawings. Clearly laid out, making good use of different typefaces and symbols. Entries include pronunciation of headword (with US variants), grammatical information, usage notes in many cases, and cross-references. Appendices include some Duden-style labelled drawings and lists of geographical and personal names, and are followed by a detailed guide to the use of the dictionary (35p.). *Class No:* 802.0-089

[2142]

Longman dictionary of contemporary English. Rundell, M., *ed.* 2nd ed. Harlow, Longman, 1987. 1248p. ISBN: 0582842220.

1st ed. 1978.

One of the best dictionaries for learners of English as a foreign language, with *c.*56,000 words and phrases, compounds always being treated as separate headwords. Definitions use a basic 2,000-word vocabulary and illustrative quotations are drawn from a computerized corpus. 500 illustrations are used to help define difficult concepts and confusable words. British and American pronunciation given, using IPA symbols. Supplementary material includes 20 sets of 'language notes' distributed throughout the text and 10 tables, including geographical

....(contd.)

names, word-beginnings and word-endings. The 'Longman defining vocabulary' is listed in Table 7. *Class No:* 802.0-089

Pronunciation

[2143]

WELLS, J.C. Longman pronunciation dictionary. Harlow, Longman, 1990. xxviii,802p. ISBN: 0582964113.

Gives recommended British *and American* pronunciations plus variants (including those considered to be incorrect, clearly labelled) for 75,000 words, including technical vocabulary and many proper names. For British English, recommended pronunciations are based on a modernized version of Received Pronunciation, and for American English on the accent known as General American. Transcription system is the same as that used in *Everyman's English pronouncing dictionary* (14th ed.) with a few minor variations. Usage notes on 33 important pronunciation features (*e.g.* elision, glottal stop, stress) are scattered through the dictionary in boxes.

Excellent use of colour, typefaces and symbols (typical of Longman language books) and good value for money. Particularly useful for students and teachers of English as a foreign language. *Class No:* 802.0-15

Dictionaries & Vocabularies

Illustrated Works

[2144]

CORBEIL, J-C. and MANSER, M. The Facts on File visual dictionary. Oxford, Facts on File, 1988. 795p. illus. ISBN: 0948894067.

American ed. published New York, Facts on File, 1986. ISBN: 0828819262.

A British edition of a dictionary developed in Canada by scholars working in English and French and aimed at 'the active member of the modern industrial society who needs to be acquainted with a wide range of technical terms from many assorted areas, but not to be a specialist in any' (*Introduction*). It comprises over 3,000 labelled illustrations arranged thematically under 28 main headings (*e.g.* Weapons, Clothing), followed by a general index to the 25,000 terms illustrated, plus thematic and specialized indexes. The drawings are of high quality and include detailed cutaways and cross-sections. Particularly useful for technological subjects. *Class No:* 802.0-3(0.025)

Unabridged Dictionaries

[2145]

The Oxford English dictionary. Prepared by J.A. Simpson and E.S.C. Weiner. 2nd ed. Oxford, Clarendon Press, 1989. 20v.(21,728p.). ISBN: 0198611862.

The definitive dictionary of the English language began life as the *New English dictionary on historical principles; founded mainly on the materials collected by the Philological Society*, ed. by Sir J.A.H. Murray, H. Bradley, Sir W.A. Craigie, and C.T. Onions, and issued in parts from Jan. 1884 to April 1928. This work is often referred to as *Murray's Dictionary* or *NED*, and includes 414,825 words and phrases.

The first edition of the *Oxford English dictionary* (a title which had been used on individual parts since July, 1895) was published in 1933 (12v. and suppl.), being 'a corrected reissue, with an introduction, supplement and bibliography' of *NED*. Cited as *OED*.

A Supplement to the Oxford English dictionary, ed. by R.W. Burchfield, was published over the period 1972-86 in 4 vols., subsuming the 1933 *Supplement*, and adding *c.*69,000 entries.

....(contd.)

The 2nd ed. integrates the original 12-vol. *OED* and the 4-vol. *Supplement* into a single 20-vol. sequence, and incorporates a further 5,000 words and meanings which have been recorded since completion of the *Supplement*. It has 291,627 entries, defining over 500,000 words, supported by 2,435,671 quotations. Entries range from a single line to several pages, that for the verb 'set' taking *c.*60,000 words to explain its 430 senses and subsenses.

Statistics apart, *OED2* is mightily impressive. Each entry-word is followed by pronunciation (IPA replacing Murray's original system); part of speech; variant spellings arranged chronologically; detailed etymological history; and numbered senses, arranged chronologically, each one accompanied by a series of quotations (with precise references) illustrating the use of the term from its first known occurrence to the modern period. Early quotations are given in the original spelling. 'The collection of quotations ... remains the centre and the glory of this dictionary' (*Review of English Studies*, v.41(161), Feb. 1990, p.87). A staggering 33,150 are from Shakespeare, with Sir Walter Scott an unlikely, but distant, runner-up. Bibliography of sources (143p.) in v.20.

The CD-ROM version, published by Oxford Univ. Press and TriStar Publishing, is currently limited to the contents of the *original* 12-vol. *OED*, with 252,000 main entries which may be searched by etymology, definition, part of speech, topic, register, usage, frequency, and quotations (by date, author, work, and text). This is a powerful research tool, particularly for etymology, and is also a vast dictionary of quotations (over 1,800,000 entries). The 2nd ed. is due to appear on CD-ROM in mid-1992 (ISBN: 0198612605).

The Compact Oxford English dictionary (New ed. 1991. 2416p. ISBN: 0198612583) reproduces micrographically in a single vol. the complete text of the 20-vol. 2nd ed. It is supplied in a slipcase with a magnifying glass and *User's guide* (71p.). *Class No: 802.0-30*

[2147]
Webster's third new international dictionary of the English language, unabridged. Grove, P.B., *ed.* Springfield, Mass., Merriam, 1961. 2662p. illus. ISBN: 0877792011.

Webster's Dictionary first published 1828. *New international* first published 1909; 2nd ed. 1934, with later reissues including corrections.

Webster's Third (also known as *W3*) was published amid much controversy because it differed radically from its predecessors in adopting a descriptive rather than prescriptive approach, presenting the language as actually used and including, without qualification, many terms that might be regarded as vulgar or incorrect.

*c.*450,000 entries (a significant reduction from *W2's* 600,000), giving definitions in chronological order (earliest first); etymology; pronunciation (including regional variations), using the publisher's own (over-complicated) system; and illustrative quotations. There are over 200,000 of the latter, mainly from contemporary sources, but they are undated and citations are to author only. Abbreviations are included in the main sequence, but proper names are excluded, except as eponyms, and *W2's* biographical and geographical sections have been dropped. 3,000 illustrations.

Essential for contemporary American English, but most reviewers have advised libraries to retain *W2* for its comprehensive coverage of the language since Chaucer's day and its treatment of obsolete and rare words, foreign terms and proverbs, using a split-page layout. 'Some people who look to Merriam-Webster as the ultimate lexicographic authority refuse to use *W3*, preferring to rely instead on a cherished, dog-eared copy of the now long out-of-print *W2*' (*Wilson Library Bulletin*, v.62(6), Feb. 1988, p.40).

12,000 words: a supplement to 'Webster's Third new international dictionary' (1986. 212p. ISBN: 0877792070) lists new words and meanings which have become established since the publication of *W3*, with scientific and technical terms predominant. *Class No: 802.0-30*

Desk Dictionaries

[2146]
The Random House dictionary of the English language. Flexner, S.B., *and others, eds.* 2nd ed., unabridged. New York, Random House, 1987. 2478p. ISBN: 0394500504.

1st ed. 1966.

A massive and unwieldy single-vol. unabridged dictionary with over 315,000 entries in the main sequence, plus a great deal of encyclopedic information in nearly 300p. of supplements. The basic format of the 1st ed. (which had *c.*260,000 entries) is retained, *i.e.* 3 columns per page, with entries in bold type and definitions in order of frequency from the commonest sense to archaic and obsolete meanings. Illustrative phrases have been specially created rather than drawn from printed sources. Entries include etymology (with approx. dates of entry into the language) and pronunciation, and many have appended synonym lists and notes on alternative pronunciations, usage, and regional variations. 2,500 black-and-white illustrations.

Supplementary material includes concise 2-way lexicons of French, Spanish, German and Italian, various tables, a directory of North American colleges and universities, the texts of the Declaration of Independence and the US Constitution, and an atlas, all of which can be found elsewhere and which add significantly to the work's size, although only changing to a 2-vol. format would make it easier to handle.

Reviewing *RHD-2* at length, *Choice* (v.25(6), Feb. 1988, p.868-69) commends its 'relative comprehensiveness, currency, and clarity' but expects *Webster's Fourth*, when it eventually appears, to become the pre-eminent unabridged dictionary of American English. *Class No: 802.0-30*

[2148]
Collins English dictionary. 3rd ed. Glasgow, HarperCollins, 1991. xxxi,1791p. ISBN: 0004332865.

1st ed. 1979; 2nd ed. 1986.

A relative newcomer to the UK desk-dictionary scene which has quickly established itself as one of the leaders in the field. This ed. has *c.*180,000 entries, including *c.*16,000 encyclopedic entries — enough to be useful, but not so many as to deflect from the dictionary's main purpose or to make it unwieldy. Coverage of science, technology, commerce and culture is strong and the English used outside the UK is very well represented and clearly labelled.

Derivatives and compounds are usually entered as separate headwords. Definitions are clearly written, and numbered, and the most common sense in current usage is placed first, with illustrative phrases and notes on usage in many cases. IPA is used for pronunciation and the etymologies which follow most entries include century of first recorded occurrence. Abbreviations are included in the main sequence. Biographical entries cover both historical and contemporary figures and include birth and death dates; geographical entries include population figures for towns, length for rivers, etc. Excellent explanatory notes on use of the dictionary (9p.) plus essays on the pronunciation of British English and the development of English as a world language. The more generous page-size adopted for this ed. has allowed 6,000 new words and meanings to be incorporated without any loss of clarity. *Class No: 802.0-300*

[2149]

Concise Oxford dictionary. Allen, R.E., *ed.* 8th ed. Oxford, Oxford Univ. Press, 1990. xxxix,1454p. ISBN: 0198612001.

First published 1911, edited by H.W. and F.G. Fowler. 7th ed. 1982, edited by J.B. Sykes. Earlier eds. were entitled *The Concise Oxford dictionary of current English.*

A completely revised and greatly expanded edition of a standard British desk dictionary which is based on the files used to produce the 2nd ed. of the *OED.* Claims 120,000 entries (of which 20,000 are new) and 190,000 definitions, the new material including many terms from science, technology, computing and ecology. Changes include adoption of IPA for pronunciation; systematic numbering of definitions (in order of comparative familiarity); use of continuous everyday prose for the definitions rather than 'telegraphese'; reduced use of symbols and abbreviations; and the provision of more information on grammar, inflection and usage; all of which make the dictionary easier to use. In terms of content, there is evidence of increased emphasis on currency as the criterion for selection and more attention has been paid to derivatives, idioms, colloquialisms, and international varieties of English. The label 'offens.' has been introduced to denote words and uses that can be regarded as offensive to particular groups of people. Brief etymologies are given in square brackets at the end of entries. Introductory essays cover the history of English and of the dictionary itself and 9 appendices include lists of countries, UK counties and US states, and the Greek and Russian alphabets.

Electronic edition available in PC and Mac versions, for use either as a stand-alone program or as a pop-up utility, accessible from other programs such as word-processing packages. *Class No:* 802.0-300

[2150]

Longman dictionary of the English language. 2nd ed. Harlow, Longman, 1991. xxv,1890p. ISBN: 0582070384.

A dictionary noted for its comprehensive coverage of contemporary English throughout the world (members of the public collect new words and meanings for Longman under the 'Wordwatch' scheme) and for the extent and clarity of its advice on grammar and usage, the latter quality almost certainly a result of the publisher's long and successful involvement in the EFL field.

Nearly 100,000 headwords and over 220,000 definitions, most compounds being entered separately. Generous use is made of illustrative phrases taken from the publisher's own database and the Longman/Lancaster Corpus of representative 20th-century texts, the latter source providing direct quotations from named authors. Pronunciation is indicated by a simple re-spelling system and etymologies are provided.

For the 2nd ed., which includes *c.*6,000 new words and meanings, abbreviations have been absorbed into the main sequence; biographical and geographical entries have been expanded and also absorbed; and information on grammar, usage and the discrimination of synonyms is provided within 1,000 boxes scattered throughout the dictionary. *Class No:* 802.0-300

[2151]

The Oxford encyclopedic English dictionary. Hawkins, J. *and* Allen, R., *eds.* Oxford, Clarendon Press, 1991. xvii,1786p. illus. maps. ISBN: 0198612486.

Supersedes *The Oxford reference dictionary* (1986) and has *c.*60,000 entries, of which 10,000 are encyclopedic articles covering current affairs, science and technology, history, people and places. These are longer than in most desk dictionaries, providing, for example, potted biographies for major historical figures and concise histories for every independent country. The dictionary entries (200,000 definitions claimed) include pronunciation (IPA); part of speech; inflection; numbered definitions in order of

....(contd.)

comparative familiarity and importance, accompanied in many cases by grammatical information and illustrative examples; phrases and derivatives; and etymology. Geographical, register and subject labels used extensively to indicate restricted usage. Further encyclopedic information appended, including chronologies of world events and scientific developments; lists of monarchs, prime ministers and presidents; 8 alphabets; anatomical and architectural diagrams; and 16 coloured maps. *Class No:* 802.0-300

[2152]

Webster's ninth new collegiate dictionary. Springfield, Mass., Merriam-Webster, 1983 (repr. 1990). 1564p. illus. ISBN: 0877795088.

1st ed. 1898; 8th ed. 1973.

A major American desk dictionary based on the extensive citation files (over 13 million examples) of Merriam-Webster. Claims to have nearly 160,000 entries and 200,000 definitions in this ed., supported by *c.*1,400 drawings. Entries give pronunciation (using a combination of IPA and Webster's symbols); etymology in most cases; date of first recorded instance (a new feature in this ed. and one which is unique in a desk dictionary); and numbered definitions, the senses being ordered historically with the earliest first. Notes on usage and lists of synonyms follow some entries. The dictionary proper is followed by a great deal of useful supplementary material, including lists of abbreviations; foreign words and phrases; biographical entries (nearly 6,000); geographical entries (over 9,000); US and Canadian colleges; and a handbook of style (25p.).

A CD-ROM version, which is capable of pronouncing words using voice technology on an Apple Macintosh computer, is published by Highlighted Data Inc., Arlington, Va.

Webster's New ideal dictionary (2nd ed. 1989. ISBN: 0877794499) is an abridged version for home and office use. 60,000 entries, omitting obsolete, rare, and highly technical words, dates of first recorded use and most of the etymologies.

An alternative American desk dictionary is the *Random House Webster's College dictionary* (New York, Random House, 1991. 1568p. illus. ISBN: 0679401105), with 180,000 entries edited online from *The Random House dictionary of the English language* (2nd ed., unabridged. 1987). *Class No:* 802.0-300

Synonyms

[2153]

ROGET, P.M. Roget's Thesaurus of English words and phrases. New ed., prepared by B. Kirkpatrick. Harlow, Longman, 1987. l, 1254p. ISBN: 0582893631.

1st ed. 1852, by Peter Mark Roget. Frequently revised; latest previous revision by S.M. Lloyd, 1982.

Roget's Thesaurus, one of the best-known of all English-language reference books, 'is essentially a collection of words and phrases classified according to underlying concepts and meanings' (*Preface*). Kirkpatrick has retained Roget's original scheme of grouping terms within 6 main 'classes' (1. Abstract relations - 2. Space - 3. Matter - 4. Intellect - 5. Volition - 6. Emotion, religion and morality), which are in turn subdivided into numbered 'sections', and 'heads'. The latter form the basic units of the book and there are 990 in this ed., compared with 1,000 in Roget's first ed. The 'heads' are divided into paragraphs, grouped according to part of speech and beginning with an italicised keyword. Within each paragraph, terms are grouped between semicolons according to meaning, context or stylistic level, and there are numerous cross-references to other 'heads'. An alphabetical index of *c.*45,000 terms provides access via references to head-numbers and keywords.

....*(contd.)*

This ed. has over 11,000 new terms among its 250,000 words and phrases, and includes Roget's original introduction (14p.), instructions on use (4p.) and a detailed plan of classification (27p.). Although synonymous with thesauri, *Roget's* is by no means easy to use (still less to describe) and a simple alphabetical listing may often provide a quicker answer to a synonym enquiry. *Class No:* 802.0-314

[2154]
URDANG, L. The Oxford thesaurus: an A-Z dictionary of synonyms. Oxford, Clarendon Press, 1991. xii,1042p. ISBN: 0198691513.

A major new thesaurus which lists *c.*275,000 synonyms under *c.*8,500 headwords. Each entry includes lists of synonyms for each sense of the headword, with an illustrative sentence for each sense-group and with words typical of a particular geographical or stylistic variety of English clearly labelled. The comprehensive index (482p.) provides access to each occurrence of every term, whether as headword or synonym. Does not include antonyms. Electronic edition due mid-1992. *Class No:* 802.0-314

[2155]
Webster's new dictionary of synonyms: a dictionary of discriminated synonyms, with antonyms and analogous and contrasted words. [2nd ed.]. Springfield, Mass., Merriam, 1968. 909p.

First published 1942 as *Webster's Dictionary of synonyms,* this ed. being 'newly edited and entirely reset'.

One of the most useful dictionaries of synonyms because it explains the differences in meaning between related words, often at considerable length, and illustrates these differences with example sentences and quotations from literature. Over 7,000 main entries, A-Z, with many thousands of terms explained, and numerous cross-references. Entries also include lists of antonyms. List of authors quoted (23p.). *Class No:* 802.0-314

Neologisms

[2156]
The Oxford dictionary of new words. Tulloch, S., *comp.* Oxford, Oxford Univ. Press, 1991. xi,332p. ISBN: 019869170x.

Provides information on *c.*2,000 'high-profile words and phrases which have been in the news during the past decade' (*Preface*) in 750 entries. The lengthy entries include pronunciation (IPA), part of speech, alternative spellings, definition, etymology, an account of history and usage (including details of compounds, derivatives and related terms) and illustrative quotations, chronologically arranged, from 500 newspapers, magazines and works of fiction from the English-speaking world. Cross-reference entries lead to all terms treated within main entries. An excellent reference work, marred only by the largely incomprehensible graphic 'subject icons' attached to each headword. *Class No:* 802.0-316.1

[2157]
Third Barnhart dictionary of new English. Barnhart, R.K., *and others, eds.* New York, Wilson, 1990. 565p. ISBN: 0824207963.

Supersedes *The Barnhart dictionary of new English since 1963* (Bronxville, N.Y., Barnhart/Harper & Row, 1973), which was published in the UK by Longman as *A Dictionary of new English, 1963-1972,* and *The Second Barnhart dictionary of new English* (1980), which included new terms appearing 1973-79.

Lists *c.*12,000 new words and phrases which have entered the vocabulary of the English-speaking world since *c.*1960, and new meanings for existing terms. Uses the same basic format as its predecessors, providing brief definitions, backed up by substantial quotations (with full bibliographical references); etymology where not obvious; date when the term became current; pronunciation (adapted IPA) for difficult words; and notes on usage, history, etc. Unfortunately, no indication is given as to how many entries have been retained from the earlier dictionaries and how many are new.

Updated by *The Barnhart Dictionary Companion* (New York, Springer-Verlag. Quarterly. ISSN: 07361122), which claims to be 'the only publication of its kind in the world devoted to updating general dictionaries'. *Class No:* 802.0-316.1

Loan Words

[2158]
BLISS, A. Dictionary of foreign words and phrases in current English. London, Routledge, 1966. x,389p. ISBN: 071009521x.

More than 5,000 entries, giving original meanings, definition or translation, current usage, pronunciations, plurals, variant forms, etc., and, where possible, date of first introduction. Specific references to sources of quotations illustrating use. Much more than a dictionary, in that it discusses how to distinguish the foreign from the naturalized; how to deal with them grammatically; how they should be spelt or transliterated. A classified table shows when and what was borrowed. *Class No:* 802.0-316.3

Idioms

[2159]
COWIE, A.P. *and* **MACKIN, R. Oxford dictionary of current idiomatic English.** London, Oxford Univ. Press, 1975-83. 2v.

V.1 *Verbs with prepositions & particles.* 1975. lxxxi,396p. ISBN: 0194311457.

V.2 *Phrase, clause & sentence idioms.* 1983. lxiii,685p. ISBN: 0194311503.

The most comprehensive dictionary of its kind, with *c.*15,000 idioms recorded and described. Each entry is supported by illustrative sentences, many of them drawn from *c.*90 works of modern literature and from the news media, although references are not given. Each vol. has a lengthy introduction, list of sources, and keyword index. *Class No:* 802.0-318

Grammar

[2160]
QUIRK, R., *and others.* **A Comprehensive grammar of the English language.** Harlow, Longman, 1985. 1792p. ISBN: 0582517346.

The largest and most detailed grammar available, clearly presented and illustrated with numerous vivid and up-to-date examples. Ch. 2 gives a general outline of the concepts and categories of English grammar; chs. 3-11 discuss sentence constituents in detail; chs. 12-19 deal with the more complex structure and discuss how constituents are arranged to form a message and how a whole text is constructed. Appendices cover word-formation, stress, rhythm, intonation, and punctuation. Detailed index.

Part or all of the same team (Quirk, Greenbaum, Leech and Svartvik) have produced the following shorter (but equally well arranged) grammars, all published by Longman:

A Student's grammar of the English language (1990. 528p. ISBN: 0582075696).

A University grammar of English (1973. 496p. ISBN: 0582552079).

A Grammar of contemporary English (1972. 1132p.

....(contd.)
ISBN: 058252444x).
A Communicative grammar of English (1975. 324p.
ISBN: 0582552389). *Class No:* 802.0-5

Etymology

[2161]
The Barnhart dictionary of etymology. Barnhart, R.K., *ed.*
New York, Wilson, 1988. xxvii,1284p. ISBN: 0824207459.
Over 30,000 entries written in a superbly accessible style,
avoiding technical terminology and confusing abbreviations.
Entries comprise headword, part of speech, brief definition,
date of earliest recorded appearance and account of
development through time. Particular attention paid to
word elements, with entries for all living prefixes and
suffixes. Based on contemporary American English and
consequently has entries for many words not covered in the
standard English etymological dictionaries.
Introductory essays on the history of English and on
Proto-Germanic and Indo-European. Excellent annotated
glossaries of language names and linguistic terms and of
literary works cited. Bibliography (2p.). *Class No:* 802.0-54

[2162]
The Oxford dictionary of English etymology.
Onions, C.T., *and others, eds.* Oxford, Clarendon Press,
1966. xvi,1025p. ISBN: 0198611129.
The standard etymological dictionary, with *c.*24,000
entries, the total number of words treated being over
38,000. Entries include the word's pronunciation, present
meaning, century when first recorded in English and any
developments in form and sense since then. Many entries
for prefixes and suffixes.
The Concise Oxford dictionary of English etymology, ed.
by T.F. Hoad (Oxford, Clarendon Press, 1986. xvi,552p.
ISBN: 019861182x) deals with *c.*17,000 words used in
modern English. *Class No:* 802.0-54

803 Germanic Languages

German Language

[2163]
Brockhaus Wahrig deutsches Wörterbuch in sechs Bänden. Wahrig, G., *and others, eds.* Wiesbaden, Brockhaus, 1980-84. 6v.
Based on Wahrig's *Deutsches Wörterbuch*, first published 1967; latest ed. 1975.
A major dictionary of contemporary German with 220,000 headwords and 555,000 definitions. Strong on scientific and technical terms, each of which is assigned to one of 180 categories. Syllabification is indicated in headwords and entries include numbered applications with examples of usage. *Class No:* 803.0

[2164]
The Collins German dictionary: German-English/English-German. Terrell, P., *and others, eds.* 2nd ed. Glasgow, HarperCollins, 1991. xxvi,902p. ISBN: 0004335538.
1st ed. 1980.
Over 280,000 headwords and 460,000 translations, with the emphasis on *current* spoken and written language. Good coverage of US English and of Swiss, Austrian and East German varieties of German. Notable for its extensive and consistent use of style labels to indicate specific contexts and types of usage. 'Language in use' is a very useful thematically-arranged supplement (72p.) on the grammar of both languages. Exceptional value for money. *Class No:* 803.0

[2165]
Langenscheidt's New Muret-Sanders encyclopedic dictionary of the English and German languages, based on the original work by E. Muret and D. Sanders. Springer, O., *ed.* Completely rev. ed. Berlin, Langenscheidt; London, Hodder & Stoughton, 1962-75 (repr. London, Harrap, 1989). 4v.
Pt. 1 *English-German (A-M, N-Z).* 1962-63. 2v.(xxxvii,1844p.).
Pt. 2 *German-English (A-K, L-Z).* 1974-75. 2v.(xxxvii,2024p.).
With the demise of *Harrap's Standard German and English dictionary, Muret-Sanders* is unrivalled as the most comprehensive bilingual dictionary. It has *c.*380,000 main entries, in a 3-column arrangement, with numerous compounds, derivatives and phrases. Entries include pronunciation guide (IPA) and numbered applications, with different styles and registers labelled. According to the *Preface,* 'American English is treated with the same degree of completeness and accuracy as British English' in terms of pronunciation, spelling and vocabulary. Appendices to each part include lists of abbreviations and proper names.
Langenscheidt's Condensed Muret-Sanders German dictionary: German-English/English-German, ed. by H. Messenger and others (Berlin, Langenscheidt; London, Hodder & Stoughton, 1982-85. 2v.) has *c.*270,000 entries. It

....(contd.)
is based on the 4-vol. work, but includes many new entries while others have been revised where necessary. *Class No:* 803.0

[2166]
Oxford-Duden German dictionary: German-English/English-German. Scholze-Stubenrecht, W. *and* Sykes, J.B., *eds.* Oxford, Clarendon Press, 1990. 1696p. ISBN: 0198641419.
The product of nearly 10 years joint work by OUP and the Dudenverlag and claims to be the first bilingual dictionary produced by a team based in *both* language areas. *c.*60,000 entries in each section arranged in 3 rather cramped columns. Many illustrative phrases. Indicates regional usage of English in Britain and the US, and of German in East and West Germany, Austria and Switzerland. Many useful appendices relating to both languages, including grammar, usage and letter-writing. *Class No:* 803.0

Yiddish

[2167]
GALVIN, H. and TAMARKIN, S. The Yiddish dictionary sourcebook: a transliterated guide to the Yiddish language. Hoboken, N.J., Ktav, 1986. x,317p. ISBN: 0870687153.
A popular introductory guide to Yiddish consisting mainly of a dictionary (English-Yiddish/Yiddish-English) of common words, giving English transliteration of the Yiddish, phonetic rendering of Yiddish pronunciation, and spelling in Yiddish using Hebrew characters. Appendices list popular expressions and proverbs. Introductory notes on history and grammar. Over 8,500 words and phrases covered. *Class No:* 803.0-088

Dutch

[2168]
VAN DALE, J.H. Groot woordenboek der Nederlandse taal. lle., herziene druk. Utrecht, Van Dale Lexicografie, 1984. 3v.(l, 3730p.). ISBN: 9066484012.
1st ed. 1864; 10th ed. 1976.
About 180,000 entries, conforming to the new simplified spelling of the Dutch language officially adopted in 1946/47. For each entry-word, gives meaning, special forms, derivatives, usage in expressions, origins (if an unusual word), but not pronunciation. Exhaustive treatment of many verbs and prepositions. Appendices include Greek and Roman names, foreign phrases, and Biblical names. *Van Dale* has become the authoritative, practical source of information on all aspects of the Dutch language.
Van Dale Lexitron is a CD-ROM dictionary first published in 1989 and based on *Groot woordenboek hedendaags Nederlands.* 102,000 dictionary entries, 273,000 inflected forms and 225,000 encyclopedic entries. *Class No:* 803.93

[2169]

Van Dale. Groot woordenboek Engels-Nederlands. Martin, W. *and* Tops, G.A.J., *and others,* eds. Utrecht, Van Dale Lexicografie, 1984. 1594p. ISBN: 906648103x.

Easily the most comprehensive English-Dutch dictionary available, with over 100,000 entries, including a great deal of technical vocabulary. Not easy to use at first because it employs a new, somewhat complicated, numerical code to distinguish between the various applications of each word and also labels words according to their frequency. The very small type-face is also inconvenient. Appendices include a compendium of English grammar (75p.) and a list of 776 English proverbs with translations. *Class No:* 803.93

[2170]

Van Dale. Groot woordenboek Nederlands-Engels. Martin, W. *and* Tops, G.A.J., *and others,* eds. Utrecht, Van Dale Lexicografie, 1986. 1560p. ISBN: 9066481072.

Similar in size and scope to the English-Dutch volume and, therefore, the fullest available dictionary of its kind. Uses the same numerical coding system. Packed with examples of usage, but does not give pronunciation for Dutch headwords. Appendices include lists of English words used in Dutch (4p.) and of 692 Dutch proverbs with translations. *Class No:* 803.93

Afrikaans Language

[2171]

BOSMAN, D., *and others.* **Tweetalige woordeboek:** Afrikaans-Engels/Engels-Afrikaans. 7. verbeterde uitg. Capetown, Tafelberg, 1967. xviii,1902p. (8. uitg. 1984).

1st ed. 1931-36, in 2 vols.

A comprehensive bilingual dictionary with over 50,000 entry-words in each half. Many examples and idioms. The English word-list is based on the *Concise Oxford dictionary.* No pronunciation, but stress is marked. Lists of abbreviations after each section. *Class No:* 803.936

Scandinavian Languages

Icelandic

[2172]

CLEASBY, R. An Icelandic-English dictionary. 2nd ed., with a supplement by Sir W.A. Craigie. Oxford, Clarendon Press, 1957. xlv,833p. ISBN: 0198631030.

1st ed. 1874, initiated by Cleasby and subsequently revised, enlarged and completed by E. Vigfusson. 2nd ed. is a reprint with supplement (p.781-833).

A scholarly dictionary of classical Old Icelandic, giving etymology, English translation and numerous quotations from literary works. Lengthy introduction includes list of sources and outline of grammar.

For modern Icelandic, see *Ensk-islensk ordabók,* by S. Sörenson (Reykjavík, 1984) and *Islensk-ensk ordabók,* by S.Hólmarsson and others (Reykjavík, 1989). *Class No:* 803.959

Norwegian

[2173]

HAUGEN, E. Norwegian-English dictionary: a pronouncing and translating dictionary of modern Norwegian (bokmål and nynorsk). 3rd ed. Bergen, Universitetsforlaget, 1984. 506p. ISBN: 8200065464.

1st ed. 1965.

Intended 'primarily as a tool for the learning of Norwegian by American students' (*Preface*) and claims to be the first such dictionary to include both forms of Norwegian, to give pronunciation of Norwegian words, and to label areas of usage and include quotations from

....(contd.)

Norwegian authors. Over 65,000 headwords with American English glosses. Lengthy introduction (34p.) including grammar, historical background and bibliography. *Class No:* 803.96

[2174]

KIRKEBY, W.A. English-Norwegian dictionary. Oslo, Norwegian Univ. Press, 1989 (distributed by Oxford Univ. Press). xv,810p. ISBN: 8200182932.

*c.*40,000 entries, with pronunciation guide for English words and translation into *bokmål.* Many Americanisms included and extensive use of labels to indicate stylistic differences. Many illustrative phrases. *Class No:* 803.96

Swedish

[2175]

The Standard Swedish-English/English-Swedish dictionary. Petti, V., *ed.* Stockholm, Esselte Studium, 1983; London, Cassell, 1985. 758;480p. ISBN: 0304340340, UK.

A handy 2-way dictionary with *c.*60,000 English-Swedish entries and 50,000 Swedish-English. *Class No:* 803.97

[2176]

Stora engelsk-svenska ordboken / A Comprehensive English-Swedish dictionary. Santesson, R., *and others,* eds. Stockholm, Esselte Studium, 1980. xxvii,1071p. ISBN: 9124298247.

Supersedes Kärre's *Engelsk-svensk ordbok* (first published 1935), which was previously regarded as the standard work, and is some 60% larger with *c.*120,000 words and phrases treated. Has *c.*60,000 headwords, derivative forms all being entered separately rather than under the headword, and numerous compounds and idioms from both British and American English. Stylistic values and specialist registers are clearly labelled. Pronunciation is indicated (IPA) for English headwords. A bibliography (2p.) and a very clear guide to use precede the dictionary. *Class No:* 803.97

[2177]

Svensk-engelsk ordbok. Santesson, R., *and others,* eds. Stockholm, Esselte Studium, 1968 (repr. 1976). xvi,979p.

1st ed. 1968.

A comprehensive Swedish-English dictionary with *c.*16,000 headwords and numerous compounds and phrases. Very clearly laid out, making good use of bold and italic type. *Class No:* 803.97

Danish

[2178]

NIELSEN, B.K. Engelsk-dansk ordbog. 2. udg. Copenhagen, Gyldendal, 1981. 1273p. ISBN: 8701449710.

1st ed. 1964.

A companion to Vinterberg and Bodelsen, with *c.*70,000 entry-words and translations for numerous derivatives, compounds and idioms. Pronunciation given for most of the English headwords. A very comprehensive dictionary, including Americanisms, scientific and technical terms, proper names and abbreviations. *Class No:* 803.98

[2179]

VINTERBERG, H. *and* **BODELSEN, C.A. Dansk-engelsk ordbog.** 2. udg. (5. oplag med tillaeg). Copenhagen, Gyldendal, 1981. 2v. ISBN: 8700671614.

1st ed. 1954-56; 2nd ed. 1966.

The most comprehensive Danish-English dictionary, with *c.*50,000 headwords and numerous examples of usage clearly set out. Includes colloquial and obsolete meanings and many technical terms. Pronunciation not indicated for Danish headwords. *Class No:* 803.98

804/806 Romance Languages

French Language

[2180]
Collins-Robert French-English/English-French dictionary. Atkins, B.T., *and others, eds.* 2nd ed. Glasgow, HarperCollins; Paris, Robert, 1987. xxix,768;929p. ISBN: 0004334515.

Published in France as *Robert-Collins dictionnaire ... .*

An outstanding single-vol. bilingual dictionary resulting from collaboration between French and English lexicographers. Over 100,000 headwords and over 100,000 phrases and idioms, with the emphasis firmly on contemporary usage. For the 2nd ed. many new words and meanings have been added, particularly from specialist fields, and abbreviations incorporated in the main text. The dictionary is particularly notable for its systematic use of labels and symbols to indicate the style, register, etc.; *e.g.*, one to three asterisks attached to a term, from slightly informal to taboo. 'Language in use: a grammar of communication in French and English' forms a very useful appendix (71p.). *Class No:* 804.0

[2181]
Harrap's Shorter French and English dictionary: French-English/anglais-français. Goldie, J., *and others, eds.* New ed., entirely re-set. London, Harrap, 1991. 2072p. in various pagings. ISBN: 0245550461.

1st ed. 1982.

A condensed version of *Harrap's Standard French and English dictionary,* which has been thoroughly revised, expanded (30% larger than previous ed.), and re-set to give a clearer layout.

*c.*45,000 English-French entry-words and *c.*36,000 French-English, with numerous compounds, phrases and idioms, the total number of translations claimed to be 460,000. Entries include pronunciation (IPA) in both sections, context indicators, style/register labels, and grammatical information. American English and Canadian French usage are well covered and clearly indicated. Appended, separately-paged sections on English grammar (76p.), English conversation (32p.), French grammar (64p.), and French conversation (32p.). *Class No:* 804.0

[2182]
MANSION, J.E. Harrap's New standard French and English dictionary, rev. and ed. by D.M. and R.P.L. Ledésert. Rev. ed. London, Harrap, 1977-80. 4v.

Vols. 1-2, *French-English*; vols. 3-4, *English-French.*

French-English section first published 1934; English-French section first published 1939. Later published together as *Harrap's Standard French and English dictionary,* a title which has also been used on recent reprints of the new ed.

A complete revision of a dictionary which has come to be regarded as the most comprehensive and authoritative of its kind. Nearly 250,000 headwords, embracing all aspects

....(contd.)
of modern spoken and written French, including technical terms, slang, neologisms, and the French of Canada, Belgium, etc. Numerous idiomatic phrases. Entries give pronunciation but not etymology. The English word-list includes many US and Commonwealth terms. Lists of abbreviations in vols. 2 and 4. *Class No:* 804.0

[2183]
Petit Larousse illustré, 1989: dictionnaire encyclopédique pour tous. Paris, Larousse, 1988. xxxi,1808p.

One of the most famous of all reference works, first published in 1856 and now appearing annually in a well-established format: dictionary (52,500 headwords in this ed.); classical and foreign quotations; encyclopedia (24,500 entries), giving brief biographical, historical and geographical data; and concise atlas. Over 4,000 illustrations.

The deluxe version, *Petit Larousse en couleurs,* also appears annually. *Class No:* 804.0

[2184]
ROBERT, P. Le Grand Robert de la langue française: dictionnaire alphabétique et analogique de la langue française. 2e. éd., entièrement revue et enrichie par A. Rey. Paris, Robert, 1985. 9v. ISBN: 2850360996.

1st ed. 1951-64 (6v.); *Supplément,* 1970.

An outstanding dictionary, compiled on historical principles and giving comprehensive coverage of French from the 15th century to the present. Over 80,000 entries, showing etymology, pronunciation, analogies, synonyms and antonyms, and the history of the word's development. *c.*160,000 quotations, with precise references. Bibliography (49p.) in v.9.

A CD-ROM version, *Le Grand Robert électronique,* became available in 1989, and is distributed in the UK and US by Chadwyck-Healey. *Class No:* 804.0

Catalan

[2185]
Vox diccionari anglès-català/català-anglès. Barcelona, Bibliograf, 1988. xl,339p.; xxiii,269p.

18,000 entries in each section, including idioms. Pronunciation (IPA) indicated for both Catalan and English headwords. Proper names and abbreviations incuded in the main sequences. Includes summary of Catalan grammar (23p.). *Class No:* 804.99

Italian Language

[2186]
The Collins Sansoni Italian dictionary: English-Italian/Italian-English. Macchi, V., *ed.* 3rd ed. Firenze, Sansoni; London, Collins, 1988. 2277p. ISBN: 0004335759.

1st ed. 1975; 2nd ed. 1981.

Has *c.*156,000 entry-words, with a total of *c.*570,000 translations. Good coverage of contemporary idiomatic usage. Strong on neologisms, with 12,000 new entries collated since 2nd ed. Includes abbreviations and proper names. Pronunciation given for English headwords (IPA), with stress indicated for Italian, plus values of e, o, s, and z. Like most Collins bilingual dictionaries, represents good value for money. *Class No:* 805.0

[2187]
Il Grande dizionario Garzanti della lingua italiana. Felici, L., *ed.* Milano, Garzanti, 1987. xv,2270p. ISBN: 8811102014.

Supersedes *Dizionario Garzanti della lingua italiana* (1965).

The largest single-vol. dictionary, with *c.*270,000 words, including many neologisms and foreign words. There are numerous Duden-style line drawings and many of the entries include etymologies. Appendices include 62 tables of specialist vocabulary and list of abbreviations. *Class No:* 805.0

[2188]
Harrap's Shorter Italian dictionary / Il Nuovo Ragazzini. Ragazzini, G., *ed.* 2. ed. Bologna, Zanichelli, 1988; London, Harrap, 1989. 2144p. ISBN: 0245548378.

Supersedes Ragazzini's *Dizionario inglese-italiano/italiano-inglese* (Bologna, Zanichelli, 1968).

A highly-regarded, up-to-date bilingual dictionary with over 60,000 entries in each section and numerous illustrative phrases and idioms. Includes proper names within the main sequences but also has appended lists. *Class No:* 805.0

[2189]
Il Nuovo dizionario Hazon Garzanti: inglese-italiano/italiano-inglese. Milano, Garzanti, 1990. 2430p. ISBN: 8811103219.

1st ed. 1961 as *Grande dizionario, inglese-italiano/italiano-inglese.*

This long overdue revision puts *Hazon* back at the forefront of modern English-Italian dictionaries. Primarily intended for Italian users, it provides phonetic transcription for the English entries only. Noted for its comprehensiveness, reviewers suggesting that there is very little in other major dictionaries which is absent from *Hazon.* 135,000 headwords, including over 58,000 specialist terms. Includes *c.*2,000 quotations from literary sources. *Class No:* 805.0

[2190]
Sansoni-Harrap standard Italian and English dictionary. Macchi, V., *ed.* 2nd ed. Firenze, Sansoni; London, Harrap, 1970-76. 4v.

Pt.1 *Italian-English.* 1970-72. 2v.

Pt.2 *English-Italian.* 1973-76. 2v.

Claims to be the most comprehensive Italian and English dictionary ever compiled, with *c.*150,000 headwords in pt.1 and *c.*170,000 in pt.2, plus numerous phrases. Includes proper names, abbreviations, scientific and technical terms, neologisms, colloquialisms, slang, and regionalisms. Pronunciation indicated for English headwords (IPA). Stress given for Italian headwords, with value of e, o, s, and z. American and British English given equal treatment. All botanical and zoological terms accompanied by Latin name. *Class No:* 805.0

Rumanian

[2191]
PANOVF, I. New Pocket Rumanian dictionary: Rumanian-English/English-Rumanian. New York, Hippocrene, 1983. 828p.

Originally published Bucharest, 1982.

Small in size, but contains *c.*30,000 entries and an extensive guide to Romanian grammar and pronunciation. *Class No:* 805.90

Spanish Language

[2192]
Larousse gran diccionario, español-inglés / English-Spanish. García-Pelayo y Gross, R., *ed.* Paris, Larousse, 1983. viii,1542,xiip. ISBN: 2034513312.

Has *c.*40,000 entries in each half and differentiates Latin American Spanish and North American English terminology. Includes scientific and technical terms, as well as colloquialisms. Some 90 category labels are applied to headwords. Many examples used to define precise meaning. Specalized vocabulary lists in boxes within each section. *Class No:* 806.0

[2193]
REAL ACADEMIA ESPAÑOLA. Diccionario de la lengua española. 20. ed. Madrid, Espasa-Calpe, 1984. 2v.(xxvi,1417p.). ISBN: 8423947777.

1st ed. 1726-39 in 6 vols.; 19th ed. 1970.

About 50,000 headwords. The authority for current Spanish usage, as well as for etymology. The different meanings and applications of words are noted, with many examples. Scientific and technical words in current use are included, as well as many Latin-American words and phrases, but generally conservative in accepting new words. This ed. has improved etymologies and many new technical terms. *Class No:* 806.0

[2194]
SMITH, C., *and others.* **Collins Spanish-English/English-Spanish dictionary.** 2nd ed. Glasgow, Collins; Barcelona, Grijalbo, 1988. xxxv,1554p. ISBN: 0004335341, UK; 8425320119, Spain.

1st ed. 1971.

One of the best desk dictionaries, with *c.*45,000 entries in each part and *c.*390,000 translations in total. Latin American Spanish and North American English usage well covered and clearly indicated. Many idioms. Style labels for all non-standard terms. Lengthy notes on 'the grammar of communication in Spanish and English'. Excellent value. *Class No:* 806.0

[2195]
University of Chicago Spanish dictionary: a new concise Spanish-English and English-Spanish dictionary of words and phrases basic to the written and spoken languages of today, plus a list of 500 Spanish idioms and sayings, with variants and English equivalents. Castillo, C. *and* Bond, O.F., *comps.* 4th ed., rev. and enl. by D.L. Canfield. Chicago, Univ. of Chicago Press, 1987. 475p. ISBN: 0226104001.

1st ed. 1948; 3rd ed. 1977.

A handy desk dictionary 'compiled for the general use of the American learner of Spanish and the Spanish-speaking learner of English, with special reference to New World usages as found in the United States and Spanish America' (*Foreword*).

35,000 entry-words, with much new vocabulary in the 4th ed. Pronunciation given for all headwords. Very useful introductory sections to each part, both covering grammar and that to the first part including a history of the Spanish language in America. *Class No:* 806.0

Portuguese Language

[2196]
Dicionário inglês-português. Houaiss, A., *ed*. Rio de Janeiro, Record; New York, French & European, 1982. 928p. ISBN: 8510165017, Brazil; 0828804923, US.

US title is *Webster's Diccionario inglês-portugês*.

Over 100,000 entries, with the emphasis on Brazilian Portuguese. Many idiomatic phrases. Clearly-signalled explanatory entries for English prefixes and suffixes. *Class No:* 806.90

[2197]
FERREIRA, A.B. de Holanda. Novo dicionário da língua portuguesa. 2. ed. Rio de Janeiro, Nova Fronteira, 1986. xxiii,1838p.

1st ed. 1975.

A third larger than the 1st ed., with over 100,000 definitions, including many neologisms and slang terms. 'Perhaps the best dictionary of the Portuguese language available in a single volume' (Chamberlain, B.J., *Portuguese language and Luso-Brazilian literature*, 1989, p.13). *Class No:* 806.90

[2198]
Novo Michaelis dicionário ilustrado / The New Michaelis illustrated dictionary. São Paulo, Melhoramentos; Wiesbaden, Brockhaus, 1958-61 (frequently reprinted). 2v.

Based on a dictionary originally published in 1893.

V.1 *English-Portuguese*. 45th ed. xxxiii,1151p.

V.2 *Portuguese-English* 43rd ed. li,1328p.

One of the best bilingual dictionaries available, with over 73,000 entries and over 4,000 Brockhaus-style illustrations in v.1. Many idiomatic phrases and technical terms. V.2 has over 78,000 entries and includes list of Portuguese abbreviations, verb conjugations, and table of weights and measures.

A concise edition is published as *Pequeno dicionário Michaelis* (São Paulo, Melhoramentos, 1988. xii,642p.). *Class No:* 806.90

[2199]
TAYLOR, J.L. Portuguese-English dictionary. Rev. ed. Stanford, Calif., Stanford Univ. Press; London, Harrap, 1970. xxii,662p. ISBN: 0804704805, US; 0245572287, UK.

First published 1959.

Entries for *c*.60,000 Portuguese terms, giving English equivalent, synonyms, and (often) examples of usage. Follows official Brazilian orthography. Includes many technical terms, with usage labels. Appendix of Portuguese verb models. *Class No:* 806.90

807/808 Classical & Slavonic Languages

Classical Languages

Latin Language

[2200]
LEWIS, C.T. *and* SHORT, C. **Latin dictionary**, founded on Andrews' edition of Freund's Latin dictionary. Rev., enl. and in greater part rewritten. Oxford, Clarendon Press, 1879 (frequently reprinted). xiv,2019p. ISBN: 0198642016.

Andrews' edition of Freund's dictionary was published in 1850.

The standard Latin-English dictionary for Latin up to *c.*1000AD and including patristic writings. About 60,000 entries, including proper and geographical names. Capital letters and figures (arabic and roman), in bold, introduce different meanings and applications of words. Very small type. Includes many quotations from classical authors, with adequate source references. List of authors and works cited, p.vii-xi.

C.T. Lewis's *Latin dictionary for schools*, first published 1889 (1204p.) is also frequently reprinted. *Class No:* 807.1

[2201]
Oxford Latin dictionary. Glare, P.G.W., *ed.* Oxford, Clarendon Press, 1982. 2150p. ISBN: 0198642245.

Originally published in 8 fascicules, 1968-82.

About 40,000 Latin headwords, based on a collection of over one million quotations from literary, epigraphic and other sources, with exact references. Different meanings are numbered. Includes proper names. Brief etymological notes, with articles on the principal suffixes — an innovation in Latin lexicography. Covers the language from the earliest recorded word up to AD200, omitting patristic writings. Fasc. 1 includes a list of references ('Authors and works', p.ix-xx), and a 'Supplementary list of modern collections', p.xx-xxi. Aims to be 'a dictionary independent alike of Lewis & Short on the one hand and of the *Thesaurus linguae latinae* on the other ... and which aims to be approximately one-third longer than Lewis & Short'. Hailed by reviewers as a major work of modern scholarship. *Class No:* 807.1

Mediaeval Latin

[2202]
LATHAM, R.E. **Revised medieval Latin word-list** from British and Irish sources. Prepared under the direction of a committee appointed by the British Academy. London, Oxford Univ. Press, 1965. xxiii,524p. ISBN: 0197258913.

Revision of *Medieval Latin word-list*, by J.H. Baxter and C. Johnson (1934 and revised reprints) which deal with *c.*20,000 words (excluding classical words unless their meanings have altered). About 40,000 entry-words and references, with English equivalents and dated citations (sources listed p.xxi-xxiii). Words are selected for inclusion

....(contd.)
'in so far as they are non-classical either in form or in meaning' (*Introduction*), those in regular occurrence during the period being asterisked. *Class No:* 807.33

Greek Language

[2203]
LIDDELL, H.G. *and* SCOTT, R. **A Greek-English lexicon ...** . New [9th] ed., rev. and aug. throughout by H.S. Jones (and others). Oxford, Clarendon Press, 1925-40. *Supplement*, 1968. 2v. ISBN: 0198642148.

1st ed. 1843. This ed. published in 10 pts., 1925-40.

The standard classical Greek-English dictionary, based on F. Passow's *Handwörterbuch der griechischen Sprache* (5th ed. Leipzig, Vogel, 1841-57. 2v. in 4). Etymological comment is deliberately reduced to a minimum; place names and many proper names are omitted, so that it is necessary to use Passow for this purpose. About 10,000 entries. Words beginning with the same element are usually grouped together. Latin and Semitic words in Greek form are included, but Byzantine and patristic literature is not covered, the dictionary limiting its period roughly to AD600. New words and new meanings are included in an Addendum. List of authors and works referred to precedes the dictionary.

Supplement, ed. by E.A. Barber and others (Oxford, Clarendon Press, 1968. xi,153p. ISBN: 0198642105), incorporates revised Addenda and Corrigenda from 9th ed., adds new words, and amends earlier entries. List of sources (5p.), including recently published inscriptions and papyri. Available separately or bound with reprinted 9th ed. *Class No:* 807.5

New Testament Greek

[2204]
BAUER, W. **A Greek-English lexicon of the New Testament and other early Christian literature;** a translation and adaptation of W. Bauer's *Griechisch-deutsches Wörterbuch zu den Schriften des Neuen Testaments und der übrigen urchristlichen Literatur* (4th ed. 1952) by W. F Arndt and F.W. Gingrich. 2nd ed., rev. and aug. from Bauer's 5th ed., 1958. Chicago, Univ. of Chicago Press, 1979. 900p. ISBN: 0226039323.

1st ed. Cambridge, Cambridge Univ. Press, 1957.

Gives exact references to sources, which include periodicals, collections and modern authors. List of sources (10p.). References to scholarly literature extend to late 1954.

J.R. Alsop's *An Index to the revised Bauer-Arndt-Gingrich Greek lexicon, second edition* (Grand Rapids, Mich., Zondervan, 1981. 525p. ISBN: 0310440319) lists the entries in the order in which they appear in the New Testament, from Matthew to Revelation, with references to page numbers in the lexicon and English translations. *Class No:* 807.7:225

Modern Greek

[2205]
PRING, J.T. The Oxford dictionary of modern Greek: Greek-English and English-Greek. Single-vol. reprint. Oxford, Clarendon Press, 1986. xx,602p. ISBN: 0198641370.
Originally published 1982, in 2 vols.
'Designed to meet the need for a compact, up-to-date dictionary suitable both for general reference and the language student' (*Preface*) and therefore concentrates on the vocabulary of everyday affairs and general literature. Many idioms and illustrative phrases included, with points of Greek style and usage explained in English. *c.*37,000 entries in all. Appendices list place names, personal names and principal parts of Greek verbs. 'Scores outstandingly well in comparison with others of its size'. (*TLS*, no.4144, Sept. 3rd, 1982, p.953). *Class No:* 807.74

[2206]
STAVROPOULOS, D.N. and HORNBY, A.S. The Oxford Greek-English learner's dictionary. Oxford, Oxford Univ. Press, 1989. iv,1019p. illus. ISBN: 0194311996.
Intended for Greek speakers (whereas Pring's dictionary is aimed at English speakers) and regarded as the best Greek-English dictionary available. 45,000 entries, with many examples of usage. Code numbers with inflected words refer to declension and conjugation tables.
The companion vol. is the same authors' *Oxford English-Greek learner's dictionary* (1977; repr. 1988. xxiv,839p. ISBN: 0194311473), which is based on Hornby's *Oxford advanced learner's dictionary of current English* with all the definitions and illustrative sentences adapted and translated into Modern Greek. Over 20,000 entry-words. Appended lists of abbreviations, geographical names, and classical names. All introductory material in Greek. *Class No:* 807.74

Slavonic & Baltic Languages

Russian Language

[2207]
Bolshoi anglo-russkii slovar'/ New English-Russian dictionary. Galperin, I.R. *and* Mednikova, E.M., *eds.* 4. izd. Moskva, Russkii Yazik, 1987 (distr. in UK by Collets). 2v.(1038;1072p.). ISBN: 0569090229.
1st ed. Moskva Sovetskaya Entsiklopediya, 1972. Supplement, 1980.
The biggest English-Russian dictionary available, with *c.*150,000 entry-words. The emphasis is on current vocabulary, with many scientific and technical terms and idioms. Intended for Russians, with pronunciation given for English headwords, but the preface and introduction are in English and Russian. Supplement (now incorporated) lists *c.*12,000 new words and phrases. Appended lists of forenames, place names, and abbreviations. 'For sheer detail of coverage and range of usage, this work is almost unparalleled, and must long remain a true lodestar' (*Language Monthly*, April 1986, p.19, on the previous ed.). *Class No:* 808.2

[2208]
The Oxford Russian-English dictionary. Wheeler, M., *ed.* 2nd ed. Oxford, Clarendon Press, 1984. xiv,927p. ISBN: 0198641540.
1st ed. 1972.
A comprehensive dictionary, primarily intended for English speakers. *c.*54,000 entries, each word being entered separately, with English translations rather than definitions. Stress indicated for all Russian words, with genitive singular and gender given for nouns. Many idioms, but no literary quotations. Appended lists of abbreviations and

....(contd.)
geographical names. Index of new material in 2nd ed. lists 205 additional entries and 107 additional meanings of existing entries. *Class No:* 808.2

[2209]
—The Oxford English-Russian dictionary. Falla, P.S., *ed.* Oxford, Clarendon Press, 1984. xvi,1053p. ISBN: 0198641176.
Unlike its Russian-English counterpart, this is not the largest dictionary in its field, having fewer than 35,000 headwords, but the vocabulary is up-to-date, the dictionary is clearly laid out, and — unlike Galperin's larger *Bolshoi anglo-russkii slovar'* — it is intended for English speakers, with bracketed English glosses to facilitate the choice between alternative Russian equivalents. However, 'the rendering of obscure words or the need for a wider range of examples will make recourse to Galperin essential' (*Modern Language Review*, v.81(1), Jan. 1986, p.262-3). The English vocabulary is based on the *Concise Oxford dictionary* and the *Oxford advanced learner's dictionary of current English,* and includes some Americanisms. Proper names are included in the main sequence. *Class No:* 808.2

[2210]
WILSON, E.A.M. The Modern Russian dictionary for English speakers: English-Russian. Oxford, Pergamon; Moskva, Russkii Yazyk, 1982. 716p. ISBN: 0080205542.
'The vocabulary comprises the words which the average educated man might want to use in speaking or writing Russian, including the simple technical terms in common use' (*Introduction*). Over 22,000 entry-words, with excellent coverage of idiomatic usage, the English being 'real and everyday, as it was conspicuously not in some earlier Soviet dictionaries' (*Language Monthly*, April 1986, p.19). Consequently, there are very extensive entries for verbs like 'be', 'get' and 'do', and for prepositions. Good use of stylistic and field labels. Stress indicated for Russian words and some grammatical information provided. *Class No:* 808.2

Ukrainian

[2211]
ANDRUSYSHEN, C.H. and KRETT, J.N. Ukrainian-English dictionary. Toronto, Univ. of Toronto Press, for the Univ. of Saskatchewan, 1957 (paperback ed. 1981). xxix,1163p. ISBN: 0802064213.
A comprehensive dictionary of *c.*130,000 words and phrases. Shows tonic stress on Ukrainian words and provides examples of usage. Includes proper names in main sequence. Uses the system of orthography accepted in 1928. *Class No:* 808.3

Polish Language

[2212]
STANISLAWSKI, J. Wielki slownik angielsko-polski, z suplementem. [The Great English-Polish dictionary, supplemented.] Warszawa, Wiedza Powszechna, 1982. 2v.(xvi,692;715p.). ISBN: 832140314x.
First published 1964.
The most comprehensive English-Polish dictionary, with over 100,000 words and phrases, including many scientific and technical terms, plus dialect, colloquial, American and Commonwealth expressions. Entries give pronunciation of English headword and numbered applications. Appendices include lists of geographical names, forenames, literary characters, and abbreviations. This ed. has supplementary lists of new words and meanings in each vol., adding *c.*12,000 entries. *Class No:* 808.4

[2213]
STANISLAWSKI, J. **Wielki słownik polsko-angielski,** z suplementem. [The Great Polish-English dictionary, supplemented.] Warszawa, Wiedza Powszechna, 1983. 2v.(xvi,800; 928p.). ISBN: 8321401074.
First published 1969.
Like its counterpart, the leader in its field with *c.*180,000 Polish words, phrases and expressions, including technical and scientific terms, colloquial, dialectal and historical terms, and many idiomatic phrases. Makes good use of qualifying labels and different typefaces. Appendices include lists of geographical names and abbreviations, and a summary of Polish grammar (52p.).
This ed. has supplementary lists of new words and meanings in each vol., adding *c.*10,000 entries. *Class No:* 808.4

Czech

[2214]
HAIS, K. *and* HODEK, B. **Velký anglicko-český slovník** / English-Czech dictionary. Praha, Academia, 1984-85 (distr. in UK by Collets). 3v.(2843p.). ISBN: 0569089204.
The most comprehensive English-Czech dictionary, with *c.*100,000 entries - the high figure due to the fact that each compound form has a separate entry. Entries comprise headword, pronunciation (IPA), numbered applications, and phrases. Usages specific to the US or UK are clearly labelled. Bibliography (3p.) Appended lists of place-names, personal names, and abbreviations. *Class No:* 808.50

[2215]
POLDAUF, I. **Česko-anglický slovník,** středního rozsahu/ Czech-English dictionary, medium. [6. vyd.]. Praha, Státní Pedagogické Nákl., 1986 (distr. in UK by Collets). 1134p. ISBN: 0569004047.
1st ed. 1959.
A standard Czech-English dictionary, which is aimed at both Czech and English users. *c.*30,000 entry-words, plus many idioms. Appended summary of Czech grammar in tables.
Poldauf's *English-Czech and Czech-English dictionary* (Praha, SPN, 1985. 1224p.) is a useful 2-way dictionary. *Class No:* 808.50

Slovak

[2216]
ŠIMKO, J. **Anglicko-slovenský slovník** / English-Slovak dictionary. 3. vyd. Bratislava, Slovenské Pedagogické Nakladateľstvo, 1971. 1443p.
1st. ed. 1967.
Approx. 12,500 English entry-words (with pronunciation indicated) and many idioms and phrases. *Class No:* 808.54

[2217]
VILIKOVSKÁ, J. *and* VILIKOVSKÝ, P. **Slovensko-anglický slovník** / Slovak-English dictionary. 4. vyd. Bratislava, SPN, 1984. 524p.
1st ed. 1959.
Over 23,000 entry-words. *Class No:* 808.54

Serbo-Croat

[2218]
BENSON, M. **English-Serbocroatian dictionary.** 3rd ed. Cambridge, Cambridge Univ. Press, 1990. 770p. ISBN: 0521384966.
1st ed. Beograd, Prosveta, 1978; Philadelphia, Univ. of Pennsylvania Press, 1979; 2nd ed. Prosveta, 1984.
The most comprehensive and up-to-date dictionary of its kind, providing Serbo-Croatian equivalents for nearly 60,000 English headwords and 100,000 phrases and

....(contd.)
collocations. Provides phonetic transcription of both US and British pronunciations for all headwords and indicates differences in US and British usage. Includes scientific and technical terms. *Class No:* 808.61/.62

[2219]
BENSON, M. **Serbocroatian-English dictionary.** Cambridge, Cambridge Univ. Press, 1990. 844p. ISBN: 0521384958.
1st ed. Philadelphia, Pennsylvania Univ. Press, 1971; 2nd ed. Beograd, Prosveta, 1985.
Like Benson's *English-Serbocroatian dictionary,* a comprehensive and up-to-date work with *c.*60,000 headwords and *c.*100,000 compounds and phrases. Shows accents for all headwords and forms, and distinguishes between Eastern and Western variants of Serbo-Croat, as well as between US and British terms in the definitions. Bibliography of sources (5p.). *Class No:* 808.61/.62

Slovenian

[2220]
KOTNIK, J. **Slovensko-angleški slovar** / Slovene-English dictionary. 8. izd. Ljubljana, Državna Založba Slovenije, 1978 (repr. 1982). 831p.
1st ed. 1945.
Over 30,000 entry-words. Chiefly equivalents with some idioms and compounds. Appended lists of forenames, geographical names and proverbs.
The companion *Angleško-slovenski slovar* by R. Skerlj (6th ed. 1965. viii, 812p.) has a similar number of entries. *Class No:* 808.63

Bulgarian

[2221]
ATANASSOVA, T., *and others.* **Bulgarian-English dictionary.** 3rd. ed. Sofia, Nauka i Izkustvo, 1988. 2v. (1050p.).
The fullest Bulgarian-English dictionary available, with over 40,000 entries. Many idioms and phrases.
The companion *English-Bulgarian dictionary* (3rd ed. 1985. 2v.) is a very comprehensive dictionary, covering the English literary language from the 18th century to the present, with some dialect and slang words and technical terms of a general nature. Over 70,000 headwords, with pronunciation indicated, and numerous idioms and phrases. *Class No:* 808.67

Baltic Languages

Lithuanian

[2222]
Anglu-lietuviu kalbu žodynas. Laucka, A., *and others, eds.* 3rd ed. Vilnius, Mokslas, 1986. 1096p.
English-Lithuanian dictionary containing *c.*60,000 words. *Class No:* 808.82

[2223]
PETERAITIS, V. **Lietuviškai angliškas žodynas.** 2. laida. [Chicago], Letuviskos Knygos Klubas, 1960. xv,586p.
1st ed. 1948.
A Lithuanian-English dictionary, primarily intended for Lithuanians living in English-speaking countries. *Class No:* 808.82

Latvian

[2224]
RAŠKEVIČS, J., *and* *others.* **Anglu-latviešu vārdnīca** /
English-Latvian dictionary. 4. izd. Riga, Avots, 1985. 819p.
  Approx. 22,000 entries. Pronunciation given for English
headwords. Appended lists of geographical names, personal
names, and abbreviations. *Class No:* 808.83

[2225]
TURKINA, E. Latviešu-anglu vārdnīca / Latvian-English
dictionary. 4. izd. Riga, Avots, 1982. 638p.
  3rd ed. 1963.
  Over 30,000 entry-words. Appendices include list of
geographical names. *Class No:* 808.83

Indian Languages

Sanskrit

[2226]
MACDONNELL, A.A. A Practical Sanskrit dictionary, with transliteration, accentuation and etymological analysis throughout. London, Oxford Univ. Press, 1924. xii,382p. ISBN: 0198643039.

First published 1893, based on the monumental *Sanskrit-Wörterbuch* by O. von Böhtlingk and R. Roth (St. Petersburg, 1855-75. 7v.).

Aims 'to satisfy, within the compass of a comparatively handy volume, all the practical wants not only of learners of Sanskrit, but also of scholars for the purposes of ordinary reading' (*Preface*). Over 16,000 entries, giving Sanskrit form, transliterated form, English translation, derivatives, and compounds. Thorough coverage of Vedic literature, plus some selections from post-Vedic texts. *Class No:* 809.12

Hindi

[2227]
PATHAK, R.C. Bhargava's Standard illustrated dictionary of the Hindi language (Hindi-English ed.). Rev. ed. Varanasi, Bhargava, 1964.

*c.*120,000 entry-words.

The companion vol. is *Bhargava's Standard illustrated dictionary of the English language (Anglo-Hindi ed.)* (12th ed. 1972. 1412p.), with *c.*100,000 entries. Both dictionaries are frequently reprinted. *Class No:* 809.143.2

Urdu

[2228]
Ferozsons' Urdu-English dictionary: a comprehensive dictionary of current vocabulary. Rev. ed. Lahore, Ferozsons, [1979?]. 831p. ISBN: 969005081.

1st ed. 1960.

About 30,000 entries, giving Urdu form, romanized form and English translation, with an indication of language of origin for each new headword.

A 2-way dictionary has been published as *Ferozsons' English-Urdu/Urdu-English dictionary* (1989. 1124p. ISBN: 9690005103). *Class No:* 809.143.3

Bengali

[2229]
DEV, A.T. Students' favourite dictionary (English-to-Bengali). 28th ed. Calcutta, Dev Sahitya Kutir, 1977. x,1616p.

1st ed. 1934.

*c.*35,000 entry-words, plus compounds and phrases. Many appendices with miscellaneous information: dates, proverbs, biographies, etc.

There is a corresponding *Students' favourite dictionary (Bengali-English)* (27th ed. Calcutta, Dev Sahitya Kutir, 1978. x,1391p.). *Class No:* 809.144

Gujarati

[2230]
DESHPANDE, P.G. Universal English-Gujarati dictionary. Bombay, Oxford Univ. Press, 1988. 959p. ISBN: 0195618289.

Provides Gujarati definitions for *c.*34,000 English words and phrases.

Deshpande's *Concise English-Gujarati dictionary* (Bombay, Oxford Univ. Press, 1986. 466p. ISBN: 0195618270) translates *c.*15,000 terms.

Deshpande has also compiled a *Gujarati-English dictionary* (Ahmadabad, University Book Production Board, 1974). *Class No:* 809.147

Iranian (Persian) Languages

[2231]
HAYYĪM, S. The New Persian-English dictionary, complete and modern, designed to give the English meanings of over 50,000 words, terms, idioms and proverbs in the Persian language, as well as the transliteration of the words in English characters. Together with a sufficient treatment of all the grammatical features of the Persian language. Tehran, Bëroukhim, 1934-36 (repr. 1975). 2v. (xvi,1078p.; xv,1246p.).

Hayyim's *The Shorter Persian-English dictionary* (3rd ed. Tehran, Bëroukhim, 1963. xvi,814p.) is an abridgement with *c.*30,000 entry-words. *Class No:* 809.15

[2232]
STEINGASS, F. A Comprehensive Persian-English dictionary, including the Arabic words and phrases to be met with in Persian literature, being Johnson's and Richardson's *Persian and Arabic dictionary,* revised, enlarged and entirely reconstructed. London, Kegan Paul, Trench, Trubner, 1892 (repr. Routledge, 1990). viii,1539p. ISBN: 0415025435.

First published 1892.

Regarded as still the best dictionary for the classical Persian language. Arabic terms are given in Arabic script and in transliterated form. Over 30,000 entry-words. *Class No:* 809.15

Celtic

Irish

[2233]
DE BHALDRAITHE, T. English-Irish dictionary. Dublin, Stationery Office, 1959 (repr. 1977). xii,864p.
Aims to provide romanized Irish equivalents for English words and phrases in common use. Not an exhaustive dictionary of the Irish language, because many thousands of words and phrases in common use in the Gaeltacht are not the equivalents of common English. Primarily based on current Irish usage, but draws on the older literary language when necessary. Proper names are included. *Class No:* 809.162

[2234]
Ó' DÓNAILL, N. Foclóir Gaeilge-Béarla. Baile Átha Cliath, Oifig an tSoláthair, 1977. xii,1309p.
A comprehensive Irish-English dictionary, which effectively supersedes Dinneen's *Irish-English dictionary* (New ed. Dublin, 1927). Over 45,000 entry-words, with numerous idiomatic phrases. Very clearly laid out, making good use of category labels and different typefaces. *Class No:* 809.162

Welsh

[2235]
The Collins Spurrell Welsh dictionary. Thorne, D.A., *and others, eds.* Rev. ed. Glasgow, HarperCollins, 1991. xii,372p. ISBN: 000433549x.
Spurrell's Welsh-English dictionary first published Carmarthen, 1848. *Collins-Spurrell Welsh dictionary* first published London, Collins, 1960, ed. by H. Lewis.
A revision of a popular and well-established dictionary. Over 13,000 Welsh-English entries and over 14,000 English-Welsh. Lists of personal and place names. Notes on Welsh pronunciation. *Class No:* 809.166

[2236]
EVANS, H.M. and THOMAS, W.O. Y Geiriadur mawr: the complete Welsh-English/English-Welsh dictionary. 8th ed. Abertawe, C. Davies, 1987. 492;367p. ISBN: 0715405438. 1st ed. 1958.
Far more than a revised and enlarged ed. of its predecessor, the *New Welsh dictionary* (1953), with the inclusion of many technical terms and also obsolete words. *c.*30,000 entries in Welsh-English section and *c.*20,000 in English-Welsh section, with terms new to this ed. appended to each section. *Class No:* 809.166

Armenian

[2237]
KOUSHAKDJIAN, M. and KHANTROUNI, D. Modern dictionary: English-Armenian/Armenian-English. Beirut, Doniguian, 1976. 949;416p.
A combination of *English-Armenian modern dictionary* (2nd ed. 1976), with *c.*18,000 entry-words, and *Armenian-English modern dictionary* (1970) with *c.*16,000 entry-words. Armenian terms not transliterated. *Class No:* 809.198.1

Albanian

[2238]
KICI, G. Albanian-English dictionary. [Washington, D.C.], G. Kici, 1976. 448p. ISBN: 0686179048.
Aimed at students of literary Albanian, but also includes some scientific terms. Omits regionalisms. *c.*26,000 entry-words, with many idioms and illustrative phrases. Lists of abbreviations and geographical names. *Class No:* 809.198.3

[2239]
KICI, G. and ALIKO, H. English-Albanian dictionary. [Washington, D.C.], G. Kici, 1969. xi,627p. ISBN: 0686049144.
Over 24,000 entry-words, with many idiomatic phrases. *Class No:* 809.198.3

Semitic

Hebrew

[2240]
ALCALAY, R. The Complete English-Hebrew dictionary. Tel Aviv, Massadah, 1959-61. 4v.(4270 cols.).
140,000 English words and expressions with Hebrew equivalents. Includes new words approved by the Hebrew Language Academy, all new words appearing in the *Reshumot* (Official Gazette), and new slang and colloquialisms; also cites numerous quotations from the Bible, proverbs, idioms, etc.
A 3-vol. edition is advertized by Kuperard (London, 1990. ISBN: 1870668197). *Class No:* 809.24

[2241]
—ALCALAY, R. The Complete Hebrew-English dictionary. Tel Aviv, Massadah, 1964-65. 4v.(2883 cols.).
About 100,000 entry-words. The English equivalents are accompanied by synonyms, and explanations, where considered necessary. Many idioms. *Class No:* 809.24

[2242]
GESENIUS, H.F.W. A Hebrew and English lexicon of the Old Testament, with an Appendix containing the Biblical Aramaic. Brown, F., *and others, eds.* Oxford, Clarendon Press, 1907 (repr. with corrections, 1962). xix,1127p. ISBN: 0198643012.
Based on Gesenius's lexicon, as translated by E. Robinson.
The standard Hebrew-English dictionary of Biblical Hebrew, and virtually a Hebrew concordance to the Old Testament. Often referred to as Brown-Driver-Briggs, after the English editors. *Class No:* 809.24

[2243]
ZILKHA, A. Modern Hebrew-English dictionary. New Haven, Conn., and London, Yale Univ. Press, 1989. vi,305p. (*Yale language series.*) ISBN: 0300046472.
Over 20,000 entries (just headword and English equivalent) covering the language of contemporary Israel, with special attention paid to the vocabulary of the media. Appendix lists over 300 common abbreviations. *Class No:* 809.24

Arabic

[2244]
HINDS, M. and BADAWI, E.-S. A Dictionary of Egyptian Arabic: Arabic-English. Beirut, Librairie du Liban, 1986. 999p. ISBN: 1853410039.
A dictionary of spoken Arabic. 'The compilers have organized their material in the traditional way under the ... root-forms in the cursive Arabic script, but the headwords entered under the root-forms are rendered phonetically and, in thousands of cases, the English definitions ... are accompanied by illustrative examples of the words' idiomatic use' (*TLS*, no.4424, Jan. 15, 1988, p.67). *Class No:* 809.27

[2245]
The Oxford English-Arabic dictionary of current usage. Doniach, N.S., *ed.* Oxford, Clarendon Press, 1972. xii,1392p. ISBN: 0198643128.
About 40,000 headwords, the English word-list being

....(contd.)

based on the *Concise Oxford dictionary* and the *Oxford advanced learner's dictionary of current usage*. Includes both formal and colloquial terms and gives Arabic equivalents, indicating regional variations. Particularly valuable for its translations of English idioms and phrases. Intended for both Arabic- and English-speaking readers.

The Concise Oxford English-Arabic dictionary of current usage, ed. by N. Doniach and others (Oxford, Clarendon Press, 1983. x,461p. ISBN: 0198643217), is a shortened and updated version. *Class No:* 809.27

[2246]
WEHR, H. A Dictionary of modern written Arabic (Arabic-English). Cowan, J.H., *ed.* 4th ed., considerably enl. and amended. Wiesbaden, Harrassowitz, 1979. xvii,1301p. (5th ed. New York, French & European, 1985. 1452p. ISBN: 082880995x).

1st English ed., 1961, was a translated and enlarged version of *Arabisches Wörterbuch für die Schriftsprache der Gegenwart* (3. Aufl. 1958) and its *Supplement* (1959).

The standard dictionary for the modern written language, with *c.*100,000 entries including scientific and technical terms, neologisms, foreign loanwords, and colloquialisms. Entry-words are given in both Arabic and romanized script and arranged according to Arabic roots. *Class No:* 809.27

Turanian (Ural-Altaic)

Turkish

[2247]
ALDERSON, A.D. *and* IZ, F. The Oxford English-Turkish dictionary. 2nd ed. Oxford, Oxford Univ. Press, 1978. xvi,619p. ISBN: 0198641230.

1st ed. 1952, by F. Iz and H.C. Hony.

About 27,000 entry-words, an increase of 50% over the 1st ed., including basic scientific vocabulary, geographical and historical terms, and some American and Australian terms. Abbreviations included in main sequence. Spelling in accordance with the rules of the Turkish Language Institute. 'Compiled mainly with a view to the needs of the Turkish student' (*Preface* to 1st ed.) and thus all guidance material is in Turkish. *Class No:* 809.435

[2248]
ALDERSON, A.D. *and* IZ, F. The Oxford Turkish-English dictionary. 3rd ed. Oxford, Clarendon Press, 1984. xviii,526p. ISBN: 0198641249.

1st ed. 1947; 2nd ed. 1957, both by H.C. Hony and F. Iz.

About 25,000 entry-words, including thousands of everyday neologisms which have replaced loan-words from Arabic and Persian in recent decades, and much new scientific terminology based largely on Western European languages. Much idiomatic material, completely rearranged so that all idioms are now found under the first word of the phrase. Includes cross-references to appropriate sections of G.L. Lewis's *Turkish grammar* (Oxford, 1967). *Class No:* 809.435

Finno-Ugrian Languages

Hungarian

[2249]
MAGAY, T. *and* ORSZÁGH, L. A Concise Hungarian-English dictionary. New ed. Oxford, Oxford Univ. Press; Budapest, Akadémiai Kiadó, 1990. 1152p. ISBN: 0198641699.

The first completely revised ed. since 1959 of this standard concise dictionary contains over 30,000 new items, with translations for over 95,000 Hungarian words and

....(contd.)

phrases. Many illustrative sentences, including good coverage of US usage. Comprehensive and lucid explanatory notes for users (4p.). *Class No:* 809.451

[2250]
—ORSZÁGH, L. A Concise English-Hungarian dictionary. Oxford, Oxford Univ. Press; Budapest, Akadémiai Kiadó, 1990. 1052p. ISBN: 0198641702.

A British edition of the 14th ed. of the standard concise dictionary, with *c.*40,000 entry-words and *c.*20,000 phrases drawn from comtemporary vocabulary. American usage well covered. Abbreviations and proper names included in main sequence. *Class No:* 809.451

Finnish

[2251]
WUOLLE, A. The Standard Finnish-English/English-Finnish dictionary. Eastbourne, Holt, Rinehart and Winston, 1986. 1004p. ISBN: 0039107043.

Originally published in 2 vols. Helsinki, Söderström, 1978 and 1981.

A well-established and frequently revised (this is the 6th ed.) concise dictionary made available in the UK for the first time. *c.*10,000 Finnish and 15,000 English headwords, with many examples of usage. *Class No:* 809.454.1

Estonian

[2252]
SAAGPAKK, P.F. Eesti-inglise sõnaraamat / Estonian-English dictionary. New Haven, Conn., Yale Univ. Press, 1982. 1180p.

Claims to be the largest bilingual dictionary of Estonian ever compiled. Aimed at both Estonians learning English and students of Estonian language and literature. Introduction includes an English-language survey of Estonian grammar (51p.). *Class No:* 809.454.5

Caucasian

Georgian

[2253]
CHERKESI, E. Georgian-English dictionary. Oxford, Printed for the Trustees of the Marjory Wardrop Fund, Univ. of Oxford, 1950. 275p.

'A first attempt to make the Georgian language and literature available to English students' (*Foreword*), which includes important ancient terms as well as modern Georgian. The *Russian-Georgian dictionary* by D. Chubinashvili (1886) was used as a standard book of reference. Over 12,000 entry-words. *Class No:* 809.463.1

Sino-Tibetan Languages

Chinese

[2254]
HORNBY, A.S. The Oxford advanced learner's English-Chinese dictionary (simplified characters). 3rd ed. Hong Kong, Oxford Univ. Press, 1989. 1456p. ISBN: 0195839544.

Based on *The Oxford advanced learner's dictionary of current English*, with definitions and examples of usage in English and Chinese and full coverage of American English. Pronunciation indicated using both the Jones and Kenyon & Knott phonetic systems.

Concise English-Chinese/Chinese-English dictionary (Hong Kong, Oxford Univ. Press, 1987. 606p. ISBN: 0195840488) is a pocket 2-way dictionary ideal for learners of both English and Chinese. *Class No:* 809.51

[2255]
A New English-Chinese dictionary. Ge Chuan-gui, *and others, comps.* Rev. and enl. ed. Seattle, Univ. of Washington Press, 1988. 1770p. ISBN: 0295966092.
1st ed. Hongkong, Joint Publishing Co., 1975.
Translates over 80,000 English and foreign words, including derivatives and compounds, and over 14,000 idioms and proverbs. Supplement includes over 4,000 new words, many of them scientific and technical terms, and words whose meanings have changed. Abbreviations and proper names in main sequence. 9 appendices, including list of British and American forenames. No transliteration.
The companion work is *A New Chinese-English dictionary*, ed. by Ding Guang-xun (Seattle, Univ. of Washington Press, 1986. 1448p. ISBN: 0295963360), with 4,600 Chinese characters and 36,000 phrases, arranged alphabetically by the Hanyu Pinyin system. *Class No: 809.51*

[2256]
The Pinyin Chinese-English dictionary. Wu Jingrong, *ed.* Reprint of 1979 ed. New York, Wiley, 1982. 976p. ISBN: 0471867969.
Originally published Hong Kong, Commercial Press, and London, Pitman, 1979.
The work of over 50 compilers at the Beijing Foreign Languages Institute. 'Over 6,000 single-character entries, over 50,000 compound character entries and over 70,000 compound words, set phrases and examples' (*Foreword*). Emphasis on modern Chinese, but includes some common classical Chinese words, dialect words and proverbs. Arranged in Chinese phonetic alphabetical order, with radical index and phonetic index of syllables. 10 appendices, including geographical terms and conversion table to the Wade system. *Class No: 809.51*

Thai

[2257]
MCFARLAND, G.B. Thai-English Dictionary. Stanford, Calif., Stanford Univ. Press, 1944 (repr. 1969). xxii;1019;39p. ISBN: 0804703833.
Originally published Bangkok, Times Press, 1941.
The classic Thai-English dictionary, giving headword in Thai script, romanized form and English translation. *c.*10,000 entry-words, with idioms and phrases, often accompanied by lengthy explanatory notes. List of the 1,000 most frequently used words. Lists of birds, fishes, shells, flora, and snakes, arranged by Latin name with Thai translation and page reference. *Class No: 809.523*

Japanese

[2258]
Basic Japanese-English dictionary. Reprint of Japanese ed. Oxford, Oxford Univ. Press, 1989. xvi,958p. ISBN: 0198641621.
Originally published Tokyo, Bonjinsha, 1986.
A concise beginners' dictionary specially designed for English speakers (rather than for Japanese students of English) by The Japan Foundation and published under licence by Oxford Univ. Press. 2,873 entries in roman script, with standard Japanese script alongside, followed by example sentences, idioms and compounds. English translations clearly set out on opposite side of each page. Useful introduction to Japanese grammar appended (33p.). *Class No: 809.56*

[2259]
Kenkyusha's New English-Japanese dictionary, on bilingual principles. Koine, Y., *ed.* 5th ed. Tokyo, Kenkyusha, 1980. 2477p. ISBN: 0317593161.
1st ed. 1927.

....(contd.)
Over 126,000 main entries, with Japanese terms not transliterated. Many phrases and compounds. Some line drawings. Appendix on the discrimination of synonyms (52p.). *Class No: 809.56*

[2260]
Kenkyusha's New Japanese-English dictionary. Masuda, K., *ed.* 4th ed. Tokyo, Kenkyusha, 1974. xiii,2110p. ISBN: 031759317x.
1st. ed. 1918; 3rd ed. 1954.
A comprehensive dictionary with *c.*80,000 entries, comprising transliterated form, Japanese characters, meaning, and phrases (in Japanese characters plus translation). *Class No: 809.56*

Korean

[2261]
MARTIN, S.E., *and others.* **A Korean-English dictionary.** New Haven, Conn., Yale Univ. Press, 1967. xviii,1902p. ISBN: 0300007531.
Contains *c.*100,000 entry-words, with the emphasis on the basic native Korean vocabulary. Limited entries for Chinese loanwords and very few for European loans. Headwords in Korean script, followed by transliterated form, English translations, and illustrative phrases. Etymologies indicated where known. Notes on pronunciation provided where not predictable from spelling. Notes on Yale romanization plus table of 5 romanization systems. Guide to pronunciation (5p.). *Class No: 809.57*

Austroasiatic Languages

Cambodian

[2262]
Cambodian-English dictionary. Headley, R.K., *and others, eds.* Washington, D.C., Catholic Univ. of America Press, 1977. 2v.(1495p.). ISBN: 0813205093.
Includes 'not only current literary and standard spoken forms of Khmer, but also archaic, obsolete, obsolescent, dialectal, and argot forms' (*Preface*). *Class No: 809.595.12*

[2263]
HUFFMAN, F.E. and PROUM, I. English-Khmer dictionary. New Haven, Conn., Yale Univ. Press, 1978. xix,690p. ISBN: 0300022611.
Contains *c.*40,000 English entries and subentries, the aim being 'to provide a corpus of basic words and phrases which it would be useful for Western students of Khmer to know how to say (or write) in standard Khmer' (*Introduction*). A secondary objective is 'to provide the first comprehensive English-Khmer dictionary for Khmer students learning English', this being based on American English. Appendix has transcription system for standard Khmer and transliteration system for Khmer script. Bibliography (2p.). *Class No: 809.595.12*

Vietnamese

[2264]
NGUYÊN-DÌNH-HÒA. **Essential English-Vietnamese dictionary.** Rutland, Vt., and Tokyo, Tuttle, 1983. xii,316p. ISBN: 0804814449.
A dictionary which grew out of the glossary for the author's text book series, *Speak Vietnamese*. 16,000 entries. Romanised Vietnamese. *Class No: 809.597*

[2265]
NGUYÊN-DÌNH-HÒA. Vietnamese-English student dictionary. Rev. and enl. ed. Saigon, Vietnamese-American Assoc., 1967; Carbondale, Ill., Southern Illinois Univ. Press, 1971.

....(contd.)
xvi,674p.

1st ed. Saigon, Binh-Minh, 1959, as *Vietnamese-English dictionary*, being an enlargement of *Vietnamese-English vocabulary* (1954).

Over 20,000 romanized entry-words with English equivalents, plus some compounds and phrases. Includes guide to Vietnamese pronunciation, with regional variations. *Class No:* 809.597

African Languages

Congo-Kordofan Languages

Swahili, Luganda, etc.

[2266]
INTER-TERRITORIAL LANGUAGE (SWAHILI) COMMITTEE TO THE EAST AFRICAN DEPENDENCIES. **A Standard Swahili-English dictionary** (founded on Madan's Swahili-English dictionary). Johnson, F., *ed.* London, Oxford Univ. Press, 1939. viii,548p. ISBN: 0198564035.

Still the most comprehensive dictionary of its kind. The companion vol., *A Standard English-Swahili dictionary*, also based on Madan and prepared under Johnson's direction (London, Oxford Univ. Press, 1939. x,654p.) is currently out of print (Feb. 1992).

C.W. Rechenbach's *Swahili-English dictionary* (Washington D.C., Catholic Univ. of America Press, 1967. 641p.) is based on the above dictionary and includes much postwar vocabulary, including loanwords. *Class No:* 809.635.4

Xhosa, Zulu, etc.

[2267]
DOKE, C.M., *and others.* **English-Zulu dictionary.** Reprint of 1958 ed. Johannesburg, Witwatersrand Univ. Press, 1958. xiv,572;vi,342p. ISBN: 0854940103.

Includes in the same vol. an abridged version of *Zulu-English dictionary* (1948). *c.*34,000 English-Zulu entries and *c.*24,000 Zulu-English. *Class No:* 809.635.72

Sudanic Languages

Hausa

[2268]
ABRAHAM, R.C. **Dictionary of the Hausa language.** 2nd ed. London, Univ. of London Press, 1962. xxvii,992p.

1st ed. Lagos, Govt. of Nigeria, by R.C. Abraham and M.M. Kano.

A Hausa-English dictionary with *c.*20,000 entries comprising headword (with pronunciation indicated), part of speech, English gloss and examples of usage. Preliminaries include a verb table which is referred to by index numbers in the dictionary. *Class No:* 809.668

[2269]
NEWMAN, R.M. **An English-Hausa dictionary.** New Haven, Conn., and London, Yale Univ. Press, 1990. xxi,327p. (*Yale language series.*) ISBN: 0300047029.

*c.*9,500 entries, giving the basic vocabulary needed for everyday use. Phrases and full sentences frequently used to illustrate Hausa usage. Includes loanwords from English and French. 6 appendices include Hausa pronoun paradigms and guides to pronunciation of personal and geographical names. Welcomed 'in spite of its flaws' by *TLS* (no. 4543, April 27, 1990, p.451) as the first new English-Hausa dictionary for 25 years. *Class No:* 809.668

Australasian & Austronesian Languages

Indonesian

[2270]
ECHOLS, J.M. *and* SHADILY, H. **An Indonesian-English dictionary.** 3rd ed., rev. and enlarged. Ithaca, NY., Cornell Univ. Press, 1989. 624p. ISBN: 0801421276.

1st ed. 1961; 2nd ed. 1963.

The standard Indonesian dictionary, with many technical terms included and numerous illustrative phrases. 1st ed. had *c.*9,500 headwords.

The same pair's *An English-Indonesian dictionary* (Ithaca, N.Y., Cornell Univ. Press, 1975. xii,660p. ISBN: 0801407281) has *c.*21,000 entries. *Class No:* 809.92

Filipino

[2271]
ENGLISH, L.J. **Tagalog-English dictionary.** [Manila], Congregation of the Most Holy Redeemer, 1986. 1583p. ISBN: 971910550x.

16,000 headwords, 21,000 derivatives and 30,000 illustrative sentences. List of English loanwords in Tagalog (7p.).

L.J. English has also compiled *English-Tagalog dictionary* (Manila, Dept. of Education, 1965. 1211p.), with 14,000 main entries, 40,000 'nuances' and 30,000 illustrative sentences. *Class No:* 809.921

Malay

[2272]
WINSTEDT, R.O. **An Unabridged Malay-English dictionary.** 5th ed. Kuala Lumpur, Marican, 1963. 390p.

1st ed. 1957.

Nearly 30,000 entry words, including scientific and technical vocabulary. Includes idioms, explanations, and language of origin of many terms.

The companion vol. is Winstedt's *An Unabridged English-Malay dictionary* (3rd ed. Singapore, Marican, 1958. 398p.). *Class No:* 809.922.1

Javanese

[2273]
HORNE, E.C. **Javanese-English dictionary.** New Haven, Conn., and London, Yale Univ. Press, 1974. xl,728p. ISBN: 0300016891.

Over 20,000 entries, consisting of a root as citation form followed by derivatives and phrases (if any) plus English translation. Many illustrative sentences. Detailed introduction in 9 sections, including phonology, spelling and morphology. *Class No:* 809.922.2

Oceanian (Melanesian & Polynesian)

Hawaiian

[2274]
PUKUI, M.K. *and* ELBERT, S.H. **Hawaiian dictionary: Hawaiian-English/English-Hawaiian.** Rev. and enl. ed. Honolulu, Univ. of Hawaii Press, 1986. 600p. ISBN: 0824807030.

Hawaiian-English dictionary first published 1957; 2nd ed. 1961; 3rd ed. 1965. *English-Hawaiian dictionary* first published 1964. Single-vol. ed. first published 1971.

*c.*26,000 Hawaiian-English entries and *c.*12,500 English-Hawaiian entries. Glossary of Hawaiian gods. Bibliography. *Class No:* 809.923.0

82/89 Literature

Literature

Bibliographies

[2275]
Contemporary authors: bibliographical series. Detroit, Gale, 1986- . v.1- (in progress). ISSN: 08873070.
V.1 *American novelists.* 1986. xvii, 431p.
V.2 *American poets.* 1986. xv, 387p.
V.3 *American dramatists.* 1989. xvii, 484p.
A companion to the main *CA* series, which is intended to provide a guide to the best critical studies about major postwar writers. Although only American authors have been treated so far, the scope is to be international, with each vol. having entries on 10 authors representing a particular nationality and genre. Entries are signed by specialists and comprise primary and secondary bibliographies and a lengthy, analytical bibliographical essay. Authors in v.1 include Baldwin, Bellow, Heller, Mailer and Updike. Cumulative indexes of authors and critics. *Class No:* 82(01)

Encyclopaedias & Dictionaries

[2276]
BENET, W.R. Benet's Reader's encyclopedia. 3rd ed. New York, Harper and Row, 1987; London, Black, 1988. vii,1091p. ISBN: 0061810886, US; 071362972X, UK.
1st ed. 1948; 2nd ed. 1965. Both have the title *The Reader's encyclopedia,*which is retained for the 3rd ed. in the UK.
A major literary companion which also contains much valuable information on other branches of the arts. 9,000 entries, arranged A-Z, include biographies of writers, artists and musicians; plot summaries of literary works; sketches of literary characters; explanations of biblical and classical allusions; and descriptions of literary schools, movements and terms. The 3rd ed. is the work of numerous contributors (Benet died in 1950) and represents a major revision with many brief entries discarded. While agreeing that Benet is an essential item in any reference collection, reviewers have noted some serious omissions. See *Choice,* v.25(7), March 1988, p.1061, and *Booklist,* v.84(13), March 1, 1988, p.1102. The latter particularly regrets the dropping of the illustrations of title pages and reproductions of manuscripts and also of the 'Preface to the first edition', with its account of how Benet came to compile the work whose title now includes his name, putting him on a par with Roget and Webster. *Class No:* 82(03)

[2277]
Columbia dictionary of modern European literature. Bédé, J.A. *and* Edgerton, W.B., *eds.* 2nd ed., fully rev. and enl. New York, Columbia Univ. Press, 1980. xxi,895p. ISBN: 0231037171.
1st ed. 1947.

....(contd.)
Covers the 20th century and the latter part of the 19th, with over 1,800 signed biocritical articles on individual authors (brief bibliographies appended), plus survey articles on the national literatures (English excluded). The work of over 500 scholars. *Class No:* 82(03)

[2278]
Encyclopedia of world literature in the 20th century. Klein, L.S., *ed.* 2nd, rev. ed. New York, Ungar, 1981-84. 4v. plus index.
1st ed. 1967-71 (3v.) by W.B. Fleischmann, plus *Supplement* (1975), based on *Lexikon der Weltliteratur* (Freiburg, 1960-61. 2v.).
A thorough revision, with all the retained entries updated and a more truly international coverage achieved. Consists mainly of signed biocritical entries on authors, with primary and secondary bibliographies and occasional critical excerpts appended, but there are also survey articles on national literatures and literary movements. Over 1,700 entries, A-Z, with separate index volume. *Class No:* 82(03)

[2279]
Kindlers neues Literatur Lexikon. Jens, W., *ed.* München, Kindler, 1988-. v.1- (in progress). ISBN: 346343000x.
1st ed. Zurich, 1965-72 (7v.).
The new Kindler is due to be completed in 1992 and will comprise 20 vols. Whereas the 1st ed. had entries for literary works arranged by title, the plan now is to have entries on authors, A-Z, in vols.1-17, and on anonymous works in vols.18-19, with essays on national literatures and the indexes in v.20. Extensive bibliographies are a feature of the work. *TLS* (no. 4515, Oct. 13, 1989, p.1136) regrets the dropping of the earlier edition's lavish illustrations, but welcomes the much improved treatment of poetry, the expanded coverage of Third World, Latin American, and women's literature, and the inclusion of some 2,000 contemporary authors. 'It will undoubtedly ... serve as the definitive reference work in its field for many years to come.' *Class No:* 82(03)

[2280]
SEYMOUR-SMITH, M. Macmillan guide to modern world literature. 3rd ed. London, Macmillan; New York, Bedrick, 1985. xxviii,1396p. ISBN: 0333334647, UK; 0872260003, US.
1st ed. London, Wolfe, 1973, as *Guide to modern world literature,* with US ed. as *Funk & Wagnall's Guide to modern world literature* (1973); 2nd ed. 1976. US title of 3rd ed. is *The New guide to modern world literature.*
Essays on the literature of 33 countries/regions of the world, with 1000s of individual writers and works discussed by a compiler who claims to have reading knowledge of 20 languages. Restricted to writers who were active after 1899. For each work discussed, a literal translation of the title and the original title with publication date are provided,

....(contd.)

plus title and date of any published English translation. Emphasis is on the major literatures (but it is nevertheless invaluable for minor literatures like Catalan) and on the first half of the 20th century. Index of authors, titles and movements. Select bibliography of reference sources and standard histories. A remarkable achievement which has been acclaimed by reviewers for its highly personal, often controversial, approach. *Class No:* 82(03)

Yearbooks & Directories

[2281]
Dictionary of literary biography yearbook, 1980-. Detroit, Gale, 1981- . Annual. illus.

Now in 2 main parts, articles on literary events of the year and lengthy obituaries, but prior to the 1988 vol. it contained new entries and updates of existing entries in the regular *DLB* series (*q.v.*). Also has lists of the year's award winners, a checklist of major publications in literary history and biography, and necrology. Cumulative index to all *DLB* vols. and yearbooks. *Class No:* 82(058)

Awards & Prizes

[2282]
STRACHAN, A.E. Prizewinning literature: UK literary award winners. London, Library Assoc., 1989. xiii,267p. ISBN: 0853655588.

Lists the winners of 60 current awards based in the UK, giving bibliographic information and an indication of whether in print at June, 1989. Contact address provided for each award. Author index. Subject index to prizes. List of sources of information on other literary awards. Children's literature excluded. *Class No:* 82(079.2)

[2283]
—Guide to literary prizes, grants and awards in Britain and Ireland. Robinson, S., *comp.* 6th ed. London, Book Trust, 1990. 60p. ISBN: 085353439x.

1st ed. 1979, as *Guide to literary prizes.*

Lists awards A-Z by title, giving the address of the organizers, the scope of the award, the amount of money involved, and relevant dates. Category index. *Class No:* 82(079.2)

Quotations

[2284]
BARTLETT, J. Familiar quotations: a collection of passages, phrases and proverbs traced to their sources in ancient and modern literature. Beck, E.M., *ed.* 15th and 125th anniversary ed., rev. and enl. Boston, Mass., Little, Brown, 1980. lviii,1540p. ISBN: 0316082759.

1st ed. 1855; 14th ed. 1968.

One of the standard collections, with over 22,500 quotations arranged by authors chronologically. Separate sections for anonymous quotations (expanded with African and Native American chants, poems and proverbs) and those from the Bible, Koran, Book of Common Prayer, Buddhist and Sanskrit sources (all these also expanded). Gives exact references, with frequent footnotes for parallel usages and versions, interesting historical details, etc. Highly accurate, well researched, and exceptionally thoroughly indexed by authors and keywords. 16th ed. due 1992. *Class No:* 82(082.2)

[2285]
The Oxford dictionary of modern quotations. Augarde, T., *ed.* Oxford, Oxford Univ. Press, 1991. xi,371p. ISBN: 019866141x.

Over 5,000 20th-century quotations, arranged A-Z by author with an index of keywords. Entries include exact

....(contd.)

references to sources. Foreign quotations appear in the original language followed by English translation. According to *Booklist* (v.87(17), May 1st, 1991, p.1742) about half the people quoted are British. *Class No:* 82(082.2)

[2286]
The Oxford dictionary of quotations. 3rd ed. Oxford, Oxford Univ. Press, 1979. xx,907p. ISBN: 019211560x.

1st ed. 1941; 2nd ed. 1953.

3rd ed. represents a substantial revision, and as only 60% of the 2nd ed. has been retained both have a place on the shelves. Many 20th-century authors appear for the first time, whilst proverbs and nursery rhymes have been omitted as they can be found in specialist dictionaries published by OUP. Contains *c.*16,000 quotations, arranged under authors, A-Z, with English literature particularly well represented. Precise citations. Foreign quotations appear in the original with English translation. Keyword index has been reduced for this ed. but still contains *c.*70,000 entries, keyed to page, item no., and abbreviated form of author's name. Separate Greek index. An online version, *Quotations database (QD),* is available via DIALOG.

The *Concise Oxford dictionary of quotations* (2nd ed. 1981. 480p. ISBN: 019211588x) is an abridged version with *c.*6,000 quotations from 1,100 authors. *Class No:* 82(082.2)

[2287]
The Quotable woman, from Eve to 1799. Partnow, E., *ed.* New York, Facts on File, 1985. xv,533p. ISBN: 0871963078.

6,000 quotations by 804 women, chronologically arranged by year of birth, the women and their quotations being numbered with the women's numbers as running heads. Name index, which also gives useful biographical information including dates, nationality, profession, other names, relationship to other famous people, awards, etc. Subject index with extensive cross-referencing. Source information provided for quotes wherever possible, including 'quoted in ...' references.

Followed by *The Quotable woman, 1800-1981* (Rev. ed. New York, Facts on File, 1982. xvii,602p. ISBN: 0871965801), which lists nearly 9,000 quotations by 1,450 women, the majority British and American. Biographical and subject indexes. *Class No:* 82(082.2)

[2288]
SHIPPS, A.W. The Quote sleuth: a manual for the tracer of lost quotations. Champaign, Ill., Illinois Univ. Press, 1990. 194p. ISBN: 0252016955.

Gives advice on quotation-hunting and evaluates a wide range of sources, including general quotations dictionaries, specialized and thematic compilations, single-author quotation books, and concordances. An annotated bibliography (63p.) lists all the works discussed in the text. Index. 'This book should not just be added to public and academic library reference collections but should also be read by reference librarians' (*Booklist,* v.86(20), June 15, 1990, p.2033). *Class No:* 82(082.2)

[2289]
STEVENSON, B.E. The Home book of quotations, classical and modern. 10th ed., rev. New York, Dodd; London, Cassell, 1974 (repr. New York, Greenhouse, 1984). xliii,2816p.

1st ed. 1934. 10th ed. published in UK as *Stevenson's Book of quotations.*

One of the standard collections, along with Bartlett and *The Oxford dictionary,* but unlike them it has a subject arrangement. Over 50,000 quotations listed under subject headings, A-Z, often with further, more specific, subdivisions. Usually gives exact citation. Indexes of authors and keywords. 10th ed. has 2 appendices (27p.) which are separately indexed. *Class No:* 82(082.2)

Biographies

[2290]
Contemporary authors: a bio-bibliographical guide to current writers in fiction, general nonfiction, poetry, journalism, drama, motion pictures, television, and other fields. Detroit, Gale, 1962-. ISSN: 00107468.

V.1-132 (main series), 1962-91 (in progress). Individual physical vols. numbered as 4-vol. units from 1-4 to 97-100. Single numbering system begins with v.101.

First revision series. 1967-79. V.1-44 in 11 vols., representing an updating and cumulation of the corresponding vols. in the original series.

Permanent series. 1975-78. V.1-2, with entries for writers in the original series who have died or who have ceased publishing.

New revision series. 1981-91. V.1-23 (in progress). Whereas in the *First revision series,* whole vols. from the original series were updated, the *New revision series* vols. contain updated articles from a number of different vols. on active writers whose original entries require significant revision.

The most comprehensive source of biographical information on writers of all kinds, which, because of its wide remit, may be considered as a general biographical source. There are entries for artists, biographers, musicians, theologians, scientists, politicians, film directors, journalists, etc., and although coverage is international, American representation is particularly strong. Each vol. has *c.*900 entries, arranged A-Z, with sections for personal and career data (including biography, address, memberships, awards, etc.); writings; work in progress; sidelights (review of career and critical reception, often including comments by the subject); and biographical/critical sources. Nearly 96,000 authors covered to date.

Cumulative indexes in even-numbered vols. up to and including v.126, covering all *CA* series and including references to other Gale biographical series (*DLB, CLC,* etc.). Separate cumulative indexes are published from time to time, the latest in 1991 covering vols. 1-132 (372p. ISBN: 0810375877). *Class No:* 82(092)

[2291]
Cyclopedia of world authors. Magill, F.N. *and* Kohler, D., *eds.* Rev. ed. Englewood Cliffs, N.J., Salem Press, 1974. 3v. ISBN: 0893561258.

1st ed. 1958.

Entries on nearly 1,000 authors, giving place and date of birth and death, list of principal works, biocritical sketch (200-1,000 words), and references to biographical sources.

Supplemented by *Cyclopedia of world authors II* (1989. 4v. ISBN: 0893565121), which has entries for 705 writers. 560 of them are new to this set and the remaining entries provide updated information on authors covered previously. Most of the writers included are English-language literary authors who have been active in the 20th-century. 'Most of the major contemporary writers one would expect to find are here' (*Booklist,* v.86(13), March 1, 1990), but some surprising omissions are noted (*e.g.* Ayckbourn, Heaney, Cela, Levertov). Index in v.4. *Class No:* 82(092)

[2292]
Major 20th-century writers: a selection of sketches from *Contemporary authors.* Ryan, B., *ed.* Detroit, Gale, 1991. 4v. ISBN: 0810377667.

Another spin-off from *Contemporary authors* (*cf. Black writers* and *Hispanic writers*) offering libraries which cannot afford to subscribe to *CA* the opportunity to acquire comprehensive biobibliographical information on over 1,000 modern writers. Entries are arranged A-Z and concentrate on literary authors (including writers for children and genre fiction authors), although several philosophers (*e.g.* Russell, Freud), politicians (*e.g.* Kennedy, Churchill), critics (*e.g.*

....(contd.)
Frye, Leavis), journalists (*e.g.* Hunter S. Thompson, Malcolm Muggeridge) and other influential non-literary authors are also included. Entries follow the standard *CA* format and have been completely updated for this publication, with 40 newly-written articles which will appear in later *CA* vols. Coverage of British and European authors is better than is often the case in American literary reference works, a special effort having been made to cover the authors regularly studied in schools and colleges on both sides of the Atlantic. Nationality index (over 60 countries) and genre index. *Class No:* 82(092)

[2293]
Twentieth-century authors: a biographical dictionary of modern literature. Kunitz, S.J. *and* Haycraft, H., *eds.* New York, Wilson, 1942. vii,1577p. illus. ISBN: 0824200497.

Biographical sketches of 1,850 authors, from all countries, whose work has been published in English and who were active between 1900 and 1942. Nearly all entries include a photograph and all have a list of principal works and references to selected secondary literature.

First supplement, ed. by S.J. Kunitz (1955. 1123p. ISBN: 082420050) updates the information on most of the authors covered in *TCA* and includes entries on *c.*700 writers who came to prominence between 1942 and 1955. *Class No:* 82(092)

[2294]
—**World authors, 1950-1970:** a companion volume to *Twentieth century authors.* Wakeman, J., *ed.* New York, Wilson, 1975. 1594p. illus. ISBN: 0824204290.

Biocritical entries on 959 authors whose work is available in English and who gained attention between 1950 and 1970. Similar in style to *TCA,* but is more truly international in coverage as more translations have become available. Entries contributed by *c.*75 specialists, but not signed, with many of the authors covered having provided autobiographical articles. Supplemented by:

World authors, 1970-75, ed. by J. Wakeman (1980. 893p. ISBN: 082420641x), with 348 new entries;

World authors, 1975-80, ed. by V. Colby (1985. 831p. ISBN: 0824207157), with 379 entries;

World authors, 1980-85, ed. by V. Colby (1990. 1000p. ISBN: 0824207971), with 320 entries. Entries in the supplementary vols. are longer, varying from 1,500 to 6,000 words. *Class No:* 82(092)

[2295]
The Writers directory, 1992-94. Chicago and London, St. James Press, 1991. A73, 1088p. ISBN: 1558620931.

First ed. 1971-72.

The 10th ed. of this biennial publication provides biographical information on over 17,000 living writers who have had published at least one full-length book in English. Entries comprise: name, pseudonyms, citizenship, year of birth, genres, past and present appointments, list of all published books. A 'yellow pages' section classifies writers by genre/subject. Very useful for minor and non-literary authors. *Class No:* 82(092)

Europe

[2296]
An Encyclopedia of Continental women writers. Wilson, K.M., *ed.* New York, Garland; London, St. James Press, 1991. 2v.(xii,1389p.). ISBN: 0824085477, US; 1558621512, UK.

Complements Garland's *Encyclopedia of British women writers* (1988) and contains *c.*1,800 signed entries on writers from Ancient Greece to the present day. Entries include birth and death dates, languages and genres of the writings, biocritical essay, and lists of works (including

....(contd.)

English translations) and critical studies. Includes many women whose writings have yet to be translated into English. Cross-references from alternative names but, disappointingly, no indexes of languages (over 30 are represented) or nationalities. The work of *c*.270 contributors. *Class No:* 82(092)(4)

[2297]
European authors, 1000-1900: a biographical dictionary of European literature. New York, Wilson, 1967. ix,1016p. ISBN: 0824200136.

Biographical sketches of 967 authors from 31 different literatures. Appended bibliographies stress English translations and studies. *Class No:* 82(092)(4)

[2298]
European writers. Stade, G., *ed.* New York, Scribner, 1983-89. 14v. ISBN: 0684192675.

V.1-2 *The Middle Ages and the Renaissance.* 1983.
V.3-4 *The Age of Reason and the Enlightenment.* 1984.
V.5-7 *The Romantic century.* 1985.
V.8-13 *The Twentieth century.* 1989-91.
V.14 *Index.* 1991.

Follows the same format as the publisher's *American writers* and *British writers* series, with a lengthy (*c*.15,000 words), signed critical essay on each author, followed by a select bibliography of primary and secondary literature. Entries are arranged chronologically by birth-date within each vol.

The vols. on the 20th century cover over 120 writers, from Freud (born 1856) to Kundera (born 1929). *Class No:* 82(092)(4)

Hispanic Peoples

[2299]
Hispanic writers: a selection of sketches from *Contemporary authors.* Ryan, B., *ed.* Detroit, Gale, 1991. xxvi,514p. ISBN: 0810376881.

A single-volume compilation of entries from Gale's *Contemporary authors* series (*q.v.*) on over 400 20th-century Hispanic writers, most of them from the US and 20 countries of Hispanic America, but including 'a limited number of authors from Spain who have influenced the literature of the New World' (*Introduction*). 40% of the entries have been taken from *CA* and updated; the rest were written specially for this work and many will appear later in *CA*. Entries provide personal and career data, bibliographies, works in progress, references to biographical and critical sources, and a review of the author's critical reception. Includes some non-literary figures, *e.g.* Ché Guevara, Joan Baez, Luis Buñuel. Nationality index. *Class No:* 82(092)(=06)

Black Races

[2300]
Black writers: a selection of sketches from *Contemporary authors.* Metzger, L., *ed.* Detroit, Gale, 1989. xxiv,619p. ISBN: 0810327724.

A one-volume compilation of entries from Gale's *Contemporary authors* series (*q.v.*) on over 400 Black (*i.e.* Afro-Caribbean) writers active during the twentieth century. All entries have been updated and over 100 were written specially for this volume and will appear later in *CA*. Entries provide personal and career data, bibliographies, works in progress, references to sources of further information and a 'Sidelights' section, which includes the writer's critical reception. Includes many non-literary figures, *e.g.* Desmond Tutu, Marcus Garvey, Nelson Mandela, Martin Luther King. Most entries are for Americans, with some African and Caribbean Blacks

....(contd.)

included, but the omission of British Blacks (*e.g.* James Berry, Grace Nichols, Linton Kwesi Johnson) is disappointing. *Class No:* 82(092)(=96)

Writing & Writing Techniques

[2301]
The Chicago manual of style, for authors, editors, and copywriters. 13th ed., rev. and expanded. Chicago, Univ. of Chicago Press, 1982. 737p. ISBN: 0226103900.

1st ed. 1906; 12th ed. 1969. All previous eds. entitled *A Manual of style.*

Considered the standard reference tool in the US. 3 sections (Bookmaking; Style; Production and printing), each with a detailed table of contents, covering all aspects of book production. The section on style makes up over half the book. Glossary of technical terms. Bibliography. Thorough index, with references to paragraph numbers. *Class No:* 82-081

[2302]
MHRA style book: notes for authors, editors, and writers of theses. 4th ed. London, Modern Humanities Research Assoc., 1991. viii,84p. ISBN: 0947623396.

1st ed. 1971; 3rd ed. 1981.

A concise, inexpensive guide to writing and editing, which has been extensively revised to take account of changes in printing technology and modern editorial practice. New sections have been added dealing with the preparation of indexes and book reviews, and several of the others expanded. *Class No:* 82-081

[2303]
The Oxford writers' dictionary. Allen, R.E., *comp.* Reprint, with corrections, of 1981 ed. Oxford, Oxford Univ. Press, 1990. xvi,448p. ISBN: 0192826697.

First published 1981 as *The Oxford dictionary for writers and editors.*

Presents the house style of the Oxford Univ. Press, providing guidance, in a single A-Z sequence, on questions of usage, spelling, abbreviations, etc. Many proper names and foreign words and phrases included. *Class No:* 82-081

[2304]
Writers' and artists' yearbook, 1906-. A directory for writers, artists, playwrights, writers for film, radio and television, photographers and composers. London, Black, 1906-. Annual.

The 1991 ed. (599p. ISBN: 0713632798) is in 2 main parts with 14 subsections. Part 1, Markets, has lists of UK and Commonwealth newspapers, magazines, book publishers, radio and TV companies, literary agents, etc., with addresses and details of material accepted and payment rates. Selective list of US publishers. Over 3,000 addresses in this ed. Part 2, General information, contains practical articles on finance, copyright, publishing practice, preparing material for publication, etc., which are regularly revised, plus lists of literary societies, awards, and prizes. Subject index. Classified index of magazines. *Class No:* 82-081

[2305]
The Writer's handbook. Turner, B., *ed.* London, Macmillan, 1987-. Annual.

A directory which claims to cover every possible market for writing, listing UK publishers, literary agents, national and regional newspapers, magazines, TV and radio companies, and film, video and theatre producers. Also lists professional associations, regional arts associations, libraries, and literary prizes. Selective list of US publishers. Companies index and thorough subject index.

Differs from most directories in its inclusion of personal,

....(contd.)

often provocative, comments in many of its entries, based on the experience of professional writers, and in giving key contact names wherever possible. The 1991 paperback ed. (1990. 576p. ISBN: 0333538110), with new sections on writers' courses, small presses and literature festivals, and a who's who of fiction editors, is excellent value. *Class No:* 82-081

[2306]
The Writer's handbook, 1936-. Boston, The Writer, 1936-. Annual. ISSN: 00842710.

The standard guide to American literary publishing, comprising articles on the technique of writing (often by well-known authors) and on the practicalities of getting published, followed by a market guide which provides relevant information on periodicals, book publishers, and other outlets, *e.g.* radio, TV. Also lists literary prizes, grants and fellowships, and organizations for writers. Index to markets. *Class No:* 82-081

[2307]
Writer's market. Cincinnati, Ohio, Writer's Digest, 1926- . Annual. ISSN: 00842729.

Subtitle: *Where and how to sell what you write.*

A directory for writers hoping to get published in the US. 1990 ed. (1046p.) includes entries for over 4,000 publishers and publications in classified lists, giving addresses, contact names, editorial needs, pay rates, submission requirements, and tips from editors. Also contains practical advice on marketing manuscripts, tax, copyright, etc. and lists of author's agents and literary awards. Subject indexes to publishers and agents, and general index. *Class No:* 82-081

Literary Criticism

[2308]
BORKLUND, E. Contemporary literary critics. 2nd ed. London, St. James Press, 1982. 600p. ISBN: 0912289333.

1st ed. 1977.

Entries on 124 British and American critics, comprising biographical notes, full list of publications, list of critical studies and a critical essay. This ed. has 9 new entries and most other entries have been revised and updated. Unlike the rest of St. James's excellent *Contemporary writers* series, this is the work of a single scholar. *Class No:* 82-09

[2309]
The Cambridge history of literary criticism: vol.1, Classical criticism. Kennedy, G.A., *ed.* Cambridge, Cambridge Univ. Press, 1989. xviii,378p. ISBN: 0521300061.

The first of a planned 9-vol. history of literary theory and practice. 11 signed essays by 7 scholars cover the Classical period up to approx. A.D.325. Extensive bibliography of primary sources and modern scholarship (22p.). Index. *Class No:* 82-09

[2310]
Contemporary literary criticism: excerpts from criticism of today's novelists, poets, playwrights, short story writers, scriptwriters, and other creative writers. Detroit, Gale, 1973- . v.1- (in progress). illus. ISSN: 00913421.

Each vol. contains selected, often lengthy, excerpts from criticism of a wide range of authors (as indicated by the subtitle), with English-language authors predominant. Entries are arranged A-Z, with excerpts appearing chronologically under each author, and also include a biocritical introduction to the author, photograph, list of principal works, and select bibliography of further critical and biographical studies. Authors may be re-introduced in later vols. as new works become the subject of criticism.

....(contd.)

Cumulative indexes in each vol. to all of Gale's literary criticism series.

67 vols. published by the end of 1991. Recent vols. contain *c.*50 author entries with many excerpts, whereas earlier vols. had more entries (over 150) with fewer excerpts.

Gale publish a number of similarly organized general series, including *Classical and medieval literature criticism* (1988-), *Literature criticism from 1400 to 1800* (1984-), *Nineteenth-century literary criticism* (1981-), *Twentieth-century literary criticism* (1978-) and *Black literature criticism* (1991-). For series with more specific coverage, see separate entries on *Poetry criticism* (1990-), *Drama criticism* (1991-), *Shakespearean criticism* (1984-) and *Short story criticism* (1988-). *Class No:* 82-09

[2311]
Encyclopedia of literature and criticism. Coyle, M., *and others, eds.* London, Routledge, 1990. xix,1299p. ISBN: 0415020654.

As with the same publisher's *Encyclopedia of language* (*q.v.*) the title is misleading. This is actually a collection of 90 essays (average length 14p.) reviewing 20th-century thinking on different aspects of the criticism of *English* literature. They cover genres, critical schools, book production, contexts (*e.g.* literature and music) and various national literatures in English, and each has a list of recommended further reading (only *c.*12 titles) and of works cited. 90 contributors. Index. *Class No:* 82-09

[2312]
WELLEK, R. A History of modern criticism, 1750-1950. New Haven, Conn., Yale Univ. Press; London, Cape, 1955-86. 6v.

V.1 *The Later eighteenth century.* 1955. vii,358p.

V.2 *The Romantic age.* 1955. 459p.

V.3 *The Age of transition.* 1966. xvi,389p.

V.4 *The Later nineteenth century.* 1966. vi,671p.

V.5 *English criticism, 1900-1950.* 1986. 343p. ISBN: 0300033788.

V.6 *American criticism, 1900-1950.* 1986. viii,345p. ISBN: 0300034865.

V.7 *German, Russian, and East European criticism, 1900-1950.* 1991. 476p. ISBN: 0300050399.

A scholarly work which has been described as 'one of the great monuments of modern literary history' (*TLS*, no.4420, Dec. 18-24, 1987, p.1406). Chapters on critical schools and individual critics. Each vol. has extensive bibliographies, chronological table, and indexes of names and topics. *Class No:* 82-09

Literary Allusions

[2313]
BREWER, E.C. Brewer's Dictionary of phrase and fable. 14th ed., rev. by I.H. Evans. London, Cassell, 1989. xxi,1220p. ISBN: 0304318353.

1st ed. 1870.

Subtitle of 1894 ed.: 'giving the derivation, source or origin of common phrases, allusions and words that have a tale to tell'. Evans, the editor since 1963, has tried to keep to these terms of reference.

The core of Dr. Brewer's highly personal reference work remains, but the 1970 centenary ed. represented a complete revision. The 14th ed. has *c.*20,000 entries, of which 300 are new and many revised, with more illustrative quotations and, for the first time, an index (p.1201-1220) to supplement the many cross-references. A work which is difficult to categorize, but which is invaluable for its coverage of phrases and adages (grouped under keywords), its lists (*e.g.* national anthems, patron saints), and for the fact that it contains an extraordinarily wide range of

....(contd.)

information within one volume.

Also useful are *Bloomsbury dictionary of phrase and allusion* by N. Rees (London, Bloomsbury, 1991. 400p. ISBN: 0747507899) and *Brewer's Dictionary of twentieth-century phrase and fable*, ed. by D. Pickering and others (London, Cassell, 1991. 662p. ISBN: 0304340596). *Class No:* 82-090.2

[2314]
GROTE, D. **Common knowledge**: a reader's guide to literary allusions. New York and London, Greenwood, 1987. xv,437p. ISBN: 031325757.

'An attempt to present in one place the fundamental names in mythology, theater, literature, religion, history and popular culture that reasonably educated persons might be expected to know ...' (*Introduction*). Over 4,000 entries arranged A-Z (Aaron-Zuleika) - mainly for characters but with a few events, concepts and places (*e.g.* Crucifixion, Noble Savage, Zion) - designed to explain briefly with what trait, activity or type that name is usually associated. Sources are given, with dates, in most entries. Copious cross-references. No bibliography, but major sources are listed in the Introduction. Unlike some similar works, it includes contemporary allusions from film, TV and popular literature. *Class No:* 82-090.2

Literary Terms

[2315]
CUDDON, J.A. **A Dictionary of literary terms and literary theory.** 3rd ed. London, Blackwell, 1991. xviii,1051p. ISBN: 0631172149.

1st ed. 1977; 2nd ed. 1979 (both published London, Deutsch; New York, Doubleday).

Nearly 3,000 entries (a substantial increase), varying considerably in length, which fall into 12 categories explained in the Preface, *e.g.* technical terms, genres, forms, schools and movements, concepts, etc. Entries include definition, explanation, etymology (where necessary) and examples, but no bibliographies, although there are references in some cases to definitive works on the subject. Fully cross-referenced. Many foreign-language terms. New ed. has expanded coverage of fiction genres (with lengthy lists of representative titles) and much new material on critical theory. *Class No:* 82-090.3

[2316]
HOLMAN, C.H. *and* HARMON, W. **A Handbook to literature.** 5th ed. New York, Macmillan, 1986. 647p. ISBN: 0025534300.

1st ed. 1936, by W.F. Thrall and A. Hibbard; 4th ed. 1980.

A well-established reference work which is basically a dictionary of literary terms, providing definitions of over 1,500 words and phrases encountered in the study of English and American literature. Entries vary from a couple of lines to several pages and are well cross-referenced. This ed. has 100 new entries, many others have been revised, and references to sources are included for the first time. Also includes a chronology of literary history and lists of Nobel and Pulitzer Prize winners. *Class No:* 82-090.3

Literary Characters

[2317]
Cyclopedia of literary characters. Magill, F.N., *ed.* New York, Harper & Row, 1963 (now published by Salem Press). viii,1280,xiv,50p. ISBN: 0893561401.

Also appears as *Masterplots cyclopedia of literary characters*.

Lists *c.*16,000 characters from 1,300 books of all countries and all periods. Arranged by title, A-Z, with all characters from each work identified and described. Lengthy analysis of major characters. Pronunciation indicated for many names. Indexes of authors and characters.

Cyclopedia of literary characters II (Englewood Cliffs, N.J., Salem Press. 1990. 4v. ISBN: 0893565172) has entries for *c.*12,000 characters in over 1,400 works, arranged like the 1963 vol., but with generally lengthier comments on individual characters. Most of the works covered feature in the *Masterplots II* series. *Class No:* 82-090.6

[2318]
SEYMOUR-SMITH, M. **The Dent dictionary of fictional characters.** [4th ed.]. London, Dent, 1991. xv,598p. ISBN: 0460030353.

1st ed. 1963, by W. Freeman; 2nd ed. 1967; 3rd ed. 1973, rev. by F. Urquhart. All earlier eds. entitled *Everyman's dictionary of fictional characters.*

A thorough revision of a standard reference book, which now lists over 50,000 characters created by some 3,000 authors, giving brief descriptions with references to the works in which they appear. Main sequence is followed by a list of authors and works covered.

Seymour-Smith has retained Urquhart's additions while restoring some of the Victorians he dropped; omitted many characters from obscure works (especially plays) which Freeman originaly included; added many more from the works of Commonwealth, US and women writers; and introduced a selection from foreign-language works popular in translation. The larger format and improved layout make this ed. easier to use. *Class No:* 82-090.6

Literary Genres

Poetry

[2319]
The Columbia Granger's Index to poetry. Hazen, E.P. *and* Fryer, D.J., *eds.* 9th ed. New York, Columbia Univ. Press, 1990. 2048p. ISBN: 0231071043.

1st ed. 1904, by E. Granger; 8th ed. 1986. Previous eds. entitled *Granger's Index to poetry.*

An indispensable reference book which has provided access to the major British and American poetry anthologies since early in the century. As each ed. drops some anthologies in order to make way for new ones, it is worth retaining as many eds. as space allows, although standard anthologies are generally covered.

The 9th ed. breaks new ground by indexing anthologies of English translations of foreign poetry among the 400-plus anthologies covered. The main sequence of titles and first lines has over 100,000 entries keyed to abbreviations for the relevant anthologies. The subject sequence lists poem titles and authors under *c.*3,500 headings and the author index lists each poet's titles. The list of anthologies gives publishing details and highlights 40 key collections recommended for libraries with limited funds.

The Columbia Granger's World of poetry is a CD-ROM (ISBN: 023107672x) with the full text of 8,500 poems plus 3,000 quotations from a further 1,500 poems; anthology locations for 70,000 poems by 12,000 poets; indexing for 550 anthologies; and evaluation of the 400 most important anthologies. Searching may be carried out by author, title, first line, keyword or subject. *Class No:* 82-1

[2320]
Contemporary poets. Chevalier, T., *ed.* 5th ed. Chicago and London, St. James Press, 1991. xv,1179p. ISBN: 1558620354.

1st ed. 1970; 4th ed. 1985.

Entries on over 800 English-language poets, comprising biographical notes, full list of publications, information

....*(contd.)*

about published bibliographies, manuscript locations, and critical studies, plus signed critical article by one of over 200 contributors. Many entries include comment by the subject. Title index to all poems referred to in the text. Over 120 new entrants in this ed., with most of the existing entries revised. *Class No: 82-1*

[2321]
MYERS, J. *and* **SIMMS, M. Longman dictionary of poetic terms.** Paperback reprint of 1985 ed. New York and London, Longman, 1989. xv,366p. ISBN: 0801303443.

First published as *Longman dictionary and handbook of poetry*, New York, 1985.

Aimed at both poets and students, to provide '(1) a catalogue of definitions, (2) a companion reader to traditional and contemporary poetry, and (3) a catalyst to the reader's own critical or creative writing' (*Preface*). 1,500 entries define terms relating to poetic techniques, devices, criticism, schools and movements, with ample illustrations and many cross-references. Within the single A-Z sequence are several lengthy essays on key terms, *e.g.* 9p. on Metaphor.

Appendix 1. classifies terms under 26 subject headings; Appendix 2. groups poetical devices under 6 headings; Appendix 3. is a selected bibliography, listing some 150 titles under 17 subject headings. *Class No: 82-1*

[2322]
Poetry criticism. Detroit, Gale, 1990-. v.1-. (in progress).

A new series following the successful format of *Contemporary literary criticism* (*q.v.*). Will concentrate on English-language poets, although some major foreign poets whose work has been translated will also be covered. 12-15 entries per vol., A-Z, comprising biographical sketch, excerpts from critical analyses of major poems, and bibliography of further reading.

V.1, ed. by R.V. Young (1990. 560p. ISBN: 0810354500), has entries on 13 poets of all periods, including John Donne, W.H. Auden and Langston Hughes. *Class No: 82-1*

[2323]
Princeton encyclopedia of poetry and poetics. Preminger, A., *ed.* Enlarged ed. Princeton, N.J., Princeton Univ. Press, 1974; London, Macmillan, 1975. xxiv,992p. ISBN: 0691062803, US; 0333181220, UK.

A reprint, with the addition of a Supplement (p.909-92), of the *Encyclopedia of poetry and poetics* (Princeton, 1965).

The main work 'consists of about 1,000 individual entries ranging from twenty to more than 20,000 words, dealing with the history, theory, technique, and criticism of poetry from earliest times to the present' (*Preface*) and the Supplement adds a further 40 entries plus cross-references to the main text. The signed articles have been compiled by a team of 240 scholars and most have bibliographies appended. A strong international flavour, with lengthy essays on the poetry of many nations and ethnic groups. All quotations from non-English poetry have translations alongside. Adequate cross-references but the lack of a name index lets down an otherwise excellent reference book. No entries for individual writers or works.

The Princeton handbook of poetic terms (Rev. ed. 1986. xv,309p. ISBN: 0691066590) has 402 entries, most of them derived from the *Princeton encyclopedia*, on poetic genres, prosody, rhetorical figures, etc. Bibliographies with entries, plus a classified reading list (9p.). *Class No: 82-1*

Drama

[2324]
Contemporary dramatists. Kirkpatrick, D.L., *ed.* 4th ed. Chicago and London, St. James Press, 1988. xii,785p. ISBN: 0912289627.

1st ed. 1973; 3rd ed. 1982.

Main A-Z sequence has entries for 380 English-language dramatists (an increase of 70 over previous ed.) comprising biographical notes, full list of publications, information about published bibliographies, critical studies and manuscript locations, and signed critical article by one of 200 contributors. Supplements have briefer entries (bibliography only) for 300 screenwriters, radio and TV writers, musical librettists and theatre groups. Title index of all plays cited has over 13,000 entries with author and date and is a useful reference tool in its own right. *Class No: 82-2*

[2325]
Drama criticism. Detroit, Gale, 1991-. v.1-. (in progess).

Yet another series following the format of *Contemporary literary criticism* (*q.v.*). Each vol. will have entries on 12-15 dramatists of all periods, comprising biographical sketch, list of major works, substantial excerpts from critical studies, and bibliography of further reading. V.1, ed. by L.J. Trudeau (1991. 500p. ISBN: 0810379112) includes entries on Sophocles, Marlowe, Gogol, Hellman, Miller and Capek, and has *c.*50 illustrations. Author, title and nationality indexes. *Class No: 82-2*

[2326]
GRIFFITHS, T.R. *and* **WODDIS, C. Bloomsbury theatre guide.** London, Bloomsbury, 1988. 373p. illus. ISBN: 0747500916.

Over 3,000 entries arranged A-Z, the majority being for dramatists with some for directors, theorists, theatre companies and types of drama. 'It concentrates on the writers, the plays and the companies you are actually likely to see in the theatre now, rather than those who get into theatre reference books because they have always been in theatre reference books' (*Introduction*) and is therefore especially good on contemporary British theatre, with women, ethnic minority and gay writers well represented. Entries on each writer comprise list of plays (not meant to be comprehensive), literary analysis and discussion of a key play. Excellent cross-referencing system using margins. Comprehensive index. *Class No: 82-2*

[2327]
Harrap's Book of 1000 plays: a comprehensive guide to the most frequently performed plays. Fletcher, S. *and* Jopling, N., *comps.* London, Harrap; New York, Facts on File, 1989. 352p. ISBN: 0245547835, UK; 0816021228, US.

US title is *The Book of 1000 plays.*

Arranged A-Z by title, each entry comprising author, genre, date and place of first production, plot summary, and list of characters. Selection is based upon 4 criteria: longest runs in London and New York; most popular plays in British and American repertory theatre; most popular plays with British and American dramatic societies; most frequently studied plays in schools and colleges. Includes musicals and operettas. Author index. *Class No: 82-2*

[2328]
McGraw-Hill encyclopedia of world drama. Hochman, S., *ed.* 2nd ed. New York, McGraw-Hill, 1984. 5v. ISBN: 0070791694.

1st ed. 1972 in 4 vols.

Contains *c.*2,500 lengthy entries (the work of numerous contributors), mainly on dramatists but also on dramatic genres and terms, and includes for the first time in this ed. survey articles on regional, national and ethnic-linguistic

....(contd.)

dramas. Author entries include: biography; critical analysis; synopses of major plays; play list, giving dates of writing, publication and first production, type, and number of acts; bibliography of primary works and selected criticism. A-Z arrangement, with general index of names, subjects and titles in v.5, plus glossary (48p.) and invaluable list of *c.*17,500 play titles, which is keyed to authors and includes plays *not* discussed in the text. Profusely illustrated. *Class No: 82-2*

[2329]
Masterplots II: drama series. Magill, F.N., *ed.* Englewood Cliffs, N.J., Salem Press, 1990. 4v. ISBN: 0893564915.

Covers 327 plays by 148 20th-century authors, most of them written in English although some major foreign works (mainly French) are included. Signed entries are arranged A-Z by title, average 5p., and include brief details of authorship, setting, dates of first performance and publication, and list of main characters, followed by plot summary and critical evaluation, in which themes, dramatic devices, and contexts are discussed. References to a few sources of further information are appended. Author index. Does not duplicate any of the entries in the original *Masterplots* series. *Class No: 82-2*

[2330]
Play index, 1949/52-. New York, Wilson, 1953-. ISSN: 05543037.

Play index, 1949-1952: an index to 2,616 plays in 1,138 volumes, ed. by D.H. West and D.M. Peake. 1953. 239p.

Play index, 1953-1960: an index to 4,952 plays in 1,735 volumes, ed. by E.A. Fidell and D.M. Peake. 1963. 464p.

Play index, 1961-1967: an index to 4,793 plays, ed. by E.A. Fidell. 1968. 464p.

Play index, 1968-1972: an index to 3,848 plays, ed. by E.A. Fidell. 1973. 403p.

Play index, 1973-1977: an index to 3,878 plays, ed. by E.A. Fidell. 1978. 475p.

Play index, 1978-1982: an index to 3,429 plays, ed. by J. Yaakov. 1983. 480p.

Play index, 1983-1987: an index to 3,964 plays, ed. by J. Yaakov and J. Greenfieldt. 1988. 522p.

Each vol. has 4 sections: 1. Main sequence of author, title and subject entries, A-Z, with main entries under author giving brief synopsis and details of acts and casts - 2. Cast analysis (groups of plays according to sex and number of cast) - 3. List of collections indexed, with bibliographical details - 4. Directory of publishers and distributors. Covers plays written in or translated into English, including plays for children. *Class No: 82-2*

[2331]
SALEM, J.M. Drury's Guide to best plays. 4th ed. Metuchen, N.J., and London, 1987. viii,480p. ISBN: 0810819805.

1st ed. 1953 by F.K.W. Drury; 3rd ed. 1978 by J.M. Salem.

Aimed at play-givers, play-goers, play-readers and librarians, and provides information on *c.*1,500 non-musical, full-length plays in English. Arranged by author, giving title, date, publisher, citations to anthologies, synopsis, number of acts, cast, sets, and royalty details. Indexed by numbers of characters and by subjects. Lists of prize-winning plays and of most popular plays for amateur and school production. List of anthologies. *Class No: 82-2*

Fiction

[2332]
Contemporary novelists. Henderson, L., *ed.* 5th ed. Chicago and London, St. James Press, 1991. 1050p. ISBN: 1558620362.

1st ed. 1972; 4th ed. 1986.

Entries on over 600 living English-language novelists (80 new for this ed.), comprising biographical notes, full list of publications, information about published bibliographies and mansucript collections, plus a signed critical essay (800-1000 words) by one of a large team of contributors. Title index of all novels mentioned. *Class No: 82-31*

[2333]
Cumulated fiction index, 1945/1960-. London, Assoc. of Assistant Librarians, 1960-. Irregular.

The first vol. (also known as *Fiction index three* because it superseded *Fiction index 1,* covering 1945-53, and its 1957 supplement) listed over 25,000 works of fiction, including short story collections, under 3,000 subject headings. Compiled by G.B. Cotton and A. Glencross.

Supplementary vols. have appeared as follows:

Cumulated fiction index, 1960-1969, comp. by R.F. Smith (1970. xii,307p. ISBN: 090009205x).

... 1970-1974, comp. by R.F. Smith and A.J. Gordon (1975. 192p. ISBN: 0900092246).

... 1975-1979, comp. by M.E. Hicken (1980. viii,225p. ISBN: 0900092335).

... 1980-1989, comp. by M.E. Hicken (1990. 495p. ISBN: 0900092785).

Fiction index: a guide to works of fiction available during the year ... appears annually between cumulations. *Class No: 82-31*

[2334]
Fiction catalog. 12th ed. New York, Wilson, 1991. 956p. ISBN: 0824208048.

1st ed. 1908; 11th ed. 1986.

An annotated list of over 5,100 works of fiction in English, including some translations of major foreign-language authors, selected with the assistance of several American public librarians. Entries are arranged by author, A-Z, and give full bibliographic data, price, plot summary, extract from a review, and contents list in the case of short story collections. Includes out-of-print titles. Index gives access by title and subject, the latter feature being particularly valuable. Subscription includes 4 annual paperbound supplements which appear between the 5-yearly editions. *Class No: 82-31*

[2335]
HICKEN, M. Sequels, volume 1: adult books. 9th ed. London, Assoc. of Assistant Librarians, 1989. 289p. ISBN: 0900092998.

1st ed. 1922; 8th ed. 1982.

A well-established guide which lists novels in which the same characters appear; sequences of novels connected by theme; sequences of novels with a historical or geographical connection; and non-fiction (mainly autobiography) intended to be read in sequence. Arranged by author, A-Z, with index of series titles and characters. For the 9th ed., some works have been renumbered within their series to take account of 'prequels' and some out-of-print material has been dropped, so the 8th ed. should be retained. *Class No: 82-31*

[2336]
HUSBAND, J. and HUSBAND, J.F. Sequels: an annotated guide to novels in series. 2nd ed. Chicago, American Library Assoc., 1990. 576p. ISBN: 0838905331.

1st ed. 1982.

A much-expanded edition in which continuing series have

....(contd.)
been updated to the end of 1989 and series created since 1982 have been added. Like Hicken's similarly-titled work it is arranged by author, A-Z, but it differs in including a one-sentence plot summary for each novel listed. Indexes of titles and subjects, the latter including main characters. According to *Booklist* (v.87(14), March 15, 1991, p.1525), genre fiction is not well covered, although coverage of detective fiction has been expanded for this ed. *Class No:* 82-31

[2337]
MCLEISH, K. Bloomsbury good reading guide. New ed., completely rev. and updated. London, Bloomsbury, 1990. x,322p. ISBN: 0747506175.
1st ed. 1988.
'The bulk of the text is articles on some 320 authors, describing the kind of books they wrote, listing titles and suggesting books, by the same authors and by others, which might make interesting follow-ups' (*Introduction*). In addition, listed alphabetically alongside the author-articles, are over 80 'menus', *i.e.* subject lists of suggested reading varying from 'Action Thrillers' to 'Weepies', with 7-8 books per list. Restricted to prose fiction available in English and includes popular as well as literary novelists. Keep at the lending counter for the guidance of readers but treat the follow-up suggestions with caution as these are inevitably subjective. Author and title index. 2nd ed. has over 50 new entries and references to over 150 new titles. *Class No:* 82-31

[2338]
What do I read next? a reader's guide to current genre fiction. Barron, N., *and others, eds.* Detroit, Gale, 1991. 547p. ISBN: 0810375559.
The first of what is intended to be an annual guide to genre fiction for librarians involved in readers advisory work lists *c.*1,500 1988-90 US publications, A-Z by author within sections for mysteries, science fiction, fantasy, horror, romance, and westerns. Entries include list of major characters, time period, locale, brief synopsis, references to up to 5 reviews, list of up to 5 recent titles by the author in the same genre, and list of similar works by other writers. 8 indexes (author, title, series, character, character description, time period, geographic setting, and genre/sub-genre) provide full access. *Class No:* 82-31

Romantic Fiction

[2339]
Twentieth-century romance and historical writers. Henderson, L., *ed.* 2nd ed. Chicago and London, St. James Press, 1990. xxiv,856p. ISBN: 091228997x.
1st ed. Detroit, Gale, 1982, as *Twentieth-century romance and gothic writers* (ed. J. Vinson).
Expanded from 300 to 500 entries to include historical fiction writers. Entries by over 200 contributors are arranged A-Z and comprise biographical notes, complete bibliography (including non-fiction works) with details of first UK and US editions, list of critical studies, manuscript locations, and signed critical essay. Reading list of over 100 general critical works. Title index has *c.*16,000 entries. Confined to English-language writers. *Class No:* 82-311

Crime Fiction

[2340]
Twentieth-century crime and mystery writers. Henderson, L., *ed.* 3rd ed. London, St. James Press, 1991. 1094p. ISBN: 1558620311.
1st ed. New York, St. Martin's Press, 1980; 2nd ed. London, St. James Press, 1985, edited by J.M. Reilly.
Entries by 180 contributors are arranged A-Z, cover *c.*600 writers (mainly British and American, but including a few foreign writers whose works are available in English), and comprise biographical notes, complete bibliography (including non-crime works), list of critical studies, manuscript locations, and signed critical essay. 120 writers have been included for the first time in this ed. while another 120 have been dropped. Bibliography of general studies of crime fiction (6p.). Comprehensive index of titles (140p.). 'In the world of crime and mystery fiction, this work is the Bible' (*Public Library Journal*, v.6(6), Nov/Dec. 1991, p.174-5). *Class No:* 82-312

Science Fiction

[2341]
Anatomy of wonder: a critical guide to science fiction. Barron, N., *ed.* 3rd ed. New York and London, Bowker, 1987. xvii,874p. ISBN: 0835223124.
1st ed. 1976; 2nd ed. 1981.
Part 1, English Language Science Fiction, has 4 chapters on the history of the genre plus one on SF for young people. Part 2 has chapters on SF from 13 countries, with Danish, Swedish, Norwegian, Dutch, Belgian, Romanian, Yugoslav and Hebrew SF new to this ed. Part 3, Research Aids, has 10 chapters on a wide range of topics, including reference works, histories, criticism, illustrations, magazines and major collections. Every chapter is followed by a well annotated bibliography, with over 2,000 SF works listed (700 new to this ed.) and 550 research aids (300 new). Core collection titles asterisked. Author/subject index and title index. Invaluable. *Class No:* 82-315

[2342]
Twentieth-century science-fiction writers. Watson, N. *and* Schellinger, P.E., *eds.* 3rd ed. Chicago and London, St. James Press, 1991. 950p. ISBN: 1558621113.
1st ed. New York, St. Martin's Press, 1981; 2nd ed. Chicago and London, St. James Press, 1986.
Entries by a large team of contributors are arranged A-Z, cover *c.*600 English-language writers and comprise biographical notes, complete bibliography (including non-SF works), list of critical studies, details of published bibliographies and manuscript collections, plus a signed critical essay (800-1,000 words). Appendix has shorter entries on a selection of major foreign-language SF writers. This ed. includes several new entries and new essays on many writers previously included. Complete title index to works mentioned, with over 6,000 entries. *Class No:* 82-315

Short Stories

[2343]
Short story criticism. Detroit, Gale, 1988-. v.1-. (in progress). illus.
Covers short story writers of all nationalities and all periods, using the same format as Gale's *Contemporary literary criticism* series (*q.v.*). Each vol. covers 10-12 authors, the entries including critical introduction, list of major short story collections, excerpted criticism chronologically arranged, and additional bibliography of critical books and articles. Photographs of each author plus reproductions of title pages, dust jackets, etc. Cumulative author index in each vol. to all of Gale's literary criticism

....*(contd.)*

series and cumulative nationality and title indexes to the *SSC* series. Beginning with v.6, excerpted comments by authors have been added wherever possible and an appendix of general information sources on short fiction (updated each vol.) has been included.

8 vols. published by the end of 1991. *Class No:* 82-32

[2344]
Short story index: an index to 60,000 stories in 4,320 collections. New York, Wilson, 1953. iv,1553p. ISSN: 03609774.

Supersedes *Index to short stories* by I.T.E. Firkins (2nd ed. 1923) and its Supplements (1929 and 1936).

A single-sequence listing of stories by author, title, and subject. Includes translations of stories by foreign writers, but excludes stories for young children. List of collections indexed. Covers collections published 1900-49. Supplements have been published covering the following periods: 1950-54 (1956); 1955-58 (1960); 1959-63 (1965); 1964-68 (1969); 1969-73 (1974); 1974-78 (1979); 1979-83 (1984); 1984-88 (1989). Over 162,000 stories have been indexed to date with coverage extended to selected periodicals in recent years.

Short story index: collections indexed, 1900-1978 (1979. 349p. ISBN: 0824206436) is an author/editor and title index to 8,400 collections. *Class No:* 82-32

Fantasy Fiction

[2345]
Fantasy literature: a reader's guide. Barron, N., *ed.* New York, Garland, 1990. 586p. ISBN: 0824031482.

An outstanding guide to the genre, arranged on similar lines to Barron's definitive science fiction reference book, *Anatomy of wonder* (*q.v.*). Signed essays on periods in the development of fantasy (to 1811; 1812-1899; 1900-56); modern fantasy for adults; and modern fantasy for young adults — each followed by a critically annotated bibliography of key works. A section on research aids has 9 chapters covering reference works, author studies, magazines, fantasy on film and TV, library collections, etc. Recommended titles are asterisked. Many cross-references. Author, title and theme indexes. Over 1,700 works and studies evaluated. *Class No:* 82-34

Horror Fiction

[2346]
Horror literature: a reader's guide. Barron, N., *ed.* New York, Garland, 1990. 596p. ISBN: 0824043472.

A companion to Barron's *Fantasy literature* (*q.v.*), with chapters on the following subjects appearing in the 'Research Aids' section of each book: fantasy and horror fiction in libraries; general reference books; fantastic art and illustration; fantasy and horror magazines; and library collections. Survey chapters cover the periods 1762-1824, 1825-96, 1897-1949, and 1950-1989, each with critically annotated bibliographies. Author, title, and theme indexes. *c.*1,500 works and studies evaluated. *Class No:* 82-35

Western Fiction

[2347]
Twentieth-century western writers. Sadler, G., *ed.* 2nd ed. Chicago and London, St. James Press, 1991. 800p. ISBN: 0912289988.

1st ed. London, Macmillan, 1982, edited by J. Vinson.

Entries by a large team of contributors are arranged A-Z, cover over 450 authors, and comprise biographical notes, primary bibliography, list of critical studies, details of published bibliographies and manuscript collections, plus a signed critical essay (800-1,000 words). 2nd ed. is published

....*(contd.)*

in a more readable format, with larger page- and type-size, and has entries on 150 writers including 35 women. Essays on many writers previously included have been rewritten. Complete title index to all works mentioned. *Class No:* 82-36

Speeches

[2348]
SUTTON, R.B. Speech index: an index to 259 collections of world famous orations and speeches for various occasions. 4th ed., rev. and enl. New York, Scarecrow, 1966. vii,947p. ISBN: 0810801388.

Speeches found in books are indexed by orator, subject, and type of speech, in a single A-Z sequence. Covers collections in English, 1900-65, and includes all entries in 3 previous eds. published 1935, 1956, and 1962.

Supplement, 1966-1980, by C. Mitchell (Metuchen, N.J., Scarecrow, 1982. 466p. ISBN: 0810815184), indexes over 130 recent collections, cumulating 2 earlier supplements (1966-70; 1971-75) and adding new material published 1975-80. *Class No:* 82-5

820 English Literature

English Literature

Bibliographies

[2349]
Annual bibliography of English language and literature, 1920-. London, Modern Humanities Research Assoc., 1921-. v.1-. ISSN: 00663786.

Earlier published by Cambridge Univ. Press for M.H.R.A.
V.61: *1986* (1990. xliv,915p.) has 14,892 entries for books, pamphlets and periodical articles (from *c.*1400 journals), as well as unpublished British and Irish theses, covering the English language and English, American and Commonwealth literature. 1. *Festschriften* and other collections - 2. Bibliography (book production, publishing, etc.) - 3. Scholarly method - 4. Language, literature, and the computer - 5. Newspapers and other periodicals - 6. English language - 7. Traditional culture, folklore and folklife - 8. English literature (p.175-839). Literature chapter has general section followed by sections on Old English, Middle English, and each century from 16th to 20th; each period-section has subsections for genres, followed by individual authors, A-Z. Cross-references. Index of authors and subjects. Index of scholars. More comprehensive than *The Year's work in English studies* (q.v.), but not annotated. *Class No: 820-0(01)*

[2350]
The New Cambridge bibliography of English literature. Watson, G., *and others, eds.* Cambridge, Cambridge Univ. Press, 1969-77. 5v.

1st ed. 1940, as *The Cambridge bibliography of English literature*(4v.). Supplement. 1957.
V.1 *600-1660*, ed. by G. Watson. 1974. ISBN: 052120040.
V.2 *1660-1800*, ed. by G. Watson. 1971. ISBN: 0521079349.
V.3 *1800-1900*, ed. by G. Watson. 1969. ISBN: 0521072557.
V.4 *1900-1950*, ed. by I.R. Willison. 1972. ISBN: 0521085357.
V.5 *Index*, comp. by J.D. Pickles. 1977. ISBN: 052121310x.
Designed to replace *CBEL*, following the same chronological arrangement with subdivisions within periods for literary forms and genres and author bibliographies (primary and secondary) for hundreds of major and minor figures. The main changes are as follows: coverage now extends to 1950; Commonwealth literatures are no longer covered (author listings now being confined to 'literary authors native to or mainly resident in the British Isles'); Celtic literature is excluded; some non-literary sections (*e.g.* those on political and social backgrounds) have been dropped, although others (*e.g.* travel, sport) have been retained.
V.4 has the following sections: 1. Introduction (covering *....(contd.)* general works and book production) - 2. Poetry - 3. The Novel - 4. Drama - 5. Prose (including critics, essayists, humorists, historians, philosophers, and writers on travel, theology, natural science, sport and the countryside) - 6. Newspapers and magazines. Skeleton index of primary authors and subject headings.

V.5 has a comprehensive single-sequence index of primary authors, subjects, anonymous titles, newspapers and periodicals, etc., with cross-references.

The Shorter new Cambridge bibliography of English literature, ed. by G. Watson (1981. xivp., 1622 cols. ISBN: 0521226007) has the same structure as the parent work. It retains the primary material for all major authors and some minor ones, whilst secondary entries have been reduced to only the most important studies. Some marginal sections (*e.g.* book production) are omitted. *Class No: 820-0(01)*

[2351]
The Year's work in English studies, 1919-. Oxford, Blackwell; Atlantic Highlands, N.J., Humanities Press, for The English Association, 1921-. v.1-. Annual. ISSN: 00844144.

Earlier published by Oxford Univ. Press and J. Murray.
V.68: *1987* (1990. lvii,933p.) has 19 chapters in which subject specialists survey the year's output of books and articles (from over 950 journals) on the English language and English, American and Commonwealth literature. References to periodical articles in the text, with books listed at the end of each chapter (rather than in footnotes, as previously). Chapters include: 1. Reference, literary history and bibliography - 2. Literary theory - 3. English language - 4-16. English literature by period, from Old English to 20th century, with separate chapters devoted to Chaucer, Shakespeare and Milton - 17-18. American literature - 19. New literatures in English. List of best books and articles. Index of critics. Index of authors and subjects. *Class No: 820-0(01)*

Encyclopaedias & Dictionaries

[2352]
Bloomsbury guide to English literature: the *new* authority on English literature. Wynne-Davies, M., *ed.* London, Bloomsbury, 1989; Englewood Cliffs, N.J., Prentice-Hall, 1990. x,1066p. illus. ISBN: 0747501696, UK; 0130836192, US.

US title is *Prentice-Hall guide to English literature.*
12 essays (average 24p.) outlining the development of major genres are followed by an A-Z reference section in *Oxford companion* style, with approx. 4,000 entries on authors (800+), works (1,000+), allusions, historical events and personages, literary terms, schools, movements and genres. Over 150 illustrations. Chronology of literary and historical events, 1066-1989. Many cross-references in both essays and reference section. Author entries largely restricted to British-based writers. Entries not signed but

....(contd.)

list of 19 contributors indicates areas of interest. A useful complement to the *Oxford companion* because of its coverage of contemporary writers and recent developments in criticism, but the omission of many names from the past means it should not be seen as a replacement. *Class No:* 820-0(03)

[2353]

The Cambridge guide to literature in English. Ousby, I., *ed.* Cambridge, Cambridge Univ. Press, 1988. 1110p. illus. ISBN: 052126751x.

'Aims to provide a handy reference guide to the literature in English produced by all the various English-speaking cultures' (*Editor's note*). Over 4,000 entries, arranged A-Z, cover authors, major works, genres, literary movements, critical concepts, etc. Numerous cross-references. Over 300 illustrations. Like the *Bloomsbury guide*, it complements rather than replaces the *Oxford companion*. Coverage of contemporary writers, children's literature and Commonwealth literature is particularly strong but it lacks the *Oxford companion*'s useful bibliographical notes. Warmly received by reviewers, in contrast to its disappointing predecessor, the *Cambridge guide to English literature* (1983), to which no reference is made in this work. *Class No:* 820-0(03)

[2354]

The Oxford companion to English literature. Drabble, M., *ed.* 5th ed. Oxford, Oxford Univ. Press, 1985. xii,1155p. ISBN: 0198661304.

1st ed. 1932, by Sir P. Harvey; 4th ed., rev. by D. Eagle, 1967.

A major revision of Harvey's standard work, with over 7,000 entries on authors, works, literary schools and movements, genres, terms, characters, and periodicals. All entries have been revised and updated, and many new ones added for authors previously omitted, contemporary authors (but no one born after 1939 is included), modern critics and critical schools, popular literary genres, and influential foreign authors, critics, artists, and composers. Omitted, however, are Harvey's many entries on allusions likely to be encountered in literature and on classical mythology, whilst the entries on classical authors have been very thoroughly revised, on account of the fact that 'fewer readers have the benefit of a classical education' (*Preface*), and their links with English literature are more strongly emphasized. Entries on major authors include references to selected biographical and critical studies. Thoroughly cross-referenced throughout.

An indispensable reference book, which covers a far wider field than its title suggests, and is therefore particularly valuable in smaller libraries.

The Concise Oxford companion to English literature, ed. by M. Drabble and J. Stringer (1987. vi,632p. ISBN: 0198661401) has over 5,000 entries, with references to many artists, musicians and foreign writers omitted. The relatively narrow price differential makes the parent volume a better purchase. *Class No:* 820-0(03)

[2355]

Reference guide to English literature. Kirkpatrick, D.L., *ed.* 2nd ed. London, St. James Press, 1991. 3v. ISBN: 155862080x.

1st ed. published under the same title as a series of 8 vols. by St. James Press, 1984, and also included in Macmillan's 14-vol. series entitled *Great writers student library*, which also included 1st ed. of *Reference guide to American literature.*

Vols. 1-2, *Writers,* include entries (arranged A-Z) on over 800 UK, US and Commonwealth writers from Beowulf to the present day. These comprise biographical notes; complete bibliography organized by genre; selected list of

....(contd.)

critical studies; and a signed critical essay by one of over 400 contributors. V.1 also contains 12 survey articles and general reading lists on the main genres and periods of English literature.

V.3, *Works,* is new to the 2nd ed. and comprises analytical essays on 600 of the most important poems, stories, essays, novels and plays, and a complete title index to all 3 vols. *Class No:* 820-0(03)

Handbooks & Manuals

[2356]

HARNER, J.L. Literary research guide: a guide to reference sources for the study of literatures in English and related topics. New York, Modern Language Assoc. of America, 1989. 737p. ISBN: 087352182x.

Supersedes M. Patterson's *Literary research guide* (2nd ed. MLA, 1984).

21 chapters in 2 groups, the first describing general reference works such as biographical sources, guides to manuscripts, etc., and the second covering works on particular literatures in English. Annotations tend to be longer than Patterson's, describe and evaluate each work, occasionally cite reviews, and can be bluntly critical. The 'related topics' covered include children's literature, film and literature, and literary theory. Name, title and subject indexes. Reviewers have suggested that as Harner states his opinions very vigorously users may sometimes feel the need to seek a second opinion. *Class No:* 820-0(035)

[2357]

MARCUSE, M.J. A Reference guide for English studies. Berkeley, Calif., Univ. of California Press, 1990. 790p. ISBN: 0520051610.

Provides bibliographical information and evaluative annotations on reference sources for all periods and genres of English and American literatures. Classified arrangement with thorough indexes (which occupy a quarter of the book) to authors, titles, and subjects. Over 2,700 entries in 24 sections. Current through 1985. Unlike Harner (*q.v.*), Marcuse does not provide an annotation for every item and is less likely to be critical. 'Although the scope ... is extremely ambitious, there are inexplicable lacunae that reduce its reliability' (*Choice,* v.28(6), Feb. 1991, p.916-17). *Class No:* 820-0(035)

Reviews & Abstracts

[2358]

Abstracts of English studies. Boulder, Colo., National Council of Teachers of English (later Alberta, Univ. of Calgary Press), 1958-. v.1-. Quarterly. ISSN: 00013560.

Originally published monthly.

Abstracts of articles on the English language, English literature, American literature, and World literatures in English from 500 periodicals. Classified arrangement, with quarterly and annual indexes of names and subjects. *Class No:* 820-0(048)

Gazetteers

[2359]

OUSBY, I. Blue guide: literary Britain and Ireland. 2nd ed. London, Black; New York, Norton, 1990. ISBN: 071363152x, UK; 0393304906, US.

1st ed. 1985.

Unlike most literary guide-books, this is arranged by writer rather than by place. 5 lengthy sections on Dickens, Hardy, Joyce, the Lake Poets, and Shakespeare (p.17-151), have detailed itineraries. *c.*180 writers are dealt with in briefer sections, arranged A-Z, in which reference is made to places in the course of biographical surveys. 37p. of

....(contd.)

maps. Indexes of Greater London locations and of other places. For 2nd ed., practical information (opening hours, telephone numbers, etc.) has been updated and new illustrations added. *Class No: 820-0(083.86)*

[2360]
The Oxford illustrated literary guide to Great Britain and Ireland. Eagle, D. *and* Carnell, H., *eds.* 2nd ed. Oxford, Oxford Univ. Press, 1981. vi,312p. illus. maps. ISBN: 0198691254.

1st ed. 1977, as *The Oxford literary guide to the British Isles.*

1,232 entries for places, A-Z, with details of their literary associations, followed by a list of 913 authors keyed to the main sequence. Living writers are excluded. Well illustrated throughout, including 32 colour plates. All places listed have references to the 13 appended maps.

New ed. announced for 1992 (ISBN: 0192129880), with entries for 105 new places and 137 extra authors covered. *Class No: 820-0(083.86)*

Histories

[2361]
The New Pelican guide to English literature. Ford, B., *ed.* Harmondsworth, Penguin, 1982-88. 9v. in 10, plus *A Guide for readers.*

1st ed. 1954-64, as *The Pelican guide to English literature* (7v.).

V.1, pt. 1, *Medieval literature: Chaucer and the alliterative tradition.* 1982. 656p. ISBN: 0140222642.

V.1, pt. 2, *Medieval literature: the European inheritance.* 1983. 640p. ISBN: 01422273.

V.2 *The Age of Shakespeare.* 1982. 608p. ISBN: 014222650.

V.3 *From Donne to Marvell.* 1982. 432p. ISBN: 014222669.

V.4 *From Dryden to Johnson.* 1982. 528p. ISBN: 014222677.

V.5 *From Blake to Byron.* 1982. 448p. ISBN 014222685.

V.6 *From Dickens to Hardy.* 1982. 528p. ISBN: 014222693.

V.7 *From James to Eliot.* 1983. 592p. ISBN: 014222707.

V.8 *The Present.* 1983. 624p. ISBN: 0140222715.

V.9 *American literature.* 1988. 816p. ISBN: 014225668.

Each vol. includes a survey of the social context of literature in the period concerned; a literary survey of the period; detailed studies of some of the chief writers and works; and an appendix comprising bio-bibliographies of the major authors and lists of further reading on the literature of the period and its background. Many specialists contribute chapters and sub-sections. Index in each vol.

A Guide for readers (2nd ed. 1991. 566p. ISBN: 0140138161) brings together the appendices from vols. 1-8 and forms a handy bibliography of English literature. *Class No: 820-0(091)*

[2362]
The Oxford history of English literature. Oxford, Clarendon Press, 1945-91. v.1-5, 7-15 (in progress).

V.1 *Middle English literature,* by J.A.W. Bennett; ed. and completed by D. Gray. 1986. xii,496p. ISBN: 0198122284.

V.2 *Chaucer and fifteenth-century verse and prose,* by H.S. Bennett. 1947. viii,327p. ISBN: 0198122292.

V.3 *Malory and fifteenth-century drama, lyrics, and ballads,* by E.K. Chambers. 1945. vi,248p. ISBN: 0198122306.

V.4 *Poetry and prose in the sixteenth century,* by C.S. Lewis. 1954. viii,696p. ISBN: 0198122314.

V.5 *English drama, 1485-1585,* by F.P Wilson; ed. with a bibliography by G.K. Hunter. 1969. 244p. ISBN:

....(contd.)

0198122322.

V.6 *English drama, 1586-1642: Shakespeare and his age* (not yet published).

V.7 *The Early seventeenth century, 1600-1660: Jonson, Donne and Milton,* by D. Bush. 2nd ed. 1962. viii,680p. ISBN: 0198122330.

V.8 *Restoration literature, 1660-1700: Dryden, Bunyan and Pepys,* by J. Sutherland. 1969. vii,569p. ISBN: 0198122349.

V.9 *The Early eighteenth century, 1700-1740: Swift, Defoe and Pope,* by B. Dobrée. 1959. xii,701p. ISBN: 0198122357.

V.10 *The Age of Johnson, 1740-1789,* by J. Butt; ed. and completed by G. Carnall. 1979. vii,671p. ISBN: 0198122365.

V.11 *The Rise of the Romantics, 1789-1815: Wordsworth, Coleridge and Jane Austen,* by W.L. Renwick. 1963. viii,293p. ISBN: 0198122373.

V.12 *English literature, 1815-1832: Scott, Byron and Keats,* by I. Jack. 1963. xii,643p. ISBN: 0198122381.

V.13 *The Victorian novel,* by A. Horsman. 1991. vii,465p. ISBN: 0198122160.

V.14 *Victorian poetry, drama, and miscellaneous prose, 1832-1890,* by P. Turner. 1989. x,522p. ISBN: 019812239x.

V.15 *Writers of the early twentieth century: Hardy to Lawrence,* by J.I.M. Stewart. 1963. viii,704p. ISBN: 0198122403.

A standard history, many of whose vols. originally appeared under different titles and with different numbers. Each vol. is by a specialist, and has very extensive bibliographies. Like the *Cambridge history,* it interprets literature in the widest sense to include biography, history, travel writing, religious writing etc.

V.1, *Middle English literature,* is described as 'traditional literary scholarship and criticism at its best' by *Review of English Studies* (v.39(153), Feb. 1988, p.97-99), whose reviewer 'has to work hard to find fault'. *Class No: 820-0(091)*

Biographies

[2363]
Dictionary of literary biography. Detroit, Gale, 1978-91. v.1-101 (in progress).

Titles relating to British literature:

10: *Modern British dramatists, 1900-1945.* (2 parts); 13: *British dramatists since World War II.* (2 parts); 14: *British novelists since 1960.* (2 parts); 15: *British novelists, 1930-1959.* (2 parts); 18: *Victorian novelists after 1885;* 19. *British poets, 1880-1914;* 20: *British poets, 1914-1945;* 21; *Victorian novelists before 1885;* 27: *Poets of Great Britain and Ireland, 1945-1960;* 32: *Victorian poets before 1850;* 34: *British novelists, 1890-1929: Traditionalists;* 35: *Victorian poets after 1850;* 36: *British novelists, 1890-1929: Modernists;* 39: *British novelists, 1660-1800.* (2 parts); 40: *Poets of Great Britain and Ireland since 1960.* (2 parts); 55: *Victorian prose writers before 1867;* 57: *Victorian prose writers after 1867;* 58: *Jacobean and Caroline dramatists;* 62: *Elizabethan dramatists;* 70: *British mystery writers, 1860-1919;* 77: *British mystery writers, 1920-1939;* 80: *Restoration and eighteenth-century dramatists,* First series; 84: *Restoration and eighteenth-century dramatists,* Second series; 87: *British mystery and thriller writers since 1940,* First series; 89: *Restoration and eighteenth-century dramatists,* Third series; 93: *British Romantic poets, 1789-1832,* First series; 95: *Eighteenth-century British poets,* First series; 96: *British Romantic poets, 1789-1832,* Second series; 98: *Modern British essayists,* First series; 100: *Modern British essayists,* Second series; 101: *British prose writers, 1660-1800,* First series.

A major reference series, which has broadened its scope in recent vols. from British and American literature to

....(contd.)

cover Canadian, French and German literature. Each vol. contains lengthy, signed articles on the main authors of a particular genre or period, lavishly illustrated with photographs of the writer and his/her works, including manuscripts. The essays are 'career biographies, tracing the development of the author's canon and the evolution of his reputation' (*Plan of the series*), and all include primary and secondary bibliographies. Cumulative index in each vol.

Full subscription to the series is beyond the means of smaller libraries, but individual vols. should always be considered for purchase as they usually rank among the best sources in their field. *Class No:* 820-0(092)

Women

[2364]

BLAIN, V., and others. The Feminist companion to literature in English: women writers from the Middle Ages to the present. London, Batsford; New Haven, Conn., Yale Univ. Press, 1990. xvi,1231p. ISBN: 0713458488, UK; 0300048548, US.

Over 2,700 biographical entries on women writers plus (in the same A-Z sequence) 65 topic entries for genres, events and institutions important in the development of women's writing (*e.g.* 'Suffrage', 'Gothic', 'Lesbian feminist criticism'). Author entries are not confined to literary writers, covering pamphleteers, diarists, travellers, etc.; are limited to *c.*500 words regardless of the status of the subject; and emphasize the conditions in which the women lived and wrote. Works are mentioned (with dates) and commented on in the author articles, but there are no separate entries for major works. Most author entries have references to other biographical sources. 58 contributors (all female) but entries are not signed and it is necessary to consult the Introduction to find out who covered which period or country. List of frequently cited works (4p.). Index of cross-references (pseudonyms, married names, etc.). Index of topic entries. Lists of writers by birth-date, in century, half-century, or quarter-century groups.

A lengthy review in *TLS* (no. 4581, 18th Jan. 1991, p.8) suggests that the strictly feminist approach has led to some serious omissions: 'Women writers associated with male dominated movements, or working with men, or published by non-feminist avant-garde presses are less likely to be included'. *Class No:* 820-0(092)-0055.2

[2365]

British women writers: a critical reference guide. Todd, J., *ed.* New York, Continuum, 1989. 762p. ISBN: 0804433348.

A companion to Ungar's *American women writers* (*q.v.*), with essays on 447 women writers from the Middle Ages to the present; including some from the Commonwealth. Signed entries are arranged A-Z and include biographical information, critical commentary, list of works, and select list of critical studies. Thorough index of names and subjects. N.B. There is a very strong overlap with P. and J. Schlueter's *Encyclopedia of British women writers* (New York, Garland, 1988). According to *Choice* (v.27(2), Oct. 1989, p.280), 273 writers are covered in both works and in 38 cases the entries are by the same contributor. *Class No:* 820-0(092)-0055.2

Manuscripts & Incunabula

[2366]

Index of English literary manuscripts. London, Mansell; New York, Bowker, 1980-. v.1-. (in progress).

V.1 *1450-1625, Parts 1 and 2,* by P. Beal. 1980. 2 pts. (1258p.). £220. ISBN: 0720108071.

V.2 *1625-1700, Part 1, Behn-King,* by P. Beal. 1987. 616p. £180. ISBN: 0720118557.

V.3 *1700-1800, Part 1, Addison-Fielding,* by M. Smith.

....(contd.)

1986. 396p. £150. ISBN: 0720117798.

V.3 *1700-1800, Part 2, Gay-Phillips,* by M. Smith. 1989. 480p. £150. ISBN: 0720119987.

V.4 *1800-1900, Part 1, Arnold-Gissing,* by B. Rosenbaum and P. White. 1982. 864p. £150. ISBN: 0720115876.

V.4 *1800-1900, Part 2, Hardy-Lamb,* by B. Rosenbaum. 1990. 730p. £225. ISBN: 0720116600.

Aims 'to list and describe briefly the extant manuscripts of literary works by a select number of British and Irish authors who flourished between 1450 and 1900' (*General introduction*). The original intention was to include all authors listed in the *Concise Cambridge bibliography of English literature*, but 'the unexpectedly large numbers of papers of nineteenth century writers necessitated a severe restriction on the number of authors that could practicably be included' (*Preface* to v.4, pt. 2). Those omitted include A.E. Housman, Charles Kingsley, Thomas Hood and Leigh Hunt.

For each author, there is an introductory essay on the extent and distribution of existing manuscripts, followed by a descriptive listing of the manuscripts, arranged by genre, then A-Z by title, with details of locations including private collections. Includes corrected proofs, diaries, notebooks, marginalia, etc., but letters are excluded. V.5 will contain indexes to the whole set.

'No other single work has ever contributed so much to the study of the primary sources of English literature' (*Library Review*, v.29(4), Winter 1980, p.487-96). *Class No:* 820-0(093)

[2367]

Location register of twentieth century English literary manuscripts and letters: a union list of papers of modern English, Irish, Scottish and Welsh authors in the British Isles. London, British Library; Boston, Hall, 1988. 2v. (x,1054p). ISBN: 0712301461, UK; 0816189811, US.

V.1 *A-J*; V.2 *K-Z*.

A computer-generated listing of over 40,000 items relating to over 2,000 authors. Arranged in a triple-column layout, with manuscripts listed by title under each author followed by correspondence in date order. Entries include brief description, dates, name of owning or depository institution, call numbers and any access restrictions. Includes non-native authors who spent a long time in Britain (*e.g.* Tagore, Soyinka), popular as well as literary writers, and Victorians (*e.g.* Meredith, Ruskin) who lived beyond 1899. Reference is made to 'personalia' (photographs, tape recordings, etc.) as well as to the usual papers, and also (in notes at the head of author entries) to material held overseas. Appendix gives full addresses of all institutions listed.

The *Location register* is maintained as a computer-readable database on BLAISE-LOCAS. *Class No:* 820-0(093)

Old English Literature

[2368]

The Cambridge companion to Old English literature. Godden, M. *and* Lapidge, M., *eds.* Cambridge, Cambridge Univ. Press, 1991. xiii,298p. maps. ISBN: 0521374383.

15 signed essays by specialists on various aspects of Anglo-Saxon (*e.g.* prose, verse, Biblical literature, the Old English language, etc.), each with references appended. Select bibliography, arranged according to chapters, with commentary (10p.). *Class No:* 820-022

[2369]

GREENFIELD, S.B. *and* **CALDER, D.G. A New critical history of Old English literature,** with a survey of the Anglo-Latin background by M. Lapidge. [2nd ed.]. New York and London, New York Univ. Press, 1986. xiii,372p.

....(contd.)
illus. maps. ISBN: 0814730027.

An extensively revised and updated edition of Greenfield's *A Critical history of Old English literature* (New York, 1965).

'The book is three things - a synopsis, a critical reading of texts, and a history of the criticism' (*Introduction*). Lapidge's background chapter is new to this ed., the space devoted to prose is tripled, and many texts are covered which were not in the first ed. Many quotations in modern English translation by the authors. The extensive bibliography (56p.), arranged A-Z by author and keyed to the numerous footnotes, includes many items that postdate the first ed. and is 'an extraordinarily helpful guide to the wealth of studies beyond' (*Modern Language Review*, v.83(3), July 1988, p.660-1). *Class No: 820-022*

Middle English Literature

[2370]
MODERN LANGUAGE ASSOCIATION OF AMERICA. Middle English Group. **A Manual of the writings in Middle English, 1050-1500.** Severs, J.B. *and* Hartung, A.E., *eds.* New Haven, Conn., Connecticut Academy of Arts and Sciences, 1967-89. v.1-8 (in progress).

Based on *A Manual of the writings in Middle English, 1050-1400*, by J.E. Wells, and its Supplements, 1-9 (New Haven, Conn., Yale Univ. Press, 1916-51).

V.1 *Romances*. 1967.

V.2 *The Pearl poet. Wyclyf and his followers. Translations and paraphrases of the Bible, and commentaries. Saints' legends. Instructions for religious.* 1970.

V.3 *Dialogues, debates and catechisms. Thomas Hoccleve. Malory and Caxton.* 1972.

V.4 *Middle Scots writers. The Chaucerian apocrypha.* 1973.

V.5 *Dramatic pieces. Poems dealing with contemporary conditions.* 1975.

V.6 *Carols. Ballads. John Lydgate.* 1980.

V.7 *John Gower. Piers Plowman. Travel and geographical writings. Works of religious and philosophical instruction.* 1986.

V.8 *Chronicles and other historical writing.* 1989.

A revision and expansion of Wells's *Manual*, with sections by specialists who provide the following information for each piece of literature: date; manuscripts; dialect of original work; sources; form and extent; content; commentary; summary of scholarly views; and extensive bibliography of manuscripts and critical studies. *Class No: 820-023*

English Poetry

[2371]
COURTHOPE, W.J. **A History of English poetry.** London, Macmillan, 1895-1910. 6v.

The outstanding reference book on the subject, covering the whole of English poetry from the beginning down to the 20th century. Detailed analysis of contents prefaces each volume; some footnote references. Combined index at end of v.6. *Class No: 820-1*

[2372]
MARTINEZ, N.C. *and* MARTINEZ, J.G.R. **Guide to British poetry explication,** v.1: Old English — Medieval. Boston, Hall, 1991. 310p. ISBN: 0816189218.

The first of a projected 4-vol. set which is a companion to *Guide to American poetry explication* (*q.v.*). The pair jointly supersede Kuntz and Martinez's *Poetry explication* (3rd ed. Boston, Hall, 1980) and provide greatly expanded coverage.

This vol. has citations for nearly 4,500 English-language

....(contd.)
studies of Old English and Medieval poems. Further vols. will cover the Renaissance, Restoration to Victorian, and modern to contemporary periods. *Class No: 820-1*

[2373]
PERKINS, D. **A History of modern poetry.** Cambridge, Mass., Harvard Univ. Press, 1976-87. 2v.

V.1 *From the 1890s to the High Modernist mode.* 1976. xvi,623p. ISBN: 0674399455.

V.2 *Modernism and after.* 1987. xii,694p. ISBN: 0674399463.

A narrative history of English and American poetry, with sections on numerous individual poets and many quotations. Index in each vol. According to *World Literature Today* (v.62(1), Winter 1988, p.131), v.1 'has been widely acclaimed as the definitive work on the topic' and 'that definitiveness holds true for its sequel', but it lacks a bibliography. *Class No: 820-1*

English Ballads

[2374]
CHILD, F.J. **The English and Scottish popular ballads.** Boston, Houghton; London, Stevens, 1882-98 (repr. New York, Dover, 1965). 5v.

The standard collection of ballads. Gives the text of 305 ballads in their different versions, with valuable introduction to each ballad. V.5 includes a glossary, index of published airs, index of titles, titles of collections, and an extensive bibliography (p.455-68).

The abridged, Cambridge ed. of Child, edited by H.C. Sargent and G.L. Kittredge (London, Nutt, 1905. xxxi, 729p.) is intended for the general reader, giving the text of almost all the ballads without the *apparatus criticus*. *Class No: 820-14*

English Drama

[2375]
The Cambridge companion to English Renaissance drama. Braunmuller, A.R. *and* Hattaway, M., *eds.* Cambridge, Cambridge Univ. Press, 1990. xvi,456p. illus. ISBN: 0521346576.

Chapters by 10 British and North American scholars on English drama, 1580-1642. 3 introductory chapters on theatres, dramaturgy, and the social, cultural and political background, are followed by surveys of various theatrical genres, *e.g.* burlesque, political drama, comedy, and tragedy. Chronological table lists plays first performed 1497-1642, with parallel lists of political and theatrical events (28p.). Bibliography of general studies (6p.), followed by very useful bibliographies of *c.*60 dramatists. Indexes of dramatists and play titles. *Class No: 820-2*

[2376]
NICOLL, A. **A History of English drama, 1660-1900.** Cambridge, Cambridge Univ. Press, 1952-59. 6v.

V.1 *Restoration drama, 1660-1700.* 4th ed. 1952. viii,462p. ISBN: 0521058279.

V.2 *Early eighteenth century drama, 1700-1750.* 3rd ed. 1952. viii,468p. ISBN: 0521058287.

V.3 *Late eighteenth century drama, 1750-1800.* 2nd ed. 1952. vi,424p. ISBN: 0521058295.

V.4 *Early nineteenth century drama, 1800-1850.* 2nd ed. 1955. x,668p. ISBN: 0521058309.

V.5 *Late nineteenth century drama, 1850-1900.* 2nd ed. 1959. vi,901p. ISBN: 0521058317.

V.6 *A Short-title alphabetical catalogue of plays produced or printed in England from 1600 to 1900.* 1959. xii,565p. ISBN: 0521058325.

All volumes contain handlist of plays, plus date and place of first performance. Includes Italian operas and

....(contd.)
repertoire of French and Italian comedians presented in London in early 18th century.

V.6 is a guide to v.1-5, giving a title index of the plays in text and handlists, indicating authors (where known), date of original production or publication, and listing subtitles and alternative titles. It adds titles and information not included in the separate handlists. *Class No: 820-2*

[2377]
The Revels history of drama in English. Potter, L., *and others, eds.* London, Methuen, 1975-83. 8v. illus.

V.1 *Medieval drama*, by A.C. Cawley and others. 1983. xlviii,348p. ISBN: 0416130208.

V.2 *1500-1576*, by N. Sanders and others. 1980. xxxvii,290p. ISBN: 0416130305.

V.3 *1576-1613*, by J.L. Barroll and others. 1975. xxxiii,526p. ISBN: 0416130402.

V.4 *1613-1640*, by P. Edwards and others. 1981. lvii,337p. ISBN: 041613050x.

V.5 *1660-1750*, by J. Loftis and others. 1976. xxxi,331p. ISBN: 0416130607.

V.6 *1750-1880*, by M.R. Booth and others. 1975. lxii,304p. ISBN: 0416130704.

V.7 *1880 to the present day*, by H. Hunt and others. 1978. xlv,298p. ISBN: 0416130801.

V.8 *American drama*, by T. Bogard and others. 1977. xlix,324p. ISBN: 0416130909.

Each vol. has sections on the social and literary context; theatres and actors; and playwrights and plays; plus detailed chronological table of plays, theatrical events and historical events. Extensive chapter bibliographies with commentary. Well illustrated throughout. Index in each vol. *Class No: 820-2*

Shakespeare

[2378]
BARTLETT, J. A Complete concordance to Shakespeare. Reprint of 1894 ed. London, Macmillan, 1990. 1918p. ISBN: 0333042751.

Originally published 1894, as *A New and complete concordance or verbal index to words, phrases & passages in the dramatic works of Shakespeare with a supplementary concordance to the poems.*

Prepared from the 1875 Globe edition but revised and collated with the 1891 ed., for which it gives exact references to act, scene and line. Index words do not include articles but select examples of the verbs 'to do', 'to be', 'to have', etc. are included, as are many prepositions, pronouns, conjunctions, etc. *Class No: 820-2SHA*

[2379]
Shakespeare: a bibliographical guide. Wells, S., *ed.* 2nd ed. Oxford, Clarendon Press, 1990. x,431p. ISBN: 0198710364. 1st ed. 1973.

'The aim is to provide a selectively critical guide to the best in Shakespeare scholarship and criticism' (*Introduction*). Comprises 19 bibliographic essays (9 of them entirely new, the rest revised) by distinguished scholars who 'have been encouraged to recommend the good rather than castigate the bad'. Ch.1, 'The Study of Shakespeare' by Wells, is a guide to general reference books, bibliographies, concordances, periodicals, etc., while the remaining chapters cover individual works, groups of works or particular aspects of Shakespearean studies. Each chapter is followed by a full bibliography of recommended works, but there is no index. *Class No: 820-2SHA*

[2380]
A Shakespeare encyclopaedia. Campbell, O.J. *and* Quinn, E.G., *eds.* London, Methuen; New York, Crowell, 1966. xviii,1014p. illus. ISBN: 0416951805.

....(contd.)
US title is *The Reader's encyclopedia of Shakespeare.*

Over 2,700 entries arranged in a single A-Z sequence but falling into 7 main categories: Shakespeare the man; Shakespeare's works; Elizabethan life; Characters in the plays; Production; Scholarship and criticism; Documents. Longer articles are signed by one of the 66 contributors. Those on individual plays run to several pages and include notes on text, date and sources; plot synopsis; commentary; stage history; bibliography; and excerpts from selected criticism arranged chronologically. Appendices include chronology of events, 1552-1623 (8p.) and selected bibliography of criticism and works (32p.). Invaluable. *Class No: 820-2SHA*

[2381]
Shakespeare survey: an annual survey of Shakespearian study and production, v.1-. Cambridge, Cambridge Univ. Press, 1948-. Annual.

Each vol. carries scholarly articles on a particular theme, but, more significantly from a bibliographical point of view, there is a critical review of the year's contributions to Shakespeare studies. That in v.41 (1989. ix,299p. ISBN: 0521360714) occupies 53p. and has 3 sections on critical studies; Shakespeare's life, times, and stage; and editions and textual studies, each by a different specialist. *Class No: 820-2SHA*

[2382]
Shakespearean criticism: excerpts from the criticism of William Shakespeare's plays and poetry, from the first published appraisals to current evaluation. Detroit, Gale, 1984-. v.1- (in progress). ISSN: 08839123.

Each vol. contains excerpts from critical studies, chronologically arranged, of 3-6 plays, in the familiar Gale format as used in *Contemporary literary criticism*, etc. Cumulative indexes. 15 vols. published by the end of 1991. *Class No: 820-2SHA*

English Fiction

[2383]
Masterplots II: British and Commonwealth fiction series. Magill, F.N., *ed.* Englewood Cliffs, N.J., Salem Press, 1987. 4v. ISBN: 0893564680.

Plot summaries and critical essays on works of British and Commonwealth fiction. See entry on *Masterplots II: American fiction series* for format. *Class No: 820-31*

[2384]
SUTHERLAND, J. The Longman companion to Victorian fiction. London, Longman, 1988; Stanford, Calif., Stanford Univ. Press, 1989. 696p. ISBN: 0582490405, UK; 0804715289, US.

US title is *The Stanford companion to Victorian fiction.*

1,606 entries, the work of one author, are arranged in a single A-Z sequence and break down as follows: 878 novelists (566 men, 312 women), 554 novels, 47 periodicals, 63 publishers, 26 illustrators and 38 miscellaneous entries on literary genres and schools. Author profiles include references to entries in major biographical and bibliographical sources such as *DNB*. Appendices listing pseudonyms/proper names and maiden/married names, plus ample cross-references, make access simple.

Invaluable for minor writers and universally acclaimed by reviewers for both content and style. 'A remarkable achievement, an invaluable tool for understanding the Victorian literary milieu' (*TLS*, no. 4504, July 28th. 1989, p.817). *Class No: 820-31*

Commonwealth Literature

[2385]
International literature in English: essays on the major writers. Ross, R.L., *ed.* Chicago and London, St. James Press, 1991. xvi,762p. ISBN: 1558621628.

Covers 60 writers (mainly novelists) from countries other than the UK and US. Signed entries by international scholars average 12p. and comprise brief biography, critical essay, list of works and annotated list of selected critical studies. General bibliography (7p.). Index. *Class No:* 820.41-44

[2386]
JAMES, T. English literature from the Third World. Harlow, Longman; Beirut, York Press, 1986. 207p. (*York handbooks.*) ISBN: 0582792770.

A handy, paperback guide to the many new national literatures written in English. Chapters on The Caribbean, Africa, The Indian subcontinent, Malaysia and Singapore, The Philippines, and Oceania, with notes on numerous individual authors and their works. Bibliography (25p.) covers general reference works, anthologies, periodicals and individual writers by region. Index. *Class No:* 820.41-44

[2387]
Journal of Commonwealth literature. Oxford, Zell, 1965-. 2 per year. ISSN: 00219894.

The second issue of each year (usually published in December) is wholly devoted to the 'Annual bibliography of Commonwealth literature' for the previous year. Arranged by region (Africa: East and Central; Africa: Western; Australia, with Papua New Guinea; Canada; India; Malaysia and Singapore; New Zealand, including South Pacific Islands; Sri Lanka; West Indies; with Pakistan and South Africa appended) with unannotated entries for primary and secondary material and a short introductory essay by the regional compiler. *Class No:* 820.41-44

Scottish Literature

[2388]
AITKEN, W.R. Scottish literature in English and Scots: a guide to information sources. Detroit, Gale, 1982. xxiv,421p. ISBN: 0810312492.

Lists 3,956 sources in 6 main sections: 1. General works - 2. Medieval-Renaissance - 3. 1660-1800 - 4. 1800-1900 - 5. 1900-1980 - 6. Popular and folk literature. Each section has many subdivisions, with the period sections each having bibliographies of works by and about individual authors, arranged chronologically by birth-date, as well as lists of general bibliographies, studies, histories and anthologies. Over 200 authors covered, with brief biographical notes in most cases. Some entries are briefly annotated. Author, title, and subject indexes. *Class No:* 820.411

[2389]
The History of Scottish literature. Craig, C., *ed.* Aberdeen, Aberdeen Univ. Press, 1987-8. 4v.

V.1. *Origins to 1660*, ed. by R.D.S. Jack. ix,310p. ISBN: 0080350542.
V.2. *1660-1800*, ed. by A. Hook. ix,337p. ISBN: 0080350550.
V.3. *Nineteenth century*, ed. by D. Gifford. 471p. ISBN: 0080350569.
V.4. *Twentieth century*, ed. by C. Craig. xiv,399p. ISBN: 0080350577.

Essays by over 80 contributors on the major genres and movements of each period and on important individual writers. The 80 chapters average 17p. and include reading lists. Each vol. has editor's introduction, short general bibliography and index. A lengthy review in *TLS* (no. 4465,

....(contd.)
28th Oct. 1988, p.1198-9) suggests that over-hasty compilation has led to unfortunate choice of contributors, poor design, deficient bibliographies and inaccuracies, although a third of the essays are 'of a high standard'. *Class No:* 820.411

[2390]
ROYLE, T. The Macmillan companion to Scottish literature. London, Macmillan, 1983. xi,322p. ISBN: 0333285085.

Over 1,000 entries of which more than 600 are on writers (not confined to literary writers), the rest covering works, institutions, movements, historical events and personalities, publishing, folklore, etc. Bibliographies of primary and secondary material appended to all major author entries. Fully cross-referenced. Includes references to Gaelic literature, but the author admits that these are limited. *Class No:* 820.411

Anglo-Irish Literature

[2391]
BRADY, A.M. and CLEEVE, B. A Biographical dictionary of Irish writers. [2nd ed.]. Mullingar, Lilliput Press; New York, St. Martin's Press, 1985. xii,388p. ISBN: 0946640033, Ireland; 0312078714, US.

1st ed. Cork, Mercier Press, 1967-71, as *Dictionary of Irish writers* (3v.) by B. Cleeve.

1,800 entries in 2 A-Z sequences: Writers in English and Writers in Irish and Latin. Includes many non-literary writers (*e.g.* politicians, theologians, historians, etc.) and gives strong emphasis to contemporary figures. Entries include biographical notes, critical comments and lists of principal works. *Class No:* 820.415

[2392]
The Macmillan dictionary of Irish literature. Hogan, R., *ed.* Westport, Conn., Greenwood, 1979; London, Macmillan, 1980. xviii,815p. ISBN: 0313207186, US; 0333270851, UK.

US title is *Dictionary of Irish literature.*

'The bulk of the dictionary is made up of biographical and critical essays on approximately 500 Irish authors who wrote mainly in the English language' (*Preface*). Also has entries for some foreign authors who 'have made a rich and lasting contribution to Irish literature' and on a few general topics (*e.g.* folklore), plus literary institutions and publications. Entries are signed (60 contributors), range from 25 to 10,000 words, and include bibliographies of primary and secondary material. Introductory essays on Gaelic literature (48p.) and on the history of Irish writing in English (10p.). Chronology of literary and historical events, 432-1977. General bibliography (5p.). Index. *Class No:* 820.415

[2393]
Modern Irish literature. Lane, D. and Lane, C.M., *eds.* New York, Ungar, 1988. xv,736p. (*A Library of literary criticism.*) ISBN: 0804431442.

Substantial excerpts from works of criticism published 1900-1985 in the USA and UK about 87 twentieth century Irish writers (north and south) are arranged chronologically under each writer in one A-Z sequence. Very useful bibliographies for each writer list all major works, selected minor works and one published bibliography where available. Index to critics. Includes only one Irish-language writer: Pádraic Ó Conaire. *Class No:* 820.415

Anglo-Welsh Literature

[2394]
The Oxford companion to the literature of Wales. Stephens, M., *ed.* Oxford, Oxford Univ. Press, 1986. xviii,682p. ISBN: 0192115863.

Covers literature in Welsh and English from the 6th century to the present. Over 2,800 entries, of which 1,200 are for writers, the majority of them users of the Welsh language and by no means all literary authors. No one born after 1950 is included. Entries for major writers carry substantial bibliographical notes. Other entries cover historical figures (royalty, politicians, sportsmen, clerics, etc.); literary movements, genres and periodicals; myths, legends and folklore; places and events of literary significance; and all aspects of Welsh culture, *e.g.* Rugby, Methodism, Nationalism. Many cross-references. Chronology of Welsh history, AD43-1985 (8p.). 222 contributors listed, but entries not signed. 'A reliable and indispensable reference-book ... its factual material invariably accurate and up to date' (*Modern Language Review,* v.83(3), July 1988, p.713-5). A Welsh edition, *Cydymaith i Lenyddiaeth Cymru* (Cardiff, Univ. of Wales Press, 1986. £17.50. ISBN: 0708309151), has more and lengthier articles on the traditional rules of poetic art. *Class No: 820.429*

Asian Literature in English

Indian Literature in English

[2395]
SINGH, A., *and others.* **Indian literature in English, 1827-1979:** a guide to information sources. Detroit, Gale, 1981. xxii,631p. (*American literature, English literature and World literatures in English.*) ISBN: 0810312387.

Part 1 lists general sources under 4 main headings: Backgrounds; Reference works; Criticism and literary history; Anthologies. Part 2 lists primary and (where appropriate) secondary material for individual authors grouped by genre. A few brief annotations. Appendices list relevant journals and Indian publishers. Primary author index in genre groupings, plus general author and title indexes. Includes works written in Indian languages and translated into English by their author. *Class No: 820.54*

African Literature in English

[2396]
LINDFORS, B. Black African literature in English: a guide to information sources. Detroit, Gale, 1979. xxx,482p. (*American literature, English literature, and World literatures in English.*) ISBN: 0810312069.

Lists over 3,300 items in 2 sections: 1. Genre and Topical Studies and Reference Sources (26 sub-sections) - 2. Individual Authors (biographical and critical material on over 600 writers). Some brief annotations. Many cross-references. Author, title, subject and geographical indexes.

Continued by *Black African literature in English: 1977-1981 supplement* (New York, Africana, 1986. xxx,382p. ISBN: 0841909628), which adds another 2,831 items, and by *Black African literature in English, 1982-1986* (London and New York, Zell, 1989. xxviii,444p. ISBN: 0905450752), which adds a further 5,825. Both supplements follow the same format as the original and continue its numbering system. *Class No: 820.6*

South African Literature in English

[2397]
Companion to South African literature. Adey, D., *and others, comps.* Craighall, S.A., Donker, 1986. 220p. illus. ISBN: 086852039x.

A single A-Z sequence with entries for authors (450), works and journals, plus 39 'composite articles' on genres, themes and topics (*e.g.* Prison literature, Banned books). Author entries do not claim to provide full bibliographies but have lists of book-length studies appended. Essentially a guide to English-language writing, 1795-1986, but 'composite articles' cover Afrikaans and African-language literature. Some writers from neighbouring countries (Botswana, Lesotho, Swaziland, Zimbabwe) are included. Well illustrated. *Addendum* lists over 220 writers not covered in the main text, with lists of representative works. *Class No: 820.680*

820.7/820.9 American & Australasian Literature

Canadian Literature

[2398]
Dictionary of literary biography. Detroit, Gale, 1978-91. v.1-101 (in progress).

The following vols., all ed. by W.H. New, give excellent coverage of Canadian literature:
V.53 *Canadian writers since 1960: first series.* 1986. 445p. ISBN: 0810317311.
V.60 *Canadian writers since 1960: second series.* 1987. 470p. ISBN: 0810317389.
V.68 *Canadian writers, 1920-1959: first series.* 1988. 417p. ISBN: 081031746x.
V.88 *Canadian writers, 1920-1959: second series.* 1989. 442p. ISBN: 0810345668.
V.92 *Canadian writers, 1890-1920.* 1990. 472p. ISBN: 0810345722.
V.99 *Canadian writers before 1890.* 1990. 434p. ISBN: 081034579x.

For a description of the series, see entry at 820-0(092) or 820.73. *Class No: 820.72*

[2399]
Literary history of Canada: Canadian literature in English. Klinck, C.F., *ed.* 2nd ed. Toronto, Univ. of Toronto Press, 1976-90. 4v. ISBN: 0802022111, v.1; 0802022138, v.2; 0802022146, v.3; 0802056857, v.4.

1st ed. 1965.

Vols. 1 and 2 are a revised version of the single-vol. first ed., which went from earliest times to 1960, v.1 covering the years to 1920 and v.2 from 1920 to 1960. V.3 covers 1960-72 and v.4 (published separately in 1990 and ed. by W.H. New) from 1972 to 1984. 70 chapters in all, by over 40 scholars, treat literature in the broadest sense, to include scientific writing, folk song, religious literature, etc. Index of names and titles in each vol.

The bibliographical apparatus leaves something to be desired as the notes at the end of each vol. are 'brief and highly selective; they were appended only if the author of a chapter felt that they were essential. The entire omission of notes for certain other chapters means only that these contributors rely upon the reader to seek out the numerous sources recorded in bibliographies of Canadian literature' (*Introduction*). Klinck recommends Watters' *Checklist* (q.v.) as 'virtually a companion volume'. *Class No: 820.72*

[2400]
The Oxford companion to Canadian literature. Toye, W., *ed.* Toronto and Oxford, Oxford Univ. Press, 1983. xx,843p. ISBN: 0195402839.

Supersedes the literary element of *The Oxford companion to Canadian history and literature* (1967) and its *Supplement* (1973).

By far the fullest single-volume guide to the subject, with 750 signed entries by 192 contributors. As well as the expected concise Oxford-style entries on writers and works,

....(contd.)
there are many lengthy contributions devoted to genres (*e.g.* nature writing, children's literature), regions (*e.g.* Newfoundland, The Maritimes) and ethnic minority literatures (*e.g.* Inuit, Ukrainian). Particularly good coverage of French-language writing and modern literature. Substantial bibliographies included in many entries. Extensive cross-references. 'Well presented and remarkably free from errors' (*Modern Language Review*, v.82(4), Oct. 1987, p.946-7). *Class No: 820.72*

[2401]
WATTERS, R.E. A Checklist of Canadian literature and background materials, 1628-1960. 2nd ed. rev. and enlarged. Toronto, Univ. of Toronto Press, 1972. xxiv,1085p. ISBN: 0802018661.

1st ed. 1959, covering 1628-1950.

Lists about 16,000 titles (4,000 more than in 1st ed.) by 7,000 Canadian authors. Part 1 'attempts to record all known titles in the recognized forms of poetry, fiction and drama that were produced by English-speaking Canadians' (*Preface*), with authors listed A-Z under each literary form. Part 2 'is a more or less selective listing of books by Canadians which seem likely to be of value to anyone studying the literature or culture of Canada' (*Preface*), arranged in 7 sections: biography; essays and speeches; local history and description; religion and monarchy; social history; scholarship; travel and description. No annotations. Library locations. Index of anonymous titles. General index of names, initials and pseudonyms. A necessary companion to Klinck's *Literary history* (q.v.). *Class No: 820.72*

Caribbean Literature

[2402]
Caribbean writers: a bio-bibliographical-critical encyclopedia. Herdeck, D.E., *and others, eds.* Washington, D.C., Three Continents, 1979. xiv,943p. illus. ISBN: 0914478745.

Covers all the islands plus Belize and the Guianas. Arranged in 4 'volumes' for English, French, Dutch and Spanish language writers, each including introductory essays, portraits of writers A-Z, and bibliographies of critical studies and anthologies. Author portraits range from single paragraphs to several pages for major names and include primary and secondary bibliographies. Over 2,000 mainly literary authors covered, with 15,000 works cited. 150 illustrations. Lists of authors by country and of those born outside the West Indies. *Class No: 820.729*

[2403]
Fifty Caribbean writers: a bio-bibliographical critical sourcebook. Dance, D.C., *ed.* New York and London, Greenwood, 1986. xii,530p. $67.95. ISBN: 0313239398.

Follows the format successfully used by Greenwood Press in their bio-bibliographical sourcebooks on regional writers of the USA. (*Fifty Western writers*, etc.). Each entry is

....(contd.)

written by a named scholar, averages 10p. and comprises: biography, discussion of the subject's major works and themes, survey of critical reception, and bibliography of primary and secondary works. General bibliography (1p.), index and notes on the 35 contributors. Covers all the major Caribbean writers and provides the first extended studies of some less well-known names. *Class No: 820.729*

American Literature

[2404]

BLANCK, J. **Bibliography of American literature,** compiled for the Bibliographical Society of America. New Haven, Conn., Yale Univ. Press, 1955-91. v.1-9 (in progress).

A selective bibliography of *c.*300 American authors from the beginning of the Federal period up to the early 20th century (anyone living beyond 1930 is excluded), which should eventually include some 35,000 items. Completed vols. cover Henry Adams to Elinor Wylie, giving all first eds. in date order with full collation, plus bibliographical references for each work. Also listed are variants, revised reprints, first appearances in books and pamphlets, etc., and selected biographical, bibliographical and critical material, but excluded are periodical and newspaper publications, translations, and volumes containing isolated correspondence. Gives US library locations. Appendix of initials, pseudonyms, and acronyms in each vol. Title page facsimiles.

Following Blanck's death, v.7 was edited by V.L. Smyers and M. Winship, and vols. 8 and 9 by M. Winship. *Class No: 820.73*

[2405]

Columbia literary history of the United States. Elliott, E., *ed.* New York, Columbia Univ. Press, 1988. xxviii,1263p. ISBN: 0231058128.

The first major history of American literature since that edited by Spiller and co. in 1948 is arranged in five parts (Beginnings to 1810; 1810-1865; 1865-1910; 1910-1945; 1945 to the present), each being the responsibility of one of five associate editors. Each part contains a general essay introducing the period and a number of signed essays on genres, movements and major figures. 85 essays in all by over 70 scholars. The decision not to include even a selective bibliography is a disappointment and footnotes have also been avoided, although a few essential sources are directly referred to in the essays. Index.

Given 'a modified welcome' by *TLS* (no. 4440, May 6-12, 1988, p.497) in a lengthy review which criticises the widely varying quality of the essays; some are 'outstanding panoramic surveys' while others are 'very thin'. *Class No: 820.73*

[2406]

Dictionary of literary biography. Detroit, Gale, 1978-91. v.1-101 (in progress).

Titles relating to American literature:

1: *The American Renaissance in New England;* 2: *American novelists since World War II;* 3: *Antebellum writers in New York and the South;* 4: *American writers in Paris, 1920-1939;* 5: *American poets since World War II.* (2 parts); 6: *American novelists since World War II, Second series;* 7: *Twentieth-century American dramatists.* (2 parts); 8: *Twentieth-century American science-fiction writers.* (2 parts); 9: *American novelists, 1910-1945.* (3 parts); 11: *American humorists, 1800-1950.* (2 parts); 12: *American Realists and Naturalists;* 16: *The Beats: literary Bohemians in postwar America.* (2 parts); 17: *Twentieth-century American historians;* 22: *American writers for children, 1900-1960;* 23: *American newspaper journalists, 1873-1900;* 24: *American colonial writers, 1606-1734;* 25: *American newspaper journalists, 1901-1925;* 26: *American*

....(contd.)

screenwriters; 28: *Twentieth-century American-Jewish fiction writers;* 29: *American newspaper journalists, 1926-1950;* 30: *American historians, 1607-1865;* 31: *American Colonial writers, 1735-1781;* 33: *Afro-American fiction writers after 1955;* 37: *American writers of the Early Republic;* 38: *Afro-American writers after 1955: dramatists and prose writers;* 41: *Afro-American poets since 1955;* 42: *American writers for children before 1900;* 43: *American newspaper journalists, 1690-1872;* 44: *American screenwriters, Second series;* 45: *American poets, 1880-1945,* First series; 46: *American literary publishing houses, 1900-1980: trade and paperback;* 47: *American historians, 1866-1912;* 48: *American poets, 1880-1945,* Second series; 49: *American literary publishing houses, 1638-1899.* (2 parts); 50: *Afro-American writers before the Harlem Renaissance;* 51: *Afro-American writers from the Harlem Renaissance to 1940;* 52: *American writers for children since 1960: fiction;* 54: *American poets, 1880-1945,* Third series. (2 parts); 59: *American literary critics and scholars, 1800-1850;* 61: *American writers for children since 1960: poets, illustrators, and nonfiction authors;* 63: *Modern American critics, 1920-1955;* 64: *American literary critics and scholars, 1850-1880;* 67: *Modern American critics since 1955;* 71: *American literary critics and scholars, 1880-1900;* 73: *American magazine journalists, 1741-1850;* 74: *American short-story writers before 1880;* 76: *Afro-American writers, 1940-1955;* 78: *American short-story writers, 1880-1910;* 79: *American magazine journalists, 1850-1900;* 82: *Chicano writers,* First series; 86: *American short-story writers, 1910-1945,* First series; 91: *American magazine journalists, 1900-1960,* First series.

A major reference series, which has broadened its scope in recent vols. from British and American literature to cover Canadian, French and German literature. Each vol. contains lengthy, signed articles on the main authors of a particular genre or period, lavishly illustrated with photographs of the writer and his/her works, including manuscripts. The essays are 'career biographies, tracing the development of the author's canon, and the evolution of his reputation' (*Plan of the series*), and all include primary and secondary bibliographies. Cumulative index in each vol.

Full subscription to the series is beyond the means of smaller libraries, but individual vols. should always be considered for purchase as they usually rank among the best sources in their field. *Class No: 820.73*

[2407]

—Concise dictionary of American literary biography. Detroit, Gale, 1987-89. 6v. illus. ISBN: 0810318180.

Colonization to the American Renaissance, 1640-1865. 1988. ISBN: 0810318199.

Realism, Naturalism and local color, 1865-1917. 1988. ISBN: 0810318210.

The Twenties, 1917-1929. 1989. ISBN: 0810318245.

The Age of maturity, 1929-1941. 1989. ISBN: 0810318202.

The New consciousness, 1941-1968. 1987. ISBN: 0810318229.

Broadening views, 1968-1988. 1989. ISBN: 0810308237.

Contains 200 entries for the authors most frequently studied in high school and college literature courses, selected from 2,300 American author entries in the regular *DLB* series (*q.v.*). Entries have been updated and expanded to include discussion of works published since the original entry was written and an annotated bibliography of secondary sources. *Class No: 820.73*

[2408]

Disclit: American authors. Twayne's United States Authors series and OCLC Subject Bibliography on CD-ROM. Boston, Hall, 1990. ISBN: 0816116504.

A CD-ROM with the full texts of 143 vols. in Twayne's

....(contd.)
well-known series of critical introductions to the lives and works of major authors, plus OCLC Electronic Publishing's subject bibliographies with over 100,000 citations. Requires a PC-compatible microcomputer with 640K of RAM and a 20MB hard disc, plus CD-ROM drive. *Class No:* 820.73

[2409]
GOHDES, C. *and* MAROVITZ, S.E. Bibliographical guide to the study of the literature of the USA. 5th ed., completely rev. and enl. Durham, N.C., Duke Univ. Press, 1984. xv,256p. ISBN: 0822305925.
1st ed. 1959; 4th ed. 1976. All previous eds. by C. Gohdes.
A well-established and regularly updated guide for the student of American literature. Arranged in 35 sections, the titles of which indicate the breadth of coverage, *e.g.* Newspapers, Psychology, Religion in the US, Racial and other minorities, Relations with other countries. Numbered entries arranged A-Z within sections and subsections with brief but pertinent annotations. Indexes of subjects and authors/editors. Very useful appendix lists the principal biographies of 135 American authors. Many cross-references within annotations and at section ends.
5th ed. adds 850 revised eds. and new titles to give a total of 1,900 entries and has a new section entitled Women's Studies and several new subsections, including Computer Aids, Film and Literature, and Science Fiction and Utopian Writings. *Class No:* 820.73

[2410]
HART, J.D. The Oxford companion to American literature. 5th ed. New York, Oxford Univ. Press, 1983. 896p. ISBN: 0195030745.
First published 1941; 4th ed. 1965.
The bulk of the A-Z entries are for authors (short biographies with bibliography and some critical comments) and literary works (over 1,100 are summarized), but also covered are fictional characters, literary schools and movements, literary awards, societies, magazines, etc., and there are numerous subject entries, ranging from 'Abolitionist' to 'Zuni Indians', on matters related to literature. 5th ed. includes 240 new authors and 115 new book summaries and many other entries have been extensively revised. Canadian literature no longer included. Chronology of literary and historical events, 1577-1982.
The Concise Oxford companion to American literature (1986. viii,497p. ISBN: 0195039823) has *c.*2,000 entries, with particular emphasis on contemporary writers. *Class No:* 820.73

[2411]
Reference guide to American literature. Kirkpatrick, D.L., *ed.* 2nd ed. Chicago and London, St. James Press, 1987. xviii,816p. ISBN: 0912289619.
US title is *St. James reference guide to American literature.*
No 1st ed. as such, but based on *American literature to 1900* and *20th century American literature*, both published New York, St. Martin's Press, and London, Macmillan, 1980.
The major part of the guide (p.37-603) is a dictionary of over 430 authors, formed by amalgamating updated entries from the 2 earlier works with over 50 new ones. Entries comprise biographical notes, complete list of publications, selected list of bibliographies and critical studies, and a signed critical essay by one of a long list of contributors. This is followed by a sequence of essays (new to this ed.) on 116 major works, a chronology of literary and historical events, and an index of works mentioned in the author entries. Introductory essays on the history of American literature by L. Leary (pre-1900) and W. French (post-1900)

....(contd.)
are accompanied by a very useful general bibliography formed by expanding and revising the reading lists in the earlier works. *Class No:* 820.73

Women

[2412]
American women writers: a critical reference guide from Colonial times to the present. Mainiero, L., *ed.* New York, Ungar, 1979-82. 4v.
V.1 *A-E.* 1979 (xlviii,601p. ISBN: 0804431515). V.2 *F-Le.* 1980 (xlii,575p. ISBN: 0804431523). V.3 *Li-R.* 1981 (xliii,522p. ISBN: 0804431531). V.4 *S-Z.* 1982 (xv,544p. ISBN: 0804431558).
Covers *c.*1,300 writers from a wide range of fields, including children's literature, religion, history and politics as well as mainstream literature. Signed entries by a long list of contributors range from 400-5,000 words and include biographical notes (particularly good on names and pseudonyms), critical essay, primary bibliography and selected secondary bibliography. Index of names and subjects in v.4. Each vol. has list of *all* writers included, with ample cross-references. Especially useful for less well-known figures, although the publishers admit that many contemporary Black and lesbian writers have been omitted and might 'best be covered in a supplementary volume' (*Publishers' foreword*).
Abridged ed. published in one vol. (xxi,899p. ISBN: 0804431574) by Ungar in 1988; edited by L.L. Faust, with articles updated and revised where necessary and a few added. *Class No:* 820.73-0055.2

American Poetry

[2413]
Guide to American poetry explication. Boston, Hall, 1989. 2v.
V.1 *Colonial and nineteenth-century* by J. Ruppert. 252p. ISBN: 0816189196.
V.2 *Modern and contemporary* by J.R. Leo. 546p. ISBN: 0816189188.
The first 2 vols. of a planned 5-vol. set which will supersede J.M. Kuntz and N.C. Martinez's *Poetry explication: a checklist of interpretation since 1925 of British and American poems past and present* (3rd ed. Boston, Hall, 1980). A further 3 vols. will cover British poetry. Both vols. are arranged by poet, A-Z, then by poem, then by critic, and include references that were found in the three eds. of the earlier work plus new material published up to 1987. Both vols. contain references to many lesser-known poets and v.2 covers Canadian poets and many from minority groups, *e.g.* Native Americans, Hispanic Americans, gays, etc. *Class No:* 820.73-1

[2414]
Roth's American poetry annual, 1988-. Great Neck, N.Y., Roth, 1989-. Annual.
Combines 3 formerly separate Roth publications, *American poetry index* (1981-86. 4v.), *Annual index to poetry in periodicals* (1984-86. 3v.), and *Annual survey of American poetry* (1985-86. 2v.), to form a single sourcebook. Contents include a survey of the previous year's poetry, with a selected anthology; an index to poetry in selected journals (108 in the 1989 vol.) and single-author collections; a list of poetry award winners; a bibliography of books and articles on poetry and poets; directories of grants, fellowships, organizations, newsletters, etc.; and a list of periodicals and publishers. *RQ* (v.30(1), Fall 1990, p.136-7) suggests that the work's importance lies in its combined author/title/first-line index, whose coverage of single-author collections is unique, whereas the information in its bibliography and directories is too selective.

....(contd.)

For poetry in multi-author anthologies, see Roth's *Poetry index annual*, which remains a separate publication. *Class No:* 820.73-1

American Drama

[2415]
American playwrights since 1945: a guide to scholarship, criticism, and performance. Kolin, P.C., *ed.* New York and London, Greenwood, 1989. xiii,595p. ISBN: 0313255431.

Essays by different scholars describing the state of research on and the history of performances of 40 dramatists. Contributions average 14p. and are divided as follows: Assessment of reputation; Primary bibliography; Production history (including screen adaptations); Survey of secondary sources (a sub-divided, analytical account); Future research opportunities; Secondary sources cited (checklist). Name index. Play and screenplay index. Covers all the big names (Miller, Williams, Simon, etc.) but particularly useful for emerging writers. *Class No:* 820.73-2

[2416]
BIGSBY, C.W.E. A Critical introduction to twentieth-century American drama. Cambridge, Cambridge Univ. Press, 1982-85. 3v. illus.

V.1 *1900-1940.* 1982. ix,342p. ISBN: 0521271169.

V.2 *Tennessee Williams. Arthur Miller. Edward Albee.* 1984. viii,355p. ISBN: 0521277175.

V.3 *Beyond Broadway.* 1985. x,485p. ISBN: 0521278961.

An authoritative survey, with select bibliographies and indexes in each vol. V.3 includes chapters on Black theatre, women's theatre and gay theatre. 'Their extensive, consistent, and coherent treatment of twentieth-century American drama makes these volumes worthy of becoming the standard critical introduction to the subject' (*American Literature*, v.58(2), May 1986, p.463-65). *Class No:* 820.73-2

[2417]
PETERSON, B.L. Contemporary Black American playwrights and their plays: a biographical directory and dramatic index. New York and London, Greenwood, 1988. xxvi,625p. ISBN: 0313251908.

A-Z listing of over 700 black playwrights (including radio, film and TV writers, musical theatre collaborators, etc.) resident and writing in the US between 1950 and 1985. Entries include biographical details and annotated lists of plays, with lengthy annotations for representative plays by major writers. Appendix A. lists another 100 playwrights whose scripts are located in special repositories. Appendix B. lists over 75 other playwrights known to have had work produced in the US since 1950. Extensive bibliography (20p.) lists libraries, anthologies, reference and critical books, dissertations and theses, periodicals. Title index. General index of theatrical names, organizations and awards. Particularly useful for unpublished writers.

A companion vol. appeared in 1990 entitled *Early Black American playwrights and dramatic writers: a biographical directory and catalog of plays, films, and broadcasting scripts* (298p. ISBN: 0313266212). *Class No:* 820.73-2

American Fiction

[2418]
Masterplots II: American fiction series. Magill, F.N., *ed.* Englewood Cliffs, N.J., Salem Press, 1986. 4v. ISBN: 0893564567.

Covers over 360 20th-century works by 198 authors, of whom 34 are Latin Americans. In contrast to the original *Masterplots* series (which is not duplicated here), the signed entries now contain a shorter plot summary and a longer

....(contd.)

critical essay dealing with structure, characterization, themes, style, etc. A few references are made to other sources. Entries are arranged by title, with author index.

The *British and Commonwealth fiction series* (1987. 4v. ISBN: 0893564680) and *World fiction series* (1988. 4v. ISBN: 0893564737) are similar in format. *Class No:* 820.73-31

New Zealand Literature

[2419]
The Oxford history of New Zealand literature in English. Sturm, T., *ed.* Auckland, Oxford Univ. Press, 1991. xviii,748p. ISBN: 019558211x.

The most comprehensive work on the subject, with 9 signed thematic chapters: 1. Maori literature - 2. Non-fiction - 3. The Novel - 4. The short story - 5. Drama - 6. Poetry - 7. Children's literature - 8. Popular fiction - 9. Publishing, patronage, literary magazines. Comprehensive, discursive bibliography (107p.) in 5 sections: 1. Bibliographies and reference works - 2. Literary history and criticism - 3. Anthologies - 4. Periodicals - 5. Authors, A-Z (primary and secondary material). References (25p.). Thorough index. The work of 11 contributors. *Class No:* 820.931

Australian Literature

[2420]
LOCK, F. and LAWSON, A. Australian literature: a reference guide. 2nd ed. Melbourne and Oxford, Oxford Univ. Press, 1980. xiv,120p. (*Australian bibliographies.*) ISBN: 0195542142.

1st ed. 1977.

417 annotated entries (an increase of 84 over 1st ed.) in 7 main sections: 1. Bibliographical aids - 2. Other reference sources - 3. Authors (reference sources for 48 individuals) - 4. Periodicals - 5. Library resources - 6. Literary studies (*i.e.* guides to general literary research) - 7. Organizations (new section in 2nd ed.). A very useful, compact guide. *Class No:* 820.94

[2421]
The Oxford history of Australian literature. Kramer, L., *ed.* Melbourne and Oxford, Oxford Univ. Press, 1981. vi,509p. ISBN: 0195505905.

Introduction by editor followed by chapters on fiction, drama and poetry by A. Mitchell, T. Sturm and V. Smith, and bibliography (62p.) in semi-narrative form by J. Hooton, subdivided as follows: Bibliographical and reference aids; General studies; Individual authors (71 names). Index to the text but not to bibliography. Does not cover non-fictional prose or popular literature. *Class No:* 820.94

[2422]
WILDE, W.H., *and others.* The Oxford companion to Australian literature. Melbourne and Oxford, Oxford Univ. Press, 1986. x,760p. ISBN: 0195542339.

Over 3,000 entries covering authors (including many non-literary figures, such as historians, journalists and entertainers) and works; literary movements, awards and societies; publishers and libraries; influential foreign writers; and places, events and traditions crucial to Australian literature. Entries for major authors include lists of critical studies. Both *TLS* (no. 4388, May 8, 1987, p.499) and *Review of English Studies* (v.39 (154), May 1988, p.334-5) praise the subject entries (*e.g.* War Literature; Folk Song and Ballad; Criticism) and their meticulous cross-references. A worthy addition to the *Oxford companion* series. *Class No:* 820.94

83 Germanic Literatures

German Literature

[2423]
Dictionary of literary biography. Detroit, Gale, 1978-91. v.1-101 (in progress).

The following vols. cover German literature:
V.56 *German fiction writers, 1914-1945*, ed. by J. Hardin. 1987. 382p. ISBN: 0810317346.
V.66 *German fiction writers, 1885-1913*, ed. by J. Hardin. 1988. 2v.(715p.). ISBN: 0810317443.
V.69 *Contemporary German fiction writers: first series*, ed. by W.D. Elfe and J. Hardin. 1988. 413p. ISBN: 0810317478.
V.75 *Contemporary German fiction writers: second series*, ed. by W.D. Elfe and J. Hardin. 1988. 367p. ISBN: 0810345536.
V.90 *German writers in the Age of Goethe, 1786-1832: first series*, ed. by J. Hardin and C.W. Schweitzer. 1990. 435p. ISBN: 0810345684.
V.94 *German writers in the Age of Goethe: Sturm und Drang to Classicism*, ed. by J. Hardin and C. Schweitzer. 1990. 427p. ISBN: 0810345749.
V.97 *German writers from the Enlightenment to Sturm und Drang, 1720-1764*, ed. by J. Hardin and C. Schweitzer. 1990. 399p. ISBN: 0810345773.

For a description of the series, see entry at 820-0(092) or 820.73. *Class No: 830*

[2424]
FAULHABER, U.K. and GOFF, P.B. German literature: an annotated reference guide. New York, Garland, 1979. x,398p. ISBN: 0824098315.

Lists 2,046 information sources on German literature and related subjects (folklore, philosophy, etc.) in 13 sections. Pays particular attention to works in English and evaluates each one 'from the standpoint of quality, reliability, currency and usefulness' (*Preface*). Index of authors, titles and subjects. *Class No: 830*

[2425]
FURNESS, R. and HUMBLE, M. A Companion to twentieth-century German literature. London, Routledge, 1991. 305p. ISBN: 0415019877.

Provides information on over 400 writers from Germany, Austria and Switzerland. Entries are arranged A-Z and include critical comments on major works, but there are no references to translations or critical studies. Useful for coverage of minor writers, but very limited on the major figures. *Class No: 830*

[2426]
GARLAND, H. and GARLAND, M. The Oxford companion to German literature. 2nd ed. Oxford, Oxford Univ. Press, 1986. x,1020p. ISBN: 0198661398.

1st ed. 1976.
Aims 'to produce a Companion to the historical and

....(contd.)
cultural background to German literature as well as to the writers and works themselves' (*Preface to 1st ed.*). c.4,000 entries, in a single A-Z sequence of authors, works, literary movements, genres, events, places, etc. (but no characters), covering the literature of German-speaking countries since c.800AD. Brief bibliographies with some author entries. *Modern Language Review* (v.83(3), July 1988, p.777-9) enthusiastically endorses the revisions made for the 2nd ed.: 'Such adjustments, reflecting changing perceptions of German post-war literature, naturally enhance the value of the *Companion*'. *Class No: 830*

[2427]
Germanistik: internationales Referatenorgan mit bibliographischen Hinweisen. Tübingen, Niemeyer, 1960-. v.1-. Quarterly. ISSN: 00168912.

An international bibliography of books, articles, and dissertations on German language and literature. Books are usually given signed reviews, but periodical articles are not annotated. Classified arrangement, with annual name and subject indexes in part 4. V.30, *1989*, has 8,009 entries in 34 sections. 'The most valuable source available to German scholars for keeping abreast of developments in the field' (Faulhaber and Goff, *German literature*, 1979, p.38). *Class No: 830*

[2428]
KOSCH, W. Deutsches Literatur-Lexikon: biographisch-bibliographisches Handbuch. Berger, B., *and others*, eds. 3., völlig neu bearb. Aufl. Bern, Francke, 1968-1992. v.1-14 (in progress).

1st ed. 1927-30 (2v.); 2nd ed. 1947-58 (4v.).
Whereas earlier eds. contained entries for literary terms, place-names, allusions, etc., this is essentially a biobibliographical dictionary of German authors. The signed entries are arranged A-Z, have reached Schilling with v.14 (1992), and comprise outline biography (no commentary), comprehensive primary bibliography, and selected secondary bibliography. Includes non-literary writers, such as historians, theologians, philosophers, etc., and some anonymous works under titles. Over 5,000 entries per vol.

Deutsches Literatur-Lexikon: Ausgabe in einem Band (Bern, Francke, 1963. 511p.) is a single-vol. abridgement of the 2nd ed., edited by B. Berger, which omits most of the subject entries. *Class No: 830*

[2429]
ROBERTSON, J.G. A History of German literature. 6th ed., by D. Reich and others. Edinburgh, Blackwood, 1970. xxvii,817p.

1st ed. 1902; 5th ed. 1968.
A standard single-vol. history in English, with 6 sections for the main literary periods. Quotations in German. Cue-words in margins facilitate quick reference. Detailed chronological table. Extensive chapter bibliographies appended. Index. *Class No: 830*

Women

[2430]
Women writers of Germany, Austria, and Switzerland: an annotated bio-bibliographical guide. Frederiksen, E., *ed.* Westport, Conn., Greenwood, 1989. 323p. ISBN: 031324989x.

Entries for 185 women writers from all periods, giving biographical sketch, critical evaluation, and list of works with summary and commentary. Chronological and geographical lists of authors appended. Bibliography of critical and biographical studies. Indexes to German and English titles. *Class No: 830-0055.2*

Yiddish Literature

[2431]
LIPTZIN, S. A History of Yiddish literature. New York, J. David, 1972 (reprinted 1985). x,521p. ISBN: 0824603079.

From the origins of Yiddish to the present in 24 chapters, with special emphasis on the contemporary period and including several chapters on Yiddish in different parts of the world. Numerous individual authors covered. Bibliography (7p.) of English-language reference material and translations of literary works. Detailed contents list. Index. *Class No: 830-088*

Austrian Literature

[2432]
Dictionary of literary biography. Detroit, Gale, 1978-91. v.1-101 (in progress).

The following vols., both edited by J. Hardin and D.G. Daviau, cover Austrian literature:
V.81 *Austrian fiction writers, 1875-1913.* 1989. 405p. ISBN: 0810345595.
V.85 *Austrian fiction writers, after 1914.* 1989. 394p. ISBN: 0810345633.
For a description of the series, see entry at 820-0(092) or 820.73. *Class No: 830-9436*

[2433]
Handbook of Austrian literature. Ungar, F., *ed.* New York, Ungar, 1973. 296p. ISBN: 0804429294.

Bio-critical essays on 80 Austrian writers, most of them selected from H. Kunisch's *Handbuch der deutschen Gegenwartsliteratur* and translated. Some new essays on non-contemporary writers. Bibliographies of primary and selected secondary works with each essay. *Class No: 830-9436*

Dutch Literature

[2434]
MEIJER, R.P. Literature of the Low Countries: a short history of Dutch literature in the Netherlands and Belgium. 2nd ed. Cheltenham, Thornes, 1978. ix,402p. ISBN: 0859500993.

1st ed. Assen, Van Gorcum, 1971.
Concise chronological narrative in 8 chapters from the 12th century to the 1970s. Quotations in Dutch with translations in footnotes. Select bibliography of works on Dutch literature in English, French and German (4p.). Index of names and titles. *Class No: 839.3*

[2435]
Winkler Prins lexicon van de Nederlandse letterkunde: auteurs, anonieme werken, periodieken. Lissens, R.F., *and others, eds.* Amsterdam, Elsevier, 1986. 477p. ISBN: 9010058689.

c.2,300 entries, A-Z, the great majority being for authors, with bibliographies of works and studies after each entry. Brief general bibliography of reference sources on Dutch literature. Index. *Class No: 839.3*

Scandinavian Literature

[2436]
Dictionary of Scandinavian literature. Zuck, V., *ed.* New York and London, Greenwood, 1990. xi,792p. ISBN: 0313214506.

A long-standing gap in literary reference coverage is filled by the appearance of this English-language dictionary of the literature of Scandinavia (including Finland), with *c.*700 signed entries (by some 120 contributors) on authors and subjects. Author entries range from 300 to 1,600 words and comprise biographical notes; analysis of major works; assessment of impact on the literary history of the writer's country; list of works (including English translations) and critical studies. Topical entries have 1,000-1,500 words and are followed by references to mainly English-language studies. Chronology, 400-1985. Bibliography of reference sources, periodicals, literary histories and anthologies for each country (16p.). Index of names, works, etc. *Class No: 839.5*

Icelandic Literature

[2437]
Old Norse-Icelandic literature: a critical guide. Clover, C.J. and Lindow, J., eds. Ithaca, N.Y., and London, Cornell Univ. Press, 1985. 387p. (*Islandica; 45.*) ISBN: 0801417554.

Essays by 6 scholars on the major branches of the literature: Mythology, Eddic poetry, Skaldic poetry, Kings' sagas, Family sagas and Norse romance. The comprehensive, classified bibliographies following each essay (*e.g.* 30p. for Eddic poetry) make this an invaluable reference work. Indexes of texts and their authors, critics, and topics. *Class No: 839.59*

Norwegian Literature

[2438]
BEYER, H. A History of Norwegian literature. Haugen, E., *tr. and ed.* New York, N.Y. Univ. Press, for The American-Scandinavian Foundation, 1956. ix,370p. illus.

Translation of 1st ed. of Beyer's *Norsk litteratur historie* (Oslo, 1952). Quotations in English. Footnote references to available translations. Bibliography (5p.) confined to English-language studies. Name and title indexes.

A 4th ed. of the original Norwegian work, by H. and E. Beyer, was published Oslo, Aschehoug, 1978.

See also *Modern Norwegian literature, 1860-1918,* by B.W. Downs (Cambridge, Cambridge Univ. Press, 1966. vii,276p.), which covers the 'classic' period of Norwegian literature. References to English translations in the text and to further reading in footnotes. Chapter bibliographies, with running commentary, are appended (8p.). *Class No: 839.6*

[2439]
DAHL, W. Norges litteratur. Oslo, Aschehoug, 1981-9. 3v. illus. ISBN: 8203105734.

V.1 *Tid og tekst 1814-1884.* 1981. 340p.
V.2 *Tid og tekst 1884-1935.* 1984. 430p.
V.3 *Tid og tekst 1935-1972, med et sluttkapitel om tekstere i 70- og 80-årene.* 1989. 375p.

A profusely illustrated history (many in colour) with many quotations, and biographies of major authors enclosed in boxes throughout the text. No bibliographies. Indexes to subjects and to names and titles in v.3. Invaluable for recent literature. *Class No: 839.6*

Swedish Literature

[2440]
GUSTAFSON, A. A History of Swedish literature.
Minneapolis, Univ. of Minnesota Press for the American-
Scandinavian Foundation, 1961. xv,708p. illus. ISBN:
0816602360.
   Comprehensive history in 12 chapters from origins to
1950s. Quotations in English. Excellent bibliographic guide
(77p.) has general section followed by surveys for the
periods covered by each chapter. Selective list of English
translations (15p.) with critical and explanatory notes. Index
of names, titles and subjects. *Class No:* 839.7

[2441]
OLSSON, B. *and* **ALGULIN, I. Litteraturens historia i**
Sverige. Stockholm, Norstedt, 1987. 605p. illus. ISBN:
9118730221.
   A well-illustrated, narrative history in 11 chapters with
numerous subsections. Biographical data on authors can be
found (with portraits) in the margins throughout. Good
bibliography (18p.) of critical studies (general and on
specific authors) with running commentary. Name and title
indexes. *Class No:* 839.7

Danish Literature

[2442]
Litteraturhåndbogen. Hansen, I.F., *and others, eds.* 2. udg.
Copenhagen, Gyldendal, 1985. 582p. illus. ISBN:
8700731765.
   1st ed. 1981.
   An extremely useful handbook in 3 main sections: 1. A
literary history of Denmark (p.31-367), comprising 7 signed
chapters on periods plus 2 on Faroese and Greenland
literature - 2. A biographical dictionary of authors (p.371-
508), with *c.*140 entries which include a portrait - 3. A
dictionary of *c.*70 literary terms (p.511-77), giving lengthy
explanations with examples. Index. *Class No:* 839.8

[2443]
MITCHELL, P.M. A History of Danish literature. 2nd, aug.
ed. New York, Kraus-Thomson, 1971. 339p. illus. ISBN:
0527642002.
   1st ed. Copenhagen, Gyldendal, 1957.
   16 chapters from the earliest times to 1970, with ch.16
new for this ed. and minor changes to the other chapters.
Quotations in English. Bibliography (5p.) of anthologies and
critical works in English. Index of authors, translators and
titles. *Class No:* 839.8

84 Romance Literatures

French Literature

[2444]

BASSAN, F., *and others*. **French language and literature:** an annotated bibliography. [2nd ed.]. New York and London, Garland, 1989. xix,365p. ISBN: 0824047982.

1st ed. 1976, as *An Annotated bibliography of French language and literature*.

1,253 entries (old ones revised and updated; many new ones added) in 3 parts and 20 chapters: 1. General bibliographies and reference works - 2. General studies on the French language - 3. Bibliographies and studies of literature (but individual authors not covered). Succinct descriptive annotations for all items. Largely confined to works in English and French 'which one can reasonably expect will be in an academic library, responsible for supporting a program of study in French language and literature' (*Preface*). Author-title index. A very useful handbook. *Class No:* 840

[2445]

A Critical bibliography of French literature. Cabeen, D.C., *and others, eds.* Syracuse, N.Y., Syracuse Univ. Press, 1947-. v.1-. (in progress).

V.1 *The Mediaeval period*, ed. by U.T. Holmes. 1947. xxvi,256p.; enl. ed. 1952.

V.2 *The Sixteenth century*, ed. by A.H. Schutz. 1956. xlii,365p.; rev. ed., ed. by R.C. La Charité, 1985. xxxii,847p. ISBN: 0815623089.

V.3 *The Seventeenth century*, ed. by N. Edelman. 1961. xlii,638p. ISBN: 0815620071.

V.3A *The Seventeeth century. Supplement*, ed. by H.G. Hall. 1983. xxviii,460p. ISBN: 0815622759.

V.4 *The Eighteenth century*, ed. by G.R. Havens and D.F. Bond. 1951. xxx,411p. ISBN: 081562008x. *Supplement*,ed. by R.A. Brooks. 1968. xxiv,283p. ISBN: 0815620098.

V.6 *The Twentieth century*, ed. by D.W. Alden and R. Brooks. 1980. 3pts. (lvii,2073p.). ISBN: 081562204x.

An invaluable selective, evaluative bibliography, arranged by chronological periods, with each section contributed by a specialist who critically appraises books, dissertations and articles, and frequently cites reviews. Index in each vol.

It should be noted that the 'revised' ed. of v.2 (1985) actually represents a complete reappraisal by 38 scholars of French Renaissance studies. The Introduction states that 'it is an entirely new and comprehensive work', but that the first ed. (1956) should not be dismissed as many entries in the rev. ed. refer specifically by number to entries therein.

The 3 parts of v.6, which contain nearly 18,000 entries, are: 1. *General subjects and principally the novel before 1940* - 2. *Poetry, theater, and criticism before 1940, and essay* - 3. *All genres since 1940. Index.* V.5, covering the 19th century, is still awaited. *Class No:* 840

[2446]

Dictionary of literary biography. Detroit, Gale, 1978-91. v.1-101 (in progress).

The following vols., all edited by C.S. Brosman, cover French literature:

V.65 *French novelists, 1900-1930.* 1988. 381p. ISBN: 0810317435.

V.72 *French novelists, 1930-1960.* 1988. 478p. ISBN: 0810345501.

V.83 *French novelists since 1960.* 1989. 413p. ISBN: 0810345617.

For a description of the series, see entry at 820-0(092) or 820.73. *Class No:* 840

[2447]

Dictionnaire des littératures de langue française. Beaumarchais, J.-P. de, *and others, eds.* 2e éd. Paris, Bordas, 1987. 4v.(xv,2874p.). illus. ISBN: 2040163514.

1st ed. 1984, in 3 vols.

Covers French literature from the 9th century to the present, with *c.*2,200 signed articles, arranged A-Z, on authors, anonymous works, literary reviews, and French-language literatures of other countries. Entries on major authors are very comprehensive, including survey of life and works (with extremely useful chronological tables), critical commentary, plot synopses of key works, and bibliography. Illustrations (many in colour) are grouped thematically and indexed in v.4, which also has index of 21,000 titles cited in the text, index of literary terms, and lists of Academy members and literary prize-winners. *Class No:* 840

[2448]

DOLBOW, S.W. Dictionary of modern French literature: from the Age of Reason through Realism. New York and London, Greenwood, 1986. x,365p. ISBN: 0313237840.

Nearly 300 entries, arranged A-Z, covering the major writers, works, and literary movements of the period 1715-1880. Bibliographies appended to each entry are largely confined to books and articles published in English, 1980-85. Plenty of cross-references. Appendix A lists historical and literary events and B groups entries by subject matter or period. Index. A companion vol. will cover 1880 to the present. *Class No:* 840

[2449]

A New history of French literature. Hollier, D., *ed.* Cambridge, Mass., and London, Harvard Univ. Press, 1989. xxv,1150p. illus. ISBN: 0674615654.

165 signed essays by different (mainly American) contributors are arranged chronologically from 778 to 1985, each headed by a date and a headline, 'evoking an event, which specifies not so much the essay's content as its chronological point of departure' (*Introduction*). Essays range from 1,500 to 4,000 words and cover genres, individual books, literary movements, periods, etc. but none

....(contd.)
are devoted to specific authors. English title given for each French work mentioned and all quotations in English. Bibliography after each essay. Chronology (13p.). Map. Index.

Well received in a lengthy review in *TLS* (no. 4531, Feb. 2nd, 1990, p.107-8) but 'not to be thought of as an exhaustive reference book'. *Class No: 840*

[2450]
The Oxford companion to French literature. Harvey, P. *and* Heseltine, J.E., *eds.* Oxford, Clarendon Press, 1959. x,771p. maps. ISBN: 0198661045.

Covers French literature (interpreted broadly, to include writers in many subject fields, *e.g.* history, theology, science) from *c.*400AD to World War Two, with *c.*6,000 entries, A-Z, on authors, works, allusions, institutions, literary movements, etc. No bibliographies with articles, but Appendix 1 is an annotated list of 'Pointers to the study of French literature and its background' (7p.) The *Oxford companion* which is most in need of updating.

The Concise Oxford dictionary of French literature, ed. by J.M.H. Reid (Oxford, Clarendon Press, 1976. 670p. ISBN: 0198661185) is a revised and condensed version with over 3,000 entries, including some additional material. *Class No: 840*

Belgian Literature

[2451]
FRICKX, R. *and* TROUSSON, R. **Lettres françaises de Belgique:** dictionnaire des oeuvres. Paris, Duculot, 1988-89. 3v. ISBN: 2801107824.

V.1 *Le Roman.* 1988, 539p.
V.2 *La Poésie.* 1988. 607p.
V.3 *Le Théâtre. L'Essai.* 1989. 484p.
Signed entries for over 3,000 literary works, published 1830-1980, are arranged A-Z by title within each vol. and comprise synopsis, brief critical evaluation and bibliography of critical studies. Each vol. has author index and index of titles which are not entry-terms. General bibliography in v.3(4p.). *Class No: 840.493*

African-French Literature

[2452]
Dictionnaire des oeuvres littéraires négro-africaines de langue française, des origines à 1978. Kom, A., *ed.* Québec, Naaman; Paris, Agencie de Coopération Culturelle et Technique, 1983. 672p. ISBN: 2890402428.

Signed articles by 93 scholars from 20 countries on *c.*650 literary works by Black African French-language authors. Arranged A-Z by title, giving plot summary, critical analysis, and bibliographical details of 1st ed. Most entries have 500-1,000 words, but those for major works have up to 2,000. Covers all literary genres, plus songs and screenplays. Indexes of African authors (giving year and country of birth) and of genres. *Class No: 840.96*

Canadian French Literature

[2453]
Dictionnaire des oeuvres littéraires du Québec. Lemire, M., *ed.* Montréal, Fides, 1978-87. 5v.

V.1 *Des origines à 1900.* 1978.
V.2 *1900 à 1939.* 1980.
V.3 *1940 à 1959.* 1982.
V.4 *1960 à 1969.* 1984.
V.5 *1970 à 1975.* 1987.
Each vol. lists works A-Z by title, with author index, and has general and author bibliographies for the period concerned. *Class No: 840.971*

[2454]
HAMEL, R., *and others.* **Dictionnaire des auteurs de langue française en Amérique du Nord.** Montréal, Fides, 1989. xxvi,1364p. illus. ISBN: 2762114756.

Supersedes the same authors' *Dictionnaire pratique des auteurs québécois* (1976) and broadens the scope to include US-based writers. Entries for over 1,600 authors of all periods, comprising biography, critical evaluation, and primary and secondary bibliography, plus photograph in many cases. Very useful bibliography of general reference sources (6p.). Includes non-literary authors. *Class No: 840.971*

Catalan Literature

[2455]
Història de la literatura catalana. Riquer, M. de, *and others,* eds. Barcelona, Ariel, 1964-88. 11v. illus. ISBN: 8434476002.

Splendidly produced history in 2 parts: *Part Antiga* (v.1-4, ed. by M. de Riquer) and *Part Moderna* (v.5-6, ed. by A. Comas, and v.7-11, ed. by J. Molas).

Each vol. comprises lengthy, signed essays by several scholars on genres, periods, authors, etc., with numerous quotations and bibliographical notes. Sumptuously illustrated throughout (many in colour), with index of illustrations in each vol. Detailed tables of contents provide access to each vol. and there is a cumulative index of names and titles (174p.) in v.11, with a separate index of periodical titles. *Class No: 849.9*

Italian Literature

[2456]
Dizionario critico della letteratura italiana. Branca, V., *ed.* 2. ed. Torino, Unione Tipografico-Editrice Torinese, 1986. 4v. illus. ISBN: 8802040184.

1st ed. 1974 in 3 vols.
Lengthy, signed articles (*e.g.* 7p. on Calvino, 17p. on Boccaccio) by over 200 contributors, mainly on authors but also on literary topics and movements, in a single A-Z sequence, with extensive bibliographies of primary and secondary material appended. Index of names (124p.) in v.4. *Class No: 850*

[2457]
The Macmillan dictionary of Italian literature. Bondanella, P. *and* Bondanella, J.C., *eds.* London, Macmillan; Westport, Conn., Greenwood, 1979. xxviii,621p. ISBN: 0333268377, UK; 0313204217, US.

US title is *Dictionary of Italian literature.*
Over 350 entries, mainly for writers, but also for genres, literary movements and schools, etc., each with a bibliography which is aimed at the reader with little or no knowledge of Italian. Chronology (40p.). Lists of entries by subject matter or period. Selected list of reference aids (3p.). Index. 35 contributors. *Class No: 850*

[2458]
WILKINS, E.H. **A History of Italian literature.** 2nd ed., rev. by T.G. Bergin. Cambridge, Mass., Harvard Univ. Press, 1974. xi,570p. map. ISBN: 0674397010.

1st ed. 1954.
Covers 1200 to the present in 53 chapters, many of them devoted to individual writers. Quotations in English translation. List of additional writers not treated in main text. Bibliography of English translations and English-language works on the literature (20p.). Chronology of literary and historical events. Index. *Class No: 850*

Rumanian Literature

[2459]
BĂLAN, I.D. **A Concise history of Rumanian literature.**
Bucureşti, Editura ştiinţifică şi enciclopedică, 1981. 119p.

A history comprising biographical articles on Romanian authors, arranged chronologically and often including translated passages from their work. 'A balanced introduction to the principal figures of Romanian literature and the anonymous masterpieces of Romanian oral literature' (Deletant, A. and Deletant, D., *Romania*, 1985, p.132), but lacks bibliography. *Class No:* 859

Spanish & Portuguese Literature

[2460]
Modern Spanish and Portuguese literatures. Schneider, M.J. and Stern, I., eds. New York, Continuum, 1988. xxxii,615p. (*A Library of literary criticism*.) ISBN: 0804432805.

Presents lengthy excerpts from critical writings about 80 20th-century authors writing in Spanish, Catalan, Galician and Portuguese, with some excerpts newly translated by the editors. Two A-Z sequences (Spain and Portugal) with criticism arranged chronologically under each author. Nearly 800 excerpts in all. Lists of works mentioned (including English translations) constitute useful primary bibliographies for the authors concerned. Index to critics. *Class No:* 860+869

Spanish Literature

[2461]
DIAZ-PLAJA, G. **Historia general de las literaturas hispánicas.** Barcelona, Barna, 1949-67. 6v. in 7. illus.

V.1 *Desde les origenes hasta 1400.* 1949.
V.2 *Pre-renacimiento y renacimiento.* 1951.
V.3 *Renacimiento y barroco.* 1953.
V.4(2 pts.) *Siglos XVIII y XIX.* 1956.
V.5 *Post-romanticismo y modernismo.* 1958.
V.6 *Literatura contemporanea* (Barcelona, Vergara, 1967).

Resembles *Cambridge history of English literature* in scope and style, with each chapter written by a specialist and accompanied by an extensive bibliography. Coverage includes literatures in other languages of Spain (*e.g.* Basque, Catalan), Spanish-American literature, and literatures of other Spanish-speaking countries (*e.g.* Philippines).

A History of Spanish literature (New York, N.Y. Univ. Press, 1971. xxii,374p. ISBN: 0814717756) is a translation by H.A. Harter of a single-vol. history by Diaz-Plaja. It contains extensive quotations and a bibliography of English translations of classic Spanish drama, poetry and prose. *Class No:* 860

[2462]
The Oxford companion to Spanish literature. Ward, P., *ed.* Oxford, Clarendon Press, 1978. viii,629p. ISBN: 0198661142.

Approx. 3,000 entries in one A-Z sequence, mainly for authors (not limited to literary writers) and works, but also for literary institutions, movements, terms and styles. Covers Spanish-American literature and also non-Spanish literature of Spain: Basque, Catalan, Galician. Rather more bibliographical information included than is traditional in *Oxford companions*, rather less on historical and political background, with references to other sources at the end of most author entries. *Class No:* 860

[2463]
SIMÓN DÍAZ, J. **Manual de bibliografía de la literatura española.** 3rd ed., refundida, corr. y aum. Madrid, Gredos, 1980. 1156p. ISBN: 8424900235.
1st ed. 1963.

....(contd.)

Selective, unannotated bibliography (not an abridgement of the author's multi-volume work *Bibliografía de la literatura hispánica*) of nearly 27,000 items. General section followed by chronological sections covering Middle Ages, Golden Age, 18th, 19th, and 20th centuries, listing general works followed by works by and about specific authors. Excellent name and subject indexes. *Class No:* 860

[2464]
WOODBRIDGE, H.C. **Guide to reference works for the study of the Spanish language and literature and Spanish American literature.** New York, Modern Language Assoc. of America, 1987. xvi,183p. (*Selected bibliographies in language and literature.*) ISBN: 0873529588.

A greatly enlarged version of Woodbridge's *Spanish and Spanish-American literature: an annotated guide to selected bibliographies* (New York, MLA, 1983).

908 well-annotated entries on reference works published 1950-85, confined in general 'to the latest and best sources available' (*Introduction*). Excellent classified arrangement, clearly demonstrated in the table of contents, based on 4 main sections: 1. The Spanish of Spain - 2. American Spanish - 3. Spanish literature of Europe - 4. Spanish literature of the western hemisphere. Index of authors, editors and compilers. Index to author bibliographies, glossaries and concordances. *Class No:* 860

Women

[2465]
Women writers of Spain: an annotated bio-bibliographical guide. Galerstein, C.L., *ed. (non-Castilian materials ed. by K. McNerney).* New York and London, Greenwood, 1986. xxi,389p. (*Bibliographies and indexes in women's studies.*) ISBN: 0313249652.

300 entries by 79 contributors are arranged A-Z and provide biographical data and an alphabetical list of major works with annotations, in most cases, which aim to 'evaluate the contribution made by each author and her work to the development of a particular genre and to the literary representation of the historical period in which whe wrote' (*Preface*). Confined to creative literary writers, with the emphasis on the feminist movement. 4 appendices: 1. Chronological list of authors - 2. Authors in Catalan - 3. Authors in Galician - 4. Translated titles. Title index. *Class No:* 860-0055.2

Spanish-American Literature

[2466]
Handbook of Latin American literature. Foster, D.W., *comp.* New York, Garland, 1987. xviii,608p. ISBN: 0824085590.

Signed essays in English (several of them translated) on the national literature of 21 Latin American countries, with the emphasis on the internal coherence of each national tradition. Important literary works are cited in the text and each essay is followed by a short, annotated bibliography of literary histories and surveys relating to that country. Bibliography of material on Latin America in general (8p.). Index of names. *Class No:* 860.7

[2467]
Latin American writers. Solé, C.A., *ed.* New York, Scribner's, 1989. 3v. ISBN: 068418463x.

Substantial essays on 176 authors (149 writing in Spanish and 27 from Brazil) are arranged chronologically by birthdate, from 1474 to the 20th century, and include brief biography, survey of output (including plot summaries of major works and quotations in the original language and/or in English), and bibliography of first eds., modern eds., translations, biographies, critical studies, and bibliographies. Chronological table of literary and historical events. General

....(contd.)
index, list of writers by country, and alphabetical index of writers partly compensate for the inconvenience of the chronological arrangement. *Class No:* 860.7

[2468]
RELA, W. A Bibliographical guide to Spanish American literature: twentieth century sources. New York and London, Greenwood, 1988. xiv,381p. (*Bibliographies and indexes in world literature.*) ISBN: 0313258619.

1,884 annotated entries in 4 sections (Bibliographies; Dictionaries; History and Criticism; Anthologies), each section having general items followed by subsections on the 14 national literatures, arranged A-Z, with further subdivision by genre in most cases. Author index. Confined to books and excludes works on individual authors.

Essentially a selective integration of Rela's mammoth *Guía bibliográfica de la literatura hispanoamericana desde el siglo XIX hasta 1970* (Buenos Aires, Casa Pardo, 1971) and *Spanish American literature: a selected bibliography... 1970-1980* (East Lansing, Mich., Michigan State Univ., 1982) with the addition of material from the 1980s. *Class No:* 860.7

Women

[2469]
Women writers of Spanish America: an annotated bio-bibliographical guide. Marting, D.E., *ed.* New York and London, Greenwood, 1987. xvi,448p. (*Bibliographies and indexes in women's studies.*) ISBN: 0313249695.

A companion vol. to *Women writers of Spain* (*q.v.*) but less consistent in approach, with many authors and works merely listed without annotation. Approx. 1,200 entries by 72 contributors are arranged A-Z and cover literary authors who write principally in Spanish and who were born or have lived most of their lives in Spanish America, plus those of Spanish-American background born or living in the USA. 5 useful appendices: 1. Partially annotated list of anthologies - 2. Authors born before 1900 - 3. Classified list of authors by country - 4. Dramatists - 5. Translations and bilingual editions.

Followed by *Spanish American women writers: a bio-bibliographical source book* (New York, Greenwood, 1990. 645p. ISBN: 0313251940), which, according to *Choice* (v.28(4), Dec. 1990, p.616) 'does more than improve on its predecessor', providing information on the lives and works of 50 major writers. Appended essays cover Indian women writers of Spanish America and Latina writers of the US. *Class No:* 860.7-0055.2

Cuban Literature

[2470]
Dictionary of twentieth-century Cuban literature. Martínez, J.A., *ed.* New York, Greenwood, 1990. 537p. ISBN: 0313251851.

A biobibliographical dictionary of 113 authors, including exiles, with entries which provide biography, critical evaluation, and bibliography of primary and secondary materials. Also includes information on 45 critics, essays on the major genres, information on literary journals, and general bibliography. Index. 'Should be the first choice as a reference guide to writers in Cuba or in exile therefrom' (*Choice*, v.27(10), June 1990, p.1648). *Class No:* 860.729.1

Mexican Literature

[2471]
FOSTER, D.W. Mexican literature: a bibliography of secondary sources. Metuchen, N.J. and London, Scarecrow, 1981. xxv,386p. ISBN: 0810814498.

Part I has nearly 1,100 general references in 28 sections. Part II covers 50 authors with between 13 and 333 entries per individual. Cut-off date 1978-79. No annotations. Index of critics. *Class No:* 860.972

Argentine Literature

[2472]
FOSTER, D.W. Argentine literature: a research guide. 2nd ed., rev. and exp. New York, Garland, 1982. xliii,778p. ISBN: 0824093976.

1st ed. 1970, by D.W. and V.R. Foster, as *Research guide to Argentine literature.*

General references in 30 sections followed by listings for 73 authors, giving bibliographies, critical monographs and dissertations, and critical essays for each, with the emphasis on material likely to be accessible in the US and Latin America. Index of critics. 2nd ed. shows very considerable expansion. *Class No:* 860.982

Chilean Literature

[2473]
FOSTER, D.W. Chilean literature: a working bibliography of secondary sources. Boston, Hall, 1978. xxii,236p. ISBN: 0816181802.

Part 1., General References, has 28 sections covering genres, periods and special topics (*e.g.* Women authors); Part 2., Authors, lists bibliographic and critical material on 46 individuals. 2,777 entries in all (500 on Neruda). No annotations. Index of critics. *Class No:* 860.983

Peruvian Literature

[2474]
HIGGINS, J. A History of Peruvian literature. Liverpool, Cairns, 1987. xiv,379p. (*Liverpool monographs in Hispanic studies.*) ISBN: 0905205359.

Covers literature in Spanish and Quechua (the language of the indigenous population) from the Renaissance onwards, with two-thirds of the book devoted to the twentieth century. 6p. of general bibliography plus bibliographies for each cited author in footnotes throughout the text. These include works and critical material and except in the case of major authors are comprehensive. Indexes of authors and works plus a short glossary. All quotations are accompanied by an English translation. 'A necessary and trustworthy guide' (*TLS*, no. 4405, 4th-11th September, 1987, p.961). *Class No:* 860.985

Portuguese Literature

[2475]
BELL, A.F.G. Portuguese literature. Oxford, Oxford Univ. Press, 1922 (repr. 1970). 395p.

General history in 6 period divisions: 1185-1325; 1325-1521; 1502-80; 1580-1706; 1706-1816; 1816-1910. Appendix 1. Literature of the People - 2. The Galician Revival. Select bibliography (20p.) of texts and critical works has been added by B. Vidigal for the reprint and includes a section on contemporary writing. *Class No:* 869

[2476]
CHAMBERLAIN, B.J. Portuguese language and Luso-Brazilian literature: an annotated guide to selected reference works. New York, Modern Language Assoc. of America, 1989. xii,95p. (*Selected bibliographies in language and*

....*(contd.)*
literature.) ISBN: 0873529561.

A classified, well-annotated guide, similar in style and format to Woodbridge's work on Spanish language and literature (*q.v.*). 538 entries in 4 main sections (Portuguese language; Portuguese literature; Brazilian literature; Luso-African and other Lusophone literatures) with numerous sub-sections. Index of authors, editors and compilers. *Class No:* 869

Brazilian Literature

[2477]
Dictionary of Brazilian literature. Stern, I., *ed.* New York and London, Greenwoood, 1988. l, 402p. ISBN: 0313249326.

300 signed entries, arranged A-Z, 'covering the most significant writers, literary schools, and related cultural movements in Brazilian literary history, with an emphasis on twentieth-century and very contemporary figures' (*Preface*). Author entries include citations for major works and are followed by bibliography of selected additional works, translations and criticism, the latter comprising primarily English-language sources where available. Introductory essay with general bibliography (14p.); map; chronology of historical and literary events (11p.); glossary of Brazilian words (1p.). Index. 46 contributors. *Class No:* 869.981

[2478]
FOSTER, D.W. *and* **RELA, W. Brazilian literature: a research bibliography.** New York, Garland, 1990. 426p. ISBN: 0824034422.

General studies (arranged under 11 subject headings) are followed by bibliographies for many individual authors. *Choice* (v.28(4), Dec. 1990, p.608) regrets several omissions, particularly of women writers, but 'for those authors included, this is now the *first* recourse'. Author index. *Class No:* 869.981

87 Classical Literature

Classical Literature

[2479]
GRANT, M. Greek and Latin authors, 800BC-AD1000. New York, Wilson, 1980. xiv,490p. illus. ISBN: 0824206401.

A biographical dictionary with entries for 376 authors, giving an account of the life, description of and commentary on the works, discussion of the writer's influence on later works, and select bibliography of editions, translations and studies. Appendix A. lists 16 works of doubtful attribution. Appendix B. groups authors by century. *Class No: 870*

[2480]
The Oxford companion to classical literature. Howatson, M.C., *ed.* 2nd ed. Oxford and New York, Oxford Univ. Press, 1989. vii,615p. maps. ISBN: 0198661215.

1st ed. 1937, by Sir P. Harvey.

Long-awaited revision and expansion of Harvey's work, which no longer assumes a knowledge of Greek and Latin on the part of the reader. Approx. 3,000 entries covering authors, works, characters, literary forms and the historical, political and religious background basic to an understanding of the classics. Ample cross-references. Chronological table of historical and literary events from 2200BC to AD529. 6 maps. First ed. is still available in paperback (ISBN: 0192814907). *Class No: 870*

Latin Literature

[2481]
The Cambridge history of Classical literature, vol.2: Latin literature. Kenney, E.J. *and* Clausen, W.V., *eds.* Cambridge, Cambridge Univ. Press, 1982. xviii,973p. plates. ISBN: 0521210437.

42 signed chapters arranged in 7 parts: Readers and Critics; Early Republic; Late Republic; The Age of Augustus; Early Principate; Later Principate; Epilogue. The essays concentrate on discussion of the literary texts, with material relating to biography, chronology and bibliography presented mainly in the very thorough 'Appendix of Authors and Works' (137p.). Another appendix (4p.) covers metrics. Bibliography of works cited in the text (19p.). Index. *Class No: 871*

Greek Literature

[2482]
The Cambridge history of Classical literature, vol 1: Greek literature. Easterling, P.E. *and* Knox, B.M.W., *eds.* Cambridge, Cambridge Univ. Press, 1985. ISBN: 0521210429.

21 chapters by several named scholars are arranged in broadly chronological order from Homer to the 3rd century A.D. As in the companion vol. on Latin literature (*q.v.*)

....(contd.)
these are followed by the 'Appendix of Authors and Works' (172p.), which provides biographical and bibliographical material on all the major writers. Further appendix on metrics (7p.) and bibliography of works cited in the text (19p.). Index. *Class No: 875*

Modern Greek Literature

[2483]
POLITIS, L. A History of modern Greek literature. Oxford, Clarendon Press, 1973. xi,338p. ISBN: 0198157215.

Part 1 covers 11th to 18th centuries in 5 chapters; Part 2 covers 19th and 20th centuries in 12 chapters. Quotations in English in the text with originals in Appendix. Chronological tables of literary and historical events. Selected bibliography of general works, texts and critical studies (22p.). Index. *Class No: 877*

88 Slavonic Literatures

Slavonic Literatures

[2484]
Modern Slavic literatures. Mihailovich, V.D., *and others*, *comps.* New York, Ungar, 1972-76. 2v. (*A Library of literary criticism.*) ISBN: 0804431752.
    V.1 *Russian literature* (xii,424p.). V.2 *Bulgarian, Czechoslovak, Polish, Ukrainian and Yugoslav literatures* (xvi,720p.).
    V.1 has excerpts from criticism on 69 20th-century authors, arranged A-Z, concentrating on those whose work is available in translation. Criticism is arranged chronologically under each author and is mainly from the US and UK, with some Russian and European critics included.
    V.2 covers 196 authors in separate sections (with different editors) for each literature. Most of the criticism excerpted is by Slavic scholars and is here translated for the first time, but there are also excerpts from English-language and European critics. A proposed section on Byelorussian literature had to be omitted for lack of critical material. Both vols. cover émigré authors. Index to critics in each vol. *Class No: 880*

[2485]
TERRY, G.M. East European languages and literatures: a subject and name index to articles in English-language journals, 1900-77. Oxford and Santa Barbara, Calif., Clio, 1978. xxv,275p. ISBN: 0903450216.
    Expanded version of an index published privately in 1976 for staff and students at Nottingham University.
    Covers Slavic countries plus Finland, Baltic States, Hungary and Romania. Indexes over 9,500 articles from 800 journals in a single A-Z sequence of names and subjects.
    Further vols. have been published by Astra Press, Nottingham, as follows: *1978-81, with articles in festschriften, conference proceedings and collected papers, 1900-81.* 1982 (xxx,218p. ISBN: 0946134006); *1982-84.* 1985 (xviii,152p. ISBN: 0946134057); *1985-87.* 1988 (xviii,130p. ISBN: 0946134138); *1988-90.* 1991 (xxii,150p. ISBN: 0946134251). *Class No: 880*

Russian Literature

[2486]
The Cambridge history of Russian literature. Moser, C.A., *ed.* Cambridge, Cambridge Univ. Press, 1989. ix,685p. ISBN: 0521309948.
    Narrative history from 988 to 1980 in 10 chapters by different scholars. The 2 chapters on the 20th century treat literature published within and outside the Soviet Union equally. Bibliography (36p.) of secondary works in book form, with the emphasis on 20th century publications. 'Thoroughly traditional in approach and form, the volume offers a solid introduction to its subject matter' (*Choice*,

....(contd.)
v.28(1), Sept. 1990, p.122). However, a lengthy review in *Modern Language Review* (v.86(2), April 1991, p.536-541) is critical of the traditional approach ('This weighty volume is completely uninformed by the developments that have taken place in critical theory during the last twenty years') and asserts that the bibliography 'contains an unacceptably high proportion of outdated works'. *Class No: 882*

[2487]
Handbook of Russian literature. Terras, V., *ed.* New Haven, Conn., and London, Yale Univ. Press, 1985. xix,558p. ISBN: 0300031556.
    Approx. 1,000 signed entries by 106 (mainly American) scholars are arranged A-Z and cover authors, journalists and critics; literary movements and schools; periodicals and publishing houses; genres, styles and themes; and literary and historical terms. Titles of Russian works are given in translation, usually followed by Russian title in parentheses, and names are given in their familiar English spelling. Brief bibliographies appended to most articles are intended 'to give the reader a head start, no more' (*Preface*) and are largely restricted to material in Russian and English. Excellent classified general bibliography (7p.). Ample cross-references and thorough index. The best single-volume source available, it is 'unlikely to be surpassed for a long time...[and] deserves to be acquired by libraries everywhere' (*Modern Language Review*, v.82(1), Jan. 1987, p.264-5). *Class No: 882*

[2488]
An Introduction to Russian language and literature. Auty, R. and Obolensky, D., *eds.* Cambridge, Cambridge Univ. Press, 1977. xiii,300p. (*Companion to Russian studies, v.2.*) ISBN: 0521280397.
    Chapters on Russian language (p.1-40) and Russian writing and printing (p.41-55) are followed by a history of the literature from AD1000 to 1975 in 5 chapters and a history of Russian theatre in 3 chapters. Each chapter is by an acknowledged specialist and is followed by extensive lists, with commentary, of recommended general studies and reference works, and of works by and about individual authors. Index. *Class No: 882*

[2489]
KASACK, W. Dictionary of Russian literature since 1917. New York, Columbia Univ. Press, 1988. xvi,502p. ISBN: 0231052421.
    Translation and amalgamation of Kasack's *Lexikon der russischen Literatur ab 1917* (Stuttgart, Kröner, 1976) and its supplement, *Ergänzungsband* (Munich, Sagner, 1986), by M. Carlson and J.T. Hedges, with bibliographical revision by R. Atack.
    706 entries covering the whole field of Russian literature (not merely Soviet literature) since the Revolution, are arranged A-Z by transliterated names. 619 author entries

....(contd.)

comprise biographical sketch, critical evaluation of works and selected bibliography of works and criticism. 87 subject entries cover journals, associations, literary movements and topics essential to an understanding of modern Russian literature, e.g. Emigration, Censorship, Gulag. Indexes of names and subjects. List of place name changes. Numerous cross-references. The original 1976 ed. was praised for its 'authoritative, comprehensive and nonideological coverage' (World Literature Today, v.51(1), Winter, 1977, p.637-8). Class No: 882

Ukrainian Literature

[2490]
ČYŽEVS'KYJ, D. A History of Ukrainian literature, (from the 11th to the end of the 19th century). Littleton, Colo., Ukrainian Academic Press, 1975. xii,681p. ISBN: 0872870936.

Originally published 1956, as Istoriia ukrains'koi literatury vid pochatkiv do doby realizmu.

The first comprehensive survey in English, with 14 chapters covering periods and many subsections for genres. Chapter bibliographies appended (19p.). Index of names and titles. Class No: 883

Polish Literature

[2491]
MILOSZ, C. The History of Polish literature. 2nd ed. Berkeley, Calif., and London, Univ. of California Press, 1983. xix,583p. plates. ISBN: 0520044657.

1st ed. 1969.

Definitive history by the 1980 Nobel Prize winner. 11 chapters on the main periods, with sub-sections on particular genres, movements and individual writers. All quotations are accompanied by translations. Substantial bibliography (17p.). Index of names and titles.

2nd ed. is reproduction of original ed. with the addition of an epilogue (7p.) covering the late 1960s and 1970s and an updated bibliography. Class No: 884

Czechoslovak Literature

[2492]
KOVTUN, G.J. Czech and Slovak literature in English: a bibliography. 2nd ed. Washington, D.C., Library of Congress, 1988. viii,152p. ISBN: 0844405787.

1st ed. 1984.

Lists translations into English and English-language studies of the 2 literatures in 5 sections: A. Anthologies (prose and poetry) - B. Anthologies (folklore) - C. General history and criticism - D. Czech authors, A-Z (233 authors) - E. Slovak authors, A-Z (93). US library locations given. Index of authors, editors and critics; index of translators. Class No: 885

Yugoslav Literature

[2493]
MIHAILOVICH, V.D. and MATEJIC, M. A Comprehensive bibliography of Yugoslav literature in English, 1593-1980. [2nd ed.]. Columbus, Ohio, Slavica, 1984. xii,586p. ISBN: 0893571369.

1st ed. 1976, entitled Yugoslav literature in English: a bibliography of translations and criticism (1821-1975).

Lives up to its title, with 5,255 entries covering all the literatures of Yugoslavia. Part 1, Translations, has sections on folk literature and individual authors. Part 2 lists criticism under 4 headings: Entries in reference works; Books and articles; Reviews; Dissertations. Easy access via 4 indexes: English titles; original titles; periodicals and newspapers; subjects and names. The planned 5-yearly

....(contd.)

updates 'will be eagerly awaited and welcomed by all in the field' (Modern Language Review, v.81(1), Jan. 1986, p.272).

First supplement, covering 1981-85, published 1989 (338p. ISBN: 0893571881), is similarly arranged. Class No: 886.1

Bulgarian Literature

[2494]
MATEJIC, M., and others. A Biobibliographical handbook of Bulgarian authors. Black, K.L., ed. Columbus, Ohio, Slavica, 1981. 347p. illus. ISBN: 0893570915.

Covers 88 authors chronologically in 5 periods from 580 to the present, giving biographical sketch and bibliography of works and critical studies (in English and Bulgarian). Some entries have photographs. Lacks index. Class No: 886.7

Baltic Literatures

[2495]
RUBULIS, A. Baltic literature: a survey of Finnish, Estonian, Latvian, and Lithuanian literatures. Notre Dame, Ind., Univ. of Notre Dame Press, 1970. xv,215p.

Separate sections for each national literature comprising introduction to the ethnic characteristics of their respective folklores and the origins of their written literatures, followed by discussion of the main literary movements and major individual authors. Many quotations in English translation. Bibliography (3p.). Lacks index. Class No: 888

89 Oriental, African, etc. Literature

Oriental Literature

[2496]
ANDERSON, G.L. **Asian literature in English:** a guide to
information sources. Detroit, Gale, 1981. 336p. ISBN:
0810313626.
A bibliography of translations into English of Asian-
language literary works and of English-language studies of
those works. Covers China, Japan, Korea, Burma,
Cambodia, Indonesia, Laos, Malaysia, Singapore, Thailand,
Vietnam, Mongolia, Tibet and Turkey. Over 2,200 entries.
For India, see A. Singh's *Indian literature in English* in the
same series. *Class No: 890*

[2497]
Dictionary of Oriental literatures. Průšek, J., *ed.* London,
Allen & Unwin; New York, Basic Books, 1974. 3v.
V.1 *East Asia*, ed. by Z. Slupski (xxiii,226p. ISBN:
0048900044). V.2 *South and South-east Asia*, ed. by D.
Zbavitel (xv,191p. ISBN: 0048900052). V.3 *West Asia and
North Africa*, ed. by J. Becka (xvii,213p. ISBN:
0048900060).
2,000 concise, signed articles by over 150 scholars from
many countries. Most entries give biographical information
and critical evaluation on individual writers from classical
to modern times and many have brief bibliographies
appended. Other entries cover literary terms, genres,
schools, movements, etc. Lists of entries at the end of each
vol., grouped according to national literatures. N.B. Vol.3
includes the Arab countries of North Africa. *Class No:*
890

[2498]
Far Eastern literatures in the 20th century: a guide.
Klein, L.S., *ed.* New York, Ungar, 1986; Harpenden,
Oldcastle, 1988. ix,195p. ISBN: 0804463522, US;
0948353171, UK.
Handy guide based on Ungar's 5-vol. *Encyclopedia of
world literature in the 20th century*, rev. ed., 1981-84
(*q.v.*). All entries on the literatures of East and Southeast
Asia plus the major Pacific islands (Fiji, Western Samoa
and Papua New Guinea) are reproduced with some minor
revisions and corrections, but unfortunately not updated. 15
national/regional surveys are arranged A-Z, with 9 followed
by articles on the major authors (60 in all). All articles and
surveys are signed and include bibliographies. Index to
author articles. *Class No: 890*

Indian Literature

[2499]
Encyclopaedia of Indian literature. Datta, A., *ed.* New Delhi,
Sahitya Akademi (distributed in US by South Asia Books),
1987-89. (in progress). v.1-3 (2924p.).
V.1 *A-Devo.* 1987. ISBN: 083642283x.
V.2 *Devraj-Jyoti.* 1988. ISBN: 0836423860.
V.3 *K-Navalram.* 1989. ISBN: 0836424875.
Aims to cover in 6 or more vols. the growth and
development of Indian literature in 22 languages. Signed
entries on authors (born up to 1947), genres, movements
and works are arranged A-Z, and some have short
bibliographies. *Choice* (v.26(8), April 1989, p.1304, and
v.27(3), Nov. 1989, p.458) notes some serious omissions
and the lack of an index in the early vols. (presumably a
cumulative one is planned), but nevertheless welcomes it as
'a scholarly, authoritative reference work'. *Class No: 891.1*

Sanskrit Literature

[2500]
BANERJI, S.C. **Companion to Sanskrit literature.** 2nd ed.
Delhi, Motilal, 1989. xviii,810p. ISBN: 812080063x.
1st ed. 1971.
A very useful encyclopedic work, with sections on
authors, works, characters, technical terms, geographical
names, and the principal figures in myths and legends.
Entries for literary works have references to editions and
translations. 16 appendices (4 added for 2nd ed.), including
a classified list of Sanskrit works and a select, classified
bibliography of western-language studies (24p.). *Class No:
891.2*

Urdu Literature

[2501]
SADIQ, M. **A History of Urdu literature.** 2nd ed., rev. and
enl. Delhi, Oxford Univ. Press, 1984. xv,652p. ISBN:
0195615581.
1st ed. 1964.
A critical survey from the early 17th century to the
present. Quotations in Urdu and English. References and
notes. Index. 2nd ed. contains many revisions and much
new material on post-Iqbal literature. *Class No: 891.43*

Persian Literature

[2502]
BROWNE, E.G. **A Literary history of Persia.** Cambridge,
Cambridge Univ. Press, 1928 (re-issue). 4v. illus.
Originally published 1902-24; vols.1-2 by Fisher Unwin,
vols.3-4 by Cambridge Univ. Press.
V.1 *From the earliest times until Firdawsí.* ISBN:
0521043441.
V.2 *From Firdawsí to Sa'dí.* ISBN: 052104345x.

....(contd.)
V.3 *The Tartar dominion (1265-1502).* ISBN: 0521043468.

V.4 *Modern times (1500-1924).* ISBN: 0521043476.

The standard history, it contains many original quotations with English translations and biographies of poets and prose-writers. Numerous detailed footnote references. Analytical index in each vol. *Class No:* 891.5

Celtic Literatures

Irish Literature

[2503]
A Bibliography of modern Irish and Anglo-Irish literature. Kersnowski, F., *ed.* Dublin, Trinity Univ., 1976. 156p.

Concentrates on writers of the Irish literary renaissance, arranged A-Z with data on writer's creative work, biography, autobiography, travel, criticism (except in periodicals), and major works about him/her. Long list of background titles in Preface. *Class No:* 891.62

[2504]
HYDE, D. A Literary history of Ireland: from earliest times to the present day. New ed., with introduction by B. Ó Cuív. London, Benn; New York, Barnes & Noble, 1967. xlii,654p.

First published London, Fisher Unwin, 1899.

A pioneering work in 44 chapters, with many (often lengthy) quotations in translation. Analytical index. New ed. has bibliography of 20th-century studies of Irish literature, but, according to the new introduction, none has superseded Hyde's work. *Class No:* 891.62

Welsh Literature

[2505]
A Guide to Welsh literature. Jarman, A.O.H. *and* Hughes, G.R., *eds.* Swansea, C. Davies, 1976-.

V.1. 1976. 295p. illus. ISBN: 0715401246.

V.2. 1979. 400p. illus. ISBN: 0715404571.

2 vols. have appeared so far of a projected 6-vol. set, which aims 'to outline the history and development of Welsh literature from its beginnings in the sixth century to the present day' (*Preface*). V.1 (11 chapters by 6 contributors) covers 6th to 13th centuries; V.2 (16 chapters by 10 contributors) continues to 1527 (somewhat later for prose). Almost all quotations are in English translation. Bibliographies after each chapter. Index in each vol. *Class No:* 891.66

[2506]
PARRY, T. A History of Welsh literature; translated from the Welsh by H. Idris Bell. Oxford, Clarendon Press, 1955. xii,534p.

Originally published 1944 as *Hanes llenyddiaeth Gymraeg hyd 1900* (Reprinted 1979 by Univ. of Wales Press. ISBN: 0708307280).

Comprehensive survey from the 6th century to 1900, to which the translator has added an appendix (125p.) on the 20th century and many footnotes on technical terms, geographical names and allusions likely to confuse non-Welsh readers. All quotations have been translated. The original's comprehensive bibliography is replaced by brief notes on a selection of English-language publications. Author and subject indexes. *Class No:* 891.66

Albanian Literature

[2507]
ELSIE, R. Dictionary of Albanian literature. New York and London, Greenwood, 1986. viii,170p. ISBN: 031325186x.

A welcome guide to a little-known literature, containing over 500 entries on writers and literature-related topics, including basic biographical and bibliographical data. Translations provided for all titles mentioned. Bibliography of general sources (3p.). Index. *Class No:* 891.983

Hebrew Literature

[2508]
WAXMAN, M. A History of Jewish literature. 2nd ed. New York and London, Yoseloff, 1960. 5v. in 6. maps.

1st ed. in 4 vols. as *A History of Jewish literature from the close of the Bible to our own days* (New York, Bloch, 1930-41); v.2 and v.4 appeared in enlarged and corrected eds., 1943-7.

V.1 *From the close of the canon to the end of the twelfth century.* xvi,539p.

V.2 *From the twelfth century to the middle of the eighteenth century.* xiii,712p.

V.3 *From the middle of the eighteenth century to 1880.* xii,767p.

V.4 *From 1880 to 1935.* 2pts. (xv,1312p.).

V.5 *From 1935 to 1960.* 361p.

Covers literature in the widest sense, including theology, philosophy, history, biography, etc., with chapters devoted to genres and periods. Chapter bibliographies at the end of each vol. Index to whole set in v.5. *Class No:* 892.4

Arabic Literature

[2509]
The Cambridge history of Arabic literature. Cambridge, Cambridge Univ. Press, 1983-90. v.1-2 (in progress).

V.1 *Arabic literature to the end of the Umayyad period,* ed. by A.F.L. Beeston and others, 1983. xvi,547p. ISBN: 0521240158.

V.2 *Religion, learning and science in the Abbasid period,* ed. by M.J.L. Young and others, 1990. xxi,587p. ISBN: 0521327636.

Each vol. contains over 20 signed essays by international scholars. Many quotations in English translation. V.1 has extremely useful bibliography of translations of the Koran into European languages (19p.). V.2 has extensive chapter bibliographies (25p.). Glossary of Arabic terms and index in each vol. *Class No:* 892.7

[2510]
Modern Arabic literature. Allen, R., *comp. and ed.* New York, Ungar, 1987. xxxiii,370p. (*A Library of literary criticism.*) ISBN: 0804430241.

Presents substantial excerpts from literary criticism on about 71 writers from Algeria, Egypt, Iraq, Lebanon, Palestine, Sudan, Syria and Tunisia, many of them translated from Arabic by the editor. Single A-Z sequence of writers, with excerpts arranged chronologically under each one. Bibliography of works mentioned lists full-length books by each author and available English translations. Index to critics. *Class No:* 892.7

Turkish Literature

[2511]
MITLER, L. Contemporary Turkish writers: a critical bibliography of leading writers in the Turkish Republican period up to 1980. Bloomington, Ind., Research Institute for Inner Asian Studies, 1988 (distributed by Indiana Univ. Press). 325p. ISBN: 0933070144.

An A-Z listing of authors active since 1923, giving pseudonyms, subject areas, birth and death dates, biographical notes, critical evaluation, and list of works which includes translations of all Turkish titles. Some entries include translated passages from the writer's works. Glossary. List of literary award winners. Select bibliography of European-language works on Turkish literature. 'The only work on modern Turkish writers in a Western language' (*Choice*, v.26(5), Jan. 1989, p.786). *Class No: 894.35*

Hungarian Literature

[2512]
CZIGÁNY, L. The Oxford history of Hungarian literature: from the earliest times to the present. Oxford, Clarendon Press, 1984. x,582p. ISBN: 0198157819.

25 chapters, of which 18 cover the 19th and 20th centuries. Major authors and works discussed in detail, with quotations in translation. Special attention paid to literary relations with Britain and the USA and good coverage of émigré writers. Annotated bibliography (46p.). Glossary of Hungarian literary and geographical terms (17p.). 'The comprehensive index ... adds to the general usefulness of what is likely to remain a standard work' (*Modern Language Review*, v.82(1), Jan. 1987, p.270-272). *Class No: 894.511*

[2513]
TEZLA, A. Hungarian authors: a bibliographical handbook. Cambridge, Mass., Belknap Press of Harvard Univ. Press, 1970. xxviii,792p. ISBN: 0674426509.

An extension of Tezla's *An introductory bibliography to the study of Hungarian literature* (Cambridge, Mass., Harvard Univ. Press, 1964. xxvi,290p. ISBN: 0674463501), which aims at a complete record of first editions, an extensive list of later editions and a selection of the major bibliographical, biographical and critical works for 162 authors. Two A-Z sequences for authors 1450-1945 and 1945-present. Biographical notes on each author. Library locations for most items. Appendix A. updates the *Introductory bibliography* with material published 1960-65; B. lists literary awards, societies, newspapers and periodicals mentioned in biographical notes; C. lists periodicals from which articles are cited; D. lists authors by literary period; E. lists libraries. Name index. Fine annotations throughout. Over 4,600 entries in all. *Class No: 894.511*

Finnish Literature

[2514]
AHOKAS, J. A History of Finnish literature. Bloomington, Ind., Indiana Univ. Research Center for the Language Sciences, for the American-Scandinavian Foundation, 1973. ix,568p. ISBN: 0877501726.

Arranged by period, with notes on individual authors and works. Index of names and titles. *Class No: 894.541*

Estonian Literature

[2515]
NIRK, R. Estonian literature: historical survey with biobibliographical appendix. Hone, A.R. *and* Mutt, O., *tr.* 2nd ed. Tallinn, Perioodika, 1987. 416p. illus. ISBN: 0828537720.

1st ed. 1970.

Two-thirds of the survey is devoted to the 20th century. Bibliography of Estonian literature in English (7p.). Still not entirely free of Soviet control (very little coverage of émigré writers) but nevertheless 'in many ways more sensible than the five-volume official academic history of Estonian literature' (*World Literature Today*, v.62(3), Summer 1988, p.482-3). *Class No: 894.545*

Chinese Literature

[2516]
The Indiana companion to traditional Chinese literature. Nienhauser, W.H., *and others*, eds. Bloomington, Ind., Indiana Univ. Press, 1985. 1052p. ISBN: 0253329833.

Covers literature up to 1911 and is the work of 200 contributors, who have produced 10 survey essays on the major types of literature and over 500 signed articles on authors, works, genres, literary movements, etc. Selective bibliographies of editions, translations and studies with each entry. Indexes of names, titles and subjects. 'A stunning example of what careful coordination of effort and painstaking editorial supervision can achieve; ... a work that far surpasses anything now available' (*Choice*, v.23 (11/12), July/Aug. 1986, p.656-8). *Class No: 895.1*

[2517]
A Selective guide to Chinese literature, 1900-1949. Malmqvist, N.G.D., *and others*, eds. Leiden, Brill, 1988-90. 4v.

V.1 *The Novel*, ed. by M. Doleželová-Velingerová. 1988. xvii,238p. ISBN: 9004078800.

V.2 *The Short story*, ed. by Z. Slupski. 1988. xiii,300p. ISBN: 9004078819.

V.3 *The Poem*, ed. by L. Haft. 1989. xi,301p. ISBN: 9004089608.

V.4 *The Drama*, ed. by B. Eberstein. 1990. xi,347p. ISBN: 9004090983.

The work of over 100 scholars from 16 countries, this series is intended to 'facilitate the first stage of research for anyone interested in 20th century Chinese literature' (*Preface*). Each vol. has an introductory essay and general bibliography, followed by signed entries for *c*.100 major works. These are arranged A-Z by author (romanized name) and include bibliographical details of 1st ed., synopsis, commentary, and lists of critical studies and translations into European languages. Author index and index of journals, publishers and literary series. *Class No: 895.1*

Japanese Literature

[2518]
KONISHI, J. A History of Japanese literature. Miner, E., *ed.* Princeton, N.J., Princeton Univ. Press, 1984- (in progress).

Originally published Tokyo, 1985-7, as *Nihon bungei shi* (5v.).

V.1 *The Archaic and Ancient Ages,* trans. A. Gatten and N. Teele, 1984 (xx,475p. ISBN: 0691065926).

V.2 *The Early Middle Ages,* trans. A. Gatten, 1986 (xv,461p. ISBN: 0691066558).

V.3 *The High Middle Ages,* trans. A. Gatten and M. Harbison, 1991 (xix,654p. ISBN: 0691066566).

The first 3 vols. to appear in English of a comprehensive 5-vol. history which is primarily concerned with the technical aspects of the literature (original title literally means 'A History of Japanese literary art'). Romanized

....(contd.)

Japanese quotations have parallel English translations. Each vol. has chronological table, select bibliography of editions and critical material in Japanese and other languages, and index.

TLS (no. 4419, Dec. 11th, 1987, p.1382) commends Konishi's international perspective and transcendence of parochial barriers: 'He ... sets Japanese literature in the broad context of East Asian literary history, something not systematically attempted in Western accounts before.' *Class No: 895.6*

[2519]
The Princeton companion to classical Japanese literature. Miner, E., *and others, eds.* Princeton, N.J., Princeton Univ. Press, 1985. xxi,570p. illus. ISBN: 0691065993.

Definitive handbook to Japanese literature from its beginnings to 1868 in 10 parts. Part 3 (127p.) is a dictionary of major authors (325 entries) and works (110). Other useful features include a brief history (60p.), chronologies, glossary of literary terms, and lists of placenames, ranks and offices. Well-illustrated sections on theatre, architecture, costume and armour. Comprehensive index and extensive cross-referencing. Bibliography (5p.). *Class No: 895.6*

Korean Literature

[2520]
KIM DONGUK. History of Korean literature. Hurvitz, L., *tr.* Tokyo, Centre for East Asian Cultural Studies, 1980. xi,321p.

Intended for Japanese readers and originally published by the Japan Broadcast Publishing Co., 1974, as *Chosen bungaku-shi.*

4 main sections (1. Ancient literature - 2. Medieval literature - 3. Early modern literature - 4. Modern literature) with subsections on genres and major works. Quotations in English. No index or bibliography, but the appended 'History of the study of Korean literature' (26p.) has many references to sources. *Class No: 895.7*

Vietnamese Literature

[2521]
DURAND, M.M. *and* **NGUYEN TRAN HUAN. An Introduction to Vietnamese literature.** Hawke, D.M., *tr.* New York, Columbia Univ. Press, 1985. xiii,213p. ISBN: 0231058527.

Originally published in French in 1969. This ed. has extra sections in 2 chapters covering 1969-75.

13 chapters tracing the development of the literature from earliest times to 1975. Quotations in English translation. Very useful bibliography of general sources and French and English translations of Vietnamese literary works (9p.). Index. *Class No: 895.97*

African Literature

[2522]
European-language writing in Sub-Saharan Africa. Gérard, A., *ed.* Budapest, Akadémiai Kiadó, 1986. 2v.(1289p.). (*A Comparative history of literatures in European languages.*) ISBN: 9630538326.

A comprehensive survey by over 60 scholars from 25 countries, which is arranged in 4 chronologically-ordered parts, 18 chapters, and numerous subsections devoted to individual writers, countries and genres. Bibliographical essay by the editor (19p.). Index. 'If one tries to find omissions, one will try in vain' (*World Literature Today*, v.62(1), Winter 1988, p.168). *Class No: 896*

[2523]
HERDECK, D.E. African authors: a companion to Black African writing. Volume 1: 1300-1973. Washington, D.C., Black Orpheus Press, 1973. x,605p. illus. maps. ISBN: 0810300761.

Provides information on 594 authors from Sub-Saharan Africa (plus Malagasy and Mauritius) writing in 37 African languages, Afrikaans and the major West European languages. One A-Z sequence of entries, which comprise biographical notes, critical comments and lists of writings, with secondary bibliography for major figures. 16 appendices include lists of authors by category and language, lists of journals and publishers, and bibliographies of critical studies and anthologies. *Class No: 896*

[2524]
JAHN, J. and DRESSLER, C.P. Bibliography of creative African writing. Nendeln, Liechtenstein, Kraus-Thomson, 1971. xl,446p. maps. ISBN: 0527451509.

Covers creative literature written in all languages in Black Africa and published in book form or performed on stage. Plays published in journals included, but not poems and stories. General section (bibliographies, periodicals, criticism, anthologies) followed by 4 regional sections (Western, Central, Eastern, Austral), with each having subsections for secondary literature, anthologies, and works of individual authors. Introductory material in English, French and German. General index plus indexes to books in African languages, translations and countries. Over 2,800 unannotated entries.

Supersedes Jahn's *A Bibliography of Neo-African literature from Africa, America and the Caribbean* (New York, Praeger; London, Deutsch, 1965) - which was not restricted to Africa proper and was thus unable to include secondary material - and the supplements to its African section later compiled by P. Páricsy. *Class No: 896*

[2525]
A New reader's guide to African literature. Zell, H.M., *and others, eds.* 2nd ed., completely rev. and expanded. London, Heinemann; New York, Holmes and Meier, 1983. xvi,553p. illus. (*Studies in African literature.*) ISBN: 0435919997, UK; 0841906394, US.

First published 1971 as *A Reader's guide to African literature.*

Comprehensive guide to literature by Black authors from south of the Sahara writing in English, French and Portuguese. General bibliography (125p.) in 5 sections. (Bibliographies and reference works; General criticism; Criticism of individual authors; Collections; Folklore and oral tradition), followed by primary bibliographies for individual authors from 43 countries grouped by language and region, with over 3,000 titles (a vast increase over first ed.) listed and annotated. Selective bibliography of children's literature (21p.). List of relevant magazines (16p.). Biographical sketches (average 1½p.) of 95 authors, 50 of them new to this ed., many with photographs. Directory of specialist booksellers and publishers and libraries with African collections. Index of authors, editors, critics and journal titles. Indispensable in its field. *Class No: 896*

Amerindians, North—Literature

[2526]
RUOFF, A.L.B. American Indian literatures: an introduction, bibliographic review, and selected bibliography. New York, Modern Language Assoc. of America, 1990. viii,200p. ISBN: 0873521919.

Introductory section surveys oral literature, autobiography, and written literature since the 18th century. Bibliographic review comprises essays on bibliographies and research guides; anthologies and collections; and scholarship and

....(contd.)
criticism. Classified bibliography lists all works mentioned plus additional material. List of significant dates. Index of people, events, and subjects. 'This scholarly volume is the most comprehensive introduction currently available to the genres and major authors of native American oral and written literature' (*Booklist*, v.87(13), March 1, 1991, p.1419). *Class No:* 897

Indonesian Literature

[2527]
TEEUW, A. Modern Indonesian literature. The Hague, Nijhoff, 1967. xv,308p., illus.
In 2 parts, covering pre- and post-war literature. 2 bibliographies, one giving details of Indonesian literary works and the other of references cited in the text. Many quotations in translation. Detailed index. *Class No:* 899.2

Malayan Literature

[2528]
WINSTEDT, R.O. A History of classical Malay literature. Reprint of 2nd ed. Kuala Lumpur, Oxford Univ. Press, 1969. x,323p.
First published in *Journal of the Malayan Branch of the Royal Asiatic Society*, v.31, pt.3, no.183, 1939; 2nd ed. 1961.
Standard history in 13 chapters with extensive bibliography (12p.). Appendix gives outlines of 12 Malay Hikayat. *Class No:* 899.221

9 GEOGRAPHY, BIOGRAPHY, HISTORY
90 Archaeology

Archaeology

[2529]
Ancient peoples and places. London, Thames & Hudson, 1957-. illus., tables, maps, bibliogs.

A series of concise and well-illustrated surveys by distinguished archaeologists and historians, examining what has been discovered and what has been deduced about ancient civilizations. 'They're not gee-whiz books, but are directed at the literate general reader, as well as providing up-to-date material for scholars in other fields' (*Sunday Telegraph*, 22 December 1968). V.100 in the series was Glyn Daniel's *A short history of archaeology* (1981). *Class No: 902*

Bibliographies

[2530]
WOODHEAD, P. Keyguide to information sources in archaeology. London, Mansell, 1985. xiv,219p. diagr. ISBN: 0720117453.

Part 1. Overview of archaeology and its literature in 7 chapters: 1. History and scope - 2. Archaeological information - 3. Who, what, where? - 4. Keeping up to date with current publications, developments and events - 5. Finding out about the literature - 6. The literature of archaeology - 7. Other sources of information. Pt. 2 Bibliographical listing (an annotated bibliography of reference sources). Pt. 3 List of selected organizations. 'A work of great interest and quite widespread usefulness' (*Library Review*, v.35, no.2, Summer 1986, p.136-7). *Class No: 902(01)*

Encyclopaedias

[2531]
The Cambridge encyclopedia of archaeology. Sherratt, A., *ed.* Cambridge, Cambridge Univ. Press, 1980. 495p. illus., charts, maps, plans.

55 contributors. 3 parts (10 sections; 62 chapters): 1/1. The development of modern archaeology ... 2/2. Man the hunter; 2/3. The postglacial revolution; 2/4.The early empires of the western Old World; 2/5. Empires in the eastern Old World; 2/6. Old empires and new forces; 2/7. On the edge of the Old World; 2/8. The New World (*e.g.* chapter 59: Andean South America); 2/9. Pattern and process ... 3/10. Framework; dating and distribution. Chronological atlas, p.437-52 (36 col. maps). Bibliography (by chapters), p.453-65. Further reading (by parts and sections), p.416-7. Analytical index, p.468-95. 500 illus. (150 col.), with descriptive captions. Omits industrial archaeology.'The selection of topics is excellent and as comprehensive as positive' (*Choice*, v.18, no.2, October 1980, p.220). 'A volume with wide appeal' (*Nature*, v.288, 6 November 1980, p.42). 'More likely to be used for browsing than for quick reference' (*College & Research Libraries*, January 1981, p.49). *Class No: 902(031)*

Dictionaries

[2532]
WHITEHOUSE, R.D., *ed.* **The Macmillan dictionary of archaeology.** London, Macmillan Press, 1983. xi,597p. bibliog., index. ISBN: 0333271904.

Over 3500 entries covering the themes, concepts, and discoveries in archaeology. Bibliography p.592-97. Subject index. *Class No: 902(038)*

Maps & Atlases

[2533]
Past worlds The Times atlas of archaeology. Scarre, C., *ed.* London, Times Books, 1989. Distributed in the US by Hammond Inc. 320p. col. illus., col. maps, tables, bibliog, index. ISBN: 0723003068.

90 academic contributors (31 from Cambridge University). 122 double page pictorial and cartographic features arranged in 7 main sections: 1. Understanding the past - 2. Human origins 16 million-10,000BC. - 3. The agricultural revolution 10,000-4,000BC. - 4. The first cities and states 4000-1000BC. - 5. Empires of the Old World 1000BC-AD650 - 6. The New World 10,000BC-AD1600 - 7. Towards the modern world AD650-1800. Chronology in 5 colour code for geographical regions p.11-21. Glossary p.281-4. Bibliography p.285-8. 750 col. illus.

A series of articles by George Hill appeared in *The Times* immediately prior to publication *viz* 1. Uncovering the secrets, 27 Sep, 1988, p.10-11; The Age of the great explorers, 28 Sep, p.11; Separate worlds, same ideas, 29 Sep, p.12; and Man and the fathers of invention, 30 Sep, p.12. 'Without question, this is now the standard archaeological atlas' (*Wilson Library Bulletin*), v.63, no.5, January 1989, p.127). *Class No: 902(084.3)*

Pacific Ocean

[2534]
BELLWOOD, P. Man's conquest of the Pacific the prehistory of Southeast Asia and Oceania. Auckland, Collins, 1978. 462p. illus., maps, bibliog., index. ISBN: 0002169118.

13 chapters: 1. Introduction; 2. Human populations - past and present; 3. Cultural foundations; 4. The cultures of Southeast Asia and Oceania; 5. The linguistic history of the Pacific area; 6. Subsistence pattern and the prehistoric implications; 7. Neolithic and Early Metal Age cultures on the Southeast Asian mainland; 8. Neolithic and Early Metal Age Inland Southeast Asia; 9. The prehistory of Melanesia; 10. Prehistory of Micronesia; 11-12. Prehistory of Polynesia; 13. Prehistory of New Zealand. Glossary p.424. Important bibliography p.425-451. *Class No: 902(265)*

Ancient Egypt

Bibliographies

[2535]
Annual Egyptological bibliography/Bibliographie Egyptologique annuelle/Jährbuch Agyptologische bibliographie. Zonhoven, L.M.J., *ed.* Leiden, International Association of Egyptologists in cooperation with the Nederlands Instituut voor het Nabije Oosten, 1948-. Annual.

The 1984v. (1987. xi, 251p. 9072147030) has 1331 numbered abstracts sytematically classified in 10 sections: 1. General (History of Egyptology, Obituaries, Present day Egyptology, Reports, Methodology, Research tools) - 2. Scripts and language - 3. Texts and philology - 4. History - 5. Art and archaeology - 6. Religion - 7. Society and culture - 8. Science and technology - 9. The country and neighbouring areas - 10. Nubian studies. Author and title indexes. Published on the recommendation of the International Council for Philosophy and Humanistic Studies, with the financial assistance of UNESCO and the Nederlandse organistie voor zuiver-wetenschappenijk onderzoek ZWO.

Janssen, J.M.A. *Annual Egyptological Bibliography indexes 1947-1956.* Leiden, E.J. Brill, 1960. xviii, 475p. *Class No:* 902(32)(01)

Ancient Greece & Rome

[2536]
STILLWELL, R., *and others eds.* **The Princeton encyclopaedia of classical sites.** Princeton, New Jersey, Princeton Univ. Press, 1976. xxi, 1019p. ISBN: 0691035423.

Data on over 2,800 archaeological sites. Aardenburg ... Zoster. About 400 contributors. Period: 750BC-AD565. All entries, however, short, have references, ('Corinth'; 6 columns; $\frac{2}{3}$ col. of bibiliography; 'Carthage': $1\frac{1}{4}$ cols., 5 references; 'Katana' (Catania, Sicily); $2\frac{1}{3}$ cols. of bibliography). Map references to 24p. of 3-colour maps; map indexes, p.1011-19. Glossary of technical terms. Scholarly, readable text. A handsome volume. 'This first-class reference book' (*Library Journal*, v.101, 1 October 1976, p.2050). *Class No:* 902(37/38)

Maps & Atlases

[2537]
HEYDEN, A.A.M. *and* **SCULLARD, H.,** *eds.* **Atlas of the Classical World.** London, Nelson, 1959. 221p. illus., maps, index.

'Not intended primarily for professional scholars' (*Foreword*). 70 coloured maps, plus insets; 475 photogravure plates, including many aerial photographs. It illustrates the centuries from prehistoric Greece to the decline of the Roman Empire before the barbaric immigrations of the 4th century. Information is presented in three ways: maps, giving religious, economic, military, literary, artistic and political statistics; illustrations (line-drawings and photographs); descriptive articles, covering geography, history and culture. Maps include town plans, and a number have lengthy legends; scales are not often indicated. *Shorter atlas of the Classical world,* compiled by H.H. Scullard and A.A.M. van der Heyden (London, Nelson, 1962 [*i.e.* 1963] 239p. illus., maps.) is not a mere abridgement. Prof. Scullard has provided a new 40,000 word account of the Greek and Roman civilizations. But the chief features are the 200 or so excellent illustrations of landscape and culture. The 10 coloured maps occupy a rather inconspicuous place. *Class No:* 902(37/38)(084.3)

Europe

[2538]
CHAMPION, T., *and others.* **Prehistoric Europe.** London, Academic Press, 1984. x, 359p. illus., maps, bibliog., index.

Comprehensive synthesis of new interpretations (based on recent archaeological data) in 9 chronological chapters each equipped with numerous maps and drawings. References p.327-35. 'It will at once take its place as a new standard work, for it is quite simply the best introduction to European prehistory which is currently available' (*Nature*, v.314, no.6006, 7 March 1985, p.28-29). *Class No:* 902(4)

[2539]
GAMBLE, C. The Palaeolithic settlement of Europe. Cambridge, Cambridge Univ Press, 1986. xix, 471p. illus., tables, bibliog. ISBN: 0521245141.

Surveys the hunter-gatherer societies of Europe in 9 chapters (1. European paleolithic studies: history and approaches; 9. The palaeolithic settlement in Europe). Extensive bibliography p.411-459. Site index p.460-462. General index p.463-471. *Class No:* 902(4)

Great Britain

[2540]
CUNLIFFE, B. Iron Age communities in Britain an account of England, Scotland and Wales from the seventh century BC until the Roman Conquest. 3rd ed. London, Routledge, 1991. xii,685p. illus., maps, drawings, bibliog., index. ISBN: 0415054168.

1st ed. 1974; 2nd ed. 1979.

Comprehensive account of the British Iron Age. 21 chapters in 4 parts: 1. Introduction (development of Iron Age studies) - 2. Space & time (from a chronological and regional standpoint) - 3. Themes (pattern of settlement, development of hill-forts etc.) - 4. Systems (Iron Age society and social change). Appendix A. Pottery - B. Selected radiocarbon dates - C. List of principal sites (p.609-23). Chapter notes p.624-6. Bibliography p.631-73. This edition is substantially revised. *Class No:* 902(410)

[2541]
HAWKES, J. The Shell guide to British archaeology. London, Michael Joseph, 1986. 320p. illus. (some col.), maps, bibliog. ISBN: 0718124480.

"A History of archaeology in Britain" and "Prehistoric and Roman Britain" precede a gazetteer of sites divided regionally. A general survey of the prehistory and archaeology of each region opens each section. Site entries explicate its archaeological age, importance, plan, and use, noting significant artifacts found and their present whereabouts. Regional maps, a glossary, and a list of the most important museums complete a compact and comprehensive guide. *Class No:* 902(410)

Reviews & Abstracts

[2542]
British archaeological abstracts. London, Council for British Archaeology, 1967-. no.1-. 2 *pa.* ISSN: 00070270.

1989: 1892 abstracts on the archaeology of Great Britain and Ireland. Arranged by periods: 1. General, multi-period undated - 2. Palaeolithic and Mesolithic - 3. Neolithic - 4. Bronze Age - 5. Iron Age - 6. Roman Britain - 7. Migration/Early medieval - 8. Medieval - 9. Post-medieval/Industrial. Recent, then by subjects. Annual author and subject indexes. When CBA's *Archaeological bibliography for Great Britain and Ireland* folded with the 1980 issue coverage of abstracts ceased to be selective and comprehensivity is now attempted from *c.*165 British and 130 foreign journals. There is a microfiche edition. *Archaeological site index to radiocarbon dates for Great*

....(contd.)
Britain and Ireland, 1971-1982 is a supplement to *British archaeological abstracts*. Lavell, C. *British archaeological thesaurus for use with British archaeological abstracts and other publications in British archaeology* (CBA, 1989). 69p. refs., pbk. £4.95. ISBN 0906780772 is 'a standard list of words in current use in British archaeology' (*British archaeological abstracts* Entry 89/893). *Class No:* 902(410)(048)

Scotland

[2543]
HANSON, W.S. *and* **SLATER, E.A.**, *eds.* **Scottish archaeology** new perceptions. Aberdeen Univ. Press, 1991. xi,228p. illus., maps, tables, bibliogs., index. limp cover. ISBN: 0080412122.
13 papers by different hands, each ending with a bibliography, provide authoritative overviews on the current state of knowledge of all periods of Scottish archaeology e.g. 2. Skara Brae: revisiting a Neolithic village in Orkney ... 4. Future of Roman Scotland ... 7. Surveying for the future: RCAHMS archaeological survey ... 13. Managing output rather than input? The implications of computerising the National Museum of Scotland's archaeological information. *Class No:* 902(411)

[2544]
Reports and inventories. Great Britain. Royal Commission on the Ancient and Historical Monuments of Scotland. Edinburgh, H.M. Stationery Office, 1909-.
1.*Berwick*, 1909. 2. *Sutherland*. 1911. 3. *Caithness*. 1911. 4/5. *Galloway*. 1912-14. 2v. 6. *Berwick*. Rev. issue. 1915. 7. *Dumfriesshire*. 1920. 8. *East Lothian*. 1924. 9. *Outer Hebrides, Skye and the Small Isles*. 1928. 10. *Midlothian and West Lothian*. 1929. 11. *Fife, Kinross and Clackmannan*. 1933. 12. *Orkney and Shetland*. 1946. 3v. 13. *City of Edinburgh*. 1951. 14. *Roxburghshire*. 1956. 2v. 15. *Selkirkshire*. 1957. 16. *Stirlingshire*. 1963. v.1-2. £15. 17. *Peeblesshire*. 1967. 2v. £10; £17.50; $20.00. 18. *Argyle*. v.1: *Kintyre*. 1972; v.2: *Lorn*. 1975; v.3: *Mull, Tiree, Coll & N. Argyle*; v.4: *Iona*. 1982; v.5: *Islay, Jura, Colonsay & Oronsay*. 1984. £45. 0114917280; v.6: *Mid-Argyll & Cowal*. 1988. 19/20. *Lanarkshire*. 1978. (v.20. £20). Occasional Publications, designed to give fuller treatment to subjects which cannot be embraced within the normal course of the Commission's publication programme include: *Late medieval monumental sculpture in the West Highlands*. 1977. 230p.+45p., plates. £14.50. *Monuments of industry: an illustrated historical record*. 1986. xiii, 248p. £28.00. 0114924570.
In the numbered series descriptions are arranged by parish. Until 1938 monuments erected up to 1707 were included; in 1938 The Commissioners were empowered to cover up to 1815; after 1948 the terminal date has been left to their discretion. *Class No:* 902(411)

Ireland

[2545]
O'KELLY, M.J. **Early Ireland:** an introduction to Irish prehistory. Cambridge, Cambridge Univ. Press, 1989. xiii, 375p. illus., maps, plans, bibliog., index. ISBN: 0521334896.
12 chronological and thematic chapters: 1. The Ice Age ... 10. The Iron Age - 11. Later prehistoric settlement - 12. Iron Age burial. 4 Appendices: Radio-carbon dating; Dendochronology; Pollen analysis; and Calibration of radio-carbon dating. Bibliography p.353-70. *Class No:* 902(415)

France

[2546]
SCARRE, C., *ed.* **Ancient France 6,000-2,000 BC** Neolithic societies and their landscape. Edinburgh, Edinburgh Univ. Press, 1984. viii, 390p. illus., maps, bibliog. ISBN: 085224441x.
8 regional chapters relate the story of France's early farming societies. Each chapter includes a brief geographical account and a short history of previous research. Important bibliography p.344-380. Index p.383-390. 'An excellently factual and stimulating reference work' (*Antiquity*, LXVIII, no.223, July 1984, p.146). *Class No:* 902(44)

China

[2547]
CHANG, Kwang-Chih. The Archaeology of ancient China. 4th ed. New Haven, Yale Univ. Press 1987. xxv, 450p. illus., maps, tables, bibliog. ISBN: 0300037821.
First published 1963. 'This edition ... bears very little resemblance to its previous incarnations ... I no longer intend to cover the whole field and cite every available reference ... now ends with the rise of civilization and no longer includes the very rich and complex period of ancient history after about 1000 BC.'
Introduction (geographical review, traditional historiography and antiquarianism, modern and contemporary archaeology) - 1. Palaeolithic foundations - 2. The early farms - 3-4. Neolithic developments - 5. The Chinese interaction sphere and the foundations of civilization - 6-7. The first Chous. Glossary of Chinese characters p.423-438. Bibliography p.443-450. *Class No:* 902(510)

Antiquities

Ancient Greece & Rome

Dictionaries

[2548]
SEYFFERT, O. A Dictionary of Classical antiquities: mythology - religion - literature - art. Nettleship, H. *and* Sandys, J.E., *Rev. and ed.* London, Allen & Unwin, 1957; Magnolia, Montana, Peter Smith. vi, 716p. illus. index.
Founded on Seyffert's *Lexikon der classicher Altertumskunde* (1882). The 1957 edition is a reprint of the 3rd ed. (1894) of the English translation.
A standard work, compact yet readable. Adequate cross-references; some references to sources. *Class No:* 904(37/38)(038)

Great Britain

Roman Times

[2549]
WILSON, R.J.A. A Guide to the Roman remains in Britain. 3rd ed. London, Constable, 1988. xvi, 453p. illus., maps, bibliog., indexes. ISBN: 0094686507.
1st ed. 1978.
Survey of all visible antiquities in 10 regional chapters. Sites are grouped according to their nature and not to their proximity. Introduction (p.1-30) includes sections on Roman army in Britain; Military remains (by type); Historical outline; and Glossary (p.26-30). Appendix 1. Gazetteer of visible remains not mentioned in text p.408-19 - 2. Some museums displaying Romano-British material (p.420-1) - 3. Bibliography p.422-444. Index of sites and types of monument. Designed primarily for the ordinary individual who has an interest in the Roman past but no prior specialized knowledge. *Class No:* 904(410)"0055-0449"

Scotland

[2550]
MACSWEEN, A. *and* SHARP, M. **Prehistoric Scotland.**
London, Batsford, 1989. 208p. illus., maps, bibliog., index.
ISBN: 071346173x.
A lavishly illustrated guide to over 100 outstanding
prehistoric sites to stand as exemplars of the various types:
settlement, defence, tombs and burial; ritual, and stones &
henges. An introductory chapter summarizes the periods of
Scottish prehistory. Glossary p.195-8. Gazetteer p.199-203.
Bibliography p.204. *Class No:* 904(411)

Eire

[2551]
HARBISON, P. **Guide to the national monuments in the**
Republic of Ireland: including a selection of other
monuments not in state care. 2nd ed. Dublin, Gill and
Macmillan, 1982. 284p.+8p. maps, bibliog., index. ISBN:
717107582.
First published 1970. May be regarded as a very much
altered and expanded edition of *The national monuments*
of Ireland published by *Bord Failte* (Irish Tourist Board)
and now out of print.
Arranged A-Z by counties (p.1-260). Entries provide a
map reference, access details, a description, and references
to relevant publications. Glossary p.261-264. Bibliography
p.269. List of selected museums and folk parks p.270.
Class No: 904(417)

England & Wales

[2552]
HAWKES, J. **A Guide to the prehistoric and Roman**
monuments in England and Wales. 2nd ed. London, Chatto
& Windus, 1973.
First published 1951.
'Attempts to reveal the monuments always in their proper
setting of the countryside' (*Preface*). Arranged by areas (*e.g.*
South-east; Wessex; South-west; Oxfordshire to the Forest of
Dean; Wales and Monmouthshire; Eastern England; North
of England). 'Gazetteer of sites described in this Guide',
p.291-315 (name of site and page references; national grid
reference), - over 600 sites. General index. 16 colour pl.,
24 illus.; 5 maps as loose inserts. *Class No:* 904(42)

England

[2553]
GREAT BRITAIN. ROYAL COMMISSION ON THE
ANCIENT AND HISTORICAL MONUMENTS OF
ENGLAND. **Inventories.** London, H.M. Stationery Office,
1910-. illus., maps, plans.
Buckinghamshire, 2v., 1912-13. *City of Cambridge,* 2v.,
1959. reprinted 1988. 500p. pbk. £35. ISBN 0113000235.
County of Cambridge, 2v., 1968-72. *Dorset,* 5v., 1952-75.
Essex, 4v., 1916-23. *Hertfordshire,* 1911. *Huntingdonshire,*
1926. *London,* 5v., 1924-30 including v.3 *Roman London,*
1928. *Middlesex,* 1937. *Lincolnshire: Town of Stamford,*
1977. 0117007129. *County of Northamptonshire,* 6v., 1975-
84. *City of Oxford,* 1939. *City of Salisbury,* v.1. 1980.
0117008494. *Shielings and Bastles,* 1970. *Westmorland,*
1936. *City of York,* 5v., 1962-81. *County of*
Cambridgeshire, v.1: *West Cambridge* (1968. lxix,256p.)
covers 37 civil parishes, each with village plan, description,
parish church, etc. Sectional preface (natural background,
building materials, ecclesiastical buildings, earthworks, etc.).
Armorial index; glossary; analytical index. 120 maps, plates,
ground plans.
The Royal Commissions on Historical Monuments of
England, Scotland and Wales were set up to make an
inventory of the ancient and historical monuments and

....(contd.)
constructions connected with or illustrative of the
contemporary culture, civilization and living conditions of
ordinary people. *Class No:* 904(420)

Wales

[2554]
BARBER, C. *and* WILLIAMS, J.G. **The Ancient stones of**
Wales. Abergavenny, Gwent, Blorenge Books, 1989. 192p.
illus., bibliog., index. ISBN: 095104446x.
Guide to all known Welsh prehistoric stone monuments
classified into 3 main groups (standing stones, stone circles,
dolmens) but with separate sections on Legends, Arthurian
monuments, The Church and the stones, Preservation *etc.*
Gazetteer A-Z by 'new' counties p.101-85. Data: name of
parish, monument, short description, O.S. map reference
number. Glossary p.188. Bibliography p.189. Index of sites
p.190-2. *Class No:* 904(429)

[2555]
GREAT BRITAIN. ROYAL COMMISSION ON ANCIENT
AND HISTORICAL MONUMENTS IN WALES.
Inventories. Cardiff, H.M. Stationery Office, 1911-.
1. *Montgomery* 1911. 2. *Flint* 1912. 3. *Radnor* 1913. 4.
Denbigh 1914. 5. *Carmarthen* 1917 6. *Merioneth* 1921. 7.
Pembroke 1925. 8. *Anglesey* 1937. 9. *Caenarvon* 3v., 1956-
64.
Glamorgan: v.1: *Pre-Norman. Pt.1. The Stone and Bronze*
Ages. 1976. xxx,144p. ISBN 0117005886. *Pt.2 The Iron*
Age and the Roman occupation. 1976. xxx,135p.16p.pl.
0117005894. *Pt.3. The early Christian period.* 1976.
xxx,80p. 15p.pl. 0117005908. *V.3: Medieval secular*
monuments. Pt.2. Non-defensive. 1982. xxxviii,397p. 44p.pl.
011701141x. *V.4: Domestic architecture from the*
Reformation to the Industrial Revolution. Pt.1. The Greater
houses. 1981. xl,379p. 0117007544. *Pt.2. Farmhouses and*
cottages. 1988. xviii,661p. 0113000200.
11. *Brecknock. V.1: The prehistoric and Roman*
monuments. Part 2. Hill forts and Roman remains. 1987.
xxxii,196p. 18p.pl. £45.00. 0113000030. All volumes
arranged by parishes with glossaries, numerous illustrations
and maps. *Class No:* 904(429)

Italy

Bibliographies

[2556]
MCILWAINE, I.C. **Herculaneum: a guide to printed sources.**
Napoli, Bibliopolis, 2v., 1988. 1029p. maps, plans, index.
ISBN: 8870882099.
Monumental work with 3 chaps: 1. Excavation of
Herculaneum - 2. Papyri - 3. Impact of the discovery - and
14 sections: 1. Source materials - 2. Campania, Naples and
Vesuvius - 3. Herculaneum: history and excavation - 4. The
town and its buildings - 5. People - 6. Neapolitan
Academies - 7. National Museum - 8. Art in general - 9.
Paintings and mosaics - 10. Sculpture - 11. Other fine and
applied arts and technologies - 12. Epigraphy and wax
tablets - 13. Papyri - 14. Biographical sources. 12
Appendices. Chronology p.27-29. Name and subject indexes
p.917-1028. A scholarly work of high distinction. *Class*
No: 904(450)(01)

Asia—Near East

[2557]
CANBY, C. **A Guide to the archaeological sites of Israel, Egypt and North Africa.** New York and Oxford, Facts On File, 1990. vi,272p. illus., maps, plans, index. ISBN: 0816010544.

Description of 300+ sites in Israel, Egypt, Libya, Tunisia, Algeria and Morocco. Data: location; history and excavations; important finds; museums. Introductory essays provide a chronological framework. 'Suffers from a lack of chronological and geographic coherence and sufficient detail for the serious traveller' (*Booklist*, v.86,n o.19, 1 June 1990, p.1923-4). *Class No:* 904(56)

Maps & Atlases

[2558]
ROAF, M. **Cultural atlas of Mesopotamia and the Ancient Near East.** New York and Oxford, Facts On File, 1990. 238p. col. illus., col. maps, bibliog., index. ISBN: 0816022186.

Pictorial atlas covers the geography, history, archaeology of the Near East from prehistory to 330 BC, combining text, maps and photographs in 3 parts: 1. Villages - 2. Cities - 3. Empires. Also 24 special features (*e.g.* Archaeology in the Near East ... Origins of writing ... Discovery of Mesopotamia); 20 site features (*e.g.* Jericho ... Nineveh ... Persepolis); 16 King Lists; and 46 maps. Chronological table p.8-9. Bibliography p.224. Glossary p.225. Gazetteer p.230-2. The author was Director of the British School of Archaeology in Iraq 1981-85. *Class No:* 904(56)(084.3)

Industrial Antiquities

[2559]
HUDSON, K. **World industrial archaeology.** Cambridge, Cambridge Univ. Press. 1979. 247 p. illus. maps, bibliog. index. (*New Studies In Archaeology*..) ISBN: 0521219914.

Introduction. The aims and state of industrial archaeology. Section 1. The techniques appropriate to the study. 2. The range of current work (by industry). Select bibliography p.237 - 241 especially useful for list of periodicals containing articles on various aspects of the study. Limited to Europe, North and South America, and South Africa. 'As an international survey this book will be of great value' (*Industrial Archaeology Review*, v.5. no.1. Winter 1980-81, p.60-61). *Class No:* 904:6

Great Britain

[2560]
BUCHANAN, R. A. **Industrial archaeology in Britain.** 2nd ed. London, Allen Lane, 1980. 475 p. illus(inc 86 plates). maps. bibliog. index. ISBN: 0713909560.

First published in Pelican Books, 1972.

Part handbook, part gazetteer organized in 4 sections (16 chapters)and a regional survey: 1. Introduction (1. Definitions and techniques; 2. The Historical framework) - 2. The industrial categories - 3. Power, transport, and public services - 4. The progress of industrial archaeology (15. The organization of the subject; 16. The study of industrial archaeology) - 5. Regional survey: Scotland, North England,Wales, English Midlands, South-East England, and South-West England each with map and bibliography. Notes and bibliographical references. p.437-452. *Class No:* 904:6(410)

[2561]
COSSON, B.P. **The BP book of industrial archaeology.** 2nd ed. Newton Abbot, Devon, David & Charles, 1987. 384p. illus. bibliog. ISBN: 0715389319.

....(contd.)
First published 1975.

17 chapters: 1. Nature of industrial archaeology; 2. The industrialization of Britain; 3. Wind and water power; 4. Steam and internal combustion engines; 5. Coal; 6. Iron and steel; 7. Engineering 8. Non-ferrous metals; 9. Stone, clay and glass; 10. Textiles; 11. The chemical industries; 12. Public utilities; 13. Roads and bridges; 14. Rivers and canals; 15. Railways; 16. Ports and shipping; 17. Conclusion.

4 Appendices: 1. Gazetteer of sites p.323-350; 2. Museums of industry p.351-360; 3. Useful addresses p.361-364; 4. Bibliography p.365-376. Index p.377-384. 246 illus. 'A vast amount of information both verbal and visual, both for the casual reader and for the dedicated student' (*Industrial Archaeology Review*, v.10, no.1, Autumn 1987, p.100-101. *Class No:* 904:6(410)

Scotland

[2562]
GREAT BRITAIN. Royal Commission on the Ancient and Historical Monuments of Scotland. **Catalogue of records, Scottish Industrial Archaeology Survey 1977-85.** Edinburgh, Royal Commission on the Ancient and Historical Monuments of Scotland, 1989. 106p. ISBN: 0748003053.

1500 industrial sites arranged in 3 sections: Topographical; Industrial classification; Thematic surveys. Data: site name, industrial classification, type of site, National Grid reference, and parish or burgh. 'Whilst the book is not a comprehensive gazetteer it presents a useful record of demolished or threatened sites on mainland Scotland ... and as such will be a valuable source of reference' (*Industrial Archaeology Review*, v.12,no.2, Spring 1990, p.223-4). *Class No:* 904:6(411)

Institutions & Associations

[2563]
'Industrial Archaeology institutions and societies' *Industrial Archaeology* Index to v.1-15. (1964-1980).1984.

Directory and activity information of 17 of the most influential institutions, associations and societies. *Class No:* 904:6:061:061.2

908 Area Studies

Worldwide

Bibliographies

[2564]
The World bibliographical series. Santa Barbara, California and Oxford, Clio Press, 1978-.
'A series of selective national bibliographies which will eventually include every country in the world. Each critically annotated bibliography covers the literature on a single country and reflects the culture, unique qualities and background to that country'.
'The series has a uniform format that enables readers to compare countries and to locate literature on similar subjects throughout a range of countries. This format is nevertheless flexible enough to reflect national idiosyncracies and to impart the genuine 'flavour' of each country'.
'Each bibliography contains: a Table of Contents; an Introduction; 600-1000 Entries; an extensive index; and a Map. Where necessary, cross-references are provided at the end of chapters and a Glossary is sometimes included. Subjects covered include: The Country and its People; Geography; Flora and Fauna; History; Population and Social Structure; Customs and Folklore; Social Change; Religion; Education; Politics and Government; Law and Constitution; Foreign Relations; Military Affairs and Defence; Economy; Agriculture; Industry; Housing; Newspapers and Periodicals; Transport and Communications; Language and Literature; Art; Music; The Media; Reference Works and Bibliographies'. (*Clio Press catalogues*). *Class No:* 908(100)(01)

Encyclopaedias

[2565]
KURIAN, G.T., *ed.* **The Encyclopedia of the First World.** New York and Oxford, Facts On File, 2v., 1990. 1,000p. Charts, tables, bibliogs. ISBN: 0816012334.
National chapters for 25 economically advanced countries offer social, political and economic information (*e.g.,* geographic features; ethnic composition; historical background; freedom and human rights; languages; constitution and government *etc.,*) supported by comparative data, chronologies of major events, and bibliographies. *Class No:* 908(100)(031)

Yearbooks & Directories

[2566]
The Europa world year book 1992. 33rd ed. London, Europa Publications, 2v., 1992. Available in North America from Gale Research Co. xx,3139p., maps, tables, index. ISBN: 0946653763. ISSN: 00712302.
First published 19236. Under various titles, latterly *Europa yearbook: a world survey.* From 1960 as an annual publication in 2v.
1. Pt.1. International organizations. Pt.2. Country surveys Afghanistan-Jordan. 2. Kampuchea-Zimbabwe. Pt.1. encompasses more than 1650 organizations *e.g.* The United Nations ... The Commonwealth ... The European Communities. Data includes history, publications and activities. Pt.2. consists of surveys of over 200 countries which follow a set pattern: 1. Introductory survey covering recent history, economic affairs, social welfare and brief geographical details - 2. Statistical survey retrospective and, up to 1988 or 1989) - 3. Directory information on the consitution, government, legislature, political organizations, diplomatic representation, judicial system, religion, press, radio and television, finance, trade and industry, transport, tourism, atomic energy. 'A consistently reliable and comprehensive reference work, essential to both general and special libraries' (*International Affairs,* v.61, no.4, Autumn 1985, p.737). *Class No:* 908(100)(058)

[2567]
The Statesman's year-book statistical and historical annual of the states of the world for the year 1992-1993. Hunter, B. 129th ed. London, Macmillan Reference Books, 1992. *c.*1730p. tables, diagrs., maps. ISBN: 0333558367.
Pt.1. International organizations. Pt.2. Countries of the world A-Z. Federal Republic of Germany (p.434-62) has sections History; Area and population; Climate; Constitution; Government; Defence; International relations; Energy and natural resources; Justice, religion, education and welfare; Diplomatic representatives; Further reading; The Länder A-Z. *Class No:* 908(100)(058)

Maps & Atlases

[2568]
BOYD, A. **An Atlas of world affairs.** 9th ed. London, Routledge, 1991. 240p. maps, index. ISBN: 0415066247.
1st ed. 1957 published by Methuen; 8th ed. by Routledge in 1987.
Arranged in 10 thematic sections (*e.g.* oil, nuclear geography) and 63 geo-political sections (*e.g.* Russia's territorial gains, Northern Seas, Suez and Indian Ocean). Long-serving general guide to international affairs since 1945. Still no mention of international terrorism or maritime piracy. Appendix: Countries and currencies p.219-23. 97 maps. *Class No:* 908(100)(084.3)

Developing Countries

Handbooks & Manuals

[2569]
Third world guide 91/92 the world as seen by the Third World: facts-figures-opinions. Montevideo, Instituto del Tercer Mundo, 1990. Available in UK, Oxford, Oxfam Publications. 612p. maps, diagrs., tables. ISBN: 0855981644, UK.

Published 1979, 1981, 1984-86, 1988 as a cumulative project. First English language edition 1985.

Introductory essays on demography, children and education, food, labour, migration, human rights, indigenous peoples, sport, health, pollution and degradation, resources depletion, power and poverty, debt, non-alignment, cartography *etc.* Countries of the world A-Z p.191-583. Profiles (external debt, history, geography, demography) and Indicators (population, education, commerce, armed forces, economy public expenditure). '*Third World Guide* can be characterized as a *Europa Yearbook* written from a Third World perspective. Clearly, it does not provide an objective treatment, but libraries seeking an alternative perspective may find this volume useful.' (*Booklist*, v.86, no.12, 15 February 1990, p.119). *Class No: 908(4/9-77)(035)*

Maps & Atlases

[2570]
Atlas of the Third World. Kurian, G. 2nd ed. New York and Oxford, Facts on File, 1989. 400p. maps, tables, bibliog., index. ISBN: 0816019304.

1st ed. 1983. Companion to *Encyclopaedia of the Third World.*

Comprehensive selection of maps and statistical information in graphic form. 1. Introduction provides a review and interpretation of the data presented - 2. Thematic profiles: 14 topics identified as critical issues in Third World development - 3. 80 Country profiles A-Z concentrating on natural resources, population, and social and economic performance. Over 600 maps and 2000 charts and graphs. 'Because of the mamy revisions and the new countries that were not in existence in 1982, the *Encyclopedia* is a worthwhile purchase even for libraries that own the earlier edition. The dynamic conditions in much of the Third World merit the publication and purchase of a new edition every five years'. (*Reference Books Bulletin 1987-1988*, p.140). *Class No: 908(4/9-77)(084.3)*

Europe—Western

[2571]
Western Europe 1989 a political and economic survey. London, Europa Publications, 1988. Distributed in North America by Taylor & Francis. xiv, 545p. ISBN: 094665347x. ISSN: 09536906.

Section 1. 8 introductory essays presenting an overview of important and topical issues relating to the region as a whole. Section 2. Analytical surveys A-Z by country or territory under 8 subject headings: Geography; Recent history and politics; Economy; Social (health and welfare, immigration, education, religion); Media; Transport; Tourism; and a select bibliography. Covers all member countries of the European Communities and of the European Free Trade Association plus Cyprus, Malta and Turkey. Revised editions are expected every 2 years. 'Much of the factual information in this volume is easily obtainable from other sources' (*Reference Reviews*, v.3, no.1, March 1989, p.10-11). *Class No: 908(400)*

Europe—Eastern

Encyclopaedias

[2572]
Encyclopedia of the Second World. Kurian, G. *and* Karch, J., *eds.* New York and Oxford, Facts On File, 1991. 614p. maps,. charts, tables, bibliog., index. ISBN: 0816012326.

National profiles (at Janaury 1990) of Albania, Bulgaria, China, Czechoslovakia, East Germany, Hungary, Mongolia, Poland, Rumania, Soviet Union, and Yugoslavia, provide information on over 30 subject fields (*e.g.* geographical features, historical background, human rights, defence, foreign policy). By virtue of unfortunate timing now largely outdated by events although it remains 'a valuable source of historical information on the rise and reign of communism in these eleven countries' (*Wilson Library Bulletin*, v.65,no.10, June 1991, p.134). *Class No: 908(401)(031)*

Yearbooks & Directories

[2573]
Eastern Europe and the Commonwealth of Independent States 1992. London, Europa, 1991. Distributed in North America by Gale Research Co. 512p. maps, tables, bibliogs. (*Regional Surveys of the World.*) ISBN: 0946653771.

Over 30 specialist contributors. Part 1. Background to the region *i.e.* introductory essays *e.g.* Nationalism in the USSR - 2. Eastern Europe. Individual country chapters A-Z on Albania, Bulgaria, Czechoslovakia, Hungary, Poland, Romania and Yugoslavia, with sections on the constituent republics within federal countries, including a geographical profile, chronology, essays on recent history and the economy, statistical survey and directory material on the constitution, government, defence and military, foreign embassies, judicial system, news media, finance, trade, tourism, industry, *etc.* and a bibliography - 3. USSR containing 11 essays covering political and economic affairs and similar sections to those in Part 2. - 4.Key personalities of the region, brief biographical details of major political figures. *Class No: 908(401)(058)*

Great Britain

[2574]
BRITISH COUNCIL. Studying and living in Britain 1991. Plymouth, Northcote House in association with the British Council, 1991. Annual. 90p. pbk. ISBN: 0746306237.

Completely revised in 1984 and updated annually.

Information and advice for overseas students and other first-time visitors to Britain on how to make the decision to come, arriving, how to find accommodation, costs, customs and services, and on the British way of life. *Class No: 908(410)*

Dictionaries

[2575]
JACOBS, A. and MONK, J., eds. The Cambridge illustrated dictionary of British heritage. Cambridge, Cambridge Univ. Press, 1987. viii,484p. illus., maps, bibliog., index. ISBN: 0521302145.

'Encapsulates the essence of Britain and British life in 1500 entries, 200-300 words in length. Fields covered include arts; buildings; ceremonies; cuisine; customs; education; finance; geography; government; history; languages; law; monarchy; monuments; organizations; religion; societies; and sports. Bibliography (by topic) p.480-3. *Class No: 908(410)(038)*

Yearbooks & Directories

[2576]
GREAT BRITAIN. Britain 1992 an official handbook. 43rd ed. London, HM Stationery Office, 1992. Annual. 480p. col. illus., maps, diagrs., tables, index. ISBN: 0117016381.

Originally compiled for overseas distribution only; first placed on sale 1954.

'Compiled by the Central Office of Information, with the cooperation of government departments and other agencies, it is updated every year and includes the latest facts and figures on most aspects of British life. *Britain 1992* covers such topical issues as the environment, the revival of inner cities and the harnessing and efficient use of various sources of energy. Other chapters provide information on social and economic issues, overseas relations and defence, education, the legal system' (*HMSO New Book Information*). Detailed analytical index. 'Controversial issues and social problems are glossed over or dismissed in a few lines' (*The Independent,* no.1631, 9 January 1992, p.2). *Class No:* 908(410)(058)

Ireland

Bibliographies of Bibliographies

[2577]
EAGER, A.R. A Guide to Irish bibliographical material a bibliography of Irish bibliographies and sources of information. 2nd ed. London, Library Association, Westport, Connecticut, Greenwood Press, 1980. xv, 502p. ISBN: 0853659311, UK; 0313223432, US.

1st ed. 1964.

9,517 unannotated entries (5,700 more than 1st ed).

Sections: General works (bibliography; librarianship; periodicals; newspapers; directories and almanacs; museums; manuscripts; incunabula; binding; censorship) - Philosophy - Religion - Sociology - Philology - Science - Useful arts - Fine arts - Literature - Geography, travel - Biography - History (by period; Ulster, Connaught; Leinster; Munster; The Irish abroad).

Object: 'to provide a bibliographic index covering Irish enumerative bibliography and aims to serve as a quick reference guide to all who are interested in Irish studies and research studies' (*Introduction*). Includes unpublished material and work in progress. 'This excellent guide ... can be recommended enthusiastically' (*Choice*, v.18 no.9 May 1981, p.1234). *Class No:* 908(415)(009)

Commonwealth

Bibliographies

[2578]
ROYAL COMMONWEALTH SOCIETY. Subject catalogue of the Library of the Royal Empire Society, formerly the Royal Colonial Institute. Lewin, E., *comp.* London, The Society, 4v., 1930-37. Reprinted Dawsons Pall Mall Press 1967.

1: *British Empire generally, and Africa.*
2: *Australia, New Zealand, South Africa. General voyages and travels, Arctic and Antarctic.*
3: *Canada, Newfoundland, West Indies, Colonial America.*
4: *Mediterranean dependencies, Middle East, India, Burmah, Ceylon, Malaya, East Indies, Far East.*

The Royal Commonwealth Society Library contains an estimated 400,000 items. Geographical areas are divided by subjects; final chronological order. Although the Society's library was damaged in World War II, and the catalogue no longer strictly applies to it, the listing remains an indispensable bibliography. 'Perhaps the finest private library on imperial history in the world' (Flint, J.E. *Books on the British Empire and Commonwealth* (1968), Foreword).

....(contd.)

Supplemented by: *Biography catalogue of the Library of the Royal Commonwealth Society*, edited by Donald H. Simpson (1961, xxiii, 511p. and *Manuscript catalogue of the Library of the Royal Commonwealth Society*, also edited by Donald H. Simpson (London, Mansell, 1975).

The *Subject catalogue* and *Biography catalogue* are updated in *Subject catalogue of the Royal Commonwealth Society* (Boston, Mass., G.K. Hall, 1971, 7v.; *First supplement.* 1977. 2v.) reproducing a total of 157,000 catalogue cards. *Class No:* 908(41-44)(01)

Yearbooks & Directories

[2579]
The Commonwealth yearbook 1991. 5th ed. London, HMSO, 1991. 562p., col. illus., pbk. ISBN: 0115917098.

Formerly *A yearbook of the Commonwealth* (1969-1986) itself a successor to the *Commonwealth Office yearbook.*

Pt.1: The Commonwealth in 1990 (Evolution of the modern Commonwealth; Organization of British Government relations with other Commonwealth countries and administration of dependent territories) - 2. Government offices in London - 3. Commonwealth Secretariat - 4. Member countries of the Commonwealth A-Z - 5. Dependent territories. A compendious outline of member countries; history, geography, constitution, government, trade, and international policy. *Class No:* 908(41-44)(058)

Manuscripts & Incunabula

[2580]
ROYAL COMMONWEALTH SOCIETY. The Manuscript catalogue of the library ... Simpson, D.H., *ed.* London, Mansell, 1975.

'The word "*manuscript*" has been somewhat liberally interpreted' (*Introduction*) and embraces minute books, letter books, correspondence, autographs and portraits. Sections: Collections (library talks; Walter Frewen Lord Prize essays) - General material (*e.g.* Voyages and travel) - Europe - Asia - Africa (p.77-129) - The Americas - Australasia. Cross-references. Notes on character and provenance of each item. Index of names; index of subjects and organizations. The fourth supplement, 'Manuscripts newly catalogued 1983-1989', is printed in Royal Commonwealth Society *Library Notes*, no. 293 (new series), October 1989, p.1-5. Previous supplements appeared in issues nos. 217, 225 and 253. 'Certainly no research library in a Commonwealth or ex-Commonwealth country can afford to be without it' (British Book News, September 1975, p.622). *Class No:* 908(41-44)(093)

Wales

Bibliographies

[2581]
HUWS, G. *and* **ROBERTS, D.H.E.,** *comp.* **Wales.** Santa Barbara, Calif., and Oxford, Clio Press, 1991. xv,247p.+1p. map, indexes. (*World Bibliographical Series, no.122.*) ISBN: 1851091181.

876 annotated entries arranged in 33 sections: Country and its people - Geography and geology - Tourism and travel ... Prehistory and archaeology - History and genealogy ... Welsh overseas - Libraries, art galleries, museums and archives - Books ... Directories - Bibliographies. Author, subject and title indexes. *Class No:* 908(429)(01)

[2582]
JONES, S.R., *comp.* **Books of Welsh interest.** Aberystwyth, Cyngor Llyfrau Cymraeg/Welsh Books Council, 1977. 236p. ISBN: 0950230553.

908 concisely annotated entries. 2 main sections. 1. General (Bibliographies - Geography, geology and natural history ...History and archaeology ... Architecture and fine arts ... Biography and autobiography - Children's books) - 2. Literature (Cultural studies and histories - Anthologies - Works by individual authors and critical studies on them). Index of authors, translators and adaptors; title index; series index. Supplementary list of titles published between September 1976 and March 1977. *Class No:* 908(429)(01)

Germany

[2583]
PASLEY, M., *ed.* **Germany: a companion to German studies.** 2nd ed. London, Methuen, 1982. viii,690p. maps, geneal. tables, index. pbk. ISBN: 0415037042.

First published in 1972 when it was edited by J. Bithell.

A well-documented survey of the main fields of German studies in 10 chapters by different hands *e.g.* 1. The German language ... 3. German history 911 to 1618 - 4. Making of modern Germany 1618-1870 - 5. From Bismarck to the present. Chapter bibliographies. Analytical index. 'The volume should find its place readily on the library shelves' (*Modern Languages*, v.55,no.2, June 1974, p.104). *Class No:* 908(430)

Hungary

Bibliographies

[2584]
Guide to Hungarian studies. Stanford, California, Hoover Institution Press, Stanford Univ., 2v., 1973. xv, 1218p. (*Hoover Institution Bibliographical Series; no.52.*)

4,426 entries in all. 20 chapters: 1. History of the Hungarian book (special reference works; journals and monographic series; monographs; articles and minor publications) - 2. Cultural life and institutions - 3. General works - 4. Statistical research - 5. The land geography, geology, description of the country - 6. The people: demography, ethnology, folklore - 7. History and historiography - 8. Constitution and legislation - 9. Government and politics - 10. Social life and institutions - 11. Economics - 12. Religion and church affairs - 13. Hungarian language - 14. Hungarian literature - 15. Fine Arts - 16. Education - 17. Scientific research - 18. Press and publishing - 19. Hungarians abroad - 20. Hungary and the United States. Index of periodicals and serials. Index of personal names. Publications are in various European languages (including Hungarian, English, French, German and Latin). *Class No:* 908(439)(01)

France

Handbooks & Manuals

[2585]
CHARLTON, D.G., *ed.* **France: a companion to French studies.** 2nd rev. ed. London, Methuen, 1983. 690p. illus., map, pbk. ISBN: 0416723101.

1st ed. 1972.

11 contributors. 'Seeks to provide a detailed introduction and guide to the history and culture of France from the time of the Renaissance to the present day' (*Preface to the first edition*). Chapters: 1. Introduction - 2. The Renaissance in France: history, thought and literature - 3. French history and society from the Wars of Religion to the Revolution ... 6. French thought in the nineteenth and twentieth centuries ... 9. French literature since 1870 - 10.

....*(contd.)*
French painting, sculpture and architecture since 1500 - 11. French music since 1500 - 12. Contemporary France; politics, society and institutions. French language is not covered. The short chapter-bibliographies in the 1st ed. are replaced by more extended bibliographical essays (*e.g.* 4. 'French history and society from the Revolution to the Fifth Republic', p.119-221, has 4½ pages of bibliography, 2, with commentary. 34 black-and-white plates. Detailed analytical index. Editor is Professor of French in the University of Warwick. A scholarly compendium, well-produced. *Class No:* 908(44)(035)

Spain

[2586]
RUSSELL, P.E., *ed.* **Spain a companion to Spanish studies.** Rev. ed. London, Methuen, 1973. xv, 592p. geneal. tables, maps.

Entirely new version of E. Allison Peers' work (1929). 12 contributors. 12 chapters, each with bibliography. 1. Spain and the Spanish language - 2. Muslim Spain (711-1492) - 3. The medieval kingdoms of the Iberian peninsula - 4. Monarchy and Empire (1474-1700) - 5. Spanish history from 1700 - 6. Spanish literature and learning to 1474-7. Medieval Catalan literature - 8/9. Spanish literature - 10. Spanish American literature - 11. The visual arts in Spain (p.473-542; nearly 7p. of bibliography). Analytical index.

'An invaluable work' (*British Book News*, January 1980, p.74-77). *Class No:* 908(460)

USSR

[2587]
AUTY, R. and OBOLENSKY, D., *eds.* **Companion to Russian studies** v.1. Introduction to Russian history. Cambridge, Cambridge Univ. Press, 1976. xvi, 403p. general tables, maps. ISBN: 0521208939.

10 academic contributors. 10 chapters, each with running commentary and 'Guide to further reading'. 1. The geographical setting - 2. Kievan Russia - 3. Appanage and Muscovite Russia - 4. Imperial Russia: Peter I to Nicholas I - 5. Imperial Russia: Alexander II to the Revolution - 6. Soviet Russia (p.272-314; 'Guide to further reading'. p.308-14: 14 sections) - 7. The Church - 8. The structure of the Soviet State: Government and politics - 9. The structure of the Soviet State: the economy - 10. The Soviet Union and its neighbours. Partly analytical index, p.393-403. 'Aims at providing a first orientation for those embarking on the study of Russian civilization, past and present, in its most important aspects' (*Preface*), although it does omit military history. 'A particularly substantial introduction to the study of Russia, whether for readers within the academic world or outside' (*Soviet Studies*, v.29, no.2, 1977, p.341). *Class No:* 908(47)

Encyclopaedias

[2588]
The Cambridge encyclopedia of Russia and the Soviet Union. Brown, A., *and others, eds.* Cambridge University Press, 1982. 492p. illus. (some col.), maps (some col.), tables, bibliog., index. ISBN: 0521231698.

112 academic contributors. Well presented encyclopedia of essential information arrayed in 12 main sections: 1. Territory and peoples - 2. History - 3. Religion - 4. Art and architecture - 5. Language and literature - 6. Music, theatre, dance and film - 7. Sciences - 8. Soviet political system - 9. Economy - 10. Society - 11. Military power and policy - 12. World role. Glossary p.11. Bibliography (by section) p.485-91. More scholarly than *Cultural atlas of Russia and the Soviet Union. Class No:* 908(47)(031)

RSFSR

[2589]
SCHOPFLIN, G., *ed.* **The Soviet Union and Eastern Europe.**
New York and Oxford, Facts On File, 1986. xviii, 637p.
illus. tables, bibliog., index. (*Handbooks To The Modern
World.*) ISBN: 0816012601.
First published by Anthony Blond in 1970.
33 contributors. 34 essays (*e.g.,* The Soviet Union and
the Warsaw Pact: military and security affairs ... Tourism
in the Soviet Union and Eastern Europe ... The Baltic
Republics) arranged in 4 parts: Historical, Political,
Economic, Social to form a concise encyclopaedia providing
basic information and informed comment about the Eastern
bloc countries. Analytical index. 'A truly indispensable
reference work for all serious libraries, academic or public'
(*Choice*, v.23, no.11-12, July-August 1986, p.1661). *Class
No:* 908(470)

Lithuania

Bibliographies

[2590]
KANTAUTAS, A. *and* KANTAUTAS, F. **A Lithuanian
bibliography:** a checklist of books and articles held by the
major libraries in Canada and the United States.
Edmonton, Univ. of Alberta Press, 1975. xxxix, 725p.
ISBN: 0888640684.
10168 entries, classified in 13 categories e.g., 4.
Bibliographic aids, general reference works, serials, locating
copies. Author and subject indexes.
*Supplement to a Lithuanian bibliography: a further
checklist...* 1979. xxviii, 316p. 0888640684. £5.50. *Class
No:* 908(474.5)(01)

Encyclopaedias

[2591]
Encyclopedia Lituanica. Sužiedélis, S. *and* Vesaitis, A., *eds.*
Boston, Encyclopedia Lituanica, 6v., 1970-1978.
Based on the same publishers *Lithuanian encyclopaedia*
(1953-1969) - the first complete general encyclopedia ever
published in Lithuania.
V.6 *V-Z* and *Supplement A-Z.* 1978. 540p. illus., map,
index. 38 contributors. Includes list of contributors to
entire work. Essential reference source to Lithuania from
the earliest times. *Class No:* 908(474.5)(031)

Ukraine

Encyclopaedias

[2592]
Encyclopedia of Ukraine. Kubijovyč, V., *ed.* Toronto, Univ.
of Toronto Press, for the Canadian Institute of Ukrainian
Studies, the Shevchenko Scientific Society, and the
Canadian Foundation for Ukrainian Studies. 1984-. illus.
maps. ports. bibliogs.
Revision of *Entsklopediia Ukrainoznavstva.* Preface
discusses earlier Soviet and non-Soviet Ukrainian
encyclopedias.
v.1 *A-F.* 1984. xv, 952p. 0802033628. v.2 *G-K* 1987.
968p. 0802034446 100 scholars are engaged worldwide on a
comprehensive guide to the life and culture of the Ukraine.
Most of the longer entries include a bibliography. To be
completed in 5v. A map/gazetteer with statistical data is
published as a supplement to v.1. *Class No:* 908(477)(031)

Scandinavia

Bibliographies

[2593]
AMERICAN SCANDINAVIAN FOUNDATION. **Index
Nordicus:** a cumulative index to English-language periodicals
on Scandinavian studies. Kvamme, J., *comp.* Boston,
Mass., G.K. Hall, 1979. 770p.
Indexes *c.*4,800 articles and 3,500 book reviews appearing
1911-76 in 6 leading English-language journals on
Scandinavian studies (*e.g., Scandinavian economic history
review* (Odense, Denmark); *Scandinavica* (London). Over
2,500 subject headings. Includes entries for English
translations of Scandinavian literature. *Class No:*
908(48)(01)

Finland

[2594]
Finnish Features. Helsinki, Ministry for Foreign Affairs, 1981-
.
Factsheets of 4-6 pages grouped in 15 categories
'produced as part of the Finnish information service
abroad' and 'intended to be used for reference purposes': 1.
The land and the people (The Finnish nature and
landscape; Population; Swedish Finland; Roots of the
Finnish language) - 2. History (Finland through the ages;
Coats of Arms) - 3. Politics - 4. Foreign Policy - 5. Legal
system - 6. Government and defence - 7. Business and
economics - 8. Social and environmental planning - 9.
Social welfare - 10. The Church and religion - 11.
Education and the media - 12. Science - 13. Culture, art
and design - 14. Leisure and sports - 15. Finnish way of
life. Updated at intervals and inserted in a spring binder.
Class No: 908(480)

Asia

Bibliographies

[2595]
LONDON UNIVERSITY. School of Oriental and African
Studies. **Library Catalogue.** Boston, Mass., G.K. Hall, 28v.,
1963 (also in 14 separate sections). First supplement 16v.,
1968. Second supplement 16v., 1973. Third supplement
19v. 1979. ISBN: 081611225; 0816107343, 1st Supplt;
0816112967, 2nd Supplt; 0816102619, 3rd Supplt.
1,053,357 catalogue cards, photolithographically
reproduced. A comprehensive catalogue (author, subject and
title entries) of material (including periodical articles and
analyticals from other collective works) on all aspects of
Asia, Oceania and Africa, but excluding the purely
scientific, medical and technical. Available as a set or in 14
sections: Author catalogue - Title index - Subject catalogues
(General. Africa. Middle East. South Asia. Southeast Asia
and Pacific Islands. Far East) - Catalogue of manuscripts
and microfilms - Chinese catalogues (Titles. Authors.
Subjects) - Japanese catalogue - Catalogue of periodicals
and series (included in the Author catalogue). No longer
available in printed form apart from 1st Supplt. Other
prices are for 96 reel microfilm edition. A *Fourth
Supplement 1978-1984* (1985) is published in microfiche
format by IDC of Zug, Switzerland. The record continues
in SOAS's *Monthly list of titles added to the catalogue.*
Class No: 908(5)(01)

Yearbooks & Directories

[2596]
Asia yearbook. Hong Kong, Far Eastern Economic Review, 1960-. Annual. 356p. tables, softcover. ISBN: 9627010332.
Formerly *Far Eastern Economic Review Yearbook.*
An overview of the previous year is followed by a general section (the power game, food and population, refugees, development banks *etc.*) and analyses of events and developments in 31 countries including Soviet Asia, the Maldives, Australia, New Zealand, Papua New Guinea and Fiji. Obituaries p.254-6. *Class No:* 908(5)(058)

Asia—Far East

Yearbooks & Directories

[2597]
The Far East and Australasia 1992. 23rd ed. London, Europa, 1991. 1100p. maps, tables, bibliogs. Annual. (*Regional Surveys of the World.*) ISBN: 0946653739.
First published 1969.
Over 50 contributors provide a compendium guide and systematic political and economic guide to all the countries and territories of East Asia, Southeast Asia, the Asiatic countries of the former USSR, Australia, New Zealand, and the Pacific Islands. Pt.1 General survey comprises a series of introductory essays (*e.g.* Development problems of Asia; the Pacific century: progress towards the integration of the Pacific Basin) - 2. Country surveys including Physical and social geography, History, Economy, Statistical survey, Directory (*i.e.* constitution, government, political organizations, diplomatic representation, judiciary, religion, the media, finance, tourism, *etc.* with a bibliography) - 3. Regional organizations (*i.e.* comprehensive information on the major organizations active within the region). 'Quite simply it must be regarded as an obligatory annual purchase for all reference and research libraries determined to keep up with world affairs' (*Reference Reviews,* v.5,no.2, 1991, p.40). *Class No:* 908(51/52+57)(058)

China

[2598]
China facts and figures. Scherer, J.L., *ed.* Gulf Breeze, Florida, Academic International Press, 1978 - Annual. (v.9. 1986). x, 390p. maps, bibliog., tables. ISBN: 0875690939.
Reviews developments in the Peoples' Republic. V.9 has 19 sections: 1. Survey - 2. Industrial and agricultural production - 3. Government - 4. Party - 5. Armed forces - 6. Demography - 7. Economy - 8. Energy - 9. Industry - 10. Agriculture - 11. Foreign trade - 12. Foreign aid - 13. Transportation - 14. Institutions - 15. Science - 16. Culture and communications - 17. Health, education and welfare - 18. Provinces and cities - 19. Special topics (1985 calendar of events; Space news; Tourism; Obituaries; Key works on the Peoples Republic p.386-390). *Class No:* 908(510)

Encyclopaedias

[2599]
The Cambridge encyclopedia of China. Hook, B. *and* Twitchett, D., *eds.* 2nd ed. Cambridge Univ. Press, 1991. 512p. illus. (some col.), maps, bibliog., index. ISBN: 052135594x.
1st ed. 1982.
Covers all aspects of China: history, geography, economics, politics, the arts, wildlife, customs, food and drink, social organization, law, education, literature etc. Arranged thematically, this edition charts the political unrest of 1989. 60 maps. *Class No:* 908(510)(031)

[2600]
THE CHINESE ACADEMY OF SOCIAL SCIENCES. Information China. James, C.V., *ed for Pergamon Press.* Oxford, New York and Beijing, Pergamon, 3v., 1989. xix, 1621p. illus., col.maps, tables, bibliog., indexes. (*Countries of the World Information Series.*) ISBN: 0080347649.
V.1: 1. China land and people - 2. History of China - 3. Sociopolitical structure and legal system. V.2: 4. The national economy - 5. Foreign trade and economic relations - 6. Living standards and social welfare - 7. The armed forces - 8. Sport - 9. Medicine and health. V.3: 10. Education - 11. Science and technology - 12. Philosophy - 13. Literature and the arts - 14. Cultural facilities - 15. Mass media - 16. Nationalities - 17. Religious beliefs - 18. Foreign policy - 19. Overseas Chinese affairs - 20. One country, two systems and the unification of the Motherland. Chronology of Chinese Historical periods p.xxix. Chinese names p.xxxiii-xxxv. China in figures p.1427-1563. Bibliography p.1565-9. Name, place-name and subject indexes. Biennial supplementary volumes are planned; the first in 1990. 'An extraordinary reference treasure, except for the lack of further sources for consultation and research' (*Choice,* v.26, no.10, June 1989, p.1664). *Class No:* 908(510)(031)

Maps & Atlases

[2601]
BLUNDEN, C. and ELVIN, M. Cultural atlas of China. Oxford, Phaidon; New York, Facts on File, 1983. 237p. illus. (mostly col.), col. maps, tables, bibliog., index. ISBN: 0714823090, UK; 0871961326, US.
1. Space (geographic and demographic context) - 2. Time (survey of Chinese culture from Beijing Man to the present) - 3. Symbols and society (thematic coverage). Bibliography p.225-27. Gazetteer p.229-34. 58 maps. 204 col.illus. *Class No:* 908(510)(084.3)

Hong Kong

Yearbooks & Directories

[2602]
Hong Kong 1991 a review of 1990. Roberts, D., *ed.* Hong Kong, Government Information Services, 1991. viii,467p. col. illus., tables, map, index. ISBN: 9620200977.
24 chapters: 1. Shaping up for the 21st century ... 24. History. 46 appendices (mostly statistical). Calendar of events in 1990 p.1-3. Attractive example of an official handbook. *Class No:* 908(512.317)(058)

Mongolia

Encyclopaedias

[2603]
Information Mongolia the comprehensive reference source of the People's Republic of Mongolia (MPR). The Academy of Sciences MPR, *comp.* Oxford, New York, and Beijing, Pergamon Press, 1990. xxxviii,505p. illus. (some col.), col. maps, tables, bibliogs., index. (*Countries Of The World Information Series.*) ISBN: 008361935.
79 contributors. Part 1. Land and people - 2. History of Mongolia - 3. Political system of the Mongolian People's Republic - 4. The Armed Forces - 5. National economy. Each part is sustained by a substantial bibliography. 19 maps. 67 tables. Analytical subject index p.483-505. Encyclopedic coverage of all aspects of Mongolian life 'within a detailed historical framework'. *Class No:* 908(517)(031)

Japan

Encyclopaedias

[2604]
Kodansha encyclopedia of Japan. Tokyo, Kodansha International Ltd., 9v. 1983. Distributed in UK by International Book Distributors and in US by Harper & Row. V.1-8. 352p. each; v.9. 288p. ISBN: 070116207, UK; 4061445316, Japan.

680 Japanese and 524 international contributors. Covers all aspects of Japanese life: technology, economics law and business with the greatest emphasis on history, geography, fine arts, and literature. V.9 is a analytical index: list of contributors p.ix-xxii. 'The long pieces on the major aspects of Japan are of the highest quality, all of them written by top-notch scholars' (Encyclopaedia of Japan, *Choice*, v.21, no. 11-12, July-August 1984, p.1576).

Supplement/1987. 64p. illus. index. $20.00. 'Overviews and in-depth analyses of the newest developments in Japanese society'. *Class No:* 908(52)(031)

Asia—Middle & Near East

Yearbooks & Directories

[2605]
The Middle East and North Africa 1992. 38th ed. London, Europa, 1991. Annual. Distributed in North America by Gale Research Co. 990p. maps, tables, bibliogs. (*Regional Surveys of the world.*) ISBN: 0946653720.

Part 1. General survey, authoritative essays on issues of contemporary interest which, in this edition, include Prelude to the 1991 Gulf War and Iraq and Kuwait, the invasion, the war, and the aftermath - 2. Regional organizations: comprehensive information on the United Nations and the other major organizations active in the region - 3. Country surveys A-Z: Geography; History; Economy; Statistical survey; Directory (the constitution, government, legislature, political organizations, diplomatic representation, judicial system, religion, press, publishers, radio and TV, finance, trade and industry, transport, tourism, atomic energy, defence, education). 'A reference work of high standard in a remarkably consistent series' (*International Affairs*, v.61,no.2, Spring 1985, p.348). *Class No:* Class No: 908(53+56)(058)

Archives

[2606]
MATTHEWS, N. *and* **WAINWRIGHT, M.D. A Guide to manuscripts and documents in the British Isles relating to the Middle East and North Africa.** Oxford, Oxford Univ. Press, 1980. 482p.

One of a series of 4v. (the others concern the Far East, Africa south of the Sahara, and South and south-east Asia) recognised by the International Council on Archives and Unesco as the UK contribution to the 'Sources of history of the nations: Asia and North Africa' series.

Coverage: the Arab countries of Middle East and North Africa, Israel, Cyprus, Turkey, Iran and certain regions of the Caucasus, Central Asia and the Crimea. Sections: England (London, p.1-221); Rest of England (locations A-Z), Wales, Scotland, Northern Ireland, Eire. 'Papers in private custody', p.387-419. Some detail in inventories. Inclusion of material does not necessarily mean that is is available for study. Detailed index, p.421-82. An essential reference source 'until at least the end of the century' (*British book news*, July 1980, p.401). *Class No:* 908(53+56)(093.20)

Asia—South & South East

Encyclopaedias

[2607]
The Cambridge encyclopedia of India, Pakistan, Bangladesh, Sri Lanka, Nepal, Bhutan and the Maldives. Robinson, F., *ed.* Cambridge, Cambridge Univ. Press, 1989. 520p. illus., (many col.), maps, tables, index. ISBN: 0521334519.

69 contributors. 85 authoritative essays grouped in 9 sections: 1. Land - 2. Peoples - 3. History to independence - 4. Politics - 5. Foreign policy - 6. Economics - 7. Religions - 8. Societies - 9. Culture. Section bibliographies. Glossary p.505-7. 75 maps. 69 tables. Analytical index. 'The best available single-volume treatment of South Asia' (*Library Journal*, v.114, no.9, 15 May 1989, p.65). *Class No:* 908(54+59)(031)

India

Bibliographies

[2608]
GREAT BRITAIN. INDIA OFFICE LIBRARY AND RECORDS. Catalogue of European printed books, India Office Library. Boston, Mass., G.K. Hall, 10v., 1964. 7225p. ISBN: 0816106711.

110,000 photolithographed catalogue cards. Scope is every aspect of the history and culture of the peoples of the Indian subcontinent and contiguous territories of related culture. Particularly strong in art and archaeology, history, philosophy and religion, linguistics, anthropology, and economics and politics, the collection includes many official British and Indian publications. *Class No:* 908(540)(01)

Pakistan

Yearbooks & Directories

[2609]
RAFIQUE AKHTAR. Pakistan year book 1989-90. 17th ed. Karachi and Lahore, East and West Publishing Co., 1989. 702p. illus., ports., tables, index.

1st ed. 1973.

38 sections deployed under 4 headings 1. The land and people - 2. The cultural heritage (History ... Archaeology ... Tourism) - 3. The Government and its services - 4. The Economy. Analytical index. *Class No:* 908(549)(058)

Israel

Yearbooks & Directories

[2610]
The Israel year book 1990. 45th ed. Jerusalem, IBRT Translation/Documentation, 1991. 329p. ISSN: 00751413.

Incorporating *The Palestine yearbook and Israel annual*, formerly published in US for the Zionist Organization of America, and the *Anglo-Palestine year book* formerly published in UK.

30 overview articles by different hands in 7 sections: 1. Politics - 2. Immigration and absorption - 3. Education and culture - 4. Economy - 5. Social services - 6. Environment - 7. Security and defense. What made the headlines in 1990 (monthly chronology) p.7-41. *Class No:* 908(569.4)(058)

Asia—South East

Maps & Atlases

[2611]
ULACK, R. *and* PAUER, G. **Atlas of Southeast Asia.** New York Macmillan Publishing Co.; London, Collier Macmillan Publishers, 1989. xvii, 171p. col. illus., col. maps, tables, bibliog., index. ISBN: 0029332001.

Part 1. Regional overview: 1. Physical environment and resources - 2. Historical and political background - 3. Cultural characteristics - 4. Regional population and urban characteristics. Part 2: 10 chapters on the nation - states of the region. Integrated text, maps and illustrations. Bibliography p.153-157. 70 maps. 'Fills a gap that has existed in the literature for many years' (*Booklist*, v. 85, no.16, 15 April 1989, p.1442-3). *Class No:* 908(59)(084.3)

Islamic World

Encyclopaedias

[2612]
The Encyclopaedia of Islam. Prepared by a number of leading orientalists and edited by an editorial committee. Under the patronage of the International Union of Academies. New ed. Leiden, E.J. Brill, 1960-. Luzac & Co. of London were co-publishers v.1-3.

Supersedes when completed *E.J. Brill's First encyclcopaedia of Islam 1913-1936* (1987).

1. Gibb, H.G.R. and others, *eds.* 1960. xix, 1359p. Over 200 contributors. Most articles with bibliographies. Abbreviated titles of some of the most often quoted works p. viii-x. 2. Lewis, B. and others, *eds.* 1965. xxi, 1146p. 3. Lewis, B. and others, *eds.* 1971 xvi, 1270p. 4. van Donzel, E. and others, *eds.* 1978. xvi, 1188p. ISBN 9004057455. 5. Bosworth, C.C. and others, *eds.* 1986. xviii, 1263p. 9004078193. Publication continues with v.6 in fascicules 1986-89. *Supplement* in progress 1980-.

The encyclopaedia of Islam new edition/Encyclopédie de l'Islam Index to volumes (des tomes) 1-V and to the Supplement Fascicules/et du Supplément, Livraisons, edited by H. and J.D. Pearson and E. van Donzel, Leiden, E.J. Brill; Paris, Éditions G-P. Maisonneuve and Larosse, 1989. vi, 295p. ISBN 9004088490. *Class No:* 908(5.297)(031)

Africa

[2613]
ZELL, H.M. **The African studies companion** a resource guide and directory. Oxford, Hans Zell, 1989. 16p. ISBN: 0905450809.

Annotated guide to major information sources: bibliographies, journals, major libraries and documentation centres, dealers and distributors of African studies material, research foundations *etc. Class No:* 908(6)

Encyclopaedias

[2614]
OLIVER, R. *and* CROWDER, M. **The Cambridge encyclopedia of Africa.** Cambridge, Cambridge Univ. Press, 1981. 492p. illus. (some col.), maps (some col.), tables, diagrs. ISBN: 0521230969.

99 contributors. 4 sections: 1. The African continent - 2. The African past before European colonisation - 3. Contemporary Africa - 4. Africa and the World. Bibliography (by chapter) p.485-491. 'There is really no other work on the market at present that is so comprehensive and useful as this handsome publication' (*Choice*, v.19, no.10, June 1982, p.1374). *Class No:* 908(6)(031)

Yearbooks & Directories

[2615]
Africa south of the Sahara 1992. 21st ed. London, Europa, 1991. Annual. Distributed in North America by Gale Research Co. 1140p. maps, tables, bibliogs. ISBN: 0946653712. ISSN: 00653896.

First published 1971.

Part 1. Background to the continent: 20 essays by separate hands (*e.g.* Africa in historical perspective; Africa and the European Community: the Lomé conventions) - 2. Regional Organizations, all major organizations working in the region: their aims activities, publications etc. Pt.3. Country surveys A-Z: Physical and social geography; The Economy; Statistical survey; Directory (i.e. constitution; government; political organizations; diplomatic representation; religion; news media; finance; trade/industry; transport; tourism; atomic energy; power; defence; and bibliography. 'An excellent reference tool for detailed information about the countries included' (*Reference Reviews*, v.4, no.1, 1990, p.34). *Class No:* 908(6)(058)

[2616]
New African Yearbook 1991-92. 8th ed. London, IC Publications, 1991. Distributed in North America by Hunter Publishing of Edison, NJ. 402p. maps, tables, softcover. ISBN: 0905268571, UK; 1556502281, US. ISSN: 01401378.

Part 1: African organizations A-Z (Description; organization; history; members *etc.*) p.10-18. Part 2: Countries A-Z General information (area; population; capital; principal towns; date of independence; Heads of State) - Political history - Economy - Current events - Statistics. *Class No:* 908(6)(058)

Black Races

Handbooks & Manuals

[2617]
MORRISON, D.G., *and others.* **Black Africa** a comparative handbook. 2nd ed. New York, Paragon House; London, Collier Macmillan, 1989. 720p. maps, charts, tables. ISBN: 0887020429, US; 0333498631, UK.

1st ed. 1972.

Systematic data on 41 nations (32 in 1st ed.). Pt1. Comparative profiles with notes on the uses and limitations of cross-national data; measures, models and meaning in aggregate data; ethnic unit classification and analysis, *etc.* Pt2. Country profiles A-Z. Sources are given; select bibliography for each territory. 'An essential reference work for students, scholars and organizations requiring quantitive comparative information relevant to problems of development in Africa' (*Choice*, v.10, no.3, May 1973, p.429-30). *Class No:* 908(6)(=96)(035)

Africa—Southern

Yearbooks & Directories

[2618]
Southern African annual review. Pycroft, C *and* Munslow, B. Oxford, Hans Zell, 1989-.

1. 1987/88. v.1: Country reviews. 404p. £48. $85. ISBN 0905450035. v.2: Regional reviews. 470p. £48. $85. 0905450043. Set 2v. 1989. £96. $170. 0905450027.

2. 1989. v.1: Country reviews. 320p. £35. $65. 0905450747. v.2 Regional reviews. 320p. £35. $65. 0905450795. Set 2v. 1990. £70. $130. 0905450698.

Volume 1 provides extensive coverage of press sources on the region, whilst Volume 2 deals with the important issues of the period, revealing the motivating forces for regional integration, confrontation, and negotiation. Based on the

....(contd.)

Southern Africa Computerized Data/Text (SACDT) System developed by the Centre of African Studies in the University of Liverpool. 'Uneven, disjointed, patchy in quality, highly selective and difficult to use' (*Reference Reviews*, v.4,no.3, 1990, p.31-2). *Class No:* 908(68)(058)

South Africa

Yearbooks & Directories

[2619]
South Africa 1989-90 official yearbook of the Republic of South Africa. 15th ed. Pretoria, Bureau for Information on behalf of the Department of Foreign Affairs. 842p., col.illus., col.maps, tables, diagrs., bibliog., index. ISBN: 0797017291.

First published 1974.

40 chapters each ending with suggested readings: 1. Physical features - 2. History - 3. People and languages - 4. Demographic trends - 5. Citizenship and immigration - 6. Constitution - 7. Government departments - 8. Political parties - 9. Black political development - 10. Foreign relations - 11. Justice - 12. National security - 13. Railways and harbours - 14. Aviation - 15. Road transport - 16. Posts and telecommunications - 17. Energy - 18. Mining and minerals - 19. Agriculture - 20. Water - 21. Forestry - 22. Marine fisheries - 23. Manpower and industrial relations - 24. Public works and land affairs - 25. National economy - 26. Finance - 27. Guide for foreign investors - 28. Education - 29. Health and welfare - 30. Community development - 31. Research - 32. Cultural life - 33. Literature - 34. Religion - 35. Press and advertising - 36. Radio & TV - 37. Sport and recreation - 38. Wildlife and conservation - 39. Tourism - 40. Calendar 1987 and 1988. Bibliography p.793-806. 37 maps. *Class No:* 908(680)(058)

America — North

Yearbooks & Directories

[2620]
The USA and Canada 1990. London, Europa Publications, 1989. xiii+iii,511p. maps, tables, bibliogs. ISBN: 0946653550. ISSN: 09560904.

Revised every 2 years.

Separate sections for each country provide introductory historical, geographical and demographic data. There follow essays (plus bibliographies) on the political and administrative system, the economy, social issues, and international relations. Extensive statistical and directory type information is listed under Public affairs; The economy; Society; Transport and utilities; and Tourism. A group of essays examine topics currently affecting US and Canada equally. Chronology of US since colonization p.3-5; Canada p.357-58. 'It is difficult to see how any other single volume of comparable size could possibly improve its coverage' (*Reference Reviews*, v.4,no.4, 1990, p.36). *Class No:* 908(71+73)(058)

Canada

Encyclopaedias

[2621]
The Canadian encyclopaedia. Marsh, J.H., *ed.* 2nd ed. Edmonton, Alberta, Hurtig Publishers, 4v., 1988. Available in US from Gale Research Co. 2784p. illus (many col.), col. maps, bibliog., index. ISBN: 0888303262, set.

First published in 3v. 1985.

*c.*9500 signed entries, with short reading lists 'to provide coverage of all aspects of life in Canada, of all regions, over a vast time scale from the geological formation of the

....(contd.)

ancient rocks ... to the most recent political events' (*Preface to 1st ed*). Analytical index. 'There will be no new edition ... until 1992 at the earliest. We are now investigating the possibility of publishing an updated supplementary volume yearly or biennially' (*Foreword to 2nd ed*). A CD-ROM edition is available. CD-ROM Find It TM software and instruction manual. 1990. 0888303424. *Class No:* 908(71)(031)

Yearbooks & Directories

[2622]
Canada Year book 1990. A review of economic, social and political developments in Canada. Ottawa, Statistics Canada, 1989. Over 600 pages in various sequences. col. maps, tables, diagrs., index. ISBN: 0660131404E.

First published in 1867 as *Year-book and almanac of British North America.*505 23 chapters: 1. Physical setting - 2. Demography - 3. Health - 4. Education - 5. Employment - 6. Social security - 7. Housing and construction - 8. Forest, fish and furs - 9. Agriculture - 10. Mines and minerals - 11. Energy - 12. Science and technology - 13. Transportation - 14. Communications - 15. Cultural activities and leisure - 16. Manufacturing - 17. Merchandising - 18. Banking, finance and insurance - 19. Government - 20. Judicial system - 21. External relations, trade and defence - 22. Government finance - 23. Review of the economy. 5. Appendices: A. Government organizations - B. Federal legislation - C. Political update - D. Commissions of Enquiry - E. Constitution. A French edition is also published. *Class No:* 908(71)(058)

Latin America

Bibliographies

[2623]
British bulletin of publications on Latin America the Caribbean Portugal and Spain. London, The Hispanic and Luso-Brazilian Council, 1950-. v.1-. 2 *pa.* ISSN: 02682400.

Annotates 200-250 English-language books and lists a large number of periodical articles per issue. Nos.1-45 are available on a 35mm. microfilm (£20.00). *Class No:* 908(729.99)(01)

[2624]
Latin American studies a basic guide to sources. McNeil, R.A., *ed.* 2nd ed. Metuchen, N.J., Scarecrow Press, 1990. xi,458p. indexes. ISBN: 0810822369.

A rev. ed. of *Latin American bibliography: a guide* edited by L. Hallewell (1978).

36 contributors. A form-based introductory guide to research on Latin America in the humanities and social sciences divided in 6 main parts: 1. Libraries and their use (leading Latin American collections in UK, US and Europe) - 2. Bibliographies - 3. Other printed sources (encyclopedias, handbooks, guides, directories, maps and atlases etc.) - 4. Non print sources - 5. Specialised information - 6. Research and career development. Subject and reference source indexes. Prepared under the auspices of the Standing Committee of National and University Libraries' Advisory Committee on Latin American Materials. 'Essential for any library with a serious interest in Latin America' (*Choice*, v.28,no.1, September 1990, p.78). *Class No:* 908(729.99)(01)

Handbooks & Manuals

[2625]
Handbook of Latin American studies. Austin, Univ. of Texas Press, 1936-. v.1-. Annual. ISSN: 00729833.
As from v.26 (1964) coverage has been split, 'Humanities' and 'Social sciences' volumes being published in alternate years. Thus v.49 Social sciences (1989, xxii,853p. 0292730462) has 8448 concisely annotated entries for Bibliography and general works - Anthropology (including Archaeology) - Economics - Education - Geography - Government and politics - International relations - Sociology. V.50 Humanities (1990. xxviii,797p. 0292730586) has 4712 entries for Bibliography and general works - Art - Folklore - History (in 7 main divisions) Language - Literature - Music - Philosophy. *Class No:* 908(729.99)(035)

Yearbooks & Directories

[2626]
South America, Central America and the Caribbean 1991. 3rd ed. London, Europa, 1990. Distributed in North America by Gale Research Co. xv,702p. maps, tables, bibliogs. (*Regional Surveys of the World.*) ISBN: 094665364x.
Previous ed. 1988.
Over 20 specialist contributors. Part 1. Background to the region consists of 8 signed introductory essays (*e.g.* Dictatorship and democracy in South America; Sovereignty, dependency and social change in the Caribbean) - 2. Country surveys: 47 A-Z chapters on all countries and territories containing concise historical, geographical and economic information, using the latest official statistics on finance, industry, agriculture, trade, population, education, transport, tourism, and the news media. Also a government, political and constitutional directory and a bibliography for each of the major countries - 3. Regional organizations *i.e.* all principal organizations working in the region with the emphasis on United Nations activities. 'Has deservedly won generous plaudits for its comprehensive coverage of three quite distinct geopolitical areas' (*Reference Reviews*, v.5,no.2, 1991, p.39-40). *Class No:* 908(729.99)(058)

USA

[2627]
KANE, J.N., *and others, comps.* **Facts about the States.** New York, H.W. Wilson, 1989. 576p. bibliogs., tables. ISBN: 0824204077.
Chapter for each State (plus Puerto Rico and Washington DC) with information on geography and climate, demography, Government and politics, history, finances, culture and education, *etc.* and a bibliography. Comparative statistics feature population, age, income. *Class No:* 908(73)

[2628]
WELLAND, D., *ed.* **The United States:** a companion to American studies. 2nd ed. London, Methuen, 1987. xii,594p. maps, bibliog., index. ISBN: 0416415008.
1st ed 1974.
14 contributors. 15 chapters: 1. Geographical basis of American life - 2. Profile of the American city - 3. Americanism - 4. Immigration and the American economy - 5. Race in American history - 6. American wars - 7. America in world affairs - 8. The United States: constitution and government - 9. American politics, past and present - 10. Emergence of an American literature - 11. Literature of realism - 12. Fiction and poetry since 1918 - 13. Drama and the arts - 14. American media and the denial of history - 15. American thought. A checklist of essential works of reference p.574-6. 9 maps. *Class No:* 908(73)

Bibliographies

[2629]
SALZMAN, J., *ed.* **American studies** an annotated bibliography. Cambridge, Cambridge Univ. Press, 3v., 1986. xii, 2058p. ISBN: 0521266866, v.1; 0521266874, v.2; 0521266882, v.3; 0521325552, set.
Replaces *An annotated bibliography of works on the civilizations of the United States* (US Information Agency, 1982).
V.1. Anthropology and folklore; Art and Architecture; History (p.237-707). V.2. Literature; Music; Political science; Popular culture; Psychology; Religion; Science, technology and medicine. V.3. Author, title and subject indexes. Prefaces to each section introduce the basic bibliographic resources for research in that discipline. 'A valuable set because of the huge number of books it lists, the meaningful way in which they are arranged, and the prefaces that precede each section' (*Reference Books Bulletin 1986-1987*, p.156). *Class No:* 908(73)(01)

[2630]
—**SALZMAN, J.,** *ed.* American studies an annotated bibliography, 1984-1988. Cambridge University Press, 1990. xi,1085p. indexes. ISBN: 0521365597.
Interim supplements are printed in *Prospects: an annual of American Cultural Studies.*
Over 200 contributors. This supplement to the original bibliography contains 3,872 annotated items published in US. Similar supplements, a volume for material published outside US, and a volume devoted to journal articles, are planned. Author and title indexes. 'A thoroughly commendable compilation' (*Choice*, v.28,no.4, December 1990, p.614). *Class No:* 908(73)(01)

Australasia & Oceania

Yearbooks & Directories

[2631]
Pacific Islands Yearbook. Douglas, N. *and* Douglas, N., *eds.* 16th ed. North Ryde, N.S.W., Angus & Robertson, 1989. vi,717p. ISBN: 0207161143. ISSN: 00787523.
Preceded by *Stewart's Handbook of the Pacific Islands: a reliable guide to all the inhabited islands of the Pacific for tourists, traders, settlers* (Sydney, McCarren, Stewart, 1908-1929 annual). Under present title since 1932.
Descriptive gazetteer A-Z by island or island group *e.g.* French Polynesia (Government - Justice - Defence - Education - Labour - Health - The Land - Primary production - Manufacturing and Mining - Tourism - Housing - Overseas trade - Finance - Transport - Communications - Water and electricity - Major office holders - Government ministers and departments) p.145-193. Pacific chronology p.7-10. Obsolete and alternative names for Pacific Islands p.686-95. Current names (with obsolete/alternative names) p.696-705. Index of islands, atolls and inlets p.706-17. *Class No:* 908(9)(058)

Indonesia

Handbooks & Manuals

[2632]
Indonesia handbook. Dalton, B. 5th ed. Chico, California, Moon Publishers, 1991. illus., maps, index, 1100p. ISBN: 0918373727.
Survey of geography, flora and fauna, ethnology and culture of all the main Indonesian islands - Java, Sumatra, Bali, Nusa Tennggara, Moluccas, Irian Jaya, Celebes, and Kalimantan. Introduction includes sections on history, government, getting to Indonesia, customs and regulations, and money. Classified booklist p.567-572. Glossary p.573-588. *Class No:* 908(910)(035)

New Zealand

Encyclopaedias

[2633]
The Illustrated encyclopedia of New Zealand. McLauchlan, G., *ed.* Auckland, David Bateman, 1990. Distributed in North America by G.K. Hall. 1448p. ISBN: 0869530071, US.
Expanded version of *The Bateman New Zealand encyclopedia* (2nd ed. 1988).
*c.*2500 articles cover all aspects of New Zealand life. Chronology of New Zealand history to the end of 1988. Entirely redesigned with pages divided into 3 columns. 2,200 colour and 800 black and white illustrations. Good index serves cross-reference role. 'Articles are well developed, readable, and much more extensive than in *Bateman*' (*Booklist*, v.87, no.6, 15 November 1990. p.682).
Class No: 908(931)(031)

Yearbooks & Directories

[2634]
New Zealand official yearbook 1990. Auckland, Department of Statistics, 1990. xvi,707p. col.illus., diagrs., stats., tables, col. maps. ISSN: 00780170.
Preceded by *Handbook of New Zealand* 1875-. 1st published under present title 1893.
Compendium of facts and figures on all aspects of New Zealand political, social, economic, and cultural life presented in 24 sections: 1. Geography ... 4. International relations and defence ... 11. Arts, media and leisure ... 22. Overseas trade. Detailed authoritative index. This 1990 edition is published in a special enlarged quarto format to celebrate New Zealand's centenary. Besides its regular features it reprints a wealth of historical material from previous yearbooks. Brief history of the *Yearbook* p.xi-xi.
Class No: 908(931)(058)

Australia

Yearbooks & Directories

[2635]
Year book Australia 1991. 74th ed. Canberra, Australian Bureau of Statistics, 1991. xvi,790p. illus. (some col.), maps, tables, bibliogs. ISSN: 03124746.
First published 1908. Title varies.
27 chapters: 1. Prehistory to Federation - 2. Government - 3. International relations ... 5. Physical geography and climate ... 12. Culture, recreation and tourism ... 27. The territories of Australia (Northern Territory, Australian Capital Territory, Norfolk Is., Heard and McDonald Is., Australian Antarctic Territory, Cocos (Keeling) Is., Christmas Is., Coral Sea Is.) - 19. Special articles (including National Trusts of Australia and Collection and preservation of Australia's documentary heritage). List of special articles and miscellaneous matter contained in previous issues. Analytical index. 'A continuous record of government policies, international relationships and a concise statistical summary of every facet of Australia's economy and society' *Class No:* 908(94)(058)

Papua—New Guinea

Encyclopaedias

[2636]
The Encyclopedia of Papua and New Guinea. Ryan, P., *ed.* Melbourne Univ. Press in association with the Univ. of Papua and New Guinea, 2v. and index. 1231p.+83p. illus., maps and index.
About 200 contributors; signed articles. 'Art' (v.1, p.20-50): over 1 column of references; cross-references, 'Port Moresby'; 3½ cols. of bibliographies. V.3 has detailed index, p.33-83; gazetteer of place-names; 10 colour lift out maps. *Choice* (v.9, no.12, February 1973, p.1572) commends the biographical articles as being more evaluative than in most encyclopaedias. Well written and well produced. At various times the prospect of updating the encyclopedia has been discussed but to no avail. *Class No:* 908(954)(031)

Greenland

[2637]
Greenland past and present. Hertling, K., *and other eds.* Copenhagen, Edvard Henriksen, n.d. 370p. illus., (some col.pl.).
31 sections by a variety of hands: Geography of Greenland - Mapping of Greenland ... History of Greenland since the time of Hans Egede - Exploration... Life in Greenland. Internal evidence would indicate a publication date in the 1970s. *Class No:* 908(988)

Antarctic

[2638]
TRIGGS, G.D., *ed.* The Antarctic Treaty regime: law, environment and resources. Cambridge Univ. Press, 1987. xxii,239p. diagrs., tables, map, bibliog. (*Studies in Polar Research.*) ISBN: 0521327660.
24 papers from the Proceedings of a conference organized by the British Institute of International and Comparative Law, April 1985, examine the legal structure established by the Treaty and discuss the legal, political and environmental issues involved. Bibliography (by topic) p.234-5.
A similar work is *The Antarctic legal regime,* edited by C.C. Joyner and S.K. Chopra, Dordrecht, Martinus Nijhoff, 1985, xi,288p. map, index. This includes 11 papers by different hands in 2 sections: Law and politics and Resource regimes and environmental protection. *Class No:* 908(99)

91 Geography, Exploration, Travel

Geography & Travel

Bibliographies

[2639]
**GREAT BRITAIN. NATIONAL MARITIME MUSEUM.
Catalogue of the library.** London. H.M. Stationery Office,
1968-. illus., ports., facsims., maps.
1. *Voyages & travel.* 1968. xi,403p. 2. *Biography.* 2v.,
1969. 501p.475p. ISBN 0112900046. 3. *Atlases &
cartography.* 2v., 1971. vi,lx, 1166p. 0112900585. 4. *Piracy
& privateering.* 1972. ix,175p. 0112901190. 5. *Naval
history. pt.1: The Middle Ages to 1815.* 1977. 218p.
0118807609. V.1 has 1,240 numbered entries, usually with
annotations or bibliographical notes. Sections (each
preceded by a chronological table): Collective voyages -
Circumnavigations (items 17-125, chronologically) Africa -
America - East Indies - Europe and Mediterranean - Far
East - Pacific - Polar: Arctic - Polar: Antarctic - General
voyages. Detailed index; index of ships. Well produced.
Class No: 91.0(01)

Exploration & Travel

Maps & Atlases

[2640]
Atlas of Columbus and the great discoveries. Nebenzahl, K.
Chicago, Rand McNally, 1990. 168p. illus (some col.), maps
(some col.), bibliog. ISBN: 052883407x.
50 late 15th century and early 16th century maps
depicting contemporary geographical knowledge and
speculation of the world's oceans and new lands. Each map
is accompanied by a short documented essay. *Class No:*
910(084.3)

[2641]
The Times atlas of world exploration. Fernández-
Armesto, F., ed. London, Times Books, 1991. 286p. col.
illus., col. maps, facsims, index. ISBN: 0723003440.
18 contributors. 46 chapters arranged in 12 mainly
continent and ocean sections. Chronology in continent time
bands p.10-15. Glossary of technical terms p.243-4.
Biographical glossary (*c.*400 explorers) p.245-72. Index of
place-names (over 12,000 entries) p.273-86. Facsimiles of
over 180 period maps and 130 specially commissioned
topographical maps showing discovery and exploration
routes. Excellent atlas covering over 3,000 years of
exploration. Generally superior to *Royal Geographical
Society history of world exploration* (*qv*) but with
inexplicable omission of any sort of bibliographical
apparatus apart from list of antique maps reproduced in
the *Atlas* with their sources. *Class No:* 910(084.3)

Expeditions, Voyages, Travel

Handbooks & Manuals

[2642]
SHALES, M., *ed.* **The Traveller's handbook.** 5th ed. London,
Wexas Ltd., 1988. xliii, 820p. maps, soft-cover. ISBN:
0905802047.
82 contributors. 1. Where and when (places in vogue;
countries at war; climate and its relevance to travel. *etc.*) -
2. Finding out more (choosing maps; background reading; a
guide to guides) - 3. Great journeys overland - 4-6. Getting
there by air, road, and other means - 7. What type of
travel - 8. Your special needs - 9. Paperwork - 10. Money
- 11. Equipping for a trip - 12. Basic guide to health - 13.
A place to stay - 14. Communicating - 15. When things go
wrong - 16. Keeping track - 17. Maps - 18. Directory (rules
and regulations; medical requirements and advice; travel;
climate; equipment; training, help, advice?; Publications and
publishers. 'A mass of information, much of which is just
about impossible to locate easily elsewhere. An
indispensable guide for the independent traveller' (*Reference
Reviews*, v.3, no.1, March 1989, p.40-1). *Class No:*
910.4(035)

Histories

[2643]
The Royal Geographical Society history of world exploration.
Keay, J., *ed.* London, Hamlyn, 1991. 320p. illus. (some
col.), col. maps, bibliog., index.
10 sections by different hands: 1. Early exploration - 2.
Asia - 3. Africa - 4. North America - 5. Central and South
America - 6. Pacific, Australia and New Zealand - 7. Arctic
- 8. Antarctic - 9. Oceanography - 10. Exploration today.
Each consists of historical narrative with boxed features on
chief explorers, their key routes, and their equipment etc.,
and a discovery map. A running chronological frieze adorns
every page. Bibliography p.314. *Class No:* 910.4(091)

Geography

Bibliographies

[2644]
**AMERICAN GEOGRAPHICAL SOCIETY. Research
catalogue.** Boston, Mass., G.K. Hall, 15v. and map suppt.,
1962. 1043p.
V.1 & 2: General - 3. Regional North America - 4-5.
United States - 6-7. Mexico, Central America, Bermuda,
West Indies, South America - 8-10. Europe - 11. Africa -
12-13. Asia - 14. Australasia - 15. Polar regions, Oceania,
Tropics. Map supplement is merely a map key to the
classification used.
First Supplement: Regional catalogue 2v., 1972. 1414p.
$260.00 (Export $315.00). ISBN 0816109990. *Topical*

....(contd.)

catalogue, 2v. 1974. 1483p. is available on microfilm by request. $265.00 ($320.00). *Second Supplement* 2v., 1978. 1300p. $260.00 ($315.00). ISBN 0816100810.

More than 200,000 photolithographed catalogue cards. Particularly strong in periodical-article entries. Includes maps. The Library is the largest of its kind in the Western hemisphere. Updated in *Current geographical publications: additions to the Research catalogue of the American Geographical Society (qv)*. *Class No:* 911(01)

[2645]

LOCK, C.B.M. Geography and cartography: a reference handbook. London, Clive Bingley, 1976. 762p.

An integration of *Geography: a reference handbook* (1968; 2nd ed. 1972.529p.) and *Modern maps and atlases* (1969).

1,400 entries, A-Z (titles of works, forms of literature, biographies, topics), with a strong bibliographical and cartobibliographical slant. Extended entries on Cartography (p.159-95); Audio visual aids; Bibliographies, national; Classification; Education in geography and cartography; Globes; Map librarianship (p.427-51); Maps (historical); Abstracts. Extensive index, p.635-762. The work does not fully integrate *Modern maps and atlases*, which should be retained for its coverage of national, regional and thematic maps and atlases (*RQ*, v.16,no.3, Spring 1977, p.258-9). A-Z order of entry has value for quick reference, but it is apt to scatter related material and choice of entry-words can be capricious (*e.g.*, 'Man and wildlife'). Sample maps would have been an asset. A bulky but highly rewarding volume; 'for all geographical libraries' (*Library Review*, v.26,1977/ 8,p.144). *Class No:* 911(01)

Encyclopaedias

[2646]

DUNBAR, G.S., *ed.* **Modern geography: an encyclopedic survey.** New York, Garland; London, St. James Press, 1991. xx,219p. index. ISBN: 0824053435, US; 1558621229, UK.

95 contributors. 'An overview of developments in the field of geography from about 1890 to the present, with emphasis on personalities, institutions, major concepts, subfields, and the evolution of the discipline in various countries' (*Introduction*). Entries are A-Z with some cross-referencing, many have bibliographies (maximum of 6 items). 300 biographies (birth and death dates, highest academic qualification, institutional affiliation, major publications). 'Highest recommendation for all academic libraries' (*Choice*, v.28,no.8, April 1991, p.1292). *Class No:* 911(031)

Reviews & Abstracts

[2647]

Geo abstracts. Norwich, Elsevier/Geo Abstracts, 1972-.

Preceded by *Geomorphological abstracts* (1960-65) and *Geographical abstracts* (1966-71) comprising 6 sections each 6 *pa*.

1972-1988 in 7 separate sections: A. Landforms and the Quaternary - B. Biogeography and climatology - C. Economic geography - D. Social and historical geography - E. Sedimentology - F. Regional and community planning - G. Remote sensing and cartography. Annual index in 2v. Index to A.B.E. and F. and C.D. and F. These 7 sections are now replaced by:

Physical geography (1989. £210 UK; £235 or $434.75 overseas. 09540504). Monthly information source derived from over 900 leading geographical journals, books, conference proceedings, reports, theses. Provides full bibliographic coverage plus informative abstracts. Merges former sections A.B.E.G Subject and geographical indexes. Available on Geobase (*via* DIALOG file, no. 292).

....(contd.)

Human geography (1988. £165 UK; £180 or $333.00 overseas. 09539611). 6*pa*. Merges former sections C.D.F. *Class No:* 911(048)

France

[2648]

PINCHEMEL, P. France a geographical, social and economic survey. Elkins, D. *and* Elkins, T.H., *translators.* Cambridge, Cambridge Univ. Press; Paris, Editions De La Maison Des Sciences De l'Homme, 1986. xxvi,660p. illus., maps, tables, bibliog., index. ISBN: 0521249872, UK; 2735101754, Fr.

Originally as *La France* (Paris, Armand Colin, 1980).

39 chapters deployed in 8 main parts: 12. The natural environment - 2. People - 3. Actors and policies in the spatial structures of France - 4. Resources, economic activity and economic enterprises - 5. The infrastructure of spatial interaction - 6. Landscape and environment in rural France - 7. The urban environment - 8. Conclusion. Bibliography p.605-49. Analytical index. *Class No:* 911(44)

Historical Geography

Europe

[2649]

POUNDS, N.J.G. An Historical geography of Europe. Cambridge University Press, 1990. xiii,484p. maps, diagrs., tables, bibliogs., index. ISBN: 0521322170.

12 alternating chapters on the changing pattern of human history during the last 2,500 years of Europe's history. One set of 7 captures Europe at particular celebrated points, the other 5 chapters trace the changes in the intervening periods. Chapter bibliographies. Based on 3v. work of the same title (1973-85). 'A superb summary of Europe's historical geography in one succinct volume' (*Choice*, v.28,no.7, March 1991, p.1205). *Class No:* 911.0(4)

England & Wales

[2650]

DODGSHON, R.A. and BUTLIN, R.A., *eds.* **An Historical geography of England and Wales.** 2nd ed. New York, Academic Press, 1990. xxi,589p. diagrs., tables, maps, bibliog., index. ISBN: 0122192532.

14 contributors (British academics, etc.). Well documented. Extends from prehistory to date. Detailed subject index. 'A most methodical analysis of recent researches into the various themes discussed' (*British Book News*, February 1979, p.171). *Class No:* 911.0(42)

France

French

[2651]

PLANHOL, X. de. Géographie historique de la France. Paris, Fayard, 1988. 635p. maps, figs., bibliog., index.

11 chapters organized in 3 parts: 1. Genèse de la France - 2. L'Organisation traditionnelle de l'Espace Français - 3. Centralisation et diversification de l'Espace Français. Chapter notes p.537-566. Bibliography p.567-591. 'Le sujet a été délib'ment traité per grandes plages chronologiques (*Avant-propos*). *Class No:* 911.0(44)=40

Scandinavia

[2652]
MEAD, W.R. **An Historical geography of Scandinavia.** London and New York, Academic Press, 1981. xviii,313p. maps, tables, diagrs., bibliogs., index. ISBN: 0124874207.

12 chapters *e.g.,* 2. The concept of Scandinavia ... 4. From Middle Ages to Baroque Empire ... 11. Fin de siècle *c.*1900 - 12. The process and problems of fulfilment. Ch. bibliographies. *Class No:* 911.0(48)

Caribbean

[2653]
WATTS, D. **The West Indies** patterns of development, culture and environmental change since 1492. Cambridge, Cambridge Univ. Press, 1987. xxii,609p. illus., maps, tables, bibliog., index. (*Cambridge Studies in Historical Geography no.8.*) ISBN: 0521245559.

3 main themes (total removal of a large aboriginal population; development of plantation agriculture; and resulting environment changes) unravelled in 11 chapters: 1. The environment - 2. Aboriginal settlement and culture - 3. Spanish intrusion and colonization - 4. Early northwest European plantations - 5. Northwest European sugar estates 1645-1665 - 6-9. Extension of the West Indian sugar estate economy 1665-1833 - 10. Post 1833 adjustments - 11. Twentieth-century trends. Notes p.540-52. Bibliography p.553-85. Analytical index. *Class No:* 911.0(729)

USA

Bibliographies

[2654]
GRIM, R.E. **Historical geography of the United States:** a guide to information sources. Detroit, Gale Research Co., 1982. xix,291p. indexes. (*Geography and Travel Information Guide Series.*) ISBN: 0810314711.

686 annotated entries 'limited almost exclusively to the United States from the beginning of the sixteenth century until the early twentieth century' arranged in 21 chapters divided into 3 parts: Cartographic sources; Archival and other historical sources; Selected literature in historical geography. Author, title and subject indexes. Because of its emphasis on 'recent and current literature, *i.e.,* published or reprinted 1965-1980, it complements rather than duplicates D.R. McManis' *Historical geography of the United States* (1965). 'Recommended for all academic libraries (*Choice,* v.20,no.8, April 1983, p.1110). *Class No:* 911.0(73)(01)

912 Maps & Atlases

Maps & Atlases

Bibliographies

[2655]

BANCROFT LIBRARY University of California. Berkeley. **Index to printed maps.** Boston, Mass., G.K. Hall, 1964. First Supplement, 1975.
Index. 1964. 521p. $79.00 (Export $95.00). ISBN 0816107041. *First Supplement.* 1975. 581p. $110.00 ($135.00). ISBN 0816111723. Total of 23100 photolithographed catalogue cards. Maps indexed are of the New World with emphasis on the western half of North America, 16th to 20th century. *Class No:* 912.0(01)

[2656]

BOOK MARKETING COUNCIL The Publishers Association. **Catalogue of maps and guides 1990.** London, Book Marketing Council, 1983-. Now annually. viii,56p. illus. map. ISBN: 085386165x.
In 2 parts: 1. Britain p.1-20 arranged Britain, England (further subdivided into the 12 Tourist Board areas), Scotland, Wales - 2. Rest of the world A-Z by countries or areas. Each publication is listed under Atlas, Map, or Travel Guide. Data: title, imprint, ISBN, pagination, retail price, map scale. Publishers directory p.54-56. Primarily intended as a book trade tool this is a useful in print bibliography. 'Brings together a lot of material, much of which does not appear in BBIP' (*Refer*, v.2,no.3, Spring 1983, p.11). *Class No:* 912.0(01)

[2657]

BRITISH LIBRARY. Catalogue of printed maps, charts and plans. Photolithographed ed. London, Trustees of the British Museum, 15v., 1967. Corrections and additions. 1967. ISBN: 0714103241.
First published as *Catalogue of the printed maps, plans and charts in the British Museum* compiled by R.K. Douglas (London, 1885. 2v.); supplemented by the annual *Catalogue of printed maps in the British Museum: accessions* (1884-).
The 15v. ed. records British Museum holdings up to 1964 and is in the same format as the *General catalogue of printed books.* Entries have brief bibliographical notes (*e.g.,* scale, map size). Arrangement is by localities. A-Z, with subdivision (*e.g.,* London, v.9, p.13-202) as relevant.
The British Library catalogue of printed maps charts and plans Ten-year supplement 1965-1974. 1978. 690p. £45.00. ISBN 0714103667.
Catalogue of cartographic materials in the British Library 1975-1988, London, Bowker-Saur, 3v., 1989. 1500p. £36.00. 0862917654. 48,000 entries relating to atlases, single sheet maps, map series, maritime charts, plans, globes, and other relevant material acquired by the British Library Map Library. Also details of 260 digital cartographic and remote sensing databases in the UK located as a result of a British

....(contd.)
Library sponsored research project. 3 sequences: 1. Geographic names A-Z using BL Map Library headings - 2. Names/titles - 3. Subjects *i.e.* reference works, books and serials relating to all aspects of cartography. Also available on 48 x reduction microfiche. *Class No:* 912.0(01)

Europe

[2658]

AA road atlas. Europe. Basingstoke, Hants, Automobile Association, 1990. vi,154p. col. maps, index. ISBN: 0749502193.
Road maps of 27 European countries (16 countries at 16 miles to 1 inch). 24,000 place name index. *Class No:* 912.0(4)

[2659]

Map of the New Europe wallchart. Wetherby, West Yorks, Reader Services Department, The Independent, 1992. col. map.
First published in *The Independent on Sunday,* no.107, 9 February 1992, Sunday Review p.31-4.
Following the collapse of the Soviet Union and the break-up of Yugoslavia, a major part of the continent's geographical and geopolitical make-up has altered. The map and guide, with a foreword by Neal Ascherson, aims to set the scene as it is now. Data: flag (col.); constitutional status; population; national and regional capitals. *Class No:* 912.0(4)

Italian

[2660]

Atlante Enciclopedico Touring. Milano, Touring Club Italiano, 3v-. 1986-.
1. *Italia* 1986. xviii, 160p. 8836502989. Explanatory sections as how maps are made *i.e.,* impact of scale, use of satellite imagery, and Glossary. 4 Major sections: 1. Thematic maps on various scales *e.g.,* geomorphology, land use, vegetation, settlement, urban development - 2. Regional analysis: satellite, physical, political, environmental and industrial maps of each of Italy's 6 major regions - 3. National synthesis: general physical, population, migration, industrial employment, energy and regional data for Italy's 20 administrative regions - 4. International comparative maps setting Italy in its E.E.C. and world contexts. Glossary p.131-143. Bibliography p.144-45. 2. *Europa* 180p. 8836502997. 3 major sections: 1. General and thematic maps with essential geographical, economic and political features, mostly at 1:20,000,000 - 2. Principal European regions *e.g.,* Scandinavia, Iberia, Italy and the Balkans, Soviet Union at 1:5,000,000 - 3. Physical-political maps at 1:2,500,000 mostly duplicating previous information. Glossary p.135-45. Bibliography p.146-47. *Class No:* 912.0(4)=50

Europe—Eastern

[2661]
Atlas der Donauländer. [Atlas of Danubian lands.]
Breu, J., *ed.* Wien, Franz Deutike Verlagsgesellschaft for
Österreichisches Ost-und Südosteuropa Institut, 10 lieferung
in loose-leaf binder, 1970-1989. ISBN: 3700590180.

A massive and monumental thematic atlas, the work of
35 cartographers over two decades, with 48 fold-out plates
(95cm x 68cm) each accompanied by a page of text. The
area covered extends from the northern boundary of
Czechoslovakia to the southern boundary of Albania; from
just west of Regensburg in Bavaria to Odessa in the east,
thus excluding the Danube headwaters. There are 43
physical, 34 population, and 67 economic and
communication maps, whose texts end with bibliographical
references. Standard scale is 1:2,000,000. Contents table and
introduction printed in German, Russian, French and
English. 'A first-rate, innovative, most attractive atlas,
unfortunately affordable only [by] the world's leading
libraries' (*Cartographica*, v.27, no.1, Spring 1990, p.93-5).
Class No: 912.0(401)

[2662]
—Atlas der Donauländer. Register. Wien, Österreichisches
Ost-und Südosteuropa-Institut, 1989. xxv,139p. ISBN:
370050019x.
Comprehensive multilingual gazetteer of the geographical
names in the *Atlas*. *Class No:* 912.0(401)

[2663]
Atlas Ost-und Südosteuropa /Atlas of Eastern and
Southeastern Europe. Jordan, P. *and* Kelnhofer, F., *eds.*
Wien, Österreiches Ost-und Südosteuropa- Institut, 1989-. 4
sheets per year.
Map 5.1 G1. *Administrative subdivision of Eastern and
South-eastern Europe.* 1989. DM28.
Map 5.1 H1. *The expansion of tourism from Western
countries to Hungary in the eighties.* 1989. DM28.
Atlas in progress: loose-leaf collection of standard size
sheets (74 x 59cm), each sheet with one or more maps on
a particular theme. Each map sheet is accompanied by a
booklet with background text to the map's theme and with
methodological notes on its compilation and design. Aims
to provide up-to-date information on the nine former
socialist countries of Eastern Europe in 5 broad thematic
sections: ecology, population, economy, transport, and
planning. Titles, legends and text in German and English.
'Likely to become a valuable reference work'
(*Cartographica*, v.28,no.1, Spring 1991, p.118-9 from where
this information is derived). *Class No:* 912.0(401)

Great Britain

[2664]
AA road atlas of the British Isles. Basingstoke. The
Automobile Association, 1990. 48,xxiv,312p. col. illus., col.
maps, index. ISBN: 0749500794.
1. The tourists' British Isles (abbeys and cathedrals;
castles; historic houses; museums and galleries; industrial
interest and preserved railways; gardens and arboreta;
country parks; theme parks; zoos, wildlife collections and
acquaria; nature reserves, nature trails; caves, prehistoric
monuments, hillforts, and Roman antiquities; calendar). 2.
The atlas: road maps; offshore islands; Ireland and Irish
index; London; over 65 town plans p.184-249; ports and
airports p.250-5. Scale 1 inch:3 miles. Sets new standards
in map clarity and production and for the wealth of
information it contains. *Class No:* 912.0(410)

[2665]
GREAT BRITAIN Ordance Survey. **County street atlases.**
Southampton, Ordnance Survey; London, George Philip,
1988-. maps, indexes.
Berkshire 1990. *Buckinghamshire* 1990. *East Essex* 1990.
West Essex 1990. *Hertfordshire* 1990. *East Kent* 1992.
West Kent 1992. *Oxfordshire* 1992. *Surrey* 1989. *East
Sussex* 1992. *West Sussex* 1992. *Warwickshire* 1992.

All roads, streets and lanes, parks, woods, farms,
bridleways and footpaths, Post Offices, schools and
libraries, museums, government offices, hospitals, fire
stations, ferry ports and harbours are clearly marked. Lists
of towns, villages and rural localities are appended. *Class
No:* 912.0(410)

[2666]
—STACEY, M. 'Current UK street maps for libraries', *Refer,*
v.8, no.1, Winter 1992, p.1-4, 6-7.
Definitions, specifications, acquisitions *etc.* 11 major
series are noted. *Class No:* 912.0(410)

[2667]
**GREAT BRITAIN. ORDNANCE SURVEY. Routemaster
maps.** Southampton, Ordnance Survey. Sheet size: flat 49 x
37 inches; folded 5 x 9½ inches.
9 regularly revised maps cover the country. Motorways,
trunk, main and secondary routes are clearly depicted. An
inset diagram of tourist information shows National Parks,
areas of outstanding beauty, and National Trails. Scale 1
inch to 4 miles (1:250,000). *Class No:* 912.0(410)

[2668]
Reader's Digest driver's atlas of the British Isles. London,
The Reader's Digest Association Ltd., 1988. 368p. col.
illus., col. maps. ISBN: 0276417569.
Successor to Reader's Digest's *Book of the road* and *New
book of the road.*
14 sections: 3. Gazetteer (p.33-79): index of 28,000
locations shown on the road maps - 4. The British Isles by
road (p.80-81): how to use the road maps, index of maps,
and guide to the symbols - 5. Major routes (p.82-89)
including ferry information - 7. Road maps on scale of 3
miles to one inch (p.92-232) - 8. Town places (p.233-301):
street maps of 128 cities and towns - 9. Britain's
motorways (p.302-320): strip plans of the principal
motorways showing interchanges, services, and distances
between junctions - 10. Places to visit (p.321-352): a
selective guide (800 locations). A reversible fold at the end
of p.81-242 is designed to bridge one map to the next;
each flap carries local information. In a comparative review
together with *Collin's road atlas Britain 1988; O.S.
Motoring atlas of Great Britain 1988;* and *RAC motoring
atlas Britain 1988, Reference Reviews* v.2, no.4, December
1988, p.224 remarked that this atlas was 'clearest of all'
and that 'having tried all four atlases out in practice, then
(it) is definitely the one I would choose'. *Class No:*
912.0(410)

Commonwealth

[2669]
Atlas of British overseas expansion. Porter, A.N., *ed.*
London, Routledge, 1991. x,279p. maps, plans, bibliog.,
index. ISBN: 0415019184.
92 chronological map/text features chart and chronicle
Britain's growth as a maritime commercial power from the
late 15th century to the postwar withdrawal from Empire
(*e.g.* Bristol and the Atlantic 1480 to 1509 ... Exports from
the West Indies ... The Commonwealth 1931 to 1989). Also
20 shorter features on 20 towns and cities of imperial
significance. Bibliography p.238-50. 137 black/white maps.
More academic in tone and content than C. Bayly's *Atlas
of the British Empire.* *Class No:* 912.0(41-44)

London

[2670]
Master atlas of Greater London. 5th ed. Sevenoaks, Kent, Geographer's A-Z Map Co., 1988. 320p. col.illus., col.maps, index. ISBN: 0850390028.
5th ed. 1985.
1. Sectional maps on scale 3⅛ inches to the mile (p.2-188) - 2. Index to streets (p.219-310) - 3. Large scale maps Central London (p.187-207) - 4. Road maps (p.209-317). Borough boundaries map inside back cover. Also index to hospitals and clinics, and stations. 'This Atlas, with the streets re-indexed to smaller squares and its re-drawn, re-designed pages, in colours selected for legibility in the subdued lighting of a car, reflects the long experience of this publisher in the production of street maps and guides, and is to be welcomed as a useful updated Atlas of London' (*Geographical Journal*, v.152,no.1, March 1986, p. 131). *Class No:* 912.0(421)

China

[2671]
Atlas of China. Chicago, Rand McNally, 1990. 48p. illus., maps, index. pbk. ISBN: 0528833855.
Two-page maps of The World, Asia, China, and 4 regional maps of China (1:3,000,000) including Tibet followed by single page maps of areas surrounding major cities (1:1,000,000). Updated from *The international atlas* (1969) showing political capitals and boundaries with cultural, transport, hydrographic and topographic features. Detailed index of 11,000 entries. For home and school use. *Class No:* 912.0(510)

[2672]
Rand McNally illustrated atlas of China. Chicago, Rand McNally, 1972. 282p. illus., diagrs., maps.
Originally as US Central Intelligence Agency, *People's Republic of China atlas* (Washington, Government Printing Office, 1971), prepared for President Nixon's visit to China.
3 main sections: Introduction to China (p.8-31) - Administrative divisions. Population. Ethnic groups. Railroads. Roads and inland waterways. Climate agriculture. Minerals and metals. Fuel and power. Industry (p.32-71) - Human resources and economy. Historical perspective. Peking and environs. Index-gazetteer of *c*.600 place-names. Fine cartography. *Geographical Review* (v.63, no.3, July 1973), p.436-8) praises its 'professionalism and crisp production'. Page size 38 x 22.5cm. *Class No:* 912.0(510)

Japan

[2673]
The National atlas of Japan. Compiled by Geographical Survey Institute, Ministry of Information. Tokyo, Japan Map Center, 1977. x,367, illus., maps.
216 maps (50 at 1:2,500,000; 166 at 1:4,000,000), with explanatory notes and small supporting maps. Nearly half the maps are thematic, covering agriculture, industry, communications and trade. Several maps concern environmental problems. Gazetteer: List of administrative areas; Index to place names (p.359-65; *c*.5,000 entries). 'A superb example of the high standards which characterize Japanese cartography' (*Geographical Journal*, v.144, 1978, p.369). *Class No:* 912.0(52)

Asia—Middle & Near East

[2674]
Atlas of the Middle East. Brawer, M., *ed.* New York, Macmillan; London, Collier Macmillan, 1988. 140p. maps, tables, diagrs., bibliog., index. ISBN: 0029052718.
Covers 19 countries from Libya in the West to Iran in the east and Turkey to the north. A regional overview is followed by country surveys *e.g.*, Iran p.86-93 has sections on topography, climate, population, agriculture, history, government and politics, and 3 maps. *Class No:* 912.0(53+56)

India

[2675]
National atlas of India. Calcutta, National Atlas and Thematic Mapping Organization, Department of Science and Technology, Government of India, 1984.
Massive work, 25 years in the making, in 8 large loose-leaf volumes: 1. General and political maps - 2. Physical and geomorphological - 3. Climatic and biogeographical - 4. Population and transport - 5. Land use and industrial - 6. Agricultural and economic - 7. Social and regional - 8. Historical and cultural. In all 300 variously dated maps on basic scale 1:6,000,000. Format allows for extracting single or more maps for detailed scrutiny or for class use.
Despite the maps' old-fashioned and cluttered appearance, the atlas remains a colossal achievement, fully justifying the sense of pride evident in S.P. Dasgupta's preface to v.1. *Class No:* 912.0(540)

Africa

[2676]
CHI-BONNARDEL, R. van. The Atlas of Africa. Paris, éditions jeune afrique, 1973. 335p. maps. ISBN: 0903274035.
Edited jointly by the publishers of *Africa* magazine and *Jeune Afrique*. Maps prepared by L'Institut Géographique National de Paris.
138 six-colour maps (1:1M to 1:10M). Maps on Africa in general are followed by 2 maps on each country and its economy, plus text and statistical data. Gazetteer of less than 6,000 entries; bibliography. 'A timely, vitally essential reference work characterized by a high order of scholarship and cartographic portrayal' (*Best reference books*, ARBA, 1970-1976, entry 223). Page size, 40x30cm. *Class No:* 912.0(6)

Canada

[2677]
National atlas of Canada. 5th ed. Ottawa, Energy Mines and Resources Canada, 1986-.
First published as *Atlas of Canada* by the Department of the Interior in 1906. 4th ed. under the present title issued in 1974 by the Macmillan Company of Canada.
'The 5th edition is planned as a continuing serial publication of separate but related maps, collectively dealing with all aspects of Canada. When comprehensive coverage of about two hundred map subjects is eventually reached, revision of the original maps will also be underway. The production of revised versions of each map will, in general, depend on the national importance of the subject, the state of scientific and scholarly knowledge in the field, and the public demand for such information' (*The fifth edition The National Atlas of Canada. An Information System*, a brochure issued *gratis* by Energy, Mines and Resources Canada, Canada Map Office, 615 Booth Street, Ottawa, Ontario, KIA OE9). A French version, *L'Atlas National du Canada* is available.
'Eventually all National Atlas data will be stored in

....*(contd.)*

digital form to allow rapid updating and information transfer as new research material is received into the National Atlas Information System' (*ibid.*). *Class No:* 912.0(71)

Mexico

[2678]
Atlas of Mexico. Pick, J.B., *and others.* Boulder, Colo., Westview Press, 1989. xxi,367p. maps, tables, bibliog., index. ISBN: 0813376955.

135 black and white maps computer plotted from data derived from 1980 census and subsequent annual statistical reports. All but 13 maps focus on political and administrative units. 93 tables. *Class No:* 912.0(72)

USA

[2679]
The National atlas of the United States. Gerlach, A.C., *ed.* Washington, U.S. Geological Survey, 1970. xiii,417p. maps, diagrs.

765 maps, mostly in colour and many with a two-page spread. General reference maps, followed by thematic maps: physical, climatic and water (74p.); historical (24p.); economic (89p., *i.e.*, 187 maps, including sets); sociocultural (30p.; administrative (24p.); mapping and charting (34p.); political (7p.). One drawback: The tight binding prevents two-page spread maps from being visible at the inner edges. 'Ranks among the finest national atlases yet produced' (*Geographical Review*, v.62, no.1, January 1972, p.97). 'The general layout and design is quite superb' (*Cartographic Journal*, v.9, no.1, June 1972, p.65-66). Page size: 47 x 34.5cm. *Class No:* 912.0(73)

Australia

[2680]
The Reader's Digest Atlas of Australia, produced in conjunction with the Division of National Mapping, Department of National Resources. Sydney, Reader's Digest, 1977. 288p. illus., diagrs., charts, maps. ISBN: 0909486549.

14 contributors. Sections: 'Mapping Australia' - 'The land we live in' (large map of Australia, showing surface features, main cities, towns, roads and railways) - 'Our country in close-up' (150 detailed physical maps, p.12-160, scale 1:1,000,000; including islands) - 'Anatomy of Australia' (small illus., etc. giving social, economic, ethnographic, industrial and political data, p.161-216) - 'Gazetteer to the maps' (nearly 40,000 entries, with coordinates. 'The best Australian atlas ever produced' (*RSR*, v.7, no.2, April/June 1979, p.10). Page size 30 x 40cm. *Class No:* 912.0(94)

World Atlases

[2681]
'National Geographic' Atlas of the world. 6th ed. Washington, National Geographic Society, 1990. 400p. col.illus., col.maps, col.graphs, index. ISBN: 0870443992.

First published 1963.

Introductory matter includes 1: Pictorial features (universe, heavens, climate *etc.*) - Oceanic floor maps. Continental physical maps and World resources, food, energy, minerals. Nations of the World has text and maps grouped in sections: United States - Canada and Greenland - Mid America - South America - Europe - Asia - Africa - Australia, New Zealand and Antarctica - The Oceans. Geographic data (airline distances, timezones, temperatures and rainfall, population of major cities *etc.*. Glossary of foreign terms. Index of 150,000+ place names. A very attractive large atlas. *Class No:* 912.01

[2682]
The New international atlas. Chicago, Rand McNally, 1990. 560p. ISBN: 0528833146, standard; 052883214x, Deluxe ed.

First published 1969.

Rand McNally's flagship atlas. 255 map pages include world, ocean, continental maps; 50 x 16 miles to the inch (1:1,000,000) maps of key regional areas of exceptional economic importance, high density of population, or confronting complex transport needs; and 60 urban maps at scale of 5 miles to the inch (1:300,000) for major world metropolitan areas. Textual matter is in 5 languages: English, French, German, Portuguese and Spanish, with place-names in the local language (country names in English and in local official form). An unusual feature is three-dimensional shadings for mountains and valleys. 168,000 world names (including 35,800 US) are indexed. *Class No:* 912.01

[2683]
Peters atlas of the world. Harlow, Longman, 1989. 226p. illus., col. maps. bibliog. ISBN: 0582035015.

1. The world in 43 double page maps each representing 1/60 of the earth's surface. 2. Nature, man and society *i.e.*, 246 thematic maps (each showing global data by colour, not symbols). 3. Index p.189-226. Principal sources of information on thematic maps p.96. The distinctive feature of this atlas is the use of Arno Peter's own projection, designed to show the Earth in its true proportion, which lends the continental outlines an unfamiliar aspect. 'The very demerits of the Peters world projection could well be commercially helpful for sales of the atlas in developing countries but only the cartographically naive will be deceived and fail to be exasperated by the pretentious and misleading claims made for the atlas by the authors and publishers' (*Geographical Journal*, v.155,no.2, July 1989, p.295-7). *Class No:* 912.01

[2684]
—**Compact Peters atlas of the world.** Harlow, Longman, 1991. 228p. col. maps. ISBN: 0582089565.

246 thematic maps. *Class No:* 912.01

[2685]
The Times atlas of the world. Comprehensive ed. 8th ed. London, Times Books in collaboration with Bartholomew, 1990. xlvii, 122 double + 1 single plates of maps, 235p. col. maps, diagrs., index. ISBN: 0723003467.

Comprehensive ed. first published 1967; 7th ed. 1985. Preceded by *The Times atlas* (1895); *The Times survey of the world* (2v., 1920-22); and *The Times atlas of the world* (Mid-century ed. 5v., 1955-59). Foreign languages eds.: 1. München, Droemersche Verlagsanstalt, *Knaurs grosser Weltatlas* (1987); Ede, Kluwer Algemene Bocken, *De grote Times Wereldatlas* (1983); and Paris, Sélection du Readers' Digest, *L'Atlas universel* (1989).

123 plates of maps (nearly all double page spread) include 7 thematic maps *e.g.* 'World climatology and food potential; and 'World mankind', the rest physico - political printed in 8 colours. Various scales: most European countries at scales ranging from 1:5000,000 to 1:250.000; most cities and islands inset maps are at 1:250,000. 15 different styles of Times Roman lettering ensures high standards of legibility. Spelling of place names corresponds to the principles and practices of the British Permanent Committee on Geographical names. English conventional names of important places added where space permits. Chinese names in Pinyin style. Preliminaries include 'States and Territories of the World' Geographical comparisons (areas of continents, oceans and seas *etc.*); Star charts; Solar system; Space flight, map projection. Glossary and abbreviations p.1-4. Index-gazetteer *c.*210,000 place names. New to the 7th edition, published to mark the 200th anniversary of *The Times,* and continued here, is the

....(contd.)
section on Earth Sciences and Astronomy, 14p. of
continental physical maps, feature on Map Projections.
Maps prepared by John Bartholomew & Son, Edinburgh. 'It
will stand for many years to come as one of the leading
cartographic sources of reference for the major topographic,
social and economic features of our planet in the mid-
1980's (*New Scientist*, 2 January 1986, p.46). *Class No:*
912.01

Bibliographies

[2686]
KISTER, K.F. Kister's atlas buying guide General English
language world atlases available in North America. Phoenix,
Arizona, Oryx Press, 1984. xii,236p. ISBN: 0912700629.

105 Atlas profiles, A-Z by title, with a critical evaluation
based on published reviews and on the compiler's own
assessment. Appendix A: World atlases at a glance: B. Map
and atlas bibliography; C. Out of print map and atlas
dealers; D. Atlas publishers and distributors. Subject-Title
index. 'Useful information for selecting one atlas out of a
group of similar works'(*RQ*, v.24,no.1, Fall 1974, p.108).
Class No: 912.01(01)

Italian

[2687]
Atlante internazionale del Touring Club Italiano. 8th ed.
Milano, Touring Club Italiano, 2v., 1968.

First published 1927.

173 places of coloured maps, relief being shown by light
brown hachuring and hill shading. A number of the 93
maps are folded, giving a lateral spread of 85cm. 74 of the
173 plates concern Europe. Scales vary: 1:1500,000 (Italy)
to 1:10,000,000 (Australia). Many large-scale local maps.
Lettering clear: transliteration follows BGN/PCGN practice.
The separate *Indice dei nomi* locates *c.*250,000 place-names
on a close grid system usable only with the *Atlante
internazionel;* also a glossary of *c.*3,500 geographical terms.
Alone among major atlases, this atlas gives a list of
sources. 'One of the most elaborate detailed and
cartographically superior of world atlases' (Church, M., and
others, comps. and eds. *A basic geographical library* (1966),
entry no.43, on the 1956 ed.). Page size: 45x61cm. *Class
No:* 912.01=50

Russian

[2688]
Atlas Mira. Baranov, A.N., *and others eds.* 2nd ed. Moskva,
Glavnoe Upravlenie Geodezii i Kartografii, 1967. 250p. of
maps.

First published 1954.

A finely produced world atlas. 168 maps on 250 plates, a
number of them folded, giving some impressive area
spreads of for example, Indonesia and Turkey. Mainly
physical maps, relief being shown by layer colour.
Incorporates results of Soviet surveys of ocean floors.
Scores over *The Times* atlas and its Italian counterpart by
reason of its uniform scale of 1:7,500,000 (except for
Arctica and Antarctica, at 1:20,000,000). Plates 7-45 are
devoted to the USSR; 40% of the total concerns Europe.
Asia is represented by plates 102-54 (as against 82-106 in
the *Atlante internazionale*). Lettering is clear, but less so
with the more pronounced layer colouring. Transliteration
does not conform to BGN/PCGN practice, limiting the
usefulness of the atlas to non-Russian readers. Inset plans
of cities are fewer than in '*The Times*' atlas and the Italian
counterpart, but features such as main streets, parks and
districts are named. Page size, 49 x 31cm.

The separate *Ukazatel geograficheskikh nazvanii* (2. izd.
Moscow, 1968, 533p.), first published 1954, is an index-

....(contd.)
gazetteer to over 200,000 place-names in the Atlas mira.
Grid references only.

An English-language ed. of *Atlas mira* (2nd ed.), - *The
World atlas* - was published in Moscow, 1967. *Class No:*
912.01=82

914/919 Gazetteers & Guide Books

Gazetteers & Guide Books

[2689]
Blue guides. London, Ernest Benn (later A & C. Black). maps, plans.
'Blue guides', *Geographical Journal*, v.144, no.3, November 1978 gives the series' background history.
Austria; Barcelona; Belgium and Luxembourg; Channel Is; China; Corsica; Czechoslovakia; Crete; Cyprus; Denmark; Egypt; England; Florence; France; Germany; Greece; Holland; Hungary; Ireland; Istanbul; Jerusalem; Malta; Morocco; Moscow and Leningrad; New York; Northern Italy; Oxford and Cambridge; Paris and Versailles; Portugal; Rome; Scotland; Sicily; Southern Italy; Spain; Switzerland; Turkey; Venice; Wales; and *Yugoslavia* are in print. 'The whole of the Blue Guide series ... offers the best guides to have appeared since the nineteenth century Baedeckers' (*Reference Reviews*, v.5,no.11, 1991, p.43). *Class No:* 914/919.9

[2690]
The Rough guides. London, Routledge & Kegan Paul (later Harrap Columbus). col. illus., maps.
Title in US is *The Real guides.*
Intended to be 'a new kind of travel guide that would fill the gap that existed between the *Blue Guide* (which doesn't tell you where the best beaches are) and the *Place x on $20 a day* guides (which don't tell you much more than how to live cheaply' (*The Independent*, 21 January 1989, p.39). 1992 titles: *The USA, Canada, Romania, Prague, Germany,* and *Thailand. Class No:* 914/919.9

[2691]
The Stateman's year book world gazetteer. Paxton, J., *ed.* 4th ed. London, Macmillan Press, 1991. xiii,693p. ISBN: 0333525272.
1st ed. 1975; 3rd ed. 1986.
8,000 entries for towns, regions, and geographical landmarks. Data: location, description, history, industries, population. Index of 700+ geographical terms p.655-693. 'A valuable reference work, which pleasantly doubles up as a traveller's companion' (*International Affairs*, v.63,no.1, Winter 1986-87, p.177). *Class No:* 914/919.9

[2692]
UNITED STATES. BOARD ON GEOGRAPHIC NAMES. Gazetteers. Washington, Defense Mapping Agency Combat Support Center, 1955-. tables.
A world series of country gazetteers, Afghanistan-Zambia, of standard names approved by the Board on Geographic Names and unapproved variants. The single line entries include coordinates, evaluation of the quality of the names, designations (*i.e.,* cities, mountains, rivers *etc.*), and political administrative unit. Includes undersea features. By far the most comprehensive and detailed of their kind.
Foreign names decisions of the US Board on Geographic

....(contd.)
Names contains information about recent decisions. They are not cumulative. *Names of political entities of the world* is published approximately every 15 months. *Class No:* 914/919.9

[2693]
Webster's new geographical dictionary. Rev. ed. Springfield, Massachusetts, Merriam, 1984. 1568p. tables, maps. ISBN: 0877794464.
First published 1949 as *Webster's geographical dictionary.*
A gazetteer, not a dictionary of geographical terms. Over 47,000 place-names entries, plus over 15,000 cross-references. Geographical terms (over 450 in *c.*12 languages),. Entries state pronunciation, word division and basic data (location; features; history) on countries, regions, cities and natural features. 217 black-and-white maps.'US and Canada have the largest number of entries, and all incorporated places with populations in excess of 2,500 are included' (*RQ*, v.12,no.3, Spring 1973, p.324). Helpful tables (*e.g.,* Greater London). 'A must for any reference, school or public library, as well as many commercial and all newspaper offices' (*Times Educational Supplement*, no.3017,23 March 1973, p.23). *Class No:* 914/919.9

Encyclopaedias

[2694]
CANBY, C. The Encyclopaedia of historic places. New York, Facts On File; London, Mansell Publishing Ltd., 2 vols, 1984. v,1051p. illus. ISBN: 0720116902, the set; 0720116937, vol.1; 0720116945, vol.2.
Geographic locations of historic significance (towns, cities, countries, provinces and regions, empires, deserts, forts and battle sites, lakes and rivers, mountains, shrines and archaeological sites 'including many places not found in standard reference books') pinpointed in A-Z entries by most common English name. 'Should become librarians' first choice as a source of short histories' (*Wilson Library Bulletin*, v.58, no.10, June 1984, p.753). *Class No:* 914/919.9(031)

Europe

[2695]
Michelin green tourist guides. Harrow, Mdx, Michelin Tyre PLC., 1992. pbk.
English language: *Austria, Canada, England - The West Country, Germany, Great Britain, Greece, Ireland, Italy, London, Mexico, Netherlands, New England, New York City, Portugal, Quebec, Rome, Scotland, Spain, Switzerland, Washington.*
French language: *Belgique & Luxembourg, Hollande, Londres, Maroc.*
Detailed descriptions of places of interest, local culture,

....(contd.)
history and touring programmes with plans of towns and buildings. Cross referenced to corresponding Michelin Maps and Red Guides. *Class No: 914*

Great Britain

[2696]
AA book of British towns. London, Drive Publications for The Automobile Association, 1982. 432p. illus. (mostly col.), col.maps.
First published 1979.
Complete guide to 691 towns and cities (more than 20,000 population) with guided tours of 11 largest. Exploring London p.224-71. Glossary of architectural and historical terms p.430.1. 212 maps in colour. 616 colour and 248 b/w. illustrations. *Class No: 914.10*

[2697]
AA book of British villages a guide to 700 of the most interesting and attractive villages in Britain. Reprinted with amendments. London, Drive Publications for The Automobile Association, 1985. 448p. col.illus., maps, indexes. ISBN: 0903356287.
First published 1980.
A-Z gazetteer p.8-416 plus 13 special features e.g., 'Discovering village history' (R. Parker); 'How villages got their names' (M. Gelling); 'Lost villages' (W.S. Hoskins). 13 Regional maps. Gazetteer of village craft centres p.444-47. *Class No: 914.10*

[2698]
GREAT BRITAIN. ORDNANCE SURVEY. The Ordnance Survey gazetteer of Great Britain. 3rd ed. Southampton, Ordnance Survey; London, Macmillan Reference Books, 1992. xiii, 816p. ISBN: 033357897x.
1st ed. 1987, 2nd ed. 1989.
Lists 256,000 named features on O.S. Landranger Map Series (1:50,000 *i.e.* 1¼ inches to the mile) covering England, Scotland and Wales on 204 sheets. Data: Name; County; National Grid Reference; Latitude and Longitude; Feature code (antiquity, forest, hill *etc.*); and Sheet number. 'The sheer scale of the work makes it an invaluable tool' (*Refer*, v.4, no.1, Spring 1986, p.16). *Class No: 914.10*

[2699]
HUDSON, K. and NICHOLLS, A. The Cambridge guide to the historic places of Britain and Ireland. Cambridge, Cambridge Univ. Press, 1989. viii, [16]p., maps, 326p. illus. (28 col.), indexes. ISBN: 0521360773.
Descriptive gazetteer of the amenities and opening hours of 1567 monuments and buildings including all major National Trust and English Heritage sites, industrial monuments, gardens, battlefields, literary shrines, spas, shops, theatres *etc.*, 8 regional double-page location maps. Place and subject indexes. *Class No: 914.10*

Ireland

[2700]
Shell guide to Ireland. Killanin, Lord *and* Duignan, M.V., *Updated by Peter Harbison.* Rev. ed. London, Macmillan, 1989. 340p. illus. (some col.), col. maps, bibliog., index. ISBN: 0333469577.
1st ed. 1962.
This edition is substantially revised. Bibliography p.340. 'One of the very few reliable and comprehensive guides to the monuments, museums, and culture of the island' (*The Times*, no.63489, p.31). *Class No: 914.15*

England

London

[2701]
NICHOLSON, L. London: Louise Nicholson's definitive guide. Rev. ed. London, the Bodley Head, 1990. x,382p. maps, bibliog., index, pbk. ISBN: 0370314530.
1. Arriving and surviving - 2. Hotels - 3. Instant London: follow my leader - 4. Royalty and pageantry - 5. London day by day: exploring the centre on foot - 6. London on wheels - 7. Rain - 8. London entertains - 9. Food and drink - 10. Spend, spend, spend - 11. Fitness and fresh air. The London year: a month by month directory of events p.352-6. Key dates in London's history p.362-4. Bibliography p.367-9. Winner of the London Tourist Board award: Best London Guide. *Class No: 914.21*

Wales

[2702]
TOMES, J. Blue guide Wales. 7th ed. London, A & C Black; New York, W.W. Norton, 1990. 326p. illus., maps, index. ISBN: 0713631538, UK; 0393306887, US.
Formerly published as *Blue Guide Wales and the Marches.*
1A. Background information (Countries of Wales, Eisteddfod, The Flag (Red Dragon), Industrial archaeology, History p.25-42, Biographical notes p.42-53 etc.) - 1B. Practical information (Organizations like Wales Tourist Board. CADW, Welsh Development Agency) - 2. Detailed descriptions of 46 routes criss-crossing the Principality, illustrated and with maps and plans. An indispensable guide 'excellent on detailed historic and geographical background' (*Observer*, no.10,399, 3 February 1991, p.59). *Class No: 914.29*

France

[2703]
Michelin green tourist guides France Guides verts touristiques. Harrow, Mdx., Michelin Tyre PLC., 1992. pbk.
English language: *Brittany, Burgundy, Chateaux of the Loire, Dordogne, Euro Disney, France, French Riviera, Ile de France, Normandy-Contentin-Channel Islands, Normandy-Seine Valley, Paris, Provence.*
French language: *Alpes du Nord, Alpes du Sud, Alsace et Lorraine, Auvergne, Berry-Limousin, Bourgogne, Bretagne, Champagne-Ardennes, Chateaux de la Loire, Corse, Côte d'Azur, Flandres-Artois-Picardie, France, Gorges du Tarn, Ile de France, Jura, Normandie-Cotentin, Normandie-Seine, Paris, Perigord-Quercy, Poitou-Vendée-Charentes, Provence, Pyrénées-Aquitaine, Pyéénées-Roussillon, Vallée du Rhône.* *Class No: 914.4*

Canada

[2704]
CANADA. DEPARTMENT OF MINES AND TECHNICAL SURVEYS. GEOGRAPHICAL BRANCH. Gazetteers of Canada. Ottawa, Canadian Government Publishing Centre, 1952-. pbk or mircrofiche.
First published by the Canadian Permanent Committee on Geographical Names (1952-62).
List of place-names with brief description or identification, location and coordinates. *Alberta* C$19.50. ISBN 0660539842 - *British Columbia,* 3rd ed. 1985. C$22.50. 0660527731 - *Manitoba,* 3rd ed. 1981. C$8.00. 0660508486 - *New Brunswick* (Microfiche only) C$3.00 - *Newfoundland,* 2nd ed. 1983. C$12.00. 0660521911 - *Northwest Territories,* 1980. C$7.00. 0660504669 - *Nova Scotia,* 2nd ed. 1977. C$10.00. 0660016745 - *Ontario,* 3rd ed. 1988. C$ 19.95. 0660518644 - *Prince Edward Island,*

....(contd.)
2nd ed. 1973. C\$1.50 - *Saskatchewan,* 3rd ed. 1985.
C\$8.00. 0660530481 - *Yukon Territory,* 4th ed. 1981.
(Microfiche only) C\$2.00. Bilingual. *Class No:* 917.1

USA

[2705]
A Historical guide to the United States. New York, W.W.
Norton, 1986. 601p. illus., index. ISBN: 0393023834.
Short essays providing a practical guide (representative
rather than exhaustive) to places of historical interest in
every State of the Union. Well indexed (p.579-601). 'The
strength of this book is that it presents a national overview
of the major state and local museums and scenic and
historical sites in one volume' (*Choice,* v.24, no.9, May
1987, p.1380). *Class No:* 917.3

Australia

[2706]
The Heritage of Australia the illustrated register of the
national estate. Melbourne, Macmillan Company of
Australia in association with Australian Heritage
Commission, 1981. various pagination. illus., (some col.),
maps, bibliogs., index. ISBN: 0333337506.
6,600 places of historical interest (buildings and
structures, national parks, Aboriginal sites, etc.) expertly
described. Arranged State by State in 40 regional sections.
Glossary p.86-89. Analytical index. Over 7,500 photographs.
Monumental work. *Class No:* 919.4

Papua—New Guinea

[2707]
Papua New Guinea handbook : Business and travel guide. 11th
ed. Sydney, Pacific Publications, 1985. 280p. illus., maps,
plans.
First published as *The Handbook of Papua and New
Guinea* in 1954. Revised at intervals.
Geography - History - The People - Land use - Finance -
Commerce - Industry - Transport and communications -
Social services - Religion. Pt.2: Provincial directory. *Class
No:* 919.54

92 Biography

Biography

Worldwide

[2708]

The Annual obituary. Chicago and London, St. James Press, 1980-. Annual. bibliogs., indexes.

1980 and 1981 edition published by St. Martins Press (New York) and Macmillan (London).

1990 volume edited by Deborah Andrews 1991. xxv,850p. ISBN 1558620923. Contains 342 obituaries consisting of a 500-2000 word essay, a detailed bio-bibliographical section and, where relevant, a reading list. All volumes are kept in print with consolidated alphabetical and professional indexes. 'Although focussing on elite personalities, provides well-written analytical essays that supplement major biographical publications' (*Choice*, v.27,no.5, January 1990, p.761). *Class No:* 929(100)

[2709]

Chambers biographical dictionary. Magnusson, M. *and* Goring, R., eds. 5th ed. Edinburgh, Chambers, 1990. xii,1604p. ISBN: 055016040x, UK.

1st ed. 1897; 4th ed. 1961. In North America published as *Cambridge biographical dictionary* (Cambridge Univ. Press, $34.50. 0521395186).

80 contributors. Contains 20,000 profiles of famous persons from earliest times to the present day ($\frac{1}{3}$ larger than the previous edition). Now gives greater prominence to 20th century figures, especially women, and focusses more attention on areas such as art, business, films, the media, politics, sport, and theatre, with a broader international overview, particularly United States and Australia (R. Benaud 10 lines, R.B. Simpson 12 lines but no entry for A.R. Border). Entries give an essential outline of life and achievements. 'As a single-volume, worldwide, all-period biographical dictionary, this has no peers' (*Library Journal*, v.116,no.1, January 1991, p.88). *Class No:* 929(100)

[2710]

Current biography. New York, H.W. Wilson, 1940-. Monthly except December. ports. ISSN: 00113344.

Each monthly issue now contains 16-18 profiles, some 2500-3000 words in length, of people 'who make today's headlines and tomorrow's history. Biographies are rewritten and updated when necessary. In December the monthly biographies are revised and cumulated into a single A-Z sequence in the *Current biography yearbook*. *Class No:* 929(100)

[2711]

—**Current biography yearbook.** New York, H.W. Wilson, 1940-. Annual. ISSN: 00849499.

A cumulation, published in December, of all biographies printed in the previous 11 months issues of *Current*

....(contd.)

biography to which are added a list of sources consulted, a classification of the subjects profiled by their professions, and a cumulative index to the articles from all previous *Yearbooks* of the decade. *Class No:* 929(100)

[2712]

Current Biography cumulated index 1940-1990. New York, H.W. Wilson, 1991. 135p. ISBN: 0824208196.

Provides access to almost 20,000 biographies. Lists subjects of all the articles and revisions and obituaries in *Current biography*. Entries include changes in title and cross-references to variants and pseudonyms. *Class No:* 929(100)

[2713]

The International who's who 1991-92. 55th ed. London, Europa Publications, 1991. Distributed in North America by Gale Research Co. xx,1800p. ISBN: 0946653704.

1st ed. 1935.

Nearly 20,000 biographies (12,000 new to this edition). Data: date of birth, nationality, education, career, honours, personal details. Reigning royal families A-Z by country p.xiii-xvii. Obituaries (listed since previous edition) p.xviii-xx. 'Each new edition of this authoritative work of reference is the result of a thorough revision of its predecessor' (*International Affairs*, v.61,no.4, August 1985, p.736-7). *Class No:* 929(100)

[2714]

McGraw-Hill encyclopedia of world biography. New York, London, McGraw-Hill, 12v., 1973. illus., ports., maps.

5,000 biographical articles by 1,2000 specialists. The articles, international in scope, averaging *c*.800 words in length were selected - according to the prospectus - 'for their relevance to today's curriculum for pupils of 12 to 17 years. Appended bibliography in each case, often with portrait, etc. 6,000 illus. in all. V.12 forms the index (100,000 entries) and has 17 study guides, plus reference to other biographical works. *Class No:* 929(100)

[2715]

Newsworthies people in the news. Biggleswade, Beds., Clover Publications, 1987-. 2pa., annual cumulation.

1990 v. covers September 1988 to August 1989. Its mimeographed, single-line entries record obituaries, interviews and profiles drawn from *The Times, Sunday Times, Observer, The Independent, Daily Telegraph, Guardian, Financial Times* and as listed in the weekly *Clover Newspaper Index* or *Clover Information Index*. *Class No:* 929(100)

[2716]

Webster's new biographical dictionary. Springfield, Massachusetts, Merriam-Webster, 1983. xviii,1130p. ISBN: 0877795436.

....*(contd.)*

Webster's biographical dictionary first published 1943. This was updated 21 times.

Based firmly upon its predecessor but 'wholly revised and reedited'. One major change: living persons are not now included. 30,000 biographies 'present in a single volume biographical information on important, celebrated, or notorious figures from the last five thousand years, beginning with Menes, King of Egypt, *c.*3100 B.C. This new work has increased coverage of Asia, Africa and Third World countries but main emphasis remains on American, Canadian and British subjects. Biographies p.1-1090. Pronouncing lists of name elements, titles, and prenames p.1091-1130. Thumb index. *Class No:* 929(100)

[2717]
Who's who in international affairs. London, Europa, 1990. Distributed in North America by Gale Research Co. 640p. indexes. ISBN: 0946653631.

Over 7,000 biographical entries for principal figures in the spheres of international politics and economics, cultural, and scientific affairs. Data: date and place of birth; family details; education; positions held and years appointed; current position; publications *etc.* Nationality and organization indexes. 'Provides biographical information on many people who are difficult to locate elsewhere' (*Booklist,* v.87,no.18, 15 May 1991, p.1836). *Class No:* 929(100)

Bibliographies

[2718]
Bibliography of biography 1970-84. London, The British Library, Bibliographic Services, 1985. 40 x 1.8 reduction negative microfiche+binder for permanent storage.

95,000 titles (autobiographies, biographies, letters and diaries of historical and contemporary figures) published worldwide in 2 alphabetical sequences: by name of individual concerned and an author-title index. Compiled from catalogue of records created by The British Library and The Library of Congress. *Class No:* 929(100)(01)

[2719]
—**Bibliography of biography 1988.** London, The British Library. Bibliographic Services, 1988. 454p. ISBN: 0712310460. ISSN: 09554629.

List of biographical works published & worldwide extracted from MARC records created in 1988 by British Library Bibliographic Services and Library of Congress in 2 sequences *viz.* Name sequence (names as subjects) with detailed bibliographical information and Author-Title index. Entries conform to AACR2. for librarians, researchers and booksellers. *Bibliography of biography 1989.* 1990. 571p. softback. £60. (UK), £70. (overseas). ISBN 0712310517 contains information on over 7,000 titles. *Class No:* 929(100)(01)

[2720]
Biography index: a cumulative index to biographical material in books and magazines. New York, H.W. Wilson, 1946-, v.1-. Quarterly paperbound issues and an annual cumulation. ISSN: 00063053.

Based on more than 2600 periodicals regularly scanned in the Wilson indexes plus works of individual and collective (auto)biographies, and obituaries. The main section is A-Z by biographees (full name, dates, nationality, profession, and full bibliographic citation). The 2nd section is an index to professions and occupations. There are 17 biennial or triennial retrospective volumes 1946-August 1992 each $160.00 US and Canada, $190.00 elsewhere. Available on the Wilsondisc database. *Class No:* 929(100)(01)

[2721]
Dictionary of universal biography of all ages and all peoples. Hyamson, A.M., *ed.*   2nd ed. (reprint). Detroit, Gale Research Co., 1981. xii,680p. ISBN: 0810341506.

1st ed. 1916. 2nd ed. London, Routledge; New York, E.P. Dutton, 1951.

A finding list of *c.*110,000 biographies contained in the 23 most comprehensive biographical dictionaries and encyclopaedias. Does not include living persons. Entries, usually single-line, include name, nationality, profession, dates (where known) and a coded reference to original dictionary. *Class No:* 929(100)(01)

[2722]
LOBIES, J.P. Index bio-bibliographicus notorum hominum. Osnabrück, Biblio Verlag, 1972-. ISBN: 3764807261, complete work.

A. *Allgemeine Einführung.* 1972. B. List of bibliographical works 1972-73. C. *Corpus alphabeticum.* 1976-. v.1-. A (general introduction) has 3 sections: 1. Universal biographies; 2. Biographical works arranged on geographical, historical and linguistic principles (2,000 items); 3. Biographical reference works by vocations (subjects and activities). B. enumerates 5145 bibliographies cited in Part A; author and subject indexes. C. has entries under biographies A-Z. V.52 to Demetrios Demopoulos. V.23 has supplements to B. (entries 5146-5500); v.24 (entries 5501-5750; v.25 (entries 5751-6000); v.40 (entries 6001-6148); v.47 (entries 6149-6215) 1990. V.45/47. Supplement III. *Sectio Sinica cum supplemento Coreano* (v.1 1976) includes a foreword on How to use Index bibliographies for Chinese names. V.2. *Ban yong - Bo Zong* (1979). *Sectio Ameniaca. V.1A-D* (1982); *E-M* (1985); *N-V and Supplement A-V* (1987). 'The aim of this work is a world wide brief biographical presentation of all personalities - including those of the second or third rank - who have been significant in one or the other way for the history of mankind' 3-5 million entries will be listed eventually in this massive and tortuous index. *Class No:* 929(100)(01)

Awards & Prizes

[2723]
Nobel Prize winners: an H.W. Wilson biographical dictionary. Wesson, T., *ed.*   New York, H.W. Wilson, 1987. xxxiv,1165p. illus., bibliogs. ISBN: 0824207564.

566 x 1500 word profiles of Nobel Prize winners 1901-1986 offering 'a narrative overview of a laureate's life and career, while focussing on the individual's prizewinning work and attempting to assess its significance'. List of winners p.vii-xii. Winners by prize category p.xiii-xix. Alfred Nobel p.xxiii-xxviii. The Nobel Prizes and Nobel Institutions p.xxix-xxxiii. Quinquennial supplements will be published beginning in 1992. 'The work has more depth than *Who's Who of Nobel Prize Winners* ed. by Bernard S. and June H. Schlessinger (1986)' (*Choice* v.25,no.8, April 1988, p.1224). *Class No:* 929(100)(079.2)

Women

[2724]
The Macmillan dictionary of women's biography. Uglow, J.S., *ed.*   2nd ed. London, Macmillan Reference Books, 1988. xvii,534p. ports, bibliog., index. ISBN: 0333453034.

1st ed. 1982. Published in US as *The Continuum dictionary of women's biography* (Continuum Publishing Co.).

Essential details of over 2000 women drawn from all periods and cultures with emphasis on British Isles, the Commonwealth, Europe and North America although this edition has an extended treatment of women from 'Third

....(contd.)

World' countries. 'An excellent reference source. Its scope and compact nature will save users much time. Highly recommended' (*Library Journal*, v.108,no.5, 1 March 1983, p.489). *Class No:* 929(100)-0055.2

Europe—Eastern

[2725]

STROYNOWSKI, J., *ed.* Who's who in the socialist countries of Europe: a biographical encyclopedia of more than 12,600 leading personalities in Albania, Bulgaria, Czechoslovakia, German Democratic Republic, Hungary, Poland, Romania, Yugoslavia. München, New York, London, Paris, K.G. Saur, 3v., 1989. ISBN: 359810636x, set.

Formerly published as *Who's who in the socialist countries* (1978).

V.1 *A-H. Index*, lx, 461p. ISBN 3598107196. Abbreviations and terms p.ix-xiii. Name index arranged by country p.xv-lx. V.2 *I-O* v, 462-878p. ISBN 359810720x. V.3 *P-Z* v, 879-1367p. ISBN 3598107471.

Biographies of eminent individuals from the spheres of party, government, military, diplomacy, economics, literature, religion, art, and press. Also 350 dissidents. Data: full name, nationality, profession, family background, real name, detailed biography (*e.g.*, Lech Walesa 55 lines; Nicolae Ceauşescu 52 lines), publications, honours, decorations, prizes. *Class No:* 929(401)

Great Britain

[2726]

British biographical index. Bank, D. *and* Exposito, A., *comps.* London, K.G. Saur, 4v., 1990. xx,2045p. ISBN: 086291390x, set.

1. *A-C.* 08692913918. 2. *D-I.* 0869213926. 3. *J-Q.* 0869213934. 4. *R-Z* 0869213942. Index to *British biographical archive* which also stands as a biographical dictionary in its own right, listing 170,000 names from 324 biographical reference works published 1601-1929 in a single A-Z sequence. Data: full name; alternative forms of name; dates of birth and death; occupation; sources (original reference work); and exact location in the *Archive* where subject's life is documented. List of sources p.vii-ix in all 4v. Customers who have already purchased the *Archive* automatically receive a copy of this printed index gratis. *Class No:* 929(410)

[2727]

The Dictionary of national biography. Oxford, Oxford Univ. Press, 1885-.

1. *The Dictionary of national biography, from the earliest times to 1900.* Edited by Sir Lesley Stephen and Sir Sidney Lee. London, Smith, Elder, 63v., 1885-1900. *First Supplement* in 3v. 1901 for those lives accidentally ommited or who had died after their letter was in print. Using thinner paper the standard edition is now reduced to 22v. incorporating 30,000 lives in 30,500p. retaining the two alphabetical sequences. £795.00. ISBN 0198651015.

2. *The Twentieth Century DNB. The Dictionary of national biography 1901-1911,* edited by Sir Sydney Lee. 1912. 2,088p. £65.00. ISBN 0198652011.

The Dictionary of national biography 1912-1921, edited by H.W.C. Davis and J.R.H. Weaver, 1927. xxvi, 623p. £60.00. ISBN 019865202x.

The Dictionary of National Biography 1922-1930, edited by J.R.H. Weaver, 1937, xiv, 962p. £65.00. ISBN 0198652038.

The Dictionary of National Biography 1931-1940, edited by L.G. Wickham Legg, 1949, xvi, 968p. £65.00. ISBN 0198652046.

The Dictionary of National Biography 1941-1950, edited by L.G. Wickham Legg, and E.T. Williams, 1959. xxi,

....(contd.)

1031p. £65.00. ISBN 0198652054.

The Dictionary of National Biography 1951-1960, edited by E.T. Williams and Helen M. Palmer, 1971. xxvi, 1150p. £65.00. ISBN 0198652062.

The Dictionary of National Biography 1961-1970, edited by E.T. Williams and C.S. Nicholls, 1981. 1170p. £65.00. ISBN 0198652070.

The Dictionary of national biography 1971-1980, edited by Lord Blake and C.S. Nicholls, 1986. xix, 1010p. £65.00. ISBN 0198652089. With a cumulative index 1901-1980. 'De mortuis nil nisi bunkum - here was a principle which served the twentieth-century *DNB* for many years. In the latest volume, however, the new chief editor conclusively demonstrates that it has been abandoned' (*English Historical Review*, v.103, no.406, January 1988, p.156-8).

The Dictionary of national biography 1981-1985: with an index covering the years 1901-1985 in one alphabetical series, edited by Lord Blake and C.S. Nicholls, 1990. 608p. £40.00. ISBN 0198652100.

The concise dictionary of national biography: from earliest times to 1985. 3v., 1992. £125.00. Includes over 36,500 biographies.

DNB now includes some 35,000 signed entries. Bibliographies are given and the sources of the information are quoted. 'For more than a century it has furnished us with a carefully-written profile of every man or woman who has left a thumb-print on the island story. No other nation can boast a reference work so magisterially exact and yet so hypnotically readable' (*Sunday Times*, 25 March 1990, p.C7).

Further information: 1. J.L. Kirby's 'The Dictionary of National Biography', *Library Association Record*, v.60, no.6, June 1958, p. 181-91-. 2. A. Bell's Leslie Stephen and DNB', *Times Literary Supplement*, 16 December 1977, p.1478 - 3. R.H. Fritze's 'The Dictionary of National Biography and its early editors and publisher', *Reference Services Review*, v.16, no.4, 1988, p.21-29). *Class No:* 929(410)

[2728]

People of today. Ellis, P., *ed.* 4th ed. London, Debrett's Peerage, 1991. 64p+2125p+15p. ISBN: 1870520041.

1st ed. 1988. Previous editions under title of *Debrett's distinguished people of today.* This was a successor to *Debrett's Handbook* the 3rd and last edition of which appeared in 1986.

Over 40,000 entries encompassing top people in business, medicine, publishing, sport, education and academia, art and antiques, politics *etc.* 14% of whom are women (John Major: 18 lines; Neil Gordon Kinnock: 10 lines; Jeremy John Durham Ashdown: 9 lines). 64 preliminary pages include valuable reference information on The Royal Family and Royal households, Her Majesty's Officers of Arms, general tables of precedence, position of letters after the name, and forms of address of persons of title. Abbreviations include ALA, FLA and FIInfSc. 'Has caused a flap in blue-blood circles because it has seen fit to exclude 400 'superfluous gentry' and instead let in a shower of famous proletarians ... and a shoal of media darlings' (*Sunday Times*, no.8702, 2 June 1991, p.2:5). A detailed look at the selection policy for this edition appears in Geraldine Bedell's 'Bringing the best of the rest to book', *ibid;* 30 September 1990, p.5:2. *Class No:* 929(410)

[2729]

Who's who an annual biographical dictionary 1992. 144th year. 1992. London, A & C Black, 1849-. Annual. 56p+2069p.

Published originally by Bailey Bros, and later by Simpkin, Marshall, Kent, it was in its early days mainly lists of names under various headings, *e.g.* Royal Household, House of Commons, etc, without any individual

....(contd.)
biographical details. It continued in this style until it was bought by A. & C. Black in 1896. The following year it became *Who's who*, 49th year, 1897 (first year of new issue, edited by Douglas Sladen). Its aim now was 'to include all the most prominent people in the Kingdom, whether their prominence is inherited, or depending upon office, or the result of ability which singles them out from their fellows in occupations open to every educated man and women'. In 1899 the title became *Who's who, 1988, an annual biographical dictionary*. In 1901 it incorporated *Men and women of the time*, adjusted its title and has appeared in this style ever since.

Scope. An authoritative dictionary of contemporary biography, the aim being 'to furnish in as compact a form as possible a series of biographical sketches of eminent living persons of both sexes, in all parts of the civilized world'. The criterion of selection is that of 'personal achievement or prominence, and of a man's or woman's interest to the public at large or to any important section of that public'. Compilation. Initially a questionnaire is sent to a person chosen for inclusion and thereafter a proof of the entry is submitted annually to the biographee for revision. This edition has 28,000 entries (1,000 new): John Major, Neil Kinnock and John Thaw all have 15 lines. *Class No:* 929(410)

[2730]
—Who was who ... a companion to Who's who containing the biographies of those who died in the decade... London, A.C. Black, 1929-.
1897-1915. 7th ed., 1987. £40. ISBN 0713626704. *1916-1928.* 5th ed., 1992. £40. 0723601698. *1929-1940.* 2nd ed., 1967. £40. 0713601701. *1941-1950.* 5th ed., 1981. £40. 0713621311. *1951-1960.* 4th ed., 1984. £40. 0713625988. *1961-1970.* 2nd ed., 1979. £40. 0713620080. *1971-1980.* 1981. £40. 0713621761. *1981-1990.* 1992. 845p. 0713633360.

Gives birth and death dates and acts as a key to the appropriate volume. 'The entries are for the most part as they last appeared in Who's who, with the dates of death added and in some cases further additional information to bring them up to date' (*Preface*). *Who was who: a cumulated index 1897-1990.* 1991. 850p. £50. 071363457x. *Class No:* 929(410)

Micromaterials

[2731]
British and Irish biographies 1840-1940. Jones, D.L., *ed.*
Cambridge and Alexandria, Virginia, Chadwyck-Healey, 6 parts, 1985-1991. 1400 silver halide microfiche 105mmx148mm, 24xreduction with a cumulated index of names and titles on COM.
Claimed to be the largest British biographical reference work ever compiled, this collection makes available 272 general, professional, and regional biographical dictionaries, containing $6\frac{1}{2}$ million entries on 4 million people largely unrepresented in *DNB* or *Who's who*. 1. 382v. on 2218 microfiche with computer output microfiche (COM) index includes 10 general dictionaries: *Burke's handbook to the Most Excellent Order of the British Empire* (1921); *Burke's landed gentry* (1833-1947); *Celebrities of the century* (1890); *Hutchinson women's who's who* (1934); *Ladies who's who 1919-27* (1930); *Men and women of the day (1889-1894); Men of mark 1876-1873* by T. Cooper; *Men of the time 1852-87* continued as *Men and women of the time 1891-1899; People of the period* by A.T. Camden Pratt (1897); and *Women of the day* by F. Hoyt (1885). Plus 14 professional and 31 regional biographical dictionaries. 2. 168v. on 2179 microfiche includes *The biographical quarterly, recording biographical data of noteworthy citizens of the English-speaking countries 1935-36* and *Debrett's*

....(contd.)
Peerage 1900-40 plus 10 professional and 32 regional works. 3. 236v. on 2455 microfiche includes *Debrett's Peerage 1864-1899* and *The Knightage of Great Britain and Ireland 1841* plus 10 professional and 25 regional works. 4. 164v. on *c.*2400 microfiche including *The upper ten thousand: an alphabetical list of all members of noble families, bishops, privy councillors, judges ... 1875-77* continued as *Kelly's handbook to the titled, landed and official classes 1880-1937* continued as *Kelly's handbook of distinguished people 1938-40* plus 10 professional and 21 regional works. 5. Published June 1990. 6. Published June 1991. Many of the works reproduced were originally printed in small editions and access is difficult in any other form. *Class No:* 929(410)(003.5)

[2732]
British biographical archive. Baillie, L. *and* Sieveking, P., *eds.*
London, K.G. Saur, 1984-1989. 1400x1:24 negative fiches either in Diazo or Silver edition. ISBN: 0862913659, Diazo; 0862913667, Silver.
A single A-Z cumulation of full-text entries from 324 English language biographical reference works originally published 1601-1929 covering every aspect of British biography. *DNB* and *Who was who* are not included. Entries for each individual are arranged together in chronological order. 'British' is interpreted to include inhabitants of colonies born up to a year before independence or home rule and foreign nationals closely associated with Britain. Particularly useful for libraries not holding older standard biographical works. *British biographical index.* compiled by L. Baillie, 4v., 1990-1994. 1600p. £398.00. ISBN 086291390x is a printed index listing in a single sequence all 170,000 persons included in the *Archive*. C.A. Toase's 'Micro biography', *Refer*, v.4, no.3, Spring 1987, p.1-5 compares the coverage, arrangement and presentation, and access in the library of *British & Irish biographies 1840-1940* and *British biographical archive*: 'There is hardly any overlap in titles between the two works'. *Class No:* 929(410)(003.5)

Bibliographies

[2733]
MATTHEWS, W., *comp.* **British autobiographies:** an annotated bibliography of British autobiographies published or written before 1951. Berkeley, Univ. of California Press, 1955. xiv,376p.
Reprinted Hamden, Conn., Archon Books, 1968.
6,654 very briefly annotated entries for persons 'born in the British Isles' and 'naturalised British subjects'. Arranged A-Z, anonymous works under the first word of the title. Subject and locality index of biographees. *Class No:* 929(410)(01)

Scotland

[2734]
Who's who in Scotland 1990-91. 3rd ed. Ayr, Carrick Publishing, 1990. 520p. ISBN: 0946724245.
1st ed. 1986; 2nd ed. 1988.
4950 entries (800 for the first time) relating to 'people of achievement and influence from all sections of Scottish society (David Steel: 30 lines; Graeme Souness: 8 lines). Data: name, present occupation, date and place of birth, family, education, publications, recreations, address. Libraries should retain previous editions which contain entries deleted from current edition. *Class No:* 929(411)

Ireland

[2735]
A Dictionary of Irish biography.

Aidan Duggan's 'A dictionary of Irish biography', *Scholarly Publishing*, v.20,no.1, October 1988,p.39-42 is an account of the 10 year planning towards the launching in 1986 of the Royal Irish Academy's project: 'The Dictionary will contain biographies and assessments of all men and women of note who died on or before 31 December 1989 and who fall into one or other of the following four categories. i Those who were born in Ireland and who in some manner achived a reputation within their native land. ii Those who were born outside Ireland but who came to Ireland and there in some manner achieved an Irish reputation. iii Those who were born in Ireland but who left their native land and in some manner achieved a reputation overseas. iv Those who were neither born in Ireland nor resident in Ireland but who achieved reputations and who clearly liked to think of themselves as essentially Irish. It is hoped that this first volume will be ready for publication in 1992 and that five more volumes will appear at approximately intervals of two to three years'. *Class No:* 929(415)

England

[2736]
BOASE, F. Modern English biography. London, F. Cass, 6v., 1985. ISBN: 0714621188.

Originally published Truro, Netherton & Worth, 1892-1921.

A most valuable work, supplementing the *DNB*, particularly for the lesser-known personalities of the 19th century. Each volume contains an analytical index to the entries. About 30,000 short biographical sketches of persons who died between 1851 and 1900. Notes sources of portraits (photographs), lists published works, theatre performances and other facts sometimes omitted in larger works of reference, states the *Times Literary Supplement* leader (no.3,330, 23 December 1965, p.1189-90). Draws on obituaries and notices in *The Times, Illustrated London News* and journals, as well as local newspapers, records, etc., and so has a greater coverage of national and local celebrities who died in the latter part of the 19th century than *DNB* (*qv*). The sub-title of the supplement varies, stating the scope as covering those 'who have died during the years 1851-1900'.

Index to biographies of women in Boase's Modern English Biography, (Edinburgh, Peter Bell, 1986. 30 unnumbered pages, sd. ISBN 0946687072) identifies 1130 women entries. Data: birth and death dates and occupation. A number of other subject indexes will be published. *Class No:* 929(420)

Wales

[2737]
The Dictionary of Welsh biography down to 1940. London, Honourable Society of Cymmrodorion, 1959. lx,1157p.

Based on the Welsh ed. of 1953.

3,500 signed articles, covering all periods and walks of life. For inclusion the biographee or at least one parent had to be born in Wales. 'The intervening years have enabled the editors to make many corrections' (*Preface*). Appendix of additional biographies. *Class No:* 929(429)

Germany

[2738]
Neue deutsche Biographie. Hrsg. von der Historischen Kommission bei der Bayerischen Akademie der Wissenschaften. Berlin, Dunker & Humblot, 1953-. v.1-. ISBN: 3428001818, complete work.

Largely based on *Allgemeine deutsche Biographie* (1873-1912).

V.16 Maly-Melanchthon (1990. xiv,785p.). Includes all who have had an influence on German history and culture. Signed entries with bibliographies and details of portraits. Monumental work with completion many years ahead. *Class No:* 929(430)

France

[2739]
Dictionnaire de biographie française. Paris, Librarie Letouzey et Ané, 1929-. v.1-. ISBN: 2706301589, complete work.

V.1-16 (1929-1985); A-Guéroult: fasc:97-104 (1986-1990). Lengthy, authoritative, signed articles with good bibliographies and/or sources used. Includes outstanding Frenchmen and women from Metropolitan France and dependent territories, from the earliest times; also foreigners who have played an important part in the life of France. Excludes living persons. *DNB* was one of the models on which the work is based. *Class No:* 929(44)

[2740]
Who's who in France Qui est qui en France Dictionnaire biographique de personalités françaises vivant en France, dans les territoires d'Outre-mer où à l'étranger et de personalités étrangères résident en France 1990-1991. 22nd ed. Paris, Éditions Jacques Lafitte, 1990. 1708p. col. illus. ISBN: 285784025x. ISSN: 00839531.

First published 1953.

Pt.1 Les Grands Institutions. Souverains et chefs d'État depuis l'an 751. Présidents de la République ... Decorations officielles françaises . Régions, départments et villes de France - 2. Le Who's Who des Enterprises - 3. Notices biographiques (p.119-1664) - 4. Vie pratique *i.e.* 9 essays on such topics as Tourisme et voyages, Guide des vins, Guide des médias. *Class No:* 929(44)

USSR

[2741]
The Soviet Union a biographical dictionary. Brown, A., *ed.* London, Weidenfeld and Nicolson, 1990. xiv,489p. bibliog. ISBN: 0297820109.

35 contributors. 1400 initialled brief entries and longer essays on prominent figures in Soviet public life since 1917. Appendix 1. Subject and profession index ... 3. A guide to the changing Soviet institutional structure - 4. Bibliography P.486-7). The author is Professor of Politics in Oxford University. *Class No:* 929(47)

[2742]
Who's who in the Soviet Union today. Schulz-Torge, U-J. München, K.G. Saur, 2v., 1989-91. 800p. ISBN: 3598108108, set; 3598108117, v.1; 3598108125, v.2.

V.1 Chronological survey of leading officials in the party, the State, the KGB and the armed forces. V.2 *Biographical entries for 2000 personalities.* Data: full name, nationality, distinctions, party career. Identifies the key political and military figures. *Class No:* 929(47)

[2743]
—Who's who in the Soviet Union a biographical encyclopedia of 5,000 leading personalities in the Soviet Union. Lewytzkyj, B., *ed.* München, K.G. Saur, 1984. xi,428p. index. ISBN: 3598104677.

....*(contd.)*

In effect this is the 2nd ed. of *Who's who in the socialist countries* (1978) but confined to the Soviet Union.

Brief biographies, based on the editor's private archives of Party, State, Komsomol and Trade Union leaders and functionaries but with less comprehensive coverage of artists and other professional groups because of the paucity of information available. Separate lists of administrative and political figures in all 14 Soviet Socialist Republics. Also lists of authors, artists, military leaders, ecclesiastical dignitaries, jurists, journalists, cosmonauts, architects. 'A fine reference work and a very useful addition to our scanty knowledge of the Soviet élite *International Affairs,* v.61,no.2, Spring 1985,p.348). *Class No:* 929(47)

Micromaterials

[2744]
Public figures in the Soviet Union: a current biographical index 1984-1987. Bi-annual updates: 1988. Cambridge and Alexandria, Virginia, Chadwyck-Healey in association Radio Free Europe - Radio Liberty Inc. 105x148mm diazo negative reading microfiche at a reduction of 48x.

Index commences January 1984 and is updated daily.

A continuously updated cumulated index containing 150,000 entries on 100,000 people in the public eye in the Soviet Union compiled by Radio Liberty published on computer output microfiche (COM) in a storage binder with printed instructions. Entries (in Russian) give surname and patronymic, title, position, organization, place of work, source and notes. Sources include *Pravda, Izvestia,* regional newspapers, party congresses, *etc.* Retrospective material before 1984 is being added selectively to some entries. *Class No:* 929(47)(003.5)

Scandinavia

Micromaterials

[2745]
Scandinavian biographical archive. Metherell, D. *and* Guthrie, P. London, K.G. Saur, 12 instalments 1989-1991. 12 instalments: £6,000 (Diazo); £6,600 (Silver). Separately Part A or B £3,400 (Diazo); £3,600 (Silver). Index (free to subscribers) £250.00.

Pt.A. - Dano - Norwegian - Icelandic section. Pt.B. - Finno - Swedish section. 110,000 individual lives from 8th to early 20th century from 360 biographical reference works published before mid 20th century rearranged into a continuous A-Z sequence. Also includes persons in colonial territories and Scandinavian emigrants worldwide. Each part comprises 400 microfiches published in 6 instalments. On completion these will be supported by the two volumed hard copy *Scandinavian Biographical Index*. *Class No:* 929(48)(003.5)

Asia—Far East

[2746]
Who's who in Australasia and the Far East. Timothy, J., *ed.* 2nd ed. Cambridge, Melrose Press, 1991. 766p. ISBN: 0948875550.

1st ed. 1989.

*c.*5,500 brief biographies of prominent people from 32 countries and territories including Australia, New Zealand, China, Hong Kong, Japan, North and South Korea, the Philippines, Singapore, Malaysia, Vietnam and smaller states like Tonga, Tuvalu and Vanuatu. 'Another valuable publication from the International Bibliographical Centre' (*Choice,* v.27,no.1, September 1989, p.96). *Class No:* 929(51/52+57)

China

20th Century

[2747]
BARTKE, W. Who's who in the People's Republic of China. 3rd ed. London, K.G. Saur, 1990. 900p. ports., index. ISBN: 0598107714.

First published in New York by M.E. Sharpe Inc. and in Brighton, Sussex, by Harvester Press 1981. 2nd ed. published by K.G. Saur in 1987.

'Entries cover a whole range of living Chinese personalities: politicians, soldiers, academics, scientists, diplomats, religious and cultural leaders. Each biography lists posts held, thus enabling the user to assess at a glance the present importance of a party cadre, and includes a photograph where available. Names are also translated into Pinyin, together with Chinese characters... Also contains an occupation index and an appendix on the organisation of the People's Republic of China, with charts and tables detailing the composition and structure of the active leadership of todays China' (*K.G. Saur catalogue*). *Class No:* 929(510)"19"

[2748]
Who's who in China: current leaders. Beijing, Foreign Languages Press, 1990. Distributed by China Books & Periodicals. xx,1126p. illus., index. ISBN: 0835123529.

Biographical sketches of 2,100 current senior officials at central and provincial levels. Parallel Chinese/English text. Appendix: Table of major organizations and their leading officials p.1037-78. *Class No:* 929(510)"19"

Japan

[2749]
Who's who in Japan 1987-88. 2nd ed. Hong Kong, International Culture Institute, 1987. Distributed in North America by Gale Research Co. and in UK by K.G. Saur. [iv],1281p. ISBN: 9627191019, Hong Kong; 3598075251, UK.

First ed. 1984-85.

About 51,000 brief biographies on leading figures in contemporary Japanese society arranged A-Z by family name. Data: name, degree or license, position, education, birthdate, career, honours, membership, hobbies, address and telephone numbers. Biennial revisions are promised. 'Those who can justify purchase will find it to be money well spent' (*Reference Reviews,* v.3,no.1, March 1989, p.42-3). *Class No:* 929(52)

India

[2750]
India Who's who 1990-91. Inder Jit, *ed.* 21st ed. New Delhi, INFA Publications. xxxi,182,168a,196bp. index.

1st published 1969.

5,000 concise biographies (500 new to this edition) of India's leading personalities in government, the armed services; state government, business, arts, crafts, education, literature, medicine, and the sciences. *Class No:* 929(540)

[2751]
SEN, S.P., *ed.* **Dictionary of national biography.** Calcutta, Institute of Historical Studies, 4v., 1972-74.

A-D, E-L, M-R, S-Z. Biographies of *c.*1400 Indians (and also foreigners who made India their home). Covers period 1800-1947 and includes living personalities. All entries are signed. Data: personal and family details; early life; career history; personality; general estimate. 'Tagore, Rabindranath' (1861-1941): 13 columns, including 2 cols. of bibliography. *Dictionary of National Biography (Supplement)* v.1. A-D (1986). edited by N.R. Ray. Covers 1947-1972. 'It is

....(contd.)

expected that the complete set of 4 volumes will be ready for release within 2 years of the appearance of the first volume' (*Preface*). *Class No:* 929(540)

Islamic World

[2752]
Who's who in the Arab World 1990-1991. Gedeon, C.G., *ed.* 10th ed. München, K.G. Saur, Distributed in North America by Gale Research Inc. 992p. bibliog, index. ISBN: 290318805x, Lebanon & US; 3598075626, UK. ISSN: 00839752.

1st ed. 1966. Now issued biennially.

Part 1. Biographical section of *c.*6000 sketches of prominent persons in the Arab World indexed by country and profession - 2. Survey of 20 Arab countries Algeria - Yemen - 3. Outline of Arab World: General survey including The League of Arab States; Mahgreb Permanent Consultative Committee; Arab petroleum; Suez Canal; Development of Arab banks; Palestinian problem; Gulf Cooperation Council. Bibliography p.991-2. 'Although the information ... has value owing to its Arab point of view, the treatment is often shallow and the editing poor' (*Choice*, v.19,no.5, January 1982,p.612). *Class No:* 929(5.297)

Canada

[2753]
Dictionary of Canadian biography. Toronto, Univ. of Toronto Press, 20v., 1966-. bibliogs., indexes.

French ed. *Dictionnaire biographique du Canada* (Québec, Les Presses de l'Université Laval).

20 entirely self-contained volumes, each covering a specific number of years. The volume in which a biography is included is determined by the date of death or, if this is unknown, the 'floreat' date. 'Biographers should endeavour to provide a readable and stimulating treatment of their subject. Factual information should come from primary sources if possible' (*DCB's Directive to contributors*). Volumes published to date: 1. *1000 to 1700.* 1966. xxiii, 755p. ISBN 0802031420. 2. *1701 to 1740.* 1969. xli,759p. 0802032400. 3. *1741 to 1770.* 1974. xlii, 782p. 0802033148. 4. *1771 to 1800.* 1979. lvii,913p. 0802033512. *Index v.1-4.* 1981. vii,254p. 0802033261. 5. *1801 to 1820.* 1983. xxv,1044p. 0802033989. 6. *1821 to 1835.* 1987. xxiv,960p. 0802034365. 7. *1836 to 1850.* 1988. xxix,1088p. 0802034527. 8. *1851 to 1860.* 1985. xxxvii,1129p. 0802034225. 9. *1861 to 1870.* 1976. xiii,967p. 0802033199. 10. *1871 to 1880.* 1972. xxix,823p. 0802032877. 11. *1881 to 1890* 1982. xx,1092p. 0802032679. 12. *1891 to 1900.* 1990. 1200p. Can $75. 0802034608.

V.7 has 326 contributors; 538 well-documented biographies ranging from 600 to 10,000 words in length. General bibliography (Archival sources; printed primary sources, reference works; studies) p.938-76. Index of identifications (29 categories of occupations) p.991-1006. Geographical index p.1009-25. Name index p.1029-1088. 'Characterized by careful scholarship, good writing and remarkable breadth of coverage' (*Choice*, v.9, no.12, February 1973, p.1572). F.G. Halpenny's 'The Dictionary of Canadian Biography/Dictionnaire biographique du Canada', *Canadian Studies* (British Library, 1984), p.133-43, has more detail. M. Dowding's 'Dictionary side-swiped by funding cutbacks', *Quill & Quires* v.56, no.4, April 1990, p.6 reports that the future volumes are imperilled through a serious loss of funding. *Class No:* 929(71)

[2754]
Who's who in Canada 1990: an illustrated biographical record of leading Canadians from business, the professions, government and academia. Kerrigan, H.M., *ed.* 81st ed.

....(contd.)

Toronto, Global Press, 1988. xxx,1008p. ports, index. ISBN: 0771539614.

Biographies p.1-945. Cross-reference listing by company position, name p.947-1002. Federal and provincial governments and judiciary p.1002-8. *Class No:* 929(71)

Newfoundland

[2755]
Dictionary of Newfoundland and Labrador biography. St. John's, Harry Cuff Publications, 1990. vi,408p. bibliog., indexes. ISBN: 0921191510.

Basic reference information on approximately 1,500 individuals 'who have influenced the development of Newfoundland and Labrador as colony, country and province, since the European re-discovery of America in 1497' (*Foreword*). Bibliographic note p.374-9. Geographic index p.380-92. Index of identifications (*i.e.* occupation or profession) p.393-408. *Class No:* 929(718)

Latin America

[2756]
Who's who in Latin America a biographical dictionary of notable living men and women of Latin America. Hilton, R., *ed.* 3rd ed. California, Stanford Univ. Press; Chicago, Marquis, 7v., 1945-1971.

First published 1935 (1,000 entries); 2nd ed. 1940 (1500 entries) The 3rd ed. reprinted in 2v. (Detroit, Ethridge, 1971).

1. *Mexico* 1946. xiii,130p. 2. *Central America* (*i.e.,* Costa Rica, El Salvador, Guatemala, Honduras, Nicaragua and Panama) 1945. xiii,130p. 3. *Colombia, Ecuador and Venezuela* 1951. xvii,149p. 4. *Bolivia, Chile, Peru* 1947. xviii,209p. 5. *Argentine, Paraguay and Uruguay* 1950. xvii,258p. 6. *Brazil* 1948. xxii,269p. 7. *Cuba, Dominican Republic and Haiti* 1951. xvii,77p. Previously in one sequence, the 3rd ed. (8,000 entries) is arranged on a regional basis, which diminishes ease of reference if the country of the biographee is not known. Includes entries for 20 republics; 'qualification for admission... is residence, not nationality'. Ronald Hilton was Director of Hispanic Area Studies, Stanford Univ. *Class No:* 929(729.99)

USA

[2757]
Dictionary of American biography. Sponsored by the American Council of Learned Societies, New York. New York, Charles Scribner's Sons, 17v. set, 1985. 19498p. ISBN: 0684173239.

First published New York, Scribners; London, Oxford Univ. Press, 20v. and Index, 1928-37. Supplements 1-7. 1944-81.

The main work carries 13,633 signed articles by 2,243 contributors. *DAB* includes 'in general only those ... who have made some significant contribution to American life in all its manifold aspects'. Article length is determined by relative importance of the person, amount of available authentic material, the nature of his career, and completeness of biographies already published; and this also applies to the appended bibliographies. The index (1937) has 6 pts.: 1. Biographies, with contributors' names; 2. Contributors, with biographies written by them; 3. Birthplaces, (a) State; (b) foreign countries; 4. Schools and colleges attended by biographee; 5. Occupations of biographee; 6. Topics. 'The monumental *D.A.B.*' (*RQ*, v.14, no.2, Winter 1974, p.169). W.K. McCoy's 'Dictionary of American Biography', *Reference Services Review*, v.11, no.3, Fall 1983, p.17-20. refs. is a good history and evaluation.

Dictionary of American biography. Supplement 8 1960-

BIOGRAPHY

....(contd.)
1970. 1989. 624p. £60.00. ISBN 0684186187 adds 454 biographies.
Dictionary of American biography. Comprehensive index. 1989. 800p. $80.00. ISBN 0684191146. Indexes subjects from original base volumes and all 8 supplements A-Z by occupation, by school/college, and by contributor.
This series of volumes is now at an end. 'ACLS has announced a successor series, *American National Biography,* to be published by Oxford. The first volume is to be available in both printed and electronic form in about five years' (*Booklist,* v.85, no.12, 15 February 1989, p.979). *Class No:* 929(73)

[2758]
—Concise dictionary of American biography. 4th ed. New York, Scribner, 1990. 1536p. index. ISBN: 0684191881.
1st ed. 1964. 2nd ed. 1977. 3rd ed. 1980 was a reprint of 2nd ed. with an 101p. supplement for those who died 1951-60.
Concise version (at an average reduction of 14:1) of all 18,110 biographies included in the full *Dictionary of American biography* and its eight supplements extending coverage to 1970 in a single A-Z sequence. Occupations index. *Class No:* 929(73)

[2759]
Who's who in America 1990-1991. 46th ed. Wilmette, Illinois, Marquis Who's Who Macmillan Directory Division, 2v., 1990. 3300p. bibliogs., index. Biennial.
First published 1899.
More than 79,000 biographies (14,000 of them 'emerging figures' new to this edition). Each biennial edition is thoroughly revised and features a retiree index, *i.e.* biographies deleted because of career retirement; obituaries; and regional and topical listings. 'A unique reference source with no close competitor' (A. Ricker's Who's Who in America', *Reference Service Review,* v.8,no.4, October/December 1980, p.7-13). *Who's who in America geographic/professional index 1988-1989,* 1988. *c.*450p. $72.00. 0837915058 facilitates access by country, state, or province (of Canada) or by one of 39 professional categories. Names are listed by location under each professional heading. *Class No:* 929(73)

[2760]
—Index to Marquis who's who books 1991. Wilmette, Illinois, Marquis Who's Who, 1991. 350p.
Successor to *Marquis who's who publications: index to all books* first published 1978; in 2v. 1984.
Referral tool to more than 280,000 individuals listed in the latest editions of Marquis who's who publications. *Class No:* 929(73)

[2761]
—KENNEDY, S. 'First look': the Marquis Who's who database, *Online,* v.8,no.2, March 1984, p.31-35.
Scope and standards; database development; unique capabilities; upcoming enhancements; user participation; database specifications. *Class No:* 929(73)

Bibliographies

[2762]
Biography and genealogy master index: a consolidated index to more than 3,200,000 listings in over 350 current and retrospective biographical dictionaries. Herbert, M.C. *and* McNeil, B., *eds.* 2nd ed. Detroit, Gale Research Co., 8v., 1980-1981. 6000p. (*Gale Biographical Index Series.*) ISBN: 0810310945. ISSN: 07301316.
First edition published 1975-76 *Biographical dictionaries master index* edited by D. Labeau and G.C. Tarbert.
More than 3.2 million citations to biographical articles

....(contd.)
from more than 350 sources. 'Entries give the individual's name, birth and death dates when provided by the indexed source, and a coded citation locating the indexed material ... However, this is neither a "genealogical" index (*e.g.* passenger and cemetery lists are absent) nor a "master" index (coverage is too narrow and selective, and the emphasis is mainly on the US) [nevertheless] 'when used with care and an understanding of its limitations, the index serves as an important and valuable aid' (*Choice,* v.19, no.1, September 1981, p.45). English language sources only.
McNeil, B. ed. *Biography and genealogy master index 1981-1985 cumulation,* 5v., 1985. 4177p. £568. 0810315068. A cumulation of the 5 annual supplements that updated the base set. An additional 2.3 million citations are recorded. *Biography and genealogy master index 1986-90 cumulation,* 3v., 1990. 3387p. £602. 0810348039. Adds 1,895,000 citations to biographical articles appearing in more than 500 editions and volumes of over 250 sources. Since 1980 over 4 million citations have been added to the base record. *Class No:* 929(73)(01)

[2763]
—Abridged biography and genealogy master index. McNeil, B. *and* Unterburger, A.L., *eds.* Detroit, Gale Research Co., 3v., 1988. 3537p. $431.25. £299. ISBN: 0810321491.
1.6 million citations from 115 current and retrospective dictionaries, subject encyclopaedias *etc.* An updated edition is expected after 5 years. 'Libraries unable to afford the full Biography and Genealogy Master Index should consider purchasing the abridged version. Highly recommended' (*Choice,* v.25, no.11/12, July/August 1988, p.1671). *Class No:* 929(73)(01)

New Zealand

[2764]
The Dictionary of New Zealand biography. Wellington, Allen & Unwin New Zealand and Department of Internal Affairs, 1990-.
V.1: 1769-1869. 1990. xviii,674p. indexes. ISBN 004641052x. 572 biographical essays (20% of women; 30% Maoris). 'As well as for eminence on a national scale, the people in this Dictionary have been chosen for their standing within less extensive milieux, for their representativeness and for the balance their presence will give to the volume as a whole' (*Introduction*). Glossary of Maori words p.xiv-xv. Categories index (*i.e.* professions and occupations) p.615-25. Tribal and Hapu index p.627-9. Name index p.631-74. Next volume will be in the Maori language and will contain those Maori biographies printed in v.1. Further volumes of *DNZB* will be published in the 1990s covering successive chronological periods. *Class No:* 929(931)

Australia

[2765]
Australian dictionary of biography. Melbourne Univ. Press, 1966-. Distributed in UK by Europa Publications. ISBN: 0522842364.
Period I - 1788-1850 Vol. 1: A-H; Vol. 2: I-Z. Period II - 1851-1890 Vol. 3: A-C; Vol. 4: D-J Vol. 5: K-Q; Vol. 6: R-Z. Period III - 1891-1939 Vol. 7: A-Ch; Vol. 8: Cl-Gib Vol. 9: Gil-Las; Vol. 10: Lat-Ner Vol. 11: Nes-Smi; Vol. 12: Smy-Z. *Index volume 1788-1939* published September 1991. Beginning in 1993, a new four-volume series will cover the lives of Australians whose *floruit* came after 1939. *Class No:* 929(94)

[2766]

GIBBNEY, H.J. *and* SMITH, A.G., *comps.* **A Biographical register 1788-1939. Notes from the name index of the Australian Dictionary of Biography.** Canberra, Australian National University, Australian Dictionary of Biography, 2v., 1987. xviii,403p.+429p. bibliog., index. ISBN: 0731501047, set.

  1. *A-K.* 07351500989. 2. *L-Z.* 0731501039.

  8100 entries. Data: name; leading occupation; main place associated with; birth, marriage, death details; biographical outline; and bibliographical references. By-product of 1st 12v. of *Australian dictionary of biography.* Based on a card index maintained since late 1950s which 'as an aid to the publication of the *Dictionary,* now extends far beyond this basic function and encompasses material on many thousands more men and women than those deemed appropriate for a *Dictionary* entry' (*Introduction*). Bibliography of collective biographical material p.xiii-xvii. Occupational index. p.361-429. *Class No:* 929(94)

[2767]

—Occupational index to the Australian Dictionary of Biography (1788-1890) Volumes 1-6. Marshall, J.G. *and* Trahair, R.C.S., *comps.* Bundoora, Victoria, Department of Sociology; School of Social Sciences, La Trobe Univ. 1979. 139p. softcover. ISBN: 0858162156.

  Based on the occupations that follow names and dates of each entry. Reproduced from typsescript. *Class No:* 929(94)

[2768]

Who's who in Australia: an Australian biographical dictionary and register of prominent people with which is incorporated John's Notable Australians. 1991. Howie, A.C., *ed.* 27th ed. Melbourne, The Herald & Weekly Times, 1991. 1267p. ISSN: 08108226.

  1st ed. *John's notable Australians* 1906. 3rd ed. *Fred John's annual* 1912. 6th ed. *Who's who in Australia* 1922. Previous ed. 1988.

  8219 biographies p.89-1267. Preliminaries include words and music *Advance Australia Fair,* Royal style and titles. Orders of precedence, Australian decorations, Australian winners of Nobel prizes, Diplomatic Corps in Australia *etc.* State governments directory p.52-59. *Class No:* 929(94)

929.5/.9 Genealogy & Heraldry

Genealogy & Heraldry

USA

Bibliographies

[2769]
FILBY, P.W., *comp.* **American and British genealogy and heraldry:** a selected list of books. 3rd ed. Boston, New England Historic Genealogical Society, 1983. xix, 940p. ISBN: 0880820047.
First two editions published by the American Library Association in 1970 and 1975.
Almost 10,000 entries citing books and definitive periodical articles on genealogy, heraldry, and North American local history with a genealogical slant. Scope enlarged to almost double that of the previous edition. Extensive index of 20,000 entries. Treatment of black and ethnic genealogy is greatly expanded and a completely new section appears listing works in English covering non-English speaking countries. Described as 'unmatched in the field' by Evelyn Haynes' 'Encore Filby!' *Reference Services Review*, v.12, no.3, Fall 1984, p.70-72 which reports that compiler and publisher are contemplating annual or biennial supplements. *Class No: 929.50/.9(73)(01)*

Genealogy

Archives

[2770]
BEVAN, J. *and* DUNCAN, A. **Tracing your ancestors in the Public Record Office.** 4th ed. London, HMSO, 1990. 244p. illus. bibliog., pbk. (*PRO Handbooks, no.19.*) ISBN: 0114402221.
First published by Cox, J. and Padfield, T. in 1981.
1. For the beginner - 2. What to use in the PRO. - 3. Some useful groups of records - 4. Special groups of people - 5. Pre-Parish Register genealogy - 6. Sources of help - 7. Useful addresses. Appendix: How to find a record of a birth or baptism (series of questions, yes or no answers referal to text). Biography p.23-4. Invaluable practical guide for all researchers and indispensable to the inexperienced visitor to the PRO. Completely revised and expanded for this edition. 'This is a wonderful book that should be in the library of every archive office and serious researcher, not just genealogists. And make sure it replaces any earlier edition. This is effectively a new book ... double the length of the third edition and better in every way' (*Journal of the Society of Archivists*, v.12,no.2, Autumn 1991, p.162-3). *Class No: 929.50(093.20)*

Worldwide

[2771]
JOHNSON, K.A. *and* SAINTY, M.R., *eds.* **Genealogical research directory national and international 1989.** North Sydney, Genealogical Research Directory, 1985-. Annual. Available in UK from SPA Books, Stevenage. 848p. maps. ISBN: 0908120737.
Originally published by Library of Australian History, 1981, as *Genealogical research directory (Australasian ed.)*.
A medium by which family historians may exchange research data with distant relatives and others. 1989 edition has 5100 participants from 30 countries who submitted over 100,000 entries. Intended to further and to avoid duplication of research. Subsidiary material includes Research repositories (Australia, Canada, France, UK, New Zealand and US) p.21-4; Calendar of genealogical events p.26-7; Directory of genealogical societies p.696-785. The carry over rate of entries in the main sequences from year to year is very low and libraries are advised not to discard previous years' editions. *Class No: 929.50(100)*

Europe

Handbooks & Manuals

[2772]
BAXTER, A. **In search of your European roots:** a complete guide to tracing your ancestors in every country in Europe. Baltimore, Genealogical Publishing Co., 1985. xix, 289p. bibliog. index, pbk. ISBN: 0806311142.
A-Z guides of 30 European countries (excluding the United Kingdom) are designed to guide the reader through the complexities of genealogical research. Up-to-date information on church, state, and provincial archives. European Jewish records p.11-20. Bibliography p.279-83. Genealogical organizations p.284-6. *Class No: 929.50(4)(035)*

Great Britain

Dictionaries

[2773]
FITZHUGH, T.V.H. **The Dictionary of genealogy.** 3rd ed. London, A & C Black, 1991. 313p. illus., facsims. ISBN: 0713633484.
1st ed. 1985; 2nd ed. 1988.
Part 1. Guide to ancestry research 'outlines the various choices open to the researcher and describes step by step, the main sources of information and the techniques to be used in tracing the family back through time'. (*Foreword*). Part 2. The Dictionary (p.25-312) contains over 1,000 descriptions, definitions and locations of virtually all the historical records likely to be examined by genealogists.

....(contd.)

Scholarly, informative, practical. 'Clearly the result of many years of research' (*Reference Reviews,* v.3,no.3, September 1989, p.140-1). *Class No:* 929.50(410)(038)

Scotland

Handbooks & Manuals

[2774]
HAMILTON-EDWARDS, G. In search of Scottish ancestry. 2nd ed. Chichester, Sussex, Phillimore, 1983. x, 252p. illus., bibliog. ISBN: 0850335132.

First published 1972.

22 Chapters (3. Parish and Nonconformist registers; 4. Surnames and Christian names; 9. Registers of deeds; 10. Other Court registers; 12. The clans and Scottish titles; 15. Migration and the Scotsman abroad; 16. The Scottish Record Office; 17. Scots heraldry and the Lyon Office; 18. Societies and libraries). Appendices A-E: C. Glossary of terms found in earlier legal and other documents p.194-200. D. List of pre-1855 parishes showing county and Commissariat p.201-214. Notes and references. Bibliography p.218-233. 'Much of the second edition ... is concerned with various changes in the location of records' (*Foreword*). 'Written primarily for the researcher with access to archives and libraries of Scotland' (*Library Journal,* v.98, no.2, 15 January 1973, p.151). *Class No:* 929.50(411)(035)

Ireland

Handbooks & Manuals

[2775]
BEGLEY, D.F., *ed.* **Irish genealogy** a record finder. Dublin, Heraldic Artists Ltd., 1981. 257p. illus. index. ISBN: 0950245577.

Sequel to *Handbook on Irish genealogy* (6th ed, 1984).

1. The peoples of Ireland - 2. Historical and administrative divisions of Ireland - 3. Irish census returns - 4. Guide to Irish directories - 5. Genealogical matter in the publications of the Irish Manuscript Commission - 6. Newspapers as a genealogical source - 7. The Registry of Deeds for genealogical purposes - 8. Wills and administrations; 9. Early genealogical sources for attornies and barristers. 10. R.E. Matheson's special report on surnames in Ireland. Gravestone inscriptions recorded in printed sources (arranged by parish) p.233-240; Miscellaneous genealogical sources p.241-248; List of libraries, archives and record offices p.249-251. *Class No:* 929.50(415)(035)

England & Wales

Handbooks & Manuals

[2776]
GARDNER, D.E. *and* **SMITH, F. Genealogical research in England and Wales.** Salt Lake City, Utah, Bookcraft Publishers, 3v., 1956-65. illus., facsims., maps.

V.1 (1956). 1. Brief historic and economic background - 2. Family sources ... - 3. Cemeteries, burial grounds and churchyards - 4. Civil registration of births, marriages and deaths - 5. Examples of civil registration - 6. The census records of England and Wales - 7. How to trace place and family in the 1841-1851 census records - 8. Street and local addresses in the 1851 census returns - 9. The parish and its administration - 10. The parish registers - 11. Laws relating to the keeping of parish registers - 12. How to use parish registers - 13. Bishop's transcripts and their value - 14. Marriage licences and the intention to marry - 15. The Nonconformists, their history and records - 16. The Jews in Great Britain and the Commonwealth - 17. The Roman

....(contd.)

Catholics and their records - 18. Surnames. Given names. Dialect.

V.2 (1959). 1. Planning research and recording research results - 2. An introduction to probate records - 3. Wills, administrations and inventories - 4. Probate calendars or indexes and act books - 5. Miscellaneous probate records - 6. Examples of the value of probate records - 7. Naval and military records. Merchant shipping records. Churches on foreign soil - 8. Historical events related to genealogical research - 9. The counties of England and Wales.

V.3 (1965) includes a discussion of apprentice and freeman records; reading early English script; Chancery proceedings, schools and university registers; poll books; feet of fines; inquisitions, post-mortems, and manor court rolls.

Gathers together a mass of data, simply explained; many footnote references and facsimiles. Each volume has an analytical index. Chapter 9 of v.2, 'The counties of England' (p.195-307) is supported by numerous black-and-white maps, but the lettering on these is far from clear in many cases, and there is no gazetteer. 'Contains the most up-to-date guide to the whereabouts of the genealogist's main series of records that there is' (*Genealogist's Magazine,* v.13, no.11, September 1961, p.345). The same review states that on probate records it is 'undoubtedly the best that has ever appeared in print'. *Class No:* 929.50(42)(035)

USA

Handbooks & Manuals

[2777]
EAKLE, A. *and* **CERNY, J.,** *comps.* **The Source** a guidebook of American genealogy. Salt Lake City, Ancestry Publishing Co., 1984. xii, 786p. illus., facsims., maps., tables. ISBN: 0916489000.

16 contributors. 23 chapters arranged in 3 parts: 1. Major record sources - 2. Published general sources - 3. Special records (immigrant, urban, Indian, Spanish, Negro, Asian, Jewish). Appendix A. Regional Federal archives and record centres - B. State historical archives and record depositories - C. Historical societies and agencies in the US - D. Genealogical Society of Utah and branches - E. Selected research libraries - F. Where to write for vital records - G. Genealogical societies of the US - H. Genealogy book publishers. Chapter bibliographies. Glossary p.742-748. Bibliographic index (material not cited in chapter bibliographies) p.750-9. Subject index p.760-86. 'Compact yet wide-ranging, this authoritative work must surely remain the definitive textbook on genealogy in the United States for much time to come' (*Genealogists Magazine,* v.21, no.7, September 1984, p.256). *Class No:* 929.50(73)(035)

Glossaries

[2778]
BENTLEY, E.P. The Genealogist's address book. Baltimore, Md., Genealogical Publishing Co., 1991. 408p. pbk. ISBN: 0806312920.

Directory information and publications of over 7,000 organizations and institutions that can assist with genealogical research: 1. National (including National Archives and its regional centres, government departments and agencies) - 2. State listings of vital records offices, county and regional archives, libraries and societies - 3. Ethnic archives *etc.* - 4. Special resources (hereditary societies, adoption information, immigration research centres *etc.*) - 5. Periodicals and newsletters. 'Essential for institutions or individuals seriously pursuing genealogical research' (*Library Journal,* v.116,no.1, January 1991, p.88). *Class No:* 929.50(73)(038.1)

Australia

Handbooks & Manuals

[2779]
HAWKINGS, D.T. **Bound for Australia.** Chichester, Sussex, Phillimore, 1987. xvi, 269p. illus., facsims., tables, bibliog., index. ISBN: 0850336147.

Guide in 9 chapters 'to enable the descendent of a convict to trace his ancestor and to discover as much as possible about that individual's personal life and crime; his (or her) journey to New South Wales; and his (or her) life in the colony' (*Preface*). Favourably received in *Archives* v.18, no.79, April 1988, p.175-6. *Class No:* 929.50(94)(035)

Family Histories

Worldwide

Handbooks & Manuals

[2780]
CURRER-BRIGGS, N. **Worldwide family history.** London, Routledge & Kegan Paul, 1982. ix, 230p. maps. ISBN: 0710009348.

Explains how English-speaking people of foreign descent can begin tracing their ancestors. Part 1. describes the history and archives of Europe, Islam, China, and Japan. Part 2. deals with colonial shipping in the seventeenth and eighteenth centuries, the settlement of the Americas, including chapters on Anglo-Saxon, Dutch, Scandinavian, German, Polish, French, Spanish, Italian, Greek and Slav emigrants, and a record of the early European settlement of South Africa, Australia, and New Zealand. Appendix 1. Heraldry and genealogical research; 2. Chief sources of information in the form of a combined bibliography and list of addresses for Europe and the United States. *Class No:* 929.52(100)(035)

Scotland

Handbooks & Manuals

[2781]
ADAM, F. **The Clans, septs and regiments of the Scottish Highlands.** 8th ed. revised by Sir Thomas Innes of Learney. Edinburgh & London, Johnston & Bacon, 1970. 692p. illus. (pl.), map. ISBN: 0717945006.

First published 1908.

6 parts: 1. History of the clan system - 2. Structure of the clan system - 3. Celtic culture - 4. Highland forces - 5. Clan insignia and heraldry - 6. Clan lists and culture. 17 plates and 56p. of tartans (112). Clan map of Scotland. A standard, well-documented account. *Class No:* 929.52(411)(035)

Parish Registers

Great Britain

[2782]
National Index of parish registers. Chichester, Sussex, Phillimore for the Society of Genealogists, 1966-. v.1-.

1: *General sources of births, marriages and deaths before 1837.* 1966. Rev.ed. 1976. 2: *Sources for Nonconformist genealogy and family history.* 1973. 3. *Sources for Roman Catholic and Jewish genealogy and family history.* 1974. 4: *South-east England* 1980. 5: *South Midlands and Welsh Border*, 1966. New ed. 1977. 11,pt.1: *Durham and Northumberland.* 1979. £4.20. 12: *Sources for Scottish genealogy and family history.* 1970. V.12, by D.J. Steel (1970, xiii,32p.) has sections: Historical background -

....(contd.)
Catholic nomenclature - Parish registers - Ancillary sources (*e.g.*, Monumental inscriptions; Court records) - Nonconformists - Bibliography, p.249-76 (A. Bibliographies; B. Genealogy and archives; C. History). Index. *Class No:* 929.53(410)

England & Wales

Maps & Atlases

[2783]
The Phillimore atlas and index of parish registers. Humphery-Smith, C.R., *ed.* Chichester, Sussex, Phillimore, 1984. v, 92p. maps, 91-281p. index. ISBN: 0850333989.

'Phillimore & Co. Ltd., had the idea of publishing a consolidated guide to parish records at the same time as the Institute of Heraldic and Genealogical Studies was considering a new edition of its book of parish maps with improved new maps and an index to parishes and research sources. The two ideas have been brought together'.

Atlas contains 42 full page historical county genealogical maps of pre-1832 parishes each accompanied by a reproduction of a topographical map from J. Bell's *A new and comprehensive gazetteer of England and Wales* (1834). 'Each parish map shows the ancient parochial boundaries, the probate court jurisdiction affecting each area by colour coding, the situation of churches and chapels where relevant, and the dates of commencement of the original registers of the parish that have survived'. The index is A-Z by county and is linked to the county maps by grid references and indicates whether parishes are included in the *International Genealogical Index*. A glowing review in *Genealogists Magazine*, v.21,no.7, September 1984, p.255 describes this as 'a genealogist's dream index'. *Class No:* 929.53(42)(084.3)

Heraldry

Handbooks & Manuals

[2784]
BOUTELL, C. **Boutell's heraldry** revised by J.P. Brooke-Little. Rev. ed. London, Warne, 1983. x,368p. illus. (inc.pl.). ISBN: 0723230935.

First published 1950. Based on Boutell's *The manual of heraldry* (1863) and *English heraldry* (1867).

27 chapters (1. The beginning and growth of heraldry - 2. Definitions, heraldic language and blazonry ... 8. Heraldic charges ... 22. Flags ... 26. Recent trends and developments - 27. Heraldic authorities and sources. 28 col.pl. Critical bibliography (p.302-313) 'designed to be read as part of the book rather than used simply as a catalogue for reference'. Glossary and index p.314-68. 'A must for all heraldry addicts' (*TLS*, no.3755, 22 February 1974, p.189 on the 1973 ed.). *Class No:* 929.6(035)

Dictionaries

[2785]
FRANKLYN, J. and TANNER, J. **An encyclopaedic dictionary of heraldry.** Oxford, Pergamon Books, 1970. xiv,307p. illus. (inc.pl.); facsims.

The glossary, p.1-355, has *c*.8,000 entries and cross-references, 474 illus.; 18p. of colour plates; text facing illus. Appendix 2: Analysis of blazon, p.350-67. 'Even if Gough & Parker's *A Glossary of terms used in heraldry* (1967) is held, this work's illustrations make it indispensable' (*Library Journal*, v.95,no.15, 1 September 1970, p.2788). *Class No:* 929.6(038)

Europe

French

[2786]
RIETSTAP, J.B. Armorial général: précédé d'un dictionnaire des termes du blason. 2nd ed. Gouda, Van Goor, 2v. , 1884-87. Reprinted Paris, Dupont, 1904; Institut Héraldique, 1905-14; The Hague, Nijhoff, 1926-34; New York, Barnes & Noble, 1965. illus.
First published 1861.
The standard encyclopaedia of European arms with entries arranged A-Z by families.
Supplément par V. Rolland and H. Rolland (The Hague, Nijhoff, 7v. in 8, 1926-54; London, Heraldry Today, 1965).
Table du Supplément par H. Rolland (Lyon, Société Sauvegarde Historique, 1951. 190p.).
Plates illustrating the arms in Riestap's original work were published under the title *Armories des familles contenues dans l'Armorial Général* (Paris, Institut Héraldique Universel, 6v., 1903-26; The Hague, Nijhoff, 1938). A 3rd. ed. of these plates edited by V. Rolland and H. Rolland (with text in English) was published under the title of *General illustrated armorial* (Lyon, Sauvegarde Historique, 6v., 1953). This was reprinted as *Illustrations to the 'Armorial Général' of J.B. Rietstap* (London, Heraldry Today, 3v., 1967). *Class No: 929.6(4)=40*

Great Britain

Handbooks & Manuals

[2787]
FOX-DAVIES, A.C. A Complete guide to heraldry: revised and annotated by J.P. Brooke-Little. London, Orbis Books, 1985. xii,528p. illus., bibliog., index.
First published 1909. Rev. ed. 1949.
A comprehensive, authoritative guide to the rules, practice and art of heraldry, revised by the Richmond Herald of Arms. Arranged in 42 systematic, short chapters, lavishly illustrated (nearly 800 drawings; 26 new coloured pl.). Comprises the history of armory; a detailed description of the treatment of charges used, regalia, seals, badges, cadency, the law of armorial bearings, and the artistic employment of heraldry. Bibliography, updated, p.486-8. *Class No: 929.6(410)(035)*

Nobility

Great Britain

[2788]
The Complete peerage of England, Scotland, Ireland, Great Britain and the United Kingdom extant, extinct or dormant. Cokayne, G.E. Gloucester, Alan Sutton, 6 vols. 1984. ISBN: 0904387828.
First edition published 1887-1898 in 8v.; new edition revised and enlarged in 12v. 1910-59. V.13 *Peers created 1901-1938* (1940). This present edition is reprinted photographically in reduced format enabling the complete work to be published in a 6v. boxed set.
Excellent biographical data giving fully, yet concisely, particulars of parentage, birth, honours, officers, public services, marriage, death and burial of every holder of a peerage; well documented. Throws valuable light on the whole history of the House of Lords.
According to *Genealogists' Magazine* (v.17, no.10, June 1961, p.319), there is progressively less hope of the index volume being printed. *Class No: 929.7(410)*

Handbooks & Manuals

[2789]
Burke's Peerage and Baronetage. Townsend, P., *ed.* 105th ed. London, Burke's Peerage, 1970. lxxxv,3259p. illus. (coats of arms).
First published 1826 as *Burke's Genealogical heraldic history of the peerage and baronetage of the United Kingdom.*
Peerage and baronetage (p.1-2910) - 'the genealogical history of the families holding Peerages and Baronetcies, from their earliest recorded origins down to 1969/70 set out in narrative pedigree, accompanied by armorial illustration'. 'Dartmouth': $5\frac{1}{2}$ columns; O'Neill: over 18 columns. Appendix: Lists of peerages and baronetcies in order of precedence; and notes on members of families whose titles are extinct. Index: 'Family names which differ from that of the title, and guide to subsidiary title'. 2nd impression (1975) omits sections on the Royal Family and Knightage. 3rd impression (1978) has preceding supplement: ' The successions, extinctions and creations of Peerages and Baronetcies ... 1969/70 to April 1978', p.vi-xix. *Class No: 929.7(410)(035)*

[2790]
Debrett's Peerage and Baronetage 1990. Kidd, C. *and* Williamson, D., *eds.* London, Debretts Peerage and Macmillan; New York, St. Martins Press, 1990. 123+P1336+B968p. col.port., illus., coats of arms. ISBN: 033338847x, UK; 0312046405, US.
Founded in 1769; renamed Debrett in 1802. 'Modern technology has come to Debrett at last and the complete text of the Peerage and Baronetage has now been computerized. This means we shall be able to produce amended family articles between editions, which we hope will appear every five years (Preface to 1985 ed.).
Comprises information concerning the Royal Family, the Peerage, Privy Councillors, Scottish Lords of Session, Baronets, Chiefs of clans in Scotland. Other information includes H.M. Officers of Arms; tables of general precedence; guide to the wearing of Orders; Foreign and Commonwealth Orders. Entries provide illustration of coat of arms and lists of living relatives, collateral branches and predecessors. This edition includes F.J. French's 'Debrett: Book and Man: A history of the Peerage (p.14-20). 1985 ed. included her 'A bibliographical check list of Debrett's principal publications'. *Class No: 929.7(410)(035)*

Yearbooks & Directories

[2791]
Burke's genealogical and heraldic history of the landed gentry. Townsend, P., *ed.* 18th ed. London, Burke's Peerage, 3v., 1965-72.
1st ed., *Burke's Genealogical ... history of commoners* (1833-38. 4v.); 2nd ed. *Landed gentry of Great Britain and Ireland,* with an index of about 100,000 names (1843-49, 3v.).
Contains biographical sketches of *c.*600 distinguished families of England, Scotland and Wales; 500 armorial illustrations; index of families. Gives brief biographical sketch of present head of family; name of wife and children (if any); lineage; arms (both illustration and description); seat. Perhaps one-half of the families are no longer landowning. American families with British ancestry are included in the 1939 ed., p.2539-3021, published separately in 1948 as *Burke's Distinguished families of America: the lineages of 1,600 families of British origin now resident in the United States of America.* Burke, Sir J.B. *A genealogical and heraldic history of colonial gentry* (London, Harrison, 1891-95. 2v. illus.), with excellent reproductions of 120 coats of arms, was reprinted by Genealogical Publishing Co., Baltimore, Md., in 1970. *Class No: 929.7(410)(058)*

Orders & Decorations

Europe

[2792]
HIERONYMUSSEN, P. **Orders, medals and decorations of Britain and Europe in colour.** London, Blandford Press, 1967. 256p. illus. (inc. col. pl).
Originally as *Europaeiske ordner i farver* [European orders in colour] (Copenhagen, Politikens Forlag, 1966).
The 80 coloured plates (450 photographs) of orders medals and decorations of 28 European nations are preceded by an introductory essay and followed by an encyclopaedia of orders (date of institution; to whom it may be given; classes; whether or not returnable on death of holder). 'An excellent general guide in a comparatively small volume' (*Times Literary Supplement*, no.3,414, 3 August 1967, p.713). *Class No: 929.71(4)*

Commonwealth

[2793]
JOCELYN, A. **Awards of honour:** the orders, decorations, medals and awards of Great Britain and the Commonwealth, from Edward III to Elizabeth II. London, A & C Black, 1956. xx, 276p. illus. (20 col. pl). index.
17 chapters: Introduction and definitions; Orders; Ribands of orders; Decorations and campaign medals; Long service and good conduct medals; Dominion and colonial decorations and medals; Miscellaneous decorations and medals; etc. The 20 colour-plates consist of mounted reproductions of medals and ribbons. Detailed index, p.265-76. Page size 31 x 25cm. *Class No: 929.71(41-44)*

Royalty

[2794]
Burke's Royal Families of the world. London, Burke's Peerage, 2v., 1977-80.
1: *Europe & Latin America*, 1977. xxv,594p. 2: *Africa & the Middle East*. 1980. xvi.320p. V.1 is arranged under 48 countries (Albania ... Yugoslavia). Includes princely and ducal houses. Introductory historical essays; biographies; pedigrees. Appendices: A. The mediatized sovereign states of the Holy Roman Empire - B. Principal order of knighthood - C. Ancestral tables - D. Select bibliography, p.569-70. Index of names in the pedigrees, p.571-88. Addendum. 'Comprehensive and definitive ... will become an indispensable reference book' (*The Times*, 4 July 1977, p.14). *Class No: 929.731*

Flags & Banners

[2795]
BARRACLOUGH, E.M.C. *and* CRAMPTON, W.G., *eds.* **Flags of the world.** 3rd ed. 1981 reprint. London, Warne, 1981. 264p. illus. (mostly col.). ISBN: 0723227977.
First published 1897. 3rd ed. 1978.
14 chapters: 2. The UK and N. Ireland; 3. The Commonwealth and Dependencies of the UK; 4. North America; 5. Latin America and the Caribbean; 6. Europe; 7. Africa; 8. The Middle East; 9. Asia; 10. Oceania and Australasia; 11. International organizations; 12. Signal flags; 13. Flags worn by merchant ships; 14. Yacht flags. Supplement *i.e.* updating with page references to main text p.241-252. Bibliography p.253-254; Index p.255-262. 'No other book comes forward as a serious rival' (*Library Review* v.30, Winter 1981, p.258-259). *Class No: 929.9*

[2796]
GREAT BRITAIN Ministry of Defence. Director General of Supplies & Transport (Navy). **Flags of all nations.** 2nd ed. London, H.M. Stationery Office, 1989. Variously paginated,

....(contd.)
col. illus., diagrs. ISBN: 0117725676.
First published for The Admiralty in 1956.
Authoritative illustrated description of national flags and ensigns with sections on British Royal Standards; international organizations; the Commonwealth, European countries and NATO; and the rest of the World. Flag terminology p.xi-xiii. Loose leaf in substantial ring-binder to allow the insertion of new and revised information. *Class No: 929.9*

[2797]
TALOCCI, M. **Guide to the flags of the world.** Revised and updated by Whitney Smith. London, Sidgwick & Jackson, 1989. 271p. col. illus., maps, bibliog., index, pbk. ISBN: 0283988703.
First published as *Guida alle bandiere di tutto il mondo* (Milano, Arnoldo Mondadori Editore, 1977). English edition first published 1982.
Vividly illustrated flags and arms A-Z by country within continents with final section on International flags. Glossary p.260-3. Bibliography p.271. *Class No: 929.9*

USA

[2798]
SHEARER, B.F. *and* SHEARER, B.S. **State names, seals, flags and symbols** a historical guide. Westport, Connecticut, Greenwood Press, 1987. viii, 239p. col. illus. bibliog., index. ISBN: 0313245592.
Replaces G.E. Shankle's *State names, flags, seals, songs, birds, flowers, and other symbols* (1938).
9 well-documented chapters: 1. State names and nicknames - 2. Mottoes - 3. Seals - 4. Flags - 5. Capitals - 6. Flowers - 7. Trees - 8. Birds - 9. Songs. Bibliography of State histories p.205-218. 'Should be part of the basic reference collection of every academic, public, or school library'. (*Choice*, v.25, no.9, May 1988, p.1386). *Class No: 929.9(73)*

93/99 History

History

Bibliographies

[2799]
Bibliographie internationale des sciences historiques/ International Bibliography of historical sciences. Edited for the International Committee of Historical Sciences, Lausanne. Paris, Colin; later München, K.G. Saur, 1930-. Annual. Available in North America from G.K. Hall. ISSN: 00742015.

Published with Unesco aid and under the patronage of the International Council for Philosophy and Humanistic Sciences.

V.56 *1987* (1991. xxv,614p. ISBN 3598204116) has 8473 unannotated entries arranged in Classes A-U, subdivided by countries, subjects and periods (*e.g.* A. Auxiliary historical sciences; C. Prehistory and protohistory; D. Ancient East; I. Middle Ages; K. Modern times; general works; L. Modern religious history; N. Modern economic and social history; P. International relations; modern history). Index of authors and persons; geographical index. Tardy appearance, but valuable for coverage of Africa, Asia, Eastern and Southern Europe. *Class No:* 930.0(01)

Encyclopaedias

[2800]
BLAKE, R., *ed.* **World history from 1800 to the present day.** Oxford, Oxford Univ. Press, 1988. [iv],391p. col.illus., col.maps, geneal. tables, col.chron.charts on end papers. (*Oxford Illustrated Encyclopaedia Vol.4.*) ISBN: 01986936x.

35 contributors. Over 2300 A-Z entries covering 19th and 20th century social and political changes, two world wars, the Industrial Revolution and other disasters. 350 illustrations. 'For school,, general reference and most other quick reference libraries it will prove an essential item' (*Library Review,* v.38,no.2, 1989,p.49). *Class No:* 930.0(031)

Dictionaries

[2801]
The Blackwell dictionary of historians. Cannon, J., *and others eds.* Oxford, Blackwell Reference, 1988. xiv,480p. bibliogs., index. ISBN: 063114708x.

200 contributors. Over 450 biographical entries including 50 living historians, 60 French, 40 Germans and 20 Italians. In addition there are 25 national historiographical surveys and 40 thematic entries. 'No reference library of reasonable size that lays claim to having any worthwhile coverage of British or overseas history should be without it' (*Library Association Record,* v.91, no.5, May 1989, p.291). *Class No:* 930.0(038)

[2802]
WETTERAU, B., *comp.* **Macmillan concise dictionary of world history.** New York, Macmillan, 1983. 867p. ISBN: 0026261103.

Published in UK as *The Concise dictionary of world history* (London, R. Hale, 1983. 896p. £26.95).

10,000 brief entries on prominent people, places and events from the Stone Age to the Space Age plus 136 larger chronological histories on topics such as 'Holy Roman Empire' and 'American Revolution'. *Class No:* 930.0(038)

Reviews & Abstracts

[2803]
Historical Abstracts bibliography of the world's historical literature. Santa Barbara, California, ABC-Clio; Oxford, Clio Press, 1955-. ISSN: 03632717.

1. Boehm H. ed. *Historical abstracts 1775-1945: bibliography of the world's periodical literature* v.1-16. 1955-1970. Up to 1964 this offered universal coverage but from 1965 US and Canada were removed and included in *America history and life* (*qv*). 2. V.17-. 1971-. Published in 2 parts: *Part A. Modern history abstracts 1450-1914* and *Part B. Twentieth century abstracts.* Entries relating to the period 1914-1945 appeared in both parts in v.17-20. 3. From 1980 (v.31) coverage was extended to books and dissertations. 4. 5 retrospective volumes were published 1980-1984 to include references that were previously outside *Historical Abstract's* scope and also references not available when the original volumes appeared. These retrospective volumes (26-30) can only be purchased in conjunction with the relevant current volumes *i.e.* 26/31, 27/32, 28/33, 29/34 and 30/35.

Contains abstracts and shorter annotations from over 1900 major historical journals published in 84 countries and in 45 languages. Books are selected from reviews in 13 historical and bibliographical journals whilst dissertations are derived from *Dissertation Abstracts International. Modern history abstracts 1450-1914* and *Twentieth century abstracts* are both published quarterly: nos. 1-3 contain references arranged by subject (vs. 1-2 have indexes) and no.4 contains a cumulative annual index. *Modern History Abstracts* is divided into 3 sub-parts: 1. General (*i.e.* bibliography, methodology, historiography, archive, libraries, societies *etc.*) - 2. Topics (*e.g.* international relations, wars, political history, science and technology) - 3. Area and Country (8 geographical divisions). *Twentieth century abstracts* omits sub-part 1. Bibliographic entries printed in *Historical abstracts* are available online from File 39, DIALOG Information Services.

Five year indexes are issued: V. 1-5 (1955-59) £196; vs. 6-10 (1960-64) £196; V.11-15 (1965-69) £196; vs. 16-20 (1970-74) £345; vs. 21-25 (1975-79) £345; vs. 31-35 (1980-84) £345; v.26-30 (retrospective) £250.

'Indispensable - the only comprehensive abstract service

....(contd.)
for historians' (White, C.M. *Sources of information in the social sciences*, 2nd ed. 1973, Entry B350). *Class No: 930.0(048)*

Periodicals

Bibliographies

[2804]
FYFE, J. **History journals and serials:** an analytical guide. Westport, Connecticut, Greenwood Press, 1986. xxiii,351p. index. (*Annotated bibliographies of serials: a subject approach No.8.*) ISBN: 0313239991. ISSN: 07485190.
689 entries in 35 geographical and topical sections (1. Universal history ... 7. Genealogy and family history ... 22-34. Geographical regions ... 35. Indexes and abstracts) forming a comprehensive and detailed annotated bibliography of major journals of international reputation in the English language. Aimed primarily at helping the librarian to select journals and the historian for personal reading and the submission of manuscripts. Table of abstacts, indexes and databases p.xvii-xx. Directory of microform and reprint publishers p.xxi-xxiii. 'The compiler has done a good job' (*Choice*, v.24, no.3, November 1986, p.454). *Class No: 930.0(051)(01)*

Maps & Atlases

[2805]
The Times atlas of world history. Stone, N., *ed.* 3rd ed. London, Times Books; Maplewood, New Jersey, Hammond, 1989. 358p. illus., col.maps, index. ISBN: 0723003041.
1st ed. 1978; 2nd ed. 1984.
126 succinct essays on major themes from 91 expert contributors, illustrated by over 600 maps, arranged in 7 sections (1. The world of early man - 2. The first civilizations - 3. The Classical civilizations of Eurasia - 4. The world of divided regions - 5. The work of the emerging West - 6. The age of European dominance - 7. The age of global civilization). World chronology to 1984, p.15-27. Glossary of 100,000 entries with supplementary information on individuals, peoples, events, treaties *etc.* p.297-334. Bibliography p.296. Index gazetteer p.335-360. The background to its publication is explained in Ambrose Ways's 'The visible shape of history', *Sunday Times Magazine*, 3 September 1978, p.63-6. 'Any library without this volume cannot claim a basic collection ... In a class by itself' (*Choice*, v.16,no.1, March 1979, p.62). 'A superb atlas has been meticulously updated and improved' (*Booklist*, v.86,no.113, 1 March 1990, p.1378). *Class No: 930.0(084.3)*

20th Century

Handbooks & Manuals

[2806]
COOK, C. and STEVENSON, J. **The Longman handbook of world history since 1914.** London, Longman, 1991. ix,539p. maps, bibliog., index. ISBN: 0582485886.
Essential facts and figures on major aspects of world twentieth-century history from the outbreak of the First World War organized in 6 sections: 1. Political history in 6 regions + lists of Heads of State and selected ministers/rulers A-Z by country (p.182-244) - 2. Wars and international affairs - 3. Economic and social - 4. Biographies (p.371-409) - 5. Glossary of terms (p.413-62) - 6. Bibliography (p.465-506). 10 maps. A key one-stop compendium. *Class No: 930.0"19"(035)*

Philosophy of History

Bibliographies

[2807]
FRITZE, R.H., *and others, eds.* **Reference sources in history** an introductory guide. Santa Barbara, Calif. and Oxford, ABC-Clio, 1990. 319p. index. ISBN: 0874361648.
685 cross-referenced entries for major reference works listed in 14 form chapters *e.g.* book review indexes, core journals, dissertations and theses, archives and manuscripts. Entries consist of full bibliographical citations and evaluative annotations. Author and title index. Coverage is for all historical periods and for all geographical areas although the emphasis is on English-language items relating to Anglo-American and European history. 'An accurate, current and reliable work that supersedes Helen J. Poulton's classic but dated *The Historian's Handbook*' (*Library Journal*, v.116,no.7, 15 April 1991, p.84). *Class No: 930.1(01)*

Chronology

[2808]
GRUN, B. **The Timetables of history:** a chronology of world events based on Werner Stein's *Kulturfahrplan*. Rev. ed. New York, Simon & Schuster, 1987. 688p. ISBN: 0317634356.
Kulturfahrplan first compiled 1946. This ed. first published 1975.
Information presented in 7 columns across the double page: 1. History and politics - 2. Literature, theater - 3. Religion, philosophy, learning - 4. Visual arts - 5. Music - 6. Science, technology, growth - 7. Daily life. Timetables start at 5000BC; annual from AD501. Preferred to C. McEvedy's *The Macmillan world history fact finder* by *Library Journal* 1st September 1985, p.190, largely because of its superior 82 page index. *Class No: 930.24*

[2809]
STEINBERG, S.H. **Historical tables 58BC-AD1985.** 12th ed. updated by J. Paxton. London, Macmillan Reference Books, 1991. ix,324p. ISBN: 0333566610.
First published 1939; 11th ed. 1986.
Double-page spread. 6 columns with headings: 1. Western Europe - 2. Central, Northern and Eastern Europe - 3. Countries overseas - 4-6 vary at different periods *e.g.,* 4. Constitutional history - 5. Economic history and Natural science - 6. Cultural life. Exact day is given, if available. Progressively fuller entries. This edition reassesses some entries for the early 1980s and adds an index of major events since 55BC (p.291-324). *Class No: 930.24*

Archives

Dictionaries

[2810]
Dictionary of archival terminology. Dictionnaire de terminologie archivistique English and French with equivalents in Dutch, German, Italian, Russian and Spanish. Walne, P., *ed.* 2nd ed. München, K.G. Saur, 1988. 212p. indexes. (*ICA Handbook Series, no.7.*) ISBN: 3598202792.
First published 1984 when it superseded *Lexicon of archival terminology* (Elsevier, 1964).
Lists *c.*500 specialist terms of archival science in 7 languages arranged A-Z with definitions in English language order followed by French equivalents and definitions and then by equivalent terms only for the other languages. *Class No: 930.25(038)*

HISTORY

Palaeography & Epigraphy

[2811]
BISCHOFF, B. **Latin palaeography** Antiquity and the Middle Ages. Cambridge Univ. Press in association with The Medieval Academy of Ireland, 1990. xi,291p. facsims., bibliog., indexes. ISBN: 0521364736.
First published as *Paläographie des romischen Altertums und des abendländischen Mittelalters*, Berlin, Erich Schmidt Verlag, 1979. 2nd ed. 1986.
Authoritative and comprehensive account of the history of the Latin script: A. Codicology - B. History of the Latin script - C. Manuscripts in cultural history. *Class No: 930.27*

[2812]
JENKINSON, H. **The later court hands in England,** from the 15th to the 17th century, illustrated from the Common Papers of the Scriveners' Company of London, the English Writing Masters and the Public Records. Cambridge, Cambridge Univ., 2v., 1927.
Pt.1: Text; pt.2: plates.
Standard work on English hands of the 15th, 16th and 17th centuries, containing (pt.1) valuable study on various aspects, bibliography, and transcripts and notes for the plates in pt.2. Alphabets in pt.2. *Class No: 930.27*

[2813]
JOHNSON, C. *and* JENKINSON, H. **English court hands AD1066-1500** illustrated chiefly from the Public Records. Oxford, Clarendon Press, 2v., 1915.
Pt.1: Text; pt.2: Plates.
Standard work on English medieval chancery, exchequer and legal hands, containing (pt.1) valuable study on various aspects and bibliography of development of individual letters, abbreviations, and transcripts (where necessary), with detailed notes for the plates in pt.2. *Class No: 930.27*

Ancient History & Ancient Peoples

Chronologies

[2814]
BICKERMAN, E.J. **Chronology of the Ancient World.** Rev. ed. London, Thames & Hudson, Ithaca, New York, Cornell Univ. Press, 1980. 223p. illus., tables, index. (*Aspects of Greek and Roman life.*) ISBN: 0500400393, UK; 080141282x, US.
First published in English 1968. Adopted from *Chronologie* published in Leipzig (2nd ed., 1963).
Elucidates the basic problems of ancient chronology ... 1. The Calendar - 2. Chronography (the principles of antiquity in computing the years) - 3. Applied chronology (rules derived from these principles to relate ancient dates to modern time reckoning - 4. Notes (p.96-108) - 5. The tables (p.109-218) including astronomical canon, Olympian years, Roman consuls and emperors, and ending with chronological tables of Greek and Roman history 776 BC and AD 476. Analytical index.
Note James, P. and others: *Centuries of darkness: a challenge to the conventional chronology of Old World archaeology* (London, Cape, 1991) argues for a radical shift in the currently accepted chronology of the ancient Near East and Mediterranean world. *Class No: 931(090)*

Ancient Egypt

[2815]
JAMES, T.G.H. **An Introduction to ancient Egypt.** London, British Museum Publications, 1989. 286p. illus. (some col. pl.), index. pbk. ISBN: 0714109231.
First published 1964 as *A general introductory guide to the Egyptian Collections in the British Museum.* Revised and reset, with additional illus.
8 chapters: 1. The land of Egypt and its natural resources - 2. An outline of ancient Egyptian history - 3. Language, decipherment and writing materials - 4. Egyptian literary and other writings - 5. Religious beliefs. List of principal gods - 6. Funerary beliefs and customs - 7. Arts and crafts - 8. Roman and Christian Egypt and the Kingdom of Menoe. List of the principal Kings of Egypt. Names (with hieroglyphics) of the principal kings of Egypt, including the Roman emperors. Bibliography (by chapter), p.274. 21 coloured plates; 101 black-and-white illus. - mostly of objects in the British Museum. 'Among the best of the current all-round introductions to ancient Egypt' (*British Book News*, December 1979, p.1037). *Class No: 932*

Jewish History

[2816]
GRANT, M. **The History of ancient Israel.** London, Weidenfeld and Nicolson; New York, Scribner, 1984. ix, 317p., bibliog., maps, index. ISBN: 0297783661, UK; 0684180812, US.
Definitive study in 20 chapters ordered in 7 pts: 1. Land of Canaan - 2. From Abraham to the Judges - 3. The United Kingdom - 4. The Divided Kingdoms - 5. Babylonian and Persian rule - 6. Greek rule and liberation - 7. Roman dependency. Tables of dates in 4 geographical columns p.286-91. Notes p.293-8. Bibliography p.299-302. 'An excellent introduction to a fascinating subject ... highly recommended for general and college libraries' (*Choice*, v.22, no.4, December 1984, p.601). *Class No: 933*

Maps & Atlases

[2817]
BACON, J. **The Illustrated atlas of Jewish civilization.** London, Deutsch; New York, Macmillan, 1990. 224p. illus (some col.), col. maps, index. ISBN: 0233985697, UK; 0025434152, US.
Introduction: Mapping Jewish history (by Martin Gilbert) - 1. From Abraham to the destruction of the Second Temple - 2. Age of prayer and thought C.E. 70 to the Spanish Inquisition - 3. High Middle Ages to Moses Mendelssohn - 4. Jewish enlightenment to the eve of Holocaust - 5. The dark side: anti-Semitism - 6. The Holocaust - 7. Israel and world Jewry following World War 2. No bibliography. 'A successful blend of beautiful cartography, arresting illustrations, and informative text covering the entire range of the Jewish historical experience from patriarchal times to the present' (*Library Journal*, v.116,no.4, 1 March 1991, p.84). *Class No: 933(084.3)*

North, West & East European Peoples

[2818]
JAMES, E. **The Franks.** Oxford and New York, Basil Blackwell, 1988. xii,265p., illus. maps, bibliog., index. (*The Peoples of Europe.*) ISBN: 0631148728.
Introduction 'Who were the Franks?' and 6 chapters: 1. The Sources (historical sources, archaeological and linguistic evidence) - 2. The Franks before Clovis - 3. Conquests - 4. Conversion to Christianity - 5. Frankish kings and their subjects - 6. Economy and society. Bibliography p.246-250. 'The story of how the Franks became the French and why they became so important in European history'. *Class No: 936*

[2819]
WOLFRAM, W. **History of the Goths.** New and completely revised from 2nd German ed. Berkeley and London, Univ. of California Press, 1988. xii,613p. and 7p. maps. bibliog., index. ISBN: 0520052595.

First published as *Geschichte der Goten: von den Anfängen bis zur Mitte des sechsten Jahrhunderts.* (München, Verlag C.H. Beck, 2nd ed. 1980)

Authoritative and comprehensive academic treatise arranged in 5 sections: 1. The names - 2. Formation of the Gothic tribes before the invasion of the Huns - 3. Forty-year migration and the formation of the Visigoths 376/378 to 416/418 - 4. Kingdom of Toulouse 418 to 507 - 5. The 'new' Ostrogoths. 3 Appendices: 1. Roman Emperors - 2. Survey of Gothic history p.367-71 - 3. Genealogical charts. Chapter notes p.377-534. Bibliography p.537-73. Formidable and extremely well-documented work. *Class No: 936*

Ancient Greece & Rome

[2820]
Oxford history of the classical world. Boardman, J., *and others.* Oxford, Oxford University Press, 1986. x, 882p., illus., maps, tables. ISBN: 0198721129.

Subsequently published in 2v. - 1. *Greece and the Hellenistic World.* 1988. 448p. illus., maps, bibliog., index, pbk. £9.95. ISBN 0192821652 - 2. *Rome.* 1988. 448p. illus (some col.), maps, ports., bibliog., index. pbk. £9.95. ISBN 0192821660.

32 chapters divided into three sections: Greece (8th-4th century BC); Greece and Rome; and Rome. Within each section political and social history chapters are interspersed with others relating to literature, philosophy and the arts. Chapter bibiliographies. Tables of events p.830-860. Index p.873-882. 16 col. plates. *Class No: 937/938*

Encyclopaedias

[2821]
GRANT, M. *and* KITZINGER, R. **Civilization of the Ancient Mediterranean. Greece and Rome.** New York, Charles Scribner's Sons, 3v., 1988. xxvii, xiv, xiv, 1980p. ISBN: 0684188643, v.1; 0684188651, v.2; 068418866x, v.3; 0684175940, set.

88 contributors. Historical summary of Greece (p.3-44); of Rome (p.45-85). 97 essays under broad subject headings: Land and Sea - Population - Agriculture and food - Technology - Government and society - Economics - Religion - Private and social life - Women and family life - Literary and performing arts - Philosophy - Visual arts. Each essay concludes with a bibliography. Epilogue: progress of classical scholarship p.1819-32. Chronological table p.xvii-xxiv. 'A comprehensive overview of current thinking about the classical world ... this set really stands alone as a unique source' (*Booklist*, v.84, no.20, 15 June 1988, p.1716). *Class No: 937/938(031)*

German

[2822]
PAULY, A.F. von *and* WISSOWA, G. **Pauly's Real-Encyclopädie der classichen Altertumswissenschaft.** Stuttgart, Metzler (later München, Druckenmüller, 1894-.1967. Supplement - Bänden 1-. 1903-. (Supplt. 15. 1978).

Published in 2 parallel series. 1. Reihe A-Q (24v. in 32 pts.) completed 1963; 2. Reihe R-Z (110v. in 19 pts.) completed 1967.

Comprehensive signed articles, with adequate bibliographies, cover every aspect of classical literature, history, geography, antiquities and civilization. The article 'Ptolemain als Geograph', in Suppt. 10: p.679-834; bibliography, p.819-34. 'P. Cornelius Tacitus', in Suppt. 11: adds cols. 347-511 (in 13 sections) to the original entry in

....(contd.)
v.4. An indispensable work of scholarship for any library. Gärtner H. and Wünsch A. *Pauly's Real-Encyclopädie der classicher Altertumswissenschaft Register der Nachträge Und Supplemente* (1980). xxii, 250p. *Der Kleine Pauly. Lexikon der Antike auf der Grundlage von Pauly's Real-Encyclopädie der classichen Altertumswissenschaft ... bearb. und hrsg. von K. Ziegler und W. Sontheimer, 5v., 1964-75* is the work of 99 contributors, mostly German. The article on Aristophanes: nearly 5 columns (against 23 in the original), with 10 lines of references. Well produced. 'Indispensable supplement to the original and much easier to use' (*Papers of the Bibliographical Society of America*, v.70, no.2, 1976, p.303). *Class No: 937/938(031)=30*

Dictionaries

[2823]
The Oxford classical dictionary. Hammond, N.G.L *and* Scullard, H.H. 2nd ed. Oxford, Oxford University Press, 1970. xxii, 1176p. ISBN: 0198691173.

First published 1948. Modelled on Lübker's *Reallexicon* (8th ed. 1914).

About 350 contributors. All articles are signed; appended bibliographies ('Spain': $1\frac{3}{4}$ cols. in 3 sections, 24 lines of bibliography; 'Sparta': 3 cols., including lists of Agiads and Eurypontids; 'Origen': $1\frac{1}{2}$ cols., 16 lines of bibliography). Designed to cover the same ground as the older dictionaries by Sir William Smith. 'The editors have introduced only a few changes. They have allowed a little more space for the achaeological background ... They have included more people, places and persons (for example, lesser rulers ...). They have paid more attention to the later Roman Empire' (*Preface*). Sources, p.ix-xxii. 'Index of names which are not titles of entries in the dictionary', p.1154-73. The essential one-volume reference work in this field, although Sir P. Harvey's *Oxford companion to Classical literature* has proved more practical for quick reference. *Class No: 937/938(038)*

Ancient Greece

Dictionaries

[2824]
TRAVLOS, J. **Pictorial dictionary of ancient Athens.** London, Thames & Hudson, 1971. xvi, 590p. illus. (inc. pl.), maps. ISBN: 087817267x.

Originally published by the German Archaeological Institute 1970.

A monumental work on the typography and architecture of Athens, 3000BC-AD300, arranged A-Z (Agora ... Zeus Phratios). Admirably illustrated and well documented (*e.g.* 'Agora': p.1-29; 37 figures; 20 references. 'Stadium': p.498-504; 8 illus.; 13 references. 722 references, ground plans and photographs. Sources p.xi-xii. Also references in text. *Class No: 937(038)*

Ancient Rome

Encyclopaedias

[2825]
WACHER, J., *ed.* **The Roman world.** London, Routledge & Kegan Paul, 2v., 1987. l,478+xiv,479-872p. maps, plans, diagrs., bibliog., index. ISBN: 0710208944, v.1; 0710208952, v.2; 0710099754, set.

Encyclopaedic survey by 33 archaeologists and historians on all aspects of the Roman world organized in 11 parts each ending with an extensive bibliography: 1. Introduction - 2. The rise of the Empire - 3. The Army - 4. The Frontiers - 5. Cities, towns and villages - 6. Government and law - 7. Rural life - 8. Economy - 9. Society - 10.

....(contd.)

Religion and burial - 11. Postscript. General Bibliography p.xxv-xxx. Chronological table p.xxiv-xliii. Glossary p.xliv-l. *Class No:* 938(031)

Maps & Atlases

[2826]
CORNELL, T. *and* MATTHEWS, J. **Atlas of the Roman world.** Oxford, Phaidon; New York, Facts on File, 1982. 240p. col. illus., col., maps, bibliog., index. ISBN: 0714821527, UK; 0871966522, US.

Pt.1. Early history and the Republic - 2. From Republic to Empire - 3. Provinces of the Empire - 4. The Empire in Decline. 21 special features *e.g.*, Roman patriotism, The city of Constantine, The Roman legacy. Chronological table p.6-7. Bibliography p.228-230. Gazetteer p.231-236. Analytical index. 62 maps. 470 illustrations (257 in colour). 'Superior to most other introductory surveys of Rome' (*Choice*, v.20, no.3, November 1982, p.406). *Class No:* 938(084.3)

Ancient Central America

[2827]
DAVIES, N. **The Ancient kingdoms of Mexico.** London, Allen Lane, 1982. 272p. illus., maps, bibliog., index. ISBN: 0713912456.

Covers the period 1500BC-AD1500 focussing on the Olmec, Teotihuacan, Toltec and Aztec civilizations. Popular work but useful for its Comparative chronology p.11; Principal Archaeological Sites of Mexico p.255-6; and Bibliography p.257-64. *Class No:* 939.728

Mediaeval & Modern History

[2828]
The New Cambridge modern history. Cambridge, Cambridge Univ. Press, 14v., 1957-79.

Reappraisal of the period covered by *Cambridge modern history* (13v. and atlas, 1902-26) omitting chapter bibliographies. These were eventually published subsequently: J. Roach, *A Bibliography of modern history* (1968) (*qv.*).

1. *The Renaissance 1483-1520* edited by G.R. Potter. 1957. xxxvi, 532p. £55.00. ISBN 0521045414. 2nd ed. planned for 1991. 2. *The Reformation 1520-1559* edited by G.R. Elton. 2nd ed., 1990. 750p. £35.00. 0521345367. 3. *The Counter-Reformation and price revolution 1559-1610* edited by W.B. Wenham. 1968. xvi, 599p. £55.00. 0521045436. 4. *The Decline of Spain and the Thirty Years' War 1609-48/59* edited by J.P. Cooper. 1970. xxi, 832p. £75.00. 0521076188. 5. *The Ascendancy of France 1648-88* edited by F.L. Carsten. 1961. £65.00. 0521045444. 6. *The Rise of Great Britain and Russia 1685-1715/25* edited by J.S. Bromley. 1970. xxxiv, 947p. £75.00. 0521075246. 7. *The Old Régime 1713-63* edited by J.O. Lindsay. 1957. xx, 625p. £65.00. 0521045452. 8. *The American and French Revolutions 1763-93* edited by A. Goodwin. 1965. xxiii, 747p. £65.00. ISBN 0521045460. 9. *War and peace in an age of upheaval 1793-1830* edited by C.W. Crawley. 1965. xiv, 748p. £75.00. 0521045479. 10. *The Zenith of European power 1830-70* edited by J.P.T. Bury. 1960. xxii, 765p. £75.00. 0521045487. 11. *Material progress and world-wide problems 1870-1898* edited by F.H. Hinsley. 1962. xi, 743p. £75.00. 0521045495. 12. *The Shifting balance of world forces 1898-1945* edited by C.L. Mowat. 2nd ed. 1968. xxvii, 845p. £75.00. 0521045517. 13. *Companion volume* edited by P. Burke. 1979. vi, 378p. £45.00. 0521221285. 14 contributors. 12 overview essays on specific themes to complement v.6-12. *e.g.* 2. The environment and the economy ... 9. The scientific revolution ... 12. On the last

....(contd.)

2,500 years in Western history, and some remarks on the coming 500. 14. *The Atlas* edited by H.C. Darby and H. Fullard. 1970. 319p. £65.00. 0521077087. *Class No:* 94

Yearbooks & Directories

[2829]
The Annual register a record of world events, 1991. Day, A.J. *and* Hoffman, V., *eds.* Harlow, Essex, Longman, 1989. xvi, 632p., illus. (pl) tables, map, index. ISBN: 0582079268.

First edited in 1758 by Edmund Burke as *The Annual register: a review of public events at home and abroad for the year ...*

88 contributors to the 1988 ed. Running commentary in 19 subdivided sections: 1. United Kingdom - 2. The Americas and Caribbean - 3. The USSR and Eastern Europe - 4. Western, Central and Southern Europe - 5. Middle East and North Africa - 6. Equatorial Africa - 7. Central and Southern Africa - 8. South Asia and Indian Ocean - 9. South-East and East Asia - 10. Australasia and South Pacific - 11. International organizations - 12. Defence and arms control - 13. Religion - 14. The Sciences - 15. The Law - 16. The Arts - 17. Sport - 18. Economic and social affairs - 19. Documents and reference. Obituary. Chronicle of principal events in 1989. p.595-609. Analytical index. *Class No:* 94(058)

Almanacs

[2830]
The Statesman's year-book historical companion. Paxton, J., *ed.* London, Macmillan Reference Books, 1988. xi, 356p. index. ISBN: 0333436598.

Celebrates the 125th anniversary of *The stateman's yearbook* (*qv*).

Records the salient constitutional and political events of each country (extracted from various editons of *The Statesman's year-book*). 'Particular attention has been given to the turbulent political histories of countries becoming independent in this century' (*Preface*). Arrangement is A-Z by country. Further readings. *Class No:* 94(059)

Maps & Atlases

[2831]
The New Cambridge modern history. v.14. The Atlas. Darby, H.C. *and* Fullard, H. Cambridge, Cambridge Univ. Press, 1970. xxiv,319p. maps (some col.). ISBN: 0521077087.

Supersedes *The Cambridge modern history atlas* (2nd ed., 1924).

288 pages of coloured maps; no text. Three groups: the first depicts exploration and political acquisition of parts of the world, plus achievement of independence, 1945-68; the second group covers wars and treaty settlements, from the Peasants' War of 1524-6 to World War II. The third group is of regional maps, each sub-group in chronological order. Well balanced: 15 areas are covered. 'Although it is designed to serve the need of readers of the *New Cambridge modern history*, the atlas is also intended to illustrate school or university courses on modern history' (*Geo Abstracts*, 1972/1, entry 72D/0321). 'One of the most informative and best historical atlases, but also one of the most compact and easiest to handle' (*Library Journal*, v.97, no.18, 15 April 1972, p.1386), giving fuller coverage than does Shepherd's *Historical atlas* (*qv*). Page size, 20x28.5cm. *Class No:* 94(084.3)

Bibliographies

[2832]
HAVLICE, P.P. **Oral history** a reference guide and annotated bibliography. Jefferson, North Carolina, McFarland, 1985. 144p. indexes. softcover. ISBN: 0899501389.

773 entries (abstracts, indexes, catalogues, journals, colloquia *etc.*) range over entire field. Main emphasis is on North American material but European and African items are included. Subject and title indexes allow easy access. 'An important reference tool, superior to the less comprehensive and less up-to-date bibliographies currently available' (*Choice*, v.23,no.2, October 1985,p.171). *Class No:* 94(086.7)(01)

20th Century

Encyclopaedias

[2833]
Chronicle of the 20th century. Mercer, D., *editor in chief.* London, Longman/Chronicle, 1988. 1359p. illus. (some col.), col. maps, ports, index. ISBN: 0582039193.

Published in 13 language editions and in 15 countries, the editorial content being adapted to suit each national readership. Belgium: Éditions Chronique; Denmark: Ladewman Forlageaktieslskab; Finland: Gummerus Kustannus OY; France: Librairie Larousse Éditions Chronique; Federal Republic of Germany: Harenberg Kommunikation; Iceland: Swart a huitu Bokaforlag; Japan: Kodansha Ltd.; Netherlands: Elsevier Boeken B.V./Agon; Norway: J.W. Cappelens Forlag A/S; Spain: Plaza & Janes; Sweden: Bonnier Fakla Bokförlag AB; Switzerland: Ex Libris; Taiwan: Chin Show Cultural Enterprises; USA: Chronicle Publications Inc.

16 contributors are listed: all well-known journalists. Concerns itself entirely with events, devoting 1-3 pages (each 11 in. x 9 in.) to each month from January 1900 - December 1987, presenting a monthly calendar, a diary of events, and illustrated 'news reports'. Cross-references point forward in time, linked previous events are traced by means of the detailed analytical index (p.1296-1356). 'The best new reference book of the year ... reduces the history of the last 88 years to monthly news summaries as they might have appeared in a middle brow tabloid ... It is a brilliant book for finding out when things happened and what exactly happened, almost as good as an entire newspaper cuttings library' (*The Independent*, no.665, 26 November 1988, p.32). *Class No:* 94"19"(031)

Glossaries

[2834]
BBC World Service glossary of current affairs. Williams, T.G., *ed.* Harlow, Essex, Longman Current Affairs; Chicago, St. James Press, 1991. 813p. index. ISBN: 0582068479, UK; 1558621083, US.

Explanations and meanings of over 7,000 legal, political, financial, administrative, media, constitutional, judicial, measurement, religious, terms etc., including abbreviations and acronyms, particular to individual countries listed A-Z with an international section. Index p.775-813. *Class No:* 94"19"(038.1)

[2835]
The Cambridge medieval history. Gwatkin, H.M., *and others,* eds. Cambridge, Cambridge Univ. Press, 8v., 1911-36. illus., tables, maps, bibliogs, indexes.

1. *The Christian Roman Empire and the foundation of the Teutonic Kingdoms.* 1911. xxiii,754p. ISBN 0521045320. 2. *The Rise of the Saracens and the foundation of the Western Empire.* 813. xxiii,889p. 0521045339. 3. *Germany and the Western Empire.* 1922. xxxviii,700p. 0521045347. 4. *The Eastern Roman Empire (717-1453).* 1923. 2nd ed. as *The Byzantine Empire. Pt.1. Byzantium and its neighbours.* 1966. xl,1168p. £90. 0521045355. *Pt.2. Government, church and civilisation.* 1967. xlii,517p. £60. 0521045363. 5. *Contest of Empire and Papacy.* 1926. xliv,1005p. 0521045371. 6. *Victory of the Papacy.* 1929. xli,1047p. £90. 052104538x. 7. *Decline of Empire and Papacy.* 1932. xxxviii,1073p. 0521045398. 8. *The Close of the Middle Ages.* 1936. xxviii,1079p.

A closely-packed survey, each chapter being an authoritative statement by a scholar of repute. An important feature of each volume is the very full bibliography. The 2nd ed. of v.4(2v.xl,1168p.; xlii,517p.) shows a considerable expansion, with 42 plates, 18 maps, numerous tables; general and chapter bibliographies, p.808-1041 p.377-476); analytical indexes.

'By far the most useful and comprehensive work in English' (Davis, R.H.C. *Medieval European history*, p.5). *Class No:* 940.1

Bibliographies

[2836]
International medieval bibliography bibliography for the study of the European Middle Ages (450-1500). School of History, Univ. of Leeds, 1967-. Annual, then 2pa. ISSN: 00207980.

v.24, no.1 *1990* (1991, lii,393p.) has 5,177 entries: General bibliography; general culture and history, then by 57 A-Z topics *e.g.* Archaeology (general, artefacts, sites), Genealogy, Heraldry, Historiography, Local history, subdivided by geographical areas. Works on Africa, the Near East, and the Orient are included only when they bear directly on Europe. Author and general indexes. *Class No:* 940.1(01)

Dictionaries

[2837]
STRAYER, J.R., *ed.* **Dictionary of the Middle Ages.** New York, Charles Scribner's Sons, 13v., 1982-1989. Distributed in UK by Macmillan. illus., maps.

v.13 *Index.* 1989. 0684182793. Over 5000 commissioned articles, mostly from US and Canadian academics, cover all aspects of medieval life in Christendom and Islam. Entries range from 500 word definitions to critical essays of 10,000 words on major figures and topics. All are signed and end with bibliogs., and cross-references. More than 1000 illustrations, charts, and maps. Published under the auspices of the American Council of Learned Societies. The Dictionary receives a grant from the National Endowment for the Humanities. *Class No:* 940.1(038)

Maps & Atlases

[2838]
MATTHEW, D. **Atlas of medieval Europe.** Oxford, Phaidon; New York, Facts on File, 1986. 240p. illus. (some col.), col.maps, bibliog., index. ISBN: 0714823023, UK; 0871961334, US.

First published 1983.

26 topics presented in map form and arranged in 4 parts: 1. Disintegration of the Ancient World - 2. Breaking new ground - 3. The fruits of civilization - 4. Consolidation of the land. 9 Special features including 'The invention pf printing' and 'Medieval mapmaking'. Chronology p.8-9. Glossary p.226-7. Bibliography p.229-231. Gazetteer p.231-7. 224 maps. 'Makes a misunderstood period intelligible to a popular audience' (*Wilson Library Bulletin,* v.58,no.3, November 1983, p.224). *Class No:* 940.1(084.3)

Crusades

[2839]
SETTON, K.M., *ed.* **A History of the Crusades.** Madison, Univ. of Wisconsin Press, 6v., 1969-1990.

V.1-2 first published by Univ. of Pennsylvania Press 1955-1962.

1. *The first hundred years* edited by M.W. Baldwin, 1969. xxxi,707p. ISBN 0299048314. 2. *The later Crusades 1189-1311* edited by R.L. Wooff and H.W. Hazard. 2nd ed. 1969, xxii,859p. 0299048411. 3. *The fourteenth and fifteenth centuries* edited by H.W. Hazard. 1975. xxi,819p. 0299066703. 4. *The art and architecture of the Crusader states* edited by H.W. Hazard. 1977. xxvii,414+10p. 029906820x. 5. *The impact of the Crusades on the Near East* edited by N.P. Zacour and H.W. Hazard. 1985. xxii,599p. 0299091406. 6. *The impact of the Crusades on Europe* edited by N.P. Zacour and H.W. Hazard. 1990. xxiii,703p. 029910740x. V.5 has 10 chapters (*e.g.* 1. Arab culture in the twelfth century ... 2. Impact of the Crusades on Moslem lands ... 8. The Teutonic Knights in the Crusader states); gazetteer and notes on maps, p.519-552; and 13 maps V.4 carries 'Addenda and corrigenda' to v.1-4. V.6 has H.E. Mayer and J. McLellans' Select bibliography of the Crusades (p.511-644). This immense compilation includes A. General works, research aids, historiography - B. Narrative sources in many Western and Near Eastern languages - C. Secondary Works. Also Gazetteer and note on maps p.483-510. *Class No:* 940.1"1095-13"

Maps & Atlases

[2840]
The Atlas of the Crusades. Riley-Smith, J., *ed.* London, Times Books, 1990; New York, Facts on File, 1991. 192p. col. illus., col. maps, bibliog., index. ISBN: 0723003610, UK; 0816021864, US.

19 contributors. 22 narrative chapters arranged in 4 parts: 1. The way of God - 2. Defence of Christendom - 3. Crusading and the world of Chivalry - 4. The last crusaders. Chronology (in 3 cols: The East; Europe and North Africa; Background events) p.10-19. Glossary p.176-9. Bibliography p.173. History ranges from Urban II's. First crusade 1095 AD to the late eighteenth century. *Class No:* 940.1"1095-13"(084.3)

Renaissance

Bibliographies

French

[2841]
Bibliographie internationale de l'Humanisme et de la Renaissance: ouvrage publié sur la recommandation du Conseil International de la Philosophie et des Sciences Humaines avec le concours de l'UNESCO. Genève, Droz, 1966-. v.1-. Annual.

V.20 Travaux parus en 1984. 1988. cxi, 835p. has *c.*5000 unannotated entries organized in 2 parts: 1. Personnages et oeuvres anonymes - 2. Subjects divided by countries (Histoire - Religion et vie religieuse, doctrines philosophiques, politiques et juridiques - Littérature, enseignement et pédagogie, grammaire et linguistique, théâtre, technique du livre, bibliothèques - Arts - Sciences et techniques. About 2000 periodicals are now scanned. Author index. A valuable research tool, even if slow to appear. *Class No:* 940.1"1095-1300"(01)=40

Encyclopaedias

[2842]
BERGIN, T.G. *and* SPEAKE, J., *eds.* **Encyclopedia of the Renaissance.** New York, Facts on File, 1987. London, B.T. Batsford Ltd. 1988. 454p., illus., geneal. tables, bibliog. ISBN: 0816013152, US; 0713459670, UK.

28 contributors. 2500 A-Z cross-referenced entries relating to individuals, issues and events in all fields of human endeavour in 14th-16th century Europe. Bibliography (in subject categories) p.433-440. Sparse chronological table p.441-454. 32 col. plates. 'Easily the best one-volume reference available' (*Choice,* v.25, no.8, April 1988, p.1219). *Class No:* 940.1"1095-1300"(031)

Modern History—Europe (1492-)

Handbooks & Manuals

[2843]
COOK, C. *and* STEVENSON, J. **The Longman handbook of modern European History 1763-1991.** 2nd rev. ed. London and New York, Longman, 1992. 464p. maps, bibliog., general tables, index. ISBN: 0582072905.

Quick reference guide organized in 7 sections: 1. Principal rulers and ministers - 2. Political events (chronology in 27 topics *e.g.* 19. Italian Fascism ... 23. Spain 1909-1939 ... 27. The movement for European unity) - 3. War, diplomacy and imperialism - 4. Economic and Social - 5. Biographies - 6. Glossary (p.301-330) - 7. Topic Bibliography (p.335-394). Maps p.396-412. Analytical index. Companion volume to *The Longman handbook of modern British history 1714-1987* (*q.v.*). 'An outstanding reference work, containing much information not available elsewhere in a single volume' (*Reference Reviews,* v.2, no.4, December 1988, p.224-5). *Class No:* 940.2(035)

20th Century

Bibliographies

[2844]
MEYER, J.A. **An Annotated bibliography of the Napoleonic era:** recent publications, 1945-1985. Westport, Connecticut, Greenwood Press, 1987. xvii,288p.index. (*Bibliographies and Indexes in World History.*)

1754 entries with indicative rather than critical annotations in 10 chapters: 1. Research aids - 2. Printed primary sources - 3. General histories - 4. Napoleon - 5. Napoleon's family - 6. Personal lives - 7. France and the

....(contd.)

world - 8. The art of war on land - 9. Naval affairs - 10. Supplement (1736-1754). Excludes journal articles. Intended as a companion volume to O'Connelly's *Historical dictionary of Napoleonic France 17990-1815.* 'A valuable current source for history in the early 19th Century' (*Choice,* v.25,no.4, December 1987, p.602). *Class No:* 940.2"19"(01)

World Wars 1 & 2

World War 1

[2845]
History of the Great War : based on official documents by direction of the Historical Section of The Committee of Imperial Defence. London, HMSO, 1922-1987.

Military Operations. East Africa August 1914 - September 1916 by C. Hordern. *Egypt and Palestine* (2v.). 1. *From the outbreak of war with Germany to June 1917* by G. Macmunn and C. Falls. 1928. xvii, 445p. 2. *From June 1917 to the end of war* by C. Falls. 1930. 395-748p. (*sic*). *France and Belgium* compiled by J.E. Edmonds (13v). *1914.* 1925. xxv, 548p. *1914* October to November, xxviii, 548p. *1915.* 1927. xliii, 433p. *1915.* 1928. xliv, 488p. *1916* 1932. xxxvi, 523p. *Appendices.* 1932. 232p. *1916 2nd July 1916 to the end of the Battle of the Somme* by W. Miles. 1938. xlv, 601p. *Maps and appendices.* 1935. x, 119p. *1917 The German retreat to the Hindenburg line and the Battle of Arras* by C. Falls. 1940. xxxix, 586p. *Appendices.* 1940. xi, 158p. *1917 The Battle of Cambrai* by W. Miles. 1948. xvi, 399p. *1918 v1. The German offensive and its preliminaries.* 1935. xxx, 569p. *Appendices.* 1935. viii, 148p. 2.*The Continuation of the German offensive.* 1937. xxviii, 550p. 3. *May-July. The German offensives and the first Allied counter-offensive.* 1939. xxxii, 385p. 4. *26th September - 11th November. The Advance to victory.* 1947. xxix, 675p. 5. *September 26 - November 11. The Advance to victory.* 1947. xxix, 675p.
Italy, 1915-1919 by J. Edmonds and others. 1949. xxix, 450p. *Macedonia* (2v). by C. Falls. V.1. *From the outbreak of war to the Spring of 1917.* 1933. xvi, 409p. V.2. *From the Spring of 1917 to the end of the war.* 1935. xvi, 365p. *The Campaign in Mesopotamia 1914-1918* (4v). by F. Moberly. 1924-1927. vii, 402p.+xiv, 581p.+xiii, 460p.+xiii, 447p. *Togoland and the Cameroons 1914-1916* by F. Moberly. 1931. xxv, 469p. *Gallipoli* (2v). by C.F. Aspinall-Oglander. V.1 *Inception of the campaign to May 1915.* 1929. xvii, 380p. 2. *May 1915 to the evacuation* 1932. xv, 517p. *Operations in Persia 1914-1919* by F.J. Moberly. 1987. xxii, 490p. ISBN 011290453x. *Transportation on the Western Front 1914-1918* by A.M. Henniker. 1937. xxxiv, 531p. *The Occupation of the Rhineland 1918-1939.* by J.E. Edmonds. 1987. xxv, 444p. ISBN 0112904548. *A history of the blockade of Germany and of the countries associated with her in the great war Austria-Hungary, Bulgaria, and Turkey 1914-1918* by A.C. Bell. xvi, 845p. *Class No:* 940.3

Maps & Atlases

[2846]
GILBERT, M. First World War atlas. Cartography by Arthur Banks and Terry Bicknell. 2nd ed. London, Weidenfeld and Nicolson, 1985. xvl, 159, xxxviip. maps, bibliog., index. ISBN: 0297786172.

First published 1970.

Over 150 annotated black-and-white maps, covering military, naval, aerial, diplomatic, technical and economic aspects in 9 sections. Excellent classified bibliography p.xvii-xxvii. *Class No:* 940.3(084.3)

Chronologies

[2847]
GRAY, R. *and* **ARGYLE, C. Chronicle of the First World War.** New York and Oxford, Facts On File, 2v., 1990-91. ISBN: 0816025975, set.

1. *1914-1916.* 1990. 352p. maps, bibliog., tables, index. £21.95. ISBN 0816021392. Preliminary sections, 'Prelude to Sarajevo' p.8-9; 'Sarajevo to the Outbreak of War', p.9-10. Glossary (of abbreviations and First World War terminology) p.314-35. Bibliography p.309-13. 19 maps.

1917-1921. 1990. 383p. maps, bibliog., tables, index. £21.95. 0816025959. Supplementary material: Armistice Terms 11 Nov. 1918, p.264. Chronology: towards peace 1919-1921, p.265-78. The Peace process 1918-1923, p.279-80. Who's who in the First World War p.298-318. Glossary p.339-60. Bibliography p.334-38. 15 maps.

Definitive day-by-day outline of events, 28 July 1914 - 31 December 1916 and 1 January 1917 - 31 December 1918, presented in 9 vertical columns: 1. Western Front - 2. Eastern Front - 3. Southern Fronts - 4. Turkish Fronts - 5. African operations - 6. Sea war - 7. Air war - 8. International events - 9. Home Fronts. *Class No:* 940.3(090)

Biographies

[2848]
HERWIG, H.H. *and* **HEYMAN, N.M. Biographical dictionary of World War I.** Westport, Connecticut, Greenwood Press, 1982. xiv, 624p. bibliog. ISBN: 0313213569.

Introduction (p.1-59) covers the origins of war, the Western front, the war in the East, the war at sea, the home front, and the Peace. Dictionary of biographical sketches p.61-365. Chronology p.367-376. Bibliography (p.395-406) lists works in 6 languages. Index. p.407-424. 'A model of its genre in both form and content and will likely become for all large libraries the standard reference work on the subject' (*RQ,* v.22, no.2, Winter 1982, p.196-197). *Class No:* 940.3(092)

Europe (From 1919)

Europe—Eastern

[2849]
The Times guide to Eastern Europe inside the other Europe. A comprehensive handbook. Sword, K., *ed.* 2nd ed. London, Times Books, 1990. 270p. maps, index. ISBN: 0723004382.

10 contributors. Part 1. (8 chapters on each of Eastern bloc countries plus Albania and Yugoslavia). Part 2. The Soviet Union (9. An overview: from dogmatism to uncertainty - 10. Russia - 11. The Baltic States - 12. Byelorussia - 13. Ukraine - 14. Moldavia. 12 Appendices: 1. Warsaw Pact 1955 - 2. Helsinki Conference 1973-75 ... 6. Eastern Europe after the First World War ... 8. Languages and Nations of Eastern Europe - 9. Nationalities in the USSR ... 11. 1990 Election results. Attempts to present a considered assessment of the history and development of Eastern Europe from the end of World War 2. *Class No:* 940.5(401)

World War 2

[2850]
History of the Second World War. London, H.M. Stationery Office, 1949-. tables, charts, maps.

Certain volumes have been reprinted by Kraus-Thomson Organization Ltd.

United Kingdom. Military histories edited by Sir J.R.M. Butler. Grand strategy (6v.). Campaigns: The campaign in Norway - France and Flanders, 1939-40 - The

....(contd.)

Mediterranean and Middle East (6v.) - The war against Japan (5v.) - Victory in the West (2v.) - The defence of the United Kingdom - The war at sea (3v.) - The strategic air offensive against Germany 1939-1945 (4v.) - Civil affairs and military government (4v.).

United Kingdom. Civil series, edited by Sir K. Hancock. Introductory (4v., including Statistical digest of the war) - General series (16v.) - War production series (8v.).

United Kingdom. Medical series, Editor-in-chief, Sir A.S. McNalty Clinical volumes (3v.) - Fighting services: Royal Navy (2v.); Army (7v.); Royal Air Force (4v.) - Medical services in wars - Civilian services (4v.).

British Foreign Policy in the Second World War by L. Woodward (5v.).

British intelligence in the Second World War by F.H. Hinsley and others (5v. in 6, 1979-1990).

S.O.E. in France: an account of the work of the British Special Operations Executive in France 1940-1944 by M.R.D. Foot.

Sir J.R.M. Butler's 'The British Military Histories of the War of 1939-45' and Sir K. Hancock's 'British Civil Histories of the Second World War', p.511-14 and p.518-25, Robin Higham's *Official histories* (Kansas State University Library, 1970) offer interesting insights. *Class No:* 940.53

Encyclopaedias

[2851]

SNYDER, L.L. **Historical guide to World War II.** Westport, Connecticut, Greenwood Press, 1982. xii, 838p. ISBN: 0313232164.

Almost 900 entries (mostly) relating to non-military aspects (unlike Marcel Baudot's *Historical encyclopaedia of World War II*) with emphasis on economic, political, social, cultural and psychological aspects. Dunkirk: 49 lines+3 refs; Pearl Harbour 114+6; Dieppe 113+3; Stalingrad 90+5. Gracie Fields 15+0; Vera Lynn 0; Marlene Dietrich 11+2; Tokyo Rose 39+0. Abbreviations WW II acronyms p.ix-xii. Appendix 1 Chronology p.785-789; 2. Ten basic books (5 UK, 5 US) p.790. Index p.791-838. 'For the professional historian, the amateur scholar, the WW II buff, and especially for the student essayist' (*Preface*). *Class No:* 940.53(031)

Maps & Atlases

[2852]

The Times atlas of the Second World War. Keegan, J., *ed.* London, Times Books, 1989. 254p. col. illus., col. maps, col. diagrs., bibliog., index. ISBN: 0723003173.

13 contributors. 90 double-page geographic, thematic and chronological features (maps, text, illustrations) delineating every theatre of war. Military formations and units and key to map symbols p.13. Chronology (6 colour coded geographic bands) p.14-27. Bibliography p.208. Glossary p.209-19. 450 full-colour maps and major battle reconstructions. 150 photographic illustrations and diagrams. 'Conceived as a means of conveying to its users both the totality and complexity of the Second World War ... its coverage is not exclusively military' (*Introduction*). *Class No:* 940.53(084.3)

Biographies

[2853]

MASON, D. **Who's who in World War II.** London, Weidenfeld & Nicolson, 1978. 363p. illus., ports., maps. ISBN: 0297773763.

About 175 biographies, with 154 good illus. and portraits. (General Alexander ... General Zhukov). 'Rommel': p.255-62; 5 illus. Glossary, p.351-63. 4p. of maps appended. British, American and German biographies predominate. 'A very interesting and well produced work of reference on the War' (*Library Review,* Autumn 1979, p.186). *Class No:* 940.53(092)

Commonwealth

[2854]

The Cambridge history of the British Empire. Cambridge, Cambridge Univ. Press, 8v., 1929-1988.

1: *The old Empire, from the beginnings to 1783.* 1929. 2: *Growth of the new Empire, 1783-1870.* 1940. 3: *The Empire-Commonwealth, 1870-1919;* edited by E.A. Benians. 1959. 4: *British India, 1497-1858;* edited by H.H. Dodwell. 1929. 5: *Indian Empire, 1858-1918, with chapters on the development of administration, 1818-1858;* edited by H.H. Dodwell, 1932. 6: *Canada and Newfoundland.* 1930. 7: pt.1: *Australia;* edited by E. Scott. Reissued 1988. xxv,759p. £35.00. ISBN 0521356210. 7: pt.2: *New Zealand* 1933. 8: *South Africa, Rhodesia and the Protectorates.* 2nd ed. 1963. Each volume carries some 20-30 chapters by specialists. The lengthy, valuable bibliography appended to each volume is divided into pt.1, Collections of MSS in public and private archives and official papers and publications, and pt.2, Other works. *Class No:* 941-44

Bibliographies

[2855]

CATTERALL, P. 'The Empire, the Commonwealth and the Mandated Territories' *British history 1945-1987: an annotated bibliography* (q.v.).

'External relations', chapter 3 of *British history 1945-1987: an annotated bibliography* (1980) includes 1080 items listed in the following sub-divided sections: B. The Empire ... General - C. Empire and Commonwealth in Asia - D. Middle East - E. Sub-Saharan Africa - F. Caribbean - G. Australasia and the Pacific - H. Canada - I. Gibraltar and Malta - J. Atlantic and Antarctic (p.102-95). The aim of these sections 'has been to provide an extensive guide to the nature of the literature on the demission of power, both generally and area by area, and, where appropriate, on the continuation of Commonwealth relations' (*Preface*). *Class No:* 941-44(01)

[2856]

ROYAL COMMONWEALTH SOCIETY. **Biography catalogue of the Library** of the Royal Commonwealth Society. Simpson, D.H. London, Royal Commonwealth Society, 1961. xxiii,511p. ISBN: 0905067355.

'The aim has been to list all the Library's biographical material. Books published up to the autumn of 1960 and periodicals to the close of 1959 have been included' (*Preface*). Some 12,000 entries for over 6,500 individuals, embracing periodical articles and analytical entries from volumes of collective biography, as well as books and pamphlets. The main sequence, 'Individual biographies' (p.-388) is followed by 'Collective biography and country indexes' (p.388-431), 'Addenda' (p.433-5) and 'Supplementary list of authors' (p.441-511). 'The men and women included are in the main, those born in, or actively connected with, countries of the Commonwealth, and persons in the United Kingdom who have been of significance in Imperial affairs' (*Preface*). There are also

HISTORY

HISTORY

HISTORY

HISTORY

(contd)

HISTORY

....(contd.)

numerous entries for explorers and travellers of many countries. Items asterisked represent books or periodicals destroyed by enemy action but inserted for their bibliographical value. Entries include full name, dates of birth and death and a brief description of the biographee; they indicate the presence of portraits and illustrations. Supplemented in v.7 of the RCS *Subject catalogue of the Royal Commonwealth Society* (Boston, Mass., G.K. Hall, 1971). *Class No:* 941-44(01)

Great Britain

[2857]
English historical documents. Douglas, D.C., *ed.* London, Eyre Methuen; New York, Oxford Univ. Press, 1953-. v.1-. diagrs. maps.

1. *c.500-1042* edited by D. Whitelock. 2nd ed., 1979. xxxii,960p. ISBN 0413324907. 2. *1042-1189* edited by D.C. Douglas and G.W. Greenaway. 2nd rev. ed., 1980. xxiv,1064p. £65. 0413325008. 3. *1189-1327* edited by H. Rothwell. 1975. xxiv,1032p. £65. 0413233006. 4. *1327-1485* edited by A.R. Myers. 1969. lxviii,1236p. £65. 0413233103. 5. *1485-1558* edited by C.H. Williams. 1967, xviii,1082p. £65. 0413233200. 6. *1558-1603* In preparation. 7. (1) *1603-1640*; (2) *1640-1660* In preparation. 8. *1660-1714* edited by A. Browning. 1953. xxxii, 966p. £65. 0413206505. 9. *American colonial documents to 1776* edited by Jensen. 1955. xxiv, 888p. £65. 0413206602. 10. *1714-1783* edited by D.B. Horn and M. Ransome. 1957. xxviii, 972p. £65. 0413233502. 11. *1783-1832* edited by A. Aspinall and E.A. Smith. 1959. xxx,992p. £65. 041323360x. 12. (1) *1833-1874* edited by G.M. Young and W.D. Handcock. 1956. xxiv,1018p. 12. (2) *1874-1914* edited by W.D. Handcock. 1977. xxiv,726p. £65. 0413233707.

Aims 'to make generally accessible a wide selection of the fundamental sources of English history' (*General preface*, v.12, pt.1). Each volume has a lengthy general introduction and a select bibliography; each of its parts has its own introduction and select bibliography. All documents (or selections from documents) are translated into English (as necessary), the text being well footnoted. V.12, pt.1 (12 parts has 269 items, including departmental and Royal Commission reports, *Times* leaders, legislation and statistical data. V.12, pt.2 (12 parts) covers such subjects as economic structure and development; religion and the churches; imperialism and foreign affairs; law penal system and courts; central and local government; education; poor law and problem of poverty; factories, health and housing; trade unions and socialism. *Class No:* 941.0

[2858]
The Oxford history of England. Oxford, Clarendon Press, 1936-1981.

1A: *Roman Britain* by P. Salway. 1981. ISBN 019821717x. This replaced the first part of *Roman Britain and the English settlements* by R.G. Collingwood and J.N.L. Myres, 2nd ed., 1937. 1B: *The English settlements* by J.N.L. Myers. £17.50. 2. *Anglo-Saxon England* by F.M. Fenton, 3rd ed. 1971. 0198217161. 3. *From Domesday Book to Magna Carta 1087-1216* by A.L. Poole, 2nd ed. 1955. 0198217072. 4. *The thirteenth century 1216-1307* by M. Powicke, 2nd ed. 1962. 0198217080. 5. *The fourteenth century 1307-1399* by M. McKisack. 1964. 0198217129. 6. *The fifteenth century 1399-1485* by E.F. Jacob. 1964. 0198217145. 7. *The earlier Tudors 1485-1558* by J.D. Mackie. 1964. 0198217064. 8. *The reign of Elizabeth 1558-1603* by J.B. Black. 2nd ed. 1959. 0198217013. 9. *The early Stuarts 1603-1660* by G. Davies. 2nd ed. 1959. 0198217048. 10. *The later Stuarts 1660-1714* by G. Clark. 2nd ed. 1956. 0198217021. 11. *The Whig supremacy 1714-1760* by B. Williams. 2nd ed. revised by C.H. Stuart 1962. 0198217102. 12. *The reign of George III 1760-1815* by J.S.

....(contd.)
Watson. 1964. 0198217137. 13. *The age of reform 1815-1870* by L. Woodward. 2nd ed. 1962. 0198217110. 14. *England 1870-1914* by R.C.K. Ensor. 1964. 0198217056. 15. *English history 1914-1945* by A.J.P. Taylor. 1965. 0198217153. *Consolidated index* edited by R. Raper 1991. vi,622p. 0198217862.

Standard introduction to the periods concerned with valuable critical bibliographies. V.15, brilliantly and occasionally controversially written (see *Times Literary Supplement*, no.3329, 16 December 1965, p.1169-70, 'History Taylor-made'), has a lengthy bibliography in the form of a running commentary (p.602-39). *Class No:* 941.0

Bibliographies

[2859]
Annual bibliography of British and Irish history. London, Harvester Wheatsheaf; since 1990 Oxford Univ. Press, 1976-. Annual.

Published for Royal Historical Society.

Comprehensive and authoritative survey of books and articles published in a calendar year. Arranged in 14 subdivided sections: A. Auxiliary (Archives, Bibliography, Works of reference) - B. General - C/I. by historical period - J. Medieval Wales - K. Scotland before the Union - L/M. Ireland - N. Empire & Commonwealth post-1783. Each section is edited by a specialist in the period. Separate author, personal name, place, and subject indexes. *1990* volume (1991,xii,275p. ISBN 0198202946) lists 1221 books and 2948 articles and also prints a history of the *Annual Bibliography* (p.x-xi) by G.R. Elton, its erstwhile editor. *Class No:* 941.0(01)

[2860]
Bibliography of British history. Oxford, Clarendon Press, 1928-. Issued under the direction of the American Historical Association and the Royal Historical Society of Great Britain.

1. *A bibliography of English history to 1485* edited by E.B. Graves. 1975, xxiv,1103p. £60.00. ISBN 0198223919 (7,221 entries). Basically a revision of C. Gross' *Sources and literature of English history from the earliest times to about 1485* (London, Longmans, 2nd ed. 1915). 2. *Tudor period 1485-1603* edited by C. Read. 2nd ed. 1959. xxviii,624p. Reprinted Hassocks, Sussex, Harvester Press; Totowa, New Jersey, Rowan & Littlefield. 0855276843 (UK). 0847660745 (US) (6,543 entries). First published 1933. 3. *Stuart Period 1603-1714* edited by G. Davies and M.F. Keeler. 2nd ed., 1970. xxxv,734p. £60.00. 0198213719. (4,350 entries). First published 1928. 4. *The Eighteenth Century 1714-1789* edited by S. Pargellis and J.D. Medley. Harvester Press and Rowan and Littlefield. 1971. xxvi,642p. 0855271361 (UK) (4,558 entries). 5. *1789-1851* edited by L.M. Brown and I.R. Christie. 1977, xxxi,759p. £55.00. 0198223900. (4,782 entries). 6. *1851-1914* edited by H.J. Hanham. 1978. xxvii,1606p. £70.00. 019823897. (10,829 entries).

Each volume has entries (mostly annotated) in sections, and usually with section introductions. *Stuart period, 1603-1714* is invaluable for its references to MS sources. The *1789-1851* volume has 15 sections: 1. General reference works - 2. Political history - 3. Constitutional history - 4. Legal history - 5. Ecclesiastical history - 6. Military history - 7. Naval history - 8. Economic history - 9. Social history - 10. Cultural history - 11. Local history - 12. Wales - 13. Scotland - 14. Ireland - 15. The British Empire. Index, p.603-759. The 1851-1914 volume, with its massive index (p.1239-1606), lacks section introductions. Alan Day's 'Birthpangs of a bibliography', *New Library World*, v.79, no.938, August 1978, p.154-7, is a brief account of this monumental and invaluable series. *Class No:* 941.0(01)

CONCISE

[2861]
Writings on British History. London, Institute of Historical Research, annual.

1901-1933 (1968-70). 5v. in 7 (Williams Dawson): 1. *The auxiliary sciences and general works* - 2. *The Middle Ages* - 3. *The Tudor and Stuart periods* - 4. *The eighteenth century* - 5. *1815-1914. 1934-1945* (1937-60). 8v. (William Dawson). *1946-1948* (1973). (Inst. Hist. Res.) *1949-1951* (1975). *1952-1954* (1975). *1955-1957* (1977). *1958-1959* (1977). *1960-1961* (1978). *1962-1964* (1979). *1965-1966* (1981). *1967-1968* (1982). *1969-1970* (1984). *1971-1972* (1985). *1973-1974* (1986).

The 1973-74 v. has sub-title: 'a bibliography of books and articles on the history of Great Britain from *c.*450AD to 1939 published during the year 1973-74 inclusive with appendix containing a select list of publications in these years on British history since 1939' (xix, 283p.). It has 5193 numbered entries, unannotated, but references to reviews are included. Over 400 journals scanned. Part 1. General works (Auxiliary sciences; Bibliographies and indexes; Archives and collections; Historiography, study and teaching; British history in general; English local history and topography; Wales and Monmouthshire; Scotland; Ireland; British Empire and Commonwealth; Genealogy and family history; Collected biography) - 2. Period histories (7 periods: Pre-conquest: Medieval; Tudor; Stuart; 18th century; 19th century; 20th century). Appendix: Select list of works published in the years 1973-74 on British history since 1939. Analytical index p.207-283. Slow progress is being made on the time-lag in publication. 'The *Writings* should be available, not only in every academic library, but also in every city and county reference library that claims to cater for serious historical study' (*History*, v.41, Feb-June-October 1956, p.361-363). *Class No:* 941.0(01)

Maps & Atlases

[2862]
FALKUS, M. *and* **GILLINGHAM, J.,** *eds.* **Historical atlas of Britain.** Rev. ed. London, Kingfisher Books, 1987. 223p. col. illus., col. maps. ISBN: 0862722950.
First published London, Granada, 1981.
21 academic contributors. Arranged in 6 chronological chapters 4000 BC to the present day dealing with political changes and 2 chapters on social and economic developments. Chronology of world history p.216-217. Index p.218-223. 'Although much more expensive and ambitious than G.S.P. Freeman-Grenville's *Atlas of British History* (London 1879), it is a much superior work' (*Choice*, v.19, no.9, May 1982, p.1216). *Class No:* 941.0(084.3)

Chronologies

[2863]
FRYDE, E.B., *and others.* **Handbook of British chronology.** 3rd ed. London, Royal Historical Society 1986. xxxix, 605p. (*R.H.S. Guides And Handbooks.*) ISBN: 0861931068. ISSN: 00804398.
First published in 1939 edited by F.M. Powicke; second edition in 1961 edited by Powicke and E.B. Fryde.
Lists of rulers, with style and significant dates, of officers of state, bishops, dukes, marquesses and earls; tables of parliament and councils. The 3rd ed. adds the names of Chancellors and Under-Treasurers of the Exchequer 1559-1713, First Secretaries of State 1962-1968, and Commanders-in-chief of land forces 1642-1904. Bibliographical guide to the lists of English office-holders p.xxiii-xxxix. 'Clearly the editors have produced a most co-ordinated work of reference' (*Archives*, v.18, no.78). *Class No:* 941.0(090)

Biographies

[2864]
Who's who in British history. Treasure, G.R., *ed.* London, Shepheard-Walwyn; New York, St. James Press, 8v., 1988-. maps, bibliog., index.
Replaces 'Who's who in history' series published by Basil Blackwell (5v. 1960-1975).
1. Fletcher R. *Roman Britain and Anglo-Saxon England.* 1989. xxv,245p. ISBN 0856830895 - 2. Tyerman, C. *Early medieval England* - 3. Hicks, M. *Late medieval England.* 1991. 400p. 0856830925 - 4. Routh, C.R.N. *Tudor England.* 1990. 476p. 0856830933 - 5. Hill. C.P. *Stuart Britain.* 1988. xiv,466p. 0856830755 - 6. Treasure, G.R. *Early Hanoverian Britain.* 1991. 0856830763 - 7. Treasure, G.R. *Late Hanoverian Britain.* 1991. 480p. 0856830941 - 8. *Victorian Britain.* (to be announced) 1992. 'Each volume paints a portrait of an age. The persons selected are not confined to those who made their mark on church or state, but extended to a wider cross-section of society, including artists, explorers, scientists, entrepreneurs and eccentrics. The series differs from the conventional *Who's Who* in two major respects: 1. entries are arranged in a broadly chronological rather than alphabetical sequence to facilitate reading about contemporaries; 2. each essay conveys more than the bare facts of the subject's life; it places him in the context of his age and evokes what was distinctive and interesting in his personality and achievement' (*Publisher's announcement*). *Class No:* 941.0(092)

Archives

[2865]
The Records of the nation The Public Record Office 1838-1988. The British Record Society 1888-1988. Martin, G.H. *and* Spufford, P., *eds.* Woodbridge, Suffolk, Boydell Press/The British Record Society, 1990. viii,312p. tables, index. ISBN: 0851155383.
21 chapters by different hands in 4 sections: 1. The history and development of the PRO- - 2. Calendars and indexes - 3. Contrasting consumers - 4. The probate records of the nation: new approaches to wills, inventories and accounts. Includes chapter 8. The thirty-year rule and freedom of access ... 11. National Register of Archives and other nationwide finding aids ... 14. A genealogist's view of the Public Records. Edited texts of papers given at the historical conference in London to mark the PRO's 150th anniversary and the British Record Society's centenary. *Class No:* 941.0(093.20)

Micromaterials

[2866]
The National inventory of documentary sources in the United Kingdom and Ireland. Cambridge and Alexandria, Virginia, Chadwyck-Healey, 1985-. Silver halide positive microfiche at 24 x reduction.
NIDS is an open-ended series published in units (each containing several hundred finding aids) at the rate of 8 per annum. Units 25 x 32 are published 1988/89.
Provides immediate access to over 12000 archives and manuscript collections in national and local government records offices, government academic and public libraries, museums, specialist research institutions, and private collections, by reproducing their finding aids on microfiche. The indexing apparatus offers 3 possible access routes; a list of finding aids; a names and subjects index; and also by titles. A free handbook, *How to use the National Inventory of Documentary Sources in the United Kingdom and Ireland in your research*, is available to prospective users and purchasers. G. Palmer's 'The National Inventory and local history', *Local History*, no.6, May 1985, p.10-11 stresses its usefulness in that area. *Class No:* 941.0(093.20)(003.5)

Bibliographies

[2867]
GREAT BRITAIN. PUBLIC RECORD OFFICE. Guide to the contents of the Public Record Office. London, H.M. Stationery Office, 3v., 1963-69.

Supersedes M.S. Guiseppi's *Guide to the manuscripts preserved in the Public Record Office* (1923-24. 2v.), of which it is largely a revision.

The Records transferred to the PRO between 1923 and 1960 'have not only lengthened previously existing series but have added upwards of two thousand classes not known to Guiseppi's *Guide* (*Preface*). Arrangement is by administrative provenance. General classes (*e.g.*, Records of the High Court of Admiralty) are allotted separate sections, with introductions. Each type of record (*e.g.*, Prize Appeal Records) is briefly annotated. Each volume has a key to regnal numbers; chronological index to statutes cited in text; index of persons and places; index of subject. V.1 has a glossary. V.3 has corrigenda and addenda to v.102. *Class No:* 941.0(093.20)(01)

Yearbooks & Directories

[2868]
FOSTER, J. and SHEPPARD, J. British archives: a guide to archive resources in the United Kingdom. 2nd ed. London, Macmillan; New York, Stockton Press, 1989. lviii, 834p. bibliog., index. ISBN: 0333443470.

1st ed. 1982.

1048 entries (340 more than 1st ed.). Data: address; telephone; enquiries to (*i.e.* named officer), hours, access, historical background, acquisition policy, major collections, significant non-manuscript material, finding aids, facilities, and publications. Index to collections p.797-828. Guide to key subjects p.829-34. Useful addresses p.xlvii-lii. Useful publications p.liii-lvii. 'Aims to consolidate information for the historian and archivist and provide a starting point for the first-time user of archives' (*Introduction*). Definitive work much improved in this edition. *Class No:* 941.0(093.20)(058)

Roman & Anglo Saxon Period

Maps & Atlases

[2869]
JONES, B. and MATTINGLY, D. An Atlas of Roman Britain. Oxford, Blackwell Reference, 1990. x,341p. illus., maps, bibliog., index. ISBN: 0631137912.

Presents in cartographic form the whole corpus of knowledge of Romano - British studies: 1. Physical context - 2. Britain and the Roman geographers - 3. Britain before the conquest - 4. Conquest and garrisoning of Britain - 5. Development of the Provinces - 6. Economy - 7. Countryside - 8. Religion - 9. Devolution. Bibliography (by chapter) p.321-32. 273 maps. 'Perceptively abreast of the latest archaeological and literary discoveries' (*Choice*, v.28,no.9, May 1991, p.1546). *Class No:* 941.01(084.3)

Victorian Age

Encyclopaedias

[2870]
MITCHELL, S., ed. Victorian Britain: an encyclopedia. New York, Garland, 1988; London, St. James Press, 1991. xxi,986p. illus., bibliog., index. ISBN: 0824015134, US; 1558621059, UK.

Signed articles covering persons, events, institutions, topics, groups, and artifacts in Great Britain 1837-1901 are enhanced with individual authoritative bibliographies. Chronology p.xi-xxi. Research Materials for Victorian

....(contd.)
Studies p.887-93. Analytical index. 'Intended to serve as an overview and point of entry into the complex interdisciplinary field of Victorian studies' (*Preface*). *Class No:* 941.08(031)

20th Century

Bibliographies

[2871]
CATTERALL, P. British history 1945-1987 an annotated bibliography. Oxford, Basil Blackwell for the Institute of Contemporary British History, 1990. xxxii,843p. indexes. ISBN: 0631170499.

8644 entries record the significant literature on events between the 1945 and 1987 general elections. They are marshalled into 15 heavily sub-divided chapters: 1. General - 2. Political and constitutional history - 3. External relations - 4. Defence - 5. Legal system - 6. Religion - 7. Economic history - 8. Environmental history - 9. Social history - 10. Education - 11. Intellectual and cultural history - 12. Local history - 13. Wales - 14. Scotland - 15. Northern Ireland. Chapter 2 has 10 sub-categories (General; Histories of Post-war administrations; Constitution; Monarchy; Administration and central government; Parliament; Party history and political biography; Political thought; Electoral history; Pressure groups). Official publications, specialist articles from academic journals, bibliographies and databases are included. 'There can hardly be a research library in the country, or further afield for that matter, that will not need to order it despite its ton-up price' (*Reference Reviews*, v.5,no.3, 1991, p.41). *Reference Reviews* Best Generalist Reference Work 1991. *Class No:* 941.082(01)

Scotland

[2872]
The New history of Scotland. Wormald, J., *ed.* London, Edward Arnold, 1978-. maps, geneal tables, bibliogs., indexes.

1. *Warlords and holy men AD800-1000* by A.P. Smyth. 2. *Kingship and unity 1000-1306* by G.W.S. Barrow. 3. *Independence and nationhood 1306-1469* by A. Grant. 4. *Court, Kirk and community 1470-1625* by J. Wormald. 5. *Lordship to patronage 1603-1745* by R. Mitchison. 6. *Integration, enlightenment, and industrialization 1746-1832* by B. Lennan. 7. *Industry and ethos 1832-1914* by S. Checkland and O. Checkland. 8. *No gods and precious few heroes 1914-1980* by C. Harvie. Presents the latest research on Scottish history from the earliest period to the present day. *Class No:* 941.1

Encyclopaedias & Dictionaries

[2873]
DONNACHIE, J. and HEWITT, G. Companion to Scottish history: from the Reformation to the present. London, B.T. Batsford, 1989. 268p. illus., maps.

Major events and personalities in essays ranging from less than 100 to more than 3000 words arranged A-Z but is 'neither a dictionary nor an encyclopedia' (*Preface*). Selection of topics 'governed partly by the relative historical importance of each entry and partly by the findings of recent research.' 13 Appendices including 1. Chronological table (p.217-23) ... 11. Principal surnames and territorial titles. 17 maps. *Class No:* 941.1(03)

Yearbooks & Directories

England & Wales—Local History

[2874]

COX, M. **Exploring Scottish history:** a directory of resource centres for local history. Aberdeen Univ. Press, 1991. 120p. pbk. ISBN: 0080412149.

Guide to the collections and services of over 250 archive and record offices. Data: hours, facilities, and other directory information. *Class No: 941.1(058)*

Ireland

[2875]

A New history of Ireland. Moody, T.W., *and others.* Oxford, Clarendon Press, 10v., 1976-.

1. *Prehistoric and early Ireland* 2. *Medieval Ireland 1169-1534* edited by A. Cosgrove. 1987. xlviii, 982p.+42p. plates. £75.00. 0198217412. 3. *Early modern Ireland 1534-1691* edited by T.W. Moody and others. 1976. lxiii, 736p. £55.00. 0198217390. 4. *Eighteenth-century Ireland 1691-1800* edited by T.W. Moody and W.E. Vaughan. 1985. 914p. £70.00. ISBN 0198217420. 5. *Ireland under the Union 1. 1801-70* edited by W.E. Vaughan. 1988. lxv, 850p. £75.00. ISBN 0198217439. 6. *Ireland under the Union 2. 1870-1921* 7. *Ireland 1921-1984* And 3 Companion volumes: 8. *A chronology of Irish history to 1976* edited by T.W. Moody and others. 1987. xii, 591p. £60.00. ISBN 0198217447. 9. *Maps, genealogies, lists: a comprehensive guide to Irish history* edited by T.W. Moody and others. 1982. xii, 59'p. £95.00. ISBN 0198217455. 10 *Illustrations, statistics, bibliography, documents.* Authoritative large-scale, cooperative history to be completed in 10v. with some 70 contributors, published under the auspices of the Royal Irish Academy. T.W. Moody's 'A New History of Ireland' *Irish Historical Studies*, v.XVI, no.63, March 1969, p.1-17 outlines its genesis and planning. *Class No: 941.5*

[2876]

NEWMAN, P.R. **Companion to Irish history 1603-1921** from the submission of Tyrone to Partition. Oxford & New York, Facts On File, 1991. xi,244p. maps, bibliog. ISBN: 081602572x.

Compendium of cross-referenced A-Z entries relating to the personalities, organizations, policies, legislation, battles, philosophies, and beliefs which shaped Irish history. Appendices gives names of Viceroys of Ireland 1603-1921; Deputies in Ireland 1603-1880; and Chief Secretaries in Ireland 1603-1921. Chronology p.230-3. Bibliography p.234-6. 6 maps. *Class No: 941.5*

Chronologies

[2877]

A Chronology of Irish history to 1976. Moody, T.W., *and others.* Oxford, Clarendon Press, 1982. xii, 591p. index. (*A New History of Ireland.*) ISBN: 0198217447.

All dateable important events in the text of the *New history* are included along with others which do not find a place there, allowing the *Chronology* to stand as an independent reference work. Arranged in periods (each furnished with an introduction and glossary) corresponding with the primary divisions of the *New history* (*qv*). Analytical index p.473-591. *Class No: 941.5(090)*

[2878]

The Darwen County Histories. Chichester, Sussex, Phillimore.

Bristol and Gloucestershire by B. Smith and E. Ralph. - *Buckinghamshire* by K. Tiller - *Cambridgeshire* by B. Galloway - *Cheshire* by D. Sylvester - *Cornwall* by I. Soulsby. 1986. - *Cumberland and Westmorland* by W. Rollinson - *Derbyshire* by J. Childs. 1987. - *Devon* by R. Stanes - *Dorset* by C. Cullingford - *County Durham* by D. Pocock and R. Norris - *Essex* by A.C. Edwards - *Gwynedd* by D. Sylvester - *Hampshire* by B. Carpenter-Turner - *Herefordshire* by J. and M. West - *Hertfordshire* by T. Rook - *Huntingdonshire* by M. Wickes - *Kent* by F. Jessup - *Lancashire* by J.J. Bagley - *Leicestershire and Rutland* by R. Millward - *Lincolnshire* by A. Rogers - *Norfolk* by S.W. Martins - *Northamptonshire* by R.L. Greenall - *Northumberland and Newcastle* by L. Hepple - *Nottinghamshire* by D. Kaye - *Oxfordshire* by M. Jessup - *Shropshire* by B. Trinder - *Somerset* by R. Dunning - *Staffordshire* by M.W. Greenslade - *Suffolk* by D. Dymond and P. Northeast - *Surrey* by P. Brandon - *Sussex* by J.R. Armstrong - *Warwickshire and Birmingham* by T. Slater - *Wiltshire* by B. Watkin - *Worcestershire* by D. Lloyd.

'In contrast to *The Victoria history of the counties of England* the objective is to produce a concise and readable synopsis of the history of each county from prehistory to the present day'. Each volume has about 40,000 words of text and between 16 and 20 maps. 'All the authors show their ability to absorb local detail and recent research into a general narrative' (*Local Historian*, v.17, no.5, Febuary 1987, p.299). *Class No: 942.1/.9*

[2879]

A Regional history of England. Cunliffe, B. *and* Hey, D., *eds.* London, Longman, 1986-. illus.

10 regions each covered by two linked but independent volumes written by authors who have been actively involved in local research. The first relying on archaeological data covering the period up to 1000 AD; and the second extending the coverage to the present day. Higham, N. *The northern counties to AD 1000.* 1986. 404p. £25.00. ISBN 0582492750. McCord, N. and Thompson, R. *The northern counties from AD 1000.* Jones, G.D.B. *The Lancashire/Cheshire region to AD 1000.* Smith, J. *The Lancashire/Cheshire region from AD 1000.* Manby, T.G. *Yorkshire to AD 1000.* Hey, D. *Yorkshire from AD 1000.* 1986. 360p. pbk. £11.50. 0582492122. Rowley, R.T. *The Severn Valley and West Midlands to AD 1000.* Rowlands, M.B. *The West Midlands from AD 1000* 1987. 464p. £26.00. 0582492157. Rowley, R.T. *The Welsh borders from AD 1000.* May, J. *The East Midlands to AD 1000.* Beckett, J.V. *The East Midlands from AD 1000.* 1988. 448p. £25.00. 0582492696. Miles, D. *The South Midlands and upper Thames to AD 1000.* Broad, J. *The South Midlands and upper Thames from AD 1000.* Rodwell, W.J. *The Eastern counties to AD 1000.* Holderness, B.A. *The Eastern counties from AD 1000.* Todd, M. *The South West to AD 1000.* 1987. 360p. £25.00. 0582492734. Coleman, B. and Higham, R.A. *The South West from AD 1000.* Cunliffe, B. *Wessex to AD 1000.* Bettey J.H. *Wessex from AD 1000.* 1986. 336p. £25.00. 0582492076. Drewett, P. *The South East to AD 1000.* 1988. 394p. £25.00. 0582492718. Brandon, P. and Short, B. *The South East from AD 1000.* 1989. 0582492467. 'The new Longman series ... is ambitious and deserves to succeed' (*Antiquity*, v.62, no.234, March 1988, p.194). *Class No: 942.1/.9*

[2880]

The Victoria history of the counties of England. London, Constable and St. Catherine Press; subsequently London, Oxford Univ. Press, for the Institute of Historical Research,

....*(contd.)*

1901-. (Many volumes reprinted by Dawson (Folkestone, Kent).

General introduction (1970). xi,281p. ISBN 0197227163. Contains a history of the project founded in 1899 and a bibliographical excursus *i.e.* a list of volumes published to date together with the names of their editors; year of publication; and contents lists for all volumes augmented with author and title indexes.

General introduction: supplement 1970 - 1990 (1990). 67p. 0197227775. Includes The *VCH* 1970-90 (p.1-8); State of *VCH* as at December 1990; Counties completed, in progress, dormant or unstarted (p.9-14); Contents lists of volumes published 1971-90 (p.15-56); Indexes of titles and authors; Corrigenda to *General Introduction*.

An indispensable series. Only Northumberland and Westmorland have still to be attempted. Each volume is by various hands and is heavily footnoted. General articles on each county usually occupy v.1-2 or v.1-3, with topography or history of parishes, boroughs and hundreds in later volumes. 'The history of each county will be complete in itself, beginning with the natural features and the flora and fauna, followed by the antiquities, pre-Roman and post-Roman; a translation and critical study of the Domesday Survey, and articles upon political, ecclesiastical, social and economic history; architecture, arts, industries, biography, folklore and sport' (*Introduction*). The evolution of VCH 'from antiquarianism to professionalism' is traced in *Times literary supplement,* 13 November 1970, p.1327. Other useful commentaries include W.R. Powell's 'The Victoria History of the Counties of England', *Library Association Record,* v.59,no.8 August 1957, p.259-262; R.B. Pugh's 'The Victoria County Histories', *History Today* v.20,no.12, December 1970, p.885-887; and C.R.J. Currie's 'Victoria County History'. *The Historian,* no.8, Autumn 1985, p.16-18. *Class No:* 942.1/.9

Bibliographies

[2881]
STEPHENS, W.B. **Sources for English local history** studies in the use of historical evidence. 2nd ed. Cambridge, Cambridge Univ. Press, 1981. xv, 342p. facsims., tables, index. (*Sources of History.*) ISBN: 0521237637.

Revised and expanded edition of book of same title published by Manchester Univ. Press, in 1973.

9 chapters. 1. Introduction (146 footnotes, citing many of the sources) - 2. Population and social structure - 3. Local government and politics - 4. Poor relief, charities, prices and wages - 5. Industry, trade and communications - 6. Agriculture - 7. Education - 8. Religion - 9. Houses, housing, and health. Analytical index p.326-342. 'An indispensable research tool, both for beginners and scholars' (*British Book News,* January 1982, p.62). *Class No:* 942.1/.9(01)

Handbooks & Manuals

[2882]
CAMPBELL-KEASE, J. **A Companion to local history research.** London, A & C Black, 1989. 384p. maps, illus., index. ISBN: 0713631457.

33 chapters in 5 sections: 1. Outline history and sources for the local historians - 2. Basic record sources - 3. More detailed records by period - 4. Specialist topics, archives and collections (16 chapters) - 5. Writing a local history. Appendix 1. Publications of the Royal Commission on the Historical Monuments in England - 2. Status of the Victoria County History programme. Major study which 'identifies and describes the principal material available for the study of local history, indicates where it may be found, and set it against the broader framework of national, as

....*(contd.)*

well as regional events'. The author writes at length of his book in *Local History,* no.26, November 1989, p.11-13. *Class No:* 942.1/.9(035)

[2883]
FRIAR, S. **The Batsford companion to local history.** London, Batsford, 1991. ISBN: 0713461810.

Over 2,000 cross-referenced A-Z entries ranging from brief definitions to short essays on major subjects covering such topics as architecture, education, genealogy, legal and ecclesiastical terms, place-names *etc. Class No:* 942.1/.9(035)

Yearbooks & Directories

[2884]
MAXTED, I., *comp.* **British national directories 1781-1819:** an index to places in the British Isles included in trade directories with general provincial coverage. Exeter, J. Maxted, 1989. vii,34p. map. A4 pbk. (*Exeter Working Papers in British Book Trade History. Special series, no.2.*) ISBN: 0951275216.

Listing by place p.1-23 (data: county, place, date code to one of 13 county based directories). County index p.24-31. 'Before the series of county based directories introduced by Pigot in 1820 there was a series of national directories, normally issued as supplements to London directories, which covered over one thousand places throughout the British Isles, the majority of which had no directory of their own. This index records the coverage in two tables, one in a single alphabetical sequence of places and the other arranged by county' (*Introduction*). *Class No:* 942.1/.9(058)

Bibliographies

[2885]
SHAW, G. *and* TIPPER, A. **British directories:** a bibliography and guide to directories published in England and Wales (1850-1950) and Scotland (1773-1950). Leicester, Leicester Univ. Press, 1988. ix,440p. illus., bibliog., index. ISBN: 0718512928.

Extends coverage and complements (1) Goss, C.W.F. *The London directories 1677-1855* (1932) and Norton, J.E. *Guide to the national and provincial directories of England and Wales, excluding London* (1950).

1. Introduction and guide (previous works and guides) - 2. Bibliography (English, Welsh, Scottish directories and British directories of commerce, industry and trades) - 3. Library holdings and index. 2,200 titles arranged by county and then chronologically. Publishers, place, and subject indexes. 'To be revered for years to come by local, family and industrial historians, librarians, archivists and many others. An essential purchase for every large reference collection or historical research centre' (*Reference Reviews,* v.3,no.3, September 1989, p.139-40). *Class No:* 942.1/.9(058)(01)

London

[2886]
ATKINS, P.J. **The Directories of London 1677-1977.** London, Mansell, 1990. xii,732p. illus., bibliog., indexes. ISBN: 0720120632.

Not so much a revision or update of C.W.F. Goss's *The London directories 1677-1855: a bibliography with notes on their origin and development* (1932) as a replacement work.

A magisterial guide to the history and development of printed London directories (directory types; history; compilation; and uses) together with a comprehensive bibliography (5800 items) and a list of the holdings of 65 libraries. Appendix: Bibliography of Directory titles (entries

....(contd.)

carry coded location guide) p.1-3. Title, publisher, and topographical indexes. 'Scholars, researchers and librarians - all will be grateful ... a fine example for future bibliographers to follow' (*Library Association Record*, v.92, no.8, August 1980. p.599). Library Association McColvin Medal commendation 1991. *Class No:* 942.1

[2887]
GREATER LONDON COUNCIL. The Survey of London. London, London County Council (then Athlone Press), 1900-.

Out of print volumes are being reprinted by AMS Press (New York).

1. *Bromley-by-Bow* (1900); 2, 4, 7, 11. *Chelsea* (1909-1927) v.7. £27.50. ISBN 048548027x; 3, 5. *St. Giles in the Fields* (1912-14); 6. *Hammersmith* (1915); 8. *St. Leonard, Shoreditch* (1922); 9. *St. Helen, Bishopgate* (1924); 10, 13, 14. *St. Margaret, Westminster* (1926-30); 12, 15. *All Hallows, Barking* (1929-34) v.15. £45. 0485482150; 16, 18, 20. *St. Martins-in-the-Fields* (1935-40); 17, 19, 21, 24. *St Pancras* (1936-52); 22. *St. Saviour and Christchurch, Southwark* (1950); 23, 26. *St. Mary, Lambeth* (1951-56); 25. *St. George the Martyr, Southwark* (1955) £35. 0485482258; 27. *Spitalfields and Mile End New Town* (1957); *Hackney,* pt.1 (1960) £35. 0485482282; 29-32. *St. James, Westminster* (5v., 1960-63) v.31-32 £65. 0485482312; 33-34. *St. Anne, Soho* (1966) £75. 0485482339; 35. *Theatre Royal, Drury Lane and the Royal Opera House, Covent Garden* (1970) £50. 0485482355; 36. *St. Paul, Covent Garden* (1970) £55. 0485482363; 37. *Northern Kensington* (1973) £55. 0485482371; 38. *The Museums area of South Kensington and Westminster* (1975) £60. 048548238x; 39-40. *The Grosvenor Estate* (1977-80) £55 and £70. 0485482398 and 0485482401; *Southern Kensington-Brompton* (1983) £55. 0485482241x; 42. *Southern Kensington-Kensington Square to Earls Court* (1986) £65. 0485482428. An historical survey of the administrative county of London. Each volume gives a detailed history of a parish, or part of a parish, with descriptions and illus. of historically important buildings. V.42 has 152p. plates, chapter references p.414-59, index p.461-502. *Class No:* 942.1

Encyclopaedias

[2888]
The Book of London. Leapman, M., *ed.* London, Weidenfeld & Nicolson, 1989. 320p. illus. (many col.), maps, bibliog., index. ISBN: 0297796240.

27 contributors. Every aspect of London's past and present is covered in this encyclopedic work arranged in 5 main parts and divided into 37 distinct sections: 1. The Growth of London (Londinium, Medieval London ... From the Great Fire to the Regency ... Twentieth-Century London, Chronology p.42) - 2. The Areas of London (*e.g.* The Thames, The City of London) - 3. A Place to live (*e.g.* Georgian terraces and Regency villas, Victorian houses for the masses, The growth of the suburbs) - 4. A Place to work - 5. A Place to enjoy (Theatre, Music ... A London Calendar). The Makers of London (architects and builders) p.302-6. Glossary of place names p.307. Bibliography p.308-10. *Class No:* 942.1(031)

[2889]
WEINREB, B. *and* **HIBBERT, C. The London encyclopaedia.** London, Macmillan, 1983. ix, 1029p. illus., indexes. ISBN: 0333300246.

164 contributors. Approximately 500 cross-referenced entries form a complete portrait of the whole of Greater London: history, tradition, streets and buildings, people and events. 'An attractive and fascinating compilation' (*Reference Reviews*, v.2, no.2, June 1988, p.93-4). *Class No:* 942.1(031)

Wales

[2890]
The History of Wales. Oxford, Clarendon Press; Univ. of Wales Press, 6v., 1981-.

2. *Conquest, coexistence, and change: Wales 1063-1415* by R.R. Davies. 1987. £40.00. ISBN 0198217323. 3. *Recovery, reorientation, and reformation: Wales 1415-1642* by G. Williams. 1987. £40.00. 019888217331. 4. *The foundation of modern Wales 1642-1780* by G.H. Jenkins. 1988. £40.00. 0198217734x. 6. *Rebirth of a nation: Wales 1880-1980* by K.O. Morgan. 1981. £27.50. 0198217366. Major history of the Principality. *Class No:* 942.9

Bibliographies

[2891]
JONES, P.H. A Bibliography of the history of Wales. Cardiff, University of Wales Press, 1989. Compiled for the History and Law Committee of the University of Wales Board of Celtic Studies. 75p. pbk. + 21 microfiche with a holder. ISBN: 0708310370.

1st ed. 1931; 2nd ed. 1962 and 4 supplements 1962-1972.

Includes 22,000 items (5,400 in previous ed. and supplements). Now computerized so that it consists of 3 sets of microfiche (48 x reduction): main classified sequence, author-title index, and KWIC index to titles of records in the classified sequence. 'Without the help of the accompanying printed handbook both historians and librarians would have difficulty in getting to grips with the layout of various indexes. Indeed the handbook is essential, and provides a comprehensive and thorough guide to using the Bibliography and also, for those who are unacquainted with indexing methods, a good description of a Key Word in Context index... The editor has to be praised on the scope, accuracy detail and amount of material included'. (*Reference Reviews*, v.3, no.3, September 1989, p.137-8). *Class No:* 942.9(01)

Germany

Encyclopaedias

German

[2892]
GEBHARDT, B. Handbuch der deutschen Geschichte. 9. neu bearb. Auf. hrsg. von H. Grundmann. Stuttgart, Ernst Klett Verlag., 1970-, v.1.

First published 1891-92. 1954-68. 5v.

1. *Frühzeit und Mittelalter.* 1970. xxiv,898p. ISBN 3129025103. 2. *Von der Reformation bis zum Ende der Absolutismus.* 1970. xvii,905p. 3129025200. 3. *Von der Französischen Revolution bis zum Ersten Weltkrieg.* 1973. x,583p. 3129025308. 4/1. *Die Zeit der Weltkriege. Der erste Weltkriege. Die Weimaren Republik.* 1973. xii,329p. 3129025405. 4/2. *Die Zeit der Weltkriege. Deutschland unter der Herrschaft des Nationalsozialismus 1933-1939. Der Zweite Weltkrieg. Das Ende des Reiches und die Entstehung der Republik Österreich, der Bundesrepublik Deutschland und der Deutschen Demokratischen Republik.*

To be completed in 5v. Arranged by period and subject, the contributions by specialists in this massive compendium 'provide an invaluable bibliography and framework of facts for German history from prehistoric times ...' (White, C.M., and others. *Sources of information in the social sciences* (2nd ed., 1973, entry B473, on the 8th ed.). *Class No:* 943.0(031)=30

Dictionaries

[2893]
FEST, W. Dictionary of German history 1806-1945. London, George Prior, 1978. 189p. ISBN: 0860431088.

Entries A-Z for c.700 topics, with emphasis on the political angle and 20th century. Most articles have short bibliographical notes, covering writings published 1950-77. Cross-references. Intended as 'an aid to study, not as a substitute for it' (*Preface*). 'This is the first dictionary of modern German history in the English language' (*Library review*, Autumn 1979, p.193). 'A valuable reference book that should be in every undergraduate library' (*Choice*, v.16, no.4, June 1979, p.508). *Class No:* 943.0(038)

Nazi Germany

Encyclopaedias

[2894]
The Encyclopedia of the Third Reich. Zentner, C. *and* Bedürftig, F., *eds.* New York, Macmillan, 2v., 1991. 1120p. illus., bibliog., index. ISBN: 0028975006.

Translated from *Das grosse Lexikon des Dritten Reiches* (1985).

40 contributors to this scholarly compendium of over 3,000 entries for events, people, culture, ideology, and almost every facet of Nazi Germany. 1,200 illustrations. 'The currently definitive reference source' (*Library Journal*, v.116,no.7, 15 April 1991, p.82). *Class No:* 943.0"1933-1945"(031)

Jews

[2895]
GUTMAN, I., ed. Encyclopedia of the Holocaust. New York, Maxwell Macmillan, 4v., 1989. 1,1905p. illus., maps, bibliog., index. ISBN: 0028960904, set; 0028971639, v.1; 0028971647, v.2; 0028971655, v.3; 0028971663, v.4.

950 signed and well-documented A-Z cross-referenced articles (most have reading lists of 2-12 items), contributed by 207 leading international scholars, cover all aspects of the Holocaust, including the history, politics and major figures of the Third Reich; the ideological roots of racism and anti-Semitism; Nazi medical practices and experiments; and the organization of genocide. Appendices include a glossary (p.1751); a detailed chronology 1920-1945 (p.1759); a list of major Jewish organizations in Germany 1893-1943; the structure of the Einsatzgruppen from June 1941; a summary of the Nuremburg Trial and subsequent trials with lists of defendants, and a country by country analysis of estimated Jewish losses in the Holocaust. V.4 has a detailed index. 'This wealth of information about one of the major events in the history of western civilization belongs in all public and academic libraries' (*Booklist*, v.86,no.13, 1 March 1990, p.1375+8). *Class No:* 943.0"1933-1945"(=924)

Bibliographies

[2896]
EDELHEIT, A.J. *and* **EDELHEIT, H. Bibliography on holocaust literature.** Boulder, Colorado, Westview Press, 1986. xxxvi,842p. index. ISBN: 081337233x.

More than 9000 items relating to English language books, pamphlets, periodical articles and dissertations arranged in 20 minutely subdivided chapters organized in 4 major sections: 1. Before the storm - 2. The perpetrators - 3. The crucible - 4. Aftermath. Author index. Absence of a subject index leads to difficulties with a subject approach although there is a detailed table of contents. 'The most comprehensive list of materials on the Holocaust yet

....(contd.)
published' (*Reference Books Bulletin 1986-87*, p.154). *Supplement* published 1990. *Class No:* 943.0"1933-1945"(=924)(01)

Federal Republic of Germany

German

[2897]
BRACHER, K.D., *eds.* **Geschichte der Bundesrepublik Deutschland.** Mannheim, F.A. Brockhaus, 5v., in 6, 1981-87. ISBN: 3765307408.

1. *Jahre der Besatzung 1945-1949* (1981) ed. by T. Eschenburg. ISBN 3765307416. 2. *Die Ära Adenauer 1949-1957* (1981) ed. by H.P. Schwarz. 3765307424. 3. *Die Ära Adenauer 1957-1963* (1983) ed. by H.P Schwarz. 3765307432. 4. *Von Erhard zur Grossen Koalition 1963-1969* (1984) ed. by K. Hildebrandt. 376530440. 5/1. *Republik in Wandel 1969-1974. Die Ära Brandt.* (1985) ed. by K.D. Bracher. 3765307459. 5/2. *Republik im Wandel 1974-1982. Die Ära Schmidt* (1987) ed. by W. Jäger and W. Link. Text is abundantly supported by statistics, tables, maps, chronologies and bibliographies to form 'a coherent, well-written, informative and balanced account of recent German history' (*TLS*, no.4246, 17 August 1984, p.921). *Class No:* 943.01=30

German Democratic Republic

[2898]
MCCAULEY, M. The German Democratic Republic since 1945. London, Macmillan Press in association with the School of Slavonic and East European Studies, Univ. of London, 1983. xiv,282p. maps, bibliog., tables, index. (*Studies in Russia and East Europe*.)

Outline study with impressive bibliography mainly consisting of German items (p.265-273) and a useful Chronology (p.195-264). *Class No:* 943.02

Austria

[2899]
JELAVICH, B. Modern Austria empire and republic 1915-1986. Cambridge, Cambridge Univ. Press, 1986. xvii, 346p. illus. maps., bibliog. index. ISBN: 0521316251.

7 chronological chapters concerned mainly with political history. Bibliography p.331-337. 'Her judgements of a host of complex and controversial issues are sensible and balanced' (*Choice* v.25, no.8, April 1988, p.1296). *Class No:* 943.6

Czechoslovakia

20th Century

[2900]
RENNER, H. A history of Czechoslovakia since 1945. London and New York, Routledge, 1989. xi, 200p. bibliog., index. ISBN: 0415003636.

9 well-documented chronological chapters. Ch. notes p.162-92. Bibliography p.193-6. *Class No:* 943.7"19"

Poland

[2901]
GIEYSZTOR, A., *and others.* **A History of Poland.** 2nd ed. Warsaw, PWN-Polish Scientific Publishers, 1980. Distributed by Hippocrene Books of New York. 668p. illus. maps, bibliog., index. ISBN: 8301003928.

5 contributors. 4 parts (25 chapters, plus 'Conclusion'): Medieval Poland - The Commonwealth of gentry - Poland under foreign rule - Poland 1918-1939. Bibliography, p.727-

....(contd.)

40 (A. Bibliographical works; B. More important textbooks and synthetic works - C. Textbooks covering longer periods; D. History of various regions and towns). Chronological tables. Well illustrated. Non-analytical index, 42 maps. 'A reference work deserving a place alongside the *Cambridge history of Poland* (*Choice*, v.18, no.1, September 1980, p.148+150). *Class No:* 943.8

Hungary

[2902]
PAMLÉNYI, E., ed. **A History of Hungary.** London, Collet's, 1975. 676p. illus., tables, maps. ISBN: 0569077001.

Compiled under the auspices of the History Institute of the Hungarian Academy of Sciences.

10 chapters (1. The origins of the Hungarian people and state - 2. The independent Hungarian feudal monarchy, to the battle of Mohács (1000-1526) ... 9. The Horthy regime (1919-44) - 10. People's Democracy in Hungary. Comparative chronology. Biographies, p.606-33. Bibliographies (p.634-44; grouped). Non-analytical index. Consistently high standard by a team of leading Hungarian historians. Favourably reviewed in *Soviet studies* v.28, July 1976, p.465-7. *Class No:* 943.9

France

[2903]
The Cambridge history of modern France. Cambridge, Cambridge Univ. Press; Paris Éditions de la Maison des Sciences de l'Homme, 8v. 1983-.

Each volume is a translation of a title or titles from the series *Nouvelle histoire de la France contemporaine* published by Éditions de Seuil of Paris 1972-.

1. *Restoration and reaction 1815-1848* by A. Jardin and A-J. Tudesq. 1983. xviii, 409p. £42.50. 0521252415 (UK). 2735100383 (Fr). 2. *The Republican experiment 1848-1852* by M. Agulhon. 1983. xiv, 211p. £27.50. 0521248299 (UK). 2735100286 (Fr). 3. *The Rise and Fall of the Second Empire 1852-1871* by A. Plessis. 1985. xvii, 193p. £27.50. 0521252423 (UK). 2735100758 (Fr). 4. *The Third Republic from its origins to the Great War 1871-1914* by J-M. Mayeur and M. Reberioux. 1984. xxi, 392p. £40.00. 0521249317 (UK). 2735100677 (Fr). 5. *The Decline of the Third Republic 1914-1938* by P. Bernard and H. Dubief 1985. xviii, 358p. £35.00. 0521252407 (UK). 2735100766 (Fr). 6. *From Munich to the Liberation 1938-1944* by J-P. Azema. 1984. xxxix, 294p. £30.00. 0521252377 (UK). 2735100782 (Fr). 7. *The Fourth Republic 1944-1958* by J-P. Rioux. 1987. xv, 531p. £40.00. 0521252385 (UK). 2735101665 (Fr).

Authors are either established historians or young scholars currently involved in the field. *Class No:* 944

Bibliographies

[2904]
CENTRE NATIONAL DE LA RECHERCHE SCIENTIFIQUE. INSTITUT D'HISTOIRE MODERNE ET CONTEMPORAINE. **Bibliographie annuelle de l'histoire de France** du cinquième siècle à 1958. Paris, Éditions du CNRS, 1956-. Annual. ISSN: 00676918.

Continues *Répertoire de l'histoire de France*, by P. Caron and H. Stein (années 1920/21-1930-31. Paris, Picard, 1923-38, 6v.), itself preceded by Répertoire méthodique de l'histoire moderne et contemporaine de la France pour l'année 1898-1912/12.

Année 1989 (1990. xciv,1231p. ISBN 2222044561) has 13657 entries. Systematic arrangement in 9 broad groups: 1. Manuels généraux et sciences auxiliaires de l'histoire - 2. Histoire politique de la France - 3. Histoire des institutions - 4. Histoire économique - 5. Sociale - 6. Histoire religieuse

....(contd.)

- 7. La France outre-mer 8. Histoire de la civilization - 9. Histoire locale. Liste des périodiques dépouillés et des leurs abbréviations p.xv-xciv. Subject and author indexes. *Class No:* 944(01)

Dictionaries

[2905]
Historical dictionaries of France. Westport, Connecticut, Greenwood Press; London, Aldwych Press, 1985-1987. bibliogs., indexes.

1. Scott, S.F. and Rothaus, B. eds. *Historical dictionary of the French Revolution 1789-1799*. 2v. 1985. xvii, 1143p. $95.00. ISBN 0313211418, US. 0861720431, UK. 2. Connelly, O. ed. *Historical dictionary of Napoleonic France 1799-1815*. 1985. xiii, 586p. $65.00. £53.50. 0313213216, US. 0867120423, UK. 3. Newman, E.L. ed. *Historical dictionary of France from the 1815 Restoration to the Second Empire*. 2v., 1987. xvii, 1241p. $135.00. £115.00. 0313227519, US. 0861720474, UK. 4. Echard, W.E. ed. *Historical dictionary of the French Second Empire 1952-1870*. 1985. xvi, 829p. $87.50. £68.50. 0313211361, US. 086172044x, UK. 5. Hutton, P.H. ed. *Historical dictionary of the Third French Republic 1870-1940*. 2v., 1986. xvi, 1206p. $125.00. £115.00. 0313220880, US. 0861720466, UK.

A multitude of contributors. Well-documented signed entries relating to leading personalities, events, constitutional developments, chronologies *etc.* R.A. Jonces and D.A. Pinkney's 'The Greenwood Press' historical dictionaries of French history', *French Historical Studies*, v.15, no.2, Fall 1987, p.345-57 subjects them to a detailed scrutiny. *Class No:* 944(038)

French

[2906]
DUBY, G., ed. **Histoire de la France.** Paris, Références Larousse, 1986-1987. illus., diagrs., plans, tables, maps, bibliogs. ISBN: 2037200110.

First published 1970-72.

1. *naissance d'une nation des origines à 1348*. 1986. 483p. 2037200102. Chronology p.445-461. Chapter bibliographies p.473-483. 2. *dynasties et révolutions de 1348 à 1852*. 1986. 543p. 2037200129. Chronology p.485-507. Bibliography p.521-543. 3. *Les temps nouveaux de 1852 à nos jours*. 1987. 2037200137. Chronology p.583-621. Bibliography p.633-652. An attractive production, including cultural, social and economic aspects of French history. *Class No:* 944=40

French Revolution

[2907]
LEFEBVRE, G. **The French Revolution.** London, Routledge & Kegan Paul; New York, Columbia Univ. Press. 2v., 1962-64.

Originally as *La Révolution Française* (Paris, Presses Universitaires de France, 1957).

1: *From its origins to 1793*. Translated by E.M. Evanson. 1962. xviii, 366p. $36.00. ISBN 0231023421 US. 2: *From 1793 to 1799*. Translated by J.H. Stewart and J. Friguglietti. 1964. xiv, 430p. $36.00. ISBN 023102519x US. V.2 has 3 parts (17 chapters): 1. The Coalition and the Revolution, to the treaties of 1795 - 2. The victorious offensive of the Revolution - The world at the advent of Napoleon. Conclusion. Bibliography, p.361-95 (by chapters and sections). Analytical index. Balanced and thorough. 'Lefebvre may very well be the greatest historian of the Revolution' (F. Chamber. *France*, 1980. Entry 86). *Class No:* 944"1789-1799"

Encyclopaedias

[2908]
JONES, C. The Longman companion to the French Revolution. London and New York, Longman, 1988. xiii, 473p. maps, geneal. table, bibliog., index. ISBN: 0582494184.

Compendious reference work organized in 13 sub-divided sections covering the period 1787-1799: 1. Political chronology - 2. Framework of government - 3. The Executive - 4. Structure of the Terror: the institutions of revolutionary government 1792-1795 - 5. International relations and war - 6. Politics - 7. Administration, justice and finance - 8. Religion and ideas - 9. Society and the economy - 10. Biographies (over 500 *dramatis personae* highlighting minor figures) - 11. Glossary of over 400 terms (p.401-424) - 12. The Revolutionary Calendar - 13. Bibliography (p.432-5). For all scholars, students and general readers requiring detailed factural data. *Class No:* 944"1789-1799"(031)

19th Century

[2909]
CALDWELL, R.J. The Era of Napoleon a bibliography of the history of Western civilization 1799-1815. New York, Garland, 2v., 1991. xxi,1447p. ISBN: 0824056442.

48,000 entries, some annotated, relating to books, periodicals, and dissertations. More than 50% cover France (French biography and local history account for some 14,000 entries). The majority of the items cited are non-English language works. Many of the chronological and thematic sections have introductions signalling the most valuable items. *Class No:* 944"18"

Italy

[2910]
Longman history of Italy. Hay, D., *ed.* Harlow, Essex, Longman, 1980-. illus., tables, maps.

1. *Italy in the early Middle Ages 600-1216* by T.S. Brown. 2. *Italy in the age of Dante and Petrarch 1216-1380* by J. Larner. 1980. 3. *Italy in the age of the Renaissance 1380-1530* by D. Hay and J. Law. £19.95. ISBN 0582483581. 4. *Italy 1530-1630* by E. Cochrane. 1988. £19.95. ISBN 0582483646. 5. *Italy in the Age of Reason 1685-1789* by D. Carpanetto and G. Ricuperati. 1987. £19.95. ISBN 0582483387. 6. *Italy in the seventeenth century* by D. Sella - 7. *Italy in the age of the Risorgimento 1790-1870* by H. Hearder. ISBN 0582491460. 8. *Modern Italy 1871-1982* by M. Clark. 1985. ISBN 058248362x.

V.2 has 12 chapters, each with chapter notes (*e.g.* 8. The countryside, p.153-227, has 1¼p. of running bibliographical commentary, with 6 references). Scholarly. 'To appreciate this book fully, at least a basic knowledge of medieval history is required ... Maps and illustrations need to be used more imaginatively' (*British Book News*, January 1981, p.61-62, on v.2). *Class No:* 945.0

Bibliographies

[2911]
COPPA, F.J. and ROBERTS, W. Modern Italian history an annotated bibliography. Westport, Conn., Greenwood Press, 1990. ix,226p. indexes. (*Bibliographies and Indexes in World History, no. 18.*) ISBN: 0313248125. ISSN: 07426852.

865 entries deployed in 7 sections: 1. General and reference works - 2. Monographic studies - 3. 18th century Italy - 4. The Risorgimento 1796 to 1861 - 5. Liberal Italy 1861 to 1922 - 6. Facist Italy 1922 to 1945 - 7. Italian Republic, 1945 to present. Author and subject indexes. *Class No:* 945.0(01)

Dictionaries

[2912]
COPPA, F.J., *ed.* **Dictionary of modern Italian history.** Westport, Connecticut, Greenwood Press, 1985. xxvi, 496p. bibliogs., index. ISBN: 031322983x.

58 contributors survey 'the chief events, personalities, institutions, systems and problems of Italy from the eighteenth century to the present' in dictionary form. Longer entries end with bibliogaphical references. Appendix A. Chronology p.459-468. 'An excellent and much needed book' (*Choice*, v.23, no.4, December 1985, p.580). *Class No:* 945.0(038)

20th Century

Dictionaries

[2913]
CANNISTARO, P.V., *ed.* **Historical dictionary of Fascist Italy.** Westport, Connecticut, Greenwood Press, 1982. xxix, 657p. maps, index. £63.75. ISBN: 0313213278.

56 contributing scholars provide mini-essays on political, military, diplomatic, economic, cultural, intellectual history. Biographical entries feature prominently and each entry ends with bibliographical references. Appendix A. Chronology p.579-582. J. Italian place-names altered during the Fascist regime p.607-630. 'The most comprehensive reference work on Italian fascism and a most welcome one' (*Choice*, v.20, no.5, January 1983. p.690). *Class No:* 945.0"19"(038)

Spain

[2914]
LYNCH, J., *ed.* **A History of Spain.** Oxford, Basil Blackwell, 14v., 1989-.

Collins. R. *The Arab conquest of Spain 710-797.* 1989. 208p. £29.50. ISBN 0631159231. Lynch, J. *Bourbon Spain 1700-1708.* 1989. xiv,450p. £45.00. 0631145761. Other titles to follow: Cestro. M.C.F. *The prehistory of Spain; Roman Spain;* Collins, R. *The Umayyad State and its rivals: Spain 797-912* and *Caliphs and Kings: Spain 912-1035;* Reilly, B. *The contest of Christian and Muslim Spain 1031-1157;* Linehan, P. *Spain 1157-1300;* Mackay, A. *Spain: centuries of crisis 1300-1474;* Edwards, J. *The Spain of the Catholic monarchs 1474-1520;* Lynch, J. *Spain under the Hapsburgs 1516-1598* (2nd ed. 1981) and *1598-1700* (2nd ed. 1981); Blinkhorn, M. *The emergence of modern Spain 1808-1939;* Robinson, R. *Spain since 1939.*

Scholarly and well-documented multi-volume history 'designed to advance research and thinking on the subject as well as to represent its current state'. *Class No:* 946.0

Dictionaries

[2915]
KERN, R.W. and DODGE, M.D., *eds.* **Historical dictionary of modern Spain 1700-1988.** Westport, Connecticut, Greenwood Press, 1990. bibliog., index. ISBN: 0313259712.

70 contributors. Entries cover important personalities and events in 6 major areas: politics, government, diplomacy; institutions, culture; society and the armed forces. *Class No:* 946.0(038)

20th Century

Dictionaries

[2916]
CORTADA, J.W., *ed.* **Historical dictionary of the Spanish Civil War** 1936-1939. Westport, Connecticut, Greenwood Press, 1982. xxviii, 571p. maps, bibligo. ISBN: 0313220549.

800 signed entries of varying length by 40 contributors on all aspects of the Civil War. Appendix A. Chronology 1930-1939; B. Military History; C. Civil War governments; D. Compendium of archives and libraries (A-Z by country) p.537-543; Selected bibliography of bibliographies p.544-546; Analytical index p.547-571. 'The long entries written by various experts and the inclusion of some rather unusual topics enhance the value of this reference tool' (*Choice* v.21, no.1, September 1983, p.62). *Class No:* 946.0"19"(038)

Portugal

[2917]
OLIVEIRA MARQUES, A.H. de. **History of Portugal.** 2nd ed. New York and London, Columbia Univ. Press, 2v., 1976. illus., ports., maps, bibliog..

1. From Lusitania to Empire. 2. From Empire to Corporate State. 'The most important book on Portuguese history in English ... it concludes with a good and partially annotated bibliography' (P.T.H. Unwin. *Portugal*, 1987. Entry 174). *Class No:* 946.9

Russia up to 1918

[2918]
PIPES, R. **The Russian Revolution 1899-1919.** London, Collins Harvill, 1990. xxvii,946p. ISBN: 0679400745.

Continues the author's *Russia under the old regime.*

Comprehensive overview of the Revolution and of the events that preceded it in 18 chapters divided into 2 parts: 1. Agony of the Old Regime - 2. Bolsheviks conquer Russia. Chronology p.847-56. Chapter notes p.857-914. 100 works on the Russian Revolution (bibliographical essay) p.915-9. 4 maps. Widely acclaimed for its scholarly analysis. *Class No:* 947/

USSR & Russia

Archives

[2919]
HARTLEY, J.M., *ed.* **The Study of Russian history from British archival sources.** London, Mansell Publishing Ltd., 1986. lx, 184p. ISBN: 0720117844.

11 papers read at a conference organized by the London School of Slavonic and East European Studies in 1984 as part of a project to prepare a comprehensive guide to sources in the British Isles. P.H. Grimsted's 'Foreign collections and Soviet archives' comments on the need to be aware of the corresponding papers in the Soviet Union. 'The hope she expresses, that other western countries will follow the British example and draw up a guide along the lines promised here will be widely shared' (*Archives*, v.18, no.78, 1987, p.115-116). *Class No:* 947(093.20)

[2920]
—HARTLY, J.M. Guide to documents and manuscripts in the United Kingdom relating to Russia and the Soviet Union. London, Mansell Publishing Ltd., 1987. xxiii, 526p. bibliog., index. ISBN: 0720118050.

The product of a three-year project undertaken at the School of Slavonic and East European Studies 'to record systematically for the first time the location of documentary material relating to Russia and the Soviet Union in the

....*(contd.)*
United Kingdom' 331 repositories and their collections are listed A-Z by town. Bibliography p.xxiii. Does not cover material in the Public Record Office, the House of Lords, or the India Office Library and Records, whose collections were judged to be generally known. Unfortunately questionnaires to almost 400 institutions reasonably expected to hold important material either failed to elicit a reply or else resulted in a nil return. But Appendix 1. Privately held papers described in the printed reports of The Royal Commission on Historical Manuscripts, or listed in the National Register of Archives and the National Register of Archives of Scotland p.409-418. Appendix 2. Unrecorded papers in private ownership p.418-421. 'Of crucial value to historians, particularly as so much material in Russia is inaccessible' (*Archives*, v.18, no.78, 1987, p.124-125). *Class No:* 947(093.20)

RSFSR

[2921]
BOHDAN NAHAYLO *and* SWOBODA, V. **Soviet disunion** a history of the Nationalities Problem in the USSR. London, Hamish Hamilton, 1990. xvi,432p. illus., maps, bibliog., index. ISBN: 0241125405.

History of the non-Russian nationalities in the Soviet Union since the Russian Revolution. 18 chaps: 1. Nations of the Russian Empire ... 3. 1919: Sovereign Soviet Republics - 4. Moslem nations ... 17. Crisis in the Empire - 18. Waiting for Gorbachev. Appendix (National structure of the USSR in early 1990 and The Union Republics) p.360-8. Chapter notes p.369-411. Bibliography p.412-7. 6 maps. *Class No:* 947.0

[2922]
CARR, E.H. **A History of Soviet Russia.** London, Macmillan, 10v. in 15, 1917-1958. ISBN: 0333242165.

1. *The Bolshevik Revolution 1971-1923.* 1. *1917-1923* 1978. 430p. £35.00 ISBN 0333085663 - 2. *The economic order.* 1951. 400p. £35.00. ISBN 0333022858 - 3. *Soviet Russia and the World.* 1978. £35.00. ISBN 0333060040.

2. *The Interregnum 1923-1924* 1978. 392p. £35.00 ISBN 0333097238. First published 1954.

3. *Socialism in one country 1924-1926.* 3v. in 4. 1. 1978. 588p. £35.00. ISBN 0333034422. First published 1958. 2. 1978. 494p. £35.00. ISBN 0333071611. First published 1959. 3. Pt.1. 1978. £35.00. ISBN 0333245687. First published 1964. 3. Pt.2. 1978. £35.00. ISBN 0333245695. First published 1964.

4. *Foundations of a planned economy 1926-1929* 3v. in 6. 1. Pt.1. 1978. £35.00. ISBN 0333245709. First published 1969. 1. Pt.2. 1978. £35.00. ISBN 0333245717. First published 1969. 2. 1978. 530p. £35.00. ISBN 0333111338. First published 1971. 3. Pt.1. 1979. £35.00. ISBN 0333132041. First published 1976. 3. Pt.2. 1979. £35.00. ISBN 0333192702. First published 1976. 3. Pt.3. 1978. £35.00. ISBN 0333194934. These volumes written jointly by E.H. Carr and R.W.Davies.

A monumental study of Soviet Russian history during the period; footnotes and bibliographies. 'A work of the greatest value for its masterly ordering and analysis of official documentation, and its unfailing clarity and readability' (Auty, R. and Obolensky, D., eds. *Companion to Russian studies.* 1: *An introduction to Russian history* (1976), p.308-9). *Class No:* 947.0

[2923]
DE MOWBRAY, S.A. **Key facts in Soviet history.** Volume 1. 1917 to 22 June 1941. Boston, Massachusetts, G.K. Hall; London, Pinter Publishers in association with John Spiers, 1990. xiii,386p. maps, bibliog., index. ISBN: 0816118205, US; 0861870131, UK.

Short accounts of the main events in Soviet history

....(contd.)

month by month emphasising internal developments in political, economic, military, and social affairs but also including cultural, scientific and technological fields. List of sources p.361-75. To be completed by a second volume continuing the course of Soviet history to the present and an index volume. Based largely on English-language sources. *Class No:* 947.0

Encyclopaedias

[2924]
The Blackwell encyclopaedia of the Russian Revolution. Shukman, H., *ed.* Oxford, Blackwell Reference, 1988. xiv,418p., maps on endpapers, bibliogs., index. ISBN: 0631152385.

Part 1 consists of 128 cross-referenced, initialled articles, from 45 contributors, arranged in an approximate chronological sequence 1860-1921. Part 2 comprises 174 biographies, long enough to be useful, including Sir Robert Bruce Lockhart, Josef Pilsudski, John Reed, and Sidney Reilly. Short reading lists are appended to all Pt.1 articles and to many of the biographies. Designed as a reference source for students and teachers and for general readers interested in 20th century history. The editor is Director of the Russian and East European Centre, St. Anthony's College, Oxford. 'Unique as a reference source devoted to this topic' (*Booklist*,v.88,no.5, 1 November 1988, p.460). *Class No:* 947.0(031)

Reviews & Abstracts

[2925]
The Current digest of the Soviet press. Columbus, Ohio, Current Digest of the Soviet Press, 1949-. Weekly. ISSN: 00113425.

Founded by the American Council of Learned Societies and the Social Sciences Research Council in 1949.

Quarterly indexed weekly extracts and abstracts in English from the Soviet press offered as documentary material without editorial comment for use in teaching and research. Annual indexes from v.28 (1976). Online version (DIALOG File 645. $84./hr. $0.25. per offline print. *Class No:* 947.0(048)

USSR in Europe

Ukraine

[2926]
SUBTELNY, O. Ukraine: a history. Toronto, Univ. of Toronto Press in association with the Canadian Institute of Ukrainian Studies, 1988. xii, 666p.+58p. plates, illus., maps, bibliog., index. ISBN: 0802058086.

28 ch. organized in 5 pts: 1. Kievian Rus' - 2. The Polish-Lithuanian period - 3. The Cossack era - 4. Ukraine under Imperial rule - 5. Twentieth-century Ukraine. Notes p.573-87. Glossary p.589-90. Bibliography p.591-620. 29 maps. Massive work of scholarship covering from the earliest period. 'No other one-volume English-language work can surpass this well-balanced survey' (*Choice*, v.26, no.11-12, July/August 1989. p.1890). *Class No:* 947.7

Scandinavia

Dictionaries

[2927]
NORDSTROM, B.J. Dictionary of Scandinavian history. Westport, Connecticut, Greenwood Press, 1986. xix, 703p. bibliog. index. $75.00; £73.50. ISBN: 0313228876.

400 initialled entries contributed by 77 scholars cover the major events and personalities in the history of Denmark, Finland, Iceberg, Norway and Sweden, with some information on Greenland and the Faroe Islands from A.D. 1000 to the present day. Entries on major topics open with a general introduction followed by a detailed study in some or all of the Nordic countries. 5 Appendices. Bibliography (p.661-663); Monarchs; Presidents; Prime ministers and governments; and a chronology. Index p.685-703. 'Fills a serious gap in English-language reference sources on the Scandinavian countries' (*Choice*, v.23, no. 10, June 1986, p.1519). *Class No:* 948(038)

Netherlands

Bibliographies

[2928]
The Low Countries History Yearbook. The Hague, Martinus Nijhoff, v.11-15, 1979-1982.

Formerly *Acta Historiae Neerlandica* v.1-10, 1966-1978 published in Leiden by E.J. Brill (v.1-5, 1966-1971) and subsequently at The Hague (v.6-10, 1973-1978) by Martinus Nijhoff.

Founded to end the isolation of Dutch historians imposed by their language and to enable them 'to participate to a greater extent in international discussion' (*Introduction to v.1*). Extremely valuable bibliographical surveys were a regular feature 1973 onwards *viz.* v.6 (1973): A.C. Carter: 'Survey of recent Dutch historiography' p.175-199; J. Dhondt: 'Belgian historiography written in Dutch 1969-1971', p.201-19. V.7 (1974): W. Blockmans and others: 'Belgian historiography written in Dutch 1971-1973', p.253-65. 'Survey of Recent Historical Works on Belgium and the Netherlands Published in Dutch', with various editors, in v.8 (1975) p.159-200; v.10 (1978) p.195-254; v.11 (1979) p.181-215; v.12 (1979) p.126-64; v.13 (1980) p.133-191; v.14 (1981) p.182-220; v.15 (1982) p.137-204. All these surveys, 1973-1982, ended with a section 'Recent Works on the History of the Low Countries published in English' (slightly variant titles). A.C. Carter and others *Historical research in the Low Countries 1970-1975: a critical survey* (The Hague, Martinus Nijhoff, 1981. 275p. bibliog., indexes). is a collection of bibliographical surveys first printed in *Acta Historiae Neerlandica*, 1973-77 and is continued by J. Kossman-Putto and E. White's *Historical research in the Low Countries 1981-83: a critical survey* (Leiden, E.J. Brill, 1985. 117p. bibliog). *Class No:* 949.2(01)

Belgium

Encyclopaedias

French

[2929]
Chronique de la Belgique. Bruxelles, Éditions Chronique, 1987.

A Flemish edition. *Kroniek van België* is also published by Elsevier (subsequently Agon).

Belgian history reported on a chronological basis as if in a contemporary newspaper with chronologies, summary articles, and closely interwoven illustrations. *Class No:* 949.3(031)=40

Switzerland

[2930]
LUCK, J.M. A History of Switzerland the first 100,000 years. Before the beginnings to the days of the present. Palo Alto, California, The Society for the Promotion of Science and Scholarship, 1985. xiv, 887p. illus., maps, tables, bibliog., index. ISBN: 093066406x.

11 chronological heavily sub-divided chapters. Glossary p.846-7. Bibliography (425 items) p.849-59. 80p. plates. Analytical index. *Class No:* 949.4

Greece

[2931]
CLOGG, R. A Short history of modern Greece. 2nd ed. Cambridge, Cambridge Univ., Press, 1986. viii, 242p. map. bibliog., index. ISBN: 0521328373.

8 chapters (1. 'Waiting for the barbarians': the downfall of Byzantium, 1204-1453 ... 8. From authoritarianism to democracy, 1974-. Bibliography, 8. Cyprus). Analytical index. 'Greatly to be recommended ... An honest and authoritative attempt to be fair-minded' (TLS, No.4001, 23 November 1979, p.5). *Class No:* 949.5

Balkans

[2932]
JELAVICH, B. History of the Balkans. v.1. Eighteenth and nineteenth centuries. v.2. Twentieth century. Cambridge, Cambridge University Press, 1983. xiv, 407p.+xi, 476p. illus., maps, bibliog., index. ISBN: 0521252490, V.1; 0521254485, V.2.

Considers the history of the major Balkan nationalities - the Albanians, Bulgars, Croats, Greeks, Romanians, Serbs and Slovenes. An introdcution to v.1 presents the historical background up the beginning of the 18th century. Bibliography p.457-460 (v.2). 'This set can be highly recommended to undergraduate and graduate students, faculty, government experts, information services, and the general public' (*Choice*), v.21, no.6, February 1984, p.873). *Class No:* 949.7

Asia

[2933]
The Cambridge history of early Inner Asia. Sinor, D., *ed.* Cambridge, Cambridge Univ. Press, 1990. x,518p. maps, bibliog., index. ISBN: 0521243041.

1. The concept of Inner Asia - 2. Geographic setting - 3. Inner Asia at the dawn of history - 4. Scythians and Sarmatians - 5. The Hsiung-nu - 6. Indo-Europeans - 7. Hun period - 8. The Avars - 9. Peoples of the Russian forest belt - 10. Peoples of the South Russian steppes - 11. Establishment and dissolution of the Türk empire - 12. The Uighurs - 13. The Karakhanids and early Islam - 14. Early medieval Tibet - 15. Forest people of Manchuria: Kitans and Jurchens. Bibliography p.424-94. 'This volume is a splendid synthesis of narrative and analytical history, and a definitive work of reference' (*Choice*, v.28,no.1, September 1990, p.190). *Class No:* 95

Encyclopaedias

[2934]
Encyclopedia of Asian history. Embree, A.T., *editor in chief.* New York, Charles Scribner's Sons; London, Collier Macmillan, 4v., 1988. xiii, 528+538+516+478p. ISBN: 0684186195.

The history of the project is well told in D.C. Smith's 'The Encyclopedia of Asian history'. *Scholarly Publishing*, v.19, no.4, July 1988, p.202-209.

Covers all aspects of Asian civilization from the earliest

....(contd.)
period to the present. Excludes the Arabian peninsula, the Middle East and the Soviet Union except for the Central Asian republics. 1200 biographies of living and dead including Europeans closely involved with Asia. All entries are signed and most carry a bibliography. V4. includes list of entries p.319-356; Directory of (over 430) contributors p.357-371; synoptic outline; and an analytical index. Prepared under the auspices of the The Asia Society and intended 'to make available the highest level of contemporary scholarship on Asia to a nonspecialist audience'. 'An excellent overview of the subject ... large academic libraries will find it a must purchase, and others should consider it for its valuable scholarship and broad coverage' (*Booklist*, v.85, no.1, 1 September 1988, p.45). *Class No:* 95(031)

Islamic World

[2935]
The Cambridge history of Islam. Holt, P.M., *and others, eds.* Cambridge, Cambridge Univ. Press, 2v. in 4, 1970. illus.

1A: *The Central Islamic lands from pre-Islamic times to the First World War.* 1B: *The Central Islamic lands since 1918.* 2A: *The Indian sub-continent, South-East Asia, Africa and the Muslim West.* 2B: *Islam society and civilisation.* Aims 'to present the history of Islam as a whole cultural whole' (*Preface*). V.1 includes dynastic lists, a bibliography (p.737-50), glossary and detailed index (p.755-815). V.2 has a bibliography (p.891-905), glossary and equally lengthy index (p.911-66). 'Not at all conducive to continuous reading and yet not quite reference articles ... But ... will remain a standard work for many years to come' (*International Affairs*, v.47,no.4, October 1971, p.838-9). *Class No:* 95.297

[2936]
HITTI, P.K. History of the Arabs from earliest times to the present. 10th rev. ed. London, Macmillan, 1970. xxiv,822p. illus., maps, index.

6 parts (52 charts): 1. The pre-Islamic age - 2. The rise of Islam and the Caliphal State - 3. The Umayyad and the Abbasid Empires - 4. The Arabs in Europe; Spain and Sicily - 5. The last of the medieval Moslem states - 6. Ottoman rule and independence. No bibliography, but heavily footnoted. 21 maps. A standard text. *Class No:* 95.297

Dictionaries

[2937]
SHIMONI, Y., *ed.* **Political dictionary of the Arab World.** Jerusalem, The Jerusalem Publishing House; New York, Macmillan; London, Collier-Macmillan, 1987. 520p. maps. ISBN: 0029164222.

A revised and updated version of *Political dictionary of the Middle East in the twentieth century* (2nd ed., 1974).

About 500 A-Z informative essays and articles (up to 2000 words long) on the leading personalities, institutions, general issues, and political movements of the 20th century up to the mid-1980s. Excludes Cyprus, Turkey and Iran. *Class No:* 95.297(038)

Maps & Atlases

[2938]
An Historical atlas of Islam. Leiden, E.J. Brill, 1981. viii, 71p. maps, index. ISBN: 9004061169.

Forms part of *The Encyclopaedia of Islam*, new edition (*qv*).

73 coloured maps grouped in 9 sections: 1. The Early Muslim earth and sky - 2. The extension of the Muslim world - 3. Early Arabia - 4. The Near and Middle East -

....(contd.)
5. Anatolia and the Balkans - 6. Muslim Spain - 7. North Africa - 8. India and the Indian seas - 9. The Far East. Index of place names p.58-70. Introduction carries bibliographical references. *Class No: 95.297(084.3)*

Asia—Middle & Near East

[2939]
A History of the Near East. Holt, P.M., *ed.* London, Longman, 7v., 1986-. maps, bibliogs., tables, index.
A history of the region from the coming of Islam to the present day. Noteworthy for the excellent bibliographical surveys in each volume. Titles 1. *The Prophet and the age of Caliphates: the Islamic Near East from the sixth to the eleventh century* by Hugh Kennedy. 1986. 440p. £24.00. 0582493129. 2. *The Age of the Crusades: the Near East from the eleventh century to 1517* by P.M. Holt. 1986. xiii, 250p. £15.95. 058249303x. 3. *The Rise of the Ottoman Empire 1300-1574* by Colin Imber. 4. *The Decline of the Ottoman Empire 1574-1792* by R.C. Ropp. 5. *The Making of the modern Near East 1792-1923* by M.E. Yapp. 1987. xii, 404p. £25.00. 0582013666. 6. *The Near East since the First World War* by M.E. Yapp. 7. *Medieval Persia 1040-1797* by David Morgan. 1988. x, 197. £17.95. 0582014832. *Class No: 95.3/.6*

Asia—South & South-East

Maps & Atlases

[2940]
SCHWARTZBERG, J.E., *with others eds.* **A Historical atlas of South Asia.** 2nd ed. New York, Oxford Univ. Press, 1992. xxxix, 369p. illus., maps. ISBN: 0195068696.
149p. of maps (mostly coloured); 117p. of historical narrative, 'South Asia' extends from Afghanistan through the Indian sub-continent, to Burma. 14 sections of maps, including geopolitical, economic, social and cultural themes. (section 14; 'A geopolitical synopsis'; 60 small-scale maps). Bibliography of 38p. 48p. of index, photographs and diagrams. 'One of the very best atlases for any region of the world ... providing a distinctly *geographical* view of history' (*Bulletin*, Special Libraries Association, Geography and Map Division, no.118, December 1979, p.60, 61). *Class No: 95.4/.0(084.3)*

Archives

[2941]
MOIR, M. A General guide to the India Office Records. London, The British Library, 1988. xvl, 331p. frontis., bibliog., index. ISBN: 0712306293.
Extends W. Foster's *A guide to the India Office Records 1600-1858* (Eyre & Spottiswoode for The India Office, 1919).
1. The administrative background (p.3-124) - 2. The India Office Records (Summary list of 50 lettered classes p.129-30; Descriptive inventory A-Z p.131-275). Appendix 2. Notes on archival sources ... for areas outside British India or on its frontiers. Bibliography p.292-300. Analytical index. Authoritative, comprehensive and well-documented account of IOR holdings. IOR is 'the most important accumulation of historical source material in Britain for the study of politics, administration and commerce in South Asia and related areas from the early seventeenth to the mid-twentieth century' (*Preface*). *Class No: 95.4/.0(093.20)*

[2942]
PEARSON, J.D. A Guide to manuscripts and documents in the British Isles relating to South and South-East Asia. London, Mansell, 2v., 1989-1990. ISBN: 0720119618.
Supplement to *A guide to Western manuscripts and documents in the British Isles relating to South and South East Asia* (1965).
1. *London.* 1989. vii,319p. index. £60.00. ISBN 0720119618. 2. *British Isles.* 1990. xvi,384p. index. £70.00. ISBN 072012011x. J.D. Pearson writes on 'The supplement to Wainwright and Matthews', *South Asian Studies* (British Library, 1986), p.106-8. *Class No: 95.4/.0(093.20)*

China

[2943]
The Cambridge history of China. Fairbank, J.K. *and* Twitchett, D., *eds.* Cambridge Univ. Press, 1978-.
1. *The Ch'in and Han Empires 221BC-AD20.* 1986. xli,981p. ISBN 0521243270. 2. *Sui and T'ang China 589-906 Pt.1.* 1979, xx,850p. £65.00. 052124467. 7. *The Ming Dynasty 1368-1644 Pt.1.* 1988. xxv,976p. £50.00. 0521243327. 8. Will be a topical volume of Ming history. 10. *Late Ch'ing 1800-1911 Pt.1.* 1978. xvi,313p. £60.00. 0521214475. 11., *Late Ch'ing 1800-1911 Pt.2.* 1980. 754p.. £60.00. 0521220297. 12 *Republican China 1912-1949 Pt.1.* 1983. xviii,1002p. £65.00. 0521235413. 13. *Republican China 1912-1949 Pt.2.* 1986. xix,1092p., £60.00. 0521243386. 14. *The People's Republic Pt.1. The emergence of revolutionary China 1949-1965.* 1987. xvii,722p. £60.00. 052124336x. All volumes have extensive bibliographies, most have bibliographical essays and all have a glossary. The maps have been prepared on the basis of the historical reconstruction of the most up-to-date historical atlas of China, the *Chung-kuo li-shih ti-t'u-chi* (Shanghai 1975). 'When the CHofC was first planned in 1966, the aim was to provide a substantial account of the history of China as a benchmark for the Western history - reading public: an account of the current state of knowledge in six volumes. Since then the outpouring of current research, the application of new methods, and the extension of scholarship into new fields have further stimulated Chinese historical studies. This growth is indicated by the fact that the history has now become a planned 15 vols., but will still leave out such topics as the history of art and of literature, many aspects of economics and technology, and all the riches of local history' (*General Editor's Preface*). Note Eastman, L.E. and others. *The Nationalist era in China 1927-1949* (1991. x,406p. index. £35.00. 052139273x) was originally published as V.13 of *Cambridge history of China. Class No: 951*

Dictionaries

[2944]
DILLON, M. Dictionary of Chinese history. London, Cass, 1979. ix,240p. chron. table, map. ISBN: 0714631078.
Aims 'to provide a quick and easy reference to the names and terms which occur most frequently in English-language works on China and which can be usefully explained in a few hundred words' (*Preface*). Entries cover the period from pre-history to the end of 1977. 'Mao Tse-tung': over 1p.; 'Congress of the Chinese Communist Party': nearly 2p. Cross-references. *Class No: 951(038)*

Chronologies

[2945]
MACKERRAS, C. Modern China: a chronology from 1842 to the present. London, Thames & Hudson, 1982. 703p. maps, index. ISBN: 0500250847.
Left hand pages chronicles major political or general incidents, military or civilian, domestic or foreign relations. Right hand pages divided into 6 categories: economy; official appointments, dismissals, resignations; cultural and social; publications; natural disasters; births and deaths. Introduction (p.7-20) describes the sources, lists general

....(contd.)

works, and specific topic chronologies. Glossary of titles and technical terms p.644-646. General index p.647-694. Geographical index p.695-703. 'Aims to present a classified and factually detailed chronology of modern China'. *Class No:* 951(090)

Tibet

[2946]
GOLDSTEIN, M.C. **A History of modern Tibet** 1913-1951: the demise of the Lamaist state. Berkely, Univ. of California Press, 1989. xxxvi,898p. illus., maps, bibliog., index. ISBN: 0520061403.

A detailed history (21 chapters) in 2 parts: 1. Era of the 13th Dalai Lama and Reting 1913-1940 and 2. Era of the Taktra and the 14th Dalai Lama. Appendix A. Anglo-Chinese Convention of 1906 - B. Anglo-Russian Convention of 1907 - C. The Simla Agreements of 1914. Glossary of Tibetan terms p.843. Bibliography p.845-54. 11 maps. 'Examines what happended and why, and balances the traditional focus on international relations with an emphasis on the intricate web of internal affairs and events' (*Preface*). 'This book deserves high praise as the first attempt at an unbiased comprehensive account of Tibetan politics from 1913-1951', (*Journal of Asian studies*, v.49,no.4, November 1990, p.901). *Class No:* 951.5

Mongolia

[2947]
BAWDEN, C.R. **The Modern history of Mongolia.** 2nd rev. ed. London, Kegan Paul International, 1989. xiv,476p. 24p. pl. illus., maps, bibliog., index. pbk. ISBN: 0710303262.

First published London, Weidenfeld & Nicolson, 1968. In fact this 'revised' edition has the text of the 1st ed. reprinted without alteration. Only revision is the incoporation of a Supplementary bibliography p.455!.

Narrative in 9 chapters from loss of Mongol independence to post-Second World War achievements. Chapter notes p.439-47. Bibliographical note. p.451-4. *Class No:* 951.7

Japan

[2948]
The Cambridge history of Japan. Cambridge, Cambridge Univ. Press, 6v., 1989-1991.

1. Brown, D.M. *ed. Ancient Japan*, 1990. 2. McCullough, W. and Shiveley, D.H. *eds. Heian Japan* 1991. 3. Yamamura, K. *ed. Medieval Japan* 1989. 992p. tables, diagrs., bibliog., £65.00 0521223547. 4. Hall, J.W. *ed. Sengoku and Edo* 1990. 5. Jansen, M.B. *ed. The nineteenth century* 1990. 992p. maps, bibliog., £60.00. 0521223563. 6. Duus, P. *ed. The twentieth century* 1989. 896p. maps, tables, diagrs., bibliog., £60.00. 0521223571. 14 chapters arranged in 4 pts: 1. Domestic politics - 2. External relations - 3. Economic development - 4. Social and intellectual change. Multi-volume cooperative history on the familiar Cambridge pattern providing a summary of the state of present knowledge of Japanese history for students and scholars. Supported by The Japan Foundation. *Class No:* 952

Bibliographies

[2949]
DOWER, J.W. **Japanese history and culture from ancient to modern times: seven basic bibliographies.** Manchester, Manchester Univ. Press, 1986. vi,232p. ISBN: 0719019141, UK; 0910129207, US.

1. Ancient and medieval Japan - 2. Early modern and modern Japan 1600-1945 - 3. Japan abroad - 4. Japan and the crisis in Asia 1931-1945: primary materials in English - 5. Occupied Japan and the cold war in Asia - 6. Bibliographies and research guides - 7. Journals and other serial publications. Compiler holds the Joseph Naiman Endowed Chair in Japanese Studies, University of California. 'Dower's selection of English-language primary sources ... includes many unusual, elusive, but valuable sources' (*Choice*,v.24, no.11-12, July/August 1987,p.1674). *Class No:* 952(01)

Dictionaries

[2950]
HUNTER, J. **Concise dictionary of modern Japanese history.** Berkeley, Univ. of California Press, 1984. xvi, 347p. map, index. ISBN: 0520043901.

Information on the individuals and political, diplomatic and socioeconomic events, and institutions that have played a significant role in Japan's modern history 1853-1980. Aimed primarily at non-Japanese speakers, non-specialists, and undergraduate students. Japanese - English glossary of historical terms. 'The special virtue of Hunter ... is the reliable citation of additional accessible sources in English' (*Choice*, v.22, no.6, February 1985, p.795). *Class No:* 952(038)

Persian Gulf

United Arab Emirates

[2951]
TARYAM, A.O. **The establishment of the United Arab Emirates 1950-1985.** London, Croom Helm, 1987. [vi], 290p. maps, index. ISBN: 070994330x.

7 well-documented chapters: 1. Internal and External influences and their impact on the Arab Emirates 1950-60 - 2. Oil and the Change in British Policy - 3. The British Withdrawal Decision and Local, Regional and International Reactions - 4. The Dubai Agreement and Talks over the Proposed Nine-member Union - 5. Failure of Talks about the Nine-member Union and the Success of the Seven-member Union - 6. The Federation of the Emirates and the Conflict between the Constitutional Structure and Regional Authorities - 7. Evaluation of the Economic and Social Development in the United Arab Emirates. The Introduction (p.1-8) is a literature review of recent books and a list of sources. *Class No:* 953.62

India

[2952]
BASHAM, A.L., *ed.* **A Cultural history of India.** Oxford, Clarendon Press, 1984. xx,585p.+xp. illus., tables, maps. ISBN: 0195615204.

A new ed. of *Legacy of India* edited by G.T. Garratt (1937). First published under this title 1975.

28 contributors. 4 main parts (34 chapters): 1. The ancient heritage - 2. Age of Muslim dominance - 3. Challenge and response: the coming of the West - 4. India and the world outside. Footnotes. 'Books for further reading', p.507-17. Detailed, analytical index. Scholarly. *Class No:* 954.0

[2953]
The New Cambridge history of India. Johnson, G., *ed.*
Cambridge Univ. Press, 30v., 1988-. Available in India
through Orient Longman of Bombay. bibliogs., maps.

The original *Cambridge history of India* (1922-1953)
(*q.v.*) formulated a chronology for Indian history and
described the administrative structures of government. This
new series consists of 30 self-contained thematic volumes in
4 distinct parts: 1. The Mughals and their contemporaries -
2. Indian States and their transition to colonialism - 3. The
Indian Empire and the beginnings of modern society - 4.
The evolution of contemporary South Asia.

Volumes published to date: Part 1: 1. Pearson, N.M. *The
Portuguese in India*, 1988. 178p. xiv,244p. 0521266939.
Part 2: 1. Bayly, C.A. *Indian society and the making of the
British Empire.* 1988. xi,230p. 0521250927 - 2. Marshall,
P.J. *Bengal: the British bridgehead. Eastern India 1740-
1828.* 1988 xv,195p. 0521253306 - 3. Grewal, J.S. *The
Sikhs of the Punjab.* 1991. 272p. 0521268842. Part 3: 1.
Jones, K.W. *Socio-religious reform movements in British
India.* 1990. xi,243p. 0521249864. Part 4: 1. Brass, P. *The
politics of India since independence.* 1990. 368p.
0521266130.

'We do not expect the *New Cambridge History of India*
to be the last word on the subject but an essential voice in
a continuing discourse about it' (Johnson, G. The New
Cambridge History of India', p.113-116, *South Asian
Studies*, The British Library, 1986. *Class No:* 954.0

[2954]
WINK, A. Al-Hind The Making of the Indo-Islamic world.
Leiden & Kinderhook (NY), E.J. Brill, 5v., 1990-1998.
maps,bibliogs.

1. *Early medieval India and the expansion of Islam 7th-
11th centuries.* 1990. viii,396p. Gld.165. US$82.50. ISBN
9004092498. 2. *The Slave Kings and the Islamic conquest
of India 11th-13th centuries. c.*1991. 3. *Indo-Muslim society
14th-15th centuries. c.*1994. 4. *Imperial formations 16th-
17th centuries. c.*1996. 5. *State and society in the
eighteenth century. c.*1998. Encyclopedic work 'which aims
to analyze the process of momentous and long-term change
which came with the Islamization of the regions which the
Arabs called AL-HIND, that is India and large parts of its
Indianized hinterland' (*Publisher's brochure*). *Class No:*
954.0

Iran

[2955]
The Cambridge history of Iran. Cambridge, Cambridge Univ.
Press, 1986-. v.1-. illus., diagrs., tables, maps.

1. *The Land of Iran* edited by W.B. Fisher. 1986. 804p.
£55. ISBN 0521069351. 2. *The Median and Archaemenian
periods* edited by I. Gershevitch. 1985. 3. *The Seleucid,
Parthian and Sasanid periods*, 2pts., edited by E. Yar-
Shater. 1983. 1488p. £50. £55. 0521246938 and
0521246997. 4. *From the Arab invasion to the Saljuqs*
edited by R.N. Frye. 1975. 747p. £50. 0521200938. 5. *The
Saljuq and Mongol periods* edited by J.A. Boyle. 1968.
778p. £55. 052106936x. 6. *The Timurid and Sefavid
periods* edited by P. Jackson and L. Lockhart. 1986. 1120p.
£65. 0521200946. 7. *From Nadir Shah to the Islamic
Republic* edited by P. Avery and G.R.G. Hambly. 1989.
£65. 0521200954. 8. Bibliography. *Class No:* 955

Byzantium

Dictionaries

[2956]
The Oxford dictionary of Byzantium. Kazhdan, A.P., *ed.* New
York, Oxford Univ. Press, 3v., 1991. li,2232p. illus., geneal.
tables, maps. ISBN: 0195046528.

Over 5,500 initialled entries from 128 contributors
relating to all aspects of Byzantine history and civilization
from the 4th to the 15th century and covering all regions
that at any time formed part of the Byzantine Empire or
had significant connections with Byzantium. Average length
of entries is 200 words although major thematic entries go
up to 1,000 words. Most end with a list of bibliographic
references. 24 maps. 'For its coverage and authority it will
last for many years as the most significant reference item
covering the whole vast field of Byzantine studies'
(*Reference Reviews*, v.5,no.4, 1991, p.34-5). *Reference
Reviews* Best Specialist Reference Work 1991. *Class No:*
956+949.61(038)

Turkey

[2957]
**SHAW, S.J. and SHAW E.K. History of the Ottoman Empire
and modern Turkey.** Cambridge, Cambridge Univ. Press,
2v., 1977.

1: *Empire of the Gazis: the rise and decline of the
Ottoman Empire*, 1280-1808. xiii, 351p.

2: *Reform, revolution and republic: the rise of modern
Turkey*, V.1 has 2 parts: 1. Rise of the Ottoman Empire,
1280-1566; 2. Decentralisation and traditional reform in
response to challenge. Bibliography: 'Ottoman history to
1808', p.302-24 (1. General histories - 2. Bibliographies - 3.
General reference works - 4/11. Periods), with brief running
commentary. Non-analytical index. V.2 is based on both
Ottoman and European sources. 'Will remain an
outstanding reference work ... excellent bibliographies at the
end of each volume list all major works both in Turkish
and English' (M. Güçlü. *Turkey*, 1981, Entry 674). *Class
No:* 956

Israel & Palestine

[2958]
SACHAR, H.M. A History of Israel.

1. *From the rise of Zionism to our time* Oxford, Basil
Blackwell, 1977. xix, 883, xlix p. bibliog., maps, index.
0613117870. 2. *From the aftermath of the Yom Kippur
War* New York and Oxford, Oxford Univ. Press, 1987. xv,
319p. bibliog. maps, index. $19.95. £19.50. 0195043863.
Extremely well-documented standard history with extensive
bibliographies. *Class No:* 956.94

Dictionaries

[2959]
ROLEF, S.H., *ed.* Political dictionary of the state of Israel.
New York, Macmillan; London, Collier Macmillan, 1987.
351p. ISBN: 0029164214.

53 contributors. 450 initialled A-Z articles on prominent
personalities, events, political parties, relations with great
powers *etc.* (Arab-Israeli conflict: 17½p., 2 maps). Analysis
of events and interpretations seem to *Reference Reviews*,
v.3, no.1, March 1989, p.11-12 'to be fair and unbiased'.
Class No: 956.94(038)

Thailand

[2960]
WYATT, D.K. **Thailand a short history.** New Haven, Connecticut, Yale Univ. Press 1983. xviii, 351p. illus., maps, bibliog., index. ISBN: 0300030541.

10 chapters: 1. Beginnings of Tai history - 2. The Tai and the Classical Empires AD1000-1200 - 3. A Tai century 1200-1351 - 4. Ayudhya and its neighbors 1351-1569 - 5. The Empire of Ayudhya 1569-1767 - 6. The early Bangkok Empire 1767-1851 - 7. Mongkut and Chulalongkorn 1851-1910 - 8. Rise of elite nationalism 1910-1932 - 9. The military ascendant 1932-1957 - 10. Development and revolution 1957-1982. Appendix A. Kings of Sukhothai - B. Kings of Lan Na - C. Kings of Ayudhya, Thonburi and Bangkok - D. Prime Ministers of Thailand. Chapter notes p.315-19. Bibliography p.321-32. Analytical index. 'The discursive bibliography is the best available introduction to the historiography of Thailand in English and some other Western languages, and includes a guide to primary sources' (M. Watts. *Thailand*, 1986. Entry 229). *Class No:* 959.3

Malaysia

[2961]
ANDAYA, B.W. *and* ANDAYA, L.Y. **A History of Malaysia.** London, The Macmillan Press; New York, St. Martin's Press, 1982. xx,350p. maps,bibliog., index. (*Macmillan's Asian Histories.*) ISBN: 0333276728, UK; 0213381204, US.

Contents: Introduction: Environment and peoples - 1. Heritage of the past - 2. Melaka and its heirs - 3. Demise of the Malay entrepot state 1699-1819 - 4. A new world is created 1819-74 - 5. The making of British Malaya 1874-1919 - 6. The functioning of colonial society 1919-57 - 7. The forging of a nation 1957-80 - Conclusion: some themes in Malaysian history. Notes and further readings p.305-329. Glossary p.330-336. Analytical index. 'Beyond question the best general history of Malysia in print' (*Choice*, v.20,nol.7, March 1983, p.1042). *Class No:* 959.5

Vietnam

Dictionaries

[2962]
DUICKER, W.J. **Historical dictionary of Vietnam.** Metuchen, New Jersey, Scarecrow Press, 1989. xiv, 269p. maps, tables, bibliog. (*Asian Historical Dictionaries, no.1.*) ISBN: 0810821648.

A-Z cross-referenced entries (191p.) give details of prominent persons and important orgnizations in addition to broad themes of current and historical significance. A bibliographical essay of key books in English and a thematically arranged bibliography (p.203-46) contribute to 'a valuable reference tool for students and nonspecialists' (*Choice*, v.27, no.2, October 1989, p.284). *Class No:* 959.7(038)

Vietnam War

[2963]
DAVIDSON, P.B. **Vietnam at war:** the history 1946-1975. Novato, California, Presidio Press; London, Sidgwick & Jackson, 1988. cxii, 838p. illus., maps, bibliog., index. ISBN: 0283997125, UK; 0891413065, US.

27 well-documented chapters: 2. The French campaign 1946-47 ... 11. Dien Bien Phu: a critique ... 18. The Tet offensive ... 26. Defeat - 27. Why we lost the war. Glossary p.795-818. Bibliography p.819-27. Analytical index. 'This fascinating book is the finest military history of the Vietnam War now available' (*Choice*, v.26 no.1 September 1988, p.217). *Class No:* 959.70

[2964]
SMITH, R.B. **An International history of the Vietnam war.** London, Macmillan, 4v., 1983-.

1. *Revolution versus containment, 1955-61.* 1983. xiii, 301p. £38. 0333242467. 2. *The struggle for South-East Asia, 1961-65.* 1985. xii, 492p. £38. 0333339576. 3. *The making of a limited war, 1965-66* 1991. xiv,490p. £38. 033339584. 4. 033339592. V.2 has 19 chapters organized in 5 chronological sections with a bibliography, notes, and index. The author is Reader in the History of South-East Asia, School of Oriental and African studies, University of London. 'Examples of modern historical writing at its best and inspire the confident expectation that the five volume work, when complete, will constitute a standard and indispensable historical record of the Vietnam War' (*International Affairs*, v.67,no.4, October 1991, p.803). *Class No:* 959.70

Africa

[2965]
The Cambridge history of Africa. Cambridge, Cambridge Univ. Press, 8v., 1975-1986. illus., maps, tables, bibliogs.

1. *From the earliest times to c.500B.C.* edited by J. Desmond Clark, 1982. xxiii,1157p. £85.00 ISBN 052122215x. 2. *From c.500B.C. to A.D.1050* edited by J.D. Fage. 1978. xvii,840p. £80.00. 0521215927. 3. *From c.1050 to c.1600* edited by Roland Oliver. 1977. xii,803p. £80.00 0521209811. 4. *From c.1600 to c.1790* edited by Richard Gray. 1975. xiv,738p. £80.00. 0521204135. 5. *From c.1790 to c.1870* edited by John E. Flint. 1976. xv,617p. £70.00. 0521207010. 6. *From 1870 to 1905* edited by Roland Oliver and G.N. Sanderson. 1985. xvi,956p. £80.00. 0521228034. 7. *From 1905 to 1940* edited by A.D. Roberts. 1986. xix,1063p. £80.00. 0521225051. 8. *From c.1940 to c.1975* edited by Michael Crowder. 1984. xvi,1011p. £80.00. 0521224098. *Class No:* 96

Maps & Atlases

[2966]
ADE AJAYI, J.F. *and* CROWDER, M., *eds.* **Historical atlas of Africa.** Harlow, Essex, Longman, 1985. 72p. maps + 72p. 22 plates. ISBN: 058264335x.

72 maps of 3 types: event maps concerning historical events and locations of towns, battles, trade routes; process maps forming a visual interpretation of historical processes; and quantitative maps consisting of numerical data characterizing historical relationships. Ten years in the planning this is a more ambitious atlas than Fage and Verity's *The atlas of African history*. 'An invaluable and accurate source for ... the development of the continent during the last three thousand years' (*African Affairs* v.85,no.339, June 1986, p.301-302). *Class No:* 96(084.3)

Africa—North

Egypt

Dictionaries

[2967]
KING, J.W. **Historical dictionary of Egypt.** Metuchen, New Jersey, Scarecrow Press, 1984. xiii, 719p. map, bibliog. (*African Historical Dictionaries, no.36.*) ISBN: 0810816709.

Chronology p.26-88. Dictionary p.89-650. Bibliography p.651-719. 'A work of considerable value for all students of Egypt' (*International Affairs*, v.61, no.3, Summer 1985, p.368). *Class No:* 962.0(038)

Africa—West

Nigeria

[2968]
ISICHEI, E. **A History of Nigeria.** London, Longman, 1983. xix,517p. illus. maps. bibliog. index. ISBN: 0582643317.
20 meticulously documented thematic chapters with an emphasis on the pre-colonial period. Bibliography p.488-503. The author is Professor of History at the University of Jos. *Class No: 966.9*

Africa—East & Equatorial

[2969]
LOW, D.A. *and* SMITH, A., *eds.* **History of East Africa.** Oxford, Clarendon Press, 3v., 1963-76. xiii,500p. li,766p. xii,691p. tables, maps, bibliogs.
1 [to 1898], edited by R. Oliver and G. Matthew. 1963. 2 [from 1890s to close of world War II], edited by V. Harlow and E.M. Chilver. 1965. 3 [1945-1963], edited by D.A. Low and Alison Smith. 1976. V.1 (12 chapters; 10 contributors) 'directly surveys results of original research' (*Prefatory note*). Bibliographies, p.457-80; analytical index. While conceding that it is an indispensable work of reference, the reviewer in *Commonwealth Journal* (v.6,no.5, October 1963, p.218) complains of unevenness of treatment and lack of general maps. V.3 (14 chapters, footnoted) has 40p. of statistical tables and a select bibliography in 4 sections. Analytical index, p.665-91). Studied from an African as well as a European standpoint. *Class No: 967*

Africa—Southern

[2970]
OMER-COOPER, J.D. **History of Southern Africa.** London, James Currey; Portsmouth, New Hampshire, Heinemann Educational Books Inc., 1987. xiii, 298p. illus., maps, bibliog., index. ISBN: 0852550103, UK; 0435080105, US.
9 chapters: 1. The Khoisan people and Bantu-speaking settlement ... 4. The mass migration of the mfecane & the Great Trek ... 9. The three phases of apartheid. Appendix 1. The enclave states Lesotho, Swaziland and Botswana. 2. Namibia. Bibliography (by chapter) p.278-285. Analytical index. 'The most important theme is the historical explanation of that peculiar system of systematic racial discrimination, repression and exploitation known as apartheid'. *Class No: 968*

South Africa

[2971]
DAVENPORT, T.R.H. **South Africa** a modern history. 4th ed. London, Macmillan, 1991. xxv,662p. illus., maps, tables, bibliog., index. ISBN: 0333550331.
1st ed. 1977; 3rd ed. 1987.
20 subdivided chapters in 3 parts: 1. Prelude to white dominion - 2. Consolidation of a White state - 3. Political economy of South Africa. This edition incorporates revised material on South African prehistory and focuses 'on the rapidly changing socio-economic and political scene since the mid-term crisis of P.W. Botha's Government'. Appendix: Heads of State 1652-1990 p.558-63. Bibliographical Notes (by chapter) p.568-613. *Class No: 968.0*

America

Bibliographies

[2972]
Literature guides to Columbus' voyage, 1492.
1. Metz, A. 'Christopher Columbus: a selection guide to literature 1970-1989', *Reference Services Review,* v.19, no.4, 1991, p.21-44. 91 annotated entries arranged in 5 subdivided parts: 1. European intellectual background - 2. Exploration - 3. Christopher Columbus - 4. Conquest and colonization - 5. Miscellaneous (Heraldry; Quincentennial).
2. Shreve, J. 'Christopher Columbus: a bibliographic voyage', *Choice,* v.29, no.5, January 1992, p.703-11. Bibliographical essay assessing the books 'felt to have worth as potential additions to American collections arranged in 9 sections. Biographies - Language of Columbus - Family - Columbus' log and other writings - Toscanelli Letter - Landfall and other murky waters - Reference works - Other books - Poetry and fiction. Consolidated list of works cited p.709-11.
3. French and Spanish language material is considered in 'Les éditeurs sur les pas de Christophe Colomb', *Livres hebdo,* v.13, no.20, 17 Mai 1991, p.57-60. *Class No: 97(01)*

Encyclopaedias

[2973]
The Christopher Columbus encyclopedia. Bedini, S.A., *ed.* New York, Simon & Schuster, 1991; London, Macmillan, 2v., 1992. 900p. ISBN: 0131426621, US; 033358995, UK.
About 350 signed A-Z articles (350-10,000 words) from over 150 contributors on Columbus' life; the contemporary world (social, political, economic and cultural institutions of Europe, biographies of reigning monarchs); Pre-Columbian exploration and discovery; Science and technology of discovery; The New World (archaeology, settlements, natural history); and Post-Columbian exploration and discovery. Issues raised are discussed both from the indigenous and European viewpoint. Published to mark the quincentenary of Columbus' first voyage to America in 1492. *Class No: 97(031)*

America—North & Central

Canada

Bibliographies

[2974]
A Reader's guide to Canadian history. Toronto, University of Toronto Press, 2v., 1982.
V2, is a revision of Granatstein's *Canada since 1867: a bibliographic guide* (2nd ed., 1977).
1. *Beginnings to Confederation* edited by D.A. Muise. 1982. xv, 253p. index. $12.95. 0802064426. 2. *Confederation to the present* edited by J.L. Granatstein and P. Stevens. xiv, 329p. index. $13.95. 0802064906. A literature survey composed of 19 chronological, thematic and geographical chapters each beginning with a bibliographic essay followed by annotated lists of significant titles. 'An essential purchase for any library whose patrons have an interest in Canada' (*Choice,* v.20, no.5, January 1983, p.692). *Class No: 971(01)*

Encyclopaedias

[2975]
STORY, N. **The Oxford companion to Canadian history and literature.** Toronto, Oxford Univ. Press, 1967. xx, 935p. maps, bibliog.

Parent volume contains *c.*1,900 articles (1,500 on Canadian history). Extensive bibliographies (*e.g.* 'Arcadia: bibliography': p.5-6; 'Rebellion of 1837: bibliography': p.699-700). 5 appendices (2. Governors General, etc.). List of titles referred to (title-date-author), p.866-935, *c.*6,000 entries. Important for entries on people, places, periodicals and societies of Canada. 'A very valuable reference tool' (*RQ*, v.7, no.4, Summer 1968, p.191).

W. Toye's *Supplement to the Oxford companion to Canadian history and literature* (1973) ISBN 0195402057 adds nearly 200 entries covering the period 1967-72. *Class No:* 971(031)

Maps & Atlases

[2976]
Historical atlas of Canada. maps, bibliog. Univ. of Toronto Press, 3v., 1987-.

V.1: *From the beginning to 1800.* edited by R.C. Harris. 1987. xviii,198p. ISBN 0862024955. 69 two-page cartographic presentations, *i.e.* maps and closely integrated text, arranged in 6 sections: 1. Prehistory; 2. The Atlantic realm; 3. Inland expansion; 4. The St. Lawrence settlements; 5. The Northwest; 6. Canada in 1800, each introduced by a scholarly essay. Notes (including primary and secondary sources) p.179-198. 'A magisterial work of value to all interested in Canada, general and learned readers alike, and it is difficult to imagine that it could be even remotely paralleled in the future' (*Geographical Journal*; v.154,no.2, July 1988, p.295-296. V.3: *Addressing the twentieth century 1891-1961* edited by D. Kerr and D.W. Holdsworth, 1990. [xx],197p. $95. 0802034489. 66 map and text features: Canada 1891-1961: an overview (1. Canada in 1891 - 2. Territorial evolution - 3. Economic growth - 4. Population distribution) - Part 1. The great transformation 1891-1929 and Part 2. Crisis and response 1929-1961. 'The initiators and engineers of this project should be justly proud of their efforts: we should be most appreciative of their version' (*Cartographica*, v.28,no.2, Summer 1991, p.91-4). V.2: *The Nineteenth Century* edited by R.L. Gentilcore is in active preparation. *Class No:* 971(084.3)

Mexico

[2977]
MEYER, M.C. *and* SHERMAN, W.L. **The Course of Mexican history.** 4th ed. New York, Oxford Univ. Press, 1991. xii,718,xxxviip. illus., maps, bibliog., index. ISBN: 0195065999.

First published 1979; 3rd ed. 1987.

45 chapters in 10 sections: 1. Pre-Columbian Mexico - 2. Spanish conquest ... 7. Modernization of Mexico 1876-1910 ... 10. The Revolution shifts gear: Mexico since 1940. Appendix: Mexican heads of state 1349-1988 p.i-iv. Chapter bibliographies. Select bibliography for those who read Spanish p.v-xix. Over 30 maps and charts. New to this edition: new section on US/Mexico border relations; a re-evaluation of classic Maya civilization; introduction to administration of Carlos Salinas de Gortari). 'As a summary reference volume for the general reader it is superior to all others' (*Hispanic American Historical Review*, v.60,no.1, February 1980, p.99-101). *Class No:* 972

Caribbean

[2978]
WILLIAMS, E. **From Columbus to Castro** the history of the Caribbean 1492-1949. London, Andre Deutsch, 1970; New York, Harper & Row, 1973. 576p. illus., tables, bibliog., index.

29 chapters: 26. Twentieth-century colonialism - 27. The colonial nationalist movement - 28. Castroism - 29. The future of the Caribbean. 'One of the most comprehensive studies' (R.A. Myers, *Dominica*, 1987. Entry 188). *Class No:* 972.9

Maps & Atlases

[2979]
ASHDOWN, P. **Caribbean history in maps.** London and New York, Longman, 1979. iv, 84p. maps, plans, index, pbk. ISBN: 0582765412.

77 black-and-white maps, with commentary in margins. Covers the Caribbean region up to 1978. 15 sections: 1. General - 2. The Amerindian peoples - 3. European exploration and settlement - 4. Slavery and the plantation society - 5. European rivalry and changes of ownership - 6. Revolt and revolution - 7. Emancipation - 8. The decline of sugar - 9. Problems, 1834-1900 - 10. The USA in the Caribbean - 11. Economic distress and the rise of nationalism - 12. Regional co-operation; failure and success - 13. The West Indies in the 1970s - 14. West Indian heroes (p.53-58: *c.*100) - 15. The history of individual states (maps 68-77: Cuba; Hispànola; Puerto Rico; Jamaica; the Lesser Antilles; the Bahamas; Barbados, Trinidad; Belize; Guyana). For schools. *Class No:* 972.9(084.3)

Jamaica

[2980]
BLACK, C.V. **The History of Jamaica.** Harlow, Essex, Longman Caribbean, 1988. 176p. illus., maps, index. pbk. ISBN: 0582038987.

First published Collins Educational 1958.

21 chronological chapters: 1. The first Jamaicans - 2. The discovery - 3. Jamaica under the Spaniards ... 21. Independent Jamaica. Important dates in the islands history p.7-8. *Class No:* 972.92

Latin America

[2981]
The Cambridge history of Latin America. Cambridge, Cambridge Univ. Press, 1984-.

1-2. *Colonial Latin America* v.1: 1984. xx,645p. £65. ISBN 0521232236. V.2: 1984. xx,912p. £70. 0521245168. 3. *From independence to 1870.* 1985. xx,945p. £80. 0521232244. 4-5. *1870-1930* v.1: 1986. xiii,676p. £65. 0521232252. V.2: 1986. xviii,951p. £80. 0521245176. 7. *Mexico, Central America and the Caribbean since 1930* 1990. 656p. 8. *Latin America since 1930. Spanish South America.* 1992. xiv,775p. 0521266521. All volumes are equipped with long bibliographic essays for each chapter with special emphasis on books and articles published in the last 20 years. 'This work measures up to the standards of solid scholarship that characterize other multi-volume Cambridge histories. The international contributors are all reputable specialists and present competent, up-to-date surveys' (*Choice*, v.23, no.9, May 1986, p.1446). *Class No:* 972.99

Archives

[2982]
WALNE, P., *ed.* **A Guide to manuscript sources for the history of Latin America and the Caribbean in the British Isles.** London, Oxford Univ. Press in collaboration with the Institute of Latin American Studies, Univ. of London, 1973. xx,580p.

A detailed inventory of public repositories. Appendix: 'The British in South America - an archive report'. Addenda. Index, p.521-80 (Ship's names: over 4 columns). A first-rate research tool in its field. 'This is a basic reference work' (*Library Journal*, v.98, no.14, August 1973, p.2266). *Class No: 972.99(093.20)*

USA

Bibliographies

[2983]
Harvard guide to American history. Freidel, F., *ed.* Cambridge, Mass., Harvard Univ. Press, 2v., 1974. xxx, 605p.+xxvi, 609-1290p. ISBN: 0674375602.

1st ed. 1954 succeeded E. Channing and others' *Guide to the study and reading of American history* (Boston, Ginn, 1912).

V.1 has 4 parts (29 sections): 1. Research methods and materials (including unpublished primary sources; microform materials; reference works) - 2. Biographies and personal records. 3. Comprehensive and area histories - 4. Histories of special subjects (*e.g.* physical environment; economic history; intellectual history; the arts; pure and applied sciences), about 20,000 entries. No annotations, but each section has an introduction.

V.2 has 5 parts, arranged chronologically: 5. America, to 1789 - 6. United States, 1789-1860 - 7. Civil War and reconstruction - 8. Rise of industry and empire - 9. Twentieth century (p.927-1067). Cumulated index of names (p.107-1274) and subject index (p.1275-90; in small type). 'Remains the best single source for those studying the history of the US' (*RQ*, Spring 1975, v.14, no.3, p.261). *Class No: 973(01)*

[2984]
Writings on American history : a subject bibliography of articles 1962-1983/84. Washington and White Plains, New York, Kraus International Publications and the American Historical Association, 15v., 1974-1985.

Succeeds the annual *Writings on American history* 1902-1960 (1930-72; various publishers). *Writings on American history 1961* filling the gap in 2v. 1979. $60.00. ISBN 0527982520. *Class No: 973(01)*

[2985]
—Writings on American history, 1962-73 a subject bibliography of books and monographs. White Plains, New York, Kraus International Publications and the American Historical Association, 10v., 1985. 6530p. index. ISBN: 0527982687.

Cites more than 50,000 books and monographs and is compiled from Library of Congress catalogue cards. V.1 includes sections on history and historians and a chronological classification. V.7(pt), v.8 and v.9(pt) comprise a geographical classification. The added emphasis on biography and genealogy in this set is reflected in the rest of v.9. V.10 is the index. *Class No: 973(01)*

Encyclopaedias

[2986]
MORRIS, R.B., *ed.* **Encyclopedia of American history.** 6th ed. New York, Harper & Row, 1981. 1328p. ISBN: 0061816051.

First published 1953; 5th Bicentennial ed. 1976.

3 parts: 1. Basic chronology, to 1975 - 2. Topical chronology (The expansion of the nation - Population, immigration and ethnic stock - Leading Supreme Court decisions - The American economy - Science, invention and technology - Thought and culture - Mass media) - 3. Five hundred notable Americans, p.961-1191 (George Washington; $1\frac{1}{2}$ columns). 42 maps and charts. Analytical index. p.1193-1245. In this ed. more space is devoted to minorities, ethnic groups and women. *Class No: 973(031)*

Dictionaries

[2987]
Dictionary of American history. New York, Scribner, 7v. & Index, 1976-77. 3344p. ISBN: 0684138565.

First published 1940 (5v. & Index).

800 contributions; 7,200 signed entries, A-Z (Aachen ... Zwaanendael colony). Brief bibliographies (*e.g.*, 'Alaska' (4 sections): 12 columns; 4 references; 'Mexican War (1846-1848)': $3\frac{1}{2}$ columns. 3 references; 'Afro Americans': over 12 columns, 8 references; 'Antitrust laws ': $2\frac{1}{2}$ cols., 5 references). Coverage of science and technology has been improved; lack of treatment of the arts is corrected (*e.g.*, 'Theater': $9\frac{1}{2}$ columns, 10 references); and coverage of native American Indians and Afro-Americans made more adequate, according to the *Preface*. No biographies. Index v. (xviii, 503p.) - *c.*90,000 entries. A standard, basic work. 'Most highly recommended' (*Library Journal*, v.102,no.13, July 1977, p.1480).

Concise dictionary of American history. Rev. ed. 1983, 1140p. $60.00. ISBN 0684173212. Adds new articles and revises others. 'A handy addition at reference desks far from the main set (*Choice*, v.20,no.11-12, July-August 1983, p.1572). *Class No: 973(038)*

Reviews & Abstracts

[2988]
America history and life article abstracts and citations of reviews and dissertations covering the United States and Canada. Santa Barbara, California, ABC Clio; Oxford, Clio Press, 1964-.

1954-1963 Abstracts of the world's periodical literature relating to the history of the United States and Canada included in *Historical Abstracts*. These were subsequently published as Vol.0 of *America history and life*. V. 1-10 (1964-1978) limited to abstracts. V. 11-25 (1979-1988) published in 4 parts: A. Articles, abstracts and citations (3 issues) - B. Index to book reviews (2 issues) - C. American history index (books, articles and dissertations) - D. Annual index. V.26-. (1989-) 5 issues a year: issues 1-4 carry abstracts, reviews and dissertations, issue 5 is a cumulative annual index.

V.26, no.1 1989 has 3536 entries from listed journals February-May 1988 arranged in 6 parts subdivided under subject classification headings: 1. North America - 2. Canada - 3. United States national history to 1945 - 4. United States national history 1945 to present - 5. United States regional, state and local history (in 7 regional subdivisions) - 6. History. The Humanities and Social Sciences (*e.g.*, Archives, libraries, museums; General bibliography; Historiography; Methodology; Teaching and study of history). Subject, author, book and film title and reviewer indexes. Comprehensive worldwide coverage drawing upon more than 2000 journals in 45 languages. Cumulative quinquennial indexes are available: V.1-5 (1964-1968)

....(contd.)
£197.00; v.6-10 (1969-1973) £197.00; v.11-15 (1974-1978) £340.00; v.16-20 (1979-1983) £388.00. Falk, J.D. and Kinnell, S. *Searching America history and life and Historical abstracts on DIALOG*, rev. ed., 1987. 116p. (ABC-Clio Guides to Online Searching), £27.05. ISBN 0874360919. *Class No: 973(048)*

Maps & Atlases

[2989]
Atlas of American history. Ferrell, R.H. *and* Natkiel, R. New York and Oxford, Facts on File Publications, 1987. 192p. illus., (some col.), col. maps, facsims., col. plans. index. ISBN: 0816010285.

A useful single volume atlas of *c.*200 x 2 or 4 colour maps drawn in 1986-7 not too happily married to a superfluous illustrated history arranged in 6 chronological sections *e.g.* 1. The colonial era ... 5. The two World Wars ... 6. America in a divided world. 3 Map essays: Territorial expansion of the USA, Population; Presidential elections. 143 historical paintings, drawings and photographs. 'For the modern period the Facts on File atlas has much broader and more up-to-date coverage than its predecessors' (*Booklist*, v.84, no.13, 1 March 1988, p.1102). A revised edition published in 1990 merely adds one map, 1988 election figures, and the name of George Bush to the list of US presidents. *Class No: 973(084.3)*

Amerindians, North

Handbooks & Manuals

[2990]
HEARD, J.N. Handbook of the American frontier: four centuries of Indian-White relationships. Metuchen, NJ., Scarecrow Press, 5v., 1987-. Distributed in UK by Shelwing Ltd. of Folkestone, Kent. (*Native American Resources Series, no.1*.)

1. *Southeastern Woodlands.* 1987. 2. *Northeastern Woodlands.* 1990. xi,403p. £31.90. 0810823241. Future volumes: will cover the Great Plains (v.3) and the Rocky Mountains, southwestern districts and the Pacific coast (v.4). V.5 will be a general index, choronology and bibliography.

Series of brief articles (up to 2p. in length with a few slightly longer), ending with source attributions, concerning American Indian tribes and leaders, explorers, traders, frontier settlers, soldiers, missionaries, mountain men, battles, massacres, forts, treaties, and other topics of interest in the history of the first 48 United States from the arrival of the earliest seafarers to the end of the Indian wars four hundred years later, arranged in 4 A-Z sequences. *Class No: 973(=97)(035)*

Colonial Period

Encyclopaedias

[2991]
The Encyclopedia of colonial and revolutionary America. New York and Oxford, Facts On File, 1980. 484p. ISBN: 0816017441.

Covering US history to 1785, this quick-reference guide includes 1500 A-Z entries on prominent native, African and European Americans (50% of the entries are biographical), geographical locations, religion, politics, and economics *etc.* 16 topic guides (*e.g.* on agriculture, geography, Spanish colonies) signpost the encyclopedia's contents. 'A superb ready reference tool for all levels' (*Choice*, v.27,no.11-12, July-August 1990, p.1804). *Class No: 973.02(031)*

America—South

Brazil

Dictionaries

[2992]
LEVINE, R.M. Historical dictionary of Brazil. Metuchen, New Jersey, Scarecrow Press, 1979. xi,297p. (*Latin American Historical Dictionaries no.19.*) ISBN: 0810811782.

Dictionary p.1-228. Bibliography p.229-97. Definitions 'treat not only people and events but Brazilian civilization in several dimensions'. 'A most helpful reference work' (S.V. Bryant. *Brazil*. 1985. Entry 145). *Class No: 981(038)*

Argentina

[2993]
ROCK, D. Argentina 1516-1982: from Spanish colonization to the Falklands War and Alphonsin. Los Angeles, Univ. of California Press, 1985. London, I.B. Tauris, 1986. xxix, 478p. illus., maps, bibliog., index. ISBN: 0520051890, US; 1850430861, UK.

'A standard work: undramatic but judicious and convincing' (*International Affairs*, v.62, no.4, Autumn 1986, p.717). *Class No: 982*

Australasia

Oceania

[2994]
CAMPBELL, I.C. A History of the Pacific Islands. St. Lucia, Univ. of Queensland Press, 1990. 239p. maps, tables, bibliog., index. pbk. ISBN: 0702222917.

First published Christchurch, Univ. of Canterbury Press, 1989.

Narrative history in 17 chapters of Polynesian, Melanesian, Micronesian and European cultures and activities in the Pacific Ocean *e.g.* 1. The original inhabitants - 2. Austronesian colonization - 3. Polynesia: the age of European discovery ... 15. Attaining independence. Glossary p.229-31. Bibliography p.232-5. 8 maps. *Class No: 993*

[2995]
SPATE, O.H.K. The Pacific since Magellan. Canberra, Australian National Univ. Press; London, Croom Helm, 3v. 1979-1988.

1. *The Spanish Lake.* 1979, xxiv,372p. £40.00. Chapter notes p.293-354. illus. 25 maps. ISBN 0708107272 Aust. 070990049x UK. 2. *Monopolists and freebooters.* 1983. xxi,426p. £35.00. Notes p.337-412. illus. 28 maps. 0708118445 Aust. 0709923716 UK. 3. *Paradise found and lost.* 1988. xxi,410p. £40.00. Notes p.325-95. illus. 28 maps. 0080344003 Aust. 0415025656 UK. Aim is 'to seek to explicate the process by which the greatest blank on the map became a nexus of global commercial and strategic relations' (*Preface to v.1*). 'An excellent survey of the scholarship about this area ... but the work suffers seriously from lack of a bibliography' (*Choice*, v.27,no.1, September 1989, p.198). *Class No: 993*

Dictionaries

[2996]
CRAIG, R.D. *and* **KING, F.P.,** *eds.* **Historical dictionary of Oceania.** Westport, Connecticut, Greenwood Press, 1981. xxxv, 392p. maps, bibliog., index. ISBN: 0313210608.

106 contributors and almost 500 entries cover the exploration, European settlement, and government of the islands of Melanesia, Micronesia and Polynesia. 7

....(contd.)
Appendices (2. Historical chronology ... 3. Prehistoric settlements ... 4. European explorers). Bibliography p.373-375. 19 maps. *Class No: 993(038)*

New Zealand

[2997]
OLIVER, W.H. *and* **WILLIAMS, B.R. Oxford history of New Zealand.** Wellington, Oxford Univ. Press; Oxford, The Clarendon Press, 1981. xiii, 572p. maps, tables, bibliog., index. ISBN: 0195580621.

Single volume cooperative history (by 16 scholars) whose structure 'combines a broad chronological shape with a detailed thematic analysis' (*Introduction*). Chapter references p.479-512. Select bibliographies p.513-551. Glossary of Maori terms p.463. Analytical index. *Class No: 993.1*

Australia

[2998]
CLARK, C.M.H. A History of Australia. Melbourne, Melbourne Univ. Press, 6v., 1962-87. illus., tables, maps, indexes.

1. *From the earliest times to the age of Macquarie.* 1962. (new ed. 1977). xii, 422p. £25.00. ISBN 0522840056. 2. *New South Wales and Van Diemen's Land 1822-38.* 1968. xiii, 364p. £25.00. 0522838219. 3. *The Beginning of an Australian civilization 1824-51.* 1973. 491p. £25.00. 0522840544. 4. *The Earth abideth for ever 1851-88.* 1978. 427p. 0522841473. 5. *The People make laws 1888-1915.* 1981. 964p. 0522842232. 'The most comprehensive survey of our past' (Borchardt, D.H. *Australian bibliography* (1974), p.58). C.M.H. Clark is considered by many to be Australia's leading historian, though his strong and avowed bias against authoritarianism, the bourgeoisie, the church, the cult of heroes, and his fight against empty traditions have aroused much criticism' (*RSR*, v.7, no.2, April/June 1979, p.9). *Class No: 994*

[2999]
The Oxford history of Australia. Bolton, G., *ed.* Melbourne, Oxford University Press, 5v., 1986-90. maps, bibliogs., tables, indexes.

1. Murray, T. *Aboriginal Australia.* 2. Kociumbras, J. *Colonial Australia 1770-1860.* 3. Kingston, B. *Time of hope 1880-1900.* 4. MacIntyre, S. *The succeeding age 1901-1942.* 5. Bolton, G. *The Middle Way 1942-1988.* 'A very solid contribution to the understanding of Australia's historical development' (*Choice*, v.27,no.2, October 1989, p.366+8). *Class No: 994*

Bibliographies

[3000]
Index to journal articles on Australian history. Hogan, T., *and others eds.* Armidale, New South Wales, Univ. of New England Publishing Unit, 1981-. vii, 203p. ISBN: 0858341379.

3 sections: 1. List of journals indexed - 2. A-Z subject index - 3. 4,019 entries from 50 journals A-Z by author. Coverage to the end of 1973. The intention was to issue a supplement every 5 years.

Continued by Crittenden, V. and Thawley, J: *Index to journal articles on Australian history for 1979.* Kensington, Univ. of New South Wales, 1981. 90p. softcover. $4.50. 0949776017. At this point it was decided to prepare an annual compilation for the years 1980-1988 and finally to cumulate them into a single Bicentennial volume.

Crittenden, V. and Thawley, J.: *Index to journal articles on Australian history 1974-1978.* 1981. 238p. $A6.75. 0949776033. Over 2000 entries including book reviews appearing in the indexed journals. 'This listing in effect

....(contd.)
constitutes a bibliography of the vast majority of Australian monographs which were received during those years' (*Introduction*). Crittenden, V. and others: *Index to journal articles on Australian history for 1980.* 1981. 161p. $A9.25. 0949776157.

Crittenden, V. and Thawley: *Index to journal articles on Australian history for 1981.* 1982. 110 0949776068.

Crittenden, V. and others: *Index to journal articles on Australian history for 1982*, North Balwyn, Victoria, Austalian Reference Publications History Project, 1987. 186p. $A16.00. 0958787603. *Class No: 994(01)*

Encyclopaedias

[3001]
Australians a historical library. Broadway, New South Wales, Fairfax, Syme and Weldon; Cambridge, Cambridge Univ. Press, 11v., 1988. illus. tables, bibliog., index. ISBN: 0949288098, Australia; 052134073x, UK.

Cooperative history, 10 years in the making, involving 400 scholars and researchers, consisting of 5 history books, 5 reference works and a Guide and Index volume. *Titles*: 1. *Australians to 1788*; 2. *Australians 1838*; 3. *Australians 1888*; 4. *Australians 1938*; 5. *Australians from 1939.* Volumes 2-4 are instances of the distinctive 'slicing' method of writing history whereby single years are examined to explore every aspect of national life. Graeme Davison, an editor and contributor, expands on this in 'Slicing History. Nationhood And The Bicentennial', *History Today*, v.38. January 1988, p.25-32.

Reference Works: 6. *Australians: A historical atlas* (the first large-scale historical atlas of Australia). 7. *Australians: A historical dictionary.* xx, 462p. illus. index. A succinct overview of Australian history in 1233 entries encompassing historical episodes, concepts, institutions, industries, movements, achievements and failures and biography. 8. *Australians: Events and places.* xvi, 476p. col. illus. col. maps, index. 1. A chronology 1788-1984 accompanied by 2 'timeline' page features: Aboriginal Australia and European exploration to 1788. 2. A historical gazetteer and descriptive account of places that centres on their historical significance grouped in 32 regions. 9. *Australians: Historical statistics.* 17 chapters each with a brief introductory essay. 10. *Australians: A guide to sources.* xviii, 473p. 55 chapters in 10 sections: 1. The writing of Australian history ... 2. Archives ... 19. Genealogy ... 20. Biography. 11. *Australians. The Guide and Index.* 112p. Links the individual volume indexes and connects the more detailed information in individual volumes with the broader themes of Australian history. 'Prepared with great scholarly care from original sources ... can be recommended for public and academic libraries' (*Booklist*, v.85, no.2, 15 September 1988, p.128-130). *Class No: 994(031)*

Maps & Atlases

[3002]
Australians: a historical atlas. Camm, J.C.R. *and* McQuilton, J., *eds.* Broadway, NSW., Fairfax, Syme and Weldon, 1987. xiii,290p. illus. (mostly col.), col. maps, col. graphs, col. tables, index. ISBN: 0949288187.

Forms part of *Australians a historical library (q.v.).*

15 chapters with text, illustrations and maps closely integrated. *I. Place*: I. Environment - 2. Aboriginal landscapes - 3. European discovery and exploration - 4. Rural landscapes - 5. Urban - 6. Mining, manufacturing and transport. *II. People*: 7. Immigrant nations - 8. Life and death - 9. Religion and education - 10. Convicts, bushrangers, larrikins - 11. Australians and war - 12. Great Depression - 13. Government. *III. Landscapes*: 14. City - 15. Country. 'The atlas in its design, lay-out, cartography, photography and quality of reproduction, diagrams, printing

....(contd.)

and binding, is as nearly perfect as it is possible to imagine' (*Geographical Journal*, v.155,no.2, July 1989, p.290-1). *Class No:* 994(084.3)

Archives

[3003]

Guide to collections of manuscripts relating to Australia a selective union list. Canberra, National Library of Australia, 1986. 21 microfiche set. 42 x reduction. ISSN: 07259107.

First published 1965.

Lists collections of private papers, business records, certain restricted collections and 'fugitive' official collections (*i.e.* hard to find official records held outside the national or State archives offices). Includes some entries relating to other geographic regions notably the Pacific Islands and areas neighbouring Australia. Arranged in 2 pts: entries in numerical order and a consolidated name index of collections and sub-groups within collections. An invaluable tool for all those engaged in historical prime source material. *Class No:* 994(093.20)

Polar Regions

Bibliographies

[3004]

DAY, A.E. Search for the Northwest Passage an annotated bibliography. New York, Garland, 1986. xiv,632p. index. (*Garland Reference Library Of Social Science, no.186.*) ISBN: 0824092880.

5160 entries arranged in 11 chapters: 1. Encyclopaedic works, maps and atlases *etc.* - 2. The search begins (1497-1553) - 3. Strait of Anian (1542-1677) - 4. Elizabethan/Stuart trading ventures (1566-1634) - 5. Hudson's Bay Company (1668-1791) - 6. Pacific search resumed (1761-1795) - 7. Royal Navy by land and sea (1815-1839) - 8. Sir John Franklin (1845-1848) - 9. Search for Franklin (1847-1880) - 10. The Passage navigated (1903-1984) - 11. Reference works. 'An excellent bibliographic source and a valuable addition to any reference collection' (*Association of Canadian Map Libraries And Archives Bulletin*, no.68, September 1988, p.25-26). *Class No:* 998/999(01)

Encyclopaedias

[3005]

STEWART, J. Antarctica an encyclopedia. Jefferson, N.C., McFarland, 2v., 1990. xxii,v,1193p. bibliog. ISBN: 0899504701, set; 089950597x, v.1; 0899505988, v.2.

A-Z encyclopedia, with 15,000 cross-referenced entries on geographical features, expeditions, people, scientific subjects, and general interest items, with distinct historical and geographical bias. A Capsule history p.xv-xviii. Chronology (1502 to 1990) p.1133-60. Expeditions p.1161-70. Bibliography p.1173-93. A major work. *Class No:* 998/999(031)

Chronologies

[3006]

HEADLAND, R.K., *comp.* **Chronological list of Antarctic expeditions** and related historical events. Cambridge, Cambridge Univ. Press, 1989. vii, 730p. illus., maps, bibliog., index. (*Studies in Polar Research.*) ISBN: 0521309034.

Based on B. Roberts' 'Chronological list of Antarctic expeditions', *Polar Record*, v.59, no.8, May 1958, p.97-134 and v.9, no.60, September 1958, p.191-239. Material in these lists had already appeared in the *Antarctic Pilot* (London, Hydrographic Department, 2nd ed., 1948).

Over 3,200 entries covering the period 700BC-1988. The

....(contd.)

region covered is the far south in general and Antarctica in particular. Bibliography p.604-21. Authoritative and well-researched record. *Class No:* 998/999(090)

Greenland

[3007]

GAD, F. The History of Greenland. London, C. Hurst, 2v. 1970-1973.

V.3 published in København by Nyt Nordisk Forlag (1982).

1. *Earliest times to 1700.* 1970. xiii, 350p. £30.00. ISBN 0900966238. 2. *1700-1782.* 1973. xviii, 446p. £35.00. 0900966572.

3. *1782-1808* V.1 ranges over 4,000 years in 9 chapters. Notes and references p.319-33; literature p.334-9; glossary p.340. V.2 deals with Greenland's connection with the Danes in 23 chapters. Note on source material p.430-2; glossary p.433-5. A third volume was to have covered Greenland until the end of the first decade of the 20th century but this has not so far appeared in English translation. 'This comprehensive, detailed and solidly documented history of Greenland from the first inhabitants to 1808' (K.E. Miller. *Denmark*, 1987. Entry 717). *Class No:* 998.8

Author-Title Index

The index reference is to the running number given to each item. The running numbers are in one sequence throughout the volume and can be found at the top right-hand corner of the entry for each item.

This index is of authors and titles in one sequence. The names of the authors are printed in bold type. Where works are jointly authored, only the first name is indexed. All books and periodicals listed or mentioned in the text, except where cited as the source of review quotations or for purposes of comparison, are entered under the headings given. All entries in *Walford* have title entries in the index; where the main heading in *Walford* is under title, added entries to the index have usually been made for an editor or compiler.

Filing is word by word, with groups of initials counted as single words. Since *Walford* uses only initials and not forenames it may occasionally happen that titles by different authors with the same surname and initials are found grouped together.

The arrangement of entries under an author is alphabetical by title. To save space, most sub-titles have been omitted, and many lengthy titles have been shortened.

12,000 words **2147**
5001 hard-to-find publishers and their addresses **1590**
A-Z of European brands **1229**
AA book of British towns **2696**
AA book of British villages **2697**
AA road atlas. Europe **2658**
AA road atlas of the British Isles **2664**
Abbott, D.
The Biographical dictionary of scientists **888**
Abbreviations dictionary **18**
ABC rail guide **1607**
ABC world airways guide **1625**
Abercrombie, N.
Contemporary British society **447**
ABHB **1575**
Abingdon dictionary of living religions **340**
Aboriginal tribes of Australia **1092**
Abraham, G.
The Concise Oxford history of music **1932**
Abraham, R.C.
Dictionary of the Hausa language **2268**
Abridged biography and genealogy master index **2763**
Abridged readers' guide to periodical literature **213**
Abstracts of English studies **2358**
Aby, S.H.
Sociology: a guide to reference and information sources **441**
Access to information in local government **692**
Acid rain abstracts annual **1464**
Acoustics abstracts **968**
Acronyms and abbreviations in library and information work **93**
Acronyms, initialisms & abbreviations dictionary **16**
The ACS style guide **988**
The Actor's handbook, 1989 **2036**
Adam, F.
The Clans, septs and regiments of the Scottish Highlands **2781**

Adam, J.H.
Longman dictionary of business English **603**
Adams, C.
Guide to the antique shops of Britain - 1991 **1815**
Adams, C.J.
A Reader's guide to the great religions **333**
Adams, R.W.
Directory of European professional and learned societies **223**
Adamson, P. and Adamson, L.
State of the world's children, 1992 **747**
Ade Ajayi, J.F. and Crowder, M.
Historical atlas of Africa **2966**
Adey, D.
Companion to South African literature **2397**
Adkins, R.T.
Information sources in polymers and plastics **1710**
Admiralty list of lights and fog signals **1619**
Admiralty list of radio signals **1618**
Admiralty manual of navigation **936, 1614**
Admiralty manual of seamanship **1615**
Admiralty notice to mariners **936, 1614**
Adult education **766**
Advances in periglacial geomorphology **1031**
Advances in underwater technology, ocean science and offshore engineering **1451**
Advertiser's annual **628**
Africa south of the Sahara 1992 **2615**
African authors **2523**
The African political dictionary **491**
The African studies companion **2613**
Africa's three religions **428**
Afro-American experience **1088**
The Agricultural notebook
See
Primrose McConnell's 'The agricultural notebook'
Agricultural research centres **1502**

Agricultural statistics for the United Kingdom **1501**
Ahokas, J.
A History of Finnish literature **2514**
AIDS information sourcebook **1316**
Ainsworth & Bisby's dictionary of the fungi **1161**
Ainsworth, G.C.
Ainsworth & Bisby's dictionary of the fungi **1161**
Ainsworth, G.C. and Sussman, A.S.
The Fungi **1162**
The Air almanac **937**
The Air Force List, 1991 **717**
Aird, A.
The Good pub guide **1554**
Aitken, W.R.
Scottish literature in English and Scots **2388**
Al-Hind The Making of the Indo-Islamic world **2954**
Al-Khatib, A.Sh.
A New dictionary of scientific and technical terms, English-Arabic, with illustrations **871**
Albanian-English dictionary **2238**
Albion, R.G.
Naval and maritime history **724**
Alcalay, R.
The Complete English-Hebrew dictionary **2240**
The Complete Hebrew-English dictionary **2241**
Alcock, S.
Historic houses, castles and gardens **1845**
Alderson, A.D. and Iz, F.
The Oxford English-Turkish dictionary **2247**
The Oxford Turkish-English dictionary **2248**
Alderson, M.
International mortality statistics **478**
Alexander, M.
British folklore, myths and legends **822**
All England law reports **640**

Allaby, A. and Allaby, M.
The Concise Oxford dictionary of earth sciences **1006**
Allaby, M.
A Dictionary of zoology **1172**
Macmillan dictionary of the environment **1106**
The Oxford dictionary of natural history **1124**
Allan, E.
A Guide to world cinema **2011**
Allen, C.W.
Astrophysical quantities **924**
Allen, G.F.
Jane's World railways, 1991/92 **1443**
Allen, R.
Modern Arabic literature **2510**
Allen, R.E.
Concise Oxford dictionary **2149**
The Oxford writers' dictionary **2303**
Allgemeines Lexikon der bildenden Künstler **1787**
Allin, C.W.
International handbook of national parks and nature reserves **1130**
An Almanack for the year of Our Lord ... 1868- **437**
Alsop, J.R.
An Index to the revised Bauer-Arndt-Gingrich Greek lexicon **2204**
Alston, Y.R.
The International biotechnology directory, 1991 **1217**
Altaner, B.
Patrology **376**
Alternative medicine: a guide to natural therapies **1292**
Altman, P.L. and Katz, D.D.
Human health and disease **1296**
Aluminum: Properties and physical metallurgy **1686**
Amateur astronomer's handbook **917**
Amateur theatre yearbook 1989-90 **2050**
America history and life **2988**
American and British genealogy and heraldry **2769**
American art directory 1991-1992 **1798**
American bibliography **69**
American bibliography: a preliminary checklist .. **65**
American book prices current **91**
American book publishing record **71**
American book publishing record cumulative 1876-1949 **67**
American book publishing record cumulative 1950-1977 **68**
American book trade directory **1587**
American Ceramic Society
Ceramic abstracts **1672**
American Chemical Society
The ACS style guide **988**
American electricians' handbook **1361**
American folklore **827**
American furniture, 1620 to the present **1887**
American Geographical Society
Research catalogue **2644**
American given names **2110**
American Indian literatures **2526**
American Library Association.
Government Documents Round Table
Guide to official publications of foreign countries **268**

American library directory **119**
American library history **104**
American men and women of science, 1989-90 **889**
American musical theatre **2052**
American naval history **726**
American Physiological Society
Handbook of physiology **1268**
American playwrights since 1945 **2415**
American popular music and its business **1964**
American Psychiatric Association. Joint Commission on Public Affairs
A Psychiatric glossary **1312**
American reference books annual **140**
American Scandinavian Foundation
Index Nordicus **2593**
American Society for Metals
Aluminum: Properties and physical metallurgy **1686**
METADEX database **1678**
Metals abstracts **1682**
Metals handbook **1680**
World aluminum abstracts **1687**
American Society of Heating, Refrigerating and Air-conditioning Engineers
ASHRAE handbook **1762**
American songwriters **1959**
American studies **2629-2630**
American universities and colleges **783**
American Welding Society
Welding handbook **1409**
American women writers: a critical reference guide **2412**
Americanisms **2138**
Amin, K.
Racism and discrimination in Britain **453**
Amos, S.W.
Dictionary of electronics **1375**
Amphibian species of the world **1195**
Analog electronics handbook **1372**
Analytical abstracts **992**
Analytical instrumentation handbook **1719**
Anatomy of wonder **2341**
The ANBAR management bibliography **616**
Ancient France 6,000-2,000 BC **2546**
The Ancient kingdoms of Mexico **2827**
Ancient peoples and places **2529**
The Ancient stones of Wales **2554**
Andaya, B.W. and Andaya, L.Y.
A History of Malaysia **2961**
Anderson, G.L.
Asian literature in English **2496**
Anderson, H.L.
A Physicist's desk reference **960**
Anderson, J.
Bloomsbury dictionary of opera and operetta **1948**
Andrews, J.A. and Hines, W.D.
Keyguide to information sources on the international protection of human rights **675**
Androuet, P.
Guide to world cheeses **1539**
Andrusyshen, C.H. and Krett, J.N.
Ukrainian-English dictionary **2211**
Angel, W.D.
Youth movements of the world **749**

Angerer, M.
Harrap's five-language business dictionary **548**
Anglesko-slovenski slovar **2220**
Anglicko-slovenský slovník **2216**
Anglo-American cataloguing rules **108**
Anglo-russkiĭ politekhnicheskiĭ slovar' **870**
Anglo-Saxon dictionary **2122**
Anglu-latviešu vārdnica **2224**
Anglu-lietuviu kalbu žodynas **2222**
Animal identification **1171**
Annotated bibliographies of mineral deposits in Europe **1061**
Annotated bibliographies of mineral deposits in the Western Hemisphere **1062**
An Annotated bibliography of the Napoleonic era **2844**
An Annotated guide to current national bibliographies **36**
Annual abstract of statistics, 1991 **468**
Annual bibliography of British and Irish history **2859**
Annual bibliography of English language and literature **2119, 2349**
Annual bibliography of the history of the printed book and libraries **1575**
Annual Egyptological bibliography/Bibliographie **2535**
Annual index to motion picture credits **2019**
The Annual obituary **2708**
The Annual register **2829**
Annual review of microbiology **1120**
Anson, R.
World textile trade and production trends **1701**
Ansteinsson, J.
English-Norwegian technical dictionary **857**
Norsk-engelsk teknisk ordbok **858**
Antarctic bibliography **1032**
The Antarctic Treaty regime **2638**
Antarctica **3005**
Anthony, L.J.
Information sources in energy technology **1336**
Information sources in engineering **1323**
Anthony, P. and Arnold, J.
Costume: a general bibliography **784**
Anthropological index to current periodicals in the Museum of Mankind Library **1081**
Apes of the world **1215**
Applied science and technology index **1222**
Aqualine abstracts **1461**
Aquatic sciences and fisheries abstracts **1046, 1112**
The Archaeology of ancient China **2547**
Archbold, T.
Engineering research centres: a world directory **1329**
Archival collections of non-book materials **260**
Ardis, S.B.
A Guide to the literature of electrical and electronics engineering **1355**
Arduini, P. and Teruzzi, G.
The Macdonald encyclopedia of fossils **1066**

Argentina 1516-1982: from Spanish colonization to the Falklands War and Alphonsin **2993**
Argentine literature **2472**
Arlott, J.
The Oxford companion to sports and games **2068**
The Armies of Britain, 1485-1980 **714**
Armorial général **2786**
The Arms control, disarmament and military security dictionary **663**
Armstead, H.C.
Geothermal energy **1015**
Armstrong, C.J. and Large, J.A.
Manual of online search strategies **8**
Armstrong, M.
A Handbook of management techniques **612**
A Handbook of personnel management **618**
The Army list. 1814- **713**
Armytage, W.H.G.
Four hundred years of English education **760**
Arnold, D.
The New Oxford companion to music **1925**
Arnold, E.N. and Burton, J.A.
A Field guide to the reptiles and amphibians of Britain and Europe **1194**
Arnold, J.
A Handbook of costume **785**
Arntzen, E.M. and Rainwater, R.
Guide to the literature of art history **1764**
Aronson, J.
The Encyclopedia of furniture **1883**
Art across America **1895**
Art documentation **1775**
Art index **1765**
Art libraries journal **1776**
Art library manual **1804**
Art of the Western World **1781**
Art sales index **1813**
Artificial intelligence and expert systems sourcebook **1743**
Artificial intelligence from A to Z **1744**
Artist's handbook of materials and techniques **1772**
Arts address book **1793**
Arts and humanities citation index **22**
Arts festivals in Britain and Ireland 1989/90 **1791**
Arts in America **1797**
Arts Review yearbook 1992 **1777**
Ash, M. and Ash, I.
Concise encyclopaedia of industrial chemical additives **1642**
The Thesaurus of chemical products **1643**
What every chemical technologist wants to know **1644**
Ashdown, P.
Caribbean history in maps **2979**
ASHRAE handbook **1762**
Ashwin, C.
Encyclopedia of drawing **1870**
Ashworth, W.
The Encyclopedia of environmental studies **1454**
Asia yearbook **2596**
Asian literature in English **2496**

Aslib book list **875**
The Aslib directory of information sources in the United Kingdom **115**
Aster, S.
British foreign policy, 1918-1945: a guide to research and research materials **504**
Astrologer's handbook **314**
The Astronomical almanac **935**
Astronomy and aeronautics **913**
Astronomy and astrophysics: a bibliographical guide **911**
Astronomy and astrophysics abstracts **920**
The Astronomy encyclopaedia **915**
Astrophysical quantities **924**
Astrophysics and twentieth-century astronomy to 1950 **921**
Atanassova, T.
Bulgarian-English dictionary **2221**
Atkins, B.T.
Collins-Robert French-English/English-French dictionary **2180**
Atkins, P.J.
The Directories of London 1677-1977 **2886**
Atlante Enciclopedico Touring **2660**
Atlante internazionale **2687**
Atlas der Donauländer **2661**
Atlas der Donauländer. Register **2662**
Atlas Mira **2688**
The Atlas of Africa **2676**
Atlas of American history **2989**
Atlas of British overseas expansion **2669**
Atlas of British social and economic history since c.1700 **460**
Atlas of China **2671**
Atlas of Columbus and the great discoveries **2640**
Atlas of Danubian lands **2661**
Atlas of dog breeds of the world **1536**
Atlas of medieval Europe **2838**
Atlas of Mexico **2678**
Atlas of naval warfare **723**
Atlas of palaeobiogeography **1069**
An Atlas of Roman Britain **2869**
Atlas of rugs and carpets
World rugs and carpets **1874**
Atlas of Southeast Asia **2611**
Atlas of the Classical World **2537**
The Atlas of the Crusades **2840**
Atlas of the environment **1460**
Atlas of the living resources of the seas **1544**
Atlas of the Middle East **2674**
Atlas of the Roman world **2826**
Atlas of the Third World **2570**
An Atlas of world affairs **2568**
Atlas of world cultures **1085**
Atlas Ost-und Südosteuropa **2663**
Audio engineering handbook **1748**
Audio, video and data telecommunications **1384**
Audouze, J. and Israël, G.
The Cambridge atlas of astronomy **932**
The Audubon Society encyclopedia of animal life **1178**
The Audubon Society encyclopedia of North American birds **1205**

Augarde, T.
The Oxford dictionary of modern quotations **2285**
Auger, C.P.
Information sources in grey literature **171**
Austin, M.
The ISTC handbook of technical writing and publication techniques **895**
Australian books in print **78**
Australian dictionary of biography **2765**
Australian literature: a reference guide **2420**
Australian national bibliography **79**
The Australian national dictionary **2140**
Australian periodicals in print **202**
Australians **3001**
Australians: a historical atlas **3002**
Automation encyclopedia **1739**
Automobile abstracts **1470**
Automobile Association
AA book of British towns **2696**
AA book of British villages **2697**
Automotive handbook **1471**
Auty, R. and Obolensky, D.
Companion to Russian studies **2587**
An Introduction to Russian language and literature **2488**
Aveynon, E.A.
Dictionary of finance **560**
Aviation: an historical survey **1482**
Avis, W.S.
A Concise dictionary of Canadianisms **2136**
A Dictionary of Canadianisms on historical principles **2136**
Gage Canadian dictionary **2136**
AVMARC **258**
Awards of honour **2793**
Bacon, J.
The Illustrated atlas of Jewish civilization **2817**
Baillie, G.H.
Clocks and watches **1717**
Baillie, L. and Sieveking, P.
British biographical archive **2732**
Baillière's comprehensive veterinary dictionary **1525**
Baillière's encyclopaedic dictionary of nursing and health care **1303**
Baillière's handbook of first aid **1284**
Bajay, Y.P.S.
Biotechnology in agriculture and forestry **1216**
Baker, D.B.
Political quotations **486**
Baker, M.J.
Macmillan dictionary of marketing and advertising **624**
Baker, S.
Endangered vertebrates **1134**
Bălan, I.D.
A Concise history of Rumanian literature **2459**
Balanchine, G. and Mason, F.
Balanchine's festival of ballet **2054**
Balanchine's festival of ballet **2054**
Ball, A.R.
British political parties **510**
Ball, N.
World hunger **458**

Ball, S.
The Directory of international sources of business information **543**

Ballentyne, D.W.G. and Lovett, D.R.
A Dictionary of named effects and laws in chemistry, physics and mathematics **849**
Ballroom dancing **2062**
Baltic literature **2495**

Bancroft Library University of California. Berkeley
Index to printed maps **2655**

Banerji, S.C.
Companion to Sanskrit literature **2500**

Banham, M.
The Cambridge guide to world theatre **2033**

Bank, D. and Exposito, A.
British biographical index **2726**
Bank of England quarterly bulletin **527**

Banks, A.S.
Political handbook of the world, 1990. Annual **484**

Bannerman, D.A.
The Birds of the British Isles **1203**

Bannister, A. and Raymond, S.
Surveying **940**

Bannock, G.
Dictionary of economics **519**

Bannock, G. and Manser, W.
International dictionary of finance **561**

Baranov, A.N.
Atlas Mira **2688**

Barber, A.
Pneumatic handbook **1395**

Barber, C. and Williams, J.G.
The Ancient stones of Wales **2554**

Barber, M.J.
Handbook of power cylinders, valves and controls **1398**

Barber, R. and Riches, A.
A Dictionary of fabulous beasts **830**

Barbour, S.
Arts festivals in Britain and Ireland 1989/90 **1791**
British performing arts yearbook, 1991 **1999**
Bare ruined choirs: the dissolution of the English monasteries **375**

Barlow, H. and Morgenstern, S.
A Dictionary of opera and song themes **1952**

Barnard, S. and Hardy, P. and Laing, D.
Encyclopaedia of rock **1977**

Barnes, R.D.
Invertebrate zoology **1181**
The Barnhart dictionary companion **2157**
The Barnhart dictionary of etymology **2161**

Barnhart, R.K.
The Barnhart dictionary of etymology **2161**
Third Barnhart dictionary of new English **2157**

Barnouw, E.A.
A History of broadcasting in the United States **2000**

Barraclough, E.M.C. and Crampton, W.G.
Flags of the world **2795**

Barrett, D.B.
World Christian encyclopedia **351**

Barrett, F.A.
Old English porcelain **1858**

Barron, N.
Anatomy of wonder **2341**
Fantasy literature: a reader's guide **2345**
Horror literature: a reader's guide **2346**
What do I read next? **2338**

Barthorp, M.
The Armies of Britain, 1485-1980 **714**

Bartke, W.
Who's who in the People's Republic of China **2747**

Bartlett, J.
A Complete concordance to Shakespeare **2378**
Familiar quotations **2284**

Barton, Sir D. and Ollis, W.D.
Comprehensive organic chemistry **995**

Basham, A.L.
A Cultural history of India **2952**
Basic Japanese-English dictionary **2258**

Bassan, F.
French language and literature **2444**

Bate, J. St. J.
Management guide to office automation **606**

Bates, E.B. and Fairbanks, J.L.
American furniture, 1620 to the present **1887**

Bates, R.L. and Jackson, J.A.
Glossary of geology **1020**
The Batsford companion to local history **2883**
The Batsford dictionary of drama **2037**
Batsford encyclopedia of embroidery techniques **1878**
Battery reference book **1365**

Bauer, W.
A Greek-English lexicon of the New Testament and other early Christian literature **2204**

Baugh, A.C. and Cable, T.
A History of the English language **2121**

Bawden, C.R.
The Modern history of Mongolia **2947**

Baxter, A.
In search of your European roots **2772**
BBC World Service glossary of current affairs **2834**
BDS **1269**

Beale, P.
A Concise dictionary of slang and unconventional English **2131**
A Dictionary of catch phrases **2130**
A Dictionary of slang and unconventional English **2131**

Bean, W.J.
Trees and shrubs hardy in the British Isles **1506**

Beatty, J.K. and Chaikin, A.
The New solar system **926**

Beaudiquez, M.
Inventaire général des bibliographies nationales rétrospectives **37**

Beaumarchais, J.-P. de
Dictionnaire des littératures de langue française **2447**

Beaver, P.
Encyclopaedia of the modern Royal Navy **719**

Beck, E.M.
Familiar quotations **2284**

Bédé, J.A. and Edgerton, W.B.
Columbia dictionary of modern European literature **2277**

Bedini, S.A.
The Christopher Columbus encyclopedia **2973**

Bednar, H.H.
Pressure vessel design handbook **1408**
Bees and beekeeping **1541**

Begley, D.F.
Irish genealogy **2775**
Beiträge zur regionalen Geologie der Erde **1024**
Belgische bibliografie **60**

Bell, A.F.G.
Portuguese literature **2475**

Bell, B.L.
An Annotated guide to current national bibliographies **36**

Bell, F.G.
Ground engineer's reference book **1432**

Bell, P.
Strassburger's textbook of botany **1139**

Bellini, M.
The International design yearbook 1990/1991 **1808**

Bellwood, P.
Man's conquest of the Pacific **2534**

Bender, A.E.
Dictionary of nutrition and food technology **1271**

Benedict, G.F.
Nontraditional manufacturing processes **1403**

Benet, W.R.
Benet's Reader's encyclopedia **2276**
Benet's Reader's encyclopedia **2276**

Bennett, H.
The Chemical formulary **1638**
Concise chemical and technical dictionary **981**
Benn's media directory **239**

Benson, E. and Conolly, L.W.
The Oxford companion to Canadian theatre **2044**

Benson, K.B.
Audio engineering handbook **1748**

Benson, M.
English-Serbocroatian dictionary **2218**
Serbocroatian-English dictionary **2219**

Bentley, E.P.
The Genealogist's address book **2778**

Benton, R.
Directory of music research libraries **1943**

Beresford, A.K.C.
Lloyd's maritime atlas of world ports and shipping places **1620**

Berger, B.
Deutsches Literatur-Lexikon **2428**
Bergey's manual of systematic bacteriology **1122**

Bergin, T.G. and Speake, J.
Encyclopedia of the Renaissance **2842**

Bernhardt, R.
Encyclopedia of public international law **651**
Berry, R.
How to write a research paper **1**
Besançon, R.M.
The Encyclopedia of physics **957**
Best books for children **130**
Best encyclopedias **144**
Besterman, T.
A World bibliography of bibliographies **27**
Betjeman, J.
Collins guide to parish churches of England and Wales **1843**
Bevan, J. and Duncan, A.
Tracing your ancestors in the Public Record Office **2770**
Beyer, H.
A History of Norwegian literature **2438**
Beyer, M.B.
Encyclopedia of materials science and engineering **1331**
Beyer, W.H.
CRC handbook of mathematical sciences **909**
The BFI Companion to the Western **2028**
Bhargava's Standard illustrated dictionary of the Hindi language **2227**
Bibliographia cartographica **944**
Bibliographic guide to psychology **319**
Bibliographic index **29**
A Bibliographical companion **26**
A Bibliographical guide to Spanish American literature **2468**
Bibliographical guide to the study of the literature of the USA **2409**
Bibliographie annuelle de l'histoire de France **2904**
Bibliographie de Belgique **60**
Bibliographie internationale d'anthropologie sociale et culturelle **1078**
Bibliographie internationale de l'Humanisme et de la Renaissance **2841**
Bibliographie internationale des sciences historiques/International Bibliography of historical sciences **2799**
Bibliographie nationale française **54**
Bibliographie nationale française. Supplément I. Publications en série **199**
Bibliography and index of geology **1003**
Bibliography of agriculture **1495**
Bibliography of American literature **2404**
Bibliography of biography 1970-84 **2718**
Bibliography of biography 1988 **2719**
Bibliography of British history **2860**
A Bibliography of British municipal history **695**
Bibliography of British newspapers **246**
A Bibliography of British railway history **1604**
A Bibliography of Christian worship **364**
Bibliography of creative African writing **2524**
Bibliography of economic geology **1059**

Bibliography of fossil vertebrates, 1928/1933- **1074**
A Bibliography of medical and biomedical biography **1264**
A Bibliography of modern Irish and Anglo-Irish literature **2503**
Bibliography of nautical books, 1991 **721**
Bibliography of the history of art **1766**
A Bibliography of the history of Wales **2891**
Bibliography on holocaust literature **2896**
Bibliography on Soviet intelligence and security services **509**
Bickerman, E.J.
Chronology of the Ancient World **2814**
Bigsby, C.W.E.
A Critical introduction to twentieth-century American drama **2416**
Bilboul, R.R.
Retrospective index to theses of Great Britain and Ireland **170**
Bindman, D.
Thames and Hudson encyclopaedia of British art **1789**
Binns, D.
A Gypsy bibliography **819**
A Biobibliographical handbook of Bulgarian authors **2494**
Biographical dictionary of artists **1786**
Biographical dictionary of dance **2061**
A Biographical dictionary of Irish writers **2391**
Biographical dictionary of Marxism **317**
Biographical dictionary of modern European radicals and socialists **514**
Biographical dictionary of Neo-Marxism **318**
The Biographical dictionary of scientists **888**
Biographical dictionary of the extreme right since 1890 **513**
Biographical dictionary of World War I **2848**
Biographical encyclopedia of photographic artists and innovators **1913**
A Biographical register 1788-1939. Notes from the name index of the Australian Dictionary of Biography **2766**
Biography and genealogy master index **2762**
Biography catalogue of the Library **2856**
Biography index **2720**
Biological abstracts **1099**
Biological abstracts/RRM **1100**
Biotechnology in agriculture and forestry **1216**
The Biotechnology marketing sourcebook **1219**
The Birds of the British Isles **1203**
Birkeland, P.W. and Larson, E.E.
Putnam's geology **1018**
Birnes, W.J.
Microcomputer applications handbook **1730**
Bischoff, B.
Latin palaeography **2811**
Black Africa **2617**
Black African literature in English **2396**

Black, C.V.
The History of Jamaica **2980**
Black, D.
World rugs and carpets **1874**
Black, G.F.
The Surnames of Scotland **2113**
Black, K.L.
A Biobibliographical handbook of Bulgarian authors **2494**
Black literature criticism **2310**
Black slavery in the Americas **501**
Black writers **2300**
Blackmore, H.L.
A Dictionary of London gunmakers 1350-1850 **1868**
Black's agricultural dictionary **1494**
The Blackwell biographical dictionary of British political life in the twentieth century **511**
The Blackwell dictionary of historians **2801**
The Blackwell encyclopaedia of political thought **493**
The Blackwell encyclopaedia of the Russian Revolution **2924**
The Blackwell encyclopedia of political institutions **492**
Blackwell guide to blues records **1992**
Blackwell guide to recorded jazz **1991**
The Blackwell guide to the musical theatre on record **1990**
Blain, V.
The Feminist companion to literature in English **2364**
Blake, B.
Jane's Weapon systems, 1988-89 **1427**
Blake, G.N. and Clark, A.N.
Chisholm's handbook of commercial geography **571**
Blake, J.B. and Roos, C.
Medical reference works, 1679-1966 **1247**
Blake, R.
World history from 1800 to the present day **2800**
Blakemore, K.
The Retail jeweller's guide **1689**
Blamey, M. and Grey-Wilson, C.
The Illustrated flora of Britain and Northern Europe **1147**
Blanck, J.
Bibliography of American literature **2404**
Bland, A.
The Royal Ballet **2059**
Blaustein, A.P. and Flanz, G.H.
Constitutions of the countries of the world **666**
Blazek, R.
The Humanities: a selective guide to information sources **23**
Bledsoe, R. and Boczek, B.A.
The International law dictionary **650**
Bliss, A.
Dictionary of foreign words and phrases in current English **2158**
Blom, E.
The New Everyman dictionary of music **1921**
Blood, D.C.
Baillière's comprehensive veterinary dictionary **1525**
Veterinary medicine **1526**

Bloom, K.
Broadway **2051**
Bloomsbury dictionary of contemporary
slang **2132**
Bloomsbury dictionary of opera and
operetta **1948**
Bloomsbury dictionary of phrase and
allusion **2313**
Bloomsbury good reading guide **2337**
Bloomsbury guide to English literature
2352
Bloomsbury theatre guide **2326**
Blow, C.M. *and* Hepburn, C.
Rubber technology and manufacture
1707
Blue guide: literary Britain and Ireland
2359
Blue guide Wales **2702**
Blue guides **2689**
Blum, A.A.
International handbook of industrial
relations **534**
Blum, E. *and* Wilhoit, F.G.
Mass media bibliography **240**
Blunden, C. *and* Elvin, M.
Cultural atlas of China **2601**
BMT [British marine technology]
abstracts **1477**
BNF **1288**
BNI: British newspaper index **248**
Boardman, J.
Oxford history of the classical world
2820
Boase, F.
Modern English biography **2736**
Bodensieck, J.H.
The Encyclopedia of the Lutheran
Church **391**
Bogdanor, V.
The Blackwell encyclopedia of political
institutions **492**
Bogue, D.J.
The Population of the United States
475
Bohdan Nahaylo *and* Swoboda, V.
Soviet disunion **2921**
Bolshoi anglo-russkii slovar' **2207**
Bolton, G.
The Oxford history of Australia **2999**
Bolton, W.
Newnes engineering materials pocket
book **1333**
Bomford, G.
Geodesy **941**
Bond, D.
The Guinness guide to 20th-century
fashion **792**
Bondanella, P. *and* Bondanella, J.C.
The Macmillan dictionary of Italian
literature **2457**
Book-auction records **92**
**Book Marketing Council The Publishers
Association.**
Catalogue of maps and guides 1990
2656
The Book of 1000 plays **2327**
The Book of calendars **953**
The Book of festivals **796**
Book of hallmarks **1861**
The Book of inventions and discoveries
1233
The Book of London **2888**
The Book of theatre quotes **2039**

Book review digest **179**
Book review digest: author/title index,
1905-1974 **180**
Book review index **181**
Book review index: a master cumulation
1965-1984 **182**
Bookbinding and the conservation of
books **1750**
Booklist **175**
Books in English **38**
Books in print **73**
Books in print plus **75**
Books in series **257**
Books of Welsh interest **2582**
Booser, E.R.
CRC handbook of lubrication **1418**
Booth, G.
The Little red book **1602**
Borchardt, D.H. *and* Francis, R.D.
How to find out in psychology **320**
Bordman, G.
American musical theatre **2052**
The Concise Oxford companion to
American theatre **2046**
The Oxford companion to American
theatre **2045**
Borklund, E.
Contemporary literary critics **2308**
Bosch, R.
Automotive handbook **1471**
Bosman, D.
Tweetalige woordeboek **2171**
Boston Spa serials **188**
Bosworth, J
Anglo-Saxon dictionary **2122**
Botanical bibliographies **1137**
Botanical Latin **1140**
Botermans, J.
The World of games **2069**
Bottomore, T.
A Dictionary of Marxist thought **316**
Boulton, C.
Erskine May's Treatise on the law,
privileges, proceedings and usage of
Parliament **671**
Bound for Australia **2779**
Boutell, C.
Boutell's heraldry **2784**
Boutell's heraldry **2784**
The Bowker annual **101**
Bowker's Complete video directory 1990
2008
Boyce, M.
Zoroastrians **419**
Boyd, A.
An Atlas of world affairs **2568**
Boyer, H.E. *and* Gull, T.L.
Metals handbook **1681**
The BP book of industrial archaeology
2561
Bracher, K.D.
Geschichte der Bundesrepublik
Deutschland **2897**
BRAD/British rate and data **241, 629**
Bradbury, F.
Book of hallmarks **1861**
Bradbury, S.
Dictionary of light microscopy **970**
Bradfield, V.J.
Information sources in architecture
1826
Bradley, H.B.
Petroleum engineering handbook **1423**

Brady, A.M. *and* Cleeve, B.
A Biographical dictionary of Irish
writers **2391**
Bragdon, A.D.
The Homeowner's complete manual of
repair & improvement **1569**
Branca, V.
Dizionario critico della letteratura
italiana **2456**
Branch, A.E.
Multilingual dictionary of commercial
international trade and shipping terms
588
Brandes, E.A. *and* Brook, G.
Smithells' Metals reference book **1684**
Brandon, S.G.F.
A Dictionary of comparative religion
341
Brandrup, J. *and* Immergut, E.H.
Polymer handbook **1711**
Brandt, A., von
Fish catching methods of the world
1543
Branford, J.
A Dictionary of South African English
2135
Brant, J.G.
Medals year book 1989 **1850**
Brass bands **1969**
The Brass book **1863**
Brassey's battles **710**
Brassey's multilingual military dictionary
703
Braunmuller, A.R. *and* Hattaway, M.
The Cambridge companion to English
Renaissance drama **2375**
Brawer, M.
Atlas of the Middle East **2674**
Brazilian literature: a research
bibliography **2478**
Bremner, M.
Enquire within upon everything **1568**
Bremness, L.
The Complete book of herbs **1566**
Bressel, J.A.
Chambers dictionary of psychiatry
1312
Brett, M.
Leisure services yearbook **1995**
Brett, P.
Building terminology **1755**
Breu, J.
Atlas der Donauländer **2661**
Brewer, E.C.
Brewer's Dictionary of phrase and
fable **2313**
Brewer's Dictionary of phrase and fable
2313
Brewer's Dictionary of twentieth-century
phrase and fable **2313**
Brickell, C.
The Royal Horticultural Society
gardeners' encyclopedia of plants and
flowers **1523**
Briggs, A.
The History of broadcasting in the
United Kingdom **2001**
The Longman encyclopedia **153**
Briggs, H.M.
Modern breeds of livestock **1530**
Briggs, K.M.
A Dictionary of British folk-tales in
the English language **823**

Bright, W.
International encyclopedia of linguistics
2097
Brinkman's cumulative catalogus 59
Brio 1928
Bristol, R.P.
Supplement to Charles Evans'
American bibliography 70
Brit-line 838
Britain 1992 2576
Britannica book of the year 149
British alternative theatre directory,
1990/91 2040
British and Irish biographies 1840-1940
2731
British and Irish herbaria 1145
British archaeological abstracts 2542
British archives 2868
British art and antiques yearbook 1792
British autobiographies 2733
British battles and medals 707, 1851
British biographical archive 2732
British biographical index 2726
British book news 176
British books in print 48
British bulletin of publications on Latin
America 2623
British Caenozoic fossils (Tertiary and
Quaternary) 1070
British catalogue of audio-visual
materials 259
The British catalogue of music 1918
The British clothing industry year book.
1990-91 1751
The 1990 British club year book and
directory 224
British Council
Studying and living in Britain 1991
2574
**British Council. Libraries Books and
Information Division. Bibliographical
Section.**
Reference works (including CD-ROM)
135
British directories 2885
British education index. 1954-.v.1- 753
British exports, 92 596
British Film Institute
Film and television handbook, 1991
2004
British folklore, myths and legends 822
British foreign policy, 1918-1945: a
guide to research and research materials
504
British Geological Survey
British regional geology 1026
British government publications: an
index to chairmen and authors 270
British historical statistics 470
British history 1945-1987 2871
British humanities index 207
British Library
The British Library general catalogue
of printed books 80-81
The British Library general subject
catalogue 1975 to 1985 83
Catalogue of printed maps, charts and
plans 2657
Checklist of British official serial
publications 271
Current research in Britain: social
sciences 440

British Library (contd.)
Subject index of modern books
acquired 84
**British Library. Department of
Manuscripts**
Index of manuscripts in the British
Library 283
British Library Document Supply Centre
Journals in translation 31
The British Library general catalogue of
printed books 80
The British Library general subject
catalogue 1975 to 1985 83
British library history: a bibliography
103
British Library. Newspaper Library
Catalogue of the Newspaper Library,
Colindale 247
**British Library of Political and Economic
Science**
International bibliography of economics
517
International bibliography of political
science 482
International bibliography of sociology
.. 444
**British Library of Political and Economic
Science, at the London School of
Economics**
International current awareness
services/ICAS 430
**British Library. Science Reference and
Information Service**
International guide to official
industrial property publications 1236
Market research: a guide to British
Library holdings 625
Sources of information on alternative
energy technology held at the Science
Reference and Information Service
1339
British Library. Science Reference Library
Index to periodicals on agriculture
held by the Science Reference Library
1497
British Marine Technology
BMT [British marine technology]
abstracts 1477
The British Medical Association guide to
medicines and drugs 1290
British Mesozoic fossils 1071
British monumental brasses 1864
British mosses and liverworts 1166
British Museum
Catalogue of additions to the
manuscripts in the British Museum
282
**British Museum. Department of Printed
Books**
Catalogue of books printed in the
XVth century 286
Subject index of the modern works
added to the library 82
British Museum (Natural History)
Animal identification 1171
British Caenozoic fossils (Tertiary and
Quaternary) 1070
British Mesozoic fossils 1071
British Palaeozoic fossils 1072
The Catalogue of meteorites 1058
Seaweeds of the British Isles 1160
British music education yearbook. 1990-
91 1945

British music hall 2053
British music yearbook 1991 1938
The British musical theatre 1954
British national bibliography 45
British national directories 1781-1819
2884
British national film and video catalogue
2021
British national formulary 1288
British natural history books, 1495-1900
1123
British newspaper index 248
British outdoor amenities directory 2083
British Palaeozoic fossils 1072
British performing arts yearbook, 1991
1999
British pharmacopoeia, 1988 1287
British pharmacopoeia (veterinary) 1528
British plant communities 1149
British political facts, 1900-85 488
British political parties 510
British prints 1906
British qualifications 774
British Rail passenger timetable 1608
British rate and data 629
British regional geology 1026
British reports, translations and theses
172
British sign language 2094
British Standards Institution
BSI standards catalogue 21
Guide for graphical symbols for
electrical power, telecommunications
and electronics diagrams 1354
Specification for quantities, units and
symbols 836
Transliteration of Cyrillic and Greek
characters 15
British theatre directory 1990 2041
British theatre yearbook, 1990 2042
British union-catalogue of periodicals
184
British union-catalogue of periodicals,
incorporating 'World list of scientific
periodicals' 185
British universities guide to graduate
study, 1991-92 780
British women writers 2365
British words on tape 266
Broadcasting in the United Kingdom
2002
Broadway 2051
Brockhaus Enzyklopädie 158
Brockhaus Wahrig deutsches Wörterbuch
2163
Bronner, E.J.
The Encyclopedia of the American
theatre 2047
Brook, B.S.
Thematic catalogues in music 1947
Brooke Association (Manchester) Ltd
Open learning directory, 1989 767
Brooke, M.Z. and Buckley, P.J.
Handbook of international trade 594
Brooks, H.
Encyclopedia of building and
construction terms 1753
Brothwell, D.R.
Digging up bones 1082
Broughton, B.B.
Dictionary of medieval knighthood and
chivalry 801-802

Brown, A.
The Cambridge encyclopedia of Russia and the Soviet Union **2588**
The Soviet Union **2741**
Brown, F.
A Hebrew and English lexicon of the Old Testament **2242**
Brown, K.D.
A Social history of the Nonconformist Ministry in England and Wales, 1800-1930 **392**
Brown, P.
Electronics and computer acronyms **1368**
Brown, R.P.
Handbook of plastics test methods **1708**
Browne, E.G.
A Literary history of Persia **2502**
Browne, T. and Partnow, E.
Biographical encyclopedia of photographic artists and innovators **1913**
Brunkow, R. de V.
Religion and society in North America **373**
Bruno, T.J. and Svornos, P.D.N.
CRC handbook of basic tables for chemical analysis **993**
Bryant, E.T.
Music librarianship **1942**
Brydson, J.A.
Plastics materials **1709**
BSI standards catalogue **21**
Buchanan, R. A.
Industrial archaeology in Britain **2560**
Buckingham, J.
Dictionary of organic compounds **994**
Buczacki, S.T. and Harris, K.M.
Collins' guide to the pests, diseases and disorders of garden plants **1157**
Buettmer, G.
The Audubon Society encyclopedia of animal life **1178**
Building bridges **1442**
The Building societies facts file **569**
Building technology **1754**
Building terminology **1755**
Buildings of England series **1837**
The Buildings of Ireland **1836**
The Buildings of Scotland **1835**
The Buildings of Wales **1839**
Bulgarian-English dictionary **2221**
Bullock, A.
The Fontana dictionary of modern thought **298**
Bullock, A. and Woodings, R.B.
The Fontana biographical companion to modern thought **304**
Bulson, C.
Current cookbooks **1562**
Bunch, A.
Community information **730**
Bungay, E.W.G. and McAllister, D.
Electric cables handbook **1363**
Buranelli, V. and Buranelli, N.
Spy/counterspy **507**
Burgess, S.M.
Dictionary of Pentecostal and charismatic movements **377**
Burke's genealogical and heraldic history of the landed gentry **2791**
Burke's Peerage and Baronetage **2789**

Burke's Royal Families of the world **2794**
Busby, R.
British music hall **2053**
Buscombe, E.
The BFI Companion to the Western **2028**
Business acronyms **597**
Business information sources **599**
Business periodicals index **598**
Butcher, D.
Official publications in Britain **272**
Butcher, J.
Copy-editing **1581**
Butler, D. and Butler, G.
British political facts, 1900-85 **488**
Butler's lives of the saints **359**
Butterflies of the world **1189**
Butterworth's medical dictionary **1251**
Buttress, F.A.
World guide to abbreviations of organizations **17**
The Buyer's guide to encyclopedias **143**
Bynagle, H.E.
Philosophy **293**
Bynum, W.F.
Dictionary of the history of science **884**
CA SEARCH **977**
CAB International
Directory of research workers in agriculture and allied sciences **1498**
Cabeen, D.C.
A Critical bibliography of French literature **2445**
Cabinet Office
The Civil Service year book, 1991 **689**
CAD/CAM online **1400**
Calasibetta, C.M.
Fairchild's dictionary of fashion **786**
Caldwell, R.J.
The Era of Napoleon **2909**
Callaham, L.I.
Russian-English chemical and polytechnical dictionary **869**
Cambodian-English dictionary **2262**
The Cambridge atlas of astronomy **932**
The Cambridge companion to English Renaissance drama **2375**
The Cambridge companion to Old English literature **2368**
The Cambridge economic history of Europe **576**
Cambridge-Eichborn German dictionary **520**
The Cambridge encyclopedia **150**
The Cambridge encyclopedia of Africa **2614**
The Cambridge encyclopedia of archaeology **2531**
The Cambridge encyclopedia of China **2599**
The Cambridge encyclopedia of India, Pakistan, Bangladesh, Sri Lanka, Nepal, Bhutan and the Maldives **2607**
The Cambridge encyclopedia of language **2089**
The Cambridge encyclopedia of life sciences **1095**
The Cambridge encyclopedia of Russia and the Soviet Union **2588**

The Cambridge guide to literature in English **2353**
The Cambridge guide to the arts in Britain **1795**
The Cambridge guide to the historic places of Britain and Ireland **2699**
The Cambridge guide to the museums of Britain and Ireland **236**
The Cambridge guide to the museums of Europe **235**
The Cambridge guide to world theatre **2033**
The Cambridge history of Africa **2965**
The Cambridge history of Arabic literature **2509**
The Cambridge history of British foreign policy, 1783-1919 **505**
The Cambridge history of China **2943**
The Cambridge history of Classical literature, vol 1: Greek literature **2482**
The Cambridge history of Classical literature, vol.2: Latin literature **2481**
The Cambridge history of early Inner Asia **2933**
The Cambridge history of Iran **2955**
The Cambridge history of Islam **2935**
The Cambridge history of Japan **2948**
The Cambridge history of literary criticism **2309**
The Cambridge history of modern France **2903**
The Cambridge history of Russian literature **2486**
The Cambridge history of the British Empire **2854**
The Cambridge illustrated dictionary of British heritage **2575**
The Cambridge illustrated history of the world's science **887**
The Cambridge medieval history **2835**
The Cambridge social history of Britain, 1750-1950 **461**
Cameron, E.
Encyclopedia of pottery and porcelain **1852**
Camm, J.C.R. and McQuilton, J.
Australians: a historical atlas **3002**
Camp, C.L.
Bibliography of fossil vertebrates, 1928/1933- **1074**
Campbell, B. and Lack, E.
A Dictionary of birds **1198**
Campbell, G.L.
Compendium of the world's languages **2088**
Campbell, I.C.
A History of the Pacific Islands **2994**
Campbell-Kease, J.
A Companion to local history research **2882**
Campbell, O.J. and Quinn, E.G.
A Shakespeare encyclopaedia **2380**
Campbell, R.J.
Psychiatric dictionary **1313**
The Routledge compendium of primary education **765**
Canada. Department of Mines And Technical Surveys. Geographical Branch
Gazetteers of Canada **2704**
Canada Year book 1990 **2622**
Canadian books in print **62**
The Canadian encyclopaedia **2621**
Canadian periodical index **210**

Canadiana 63
The Canals of the British Isles 1622
Canby, C
The Encyclopaedia of historic places 2694
Canby, C.
A Guide to the archaeological sites of Israel, Egypt and North Africa 2557
Cannistaro, P.V.
Historical dictionary of Fascist Italy 2913
Cannon, J.
The Blackwell dictionary of historians 2801
CANS (Citizens Advice Notes) 731
Caplan, H.H.
The Classified directory of artists' signatures, symbols and monograms 1784-1785
Careers encyclopedia 536
Caribbean history in maps 2979
Caribbean writers 2402
Carlisle, R.
The Illustrated encyclopedia of mankind 1084
Carmichael, R.S.
CRC handbook of physical properties of rocks 1056
Carpenter, H.
The Oxford companion to children's literature 123
Carpet annual 1991 1704
Carr, E.H.
A History of Soviet Russia 2922
Carr, I. and Priestley, B. and Fairweather, D.
Jazz 1970
Carrington, B.
Subways of the world 1446
Carter, A.
British music education yearbook. 1990-91 1945
British music yearbook 1991 1938
Carter, S. and Ritchie, M.
Women's studies 807
Carvill, J.
Mechanical engineer's data book 1341
Cassidy, F.G. and Le Page, R.B.
Dictionary of Jamaican English 2137
Castillo, C. and Bond, O.F.
University of Chicago Spanish dictionary 2195
A Catalog of books represented by Library of Congress printed cards 85
Catalogo dei libri in commercio 56
Catalogue of additions to the manuscripts in the British Museum 282
Catalogue of books printed in the XVth century 286
Catalogue of British official publications not published by HMSO 273
Catalogue of European printed books, India Office Library 2608
Catalogue of maps and guides 1990 2656
The Catalogue of meteorites 1058
Catalogue of printed maps, charts and plans 2657
Catalogue of records, Scottish Industrial Archaeology Survey 1977-85 2562
Catalogue of the library 2639

Catalogue of the Newspaper Library, Colindale 247
The Catalogue of United Kingdom official publications 275
Cates, J.A.
Journalism: a guide to the reference literature 253
Catholic almanac, 1971- 382
Catholic University of America, editorial staff
New Catholic encyclopedia 385
Cattell, J.
Who's who in American music 1940
Catterall, P.
British history 1945-1987 2871
'The Empire, the Commonwealth and the Mandated Territories' 2855
Cattle: a handbook to the breeds of the world 1532
CD guide 1983
CD-ROM: a practical guide for information professionals 10
The CD-ROM directory 11
CD-ROM research collections 14
CD-ROMs in print 12
Central Statistical Office
Annual abstract of statistics, 1991 468
Financial statistics 556
Social trends 472
Centre National De La Recherche Scientifique. Institut D'Histoire Moderne Et Contemporaine
Bibliographie annuelle de l'histoire de France 2904
Centres and bureaux 230
Ceramic abstracts 1672
Česko-anglický slovník 2215
Chadwick, H. and Chadwick, O.
Oxford history of the Christian Church 371
Chaffers, W.
Marks and monograms on European and Oriental pottery and porcelain 1856
Chamberlain, B.J.
Portuguese language and Luso-Brazilian literature 2476
Chambers biographical dictionary 2709
Chambers biology dictionary 1096
Chambers book of musical quotations 1931
Chambers dictionary of psychiatry 1312
Chambers science and technology dictionary 850
Chambers sporting quotations 2077
Champion, T.
Prehistoric Europe 2538
Chandler, I.
Building technology 1754
Chaney, J.F.
Thermophysical properties research literature retrieval guide, 1900-1980 975
Chang, Kwang-Chih
The Archaeology of ancient China 2547
Chapman, R.L.
New dictionary of American slang 2129
Charities digest 727
Charles, N. and James, J.
The Rights of women 808

Charlton, D.G.
France 2585
A Checklist of American imprints 66
Checklist of British official serial publications 271
A Checklist of Canadian literature and background materials, 1628-1960 2401
A Checklist of painters 1890
Cheese: chemistry, physics and microbiology 1540
Cheese guide 1539
Chemical abstracts 983
Chemical engineering 1632
Chemical engineering abstracts 1635
The Chemical formulary 1638
Chemical industry notes 1636
Chemical information sources 979
Chemical technicians' ready reference handbook 1639
The Chemistry of clays and clay minerals 1673
Chenier, P.J.
Survey of industrial chemistry 1631
Cheremisinoff, P.N.
Encyclopedia of environmental control technology 1455
Cherkesi, E.
Georgian-English dictionary 2253
Chernow, B.A. and Vallasi, G.A.
The Reader's adviser 122
Chernukhin, A.E.
Anglo-russkii politekhnicheskii slovar' 870
Chester, K.
Nuclear energy and the nuclear industry 1348
Chester, T.R.
Children's books research 124
Sources of information about children's books 125
Chevalier, T.
Contemporary poets 2320
Twentieth-century children's writers 129
Chi-Bonnardel, R. van
The Atlas of Africa 2676
Chiarmonte, P.
Women artists in the United States 1801
The Chicago manual of style 2301
Child, F.J.
The English and Scottish popular ballads 2374
Children's books in print 131
Children's books of the year 132
Children's books research 124
Children's Britannica 154
Children's costume in England, 1300-1900 793
Children's literature: a guide to reference sources 126
Children's literature abstracts 127
Children's song index 1965
Chilean literature 2473
Chilvers, I.
The Concise Oxford dictionary of art and artists 1767
Chilvers, I. and Osborne, H. and Farr, D.
The Oxford dictionary of art 1768
China facts and figures 2598

Chinery, M.
A Field guide to the insects of Britain and Northern Europe 1188
The Chinese Academy of Social Sciences
Information China 2600
Chinese-English dictionary of engineering technology 872
Chisholm's handbook of commercial geography 571
Chitham, R.
The Classical orders of architecture 1841
Chittenden, F.J.
Dictionary of gardening 1522
Choice 177
Christensen, R.D.
Motorcycles in magazines, 1895-1983 1476
The Christian year 357
Christianity in a revolutionary age 353
Christmas carols 1956
The Christopher Columbus encyclopedia 2973
Chronicle of the 20th century 2833
Chronicle of the First World War 2847
Chronique de la Belgique 2929
Chronological list of Antarctic expeditions 3006
A Chronology of Irish history to 1976 2877
Chronology of the Ancient World 2814
The Church of England year book, 1992 388
The Church of Scotland year-book, 1990 393
CICI directory of information products and services 102
CIRIA guide to EC and international sources of construction information 1759
Civil engineering calculations reference guide 1437
The Civil Service today 690
The Civil Service year book, 1991 689
Civilization of the Ancient Mediterranean. Greece and Rome 2821
Clabburn, P.
The Needleworker's dictionary 1571
The Clans, septs and regiments of the Scottish Highlands 2781
Clapham, A.R.
Flora of the British Isles 1150
Flora of the British Isles: illustrations 1151
Clark, A.N.
Longman dictionary of geography, human and physical 1035
Clark, C.M.H.
A History of Australia 2998
Clark, G.H.
Industrial and marine fuels reference book 1647
Clark, S.P.
Handbook of physical constants 1008
Clarke, D.
The Penguin encyclopedia of popular music 1971
Clarke, M. and Crisp, C.
The History of the dance 2065
Clarke, P.B.
Finding out in education 754

Clason, W.E.
Elsevier's dictionary of library science 98
Classical and medieval literature criticism 2310
The Classical catalogue 1985
Classical mythology 409
The Classical orders of architecture 1841
The Classified directory of artists' signatures, symbols and monograms 1784-1785
Clay, H.M.
Clay's handbook of environmental health 1456
Clay's handbook of environmental health 1456
Clayton, W.D.
Genera graminum: grasses of the world 1170
Cleasby, R.
An Icelandic-English dictionary 2172
Clennett, M.A.
Keyguide to information sources in dentistry 1310
Clifford, M.
Master handbook of electronic tables and formulas 1378
Clocks and watches 1717
Clogg, R.
A Short history of modern Greece 2931
Clouds of the world 1052
Clover, C.J. and Lindow, J.
Old Norse-Icelandic literature 2437
Clover newspaper index 249
Coal abstracts 1649
The Coastline of England and Wales 1042
Cobbett, W.W.
Cyclopedic survey of chamber music 1980
Cockerell, H.
Dictionary of insurance 750
Codlin, E.M.
The Aslib directory of information sources in the United Kingdom 115
Cohen-Stratyner, B.N.
Biographical dictionary of dance 2061
Cohn-Sherbok, D.
A Dictionary of Judaism and Christianity 420
Cokayne, G.E.
The Complete peerage of England, Scotland, Ireland, Great Britain and the United Kingdom 2788
Cole, W.O. and Sambhi, P.S.
The Sikhs: their religious beliefs and practices 416
Collier's encyclopedia 145
Collin, P.H.
Dictionary of government and politics 686
Collins dictionary of music 1927
Collins dictionary of sociology 442
Collins English dictionary 2148
The Collins German dictionary 2164
Collins' guide to mushrooms and toadstools 1164
Collins guide to parish churches of England and Wales 1843
Collins' guide to stars and planets 929

Collins' guide to the pests, diseases and disorders of garden plants 1157
Collins, H.H.
Harper & Row's complete field guide to North American wildlife. Eastern edition 1128
Collins-Robert French-English/English-French dictionary 2180
The Collins Sansoni Italian dictionary 2186
Collins Spanish-English/English-Spanish dictionary 2194
The Collins Spurrell Welsh dictionary 2235
Collins, T.H.
Analog electronics handbook 1372
Colonialism in Africa, 1870-1960 499
The Color compendium 973
Colour index 972
Columbia dictionary of modern European literature 2277
The Columbia Granger's Index to poetry 2319
The Columbia Granger's World of poetry 2319
Columbia literary history of the United States 2405
Colwell, R.N.
Manual of remote sensing 1014
Comaroni, J.
Dewey Decimal Classification 111
Comas, A.
Història de la literatura catalana 2455
Commercial timbers of the world 1695
Common knowledge 2314
Commonwealth universities yearbook, 1991: a directory to the universities of the Commonwealth and the handbook of the Association 777
The Commonwealth yearbook 1991 2579
The Communications satellite 1389
Communications satellite handbook 1388
Communications standard dictionary 1574
A Communicative grammar of English 2160
Community information 730
The Compact dictionary of exact science and technology 856
The Compact Oxford English dictionary 2145
Compact Peters atlas of the world 2684
A Companion to ethics 331
Companion to Irish history 1603-1921 2876
A Companion to local history research 2882
Companion to Russian studies 2587
Companion to Sanskrit literature 2500
Companion to Scottish history 2873
Companion to South African literature 2397
A Companion to the phyiscal sciences 958
A Companion to twentieth-century German literature 2425
Compendex 1322
Compendium of marketing information sources 621
Compendium of the world's languages 2088

The Complete book of cleaning **1573**
The Complete book of herbs **1566**
Complete book of puppet theatre **2029**
The Complete book of spices **1567**
Complete British railways maps and gazetteers, 1825-1985 **1606**
A Complete checklist of the birds of the world **1199**
A Complete concordance to Shakespeare **2378**
The Complete encyclopaedia of arms and weapons **1867**
Complete encyclopedia of photography **1911**
The Complete English-Hebrew dictionary **2240**
The Complete film dictionary **2017**
A Complete guide to heraldry **2787**
The Complete guide to illustration and design **1806, 1902**
The Complete guide to modern dance **2063**
The Complete guide to painting and drawing techniques and materials **1871**
Complete guide to photography **1910**
The Complete guide to the art of modern cookery **1565**
The Complete Hebrew-English dictionary **2241**
The Complete peerage of England, Scotland, Ireland, Great Britain and the United Kingdom **2788**
The Complete practical book of country crafts **1716**
The Composition of foods **1272, 1656**
A Comprehensive bibliography of Yugoslav literature in English, 1593-1980 **2493**
Comprehensive dictionary of engineering and technology **865**
A Comprehensive dictionary of psychological and psychoanalytical terms **325**
Comprehensive dissertation index **166**
A Comprehensive English-Swedish dictionary **2176**
A Comprehensive grammar of the English language **2160**
Comprehensive organic chemistry **995**
A Comprehensive Persian-English dictionary **2232**
Compton, R.
The Illustrated dictionary of knitting **1879**
Compton's encyclopedia and fact-index **155**
Computer and control abstracts. Science abstracts. Section C **1727**
Computer & telecommunications acronyms **1721**
Computer security reference book **1737**
Computers and computing information resources directory **1728**
Computing information directory **1722**
Comrie, B.
The World's major languages **2091**
The Concise AACR2. 1988 revision **109**
A Concise Anglo-Saxon dictionary **2123**
The Concise Baker's biographical dictionary of musicians **1936**
Concise chemical and technical dictionary **981**

Concise dictionary of American biography **2758**
Concise dictionary of American literary biography **2407**
A Concise dictionary of Canadianisms **2136**
Concise dictionary of computing **1726**
A Concise dictionary of Eastern religion **412**
A Concise dictionary of Indian philosophy **307**
A Concise dictionary of Middle English **2124**
Concise dictionary of modern Japanese history **2950**
A Concise dictionary of slang and unconventional English **2131**
Concise encyclopaedia of industrial chemical additives **1642**
Concise encyclopedia of biochemistry **1117**
Concise encyclopedia of polymer science and engineering **1713**
Concise encyclopedia of traffic and transportation systems **1596**
Concise encyclopedia of wood and wood-based materials **1692**
Concise English-Chinese/Chinese-English dictionary **2254**
A Concise English-Hungarian dictionary **2250**
Concise Esperanto and English dictionary **2093**
The Concise guide to British pottery and porcelain **1855**
A Concise history of Canadian painting **1894**
A Concise history of Rumanian literature **2459**
A Concise Hungarian-English dictionary **2249**
Concise medical dictionary **1254**
The Concise Oxford companion to American literature **2410**
The Concise Oxford companion to American theatre **2046**
The Concise Oxford companion to English literature **2354**
Concise Oxford dictionary **2149**
The Concise Oxford dictionary of art and artists **1767**
The Concise Oxford dictionary of ballet **2055**
The Concise Oxford dictionary of earth sciences **1006**
The Concise Oxford dictionary of English etymology **2162**
The Concise Oxford dictionary of English place-names **2104**
The Concise Oxford dictionary of French literature **2450**
The Concise Oxford dictionary of quotations **2286**
Concise Oxford dictionary of the Christian Church **363**
The Concise Oxford English-Arabic dictionary of current usage **2245**
The Concise Oxford history of music **1932**
The Concise Scots dictionary **2134**
Concise theological dictionary **355**
Concrete technology **1676**
The Concrete year book, 1991 **1675**

Confederation of Information Communication Industries
CICI directory of information products and services **102**
The Congregationalism of the last 300 years **394**
Congressional quarterly's guide to the Congress of the United States **674**
Connors, M.
Computers and computing information resources directory **1728**
Conservation sourcebook **1824**
Considine, D.M.
Standard handbook of industrial automation **1738**
Van Nostrand's scientific encyclopedia **846**
Considine, D.M. and Considine, G.D.
Food and food production encyclopedia **1651**
Van Nostrand encyclopedia of chemistry **980**
Considine, T.
The Language of sport **2076**
Constable, G.
Medieval monasticism **374**
Constitutions of the countries of the world **666**
Construction Industry Research and Information Association
CIRIA guide to EC and international sources of construction information **1759**
Construction materials **1761**
Consumer monitor **1558**
Contemporary artists **1803**
Contemporary authors **2290**
Contemporary authors: bibliographical series **2275**
Contemporary Black American playwrights and their plays **2417**
Contemporary British society **447**
Contemporary designers **1809**
Contemporary dramatists **2324**
Contemporary graphic artists **1907**
Contemporary literary criticism **2310**
Contemporary literary critics **2308**
Contemporary musicians **1941**
Contemporary novelists **2332**
Contemporary poets **2320**
Contemporary theatre, film and television **1997**
Contemporary Turkish writers **2511**
Conway's All the world's fighting ships **1430**
Cook, C.
Sources of British political history, 1900-1951 **489**
Cook, C. and Pugh, G.
Sources in European political history **487**
Cook, C. and Stevenson, J.
The Longman handbook of modern European History 1763-1991 **2843**
The Longman handbook of world history since 1914 **2806**
The Cook's encyclopedia **1564**
Coombs, C.F.
Printed circuits handbook **1381**
Coombs, J.
The International biotechnology directory, 1991 **1217**

Coop, J.E.
Sheep and goat production **1533**
Coppa, F.J.
Dictionary of modern Italian history **2912**
Coppa, F.J. and Roberts, W.
Modern Italian history **2911**
Copy-editing **1581**
Copyright laws and treaties of the world **682**
Corbeil, J-C. and Manser, M.
The Facts on File visual dictionary **2144**
Corbet, G. and Ovenden, D.
The Mammals of Britain and Europe **1211**
Corbet, G.B. and Harris, S.
The Handbook of British mammals **1212**
Corbet, G.B. and Hill, J.E.
A World list of mammalian species **1209**
Corbitt, R.A.
Standard handbook of environmental engineering **1458**
Core list of books & journals in education **755**
Corkhill, T.
A Glossary of wood **1693**
Cornell, T. and Matthews, J.
Atlas of the Roman world **2826**
Cornish, G.P.
Archival collections of non-book materials **260**
Corsi, P.
Information sources on the history of science and medicine **885**
Corsini, R.J.
Encyclopedia of psychology **324**
Cortada, J.W.
Historical dictionary of the Spanish Civil War **2916**
Cosson, B.P.
The BP book of industrial archaeology **2561**
Costume: a general bibliography **784**
Cotterell, H.H.
Old pewter **1866**
Cotton, B.
The New guide to graphic design **1903**
Cotton, M.
Directory of world sportscars **1475**
Coulson, J.M. and Richardson, J.F.
Chemical engineering **1632**
Council for International Organizations of Medical Sciences
International nomenclature of diseases **1297**
Councils, committees & boards **220, 688**
The Counties and regions of the United Kingdom **579**
Countries of the world and their leaders, 1991 **697**
Country reports **572**
The County court practice, 1991 **684**
County street atlases **2665**
Couper, A.D.
The Times atlas and encyclopaedia of the sea **1047**
The Course of Mexican history **2977**

Courtauld Institute of Art. London
A Checklist of painters **1890**
Courthope, W.J.
A History of English poetry **2371**
Cowan, J.H.
A Dictionary of modern written Arabic (Arabic-English) **2246**
Cowell, S.
Who's who in the environment **1825**
Cowen, P.
A Guide to stained glass in Britain **1882**
Cowie, A.P. and Mackin, R.
Oxford dictionary of current idiomatic English **2159**
Cox, J.
Keyguide to information sources in CAD/CAM **1401**
Keyguide to information sources in online and CD-ROM database searching **5**
Cox, M.
Exploring Scottish history **2874**
Coyle, M.
Encyclopedia of literature and criticism **2311**
Cracknell, H.L. and Kaufman, R.J.
The Complete guide to the art of modern cookery **1565**
Cracknell, H.L. and Nobis, G.
The New catering repertoire **1546**
Craig, C.
The History of Scottish literature **2389**
Craig, R.D.
Dictionary of Polynesian mythology **406**
Craig, R.D. and King, F.P.
Historical dictionary of Oceania **2996**
Cramp, S. and Simmons, K.E.L.
Handbook of the birds of Europe, the Middle East and North Africa **1200**
Crane, E.
Bees and beekeeping **1541**
CRC atlas of spectral data **971**
CRC handbook of basic tables for chemical analysis **993**
CRC handbook of chemistry and physics **985**
CRC handbook of lubrication **1418**
CRC handbook of mariculture **1542**
CRC handbook of materials science **1334**
CRC handbook of mathematical sciences **909**
CRC handbook of medicinal herbs **1291**
CRC handbook of physical properties of rocks **1056**
CRC handbook of physiology in aging **1300**
CRC handbook of radiation chemistry **990**
CRC practical handbook of physical properties of rocks and minerals **1056**
CRIB **1104**
Crim, K.
Abingdon dictionary of living religions **340**
Criminologica Foundation, the University of Leiden, and Joint Bureaus for Dutch Child Welfare (WIJN), Utrecht.
Criminology and penology **678**
Criminology and penology **678**

A Critical bibliography of French literature **2445**
Critical guide to Catholic reference books **384**
Critical guide to music schools and conservatories throughout the world **1946**
A Critical introduction to twentieth-century American drama **2416**
Crockford's clerical directory, 1991/92 **389**
Crofton, I.
A Dictionary of art quotations **1779**
Crompton, T.R.
Battery reference book **1365**
Croner's care homes guide **738**
Crookshank, A. and Fitzgerald, D.J.V.
The Painters of Ireland **1893**
Cropley, J.
Directory of financial information sources **555**
Cross, F.L. and Livingstone, E.A.
The Oxford dictionary of the Christian Church **363**
Cross-national study of health systems - countries, world regions, and special problems **735**
Crystal, D.
The Cambridge encyclopedia **150**
The Cambridge encyclopedia of language **2089**
A Dictionary of linguistics and phonetics **2096**
Cuddon, J.A.
A Dictionary of literary terms and literary theory **2315**
The Macmillan dictionary of sports and games **2067**
Cullingworth, J.B.
Town and country planning in Britain **1816**
Cullum, R.D.
Handbook of engineering design **1330**
Culpin, C.
Farm machinery **1510**
Cultural atlas of China **2601**
Cultural atlas of Mesopotamia and the Ancient Near East **2558**
A Cultural history of India **2952**
Cummings, D.
The New Everyman dictionary of music **1921**
Cummings, D. and McIntire, D.
International who's who in music and musician's directory 1990-91 **1937**
Cumulated fiction index **2333**
The Cumulative book index **76**
Cunliffe, B.
Iron Age communities in Britain **2540**
Cunliffe, B. and Hey, D.
A Regional history of England **2879**
Cunnington, P. and Buck, A.
Children's costume in England, 1300-1900 **793**
Cureton, T.K.
Encyclopedia of physical education, fitness, and sport **2075**
Curl, J.S.
English architecture **1838**
Currell, D.
Complete book of puppet theatre **2029**
Current bibliographies in medicine **1248**

Current biography 2710
Current Biography cumulated index 1940-1990 2712
Current biography yearbook 2711
Current biotechnology abstracts 1218
Current British directories 215
Current British journals 196
Current contents: Agriculture, biology & environmental sciences 1496
Current contents: CompuMath 905
Current contents: Engineering, technology & applied sciences 1223
Current contents: Life sciences 1101
Current contents: Physical, chemical and earth sciences 1007
Current cookbooks 1562
The Current digest of the Soviet press 2925
Current information in the construction industry (CICI) 1756
Current research in Britain. Biological sciences 1104
Current research in Britain: social sciences 440
Current research in Britain. The humanities 24
Current serials received 189
Current technology index 1224
Current titles in speleology 1043
'Current UK street maps for libraries' 2666
Currer-Briggs, N.
  Worldwide family history 2780
Curtis, T.
  Lyle official arts review, 1991 1889
Curtis, W.A.
  A History of creeds and confessions of faith in Christendom and beyond 360
Cushing, H.G.
  Children's song index 1965
Cushion, J.P.
  Pocket book of British ceramic marks 1857
The Customs and ceremonies of Britain 794
Cyclopedia of literary characters 2317
Cyclopedia of world authors 2291
Cyclopedic survey of chamber music 1980
Čyževs'kyj, D.
  A History of Ukrainian literature 2490
Czaya, E.
  Rivers of the world 1064
Czech and Slovak literature in English 2492
Czigány, L.
  The Oxford history of Hungarian literature 2512
D'Abrera, B.
  Butterflies of the world 1189
Dahl, W.
  Norges litteratur 2439
Daintith, J.
  The Pan dictionary of physics 961
Daintith, J. and Isaacs, A.
  Medical quotes: a thematic dictionary 1259
Dalal-Clayton, D.B.
  Black's agricultural dictionary 1494

Dale, P.
  Guide to libraries and information units 116
  Guide to libraries in Western Europe 114
Daley, B.
  American men and women of science, 1989-90 889
Dalley, T.
  The Complete guide to illustration and design 1806, 1902
Dalton, B.
  Indonesia handbook 2632
Dance, D.C.
  Fifty Caribbean writers 2403
Dance handbook 2056
Dancing yearbook 1991 2064
Dangerous properties of industrial materials 1283
Daniells, L.M.
  Business information sources 599
Dansk-engelsk ordbog 2179
Dansk-Engelsk teknisk ordbog 862
Darby, H.C. and Fullard, H.
  The New Cambridge modern history. v.14. The Atlas 2831
Darnay, B.T. and Young, M.L.
  Life sciences organizations and agencies directory 1103
Darnborough, A. and Kinrade, D.
  Directory for the disabled 746
The Darwen County Histories 2878
Data book on the viscosity of fluids 991
Datta, A.
  Encyclopaedia of Indian literature 2499
Dauben, J.W.
  The History of mathematics, from antiquity to the present 907
Davenport, T.R.H.
  South Africa 2971
David, R. and Brierley, J.E.C.
  Major legal systems of the world today 649
Davidson, P.B.
  Vietnam at war 2963
Davies, J.G.
  A New dictionary of liturgy and worship 365
Davies, K.
  Occupations, 92 538
Davies, N.
  The Ancient kingdoms of Mexico 2827
Davies, R. and Rupp, G.
  A History of the Methodist Church in Great Britain 396
Davis, D.G.
  American library history 104
Davis, N.
  Afro-American experience 1088
Day, A.E.
  Search for the Northwest Passage 3004
Day, A.J.
  Political parties of the world 512
Day, A.J. and Hoffman, V.
  The Annual register 2829
Day, M.H.
  Guide to fossil man 1077
De Bhaldraithe, T.
  English-Irish dictionary 2233

De Carle, D.
  Watch and clock encyclopedia 1718
De Mowbray, S.A.
  Key facts in Soviet history 2923
De Munter, M. and Bauduin, C.
  Elsevier's fiscal and customs dictionary in five languages 562
De Pina Araújo, A.
  De Pina's technical dictionary 868
De Pina's technical dictionary 868
De Sola, R.
  Abbreviations dictionary 18
De Vries, L.
  French-English science and technology dictionary 864
  German-English science dictionary 852
Dearling, J.
  Dancing yearbook 1991 2064
Debrett's correct form 805
Debrett's etiquette and modern manners 803
Debrett's Peerage and Baronetage 1990 2790
Degrees and hoods of the world's universities and colleges 773
Demographic yearbook, 1989 477
Denffer, D. von
  Strassburger's textbook of botany 1139
The Dent dictionary of fictional characters 2318
Dental practitioners' formulary 1288
Denti, R.
  Dizionario tecnico, italiano-inglese, inglese-italiano 866
Department of Employment
  Employment gazette 530
  New earnings survey 535
Department of Health and Social Security Library Services
  Social service abstracts 732
Department of Social Security
  Social security statistics, 1991 752
Derbyshire, J.D. and Derbyshire, I.
  Political systems of the world 667
Derdak, T.
  International directory of company histories 589
Deshpande, P.G.
  Universal English-Gujarati dictionary 2230
Desmond, R.
  Dictionary of British and Irish botanists and horticulturists 1142
Deutsche Nationalbibliographie 50
Deutsches Literatur-Lexikon 2428
Deutschsprachige Zeitschriften 198
Dev, A.T.
  Students' favourite dictionary (English-to-Bengali) 2229
Development index 582
Devine, J. and Watts, A.
  Information pack on product liability 1402
Dewey Decimal Classification 111
Dexter, H.M.
  The Congregationalism of the last 300 years 394
Diagram Group
  Handbook of arts and crafts 1875
  Pets: every owner's encyclopedia 1534
  Rules of the game 2079

Diaz-Plaja, G.
A History of Spanish literature 2461
Historia general de las literaturas hispánicas 2461
Diccionario de la lengua española 2193
Diccionario de términos cientificos y técnicos 867
Dicionário inglês-portuguès 2196
Dictionary of accounting terms 610
Dictionary of agriculture in six languages 1493
Dictionary of Albanian literature 2507
The Dictionary of alchemy 313
Dictionary of American biography 2757
Dictionary of American diplomatic history 506
Dictionary of American history 2987
Dictionary of American medical biography 1262
A Dictionary of Americanisms on historical principles 2138
Dictionary of anonymous and pseudonymous English literature 32
Dictionary of architecture and construction 1829
Dictionary of archival terminology. Dictionnaire de terminologie archivistique 2810
A Dictionary of art quotations 1779
Dictionary of art terms 1773
Dictionary of Asian philosophies 308
Dictionary of banking 568
Dictionary of behavioral science 328
Dictionary of biomedical acronyms and abbreviations 1093
A Dictionary of birds 1198
Dictionary of Brazilian literature 2477
Dictionary of British and Irish botanists and horticulturists 1142
A Dictionary of British folk-tales in the English language 823
A Dictionary of British miniature painters 1900
Dictionary of British portraiture 1899
Dictionary of British watercolour artists 1896
Dictionary of business biography 604
A Dictionary of business quotations 550
Dictionary of Canadian biography 2753
A Dictionary of Canadianisms on historical principles 2136
A Dictionary of catch phrases 2130
Dictionary of Chinese history 2944
A Dictionary of Christian spirituality 362
Dictionary of civil engineering 1434
A Dictionary of Classical antiquities 2548
Dictionary of classical mythology 410
Dictionary of company law 681
A Dictionary of comparative religion 341
Dictionary of computing 1725
Dictionary of concepts in recreation and leisure studies 1994
Dictionary of dairy terminology 1538
Dictionary of development 525
The Dictionary of economic plants 1158
Dictionary of economics 519
A Dictionary of Egyptian Arabic 2244
Dictionary of Egyptian gods and goddesses 402

Dictionary of electrochemistry 989
Dictionary of electronics 1375
Dictionary of engineering acronyms and abbreviations 1321
Dictionary of engineering and technology 855
The Dictionary of English furniture 1886
A Dictionary of English place-names 2106
A Dictionary of English surnames 2113
Dictionary of eponyms 2115
A Dictionary of fabulous beasts 830
The Dictionary of feminist theory 809
Dictionary of finance 560
A Dictionary of first names 2109
A Dictionary of flowering plants and ferns 1168
Dictionary of foreign words and phrases in current English 2158
Dictionary of gardening 1522
Dictionary of gastronomy 1564
The Dictionary of genealogy 2773
A Dictionary of genetics 1113
Dictionary of German history 1806-1945 2893
Dictionary of gods and goddesses, devils and demons 407
Dictionary of government and politics 686
Dictionary of graphic arts abbreviations 1901
A Dictionary of Hinduism 413
A Dictionary of hymnology 366
Dictionary of insurance 750
Dictionary of international economics 521
A Dictionary of Irish artists 1796
A Dictionary of Irish biography 2735
Dictionary of Irish literature 2392
A Dictionary of Irish mythology 408
Dictionary of Italian literature 2457
Dictionary of Jamaican English 2137
A Dictionary of Judaism and Christianity 420
Dictionary of lace 1877
Dictionary of light microscopy 970
A Dictionary of linguistics and phonetics 2096
Dictionary of literary biography 2363, 2398, 2406, 2423, 2432, 2446
Dictionary of literary biography yearbook 2281
A Dictionary of literary terms and literary theory 2315
Dictionary of logical terms and symbols 330
A Dictionary of London gunmakers 1350-1850 1868
Dictionary of management 614
Dictionary of marine technology 1450
A Dictionary of Marxist thought 316
Dictionary of mathematical games, puzzles and amusements 908
Dictionary of mechanical engineering 1345
Dictionary of medical ethics 1266
Dictionary of medical quotations 1259
Dictionary of medical syndromes 1301
Dictionary of medieval knighthood and chivalry 801-802
Dictionary of microbiology and molecular biology 1121

Dictionary of military and technological abbreviations and acronyms 1426
A Dictionary of military quotations 706
A Dictionary of modern defense and strategy 712
A Dictionary of modern English usage 2125
Dictionary of modern French literature 2448
Dictionary of modern Italian history 2912
A Dictionary of modern written Arabic (Arabic-English) 2246
A Dictionary of named effects and laws in chemistry, physics and mathematics 849
A Dictionary of names and nicknames 2101
The Dictionary of national biography 2727
Dictionary of national biography 2751
Dictionary of nautical words and terms 1478
The Dictionary of New Zealand biography 2764
Dictionary of Newfoundland and Labrador biography 2755
Dictionary of non-Christian religions 399
Dictionary of nutrition and food technology 1271
Dictionary of occult, hermetic and alchemical sigils 309
A Dictionary of opera and song themes 1952
Dictionary of optometry 1319
Dictionary of organic compounds 994
Dictionary of Oriental literatures 2497
Dictionary of ornament 1811
Dictionary of painting and decorating 1763
Dictionary of Pentecostal and charismatic movements 377
A Dictionary of place-names in the British Isles 2107
A Dictionary of plants used by man 1159
Dictionary of Polynesian mythology 406
A Dictionary of pseudonyms and their origins 35
A Dictionary of psychotherapy 1293
Dictionary of Qur'ānic terms and concepts 422
A Dictionary of religious and spiritual quotations 344
Dictionary of religious quotations 345
Dictionary of robotics 1747
Dictionary of Russian literature since 1917 2489
Dictionary of Scandinavian history 2927
Dictionary of Scandinavian literature 2436
Dictionary of science and technology, English-German 854
Dictionary of science and technology, German-English 853
Dictionary of scientific biography 890
A Dictionary of scientific units 964
Dictionary of Scottish business biography, 1860-1960 605
Dictionary of Scottish painters 1892
A Dictionary of slang and unconventional English 2131

A Dictionary of South African English 2135
Dictionary of space technology 1489
Dictionary of subjects and symbols in art 1812
A Dictionary of superstitions 829
A Dictionary of surnames 2112
Dictionary of taxation 565
A Dictionary of the European Communities 659
Dictionary of the fungi 1161
Dictionary of the Hausa language 2268
Dictionary of the history of ideas 301
Dictionary of the history of science 884
Dictionary of the Middle Ages 2837
A Dictionary of the social sciences 434
A Dictionary of translated names and titles 2103
Dictionary of twentieth-century Cuban literature 2470
Dictionary of universal biography 2721
The Dictionary of Victorian painters 1897
The Dictionary of Welsh biography down to 1940 2737
The Dictionary of Western sculptors in bronze 1865
The dictionary of world politics 480
A Dictionary of zoology 1172
Dictionnaire de biographie française 2739
Dictionnaire de termes juridiques en quatre langues ... Legal dictionary in four languages 636
Dictionnaire des auteurs de langue française en Amérique du Nord 2454
Dictionnaire des littératures de langue française 2447
Dictionnaire des oeuvres littéraires du Québec 2453
Dictionnaire des oeuvres littéraires négro-africaines de langue française 2452
Diehl, K.S.
Hymns and tunes 1955
Diesel engine reference book 1394
Digging up bones 1082
Dillmont, T.
Encyclopaedia of needlework 1876
Dillon, M.
Dictionary of Chinese history 2944
Dinosaur data book 1075
Diplomatic handbook 702
The Diplomatic Service list, 1991 701
Directories in print 216
The Directories of London 1677-1977 2886
Directory for the disabled 746
Directory for the environment 1109, 1132
Directory of alternative communities in the British Isles 436
The Directory of appropriate technology 1228
Directory of architecture and planning 1817
Directory of British associations 221
Directory of British brass bands 1968
Directory of British official publications 276
Directory of Christian groups, communities and networks 368

The Directory of continuing education for nurses, midwives and health visitors 1307
The Directory of directors 590
Directory of employers; associations, trade unions, joint organisations, etc 533
Directory of European industrial and trade associations 1715
Directory of European observatories 925
Directory of European professional and learned societies 223
Directory of financial information sources 555
Directory of grant-making trusts, 1991 728
Directory of international film and video festivals 2023
The Directory of international sources of business information 543
The Directory of jobs and careers abroad 537
Directory of law libraries in the British Isles 647
Directory of medical and health care libraries in the United Kingdom and Republic of Ireland, 1990 743
The Directory of museums and living displays 233
Directory of music research libraries 1943
Directory of natural history and related societies in Britain and Ireland 1126
Directory of online databases 6
Directory of popular music 1900-1980 1963
Directory of portable databases 13
Directory of recorded sound resources in the United Kingdom 267
Directory of research workers in agriculture and allied sciences 1498
Directory of scientific directories 880
Directory of services for elderly people in the UK 450
Directory of special libraries and information centers 120
Directory of theatre resources 2048
Directory of translators and translating agencies in the United Kingdom 2092
Directory of world sportscars 1475
Directory of youth services and child care in the UK 748
Directory to the furnishing trade, 1990 1749
Dirix, A.
Encyclopaedia of sports medicine 1274
Disclit: American authors 2408
Dissertation abstracts international 167
Distribution and taxonomy of birds of the world 1201
Dizionario critico della letteratura italiana 2456
Dizionario tecnico, italiano-inglese, inglese-italiano 866
Dodd, J.S.
The ACS style guide 988
Dodgshon, R.A. and Butlin, R.A.
An Historical geography of England and Wales 2650
Dod's parliamentary companion, 1991 670

Doke, C.M.
English-Zulu dictionary 2267
Dolbow, S.W.
Dictionary of modern French literature 2448
Donald, E.B.
Debrett's etiquette and modern manners 803
Doniach, N.
The Concise Oxford English-Arabic dictionary of current usage 2245
Doniach, N.S.
The Oxford English-Arabic dictionary of current usage 2245
Donnachie, J. and Hewitt, G.
Companion to Scottish history 2873
Dorian, A.F.
Dictionary of science and technology, English-German 854
Dictionary of science and technology, German-English 853
Elsevier's encyclopaedic dictionary of medicine 1253
Dorland's illustrated medical dictionary 1252
Douglas, D.C.
English historical documents 2857
Douglas, N. and Douglas, N.
Pacific Islands Yearbook 2631
Dower, J.W.
Japanese history and culture from ancient to modern times: seven basic bibliographies 2949
Downs, B.W.
Modern Norwegian literature 2438
Downs, L.J.
The Biotechnology marketing sourcebook 1219
DPF/BNF 1288
Drabble, M.
The Concise Oxford companion to English literature 2354
The Oxford companion to English literature 2354
Drago, R.J.
Fundamentals of gear design 1416
Drama criticism 2325
Drawings of British plants 1154
Drewry, G. and Butcher, T.
The Civil Service today 690
Drodge, S.
Adult education 766
Drozda, T.J.
Tool and manufacturing engineers handbook 1404
Drury's Guide to best plays 2331
Duby, G.
Histoire de la France 2906
Duckles, V.H. and Keller, M.A.
Music reference and research materials 1919
Duffey, E.
National parks and reserves of Western Europe 1820
Duicker, W.J.
Historical dictionary of Vietnam 2962
Duke, J.A.
CRC handbook of medicinal herbs 1291
Dunbar, G.S.
Modern geography: an encyclopedic survey 2646

Duncan, A.S.
Dictionary of medical ethics **1266**
Dunhouse, M.B.
International directory of children's literature **128**
Dunmore-Leiber, L.
Book review digest: author/title index, 1905-1974 **180**
Dunning, P.H.
Sources of information on alternative energy technology held at the Science Reference and Information Service **1339**
Dupayrat, J.
Dictionary of biomedical acronyms and abbreviations **1093**
Durand, M.M. *and* Nguyen Tran Huan
An Introduction to Vietnamese literature **2521**
Eager, A.R.
A Guide to Irish bibliographical material **2577**
Eagle, D. *and* Carnell, H.
The Oxford illustrated literary guide to Great Britain and Ireland **2360**
Eakins, R.
Picture sources UK **263**
Eakle, A. *and* Cerny, J.
The Source **2777**
Early Black American playwrights and dramatic writers **2417**
Early Ireland **2545**
Earnshaw, P.
Dictionary of lace **1877**
Earth and astronomical sciences research centres **922, 1010**
The Earth sciences: an annotated bibliography **1009**
East European languages and literatures **2485**
Easterling, P.E. *and* Knox, B.M.W.
The Cambridge history of Classical literature, vol 1: Greek literature **2482**
Eastman, L.G.
The Cambridge history of China **2943**
Eastman, M.H.
Index to fairy tales, myths and legends **831**
Eatwell, J.
The New Palgrave: a dictionary of economics **518**
Ecce homo: an annotated bibliographic history of physical anthropology **1079**
Echols, J.M. *and* Shadily, H.
An Indonesian-English dictionary **2270**
The Economic history of Britain since 1700 **578**
Economic survey of Europe, 1990-1991 **577**
Economic titles/abstracts **515**
'The Economist' book of vital world statistics **462**
'The Economist' dictionary of political biography **698**
Economist Intelligence Unit
Country reports **572**
World textile trade and production trends **1701**
Ecosystems of the world **1111**

Edelheit, A.J. *and* Edelheit, H.
Bibliography on holocaust literature **2896**
Edited for the International Committee of Historical Sciences, Lausanne
Bibliographie internationale des sciences historiques/International Bibliography of historical sciences **2799**
The Education authorities directory and annual, 1991 **759**
Education index **756**
Edwards, H. *and* Hughes, D.
The London Business School small business bibliography **553**
Edwards, L.M.
Handbook of geothermal energy **1016**
Edwards, M.
Complete encyclopedia of photography **1911**
Edwards, P.
The Encyclopedia of philosophy **299**
Edwards, R.
Shorter dictionary of English furniture **1885**
The Eerdmans Bible dictionary **348**
Eesti-inglise sõnaraamat **2252**
Egon Ronay's Cellnet guide, 1991. Hotels & restaurants in Great Britain and Ireland **1551**
Eichborn, R.
Cambridge-Eichborn German dictionary **520**
Eighteenth century short title catalogue **42**
Eisenschitz, T.S.
Patents, trade marks and designs in information work **1240**
Eiss, H.E.
Dictionary of mathematical games, puzzles and amusements **908**
Ekwall, E.
The Concise Oxford dictionary of English place-names **2104**
ELCOM **1369**
Electric cables handbook **1363**
Electrical and electronics abstracts. Science abstracts. Section B **1357**
Electrical and electronics trades directory **1358**
Electrical engineer's reference book **1360**
Electronic engineers' handbook **1373**
Electronic engineer's reference book **1374**
Electronics and communications abstracts **1377**
Electronics and computer acronyms **1368**
Eliade, M.
A History of religious ideas **334**
Yoga **417**
Elkins, D. *and* Elkins, T.H.
France **2648**
Elling, R.H.
Cross-national study of health systems - countries, world regions, and special problems **735**
Elliot, J.M. *and* Elliot, R.R.
The Arms control, disarmament and military security dictionary **663**
Elliott, E.
Columbia literary history of the United States **2405**

Elliott, J.
Elliott's Guide to films on video **2009**
Elliott, S.P.
A Reference guide to the United States Supreme Court **685**
Elliott, T.C.
Standard handbook of powerplant engineering **1392**
Elliott's Guide to films on video **2009**
Ellis, J.
The Russian Orthodox Church **381**
Ellis, P.
People of today **2728**
Ellis, P. B.
A Dictionary of Irish mythology **408**
Elsevier's dictionary of library science **98**
Elsevier's dictionary of the printing and allied industries **1578**
Elsevier's encyclopaedic dictionary of medicine **1253**
Elsevier's fiscal and customs dictionary in five languages **562**
Elsie, R.
Dictionary of Albanian literature **2507**
EMBASE **1245**
Embleton, C.
Geomorphology of Europe **1039**
Embree, A.T.
Encyclopedia of Asian history **2934**
Emily Post's etiquette **804**
Employment gazette **530**
Emslie-Smith, D.
Textbook of physiology **1269**
Encyclopaedia of Australian art **1802**
Encyclopaedia of ferns **1167**
The Encyclopaedia of historic places **2694**
An Encyclopaedia of homoeopathy **1286**
Encyclopaedia of Indian literature **2499**
The Encyclopaedia of Islam **2612**
Encyclopaedia of mathematics **901**
Encyclopaedia of modern British army regiments **715**
Encyclopaedia of needlework **1876**
Encyclopaedia of occupational health and safety **1281**
An Encyclopaedia of Parliament **669**
An Encyclopaedia of philosophy **300**
Encyclopaedia of rock **1977**
Encyclopaedia of sports medicine **1274**
Encyclopaedia of the modern Royal Navy **719**
The Encyclopaedia of the United Nations and international agreements **653**
Encyclopaedia of world crime **679**
An encyclopaedic dictionary of heraldry **2785**
The Encyclopedia Americana **146**
Encyclopedia Lituanica **2591**
Encyclopedia of adolescence **449**
Encyclopedia of advertising **630**
The Encyclopedia of aging **451**
The Encyclopedia of alcoholism **1276**
Encyclopedia of American architecture **1840**
Encyclopedia of American economic history **580**
Encyclopedia of American film comedy **2024**
Encyclopedia of American history **2986**

The Encyclopedia of American intelligence and espionage **508**
Encyclopedia of American music **1939**
Encyclopedia of American religions **338-339**
Encyclopedia of anthropology **1080**
The Encyclopedia of applied geology **1017**
Encyclopedia of architects **1833**
Encyclopedia of architecture **1827**
Encyclopedia of Asian history **2934**
Encyclopedia of associations **222**
Encyclopedia of astronomy **916**
Encyclopedia of astronomy and astrophysics **914**
The Encyclopedia of atmospheric sciences and astrogeology **1048**
Encyclopedia of aviculture **1535**
Encyclopedia of banking and finance **558**
The Encyclopedia of beaches and coastal environments **1041**
Encyclopedia of British women writers **2365**
Encyclopedia of building and construction terms **1753**
Encyclopedia of business information sources **600**
Encyclopedia of chemical technology **1629**
The Encyclopedia of colonial and revolutionary America **2991**
Encyclopedia of comic characters **1872**
Encyclopedia of computer science and engineering **1723**
Encyclopedia of consumer law **1559**
An Encyclopedia of Continental women writers **2296**
Encyclopedia of crime and justice **680**
Encyclopedia of drawing **1870**
The Encyclopedia of drug abuse **1277**
Encyclopedia of early Christianity **370**
Encyclopedia of earth sciences **1005**
Encyclopedia of educational research **761**
The Encyclopedia of electronic circuits **1379**
Encyclopedia of electronics **1370**
The Encyclopedia of employment law and practice **532**
Encyclopedia of environmental control technology **1455**
The Encyclopedia of environmental studies **1454**
Encyclopedia of European Community law **655**
Encyclopedia of fashion details **787**
Encyclopedia of feminism **810**
Encyclopedia of food engineering **1655**
The Encyclopedia of furniture **1883**
The Encyclopedia of gemstones and minerals **997**
The Encyclopedia of geochemistry and environmental sciences **1012**
Encyclopedia of horror movies **2025**
Encyclopedia of human evolution and prehistory **1115**
Encyclopedia of industrial automation **1739**
Encyclopedia of library and information science **99**
Encyclopedia of literature and criticism **2311**

Encyclopedia of magic and magicians **2066**
The Encyclopedia of mammals **1207**
The Encyclopedia of management **613**
Encyclopedia of materials science and engineering **1331**
Encyclopedia of microcomputers **1729**
Encyclopedia of minerals **998**
Encyclopedia of modern physics **959**
Encyclopedia of occultism and parapsychology **310**
The Encyclopedia of oceanography **1044**
The Encyclopedia of Papua and New Guinea **2636**
The Encyclopedia of philosophy **299**
Encyclopedia of physical education, fitness, and sport **2075**
Encyclopedia of physical sciences and technology **844**
The Encyclopedia of physics **957**
Encyclopedia of polymer science and engineering **1712**
Encyclopedia of pop, rock and soul **1979**
Encyclopedia of pottery and porcelain **1852**
Encyclopedia of psychology **324**
Encyclopedia of public international law **651**
Encyclopedia of PVC **1714**
The Encyclopedia of sedimentology **1030**
The Encyclopedia of soil science **1512**
The Encyclopedia of solid earth geophysics **1011**
The Encyclopedia of structural geology and plate tectonics **1029**
Encyclopedia of terrorism and political violence **497**
Encyclopedia of the American religious experience **379**
The Encyclopedia of the American theatre **2047**
The Encyclopedia of the First World **2565**
An Encyclopedia of the history of technology **1226**
Encyclopedia of the Holocaust **2895**
The Encyclopedia of the horse **1531**
The Encyclopedia of the Lutheran Church **391**
Encyclopedia of the musical film **1950, 2026**
Encyclopedia of the Renaissance **2842**
Encyclopedia of the Second World **2572**
The Encyclopedia of the Third Reich **2894**
Encyclopedia of the world's air forces **718**
The Encyclopedia of TV science fiction **2027**
Encyclopedia of Ukraine **2592**
The Encyclopedia of unbelief **346**
The Encyclopedia of witches and witchcraft **312**
The Encyclopedia of world costume **789**
Encyclopedia of world cultures **1083**
Encyclopedia of world literature in the 20th century **2278**
The Encyclopedia of world regional geology **1025**
Encyclopedic dictionary of industrial technology **1405**

Encyclopedic dictionary of mathematics **902**
Encyclopedic dictionary of semiotics **2118**
Encyclopedic dictionary of Yoga **418**
Encyclopedic handbook of cults in America **398**
Endangered vertebrates **1134**
Energy and the environment in the 21st century **1337**
Engelsk-dansk ordbog **2178**
Engelsk-dansk teknisk ordbog **863**
Engelsk-norsk teknisk ordbok **857**
Engelsk-svensk teknisk ordbok **859**
The Engineering index monthly **1325**
Engineering mathematics handbook **903**
Engineering research centres: a world directory **1329**
Englefield, D. and Drewry, G.
  Information sources in politics and political science: worldwide **479**
English-Albanian dictionary **2239**
The English and Scottish popular ballads **2374**
English architecture **1838**
The English ceremonial book **800**
English court hands AD1066-1500 **2813**
The English dialect dictionary **2133**
The English festivals **798**
An English-Hausa dictionary **2269**
English, H.B. and English, A.C.
  A Comprehensive dictionary of psychological and psychoanalytical terms **325**
English historical documents **2857**
English-Irish dictionary **2233**
English-Khmer dictionary **2263**
An English library **121**
English literature from the Third World **2386**
English, L.J.
  Tagalog-English dictionary **2271**
English-Norwegian dictionary **2174**
English-Norwegian technical dictionary **857**
English-Serbocroatian dictionary **2218**
English-Zulu dictionary **2267**
Engström, E.
  Engelsk-svensk teknisk ordbok **859**
  Svensk-engelsk teknisk ordbok **860**
Enquire within upon everything **1568**
Ensk-islensk ordabók **2172**
Ensor, P.
  CD-ROM research collections **14**
Entomology: a guide to information sources **1184**
Entomology abstracts **1187**
ENVIROLINE **1453**
Environment abstracts **1459**
Environmental and international sciences research centres **1110**
Environmental health reference book **1457**
Environmental periodicals bibliography **1105**
Eponyms dictionary index **849**
Epstein, R.
  Law and commercial dictionary in five languages **549**
The Era of Napoleon **2909**
Eastern Europe and the Commonwealth of Independent States 1992 **2573**

Ernst, R.
Comprehensive dictionary of engineering and technology **865**
Wörterbuch der industriellen Teknik **855**
Erskine May's Treatise on the law, privileges, proceedings and usage of Parliament **671**
Escoffier, A.
The Complete guide to the art of modern cookery **1565**
Esdaile, A.
Esdaile's manual of bibliography **25**
Eshbach's handbook of engineering fundamentals **1324**
Essay and general literature index **161**
Essential English-Vietnamese dictionary **2264**
The establishment of the United Arab Emirates 1950-1985 **2951**
Estonian literature: historical survey **2515**
Euesden, M.
Introduction to biotechnology information **1220**
Euro abstracts. Section 2: Coal and steel **1685**
Europa camping + caravaning **1556**
The Europa world year book 1992 **2566**
European authors, 1000-1900 **2297**
European Business School Librarians Group
SCIMP [Selective cooperative index of management periodicals] **617**
European ceramic art **1854**
The European Communities encyclopedia and directory, 1992 **656**
The European Community **657**
European-language writing in Sub-Saharan Africa **2522**
European marketing data and statistics **622**
European Organisation for Quality Control. Glossary Committee
Glossary of terms used in quality control **619**
European Parliament
Legal terminology of the European Communities **635**
The European patent system **1241**
European research centres **898**
European sources of scientific and technical information **896**
European writers **2298**
Evans, C.
American bibliography **69**
Evans, G.
The Encyclopedia of drug abuse **1277**
Evans, G. and Newnham, J.
The dictionary of world politics **480**
Evans, H. and Evans, M.
Picture researcher's handbook **262**
Evans, H.M. and Thomas, W.O.
Y Geiriadur mawr **2236**
Evans, I.H.
Brewer's Dictionary of phrase and fable **2313**
Every man's own lawyer **641**
Everyman companion to the theatre **2035**
Everyman's Judaica **421**
Ewen, D.
American songwriters **1959**

Ewing, G.W.
Analytical instrumentation handbook **1719**
Exceptional child education resources **768**
Excerpta medica **1256**
Excerpta medica. 26. Immunology, serology and transplantation **1308**
Exploring Scottish history **2874**
Ezell, E.C. and Pegg, T.M.
Small arms of the world **1428**
Faber companion to twentieth century popular music **1972**
Facts about the States **2627**
Facts on file **254**
Facts on File dictionary of religions **342**
The Facts on File dictionary of telecommunications **1383**
The Facts on File visual dictionary **2144**
Fairbank, J.K. and Twitchett, D.
The Cambridge history of China **2943**
Fairbridge, R.W.
The Encyclopedia of atmospheric sciences and astrogeology **1048**
Encyclopedia of earth sciences **1005**
The Encyclopedia of geochemistry and environmental sciences **1012**
The Encyclopedia of oceanography **1044**
The Encyclopedia of world regional geology **1025**
Fairbridge, R.W. and Bourgeois, J.
The Encyclopedia of sedimentology **1030**
Fairbridge, R.W. and Finkl, C.W.
The Encyclopedia of soil science **1512**
Fairchild's dictionary of fashion **786**
Fairchild's dictionary of textiles **1702**
Fakhry, M.
A History of Islamic philosophy **305**
Falk, P.H.
Who was who in American art **1799**
Falkus, M. and Gillingham, J.
Historical atlas of Britain **2862**
Falla, P.S.
The Oxford English-Russian dictionary **2209**
Familiar quotations **2284**
The Families of flowering plants **1169**
Fang, J.R.
World guide to library, archive and information science associations **106**
Fantasy literature: a reader's guide **2345**
FAO production yearbook **1499**
The Far East and Australasia 1992 **2597**
Far Eastern literatures in the 20th century **2498**
Farm machinery **1510**
Farm management pocketbook **1509**
Farmer, D.H.
The Oxford dictionary of saints **358**
Farrell, S.
International pulp and paper information sources **1697**
Farrow, N.
An English library **121**
The Fashion dictionary **788**
Fashion production terms **1752**
Faulhaber, U.K. and Goff, P.B.
German literature: an annotated reference guide **2424**

Fayed, M.E.
Handbook of powder science and technology **1406**
Felici, L.
Il Grande dizionario Garzanti della lingua italiana **2187**
Feltham, R.G.
Diplomatic handbook **702**
The Feminist companion to literature in English **2364**
Fenton, T.P. and Heffron, M.J.
Third world resource directory **459**
Ferguson, E.
Encyclopedia of early Christianity **370**
Fernández-Armesto, F.
The Times atlas of world exploration **2641**
Ferney, D.
The Multilingual business handbook **609**
Ferozsons' Urdu-English dictionary **2228**
Ferreira, A.B. de Holanda
Novo dicionário da língua portuguesa **2197**
Ferrell, R.H. and Natkiel, R.
Atlas of American history **2989**
Fest, W.
Dictionary of German history 1806-1945 **2893**
Feuerstein, G.
Encyclopedic dictionary of Yoga **418**
Feutry, M.
Technological dictionary **848**
Fiber optics standard dictionary **1385**
Fiction catalog **2334**
Field crop abstracts **1516**
A Field guide to the birds of Britain and Europe **1202**
A Field guide to the insects of Britain and Northern Europe **1188**
A Field guide to the reptiles and amphibians of Britain and Europe **1194**
Fifty Caribbean writers **2403**
Filby, P.W.
American and British genealogy and heraldry **2769**
Film and television handbook, 1991 **2004**
Filmer, A.J. and Golay, A.
Harrap's Book of film directors and their films **2020**
Financial management handbook **557**
Financial statistics **556**
The Financial system today **559**
'Financial Times' Oil and gas international year book **1666**
'Financial Times' world hotel directory **1547**
Financial times world insurance year book, 1991 **751**
Finding out in education **754**
Findling, J.E.
Dictionary of American diplomatic history **506**
Fink, D.G.
Standard handbook for electrical engineers **1359**
Fink, D.G. and Christiansen, D.
Electronic engineers' handbook **1373**
Finkl, C.W.
The Encyclopedia of applied geology **1017**

Finlay, M.
  Who's who in the UK information world 1992 **105**
Finnie, H.
  Checklist of British official serial publications **271**
Finnish Features **2594**
Fintel, M.J.
  Handbook of concrete engineering **1439**
'First look' **2761**
First World War atlas **2846**
Fish catching methods of the world **1543**
Fisher, Sir R.A. *and* Yates, F.
  Statistical tables for biological, agricultural and medical research **1102**
Fishes of the world **1192**
Fitch, J.M.
  Environmental and international sciences research centres **1110**
Fitz-Simons, C.
  The Irish theatre **2043**
Fitzhugh, T.V.H.
  The Dictionary of genealogy **2773**
Five centuries of English book illustration **292**
Flags at sea **1613**
Flags of all nations **2796**
Flags of the world **2795**
Flaherty, D.H.
  Privacy and data protection **1736**
Flanagan, C.C. *and* Flanagan, J.T.
  American folklore **827**
Fleming, J.
  The Penguin dictionary of architecture **1828**
Fleming, J. *and* Honour, H.
  The Penguin dictionary of decorative arts **1869**
Fletcher, B.
  A History of architecture **1830**
Fletcher, J.
  Information sources in economics **516**
Fletcher, S. *and* Jopling, N.
  Harrap's Book of 1000 plays **2327**
Flexner, S.B.
  The Random House dictionary of the English language **2146**
Flick, E.W.
  Industrial solvents handbook **1641**
Flora europaea **1148**
Flora of the British Isles **1150**
Flora of the British Isles: illustrations **1151**
Floud, R. *and* McGloskey, D.
  The Economic history of Britain since 1700 **578**
FLUIDEX. BHRA Fluid engineering abstracts **1397**
The Focal encyclopedia of photography **1909**
Foclóir Gaeilge-Béarla **2234**
Folklore, myths and legends of Britain **824**
The Fontana biographical companion to modern thought **304**
The Fontana dictionary of modern thought **298**
Food additive user's handbook **1658**
Food and Agriculture Organization
  FAO production yearbook **1499**

Food and Agriculture Organization. Fisheries Department
  Atlas of the living resources of the seas **1544**
Food and food production encyclopedia **1651**
Food from your garden **1519**
Food science and technology abstracts **1652**
Ford, B.
  The Cambridge guide to the arts in Britain **1795**
  The New Pelican guide to English literature **2361**
Ford, D.F.
  The Modern theologians **354**
Ford, P. *and* Ford, G.
  A Guide to Parliamentary Papers **672**
Ford-Robertson, F.C. *and* Winters, R.K.
  Terminology of forest science, technology, practice and products **1503**
Foreign and Commonwealth Office
  The Diplomatic Service list, 1991 **701**
Foreign language dictionaries: specialist and general **2100**
Foreman, S.
  Consumer monitor **1558**
Forest products abstracts **1694**
The Forester's companion **1505**
Forestry abstracts **1504**
Fortey, R.
  Fossils: the key to the past **1067**
Forthcoming international scientific and technical conferences **897**
Foskett, D.
  A Dictionary of British miniature painters **1900**
Fossils: the key to the past **1067**
Foster, D.W.
  Argentine literature **2472**
  Chilean literature **2473**
  Handbook of Latin American literature **2466**
  Mexican literature **2471**
Foster, D.W. *and* Rela, W.
  Brazilian literature: a research bibliography **2478**
Foster, J. *and* Sheppard, J.
  British archives **2868**
Four hundred years of English education **760**
Fowler, H.W.
  A Dictionary of modern English usage **2125**
Fox-Davies, A.C.
  A Complete guide to heraldry **2787**
Fox, P.F.
  Cheese: chemistry, physics and microbiology **1540**
France **2585, 2648**
Franklyn, J. *and* Tanner, J.
  An encyclopaedic dictionary of heraldry **2785**
The Franks **2818**
Fream, W.
  Fream's principles of food and agriculture **1491**
Fream's principles of food and agriculture **1491**
Frederiksen, E.
  Women writers of Germany, Austria, and Switzerland **2430**

Freeman, R.B.
  British natural history books, 1495-1900 **1123**
Freeman, R.L.
  Reference manual for telecommunications engineering **1382**
Freidel, F.
  Harvard guide to American history **2983**
French, D.
  Dictionary of accounting terms **610**
French, D. *and* Saward, H.
  Dictionary of management **614**
French-English science and technology dictionary **864**
French language and literature **2444**
The French Revolution **2907**
French's index of differential diagnosis **1302**
Frey, L.
  Women in Western European history **816-817**
Friar, S.
  The Batsford companion to local history **2883**
Frickx, R. *and* Trousson, R.
  Lettres françaises de Belgique **2451**
Friday, A. *and* Ingram, D.S.
  The Cambridge encyclopedia of life sciences **1095**
Friedman, N.
  The Naval Institute guide to world naval weapons systems **1431**
Frisch, M.
  Directory for the environment **1109, 1132**
Fritze, R.H.
  Reference sources in history **2807**
Frodin, D.G.
  Guide to standard floras of the world **1146**
From Columbus to Castro **2978**
From the Titanic to the Challenger **1225**
Frost, D.R.
  Amphibian species of the world **1195**
Fryde, E.B.
  Handbook of British chronology **2863**
Fu, C.W. *and* Chang, W.
  Guide to Chinese philosophy **306**
Fuel and energy abstracts **1648**
Fulton, L.
  Small press record of books in print **291**
Fulton, R.
  The Encyclopedia of TV science fiction **2027**
Fundamentals of gear design **1416**
The Fungi **1162**
Furness, R. *and* Humble, M.
  A Companion to twentieth-century German literature **2425**
Furness, S.
  Rivers of the world **1064**
Furniss, T.
  Space flight **1485**
Fyfe, J.
  History journals and serials **2804**
Gad, F.
  The History of Greenland **3007**
Gage Canadian dictionary **2136**
Gale directory of publications and broadcasting media **242**

Galerstein, C.L.
Women writers of Spain **2465**
Gallaudet encyclopedia of deaf people
and deafness **1309**
Galperin, I.R. and Mednikova, E.M.
Bolshoi anglo-russkii slovar' **2207**
Galvin, H. and Tamarkin, S.
The Yiddish dictionary sourcebook
2167
Gambaccini, P. and Rice, J.
The Guinness book of British hit
albums **1974**
Gambaccini, P. and Rice, J. and Rice, T.
The Guinness book of British hit
singles **1975**
Gambhir, M.L.
Concrete technology **1676**
Gamble, C.
The Palaeolithic settlement of Europe
2539
Gammond, P.
The Oxford companion to popular
music **1962, 1978**
Gänzl, K.
The Blackwell guide to the musical
theatre on record **1990**
The British musical theatre **1954**
Gänzl, K. and Lamb, A.
Gänzl's Book of the musical theatre
1949
Gänzl's Book of the musical theatre
1949
García-Pelayo y Gross, R.
Larousse gran diccionario, español-
inglés **2192**
Gardening: a guide to the literature
1520
Gardner, D.E. and Smith, F.
Genealogical research in England and
Wales **2776**
Gardner, W.
Gardner's Chemical synonyms and
trade names **1634**
Gardner's Chemical synonyms and trade
names **1634**
Garland, H. and Garland, M.
The Oxford companion to German
literature **2426**
Garland, K.
Graphics, design and printing terms
1584, 1904
Garner, P.
Financial management handbook **557**
Gartside, L.
Modern business correspondence **607**
Gatland, K.W.
The Illustrated encyclopedia of space
technology **1486**
Gaylord, E.H., Jr. and Gaylord, C.N.
Structural engineering handbook **1433**
Gazetteers **2692**
Gazetteers of Canada **2704**
Ge Chuan-gui
A New English-Chinese dictionary
2255
Gear, A.
The New organic food guide **1653**
Gebhardt, B.
Handbuch der deutschen Geschichte
2892
Gedeon, C.G.
Who's who in the Arab World 1990-
1991 **2752**

Gee, P.
Spicer and Pegler's book-keeping and
accounts **611**
Geiger, A.
A History of textile art **1873**
Geigy scientific tables **1260**
Y Geiriadur mawr **2236**
Geisst, C.R.
A Guide to financial institutions **566**
Gemstones **1001**
Genealogical research directory national
and international 1989 **2771**
Genealogical research in England and
Wales **2776**
The Genealogist's address book **2778**
Genera graminum: grasses of the world
Grasses **1170**
A General guide to the India Office
Records **2941**
General navigation, coastal navigation
and pilotage **936**
Geo abstracts **2647**
GEOBASE **1002**
Geodesy **941**
Geographical abstracts. Physical
geography **1037, 1068**
A Geographical bibliography for
American libraries **1033**
Géographie historique de la France
2651
Geography and cartography **2645**
A Geolinguistic handbook **2090**
Geological abstracts **1021**
Geological dictionary **1019**
Geologists and the history of geology
1023
The Geologist's directory **1022**
Geomorphology of Europe **1039**
Georgano, N.
The New encyclopedia of motorcars
1473
Georgian-English dictionary **2253**
Geothermal energy **1015**
Gérard, A.
European-language writing in Sub-
Saharan Africa **2522**
Gerdts, W.H.
Art across America **1895**
Gerlach, A.C.
The National atlas of the United
States **2679**
German books in print **52**
The German Democratic Republic since
1945 **2898**
German-English glossary of financial and
economic terms **563**
German-English science dictionary **852**
German literature: an annotated
reference guide **2424**
Germanistik **2427**
Germany **2583**
Gesamtkatalog der Wiegendrucke **287**
Geschichte der Bundesrepublik
Deutschland **2897**
Gesenius, H.F.W.
A Hebrew and English lexicon of the
Old Testament **2242**
Gestuno **2095**
Gettings, F.
Dictionary of occult, hermetic and
alchemical sigils **309**

Gibb, H.A.R. and Kramer, J.H.
The Shorter encyclopedia of Islam
423
Gibbney, H.J. and Smith, A.G.
A Biographical register 1788-1939.
Notes from the name index of the
Australian Dictionary of Biography
2766
Gibbs-Smith, C.H.
Aviation: an historical survey **1482**
Gibilisco, S. and Slater, N.
Encyclopedia of electronics **1370**
Gibson, W.B.
Hoyle's Modern encyclopedia of card
games **2073**
Gieysztor, A.
A History of Poland **2901**
Gifford, D.
Encyclopedia of comic characters
1872
Gilbert, M.
First World War atlas **2846**
Gilbert, P. and Hamilton, C.J.
Entomology: a guide to information
sources **1184**
Gilg, A.W.
International yearbook of rural
planning **1819**
Gillespie, C.C.
Dictionary of scientific biography **890**
Gillespie, J.T.
Best books for children **130**
Gingerich, O.
Astrophysics and twentieth-century
astronomy to 1950 **921**
Gioello, D.A. and Berke, B.
Fashion production terms **1752**
Giscard d'Estaing, V-A.
The Book of inventions and
discoveries **1233**
Githens, J.
Guide to world cheeses **1539**
Glaister, G.A.
Glaister's glossary of the book **1576**
Glaister's glossary of the book **1576**
Glare, P.G.W.
Oxford Latin dictionary **2201**
Glass science and technology **1671**
Glossary for horticultural crops **1518**
Glossary of art, architecture and design
since 1945 **1774**
Glossary of automotive terms **1474**
A Glossary of botanic terms **1138**
Glossary of genetics and cytogenetics,
classical and molecular **1114**
Glossary of genetics: classical and
molecular **1114**
A Glossary of geographical terms **1036**
Glossary of geology **1020**
Glossary of health care terminology **737**
Glossary of marketing terms **623**
Glossary of terms used in quality control
619
A Glossary of wood **1693**
Godden, G.A.
The Concise guide to British pottery
and porcelain **1855**
Godden, M. and Lapidge, M.
The Cambridge companion to Old
English literature **2368**
The Gods of the Celts **424**
Goff, F.R.
Incunabula in American libraries **288**

Gohdes, C. and Marovitz, S.E.
Bibliographical guide to the study of the literature of the USA **2409**
Goldie, J.
Harrap's Shorter French and English dictionary **2181**
Goldstein, M.C.
A History of modern Tibet **2946**
The Good beer guide **1553**
The Good church guide, 1989 **378**
The Good food guide **1552**
The Good gardens guide 1990 **1823**
The Good hotel guide **1548**
The Good pub guide **1554**
Goodall, D.W.
Ecosystems of the world **1111**
Goode, P. and Lancaster, M.
The Oxford companion to gardens **1821**
Goodier, J.H.
Dictionary of painting and decorating **1763**
Gordon, L.L.
British battles and medals **707**
Gore, A.
The History of English interiors **1880**
Gorman, M.
The Concise AACR2. 1988 revision **109**
Gorman, M. and Winkler, P.
Anglo-American cataloguing rules **108**
Gorman, R.A.
Biographical dictionary of Marxism **317**
Biographical dictionary of Neo-Marxism **318**
Gorsline, D.
A History of fashion **790**
Gould, J. and Kolb, W.K.
A Dictionary of the social sciences **434**
Government reports announcements & index **874**
Gower handbook of quality management **620**
Gowing, L.
Biographical dictionary of artists **1786**
Graf, R.F.
The Encyclopedia of electronic circuits **1379**
Graham, A.L.
The Catalogue of meteorites **1058**
Graham, G.A.
Encyclopedia of industrial automation **1739**
Graham, I.
Encyclopedia of advertising **630**
Graham, J. and Lowe, S.
The Facts on File dictionary of telecommunications **1383**
A Grammar of contemporary English **2160**
Grand dictionnaire encyclopédique Larousse **159**
Le Grand Robert de la langue française **2184**
Le Grand Robert électronique **2184**
Grande dizionario enciclopedico UTET **160**
Il Grande dizionario Garzanti della lingua italiana **2187**
Grandison, A.G.C.
Snakes - a natural history **1197**

Granger's Index to poetry **2319**
Grant & Cutler Ltd
Foreign language dictionaries: specialist and general **2100**
Grant and Hackh's chemical dictionary **982**
Grant, M.
Greek and Latin authors **2479**
The History of ancient Israel **2816**
Grant, M. and Kitzinger, R.
Civilization of the Ancient Mediterranean. Greece and Rome **2821**
Grant, R.L. and Grant, A.C.
Grant and Hackh's chemical dictionary **982**
Graphic arts encyclopedia **1585**
Graphics, design and printing terms **1584, 1904**
Grasselli, J.G. and Ritchey, W.M.
CRC atlas of spectral data **971**
Grasses **1170**
Gray, I.H.
Mythology of all races **401**
Gray, R. and Argyle, C.
Chronicle of the First World War **2847**
Gray's anatomy **1267**
Grayson, L.
Recycling: energy from community waste **1340**
Great Britain
Britain 1992 **2576**
Statutory Instruments. 1890- **642**
Great Britain. Central Statistical Office
Guide to official statistics **469**
Key date **473**
Great Britain. Department of Employment
Directory of employers; associations, trade unions, joint organisations, etc **533**
Great Britain. Department of Transport
Transport statistics: Great Britain **1598**
Great Britain. Her Majesty's Stationery Office
HMSO annual catalogue **277**
Great Britain. Home Office. Fire Department
Manual of firemanship **1282**
Great Britain. Hydrographic Department
Admiralty list of lights and fog signals **1619**
Admiralty list of radio signals **1618**
Tide tables **939**
Great Britain. India Office Library and Records
Catalogue of European printed books, India Office Library **2608**
Great Britain. Meteorological Office
Meteorological glossary **1050**
Tables of temperature, relative humidity, precipitation and sunshine for the world **1053**
Great Britain. Ministry of Agriculture, Fisheries and Food
Agricultural statistics for the United Kingdom **1501**
Great Britain. Ministry of Defence
Manual of map reading and land navigation **946**

Great Britain Ministry of Defence. Director General of Supplies & Transport (Navy)
Flags of all nations **2796**
Great Britain. Ministry of Defence. Navy
Admiralty manual of navigation **936, 1614**
Admiralty manual of seamanship **1615**
Great Britain. Ministry of Defence. Navy Department
The Navy list **720**
Great Britain. National Maritime Museum
Catalogue of the library **2639**
Great Britain Ordance Survey
County street atlases **2665**
Great Britain. Ordnance Survey
The Ordnance Survey gazetteer of Great Britain **2698**
Routemaster maps **2667**
Great Britain. Public Record Office
Guide to the contents of the Public Record Office **2867**
Great Britain. Royal Commission on Ancient And Historical Monuments In Wales
Inventories **2555**
Great Britain. Royal Commission on the Ancient and Historical Monuments of England
Inventories **2553**
Great Britain. Royal Commission on the Ancient and Historical Monuments of Scotland
Catalogue of records, Scottish Industrial Archaeology Survey 1977-85 **2562**
Great Britain. Royal Commission on the Ancient and Historical Monuments of Scotland
Reports and inventories **2544**
Great Britain. Statutory Publications Office
The Public General Acts and General Synod Measures **643**
Statutes in force **644**
The Great English-Polish dictionary **2212**
Great passenger ships of the world **1480**
The Great Polish-English dictionary **2213**
The Great song thesaurus **1958**
Greater London Council
The Survey of London **2887**
Greek and Latin authors **2479**
A Greek-English lexicon ... **2203**
A Greek-English lexicon of the New Testament and other early Christian literature **2204**
The Green book **1511**
Green dictionary **1465**
Green, F.J.
Sigma-Aldrich handbook of stains, dyes and indicators **1677**
Green, M.
The Gods of the Celts **424**
Green, S.
Encyclopedia of the musical film **1950, 2026**
Keyguide to information sources in food science and technology **1654**

Greenbaum, S. *and* Whitcut, J.
The Longman guide to English usage 2126
Greenfield, E. *and* Layton, R. *and* March, I.
The Penguin guide to compact discs 1987
The Penguin guide to compact discs and cassettes, Yearbook 1991/92 1988
Greenfield, S.B. *and* Calder, D.G.
A New critical history of Old English literature 2369
Greenland past and present 2637
Greenstein, C.H.
Dictionary of logical terms and symbols 330
Grenville, J.A.S.
The Major international treaties, 1914-1945 660
Grenville, J.A.S. *and* Wasserstein, B.
The Major international treaties since 1945 661
Greuter, W.
International Code of Botanical Nomenclature 1141
Griffin, D.
Encyclopaedia of modern British army regiments 715
Griffiths, T.R. *and* Woddis, C.
Bloomsbury theatre guide 2326
Grim, R.E.
Historical geography of the United States 2654
Grimal, P.
Larousse world mythology 404
Grimes, J.
A Concise dictionary of Indian philosophy 307
Grimmett, R.F.A. *and* Jones, T.A.
Important bird areas in Europe 1135
Grogan, D.
Science and technology: an introduction to the literature 840
Groot woordenboek der Nederlandse taal 2168
Gross, C.
A Bibliography of British municipal history 695
Gross, J.S.
Webster's new world illustrated encyclopedic dictionary of real estate 541
Grote, D.
Common knowledge 2314
Ground engineering yearbook, 1991 1436
Ground engineer's reference book 1432
Grout, D. *and* Palisca, C.
A History of Western music 1933
Grout, D.J.
A Short history of opera 1953
Grove concise encyclopaedia of music 1926
Grove, P.B.
Webster's third new international dictionary of the English language 2147
Grubb, P.W.
Patents in chemistry and biotechnolgy 987
Grun, B.
The Timetables of history 2808

Grzimek, B.
Grzimek's animal life encyclopedia 1176
Grzimek's encyclopedia of ecology 1108
Grzimek's encyclopedia of mammals 1206
Grzimek's animal life encyclopedia 1176
Grzimek's encyclopedia of ecology 1108
Grzimek's encyclopedia of mammals 1206
Gschneidner, K.A. *and* Eyring, Le R.
Handbook of the physics and chemistry of rare earths 1688
Guide for graphical symbols for electrical power, telecommunications and electronics diagrams 1354
Guide to American poetry explication 2413
A Guide to British government publications 278
Guide to British poetry explication 2372
Guide to Chinese philosophy 306
Guide to Chinese religion 425
Guide to collections of manuscripts relating to Australia 3003
Guide to documents and manuscripts in the United Kingdom relating to Russia and the Soviet Union 2920
A Guide to financial institutions 566
Guide to fossil man 1077
Guide to Hungarian studies 2584
A Guide to Irish bibliographical material 2577
Guide to libraries and information units 116
Guide to libraries in Western Europe 114
A Guide to library research methods 2
Guide to literary prizes, grants and awards in Britain and Ireland 2283
A Guide to manuscript sources for the history of Latin America and the Caribbean in the British Isles 2982
A Guide to manuscripts and documents in the British Isles relating to South and South-East Asia 2942
A Guide to manuscripts and documents in the British Isles relating to the Middle East and North Africa 2606
Guide to microforms in print 264
A Guide to military museums 705
Guide to modern defense and strategy
A Dictionary of modern defense and strategy 712
Guide to official publications of foreign countries 268
Guide to official statistics 469
A Guide to Parliamentary Papers 672
A Guide to published library catalogs 90
Guide to reference books 136
Guide to reference works for the study of the Spanish language and literature and Spanish American literature 2464
Guide to reprints 165
A Guide to sources of US military history 716
A Guide to stained glass in Britain 1882
Guide to standard floras of the world 1146

Guide to the antique shops of Britain - 1991 1815
A Guide to the archaeological sites of Israel, Egypt and North Africa 2557
A Guide to the cathedrals of Britain 1844
Guide to the contents of the Public Record Office 2867
Guide to the flags of the world 2797
Guide to the literature of art history 1764
A Guide to the literature of astronomy 912
A Guide to the literature of electrical and electronics engineering 1355
Guide to the local administrative units of England 694
Guide to the national monuments in the Republic of Ireland 2551
Guide to the petroleum reference literature 1661
A Guide to the prehistoric and Roman monuments in England and Wales 2552
A Guide to the Roman remains in Britain 2549
A Guide to the sources of British military history 708
A Guide to theses and dissertations 168
A Guide to Welsh literature 2505
Guide to world cheeses 1539
A Guide to world cinema 2011
Les Guides rouges 1549
Guiley, R.E.
The Encyclopedia of witches and witchcraft 312
The Guinness book of British hit albums 1974
The Guinness book of British hit singles 1975
The Guinness book of records 151
The Guinness book of speed 967
The Guinness encyclopedia of international sports records and results 2078
The Guinness guide to 20th-century fashion 792
Gullberg, I.F.
Svensk-engelsk fackordbok för näringsliv, fövaltning, undevisning och forskning 861
Gulliver, J.S. *and* Arndt, R.E.A.
Hydropower engineering handbook 1362
Gunn, A.
CD-ROM: a practical guide for information professionals 10
Gunnemark, E.
A Geolinguistic handbook 2090
Gunston, B.
The Guinness book of speed 967
Gunston, C.A. *and* Corner, C.M.
German-English glossary of financial and economic terms 563
Gustafson, A.
A History of Swedish literature 2440
Guthrie, W. K. C.
A History of Greek philosophy 302
Gutkind, E.A.
International history of city development 696, 1818
Gutman, I.
Encyclopedia of the Holocaust 2895

Guyer, E.C.
Handbook of applied thermal design
1393
Gwatkin, H.M.
The Cambridge medieval history 2835
A Gypsy bibliography 819
Hadfield, C.
The Canals of the British Isles 1622
Hadfield, M.
A History of British gardening 1822
Haeffner, M.
The Dictionary of alchemy 313
Haensch, G. and Haberkamp de Anton, G.
Dictionary of agriculture in six
languages 1493
Hais, K. and Hodek, B.
Velký anglicko-český slovník 2214
Halkett, S. and Laing, J.
Dictionary of anonymous and
pseudonymous English literature 32
Hall, C.W.
Encyclopedia of food engineering
1655
Hall, J.
Dictionary of subjects and symbols in
art 1812
Hall, J.L.
Online bibliographic databases 839
Hall, J.R.C
A Concise Anglo-Saxon dictionary
2123
Hallam, A.
Atlas of palaeobiogeography 1069
Halley, R.J.
Primrose McConnell's 'The agricultural
notebook' 1492
Halliwell, L.
Halliwell's film guide 2012
Halliwell's filmgoer's and video
viewer's companion 2013
Halliwell's television companion 2003
Halliwell's film guide 2012
Halliwell's filmgoer's and video viewer's
companion 2013
Halliwell's television companion 2003
Halsbury's Statutes of England and
Wales 645
Halsby, J. and Harris, P.
Dictionary of Scottish painters 1892
Hamel, R.
Dictionnaire des auteurs de langue
française en Amérique du Nord
2454
Hamer, F. and Hamer, J.
The Potter's dictionary of materials
and techniques 1853
Hamilton, B. and Guidos, B.
MASA: medical acronyms, symbols
and abbreviations 1243
Hamilton-Edwards, G.
In search of Scottish ancestry 2774
Hamilton, L.
Information pack including
bibliography on advanced
manufacturing technology 1740
Hamilton, L. and Hallam, L.
Information pack on computer
integrated manufacturing 1741
Hamilton, R.J. and Bhatti, A.
Recent advances in chemistry and
technology of fats and oils 1659

Hammond, N.G.L and Scullard, H.H.
The Oxford classical dictionary 2823
Han ying kung cheng chi shu tzu hui
872
Hancox, P.J.
Keyguide to information sources in
artificial intelligence/expert systems
1742
Handbook for astronomical societies
923
Handbook of adhesives 1670
Handbook of applied meteorology 1049
Handbook of applied thermal design
1393
Handbook of arts and crafts 1875
Handbook of Austrian literature 2433
The Handbook of British birds 1204
Handbook of British chronology 2863
The Handbook of British mammals
1212
Handbook of chemical production
processes 1640
Handbook of concrete engineering 1439
A Handbook of consumer law 1560
A Handbook of costume 785
Handbook of developmental psychology
321
Handbook of engineering design 1330
Handbook of engineering fundamentals
Eshbach's handbook of engineering
fundamentals 1324
Handbook of family planning 745
Handbook of geochemistry 1013
Handbook of geothermal energy 1016
Handbook of heat transfer applications
974
Handbook of international road transport
1601
Handbook of international trade 594
A Handbook of Irish folklore 825
Handbook of Latin American literature
2466
Handbook of Latin American studies
2625
A Handbook of management techniques
612
Handbook of measurement science 966
Handbook of Middle American Indians
1090
The Handbook of non-sexist writing
2127
Handbook of North American Indians
1089
Handbook of parapsychology 311
A Handbook of personnel management
618
Handbook of petroleum refining
processes 1668
Handbook of physical constants 1008
Handbook of physiology 1268
Handbook of plastics test methods 1708
Handbook of powder science and
technology 1406
Handbook of power cylinders, valves
and controls 1398
Handbook of pseudonyms and personal
nicknames 33
Handbook of psychiatry 1314
Handbook of Russian literature 2487
Handbook of sociology 443
Handbook of South American Indians
1091
Handbook of special education 769

Handbook of sweeteners 1657
Handbook of the American frontier
2990
Handbook of the birds of Europe, the
Middle East and North Africa 1200
A Handbook of the living primates
1214
Handbook of the physics and chemistry
of rare earths 1688
Handbook of the Religious Society of
Friends, 1982 397
Handbook of toxic and hazardous
chemicals and carcinogens 1294
Handbook of vitamins 1118
Handbook of water purification 1462
The Handbook of Western philosophy
294
A Handbook to literature 2316
Handbooks for the identification of
British insects 1186
Handbuch der bibliographischen
Nachschlagewerke 139
Handbuch der deutschen Geschichte
2892
Hanks, P. and Hodges, F.
A Dictionary of first names 2109
A Dictionary of surnames 2112
Hansen, I.F.
Litteraturhåndbogen 2442
Hanson, W.S. and Slater, E.A.
Scottish archaeology 2543
Harbison, P.
Guide to the national monuments in
the Republic of Ireland 2551
Harder, K.B.
Illustrated dictionary of place names:
United States and Canada 2105
Hardon, J.A.
Modern Catholic dictionary 383
Hardy, P.
Encyclopedia of horror movies 2025
Hardy, P. and Laing, D.
Faber companion to twentieth century
popular music 1972
Harland, W.B.
Geologic time scale 1989 1055
Harmon, N.B.
The Interpreter's Bible 350
Harner, J.L.
Literary research guide 2356
Harper & Row's complete field guide to
North American wildlife. Eastern
edition 1128
Harper & Row's complete field guide to
North American wildlife. Western
edition 1129
Harper's Bible commentary 349
Harrap's Book of 1000 plays 2327
Harrap's Book of film directors and
their films 2020
Harrap's CD-ROM multilingual
dictionary database 2116
Harrap's dictionary of business and
finance 547
Harrap's five-language business dictionary
548
Harrap's New standard French and
English dictionary 2182
Harrap's Shorter French and English
dictionary 2181
Harrap's Shorter Italian dictionary
2188

Harrap's Standard Italian dictionary 2190
Harris, C.D.
A Geographical bibliography for American libraries 1033
Harris, C.D. and Fellmann, J.D.
International list of geographical serials 1038
Harris, C.M.
Dictionary of architecture and construction 1829
Shock and vibration handbook 969
Harris, T.Y.
Wild flowers of Australia 1156
Harrison, H.P.
Picture librarianship 1916
Harrison, T.
Access to information in local government 692
Harrod's librarians' glossary 100
Harrold, A.
Libraries in the United Kingdom and Republic of Ireland 118
Hart, F.D.
French's index of differential diagnosis 1302
Hart, G.
Dictionary of Egyptian gods and goddesses 402
Dictionary of taxation 565
Hart, H.
Hart's rules for compositors and readers at the University Press, Oxford 1582
Hart, J.D.
The Concise Oxford companion to American literature 2410
The Oxford companion to American literature 2410
Hart, N.A. and Stapleton, J.
Glossary of marketing terms 623
Hartley, J.M.
The Study of Russian history from British archival sources 2919
Hartly, J.M.
Guide to documents and manuscripts in the United Kingdom relating to Russia and the Soviet Union 2920
Hartnoll, P.
The Oxford companion to the theatre 2034
Hart's rules for compositors and readers at the University Press, Oxford 1582
Harvard guide to American history 2983
Harvey, A.P.
European sources of scientific and technical information 896
Harvey, J.M.
Statistics Europe 467
Harvey, P. and Heseltine, J.E.
The Oxford companion to French literature 2450
Hastings, A.
A History of English Christianity, 1920-1985 352
Hatch, J.E.
Aluminum: Properties and physical metallurgy 1686
Haugen, E.
A History of Norwegian literature 2438
Norwegian-English dictionary 2173

Haviland, V.
Children's literature: a guide to reference sources 126
Havlice, P.P.
Oral history 2832
Hawaiian dictionary 2274
Hawke, D.M.
An Introduction to Vietnamese literature 2521
Hawkes, J.
A Guide to the prehistoric and Roman monuments in England and Wales 2552
The Shell guide to British archaeology 2541
Hawkings, D.T.
Bound for Australia 2779
Hawkins, J. and Allen, R.
The Oxford encyclopedic English dictionary 2151
Hawksworth, D.L.
Ainsworth & Bisby's dictionary of the fungi 1161
Hay, D.
Longman history of Italy 2910
Haycraft, F.W.
Degrees and hoods of the world's universities and colleges 773
Hayes, C.
The Complete guide to painting and drawing techniques and materials 1871
Haynes, D.
Information sources in information technology 3
Hayward, A. and Weare, F.
Steel detailers' manual 1441
Hayyim, S.
The New Persian-English dictionary 2231
Hazen, E.P. and Fryer, D.J.
The Columbia Granger's Index to poetry 2319
Hazewinkel, M.
Encyclopaedia of mathematics 901
Headland, R.K.
Chronological list of Antarctic expeditions 3006
Headley, R.K.
Cambodian-English dictionary 2262
Health service abstracts 736
Heaney, H.J.
World guide to abbreviations of organizations 17
Heard, J.N.
Handbook of the American frontier 2990
Heath, J. and others
The Moths and butterflies of Great Britain and Ireland 1190
Heawood, R. and Larke, C.
The Directory of appropriate technology 1228
A Hebrew and English lexicon of the Old Testament 2242
Hedgecoe, J.
Complete guide to photography 1910
Hedgecoe on video 1915
Hedgecoe on video 1915
Henbest, N. and Marten, M.
The New astronomy 933
Henderson, C.A.P.
Current British directories 215

Henderson, C.A.P. (contd.)
Pan-European associations 219
Henderson, G.P. and Henderson, S.P.A.
Directory of British associations 221
Henderson, I.F.
Henderson's dictionary of biological terms 1097
Henderson, L.
Contemporary novelists 2332
Twentieth-century crime and mystery writers 2340
Twentieth-century romance and historical writers 2339
Henderson's dictionary of biological terms 1097
Herbert, M.C. and McNeil, B.
Biography and genealogy master index 2762
Herculaneum: a guide to printed sources 2556
Herdeck, D.E.
African authors 2523
Caribbean writers 2402
The Heritage of Australia 2706
Herring, S.D.
From the Titanic to the Challenger 1225
Hertling, K.
Greenland past and present 2637
Herwig, H.H. and Heyman, N.M.
Biographical dictionary of World War I 2848
Heyden, A.A.M. and Scullard, H.
Atlas of the Classical World 2537
Heyel, C.
The Encyclopedia of management 613
Heywood, C.A.
International directory of botanical gardens V 1143
Hibbert, D.B. and James, A.M.
Dictionary of electrochemistry 989
Hicken, M.
Sequels 2335
Hicks, T.G.
Civil engineering calculations reference guide 1437
Hieronymussen, P.
Orders, medals and decorations of Britain and Europe in colour 2792
Higgins, J.
A History of Peruvian literature 2474
Higham, R.
A Guide to sources of US military history 716
A Guide to the sources of British military history 708
Higher education in the European Community 771
Highway engineering 1448
Highway Research Information Service
HRIS abstracts 1447
Hildebrandt, D.M.
Computing information directory 1722
Hill, J.
The Complete practical book of country crafts 1716
Hill, M.N.
The Sea 1045
Hilton, R.
Who's who in Latin America 2756
Hinds, M. and Badawi, E.-S.
A Dictionary of Egyptian Arabic 2244

Hinnells, J.R.
Facts on File dictionary of religions 342
The Penguin dictionary of religions 342
Hirshfeld, A. and Sinnott, R.
Sky catalogue 2000.0 931
Hislop, R.
Art sales index 1813
The Picture price guide 1990 1888
Hispanic writers 2299
Histoire de la France 2906
Història de la literatura catalana 2455
Historia general de las literaturas hispánicas 2461
Historic houses, castles and gardens 1845
Historical Abstracts 2803
Historical atlas of Africa 2966
Historical atlas of Britain 2862
Historical atlas of Canada 2976
An Historical atlas of Islam 2938
A Historical atlas of South Asia 2940
Historical dictionaries of France 2905
Historical dictionary of Brazil 2992
Historical dictionary of Egypt 2967
Historical dictionary of Fascist Italy 2913
Historical dictionary of modern Spain 1700-1988 2915
Historical dictionary of Oceania 2996
Historical dictionary of the Spanish Civil War 2916
Historical dictionary of Vietnam 2962
An Historical geography of England and Wales 2650
An Historical geography of Europe 2649
An Historical geography of Scandinavia 2652
Historical geography of the United States 2654
A Historical guide to the United States 2705
Historical guide to World War II 2851
Historical tables 58BC-AD1985 2809
History journals and serials 2804
The History of ancient Israel 2816
A History of architecture 1830
A History of Australia 2998
History of ballet and modern dance 2060
A History of British gardening 1822
A History of British trade unionism 539
The History of broadcasting in the United Kingdom 2001
A History of broadcasting in the United States 2000
The History of cartography 950
A History of classical Malay literature 2528
A History of creeds and confessions of faith in Christendom and beyond 360
A history of Czechoslovakia since 1945 2900
A History of Danish literature 2443
History of East Africa 2969
A History of English Christianity, 1920-1985 352
A History of English drama, 1660-1900 2376
The History of English interiors 1880
A History of English poetry 2371

A History of fashion 790
A History of Finnish literature 2514
A History of German literature 2429
A History of graphic design 1905
A History of Greek philosophy 302
The History of Greenland 3007
A History of Hungary 2902
A History of Islamic philosophy 305
A History of Israel 2958
A History of Italian literature 2458
The History of Jamaica 2980
A History of Japanese literature 2518
A History of Jewish literature 2508
History of Korean literature 2520
A History of Malaysia 2961
The History of mathematics, from antiquity to the present 907
A History of modern criticism, 1750-1950 2312
A History of modern Greek literature 2483
A History of modern poetry 2373
A History of modern Tibet 2946
A History of Nigeria 2968
A History of Norwegian literature 2438
A History of Peruvian literature 2474
History of photography 1912
A History of Poland 2901
The History of Polish literature 2491
A History of political theory 494
History of Portugal 2917
A History of religious ideas 334
A History of Russian thought 315
The History of science and technology in the United States 893
The History of Scottish literature 2389
History of Southern Africa 2970
A History of Soviet Russia 2922
A History of Spain 2914
A History of Spanish literature 2461
A History of Swedish literature 2440
A History of Switzerland 2930
A History of technology 1227
A History of textile art 1873
History of the Arabs 2936
History of the Balkans. v.1. Eighteenth and nineteenth centuries. v.2. Twentieth century 2932
A History of the circus 2032
A History of the Crusades 2839
The History of the dance 2065
A History of the English Church 390
A History of the English language 2121
A History of the expansion of Christianity 367
History of the Goths 2819
History of the Great War 2845
A History of the League of Nations 652
A History of the Methodist Church in Great Britain 396
A History of the Near East 2939
History of the Ottoman Empire and modern Turkey 2957
A History of the Pacific Islands 2994
The History of the puppet theatre 2030
History of the Second World War 2850
A History of Ukrainian literature 2490
A History of Urdu literature 2501
The History of Wales 2890
A History of Welsh literature 2506
A History of Western music 1933
A History of Western philosophy 303
A History of Western sculpture 1846

A History of Yiddish literature 2431
Hitti, P.K.
History of the Arabs 2936
HMSO annual catalogue 277
Hoad, T.F.
The Concise Oxford dictionary of English etymology 2162
Hochman, S.
French-English science and technology dictionary 864
McGraw-Hill encyclopedia of world drama 2328
Hodgson, T.
The Batsford dictionary of drama 2037
Hodnett, E.
Five centuries of English book illustration 292
Hodson, H.V.
The International foundation directory 729
Hogan, R.
The Macmillan dictionary of Irish literature 2392
Hogan, T.
Index to journal articles on Australian history 3000
Hogarth, J.
Glossary of health care terminology 737
Holden, U. and Mathez, E.A.
The Encyclopedia of gemstones and minerals 997
Holidays and anniversaries of the world 799
Holland, A.
British theatre directory 1990 2041
Holland, R.C.
Illustrated dictionary of microelectronics and microcomputers 1380
Holland, W.W.
Oxford textbook of public health 1279
Holler, F.L.
Information sources of political science 481
Hollier, D.
A New history of French literature 2449
Hollingsworth, B.
An Illustrated guide to modern trains 1481
Hollis press & public relations annual, 1991-92 631
Holman, C.H. and Harmon, W.
A Handbook to literature 2316
Hólmarsson, S.
Islensk-ensk ordabók 2172
Holmes, A.
Holmes' principles of physical geology 1027
Holmes, D.L.
Holmes' principles of physical geology 1027
Holmes' principles of physical geology 1027
Holmgren, P.K.
Index herbariorum 1144
Holt, P.M.
The Cambridge history of Islam 2935
A History of the Near East 2939

Homburger, W.S.
Transportation and traffic engineering handbook **1597**
The Home book of quotations **2289**
The Homeowner's complete manual of repair & improvement **1569**
Honacki, J.H.
Mammal species of the world **1208**
Hone, A.R. *and* Mutt, O.
Estonian literature: historical survey **2515**
Honey, W.B.
European ceramic art **1854**
Old English porcelain **1858**
Hong Kong 1991 **2602**
Honour, H. *and* Fleming, J.
A World history of art **1780**
Hook, B. *and* Twitchett, D.
The Cambridge encyclopedia of China **2599**
Hooker, D.
Art of the Western World **1781**
Hooper, D. *and* Whyld, K.
The Oxford companion to chess **2071**
Hope, A. *and* Walch, M.
The Color compendium **973**
Hope, C.E.G.
The Encyclopedia of the horse **1531**
Hora, B.
The Oxford encyclopedia of trees of the world **1507**
Hordeski, M.
The Illustrated dictionary of microcomputers **1732**
Horn, M.
Contemporary graphic artists **1907**
Hornby, A.S.
The Oxford advanced learner's dictionary of current English **2141**
The Oxford advanced learner's English-Chinese dictionary **2254**
Horne, E.C.
Javanese-English dictionary **2273**
Horror literature: a reader's guide **2346**
Horticultural abstracts **1517**
Hospital literature index **744**
The Hospitals and health services yearbook ... and directory of hospital suppliers **739**
Hotel and motel red book **1550**
Houaiss, A.
Dicionário inglês-português **2196**
Houghton, D.D.
Handbook of applied meteorology **1049**
Houghton, W.E.
Wellesley index to Victorian periodicals **209**
Houldcroft, P.T.
Materials data sources **1335**
Hounsome, T.
New rock records **1993**
House of Commons
Manual of procedure in the public business **673**
Housing year book, 1992 **691**
How to find chemical information **978**
How to find out in psychology **320**
How to start and run your own business **554**
How to use a medical library **1249**
How to write a research paper **1**

Howard, D.
Directory of theatre resources **2048**
Howard, R. *and* Moore, A.
A Complete checklist of the birds of the world **1199**
Howatson, M.C.
The Oxford companion to classical literature **2480**
Howe, G.M.
A World geography of human diseases **1298**
Howie, A.C.
Who's who in Australia: an Australian biographical dictionary and register of prominent people with which is incorporated John's Notable Australians. 1991 **2768**
Hoyle's Modern encyclopedia of card games **2073**
HRIS abstracts **1447**
HSELINE **1280**
Hubbard, C.E.
Grasses **1170**
Hubbard, J.C.E.
Grasses **1170**
Hudson, K.
The Cambridge guide to the museums of Britain and Ireland **236**
The Cambridge guide to the museums of Europe **235**
World industrial archaeology **2559**
Hudson, K. *and* Nicholls, A.
The Cambridge guide to the historic places of Britain and Ireland **2699**
The Directory of museums and living displays **233**
Huffman, F.E. *and* Proum, I.
English-Khmer dictionary **2263**
Huffman, R.J.
Inventing and patenting sourcebook **1237**
Hugh Johnson's wine companion **1650**
Hughes, G.
Arts Review yearbook 1992 **1777**
Hugman, B.J. *and* Arnold, P.
The Olympic Games **2082**
Human health and disease **1296**
Human resources abstracts **529**
Humana, C.
World human rights guide **676**
The Humanities: a selective guide to information sources **23**
Humanities index **203**
Humm, M.
The Dictionary of feminist theory **809**
Humphery-Smith, C.R.
The Phillimore atlas and index of parish registers **2783**
Humphreys, C.A.
A Popular dictionary of Buddhism **414**
Humphries, J.
Master catalogue **1986**
Hungarian authors **2513**
Hunt, P.
The Marshall Cavendish illustrated encyclopedia of gardening **1521**
Hunt, V.D.
Artificial intelligence and expert systems sourcebook **1743**
Hunt, W.D.
Encyclopedia of American architecture **1840**

Hunter, B.
The Statesman's year-book **2567**
Hunter, D.E. *and* Whitten, P.
Encyclopedia of anthropology **1080**
Hunter, J.
Concise dictionary of modern Japanese history **2950**
Hurvitz, L.
History of Korean literature **2520**
Husband, J. *and* Husband, J.F.
Sequels **2336**
Huson, T. *and* Postlethwaite, T.N.
The International encyclopedia of education **757**
Hutchings, E.A.D.
A survey of printing processes **1586**
The Hutchinson encyclopedia **152**
Hutchinson, J.
The Families of flowering plants **1169**
Hutchinson, L.
Standard handbook for secretaries **608**
Huws, G. *and* Roberts, D.H.E.
Wales **2581**
Huxley, A.
Standard encyclopedia of the world's oceans and islands **1040**
Hyamson, A.M.
Dictionary of universal biography **2721**
Hyatt, E.
Keyguide to information sources in remote sensing **943**
Hyde, D.
A Literary history of Ireland **2504**
Hydropower engineering handbook **1362**
Hymns and tunes **1955**
Hywell-Davies, J.
The Macmillan guide to British nature reserves **1131**
ICC Business Publications Ltd.
Macmillan's unquoted companies, 1992 **551**
An Icelandic-English dictionary **2172**
Identifying antique British silver **1860**
IEEE Standard dictionary of electrical and electronic terms **1356**
IFLA directory of art libraries **1805**
Igneous rocks of the British Isles **1057**
Illingworth, V.
Dictionary of computing **1725**
The Macmillan dictionary of astronomy **919**
Illumination engineering **1469**
The Illustrated atlas of Jewish civilization **2817**
Illustrated dictionary of architecture 800-1914 **1834**
Illustrated dictionary of electronics **1376**
An Illustrated dictionary of glass **1881**
The Illustrated dictionary of knitting **1879**
The Illustrated dictionary of microcomputers **1732**
Illustrated dictionary of microelectronics and microcomputers **1380**
Illustrated dictionary of place names: United States and Canada **2105**
An Illustrated dictionary of silverware **1859**
An Illustrated dictionary of word processing **1583**
The Illustrated encyclopedia of mankind **1084**

The Illustrated encyclopedia of New Zealand **2633**
The Illustrated encyclopedia of space technology **1486**
The Illustrated flora of Britain and Northern Europe **1147**
An Illustrated guide to modern trains **1481**
An Illustrated history of jewellery **1862**
An Illustrated history of the world's religions **400**
The Illustrated reference on cacti and other succulents **1524**
IMM abstracts **1420**
Imms, A.D.
  Imms' general textbook of entomology **1185**
Imms' general textbook of entomology **1185**
Important bird areas in Europe **1135**
In search of Scottish ancestry **2774**
In search of your European roots **2772**
Incunabula in American libraries **288**
Incunabula short title catalogue **289**
Independent schools yearbook, 1991 **763-764**
Independent television in Britain **2007**
Inder Jit
  India Who's who 1990-91 **2750**
The Index and abstract directory **173**
Index bio-bibliographicus notorum hominum **2722**
Index herbariorum **1144**
Index medicus **1257**
Index Nordicus **2593**
Index of conference proceedings **226**
Index of English literary manuscripts **2366**
Index of manuscripts in the British Library **283**
Index périodiques canadiens **210**
Index to children's songs: a title, first line, and subject index **1966**
Index to dental literature **1311**
Index to fairy tales, 1949-1972 **832**
Index to fairy tales, myths and legends **831**
Index to journal articles on Australian history **3000**
Index to legal periodicals, 1908- **632**
Index to Marquis who's who books 1991 **2760**
Index to periodicals on agriculture held by the Science Reference Library **1497**
Index to personal names in the National union catalog of manuscript collections 1959-1984 **285**
Index to printed maps **2655**
Index to social sciences and humanities proceedings **228**
An Index to the revised Bauer-Arndt-Gingrich Greek lexicon **2204**
Index to The Times **251**
Index to theses: with abstracts **169**
Index to US government periodicals **279**
Index translationum **30**
Index veterinarius **1527**
India Who's who 1990-91 **2750**
Indian books in print **61**
Indian literature in English, 1827-1979 **2395**
Indian mythology **403**

The Indiana companion to traditional Chinese literature **2516**
Indonesia handbook **2632**
An Indonesian-English dictionary **2270**
Industrial and marine fuels reference book **1647**
Industrial archaeology in Britain **2560**
'Industrial Archaeology institutions and societies' **2563**
Industrial development abstracts **583**
Industrial fasteners handbook **1417**
Industrial minerals directory **1683**
Industrial research in the United Kingdom **899**
Industrial solvents handbook **1641**
Industrial statistics yearbook, 1988 **585**
Information China **2600**
Information industry directory **7**
Information Mongolia **2603**
Information pack including bibliography on advanced manufacturing technology **1740**
Information pack on computer integrated manufacturing **1741**
Information pack on product liability **1402**
Information resources in toxicology **1295**
Information sources in agriculture and food science **1490**
Information sources in agriculture and horticulture **1490**
Information sources in architecture **1826**
Information sources in economics **516**
Information sources in energy technology **1336**
Information sources in engineering **1323**
Information sources in grey literature **171**
Information sources in information technology **3**
Information sources in management and business **601, 615**
Information sources in metallic materials **1679**
Information sources in pharmaceuticals **1285**
Information sources in physics **956**
Information sources in politics and political science: worldwide **479**
Information sources in polymers and plastics **1710**
Information sources in science and technology **841**
Information sources in the earth sciences **1004**
Information sources in the life sciences **1094**
Information sources in the medical sciences **1250**
Information sources of political science **481**
Information sources on the history of science and medicine **885**
INIS Atomindex **1350**
INIS: Thesaurus **1352**
Inland waterways series **1623**
INSPEC **955**
INSPEC thesaurus **965**
Institute of Electrical and Electronics Engineers
  IEEE Standard dictionary of electrical and electronic terms **1356**

Institution of Electrical Engineers
  Computer and control abstracts. Science abstracts. Section C **1727**
  Electrical and electronics abstracts. Science abstracts. Section B **1357**
  INSPEC **955**
  INSPEC thesaurus **965**
  Physics abstracts. Science abstracts. Section A **963**
Institution of Highways and Transportation *and* Department of Transport
  Roads and traffic in urban areas **1600**
Institution of Mining and Metallurgy
  IMM abstracts **1420**
Instrumentation reference book **1364**
Inter-Parliamentary Union
  Parliaments of the world **668**
Inter-Territorial Language (Swahili) Committee to the East African Dependencies
  A Standard Swahili-English dictionary **2266**
International aerospace abstracts **1487**
International affairs **502**
The International almanac of electoral history **498**
International annual bibliography of Festschriften **164**
International Association of Universities
  International handbook of universities **778**
International Atomic Energy Agency
  INIS Atomindex **1350**
  INIS: Thesaurus **1352**
International bibliography of book reviews of scholarly literature **183**
International bibliography of economics **517**
International bibliography of Festschriften from the beginnings until 1979 **163**
International bibliography of periodical literature **205**
International bibliography of political science **482**
International bibliography of social and cultural anthropology **1078**
International bibliography of sociology .. **444**
The International biotechnology directory, 1991 **1217**
International books in print **39**
International Buddhist directory **415**
International Cargo Handling Coordination Association
  A Multilingual glossary of cargo handling terms **1452**
International civil engineering abstracts **1435**
International Code of Botanical Nomenclature **1141**
International code of zoological nomenclature **1174**
International congress calendar **225**
International current awareness services/ ICAS **430**
International Dairy Federation
  Dictionary of dairy terminology **1538**
The International design yearbook 1990/ 1991 **1808**
International development abstracts **584**

International dictionary of education 758

International dictionary of films and filmmakers 2014

International dictionary of finance 561

International dictionary of medicine and biology 1098, 1255

International dictionary of psychology Macmillan dictionary of psychology 327

An International dictionary of theatre language 2038

International directory of botanical gardens V 1143

The International directory of business information sources and services 602

International directory of children's literature 128

International directory of company histories 589

International directory of film and TV documentation centres 2022

International documentation of cartographical literature 944

International encyclopedia of abbreviations and acronyms of organizations 19

International encyclopedia of composites 1332

The International encyclopedia of education 757

The International encyclopedia of higher education 770

International encyclopedia of linguistics 2097

International Federation of Library Associations and Institutions Inventaire général des bibliographies nationales rétrospectives 37

The International foundation directory 729

International geographical glossary 1034

International Geographical Union and Commission on International Geographical Terminology International geographical glossary 1034

International guide to official industrial property publications 1236

International handbook of industrial relations 534

International handbook of national parks and nature reserves 1130

International handbook of universities 778

International history of city development 696, 1818

An International history of the Vietnam war 2964

International Labour Office Encyclopaedia of occupational health and safety 1281 Yearbook of labour statistics, 1991 531

The International law dictionary 650

International leather guide 1696

International list of geographical serials 1038

International literary market place 1588

International literature in English 2385

International medieval bibliography 2836

International mortality statistics 478

International nomenclature of diseases 1297

International nursing index 1305

International packaging abstracts 1412

International petroleum abstracts 1664

International pulp and paper information sources 1697

The International relations dictionary 503

International research centers directory 231

International Road Union Manuel du transport routier international 1601

International standards index: welding and related processes 1410

The International Stock Exchange official yearbook, 1934- 570

International tables for crystallography 996

International television and video almanac 1990 2005

International trade statistics yearbook, 1989 595

International Union of Pure and Applied Physics. Commission for Symbols, Units and Nomenclature Symbols, units, nomenclature and fundamental constants in physics 954

The International who's who 1991-92 2713

International who's who in music and musician's directory 1990-91 1937

International yearbook of educational and training technology, 1991 762

International yearbook of rural planning 1819

International zoo yearbook 1175

Internationale Bibliographie der Festschriften von der Anfängen bis 1979 163

Internationale Bibliographie der Rezensionen Wissenschaftlicher Literatur 183

Internationale Bibliographie der Zeitschriftenliteratur 205

Internationale Enzyklopädie der Abkürzungen und Akronyme von Organisationen 19

Internationale geographische terminologie 1034

Internationale Jahresbibliographie der Festschriften 164

Internationale volkskundliche Bibliographie/International folklore and folklife bibliography/... 1939/41- 820

The Interpreter's Bible 350

An Introduction to ancient Egypt 2815

Introduction to biotechnology information 1220

An Introduction to Russian language and literature 2488

An Introduction to Vietnamese literature 2521

Inventaire général des bibliographies nationales rétrospectives 37

Inventing and patenting sourcebook 1237

Inventories 2553, 2555

Inventory of abstracting and indexing services produced in the UK 174

Invertebrate zoology 1181

The Investor's dictionary 567

Ireland, N.O. Index to fairy tales, 1949-1972 832

Ireland, P.J. Encyclopedia of fashion details 787

Irish genealogy 2775

Irish publishing record 49

The Irish theatre 2043

Iron Age communities in Britain 2540

Irregular serials and annuals 194

Isaacson, R.T. Gardening: a guide to the literature 1520

Isichei, E. A History of Nigeria 2968

ISIS cumulative bibliography 886

Islensk-ensk ordabók 2172

ISMEC: mechanical engineering abstracts 1342

The Israel year book 1990 2610

The ISTC handbook of technical writing and publication techniques 895

Ivamy, E.R.H. Dictionary of company law 681 Mozley & Whiteley's law dictionary 638

Jablonski, E. Encyclopedia of American music 1939

Jackson, B.D. A Glossary of botanic terms 1138

Jackson, G. Index to periodicals on agriculture held by the Science Reference Library 1497

Jackson, K.G. and Townsend, B. Television and video engineer's reference book 1390

Jackson, K.M. Computer security reference book 1737

Jackson, M.H. Environmental health reference book 1457

Jacobs, A. The Penguin dictionary of musical performers 1935

Jacobs, A. and Monk, J. The Cambridge illustrated dictionary of British heritage 2575

Jacobs, M. and Warner, M. The Phaidon companion to art and artists in the British Isles 1794

Jacobson,, M.D. Pros and cons 448

Jacolev, L. German-English science dictionary 852

Jahn, J. and Dressler, C.P. Bibliography of creative African writing 2524

Jaine, T. The Good food guide 1552

James, C.V. Information China 2600

James, D.E. The Encyclopedia of solid earth geophysics 1011

James, E. The Franks 2818

James, J.S. Stroud's judicial dictionary of words and phrases 639

James, N.D.G. The Forester's companion 1505

James, S.
Chambers sporting quotations 2077
James, S. and Parker, R.
A Dictionary of business quotations 550
James, T.
English literature from the Third World 2386
James, T.G.H.
An Introduction to ancient Egypt 2815
Jane's All the world's aircraft 1483
Jane's dictionary of naval terms 722
Jane's Encyclopedia of aviation 1484
Jane's Freight containers, 1987 1414
Jane's Military communications, 1991-92 1429
Jane's Spaceflight directory, 1987 1488
Jane's Weapon systems, 1988-89 1427
Jane's World railways, 1991/92 1443
Japan. Agency of Cultural Affairs
Japanese religion 426
Japanese history and culture from ancient to modern times: seven basic bibliographies 2949
Japanese religion 426
Jarman, A.O.H. and Hughes, G.R.
A Guide to Welsh literature 2505
Jary, D. and Jary, J.
Collins dictionary of sociology 442
Javanese-English dictionary 2273
Jay, F.
IEEE Standard dictionary of electrical and electronic terms 1356
Jazz 1970
Jedruch, J.
Nuclear engineering databases, standards and numerical analysis 1349
Jelavich, B.
History of the Balkans. v.1. Eighteenth and nineteenth centuries. v.2. Twentieth century 2932
Modern Austria 2899
Jenkins, G.
Oil economists' handbook 1662
Jenkinson, H.
The later court hands in England 2812
Jennett, S.
The Making of books 1577
Jens, W.
Kindlers neues Literatur Lexikon 2279
Jeremy, D.J.
Dictionary of business biography 604
Jerrard, H.G. and McNeill, D.B.
A Dictionary of scientific units 964
Jervis, S.
The Penguin dictionary of design and designers 1807
Jessop, G.R.
VHF/UHF manual 1387
Jewellery: concepts and technology 1690
Jocelyn, A.
Awards of honour 2793
Johansson, E.
Official publications of Western Europe 269
Johnson, C.
Green dictionary 1465

Johnson, C. and Jenkinson, H.
English court hands AD1066-1500 2813
Johnson, F.
A Standard Swahili-English dictionary 2266
Johnson, G.
The New Cambridge history of India 2953
Johnson, H.
Hugh Johnson's wine companion 1650
Johnson, K.A. and Sainty, M.R.
Genealogical research directory national and international 1989 2771
Joint Steering Committee for the Revision of AACR
Anglo-American cataloguing rules 108
Jones, B.
Handbook for astronomical societies 923
Jones, B. and Mattingly, D.
An Atlas of Roman Britain 2869
Jones, C.
The Longman companion to the French Revolution 2908
Jones, D.B.
Oxford economic atlas of the world 575
Jones, D.L.
British and Irish biographies 1840-1940 2731
Encyclopaedia of ferns 1167
Jones' Instrument technology 1720
Jones, P.H.
A Bibliography of the history of Wales 2891
Jones, S.R.
Books of Welsh interest 2582
Jordan, P. and Kelnhofer, F.
Atlas Ost-und Südosteuropa 2663
Joslin, E.C.
British battles and medals 707, 1851
Journal of Commonwealth literature 2387
Journalism: a guide to the reference literature 253
Journals in translation 31
Joyner, C.C and Chopra, S.K.
Antarctica 3005
Julian, J.
A Dictionary of hymnology 366
Junge, E.
World coin encyclopedia 1848
The Junior bookshelf 133
Kadish, S.H.
Encyclopedia of crime and justice 680
Kalley, J.A.
South Africa under Apartheid 454
Kane, J.N.
Facts about the States 2627
Kanner, B.
The Women of England 818
Kantautas, A. and Kantautas, F.
A Lithuanian bibliography 2590
Kaplan, M.
Variety presents 1996
Karassik, I.J.
Pump handbook 1399
Karpel, B.
Arts in America 1797

Karush, W.
Webster's new world dictionary of mathematics 904
Kasack, W.
Dictionary of Russian literature since 1917 2489
Katz, B.
Magazines for libraries 186
Kaufman, M.
Dictionary of American medical biography 1262
Kaye, G.W.C. and Laby, T.H.
Tables of physical and chemical constants 883
Kazhdan, A.P.
The Oxford dictionary of Byzantium 2956
Kearns, W.H.
Welding handbook 1409
Keay, J.
The Royal Geographical Society history of world exploration 2643
Keegan, J.
The Times atlas of the Second World War 2852
Keeling, D.F.
British library history: a bibliography 103
Keesing's record of world events 255
Keesing's UK record 256
Keller, H. and Erb, U.
Dictionary of engineering acronyms and abbreviations 1321
Kelly, J.N.D.
Early Christian creeds 360
The Oxford dictionary of Popes 387
Kelly's business directory, 1992 544
Kelly's United Kingdom exports
British exports, 92 596
Kemp, D.A.
Astronomy and astrophysics: a bibliographical guide 911
Kemp, P.
The Oxford companion to ships and the sea 1610
Kempe's Engineer's year-book, 1991 1326
Kemps international music and recording industry yearbook 1990 1930
Kenkyusha's New English-Japanese dictionary 2259
Kenkyusha's New Japanese-English dictionary 2260
Kennedy, G.A.
The Cambridge history of literary criticism 2309
Kennedy, J.
Dictionary of anonymous and pseudonymous English literature 32
Kennedy, M.
The Oxford dictionary of music 1922
Kennedy, S.
'First look' 2761
Kenney, E.J. and Clausen, W.V.
The Cambridge history of Classical literature, vol.2: Latin literature 2481
Kent, A.
Encyclopedia of library and information science 99
Encyclopedia of microcomputers 1729
Kent, D.H. and Allen, D.E.
British and Irish herbaria 1145

Kern, R.W. *and* Dodge, M.D.
Historical dictionary of modern Spain
1700-1988 **2915**
Kernchen, H-J.
Handbuch der bibliographischen
Nachschlagewerke **139**
Kernfeld, B.
Blackwell guide to recorded jazz **1991**
New Grove dictionary of jazz **1973**
Kerrich, G.J
Keyworks to the fauna and flora of
the British Isles and Northwestern
Europe **1179**
Kerrigan, H.M.
Who's who in Canada 1990 **2754**
Kersnowski, F.
A Bibliography of modern Irish and
Anglo-Irish literature **2503**
Key abstracts: Electrical measurements
and instrumentation **976**
Key date **473**
Key facts in Soviet history **2923**
Keyguide to information sources in
archaeology **2530**
Keyguide to information sources in
artificial intelligence/expert systems
1742
Keyguide to information sources in
business ethics **332**
Keyguide to information sources in
CAD/CAM **1401**
Keyguide to information sources in
dentistry **1310**
Keyguide to information sources in food
science and technology **1654**
Keyguide to information sources in
museum studies **234**
Keyguide to information sources in
online and CD-ROM database searching
5
Keyguide to information sources in
remote sensing **943**
Keyguide to information sources on the
international protection of human rights
675
Keyword index to British official
publications not published by HMSO
274
Keyword index to serial titles **187**
Keyworks to the fauna and flora of the
British Isles and Northwestern Europe
1179
Kici, G.
Albanian-English dictionary **2238**
Kici, G. *and* Aliko, H.
English-Albanian dictionary **2239**
Kidd, C. *and* Williamson, D.
Debrett's Peerage and Baronetage 1990
2790
Kightly, C.
The Customs and ceremonies of
Britain **794**
Killanin, Lord *and* Duignan, M.V.
Shell guide to Ireland **2700**
Kim Donguk
History of Korean literature **2520**
Kindlers neues Literatur Lexikon **2279**
King, J.W.
Historical dictionary of Egypt **2967**
King, R.C. *and* Stansfield, W.D.
A Dictionary of genetics **1113**
Kirby, N.G.
Baillière's handbook of first aid **1284**

Kirk, R.E. *and* Othmer, D.F.
Encyclopedia of chemical technology
1629
Kirkeby, W.A.
English-Norwegian dictionary **2174**
Kirkpatrick, D.L.
Contemporary dramatists **2324**
Reference guide to American literature
2411
Reference guide to English literature
2355
Kister, K.F.
Best encyclopedias **144**
Kister's atlas buying guide **2686**
Kister's atlas buying guide **2686**
Klain, J.
International television and video
almanac 1990 **2005**
Klein, B.T.
Reference encyclopedia of the
American Indian **455**
Klein, L.S.
Encyclopedia of world literature in the
20th century **2278**
Far Eastern literatures in the 20th
century **2498**
Klinck, C.F.
Literary history of Canada **2399**
Kludas, A.
Great passenger ships of the world
1480
Knappert, J.
Indian mythology **403**
Knight, D.
A Companion to the phyiscal sciences
958
Knizhnaia letopis **58**
Knötel, H. *and* Sieg, H.
Uniforms of the world **709**
Knötel, R.
Uniforms of the world **709**
Knowles, A.S.
The International encyclopedia of
higher education **770**
Knowles, D.
Bare ruined choirs ... **375**
The Religious orders in England **375**
Kobbé's complete opera book **1951**
Kodansha encyclopedia of Japan **2604**
Koegler, H.
The Concise Oxford dictionary of
ballet **2055**
Kohls, S.
Dictionary of international economics
521
Koine, Y.
Kenkyusha's New English-Japanese
dictionary **2259**
Kolin, P.C.
American playwrights since 1945 **2415**
Kom, A.
Dictionnaire des oeuvres littéraires
négro-africaines de langue française
2452
Kommission für der Gesamtkatalog der
Wiegendrucke
Gesamtkatalog der Wiegendrucke **287**
Kompass United Kingdom **545**
Konigsberg, I.
The Complete film dictionary **2017**
Konishi, J.
A History of Japanese literature **2518**
A Korean-English dictionary **2261**

Kosch, W.
Deutsches Literatur-Lexikon **2428**
Koschnick, W.J.
Standard dictionary of the social
sciences **435**
Kotnik, J.
Slovensko-angleški slovar **2220**
Koushakdjian, M. *and* Khantrouni, D.
Modern dictionary: English-Armenian/
Armenian-English **2237**
Kovtun, G.J.
Czech and Slovak literature in English
2492
Kramer, L.
The Oxford history of Australian
literature **2421**
Krause, C.L. *and* Mishler, C.
Standard catalog of world coins **1847**
Kroschwitz, J.J.
Concise encyclopedia of polymer
science and engineering **1713**
Kubijovyč, V.
Encyclopedia of Ukraine **2592**
Kučera, A.
The Compact dictionary of exact
science and technology **856**
Kuiper, G.P. *and* Middlehurst, B.M.
The Solar system **927**
Stars and stellar systems **928**
Kunitz, S.J. *and* Haycraft, H.
Twentieth-century authors **2293**
Kurian, G.
Atlas of the Third World **2570**
Kurian, G. *and* Karch, J.
Encyclopedia of the Second World
2572
Kurian, G.T.
The Encyclopedia of the First World
2565
World press encyclopedia **245**
Kutz, M.
Mechanical engineer's handbook **1343**
Kvamme, J.
Index Nordicus **2593**
Kverneland, K.O.
World metric standards for engineering
1328
La Beau, T.
Theatre, film and television
biographies master index **1998**
Lablanc, M.L.
Contemporary musicians **1941**
Lacy, N.C.
The New Arthurian encyclopedia **828**
Laffin, J.
Brassey's battles **710**
Laing, W.
Laing's review of private health care
... and directory of independent
hospitals **740**
Laing's review of private health care ...
and directory of independent hospitals
740
Lamb, E. *and* Lamb, B.
The Illustrated reference on cacti and
other succulents **1524**
Lambert, D. *and* The Diagram Group
Dinosaur data book **1075**
Lambert, M.
Jane's All the world's aircraft **1483**
Lampkin, N.
Organic farming **1508**

Lampugnani, V.M.
Thames and Hudson encyclopedia of twentieth century architecture **1842**

Landau, S.I.
International dictionary of medicine and biology **1098, 1255**

Lane, D. and Lane, C.M.
Modern Irish literature **2393**

Lange, M. and Mora, F.B.
Collins' guide to mushrooms and toadstools **1164**

Lange, N.A.
Lange's handbook of chemistry **986**

Langenscheidt's Condensed Muret-Sanders German dictionary **2165**

Langenscheidt's New Muret-Sanders encyclopedic dictionary of the English and German languages **2165**

Lange's handbook of chemistry **986**

Langman, L.
Encyclopedia of American film comedy **2024**
An Illustrated dictionary of word processing **1583**

Language of ballet **2057**

The Language of psychoanalysis **329**

The Language of sport **2076**

Language teaching **2086**

Lapedes, D.N.
Diccionario de términos cientificos y técnicos **867**

Laplanche, J. and Pontalis, J.-B.
The Language of psychoanalysis **329**

Larousse gran diccionario, español-inglés **2192**

Larousse world mythology **404**

Laser handbook **1367**

Laszlo, E. and Yoo, J.Y.
World encyclopedia of peace **665**

The later court hands in England **2812**

Latham, R.E.
Revised medieval Latin word-list **2202**

Latin American studies **2624**

Latin American writers **2467**

Latin dictionary **2200**

Latin dictionary for schools **2200**

Latin palaeography **2811**

Latourette, K.J.
A History of the expansion of Christianity **367**

Latourette, K.S.
Christianity in a revolutionary age **353**

Latviešu-anglu vārdnica **2225**

Laucka, A.
Anglu-lietuviu kalbu žodynas **2222**

Laughton, M.A. and Say, M.G.
Electrical engineer's reference book **1360**

Law and commercial dictionary in five languages **549**

Law databases, 1988 **634**

Lawrence, E.
Henderson's dictionary of biological terms **1097**

Lawther, G.
Handbook of arts and crafts **1875**

Lax, R. and Smith, F.
The Great song thesaurus **1958**

Layton, C.W.T.
Dictionary of nautical words and terms **1478**

Le Docte, E.
Dictionnaire de termes juridiques en quatre langues ... Legal dictionary in four languages **636**

Lea, P.W.
Printed reference materials **138**

Lean, G.
Atlas of the environment **1460**

Leapman, M.
The Book of London **2888**

Lee, S.M.
International encyclopedia of composites **1332**

Lefebvre, G.
The French Revolution **2907**

Legal Aid Board
Legal aid handbook **648**

Legal aid handbook **648**

Legal terminology of the European Communities **635**

Leigh, R.
Directory of European industrial and trade associations **1715**

Leistner, O.
Internationale Bibliographie der Festschriften von der Anfängen bis 1979 **163**

Leisure services yearbook **1995**

Lemire, M.
Dictionnaire des oeuvres littéraires du Québec **2453**

Lemmon, D.
British theatre yearbook, 1990 **2042**

Lengenfelder, H.
World guide to libraries **113**

Lentner, C.
Geigy scientific tables **1260**

Leo, J.R.
Guide to American poetry explication **2413**

Leonard, D.
Pocket guide to the European Community **658**

Lerner, R.M.
Encyclopedia of adolescence **449**

Lestrange, R.
British monumental brasses **1864**

Lettres françaises de Belgique **2451**

Lever, C.
The Naturalized animals of the British Isles **1180**

Lever, J. and Harris, J.
Illustrated dictionary of architecture 800-1914 **1834**

Levine, R.M.
Historical dictionary of Brazil **2992**

Levy, R.C.
Inventing and patenting sourcebook **1237**

Lewin, E.
Subject catalogue of the Library of the Royal Empire Society **2578**

Lewis, C.T.
Latin dictionary for schools **2200**

Lewis, C.T. and Short, C.
Latin dictionary **2200**

Lewis, P. and Darley, G.
Dictionary of ornament **1811**

Lewis, R.P.W.
Meteorological glossary **1050**

Lewytzkyj, B.
Who's who in the Soviet Union **2743**

Lexique général des termes ferroviaires **1444**

LEXIS **640**

Leydon, M.
Market research: a guide to British Library holdings **625**

Lhéritier, A.
Manuel de bibliographie **137**

Libraries directory **117**

Libraries in the United Kingdom and Republic of Ireland **118**

Library and information science abstracts **94**

Library Association
Library Association yearbook **107**

Library Association. Reference, Special and Information Section
British government publications: an index to chairmen and authors **270**

Library Association yearbook **107**

Library Catalogue **2595**

Library literature **95**

Library of Congress
A Catalog of books represented by Library of Congress printed cards **85**
Index to personal names in the National union catalog of manuscript collections 1959-1984 **285**
The Library of Congress catalog. Books: subjects **89**
National union catalog **86**
National union catalog. Books **87**

The Library of Congress catalog. Books: subjects **89**

Library of Congress Classification **112**

Library of Congress. Office of Subject Cataloging Policy
Library of Congress subject headings **110**

Library of Congress. Special Materials Cataloging Division. Manuscripts Section
National union catalog of manuscript collections **284**

Library of Congress. Subject Cataloging Division. Processing Department
Library of Congress Classification **112**
Library of Congress subject headings **110**

Libros en venta **64**

Libros españoles en venta **57**

Liddell, H.G. and Scott, R.
A Greek-English lexicon ... **2203**

Lide, D.R.
CRC handbook of chemistry and physics **985**

Lietuviškai angliškas žodynas **2223**

The Life of vertebrates **1191**

Life sciences organizations and agencies directory **1103**

Lilley, G.P.
Information sources in agriculture and food science **1490**

Lilly, L.C.R.
Diesel engine reference book **1394**

Lindfors, B.
Black African literature in English **2396**

Linguistics and language behavior abstracts (LLBA) **2098**

The Linguistics encyclopedia **2099**

Linton, D.
The Newspaper press in Britain **243**

Lipinski,, A.
The Directory of jobs and careers abroad 537
Lippy, C.H. and Williams, P.W.
Encyclopedia of the American religious experience 379
Liptzin, S.
A History of Yiddish literature 2431
Lissens, R.F.
Winkler Prins lexicon van de Nederlandse letterkunde 2435
Literary history of Canada 2399
A Literary history of Ireland 2504
A Literary history of Persia 2502
Literary market place 1589
Literary research guide 2356
Literature criticism from 1400 to 1800 2310
Literature guides to Columbus' voyage, 1492 2972
Literature of the Low Countries 2434
A Lithuanian bibliography 2590
Litteraturens historia i Sverige 2441
Litteraturhåndbogen 2442
The Little red book 1602
Les Livres disponibles 55
Lloyd's maritime atlas of world ports and shipping places 1620
Lloyd's nautical year book 1612
Lloyd's ports of the world 1621
Lobies, J.P.
Index bio-bibliographicus notorum hominum 2722
Location register of twentieth century English literary manuscripts and letters 2367
Lock, C.B.M.
Geography and cartography 2645
Modern maps and atlases 947
Lock, D.
Gower handbook of quality management 620
Lock, F. and Lawson, A.
Australian literature: a reference guide 2420
Lodge, K.
Directory of architecture and planning 1817
Directory of services for elderly people in the UK 450
Logan, C.M. and Rice, M.K.
Logan's medical and scientific abbreviations 1242
Logan's medical and scientific abbreviations 1242
London art and artists guide 1790
The London Business School small business bibliography 553
The London encyclopaedia 2889
London: Louise Nicholson's definitive guide 2701
London University. School of Oriental and African Studies
Library Catalogue 2595
Long, K.
The Music of the English church 1957
Longley, D. and Shain, M.
Macmillan dictionary of information technology 4
The Longman companion to the French Revolution 2908

The Longman companion to Victorian fiction 2384
Longman dictionary of business English 603
Longman dictionary of contemporary English 2142
Longman dictionary of geography, human and physical 1035
Longman dictionary of poetic terms 2321
Longman dictionary of the English language 2150
The Longman encyclopedia 153
The Longman guide to English usage 2126
Longman Guide to world science and technology 835
The Longman handbook of modern European History 1763-1991 2843
The Longman handbook of world history since 1914 2806
Longman history of Italy 2910
Longman pronunciation dictionary 2143
Lorch, W.
Handbook of water purification 1462
Lord, M.P.
Macmillan dictionary of physics 962
Loudon, N. and Newton, J.
Handbook of family planning 745
The Low Countries History Yearbook 2928
Low, D.A. and Smith, A.
History of East Africa 2969
Lowe, L.
Directory of popular music 1900-1980 1963
Lucie-Smith, E.
Dictionary of art terms 1773
Luck, J.M.
A History of Switzerland 2930
Lum, A.
'Palaeontology' 1065
Lurker, M.
Dictionary of gods and goddesses, devils and demons 407
Lusis, A.
Astronomy and aeronautics 913
Lyle official arts review, 1991 1889
Lynch, C.T.
CRC handbook of materials science 1334
Lynch, D.B.
Concise dictionary of computing 1726
Lynch, J.
A History of Spain 2914
Lyon, C. and Vinson, J.
International dictionary of films and filmmakers 2014
Lyon, E.
Online medical databases 1244
McCabe, J.P.
Critical guide to Catholic reference books 384
McCance, R.A. and Widdowson, E.M.
The Composition of foods 1272, 1656
McCauley, M.
The German Democratic Republic since 1945 2898
Macchi, V.
The Collins Sansoni Italian dictionary 2186
Sansoni-Harrap standard Italian and English dictionary 2190

McClintock, D.
Supplement to 'The pocket guide to wild flowers' 1153
McClintock, D. and Fitter, R.S.R.
The pocket guide to wild flowers 1152
McConnell, P.
Primrose McConnell's 'The agricultural notebook' 1492
McCulloch, A.
Encyclopaedia of Australian art 1802
McDonagh, D.
The Complete guide to modern dance 2063
MacDonald, B.
Broadcasting in the United Kingdom 2002
Macdonald, D.
The Encyclopedia of mammals 1207
The Macdonald encyclopedia of fossils 1066
The Macdonald encyclopedia of shells 1182
MacDonnell, A.A.
A Practical Sanskrit dictionary 2226
McFarland, G.B
Thai-English Dictionary 2257
McGillivray, D.
British alternative theatre directory, 1990/91 2040
McGraw-Hill dictionary of scientific and technical terms 847
McGraw-Hill encyclopedia of electronics and computers 1371
McGraw-Hill encyclopedia of environmental science 1107
McGraw-Hill encyclopedia of science and technology 845
McGraw-Hill encyclopedia of world biography 2714
McGraw-Hill encyclopedia of world drama 2328
McGraw-Hill handbook of essential engineering information and data 1327
McGraw-Hill yearbook of science and technology 881
Machinery's handbook 1344
Machlin, L.J.
Handbook of vitamins 1118
McHugh, F.P.
Keyguide to information sources in business ethics 332
McIlwaine, I.C.
Herculaneum: a guide to printed sources 2556
McInairnie, E.
The Geologist's directory 1022
McIntyre, J.E.
Moncrieff's Man-made fibres 1705
Mackay, J.
The Dictionary of Western sculptors in bronze 1865
Mackenzie, I.
British prints 1906
McKeown, R.
National directory of slide collections 261
Mackerras, C.
Modern China 2945
Mackie, T.T. and Rose, R.
The International almanac of electoral history 498

McLauchlan, G.
The Illustrated encyclopedia of New Zealand 2633
McLeish, K.
Bloomsbury good reading guide 2337
Macleod, I.
The Scots thesaurus 2134
Maclysaght, E.
The Surnames of Ireland 2113
McManners, J.
The Oxford illustrated history of Christianity 372
The Macmillan & Silk Cut nautical almanac 1616
The Macmillan companion to Scottish literature 2390
Macmillan concise dictionary of world history 2802
The Macmillan dictionary of archaeology 2532
The Macmillan dictionary of astronomy 919
Macmillan dictionary of information technology 4
The Macmillan dictionary of Irish literature 2392
The Macmillan dictionary of Italian literature 2457
Macmillan dictionary of marketing and advertising 624
The Macmillan dictionary of modern economics 522
Macmillan dictionary of physics 962
Macmillan dictionary of psychology 327
Macmillan dictionary of religion 343
The Macmillan dictionary of sports and games 2067
Macmillan dictionary of the environment 1106
The Macmillan dictionary of women's biography 2724
Macmillan directory of business information sources 546
Macmillan directory of multinationals 552
The Macmillan family encyclopedia 147
The Macmillan guide to British nature reserves 1131
Macmillan guide to modern world literature 2280
Macmillan student encyclopedia of sociology 445
Macmillan's unquoted companies, 1992 551
McNeil, B. and Unterburger, A.L.
Abridged biography and genealogy master index 2763
McNeil, R.A.
Latin American studies 2624
McNeill, F.M.
The Silver bough 795
McNeill, I.
An Encyclopedia of the history of technology 1226
Macquarrie, J. and Childers, J.F.
A New dictionary of Christian ethics 361
MacQuoid, P. and Edwards, R.
The Dictionary of English furniture 1886
MacSween, A. and Sharp, M.
Prehistoric Scotland 2550

McVey, J.P.
CRC handbook of mariculture 1542
Maddox, G.L.
The Encyclopedia of aging 451
Magalini, S.I.
Dictionary of medical syndromes 1301
Magay, T. and Országh, L.
A Concise Hungarian-English dictionary 2249
Magazine index 211
Magazines for libraries 186
Magill, F.N.
Cyclopedia of literary characters 2317
Masterplots II: American fiction series 2418
Masterplots II: British and Commonwealth fiction series 2383
Masterplots II: drama series 2329
Magill, F.N. and Kohler, D.
Cyclopedia of world authors 2291
Magill, F.N. and McGreal, I.P.
World philosophy 297
Magnusson, M. and Goring, R.
Chambers biographical dictionary 2709
Mainiero, L.
American women writers: a critical reference guide 2412
Maizell, R.E.
How to find chemical information 978
Maizlish, A. and Hunt, W.S.
The World map directory, 1989 948
Major 20th-century writers 2292
Major chemical and petrochemical companies of Europe, 1991-1992 1637
Major companies of Europe, 1991/92 591
The Major international treaties, 1914-1945 660
The Major international treaties since 1945 661
The Major languages of East and South-East Asia 2091
The Major languages of Eastern Europe 2091
The Major languages of South Asia, the Middle East and Africa 2091
The Major languages of Western Europe 2091
Major legal systems of the world today 649
The Making of books 1577
Malclès, L-N.
Manuel de bibliographie 137
Malinowsky, H.R. and Perry, G.J.
AIDS information sourcebook 1316
Mallalieu, H.L.
Dictionary of British watercolour artists 1896
Malmkjaer, K.
The Linguistics encyclopedia 2099
Malmqvist, N.G.D.
A Selective guide to Chinese literature, 1900-1949 2517
Maltin, L.
TV movies and video guide, 1992 2010
Mammal species of the world 1208
Mammalian paleofaunas of the world 1076

The Mammals of Britain and Europe 1211
Management guide to office automation 606
Mandell, G.L.
Principles and practice of infectious diseases 1315
Mann, M. 445
Mann, T.
A Guide to library research methods 2
Man's conquest of the Pacific 2534
Manser, M.H.
Dictionary of eponyms 2115
Mansion, J.E.
Harrap's New standard French and English dictionary 2182
Manson-Bahrs, P.E.C.
Manson's tropical diseases 1299
Manson's tropical diseases 1299
Manual de bibliografía de la literatura española 2463
Manual of British Standards on building construction and specification 1758
Manual of firemanship 1282
Manual of map reading and land navigation 946
Manual of online search strategies 8
Manual of photogrammetry 942
Manual of procedure in the public business 673
Manual of remote sensing 1014
A Manual of the writings in Middle English, 1050-1500 2370
Manuel de bibliographie 137
Manuel du transport routier international 1601
The Manuscript catalogue of the library .. 2580
Map of the New Europe wallchart 2659
Maps and map-makers 951
Mara, T.
Language of ballet 2057
Marcan, P.
Arts address book 1793
Marchant, P.
Online patents and trademarks databases 1235
Marcus, G.J.
A Naval history of England 725
Marcuse, M.J.
A Reference guide for English studies 2357
Marie, S. and Piggott, J.R.
Handbook of sweeteners 1657
The Marine encyclopaedic dictionary 1611
Marine technology reference book 1449
A Mariner's guide to the rules of the road 1617
Mark, H.F.
Encyclopedia of polymer science and engineering 1712
Market research: a guide to British Library holdings 625
Markets yearbook 626
Marks and monograms on European and Oriental pottery and porcelain 1856
Marsh, J.H.
The Canadian encyclopaedia 2621
The Marshall Cavendish illustrated encyclopedia of gardening 1521

Marshall, J.G. *and* **Trahair, R.C.S.**
Occupational index to the Australian
Dictionary of Biography (1788-1890)
Volumes 1-6 **2767**
Marshall, W.
Nuclear power technology **1353**
Martin, G.H. *and* **Spufford, P.**
The Records of the nation **2865**
Martin, S.E.
A Korean-English dictionary **2261**
Martin, W. *and* **Tops, G.A.J.**
Van Dale. Groot woordenboek Engels-
Nederlands **2169**
Van Dale. Groot woordenboek
Nederlands-Engels **2170**
Martínez, J.A.
Dictionary of twentieth-century Cuban
literature **2470**
Martinez, N.C. *and* **Martinez, J.G.R.**
Guide to British poetry explication
2372
Marting, D.E.
Spanish American women writers
2469
Women writers of Spanish America
2469
MASA: medical acronyms, symbols and
abbreviations **1243**
Mason, D.
Who's who in World War II **2853**
Mason, T.
Sport in Britain **2080**
Masoro, E.J.
CRC handbook of physiology in aging
1300
Mass media bibliography **240**
Master atlas of Greater London **2670**
Master catalogue **1986**
Master handbook of electronic tables and
formulas **1378**
Masterplots cyclopedia of literary
characters **2317**
Masterplots II: American fiction series
2418
Masterplots II: British and
Commonwealth fiction series **2383**
Masterplots II: drama series **2329**
Masuda, K.
Kenkyusha's New Japanese-English
dictionary **2260**
Matejic, M.
A Biobibliographical handbook of
Bulgarian authors **2494**
Materials data sources **1335**
Mathematical reviews **906**
Mathematical Society of Japan
Encyclopedic dictionary of
mathematics **902**
Mathews, M.M.
Americanisms **2138**
A Dictionary of Americanisms on
historical principles **2138**
Mathfile **900**
Matthew, D.
Atlas of medieval Europe **2838**
Matthews, N. *and* **Wainwright, M.D.**
A Guide to manuscripts and
documents in the British Isles relating
to the Middle East and North Africa
2606

Matthews, P. *and* **Morrison, I.**
The Guinness encyclopedia of
international sports records and
results **2078**
Matthews, W.
British autobiographies **2733**
Mattison, C.
Snakes of the world **1196**
Maxted, I.
British national directories 1781-1819
2884
Mayer, R.
Artist's handbook of materials and
techniques **1772**
Mayhew, A.L.
A Concise dictionary of Middle
English **2124**
Mays, J.L.
Harper's Bible commentary **349**
Mazda, F.
Electronic engineer's reference book
1374
Mead, W.R.
An Historical geography of
Scandinavia **2652**
Mechanical design and systems handbook
1415
Mechanical engineer's data book **1341**
Mechanical engineer's handbook **1343**
Medals year book 1989 **1850**
Medical acronyms, symbols and
abbreviations **1243**
The Medical directory, 1991 **1258**
**Medical, Health and Welfare Libraries
Group of the Library Association**
Directory of medical and health care
libraries in the United Kingdom and
Republic of Ireland, 1990 **743**
Medical quotes: a thematic dictionary
1259
Medical reference works, 1679-1966
1247
Medical research centres **1265**
Medical sciences international who's who
1263
Medieval monasticism **374**
MEDLINE [Medical Analysis and
Retrieval Service On-Line] **1245**
Meenan, A.
Directory of natural history and
related societies in Britain and
Ireland **1126**
Meggs, P.
A History of graphic design **1905**
Meijer, R.P.
Literature of the Low Countries **2434**
Melton, J.G.
Encyclopedia of American religions
338-339
Encyclopedic handbook of cults in
America **398**
Mercer, D.
Chronicle of the 20th century **2833**
The Merck index **1645**
The Merck veterinary manual **1529**
METADEX database **1678**
Metals abstracts **1682**
Metals handbook **1680-1681**
Meteorological and geoastrophysical
abstracts **1051**
Meteorological glossary **1050**
Metford, J.C.J.
The Christian year **357**

Metherell, D. *and* **Guthrie, P.**
Scandinavian biographical archive
2745
Metzger, L.
Black writers **2300**
Mexican literature **2471**
Meyer, J.A.
An Annotated bibliography of the
Napoleonic era **2844**
Meyer, M.C. *and* **Sherman, W.L.**
The Course of Mexican history **2977**
Meyers, R.
Encyclopedia of modern physics **959**
Meyers, R.A.
Encyclopedia of astronomy and
astrophysics **914**
Handbook of chemical production
processes **1640**
Handbook of petroleum refining
processes **1668**
Meyers, R.A.M.
Encyclopedia of physical sciences and
technology **844**
Meynen, E.
International geographical glossary
1034
MHRA style book **2302**
Michelin green tourist guides **2695**
Michelin green tourist guides France
2703
Microcomputer applications handbook
1730
Microcomputer index **1733**
Micrographics and optical recording
buyer's guide **1914**
Microprocessor data book **1734**
Microwave handbook **1366**
The Middle East and North Africa 1992
2605
A Middle English dictionary **2124**
Mihailovich, V.D.
Modern Slavic literatures **2484**
Mihailovich, V.D. *and* **Matejic, M.**
A Comprehensive bibliography of
Yugoslav literature in English, 1593-
1980 **2493**
Miles, D.
British sign language **2094**
The Military balance, 1991-92 **704**
Millard, P.
Trade associations and professional
bodies **587**
Miller, C. *and* **Swift, K.**
The Handbook of non-sexist writing
2127
Miller, D.
The Blackwell encyclopaedia of
political thought **493**
Miller, J. *and* **Miller, M.**
Miller's antique price guide **1814**
Miller, J.C.
Slavery **500**
Miller's antique price guide **1814**
Millodot, M.
Dictionary of optometry **1319**
Mills, A.D.
A Dictionary of English place-names
2106
Mills, D. *and* **Vevers, G.**
The Practical encyclopedia of
freshwater tropical aquarium fishes
1545

Milne, T.
Time Out film guide **2018**
Milosz, C.
The History of Polish literature **2491**
Milton, R.
The English ceremonial book **800**
Miner, E.
A History of Japanese literature **2518**
The Princeton companion to classical Japanese literature **2519**
Mineral deposits of Europe **1061**
Mineralogical abstracts **1000**
Mining and mineral industries **1422**
The Mining directory, mines and mining equipment companies worldwide **1421**
Minorities Rights Group
World directory of minorities **495**
Mir, M.
Dictionary of Qur'ānic terms and concepts **422**
Miskin, C.
Directory of law libraries in the British Isles **647**
MIT dictionary of modern economics
The Macmillan dictionary of modern economics **522**
Mitchell, B. and Reeds, B.
Standard catalogue of British coins **1849**
Mitchell, B.R.
British historical statistics **470**
Mitchell, P.M.
A History of Danish literature **2443**
Mitchell, S.
Victorian Britain **2870**
Mitchell's Building series **1757**
Mitler, L.
Contemporary Turkish writers **2511**
Mitzel, H.E.
Encyclopedia of educational research **761**
MLA international bibliography **2084**
Modern Arabic literature **2510**
Modern Austria **2899**
Modern breeds of livestock **1530**
Modern business correspondence **607**
Modern Catholic dictionary **383**
Modern China **2945**
Modern Chinese-English technical and general dictionary **873**
Modern dictionary: English-Armenian/Armenian-English **2237**
Modern English biography **2736**
Modern geography: an encyclopedic survey **2646**
Modern Hebrew-English dictionary **2243**
The Modern history of Mongolia **2947**
Modern Indonesian literature **2527**
Modern Irish literature **2393**
Modern Italian history **2911**
Modern Language Association of America
MLA international bibliography **2084**
Modern Language Association of America. Middle English Group
A Manual of the writings in Middle English, 1050-1500 **2370**
Modern maps and atlases **947**
Modern Norwegian literature **2438**
Modern proverbs and proverbial sayings **834**
The Modern Russian dictionary for English speakers **2210**
Modern Slavic literatures **2484**

Modern Spanish and Portuguese literatures **2460**
The Modern theologians **354**
Mohr, B.
Higher education in the European Community **771**
Moir, M.
A General guide to the India Office Records **2941**
Molas, J.
Història de la literatura catalana **2455**
Moncrieff's Man-made fibres **1705**
Money, S.A.
Microprocessor data book **1734**
Newnes microprocessor pocket book **1731**
Montague-Smith, P.
Debrett's correct form **805**
Montgomery, A.C.
Acronyms and abbreviations in library and information work **93**
Monthly catalog of United States government publications **280**
Moody, M.
Property information source book, 1989 **542**
Moody, T.W.
A Chronology of Irish history to 1976 **2877**
A New history of Ireland **2875**
Moore, A.
Ballroom dancing **2062**
Moore, B.E. and Fine, B.D.
Psychoanalytic terms and concepts **326**
Moore, P.
The Astronomy encyclopaedia **915**
Moore, R.C.
Treatise on invertebrate paleontology **1073**
Móra, I.
Publisher's practical dictionary in 20 languages **1591**
Morford, M.P.O. and Lenardon, R.J.
Classical mythology **409**
Morgan, A.L. and Naylor, C.
Contemporary designers **1809**
Morgan, N.
Marine technology reference book **1449**
Morgan, T.J.
Welsh surnames **2113**
Morgan, W.L. and Gordon, G.D.
Communications satellite handbook **1388**
Morgano, M.
How to start and run your own business **554**
Morris, B.
The European Community **657**
Morris, P. and Weston, G.
Directory of translators and translating agencies in the United Kingdom **2092**
Morris, R.B.
Encyclopedia of American history **2986**
Morrison, D.G.
Black Africa **2617**
Mort, D.
The Counties and regions of the United Kingdom **579**

Mort, D. *(contd.)*
Sources of unofficial UK statistics **471**
Morton, L.T.
Morton's medical bibliography **1261**
Morton, L.T. and Godbolt, S.
Information sources in the medical sciences **1250**
Morton, L.T. and Moore, R.J.
A Bibliography of medical and biomedical biography **1264**
Morton, L.T. and Wright, D.J.
How to use a medical library **1249**
Morton's medical bibliography **1261**
Mosby's medical, nursing, and allied health dictionary **1304**
Moser, C.A.
The Cambridge history of Russian literature **2486**
Mossman, J.
Holidays and anniversaries of the world **799**
Pseudonyms and nicknames dictionary **34**
The Moths and butterflies of Great Britain and Ireland **1190**
Motif-index of folk-literature **821**
Motion picture guide **2015-2016**
Motorcycles in magazines, 1895-1983 **1476**
Mozley & Whiteley's law dictionary **638**
Muirden, J.
Amateur astronomer's handbook **917**
Observational astronomy for amateurs **918**
Muller, P.M. and Lamparsky, A.
Perfumes **1660**
The Multilingual business handbook **609**
Multilingual dictionary of commercial international trade and shipping terms **588**
A Multilingual glossary of cargo handling terms **1452**
The Municipal year book and public service directory **693**
Munn, G. G.
Encyclopedia of banking and finance **558**
Munro, D. and Day, A.J.
A World record of major conflict areas **496**
Murdoch, J.B.
Illumination engineering **1469**
Murdock, G.P.
Atlas of world cultures **1085**
Outline of cultural materials **1086**
Outline of world cultures **1087**
Murray, P. and Murray, L.
The Penguin dictionary of art and artists **1769**
Museums yearbook **237**
Musgrave, J.
A History of architecture **1830**
Mushrooms and other fungi of Great Britain and Europe **1165**
Music in British libraries **1944**
Music index **1920**
Music librarianship **1942**
Music Master
Master catalogue **1986**
The Music of the English church **1957**
Music reference and research materials **1919**

Musical instruments 1981
Musical terms, symbols and theory 1917
Myers, Allen C.
The Eerdmans Bible dictionary 348
Myers, J. and Simms, M.
Longman dictionary of poetic terms 2321
Mythical and fabulous creatures 405
Mythology of all races 401
Names and nicknames of places and things 2101
Napier, J.R. and Napier, P.H.
A Handbook of the living primates 1214
Nash, J. and Ross, S.R.
Motion picture guide 2015-2016
Nash, J. R.
Encyclopaedia of world crime 679
Nass, L.I. and Heiberger, C.
Encyclopedia of PVC 1714
National anthems of the world 1967
National Association of Health Authorities and Trusts
The NHS handbook 741
National atlas of Canada 2677
National atlas of India 2675
The National atlas of Japan 2673
The National atlas of the United States 2679
National Centre for Christian Communities and Networks
Directory of Christian groups, communities and networks 368
National directory of slide collections 261
National Federation of Consumer Groups
A Handbook of consumer law 1560
'National Geographic' Atlas of the world 2681
National Index of parish registers 2782
The National inventory of documentary sources in the United Kingdom and Ireland 2866
National newspaper index 252
National parks and reserves of Western Europe 1820
National union catalog 86
National union catalog. Books 87
National union catalog of manuscript collections 284
National union catalog, pre-1956 imprints 88
Nationalist era in China 1927-1949
The Cambridge history of China 2943
Natural history book reviews 1125
The Natural history of Britain and Northern Europe 1127
The Naturalized animals of the British Isles 1180
Naumann, St. E.
Dictionary of Asian philosophies 308
The Nautical almanac 938
Naval and maritime history 724
A Naval history of England 725
The Naval Institute guide to world naval weapons systems 1431
The Navy list 720
Nayler, G.H.F.
Dictionary of mechanical engineering 1345
Naylor, C.
Contemporary artists 1803

Nebenzahl, K.
Atlas of Columbus and the great discoveries 2640
The Needleworker's dictionary 1571
The Negro almanac 456
Nelson, B.R.
A Guide to published library catalogs 90
Nelson, J.
Fishes of the world 1192
Nelson, P.M.
Transportation noise reference book 1467
Nettleship, H. and Sandys, J.E.
A Dictionary of Classical antiquities 2548
Neue deutsche Biographie 2738
Neufeldt, V. and Guralnik, D.B.
Webster's new world dictionary of American English 2139
New African Yearbook 1991-92 2616
The New Arthurian encyclopedia 828
New, A.S.B.
A Guide to the cathedrals of Britain 1844
The New astronomy 933
The New Cambridge bibliography of English literature 2350
The New Cambridge history of India 2953
The New Cambridge modern history 2828
The New Cambridge modern history. v.14. The Atlas 2831
The New catering repertoire 1546
New Catholic encyclopedia 385
A New Chinese-English dictionary 2255
A New critical history of Old English literature 2369
New dictionary of American family names 2114
New dictionary of American slang 2129
A New dictionary of Christian ethics 361
A New dictionary of liturgy and worship 365
A New dictionary of scientific and technical terms, English-Arabic, with illustrations 871
New earnings survey 535
The New Encyclopaedia Britannica 148
The New encyclopedia of motorcars 1473
A New English-Chinese dictionary 2255
New English-Russian dictionary 2207
The New Everyman dictionary of music 1921
New Grove dictionary of jazz 1973
New Grove dictionary of music and musicians 1923
New Grove dictionary of musical instruments 1982
The New guide to graphic design 1903
The New guide to illustration 1908
The New guide to modern world literature 2280
New Harvard dictionary of music 1924
A New history of French literature 2449
A New history of Ireland 2875
The New history of Scotland 2872
The New international atlas 2682
New Larousse gastronomique 1563

New literature on old age 452
The New Macmillan guide to family health 1270
New ophthalmic literature 1320
The New organic food guide 1653
The New Oxford companion to music 1925
The New Oxford history of music 1934
The New Palgrave: a dictionary of economics 518
The New Pelican guide to English literature 2361
The New Persian-English dictionary 2231
New Pocket Rumanian dictionary 2191
A New reader's guide to African literature 2525
New rock records 1993
The New Royal Horticultural Society dictionary of gardening 1522
New serial titles 190
New serial titles: 1950-1970 191
The New solar system 926
New technical books 876
New Westminster dictionary of liturgy and worship 365
New, W.H.
Literary history of Canada 2399
New Zealand books in print 77
New Zealand official yearbook 1990 2634
Newhall, B.
History of photography 1912
Newman, A.C.D.
The Chemistry of clays and clay minerals 1673
Newman, H.
An Illustrated dictionary of glass 1881
An Illustrated dictionary of silverware 1859
Newman, H. and Robertson, R.
An Illustrated history of jewellery 1862
Newman, P.R.
Companion to Irish history 1603-1921 2876
Newman, R.M.
An English-Hausa dictionary 2269
Newnes computer engineer's pocket book 1724
Newnes engineering materials pocket book 1333
Newnes microprocessor pocket book 1731
The Newspaper press in Britain 243
Newspapers: a reference guide 244
Newsworthies 2715
Newton, D.C.
Trade names 1230
Nguyên-Dinh-Hòa
Essential English-Vietnamese dictionary 2264
Vietnamese-English student dictionary 2265
The NHS handbook 741
Nicholas, R. and Nicholas, D.
Virology: an information profile 1119
Nicholls, D. and Marsh, P.
Biographical dictionary of modern European radicals and socialists 514
Nicholson, L.
London: Louise Nicholson's definitive guide 2701

Nicoll, A.
A History of English drama, 1660-1900 **2376**
Nielsen, B.K.
Engelsk-dansk ordbog **2178**
Nienhauser, W.H.
The Indiana companion to traditional Chinese literature **2516**
Nineteenth-century literary criticism **2310**
Nineteenth century short title catalogue **44**
Nirk, R.
Estonian literature: historical survey **2515**
Nix, J. and Hill, P.
Farm management pocketbook **1509**
Nobel Prize winners **2723**
Noel, J.V.
The VNR dictionary of ships and the sea **1479**
Noltingk, B.E.
Jones' Instrument technology **1720**
Noltingk, D.E.
Instrumentation reference book **1364**
Nontraditional manufacturing processes **1403**
Nordstrom, B.J.
Dictionary of Scandinavian history **2927**
Norges litteratur **2439**
Norkett, P.
The Building societies facts file **569**
Norman, J.
The Complete book of spices **1567**
Norman, J.M.
Morton's medical bibliography **1261**
Norsk-engelsk teknisk ordbok **858**
Norton, A.P.
Norton's 2000.0 **934**
Norton's 2000.0 **934**
Norwegian-English dictionary **2173**
Norwich, J.J.
The Oxford illustrated encyclopaedia of the arts **1770**
Notes **1929**
Novo dicionário da língua portuguesa **2197**
Novo Michaelis dicionário ilustrado **2198**
Nowak, R.M. and Paradiso, J.L.
Walker's mammals of the world **1210**
Nuclear data sheets **1351**
Nuclear energy and the nuclear industry **1348**
Nuclear engineering databases, standards and numerical analysis **1349**
Nuclear power technology **1353**
Il Nuovo dizionario Hazon Garzanti **2189**
Il Nuovo Ragazzini **2188**
Nursing bibliography **1306**
Nutrition and health encyclopedia **1273**
Ó' Dónaill, N.
Foclóir Gaeilge-Béarla **2234**
O Súilleabháin, S.
A Handbook of Irish folklore **825**
Oberg, E.
Machinery's handbook **1344**
Obin, A.
Bibliography of nautical books, 1991 **721**

O'Brien, P. and Fabiano, E.
Core list of books & journals in education **755**
O'Brien, R. and Chafetz, M.
The Encyclopedia of alcoholism **1276**
Observational astronomy for amateurs **918**
Occupational index to the Australian Dictionary of Biography (1788-1890) Volumes 1-6 **2767**
Occupations, 92 **538**
Oceanic mythology **429**
Ochs, M.
Notes **1929**
Ocran, E.B.
Ocran's acronyms **837**
Ocran's acronyms **837**
O'Donnell, M.M.
Contemporary theatre, film and television **1997**
OECD economic surveys **573**
Official gazette of the United States Patent and Trademark Office: Patents **1238**
Official journal (patents) **1239**
The Official museum directory **238**
Official publications in Britain **272**
Official publications of Western Europe **269**
Offshore engineering abstracts **1424, 1667**
Ogilvie, M.B.
Women in science **891**
Oglesby, C.H. and Hicks, R.G.
Highway engineering **1448**
Oil and gas dictionary **1663**
Oil and gas international year book **1666**
Oil economists' handbook **1662**
Oilfields of the world **1425**
O'Kelly, M.J.
Early Ireland **2545**
Old English porcelain **1858**
Old Norse-Icelandic literature **2437**
Old pewter **1866**
O'Leary, T.J. and Levinson, D.
Encyclopedia of world cultures **1083**
Oliveira Marques, A.H. de
History of Portugal **2917**
Oliver, P.
Blackwell guide to blues records **1992**
Oliver, R. and Crowder, M.
The Cambridge encyclopedia of Africa **2614**
Oliver, W.H. and Williams, B.R.
Oxford history of New Zealand **2997**
Geologic time scale 1989 **1055**
Olsson, B. and Algulin, I.
Litteraturens historia i Sverige **2441**
The Olympic book of sports medicine **1274**
The Olympic Games **2082**
Omer-Cooper, J.D.
History of Southern Africa **2970**
Onions, C.T.
The Oxford dictionary of English etymology **2162**
Online bibliographic databases **839**
Online databases in the medical and life sciences **1246**
Online medical databases **1244**
Online patents and trademarks databases **1235**

Open learning directory, 1989 **767**
Ophthalmic literature **1320**
Opie, I. and Tatem, M.
A Dictionary of superstitions **829**
Opitz, H. and Strasser, K.-H.
Publishers' international ISBN directory **1592**
Oral history **2832**
Orders, medals and decorations of Britain and Europe in colour **2792**
Ordnance Survey complete guide to the battlefields of Britain **711**
The Ordnance Survey gazetteer of Great Britain **2698**
Organic farming **1508**
Organisation for Economic Co-operation and Development
OECD economic surveys **573**
Oriental economist's new Japanese-English dictionary of economic terms **523**
The Origins of modern humans **1116**
Ormond, R. and Rogers, M.
Dictionary of British portraiture **1899**
Országh, L.
A Concise English-Hungarian dictionary **2250**
Osborne, H.
The Oxford companion to twentieth century art **1810**
Osbourne, C.
International yearbook of educational and training technology, 1991 **762**
Osmánczyk, E.J.
The Encyclopaedia of the United Nations and international agreements **653**
O'Toole, G.I.A.
The Encyclopedia of American intelligence and espionage **508**
Ottley, G.
A Bibliography of British railway history **1604**
Ousby, I.
Blue guide: literary Britain and Ireland **2359**
The Cambridge guide to literature in English **2353**
Outline of cultural materials **1086**
An Outline of European architecture **1831**
Outline of world cultures **1087**
Owen, M.
The Cook's encyclopedia **1564**
Owen, T.M.
Welsh folk customs **826**
The Oxford advanced learner's dictionary of current English **2141**
The Oxford advanced learner's English-Chinese dictionary **2254**
The Oxford book of sea songs **1960**
Oxford children's encyclopedia **156**
The Oxford companion to American literature **2410**
The Oxford companion to American theatre **2045**
The Oxford companion to Australian literature **2422**
The Oxford companion to Canadian history and literature **2975**
The Oxford companion to Canadian literature **2400**

The Oxford companion to Canadian theatre **2044**

The Oxford companion to chess **2071**

The Oxford companion to children's literature **123**

The Oxford companion to classical literature **2480**

The Oxford companion to English literature **2354**

The Oxford companion to French literature **2450**

The Oxford companion to gardens **1821**

The Oxford companion to German literature **2426**

The Oxford companion to law **633**

The Oxford companion to popular music **1962, 1978**

The Oxford companion to ships and the sea **1610**

The Oxford companion to Spanish literature **2462**

The Oxford companion to sports and games **2068**

The Oxford companion to the literature of Wales **2394**

The Oxford companion to the theatre **2034**

The Oxford companion to twentieth century art **1810**

The Oxford dictionary for writers and editors **2303**

The Oxford dictionary of art **1768**

The Oxford dictionary of Byzantium **2956**

Oxford dictionary of current idiomatic English **2159**

The Oxford dictionary of English Christian names **2111**

The Oxford dictionary of English etymology **2162**

The Oxford dictionary of modern Greek **2205**

The Oxford dictionary of modern quotations **2285**

The Oxford dictionary of music **1922**

The Oxford dictionary of natural history **1124**

The Oxford dictionary of new words **2156**

The Oxford dictionary of Popes **387**

The Oxford dictionary of quotations **2286**

The Oxford dictionary of saints **358**

The Oxford dictionary of the Christian Church **363**

Oxford-Duden German dictionary **2166**

Oxford economic atlas of the world **575**

The Oxford encyclopedia of trees of the world **1507**

The Oxford encyclopedic English dictionary **2151**

The Oxford English-Arabic dictionary of current usage **2245**

The Oxford English dictionary **2145**

The Oxford English-Russian dictionary **2209**

The Oxford English-Turkish dictionary **2247**

The Oxford Greek-English learner's dictionary **2206**

The Oxford guide to card games **2072**

The Oxford history of Australia **2999**

The Oxford history of Australian literature **2421**

The Oxford history of England **2858**

The Oxford history of English literature **2362**

The Oxford history of Hungarian literature **2512**

Oxford history of New Zealand **2997**

The Oxford history of New Zealand literature in English **2419**

Oxford history of the Christian Church **371**

Oxford history of the classical world **2820**

The Oxford illustrated encyclopaedia of the arts **1770**

The Oxford illustrated history of Christianity **372**

The Oxford illustrated literary guide to Great Britain and Ireland **2360**

Oxford Latin dictionary **2201**

The Oxford Russian-English dictionary **2208**

Oxford textbook of public health **1279**

The Oxford thesaurus **2154**

The Oxford Turkish-English dictionary **2248**

The Oxford writers' dictionary **2303**

Pacey, P.
  Art library manual **1804**

Pacific Islands Yearbook **2631**

The Pacific since Magellan **2995**

Page, G.T. *and* Thomas, J.B.
  International dictionary of education **758**

The Painters of Ireland **1893**

PAIS bulletin **431**

Pakistan year book 1989-90 **2609**

The Palaeolithic settlement of Europe **2539**

'Palaeontology' **1065**

Palgrave, R.H.I.
  The New Palgrave: a dictionary of economics **518**

Palmer, J.
  Jane's dictionary of naval terms **722**

Palmer, R.
  The Oxford book of sea songs **1960**

Pamlényi, E.
  A History of Hungary **2902**

The Pan dictionary of physics **961**

Pan-European associations **219**

Panovf, I.
  New Pocket Rumanian dictionary **2191**

Pantzer, K.F.
  A Short-title catalogue of books printed in England, Scotland and Ireland: and of English books printed abroad 1475-1640 **40**

Papageorgiou, M.
  Concise encyclopedia of traffic and transportation systems **1596**

Paper and board abstracts **1698**

Papua New Guinea handbook : Business and travel guide **2707**

Parise, F.
  The Book of calendars **953**

Parker, C.C. *and* Turley, R.V.
  Information sources in science and technology **841**

Parker, H.W.
  Snakes - a natural history **1197**

Parker, S.P.
  McGraw-Hill dictionary of scientific and technical terms **847**
  McGraw-Hill encyclopedia of electronics and computers **1371**
  McGraw-Hill encyclopedia of environmental science **1107**

Parkinson, G.H.R.
  An Encyclopaedia of philosophy **300**
  The Handbook of Western philosophy **294**

Parlett, D.
  The Oxford guide to card games **2072**
  The Penguin book of word games **2074**

Parliaments of the world **668**

Parmley, R.O.
  Standard handbook of fastening and joining **1691**

Parrinder, E.G.
  A Dictionary of religious and spiritual quotations **344**

Parrinder, G.
  Africa's three religions **428**
  Dictionary of non-Christian religions **399**
  An Illustrated history of the world's religions **400**

Parry, J.
  World ballet and dance 1990-91 **2058**

Parry, R.M. *and* Perkins, C.R.
  World mapping today **945**

Parry, T.
  A History of Welsh literature **2506**

Partnow, E.
  The Quotable woman ... 1800-1981 **815**
  The Quotable woman, from Eve to 1799 **2287**

Partridge, E.
  A Dictionary of catch phrases **2130**
  A Dictionary of slang and unconventional English **2131**

Pascal **877**

Pasley, M.
  Germany **2583**

Past worlds **2533**

Patents in chemistry and biotechnolgy **987**

Patents, trade marks and designs in information work **1240**

Paterson, G.
  The European patent system **1241**

Paterson, L. *and* McCrone, D.
  The Scottish government yearbook, 1992 **687**

Pathak, R.C.
  Bhargava's Standard illustrated dictionary of the Hindi language **2227**

Patrology **376**

Patten, M.N.
  Information sources in metallic materials **1679**

Patterson, D.
  Commercial timbers of the world **1695**

Pauly, A.F. von *and* Wissowa, G.
  Pauly's Real-Encyclopädie der classichen Altertumswissenschaft **2822**

Pauly's Real-Encyclopädie der classichen Altertumswissenschaft **2822**

Paxton, J.
  A Dictionary of the European
    Communities **659**
  The Penguin dictionary of
    abbreviations **20**
  The Penguin dictionary of proper
    names **2102**
  The Stateman's year book world
    gazetteer **2691**
  The Statesman's year-book historical
    companion **2830**
Payne, C.
  Sotheby's concise encyclopaedia of
    furniture **1884**
Payton, G.
  The Penguin dictionary of proper
    names **2102**
PDR **1289**
Pearce, D.W.
  The Macmillan dictionary of modern
    economics **522**
Pearce, E.A. *and* Smith, C.G.
  The World weather guide **1054**
Pearce, J.
  Gardner's Chemical synonyms and
    trade names **1634**
Pearson, B.C.
  Guide to the petroleum reference
    literature **1661**
Pearson, J.D.
  A Guide to manuscripts and
    documents in the British Isles relating
    to South and South-East Asia **2942**
Peiersen, O.
  Norsk-engelsk teknisk ordbok **858**
Pelican history of art **1782**
Pellant, C.
  Rocks, minerals and fossils of the
    world **999**
Pelling, H.
  A History of British trade unionism
    539
Pemsel, H.
  Atlas of naval warfare **723**
The Penguin book of word games **2074**
The Penguin dictionary of abbreviations
  20
The Penguin dictionary of architecture
  1828
The Penguin dictionary of art and artists
  1769
The Penguin dictionary of decorative
  arts **1869**
The Penguin dictionary of design and
  designers **1807**
The Penguin dictionary of musical
  performers **1935**
The Penguin dictionary of proper names
  2102
The Penguin dictionary of religions **342**
The Penguin dictionary of science **851**
The Penguin encyclopaedia of popular
  music **1971**
The Penguin guide to compact discs
  1987
The Penguin guide to compact discs and
  cassettes, Yearbook 1991/92 **1988**
Penney, B.
  Music in British libraries **1944**
People in power **483**
People of today **2728**
Pepper, M.
  Dictionary of religious quotations **345**

Pequeno dicionário Michaelis **2198**
Perfumes **1660**
Periodicos y revistas españolas e
  hispanoamericanos **200**
Perkins, D.
  A History of modern poetry **2373**
Permeggiani, L.
  Encyclopaedia of occupational health
    and safety **1281**
Perry, F.E.
  Dictionary of banking **568**
Perry, R.H. *and* Green, D.W.
  Perry's chemical engineers' handbook
    1633
Perry's chemical engineers' handbook
  1633
Pest and disease control handbook **1514**
The Pesticide manual **1515**
Peteraitis, V.
  Lietuviškai angliškas žodynas **2223**
Peters atlas of the world **2683**
Petersen, D.
  Audio, video and data
    telecommunications **1384**
Peterson, B.L.
  Contemporary Black American
    playwrights and their plays **2417**
  Early Black American playwrights and
    dramatic writers **2417**
Peterson, C.S. *and* Fenton, A.D.
  Index to children's songs: a title, first
    line, and subject index **1966**
Peterson, R.
  A Field guide to the birds of Britain
    and Europe **1202**
Petit Larousse illustré, 1989 **2183**
Petroleum abstracts **1665**
Petroleum engineering handbook **1423**
Pets: every owner's encyclopedia **1534**
Petti, V.
  The Standard Swedish-English/English-
    Swedish dictionary **2175**
Pevsner, N.
  Buildings of England series **1837**
  The Buildings of Ireland **1836**
  The Buildings of Scotland **1835**
  The Buildings of Wales **1839**
  An Outline of European architecture
    1831
The Phaidon companion to art and
  artists in the British Isles **1794**
Phaidon dictionary of twentieth-century
  art **1898**
The Phillimore atlas and index of parish
  registers **2783**
Phillips, B.
  The Complete book of cleaning **1573**
Phillips, C.S.
  The African political dictionary **491**
Phillips International Paper directory,
  1990 **1700**
Phillips, R.
  Mushrooms and other fungi of Great
    Britain and Europe **1165**
The Philosopher's index **295**
Philosophy **293**
Phonetic symbol guide **2117**
Physicians' desk reference **1289**
A Physicist's desk reference **960**
Physics abstracts. Science abstracts.
  Section A **963**
Pick, J.B.
  Atlas of Mexico **2678**

Picken, C.
  The Translator's handbook **894**
Picken, M.B.
  The Fashion dictionary **788**
Pickering, D.
  Brewer's Dictionary of twentieth-
    century phrase and fable **2313**
Pickering, W.R.
  Information sources in pharmaceuticals
    1285
Pictorial dictionary of ancient Athens
  2824
Picture librarianship **1916**
The Picture price guide 1990 **1888**
Picture researcher's handbook **262**
Picture sources UK **263**
Pinchemel, P.
  France **2648**
The Pinyin Chinese-English dictionary
  2256
Pipes, R.
  The Russian Revolution 1899-1919
    2918
PIRA Abstracts **1413**
Place-names of the world **2108**
Placzek, A.K.
  Encyclopedia of architects **1833**
Planhol, X. de
  Géographie historique de la France
    2651
Plano, J.C. *and* Olton, R.
  The International relations dictionary
    503
Plastics materials **1709**
Play index **2330**
Ploski, H.A.
  The Negro almanac **456**
Pneumatic handbook **1395**
Pocket book of British ceramic marks
  1857
Pocket encyclopaedia of cacti in colour
  1524
Pocket guide to the European
  Community **658**
The pocket guide to wild flowers **1152**
Poetry criticism **2322**
Poetry index annual **2414**
Poignant, R.
  Oceanic mythology **429**
Poland, J.M.
  A Guide to the literature of electrical
    and electronics engineering **1355**
Poldauf, I.
  Česko-anglický slovník **2215**
A Political dictionary of the Arab world
  490
Political dictionary of the Arab World
  2937
Political dictionary of the state of Israel
  2959
Political handbook of the world, 1990.
  Annual **484**
Political leaders of the contemporary
  Middle East and North Africa **699**
Political parties of the world **512**
Political quotations **486**
Political science **485**
Political systems of the world **667**
Politis, L.
  A History of modern Greek literature
    2483

Pollard, A.W. and Redgrave, G.R.
  A Short-title catalogue of books printed in England, Scotland and Ireland: and of English books printed abroad 1475-1640 **40**
Pollington, C.E.
  Glossary of terms used in quality control **619**
Pollution abstracts **1466**
Polymer handbook **1711**
Polytechnic courses handbook, 1992 entry **781**
Pond, G. and Raleigh, I.
  A Standard guide to cat breeds **1537**
Poole, T.R.
  Identifying antique British silver **1860**
Poole's index to periodical literature **206**
Pooley, R. and Ryall,, W.
  Pooley's flight guide: United Kingdom and Ireland **1624**
Pooley's flight guide: United Kingdom and Ireland **1624**
Pope-Hennessy, J.
  A History of Western sculpture **1846**
Pope, R.
  Atlas of British social and economic history since c.1700 **460**
POPSI **1961, 1976**
A Popular dictionary of Buddhism **414**
Population index **476**
The Population of the United States **475**
Porter, A.N.
  Atlas of British overseas expansion **2669**
Porter, G.
  Encyclopedia of American economic history **580**
Porter, R.
  The Earth sciences: an annotated bibliography **1009**
Porter, V.
  Cattle: a handbook to the breeds of the world **1532**
Portuguese-English dictionary **2199**
Portuguese language and Luso-Brazilian literature **2476**
Portuguese literature **2475**
Post, E.P.
  Emily Post's etiquette **804**
Potter, L.
  The Revels history of drama in English **2377**
The Potter's dictionary of materials and techniques **1853**
Pounds, N.J.G.
  An Historical geography of Europe **2649**
Powder metallurgy science and technology **1407**
The Practical encyclopedia of freshwater tropical aquarium fishes **1545**
A Practical Sanskrit dictionary **2226**
Prehistoric Europe **2538**
Prehistoric Scotland **2550**
Preminger, A.
  Princeton encyclopedia of poetry and poetics **2323**
Prentice-Hall guide to English literature **2352**
Pressure vessel design handbook **1408**

Pretz, B.
  Dictionary of military and technological abbreviations and acronyms **1426**
Primrose McConnell's 'The agricultural notebook' **1492**
The Princeton companion to classical Japanese literature **2519**
The Princeton encyclopaedia of classical sites **2536**
Princeton encyclopedia of poetry and poetics **2323**
The Princeton handbook of poetic terms **2323**
Principles and practice of infectious diseases **1315**
Pring, J.T.
  The Oxford dictionary of modern Greek **2205**
Printed circuits handbook **1381**
Printed reference materials **138**
Printers yearbook **1580**
Printing abstracts **1579**
Privacy and data protection **1736**
Private press books **290**
Prizewinning literature **2282**
Proceedings in print **229**
Property information source book, 1989 **542**
Pros and cons **448**
Proverbs, sentences and proverbial phrases, from English writings mainly before 1500 **833**
Průšek, J.
  Dictionary of Oriental literatures **2497**
Prytherch, R.J.
  Harrod's librarians' glossary **100**
  Sources of information in librarianship and information science **96**
Pseudonyms and nicknames dictionary **34**
PsycBooks **322**
Psychiatric dictionary **1313**
A Psychiatric glossary **1312**
Psychoanalytic terms and concepts **326**
Psychological abstracts **323**
Public figures in the Soviet Union **2744**
The Public General Acts and General Synod Measures **643**
Publishers' international ISBN directory **1592**
Publisher's practical dictionary in 20 languages **1591**
Pugh, E.
  Pugh's Dictionary of acronyms and abbreviations **1221**
Pugh's Dictionary of acronyms and abbreviations **1221**
Pukui, M.K. and Elbert, S.H.
  Hawaiian dictionary **2274**
Pullum, G.K. and Ladusaw, W.A.
  Phonetic symbol guide **2117**
Pump handbook **1399**
Purcell, G.R. and Schlachter, G.A.
  Reference sources in library and information services **97**
Putnam, W.C.
  Putnam's geology **1018**
Putnam's geology **1018**
Pycroft, C and Munslow, B.
  Southern African annual review **2618**
Pye, M.
  Macmillan dictionary of religion **343**

Quarterly transport statistics **1598**
Quirk, R.
  A Comprehensive grammar of the English language **2160**
The Quotable woman ... 1800-1981 **815**
The Quotable woman, from Eve to 1799 **2287**
Quotations database **2286**
The Quote sleuth **2288**
RAC camping and caravanning guide **1557**
Rachow, L.A.
  Theatre and performing arts collections **2049**
Racism and discrimination in Britain **453**
Rafique Akhtar
  Pakistan year book 1989-90 **2609**
Ragazzini, G.
  Harrap's Shorter Italian dictionary **2188**
Raggett, J. and Bains, W.
  Artificial intelligence from A to Z **1744**
Rahner, K.
  Sacramentum mundi **386**
Rahner, K. and Vorgrimler, H.
  Concise theological dictionary **355**
The Railway data book **1445**
Railway directory **1603**
Ralston, A. and Reilly, E.D.
  Encyclopedia of computer science and engineering **1723**
Ramson, W.S.
  The Australian national dictionary **2140**
Rand McNally illustrated atlas of China **2672**
Randel, D.M.
  New Harvard dictionary of music **1924**
The Random House dictionary of the English language **2146**
Random House Webster's College dictionary **2152**
Ransom, J.E.
  Harper & Row's complete field guide to North American wildlife. Western edition **1129**
Raper, D.
  Law databases, 1988 **634**
RAPRA abstracts **1706**
Raškevičs, J.
  Anglu-latviešu vārdnīca **2224**
Reader, I.
  Religion in contemporary Japan **427**
The Reader's adviser **122**
The Reader's Digest Atlas of Australia, produced in conjunction with the Division of National Mapping, Department of National Resources **2680**
Reader's Digest complete guide to sewing **1572**
Reader's Digest driver's atlas of the British Isles **2668**
Reader's Digest new D-I-Y manual **1570**
Reader's Digest you and your rights **677**
The Reader's encyclopedia **2276**
The Reader's encyclopedia of Shakespeare **2380**

Readers' guide abstracts to periodical literature 214
A Reader's guide to Canadian history 2974
Readers' guide to periodical literature (Unabridged) 212
A Reader's guide to the great religions 333
Real Academia Española
 Diccionario de la lengua española 2193
Reaney, P.H.
 A Dictionary of English surnames 2113
Recent advances in chemistry and technology of fats and oils 1659
Recent advances in surgery 1318
Rechenbach, C.W.
 Swahili-English dictionary 2266
The Records of the nation 2865
Recreation management handbook 2081
Recycling: energy from community waste 1340
Reed, W.L. and Bristow, M.J.
 National anthems of the world 1967
Rees, N.
 Bloomsbury dictionary of phrase and allusion 2313
Rees, P.
 Biographical dictionary of the extreme right since 1890 513
Reference books bulletin 141
Reference encyclopedia of the American Indian 455
A Reference guide for English studies 2357
Reference guide to American literature 2411
Reference guide to English literature 2355
A Reference guide to the United States Supreme Court 685
Reference manual for telecommunications engineering 1382
Reference reviews 142
Reference sources in history 2807
Reference sources in library and information services 97
Reference works (including CD-ROM) 135
The Refrigeration and air conditioning year book 1396
A Regional history of England 2879
A Regional history of the railways of Great Britain 1605
Registered Nursing Home Association: reference book, 1990/91 742
Reich, B.
 Political leaders of the contemporary Middle East and North Africa 699
Reich, D.
 A History of German literature 2429
Reid, D.
 A Concise history of Canadian painting 1894
Reid, J.M.H.
 The Concise Oxford dictionary of French literature 2450
Reinforced concrete designer's handbook 1440
Rela, W.
 A Bibliographical guide to Spanish American literature 2468

Religion and society in North America 373
Religion in contemporary Japan 427
Religion index one: periodicals 335
Religion index two: multi-author works 336
Religious books in print 337
The Religious orders in England 375
Religious Society of Friends
 Handbook of the Religious Society of Friends, 1982 397
Remarkable animals: a unique encyclopaedia of wildlife wonders 1177
Remnant, M.
 Musical instruments 1981
Rengger, N.
 Treaties and alliances of the world 662
Renner, H.
 A history of Czechoslovakia since 1945 2900
Rensburg, W.C.J., van
 Strategic minerals 1060
Reports and inventories 2544
Research catalogue 2644
Research centers directory 232
Research into higher education abstracts 772
The Research Libraries of the New York Public Library and the Library of Congress
 Bibliographic guide to psychology 319
Retail directory 627
The Retail jeweller's guide 1689
Retrospective index to theses of Great Britain and Ireland 170
Retrospective national bibliographies an international directory 37
The Revels history of drama in English 2377
Reviews of United Kingdom statistical sources 1599
Reviews of United Kingdom statistical sources. V.7: Road passenger transport; Road goods transport 1599
Reviews of United Kingdom statistical sources. V.10: Ports and inland waterways; Civil aviation 1599
Reviews of United Kingdom statistical sources. V.14: Rail transport; Sea transport 1599
Revised medieval Latin word-list 2202
Reynolds, C.E. and Steedman, J.C.
 Reinforced concrete designer's handbook 1440
Reynolds, M.M.
 A Guide to theses and dissertations 168
Richard, S.
 British government publications: an index to chairmen and authors 270
 Directory of British official publications 276
Richards, O.W.
 Imms' general textbook of entomology 1185
Richardson, B.G.
 CIRIA guide to EC and international sources of construction information 1759
Richman, J. and Draycott, A.T.
 Stone's justice's manual, 1991 683

Rickett, H.W.
 Wild flowers of the United States 1155
The Rider encyclopedia of Eastern philosophy and religion 411
Ridge, J.D.
 Annotated bibliographies of mineral deposits in Europe 1061
 Annotated bibliographies of mineral deposits in the Western Hemisphere 1062
Ridpath, I.
 Collins' guide to stars and planets 929
 Norton's 2000.0 934
Rieger, R.O.
 Glossary of genetics and cytogenetics, classical and molecular 1114
Rietstap, J.B.
 Armorial général 2786
The Rights of women 808
Riley-Smith, J.
 The Atlas of the Crusades 2840
Rimmer, B.
 International guide to official industrial property publications 1236
Riquer, M. de
 Història de la literatura catalana 2455
Rivers of the world 1064
Roads and traffic in urban areas 1600
Roaf, M.
 Cultural atlas of Mesopotamia and the Ancient Near East 2558
Robbins, K.
 The Blackwell biographical dictionary of British political life in the twentieth century 511
Robert, P.
 Le Grand Robert de la langue française 2184
Roberts, D.
 Hong Kong 1991 2602
Roberts, M.J.
 The Spiders of Great Britain and Ireland 1183
Roberts, M.T. and Etherington, D.
 Bookbinding and the conservation of books 1750
Roberts, W.L.
 Encyclopedia of minerals 998
Robertson, A. and Hutera, D.
 Dance handbook 2056
Robertson, D.
 A Dictionary of modern defense and strategy 712
Robertson, J.G.
 A History of German literature 2429
Robinson, F.
 The Cambridge encyclopedia of India, Pakistan, Bangladesh, Sri Lanka, Nepal, Bhutan and the Maldives 2607
Robinson, M.
 The Concise Scots dictionary 2134
Robinson, S.
 Guide to literary prizes, grants and awards in Britain and Ireland 2283
Robinson, W.D.
 The Solid waste handbook 1468
Robot technology 1745
Robotics abstracts 1746

Rocca, R.G. *and* Dziak, J.J.
Bibliography on Soviet intelligence and security services **509**

Rock, D.
Argentina 1516-1982: from Spanish colonization to the Falklands War and Alphonsin **2993**

Rocks, minerals and fossils of the world **999**

Rodgers, F.
A Guide to British government publications **278**

Rodwell, J.S.
British plant communities **1149**

Roget, P.M.
Roget's Thesaurus of English words and phrases **2153**

Roget's Thesaurus of English words and phrases **2153**

Rohsenow, W.M. *and* Hartnett, J.P.
Handbook of heat transfer applications **974**

Rolef, S.H.
Political dictionary of the state of Israel **2959**

The Roman world **2825**

Ronan, C.
Encyclopedia of astronomy **916**

Ronan, C.A.
The Cambridge illustrated history of the world's science **887**

Room, A.
Dictionary of place-names in the British Isles **2107**
A Dictionary of pseudonyms and their origins **35**
Dictionary of translated names and titles **2103**
Place-names of the world **2108**

Rosaler, R.C. *and* Rice, J.O.
Standard handbook of plant engineering **1346**

Rose, A.H. *and* Harrison, J.S.
The Yeasts **1163**

Rose, G. *and* King, P.
The Good gardens guide 1990 **1823**

Rosenberg, J.M.
The Investor's dictionary **567**

Ross-Craig, S.
Drawings of British plants **1154**

Ross, R.L.
International literature in English **2385**

Rothbart, H.A.
Mechanical design and systems handbook **1415**

Rothenberg, M.
The History of science and technology in the United States **893**

Roth's American poetry annual **2414**

The Rough guides **2690**

Routemaster maps **2667**

The Routledge compendium of primary education **765**

Rowley, E.E.
The Financial system today **559**

Royal Automobile Club
RAC camping and caravanning guide **1557**

The Royal Ballet **2059**

Royal Botanic Gardens, Kew
World plant conservation bibliography **1133**

Royal College of Physicians of London
Smoking or health **1278**

Royal Commonwealth Society
Biography catalogue of the Library **2856**
The Manuscript catalogue of the library .. **2580**
Subject catalogue of the Library of the Royal Empire Society **2578**

Royal Entomological Society of London
Handbooks for the identification of British insects **1186**

The Royal Geographical Society history of world exploration **2643**

Royal Horticultural Society
Dictionary of gardening **1522**

The Royal Horticultural Society gardeners' encyclopedia of plants and flowers **1523**

Royal Society of Chemistry
Specialist periodical reports: reviews of the chemical literature **984**

Royle, T.
A Dictionary of military quotations **706**
The Macmillan companion to Scottish literature **2390**

Rubber and Plastics Research Association of Great Britain (RAPRA)
RAPRA abstracts **1706**

Rubber technology and manufacture **1707**

Rubenstein, H.
The Good hotel guide **1548**

Rubulis, A.
Baltic literature **2495**

Ruffner, J.A.
Eponyms dictionary index **849**

Rules of the game **2079**

Rundell, M.
Longman dictionary of contemporary English **2142**

Ruoff, A.L.B.
American Indian literatures **2526**

Ruppert, J.
Guide to American poetry explication **2413**

Russell, P.E.
Spain **2586**

Russian-English chemical and polytechnical dictionary **869**

The Russian Orthodox Church **381**

The Russian Revolution 1899-1919 **2918**

Rutgers, A. *and* Norris, K.A.
Encyclopedia of aviculture **1535**

Ryan, B.
Hispanic writers **2299**
Major 20th-century writers **2292**

Ryan, P.
The Encyclopedia of Papua and New Guinea **2636**

Saagpakk, P.F.
Eesti-inglise sõnaraamat **2252**

Sabine, G.H.
A History of political theory **494**

Sachar, H.M.
A History of Israel **2958**

Sacramentum mundi **386**

Sadie, S.
New Grove dictionary of music and musicians **1923**

Sadie, S. *(contd.)*
New Grove dictionary of musical instruments **1982**

Sadie, S. *and* Latham, A.
Grove concise encyclopaedia of music **1926**

Sadiq, M.
A History of Urdu literature **2501**

Sadler, G.
Twentieth-century western writers **2347**

SAE handbook **1472**

Sage race relations abstracts **457**

St. James reference guide to American literature **2411**

Sakoian, F. *and* Acker, L.S.
Astrologer's handbook **314**

Salem, J.M.
Drury's Guide to best plays **2331**

The Salvation Army year book, 1992 **369**

Salzman, J.
American studies **2629-2630**

Sanders, D.M.
Ground engineering yearbook, 1991 **1436**

Sanders, H.
British outdoor amenities directory **2083**

Sanjek, R.
American popular music and its business **1964**

Sansoni-Harrap standard Italian and English dictionary **2190**

Santesson, R.
Stora engelsk-svenska ordboken **2176**
Svensk-engelsk ordbok **2177**

Sarjeant, W.A.S.
Geologists and the history of geology **1023**

Saunders, J.B.
Words and phrases legally defined **637**

Savage, D.E. *and* Russell, D.E.
Mammalian paleofaunas of the world **1076**

Sax, I. *and* Lewis, R.J.
Dangerous properties of industrial materials **1283**

Say, M.G.
Electrical engineer's reference book **1360**

Scandinavian biographical archive **2745**

Scarne, J.
Scarne's Encyclopedia of games **2070**

Scarne's Encyclopedia of games **2070**

Scarre, C.
Ancient France 6,000-2,000 BC **2546**
Past worlds **2533**

Scherer, J.L.
China facts and figures **2598**

Schiffer, P. *and* Schiffer, N.
The Brass book **1863**

The Schirmer guide to schools of music and conservatories throughout the world **1946**

Schlueter, P.
Encyclopedia of British women writers **2365**

Schneider, M.J. *and* Stern, I.
Modern Spanish and Portuguese literatures **2460**

Schniewind, A.P.
Concise encyclopedia of wood and wood-based materials **1692**

Scholze-Stubenrecht, W. and Sykes, J.B.
Oxford-Duden German dictionary **2166**

Schopflin, G.
The Soviet Union and Eastern Europe **2589**

Schulz-Torge, U-J.
Who's who in the Soviet Union today **2742**

Schumacher, S. and Woerner, G.
The Rider encyclopedia of Eastern philosophy and religion **411**

Schwann CD **1989**

Schwartz, H.L.
The Encyclopedia of beaches and coastal environments **1041**

Schwartzberg, J.E.
A Historical atlas of South Asia **2940**

Schwarzlose, R.A.
Newspapers: a reference guide **244**

SCICAT **842**

Science and technology: an introduction to the literature **840**

Science & technology libraries **879**

Science citation index **878**

Science: invention and discovery in the twentieth century **1234**

Science Reference and Information Service catalogue **842**

Scientific and technical books and serials in print **843**

SCIMP [Selective cooperative index of management periodicals] **617**

Scopes, N.
Pest and disease control handbook **1514**

Scorer, R.
Clouds of the world **1052**

The Scots thesaurus **2134**

Scott, J.S.
Dictionary of civil engineering **1434**

Scott, T. and Eagleson, M.
Concise encyclopedia of biochemistry **1117**

Scottish archaeology **2543**

The Scottish government yearbook, 1992 **687**

The Scottish legal system **646**

Scottish literature in English and Scots **2388**

The Sea **1045**

Sea guide to whales of the world **1213**

Seal, R.A.
A Guide to the literature of astronomy **912**

Seals and sealing handbook **1347**

Search for the Northwest Passage **3004**

Seaweeds of the British Isles **1160**

Sebeok, T.A.
Encyclopedic dictionary of semiotics **2118**

Segal, A.
Careers encyclopedia **536**

Selected water resources abstracts **1063**

Selective cooperative index of management periodicals **617**

A Selective guide to Chinese literature, 1900-1949 **2517**

Sellar, L.
Centres and bureaux **230**

Sellar, L. (contd.)
Councils, committees & boards **220, 688**

Sen, S.P.
Dictionary of national biography **2751**

Sendall, B. and Potter, J.
Independent television in Britain **2007**

Sequels **2335-2336**

Serbocroatian-English dictionary **2219**

The Serials directory **192**

Serials in the British Library **193**

Setton, K.M.
A History of the Crusades **2839**

Severs, J.B. and Hartung, A.E.
A Manual of the writings in Middle English, 1050-1500 **2370**

Seyfert, C.K.
The Encyclopedia of structural geology and plate tectonics **1029**

Seyffert, O.
A Dictionary of Classical antiquities **2548**

Seymour-Smith, M.
The Dent dictionary of fictional characters **2318**
Macmillan guide to modern world literature **2280**

Shakespeare: a bibliographical guide **2379**

A Shakespeare encyclopaedia **2380**

Shakespeare survey **2381**

Shakespearean criticism **2382**

Shales, M.
The Traveller's handbook **2642**

Sharp, H.S.
Handbook of pseudonyms and personal nicknames **33**

Sharpe, C.
Kempe's Engineer's year-book, 1991 **1326**

Shaw, D.F.
Information sources in physics **956**

Shaw, G. and Tipper, A.
British directories **2885**

Shaw, R.R.
American bibliography: a preliminary checklist .. **65**

Shaw, S.J. and Shaw E.K.
History of the Ottoman Empire and modern Turkey **2957**

Shearer, B.F. and Shearer, B.S.
State names, seals, flags and symbols **2798**

Sheehy, E.P.
Guide to reference books **136**

Sheep and goat production **1533**

The Shell guide to British archaeology **2541**

Shell guide to Ireland **2700**

Shell guide to the great paintings of England **1891**

Shepard, L.A.
Encyclopedia of occultism and parapsychology **310**

Shepherd, M.
Handbook of psychiatry **1314**

Sheppard's book dealers in North America **1593**

Sheppard's book dealers in the British Isles **1594**

Sheppard's European bookdealers **1595**

Sherratt, A.
The Cambridge encyclopedia of archaeology **2531**

Shimoni, Y.
A Political dictionary of the Arab world **490**
Political dictionary of the Arab World **2937**

Shipps, A.W.
The Quote sleuth **2288**

Shock and vibration handbook **969**

A Short history of modern Greece **2931**

A Short history of opera **1953**

Short story criticism **2343**

Short story index **2344**

A Short-title catalogue of books printed in England ... 1475-1640 **40**

Short-title catalogue of books printed in England ... 1641-1700 **41**

Shorter dictionary of English furniture **1885**

The Shorter encyclopedia of Islam **423**

The Shorter new Cambridge bibliography of English literature **2350**

Showman's directory 1990 **2031**

Shugar, G.J.
Chemical technicians' ready reference handbook **1639**

Shukman, H.
The Blackwell encyclopaedia of the Russian Revolution **2924**

Sibley, C.G. and Monroe, B.L.
Distribution and taxonomy of birds of the world **1201**

Sidgwick, J.B.
Amateur astronomer's handbook **917**
Observational astronomy for amateurs **918**

Sigma-Aldrich handbook of stains, dyes and indicators **1677**

The Signal selection of children's books **134**

The Sikhs: their religious beliefs and practices **416**

The Silver bough **795**

Simkin, T.
Volcanoes of the world **1028**

Šimko, J.
Anglicko-slovenský slovník **2216**

Simmonds, K.R.
Encyclopedia of European Community law **655**

Simon, A.L.
Dictionary of gastronomy **1564**

Simón Díaz, J.
Manual de bibliografía de la literatura española **2463**

Simpson, D.H.
Biography catalogue of the Library **2856**
The Manuscript catalogue of the library .. **2580**

Simpson, I.
The New guide to illustration **1908**

Sinclair, S.
Third world economic handbook **526**

Singer, C.
A History of technology **1227**

Singer, P.
A Companion to ethics **331**

Singh, A.
Indian literature in English, 1827-1979 **2395**

Singh, S.
  Indian books in print **61**
Singleton, P. *and* Sainsbury, D.
  Dictionary of microbiology and
  molecular biology **1121**
Sinor, D.
  The Cambridge history of early Inner
  Asia **2933**
SIPRI: yearbook **664**
Sittig, M.
  Handbook of toxic and hazardous
  chemicals and carcinogens **1294**
Skeist, I.
  Handbook of adhesives **1670**
Skerlj, R.
  Anglesko-slovenski slovar **2220**
Sky atlas 2000.0 **931**
Sky catalogue 2000.0 **931**
Slama, C.C.
  Manual of photogrammetry **942**
Slaven, A *and* Checkland, S.
  Dictionary of Scottish business
  biography, 1860-1960 **605**
Slavery **500**
Slonimsky, N.
  The Concise Baker's biographical
  dictionary of musicians **1936**
Slovensko-angleški slovar **2220**
Slovensko-anglický slovník **2217**
Small arms of the world **1428**
Small press record of books in print
  291
Smelser, N. J.
  Handbook of sociology **443**
Smith, C.
  Collins Spanish-English/English-Spanish
  dictionary **2194**
Smith, E.C.
  New dictionary of American family
  names **2114**
Smith, F.H. *and* Spencer, F.
  The Origins of modern humans **1116**
Smith, G.F.H.
  Gemstones **1001**
Smith, J.
  Food additive user's handbook **1658**
Smith, J.D.
  Black slavery in the Americas **501**
Smith, M.
  Manual of British Standards on
  building construction and
  specification **1758**
Smith-Morris, M.
  'The Economist' book of vital world
  statistics **462**
Smith, R.B.
  An International history of the
  Vietnam war **2964**
Smith, S.L.J.
  Dictionary of concepts in recreation
  and leisure studies **1994**
Smith, T.
  An Encyclopaedia of homoeopathy
  1286
  The New Macmillan guide to family
  health **1270**
Smithells, C.J.
  Smithells' Metals reference book **1684**
Smithells' Metals reference book **1684**
Smoking or health **1278**
Smurthwaite, D.
  Ordnance Survey complete guide to
  the battlefields of Britain **711**

Snakes - a natural history **1197**
Snakes of the world **1196**
Snell, G.
  The Book of theatre quotes **2039**
Snyder, L.L.
  Historical guide to World War II
  2851
A Social history of the Nonconformist
  Ministry in England and Wales, 1800-
  1930 **392**
Social sciences and humanities index
  204
Social sciences index **432**
Social security statistics, 1991 **752**
Social service abstracts **732**
Social services year book, 1991/92 **733**
Social trends **472**
Society for Underwater Technology
  Advances in underwater technology,
  ocean science and offshore
  engineering **1451**
Society of Automotive Engineers
  Glossary of automotive terms **1474**
  SAE handbook **1472**
Sociological abstracts **446**
Sociology: a guide to reference and
  information sources **441**
The Software encyclopedia, 1990 **1735**
Soils and fertilizers **1513**
Sola, R. De
  See
    De Sola, R.
The Solar system **927**
Solé, C.A.
  Latin American writers **2467**
The Solid waste handbook **1468**
Sörenson, S.
  Ensk-islensk ordabók **2172**
Sotheby's concise encyclopaedia of
  furniture **1884**
Soule, J.
  Glossary for horticultural crops **1518**
The Source **2777**
Sources for English local history **2881**
Sources in European political history
  487
Sources of British political history, 1900-
  1951 **489**
Sources of information about children's
  books **125**
Sources of information in librarianship
  and information science **96**
Sources of information in the social
  sciences **433**
Sources of information on alternative
  energy technology held at the Science
  Reference and Information Service
  1339
Sources of unofficial UK statistics **471**
South Africa **2971**
South Africa 1989-90 **2619**
South Africa under Apartheid **454**
South America, Central America and the
  Caribbean 1991 **2626**
South, M.
  Mythical and fabulous creatures **405**
Southern African annual review **2618**
Soviet disunion **2921**
Soviet mathematical encyclopaedia
  Encyclopaedia of mathematics **901**
The Soviet Union **2741**
The Soviet Union and Eastern Europe
  2589

Space flight **1485**
Spain **2586**
Spanish American women writers **2469**
Sparkes, A.W.
  Talking philosophy: a wordbook **296**
Spate, O.H.K.
  The Pacific since Magellan **2995**
Speaight, G.
  A History of the circus **2032**
  The History of the puppet theatre
  2030
Specialist periodical reports: reviews of
  the chemical literature **984**
Specification for quantities, units and
  symbols **836**
Spedding, C.R.W.
  Fream's principles of food and
  agriculture **1491**
Speech index **2348**
Spencer, F.
  Ecce homo: an annotated bibliographic
  history of physical anthropology
  1079
Spicer and Pegler's book-keeping and
  accounts **611**
Spicer, D.G.
  The Book of festivals **796**
  Yearbook of English festivals **797**
Spicer, E.E. *and* Pegler, E.C.
  Spicer and Pegler's book-keeping and
  accounts **611**
The Spiders of Great Britain and Ireland
  1183
Spon's Architects' and builders' price
  book, 1992 **1760**
Spon's Civil engineering and highway
  works price book, 1992 **1438**
Sport in Britain **2080**
Sports documentation monthly bulletin
  1275
Springer, O.
  Langenscheidt's New Muret-Sanders
  encyclopedic dictionary of the English
  and German languages **2165**
Spurrell, W.
  The Collins Spurrell Welsh dictionary
  2235
Spy/counterspy **507**
Stables, L.
  Pest and disease control handbook
  1514
Stacey, M.
  'Current UK street maps for libraries'
  2666
Stade, G.
  European writers **2298**
Stafford,, D. *and* Purkis, R.
  Macmillan directory of multinationals
  552
Stafleu, F.A. *and* Cowan, R.S.
  Taxonomic literature **1136**
Stambler, I.
  Encyclopedia of pop, rock and soul
  1979
Stamp, Sir D. *and* Clark, A.N.
  A Glossary of geographical terms
  1036
Standard catalog of world coins **1847**
Standard catalogue of British coins
  1849
Standard dictionary of the social sciences
  435

Standard encyclopedia of the world's oceans and islands 1040
The Standard Finnish-English/English-Finnish dictionary 2251
A Standard guide to cat breeds 1537
Standard handbook for electrical engineers 1359
Standard handbook for secretaries 608
Standard handbook of environmental engineering 1458
Standard handbook of fastening and joining 1691
Standard handbook of industrial automation 1738
Standard handbook of plant engineering 1346
Standard handbook of powerplant engineering 1392
The Standard periodical directory 201
A Standard Swahili-English dictionary 2266
The Standard Swedish-English/English-Swedish dictionary 2175
The Stanford companion to Victorian fiction 2384
Stangos, N.
    Thames and Hudson dictionary of art and artists 1771
Stanislawski, J.
    Wielki slownik angielsko-polski 2212
    Wielki slownik polsko-angielski 2213
Stanley Gibbons Great Britain specialised stamp catalogue 1626
Stanley Gibbons simplified catalogue. Stamps of the world 1627
Stanley Gibbons stamp catalogue 1628
Stanway, A.
    Alternative medicine: a guide to natural therapies 1292
Stark, M.M.
    Mining and mineral industries 1422
Stars and stellar systems 928
State names, seals, flags and symbols 2798
State of the world's children, 1992 747
The Stateman's year book world gazetteer 2691
The Statesman's year-book historical companion 2830
Statistical abstract of the United States, 1991 474
Statistical tables for biological, agricultural and medical research 1102
Statistical yearbook/Annuaire statistique, 1987 463
Statistics Europe 467
Statutes in force 644
Statutory Instruments. 1890- 642
Stavropoulos, D.N. and Hornby, A.S.
    The Oxford Greek-English learner's dictionary 2206
Stearn, W.T.
    Botanical Latin 1140
Steel detailers' manual 1441
Steen, J.
    History of ballet and modern dance 2060
Steers, J.A.
    The Coastline of England and Wales 1042
Stein, G.
    The Encyclopedia of unbelief 346

Steinberg, S.H.
    Historical tables 58BC-AD1985 2809
Steingass, F.
    A Comprehensive Persian-English dictionary 2232
Stephens, J.
    Inventory of abstracting and indexing services produced in the UK 174
Stephens, M.
    The Oxford companion to the literature of Wales 2394
Stephens, W.B.
    Sources for English local history 2881
Stephens, W.R.W. and Hunt, W.
    A History of the English Church 390
Stern, I.
    Dictionary of Brazilian literature 2477
Stevens, P.
    Oil and gas dictionary 1663
Stevenson, B.E.
    The Home book of quotations 2289
Stevenson, G.A.
    Graphic arts encyclopedia 1585
Stevenson's Book of quotations 2289
Steward, J.H.
    Handbook of South American Indians 1091
Stewart, G.R.
    American given names 2110
Stewart, J.
    Antarctica 3005
Stewart, J.D.
    British union-catalogue of periodicals 184
Stillwell, R.
    The Princeton encyclopaedia of classical sites 2536
Stobart, T.
    The Cook's encyclopedia 1564
Stockholm International Peace Research Institute
    SIPRI: yearbook 664
Stokes, R.
    A Bibliographical companion 26
    Esdaile's manual of bibliography 25
Stone, N.
    The Times atlas of world history 2805
Stone's justice's manual, 1991 683
Stora engelsk-svenska ordboken 2176
Story, N.
    The Oxford companion to Canadian history and literature 2975
Strachan, A.E.
    Prizewinning literature 2282
Strassburger, E.
    Strassburger's textbook of botany 1139
Strassburger's textbook of botany 1139
Strategic minerals 1060
Stratmann, F.H.
    A Middle English dictionary 2124
Strayer, J.R.
    Dictionary of the Middle Ages 2837
Strickland, W.S.
    A Dictionary of Irish artists 1796
Stroud, F.
    Stroud's judicial dictionary of words and phrases 639
Stroud's judicial dictionary of words and phrases 639

Stroynowski, J.
    Who's who in the socialist countries of Europe 2725
Structural engineering handbook 1433
Students' favourite dictionary (English-to-Bengali) 2229
A Student's grammar of English 2160
Studies on women abstracts 812
Studwell, W.E.
    Christmas carols 1956
Study abroad: international scholarships and courses 776
The Study of Russian history from British archival sources 2919
Studying and living in Britain 1991 2574
Sturges, P. and Sturges, C.
    Who's who in British economics 528
Sturm, T.
    The Oxford history of New Zealand literature in English 2419
Sturtevant, W.C.
    Handbook of North American Indians 1089
Stutley, M. and Stutley, J.
    A Dictionary of Hinduism 413
Subject catalogue of the Library of the Royal Empire Society 2578
Subject guide to books in print 74
Subject guide to German books in print 53
Subject guide to major United States government publications 281
Subject index to periodicals 208
Subtelny, O.
    Ukraine: a history 2926
Subways of the world 1446
Sullivan, E.
    The Marine encyclopaedic dictionary 1611
Summers, W.I.
    American electricians' handbook 1361
Sundén, U.
    Remarkable animals: a unique encyclopaedia of wildlife wonders 1177
Supplement to Charles Evans' American bibliography 70
Supplement to 'The pocket guide to wild flowers' 1153
The Surnames of Ireland 2113
The Surnames of Scotland 2113
Survey of current business 581
Survey of industrial chemistry 1631
The Survey of London 2887
A survey of printing processes 1586
Surveying 940
Sutherland, D.S.
    Igneous rocks of the British Isles 1057
Sutherland, J.
    The Longman companion to Victorian fiction 2384
Sutherland, S.
    Macmillan dictionary of psychology 327
Sutton, M.
    Children's Britannica 154
Sutton, R.B.
    Speech index 2348
Sužiedélis, S. and Vesaitis, A.
    Encyclopedia Lituanica 2591

Svensk-engelsk fackordbok för näringsliv, fövaltning, undevisning och forskning **861**

Svensk-engelsk ordbok **2177**

Svensk-engelsk teknisk ordbok **860**

Swahili-English dictionary **2266**

A Swedish-English dictionary of technical terms used in business, industry, administration, education and research **861**

Swedish-English technical dictionary **860**

Sweetman, J.
American naval history **726**

Swift, G.
Batsford encyclopedia of embroidery techniques **1878**

Swift, L.H.
Botanical bibliographies **1137**

Sword, K.
The Times guide to Eastern Europe **2849**

SWRA **1063**

Sydenham, P.H.
Handbook of measurement science **966**

Symbols, units, nomenclature and fundamental constants in physics **954**

Synge, P.M.
Dictionary of gardening **1522**

Tabata, V.
CRC handbook of radiation chemistry **990**

Tables of physical and chemical constants **883**

Tables of temperature, relative humidity, precipitation and sunshine for the world **1053**

Tagalog-English dictionary **2271**

Talking philosophy: a wordbook **296**

Talocci, M.
Guide to the flags of the world **2797**

Tapley, B.D.
Eshbach's handbook of engineering fundamentals **1324**

Tarassuk, L. and Blair, C.
The Complete encyclopaedia of arms and weapons **1867**

Tarbert, G.C.
Book review index: a master cumulation 1965-1984 **182**

Taryam, A.O.
The establishment of the United Arab Emirates 1950-1985 **2951**

Tate, W.H.
A Mariner's guide to the rules of the road **1617**

Tattersall, I.
Encyclopedia of human evolution and prehistory **1115**

Taxonomic literature **1136**

Taylor, A.R.
Brass bands **1969**

Taylor, G.D.
Construction materials **1761**

Taylor, J.L.
Portuguese-English dictionary **2199**

Taylor, M.J.H.
Encyclopedia of the world's air forces **718**

Taylor, P.A.
Dictionary of marine technology **1450**

Technological dictionary **848**

Teeuw, A.
Modern Indonesian literature **2527**

Television and video engineer's pocket book **1391**

Television and video engineer's reference book **1390**

Tenney, M. and Barabas, S.
The Zondervan pictorial encyclopedia of the Bible **347**

Terminology of forest science, technology, practice and products **1503**

Terras, V.
Handbook of Russian literature **2487**

Terrell, P.
The Collins German dictionary **2164**

Terres, J.K.
The Audubon Society encyclopedia of North American birds **1205**

Terry, G.M.
East European languages and literatures **2485**

Tester, J.W.
Energy and the environment in the 21st century **1337**

Textbook of physiology **1269**

Tezla, A.
Hungarian authors **2513**

Thackrah, J.R.
Encyclopedia of terrorism and political violence **497**

Thai-English Dictionary **2257**

Thailand a short history **2960**

Thames and Hudson dictionary of art and artists **1771**

Thames and Hudson encyclopaedia of British art **1789**

Thames and Hudson encyclopaedia of twentieth century architecture **1842**

The Academy of Sciences MPR
Information Mongolia **2603**

The Cambridge history of Latin America **2981**

'The Empire, the Commonwealth and the Mandated Territories' **2855**

The New illustrated science and invention encyclopedia **882**

The Statesman's year-book **2567**

Theatre and performing arts collections **2049**

Theatre, film and television biographies master index **1998**

Thematic catalogues in music **1947**

Thematic list of description; political science, 1989
International bibliography of political science **482**

Theological book review. October 1988- **356**

Thermophysical properties research literature retrieval guide, 1900-1980 **975**

The Thesaurus of chemical products **1643**

Thesaurus of pulp and paper terminology **1699**

Thieme, U. and Becker, F.
Allgemeines Lexikon der bildenden Künstler **1787**

Third Barnhart dictionary of new English **2157**

Third world **2570**

Third world economic handbook **526**

Third world guide 91/92 **2569**

Third world resource directory **459**

Thomas Cook European timetable: railway and shipping services throughout Europe **1609**

Thomas Cook overseas timetable: railway, road and shipping services outside Europe **1609**

Thomas, D. St. J. and Patmore, J.A.
A Regional history of the railways of Great Britain **1605**

Thomas, W.H. and Ervine, C.
Encyclopedia of consumer law **1559**

Thompson, B.
A Bibliography of Christian worship **364**

Thompson, F.M.L.
The Cambridge social history of Britain, 1750-1950 **461**

Thompson, P.K.J.
The County court practice, 1991 **684**

Thompson, S.
Motif-index of folk-literature **821**

Thomsett, M.C.
Musical terms, symbols and theory **1917**

Thomson, P. and Salgado, G.
Everyman companion to the theatre **2035**

Thornberry, P., ed.
World directory of minorities **495**

Thorne, D.A.
The Collins Spurrell Welsh dictionary **2235**

Thorne, T.
Bloomsbury dictionary of contemporary slang **2132**

Thorpe, F.
International directory of film and TV documentation centres **2022**

Tide tables **939**

Tierney, H.
Women's studies encyclopedia **811**

Tietjen, G.L.
A Topical dictionary of statistics **910**

Time Out film guide **2018**

The Times 1000 ... 1991-1992 **592**

The Times atlas and encyclopaedia of the sea **1047**

The Times atlas of the Second World War **2852**

The Times atlas of the world. Comprehensive ed **2685**

The Times atlas of world exploration **2641**

The Times atlas of world history **2805**

The Times guide to Eastern Europe **2849**

The Times index **250**

The Times literary supplement **178**

The Timetables of history **2808**

Timothy, J.
Who's who in Australasia and the Far East **2746**

Tindale, N.B.
Aboriginal tribes of Australia **1092**

Tiratsoo, E.N.
Oilfields of the world **1425**

Tirion, W.
Sky atlas 2000.0 **931**

Titles and forms of address **806**

TLS. The Times literary supplement **178**

Toase, C.A.
Bibliography of British newspapers **246**

Todd, J.
British women writers **2365**

Tomes, J.
Blue guide Wales **2702**

Tool and manufacturing engineers handbook **1404**

Tooley, M.
Newnes computer engineer's pocket book **1724**

Tooley, R.V.
Maps and map-makers **951**
Tooley's dictionary of mapmakers **952**
Tooley's dictionary of mapmakers **952**

Toomey, A.F.
A World bibliography of bibliographies 1964-1974 **28**

The Top 3,000 directories and annuals **217**

A Topical dictionary of statistics **910**

Totok, W.
Handbuch der bibliographischen Nachschlagewerke **139**

Towell, J.E.
Business acronyms **597**

Towell, J.E. and Sheppard, H.E.
Computer & telecommunications acronyms **1721**

Town and country planning in Britain **1816**

Townsend, P.
Burke's genealogical and heraldic history of the landed gentry **2791**
Burke's Peerage and Baronetage **2789**

Toye, W.
The Oxford companion to Canadian literature **2400**

Tracing your ancestors in the Public Record Office **2770**

Trade associations and professional bodies **587**

The Trade mark journal **1231**

Trade names **1230**

Trade names dictionary **1232**

Trade unions of the world, 1992-93 **540**

The Translator's handbook **894**

Transliteration of Cyrillic and Greek characters **15**

Transport statistics: Great Britain **1598**

Transportation and traffic engineering handbook **1597**

Transportation noise reference book **1467**

Trapido, J.
An International dictionary of theatre language **2038**

Trask, W.R.
Yoga **417**

Travel trade directory **586**

The Traveller's handbook **2642**

Travlos, J.
Pictorial dictionary of ancient Athens **2824**

Treasure, G.R.
Who's who in British history **2864**

Treaties and alliances of the world **662**

Treatise on invertebrate paleontology **1073**

Trees and shrubs hardy in the British Isles **1506**

Tribos (Tribology abstracts) **1419**

Triggs, G.D.
The Antarctic Treaty regime **2638**

Tripp, E.
Dictionary of classical mythology **410**

Tropical agriculture series **1500**

Trundle, E.
Television and video engineer's pocket book **1391**

Tucker, N. and Timms, H.
The Buyer's guide to encyclopedias **143**

Tudor, J.
Macmillan directory of business information sources **546**

Tulloch, S.
The Oxford dictionary of new words **2156**

Tuma, J.J.
Engineering mathematics handbook **903**

Turkina, E.
Latviešu-anglu vārdnīca **2225**

Turner, B.
The Actor's handbook, 1989 **2036**
The Writer's handbook **2305**

Turner, R.P. and Gibilisco, S.
Illustrated dictionary of electronics **1376**

Turnill, R.
Jane's Spaceflight directory, 1987 **1488**

Tutin, T.
Flora europaea **1148**

Tuttle, L.
Encyclopedia of feminism **810**

Tuttle, R.H.
Apes of the world **1215**

TV movies and video guide, 1992 **2010**

Tver, D.F.
Encyclopedic dictionary of industrial technology **1405**

Tver, D.F. and Russell, P.
Nutrition and health encyclopedia **1273**

Tweetalige woordeboek **2171**

Twentieth-century authors **2293**

Twentieth-century children's writers **129**

Twentieth-century crime and mystery writers **2340**

Twentieth-century literary criticism **2310**

Twentieth-century romance and historical writers **2339**

Twentieth-century science-fiction writers **2342**

Twentieth-century western writers **2347**

Uglow, J.S.
The Macmillan dictionary of women's biography **2724**

Uhlmann, D.R.
Glass science and technology **1671**

UK Christian handbook, 1989/90 **380**

UKOLUG quick guide to online commands **9**

Ukraine: a history **2926**

Ukrainian-English dictionary **2211**

Ulack, R. and Pauer, G.
Atlas of Southeast Asia **2611**

Ullmann, F.
Ullmann's Encyclopedia of industrial chemistry **1630**

Ullmann's Encyclopedia of industrial chemistry **1630**

Ulrich's international periodicals directory **194**

An Unabridged Malay-English dictionary **2272**

UNDOC: current index **654**

Unesco and World Intellectual Property Organization (WIPO)
Copyright laws and treaties of the world **682**

Unesco statistical digest **465**

Unesco statistical yearbook, 1990 **464**

Ungar, F.
Handbook of Austrian literature **2433**

UNICEF
State of the world's children, 1992 **747**

Uniforms of the world **709**

Union Internationale des Chemins de Fer
Lexique général des termes ferroviaires **1444**

Union of International Associations
International congress calendar **225**
Yearbook of international organizations **218**

United Free Church of Scotland ... Handbook **393**

United Kingdom Online User Group
UKOLUG quick guide to online commands **9**

United Nations. Department of International Economic and Social Affairs
Industrial statistics yearbook, 1988 **585**
World economic survey, 1991 **574**

United Nations. Department of International Economic and Social Affairs. Statistical Office
Statistical yearbook/Annuaire statistique, 1987 **463**
Yearbook of national accounts statistics, 1988 **564**

United Nations. Economic Commission for Europe
Economic survey of Europe, 1990-1991 **577**

United Nations Educational, Scientific and Cultural Organization
Unesco statistical yearbook, 1990 **464**

United Nations Industrial Development Organization (UNIDO), Vienna
Industrial development abstracts **583**

United Nations. Statistical Office
Demographic yearbook, 1989 **477**
International trade statistics yearbook, 1989 **595**

The United Reformed Church year book, 1991/92 **395**

The United States **2628**

United States. Board on Geographic Names
Gazetteers **2692**

United States. Bureau of the Census
Statistical abstract of the United States, 1991 **474**

Universal English-Gujarati dictionary **2230**

University entrance, 1992: the official guide **782**

A University grammar of English **2160**

University of Chicago Spanish dictionary **2195**

University of Warwick Business Information Service
Sources of unofficial UK statistics 471

Untracht, O.
Jewellery: concepts and technology 1690

Upham, M.
Trade unions of the world, 1992-93 540

Uphof, J.C.T.
The Dictionary of economic plants 1158

Urdang, L.
Names and nicknames of places and things 2101
The Oxford thesaurus 2154

US Department of Commerce. Bureau of Economic Analysis
Survey of current business 581

The USA and Canada 1990 2620

Uscher, N.
The Schirmer guide to schools of music and conservatories throughout the world 1946

Usher, G.
A Dictionary of plants used by man 1159

Uvarov, E.B. and Isaacs, A.
The Penguin dictionary of science 851

Van Cleve, J.V.
Gallaudet encyclopedia of deaf people and deafness 1309

Van Dale. Groot woordenboek Engels-Nederlands 2169

Van Dale. Groot woordenboek Nederlands-Engels 2170

Van Dale, J.H.
Groot woordenboek der Nederlandse taal 2168

Van Dale Lexitron 2168

Van Nostrand encyclopedia of chemistry 980

Van Nostrand's scientific encyclopedia 846

Vance, C. and Hackworth-Young, J.
Amateur theatre yearbook 1989-90 2050

Variety presents 1996

The Vegetarian good food guide 1552

Velký anglicko-český slovník 2214

Vercoutter, P.A.J.
Directory of European observatories 925

Vernon, K.D.C.
Information sources in management and business 601, 615

Vernon, R.
Directory of research workers in agriculture and allied sciences 1498

Verzeichnis lieferbarer Bücher 52

Verzeichnis lieferbarer Bücher. Schlagwort-Verzeichnis 53

Veterinary medicine 1526

VHF/UHF manual 1387

Viaux, J.
IFLA directory of art libraries 1805

The Victoria history of the counties of England 2880

Victorian Britain 2870

Vietnam at war 2963

Vietnamese-English student dictionary 2265

Vilikovská, J. and Vilikovský, P.
Slovensko-anglický slovník 2217

Viney, N. and Piper, D.
Shell guide to the great paintings of England 1891

Vinterberg, H. and Bodelsen, C.A.
Dansk-engelsk ordbog 2179

Virology: an information profile 1119

Virology and AIDS abstracts 1317

A Visual history of costume 791

Viswanath, D.S. and Natarajan, G.
Data book on the viscosity of fluids 991

The VNR dictionary of ships and the sea 1479

Voeglin-Carleton, A.
British words on tape 266

Volcanoes of the world 1028

Vollmer, H.
Allgemeines Lexikon der bildenden Künstler 1787

Voluntary agencies directory, 1991 734

Vox diccionari anglès-català/català-anglès 2185

Wacher, J.
The Roman world 2825

Waddell, H.
London art and artists guide 1790

Wahrig, G.
Brockhaus Wahrig deutsches Wörterbuch 2163

Wakefield,, G.S.
A Dictionary of Christian spirituality 362

Wakeman, J.
World authors, 1950-1970 2294

Waldman, H.
Dictionary of robotics 1747

Wales 2581

Walford, A.J.
The Working languages of the European Community 2087

Walicki, A.
A History of Russian thought 315

Walker, D.M.
The Oxford companion to law 633
The Scottish legal system 646

Walker, J.
Halliwell's film guide 2012

Walker, J.A.
Glossary of art, architecture and design since 1945 1774

Walker, P.M.B.
Chambers biology dictionary 1096

Walker's mammals of the world 1210

Wallis, L.W.
Dictionary of graphic arts abbreviations 1901

Walne, P.
Dictionary of archival terminology. Dictionnaire de terminologie archivistique 2810

A Guide to manuscript sources for the history of Latin America and the Caribbean in the British Isles 2982

Walrond-Skinner, S.
A Dictionary of psychotherapy 1293

Walsh, M.
Butler's lives of the saints 359

Walters, F.P.
A History of the League of Nations 652

Walton, F.
The Encyclopedia of employment law and practice 532

Wang, M.C.
Handbook of special education 769

Ward A.W., Sir and Gooch, G.P.
The Cambridge history of British foreign policy, 1783-1919 505

Ward, P.
The Oxford companion to Spanish literature 2462

Warrern, A.
Dansk-Engelsk teknisk ordbog 862
Engelsk-dansk teknisk ordbog 863

Warwick Statistics Service
The Counties and regions of the United Kingdom 579

Wastes in the ocean 1463

Watch and clock encyclopedia 1718

Water Research Centre
Aqualine abstracts 1461

The Waterloo directory of Victorian periodicals 197

Waters, T.A.
Encyclopedia of magic and magicians 2066

Watson, D.
Chambers book of musical quotations 1931

Watson, E.V.
British mosses and liverworts 1166

Watson, G.
The New Cambridge bibliography of English literature 2350

Watson, L.
Sea guide to whales of the world 1213

Watson, N. and Schellinger, P.E.
Twentieth-century science-fiction writers 2342

Watters, R.E.
A Checklist of Canadian literature and background materials, 1628-1960 2401

Watts, D.
The West Indies 2653

Wauchope, R.
Handbook of Middle American Indians 1090

Waxman, M.
A History of Jewish literature 2508

The Webb Society deep sky observer's handbook 930

Webb, W.
Sources of information in the social sciences 433

Webber, S. and Baile, C.
UKOLUG quick guide to online commands 9

Webster's Diccionario inglés-portugês 2196

Webster's Dictionary of English usage 2128

Webster's new biographical dictionary 2716

Webster's new dictionary of synonyms 2155

Webster's new geographical dictionary 2693

Webster's new ideal dictionary 2152

Webster's new world dictionary of American English **2139**
Webster's new world dictionary of mathematics **904**
Webster's new world illustrated encyclopedic dictionary of real estate **541**
Webster's ninth new collegiate dictionary **2152**
Webster's third new international dictionary of the English language **2147**
Wedepohl, K.M.
Handbook of geochemistry **1013**
Weekly record **72**
Weerasinghe, L.
Directory of recorded sound resources in the United Kingdom **267**
Wehr, H.
A Dictionary of modern written Arabic (Arabic-English) **2246**
Weik, M.H.
Communications standard dictionary **1574**
Fiber optics standard dictionary **1385**
Weinreb, B. and Hibbert, C.
The London encyclopaedia **2889**
Welding abstracts **1411**
Welding handbook **1409**
Well, J.
The Directory of continuing education for nurses, midwives and health visitors **1307**
Welland, D.
The United States **2628**
Wellek, R.
A History of modern criticism, 1750-1950 **2312**
Weller, B.F.
Baillière's encyclopaedic dictionary of nursing and health care **1303**
Wellesley index to Victorian periodicals **209**
Wells, J.C.
Concise Esperanto and English dictionary **2093**
Longman pronunciation dictionary **2143**
Wells, S.
Shakespeare: a bibliographical guide **2379**
Welsh, B.W.W. and Butorin, P.
Dictionary of development **525**
Welsh folk customs **826**
Welsh surnames **2113**
Wennrich, P. and Spiller, P.
International encyclopedia of abbreviations and acronyms of organizations **19**
Wesson, T.
Nobel Prize winners **2723**
The West Indies **2653**
Western Europe 1989 **2571**
Westminster dictionary of Christian ethics
A New dictionary of Christian ethics **361**
Westrup, J.
Collins dictionary of music **1927**
Westwood, J.N.
The Railway data book **1445**
Wetterau, B.
Macmillan concise dictionary of world history **2802**

Wexler, P.
Information resources in toxicology **1295**
What do I read next? **2338**
What every chemical technologist wants to know **1644**
Wheeler, A.
The World encyclopedia of fishes **1193**
Wheeler, M.
The Oxford Russian-English dictionary **2208**
Which? **1561**
Which degree? **775**
Whistler, L.
The English festivals **798**
Whitaker, J.
An Almanack for the year of Our Lord ... 1868- **437**
Whitaker's book list **46**
Whitaker's books in print **48**
Whitaker's books of the month **47**
Whitehouse, R.D.
The Macmillan dictionary of archaeology **2532**
Whiteside, R.
Major chemical and petrochemical companies of Europe, 1991-1992 **1637**
Whiting, B.J.
Modern proverbs and proverbial sayings **834**
Whiting, B.J. and Whiting, H.W.
Proverbs, sentences and proverbial phrases, from English writings mainly before 1500 **833**
Whitrow, M.
ISIS cumulative bibliography **886**
Who owns whom, 1991 **593**
Who was who .. **2730**
Who was who in American art **1799**
Who's who **2729**
Who's who in America 1990-1991 **2759**
Who's who in American art **1800**
Who's who in American music **1940**
Who's who in art **1788**
Who's who in Australasia and the Far East **2746**
Who's who in Australia: an Australian biographical dictionary and register of prominent people with which is incorporated John's Notable Australians. 1991 **2768**
Who's who in British economics **528**
Who's who in British history **2864**
Who's who in Canada 1990 **2754**
Who's who in China: current leaders **2748**
Who's who in European politics **700**
Who's who in France **2740**
Who's who in international affairs **2717**
Who's who in Japan 1987-88 **2749**
Who's who in Latin America **2756**
Who's who in science in Europe **892**
Who's who in Scotland 1990-91 **2734**
Who's who in the Arab World 1990-1991 **2752**
Who's who in the environment **1825**
Who's who in the People's Republic of China **2747**
Who's who in the socialist countries of Europe **2725**
Who's who in the Soviet Union **2743**

Who's who in the Soviet Union today **2742**
Who's who in the UK information world 1992 **105**
Who's who in World War II **2853**
Who's who on television **2006**
Wielki slownik angielsko-polski **2212**
Wielki slownik polsko-angielski **2213**
Wiener, P.P. 301
Wiggins, G.
Chemical information sources **979**
Wignall, C.J.
Complete British railways maps and gazetteers, 1825-1985 **1606**
Wigoder, G.
Everyman's Judaica **421**
Wijnekus, F.J.M. and Wijnekus, E.F.P.H.
Elsevier's dictionary of the printing and allied industries **1578**
Wilcox, B. and Walkowicz, C.
Atlas of dog breeds of the world **1536**
Wild flowers of Australia **1156**
Wild flowers of the United States **1155**
Wilde, W.H.
The Oxford companion to Australian literature **2422**
Wilding, N. and Laundy, P.
An Encyclopaedia of Parliament **669**
Wilkes, J.A.
Encyclopedia of architecture **1827**
Wilkins, E.H.
A History of Italian literature **2458**
Williams, D.W.
Reader's Digest you and your rights **677**
Williams, E.
From Columbus to Castro **2978**
Williams, P.L.
Gray's anatomy **1267**
Williams, T.G.
BBC World Service glossary of current affairs **2834**
Williams, T.I.
Science: invention and discovery in the twentieth century **1234**
Williams, W.J.
Subject guide to major United States government publications **281**
Williamson, J.
Jane's Military communications, 1991-92 **1429**
Williamson, M.
The Communications satellite **1389**
Dictionary of space technology **1489**
Willings press guide **195**
Willis, J.C.
A Dictionary of flowering plants and ferns **1168**
Wilson, E.A.M.
The Modern Russian dictionary for English speakers **2210**
Wilson, K.M.
An Encyclopedia of Continental women writers **2296**
Wilson, R.J.A.
A Guide to the Roman remains in Britain **2549**
Wilson, R.M.
A Dictionary of English surnames **2113**

Wilson, T.
Flags at sea **1613**
Wing, D.G.
Short-title catalogue of books printed in England, Scotland, Ireland, Wales and British America and of English books printed in other countries 1641-1700 **41**
Wingate, I.B.
Fairchild's dictionary of textiles **1702**
Wink, A.
Al-Hind The Making of the Indo-Islamic world **2954**
Winkler Prins lexicon van de Nederlandse letterkunde **2435**
Winstedt, R.O.
A History of classical Malay literature **2528**
An Unabridged Malay-English dictionary **2272**
Winternitz, M.
A Concise dictionary of Eastern religion **412**
Wise, T.
A Guide to military museums **705**
Witherby, H.F.
The Handbook of British birds **1204**
Withycombe, E.G.
The Oxford dictionary of English Christian names **2111**
Wittfoht, H.
Building bridges **1442**
Woefel, C.J.
Encyclopedia of banking and finance **558**
Wolff, M.
The Waterloo directory of Victorian periodicals **197**
Wolfram, W.
History of the Goths **2819**
Wolman, B.B.
Dictionary of behavioral science **328**
Handbook of parapsychology **311**
Wolman, J.B.
Handbook of developmental psychology **321**
Wolter, J.A.
World directory of map collections **949**
Women artists in the United States **1801**
Women in science **891**
Women in Western European history **816-817**
The Women of England **818**
Women studies abstracts **813**
Women writers of Germany, Austria, and Switzerland **2430**
Women writers of Spain **2465**
Women writers of Spanish America **2469**
Women's studies **807**
Women's studies encyclopedia **811**
Women's studies index. 1989- **814**
Wood, C.
The Dictionary of Victorian painters **1897**
Wood, D.
Trade names dictionary **1232**
Wood, D.N.
Information sources in the earth sciences **1004**

Woodbridge, H.C.
Guide to reference works for the study of the Spanish language and literature and Spanish American literature **2464**
Woodhead, P.
Keyguide to information sources in archaeology **2530**
Keyguide to information sources in museum studies **234**
Woodward, B.
Annual index to motion picture credits **2019**
Woodworth, D.P.
Current British journals **196**
Words and phrases legally defined **637**
The Working languages of the European Community **2087**
The World almanac & book of facts, 1991 **438**
World aluminum abstracts **1687**
World atlas of architecture **1832**
World authors, 1950-1970 **2294**
World ballet and dance 1990-91 **2058**
World Bank
World tables, 1991 **466**
The World Bank glossary.. **524**
The World bibliographical series **2564**
A World bibliography of bibliographies **27**
A World bibliography of bibliographies 1964-1974 **28**
World book encyclopedia **157**
World ceramic abstracts **1674**
World Christian encyclopedia **351**
World coin encyclopedia **1848**
World Conservation Monitoring Centre
World plant conservation bibliography **1133**
World directory of map collections **949**
World directory of minorities **495**
World directory of social science institutions, 1990 **439**
World economic survey, 1991 **574**
The World encyclopedia of fishes **1193**
World encyclopedia of peace **665**
World energy and nuclear directory **1338**
World Federation of the Deaf
Gestuno **2095**
A World geography of human diseases **1298**
World guide to abbreviations of organizations **17**
World guide to libraries **113**
World guide to library, archive and information science associations **106**
World Health Organization
International nomenclature of diseases **1297**
World history from 1800 to the present day **2800**
A World history of art **1780**
World human rights guide **676**
World hunger **458**
World industrial archaeology **2559**
A World list of mammalian species **1209**
The World map directory, 1989 **948**
World mapping today **945**
World metric standards for engineering **1328**
World of art **1783**

The World of games **2069**
The World of learning, 1991 **779**
World philosophy **297**
World plant conservation bibliography **1133**
World press encyclopedia **245**
World radio TV handbook **1386**
A World record of major conflict areas **496**
World rugs and carpets **1874**
World surface coating abstracts **1646**
World tables, 1991 **466**
World textile abstracts **1703**
World textile trade and production trends **1701**
The World weather guide **1054**
The World's major languages **2091**
Worldwide family history **2780**
Worldwide petrochemical directory, 1992 **1669**
Wormald, J.
The New history of Scotland **2872**
Worrall, M.
Oxford children's encyclopedia **156**
Wörterbuch der industriellen Teknik **855**
Worthing, C.R.
The Pesticide manual **1515**
Woy, J.
Encyclopedia of business information sources **600**
Wright, D.J.
Directory of medical and health care libraries in the United Kingdom and Republic of Ireland, 1990 **743**
Wright, J.
The English dialect dictionary **2133**
Wrigley, G.
Tropical agriculture series **1500**
Writers' and artists' yearbook **1778, 2304**
The Writers directory **2295**
The Writer's handbook **2305-2306**
Writer's market **2307**
Writings on American history **2984**
Writings on American history, 1962-73 **2985**
Writings on British History **2861**
Wu Jingrong
The Pinyin Chinese-English dictionary **2256**
Wuolle, A.
The Standard Finnish-English/English-Finnish dictionary **2251**
Wyatt, D.K.
Thailand a short history **2960**
Wyatt, H.V.
Information sources in the life sciences **1094**
Wynne-Davies, M.
Bloomsbury guide to English literature **2352**
The Oxford classical dictionary **2823**
Yarwood, D.
The Encyclopedia of world costume **789**
Year book Australia 1991 **2635**
Yearbook of English festivals **797**
Yearbook of international organizations **218**
Yearbook of labour statistics, 1991 **531**
Yearbook of national accounts statistics, 1988 **564**

The Year's work in English studies
2120, 2351
The Year's work in modern language
studies **2085**
The Yeasts **1163**
YHA accommodation guide **1555**
The Yiddish dictionary sourcebook **2167**
Yoga **417**
York, H.E.
Political science **485**
Young, J.Z.
The Life of vertebrates **1191**
Youngs, F.A.
Guide to the local administrative units
of England **694**
Youth Hostels Association
YHA accommodation guide **1555**
Youth movements of the world **749**
Yu, D.C. *and* Thompson, L.G.
Guide to Chinese religion **425**
Zell, H.M.
The African studies companion **2613**
A New reader's guide to African
literature **2525**
Zeller, O.
Internationale Bibliographie der
Rezensionen Wissenschaftlicher
Literatur **183**
Zentner, C. *and* Bedürftig, F.
The Encyclopedia of the Third Reich
2894
Zilkha, A.
Modern Hebrew-English dictionary
2243
The Zondervan pictorial encyclopedia of
the Bible **347**
Zonhoven, L.M.J.
Annual Egyptological bibliography/
Bibliographie **2535**
The Zoological record **1173**
Zoroastrians **419**
Zuck, V.
Dictionary of Scandinavian literature
2436
Zylka, R.
Geological dictionary **1019**

Subject Index

The index reference is to the running number given to each item. The running numbers are in one sequence throughout the volume and can be found at the top right-hand corner of the entry for each item.

The index is computer generated, thus terms for the index have been largely derived from the headings and sub-headings used throughout *Walford*, but many other entries have been added, including synonyms, inverted headings, and cross-references.

The arrangement of the index is alphabetical and filing is word by word, with groups of initials counted as single words. Under each main heading will be found a resumé of all the subject terms used under that heading and the numbers of the items to which they refer. Similarly, under each narrower sub-heading there is a list of terms used. These headings are printed in bold type in the index, e.g. **Genealogy, Theatre**. Where the term in the index needs to be qualified by the broader term of which it is a sub-division, then the broader term is given in square brackets, e.g. **Abbreviations and Symbols** [Graphic Arts] or [Music]. Italics are used for some subdivisions of subjects.

Abbeys (Architecture) **1844**
England & Wales **1844**
Abbreviations 16-20
Abbreviations & Symbols 93, 836-837, 954, 1093, 1221, 1242-1243, 1321, 1354, 1368, 1721, 1901, 1917
[Biology] **1093**
[Computers] **1721**
[Electrical Engineering] **1354**
[Electronics] **1368**
[Engineering] **1321**
[Graphic Arts] **1901**
[Librarianship & Information Studies] **93**
[Medicine] **1242-1243**
[Music] **1917**
[Physics] **954**
[Science] **836-837**
[Technology] **1221**
Aborigines 1092
[Ethnology (Races)] **1092**
Abstracts 173-174
Academic Dress 773
Accountancy 610-611
Book-keeping **611**
Accounts (Public Finance) **564**
Acoustics 968-969
Acronyms
See
Abbreviations
Additives (Food Industry) **1658**
Address, Forms of 805-806
Adhesives (Chemical Industry) **1670**
Administration, Public
See
Public Administration
Adolescents (Sociology) **449**
Adult Education 766-767
Advertising 628-630
Aerodynamics 967
Africa 491, 2613-2617, 2676
Black Races **2617**
Handbooks & Manuals **2617**
Encyclopaedias **2614**
Yearbooks & Directories **2615-2616**
[Area Studies] **2613-2617**
[Maps & Atlases] **2676**
[Politics] **491**

Africa (History) **2965-2966**
Maps & Atlases **2966**
Africa—East & Equatorial (History) **2969**
Africa—North (History) **2967**
Africa—Southern 2618
Yearbooks & Directories **2618**
[Area Studies] **2618**
Africa—Southern (History) **2970-2971**
Africa—West (History) **2968**
African-French Literature 2452
African Languages 2266-2269
Congo-Kordofan Languages **2266-2267**
Swahili, Luganda, etc. **2266**
Xhosa, Zulu, etc. **2267**
Sudanic Languages **2268-2269**
Hausa **2268-2269**
African Literature 2522-2525
African Literature in English 2396-2397
South African Literature in English **2397**
African Religions 428
Afrikaans Language 2171
Aged People (Sociology) **450-452**
Ageing (Medicine) **1300**
Agricultural Machinery 1510-1511
Agriculture 1490-1524
Agricultural Machinery **1510-1511**
Bibliographies **1490**
Dictionaries **1493-1494**
English **1494**
Polyglot **1493**
Farms **1508-1509**
Management **1509**
Organic Farming **1508**
Fertilizers **1513**
Field Crops **1516**
Forestry **1503-1507**
Trees (Silviculture) **1506-1507**
Encyclopaedias **1506-1507**
Great Britain **1501**
Handbooks & Manuals **1491-1492**
Horticulture **1517-1524**
Fruit & Vegetables **1519**
Gardening **1520-1524**
Bibliographies **1520**
Cacti **1524**
Encyclopaedias **1521-1523**

Agriculture *(contd.)*
Periodicals & Progress Reports **1497**
Pests & Diseases **1514-1515**
Pesticides **1515**
Research Establishments **1502**
Reviews & Abstracts **1495-1496**
Soil Science **1512**
Tables & Data Books **1499**
Tropics **1500**
Yearbooks & Directories **1498**
AIDS 1256, 1316-1317
Air Almanacs 937-938
Air Conditioning 1762
Air Force 717-718
Air Transport 1624-1625
Airports & Airfields **1624**
Timetables **1625**
Aircraft Engineering 1482-1484
Airfields (Air Transport) **1624**
Airlines 1625
Airports (Air Transport) **1624**
Albanian Language 2238-2239
Albanian Literature 2507
Alchemy 313
Alcoholism 1276
Algae (Botany) **1160**
Allegories (The Arts) **1812**
Alliances (International Law) **660-662**
Allusions (Literature) **2313-2314**
Alternative Medicine 1292
Aluminium (Metallurgy) **1686-1687**
Amateur Theatre 2050
America 827
[Folklore & Folktales] **827**
America (History) **2972-2973**
Bibliographies **2972**
Encyclopaedias **2973**
America—Central (Ancient History) **2827**
America — North 2049, 2620
Yearbooks & Directories **2620**
[Area Studies] **2620**
[*Libraries*] **2049**
America—North & Central 1128-1129, 1205, 1550
[Birds] **1205**
[Hotels & Restaurants] **1550**
[Nature Study] **1128-1129**

America—North & Central (History) 2974-2991
America—South (History) 2992-2993
American Drama 2415-2417
American English 2138-2139
American Fiction 2418
American Indians
  See
    Amerindians
American Literature 2404-2418
  American Drama 2415-2417
  American Fiction 2418
  American Poetry 2413-2414
  Women 2412
American Poetry 2413-2414
Amerindians 455
Amerindians, North 1089-1090, 2990
  Handbooks & Manuals 2990
  [Ethnology (Races)] 1089-1090
  [USA] 2990
Amerindians, North—Literature 2526
Amerindians, South 1091
  [Ethnology (Races)] 1091
Amphibians (Zoology) 1194-1195
Amplifiers 1367
  Lasers 1367
Analysis (Mathematics) 909
  Functions 909
Analytical Chemistry 992-993
Anatomy (Medicine) 1267
Ancient Egypt 2535
  Bibliographies 2535
Ancient Greece & Rome 2536-2537,
2548
  Dictionaries 2548
  Maps & Atlases 2537
Ancient History & Ancient Peoples
2814-2827
  Ancient Central America 2827
  Ancient Egypt 2815
  Ancient Greece 2824
    Dictionaries 2824
  Ancient Greece & Rome 2820-2823
    Dictionaries 2823
    Encyclopaedias 2821-2822
      German 2822
  Ancient Rome 2825-2826
    Encyclopaedias 2825
    Maps & Atlases 2826
  Chronologies 2814
  Jewish History 2816-2817
    Maps & Atlases 2817
  North, West & East European Peoples
  2818-2819
Anglican Church 389-390
Anglo-American cataloguing rules 108-
109
Anglo-Irish Literature 2391-2393
Anglo-Saxon Language 2122-2123
Anglo-Welsh Literature 2394
Animals (Zoology) 1176-1180
  Behaviour 1178
  Geographic Distribution of Animals
  1179-1180
  Handbooks & Manuals 1176-1177
Animals, Distribution of 1179-1180
Anniversaries 799
Anonyma (Bibliographies) 32-35
Antarctic 2638
  [Area Studies] 2638
Antarctic legal regime 3005
Anthems, National 1967
Anthropology 1078-1081

Anthropology (contd.)
  Bibliographies 1078-1079
  Encyclopaedias & Dictionaries 1080
  Reviews & Abstracts 1081
Antiquarian Books 1593-1595
Antiques 1814-1815
  Great Britain 1815
Antiquities (Archaeology) 2548-2563
  Ancient Greece & Rome 2548
    Dictionaries 2548
  Asia—Near East 2557-2558
    Maps & Atlases 2558
  Eire 2551
  England 2553
  England & Wales 2552
  Great Britain 2549
    Roman Times 2549
  Industrial Antiquities 2559-2563
    Great Britain 2560-2561
    Institutions & Associations 2563
    Scotland 2562
  Italy 2556
    Bibliographies 2556
  Scotland 2550
  Wales 2554-2555
Apartheid 454
Apes (Zoology) 1215
Aquaculture 1542
Aquaria 1545
Arab World
  See
    Islamic World
Arabic Language 2244-2246
Arabic Literature 2509-2510
Archaeology 2529-2547
  Ancient Egypt 2535
    Bibliographies 2535
  Ancient Greece & Rome 2536-2537
    Maps & Atlases 2537
  Bibliographies 2530
  China 2547
  Dictionaries 2532
  Encyclopaedias 2531
  Europe 2538-2539
  France 2546
  Great Britain 2540-2542
    Reviews & Abstracts 2542
  Ireland 2545
  Maps & Atlases 2533
  Pacific Ocean 2534
  Scotland 2543-2544
Archaeology, Industrial 2559-2563
  Great Britain 2560-2561
  Institutions & Associations 2563
  Scotland 2562
Architecture 1826-1845
  Bibliographies 1826
  Biographies 1833
  Dictionaries 1829
  Encyclopaedias 1827-1828
  England 1837-1838
    Glossaries 1838
  Great Britain 1834
  Histories 1830-1832
  Ireland 1836
  Periods & Styles 1841-1842
    Classicism 1841
    Modern 1842
  Scotland 1835
  Types of Buildings 1843-1845
    Domestic Architecture 1845
      Manor Houses & Stately Homes
      1845

Architecture (contd.)
  Types of Buildings
    Domestic Architecture
      Manor Houses & Stately Homes
      Great Britain 1845
    Religious Architecture 1843-1844
      Abbeys & Cathedrals 1844
        England & Wales 1844
      Churches 1843
        England & Wales 1843
      USA 1840
      Wales 1839
Architecture, Domestic 1845
  Manor Houses & Stately Homes 1845
    Great Britain 1845
Architecture, Modern 1842
Architecture—Periods & Styles 1841-
1842
  Classicism 1841
  Modern 1842
Archives (History) 2810
  Dictionaries 2810
Argentina (History) 2993
Argentine Literature 2472
Armed Forces 703-726
  Air Force 717-718
  Army 713-716
    Great Britain 715
    Histories 714
    USA 716
  Battles & Battlefields 710-711
  Great Britain 707-708
  Navy 719-726
    Histories 724-726
  Quotations 706
  Strategy 712
  Uniforms & Insignia 709
Armenian Language 2237
Armour (Metal Arts) 1867-1868
  Encyclopaedias & Dictionaries 1867
  Firearms & Pistols 1868
Arms (Metal Arts) 1867-1868
  Encyclopaedias & Dictionaries 1867
  Firearms & Pistols 1868
Arms, Small (Military & Naval
Engineering) 1428
Army 713-716
  Great Britain 715
  Histories 714
  USA 716
Arthurian Romances 828
Artificial Intelligence (Technology) 1742-
1744
Artificial Languages 2093
  Esperanto 2093
The Arts 1764-1815
  20th Century 1803
    Biographies 1803
    Australia 1802
  Bibliographies 1764-1766
  Biographies 1784-1788
  Collectors & Collecting 1813-1815
    Antiques 1814-1815
      Great Britain 1815
  Design 1806-1809
    Biographies 1809
    Encyclopaedias & Dictionaries
    1806-1807
    Yearbooks & Directories 1808
  Dictionaries 1773-1774
  Encyclopaedias & Dictionaries 1767-
  1771
  Great Britain 1789-1795

The Arts *(contd.)*
Great Britain
Gazetteers **1794**
Histories **1795**
Yearbooks & Directories **1791-1793**
Handbooks & Manuals **1772**
Histories **1780-1783**
Ireland **1796**
Libraries **1804-1805**
Yearbooks & Directories **1805**
Ornamentation **1811-1812**
Dictionaries **1811**
Symbols & Allegories **1812**
Periodicals **1775-1776**
Periods & Styles **1810**
Modern Art **1810**
Encyclopaedias & Dictionaries **1810**
Quotations **1779**
USA **1797-1801**
Biographies **1799-1801**
Women **1801**
Yearbooks & Directories **1798**
Yearbooks & Directories **1777-1778**
Arts, Performing
See
Performing Arts
Asia **305-308, 2595-2596**
Bibliographies **2595**
Yearbooks & Directories **2596**
[Area Studies] **2595-2596**
[Philosophy] **305-308**
Asia (History) **2933-2964**
Encyclopaedias **2934**
Asia—Far East **2597, 2746**
Yearbooks & Directories **2597**
[Area Studies] **2597**
[Biography] **2746**
Asia—Middle & Near East **490, 2605-2606, 2674**
Archives **2606**
Yearbooks & Directories **2605**
[Area Studies] **2605-2606**
[Maps & Atlases] **2674**
[Politics] **490**
Asia—Middle & Near East (History) **2939**
Asia—Near East **2557-2558**
Maps & Atlases **2558**
[Antiquities] **2557-2558**
Asia—South & South East **2607**
Encyclopaedias **2607**
[Area Studies] **2607**
Asia—South & South-East (History) **2940-2942**
Archives **2941-2942**
Maps & Atlases **2940**
Asia South East **2534**
Asia—South East **2611**
Maps & Atlases **2611**
[Area Studies] **2611**
Asian Literature in English **2395**
Indian Literature in English **2395**
Asian Religions
See
Eastern Religions
Associations & Organizations **218-238**
Conferences **225-229**
Conference Proceedings **226-229**
Europe **219**
Great Britain **220-221**
Museums **233-238**
Europe **235**

Associations & Organizations *(contd.)*
Museums
Great Britain **236-237**
USA **238**
Non-Government Organizations **223-224**
Learned Societies **223**
Social, Sports & Literary Clubs & Associations **224**
Research Establishments **230-232**
USA **222**
Astrology **314**
Astronautics **1485-1489**
Astronomical Instruments **925**
Observatories **925**
Astronomy **911-935**
Astronomical Instruments **925**
Observatories **925**
Astrophysics **924**
Tables & Data Books **924**
Bibliographies **911-913**
Dictionaries **919**
Encyclopaedias **914-915**
Handbooks & Manuals **916-918**
Histories **921**
Institutions & Associations **922-923**
Reviews & Abstracts **920**
Solar System **926-927**
Stars & Galaxies **928-934**
Handbooks & Manuals **928-930**
Illustrations **932-933**
Maps & Atlases **934**
Tables & Data Books **931**
Astrophysics **920, 924**
Tables & Data Books **924**
Atlases
See also
Maps & Atlases
Atlases, World **2681-2688**
Bibliographies **2686**
Italian **2687**
Russian **2688**
Atomic Engineering **1348-1353**
Bibliographies **1348-1349**
Reactors **1353**
Reviews & Abstracts **1350**
Tables & Data Books **1351**
Thesauri **1352**
Audio-Visual (Manufactures) **1748**
Audio-Visual Materials **258-267**
Illustrations **261-263**
Microfilms **264-265**
Sound Recordings **266-267**
Australasia (History) **2994-3003**
Australasia & Oceania **1156, 2631**
Yearbooks & Directories **2631**
[Area Studies] **2631**
[Plants (Flora)] **1156**
Australasian & Austronesian Languages **2270-2274**
Indonesian **2270-2271**
Filipino **2271**
Javanese **2273**
Malay **2272**
Oceanian (Melanesian & Polynesian) **2274**
Hawaiian **2274**
Australia **78-79, 202, 1802, 2635, 2680, 2706, 2765-2768, 2779**
Handbooks & Manuals **2779**
Yearbooks & Directories **2635**
[Area Studies] **2635**
[The Arts] **1802**

Australia *(contd.)*
[Biography] **2765-2768**
[Genealogy] **2779**
[Maps & Atlases] **2680**
[National Bibliographies] **78-79**
[Periodicals] **202**
Australia (History) **2998-3003**
Archives **3003**
Bibliographies **3000**
Encyclopaedias **3001**
Maps & Atlases **3002**
Australian English **2140**
Australian Literature **2420-2422**
Austria (History) **2899**
Austrian Literature **2432-2433**
Austroasiatic Languages **2262-2265**
Cambodian **2262-2263**
Vietnamese **2264-2265**
Authorship (Literature) **2301-2307**
Automation Technology **1738-1741**
Automobile Engineering
See
Motor Vehicle Engineering
Aviary Birds **1535**
Aviation
See
Aircraft Engineering
Awards & Prizes **1996, 2282-2283, 2723**
[Literature] **2282-2283**
[Performing Arts] **1996**
[Worldwide] **2723**
Bacteria (Microbiology) **1122**
Bacteriology **1122**
Badges (Armed Forces) **709**
Balkans (History) **2932**
Ballads, English **2374**
Ballet **2054-2061**
Biographies **2061**
Dictionaries **2057**
Encyclopaedias & Dictionaries **2054-2056**
Histories **2059-2060**
Yearbooks & Directories **2058**
Baltic Languages **2222-2225**
Latvian **2224-2225**
Lithuanian **2222-2223**
Baltic Literatures **2495**
Bands, Brass **1968-1969**
Banking **568-569**
Building Societies **569**
Banners (Heraldry) **2795-2798**
USA **2798**
Batteries (Electrical Engineering) **1365**
Battles & Battlefields **710-711**
Beekeeping **1541**
Behavioural Science
See
Psychology
Belgian Literature **2451**
Belgium **60**
[National Bibliographies] **60**
Belgium (History) **2929**
Encyclopaedias **2929**
French **2929**
Bengali Language **2229**
Beverage Industry **1650**
Wines **1650**
Bible **347-350**
Commentaries **349-350**
Dictionaries **348**
Bible Commentaries **349-350**
Bibliographies **27-79**
Anonyma & Pseudonyma **32-35**

Bibliographies *(contd.)*
 Bibliographies of Bibliographies 27-29
 National Bibliographies 36-79
  Australia 78-79
  Belgium 60
  Bibliographies 36-37
  Canada 62-63
  France 54-55
  Germany 50-53
  Great Britain 40-48
   16th & 17th Centuries 40
   17th Century 41
   18th Century 42-43
   19th Century 44
   Contemporary 45-48
  India 61
  Ireland 49
  Italy 56
  Latin America 64
  Netherlands 59
  New Zealand 77
  Spain 57
  USA 65-76
   Contemporary 71-76
  USSR 58
  Worldwide 38-39
   English 38-39
  Translations 30-31
Bibliography 25-26
Biochemistry 1117-1118
 Vitamins 1118
Biographies 105, 304, 604-605, 888-892,
 952, 1023, 1142, 1262-1264, 1784-1788,
 1799-1801, 1803, 1809, 1833, 1890,
 1913, 1935-1937, 1940-1941, 1997-1998,
 2006, 2019-2020, 2061, 2290-2300, 2363-
 2365, 2848, 2853, 2864
 20th Century 1937
 Black Races 2300
 Europe 892, 2296-2298
 Hispanic Peoples 2299
 Women 1801, 2364-2365
 [20th Century] 1803, 1941
 [Architecture] 1833
 [The Arts] 1784-1788
 [Ballet] 2061
 [Botany] 1142
 [Business Methods & Organization]
  604-605
 [Cartography] 952
 [Design] 1809
 [English Literature] 2363-2365
 [Films & Videos] 2019-2020
 [Geology] 1023
 [Great Britain] 2864
 [Librarianship & Information Studies]
  105
 [Literature] 2290-2300
 [Medicine] 1262-1264
 [Music] 1935-1937
 [Painting] 1890
 [Performing Arts] 1997-1998
 [Philosophy] 304
 [Photography] 1913
 [Science] 888-892
 [Television] 2006
 [USA] 1799-1801, 1940
 [World War 1] 2848
 [World War 2] 2853
Biology 1093-1104
 Abbreviations & Symbols 1093
 Bibliographies 1094
 Dictionaries 1096-1098

Biology *(contd.)*
 Dictionaries
  English 1096-1098
 Handbooks & Manuals 1095
 Institutions & Associations 1103
 Research Projects 1104
 Reviews & Abstracts 1099-1101
 Tables & Data Books 1102
Biotechnology 1216-1220
Birds (Zoology) 1198-1205
 America—North & Central 1205
 Encyclopaedias & Dictionaries 1198
 Europe 1202
 Great Britain 1203-1204
 Tables & Data Books 1199
 Worldwide 1200-1201
Birds, Cage 1535
Birth Control (Health & Welfare
 Services) 745
Births (Statistics) 478
Black Races 1088, 2300, 2617
 Handbooks & Manuals 2617
 [Africa] 2617
 [*Biographies*] 2300
 [USA] 1088
Blues Music 1970-1973
 Encyclopaedias & Dictionaries 1970-
  1973
Boiler Making 1408
The Book 1575-1577
Book Auction Catalogues 91-92
Book-keeping 611
Book Reviews 175-183
 Indexes 179-183
Book Sales Catalogues 91-92
Book Trade 1587-1595
 Bookselling 1593-1595
  Antiquarian & Second-hand Books
   1593-1595
 Publishing 1590-1592
Bookbinding 1750
Bookselling 1593-1595
 Antiquarian & Second-hand Books
  1593-1595
Botanical Gardens 1143
Botany 1136-1145
 Bibliographies 1136-1137
 Biographies 1142
 Botanical Gardens 1143
 Dictionaries 1140
 Encyclopaedias & Dictionaries 1138
 Handbooks & Manuals 1139
 Nomenclatures 1141
 Practical Work 1144-1145
  Collections 1144-1145
Brand Names
 See
  Trade Names, Trade Marks, Brand
  Names
Brass 1863-1864
Brass Bands 1968-1969
Brazil (History) 2992
 Dictionaries 2992
Brazilian Literature 2477-2478
Bridges (Civil Engineering) 1442
British Empire
 See
  Commonwealth
Broadcasting Entertainment 2000-2002
Bronze 1865
Bronze (Metal Arts) 1863-1866
Buddhism 414-415
Building 1753-1760

Building *(contd.)*
 Dictionaries 1755
 Encyclopaedias 1753
 Estimates 1760
 Handbooks & Manuals 1754
 Information Services 1759
 Published Series 1757
 Reviews & Abstracts 1756
 Standards 1758
Building Estimates 1760
Building Materials 1761
Building Societies 569
Building Trades 1762-1763
 Heating & Ventilation 1762
 Painting & Decorating 1763
Buildings, Types of (Architecture) 1843-
 1845
 Domestic Architecture 1845
  Manor Houses & Stately Homes
   1845
   Great Britain 1845
 Religious Architecture 1843-1844
  Abbeys & Cathedrals 1844
   England & Wales 1844
  Churches 1843
   England & Wales 1843
Bulgarian Language 2221
Bulgarian Literature 2494
Business Ethics 332
Business Methods 597-605
 Biographies 604-605
 Dictionaries 603
Business Organization (Economics)
 See
  Business Relationships (Economics)
Business Relationships (Economics) 543-
 554
 Dictionaries 547-549
 Multinationals 552
 Private Firms 551
 Quotations 550
 Small Businesses 553-554
Businesses 589-593
Businesses, Small 553-554
Butterflies 1189-1190
Byzantium (History) 2956
 Dictionaries 2956
Cables (Electrical Engineering) 1363
Cacti 1524
Cage Birds 1535
Cambodian Language 2262-2263
Camp Sites 1556-1557
Canada 62-63, 210, 1894, 2044, 2621-
 2622, 2677, 2704, 2753-2754
 Encyclopaedias 2621
 Yearbooks & Directories 2622
 [Area Studies] 2621-2622
 [Biography] 2753-2754
 [Indexes] 210
 [Maps & Atlases] 2677
 [National Bibliographies] 62-63
 [Painting] 1894
 [Theatre] 2044
Canada (History) 2974-2976
 Bibliographies 2974
 Encyclopaedias 2975
 Maps & Atlases 2976
Canadian English 2136
Canadian French Literature 2453-2454
Canadian Literature 2398-2401
Canal Transport 1622-1623
Cancer 1256
Capital 567

Caravan Sites 1556-1557
Card Games 2072-2073
 Laws 2073
Careers 536-538
Cargo Handling 1452
Caribbean 2653, 2982
 [Historical Geography] 2653
Caribbean (History) 2978-2980
 Maps & Atlases 2979
Caribbean English Language 2137
Caribbean Literature 2402-2403
Caricature 1872
Carpets (Manufactures) 1704
Carpets (Textile Arts) 1874
Cars, Private 1473-1474
Cartography 944-952
 Bibliographies 944-945
 Biographies 952
 Handbooks & Manuals 946-947
 Histories 950-951
 Maps & Atlases 949
 Yearbooks & Directories 948
Cartoons 1872
Catalan Language 2185
Catalan Literature 2455
Cataloguing (Information Science &
 Librarianship) 108-109
Catch Phrases (English Language) 2130
Catering Establishments 1546-1554
 Hotels & Restaurants 1547-1550
  America—North & Central 1550
  Europe 1548-1549
  Worldwide 1547
 Inns & Public Houses 1553-1554
 Restaurants 1551-1552
Cathedrals (Architecture) 1844
 England & Wales 1844
Cats 1537
Cattle 1532
Caucasian Languages 2253
 Georgian 2253
Caves (Geology) 1043
CD-Rom Information Systems 10-14
Celtic Cults 424
Celtic Languages 2233-2236
 Irish 2233-2234
 Welsh 2235-2236
Celtic Literatures 2503-2506
 Irish Literature 2503-2504
 Welsh Literature 2505-2506
Cement Industry 1675-1676
 Concrete 1675-1676
Central Government 697-702
Ceramic Industry 1672-1674
Ceramic Marks 1856-1857
 Great Britain 1857
Ceramics 1852-1858
 Ceramic Marks 1856-1857
  Great Britain 1857
 Encyclopaedias & Dictionaries 1852-
 1854
 Great Britain 1855
 Porcelain 1858
Ceremonies, Official 800
Chamber Music 1980
Charities & Foundations 727-729
Cheese (Dairy Farming) 1539-1540
Chemical Engineering 1629-1641
 Dictionaries 1634
 Encyclopaedias 1629-1630
 Handbooks & Manuals 1631-1633
 Liquids 1641
  Solvents 1641

Chemical Engineering (contd.)
 Processes 1640
 Reviews & Abstracts 1635-1636
 Tables & Data Books 1638-1639
 Yearbooks & Directories 1637
Chemical Products 1642-1646
 Surface-active Agents 1646
Chemicals, Hazardous 1283
Chemistry 977-988
 Bibliographies 978-979
 Databases 977
 Dictionaries 981-982
 Encyclopaedias 980
 Patents 987
 Progress Reports 984
 Reviews & Abstracts 983
 Tables & Data Books 985-986
 Writing & Lecturing 988
Chess 2071
Child Welfare 747
Children 154-157
 [English] 154-157
Children's Reading - Books 130-134
Children's Reading - Criticism 123-129
Children's Songs 1965-1966
Chilean Literature 2473
China 2547, 2598-2601, 2671-2672,
2747-2748
 20th Century 2747-2748
 Encyclopaedias 2599-2600
 Maps & Atlases 2601
 [Archaeology] 2547
 [Area Studies] 2598-2601
 [Biography] 2747-2748
 [Maps & Atlases] 2671-2672
China (History) 2943-2945
 Chronologies 2945
 Dictionaries 2944
Chinese Language 2254-2256
Chinese Literature 2516-2517
Chinese Religions 425
Chivalry 801-802
Christian Church 363-376
 Church History 370-376
  Patrology (Church Fathers) 376
  Religious Orders & Communities
  374-375
 Liturgy & Worship 364-366
  Hymns 366
 Missionary Work (Christian Church)
 367
 Religious Associations & Societies
 368-369
  Salvation Army 369
Christian Churches 377-397
 Anglican 389-390
 Eastern Churches 381
 Lutheran 391
 Methodist 396
 Non-Conformist 392-394
 Other Churches & Sects 397
  Quakers (Society of Friends) 397
 Protestant 388
 Roman Catholic 382-387
 United Reformed Church 395
Christian Names 2109-2111
Christianity 351-362
 Creeds 360
 Ethics 361
 Saints 357-359
 Spirituality 362
 Theology 354-356

Chronologies 2814, 2847, 2863, 2877,
2945, 3006
 [Ancient History & Ancient Peoples]
 2814
 [China] 2945
 [Great Britain] 2863
 [Ireland] 2877
 [Polar Regions] 3006
 [World War 1] 2847
Chronology (History) 2808-2809
Church Fathers 376
Church History 370-376
 Patrology (Church Fathers) 376
 Religious Orders & Communities 374-
 375
Church Music 1955-1957
 England 1957
Church of England
 See
  Anglican Church
Churches (Architecture) 1843
 England & Wales 1843
Cinema Entertainment 2008-2028
 Biographies 2019-2020
 Dictionaries 2017
 Encyclopaedias & Dictionaries 2011-
 2016
 Film Festivals 2023
 Film Libraries 2022
 Genres of Films 2024-2028
 Great Britain 2021
 Reviews & Abstracts 2018
Circuits (Electronics) 1379-1381
 Printed Circuits 1381
Circuses 2032
Citizens Rights 677
Civic Ceremonies 800
Civil Engineering 1432-1442
 Bridges 1442
 Dictionaries 1434
 Handbooks & Manuals 1432-1433
 Reviews & Abstracts 1435
 Structures 1439-1441
  Concrete 1439-1440
  Metal 1441
 Tables & Data Books 1437-1438
 Yearbooks & Directories 1436
Civil Service 689-690
Classical Languages 2200-2206
 Greek Language 2203-2206
  Modern Greek 2205-2206
  New Testament Greek 2204
 Latin Language 2200-2202
  Mediaeval Latin 2202
Classical Literature 2479-2480
Classical Mythology 409-410
Classicism (Architecture) 1841
Classification Systems (Information
 Science & Librarianship) 111-112
Clay (Chemical Industry) 1673
Cleaning (The Home) 1573
Climate 1005, 1053-1054
Clock & Watch Making 1717-1718
Clothing 1571-1572
 Sewing & Needlework 1571-1572
Clothing Industry 1751-1752
Clouds 1052
Clutches (Engineering) 1416
Coal (Fuel Technology) 1649
Coastlines (Geology) 1041-1042
Coins 1847-1849
 Encyclopaedias & Dictionaries 1848
 Great Britain 1849

Collectors & Collecting 1813-1815
  Antiques 1814-1815
    Great Britain 1815
Colleges 777-783
  Great Britain 780-782
  USA 783
Colonial Administration 499
Colour (Chemical Industry) 1677
  Dyes & Dyeing 1677
Colours (Optics) 972-973
Comedy Films 2024
Comics 1872
Commerce 587-596
  Businesses 589-593
  Foreign Trade 594-596
    Exports 596
Commercial Finance 566-567
  Capital & Investment 567
Commercial Graphics 1908
Commercial Law 681-682
  Copyright 682
Commonwealth 2578-2580, 2669, 2793
  Bibliographies 2578
  Manuscripts & Incunabula 2580
  Yearbooks & Directories 2579
  [Area Studies] 2578-2580
  [Maps & Atlases] 2669
  [Orders & Decorations] 2793
Commonwealth (History) 2854-2856
  Bibliographies 2855-2856
Commonwealth Literature 2385-2387
Communications (Military & Naval
  Engineering) 1429
Communism
  See also
    Political Parties
Communism 316-318
Companies
  See
    Businesses
Comparative Law 649
Compounds (Organic Chemistry) 995
Computer Industry 1721-1737
  Abbreviations & Symbols 1721
  Bibliographies 1722
  Data Processing 1729-1737
    Computer Software 1735
    Micros 1729-1734
      Dictionaries 1732
      Encyclopaedias 1729
      Handbooks & Manuals 1730-1731
      Reviews & Abstracts 1733
      Tables & Data Books 1734
    Security 1736-1737
  Dictionaries 1725-1726
  Encyclopaedias 1723
  Handbooks & Manuals 1724
  Reviews & Abstracts 1727
  Yearbooks & Directories 1728
Computer Software 1735
Concrete (Cement Industry) 1675-1676
Concrete Structures (Civil Engineering)
  1439-1440
Condiments 1566-1567
Confectionery 1657
Conference Proceedings 226-229
Conferences 225-229
  Conference Proceedings 226-229
Congo-Kordofan Languages 2266-2267
  Swahili, Luganda, etc. 2266
  Xhosa, Zulu, etc. 2267
Conjuring 2066
Conservation, Wildlife 1134-1135

Constitutional Law 666-677
  Human Rights 675-677
  Citizens Rights 677
  Parliaments 668-674
    Great Britain 670-673
    USA 674
Construction Industry 1753-1763
  Building 1753-1760
    Dictionaries 1755
    Encyclopaedias 1753
    Estimates 1760
    Handbooks & Manuals 1754
    Information Services 1759
    Published Series 1757
    Reviews & Abstracts 1756
    Standards 1758
  Building Materials 1761
  Building Trades 1762-1763
    Heating & Ventilation 1762
    Painting & Decorating 1763
Consumers & Shopping 1558-1561
  Bibliographies 1558
  Great Britain 1561
  Laws 1559-1560
Containerization (Engineering) 1414
Control Engineering 1738-1741
Cookery 1562-1565
  Bibliographies 1562
  Encyclopaedias & Dictionaries 1563-
    1564
  Handbooks & Manuals 1565
Copper (Metal Arts) 1863-1866
Copy Presentation (Printing Industry)
  1581-1583
  Word Processing 1583
Copyright (Law) 682
Correspondence (Office Practice) 609
Cosmetics Industry 1660
Costume 784-793
  20th Century 792
  Children's Fashions 793
  Histories 790-791
Courts (Law) 684-685
Crafts, Country 1716
Creative Writing (Literature) 2301-2307
Creeds (Christianity) 360
Crime Fiction 2340
Criminal Justice 678-680
Crochet 1879
Crops, Field 1516
Crusades 2839-2840
  Maps & Atlases 2840
  [Mediaeval History—Europe] 2839-
    2840
Cryptogams 1160-1167
  Algae, Seaweeds, etc. 1160
  Fungi, Moulds 1161-1165
    Mushrooms & Toadstools 1164-
      1165
    Yeasts 1163
  Mosses 1166
  Vascular Plants 1167
    Ferns 1167
Crystal Ware 1881-1882
  Stained Glass 1882
    Great Britain 1882
Crystallography 996
Cuban Literature 2470
Customs 794-806
  Chivalry 801-802
  Etiquette 803-806
    Forms of Address 805-806
  Festivals 795-798

Customs (contd.)
  Official Ceremonies 800
  Special Days 799
Cybernetic Technology 1742-1747
  Artificial Intelligence. Expert Systems
    1742-1744
  Robots 1745-1747
Czech Language 2214-2215
Czechoslovak Literature 2492
Czechoslovakia (History) 2900
  20th Century 2900
Dairy Produce 1538-1540
  Cheese 1539-1540
Dancing
  See also
    Ballet
Dancing 2062-2065
  Encyclopaedias & Dictionaries 2063
  Histories 2065
  Yearbooks & Directories 2064
Danish Language 2178-2179
Danish Literature 2442-2443
Data Processing 1729-1737
  Computer Software 1735
  Micros 1729-1734
    Dictionaries 1732
    Encyclopaedias 1729
    Handbooks & Manuals 1730-1731
    Reviews & Abstracts 1733
    Tables & Data Books 1734
  Security 1736-1737
Databases 634, 838-839, 900, 955, 977,
  1002, 1235, 1244-1246, 1322, 1369,
  1400, 1453, 1678
  [Chemistry] 977
  [Earth Sciences] 1002
  [Electronics] 1369
  [Engineering] 1322
  [Law] 634
  [Mathematics] 900
  [Medicine] 1244-1246
  [Metallurgy] 1678
  [Patents] 1235
  [Physics] 955
  [Production Engineering] 1400
  [Public Health Engineering] 1453
  [Science] 838-839
Dates
  See
    Chronology (History)
Days, Special 799
Deafness (Medicine) 1309
Deaths (Statistics) 478
Decorating (Building Trades) 1763
Decoration, Interior 1880
Decorations (Civil Awards) 2792-2793
  Commonwealth 2793
  Europe 2792
Deep-Sea Fishing 1544
  Maps & Atlases 1544
Deep Sky
  See
    Stars
Degrees & Qualifications 774-775
Demography 475-478
  Births & Deaths 478
Dentistry 1288, 1310-1311
  Reviews & Abstracts 1311
Design (The Arts) 1806-1809
  Biographies 1809
  Encyclopaedias & Dictionaries 1806-
    1807
  Yearbooks & Directories 1808

Detective Fiction
See
  Crime Fiction
Developing Countries 459, 525-526, 1228, 2569-2570
  Handbooks & Manuals 2569
  Maps & Atlases 2570
  [Area Studies] 2569-2570
  [Economics] 525-526
  [Social Climate] 459
  [Technology] 1228
Development Policies (Economics) 582-584
Dewey Decimal Classification 111
Diagnosis (Medicine) 1302
Dialects (English Language) 2133
Dictionaries (English Language) 2144-2159
  Desk Dictionaries 2148-2152
  Idioms 2159
  Illustrated Works 2144
  Loan Words 2158
  Neologisms 2156-2157
  Synonyms 2153-2155
  Unabridged Dictionaries 2145-2147
Diesel Engines 1394
Dietetics 1271-1273
Dinosaurs 1075
Diplomatic service 701-702
Directories 215-217
Disabled (Health & Welfare Services) 746
Disarmament 663-665
Discography 1983-1993
  Jazz 1991-1992
  Opera 1990
  Rock Music 1993
Diseases (Medicine) 1296-1299
  Tropical Diseases 1299
  Worldwide 1298
DIY
See
  The Home
Docks & Harbours (Engineering) 1452
  Cargo Handling 1452
Dogs 1536
Dolphins 1213
Domestic Architecture 1845
  Manor Houses & Stately Homes 1845
  Great Britain 1845
Drama 2324-2331
Drama, American 2415-2417
Drama, English 2375-2382
Drawing 1870-1872
  Cartoons & Caricature 1872
  Technique 1871
Drawing Technique 1871
Dress
See
  Costume
Drinks Industry 1650
  Wines 1650
Drugs (Health & Hygiene) 1277
Dutch Language 2168-2170
Dutch Literature 2434-2435
Dyes & Dyeing (Chemical Industry) 1677
Earth Sciences 1002-1010
  Bibliographies 1003-1004
  Databases 1002
  Dictionaries 1006
    English 1006
  Encyclopaedias 1005

Earth Sciences *(contd.)*
  Histories 1009
  Institutions & Associations 1010
  Reviews & Abstracts 1007
  Tables & Data Books 1008
Earth Structure 1027
Eastern Churches 381
Eastern Religions 411-412
Ecology 1105-1111
  Bibliographies 1105
  Encyclopaedias & Dictionaries 1106-1107
  Handbooks & Manuals 1108
  Worldwide 1111
  Yearbooks & Directories 1109-1110
Economic Geology
See
  Geology, Economic
Economic Policies & Controls 582-586
  Economic Development 582-584
  Production 585
  Tourism 586
Economic Surveys 571-581
  Europe 577
  Great Britain 578-579
  Histories 576
  Maps & Atlases 575
  USA 580-581
Economics 515-529
  Developing Countries 525-526
  Dictionaries 519-524
  Great Britain 527-528
  Poverty 529
Education 753-761
  Histories 760
  Research Projects 761
  Yearbooks & Directories 759
Education Courses 1307
  [Nursing] 1307
Education, Music 1945-1946
Education, Special 768-769
Education Technology 762
Effluents, Industrial 1468
Egypt (Ancient History) 2815
Egypt (History) 2967
  Dictionaries 2967
Egypt, Ancient 2535
  Bibliographies 2535
Eire 2043, 2551
  [Antiquities] 2551
  [Theatre] 2043
Elastomers (Manufactures) 1710-1714
  PVC 1714
Elections 498
Electrical Engineering 1354-1381
  Abbreviations & Symbols 1354
  Batteries 1365
  Bibliographies 1355
  Dictionaries 1356
  Electronics 1368-1381
    Abbreviations & Symbols 1368
    Circuits 1379-1381
      Printed Circuits 1381
    Databases 1369
    Dictionaries 1375-1376
    Encyclopaedias 1370-1371
    Handbooks & Manuals 1372-1374
    Reviews & Abstracts 1377
    Tables & Data Books 1378
  Measurement 1364
  Power Supply 1362
    Hydroelectric Power 1362
  Pulses 1367

Electrical Engineering *(contd.)*
  Pulses
    Amplifiers 1367
    Lasers 1367
  Reviews & Abstracts 1357
  Tables & Data Books 1359-1361
  Transmission 1363
    Cables 1363
  Waves & Oscillations 1366
    Microwaves 1366
  Yearbooks & Directories 1358
Electricity 976
  Measurements 976
Electrochemistry 989
Electronics 1368-1381
  Abbreviations & Symbols 1368
  Circuits 1379-1381
    Printed Circuits 1381
  Databases 1369
  Dictionaries 1375-1376
  Encyclopaedias 1370-1371
  Handbooks & Manuals 1372-1374
  Reviews & Abstracts 1377
  Tables & Data Books 1378
Embroidery 1878
Employment (Economics) 530-540
  Industrial Relations 533-534
  Occupations & Careers 536-538
  Salaries & Wages 535
  Trade Unions 539-540
Endangered Species 1134-1135
Energy (Sources) 1336-1338
Energy, Alternative Sources of 1339-1340
Energy Conservation 1339-1340
  Alternative Sources 1339-1340
Engineering 1321-1330
  Abbreviations & Symbols 1321
  Bibliographies 1323
  Databases 1322
  Engineering Design 1330
  Handbooks & Manuals 1324
  Research Establishments 1329
  Reviews & Abstracts 1325
  Standards 1328
  Tables & Data Books 1326-1327
Engineering Design 1330
England (History) 2857-2932
  20th Century 2871
    Bibliographies 2871
  Archives 2865-2868
    Bibliographies 2867
    Micromaterials 2866
    Yearbooks & Directories 2868
  Bibliographies 2859-2861
  Biographies 2864
  Chronologies 2863
  Maps & Atlases 2862
  Roman & Anglo Saxon Period 2869
    Maps & Atlases 2869
  Russia up to 1918 2918
  Victorian Age 2870
    Encyclopaedias 2870
England & Wales (History) 2878-2889
  Bibliographies 2881
  Handbooks & Manuals 2882-2883
  Yearbooks & Directories 2884-2885
    Bibliographies 2885
England, Church of
See
  Anglican Church
English as a Second Language 2141-2142
English Ballads 2374

English Drama 2375-2382
English Fiction 2383-2384
English Language 2119-2162
  Bibliographies 2119-2120
  Dialects 2133
  Dictionaries & Vocabularies 2144-2159
    Desk Dictionaries 2148-2152
    Idioms 2159
    Illustrated Works 2144
    Loan Words 2158
    Neologisms 2156-2157
    Synonyms 2153-2155
    Unabridged Dictionaries 2145-2147
  English as a Second Language 2141-2142
  English Slang 2129-2132
  Grammar 2160-2162
    Etymology 2161-2162
  Histories 2121
  National Variants of English 2134-2140
    Australia 2140
    Canada 2136
    Caribbean 2137
    Scotland 2134
    South Africa 2135
    USA 2138-2139
  Origins 2122-2124
    Anglo-Saxon 2122-2123
    Middle English Language 2124
  Pronunciation 2143
  Usage 2125-2128
English Language, Australia 2140
English Language, Canada 2136
English Language, Caribbean 2137
English Language, South Africa 2135
English Language, USA 2138-2139
English Literature 2349-2384
  Bibliographies 2349-2351
  Biographies 2363-2365
    Women 2364-2365
  Encyclopaedias & Dictionaries 2352-2355
  English Ballads 2374
  English Drama 2375-2382
  English Fiction 2383-2384
  English Poetry 2371-2373
  Gazetteers 2359-2360
  Handbooks & Manuals 2356-2357
  Histories 2361-2362
  Manuscripts & Incunabula 2366-2367
  Middle English Literature 2370
  Old English Literature 2368-2369
  Reviews & Abstracts 2358
English Poetry 2371-2373
Entertainment 1996-1999
  Awards & Prizes 1996
  Biographies 1997-1998
  Great Britain 1999
Environmental Health
  See
    Public Health
Environmental Health 1256
Environmental Planning (Town & Country Planning) 1824-1825
  Great Britain 1824-1825
  Yearbooks & Directories 1824-1825
Environmental Pollution 1464-1466
Epigraphy 2811-2813
Eponyms 2115
Esperanto 2093
Espionage 507-509

Essays, General & Festschriften 161-164
Estonian Language 2252
Estonian Literature 2495, 2515
Ethics 331-332
  Business Ethics 332
Ethics (Christianity) 361
Ethics (Medicine) 1266
Ethnic Minorities (Politics) 495
Ethnology (Anthropology) 1083-1092
  Aborigines 1092
  Amerindians, North 1089-1090
  Amerindians, South 1091
  Encyclopaedias 1083-1084
  Tables & Data Books 1085-1087
  USA 1088
    Black Races 1088
Etiquette 803-806
  Forms of Address 805-806
Etymology (English Language) 2161-2162
Europe—Eastern 2572-2573, 2661-2663, 2725, 2849
  Encyclopaedias 2572
  Yearbooks & Directories 2573
  [Area Studies] 2572-2573
  [Biography] 2725
  [Europe (From 1919)] 2849
  [Maps & Atlases] 2661-2663
Europe—History, From 1919 2849-2853
Europe—Eastern 2849
Europe—History, Mediaeval 2835-2842
  Bibliographies 2836
  Crusades 2839-2840
    Maps & Atlases 2840
  Dictionaries 2837
  Maps & Atlases 2838
  Renaissance 2841-2842
    Bibliographies 2841
    French 2841
    Encyclopaedias 2842
Europe—History, Modern (1492-) 2843-3007
  20th Century 2844
    Bibliographies 2844
    Handbooks & Manuals 2843
Europe—Western 269, 1820, 2571
  [Area Studies] 2571
  [Government Publications] 269
  [National Parks] 1820
European Community 655-659
Events
  See
    Chronology (History)
Evolution (Biology) 1115-1116
Expeditions 2642-2643
  Handbooks & Manuals 2642
  Histories 2643
Expert Systems (Technology) 1742-1744
Exploration & Travel 2640-2643
  Expeditions, Voyages, Travel 2642-2643
    Handbooks & Manuals 2642
    Histories 2643
  Maps & Atlases 2640-2641
Exports 596
Fabrics (Manufactures) 1705
  Man-made Fibres 1705
Fabulous beasts 830
Fairies 830-832
Family Histories 2780-2781
  Scotland 2781
    Handbooks & Manuals 2781
  Worldwide 2780
    Handbooks & Manuals 2780

Family Names 2112-2114
Family Planning Services 745
Fantasy Fiction 2345
Far East
  See
    Asia—Far East
Far Eastern Literature
  See
    Oriental Literature
Farming, Organic 1508
Farms 1508-1509
  Management 1509
  Organic Farming 1508
Fashion, Children's 793
Fasteners (Engineering) 1417
Fasteners (Manufactures) 1691
Fats (Chemical Industry) 1659
Fauna 1176-1180
  Behaviour 1178
  Geographic Distribution of Animals 1179-1180
  Handbooks & Manuals 1176-1177
Federal Republic of Germany (History) 2897
  German 2897
Feminism (Customs & Traditions) 807-818
  Histories 816-818
  Quotations 815
  Reviews & Abstracts 812-814
Ferns (Botany) 1167-1168
Fertilizers 1513
Festivals (Customs & Traditions) 795-798
Fevers 1315-1317
  AIDS 1316-1317
Fibres, Man-made (Manufactures) 1705
Fiction 2332-2347
  Crime Fiction 2340
  Fantasy Fiction 2345
  Horror Fiction 2346
  Romantic Fiction 2339
  Science Fiction 2341-2342
  Short Stories 2343-2344
  Western Fiction 2347
Fiction, American 2418
Fiction, English 2383-2384
Field Crops 1516
Filipino Language 2271
Film Entertainment 2008-2028
  Biographies 2019-2020
  Dictionaries 2017
  Encyclopaedias & Dictionaries 2011-2016
  Film Festivals 2023
  Film Libraries 2022
  Genres of Films 2024-2028
  Great Britain 2021
  Reviews & Abstracts 2018
Film Festivals 2023
Film Libraries 2022
Film Photography 1915
  Video 1915
Finance 555-567
  Commercial Finance 566-567
    Capital & Investment 567
  Dictionaries 560-563
  Public Finance 564-565
    Accounts 564
    Taxation 565
Fine Arts
  See
    The Arts

Finland 2594
  [Area Studies] 2594
Finnish Language 2251
Finnish Literature 2495, 2514
Firearms (Metal Arts) 1868
Fires & Fire Prevention 1282
Firms
  See
    Businesses
First Aid 1284
Fish & Fisheries 1542-1545
  Aquaria 1545
  Deep-Sea Fishing 1544
    Maps & Atlases 1544
  Fishing Gear 1543
Fish, Tropical 1545
Fishes (Zoology) 1192-1193
Fishing, Deep-Sea 1544
  Maps & Atlases 1544
Fishing Gear 1543
Flags (Heraldry) 2795-2798
  USA 2798
Flags, Ships 1613
Flora 1146-1159
  Australasia & Oceania 1156
  Diseases 1157
  Economic Aspects 1158-1159
  Europe 1147-1148
  Great Britain 1149-1154
  USA 1155
  Worldwide 1146
Flowering Plants 1168-1170
  Dictionaries 1168
  Grasses 1170
  Nomenclatures 1169
Flowerless Plants 1160-1167
  Algae, Seaweeds, etc. 1160
  Fungi, Moulds 1161-1165
    Mushrooms & Toadstools 1164-1165
    Yeasts 1163
  Mosses 1166
  Vascular Plants 1167
    Ferns 1167
Fluid Sealing (Engineering) 1347
Fluids Handling Engineering 1397-1399
  Pumps 1399
  Valves & Taps 1398
Folk Songs 1960-1964
  Encyclopaedias & Dictionaries 1962-1963
  USA 1964
Folklore 820-828
  America 827
  Great Britain 822-824
  Ireland 825
  Metrical Romances 828
  Wales 826
Folktales
  See
    Folklore
Food (Health & Hygiene) 1271-1273
Food Additives 1658
Food & Drink 1562-1567
  Condiments, Garnishes & Pickles 1566-1567
  Cookery 1562-1565
    Bibliographies 1562
    Encyclopaedias & Dictionaries 1563-1564
    Handbooks & Manuals 1565
Food Engineering 1655-1656
Food Industry 1651-1658

Food Industry *(contd.)*
  Bibliographies 1654
  Food Engineering 1655-1656
  Preservation & Treatments 1658
    Additives 1658
  Sugar Industry 1657
Foreign Relations 502-509
  Espionage 507-509
  Great Britain 504-505
  USA 506
Foreign Trade 594-596
  Exports 596
Foreign Words and Phrases (English Language) 2158
Forenames 2109-2111
Forestry 1503-1507
  Trees (Silviculture) 1506-1507
    Encyclopaedias 1506-1507
Forms of Address 805-806
Fossil Invertebrates 1073
Fossil Man 1077
Fossil Vertebrates 1074-1077
  Dinosaurs 1075
  Mammals 1076-1077
  Man 1077
Fossils 1065-1072
  Bibliographies 1065
  Encyclopaedias 1066
  Great Britain 1070-1072
  Handbooks & Manuals 1067
  Maps & Atlases 1069
  Reviews & Abstracts 1068
Foundations, Charitable 727-729
France 54-55, 199, 2546, 2585, 2648, 2651, 2703, 2739-2740
  French 2651
  Handbooks & Manuals 2585
  [Archaeology] 2546
  [Area Studies] 2585
  [Biography] 2739-2740
  [Geography] 2648
  [Historical Geography] 2651
  [National Bibliographies] 54-55
  [Periodicals] 199
France (History) 2903-2909
  19th Century 2909
  Bibliographies 2904
  Dictionaries 2905
  French 2906
  French Revolution 2907-2908
    Encyclopaedias 2908
  Franks 2818
Freight
  See also
    Cargo Handling
French Canadian Literature 2453-2454
French Language 2180-2185
  Catalan 2185
French Literature 2444-2450
French Revolution 2907-2908
  Encyclopaedias 2908
  [France] 2907-2908
Fruit (Horticulture) 1519
Fuel Technology 1647-1649
  Coal 1649
Functions (Mathematics) 909
Funfairs etc. 2031
Fungi (Botany) 1161-1165
  Mushrooms & Toadstools 1164-1165
  Yeasts 1163
Furniture Industry 1749
Furniture—Interior Decoration 1883-1887
  England 1885-1886

Furniture—Interior Decoration *(contd.)*
  Styles 1887
    USA 1887
Furniture Styles 1887
  USA 1887
Further Education 770-783
  Academic Dress 773
  Degrees & Qualifications 774-775
  Scholarships & Postgraduate Awards 776
  Universities, Polytechnics & Colleges 777-783
    Great Britain 780-782
    USA 783
Galaxies 928-934
  Handbooks & Manuals 928-930
  Illustrations 932-933
  Maps & Atlases 934
  Tables & Data Books 931
Games & Sport 2067-2069
  Encyclopaedias & Dictionaries 2067-2068
  Histories 2069
Games, Word 2074
Gardening 1520-1524
  Bibliographies 1520
  Cacti 1524
  Encyclopaedias 1521-1523
Gardens (Town & Country Planning) 1821-1823
  Great Britain 1822-1823
Gazetteers & Guide Books 2689-2707
  Encyclopaedias 2694
Gears (Engineering) 1416
Gemmology
  See also
    Precious Stones
Gemmology 1001
Gems
  See
    Gemmology
Gender-free Usage (English Language) 2127
Genealogy 2770-2779
  Archives 2770
  Australia 2779
    Handbooks & Manuals 2779
  England & Wales 2776
    Handbooks & Manuals 2776
  Europe 2772
    Handbooks & Manuals 2772
  Great Britain 2773
    Dictionaries 2773
  Ireland 2775
    Handbooks & Manuals 2775
  Scotland 2774
    Handbooks & Manuals 2774
  USA 2777-2778
    Glossaries 2778
    Handbooks & Manuals 2777
  Worldwide 2771
Genealogy & Heraldry 2769
  USA 2769
    Bibliographies 2769
Genetics (Biology) 1113-1114
Genres of Films 2024-2028
Geochemistry 1012-1013
Geodesy 940-953
  Cartography 944-952
    Bibliographies 944-945
    Biographies 952
    Handbooks & Manuals 946-947
    Histories 950-951

Geodesy (contd.)
Cartography
Maps & Atlases **949**
Yearbooks & Directories **948**
Photogrammetry **942-943**
Remote Sensing **943**
Time **953**
Geodynamics **1028-1032**
Glaciology **1031-1032**
Sedimentation **1030**
Tectonics **1029**
Volcanoes **1028**
Geography **2644-2654**
Bibliographies **2644-2645**
Encyclopaedias **2646**
France **2648**
Historical Geography **2649-2654**
Caribbean **2653**
England & Wales **2650**
Europe **2649**
France **2651**
French **2651**
Scandinavia **2652**
USA **2654**
Bibliographies **2654**
Reviews & Abstracts **2647**
Geography & Travel **2639**
Bibliographies **2639**
Geology **1017-1047**
Biographies **1023**
Dictionaries **1019-1020**
English **1020**
Polyglot **1019**
Earth Structure **1027**
Encyclopaedias **1017**
Geodynamics **1028-1032**
Glaciology **1031-1032**
Sedimentation **1030**
Tectonics **1029**
Volcanoes **1028**
Geomorphology (Earth's physical
forms) **1033-1047**
Bibliographies **1033**
Caves **1043**
Coastlines **1041-1042**
Dictionaries **1034-1036**
English **1035-1036**
Polyglot **1034**
Europe **1039**
Islands **1040**
Oceanography **1044-1047**
Encyclopaedias **1044**
Handbooks & Manuals **1045**
Maps & Atlases **1047**
Reviews & Abstracts **1046**
Periodicals & Progress Reports
1038
Reviews & Abstracts **1037**
Great Britain **1026**
Handbooks & Manuals **1018**
Reviews & Abstracts **1021**
Worldwide **1024-1025**
Yearbooks & Directories **1022**
Geology, Economic **1059-1064**
Hydrology **1063-1064**
Rivers & Lakes **1064**
Minerals & Ores **1060-1062**
Geomorphology **1005, 1033-1047**
Bibliographies **1033**
Caves **1043**
Coastlines **1041-1042**
Dictionaries **1034-1036**
English **1035-1036**

Geomorphology (contd.)
Dictionaries
Polyglot **1034**
Europe **1039**
Islands **1040**
Oceanography **1044-1047**
Encyclopaedias **1044**
Handbooks & Manuals **1045**
Maps & Atlases **1047**
Reviews & Abstracts **1046**
Periodicals & Progress Reports **1038**
Reviews & Abstracts **1037**
Geophysics **1011**
Encyclopaedias **1011**
Georgian Language **2253**
Geothermal Energy **1015-1016**
Geothermal Exploration **1015-1016**
Geriatrics **1256, 1300**
German Democratic Republic (History)
2898
German Language **2163-2167**
Yiddish **2167**
German Literature **2423-2431**
Women **2430**
Yiddish Literature **2431**
Germany **50-53, 198, 2583, 2738**
[Area Studies] **2583**
[Biography] **2738**
[National Bibliographies] **50-53**
[Periodicals] **198**
Germany (History) **2892-2898**
Dictionaries **2893**
Encyclopaedias **2892**
German **2892**
Nazi Germany **2894-2896**
Encyclopaedias **2894**
Jews **2895-2896**
Bibliographies **2896**
Germany, Federal Republic of
See
Federal Republic of Germany
Gerontology
See
Geriatrics
Glaciology **1031-1032**
Glass Industry **1671**
Glass, Stained
See
Stained Glass
Glassware **1881-1882**
Stained Glass **1882**
Great Britain **1882**
Glues (Chemical Industry) **1670**
Goats **1533**
Goblins **830-832**
Goldsmiths **1859-1861**
Encyclopaedias & Dictionaries **1859**
Great Britain **1860**
Hallmarks **1861**
Goths **2819**
Government Bodies **688**
Government, Central **697-702**
Government Libraries **116**
Government, Local **692-696**
Urban Areas (Towns & Cities) **695-696**
Government Policies (Science &
Technology) **835**
Worldwide **835**
Government Publications **268-281**
Europe—Western **269**
Great Britain **270-278**
USA **279-281**

Grain Crops **1516**
Grammar (English Language) **2160-2162**
Etymology **2161-2162**
Grants (Further & Higher Education)
776
Graphic Arts **1901-1908**
Abbreviations & Symbols **1901**
Commercial Graphics **1908**
Dictionaries **1904**
Encyclopaedias & Dictionaries **1902**
Great Britain **1906**
Handbooks & Manuals **1903**
Histories **1905**
USA **1907**
Graphics (Printing)
See
Typography
Grasses (Botany) **1170**
Great Britain (History) **2857-2932**
20th Century **2871**
Bibliographies **2871**
Archives **2865-2868**
Bibliographies **2867**
Micromaterials **2866**
Yearbooks & Directories **2868**
Bibliographies **2859-2861**
Biographies **2864**
Chronologies **2863**
Maps & Atlases **2862**
Roman & Anglo Saxon Period **2869**
Maps & Atlases **2869**
Russia up to 1918 **2918**
Victorian Age **2870**
Encyclopaedias **2870**
Greece (Ancient History) **2824**
Dictionaries **2824**
Greece (History) **2931**
Greece & Rome (Ancient History) **2820-2823**
Dictionaries **2823**
Encyclopaedias **2821-2822**
German **2822**
Greece & Rome, Ancient **2536-2537,
2548**
Dictionaries **2548**
Maps & Atlases **2537**
Greek Language **2203-2206**
Modern Greek **2205-2206**
New Testament Greek **2204**
Greek Literature **2482-2483**
Modern Greek Literature **2483**
Greek Literature, Modern **2483**
Greek, Modern **2205-2206**
Greek, New Testament **2204**
Greenland **2637**
[Area Studies] **2637**
Greenland (History) **3007**
Guide Books
See
Gazetteers & Guide Books
Gujarati Language **2230**
Guns
See
Weapons
Gynaecology **1256**
Gypsies **819**
Hallmarks **1861**
Handicapped (Health & Welfare Services)
746
Handicrafts (Decorative Arts) **1875-1879**
Crochet & Knitting **1879**
Embroidery **1878**

Handicrafts (Decorative Arts) *(contd.)*
Encyclopaedias & Dictionaries 1875-1876
Lacemaking 1877
Harbours (Transport Services) 1620-1621
Harbours (Engineering)
See
Docks & Harbours (Engineering)
Hausa Language 2268-2269
Hawaiian Language 2274
Hazardous Chemicals 1283
Health (Medicine) 1270-1273
Food 1271-1273
Health Services 735-749
Child Welfare 747
Disabled & Handicapped 746
Family Planning 745
Great Britain 738-742
Hospitals 744
Libraries 743
Youth Welfare 748-749
Hearing (Medicine) 1309
Heat (Physics) 974-975
Heat Effects on Bodies 975
Heat Transfer 974
Heat Engineering 1392-1394
Internal Combustion Engines 1394
Diesel Engines 1394
Heat Transfer 974
Heating (Building Trades) 1762
Hebrew Language 2240-2243
Hebrew Literature 2508
Heraldry 2784-2787
Dictionaries 2785
Europe 2786
French 2786
Great Britain 2787
Handbooks & Manuals 2787
Handbooks & Manuals 2784
Herbals
See
Plant Medicines
Herbs (Cookery) 1566-1567
Hi-Fi Equipment (Manufactures) 1748
Higher Education 770-783
Academic Dress 773
Degrees & Qualifications 774-775
Scholarships & Postgraduate Awards 776
Universities, Polytechnics & Colleges 777-783
Great Britain 780-782
USA 783
Highway Engineering
See
Roads (Engineering)
Hindi Language 2227
Hinduism 413
Hispanic Peoples 2299
[Biographies] 2299
Historic Places 2694, 2699, 2705-2706
Historical Fiction 2339
Historical Geography 2649-2654
Caribbean 2653
England & Wales 2650
Europe 2649
France 2651
French 2651
Scandinavia 2652
USA 2654
Bibliographies 2654
Historical Places 2549
Historiography 2801

History
See also
Ancient History
History 2799-2813
20th Century 2806
Handbooks & Manuals 2806
Archives 2810
Dictionaries 2810
Bibliographies 2799
Chronology 2808-2809
Dictionaries 2801-2802
Encyclopaedias 2800
Maps & Atlases 2805
Palaeography & Epigraphy 2811-2813
Periodicals 2804
Bibliographies 2804
Philosophy of History 2807
Bibliographies 2807
Reviews & Abstracts 2803
History, Philosophy of 2807
Bibliographies 2807
The Home 1568-1573
Cleaning 1573
Clothing 1571-1572
Sewing & Needlework 1571-1572
Maintenance 1569-1570
Homeopathy 1286
Hong Kong 2602
Yearbooks & Directories 2602
[Area Studies] 2602
Honours (Civil Awards) 2792-2793
Commonwealth 2793
Europe 2792
Horology
See
Clock & Watch Making
Horror Fiction 2346
Horror Films 2025
Horses & Ponies 1531
Horticulture 1517-1524
Fruit & Vegetables 1519
Gardening 1520-1524
Bibliographies 1520
Cacti 1524
Encyclopaedias 1521-1523
Hospitals 744
Hostels 1555
Hotels & Restaurants 1547-1550
America—North & Central 1550
Europe 1548-1549
Worldwide 1547
Household Management 1546-1557
Camps & Caravan Sites 1556-1557
Catering Establishments 1546-1554
Hotels & Restaurants 1547-1550
America—North & Central 1550
Europe 1548-1549
Worldwide 1547
Inns & Public Houses 1553-1554
Restaurants 1551-1552
Clubs & Hostels 1555
Housing (Public Administration) 691
Human Rights 675-677
Citizens Rights 677
The Humanities 22-24
Hungarian Language 2249-2250
Hungarian Literature 2512-2513
Hungary 2584
Bibliographies 2584
[Area Studies] 2584
Hungary (History) 2902
Hunger 458
Hydraulic Engineering 1449-1452

Hydraulic Engineering *(contd.)*
Docks & Harbours 1452
Cargo Handling 1452
Underwater Work 1451
Hydrobiology 1112
Hydroelectric Power 1362
Hydrology 1063-1064
Rivers & Lakes 1064
Hygiene (Medicine) 1270-1273
Food 1271-1273
Hymns (Christian Church) 366
Icelandic Language 2172
Icelandic Literature 2437
Idioms (English Language) 2159
Illustrated Books 292
Illustrations 261-263
Immunology (Medicine) 1256, 1308
Incunabula 286-289
Incunabula & Manuscripts
See
Manuscripts & Incunabula
Indexing (Information Science & Librarianship) 110
India 61, 2608, 2675, 2750-2751
Bibliographies 2608
[Area Studies] 2608
[Biography] 2750-2751
[Maps & Atlases] 2675
[National Bibliographies] 61
India (History) 2952-2954
Indian Languages 2226-2230
Bengali 2229
Gujarati 2230
Hindi 2227
Sanskrit 2226
Urdu 2228
Indian Literature 2499
Indian Literature in English 2395
Indians, American
See
Amerindians
Indonesia 2632
Handbooks & Manuals 2632
[Area Studies] 2632
Indonesian Language 2270-2271
Filipino 2271
Indonesian Literature 2527
Indoor Games 2070-2074
Card Games 2072-2073
Laws 2073
Chess 2071
Word Games 2074
Industrial Antiquities 2559-2563
Great Britain 2560-2561
Institutions & Associations 2563
Scotland 2562
Industrial Health 1256
Industrial Relations 533-534
Industries, Trades & Crafts 1715-1716
Country Crafts 1716
Infections & Fevers 1315-1317
AIDS 1316-1317
Information Management 108-112
Cataloguing 108-109
Classification Systems 111-112
Indexing 110
Information Services 896, 1240, 1759
[Building] 1759
[Patents] 1240
[Science] 896
Information Studies
See
Librarianship & Information Studies

Information Technology 3-14
  CD-Rom Information Systems 10-14
  Online Information Systems 5-9
Inland Waterway Transport 1622-1623
Inns 1553-1554
Insects 1184-1188
  Bibliographies 1184
  Europe 1188
  Handbooks & Manuals 1185-1186
  Reviews & Abstracts 1187
Insignia (Armed Forces) 709
Institutions & Associations 106-107, 439,
  492, 922-923, 1010, 1103, 2563
  [Astronomy] 922-923
  [Biology] 1103
  [Earth Sciences] 1010
  [Industrial Antiquities] 2563
  [Librarianship & Information Studies]
    106-107
  [Politics] 492
  [Social Sciences] 439
Instrument Making 1719-1720
Instrumental Music 1968-1980
  Brass Bands 1968-1969
  Chamber Music 1980
  Jazz & Blues Music 1970-1973
    Encyclopaedias & Dictionaries
      1970-1973
  Pop Music 1974-1979
    Encyclopaedias & Dictionaries
      1977-1979
Insurance 750-752
  Social Security 752
Intelligence, Artificial (Technology)
  1742-1744
Interior Decoration 1880
Internal Combustion Engines (Heat
  Engineering) 1394
  Diesel Engines 1394
Internal Relations (Politics) 495-497
  Minorities 495
  Resistance & Revolution 496
  Terrorism & Persecution 497
International Affairs
  See
    Foreign Relations
International Law 650-665
  Alliances & Treaties 660-662
  Disarmament 663-665
  Law of International Organizations
    652-659
    European Community 655-659
    League of Nations 652
    United Nations 653-654
International Organizations 218
Inventions 1233-1234
Invertebrates 1181-1190
  Butterflies & Moths 1189-1190
  Insects 1184-1188
    Bibliographies 1184
    Europe 1188
    Handbooks & Manuals 1185-1186
    Reviews & Abstracts 1187
  Molluscs. Shellfish & Shells 1182
  Spiders 1183
Investment 567
Iran (History) 2955
Iranian Languages 2231-2232
Ireland 49, 408, 825, 1796, 1836, 1893,
  2545, 2577, 2700, 2735, 2775
  Bibliographies of Bibliographies 2577
  Handbooks & Manuals 2775
  [Archaeology] 2545

Ireland *(contd.)*
  [Architecture] 1836
  [Area Studies] 2577
  [The Arts] 1796
  [Biography] 2735
  [Folklore & Folktales] 825
  [Genealogy] 2775
  [Mythology] 408
  [National Bibliographies] 49
  [Painting] 1893
Ireland (History) 2875-2877
  Chronologies 2877
Irish Language 2233-2234
Irish Literature 2503-2504
Irish Literature in English
  See
    Anglo-Irish Literature
Iron & Steel Industry 1685
  Steel 1685
Islam 422-423
Islamic World 2612, 2752
  Encyclopaedias 2612
  [Area Studies] 2612
  [Biography] 2752
Islamic World (History) 2935-2938
  Dictionaries 2937
  Maps & Atlases 2938
Islands (Geology) 1040
Israel
  See also
    Jewish History
Israel 2610
  Yearbooks & Directories 2610
  [Area Studies] 2610
Israel (History) 2958-2959
  Dictionaries 2959
Italian Language 2186-2190
Italian Literature 2456-2458
Italy 56, 2556
  Bibliographies 2556
  [Antiquities] 2556
  [National Bibliographies] 56
Italy (History) 2910-2913
  20th Century 2913
    Dictionaries 2913
  Bibliographies 2911
  Dictionaries 2912
Jamaica (History) 2980
Jamaican English 2137
Japan 2604, 2673, 2749
  Encyclopaedias 2604
  [Area Studies] 2604
  [Biography] 2749
  [Maps & Atlases] 2673
Japan (History) 2948-2950
  Bibliographies 2949
  Dictionaries 2950
Japanese Language 2258-2260
Japanese Literature 2518-2519
Japanese Religions 426-427
Javanese Language 2273
Jazz 1970-1973
  Encyclopaedias & Dictionaries 1970-
    1973
Jazz (Discography) 1991-1992
Jewellery (Manufactures) 1689-1690
Jewellery (Metal Arts) 1862
Jewish History
  See also
    Holocaust
    Israel
    Palestine
Jewish History 2816-2817

Jewish History *(contd.)*
  Maps & Atlases 2817
Jewish Religion 420-421
Jews 2895-2896
  Bibliographies 2896
  [Nazi Germany] 2895-2896
Journalism 253
Judaism 420-421
Justice, Criminal 678-680
Khmer Language
  See
    Cambodian Language
Knitting 1879
Korean Language 2261
Korean Literature 2520
Laboratory Tools & Techniques 991
  Work with Liquids 991
Labour (Economics) 530-540
  Industrial Relations 533-534
  Occupations & Careers 536-538
  Salaries & Wages 535
  Trade Unions 539-540
Lacemaking 1877
Lakes (Hydrology) 1064
Land & Property 541-542
  Property Market 542
Landscape Planning 1819-1820
  National Parks 1820
    Europe—Western 1820
Language Teaching 2086-2087
Languages 2088-2095
  Artificial Languages 2093
    Esperanto 2093
  Sign Language 2094-2095
  Translation & Translators 2092
Lasers (Electrical Engineering) 1367
Lasers (Optics) 971
  Spectral Data 971
Latin America 64, 2623-2626, 2756
  Bibliographies 2623-2624
  Handbooks & Manuals 2625
  Yearbooks & Directories 2626
  [Area Studies] 2623-2626
  [Biography] 2756
  [National Bibliographies] 64
Latin America (History) 2981-2982
  Archives 2982
Latin Language 2200-2202
  Mediaeval Latin 2202
Latin Literature 2481
Latin, Mediaeval 2202
Latvian Language 2224-2225
Latvian Literature 2495
Law 632-649
  Comparative Law 649
  Databases 634
  Dictionaries 635-639
  Great Britain 640-645
  Legal Aid 648
  Libraries 647
  Scotland 646
Law of International Organizations 652-
  659
  European Community 655-659
  League of Nations 652
  United Nations 653-654
Law, Patent 1241
Laws 1402, 1559-1560, 2073, 2079
  [Bibliographies] 1402
  [Card Games] 2073
  [Consumers & Shopping] 1559-1560
  [Sport] 2079
League of Nations 652

Learned Societies 223
Leather (Manufactures) 1696
Legal Aid 648
Legal Procedures 683-685
  Courts 684-685
Leisure 1994-1995
  Dictionaries 1994
  Great Britain 1995
Leninism 316-318
Lepidoptera 1189-1190
Librarianship & Information Studies
  See also
    Information Management
Librarianship & Information Studies 93-107
  Abbreviations & Symbols 93
  Bibliographies 94-97
  Biographies 105
  Encyclopaedias & Dictionaries 98-100
  Histories 103-104
  Institutions & Associations 106-107
  Yearbooks & Directories 101-102
Libraries 647, 743, 1804-1805, 2048-2049
  America — North 2049
  Great Britain 2048
  Yearbooks & Directories 1805
  [The Arts] 1804-1805
  [Health & Welfare] 743
  [Law] 647
  [Theatre] 2048-2049
Libraries, Film 2022
Libraries, Music 1943-1944
Library Association 107
Library Catalogues 80-90
  Bibliographies 90
Library of Congress Classification 112
Library of Congress Subject Headings 110
Life Saving (First Aid) 1284
Lighting Engineering 1469
Lights & Beacons (Maritime Navigation) 1619
Linguistics 2096-2118
  Dictionaries 2100-2116
    Eponyms 2115
    Multilingual Dictionaries 2116
    Nicknames 2101
    Personal Names 2109-2114
      Family Names 2112-2114
      Forenames 2109-2111
    Place Names 2104-2108
    Proper Names 2102-2103
  Phonetics 2117
  Semantics & Semiotics 2118
Linguistics—Dictionaries 2100-2116
  Eponyms 2115
  Multilingual Dictionaries 2116
  Nicknames 2101
  Personal Names 2109-2114
    Family Names 2112-2114
    Forenames 2109-2111
  Place Names 2104-2108
  Proper Names 2102-2103
Liquids (Chemical Industry) 1641
  Solvents 1641
Liquids (Chemistry) 991
Literary Allusions 2313-2314
Literary Characters 2317-2318
Literary Clubs 224
Literary Criticism 2308-2312
Literary Terms 2315-2316
Literature 2275-2318

Literature (contd.)
  Awards & Prizes 2282-2283
  Bibliographies 2275
  Biographies 2290-2300
    Black Races 2300
    Europe 2296-2298
    Hispanic Peoples 2299
  Encyclopaedias & Dictionaries 2276-2280
  Literary Allusions 2313-2314
  Literary Characters 2317-2318
  Literary Criticism 2308-2312
  Literary Terms 2315-2316
  Quotations 2284-2289
  Writing & Writing Techniques 2301-2307
  Yearbooks & Directories 2281
Lithuania 2590-2591
  Bibliographies 2590
  Encyclopaedias 2591
  [Area Studies] 2590-2591
Lithuanian Language 2222-2223
Lithuanian Literature 2495
Liturgy (Christianity) 364-366
  Hymns 366
Livestock 1530-1537
  Cattle 1532
  Horses & Ponies 1531
  Pets 1534-1537
    Cage & Aviary Birds 1535
    Cats 1537
    Dogs 1536
  Sheep and Goats 1533
Loan Words (English Language) 2158
Local Government 692-696
  Urban Areas (Towns & Cities) 695-696
Local History (England & Wales) 2878-2889
  Bibliographies 2881
  Handbooks & Manuals 2882-2883
  Yearbooks & Directories 2884-2885
    Bibliographies 2885
Logic 330
London 2670, 2701
  [Maps & Atlases] 2670
London (History) 2886-2889
  Encyclopaedias 2888-2889
Lubrication (Engineering) 1418-1419
Luganda Language 2266
Lusophone Literature
  See
    Portuguese literature
Lutheran Church 391
Machine Elements (Engineering) 1415-1416
  Gears & Clutches 1416
Machinery, Protection of 1347
  Fluid Sealing 1347
Magic 311
Mail Ordering 1558-1561
  Bibliographies 1558
  Great Britain 1561
  Laws 1559-1560
Maintenance Engineering 1346
Malay Language 2272
Malayan Literature 2528
Malaysia (History) 2961
Mammals 1206-1213
  Encyclopaedias 1206
  Europe 1211
  Great Britain 1212
  Handbooks & Manuals 1207

Mammals (contd.)
  Tables & Data Books 1208
  Whales, etc. 1213
  Worldwide 1209-1210
Man, Fossil 1077
Man, Races of (Anthropology) 1083-1092
  Aborigines 1092
  Amerindians, North 1089-1090
  Amerindians, South 1091
  Encyclopaedias 1083-1084
  Tables & Data Books 1085-1087
  USA 1088
    Black Races 1088
Management 612-627
  Marketing & Sales 621-627
    Market Research 625
    Retail Selling 626-627
  Personnel Management 618
  Production Management 619-620
    Quality Control 619-620
  Reviews & Abstracts 616-617
Manor Houses (Architecture) 1845
  Great Britain 1845
Manuscripts 282-285
Manuscripts & Incunabula 2366-2367, 2580
  [Commonwealth] 2580
  [English Literature] 2366-2367
Maps & Atlases 2655-2680
  Africa 2676
  Asia—Middle & Near East 2674
  Australia 2680
  Bibliographies 2655-2657
  Canada 2677
  China 2671-2672
  Commonwealth 2669
  Europe 2658-2660
    Italian 2660
  Europe—Eastern 2661-2663
  Great Britain 2664-2668
  India 2675
  Japan 2673
  London 2670
  Mexico 2678
  USA 2679
Mariculture 1542
Marine Biology 1112
Marine Pollution 1463
Marine Transport 1610-1612
  Dictionaries 1611
    English 1611
  Encyclopaedias 1610
  Yearbooks & Directories 1612
Maritime Navigation
  See also
    Navigation
Maritime Navigation 1614-1619
  Handbooks & Manuals 1614-1617
  Lights & Beacons 1619
  Signals 1618
Market Research 625
Marketing 621-627
  Market Research 625
  Retail Selling 626-627
Marxism 316-318
Masers (Electrical Engineering) 1367
Mass Media 239-242
Materials (Painting) 1896
  Water-colour Painting 1896
    Great Britain 1896
Materials Handling (Engineering) 1417-1419

Materials Handling (Engineering) (contd.)
Fasteners **1417**
Lubrication **1418-1419**
Materials Science 1331-1335
Encyclopaedias **1331-1332**
Handbooks & Manuals **1333**
Tables & Data Books **1334-1335**
Mathematics 900-908
Databases **900**
Dictionaries **904**
Encyclopaedias **901-902**
Handbooks & Manuals **903**
Histories **907**
Recreational Mathematics **908**
Reviews & Abstracts **905-906**
Mathematics, Recreational 908
Measurement (Electrical Engineering) **1364**
Measurement (Physics) **966**
Mechanical Engineering 1341-1347
Maintenance Engineering **1346**
Protection of Machinery **1347**
Fluid Sealing **1347**
Mechanics 967
Aerodynamics **967**
Medals 1850-1851
Great Britain **1851**
Yearbooks & Directories **1850**
Medication (Pharmacology) **1290**
Medicine 1242-1266
Abbreviations & Symbols **1242-1243**
Bibliographies **1247-1250**
Biographies **1262-1264**
Databases **1244-1246**
Dictionaries **1253-1255**
English **1254-1255**
Polyglot **1253**
Encyclopaedias **1251-1252**
Ethics **1266**
Histories **1261**
Quotations **1259**
Research Establishments **1265**
Reviews & Abstracts **1256-1257**
Tables & Data Books **1260**
Yearbooks & Directories **1258**
Medicines (Pharmacology) **1291**
Plant Medicines **1291**
Melanesian Language 2274
Hawaiian **2274**
Metal Arts 1859-1868
Arms & Armour **1867-1868**
Encyclopaedias & Dictionaries **1867**
Firearms & Pistols **1868**
Copper, Bronze etc. **1863-1866**
Goldsmiths & Silversmiths **1859-1861**
Encyclopaedias & Dictionaries **1859**
Great Britain **1860**
Hallmarks **1861**
Jewellery **1862**
Metal Structures (Civil Engineering) **1441**
Metallurgy 1678-1688
Bibliographies **1679**
Databases **1678**
Handbooks & Manuals **1680-1681**
Iron & Steel Industry **1685**
Steel **1685**
Non-Ferrous Metals **1686-1688**
Aluminium **1686-1687**
Rare Earth Metals **1688**
Reviews & Abstracts **1682**
Tables & Data Books **1684**

Metallurgy (contd.)
Yearbooks & Directories **1683**
Metalwork (Fine Arts) **1859-1868**
Arms & Armour **1867-1868**
Encyclopaedias & Dictionaries **1867**
Firearms & Pistols **1868**
Copper, Bronze etc. **1863-1866**
Goldsmiths & Silversmiths **1859-1861**
Encyclopaedias & Dictionaries **1859**
Great Britain **1860**
Hallmarks **1861**
Jewellery **1862**
Meteorites 1058
Meteorology 1048-1054
Climate **1053-1054**
Dictionaries **1050**
Encyclopaedias **1048**
Handbooks & Manuals **1049**
Reviews & Abstracts **1051**
Vapours **1052**
Clouds **1052**
Methodist Church 396
Metrical Romances 828
Mexican Literature 2471
Mexico 2678, 2827
[Maps & Atlases] **2678**
Mexico (History) **2977**
Microbiology 1120-1122
Bacteria **1122**
Microcomputers 1729-1734
Dictionaries **1732**
Encyclopaedias **1729**
Handbooks & Manuals **1730-1731**
Reviews & Abstracts **1733**
Tables & Data Books **1734**
Microfilms 264-265
Microphotography 1914
Yearbooks & Directories **1914**
Micros (Computer Industry) **1729-1734**
Dictionaries **1732**
Encyclopaedias **1729**
Handbooks & Manuals **1730-1731**
Reviews & Abstracts **1733**
Tables & Data Books **1734**
Microscopy (Optics) **970**
Microwaves (Electrical Engineering) **1366**
Middle East
See
Asia—Middle & Near East
Middle English Language 2124
Middle English Literature 2370
Military Engineering 1426-1431
Field Engineering **1429-1431**
Communications **1429**
Navies **1430-1431**
Weapons & Arms **1427-1428**
Small Arms **1428**
Mineralogy 997-1001
Encyclopaedias **997-998**
Gemmology **1001**
Handbooks & Manuals **999**
Reviews & Abstracts **1000**
Minerals (Economic Geology) **1005, 1060-1062**
Mines, Types of 1425
Oilfields **1425**
Miniature Painting 1900
Mining 1420-1425
Methods **1423-1424**
Oil extraction **1423-1424**
Offshore **1424**
Types of Mine **1425**
Oilfields **1425**

Minorities (Politics) **495**
Modern Art 1810
Encyclopaedias & Dictionaries **1810**
Molecular Biology 1121
Molluscs (Zoology) **1182**
Mongolia 2603
Encyclopaedias **2603**
[Area Studies] **2603**
Mongolia (History) **2947**
Monkeys (Zoology) **1215**
Mosses (Botany) **1166**
Moths 1189-1190
Motion Pictures
See
Films
Motor Cycles 1476
Motor Vehicle Engineering 1470-1472
Moulds (Botany) **1161-1165**
Mushrooms & Toadstools **1164-1165**
Yeasts **1163**
Multinationals 552
Museums 233-238
Europe **235**
Great Britain **236-237**
USA **238**
Mushrooms (Botany) **1164-1165**
Music 1917-1967
20th Century **1941**
Biographies **1941**
Abbreviations & Symbols **1917**
Bibliographies **1918-1920**
Biographies **1935-1937**
20th Century **1937**
Encyclopaedias & Dictionaries **1921-1927**
Great Britain **1938**
Yearbooks & Directories **1938**
Histories **1932-1934**
Kinds of Music **1948-1957**
Opera & Operettas **1948-1954**
Dictionaries **1952**
Encyclopaedias & Dictionaries **1948-1951**
Great Britain **1954**
Histories **1953**
Sacred & Church Music **1955-1957**
England **1957**
Music Education **1945-1946**
Music Librarianship **1942-1944**
Music Libraries **1943-1944**
Music Theory **1947**
Thematic Catalogues **1947**
Periodicals & Progress Reports **1928-1929**
Quotations **1931**
USA **1939-1940**
Biographies **1940**
Encyclopaedias & Dictionaries **1939**
Vocal Music **1958-1967**
Children's Songs **1965-1966**
Folk Songs **1960-1964**
Encyclopaedias & Dictionaries **1962-1963**
USA **1964**
National Anthems **1967**
USA **1959**
Yearbooks & Directories **1930**
Music Education 1945-1946
Music Hall 2053
Great Britain **2053**
Music Librarianship 1942-1944
Music Libraries **1943-1944**
Music Libraries 1943-1944

Music Theory 1947
  Thematic Catalogues 1947
Musical Instruments 1981-1982
Musical Theatre 2051-2052
  USA 2051-2052
Musicals 1950, 2026
Mystery Fiction 2340
Mythology 401-410
  Classical Mythology 409-410
  Dictionaries 406-407
  Ireland 408
Names, Christian 2109-2111
Names, Family 2112-2114
Names, Personal 2109-2114
  Family Names 2112-2114
  Forenames 2109-2111
Names, Place 2104-2108
Names, Proper 2102-2103
Narcotics (Health & Hygiene) 1277
National Anthems 1967
National Bibliographies 36-79
  Australia 78-79
  Belgium 60
  Bibliographies 36-37
  Canada 62-63
  France 54-55
  Germany 50-53
  Great Britain 40-48
    16th & 17th Centuries 40
    17th Century 41
    18th Century 42-43
    19th Century 44
    Contemporary 45-48
  India 61
  Ireland 49
  Italy 56
  Latin America 64
  Netherlands 59
  New Zealand 77
  Spain 57
  USA 65-76
    Contemporary 71-76
  USSR 58
  Worldwide 38-39
    English 38-39
National Parks 1820
  Europe—Western 1820
Native Americans
  See
    Amerindians, North
Nature Conservation 1132-1133
Nature Reserves 1130-1131
Nature Study 1123-1129
  America—North & Central 1128-1129
  Bibliographies 1123
  Encyclopaedias & Dictionaries 1124
  Europe 1127
  Reviews & Abstracts 1125
  Yearbooks & Directories 1126
Nautical Almanacs 937-938
Naval Engineering 1426-1431
  Field Engineering 1429-1431
    Communications 1429
    Navies 1430-1431
    Weapons & Arms 1427-1428
      Small Arms 1428
Navies 1430-1431
Navigation
  See also
    Maritime Navigation
Navigation 935-939
  Air & Nautical Almanacs 937-938
  Tide Tables 939

Navy 719-726
  Histories 724-726
Nazi Germany 2894-2896
  Encyclopaedias 2894
  Jews 2895-2896
    Bibliographies 2896
  [Germany] 2894-2896
Nebulae 928-934
  Handbooks & Manuals 928-930
  Illustrations 932-933
  Maps & Atlases 934
  Tables & Data Books 931
Needlework 1571-1572
Needlework (Decorative Arts) 1875-1879
  Crochet & Knitting 1879
  Embroidery 1878
  Encyclopaedias & Dictionaries 1875-1876
  Lacemaking 1877
Neologisms (English Language) 2156-2157
Netherlands 59
  [National Bibliographies] 59
Netherlands (History) 2928
  Bibliographies 2928
New Testament Greek 2204
New Zealand 77, 2633-2634, 2764
  Encyclopaedias 2633
  Yearbooks & Directories 2634
  [Area Studies] 2633-2634
  [Biography] 2764
  [National Bibliographies] 77
New Zealand (History) 2997
New Zealand Literature 2419
Newfoundland 2755
  [Biography] 2755
News Digests 254-256
Newspapers 246-252
  Indexes 248-252
    Great Britain 248-251
    USA 252
Nicknames 2101
Nigeria (History) 2968
Nobility (Heraldry) 2788-2794
  Great Britain 2788-2791
    Handbooks & Manuals 2789-2790
    Yearbooks & Directories 2791
  Orders & Decorations 2792-2793
    Commonwealth 2793
    Europe 2792
  Royalty 2794
Noise Abatement 1467
Non-Conformist Church 392-394
Non-Ferrous Metals 1686-1688
  Aluminium 1686-1687
  Rare Earth Metals 1688
Northwest Passage 3004
Norwegian Language 2173-2174
Norwegian Literature 2438-2439
Novels
  See
    Fiction
Nuclear Engineering 1348-1353
  Bibliographies 1348-1349
  Reactors 1353
  Reviews & Abstracts 1350
  Tables & Data Books 1351
  Thesauri 1352
Nuclear Reactors 1353
Numismatics 1847-1849
  Encyclopaedias & Dictionaries 1848
  Great Britain 1849
Nursing 1303-1307

Nursing (contd.)
  Education Courses 1307
  Encyclopaedias & Dictionaries 1303-1304
  Reviews & Abstracts 1305-1306
Nutrition (Health & Hygiene) 1271-1273
Observatories 925
Obstetrics 1256
Occultism 311
Occultism & Parapsychology 309-313
  Alchemy 313
  Occultism 311
  Witchcraft & Magic 312
Occupational Health & Safety 1280-1281
  Encyclopaedias 1281
Occupations 536-538
Oceania
  See also
    Australasia & Oceania
Oceania (History) 2994-2996
  Dictionaries 2996
Oceanic Religions 429
Oceanography 1044-1047
  Encyclopaedias 1044
  Handbooks & Manuals 1045
  Maps & Atlases 1047
  Reviews & Abstracts 1046
Oceans & Seas
  See also
    Pacific Ocean
Office Practice 606-609
  Correspondence 609
Offshore Oil (Petroleum Industry) 1667
Offshore Oil Extraction 1424
Oil Extraction (Mining) 1423-1424
  Offshore 1424
Oilfields 1425
Oils (Chemical Industry) 1659
Old Age
  See
    Aged People
Old English Literature 2368-2369
Old Norse Literature
  See
    Icelandic Literature
Olympic Games 2082
Online Information Systems 5-9
Open Learning 767
Opera (Discography) 1990
Opera & Operettas 1948-1954
  Dictionaries 1952
  Encyclopaedias & Dictionaries 1948-1951
  Great Britain 1954
  Histories 1953
Ophthalmology 1319-1320
Optics (Physics) 970-973
  Colours 972-973
  Microscopy 970
  Reflection. Emission. 971
    Lasers 971
    Spectral Data 971
Orders of Chivalry 2792-2793
  Commonwealth 2793
  Europe 2792
Ores (Economic Geology) 1060-1062
Organic Chemistry 994-995
  Compounds 995
Organic Farming 1508
Organizations & Associations 218-238
  Conferences 225-229
    Conference Proceedings 226-229
  Europe 219

Organizations & Associations (contd.)
Great Britain 220-221
Museums 233-238
Europe 235
Great Britain 236-237
USA 238
Non-Government Organizations 223-224
Learned Societies 223
Social, Sports & Literary Clubs & Associations 224
Research Establishments 230-232
USA 222
Oriental Literature 2496-2498
Ornamentation (The Arts) 1811-1812
Dictionaries 1811
Symbols & Allegories 1812
Ornithology
See
Birds (Zoology)
Orthodox church 381
Otology 1309
Outdoor Pursuits 2083
Great Britain 2083
Pacific Ocean 2534
[Archaeology] 2534
Packaging (Engineering) 1412-1414
Containerization 1414
Paediatrics 1256
Painting 1888-1900
Biographies 1890
Canada 1894
Great Britain 1891
Ireland 1893
Materials & Paints 1896
Water-colour Painting 1896
Great Britain 1896
Miniature Painting 1900
Painting Subjects 1899
Portraits 1899
Great Britain 1899
Periods & Styles 1897-1898
19th Century 1897
20th Century 1898
Scotland 1892
USA 1895
Yearbooks & Directories 1888-1889
Painting (Building Trades) 1763
Painting—Periods & Styles 1897-1898
19th Century 1897
20th Century 1898
Painting Subjects 1899
Portraits 1899
Great Britain 1899
Paintings—Periods & Styles 1897-1898
19th Century 1897
20th Century 1898
Paints 1896
Water-colour Painting 1896
Great Britain 1896
Pakistan 2609
Yearbooks & Directories 2609
[Area Studies] 2609
Palaeography 2811-2813
Palaeontology 1065-1072
Bibliographies 1065
Encyclopaedias 1066
Great Britain 1070-1072
Handbooks & Manuals 1067
Maps & Atlases 1069
Reviews & Abstracts 1068

Palestine
See also
Jewish History
Palestine (History) 2958-2959
Dictionaries 2959
Pantomime 2053
Great Britain 2053
Paper Industry 1697-1700
Yearbooks & Directories 1700
Papua—New Guinea 2636, 2707
Encyclopaedias 2636
[Area Studies] 2636
Parish Registers 2782-2783
England & Wales 2783
Maps & Atlases 2783
Great Britain 2782
Parks (Town & Country Planning) 1821-1823
Great Britain 1822-1823
Parliaments (Law) 668-674
Great Britain 670-673
USA 674
Passenger Ships 1480
Patents 1235-1241
Bibliographies 1236
Databases 1235
Handbooks & Manuals 1237
Information Services 1240
Patent Law 1241
Periodicals 1238-1239
Pathology 1296-1299
Tropical Diseases 1299
Worldwide 1298
Pathology, Special 1309-1317
Communicable Infections & Fevers 1315-1317
AIDS 1316-1317
Dentistry 1310-1311
Reviews & Abstracts 1311
Hearing (Otology) 1309
Psychiatry 1312-1314
Patients (Medicine) 1300
Geriatrics 1300
Patrology 376
Performing Arts 1996-1999
Awards & Prizes 1996
Biographies 1997-1998
Great Britain 1999
Perfumery Industry 1660
Periodicals 184-214
Australia 202
France 199
Germany 198
Great Britain 196-197
Indexes 203-214
Canada 210
Great Britain 207-209
USA 211-214
Spain 200
USA 201
Periods & Styles (The Arts) 1810
Modern Art 1810
Encyclopaedias & Dictionaries 1810
Persecution (Politics) 497
Persian Gulf (History) 2951
Persian Languages 2231-2232
Persian Literature 2502
Personal Names 2109-2114
Family Names 2112-2114
Forenames 2109-2111
Personnel Management 618
Peruvian Literature 2474
Pesticides 1515

Pests & Diseases (Agriculture) 1514-1515
Pesticides 1515
Petrochemicals 1669
Petroleum Industry 1661-1669
Bibliographies 1661
Dictionaries 1663
Handbooks & Manuals 1662
Offshore Oil 1667
Petrochemicals 1669
Refining 1668
Reviews & Abstracts 1664-1665
Yearbooks & Directories 1666
Petrology 1005, 1056-1058
Meteorites 1058
Rocks 1057
Pets 1534-1537
Cage & Aviary Birds 1535
Cats 1537
Dogs 1536
Pewter 1866
Phanerogams 1168-1170
Dictionaries 1168
Grasses 1170
Nomenclatures 1169
Pharmacology 1285-1291
Homeopathy 1286
Medications & Drugs 1290
Origins of Medicines & Therapy 1291
Plant Medicines 1291
Pharmacopoeias 1287-1289
Great Britain 1287-1288
USA 1289
Pharmacopoeias 1287-1289
Great Britain 1287-1288
USA 1289
Philately
See
Postage Stamps
Philosophical Systems 315-318
Socialist Systems 315-318
Communism. Marxism. Leninism 316-318
Philosophy 293-308
Asia 305-308
Biographies 304
Encyclopaedias 298-300
Histories 301-303
Phonetics 2117
Photogrammetry 942-943
Remote Sensing 943
Photographic Collections 1916
Photography 1909-1915
Biographies 1913
Encyclopaedias & Dictionaries 1911
Film & Television Photography 1915
Video 1915
Histories 1912
Microphotography 1914
Yearbooks & Directories 1914
Physical Chemistry 989-990
Electrochemistry 989
Radiation Chemistry 990
Physical Education 1275
Physical Welfare 1274-1278
Alcoholism 1276
Drugs (Narcotics) 1277
Physical Education 1275
Smoking 1278
Sports Medicine 1274
Physics 954-966
Abbreviations & Symbols 954
Bibliographies 956

Physics (contd.)
  Databases 955
  Dictionaries 961-962
  Encyclopaedias 957-959
  Handbooks & Manuals 960
  Physical Measurement 966
  Reviews & Abstracts 963
  Tables & Data Books 964
  Thesauri 965
Physiology 1268-1269
Pickles (Cookery) 1566-1567
Pictures 261-263
Pins (Manufactures) 1691
Pistols (Metal Arts) 1868
Place Names 2104-2108
Plant Diseases 1157
Plant Medicines 1291
Plants (Botany) 1146-1159
  Australasia & Oceania 1156
  Diseases 1157
  Economic Aspects 1158-1159
  Europe 1147-1148
  Great Britain 1149-1154
  USA 1155
  Worldwide 1146
Plastics Industry 1708-1710
Plays 2324-2331
Pneumatic Energy Machines 1395
Poetry 2319-2323
Poetry, American 2413-2414
Poetry, English 2371-2373
Poisons 1294-1295
Poland (History) 2901
Polar Regions (History) 3004-3006
  Bibliographies 3004
  Chronologies 3006
  Encyclopaedias 3005
Polish Language 2212-2213
Polish Literature 2491
Political Movements 510-514
Political Parties 510-514
Political Theory 493-494
Politics 479-514
  Africa 491
  Asia—Middle & Near East 490
  Colonial Administration 499
  Elections 498
  Europe 487
  Foreign Relations 502-509
    Espionage 507-509
    Great Britain 504-505
    USA 506
  Great Britain 488-489
  Institutions & Associations 492
  Internal Relations 495-497
    Minorities 495
    Resistance & Revolution 496
    Terrorism & Persecution 497
  Parties & Movements 510-514
  Political Theory 493-494
  Quotations 486
  Slavery 500-501
Pollution, Environmental 1464-1466
Pollution, Marine 1463
Polymers (Manufactures) 1710-1714
  PVC 1714
Polynesian Language 2274
  Hawaiian 2274
Polytechnics 777-783
  Great Britain 780-782
  USA 783
Ponies 1531
Pop Music 1974-1979

Pop Music (contd.)
  Encyclopaedias & Dictionaries 1977-1979
Popes 387
Population (Statistics) 475-478
  Births & Deaths 478
Porcelain 1858
Porpoises 1213
Portraits (Painting) 1899
  Great Britain 1899
Ports & Harbours (Transport Services) 1620-1621
Ports (Engineering)
  See
    Docks & Harbours (Engineering)
Portugal (History) 2917
Portuguese Language 2196-2199
Portuguese Literature 2475-2476
Postage Stamps 1626-1628
Postal Services 1626-1628
  Postage Stamps 1626-1628
Postgraduate Awards (Further & Higher Education) 776
Pottery 1852-1858
  Ceramic Marks 1856-1857
    Great Britain 1857
  Encyclopaedias & Dictionaries 1852-1854
  Great Britain 1855
  Porcelain 1858
Poverty 529
Powder Metallurgy 1406-1407
Power Engineering
  See
    Heat Engineering
Power Supply 1362
  Hydroelectric Power 1362
Preservation (Food Industry) 1658
  Additives 1658
The Press 243-245
Presses, Small 290-291
Primary Schools 765
Primates 1214-1215
  Apes & Monkeys 1215
Printed Circuits (Electronics) 1381
Printing Industry 1578-1586
  Dictionaries 1578
  Processes & Printing Surfaces 1581-1585
    Copy Presentation 1581-1583
      Word Processing 1583
    Typography 1584-1585
  Reviews & Abstracts 1579
  Techniques 1586
  Yearbooks & Directories 1580
Printing Surfaces 1581-1585
  Copy Presentation 1581-1583
    Word Processing 1583
  Typography 1584-1585
Printing Techniques 1586
Private & Small Presses 290-291
Private Firms 551
Production Engineering 1400-1419
  Bibliographies 1401-1402
    Laws 1402
  Databases 1400
  Dictionaries 1405
  Handbooks & Manuals 1403-1404
  Workshop Practice 1406-1419
    Boiler Making 1408
    Machine Elements 1415-1416
      Gears & Clutches 1416
    Materials Handling 1417-1419

Production Engineering (contd.)
  Workshop Practice
    Materials Handling
      Fasteners 1417
      Lubrication 1418-1419
      Packaging 1412-1414
        Containerization 1414
      Powder Metallurgy 1406-1407
      Welding 1409-1411
Production Management 619-620
  Quality Control 619-620
Pronunciation (English Language) 2143
Proper Names 2102-2103
Property & Land 541-542
  Property Market 542
Property Market 542
Protestant Church 388
Proverbs 833-834
Pseudonyma (Bibliographies) 32-35
Psychiatry 1312-1314
Psychoanalysis 329
Psychology 319-328
  Dictionaries 325-328
  Encyclopaedias 324
Psychotherapy 1293
Public Administration 686-691
  Civil Service 689-690
  Government Bodies 688
  Housing 691
Public Finance 564-565
  Accounts 564
  Taxation 565
Public Health 1279-1284
  Public Safety 1280-1284
    Fires & Fire Prevention 1282
    First Aid 1284
    Hazardous Chemicals 1283
    Industrial & Occupational Safety 1280-1281
      Encyclopaedias 1281
Public Health Engineering 1453-1468
  Databases 1453
  Encyclopaedias 1454-1455
  Environmental Pollution Measures 1464-1466
  Handbooks & Manuals 1456-1458
  Industrial Effluents & Wastes 1468
  Maps & Atlases 1460
  Marine Pollution 1463
  Noise Abatement 1467
  Reviews & Abstracts 1459
  Water Supply 1461-1462
    Treatment 1462
Public Houses 1553-1554
Public Opinion (Sociology) 448
Public Relations 631
Public Safety 1280-1284
  Fires & Fire Prevention 1282
  First Aid 1284
  Hazardous Chemicals 1283
  Industrial & Occupational Safety 1280-1281
    Encyclopaedias 1281
Publicity 628-630
  Advertising 628-630
Publishers' Series 257
Publishing 1590-1592
Pulses (Electrical Engineering) 1367
  Amplifiers 1367
  Lasers 1367
Pumps (Fluids Handling Engineering) 1399
Puppets 2029-2030

Puppets *(contd.)*
  Histories 2030
PVC (Manufactures) 1714
Quakers 397
Qualifications (Further & Higher Education) 774-775
Quality Control 619-620
Quechua Literature 2474
Quotations 344-345, 486, 550, 706, 815, 1259, 1779, 1931, 2039, 2077, 2284-2289
  [Armed Forces] 706
  [The Arts] 1779
  [Business Relationships & Organization] 550
  [Literature] 2284-2289
  [Medicine] 1259
  [Music] 1931
  [Politics] 486
  [Religion] 344-345
  [Sport] 2077
  [Theatre] 2039
  [Women & Society] 815
Race Relations (Sociology) 453-457
Races (Anthropology) 1083-1092
  Aborigines 1092
  Amerindians, North 1089-1090
  Amerindians, South 1091
  Encyclopaedias 1083-1084
  Tables & Data Books 1085-1087
  USA 1088
    Black Races 1088
Radiation Chemistry 990
Radio & Television Apparatus 1386
Radio Engineering 1387-1389
  Space Radiocommunication 1388-1389
    Satellites 1388-1389
  VHF 1387
Radio Entertainment 2000-2002
Radiology 1256
Rail Vehicle Engineering 1481
Railway Engineering 1443-1446
  Underground Railways 1446
Railway Transport 1603-1609
  Great Britain 1604-1606
  Timetables 1607-1609
  Worldwide 1603
Rare Earth Metals (Metallurgy) 1688
Rationalism 346
Reactors (Engineering) 1353
Records & Tapes
  See
    Sound Recordings
Refining (Petroleum Industry) 1668
Reflection (Physics) 971
  Lasers 971
    Spectral Data 971
Refrigeration 1396
  Yearbooks & Directories 1396
Religion 333-346
  Dictionaries 340-343
  Encyclopaedias 338-339
  Quotations 344-345
  Rationalism 346
Religions, Non-Christian 398-400
Religious Architecture 1843-1844
  Abbeys & Cathedrals 1844
    England & Wales 1844
  Churches 1843
    England & Wales 1843
Religious Associations (Christian Church) 368-369
  Salvation Army 369

Religious Music 1955-1957
  England 1957
Religious Orders 374-375
Religious Societies (Christian Church) 368-369
  Salvation Army 369
Remote Sensing (Geological Techniques) 1014
Remote Sensing (Photogrammetry) 943
Renaissance 2841-2842
  Bibliographies 2841
    French 2841
  Encyclopaedias 2842
  [Mediaeval History—Europe] 2841-2842
Repairs (Household) 1569-1570
Reports 171-172
Reprints 165
Reptiles (Zoology) 1194-1195
Research Establishments 230-232
Research Establishments 898-899, 1265, 1329, 1502
  [Agriculture] 1502
  [Engineering] 1329
  [Medicine] 1265
  [Science] 898-899
Research Projects 440, 761, 1104
  [Biology] 1104
  [Education] 761
  [Social Sciences] 440
Resistance (Politics) 496
Restaurants 1551-1552
Resuscitation 1284
Retail Selling 626-627
Retirement (Sociology) 450-452
Revolution (Politics) 496
River Transport 1622-1623
Rivers (Hydrology) 1064
Road Transport 1601-1602
Roads (Engineering) 1447-1448
Robots 1745-1747
Rock Music (Discography) 1993
Rocks (Petrology) 1057
Roman Catholic Church 382-387
Roman Times 2549
  [Great Britain] 2549
Romantic Fiction 2339
Rome (Ancient History) 2825-2826
  Encyclopaedias 2825
  Maps & Atlases 2826
Royalty 2794
RSFSR 2589, 2921-2925
  Encyclopaedias 2924
  Reviews & Abstracts 2925
  [Area Studies] 2589
RSFSR (History) 2921-2925
  Encyclopaedias 2924
  Reviews & Abstracts 2925
Rubber Industry 1707
Rubbers, Synthetic (Manufactures) 1710-1714
  PVC 1714
Rumanian Language 2191
Rumanian Literature 2459
Russia (History) 2918
Russian Language 2207-2211
  Ukrainian 2211
Russian Literature 2486-2490
  Ukrainian Literature 2490
Russian Soviet Federal Socialist Republic
  See
    RSFSR
Sacred Music 1955-1957

Sacred Music *(contd.)*
  England 1957
Safety, Industrial 1280-1281
  Encyclopaedias 1281
Safety, Occupational 1280-1281
  Encyclopaedias 1281
Saints 357-359
Salaries 535
Sales Management 621-627
  Market Research 625
  Retail Selling 626-627
Salvation Army 369
Sanskrit Language 2226
Sanskrit Literature 2500
Satellites (Telecommunications) 1388-1389
Scandinavia 2593, 2652, 2745
  Bibliographies 2593
  Micromaterials 2745
  [Area Studies] 2593
  [Biography] 2745
  [Historical Geography] 2652
Scandinavia (History) 2927
  Dictionaries 2927
Scandinavian Languages 2172-2179
  Danish 2178-2179
  Icelandic 2172
  Norwegian 2173-2174
  Swedish 2175-2177
Scandinavian Literature 2436-2441
  Icelandic Literature 2437
  Norwegian Literature 2438-2439
  Swedish Literature 2440-2441
Scholarships (Further & Higher Education) 776
Schools 763-765
  Primary Schools 765
  Yearbooks & Directories 763-764
Science 836-899
  Abbreviations & Symbols 836-837
  Bibliographies 840-843
  Biographies 888-892
    Europe 892
  Conferences 897
  Databases 838-839
  Dictionaries 847-873
    Arabic 871
    Chinese 872-873
    Danish 862-863
    English 849-851
    French 864-865
    German 852-856
    Italian 866
    Norwegian 857-858
    Polyglot 848
    Portuguese 868
    Russian 869-870
    Spanish 867
    Swedish 859-861
  Encyclopaedias 844-846
  Histories 884-887
  Information Services 896
  Periodicals 879
  Reports Literature 874
  Research Establishments 898-899
  Reviews & Abstracts 875-878
  Tables & Data Books 883
  Teaching Materials 882
  Translations 894
    USA 893
  Writing & Lecturing 895
  Yearbooks & Directories 880-881
Science Fiction 2341-2342

Science Fiction Films 2027
Scotland 646, 1835, 1892, 2543-2544, 2550, 2562, 2734, 2774, 2781
  Handbooks & Manuals 2774, 2781
  [Antiquities] 2550
  [Archaeology] 2543-2544
  [Architecture] 1835
  [Biography] 2734
  [Family Histories] 2781
  [Genealogy] 2774
  [Industrial Antiquities] 2562
  [Law] 646
  [Painting] 1892
Scotland (History) 2872-2874
  Encyclopaedias & Dictionaries 2873
  Yearbooks & Directories 2874
Scots Language 2134
Scottish Literature 2388-2390
Scripts 15-20
  Abbreviations 16-20
  Transliteration 15
Sculpture 1846
  Histories 1846
Sea Fisheries 1544
  Maps & Atlases 1544
Seaweeds (Botany) 1160
Second-hand Books 1593-1595
Security (Computers) 1736-1737
Sedimentation (Geology) 1030
Seed Plants 1168-1170
  Dictionaries 1168
  Grasses 1170
  Nomenclatures 1169
Semantics & Semiotics 2118
Semiotics 2118
Semitic Languages 2240-2246
  Arabic 2244-2246
  Hebrew 2240-2243
Serbo-Croat Language 2218-2219
Serials
  See
    Periodicals
Sewing 1571-1572
Sexist Usage (English Language) 2127
Shakespeare, William 2378-2382
Sheep 1533
Shellfish (Zoology) 1182
Shells (Zoology) 1182
Shipbuilding 1477-1480
  Passenger Ships 1480
Ships' Flags 1613
Ships, Passenger 1480
Shopping 1558-1561
  Bibliographies 1558
  Great Britain 1561
  Laws 1559-1560
Short Stories 2343-2344
Sign Language 2094-2095
Signals (Maritime Navigation) 1618
Sikhism 416
Sikhs 416
Silversmiths 1859-1861
  Encyclopaedias & Dictionaries 1859
  Great Britain 1860
  Hallmarks 1861
Silviculture 1506-1507
  Encyclopaedias 1506-1507
Sino-Tibetan Languages 2254-2261
  Chinese 2254-2256
  Japanese 2258-2260
  Korean 2261
  Thai 2257
Slang, English 2129-2132

Slavery 500-501
Slavonic & Baltic Languages 2207-2225
  Baltic Languages 2222-2225
    Latvian 2224-2225
    Lithuanian 2222-2223
  Bulgarian 2221
  Czech 2214-2215
  Polish Language 2212-2213
  Russian Language 2207-2211
    Ukrainian 2211
  Serbo-Croat 2218-2219
  Slovak 2216-2217
  Slovenian 2220
Slavonic Literatures 2484-2485
Slide Collections 261
Slovak Language 2216-2217
Slovenian Language 2220
Small Businesses 553-554
Smoking (Health & Hygiene) 1278
Snails (Zoology) 1182
Snakes (Zoology) 1196-1197
Social Climate 459-461
  Developing Countries 459
  Great Britain 460-461
Social Clubs & Associations 224
Social Sciences 430-440
  Dictionaries 434-435
  Institutions & Associations 439
  Research Projects 440
  Yearbooks & Directories 436-438
Social Security 752
Social Services 730-734
Socialism 514
Socialist Systems 315-318
  Communism. Marxism. Leninism 316-318
Society of Friends 397
Sociology 441-461
  Adolescents 449
  Aged People 450-452
  Great Britain 447
  Hunger 458
  Public Opinion 448
  Race Relations 453-457
  Social Climate 459-461
    Developing Countries 459
    Great Britain 460-461
Software, Computers 1735
Soil Science 1512-1513
Solar System 926-927
Solid Waste 1468
Solvents (Chemical Industry) 1641
Somatology 1082
Songs 1958-1967
  Children's Songs 1965-1966
  Folk Songs 1960-1964
    Encyclopaedias & Dictionaries 1962-1963
    USA 1964
  National Anthems 1967
  USA 1959
Sound (Physics) 968-969
Sound Recordings 266-267
Sound Recordings (Discography) 1983-1993
  Jazz 1991-1992
  Opera 1990
  Rock Music 1993
Sound Recordings (Manufactures) 1748
South Africa 2619
  Yearbooks & Directories 2619
  [Area Studies] 2619
South Africa (History) 2971

South African English 2135
South African Literature in English 2397
Soviet Russia (History) 2926
Space Radiocommunication 1388-1389
  Satellites 1388-1389
Spain 57, 200, 2586
  [Area Studies] 2586
  [National Bibliographies] 57
  [Periodicals] 200
Spain (History) 2914-2916
  20th Century 2916
    Dictionaries 2916
  Dictionaries 2915
Spanish-American Literature 2466-2469
  Women 2469
Spanish & Portuguese Literature 2460
Spanish Language 2192-2195
Spanish Literature 2461-2465
  Women 2465
Spectral Data 971
Speeches (Literature) 2348
Speed (physics) 967
Speleology
  See
    Caves (Geology)
Spices 1566-1567
Spiders 1183
Spirituality (Christianity) 362
Sport 2075-2082
  Dictionaries 2076
  Encyclopaedias & Dictionaries 2075
  Great Britain 2080-2081
    Yearbooks & Directories 2081
  Laws 2079
  Official Records 2078
  Olympic Games 2082
  Quotations 2077
Sports Cars 1475
Sports Medicine 1274
Stained Glass (Decorative Arts) 1882
  Great Britain 1882
Standards 21
Stars 928-934
  Handbooks & Manuals 928-930
  Illustrations 932-933
  Maps & Atlases 934
  Tables & Data Books 931
Stately Homes (Architecture) 1845
  Great Britain 1845
Statistics 462-478
  Europe 467
  Great Britain 468-473
  Population 475-478
    Births & Deaths 478
  USA 474
Statistics (Mathematics) 910
Steel (Civil Engineering) 1441
Steel Industry 1685
Stock Markets & Exchanges 570
Strategy 712
Stratigraphy 1055
Structures (Civil Engineering) 1439-1441
  Concrete 1439-1440
  Metal 1441
Subject Heading Lists 110
Succulents 1524
Sudanic Languages 2268-2269
  Hausa 2268-2269
Sugar Industry 1657
Superstitions 829
Surgery 1256, 1318
Surnames 2112-2114

Surveying 935, 940-953
  Cartography 944-952
    Bibliographies 944-945
    Biographies 952
    Handbooks & Manuals 946-947
    Histories 950-951
    Maps & Atlases 949
    Yearbooks & Directories 948
  Photogrammetry 942-943
  Remote Sensing 943
  Time 953
Swahili Language 2266
Swedish Language 2175-2177
Swedish Literature 2440-2441
Switzerland (History) 2930
Symbols (The Arts) 1812
Symptoms (Medicine) 1302
Syndromes (Medicine) 1301
Synonyms (English Language) 2153-2155
Synthetic Fibres (Manufactures) 1705
Systematic Zoology (Categories of
Animals) 1181-1215
  Invertebrates 1181-1190
    Butterflies & Moths 1189-1190
    Insects 1184-1188
      Bibliographies 1184
      Europe 1188
      Handbooks & Manuals 1185-1186
      Reviews & Abstracts 1187
    Molluscs. Shellfish & Shells 1182
    Spiders 1183
  Vertebrates 1191-1215
    Birds 1198-1205
      America—North & Central 1205
      Encyclopaedias & Dictionaries
      1198
      Europe 1202
      Great Britain 1203-1204
      Tables & Data Books 1199
      Worldwide 1200-1201
    Fishes 1192-1193
    Mammals 1206-1213
      Encyclopaedias 1206
      Europe 1211
      Great Britain 1212
      Handbooks & Manuals 1207
      Tables & Data Books 1208
      Whales, etc. 1213
      Worldwide 1209-1210
    Primates 1214-1215
      Apes & Monkeys 1215
    Reptiles & Amphibians 1194-1195
    Snakes 1196-1197
Tapestries (Textile Arts) 1874
Taps (Fluids Handling Engineering)
1398
Taxation 565
Teaching Materials 762
Teaching Materials 882
Teaching Materials
  Education Technology 762
Teaching Materials
  [Science] 882
Technology 1221-1228
  Abbreviations & Symbols 1221
  Developing Countries 1228
  Histories 1225-1227
  Reviews & Abstracts 1222-1224
Technology, Information ·3-14
  CD-Rom Information Systems 10-14
  Online Information Systems 5-9
Tectonics 1029
Telecommunication Services 1574

Telecommunications 1382-1391
  Radio 1387-1389
    Space Radiocommunication 1388-
    1389
      Satellites 1388-1389
      VHF 1387
    Radio & Television Apparatus 1386
    Television 1390-1391
    Wave Signals 1385
Television Engineering 1390-1391
Television Entertainment 2003-2007
  Biographies 2006
  Great Britain 2007
  Yearbooks & Directories 2004-2005
Television Photography 1915
  Video 1915
Terrorism (Politics) 497
Textile Arts 1873-1874
  Histories 1873
  Tapestries & Carpets 1874
Textile Fibres 1705
  Man-made Fibres 1705
Textile Industry 1701-1705
  Products 1704
    Carpets 1704
  Textile Fibres 1705
    Man-made Fibres 1705
Thai Language 2257
Thailand (History) 2960
Theatre 2033-2050
  Amateur Theatre 2050
  Canada 2044
  Dictionaries 2037-2038
  Eire 2043
  Encyclopaedias & Dictionaries 2033-
  2035
  Great Britain 2040-2042
    Yearbooks & Directories 2040-2042
  Handbooks & Manuals 2036
  Libraries 2048-2049
    America — North 2049
    Great Britain 2048
  Quotations 2039
  USA 2045-2047
Thematic Catalogues (Music) 1947
Theology (Christianity) 354-356
Theoretical Chemistry 989-990
  Physical Chemistry 989-990
    Electrochemistry 989
    Radiation Chemistry 990
Therapeutic Treatments 1292-1293
  Psychotherapy 1293
Thesauri 965, 1352
  [Nuclear & Atomic Engineering] 1352
  [Physics] 965
Theses & Dissertations 166-170
  Great Britain 169-170
Third World
  See
    Developing Countries
Tibet (History) 2946
Tide Tables 939
Timber Industry 1692-1695
Time 953
Timetables (Air Transport) 1625
Timetables (Railway Transport) 1607-
1609
Toadstools (Botany) 1164-1165
Tourism 586
Town & Country Planning 1816-1818
  Great Britain 1816-1817
  Town Planning 1818
    Histories 1818

Town Planning 1818
  Histories 1818
Towns 2696
Towns & Cities (Local Government)
695-696
Toxicology 1256, 1294-1295
Trade 587-596
  Businesses 589-593
  Foreign Trade 594-596
    Exports 596
*Trade Names, Trade Marks, Brand
Names* 1229-1232
  [Patents & Inventions] 1229-1232
Trade Unions 539-540
Translation (Languages) 2092
Translations 894
  [Science] 894
Translations (Bibliographies) 30-31
Translators (Languages) 2092
Transliteration 15
Transmission (Electrical Engineering)
1363
  Cables 1363
Transport Services 1596-1625
  Air Transport 1624-1625
    Airports & Airfields 1624
    Timetables 1625
  Canal & River Transport 1622-1623
  Encyclopaedias & Dictionaries 1596
  Great Britain 1598-1599
  Handbooks & Manuals 1597
  Marine Transport 1610-1612
    Dictionaries 1611
      English 1611
    Encyclopaedias 1610
    Yearbooks & Directories 1612
  Maritime Navigation 1614-1619
    Handbooks & Manuals 1614-1617
    Lights & Beacons 1619
    Signals 1618
  Ports & Harbours 1620-1621
  Railway Transport 1603-1609
    Great Britain 1604-1606
    Timetables 1607-1609
    Worldwide 1603
  Road Transport 1601-1602
    Routes & Services 1600
    Urban Transport 1600
  Ships' Flags 1613
Transport Vehicles 1470-1476
  Motor Cycles 1476
  Motor Vehicle Engineering 1470-1472
  Private Cars 1473-1474
  Sports Cars 1475
Travel 2642-2643
  Handbooks & Manuals 2642
  Histories 2643
Treaties (International Law) 660-662
Treatment (Medicine) 1303-1307
  Nursing 1303-1307
    Education Courses 1307
    Encyclopaedias & Dictionaries
    1303-1304
    Reviews & Abstracts 1305-1306
Trees 1506-1507
  Encyclopaedias 1506-1507
Tribology 1418-1419
Tropical Diseases 1299
Tropical Fish 1545
Tropics 1500
  [Agriculture] 1500
Turanian Languages 2247-2248
  Turkish 2247-2248

Turkey (History) 2957
Turkish Language 2247-2248
Turkish Literature 2511
Typography (Printing Industry) 1584-1585
Ukraine 2592
 Encyclopaedias 2592
 [Area Studies] 2592
Ukraine (History) 2926
Ukrainian Language 2211
Ukrainian Literature 2490
Underground Railways 1446
Underwater Work (Engineering) 1451
Uniforms (Armed Forces) 709
Union of Soviet Socialist Republics
 See
 USSR
Unions, Trade
 See
 Trade Unions
United Arab Emirates (History) 2951
United Nations 653-654
United Reformed Church 395
United States of America
 See
 USA
Universities 777-783
 Great Britain 780-782
 USA 783
Ural-Altaic Languages 2247-2248
 Turkish 2247-2248
Urban Areas (Local Government) 695-696
Urban Transport 1600
Urdu Language 2228
Urdu Literature 2501
USA 65-76, 119-120, 201, 211-214, 222, 238, 252, 279-281, 474, 506, 580-581, 674, 716, 783, 893, 1088, 1155, 1289, 1797-1801, 1840, 1887, 1895, 1907, 1939-1940, 1959, 1964, 2045-2047, 2051-2052, 2138-2139, 2627-2630, 2654, 2679, 2705, 2757-2763, 2769, 2777-2778, 2798
 Bibliographies 2629-2630, 2654, 2762-2763, 2769
 Biographies 1799-1801, 1940
 Women 1801
 Black Races 1088
 Contemporary 71-76
 Encyclopaedias & Dictionaries 1939
 Glossaries 2778
 Handbooks & Manuals 2777
 Yearbooks & Directories 1798
 [Architecture] 1840
 [Area Studies] 2627-2630
 [Army] 716
 [The Arts] 1797-1801
 [Biography] 2757-2763
 [Economic Surveys] 580-581
 [Ethnology (Races)] 1088
 [Flags & Banners] 2798
 [Folk Songs] 1964
 [Foreign Relations] 506
 [Genealogy] 2777-2778
 [Genealogy & Heraldry] 2769
 [Government Publications] 279-281
 [Graphic Arts] 1907
 [Historical Geography] 2654
 [Indexes] 211-214, 252
 [Libraries] 119-120
 [Maps & Atlases] 2679
 [Museums] 238
 [Music] 1939-1940

USA (contd.)
 [Musical Theatre] 2051-2052
 [National Bibliographies] 65-76
 [Organizations & Associations] 222
 [Painting] 1895
 [Parliaments] 674
 [Periodicals] 201
 [Pharmacopoeias] 1289
 [Plants (Flora)] 1155
 [Science] 893
 [Statistics] 474
 [Styles] 1887
 [Theatre] 2045-2047
 [Universities, Polytechnics & Colleges] 783
 [Vocal Music] 1959
USA (History) 2983-2991
 Amerindians, North 2990
 Handbooks & Manuals 2990
 Bibliographies 2983-2985
 Colonial Period 2991
 Encyclopaedias 2991
 Dictionaries 2987
 Encyclopaedias 2986
 Maps & Atlases 2989
 Reviews & Abstracts 2988
USSR 58, 2587-2588, 2741-2744
 Encyclopaedias 2588
 Micromaterials 2744
 [Area Studies] 2587-2588
 [Biography] 2741-2744
 [National Bibliographies] 58
USSR (History) 2919-2925
 Archives 2919-2920
 RSFSR 2921-2925
 Encyclopaedias 2924
 Reviews & Abstracts 2925
USSR in Europe (History) 2926
Valves (Fluids Handling Engineering) 1398
Vascular Plants 1167
 Ferns 1167
Vegetables (Horticulture) 1519
Ventilation (Building Trades) 1762
Vertebrates 1191-1215
 Birds 1198-1205
 America—North & Central 1205
 Encyclopaedias & Dictionaries 1198
 Europe 1202
 Great Britain 1203-1204
 Tables & Data Books 1199
 Worldwide 1200-1201
 Fishes 1192-1193
 Mammals 1206-1213
 Encyclopaedias 1206
 Europe 1211
 Great Britain 1212
 Handbooks & Manuals 1207
 Tables & Data Books 1208
 Whales, etc. 1213
 Worldwide 1209-1210
 Primates 1214-1215
 Apes & Monkeys 1215
 Reptiles & Amphibians 1194-1195
 Snakes 1196-1197
Veterinary Medicine 1525-1529
 Encyclopaedias & Dictionaries 1525
 Handbooks & Manuals 1526
 Reviews & Abstracts 1527
 Tables & Data Books 1528-1529
VHF (Radio) 1387
Vibrations (Physics) 968-969
Video Entertainment 2008-2028

Video Entertainment (contd.)
 Biographies 2019-2020
 Dictionaries 2017
 Encyclopaedias & Dictionaries 2011-2016
 Film Festivals 2023
 Film Libraries 2022
 Genres of Films 2024-2028
 Great Britain 2021
 Reviews & Abstracts 2018
Video Photography 1915
Video Recordings (Manufactures) 1748
Vietnam (History) 2962-2964
 Dictionaries 2962
Vietnam War (History) 2963-2964
Vietnamese Language 2264-2265
Vietnamese Literature 2521
Virology 1119
Viruses (Biology) 1119
Vitamins (Biochemistry) 1118
Vocal Music 1958-1967
 Children's Songs 1965-1966
 Folk Songs 1960-1964
 Encyclopaedias & Dictionaries 1962-1963
 USA 1964
 National Anthems 1967
 USA 1959
Volcanoes (Geology) 1028
Voyages 2642-2643
 Handbooks & Manuals 2642
 Histories 2643
Wages 535
Wales 826, 1839, 2554-2555, 2581-2582, 2702, 2737
 Bibliographies 2581-2582
 [Antiquities] 2554-2555
 [Architecture] 1839
 [Area Studies] 2581-2582
 [Biography] 2737
 [Folklore & Folktales] 826
Wales (History) 2890-2891
 Bibliographies 2891
Watch Making
 See
 Clock & Watch Making
Water-colour Painting 1896
 Great Britain 1896
Water Supply 1461-1462
 Treatment 1462
Water Treatment 1462
Wave Signals (Telecommunications) 1385
Waves & Oscillations (Electrical Engineering) 1366
 Microwaves 1366
Waxes (Chemical Industry) 1659
Weapons & Arms (Engineering) 1427-1428
 Small Arms 1428
Welding (Workshop Practice) 1409-1411
Welfare Services 735-749
 Child Welfare 747
 Disabled & Handicapped 746
 Family Planning 745
 Great Britain 738-742
 Hospitals 744
 Libraries 743
 Youth Welfare 748-749
Welsh Language 2235-2236
Welsh Literature 2505-2506

Welsh Literature in English
  See
    Anglo-Welsh Lierature
West Indian English
  See
    Caribbean English
West Indies
  See
    Caribbean
Western Fiction 2347
Western Films 2028
Whales 1213
Wild Flowers 1146-1159
  Australasia & Oceania 1156
  Diseases 1157
  Economic Aspects 1158-1159
  Europe 1147-1148
  Great Britain 1149-1154
  USA 1155
  Worldwide 1146
Wildlife Conservation 1134-1135
Wine Industry 1650
Witchcraft & Magic 312
Women 1801, 2364-2365, 2412, 2430, 2465, 2469, 2724
  [American Literature] 2412
  [*Biographies*] 1801, 2364-2365
  [German Literature] 2430
  [Spanish-American Literature] 2469
  [Spanish Literature] 2465
  [Worldwide] 2724
Word Games 2074
Word Processing 1583
Words, Loan (English Language) 2158
Workshop Practice 1406-1419
  Boiler Making 1408
  Machine Elements 1415-1416
    Gears & Clutches 1416
  Materials Handling 1417-1419
    Fasteners 1417
    Lubrication 1418-1419
  Packaging 1412-1414
    Containerization 1414
  Powder Metallurgy 1406-1407
  Welding 1409-1411
World War 1 2845-2848
  Biographies 2848
  Chronologies 2847
  Maps & Atlases 2846
World War 2 2850-2853
  Biographies 2853
  Encyclopaedias 2851
  Maps & Atlases 2852
World Wars 1 & 2 2845-2848
Worship (Christian Church) 364-366
  Hymns 366
Writing & Lecturing 895, 988
  [Chemistry] 988
  [Science] 895
Writing Techniques (Literature) 2301-2307
Xhosa Language 2267
Yeasts (Botany) 1163
Yiddish Language 2167
Yiddish Literature 2431
Yoga 417-418
Youth Welfare 748-749
Yugoslav Literature 2493
Zoology 1171-1175
  Bibliographies 1171
  Dictionaries 1172
  Nomenclatures 1174
  Reviews & Abstracts 1173

Zoology *(contd.)*
  Zoos 1175
Zoos 1175
Zoroastrianism 419
Zulu Language 2267